POLICE ADMINISTRATION
STRUCTURES, PROCESSES, AND BEHAVIORS

Ninth Edition

Charles R. Swanson

University of Georgia

Leonard Territo

Saint Leo University

Robert W. Taylor

The University of Texas at Dallas

PEARSON

Boston   Columbus   Hoboken   Indianapolis   New York   San Francisco   Amsterdam
Cape Town   Dubai   London   Madrid   Milan   Munich   Paris   Montreal   Toronto
Delhi   Mexico City   São Paulo   Sydney   Hong Kong   Seoul   Singapore   Taipei   Tokyo

Editorial Director: *Andrew Gilfillan*
Portfolio Manager: *Gary Bauer*
Development Editor: *Elisa Rogers, 4-development*
Editorial Assistant: *Lynda Cramer*
Director of Marketing: *David Gesell*
Field Marketing Manager: *Thomas Hayward*
Product Marketing Manager: *Kaylee Carlson*
Senior Marketing Assistant: *Les Roberts*
Digital Content Lead: *Autumn Benson*
Creative Digital Lead: *Mary Siener*
Director Courseware and Content Producers: *Brian Hyland*
Managing Producer: *Cynthia Zonneveld*

Rights and Permissions: *Johanna Burke*
Project Manager: *Susan Hannahs, SPi Global*
Manufacturing Buyer: *Deidra Smith, Higher Ed, RR Donnelley*
Cover Designer: *StudioMontage*
Cover Art: *Jodie Coston/Getty Images*
Digital Content Producer: *Maura Barclay*
Full-Service Project Management: *Shylaja Gattupalli, SPi Global*
Composition: *SPi Global*
Printer/Binder: *Edwards Brothers*
Cover Printer: *Lehigh-Phoenix Color/Hagerstown*
Text Font: *ITC Garamond Std*

Library of Congress Cataloging-in-Publication Data

Names: Swanson, Charles R., author. | Territo, Leonard, author. | Taylor, Robert W., author.
Title: Police administration: structures, processes, and behaviors / Charles R. Swanson, University of Georgia, Leonard Territo, Saint Leo University, Robert W. Taylor, The University of Texas at Dallas.
Description: Ninth edition. | Boston : Pearson Education, [2017]
Identifiers: LCCN 2016025718| ISBN 9780133754056 | ISBN 0133754057
Subjects: LCSH: Police administration.
Classification: LCC HV7935.S95 2017 | DDC 363.2068—dc23
LC record available at https://lccn.loc.gov/2016025718

10 9 8 7 6 5 4 3 2 1

ISBN 10:   0-13-375405-7
ISBN 13: 978-0-13-375405-6

Dedication

For the exceptional women in my life: my wife Paige for her dedication to providing medical care in her free clinic to those who would otherwise have none, my wonderful daughters Traci and Kellie for their keen minds and love of family, precious granddaughters Keira and Olivia, who will help shape America's tomorrows, and Maggie, forever in our hearts.

—Mike Swanson

For my wife, Elena, the kindest and sweetest woman I have ever known, and our children, Lorraine, Kseniya, and Illia, and our grandchildren, Matthew, Branden, and Alexander.

—Leonard Territo

For my wonderful and beautiful wife, Mary, and our children, Matt, Scott, Laura, and Shawna, and our grandchildren, Madison, Olivia, Brody, Auggie, Axel, Kylie, and the many more to come.

—Bob Taylor

BRIEF CONTENTS

CONTENTS

Chapter 4   POLITICS AND POLICE ADMINISTRATION   112

PART 2 The Organization and the Leader   142

Chapter 5 ORGANIZATIONAL THEORY   144

Chapter 6   ORGANIZATIONAL DESIGN   176

PART 3 The Management of Police Organizations 344

Chapter 10 ORGANIZATIONAL AND INTERPERSONAL COMMUNICATION 346

Chapter 15 ORGANIZATIONAL CHANGE   512

PREFACE

The field of police administration is dynamic and ever changing. Laws are modified, new problems occur, and administrative practices that were once accepted as gospel are challenged, modified, and, in some cases, discarded. Beginning in the turbulent 1960s with the due process revolution, followed by the civil rights movement, the Vietnam War demonstrations, widespread riots in our largest cities, the President's Commission on Law Enforcement and the Administration of Justice, and large-scale research on policing, the somewhat static precepts of policing came under increased scrutiny. Like a ball gaining speed as it rolls down a steep hill, change has become more fast paced, urgent, and pervasive.

Even while revising this book, we returned occasionally to already "finished" chapters to include significant developments. When unarmed Michael Brown was shot to death by a Ferguson, Missouri, Police Officer, civil protests and some rioting ensued. The incident produced a call for a federal civil rights investigation, better training for the police, body cameras, and an indictment for murder. Other cities soon had their own police use of force issues, such as the death in police custody of Freddie Gay in Baltimore in 2015. How these and other events have played out they represent our effort to keep the book strong and balanced between theory and the "the real world."

Collectively, the three authors of this text have been police officers, detectives, administrators, and educators for over 100 years. We have studied, practiced, researched, taught, and consulted on police administration, and an inevitable by-product of these experiences is the development of certain perspectives. In addition to meticulous research and recent events, our own insights also undergird this book.

NEW TO THIS EDITION

This revision of *Police Administration* includes:

- Many new, revised, and updated sections, e.g., failed police leadership, supplemental budgets, and new information on the smart policing initiative;
- Coverage of timely topics, such as the guardian and harm-focused models of policing, and the Triple T Strategy;
- Important developments, such as the closer scrutiny of police officers use of deadly force;
- New photographs, figures, tables, and box items on current topics and quick fact boxes that further illuminate chapter narratives. To illustrate, Mary

Edwards Walker is the only woman to receive the Congressional Medal of Honor. She subsequently had it stripped from her, although it was restored decades after her death. What explains these contradictory actions?

Users of the book will find much that is familiar to them and carefully planned additions to continue moving it forward. The thumbnail sketches of chapters in the following section illustrates, without being exhaustive, what we have done with this revision. In forging this edition, we kept the reader, the user, the profession central at the to our efforts, and the impact of the larger society carefully in our minds.

CHAPTER 1: THE EVOLUTION OF POLICE ADMINISTRATION

- Added major section, "The New Operating Environment"
- Fresh and revised content in many sections
- More Box Items, Quick Facts, and photographs

CHAPTER 2: POLICING TODAY

- New and revised material on the impact of the decline in crime over the past decade on police departments nationally with a special focus on new, rising violent crime rates in large cities
- Revised material on the primary elements of community policing with a focus on organizational structure
- New and updated material on evaluation research and community policing, evidence-based policing, hot-spots policing, intelligence-led policing, and predictive policing.
- New material on the "Triple-T Strategy: Targeting, Testing and Tracking" proposed recently by Larry Sherman.
- A new box item on "Harm-Focused Policing"
- Updated material on community policing models in Newport News, Virginia; Chicago, Illinois; and Minneapolis, Minnesota
- New material on the use of social media and policing
- New material on the changing paradigm in policing, from the warrior to guardian philosophy.
- New and in-depth discussion on the militarization of the police

- New material on improving police-community relations in light of President Barak Obama's Crime Reduction and Prevention Initiative in 2014.
- New box item on "Youth Outreach Programs"

CHAPTER 3: INTELLIGENCE, TERRORISM, AND HOMELAND SECURITY

- New box item on "Ten Simple Steps that Assist Individual Police Agencies Become Part of the National Criminal Intelligence Sharing Plan
- New material highlighting the Nation Fusion Center Association (NFCA) and the National Counterterrorism Center (NCTC)
- New box item on the USA Freedom Act
- Updated material on the U.S. Department of Homeland Security
- Revised and updated material on Radical Islamic Terrorism, with a special focus on Al-Qaeda and the Islamic State, including an analysis of the Charlie Hebdo attack in Paris, France in 2015
- Updated information relating to radical Islamic groups operating throughout the world
- Revised information on 'homegrown' Islamic terrorists, including an analysis of the Boston Marathon bombing in 2013
- New material on terrorist groups and the use of the "deep web" for recruiting, propaganda and operational planning
- New section devoted to the analysis of recent terrorist attacks: "Crude Devises and Non-Sophisticated Weapons aimed at Mass Casualty"
- New and updated research on other international threats posed by terrorists, including discussion on Boko Harem, "El Chapo" Guzman and the Mexican Cartels, and an extensive addition on Outlaw Motorcycle Gangs
- Updated and revised material on right-wing terrorism, with a focused box item on the Charleston, South Carolina Church Massacre in 2015

CHAPTER 4: POLITICS AND POLICE ADMINISTRATION

- New discussion of the call for and use of police body-worn cameras
- Examination of some highly controversial shootings of African-American males by police officers and the political and institutional response in investigating allegations of police profiling.

- Investigation of the police rank and file backlash from the firing, indicting, and arresting of police officers on criminal charges.

CHAPTER 5: ORGANIZATIONAL THEORY

- New Sections on mechanistic and organic organizations and the Reformatted Bureaucracy
- Significant discussion of sanctuary cities
- Additional Box Items, Quick Facts, and photographs

CHAPTER 6: ORGANIZATIONAL DESIGN

- New box items on how organizational structure impact police misconduct and how bottom-up approaches improves officer performance and moral
- Updated material on the factors that influence organizational design
- New material on organizational design and the investigative function with pointed discussion on crime and police factors that impact investigation
- New focused discussion on investigative styles commonly observed within police organizations
- Revised material on the unique structure of sheriffs' offices in the United States

CHAPTER 7: LEADERSHIP

- New section on effective senior police leadership
- Rewritten section on managers and leaders
- New section "The Fall of Police Leaders," an examination of failed police leaders
- New content on sense making and other work skills
- New content on the Warrior Servant Leader
- New Box Items, Quick Facts, and photographs

CHAPTER 8: PLANNING AND DECISION MAKING

- Synoptic, Incremental, Transactive, Advocacy, and Radical (SITAR) Approaches to Planning
- Planning and Time Orientations
- Strengths, Weaknesses, Opportunities, and Threats (SWOT) Analysis
- The Pugh Decision Making Matrix
- Paired Comparisons of Planning Alternatives

- Case Study 1: The After Action Report, Navy Ship Yard, Washington D.C. Navy in 2014 (Including Lessons Learned in Active Shooter Situation)
- Case Study 2: Tampa Quick Look Analysis of Hosting the 2012 National Republication Convention
- New Box Items, Quick Facts, and photographs

CHAPTER 9: HUMAN RESOURCE MANAGEMENT

- Updated all major federal laws pertaining to Human Resource Management
- New summaries of key federal court decisions on/;p= Human Resource Management,
- New content on legal aspects of police officer pregnancies
- Additional information on the use of lie detectors in police applicant screening
- New content on internal affairs investigations
- New content on police use of force
- New Box Items, Quick Facts, and photographs

CHAPTER 10: ORGANIZATIONAL AND INTERPERSONAL COMMUNICATION

- Social media and law enforcement communications.
- Issues regarding police officers personal postings on social media sites.
- The evolution of police – media communications in the digital age.
- Communicating with people with disabilities.
- More Box Items, Quick Facts, and photographs

CHAPTER 11: LABOR RELATIONS

- Labor – management relations in the face of funding cutbacks. These include setting new priorities and making specific recommendations on how best to deal with budget reductions.
- New Box Items, Quick Facts, and photographs

CHAPTER 12: FINANCIAL MANAGEMENT

- Major rewrite of "The Economy and Police Budgets" section
- Major new section on the impact of the Stockton (CA) bankruptcy

- Additional information on Citizen Centric Reports
- New content: Five Budget Tips
- Major New Section on Budget Adjustments
- New information on Program Budgets
- Major rewrite of Asset Forfeiture section
- New information on Performance Budgets
- New content on Black Asphalt
- Major new section on the use of volunteers
- New Box Items, Quick Facts, and photographs

CHAPTER 13: STRESS AND POLICE PERSONNEL

- Police officers homicide and suicide.
- The stress of small-town policing.
- The impact of shift length on performance, health, quality of life, fatigue and extra-duty employment.
- The police psychologist's role in a psychological health/wellness initiative.
- New Box Items, Quick Facts, and photographs

CHAPTER 14: LEGAL ASPECTS OF POLICE ADMINISTRATION

- Expansive new box item on police training and liability from an officer's perspective
- Revised and updated material on the misuse of firearms and deadly force with a special focus on the impact of the 2014-15 shooting incidents in Ferguson, MO; Charleston, SC; Cincinnati, OH; and Baltimore, MD
- Revised and updated material on *Graham v. Connor (1989)* and the impact of this landmark case on police liability
- New box items on 1) the impact of police body cameras on police liability; 2) the deadly statistics associated with police pursuits and chases; 3) police sexual violence as an emerging law enforcement issue; and 4) police membership in hate groups
- New material on vehicle pursuits and the use of deadly force
- Updated material relating to case law and use of force by the police
- New and expansive material on Federal Consent Decrees
- Updated material on police officers' rights, particularly those focusing on officers who are minority, women and/or gay

CHAPTER 15: ORGANIZATIONAL CHANGE

- New introductory material on organizational change and the factors that impact successful change in policing
- New and updated material on why change occurs as a reaction to crisis, fluctuating crime rates, technological advances, funding and economic decline, politics, a changing workforce, and a changing and new paradigm shift in policing focusing on new strategies to cope with rising crime rates with less resources
- New box items that focus on: 1) organizational change in policing in wake of police-community unrest; 2) the effect of economic downturn on police agencies; 3) the race gap in America's police departments; and 4) confronting the real problem in America's inner cities
- New material on the impact of the 2015 Supreme Court landmark case, *Obergefell v Hodges*, legalizing and recognizing same-sex marriage on policing
- New and revised material on organizational change models focusing on Kurt Lewin's Three-Step Model, the Traditional Action Research Model in Organizational Development, and the Burke-Litwin Model of organization transformation
- Revise material on the role of the police culture in organizational change
- New material on John Kotter's 8-step model for successful organizational change
- New and expansive material on information technology and change
- New and expansive material on policing in the future . . . everything changes . . . with special focus on the impact of predictive policing, changes in traditional police responses, next generation 9-11 and body-worn cameras on future police agencies

Organization

The overall flow of the book starts with Chapter 1 (The Evolution of Police Administration), which explains how the field of police administration developed and is continuing to develop and ends with Chapter 15 (Organizational Change), which describes important strategies for going forward. Essentially, these two "bookend" chapters chronicle how we got here and the means to move beyond the here and now.

The chapters in this book are grouped into four parts or sections, generally moving from broader topics to more specific ones:

PART ONE: FOUNDATIONS

The four chapters in Part One are grouped together because they provide a "wide lens" view of the field of police administration. Part One is usefully characterized as providing a "base layer" of information about the field of police administration so the subject specific chapters that follow have a context in which to occur

Chapter 1, "The Evolution of Police Administration," is a historical overview of how that field developed in the United States, along with general description of where it is now. This description serves to prepare the reader for some of the important topics to be covered in more detail in the chapters that follow. Chapter 2, "Policing Today," covers current policing philosophies, their characteristics, and impact. Chapter 3, "Intelligence, Terrorism, and Homeland Security," addresses the terrorism threat and its impact on national laws and policy, as well as its effect on the role of state and local law enforcement agencies. Chapter 4, "Politics and Police Administration," Examines the political effect of various institutions, officials, and the public on law enforcement agencies, as well as some major forces impacting on law enforcement agencies, such as the increased scrutiny of police use of force cases that started with Ferguson, Missouri in 2014 and gained prominence with the series of deadly encounters between the police and unarmed African American males that followed. The short-term result is an increase in criminal charges being placed against police officers in these encounters and which seemingly is having some operational consequences.

PART TWO: THE ORGANIZATION AND THE LEADER

Organizations exists to do the things people can't do for themselves in modern society. They must be thoughtfully designed to achieve the purposes for which they are created. Leaders are responsible for ensuring organizational performance. To do so, they must plan, envision the organization's future, make decisions, select a course of action from alternatives, and direct the human resources (HR) program. HR is of substantial importance to police administration because it is the largest single class of expenditures for police services: at least 80 percent of the police operational budget is encumbered by costs for it. These connections constitute the basis for grouping five chapters together in Part Two.

Chapter Five, "Organizational Theory," traces the different ways organizations can be structured and the assumptions that different approaches make about people. To illustrate, the classical bureaucratic approach holds that subordinates must be closely watched, resulting in such effects as narrow spans of control, which in term, contribute to "tall" organizational structures that often have seven, eight, or even more horizontal layers. Chapter Six, "Organizational Design," introduces concepts and the decisions that effect how organizations are designed and structured. Chapter 7, "Leadership," is a comprehensive treatment of the subject, including definitions and theories about it, and the difference between authority and power. A major section ilustrates why police leaders fail because those lessons are often more illuminating than content about what leaders "should" do. Remember the failed leadership section as "Thou shalt nots" to be rigorously avoided. Chapter 8, "Planning and Decision Making," covers two related skills law enforcement leaders use to help create and sustain improvements. Chapter 9, Human Resource Management, provides the knowledge necessary to direct the HR program, including the maze of federal laws regulating it, as well as the numerous moving parts HR has including recruitment, testing, selection, training, and promotional testing. Law enforcement leaders need to be well versed in HR because so much is spent on it and so many things can go wrong and create liabilities.

PART THREE: THE MANAGEMENT OF POLICE ORGANIZATIONS

Part Three focuses on a trio of key, organization-wide management processes. Chapter 10, "Organizational and Interpersonal Communication," is included because nothing can be started, guided, receive corrective action, or be terminated without communication. Chapter 11, "Labor Relations," provides information regarding labor relations, including establishing the collective bargaining relationship, bargaining, and contract administration. While some law enforcement executives chafe at the existence of a union in their agency as a restriction on executive actions, others hold that a carefully negotiated contract make administration easier because so many aspects of the management-union membership relationship is regulated in clear terms. Police Chiefs and Sheriffs know that their agencies run on three things: staff, information, and money. When budgets are slashed, the result is fewer officers and deputies to protect the same area and fewer dollars to analyze information. While volunteers can be trained to perform some tasks, severe budget cuts translate into reduced or entirely eliminated functions. In the last several years, some police budgets were cut to the extent the agencies couldn't provide 24-hour police services. Such things explain why knowledge about, and skill in financial management is one of the premier attributes of law enforcement leaders and why Chapter 12, Financial Management, is so important.

PART FOUR: ORGANIZATIONAL ISSUES

This concluding part contains three chapters that are grouped together by being specific issues that touch the entire law enforcement organization. Chapter 13, "Stress and Police Personnel," effects all sworn personnel and often civilian employees as well. Negative stress degrades individual and sometimes unit and agency functioning. Chapter 14, "Legal Aspects of Administration," centers on police civil liability, which often arises out of the misuse of force and high speed pursuits. In recent decades, the old refrain that law enforcement agencies are very

traditional and resist change has been dismissed by a newer reality: The pace of change in law enforcement is brisk, if not bordering on continuous. Candidates for police chief positions in departments of roughly 30 or more are frequently specifically probed about how they would go about changing a police agency, the subject of Chapter 15, "Organizational Change."

Pedagogical Features

This book is rich with pedagogical or teaching tools which were selected based on research on what tools were helpful. The teaching tools included in this book are as follows:

- **Learning Objectives**

  At the beginning of each chapter there are behaviorally stated learning objectives which can be used to focus students on what they should learn in the chapter. In this regard learning objectives provide an important study guide. The objectives are stated in specific terms so that the learning outcome is clearly understood and students will know what they should be able to do when finished with the chapter. The learning objectives also serve as the basis for the chapter summary.

- **Key Terms and Definitions**

  The key terms in each chapter are in bold and at the end of each chapter there is an alphabetized list of key terms. At the end of the book there is an alphabetized glossary of all key terms and their definitions. This feature eliminates the need to search several previous chapters looking for the definition of a term

- **Photographs, Tables, and Figures**

  The book is replete with these three types of items learning tools. Many of the photographs have not appeared in other criminal justice books and some of the tables and figures were prepared by the authors and are unique to this work. The photographs, tables, and figures compliment the narrative content.

- **Quick Fact Boxes**

  These boxes are short, informative, and interesting supplements to the content of a chapter, e.g. in Chapter 1, "The Evolution of Police Administration," there is a biographical sketch of August Vollmer. If it appeared in the narrative, the flow of the chapter would be disrupted, but the information is illuminating and therefore deserved a place in the chapter. Each chapter contains several Quick Facts Boxes.

- **Box Items**

  These boxes contain more extended informative, than quick fact boxes and provide relevant supplemental information to the chapter. Each chapter has multiple box items.

- **Chapter Summary**

  The chapter summary is based on the learning objectives and reinforces what the student has learned in completing the chapter. Each learning objective is stated and then followed by a statement of what should have been learned by fulfilling that objective.

- **Chapter Review Questions**

  The chapter review questions call attention to other learning opportunities in the chapter that, arguably, could have been included as learning objectives. These are important points of learning that will facilitate additional student growth and can also be the basis of classroom discussions and short essay examination questions.

- **Critical Thinking Exercises**

  Critical interest exercises promote student interest and participation. Each of the 15 chapters has two or more critical thinking exercises that can be assigned to individual students or groups that report back on their conclusions. This could be done in class or as out-of-class experiences. They may also be used to stimulate class discussions and involvement.

Instructor Supplements

Instructor's Manual with Test Bank. Includes content outlines for classroom discussion, teaching suggestions, and answers to selected end-of-chapter questions from the text. This also contains a Word document version of the test bank.

TestGen. This computerized test generation system gives you maximum flexibility in creating and administering tests on paper, electronically, or online. It provides state-of-the-art features for viewing and editing test bank questions, dragging a selected question into a test you are creating, and printing sleek, formatted tests in a variety of layouts. Select test items from test banks included with TestGen for quick test creation, or write your own questions from scratch. TestGen's random generator provides the option to display different text or calculated number values each time questions are used.

PowerPoint Presentations. A PowerPoint lecture package is available for use in class.

To access supplementary materials online, instructors need to request an instructor access code. Go to www.pearsonhighered.com/irc, where you can register for an instructor access code. Within 48 hours after registering, you will receive a confirming email, including an instructor access code. Once you have received your code, go to the site and log on for full instructions on downloading the materials you wish to use.

Alternate Versions

eBooks. This text is also available in multiple eBook formats. These are an exciting new choice for students looking to save money. As an alternative to purchasing the printed textbook, students can purchase an electronic version of the same content. With an eTextbook, students can search the text, make notes online, print out reading assignments that incorporate lecture notes, and bookmark important passages for later review. For more information, visit your favorite online eBook reseller or visit www.mypearsonstore.com.

ACKNOWLEDGMENTS

Although it is insufficient compensation for their gracious assistance, we wish to recognize here the individuals and organizations who helped to make this book a reality. Unless asked to do otherwise, we have indicated their organizational affiliation at the time they made their contribution.

We thank Will Aitchison for his extensive contributions to Chapter 11, Labor Relations. He also allowed us to draw from his previous works, and for this we are greatly indebted.

We also wish to thank our long-time secretary, Sharon Ostermann, for typing considerable portions of the 9th edition, as well as providing invaluable assistance in conducting the necessary research to be certain this edition contained the most current and accurate information in policing today. Her pleasant attitude and considerable intelligence made this revision a much easier task.

We would like to thank the following reviewers for their comments and suggestions: Elizabeth Bondurant, Mercer County Community College; Frederick Crawford, Missouri Baptist University; Jay Kramer, Central Georgia Technical College; Ted Purtle, Austin Community College; Michael Raymond, New Hampshire Technical College-Concord's Community College and John Reinholz, Bryant and Stratton College.

A special thanks to these individuals: Sal Territo, Maryellin Territo, Jeannie -Griffin, Linda Pittman, Dwayne Shumate, and Donna McKnight, who provided typing and -research assistance and made innumerable contributions, not only for this edition but for many previous ones as well.

For as long as this book has been in print our colleague and long-time friend, Dr. Max Bromley, Associate Professor, Department of Criminology, University of South Florida has provided us with information about the most current research on many aspects of police administration. His generosity and friendship are much appreciated.

We also wish to thank Major Lee Bercaw of the Tampa, Florida Police Department who provided us with his agency's comprehensive after-action report on how the Tampa Police Department's handling of the 2012 Republican National Conference. This document discusses every aspect of good planning and will no doubt be a valuable document and template for other agencies planning major events. This information was incorporated into Chapter 8, Planning and Decision Making.

Many people helped strengthen this book by providing critiques, photographs, and suggestions. We have elected to indicate their organizational affiliation when they helped us, even though some have moved on to other responsibilities. We are grateful for the help of Scott Wofford, Radio Shack, Fort Worth, Texas; Special Agent Jimmy Capra (retired) and the Drug Enforcement Administration; our colleague of 20 years, Jim Campbell, East Carolina University; Chief John Kerns, Sacramento, California, Police Department; U.S. Secret Service; Bureau of Alcohol, Tobacco, Firearms, and Explosives; Deputy Superintendent Jim Finley, Illinois State Police; Drs. Walter Booth and Chris Hornickj, Multidimensional Research Association, Aurora, Colorado; Lieutenant Rick Frey, Broward County, Florida, Sheriff's Office; Captain Lawrence Akley, St. Louis, Missouri, Metro Police Department; the Maricopa, Arizona, Sheriff's Office; Inspector Vivian Edmond, Michelle Andonian, and Commander Dorothy Knox, Detroit, Michigan, Police Department; Major Herman Ingram, Baltimore, Maryland, Police Department; Commissioner Morgan Elkins and Captain Dennis Goss, Kentucky State Police; St. Paul, Minnesota, Police Department; Thomas J. Deakin, John E. Ott, editor of the *FBI Law Enforcement Bulletin*, all three with the Federal Bureau of Investigation; our good friend, Bill Tafoya, the "father" of futuristics in policing; our lifelong friend, Ron Lynch, University of North Carolina; the California Highway Patrol; Norma Kane, the Kansas City, Missouri, Police Department; the San Diego, California, Police Department; the Texas Department of Public Safety: the Philadelphia Police Department; National Tactical Officers Association; Lieutenant James B. Bolger, Michigan State Police; the Denver Police Department; Colonel Carroll D. Buracker and Scott Boatright, Fairfax County, Virginia, Police Department; Major Dave Sturtz, Ohio State Patrol; the National Consortium for Justice Information and Statistics, Sacramento, California; Phoenix, Arizona, Police and Fire Departments; Lieutenant Mark Stallo, Dallas, Texas Police Department; Don Fish, Florida Police Benevolent Association; Captain Keith Bushey, Los Angeles, California, Police Department; Deputy Chief Kevin Stoeher, Mt. Lebanon, Pennsylvania, Police Department; Karen Anderson and Lisa Bird, LAN Publications Group; Lieutenant Rex Splitt, Craig, Colorado, Police Department; Chief R. E. Hansen and Cynthia Shaw, Fayetteville, North Carolina, Police Department; Officer David Hoffman, Anchorage, Alaska, Police Department; LaNell Thornton, Chief Paul Annee, and Lieutenant Michael Spears, Indianapolis, Indiana, Police Department; Lexington-Fayette, Kentucky, Urban County Police Department; Environmental Systems Research Institute, Redlands, California; Nancy Brandon, Metro Software, Park City, Utah; Larry Yium, Director of Budget and Finance, Houston, Texas; Lois Roethel and Leslie Doak, Las Vegas, Nevada, Police Department; the Knox County, Maine, Sheriff's Department; Chief Jim Wetherington, a mentor, and Assistant

Chief Sam Woodall, Semper Fi, Columbus, Georgia, Police Department; Sergeant Mike Parker, Los Angeles County Sheriff's Office; Major John F. Meeks, Baltimore, Maryland, Police Department; Mary Foss and Chief Randall Gaston, -Anaheim, California, Police Department; Captain Tom Brennan, Newark, New Jersey, Police Department; Lieutenant Robert O'Toole, Boston, Massachusetts, Police Department; Commander Tim McBride, Los Angeles, California, Police Department; Sergeant Patrick Melvin, Phoenix, Arizona, Police Department; Officer Matthew Rastovski, Birmingham, Alabama, Police Department; Lieutenant Doug Cain, Baton Rouge, Louisiana, Police Department; Sheriff Leroy D. Baca and Natalie Salazar Macias, Los Angeles County Sheriff's Office; Chief P. Thomas Shanahan and Sergeant James Cifala, Ann Arundel County Police Department, Maryland; Chief Harold L. Hurts, Police Chief Danny Garcia (retired), Phoenix, Arizona, Police Department; Amy M. Pich, Seattle, Washington, Police Department; Deputy Chief Raymond D. Schultz, Albuquerque, New Mexico, Police Department; Sheriff Cal Henderson and Detective Herb Metzger, Hillsborough County Sheriff's Office, Tampa, Florida; Sergeant Robert J. Delaney, Chicago, Illinois, Police Department; a very special thanks to Dr. Denis Dean, Dr. John Worrall and Dr. Galia Cohen, The University of Texas at Dallas, for their continued support at UT-Dallas, and their willingness to review specific parts of this text; Sergeant Don Pahlke (retired), Portland, Oregon, Police Bureau, Bob's partner in a squad car, who taught Bob what real policing was all about; former Chief David M. Kunkle, Chief David O. Brown, Assistant Chief Floyd Simpson (rest in peace, my friend), Lt. Ronald Thomasson, Lt. Dianna Watts, and Mr. Michael Freeman, Dallas, Texas Police Department; Chief Brian Harvey, Allen Police Department, retired Chief Lowell Cannaday, Irving, Texas, Police Department; Chief Jimmy Perdue, North Richland Hills, Texas, Police Department; former Chief and good friend, Mr. Darrell Stephens, Charlotte-Mecklenburg, North Carolina Police Department, now Executive Director of Major Cities Chiefs of Police Association; former Commissioner Paul Evans, Boston Police Department; former Chief Bob Olsen, Minneapolis, Minnesota, Police Department; Mr. Gil Kerlikowske, former Director of National Drug Policy, now Commissioner of U.S. Customs and Border Protection; Sheriff Jerry Keller (retired), Las Vegas Metropolitan Police Department; Sheriff Lupe Valdez, Dallas County Sheriff's Office; Chief Bob Lehner, Elk Grove, California Police Department; Dean Victor Strecher (retired), Sam Houston State University; Mr. Bill Hill, former Dallas County District Attorney, Dallas Texas; Chief Greg Allen, Assistant Chief Pete Pacillas, and Ms. Jennifer Callan, El Paso, Texas, Police Department; Dr Kelley Stone, former Fusion Center Director at Collin County, Texas, now with IBM; Dr. David Carter, Michigan State University; Dr. John Liederbach, Bowling Green State University; Dr. Shelly Greenberg, Johns Hopkins University; Dr. Geoff Alpert, University of South Carolina; Dr. James Marquardt, Lamar University; and our colleagues and friends who have been involved in police training and education for the last forty years, Mr. Lonnie Wilder, Mr. Norm Willox,and Mr. Dave Willox.

Lieutenant Stephen Hartnett of the Tampa, Florida, Police Department -provided us with material on the psychological testing of police applicants. Chief of Police Ronald Miller and Major Roger Villanueva of the Kansas City, Kansas, Police Department provided us with information on their agency's college incentive and -college tuition assistance programs. Chief of Police Bill McCarthy of the City of Des Moines, Iowa, Police Department provided us with information on the agency's salary schedule. Cynthia Brown, publisher of *American Police Beat*, Cambridge, Massachusetts, gave us permission to use numerous articles and photographs in several of our chapters. Melonie Hamilton with *Police Magazine*, Torrence, California, assisted us in obtaining photos in relation to our discussion of assessment centers, as well as our -discussion of Internal Affairs investigations.

We would also like to thank Chief Joe Lumpkin of the Savannah, Georgia, Police Department for his continued good counsel and information on the subject of police administration and Chief Dwayne , formerly Director of Public Safety in Cordele, Georgia, Police Department for his continued work as the president of the Georgia Association of Chiefs of Police. We also thank Deanette L. Palmer, Ph.D., a psychologist with the Spokane, Washington, Police Department. We wish to thank Meredith A. Bowman of the Southeastern Public Safety Institute, St. Petersburg College, St. Petersburg, Florida, and our colleague Jim Sewell, Florida Department of Law Enforcement, who has also contributed to this book. And a very special thanks to Ms. Jennifer Davis-Lamb, Caruth Police Institute, for her outstanding research and energy on this project. Her hard work helped improve the overall quality of this book. Lastly, we would like to thank our editor, Gary Bauer, for his continued guidance, support, patience, and encouragement. It has been a pleasure working with him.

Charles R. "Mike" Swanson
Leonard Territo
Robert W. Taylor

ABOUT THE AUTHORS

Charles R. "Mike" Swanson enlisted in the Marine Corps at 17, after which he was a uniformed officer and detective with the Tampa Police Department. As Deputy Director of Florida Governor Kirk's Council on Law Enforcement and Criminal Justice he led a central and seven public safety regional offices to innovations in service delivery and also advised the Governor on policy issues.

Subsequently, he taught criminal justice courses for a year at East Carolina University and then joined the University of Georgia's Vinson Institute of Government working full-time with Georgia law enforcement agencies in solving practical problems and conducting agency assessments. In more than 200 seminars, he also trained over 10,000 police officers from over 40 states in topics ranging from advanced homicide investigation to organizational theory. Mike also designed and led training in China's Shanghai Municipal Institute for senior governmental officials and has been a consultant to agencies in the United States, ranging from Elizabeth, New Jersey to the Multnomah Department of Public Safety in Portland, Oregon. He has written over 100 consulting reports.

Mike has extensive experience in police promotional systems. Notably, as an expert, he led a state patrol agency out of federal district court, designing and administering the new promotional system he developed for some 10 years. The Commissioner of the state patrol described it as "Our agency's most important development in human resource management in the last 50 years." None of the approximately 14 agencies for which he designed promotional systems has been successfully sued. Mike has extensive experience in job analysis and test validation, developing and administering more than 100 written tests, and exercises for oral, boards and assessment centers. He has also trained assessment center assessors from more than 20 states.

Rising through the ranks to retire as the Interim Director of the Vinson Institute, Mike led its 183 faculty and staff members in a state-wide program of technical assistance, training, and research for state and local units of government in Georgia.

Among his other publications are several other co-authored books, Terrorism, Intelligence and Homeland Security (First Edition, 2015), Criminal Investigation (12th edition in preparation), The Police Personnel Selection Process (1980) Introduction to Criminal Justice, (1979) and Court Administration: Issues and Responses (1980).

Both Police Administration and Criminal Investigation were previously translated into Mandarin. The Georgia Association of Chiefs of Police twice recognized his contributions to the association. He received the first award for 20 years of service to the association and other contributions and later named their first honorary Chief of Police. Mike is the recipient of the Academy of Criminal Justice Sciences' O. W. Wilson Award for distinguished police research. The University of Georgia twice granted him Distinguished Service Awards and a Walter Bernard Hill Award for Distinguished Achievement in Public Service. The Governors of Florida, Kentucky, and Georgia have issued proclamations recognizing his contributions to law enforcement in their states.

Mike holds a B.S. and M.S. in Criminology from Florida State University and a Ph.D in Political Science with an emphasis in public administration from the University of Georgia.

Leonard Territo is presently a distinguished professor at Saint Leo University, Saint Leo, Florida, and professor emeritus in the Department of Criminology, at the University of South Florida, Tampa, Florida. He was previously the chief deputy (undersheriff) of the Leon County Sheriff's Office in Tallahassee, Florida. He also served for almost nine years with the Tampa Police Department as a patrol officer, motorcycle officer, and homicide detective. He is the former chairperson of the Department of Police Administration and director of the Florida Institute for Law Enforcement at St. Petersburg Junior College, St. Petersburg, Florida.

In addition to writing nearly 50 articles, book chapters, and technical reports, he has authored, co-authored and edited twelve books, including *Criminal Investigation*, which is going into its 12th edition; *International Sex Trafficking of Women and Children: Understanding the Global Epidemic*, which is in its 2nd edition; *Criminal Investigation of Sex Trafficking in America; The International Trafficking of Human Organs: A Multi-Disciplinary Perspective; Crime and Justice in America*, which is in its 6th edition; *Stress Management in Law Enforcement*, which is in its 3rd edition; *Police Civil Liability; College Crime and Prevention and Personal Safety Awareness; Stress and Police Personnel; The Police Personnel Selection Process; Hospital and College Security Liability*; and a crime novel, *Ivory Tower Cop*, which was inspired by a true story. His books have been used in more than a thousand colleges and universities in 50 states, and his writings have been used and referenced by both academic and police departments in 14 countries including Australia, Barbados, Canada, Chile, Czechoslovakia, England, France, Germany, Israel, the Netherlands, Poland, Saudi Arabia, South Korea, and Spain.

His teaching awards include being selected from among 200 criminal justice educators from the state of Florida as the Outstanding Criminal Justice Educator of the Year by the College of Social and Behavioral Sciences at the University of South Florida. He has been given awards by both the Florida Police Chiefs Association and the Tampa Police Academy for his years of teaching and meritorious services; he was given an award for Distinguished Scholarly Publications by Saint Leo University, Saint Leo, Florida; he has been selected for inclusion in *Who's Who in American Law Enforcement*, and he has recently been given a Lifetime Achievement Award from the Department of Criminology at the University of South Florida.

Robert W. Taylor is currently a Professor in the Criminology Program at The University of Texas at Dallas. Previous to this position, he was the Director of the Executive Masters in Justice Administration and Leadership Program and the former Program Head for the Public Affairs Program at UT-Dallas. Both are academic programs integrating the traditions of management, governmental affairs, policy analysis, and decision science in the public sector. The program hosted one of the largest graduate degree programs on campus including Doctoral (Ph.D.) and Master's Degrees in Public Affairs and Public Administration.

From January 2008 through 2010, Dr. Taylor was the Executive Director of the W.W. Caruth Jr. Police Institute at Dallas (CPI). The Institute was established through a $9.5 million grant from the Communities Foundation of Texas. Dr. Taylor was a principle party to the development of the Institute and was appointed the founding director by the University of North Texas System. The primary mission of the Institute is to provide direction and coordination of major training and research projects for the Dallas Police Department. The Institute represents a national "think tank" on policing strategies focused on major urban cities in the United States. Dr. Taylor remains a "Scholar-in-Residence" at the Institute. From 1996 to 2008, Dr. Taylor was professor and chair of the Department of Criminal Justice at the University of North Texas. He served in this capacity for thirteen years, and under his direction, the Department gained national prominence.

In 1995, Bob took a leave of absence from university administration and teaching, to join Emergency Resources International, Inc., the parent company of the famed "Red Adair" firefighters. His duties as Senior Vice-President, Crisis Management Division, included liaison with foreign governments and authorities, extensive contract negotiations, and the strategic development of a world-wide communication and information system. Bob's major project was acting as team leader on the largest oil spill in history (3 million bbls), located in the remote Nenets District of Russia, over 200 miles north of the Arctic Circle.

For the past forty years, Bob has studied criminal justice administration and specifically, police responses to crime and terrorism, focusing on issues in the Middle East. He has traveled extensively throughout the Middle East, meeting several heads of state in that region. He has acted as a consultant to numerous federal, state and local agencies, and since September 11, 2001, Dr. Taylor has been a consultant to the U.S. Department of Justice working with the Institute for Intergovernmental Research (IIR). He has also worked extensively throughout the Middle East, especially in the countries of Turkey, United Arab Emirates, Bahrain, and Lebanon. He has been an instructor for the U.S. Department of State, Anti-Terrorism Assistance –ATA Program (2001–06) and taught internationally in the Executive Seminar on Cyber Terrorism presented to executives of foreign governments. Dr. Taylor has also worked extensively with the U.S. intelligence community. He holds appropriate *top secret* national security clearances through the JPASS system (currently archived).

Dr. Taylor has authored or co-authored over two hundred articles, books, and manuscripts. Most of his publications focus on police administration and management, police procedures, international and domestic terrorism, drug trafficking, and criminal justice policy. His articles appear in numerous journals including *Defense Analysis* (University of Oxford, England Press), the *ANNALS* (American Academy of Political and Social Sciences), *Police Quarterly, Crime and Delinquency,* and the *Police Chief* (International Association of Chiefs of Police). Dr. Taylor is senior author of four best-selling textbooks, *Terrorism, Intelligence and Homeland Security* (Upper Saddle River, NJ: Pearson Publishing, 2016); *Digital Crime and Digital Terrorism*, 3rd edition (Pearson, 2014); *Juvenile Justice: Policies, Practices and Programs*, 4th edition (New York: McGraw-Hill, 2014); and *Police Patrol Allocation and Deployment* (Pearson, 2011). He is also the co-author of two truly landmark textbooks, Police Administration: Structures, Processes, and Behaviors, 8th edition (Pearson Publishing, 2012); and *Criminal Investigation* 11th edition (McGraw-Hill, 2012). These texts are used in over 700 universities, colleges, and police departments throughout the United States, Europe and China, and continue to be developed into new editions.

Bob has an extensive background in academic and professional criminal justice, having taught at four major universities and serving as a sworn police officer and major crimes detective (lateral rank of sergeant) in Portland, Oregon for over six years. In 1984, he was appointed as a Research Fellow at the International Center for the Study of Violence at the University of South Florida, Tampa, Florida, conducting various studies involving international and domestic terrorism, police training and management, public violence and homicide, computerized mapping, and international drug trafficking. He continues to conduct research in these areas and is the recipient of numerous grants and contracts (over $18 million in funded projects). His latest work has concentrated in four areas: 1) Police use of force and improved tactical/strategic improvement through advanced training, decision-making, leadership and management practices particularly addressing areas of officer violence and officer-involved shootings; 2) International terrorism, especially Middle-Eastern groups, and the spread of radical Islam; 3) Evaluation of community policing, evidence-based policing, and other predictive policing strategies in the United States; and 4) Intelligence analysis, fusion centers, and decision-making particularly during protracted conflict or crisis situations.

In 2004, Dr. Taylor was asked by the International Justice Mission in Washington, D.C. to assist in the training of the Cambodian National Police on child sex slavery and human trafficking as part of a large project funded through the U.S. Department of State ($1 million). His interest and research in this area has led to a leadership role in designing and developing training efforts in the United States aimed at raising awareness of the human trafficking tragedy for American law enforcement officers, funded in part through the U.S. Department of Justice. Dr. Taylor focuses on the nexus between human trafficking, drug trafficking and the financing of terrorist incidents internationally and domestically.

In 2003, Dr. Taylor was awarded the University of North Texas, Regent's Lecture Award for his work in the Middle East. In March 2008, the Academy of Criminal Justice Sciences presented Bob with the prestigious O.W. Wilson Award 'in recognition of his outstanding contribution to police education, research and practice.'

Dr. Taylor has been a consultant to the U.S. Army and the U.S. Marine Corp; the U.S. Department of Homeland Security, the U.S. Department of Treasury, Federal Law Enforcement Training Center, the U.S. Secret Service, the Bureau of Alcohol, Tobacco, and Firearms, the U.S. Department of Justice, the Federal Bureau of Investigation, the Drug Enforcement Administration, agencies within the U.S. intelligence community, the Police Foundation, the Police Executive Research Forum – PERF, the International Association of Chiefs of Police, and numerous state and local municipalities and private corporations. He has also conducted significant training in the United States protectorates of the U.S. Virgin Islands, Guam and Saipan, and the countries of Canada, England, France, Switzerland, Thailand, Cambodia, Barbados, Northern Cyprus, Bahrain, Venezuela, Russia, Finland, United Arab Emirates, Kenya, Singapore and Turkey. He is an active member of the Academy of Criminal Justice Sciences (elected National Chair of the ACJS Police Section - 2002) and the American Society of Criminology.

Dr. Taylor is a graduate of Michigan State University (Master of Science-1973) and Portland State University (Doctor of Philosophy-1981).

PART 1 Foundations

These first four chapters are foundational in that they tell us how law enforcement got to where it is today, explain current police operational philosophies, describe how national and domestic terrorism have impacted on the role of our police agencies, and discuss the continuing importance of politics. This section also introduces terms and concepts referred to in subsequent chapters.

Chapter 1, "The Evolution of Police Administration," differs from other histories of policing because it has a specific, rather than a general, focus. It explains policing's trials and tribulations as it morphed from a colonial night watchman system into complex organizations testing new philosophies. Also chronicled are the social, political, economic, and technological forces that continuously shape and reshape American policing. The underlying thesis of this chapter is that policing is like a sandbar in a river, being shaped and reshaped by the currents of the society in which it is embedded.

Chapter 2, "Policing Today," examines in greater detail the shifts in operational philosophies identified in the previous chapter. More specifically, as police departments came to grips with the limitations of the traditional strategies of random patrol and responding to incidents, it opened the door to new ways of delivering law enforcement services, such as community policing and evidence based policing. This chapter provides a strong understanding of the use and limitations of these different operational philosophies and strategies aimed at lowering crime and providing better police services to our communities.

Chapter 3, "Intelligence, Terrorism, and Homeland Security," addresses the significant shifts that have occurred in law enforcement in the wake of the 9/11 attacks on this country, as well as the threats posed by the Mexican drug cartels operating near our border, "homegrown" terrorists, and recent trends in radical Islamic groups, including the surging ISIS. This chapter vividly illustrates the dangers of international terrorism, domestic right-wing hate groups, left-wing anarchists, and ecoterrorists.

Chapter 4 "Politics and Police Administration," ends Part One. It explains various local forms of government and key offices. This chapter also takes a pragmatic view of how politics affects law enforcement agencies. There is a significant case study of the Baltimore Police Department, the community, the riots, and the criminal charges placed against six officers in the death of Freddie Gray, as well as coverage of other similar recent incidents. In the wake of police shootings of African American men in 2014–2015 a movement toward requiring police officers to wear body cameras emerged, which is also examined.

CHAPTER ONE

THE EVOLUTION OF POLICE ADMINISTRATION

Learning Objectives

1. List the events in England that led to the creation of the London Metropolitan Police.
2. Describe the importance of the frontier closing in 1890.
3. Define *politics* and give three reasons why it cannot be kept out of police agencies.
4. Define and describe machine politics in the 19th century.
5. Identify the most negative and positive things about the patronage/spoils system.
6. Explain why the concept of a police profession is so important.
7. Discuss the contributions of Chief Gus Vollmer.
8. Describe the impact of prohibition on policing.
9. Describe the Black Codes and Jim Crow laws.
10. State how World War II affected law enforcement.
11. Explain the unequal badge problem.
12. Describe how the police rank and file became isolated in the 1960s.
13. Define COP, ZTP, CompStat, EBP, and HSP.
14. Give three reasons why the United States has not experienced a major terrorist attack from abroad since 9/11.
15. Identify what may be the transcendent event for law enforcement over the past decade.

INTRODUCTION

STUDYING THE EVOLUTION OF *police administration is crucial because (1) the past is full of important lessons; (2) ignoring these lessons increases the probability that prior mistakes will be repeated and opportunities forfeited; (3) knowledge of the past breeds* esprit de corps, *or pride in the heritage of one's chosen profession; (4) it instills an appreciation that each of us stands on the shoulders of the men and women who served before us with dignity, compassion, and valor; (5) there is a more complete comprehension of where and why a profession is when you know where it has been; (6) concepts in this chapter are part of the vocabulary of policing; and (7) it sets the stage for discussions in some of the chapters that follow.*

THE URBANIZATION OF AMERICAN POLICING

The earliest American colonists, who were primarily English, depended on volunteer citizen night watchmen, patrolling from dusk to dawn, to alert them to threats, such as fires, crimes, and pirates. When watchmen raised an alarm, it became the collective responsibility of all residents to respond. Other offices familiar to the colonists, such as sheriff, constable, and coroner, were subsequently added, although initially their numbers were very small. In 1625, New Amsterdam, now New York City, created its office of sheriff.[1]

In 1833, Philadelphia became the first city in this country to have a paid, full-time day police force.[2] Gradually, the widespread use of volunteer citizens' night patrols was replaced by paid night police departments, which were entirely separate from the full-time day police. It was not until 1844, in New York City, that the first unified day-night police force was created (see Figure 1.1).

To no small degree, the rise of unified, full-time police departments in America was influenced by events in England. During the late 17th and early 18th centuries, England's economy made two key shifts: (1) improved agricultural methods provided significant surplus crops to support people living in cities and (2) people were drawn to cities by the industrial revolution (1760–1830),[3] which shifted production from manual labor to machine made, initially in the textile industry and then spreading to other goods. Factories surpassed homes and small workshops as employers.

As the populations of England's cities grew, so did their problems, such as slums, crime, and appalling working conditions. As a result, social unrest escalated. The old ways of dealing with crime and unrest were inadequate. In 1829, Parliament passed the Metropolitan Police Act with the strong support of **Sir Robert Peel** (1788–1850), creating a full-time police agency for London.

FIGURE 1.1 ▶ The Colorado Springs (Colorado) Police Department circa 1890–1900. The influence of Union Civil War (1861–1865) uniforms is plainly seen, including the style of several visible belt buckles. In the second row are two commanding officers, identified as such by the Union army's convention that commissioned officers wore a coat with two rows of buttons so they could be immediately recognized as leaders. Chief Dana leans slightly to the left and seated beside him is Captain Gathright. In the third row, is an African American officer, Horace Shelby. (The Denver Public Library, Western History Collection, X-14668)

Quick Facts: Sir Robert Peel's Other Accomplishments

Sir Robert Peel is a luminary just on the basis of his contributions to policing, but he is not without other significant accomplishments. Peel was twice Prime Minister of England (1834–1835 and 1841–1846). As a social reformer, he championed laws that prohibited women and children from working in mines (1842) and limiting their working hours in factories (1844). We are left to wonder what else Peel might have achieved had his life not been cut short by injuries caused by a horse fall.

New principles, such as officers should be hired on a probationary basis, were articulated for the London Metropolitan Police, stressing the need for professional conduct by the agency and its officers.[4] The effort to create a force in which the public would have confidence and would support produced grim numbers: In the first three years of its existence, 5,000 officers were dismissed and another 6,000 resigned; many of them were under pressure.[5]

American cities selectively drew on the experience of the London Metropolitan Police, gradually creating centralized, full-time police departments. However, the majority of American politicians during the 1800s had no interest in hiring quality officers, choosing instead to continue using officers to suit their own purposes: graft, control of elections, and harassment of the opposition party (see Figure 1.2).

In the history and image of America, the "wild and wooly" West looms large (see Figure 1.3), although it spans a scant 90 years, from roughly 1800 to 1890. The acclaimed Pony Express (1860–1861) is a prime example of how quickly things changed in the West. From Missouri to California, relay stations were established every 10 miles, where Pony Express riders could obtain fresh mounts. Despite riding through dangerous wilderness areas, riders couldn't carry guns in order to transport more mail. Orphans were preferred as riders because if they were killed, no one would miss them. Despite its success, the Pony Express was out of business in 18 months due to the completion of the transcontinental telegraph (1861).

Factors contributing to the settlement of the West included the discovery of gold at Sutter's Mill, California (1848), the availability of tracts of land to settlers under the Homestead Act (1862), and the

FIGURE 1.2 ▶ Satire of police corruption. "Mulberry Ring" refers to the New York City Police Department, then located at 300 Mulberry Street. (Library of Congress Prints and Photographs Division [LC-USZ62-85436])

FIGURE 1.3 ▶ "Big Ned," Con Wagner, and "Ace" Moore were lynched by vigilantes in a partially completed cabin near Laramie, Wyoming (1868). Hoisted just off the ground with no fall to break their necks, the men slowly strangled. (Denver Public Library, Western History Collection, Arundel Hull, Z-5808)

conclusion of the Civil War (1861–1865). Although there were already free African-Americans in the West, that number was increased after 1865, due to (1) assistance from the federal **Freedmen's Bureau** (1865–1872), (2) flight from the South's new sharecropper system that effectively re-enslaved the recently emancipated, (3) the repressive laws enacted to keep "Negroes" segregated and powerless, and (4) the brutality of the **Ku Klux Klan (KKK)**, which was formed in 1866 for social purposes, but quickly began using terror, violence, and lynchings to control African-Americans.

Benjamin "Pap" Singleton (1809–1892; see Figure 1.4), a former slave in Tennessee, promoted the idea of forming African-American townships in Kansas, leading to the establishment of such townships as Nicodemus (1877; see Figure 1.5). Singlehandedly, Singleton may have inspired the exodus of 20,000 people out of the South. However, other promoters established perhaps as many as 42 similar settlements in both Kansas and Oklahoma.[6] As a large organized movement, the exodus was finished by 1872, although smaller groups of African-Americans continued to regularly arrive through 1880.

The completion of the transcontinental railroad (1869) and the construction of other rail lines provided mass transportation into the West for adventurers and settlers. By the mid-1880s, cattle drives up the Chisholm and other trails from Texas to Abilene,[7] Dodge City, Wichita, and other Kansas "cow towns" were a thing of the past due to the expansion of railroads, settlements, and the use of barbwire to close off open range.

West of the Mississippi, episodic war with Native Americans is traditionally dated as lasting from 1823 to 1890, although the last battle was fought in 1918 (see Box 1.1). Eventually, the tribes were forced onto reservations, producing a need for law and order on tribal lands and protection from trespassers. Lacking any appropriated funds to create a reservation law enforcement capability, agents on various reservations scrapped together funds and recruited Native Americans as police officers. The Congress finally began appropriating money for tribal police agencies in 1879 (see Figure 1.6).[8] Tribal enforcement agencies represent an out-of-the-mainstream example of American police administration, as is the U.S. Mint Police (1792).

FIGURE 1.4 ▶ Benjamin "Pap" Singleton was a 37-year-old slave when he escaped to Detroit and began operating a secret boarding house for runaway slaves. After the Civil War ended, he returned to Tennessee and later began his work as a Moses-like figure, leading people to the promised land (State of Kansas Historical Society).

FIGURE 1.5 ▶ Prosperous African-American settlers in Nicodemus, Kansas, 1877.
(Library of Congress Prints and Photographs Division [76000820])

Box 1.1 The Battle with Yaquis Indians in Bear Valley, Arizona

Yaquis Indians living in Northern Mexico were in rebellion against their Mexican national government. Yaquis would cross into the United States, take jobs long enough to buy arms and ammunition, return to Mexico, and distributed the weapons to other Yaquis. At other times these goods were taken by raids on isolated ranches. On January 9, 1918, there was a chance encounter in Bear Valley, Arizona, between horse-mounted Yaquis headed south with newly purchased weapons and a patrol from the 10th Cavalry. The Yaquis mistook the African-American troopers of the 10th as Mexican soldiers seeking to intercept them. If caught, the penalty would be death and so they opened fire. In the skirmish that followed, at least one Yaquis was killed and nine captured. Those taken prisoner were tried on minor charges, served 30 days confinement, and were released. Because World War I was still going on, the Bear Valley engagement got little attention in the news media or officially. The 10th Cavalry was historically comprised of African-Americans with an excellent reputation as fighters. Because of the ferocity with which they fought, the Cheyenne Indians called them "Buffalo Soldiers."[9]

FIGURE 1.6 ▶ Standing Rock Reservation Dakota/Lakota (Sioux) police officers Red Tomahawk (L) and Eagle Man (R). Note that Eagle Man is wearing moccasins with his uniform. These two officers, 37 other Native American officers, and four volunteers attempted to arrest Hunkpapa Sioux spiritual leader Sitting Bull in 1890. The basis for the arrest was his rumored involvement with a potential uprising. His followers opened fire to prevent the arrest and in the ensuing 30-minute battle, eight officers and Sitting Bull and seven followers were killed, including Crow Foot, Sitting Bull's 17-year-old son. Sitting Bull had long maintained that contacts with white men could only result in the destruction of the Sioux way of life. This photograph is dated to the 1880s. (Denver Public Library, Western History Collection, D. Barry, B-836)

Western law enforcement agencies were often small, their jurisdictions were limited, the local records were inadequate for serious investigations, there was no centralized record keeping agency, marauding bandits had vast lands into which they could vanish, and communication between agencies was often sparse and slow. Opposing them was an abundance of rustlers, stagecoach and train robbers, and murderers, a small number of whom were unique. Born in England, Charles Bowles came to the United States, fought for the Union, rising to the rank of First Sergeant, was wounded while participating in General Sherman's march through Georgia to the sea, and at some point simplified his name to Boles. As "Black Bart," Boles became one of the truly unique criminals of the Old West. He pulled his robberies with an empty shotgun, only robbed Wells Fargo stagecoaches and took the company's strongbox, but never robbed passengers, some of whom remembered him as "gentlemanly" and engaging in "intellectual" conversations.[10]

Given the limitations of Western law enforcement agencies of the period, it is not surprising that the **Pinkerton National Detective Agency**, Wells Fargo detectives, and Union Pacific operatives developed a strong record in catching or killing these robbers. Unrestricted by jurisdiction, these private "lawmen" pursued bandits across jurisdictional lines and were aided by their employers' substantial record systems.

Notorious outlaws "Butch Cassidy" (Robert Parker) and the "Sundance Kid" (Harry Longaboug) were part of a loose coalition of gangs whose primary hideout was the Hole-in-the-Wall Pass in Wyoming, a place with only one entrance and other natural defense features. Parker was the leader of a loose-knit gang, called "the wild bunch" and sometimes "the-hole-the-wall gang." Determined to end the wild bunch's string of bank and train robberies, the Pinkertons "hounded" Parker and Longabough so consistently that by 1902 they ended up in Argentina and were thought to have been later killed in 1908 by Bolivian soldiers in a shootout. However, that ending is in doubt as is the Pinkerton's assertion that one of these two men was killed later, in 1911 by Uruguayan police.

The bodies of the two bandits killed in 1908 were exhumed in 1986 and it was announced that they were not Parker and Longabough. Speculation and rumors about what happened to Parker

Box 1.2 Black Bart, the Poet Bandit

Charles Boles (1829– unknown) robbed 28 Wells Fargo stage-coaches in California before being arrested. He was fond of leaving poems at the scene of his crimes, signed "Black Bart, the PO8" (poet). One of them reads:

> I've labored long and hard for bread,
> For honor and for riches
> But on my corns too long you've tread
> You fine haired sons of bitches

Finally arrested, Boles served four years and was released early for good behavior. Most sources maintain Boles dropped out of sight in 1888 and the rest of his life is unknown. However, one source, with no documentation, maintains that after Boles was released from prison, three Wells Fargo stages were robbed. The company is purported to have offered him a pension if he'd leave the country. Boles supposedly boarded the steamer Empress of China headed to that country.[11]

and Longabough continued for many decades thereafter. Some of their friends reported speaking with one or the other, or both at different locations in South America and the United States after their alleged deaths. Their actual fates remain a mystery.[12]

In 1890, the federal government announced that the frontier was closed and six states were later admitted to the union.[13] Both of the territorial governments of Arizona and New Mexico realized that their own aspirations for statehood would be impeded by their image of being populated by thieves, rustlers, and bandits. Drawing on the long experience of the Texas Rangers (1823),[14] they created the Arizona Territorial Rangers (1860) and the New Mexico Territorial Mounted Police (1905) to curb lawlessness.

The significance of the **frontier closing** in 1890 is that it marks the onset of the swift transition from a rural, agrarian society to an urbanized one in only 30 years. The Census of 1920 revealed that 51 percent of Americans lived in an urban incorporated area, *but the definition of that area was a place with a population of 2,500 or more people.*[15]

Presently, there are 17,985 state and local law enforcement agencies with at least one full-time employee or its equivalent.[16] The breakdown of this number by type of agency and full-time sworn positions includes (1) 12,501 local police departments with 461,063 officers; (2) 3,063 sheriffs' offices with 182,979 deputies; (3) 50 state primary law enforcement agencies have 60,772 enforcement positions. These agencies may be state police, highway patrol, or departments of public safety; (4) special jurisdiction entities, for example, port, river, and bay, transit, airport, and kindred enforcement authorities add another 59,968 positions; and (5) constable/marshal and related offices account for 3,464 positions, many in Texas.[17]

In practical terms, the present consequence of urbanization is that a majority of the sworn personnel identified in the preceding paragraph are deployed in urban areas and this is particularly true for local police departments. The largest of these is the New York City Police Department with 36,023 officers.[18] In contrast, 49 percent of all municipal agencies employ fewer than 10 full-time officers.[19] The number of small departments has dropped slightly over the past several years; perhaps consolidation, catastrophic judgments for police misconduct, and small towns contracting for police services are contributing to a slow erosion of small police departments. While small municipal police departments are more numerous than large ones, most officers work in large ones. Nearly two-thirds, 61 percent, of all sworn personnel work for municipal departments with 100 or more full-time officers.[20]

The pattern for the 3,063 sheriff's departments, although they involve fewer full-time sworn positions, parallels that of municipal agencies. The Los Angeles County Sheriff's Department is the largest in the country with 9,461 deputies.[21] Twenty-five percent (775) of sheriff's offices employ less than 10 sworn, which represents 2.4 percent (4,042) of all full-time deputies.[22] At the larger end of the spectrum, departments with 100 or more deputies are only 12 percent (378) of the total, but they employ 66 percent (120,909) of all full-time deputies.[23] The usual major functions of sheriff's offices include patrol of unincorporated portions of the county, follow-up investigations, operation of the county jail, court security, and serving legal process papers. In a number of states, some municipalities contract with their sheriff's department for police services. There are some variations of this. In several states, some counties have done one or more of the following: created a separate Department of Corrections in lieu of the sheriff's jail function, established a county police department thereby focusing the sheriff's office on court security and process serving, and eliminating the sheriff's department in favor of a county police department and distributing the other sheriff's functions over several existing and/or new departments. Alaska, Connecticut, Hawaii, and Rhode Island, and Washington DC do not have the traditional office of sheriff.[24]

The events highlighted in this section and those that follow illustrate the most important point of this chapter: policing cannot be understood if examined alone, as though the institution was an island in a lake. The more persuasive analogy is that policing is a sandbar in a river, subject to being changed continuously by the societal currents in which it is immersed. As a profoundly significant social institution, policing is shaped and reformed repeatedly by a multitude of forces in American society and transnationally.

POLITICS AND ADMINISTRATION IN THE 19TH CENTURY: ILLS OF THE PATRONAGE SYSTEM/ SPOILS SYSTEM

Politics is the process of acquiring and maintaining control over a government, including its policies, administration, and operations. Politics isn't inherently bad or good—these types of descriptions come from how power is used, as opposed to some intrinsic quality of power itself. There is no way to keep politics out of police departments because (1) police departments must be responsive to democratic control; (2) public policy is expressed in the laws, regulations, operating procedures, decisions, and actions taken or not taken by a governmental agency. Public policy is where politics and administration intersect, the method by which governmental agencies are guided and controlled; and (3) as a practical matter, politics flourishes in even the smallest agencies. The type of politics we do want to keep out of policing is highly partisan party politics, which has had a long and, most frequently, unhealthy relationship with policing.

During the 1800s, a **political machine** or **machine politics** was often a tightly controlled political party headed by a boss or small autocratic group whose purpose was to repeatedly win elections for personal gain, often through graft and corruption. These parties had a hierarchical structure running from the boss at the top through the precincts to each neighborhood, where block captains make sure supporters "voted right." Originating in Chicago, the phrase "vote early and often" reflects the machine politics' spirit. Loyal voters were rewarded with incentives for their support, such as jobs, promotions, transfers to more desirable positions, lucrative contracts, liquor licenses, or helping their recently arrived immigrant relatives gain citizenship and find housing. New York Senator William Marcy (1786–1857) coined the phrase "to the [election] victor belongs the spoils" [the authority to make patronage appointments and bestow other benefits].

The use of government resources by politicians to reward loyal voters is called **patronage** or the **spoils system**. The worst abuse of the patronage system was when people were rewarded for their political loyalty rather than their ability, roughly from 1820 to 1883. In reaction, the **Pendleton Act** was passed (1883), establishing the U.S. Civil Service Commission to enforce its provisions and mandating that federal employees pass a competitive examination and be appointed on the basis of merit. Even behind this progressive/reform legislation ugliness was at work: Momentum for its passage was garnered from the assassination of **President James Garfield** (1881; see Figure 1.7) in Washington, DC, by Charles Guiteau, a frustrated seeker of a patronage job as ambassador to France.[25]

However, the Pendleton Act initially only covered a small percentage of federal jobs. When **President Benjamin Harrison** (1833–1901) took office (1889),[26] he seized upon this loophole, and 31,000 postmaster jobs changed hands through patronage. This action was at odds with his avowed support for civil service reform and he received substantial criticism for his "prostitution of the public service."[27]

Under the 19th-century patronage system, a person seeking employment in a police department usually needed a letter of endorsement from a powerful politician allied with the party in power. The letters were typically written by elected officials, such as members of the city council or county commission, prominent state officials, or the chairman of a county's political party. When a new party came to power, the entire staff of a police agency was dismissed and replaced by patronage appointments.[28]

FIGURE 1.7 ▶ Artist's sketch of the assassination of President Garfield at the Baltimore and Ohio train station in Washington, DC. His assassin is being apprehended in the background. (Library of Congress Prints and Photographs Division [LC-USZ62-7622])

Machine politics and the ugly side of patronage were enhanced by the absence of an effective secret ballot at the polls in many states during much of the 19th century.[29] Each political party distributed ballot tickets for its own candidates. Because these tickets varied in size and color, carrying a ticket into a polling place made voting a public act and subjected voters to harassment and intimidation.[30] Votes were sold for drinks and money, and states began slowly enacting residency requirements to vote.[31]

According to "Boss" Tweed (William M. Tweed, 1823–1878), the mid-1800s ringleader of the most powerful New York City political machine, ballots didn't make a difference, the counters did.[32] As a final insult to the democratic process, state courts, dominated by patronage judges, consistently ruled that ballots could not be released for investigating and prosecuting abuses, such as using the names of dead people as voters in an election.[33]

Patronage that is not excessive or does not create inefficiency, however, is useful. Elected officials can appoint persons who agree with their policies, making governing easier. Patronage involves more people in the democratic process because they feel that their efforts and votes have meaning.

There are examples of resistance to corruption during the 19th century. In 1856, San Francisco citizens, outraged by election corruption, graft, and out-of-control crime, formed the Committee of Vigilance to provide "security for life and property." An earlier Vigilance Committee (1851) had only focused on rampant crime. Even with its own constitution and terms on the committee limited to three months, the committee was nonetheless a vigilante group, executing criminals, forcing corrupt elected officials to resign, and ordering people to leave the state immediately. Because the owner of the San Francisco newspaper supported the committee, its early reputation was excellent. However, as historians looked more closely at the committee, its reputation began to suffer. On the other side of the country, the **Lexow Committee** (1894–1895), named after its chairman, was established by the New York Senate to examine police corruption in the New York City Police Department. Its report, which ran some 10,000 pages, was instrumental in that city electing a reform candidate as mayor.

Nationally, some reform candidates were occasionally elected, although machine politics usually defeated them in the next election, and from time to time, the outrage of decent citizens boiled over, leading them to activities such as sacking brothels protected by politicians and engaging in election day violence. However, real progress was not made until the 20th century.

The Reformation Period

As policing entered the 20th century, our cities were staggering under the burdens of machine politics, rampant patronage, government inefficiency, poverty, corruption, crime, slums, inadequate health care, riots, and the exploitation of woman and children by industries (see Figure 1.8).[34] State and federal governments were similarly dysfunctional and scandalized. Conditions were so intolerable that they finally became the stimulus for change.

FIGURE 1.8 ▶ At the beginning of the 20th century, children were still being exploited as a labor source. Here, "coal breaker boys" (circa 1890–1910) take a break from their 14-hour days in the mines, where they separated chunks of coal. Note their lunch pails in the foreground. (Library of Congress Prints and Photographs Division [LC-D4-32069])

Change came in the form of the **Reformation Period** (1900–1926), which had two immediate needs: (1) arousing the public from its apathy and (2) creating a conceptual cornerstone or model for improvement by separating politics and patronage in the worst sense from the administration of governmental agencies.

Arousing the Public from Its Apathy: The Muckrakers

Author Lincoln Steffens exposed major corruption in Chicago, St. Louis, and other municipalities in *The Shame of the Cities* (1906). He believed that bribery was not an ordinary felony, but an act of treason that subverted democracy. Sinclair's novel, *The Jungle* (1906), called attention to major abuses in the meatpacking industry, which led to the passage of the Pure Food and Drug Act (1906). Churchill's *Coniston* (1906) addressed political corruption in New Hampshire and Phillips's *The Treason of the Senate* did likewise with that body. It was President Theodore Roosevelt (see Figure 1.9, 1858–1919) who, in a 1906 speech, labeled Steffens, Sinclair, and other writers who exposed social ills, scandals, and corruption as "**muckrakers**." Although he was a popular president, there is also evidence of him being less than fair minded.[35] The muckraker tradition continues into the present day.

FIGURE 1.9 ▶ Colonel Roosevelt standing at the middle of his troops on San Juan Hill, Cuba, during the Spanish American War (1898). He previously served as Police Commissioner of New York City (1895–1897), famous there for his "midnight ramble," checking to see that officers were working their assignments. (Library of Congress Prints and Photographs Division [LC-USZC4-7934])

The Conceptual Cornerstone

The conceptual cornerstone was provided for by Woodrow Wilson (1856–1924) while he was a faculty member at Bryn Mawr College in Pennsylvania.[36] He later served as President of the United States (1913–1921). Wilson called for a dichotomy or separation of politics, in the worst sense of the word, and administration.[37] However impractical that might seem now, the idea was then very progressive.[38]

As the work of the muckrakers and the conceptual cornerstone entwined, rapid progress was made. In 1906, the New York Bureau of Municipal Research was formed. Staunton, Virginia, appointed the first city manager in 1908, placing responsibility for day-to-day operations in the hands of a trained professional not beholding to any political party. Two years later, the **city manager movement** was well underway, and appointees were usually experienced engineers or business managers. Further impetus was created in 1914, when the International City Manager Association was founded and the University of Michigan offered a degree in municipal administration.

In 1916, the National Municipal League issued a model city charter calling for a strict separation of politics and administration, which had a trickle-down effect on the police and other departments. City managers worked hard to see that capable persons were appointed to leadership positions. The **Boston Police Strike** of 1919 was seen as incompatible with the emerging view of public service. Massachusetts and other states passed laws forbidding police unionization, which killed the movement until the 1960s (see Chapter 11, Labor Relations).

In 1922, the Cleveland Foundation completed a major study of crime in that city, which at that time was the fifth-largest in the nation.[39] Separate groups worked on different aspects of the criminal justice system. **Raymond Fosdick** (1883–1972) guided the group working on the police department, which was soundly criticized. Fosdick concluded that it was mostly just a larger version of what existed there in 1866—the record system was meager, precincts were too numerous, there was confusion in the lines of authority, and widespread corruption was common. The Cleveland study is noteworthy because it appears to be the model, albeit slowly adopted, of using outside experts to study police agencies.

As the separation of politics and administration gained traction, attention was focused on new ideas. Illustratively, scientific management sought to find the one best way to do things, the bureaucratic model was carefully articulated, and administrative theory formulated generic principles and methods of administration (see Chapter 5, Organizational Theory). The shift to these new ideas was marked by the publication of White's *Public Administration* (1926) and Willoughby's *Principles of Public Administration* (1927). The politics/administration dichotomy was not abandoned and both authors endorsed the city manager's 1924 code of political neutrality.

Box 1.3 Three Medal of Honor: Teddy Roosevelt, Mary Walker, and Buffalo Bill Cody

In 1901, President William McKinley was assassinated and his Vice-President Teddy Roosevelt (1858–1919) succeeded him at 42 years of age, serving as President (1901–1909). He is still the youngest person to rise to that office. Roosevelt used his executive power to preserve wilderness areas as parks and those lands later became part of the National Park Service when it was legislatively created in 1916. He also championed important laws, such as the establishment of the Food and Drug Administration (FDA, 1906). In 1912, Roosevelt was shot in the chest by a deranged man. However, Roosevelt delivered a 50 page speech before being treated. For negotiating an end to the Russo-Japanese War (1904–1905) President Roosevelt became the first American to receive a Nobel Prize, for peace in 1912.

In 2001, President Clinton posthumously awarded Teddy Roosevelt the Medal of Honor for leading the courageous charge up San Juan Hill, Cuba, in 1898.

The Medal of Honor has been awarded to only one woman, Dr. Mary Edwards Walker (1832–1919). A physician, she was initially forced to accept a nurse's position in the Union Army at the beginning of the Civil War. Within a short time, she was appointed as the first female surgeon in the U.S. Army and served with great distinction in battlefield medicine. While perhaps on a spy mission, she was arrested and spent four months in a confederate prison. In 1865, Dr. Walker received the Medal of Honor. In 1917, the criteria to receive the medal was changed and that recognition was rescinded for over 900 recipients of it, including Dr. Walker and William F. "Buffalo Bill" Cody (1846–1917). Cody, a frontiersman, Army scout, and proprietor of the "Wild West Show," received it for gallantry while scouting with an Army patrol that battled Cheyenne Indians along Nebraska's Platte River in 1872. President Jimmy Carter directed that Dr. Walker's Medal of Honor be reinstituted and her name restored to the roll of those who have received it. In 1989, the Army Board for the Correction of Military Records reinstated Buffalo Bill's medal.

Despite the progress that has been made, politics and administration, endures to this day as an area of practical concern for police executives and even for those farther down the chain of command:

> A detective was selected to attend a prestigious national training program. At the last minute, the newly elected mayor wanted to reward someone who turned out a block of voters that helped him win the election. The detective who was originally selected to the program was called into his commander's office and told "unpack your bags because the mayor's favorite detective is going in your slot." The replaced detective thought it stunk, but accepted it without outward rancor.

During the Reformation Period, progress was made toward reducing corruption, fraud, waste, and abuse in government; creating a cadre of qualified personnel to hold public jobs; developing the civil service system; emphasizing proper recruitment, selection, training, and promotion of governmental employees; rescuing the public's business from highly partisan/machine politics; and developing new theories, models, and practices related to organizations. The Reformation Period is more than history; it was the landmark that unleashed a process of improvement that has been continuous. Chapter 2, Policing Today, covers some of these developments.

POLICE PROFESSIONALIZATION

Profession and Professional

The word **profession** comes from the Latin *pro* (forth) and *fateri* (confess), meaning to announce a belief. At its earliest use, the word referred to public statements or declarations of faith.[40] By 1541, *profession* meant a learned occupation and 25 years later, its meaning was reduced to how a person habitually earned a living. In 1675, there was another shift, professing to be duly qualified. The serious work on professions has centered on specifying what criteria must be met to constitute a profession. Table 1.1 illustrates three different views about such criteria.

TABLE 1.1 THREE VIEWS OF THE CRITERIA MAKING UP A PROFESSION[41]	
Most Commonly Identified Criteria	**Merton's Criteria**
1. An organized body of theoretical knowledge.	1. Knowing (systematic knowledge).
	2. Doing (trained capacity and technical skill).
	3. Helping (knowing and doing).
2. Advanced study is needed to master knowledge.	
3. A code of conduct guides action.	
4. Prestige.	
5. Standards of admission.	
6. A professional association.	**Becker's Criteria**
7. Altruism is the driving force for wanting to practice the profession.	If you can get people to call you one, you are one.

Quick Facts: August Vollmer: The Father of Modern Law Enforcement

Beginning in 1829, England's London Metropolitan Police created a full-time paid police force that was "professional" in the sense of that's how officers habitually earned their living. Similar "professional" officers existed in this country from roughly 1845 onward. However, the genesis of American professional policing was the work of **August (Gus) Vollmer** in Berkley, California, during 1905–1932 (see Figure 1.10). Without detracting from the genius of his efforts, note that his successes closely parallel those of the Reformation Period of 1900–1926.

FIGURE 1.10 ▶ August Vollmer, seated second from far left. (Courtesy of the City of Berkeley Police Department-Historical Unit)

The importance to policing of being seen as a profession was fundamental to transforming the public view of officers from corrupt thugs and heavy-handed brutes to something noble—professionals. Every opportunity to develop this view was seized upon. For example, when cars first became available, they were largely purchased by people with a degree of affluence, those thought of as being upper class. Knowing that such people were influential in molding opinions, chiefs quickly assigned their best officers to traffic enforcement duties.

Carte summarized the work of this giant: Under Chief Vollmer's leadership (see Figure 1.10, the Berkeley Police Department (BPD) became the model for professional policing. He mobilized

Quick Facts: August "Gus" Vollmer

"Gus" Vollmer (1876–1955) is the father of modern law enforcement. Born in New Orleans to German immigrant parents, his formal education ended in the sixth grade. Gus served with the Marine Corps in the Philippines during the Spanish-American War (1898), fighting 25 engagements with enemy forces. He was elected Berkeley Town Marshall in 1905, and in 1909, the title was changed to Police Chief. In 1921, he was elected President of the International Association of Police Chiefs. Retiring from the Berkeley Police Department in 1932, he remained active as a consultant and writer for many years. Suffering from failing eyesight, Parkinson's disease, and cancer, this extraordinary man ended his own life at 79 years of age.

officers, moving them first to bicycles and then to patrol cars, introduced a police signal system to dispatch calls, established a modern records system, used crime analysis to establish and staff geographical beats, created the first scientific crime laboratory in the United States in 1916, and the first lie detection machine used in investigation was built in the BPD in 1921.[42]

Despite these achievements, Vollmer is better known for his tireless efforts to improve the caliber of personnel. He established police training in 1908, encouraged officers to attend college classes, introduced intelligence and psychological testing for officers, and, around 1919, began recruiting college students.[43] Although they never constituted a majority of officers, the "college cops" set the tone for the BPD over the coming decades. The most influential of these "college cops" was **O.W. Wilson**.[44]

The Pendleton Act of 1883 to the Military Model

The Pendleton Act of 1883 marked the beginning of the end for the ills of the patronage/spoils system. In the three decades following the adoption of the Pendleton Act, state and local governments also adopted similar measures, although the spoils systems lasted well into the 1900s. The federal Hatch Act (1939) placed another wedge between politics and administration by forbidding federal employees from engaging in partisan political activities, which also spurred similar measures, "Little Hatch Acts," by state and local governments.

Although the rise of federal and state civil service systems intuitively is attractive, some observers were not so enthusiastic. Fosdick, writing in 1920, concluded that it sometimes made it difficult to terminate officers who committed serious breaches because the proof did not satisfy civil service safeguards.

Civil service and Vollmer's notion of educated, professional officers also conflicted. The former's emphasis was on keeping politics out of policing, whereas Vollmer's concept of merit was competent performance. Perhaps as much as 80 percent of an agency's budget is spent on personnel and related support costs, so personnel issues continue to be prominent for chiefs today (see Chapter 7, Leadership; Chapter 9, Human Resource Management; and Chapter 12, Financial Management).

While some worked at ending the spoils system, other reformers sought to enhance professionalization by using a new model that presumably would lead to more efficient operations. They concluded the country was besieged by crime and that police, as our front line of defense against it, were analogous to the military.

The **military model** (Figure 1.11) resulted in more staff positions to do specialized work, an emphasis on both line inspection of officers and staff inspections of functions, written policies and procedures, enhanced training, increased accountability, and the widespread adoption of the bureaucratic form of organization (see Chapter 5, Organizational Theory), which remains in use today. The implementation of the military model required expanded authority for chiefs, who were then able to put an end to precincts operating so independently that they sometimes looked like completely separate agencies.

The military model was so persuasive that some jurisdictions hired military officers to head their law enforcement agencies. Illustratively, retired Marine Major General Smedley Butler was hired as Director of Public Safety in Philadelphia, serving during 1924–1925. General Butler is among an elite group of 19 men in our nation's history who were awarded two Congressional Medals of Honor for valor.

PROHIBITION TO THE 1930s

The Roaring '20s and Prohibition

The 1920s are often referred to as the "roaring '20s" because of the tremendous changes that occurred in America in that decade. Following World War I, military demobilization released hundreds of thousands of young men to work in the rapidly expanding economy as our factories shifted from the production of military necessities to consumer goods. Henry Ford made millions of affordable cars. The construction of highways quickly paralleled this development, as did the proliferation of motels, gas stations, cafes, and other businesses catering to travelers. Some state highway patrol agencies were created to foster the safe movement of vehicles along these new road systems. Suburbs, formerly limited to areas served

---

Quick Facts: O.W. Wilson

Orlando Winfield Wilson (1900–1972) both studied under Vollmer and worked for him as a patrol officer. After graduating from the University of California at Berkeley, O.W. spent the next 14 years serving as Chief of the Fullerton, California, and then the Wichita, Kansas, Police Departments. He advocated many of the things Vollmer did, earning him a reputation as a progressive leader. In 1939, he joined the Berkeley faculty as professor of police administration. From 1943 to 1947, O.W. served as an Army Colonel in England, Italy, and Germany, often helping to reorganize police agencies. He returned to Berkeley and became the Dean of the School of Criminology (1950–1960). O.W. became Superintendent of Chicago's scandal-ridden police department (1960–1967), earning him a reputation as a fair but tough-minded reformer. Well established as an advocate of professionalism, O.W. Wilson's well-regarded *Police Administration* (1950) was another jewel in his crown.

FIGURE 1.11 ▶ The military model at work in policing. A 1906 Pennsylvania State Police barracks inspection. (Courtesy of the Pennsylvania State Police)

by trolley and train lines, could spring up anywhere there were roads. Some suburbs evolved into towns, resulting in more small police departments, and big-city police agencies added more officers.

Women rebelled at the strict rules for their dress and behavior. A new sound, jazz, swept the nation, abetted by the rapid expansion of radio stations, which also created national sports heroes, such as baseball's Babe Ruth and golf's Bobby Jones. Also during the second decade of the 20th century, the first "talkie" movie was made, the rural electrification movement began, and telephone service expanded dramatically. Amid all of these changes, the "noble experiment" of **prohibition** was a defining force throughout the 1920s.

In the first half of the 19th century, ministers used their pulpits to denounce drinking, claiming that those who imbibed excessively were sinners who had lost their way with God. Thus, the **temperance movement**, which began in the second half of the 19th century, grew out of churches.

There were substantial reasons to oppose alcohol, drunkenness was made worse by other vices commonly found in saloons, such as prostitution and gambling. Drinking constituted both significant family and public health problems. In the 1800s, deaths by liver cirrhosis and chronic alcoholism were 25 per 100,000 people,[45] more than twice what it is now. Given these problems, the existence of a national prohibition law (1919–1933) can in part be viewed as pro-family legislation.[46]

In the second half of the 18th century, temperance crusaders turned from using moral persuasion to legal coercion.[47] Some 17 states adopted prohibition laws, although by 1903, all but three abandoned them.[48,49]

Making alcohol illegal was preceded by the formation and mutual support of various temperance movement organizations, including the Prohibition Party (1869), which offered candidates for election, and the Woman's Christian Temperance Union (WCTU, 1874). Perhaps the best-known WCTU temperance activist was **Carry Nation** (Figure 1.12) who went into saloons with a hatchet, ripping kegs open and scolding drinkers. She was arrested more than 30 times for these "hatchitations."

Prohibition was ratified as the 18th Amendment to the Constitution in 1919, the same year Congress passed the **National Prohibition Act**, more commonly known as the **Volstead Act**, as the legal means for enforcing the new amendment. The making, manufacturing, selling, bartering, transporting, importing, exporting, and delivery of alcohol were made illegal, with the exception that 200 gallons of alcohol could be made annually by homeowners for their own consumption. However well intended, national prohibition resulted in a large, illicit market for alcohol that gangsters fought violently to control. They smuggled "booze" from Canada and across the ocean in "rum runner" boats, set up illegal breweries and stills, and hijacked their rivals' liquor convoys. Illegal bars called **speakeasies** were established, so named because at their entrances customers spoke the password softly before entering and drinking. In New York City alone, there were an estimated 32,000 speakeasies.[50] "**Bootlegger**" was a flexible term meaning people who made, smuggled, or transported liquor. It was also used to refer to people who had a flask slipped into their boots or held one on their leg by a garter (Figure 1.13).

The prohibition era is a prime example of the law of unintended consequences. It did more to damage the image and

FIGURE 1.12 ▶ The family Bible recorded her name as Carry Nation (1846–1911), although it is habitually misspelled as "Carrie." She referred to herself as "a bulldog running along at the feet of Jesus, barking at what He doesn't like." (Library of Congress Prints and Photographs Division [LC-B2- 1131-3])

FIGURE 1.13 ▶ A 1922 "bootlegger" and "flapper." Tired of the strict roles set for "proper ladies," flappers asserted their independence during the 1920s by challenging conventional notions about how women should behave. "Shockingly," they wore make-up, danced, dressed "provocatively," wore their hair bobbed, smoked and drank in speakeasies. (Library of Congress Prints and Photographs Division [LC-USZ62-99952])

reputation of policing than any other single event. To protect their operations, gangsters bribed police, judges, and other public officials to "look the other way" on a massive scale. The police professionalization movement was hampered and law enforcement suffered a self-inflicted black eye that lingered for decades afterward. Still, officers of integrity continued to enforce the law (Figure 1.14). In Chicago, Eliot Ness, a federal Treasury agent, and 10 agents he handpicked were known as the **untouchables** because they couldn't be "bought."

Prohibition also resulted in 1,300 breweries being closed,[51] causing thousands of people to lose their jobs and fewer tax dollars flowing to governments. Less well recognized is that prohibition created the environment in which organized crime could be invented,[52] or at least systematized, and gain a tenacious grip on public officials. Because prohibition laws were widely flaunted, many people developed a diminished regard for the law and authority.

Recognizing the widespread disobedience to the Volstead Act and the many ills associated with it, Congress abolished the Volstead Act in 1931. Two years later, the 21st Amendment repealed the 18th Amendment. Still, the damage done to public

esteem for government and its officials lingered on for years, and organized crime continues to plague our society.

The Lawless Years: Late 1920s to 1930s

Overlapping with the later portion of the prohibition period, the lawless, or gangsters', era lasted from the late 1920s and into the mid-1930s, when criminals filled their pockets with spectacular bank robberies and kidnappings, known as the "**snatch racket**." These bandits operated in the same era as prohibition gangsters, but were independent of them, specializing in robbing "soft targets," small banks, and snatching wealthy people from their unprotected homes.

In the crash of October 1929, the stock market lost 80 percent of its value, wiping out billions of dollars of wealth. Millions of people became unemployed, lost their homes and farms, and consumer spending dried up. The severe droughts in the American prairie states during 1930–1936 created a "**dustbowl**" as fertile topsoil got blown away. More people lost everything and

FIGURE 1.14 ▶ New York City police pour alcohol seized in a 1921 speakeasy raid into the sewer system. (Library of Congress Prints and Photographs Division [LC-USZ62-123257])

immigrated, seeking a better life elsewhere, many going to California. Collectively, these immigrants were called **Okies** because so many of them, between 400,000 and 500,000, fled Oklahoma; the plight of these families was memorialized in John Steinbeck's *The Grapes of Wrath*[53] (1939; Figure 1.15). In response to these migrations, some cities established "**bum blockades**" manned by police officers to turn back everyone who lacked sufficient funds to support themselves[54] so they wouldn't be a drain on local resources. In California, the police sold license plates at the state line blockades as a partial test of finances. The bum blockades also created negative opinions of the police among those who were turned away.

During the depression, as a means to ensure that jobs went to local taxpayers and to help the local tax base, city and county governments enacted **residency requirements** mandating that employees live within the jurisdiction of the employing unit of government and existing employees had to meet the same standard to keep their jobs.[55] Critics of the requirement argue that it places officers in a difficult situation. They had to choose between living in better neighborhoods, which they found difficult to afford and living in lower income areas where their children may have to attend marginal schools.[56]

However difficult the 1930s, law enforcement, surprisingly, gained some momentum, moving away from its tarnished image and toward increased legitimacy and authority in society. President Hoover appointed the **National Commission on Law Observance and Law Enforcement** in 1929, the

first comprehensive study of crime and policing in America's history. It was commonly referred to as the **Wickersham Commission**, taking the name of its chairman. The Wickersham Commission issued its report in 1931, consisting of 14 volumes, much of it written by August Vollmer. Among its recommendations was support for civil service protection for the police and enhanced training and education. Major academic police programs sprang up or expanded at the University of California, Berkeley; Michigan State University; and Northwestern University.[57]

The importance of separating police and politics gained additional impetus as law enforcement associations emerged. In 1934, the **International Association of Chiefs of Police (IACP)** was formed.[58] The IACP issued a newsletter, creating a common perception of what was important to the profession. The FBI established its crime laboratory in 1932, which provide free analysis of evidence submitted by state and local police agencies. Two years later the FBI launched its prestigious **National Police Academy (NA, 1934)** to train police executives, resulting in a core of knowledgeable leaders. As the next decade began in 1940, the **National Sheriffs Association (NSA)** came into being.

The kidnapping and murder of the infant son of "Lucky Lindy" Lindbergh, the first man to complete a trans-Atlantic flight, led to the adoption of the federal Kidnapping Act (1932), which gave the Federal Bureau of Investigation (FBI) jurisdiction over such crimes.

FIGURE 1.15 ▶ Her tough life is carved into the face of this 32-year-old mother. With her seven children, she lived in a migrant pea picker camp near Nipomo, California. Note the condition of the clothes, the kerosene lantern, and the canvas tent. Because the early pea crop failed, the camp is destitute. The parents of this family have just sold the tent in order to buy food for their family. (Library of Congress Prints and Photographs Division [LC-USF34-9093-C])

In some circles, bank robbers achieved celebrity status, with colorful names such as "Pretty Boy" Floyd, "Creepy Karpis," and "Handsome Harry" Piermont. Because these bandits moved rapidly from one state to another, frustrating state and local investigators who lacked wider jurisdiction, the Congress passed the federal Bank Robbery Act (1934) and tasked the FBI with its enforcement. Fairly quickly, the FBI apprehended or killed notorious bank robbers resisting arrest, making it a very dangerous occupation. **John Dillinger** (1903–1934), who may have robbed two dozen banks, was killed in a gunfight with FBI agents outside of a Chicago theater, marking the end of the lawless era.[59]

The Ku Klux Klan: Formation to the 1930s

Like the situation in prohibition, the relationship between some law enforcement officers and the Ku Klux Klan (KKK, see Figure 1.16) was toxic, producing effects that have lingered for decades. The KKK was formed in Pulaski, Tennessee in 1866 by Confederate Army veterans who were bored and wanted to create a mysterious stir at parties.[60] They made up names for themselves such as Grand Cyclops and Imperial Wizard, and wore masks and robes made from sheets by the wife of a founding member. However, quite quickly the agenda shifted

from fun to repressing former slaves, referred to as freedmen, first by intimidation tactics and then by violence.

The KKK essentially took over some of the duties that **slave patrols** held until the end of the civil war. Those patrols, usually of three to six persons,[61] could enter any plantation and search, without warrant, slave quarters, disperse all slave meetings, hunt down fugitive slaves, and administer impromptu punishments as they saw fit.[62] Many Southerners tolerated or approved of the Klan's activities. Freeing the slaves upset the status quo and created chaos. The KKK repression of African-Americans had the potential to maintain white supremacy and "restore order,"[63] warding off feared depredations by them, creating some resemblance to the pre-1865 South.

Southern state and local legislatures quickly adopted **Black Codes** in reaction to losing the Civil War; the codes were intended to keep African-Americans "inferior." During 1880–1960, **Jim Crow laws** added more restrictions. The name Jim Crow was taken from a minstrel show character, played by white actors who blackened their faces with burnt cork and presented a grotesque caricature of African-Americans.

Together, the Black Codes and Jim Crow laws made a mockery of equality. It was all but impossible for African-Americans to vote, and they were prohibited from assembling unless a White person was present. Separate facilities, including

FIGURE 1.16 ▶ A KKK parade, circa 1921. The participation of children was intended to indoctrinate them in hate. (Library of Congress Prints and Photographs Division [LC-F81-43556])

telephone booths and cemeteries, were mandated, it was illegal to teach Blacks how to read or write, and mixed marriages were forbidden. Enforcement of these laws caused the police to drop even lower in the estimation of African-Americans.

To combat the KKK and the Black Codes, the Republican-dominated Congress passed laws to "reconstruct" the south (1865–1877) into something that approximated life in the northern states. Reformists of all types, primarily from New England, flooded the South, many with the selfless intention of helping the South "to raise itself." Others arrived with the intention of simply making profits and gaining power. The "uninvited do-gooders" that came south with their alien ideas were derisively lumped together by southerners as **carpet-baggers**, so called because their luggage was cheaply made of second-hand carpet.

The federal **Forces Act** (1870) was passed in response to the actions of the KKK. Prosecutions under the Act resulted, for the most part, in the disintegration of the Klan, although arguably state and local legislative bodies had substantially achieved White supremacy through the Black Codes. Since the reconstruction following the Civil War, the KKK has reinvented itself several times (see Figure 1.16 and Chapter 3, Intelligence, Terrorism, and Homeland Security).

Lynchings are often associated with the KKK, but were not unique to it. The term is derived from the name of Charles Lynch (1736–1796) of Virginia. During the tumultuous American Revolution, he led a group of people who took the law into their own hands to deal with criminals. At its earliest meaning, **lynching** meant rough justice and often only involved a severe beating.

Later, it became synonymous with hanging someone without the legal authority to do so.[64,65,66]

Nationally, lynching was a ferocity that was substantially race based against African-Americans, Chinese, Hispanic, and Native American victims.[67] Before these lynchings, some victims were beaten or tortured.[68] Some of these grisly acts were conducted in sight of African-American enclaves and their church congregations as a means of intimidation.[69]

Lynchings were often based on mere suspicion or an accusation. At least occasionally, law enforcement officers led the posses that apprehended and lynched the "offender." In other instances, police officials released prisoners to lynch mobs or failed to intervene when mobs seized African-Americans and executed them. An ugly truth is that some officers were also Klan members. Lynchings tainted police race relations across generations, creating a hostility toward, and an abiding suspicion of, the police, often manifested by a lack of co-operation.[70]

THE 1940S AND 1950S: WAR, FEAR OF COMMUNISM, AND THE PROFESSIONAL MODEL REASSERTED

These two decades were dominated by World War II and the Korean War (1950–1953). The mobilization of able-bodied men for military service created opportunities for women in policing and the defense industry. The police took on new responsibilities as part of the war effort, the civil rights movement was born, there was substantial fear of communism, and the publication of O.W. Wilson's **Police Administration** reaffirmed the professional model of policing.

The 1940s: World War II and Some Progress for Women in Policing

The 1940s were defined by America's involvement in World War II, which lasted some four years after Operation Z, the Japanese attack on Pearl Harbor, Hawaii (December 7, 1941).

The men in public safety agencies had no exemptions from compulsory military service and they volunteered and were drafted in great numbers. Departments quickly turned their attention to the new staffing realities: (1) the remaining officers did not meet military physical standards and/or were too old for military service. For the duration of the war, there would not be better police applicants and (2) women could be part of the staffing solution.

Although small numbers of women had been hired as police officers since 1920, the war opened the door to more of them, but they were often assigned to specialty duties such as dealing with juvenile delinquents and shoplifting. This practice was the norm for several decades thereafter (Figure 1.17). The **Civil Rights Act of 1964** invalidated Jim Crow laws. Title VII of the Act forbade businesses to discriminate in hiring, promoting, and firing on the basis of sex, race, color, religion, and national origin, but state and local units of government were excluded from this requirement until the passage of the **Equal Employment Opportunity Act of 1972**, which amended Title VII. Functionally, this opened the door for women to be used in all types of assignments, including patrol, and fostered more minority hirings. Police duties during World War II expanded to civil defense tasks in some jurisdictions as they were tasked with such responsibilities as directing the work of air wardens. Concerned about air raids and shelling from submarines, **air raid warden** units were formed around the country, staffed by women, civic and fraternal groups, Boy Scouts, and other volunteers. Among their duties were checking to make sure no lights were showing, which our enemies could see and use to navigate toward their targets. Downtown areas were dark and windows everywhere were outfitted with dark shades. Nonetheless, a few attacks did occur.[71]

Law enforcement was engaged in combating forged **ration books**, which limited the amount of commodities (e.g., butter, gas, and meat) that the public could buy in order to redirect those goods to a rapidly expanding military. Civilians supported the war effort with **victory gardens** (see Figure 1.18), planting vegetables and fruit to meet some of their own food needs.[72]

When the war ended, veterans came home, the domestic market for goods heated up, and jobs were plentiful in an expanding economy. Some numbers of veterans made a smooth transition from the military to police departments because of the preference given to military veterans in hiring and their familiarity with responsibility, wearing a uniform, a hierarchical organizational structure, and formal ranks.

Now past the pain of the depression and the war, prosperity seemed within the grasp of Americans. New highways were built, and factories that had produced tanks now churned out cars. Many people who suddenly joined the middle class left the cities for the newly developing suburbs, purchased with the help of veterans' benefits. The Levitt brothers built so many suburban homes that a generic name for any suburb became "Levitt Town."

A novelty in the 1940s, television expanded in the 1950s as quickly as radio stations did following World War I. The New York City Police Department rapidly seized on TV for administration purposes and to broadcast lineups of suspects to police precincts located conveniently for victims.

The 1950s: The Korean War, Fear of Communism, and the Professional Model Reasserted

For the most part, interest in the police waned during the 1950s, as new issues came to the fore, including urban congestion and the perception that traditional values were on the decline.[73] O.W. Wilson's *Police Administration* (1950) essentially validated the military model, whose core operational philosophy was R2I: respond to incident. Crime was thought to be prevented and apprehensions made by random, aggressive patrol in all areas of the city

---

Quick Facts: Japanese Attacks on the American Homeland

In 1942, a Japanese sub surfaced off the coast of California. Sixteen shells from a deck-mounted gun were fired at the Ellwood Oil Field near Santa Barbara, causing little damage. That same type of attack occurred again later that year when a Japanese sub followed fishing boats transiting from the Pacific Ocean up the Columbia River in Oregon.

Intending to start a forest fire, a seaplane launched from a Japanese sub dropped incendiary bombs on a heavily wooded section of Oregon. Japan also lauched 9,000 balloons into the Pacific Jet Stream. Fire bombs and/or anti-personnel mines were suspended underneath the balloons. Only 342 are known to have reached the United States. Some of the balloons were carried as far as Arizona, Kansas, and Michigan, but none caused major fires. A Sunday school teacher and five of her 13- and 14-year-old students were killed by a balloon, the only mainland American civilian casualties that occurred during World War II.

FIGURE 1.17 ▶ The door to a police career opened a little wider for these women taking the 1947 New York City Police Department entrance examination. (Library of Congress Prints and Photographs Division [LC-USZ62-136823])

FIGURE 1.18 ▶ Spring 1943, planting a victory garden for personal consumption at an unspecified location. Even small children were involved in this effort. (Library of Congress Prints & Photographs Division [LC-USE6-D-009201])

at all times. *Police Administration* quickly became the "Bible" for law enforcement executives, who were guided by it as they sought to find the optimum way to organize and staff the units in their agency and achieve the most efficient operations. Written policies and procedures manuals became more common and comprehensive.

On the streets, officers who were combat veterans watched rookie officers closely. The veterans would tolerate rookies who drank too much, ran around on their spouses, and were bill dead-beats,[74] but if a rookie couldn't be counted on in a fight, the veterans would run him off. This value may account for some portion of the belief in police circles that women were ill-equipped for patrol work. In that era and several decades that followed, it was widely thought that physically women wouldn't be able to handle the rough hands-on part of policing. The "weaker sex" continues to invalidate sterotypes of them: In 2015, two of the new graduates of the Army's Ranger School were women.

The Korean War (1950–1953) saw the recall of many World War II veterans, including some law enforcement officers, who had joined or stayed in reserve and National Guard units. Because the Korean War was confined to one peninsula and, thus, was a war fought on a smaller scale, the impact on police staffing was far less than that of World War II.

In 1953, Ethel and Julius Rosenberg were executed for divulging nuclear bomb secrets to the Soviet Union. The Soviet Union beat the United States into space in 1957 with the first satellite, Sputnik, causing concerns about communists using the bomb to rule the world from space. In addition, Castro's rise to power in Cuba (1959) put communism on our doorstep and Senator Joseph McCarthy ran roughshod, searching everywhere for communists, until he was discredited.

Rosa Parks (1913–2005), an African-American woman riding a public bus in Montgomery, Alabama, refused to give up her seat up to a White man on December 1, 1955, and was arrested (see Figure 1.19). Reverend **Martin Luther King, Jr.**, a 26-year-old minister in that city, organized a bus boycott by African-Americans that lasted 381 days and reduced bus revenues by 80 percent.[75] The incident birthed the Civil Rights movement. The next year, federal courts ordered the desegregation of the bus system.

Although African-Americans had served as lawmen in the West after the Civil War, their numbers were not large. Some municipalities with large African-American populations, including Washington, DC (1861), Chicago and New Orleans (1872), and Charleston, South Carolina (1873), began hiring minorities at the onset and after the Civil War to police their "own kind." During the 1950s, more substantial representation was achieved. In *Brown v. Board of Education* (1954), the Supreme Court ruled that segregation was illegal, although the ruling was more often ignored than followed. Nationally, real progress in the hiring and promotion of African-Americans was not made until the succession of civil rights bills previously noted was passed during the 1960s and 1970s.

During the 1950s and extending into the mid-1960s, a small number of Southern cities still had the problem of the "**unequal badge**." In those cities, African-American officers were not allowed to arrest a White person because of the fear it might trigger a riot. Therefore, minority officers could not drive patrol cars for a similar reason; it was believed that White motorists would not accept a ticket from an African-American officer.[76] This resulted in the practice of majority officers dropping their African-American counterparts off at their walking beats in minority business districts at the

FIGURE 1.19 ▶ Mourners file past the casket of Rosa Parks, the mother of the Civil Rights movement, in the Rotunda of the U.S. Capitol, Washington, DC. Honoring a private citizen in this manner is rare. She is the first woman to be so recognized. (Mandel Nfgan/AFP/Getty Images)

beginning of a shift and picking them up afterward. Minorities subtly retaliated by getting into the back seat when being picked up, making it appear White officers were their chauffeurs.

In 1959, the California **Peace Officers Standards and Training Commission (POST)** was legislatively created to set minimum standards for the selection and training of police officers. Although some states followed suit during the early 1960s, many POST units were not created until the late 1960s and early 1970s when federal grant funds from the now-defunct federal Law Enforcement Assistance Administration (LEAA) were available. POST units play an important role in police professionalization. They essentially constitute a professional licensing board and can revoke an officer's certificate to hold a job with any public law enforcement agency in the state that issued it.

THE TURBULENT 1960s: RIOTS, POLITICAL PROTESTS, ASSASSINATIONS, AND THE ISOLATION OF THE RANK AND FILE

World War II regained international attention with the trial (1961) of Adolph Eichmann in Israel for his role in the holocaust. Closer to home, the Bay of Pigs, the American-sponsored Cuban invasion (1961), intended to topple Castro, failed. Further concerns about the "commies" controlling outer space were sparked

when the Soviet Union launched the first man into orbit (1962). The Soviets ignited the Cuban Missile Crisis in October 1962 by placing nuclear weapons in Cuba, and war seemed terrifyingly imminent. Although Russian Premier Khrushchev quickly removed the weapons, the practical effect was that Castro's hand was strengthened. We agreed not to invade or sponsor further invasions of Cuba.

Domestically, the 1960s was a staggering decade for our society as smoldering racial, social, and economic tensions erupted. In 1965, these tensions boiled over in Los Angeles' Watts neighborhood. A White California Highway Patrol motorcycle officer stopped Marquette Frye, an African-American, for drunk driving. Frye's brother was also in the car and the men's mother soon appeared. Los Angeles officers arrived to assist as African-Americans congregated at the scene. Events spiraled out of control, rocks were thrown at the officers, and all three Fryes were arrested. Six days of looting, sniping, and arson followed in Watts, 34 people were killed, most of them were minorities, and losses amounted to $200 million before an uneasy peace was restored.

Over the next three years, more than two dozen major cities were struck by similar riots. The 1967 Detroit riot could not be controlled by local officers and elements of the state police and Michigan's National Guard. Ultimately, it took the presence of two brigades, one each from the 82nd and 101st Airborne Divisions to restore order. The following year in Washington, DC, a riot broke out the day the Reverend Martin Luther King was assassinated in Memphis, Tennessee. It was only quelled with the assistance of nearly 14,000 troops (see Figure 1.20), although rioters came within two blocks of the White House before being forced back.

The causes cited across all of these riots were fundamentally the same: high rates of minority unemployment; poor housing;

FIGURE 1.20 ▶ Army soldier on duty during the 1968 riot in Washington, DC. The smoldering building in the background is an indicator of the wider damage. (Library of Congress Prints & Photographs Division [LC-U9-18949-12])

White store owners who took money from the minority communities but showed no reciprocity, such as jobs for them; a segregated and unequal society; and police officers viewed as hostile and repressive, a force of occupation to maintain the status quo.

The first mass murder on an American university campus occurred at the University of Texas in 1966. In today's lexicon, there was an active shooter on campus. **Charles Whitman** brought an assortment of firearms, including a scoped rifle, to the 28th floor of a campus building and began shooting. Before he was stopped, Whitman killed 14 people and wounded 32 others. He died a few days later of wounds inflicted by the police. To some degree, the incident helped transform campus security departments from simply being unarmed watchmen to professional police agencies.

In 1967, the first national study of police since the Wickersham Report (1931) was completed. President Johnson's Commission on Law Enforcement and Administration of Justice issued a summary report, *The Challenge of Crime in a Free Society*. The study was supplemented by task force reports on the police, organized crime, and other topics. The organization of the Commission's report paralleled the Cleveland Foundation's use in 1922 of subordinate working groups to study specific areas. Among the recommendations made was that police officers should have college degrees. The 1968 report from the **National Advisory Commission on Civil Disorders**, the Kerner Commission, which also took the name of its chair, Ohio Governor Otto Kerner, simply confirmed what everyone knew were the causes of riots. It also acknowledged the confusing demands being placed on law enforcement: One side saw the police as maintaining order at the expense of justice, whereas the other demanded tougher enforcement.[77]

The Kerner Commission didn't start the role debate, but it certainly added credence, as did The *Challenge of Crime in a Free Society*, to the need to have such a discussion. As stated earlier, at the core of the military model was the belief that there was a war on crime led by the police. Their duty was ferreting out crime, conducting investigations, making arrests, and assisting with the prosecution of offenders. Others suggested that the police needed to be something more than that or risk forever being seen as the "bullies" of a culturally divided society. During the 1960s, the police, albeit slowly and under pressure, began a metamorphosis from just being crime fighters. Their role enlarged to being conflict managers, community relations specialists, and a conduit to social welfare agencies.

Meanwhile, other events in the 1960s were also changing the world-view of police officers. There were hippies, psychedelic drugs, massive demonstrations against the Vietnam War, draft evaders and military deserters, civil rights marches and demonstrations, the beginning of open emergence by gays, the burgeoning women's rights movement, the passage of civil rights legislation discussed earlier, and Supreme Court decisions, such as the restrictions placed on police interrogations by *Miranda v. Arizona* (1966). Native Americans sought more control over their lands and **Cesar Chavez** unionized mostly Mexican farm workers in the Southwest to provide them with better working conditions and wages.

Chicago police clashed repeatedly with demonstrators at the 1968 Democratic National Convention. Both sides used excessive force. The demonstrators threw apples into which razor blades had been inserted, vials containing urine, and garbage can lids at the police. Such provocations do not, however, excuse the out-of-control behavior exhibited by the police on some occasions.

Further evidence to the police that our society was unraveling during the 1960s were the assassinations of President Kennedy (1917–1963) in Dallas[78]; Robert Kennedy (1925–1968), the dead President's brother, who was campaigning for the presidency in Los Angeles; and the civil rights leader, Reverend Martin Luther King, Jr. (1929–1968), who was supporting a sanitation workers strike in Memphis. On April 4, 1968, the Reverend Martin Luther King, Jr., stepped outside of his hotel room and was shot to death by James Earl Ray (1928–1998, see Figure 1.21). The day before, in Memphis, the Reverend King gave perhaps his most notable address, "I've Been to the Mountaintop."

A new world was unfolding that the police did not understand and in which they felt isolated and unsupported. In this milieu, police professionalism took on new urgency. Before the 1960s, police departments, as an entry-level educational attainment, commonly required a tenth-grade to a high school degree, or its counterpart, the general equivalency degree (GED). The first major law enforcement agency to require a college degree was the Multnomah County Sheriff's Office (Oregon) in 1965,[79] although in most cases, if any college was required it usually amounted to 6 to 12 semester hours. Other departments hired officers with the understanding that they would complete a certain number of hours within a specified time period after appointment or forfeit their jobs. Police locker rooms were polarized as the less-educated portion of the older officers taunted younger, college-attending officers with requests to "Talk some psychology" and "Say some sociology to me." The kindest epithets hurled at officers working on a degree were "egghead" and "educated idiot." On campus degree-seeking police officers were subject to cries of "police spy" if their occupation was discovered by other students. While a very small number of departments required a college degree as an entry-level credential, the vast majority remained at a high school education or a General Equivalency Degree (GED).

Nonetheless, in policing, "professional" slowly became synonymous with "education" from roughly 1965–1967 onward. Education was seen as a means of improving community relations, which were generally poor before the urban riots and also contributed to their advent, and of reducing police violence, promoting more judicious use of police discretionary decision making, countering corruption as a competing model, and redefining the role of policing our society.[80] From the late 1960s until the mid-1970s, there was a quick proliferation of police administration and criminal justice programs in community colleges and universities.

Some impetus to college education for officers came in programs adopted by progressive communities. Those officers with college degrees got an additional 5 or 10 percent above the normal salary and those without a degree could work on a

FIGURE 1.21 ▶ The Lorraine Hotel, Memphis, Tennessee. Reverend King, a Nobel Peace Prize winner (1964), occupied room 306. (Library of Congress Prints and Photographs Division [LC-DIG-highsm-04695])

degree and get some reimbursement for the cost, based on their final grade.[81] Tuition for an "A" was reimbursed 100 percent, a "B" 50 percent, and a "C" 25 percent. Officers were not normally reimbursed for the cost of their books. Beginning in 1968, the federal Law Enforcement Education Program (LEEP), an arm of LEAA, provided up to $2,400 a year to help defray college education costs for criminal justice majors. Repayment could be accomplished by a 25 percent loan forgiveness formula for each year of service with a public criminal justice agency, up to a maximum of four years/100 percent.

Character and background checks became more robust, and the use of polygraphs and credit checks became more standard. Some psychological screening was done, although it often involved the general practitioner conducting the entry-level physical exam to simply state that no abnormalities were observed. The most important leap in the quality of applicant screening was the result of standards set by emerging POSTs.

The professionalization movement during the 1950s and 1960s shaped the role of the police and created a sense of pride and unity among officers. However, in the second half of the 1960s, police unity was redirected as a result of riots and civil rights demonstrations, Supreme Court decisions "handcuffing" the police, a spiraling crime rate, an increasingly critical press, a perceived lack of public support, and the creation of civilian review boards to investigate allegations of police misconduct fueled police suspicions of being under attack.

Officers saw administrators as trying to bring unwanted change into their world and dismissed the "bosses" as being out of touch with the realities of police work on the street. Together, these events resulted in the police rank and file feeling they were isolated and unsupported, creating a "we against them" mentality that propelled them to join unions as states began passing public sector collective bargaining laws in the 1960s. Unions created a new power center in police departments, exciting officers and alarming administrators.

THE 1970s: RESEARCH, EXPERIMENTATION, AND RISING TERRORISM

Wadman and Allisan wrote, "The 1970s are generally regarded as a period of malaise in American history . . . the Vietnam War ended without a sense of closure [1975], the **Watergate Scandal** intensified distrust of government . . . the economic downturn reduced budgets, limiting the ability of the police to innovate . . . and traditional police concepts made it difficult for communities to influence police priorities and programs."[82] President Nixon's 1974 resignation while facing impeachment grew out of the burglary of the Democratic National Committee headquarters at the Watergate Office Complex in Washington, DC. The burglary was initially tied to the Republican Committee to Reelect the President and then to members of President Nixon's staff. As a result of Watergate, 61 percent of Americans expressed distrust of government—a burden on all public agencies, including the police. Prior events may have also fed this distrust, including the killing of four Kent State University students by members of the Ohio National Guard (1970) who fired on the demonstrators[83] and disillusionment with the Vietnam War. Because police officers also tried to control protests, they were often bitterly resented by demonstrators who labeled them "pigs."[84]

Once again, the country seemed to be coming unglued. Presidential candidate George Wallace was shot and paralyzed while campaigning in Maryland (1972)[85] and there were two assassination attempts on President Ford's life in an 18-day period (1975). Against this social backdrop, important things were occurring in policing. The previously mentioned *Challenge of Crime in a Free Society* found, "There is no subject connected with crime or criminal justice into which further research is unnecessary."[86] Doig reached the same conclusion, declaring that law enforcement was a *terra incognita*, an unknown land.[87] During the 1970s, with grants from LEAA, there was a torrent of research. An early trilogy of major experiments rocked policing: (1) the **Kansas City Preventive Patrol Study**, (2) the **Rand Criminal Investigation Study**, and (3) the **team policing** experiment.

The Kansas City Preventive Patrol Study examined three types of patrol services to see what difference each made:

1. *Reactive districts* received no regular patrol; officers who responded to calls entered and left the district by the shortest routes.
2. *Proactive districts* were saturated with two to three times the normal amount of patrolling.
3. *Control districts* maintained regular or normal patrolling.

The study found no significant differences in reported crime, arrests, traffic accidents, fear of crime, or security measures among the three types of districts. As local governmental leaders learned of the results, some refused to fund requests for additional police officers. The findings were controversial and dismissed by police leaders as being a lone and methodologically flawed study.

The Rand (Corporation) Criminal Investigation Study sought to determine what factors contribute to the success of criminal investigations, and just what it is that detectives do. Focusing on serious crimes, the study concluded that the preliminary investigations conducted by patrol officers provided the information that led to the solution of most crimes. Critics of detectives said it confirmed suspicions of their value, while police leaders labeled it "one, unreplicated study." Like the Kansas City Study, the finding also became an issue in police budgets for a period of time.

Team policing was a bold reform effort to reshape how police resources were used and to reduce the amount of specialization by using patrol officers in a variety of roles, such as plainclothes assignments.[88] Roughly 20 to 30 officers were formed into teams, under the 24-hour direction of a single commander who controlled how they were deployed. By the end of the 1970s, team policing vanished due to the problems of implementation and the opposition of mid-level police managers who correctly saw that it reduced their importance. The experiment increased appreciation of the capabilities of patrol officers and helped set the stage for community policing, which exploded during the 1980s.

Around 1970, there was a movement toward new organizations. In 1969, the **International Association of Police Women (IAPW)**, with roots that date back to 1926, adopted its current name. A number of state-level women officers associations belong to IAWP. The **National Association of Women Law Enforcement Executives (NAWLEE)** also advocates for women's issues in policing. The formation of the federal **National Criminal Justice Reference Service (NCJRS**, 1972) created an easily accessible body of cutting-edge information for criminal justice students, scholars, and practitioners. **HAPCOA**, the Hispanic American Police Command Officers Association, was formed in 1973 to assist in the recruitment, training, and promotion of qualified Hispanic men and women and to advocate for Hispanic law enforcement issues. The **Police Executive Research Forum (PERF**, 1975) was formed by the largest city, county, and state agencies for the purpose of pursuing research and public policy work of particular interest to its members. The **National Organization of Black Law Enforcement Executives (NOBLE**, 1976) focuses on crime in low-income urban areas. The **Commission on Accreditation of Law Enforcement Agencies (CALEA**, 1979) was established with the support of the IACP, NSA, PERF, and NOBLE as an independent accrediting body for law enforcement agencies. CALEA accreditation can reduce liability insurance costs, be used as a tool in attracting new businesses to a community, and stimulates community pride and confidence in a community's police department. Although its formation falls in a later era, the **National Association of Asian American Law Enforcement Commanders (NAAALEC)** was created in 2002 to promote a positive police image in Asian/Pacific communities and to speak on topics of common concerns for its membership.

The **Greensboro Massacre** (North Carolina, 1979) was one of the most brutal and widely witnessed assaults on civil rights. Representatives of the Communist Workers Party, then known as the Workers Viewpoint Organization, were attempting to unionize African-American workers, when members of a KKK and American Nazi Party (ANP) caravan opened fire, killing 3 and wounding 10. A police intelligence officer and a police photographer were present, but the officer did not intervene. The incident was recorded by the news media and the nationally distributed pictures provided yet another example that the police would not protect minorities. When all-White juries in both state and federal trials failed to convict the attackers, the judicial process was also stained. Finally, at civil trial, five attackers and the police were found liable. A much larger police presence may have prevented any deaths.

Although terrorism is an ancient strategy, transnational terrorism began a march toward the present during the 1970s (see Chapter 3, Intelligence, Terrorism, and Homeland Security). On Black Sunday (1970), operatives of the **Popular Front for the Liberation of Palestine (PFLP)** hijacked four planes. The **Black September Organization (BSO)**, a Palestinian group, killed 11 Israeli athletes and team officials at the 1972 Olympic Games in Munich, some of whom died in a botched rescue attempt. Four years later, the PFLP, aided by two Germans from the Revolutionary Cells, hijacked an Air France jet and forced it to fly to the Entebbe Airport in Uganda.[89] The hijackers released all non-Jewish passengers but held their Jewish hostages in the terminal. The hijackers demanded the release of 53 Palestinians held in several countries in exchange. The Israel Defense Force (IDF) conducted a spectacular raid, freeing the hostages.[90] The success of the Entebbe raid may have encouraged President Carter to approve a military plan to free 53 American hostages held in Iran for more than a year. The raid failed and played a part in his defeat by Ronald Reagan.[91]

1980S TO THE 9/11 ATTACKS: THE COMMUNITY-ORIENTED POLICING ERA

Innovation in policing strategies occurred at a rapid pace during this 20-year period. Some came about as a result of the convergence of several phenomena, including the rise of terrorism from foreign and domestic sources, for example, al Qaeda's September 11, 2001 (9/11) attacks on the World Trade Centers and the Pentagon and **Timothy McVeigh's 1995** bombing of the federal building in Oklahoma City. The 2001 attacks produced the worst single day loss of life by American police officers: **72**. The call for more transparency in policing due to high-profile incidents involving law enforcement decision-making at **Ruby Ridge, Idaho** and in **Waco**, Texas, also produced innovations to gain and maintain community trust. Chapter 8 Planning and Decision Making addresses the impact of police decision making.

New strategies in policing also emerged. These new paradigms include **community-oriented policing (COP)**, **zero tolerance policing (ZTP)**, **CompStat**, **evidence-based policing (EBP)**, and **hot spot policing** (HSP). COP is the development of police strategies and programs in partnership with communities in order to deliver custom-tailored police services and solutions to problems, as well as a renewed focus on crime prevention rather than crime detection. ZTP was based on the premise that when small infractions of the law are ignored, it creates a climate conducive to more serious crimes being committed. The extension of this thinking was ZTP, which required non-discretionary enforcement for all crimes. CompStat, which was initially implemented in 1994 in the New York City Police Department, is a management control system designed to develop, analyze, and disseminate information about reported crime and to track efforts to deal with it.[92] Evidence-based policing (EBP) is based on data analysis of a constellation of sources, including intelligence, agency records, and scientific research. With the results of the analysis, strategies are selected or developed to attack the targeted problem.

Larry Sherman pioneered the notion of hot-spot policing by analyzing crime data. He concluded that a relatively few places/addresses in a city produced roughly half of all crimes. By concentrating on those locations, such as open air drug markets, specific bars, and other areas, crime could be reduced. Some of these new strategies, such as hot-spots, were later identified as "best practices," publicized, and adopted by many agencies.

Each of these paradigms are further discussed in detail in Chapter 2, Policing Today, along with other emerging approaches such as directed patrol and intelligence-led policing. However, it should be noted that of all of these approaches, COP had the quickest, and to date, the most widespread impact on policing. It produced an important impact on not only police operations, but also on the structure and culture of police organizations. Certainly, policing has dramatically changed since the days of August Vollmer and O.W. Wilson; policing has become much more proactive, focused on preventing not only crime but terrorism as well. Perhaps, no greater challenge confronts American policing today than the imperative to prevent the next terrorist attack on the American homeland.

THE NEW OPERATING ENVIRONMENT: POST-9/11 TO 2016

The new operating environment spans from post-9/11 to 2016. There are some periods in the history of police administration that have been fairly stable periods and others with some continuity mixed with some notable developments. The post-9/11 to 2016 period had some continuity, but there were also major events that substantially impacted law enforcement in ways that could not have been foreseen. This section touches on four subjects: (1) post-9/11 events and the war on terrorism, (2) the affect on the Great Recession of late 2007–2010 and the slow and mixed recovery that has followed, (3) police use of force issues that has shaken confidence in the police, reinvigorated the interest of the U.S. Department of Justice in investigating such incidents, and the impact of Baltimore police officers being criminally charged in the death of Freddie Gray, and (4) the Smart Policing Initiative and the Guardian Model.

(1) POST-9/11 EVENTS

Roughly six weeks after the 9/11 attacks, the Congress quickly passed major legislation, the USA Patriot Act, specifically aimed at combating terrorism. Other acts for the same purpose followed. As a result of the Patriot Act, state and local law enforcement's powers and role in combating terrorism were also expanded. These measures and other aspects of terrorism are discussed in Chapter 3, "Intelligence, Security, and Homeland Security.

A few foreign inspired attacks e.g., San Bernardino attack (2015) occurred post-9/11, but more deaths have been caused by domestic extremists. The absence of many more foreign attacks may be due to some combination of prevention, lack of potential attackers' capabilities, and absence of their present intent to conduct them. One thing is clear: Larger, more sophisticated terrorist networks with deep pockets are unlikely to abandon their zeal to strike grievous blows on American interests abroad and in our heartland. Their deep pockets are derived from: (1) quickly raiding banks and seizing all of their assets in conquered territories, (2) selling captured artwork, sculptures, and antiquities from museums, as well as those they loot from historical heritage sites, (3) sales of pirated copies of music and movies and counterfeited goods, for example, handbags by Gucci and Prada and pharmaceuticals, (4) drug production and distribution, and (5) in the particular case of the Islamic State (IS, aka ISIL), the capture in Iraq of stored oil, oil fields, and oil production facilities. ISIS also has an extensive fine and permit system, e.g., failure to correctly answer questions about Islam at a roadcheck is a $25 fine and charging people $800 to $1,000 for a permit to leave a city under its control.

In the brief sketches of terrorist attacks that follow, not all perpetrators were charged with terrorism, perhaps because murder or other significant felony crimes were easier to prove.

Among notable recent attacks are (1) a Memphis, Tennessee, American converted to Islam and murdered one person at a military recruiting station in Little Rock, Arkansas in 2009. At several points while in custody he claimed to be on jihad for al Qaeda.[93] Army Major Nidal Hasan, a Muslim who attended the same Virginia mosque as several of the 9/11 attackers and communicated with a radical Muslim cleric, went on a shooting rampage at Fort Hood, Texas, in 2009. He murdered 13 people and wounded in excess of 30 others, the largest mass murder on a military installation.[94] Tried before a military court, he received the death penalty. It is presently unclear whether he will actually be executed. Shot during his rampage, Hasan is now confined to a wheelchair. The federal government concluded that Hasan's actions were not terrorism, but workplace violence, a position with which many members of Congress and terrorism experts did not agree; (2) in 2010, smoke rising from a car in New York City's Times Square revealed a malfunctioning car bomb. The would-be bomber pleaded guilty to multiple charges, including terrorism;[95] (3) an American citizen planted a radio-controlled pipe bomb along the route of the Martin Luther King, Jr., Day memorial walk in Seattle in 2011. It was discovered in a suspicious backpack before it exploded. Three years later the perpetrator received a 32-year prison sentence;[96] (4) in the National Security Agency (NSA) Edward Snowden electronically stole American, British, and other files to which he had access in 2012. He described his motive as wanting to reveal the "illegal spying" the federal government was allegedly conducting against American citizens.[97] Some have praised him for revealing the "spying." However, those files revealed our methods, operations, capabilities, and other intelligence information. It is widely held by several countries' intelligence services, including our own, that his disclosure of some data did grave harm to national security. Presently he is thought to be in Russia and the extent of his betrayal is not fully known. He presently faces espionage charges in the United States, although Great Britain has entertained the possibility of terrorism charges based on their laws; (5) the American Consulate in Benghazi, Libya, was attacked by terrorists during 2012, and resulted in the deaths of the American Ambassador to Libya and several others. The failure of America to immediately send military support has been hotly discussed both in the military and the Congress; (6) the American Embassy

in Ankara, Turkey, was attacked in 2013 by a suicide bomber who was reportedly a member of a terrorist organization. That same year, two brothers born in the former Soviet Union were primarily responsible for detonating bombs at the Boston Marathon finish line. One brother was killed during a gun battle with the police and the other was convicted in 2015 of 30 charges, 17 of which carry the death penalty, to which he was sentenced;[98] and (7) in 2015, a married couple who were radicalized Muslims attacked a county training event/Christmas party, attended by the husband's coworkers, in San Bernardino, California, murdering 14 and wounding 22. Later that same day they were both killed in a shootout with law enforcement officers.[99]

(2) THE GREAT RECESSION

The economy has affected police departments considerably during and since the Great Recession, which lasted from December 2007 until 2010. Nationally, many law enforcement agencies have experienced deep cuts. Illustratively, Stockton, California, was in an economic boom until 2007, but subsequently was forced to lay off many of its police officers, firefighters, and other employees. The cuts were so severe that at one point the Stockton Police Department during portions of some days could only respond to crimes in progress. Chapter 12, "Financial Management," discusses the major events in Stockton's eventual bankruptcy.

As a result of the Great Recession, a number of municipalities closed their police departments, contracted with the sheriff or county police department for law enforcement services, consolidated with one or more other agencies, or entered bankruptcy. Elsewhere, some citizen groups began asking the question, "Can we afford our police department?" "Do we really need one that consumes so much of our city budget?" "Will we be better off with a smaller one?" A rule of thumb is that it takes a decade to recover from such a damaging recession.

The recovery has been slow and uneven, although here and there some cuts made have been partially restored by appropriators. Some police agencies may never return and for some time the others will be leaner with fewer services. Citizen associations have sprung up in some instances to self-police or do so with private security supplementing their efforts.

Despite some economic recovery, oil prices fell 70 percent between 2014 and 2016, producing an uneven ripple across high oil-producing states. Alaska is in fiscal turmoil over this development. In 2016, its budget was facing a $3.4 billion deficit and the state was considering enactment of a state income tax law. Cuts at all levels of Alaskan government were underway as this was written.

(3) SHAKEN CONFIDENCE IN POLICE USE OF FORCE AND PROSECUTION OF OFFICERS

Between 2014 and 2016, a series of police use of force cases were perhaps the transcendent event for law enforcement in the last decade. Some of the actions by police were highly criticized, a few produced riots, others resulted in criminal charges being levied against officers, and a few of them were convicted.

While not a comprehensive list, the following are among the most highly publicized police use of force cases during 2014–2016: (1) On August 9, 2014, a Ferguson, Missouri, White police officer shot and killed Michael Brown, a 17-year-old unarmed African-American who allegedly was trying to seize the officer's gun. The officer reported fearing for his life. Witness accounts varied and the Grand Jury declined to indict the officer. Several days of rioting occurred, during which shots were fired at police officers; (2) Eric Garner was a 43-year-old unarmed African-American man who police believed was illegally selling "loosies or singles" from cigarettes on July 17, 2014. Such sales deprive the state and city of a combined $6.95 in tax revenue on each pack and legal sellers lose business they might otherwise have had. In effecting the arrest, New York Police Department (NYPD) officers wrestled Garner to the ground. A White officer reportedly used a chokehold on him, a tactic not allowed under NYPD policy. Garner had trouble breathing and died in the hospital an hour later. The medical examiner attributed his death to several factors, including the chokehold and poor health. However, the Grand Jury also declined to indict the officer, who has received multiple death threats as a result of Garner's death. Large protestors' demonstrations occurred in New York City and several other major cities around the country, but no rioting occurred; (3) On October 20, 2014, a 17-year-old African-American male, Laquan McDonald, was walking approximately down the middle of a Chicago street brandishing a small knife, but not approaching officers. Several police officers were on the scene. When the teenager refused to obey commands to drop the knife a White officer shot him 16 times, killing him. Most of those shots were fired after the teenager lay unmoving in the road. None of the other officers fired a shot. The event was recorded by one of the police car's camera. A year later the officer was indicted for first-degree murder. The year-long delay in bringing charges against the officer resulted in the resignation of the Police Superintendent and demands for the Mayor to resign; (4) On April 4, 2015, a North Charleston, South Carolina, a police officer stopped a car driven by Walter Scott for a broken taillight. The unarmed 50-year-old African-American ran from the White police officer, who shot and killed him. An uninvolved citizen made a phone video of the shooting portion of the incident. The officer was charged with murder, but had not gone to trial as of early 2016; and (5) A small mixed race group of Baltimore, Maryland, police officers arrested a 25-year-old African-American Freddie Gray for possession of an illegal knife on April 12, 2015. In the process of arresting him he was placed face down on the pavement and his arms and legs placed in restraint.

Gray was placed in a police van to transport him to jail. However, the police wagon diverted to a hospital where he died of spinal cord injuries. The coroner's report concluded that a high-energy impact contributed to his death. This may have occurred in the police van. Days of riots followed. The officers involved were charged with various crimes and the Police Commissioner was later replaced following a surge in violent crime. The first officer tried ended in a hung jury. In 2016, the prosecution offered that officer immunity to testify against the officers whose trials were still pending. Chapter 4, "Politics and Police Administration" examines this incident and many of the related cases in detail.

As a result of these highly publicized events, the issue of police use of force became part of the conversations of Americans, for example, "This could happen here, to someone in my family." The U.S. Department of Justice quickly appeared to place more emphasis on investigating police use of force cases, particularly those involving deaths. In 2015, the University of Chicago Law School's Civil Rights and Police Accountability Clinic started an online database consisting of tens of thousands of Chicago Police Department misconduct complaints. In that same year, the Dallas, Texas, City Council approved a $1.6 million settlement to a mentally ill man who was wounded by one of its police officers. It was the largest settlement to a lone plaintiff in city history. Arguably, although the plaintiff's case had clear merit, with all the other negative media attention centered on incidents involving police use of deadly force, the city council may have wanted to make sure the suit was handled quickly and as quietly as possible. Major negative publicity about governments can hinder economic development. In such circumstances a city to which a major employee had been considering for relocating its business is sometimes eliminated and another jurisdiction selected.

Many law enforcement agencies quickly initiated reviews and made thoughtful changes to their use of force policies. In 2015, the Los Angeles, California, Police Commission began the process of creating a use of force policy that emphasized de-escalation and advocates minimum force whenever possible. In the following year, the State of Washington's legislature enacted a bill requiring a study of how officers in that state used deadly force. The Utah state legislature also took action in 2016. It created a state center at which officers would be trained in techniques to defuse situations and thereby decrease use of force incidents.

While some may argue that it appears too convenient for those few officers who make a mistake in the use of deadly force to claim were in fear of their lives under the "reasonable

Quick Facts: The "Ferguson Effect Versus the "Baltimore Effect"

The shooting death of Michael Brown and the riots that followed raised concerns that if police elsewhere have to resort to force, it might create trigger riots there too. This became known as the "Ferguson Effect." The "Baltimore Effect" is,

"I don't want to end up in prison, so I'll respond to the calls from dispatch, but other than that, I'm just going to ride around and not get involved."

Quick Facts: Fatal Shootings by Police Officers

With seven days left in 2015, U.S. police officers had fatally shot 965 people.[100] Of these, 564 were armed with a gun, 281 had another type of weapon, and 90 were unarmed. Although these numbers are large, they need to be put in context.

Based on 2008 data, one in every 67,000 face-to-face contacts with citizens in this country results in death from police use of force or approximately 0.0015 percent of the time.[101] There is a sanctity to all lives and hopefully the national media scrutiny, police-initiated changes, legislative mandates, and other actions following the events of 2014–2016 will save the lives of both citizens and officers.

officer" test established by the Supreme Court in *Graham v. Connor* (1989), it ignores two basic facts: (1) We can't really know what goes through an officer's mind under conditions of extreme stress and (2) a death caused by a police officer is always subject to investigation and arguably it should be done by a team from another agency which includes a member from the officer's department who is thoroughly familiar with its policies and practices. Perhaps the lack of indictments in police use of force cases may not be from a reluctance to do so, as much as that the test of the reasonable officer in *Graham v. Connor* may need to be revisited.

On January 16, 2016, the Police Executive Research Forum (PERF) issued its "Use of Force: Taking Policing to a Higher Standard" report, which covers 30 guiding principles for re-engineering police use of force.[102] PERF notes that about 200 chiefs, training directors, federal government representatives, academics, and mental health professionals participated in generating the 30 guiding principles.[103]

Because these principles were generated by professionals working on a crucial subject they inherently deserve careful consideration. It is therefore, somewhat surprising that the PERF report has been subject to some criticisms. The report implies that much is wrong in policing, when many agencies work hard and effectively on use of force issues. For example, PERF's Guiding Principle 1 is, "The sanctity of human life should be at the heart of everything an agency does."[104] However, even a cursory examination of this subject reveals a reverence for life by law enforcement agencies in their mission statements and use of force policies. Officers are also taught in the academy that when the need to preserve evidence at a crime scene and preserving a life are in conflict, the latter is always what is most important. In 2003, the Community Relations Service, U.S. Department of Justice, noted in its "Principles of Good Policing: Avoiding Violence Between Police and Citizens" that a police department must place its "highest value on the preservation of human life."[105] That wording appears in an unknown number of police mission statements and/or use of force policies. For many years, the American Civil Liberties Union has advocated the use of language similar to Guiding Principle 1. The PERF report is a good place to publicize use of force ideas, but pointing to already existing good practices should not have been neglected. In 2015, Ohio adopted a standard to be applied to its local and state governments, "The preservation of human life is of the highest value in the State of Ohio."

As a matter of risk management, Guiding Principle 2 also appears to miss the mark because it seeks to establish a higher standard for the use of force than the Supreme Court did in *Graham v. Connor*.[106] Adoption of this principle seemingly would expose governments to increased liability. The bottom line for government officials reading the 30 Guiding Principles is to ask key questions, such as "Is this different from what we do?" or "What value does it add?"

Thoughtful questions must be asked and carefully considered actions must be taken to reduce unnecessary and unlawful use of force cases. Some PERF principles will add to this process. There is also a larger view that cannot be ignored: Overwhelmingly law enforcement performs extremely well every day and exercises tactical restraint that doesn't show up in any statistics.

In 2015, FBI Director James Comey speculated that the rise in murders across the country over the past year may be associated with a "chill wind blowing through American law enforcement and its changing behavior . . .," officers don't want to get out of their cars and they are being taunted by people holding up smart phones with cameras. Comey went on to say that the national uproar about police officers shooting blacks is positive and a conversation that needed to be had.[107]

Criminal homicides and non-fatal shootings spiked in Baltimore following the indictments. Officers want to go home at the end of their shift and not to jail, court, or prison. Morale in Baltimore is low and officers are reluctant to do much beyond answering calls given to them. Arrests have plummeted. Some officers have quit because of the current environment and others seek "inside" jobs anywhere they can in the department.[108]

The death of Michael Brown in Ferguson may have tapped simmering rage or anger toward law enforcement officers. In just December 2014, there were multiple unprovoked attacks on peace officers: (1) shots were suddenly fired at a Los Angeles Police patrol car.[109] (2) two Pasco County (Florida) deputies were shot at while observing traffic conditions[110] and (3) two New York City police officers were murdered execution style while they sat in their car.[111]

Quick Facts: Tactical Restraint

Walking a beat in a high crime area, I turned a corner as two cars rolled past me. As a result, I didn't hear the first shot. What first drew my attention was pieces of bricks sliding down the side of the building on my left. I looked up to see what happened, heard the second shot, and saw it impact several feet above my head. As I turned back to the street, a man with a gun in his hand ran across the street in front of the store he had just robbed. He was now on my side of the street, just a short block ahead. He wheeled around, fired another shot, and took off running directly away from me like he was going to make the Olympic team. I had a sight picture on his back, but pulled my gun up. If I missed that shot, someone blocks down that sidewalk could have been killed. I chased the shooter, but he turned the next corner and vanished. His escape would have made Houdini proud. We never cleared that case.

Suppose I missed the shot and hit someone four blocks down the street. There is no do-over on it . . . you can't just wave your hand, mumble something, and un-shoot somebody. The old timers used to chuckle when they told stories about performing common law divorces by having a couple both place a hand on their badge and then saying a few solemn words to them. But, shooting at someone isn't a laughing matter . . . it's called deadly force for a reason.

A Birmingham, Alabama, plainclothes detective feared being labeled a racist and didn't counter force used against him by aggressive African-American man on a traffic stop. In this 2015 incident, the alleged assailant reportedly seized the White detective's gun and used it to beat him unconscious. The detective said he didn't use force against the man because he didn't want to be in the headlines for shooting an unarmed man. His attacker said he did it because of the recent shootings by police. Onlookers took pictures, but didn't come to the detective's assistance. One picture posted in the social media showed the detective lying on the ground under which the message was "Pistol whipped his ass to sleep" and another picture taunted the detective with a note that offered "milk and cookies for his nap."[112] A Harris County (Texas) Deputy Sheriff was executed in an unprovoked 2015 attack while he was fueling his car at a gas station. A man walked up, shot the deputy in the back of his head, and then shot at him 14 more times while the deputy was face down.[113] Other unprovoked attacks on law enforcement have also been reported, making a dangerous job all the more so.

Some state and local governments are finding difficulty in filling police officer vacancies.[114] As a result, some of these jurisdictions are waving the usual U.S. citizenship requirement and hiring green card holding immigrants legally in the country to fill the positions. Part of this difficulty may be that law enforcement jobs have become less attractive in the wake of the Baltimore indictments and the unprovoked attacks. The effect of employing immigrants who have legally entered this country remains to be analyzed. Parenthetically, green card holders are able to join the U.S. military to no apparent ill effect.[115]

(4) THE SMART POLICING INITIATIVE AND THE GUARDIAN MODEL

The Smart Policing Initiative (SPI) emerged in 2009 as a collaboration between the grant awarding federal Bureau of Justice Assistance, (BJA) and police agencies. The purpose of SPI is to encourage the refinement of existing evidence-based strategies and development of new ones. Participating law enforcement can get technical assistance from the CNA Corporation, which is under contract to the SPI. The evidence supporting evidence-based strategies is strong. However, an incomplete or flawed understanding of the strategy selected for implementation will jeopardize the success of the project.

The President's Task Force on 21st Century Policing released its final report in 2015 with a number of recommendations.[116] One of the most intriguing recommendations was that the law enforcement culture should embrace a guardian mind-set to build public trust and legitimacy. Law enforcement officers cannot do so if they cling to a "warrior" orientation as crime fighters. Plato wrote that in a republic that honors democracy, the greatest amount of power is given to those called Guardians, who protect the community from within it.

Implementing the Guardian role requires a major paradigm shift and such a shift would face some resistance. Even if policies and supervisory actions reinforce it, most police officers work without direct supervision. It is said that the street police culture has policies for lunch.[117] Nonetheless, although implementing the Guardian role will have some steep hills to climb, police executives should not be shrink from do it simply because it is hard. The implementation of community-oriented policing (COP) in the early 1980s faced a similar challenge. It may well be that COP is an effective precursor for the Guardian role. The Guardian role presently lacks a robust description. As time passes, descriptions of the Guardian role will emerge. Like some other matters in law enforcement, we should anticipate varying ways in which it is implemented, although some common core features are also likely to emerge.

Chapter Summary

Summary by Learning Objective

1. **List the events in England that led to the creation of the London Metropolitan Police.**

   These events included: (1) improved agricultural methods provided surplus crops to feed people living in cities; (2) people were drawn to cities by the industrial revolution which created jobs in cities; (3) as city populations grew, so did crime and social problems, which led to; (4) the need for the London Metropolitan Police.

2. **Describe the importance of the frontier closing in 1890.**

   The significance of the frontier closing in 1890 is that it marks the onset of the swift transition from a rural, agrarian society to an urbanized one in only 30 years.

3. **Define *politics* and give three reasons why it cannot be kept out of police agencies.**

   Politics is the process of acquiring and maintaining control over a government, including its policies, administration, and operations. The three reasons politics cannot be kept out of policing are: (1) police departments must be subject to democratic control, (2) public policy is where politics and administration intersect, and (3) politics exists, even in small police departments; what we want to do is keep the worst sort of politics—highly partisan—out of policing because of its long and most often unhealthy relationship with policing.

4. **Define and describe machine politics in the 19th century.**

   During the 1880s, machine politics was often a tightly controlled political party headed by a "Boss" or small autocratic group whose purpose was to repeatedly win elections for political gain, often through graft and corruption.

5. **Identify the most negative and positive things about the patronage/spoils system.**

   The worst abuse of the patronage/spoils system is when unqualified people are rewarded,, e.g., given a job for their political loyalty instead of their ability. Patronage that is not excessive or create inefficiencies is useful: Elected officials can appoint persons who agree with their policies, making governing easier.

6. **Explain why the concept of a police profession is so important.**

   The importance of policing being seen as a profession was fundamental to transforming the public view of the police from corrupt thugs and heavy-handed brutes to something more noble-professionals.

7. **Discuss the contributions of Chief Gus Vollmer.**

   Vollmer is the father of modern law enforcement. Under his leadership, the Berkeley (California) Police Department became a model of professional policing. He mobilized police officers, first on bikes and later in cars, created a signal system to dispatch police cars, created a modern records system, used crime analysis to establish and staff beats, created the first scientific crime laboratory, and the first lie detector machine was built in the Berkeley Police Department.

8. **Describe the impact of prohibition on policing.**

   It did more damage to the image and reputation of policing than any other event. To protect their operations, gangsters bribed judges, policemen, and other public officials to "look the other way" on a massive scale.

9. **Describe the Black Codes and Jim Crow laws.**

   In reaction to losing the civil war, southern state and local legislatures quickly passed Black Codes intended to keep African-Americans in "inferior" positions. Later, during 1880–1960 "Jim Crow" laws added more restrictions. Separate facilities for the majority and the minority were mandated, including schools, cemeteries, seating on buses, and telephone booths. At various periods in our history, it was a crime to teach minorities how to read, mixed marriages were illegal, and so many barriers were erected that voting was nearly impossible. The Black Codes and Jim Crow laws made a mockery of equality.

10. **State how World War II affected law enforcement.**

    The men in public safety agencies had no exemptions from compulsory military service and they volunteered and were drafted in great numbers. Departments quickly turned their attention to the new staffing realities: (1) the remaining officers did not meet military physical standards and/or were too old for military service. For the duration of the war, there would not be better police applicants and (2) women could be part of the staffing solution.

11. **Explain the unequal badge problem.**

    During the 1950s through the mid-1960s, a small number of Southern police departments had an informal practice that minority officers were not to arrest majorities for fear a riot would result. A variation of this was in some of those cities minorities couldn't drive a patrol car based on the reasoning that a white motorist would not accept a traffic citation from an African-American officer. A majority officer would drive a minority to his walking beat and pick him up at the end of the shift. Minorities would subtly retaliate by getting in the back seat when being picked up, so it appeared the majority officer was a chauffeur.

12. **Describe how the police rank and file became isolated in the 1960s.**

    During the 1960s, smoldering social, economic, and racial tensions erupted. A major race-based riot occurred over six days in the Watts neighborhood of Los Angeles, with exchanges of gunfire and buildings on fire, sometimes from arson. The precipitating event was a police arrest of a minority driver. In the end, 34 people were killed, most minorities, and property damages and losses amounted to $200 million. Over the next three years, more than two-dozen major cities were also shaken by television images of rioting, burning buildings, and the deployment of military units. The underlying factors across riots generally included high unemployment, poor housing, and lack of opportunities for minorities.

    The police were also tasked to provide crowd control for demonstrations against the increasingly unpopular and undeclared Vietnam War. In 1968, crowds outside the Democratic National Convention in Chicago clashed repeatedly with the police, both sides using excessive force. A few in the crowds threw apples bristling with razor blades at the police, as wells as garbage can lids and vials of urine. President Kennedy was assassinated in Dallas in 1963, his brother Senator Robert Kennedy likewise lost his life while campaigning for the presidency, and the ambush murder of the Reverend King in 1968 quickly produced more riots.

    The Supreme Court unleashed a series of decisions that "handcuffed" the police, further evidence that "people were turning against the police." Draft evaders refused to serve their country, the women's movement was underway, drug use increased, civil rights legislation was being enacted, crime was rocketing up, the news media was often critical of the police, and calls for Civilian Review Boards to investigate police misconduct were becoming more insistent.

    The net effect of these events resulted in the rank and file officers feeling that they were isolated and unsupported, creating a "we against them" mentality that propelled officers to join unions as public sector collective bargaining laws were enacted.

13. **Briefly define COP, ZTP, CompStat, EBP, and HSP.**

    COP is Community Oriented Policing and centers on developing police strategies and partnerships with communities in order to deliver custom-tailored police services and solutions to problems, as well as a renewed focus on crime prevention rather than criminal detection. ZTP is Zero Tolerance Policing is premised on ignoring minor law violations creates a climate conducive to more serious offenses. CompStat is a management control system designed to develop, analyze, disseminate crime information and track efforts to deal with it. Evidence Based Policing (EPB) is rooted on data analysis of many different sources of information, such as agency intelligence and scientific research. The results strategies selected or developed to attach the targeted problems. Hot Spot Policing (HSP) grew out of research by Larry Sherman who found that about half of all crimes come from relatively few places/addresses, such as open air drug markets and bars. By concentrating on these spots crime can be reduced.

14. **Give three reasons why the United States has not experienced a major terrorist attack from abroad since 9/11.**

    These reasons are: (1) prevention, (2) lack of capability, and (3) lack of present intent.

15. **Identify what may be the transcendent event for law enforcement over the past decade.**

    The series of highly publicized police use of deadly force during 2014–2016.

Chapter Review Questions

1. What does the dichotomy of politics and administration mean?
2. At its earliest, what did "profession" mean?
3. What did the Hatch Act and the "Little Hatch Acts" seek to accomplish?"
4. When was the gangster era and what was it?
5. What did "lynching" mean at its earliest?
6. What was the trilogy of major studies of the police?
7. Who developed the concept of hot-spot policing and what are the findings that support its use?

8. Major Nidal Hasan's shooting rampage at Fort Hood was characterized by the federal government as workplace violence. Do or don't you agree with that characterization? Why?
9. Should Edward Snowden be praised as a protector of Constitutional rights or taken into custody and tried for espionage? Why?
10. How can police use of deadly force affect economic development?
11. What did FBI Director James Comey mean when he stated that a chill wind may be blowing through law enforcement?

Critical Thinking Exercises

1. Assume that in England the improved agricultural methods never occurred, but the industrial revolution did. How might that have affected England's evolution?

2. Assume your family was fleeing from catastrophic conditions in Oklahoma during the time of the bum blockades and were turned back from town after town while seeking medicine for your diabetic younger brother. What would you do?

3. As the Chief of Police of a 100-officer department, you have been closely monitoring the unprovoked ambush-type murders of police officers. Officers in your department are on edge about this development. What actions would you take to increase the likelihood that such incidents do not occur and officers have a better chance of surviving them?

Key Terms

air raid wardens
Black Codes
Black September Organization (BSO)
bootlegger
Boston Police Strike
bum blockades
carpetbaggers
Challenge of Crime in a Free Society
Chavez, Cesar
city manager movement
Civil Rights Act of 1964
Commission on Accreditation of Law Enforcement Agencies (CALEA)
community-oriented policing
Community-Oriented Policing Services (COPS)
Dillinger, John
dustbowl
Equal Employment Opportunity Act of 1972
evidence-based policing (EBP)
Forces Act
Fosdick, Raymond
Freedmen's Bureau
frontier closing
Garfield, President
Greensboro Massacre (N.C.)
Harrison, President
Hispanic American Police Command Officers Association (HAPCOA)
Hot-Spot Policing
International Association of Chiefs of Police (IACP)
International Association of Police Women (IAPW)

Jim Crow laws
Kansas City Preventive Patrol Study
King, Martin Luther Jr., Reverend
KKK
Lexow Committee
lynching
machine politics
McVeigh, Timothy
military model
muckrakers
National Academy (NA)
National Advisory Commission on Civil Disorders
National Association of Asian American Law Enforcement Commanders (NAAALEC)
National Association of Women Law Enforcement Executives (NAWLEE)
National Commission on Law Observance and Law Enforcement
National Criminal Justice Reference Service (NCJRS)
National Organization of Black Law Enforcement Executives (NOBLE)
National Prohibition Act
National Sheriffs Association (NSA)
Nation, Carry
Okies
patronage
Peel, Sir Robert
Pendleton Act
Police Executive Research Forum (PERF)
Popular Front for the Liberation of Palestine (PFLP)

Pinkerton National Detective Agency
Police Administration
political machine
Politics
Peace Officers Standards and Training Commissions (POSTs)
profession
prohibition
Rand Criminal Investigation Study
ration books
Reformation Period
residency requirements
Ruby Ridge
Singleton, Benjamin "Pap"
slave patrols
snatch racket
speakeasies
spoils system
team policing
temperance movement
unequal badge
untouchables
victory gardens
Vollmer, August (Gus)
Volstead Act
Waco
Watergate Scandal
Whitman, Charles
Wickersham Commission
Wilson, O.W.
zero-tolerance policing
Two Medal of Honors

Endnotes

[1]New Amsterdam was settled by the Dutch. To be precise, the office they created was schout, their cultural equivalent of a sheriff.

[2]Raymond Fosdick, *American Police Systems* (Montclair, NJ: Patterson Smith reprint, 1969), pp. 63–64.

[3]These dates are for the first of three successive industrial revolutions in England. Others define the period as 1760–1840 and 1750–1850.

[4]Many sources list these principles, including the New Westminster Police Service (British Columbia, Canada),

www.NWpolice.org/Peel.html, January 9, 2010. Also see Douglas Hurd, *Sir Robert Peel: A Biography* (London: Weidenfeld & Nicolson, 2007). Susan Lentz maintains that the principles are the invention of 20th-century textbook writers, see "The Invention of Peel's Principles," *Journal of Criminal Justice*, Vol. 35, No. 1 (January 2007), pp. 69–79, January 2007.

[5]Melville Lee, *A History of Police in England* (Montclair, NJ: Patterson Smith reprint, 1971), p. 240.

[6]Perhaps 250,000 former slaves left the South for the West during the 1870s, so many they were called "exodusters" and Singleton hailed as the "Moses of the Colored Exodus." See Mike Meacham, "The Exoduster Movement," *Western Journal of Black Studies*, Vol. 27, No 2, (Summer, 2003), pp. 108–117 and The Testimony of Benjamin Singleton Before the Senate Select Committee Investigating the Negro Exodus from the South, Washington, DC: April 17, 1880. Sources identify the place of "Pap" Singleton's death alternatively as "someplace in the West" and St. Louis.

[7]At one time or another, three legendary lawmen of the West were employed in Abilene: Bat Masterson, Wyatt Earp, and Wild Bill Hickok.

[8]For an excellent summary of the development of tribal police systems, see David Etheridge, *Indian Law Enforcement History* (Washington, DC: Bureau of Indian Affairs, Division of Law Enforcement Services, February 1, 1975), p. 80.

[9]Colonel H. B. Wharfield, "A Fight with the Yaquis at Bear Valley, 1918," *Arizoniani*, Vol. 4, No. 3, (Fall 1983), pp. 1–8.

[10]Boles bio See George Hoeper, Black Bart: The Boulevardier Bandit (:Word Dancer Press, 1995). Sidney Drabkin, "Black Bart A Legendary Stagecoach Robber," Examiner.com, June 30, 2012, w.examiner.com/article/black-bart-a-legendary-stagecoach-robber,(accessed August 17, 2015), and Gail L. Jenner, Black Bart: The Poet Bandit (Affinity Publishing, 2009); the publisher's website does not list a physical address.

[11]No author, 'Black Bart," Soylent Communication, p. 1,copyright 2014, http://www.nndb.com/people/585/000207961, accessed August 16, 2015. This poem is repeatedly found, but without attribution to a source. Boles's alleged offer of a pension and trip to China is from no author, "Black Bart," Cowell Historical Society, undated, p. 2, http://cowellhistoricalsociety.org/html/bart.html, (accessed August 17, 2015).

[12]Some facts are drawn from Mac Blewer, "Butch Cassidy in Wyoming" Wyoming State Historical Society, undated, but carefully researched, http://www.wyohistory.org/encyclopedia/butch-cassidy-wyoming (accessed August 17, 2015), Jay Clarke, "The Death of Butch Cassidy Keeps Getting Curiouser and Curiouser," Chicago Tribune, December 7, 1896, http://articles.chicagotribune.com/1986-12-07/travel/8604010694_1_etta-place-butch-cassidy-robert-leroy-parker, accessed August 16, 2015, and no author, "Former Utah and Two Hole in the Wall Daring Train Robbers Are Now Terrorizing South America Republic, The Ogden Standard, February 21, 1910, p.1, http://chroniclingamerica.loc.gov/lccn/sn85058398/1910-02-21/ed-1/seq-1/#words=BRIGANDS+ARGENTINA+CASSIDY+IEADER, (accessed August 17, 2015).

[13]Only Utah (1896), Oklahoma (1907), Arizona and New Mexico (1912), Alaska (1959), and Hawaii (1959) had not yet been granted statehood.

[14]See M. David Desoucy, *Arizona Rangers* (Mount Pleasant, S.C.: Arcadia Publishing, 2008), Chuck Hornung, *Fullerton's Rangers: A History of the Mexico Territorial Mounted Police* (Jefferson, NC: McFarland & Company, 2005), and Mike Cox, *The Texas Rangers: Wearing the Cinco Peso, 1821–1900* (New York: Forge Books, 2008). "Texas Ranger" was not used in any legislation until 1874, although the term "Ranger" had been widely used by Texas citizens for many years.

[15]U.S. Census Bureau, Table 1, Urban and Rural Population 1900 to 1990, https://www.census.gov/population/censusdata/urpop0090.txt (accessed August 16, 2015).

[16]Brian A. Reaves, Census of State and Local Law Enforcement Agencies, 2008, Bureau of Justice Statistics, July 2011, p. 2.

[17]Ibid., p. 2 and Table 1.

[18]Ibid., p. 14.

[19]Ibid., p. 1.

[20]Ibid., p. 2

[21]Ibid., Appendix Table 10, p. 19.

[22]Ibid., p. 5, calculated with data from Table 4.

[23]Ibid., p. 5.

[24]Loc. cit.

[25]The site of the assassination is where the present National Gallery of Art is located, 401 West Constitution Avenue NW.

[26]The Dodge City Cow-Boy Band played at his inauguration. It was a curious choice; the bandleader was prone to tossing his baton away and directing with a loaded revolver. No author, *Band of Buckaroos, Wild West*, Vol. 22, No. 2 (August 2009), p. 16.

[27]Editorial, Nation, Vol. 48, No. 1243, (1889), pp. 338–341.

[28]Thomas A. Reppetto, *The Blue Parade* (New York: Free Press, 1978), pp. 41–42.

[29]Peter H. Argersinger, "New Perspectives on Election Fraud in the Gilded Age," *Political Science Quarterly*, Vol. 100, No. 4, (Winter 1985–1986), p. 672.

[30]Ibid., p. 672. This is the reason that in all states today, any political signs or activities on behalf of a party or candidate cannot be displayed or conducted within a specified number of feet of a polling station.

[31]Ibid., p. 672.

[32]Ibid., p. 678.

[33]Ibid., pp. 680–681.

[34]Alice B. Stone and Donald C Stone, "Early Development of Education in Public Administration:" in *American Public Administration: Past, Present, and Future*, edited by Frederick C. Mosher (Tuscaloosa: University of Alabama Press, 1975), pp. 17–18.

[35]In 1906, racial tensions between the residents of Brownsville, Texas, and members of the all-black 25th Infantry Regiment, stationed at nearby Fort Brown, were high. One evening, rifle shots were fired, which killed a white bartender. The Mayor blamed the Black soldiers. Despite the fact that every White commander of the regiment swore all of the men were in the barracks that night, President Roosevelt ordered them to be dishonorably discharged on the basis of a "conspiracy of silence" because no one came forward to identify

the "guilty." This was done without any hearing, trial, or opportunity of the regiment members to confront their accusers. Years later, on the presentation of a careful study of the matter, President Nixon reversed the dishonorable discharges. For further information on President Roosevelt's tenure as New York City Police Commissioner, see Jay Stuart Berman, *Police Administration and Progressive Reform: Theodore Roosevelt as Police Commissioner of New York* (Santa Barbara: ABC-CLIO, 1987). This work was originally published by Greenwood Press; the title passed through several publishing houses before coming to rest with ABC-CLIO on October 1, 2008.

[36]In Welsh, the name means "big hill." Bryn Mawr was the first institution of higher learning to offer graduate degrees to women. Its first Ph.D. was awarded in 1888.

[37]Woodrow Wilson, "The Study of Administration," *Political Science Quarterly* 2 (June 1887), pp. 197–222.

[38]Parenthetically, Woodrow Wilson is the only U.S. president (1913–1921) to hold an earned Ph.D. and signed the legislation making Mother's Day a national holiday.

[39]Raymond Fosdick and Others, edited by Roscoe Pound and Felix Frankfurter, *Criminal Justice in Cleveland, Report of the Cleveland Foundation* (Cleveland: The Cleveland Foundation, 1922). The 81 detectives, supposedly the "cream of the department," were substantially short of that. After administering the Army Alpha Test for Mental Ability to all officers, 25 percent of all detectives were found by Fosdick to have "inferior intelligence," and the personnel in the traffic and mounted patrol units had higher test scores.

[40]E. W. Roddenbury, "Achieving Professionalization," *Journal of Criminal Law, Criminology, and Police Science* 44 (May 1953–1954), p. 109.

[41]See Sylvia R. Cruess, Sharon Johnson, and Richard L. Cruess, "Profession," *Teaching and Learning in Medicine*, Vol. 6, No 4, (Winter 2004), pp. 74–76, Robert K. Merton, "Some Thoughts on the Professions in American Society (Address before the Brown University Graduate Convocation, Providence, R.I., June 6, 1960), and Howard Becker, "The Nature of a Profession," in the Sixty-First Yearbook of the National Society for the Study of Education (Chicago: National Society for the Study of Education, 1962).

[42]Gene Edward Carte, "August Vollmer and the Origins of Police Professionalism," *Journal of Police Science and Administration*, No. 3, (1973), p. 274.

[43]Larry T. Hoover ascribes the development of a police academic establishment to O. W. Wilson. See "From Police Administration to Police Science: The Development of a Police Academic Establishment in the United States," *Police Quarterly*, Vol. 8, No. 1, (2005), pp. 8–22.

[44]The Academy of Criminal Justice Sciences Police Section bestows an annual award in Wilson's name for distinguished police scholarship.

[45]Jack S. Blocker, "Did Prohibition Really Work," *American Journal of Public Health*, Vol. 96, No. 2, (February 2006), p. 235.

[46]Marcia Yablon, "The Prohibition Hangover," conference paper, Law & Society Annual Meeting, Humboldt University, Berlin, Germany, July 25, 2007.

[47]Holland Webb, "Temperance Movements and Prohibition," *International Social Science Review*, Vol. 74, No. 1 and 2, (1999), p. 61.

[48]No Author, "Abandoning Prohibition," *The Nation* Vol. 76, No. 1977, (May 21, 1930), pp. 409–410.

[49]Oddly, this was at the same time that Americans began drinking more; between 1900 and 1913 the annual production of alcohol grew dramatically. Beer jumped from 1.2 billion to 2 billion gallons and liquor grew from 97 to 147 million gallons. Blocker, "Did Prohibition Really Work?" p. 235.

[50]Seth Kugel, "Tell Them Seth Sent You," *New York Times*, April 29, 2007.

[51]Ibid., p. 236.

[52]Jack Kelly, "Gangster City," *American Heritage*, Vol. 46, No. 2, (April 1995), p. 65.

[53]Toni Alexander, "Welcome to Old Times: Inserting the Okie Past Into California's San Joaquin Valley Present," *Journal of Cultural Geography*, Vol. 26, No. 1, (February 2009), p. 74.

[54]Cecilia Rasmussen, "LAPD Blocked Dust Bowl Migrants at State Borders," *The Los Angeles Times*, March 9, 2003.

[55]Kevin M. O'Brien, "Do Municipal Residency Requirements Affect Labour Market Outcomes?" *Urban Studies*, Vol. 34, No. 11, (November 199)7, p. 1159.

[56]Kevin Johnson, "Police, Firefighters Challenge Residency Rules," *USA Today*, October 3, 2006.

[57]Frank J. Remington, "Development of Criminal Justice Education as an Academic Discipline," *Journal of Criminal Justice Education*, Vol. 1, No. 1, (March 1990), pp. 9–20.

[58]Its roots are traceable back to the National Chiefs of Police Union (1893), which largely focused on apprehension of fugitives.

[59]In Chicago, Dillinger dated Romanian immigrant Ana Cumpanas, a brothel operator known as Anna Sage. Subsequently, he was involved with one of her employees. Fearing deportation and perhaps stung by being dropped by Dillinger, Sage betrayed him to the FBI. According to FBI records, on July 22, 1934, Sage wore an orange skirt and a white blouse to a movie with Dillinger at the Biograph Theater to help agents identify him. This is in contrast to the numerous media reports stating she wore a red dress, which probably made better reading. Sage's betrayal did her little good. After receiving a $5,000 reward, she was deported to Romania. Annually, gangster buffs hold a ceremony on July 22 at the Biograph, complete with food, drinks, bagpipes, and speakers, to commemorate Dillinger's death. Dary Matera authored the most recent biography of him. See *John Dillinger* (New York: Carroll & Croft, 2005).

[60]Elaine Frantz Parsons, "Midnight Rangers: Costume and Performance in the Reconstruction-Era Ku Klux Klan," Vol. 93, No. 3, *The Journal of American History*, (December 2005), p. 812. Some of the founding KKK members may have earlier been part of a musical group, the "Midnight Rangers;" in that era, "rangers" were roaming groups of armed men of dubious legality. Also see, Patrick O'Donnell, *Ku Klux Klan: America's First Terrorists Exposed* (Idea Men Productions: West Orange, NJ, 2006).

[61]Occasionally, women accompanied these patrols although their role is not clear.

[62]The topic of slave patrols has received little attention. See K.B. Turner, David Giacopassi, and Margaret Vandiver, "Ignoring the Past: Coverage of Slave Patrols in Criminal Justice Texts," *Journal of Criminal Justice Education*, Vol. 17, No. 1, (March 2006).

[63]Danial Kato, "Law and (Dis)Order: Why the KKK was So Successful in 1868?" Conference Paper, Western Political Science Association, 2007, Las Vegas, Annual Meeting, pp. 35

[64]Brundage estimates that following 1865, between 4,000 and 5,000 people were lynched in the South and that 91 percent of the victims were African-Americans. W. F. Brundage, "The Ultimate Shame: Lynch-Law in the Post-Civil War American South," *Social Alternatives*, Vol. 25, No. 1, (First Quarter, 2006), pp. 28–29.

[65]A more modest number is put forth by Stovel, 1,200. See Katherine Stovel, "Local Sequential Patterns: The Structure of Lynching in the Deep South, 1880-1930," *Social Forces*, Vol. 79, No. 3, (2001), pp. 843–880.

[66]Carrigan and Webb identified 597 Mexican lynchings between 1848 and 1928, a figure that probably is substantially low. See William D. Carrigan and Clive Webb, The Lynching of Persons of Mexican Origin or Descent in the United States, 1848 to 1928, *Journal of Social History*, Vol. 37, No. 2, (Winter 2003), p. 413.

[67]Brundage, p. 29.

[68]Ibid., p. 29.

[69]Ibid., p. 29. The first and second Klans not only lynched people, but even more horrifying, also tied their victims to trees with logging chains, stacked wood around it, doused the stack with kerosene, and burnt them alive. The National Association for the Advancement of Colored People (NAACP) was founded in 1909, partially in response to lynching incidents.

[70]When the lead coauthor was working as a patrol officer he was dispatched to an African-American bar on an aggravated assault call. In addition to the bartender, there were only three patrons—two men and a woman, sitting in a booth together. The floor had just been mopped and was still drying, but nobody knew anything about an assault. One of the men was glassy eyed. When asked to stand up, he fell out of the booth. Where he had been leaning back in the booth was covered with blood from several knife wounds in his back. His assailant was the other man.

[71]In 1942, Japanese submarines shelled the oil installation at Goleta (CA) and also Ft. Stevens (OR). The first attack caused $500 in damage and the second one failed to hit its target.

[72]Unimaginable today, families collected their waste fats and grease from cooking; 3 pounds would help make a pound of explosives. Women turned in their hosiery so parachutes and powder bags for naval guns could be made. At scrap metal drives, families turned in every iron pot and aluminum pan they could to help make tanks and airplanes.

[73]Many saw the new rock'n'roll sound popularized by such performers as Little Richard, Elvis Presley, and Jerry Lee Lewis as inspired by the devil to seize the souls of our children. The emergence of doo-wop music in the mid-1950s, a smooth harmonized group sound, provided further "evidence" of the evil of rock 'n'roll.

[74]There is one exception to a bill dead-beat being accepted. Historically, many employee credit unions wouldn't issue a loan unless the applicant had cosigners. If an officer defaulted on such a loan and his cosigners had to pay it off, his reputation went to absolute zero and he might find that his backups were slow getting to him, a hint that it was time to find another occupation.

[75]One of the casualties of that boycott was a city of Montgomery White librarian, Juliette Morgan, who wrote a letter printed in the Montgomery Advertiser praising the restraint of African-Americans in protesting for equal treatment. The KKK is thought to be responsible for burning a cross on her lawn and invectives were hurled at her from all quarters. Although Juliette Morgan was not a healthy person, the intense hostility displayed toward her must have played a role in her suicide 18 months later. See Mary Stanton, *Journey Toward Justice*: Juliette Hampton Morgan (Athens, Georgia: University of Georgia, 2006).

[76]The lead author on this book was a field training officer for the first group of African-Americans Tampa Police Department officer trained for general patrol duties in 1964 and witnessed attempts by White motorists to refuse his trainee's traffic citation. Such events were not unusual. See Elliot M. Rudwick, *The Unequal Badge: Negro Policemen in the South* (Atlanta: Southern Relations Council, 1962) and Jack Kuykendall and David E. Burns, "The Black Police Officer: A Historical Perspective," *Journal of Contemporary Criminal Justice*, Vol. 1, No. 4, (1980).

[77]This quote has been restated for succinctness. See U.S. National Advisory Commission on Civil Disorders, Report of the National Advisory Commission on Civil Disorders (Washington, DC: U.S. Government Printing Office, 1968), p. 157.

[78]Some believe that it was Castro's retaliation for a Central Intelligence Agency–attempted assassination of him in 1961, coordinated by mobster "Handsome Johnny" Roselli (1905–1976). Roselli broke into crime with Capone's outfit in Chicago. The men allegedly involved in the assassination were apprehended and executed in Cuba. Several months after testifying before a Senate committee on this affair, Roselli's decomposing and legless body was found in a steel barrel near Dumfounding Bay, Florida. There is, of course, no shortage of theories about JFK's assassination. The topic continues to command attention; see Amy Zegart, "A Plot to Assassinate Castro Was Approved by CIA Director Allen Dulles," *The New York Times*, (January 26, 2007).

[79]Garr Nielsen, Multnomah County, Oregon, *The Police Chief*, Vol. 73, No. 8, (August 2006). Reviewed online, no page numbers.

[80]James Q. Wilson, "The Police and Their Problems," *Public Policy*, Vol. 12, (1963), pp. 189–216.

[81]Typically, with a final grade of "A" an officer received 100 percent of the cost of the course, 50 percent for a "B," and 25 percent for a "C."

[82]Robert C. Wadman and William Thomas Allison, *To Serve and Protect* (Upper Saddle River, NJ: Prentice Hall, 2000), p. 151.

[83]By 1973, all major American troop formations were withdrawn from South Vietnam, although advisors remained. The country fell to the North Vietnam communists in 1975.

[84]Vietnam veterans attending college often chose to conceal their service because the anti-war movement, which permeated campuses, would lead to them being spit at or reviled as "baby killers," a shameful reward for their service. At the same time, law enforcement personnel attending universities part-time did not reveal their occupation because of student "paranoia about police spies" investigating anti-war activities or drug use.

[85]His assailant was released from prison in 2007.

[86]Nicholas deB Katzenback, *The Challenge of Crime in a Free Society* (Washington, DC: Government Printing Office, 1967), p. 12.

[87]Jameson W. Doig, "Police Problems, Proposals, and Strategies for Change," *Public Administration Review*, 28, (September/October 1968), p. 393.

[88]National Research Council of the National Academies, *Fairness and Effectiveness in Policing: The Evidence* (Washington, DC: The National Academies Press, 2001), p. 176.

[89]Joe Schwartz, *Israel's Defense, First Things: A Journal of Religion and Public Life*, No. 191, (March 2009), p. 29. His assailant was released from prison in 2007.

[90]After the raid, Ugandan Army officers murdered an Israeli passenger who previously had been taken from the terminal to a hospital.

[91]It also led to U.S. Navy Seal Team 6 (ST6) being designated as a primary counter-terrorism group (1981). Six years later, ST6 was folded into the U.S. Navy Special Warfare Development Group (NSWDG) with responsibility for maritime environment terrorism.

[92]David Weisburd et. al., *CompStat and Organizational Change: A National Assessment* (Washington, DC: National Institute of Justice, 2008), p. 5.

[93]Drawn with restatement from Steve Barnes and Jmes Dao, "Gunman Kills Soldier Outside Recruiting Station," *The New York Times*, June 1, 2009, P.1, http://www.nytimes.com/2009/06/02/US/02recruit.html, accessed march 19, 2016.

[94]A portion of the description of this incident was drawn with restatement from Bill Kenber, "Nidal Hasan Sentenced to Death for Fort Hood Shooting Rampage," *The Washington Post*, August 28, 2013, www.washingtonpost.com/world/national-security/nidal-hasan-sentenced-to-death-for-fort-hood-shooting-rampage/2013/08/28/aad28de2-0ffa-11e3-bdf6-e4fc677d94a1_story.html, accessed March 19, 2016.

[95]See Al Baker and William Rashbaum, "Police Find Car Bomb in Times Square," *The New York Times*, May 1, 2010, p. 1 with restatement, www.nytimes.com/2010/05/02/nyregion/02timessquare.html?pagewanted=all, accessed march 19, 2016.

[96]See Warren Richey, "Failed MLK Dat Parade Bomber Gets 32-Year Sentence," Christain Science Monitor, December 20, 2011, http://www.csmonitor.com/USA/Justice/2011/1220/Failed-Martin-Luther-King-Day-parade-bomber-gets-32-year-sentence, accessed march 19, 2016.

[97]See Peter Finn and Sari Horwitz, "U.S. Charges Snowden with Espionage," *The Washington Post*, June 21, 2015, p. 1, https://www.washingtonpost.com/world/national-security/us-charges-snowden-with-espionage/2013/06/21/507497d8-dab1-11e2-a016-92547bf094cc_story.html, accessed March 19, 2016 and No author, "Snowden Granted 3-Yr Residence Permiy in Russia-Lawyer, August 7, 2014, www.google.com/webhp?sourceid=chrome-instant&ion=1&espv=2&ie=UTF-8#q=snowden%20in%20russia%20seeks%20asylum, accessed august 7, 2014. At various times Snowden has also mentioned to the news media he might seek political asylum in Hong Kong, Cuba, Switzerland, and South American Countries.

[98]See G. Jeffrey MacDonald, "Cops: Tsarnaev Shootout 'Non-Stop' for 8 Minutes," *USA Today*, March 17, 2017, p. 1, http://www.usatoday.com/story/news/2015/03/16/boston-marathon-trial/24843547 and accessed March 19, 2016 and No author, ?Boston Marathon Bomber Sentenced to Death," CBS News, p. 1, http://www.cbsnews.com/news/boston-marathon-bomber-dzhokhar-tsarnaev-sentencing, accessed March 19, 2016.

[99]See Krishhnadev Calamur, Marina Koren, and Matt Ford, "A Day After the San Bernardino Shooting," *The Atlantic*, December 3, 2015, http://www.theatlantic.com/national/archive/2015/12/a-shooter-in-san-bernardino/418497, accessed march 19, 2015.

[100]Kimberly Kindy, Marc Fisher, Julie Tate, and Jennifer Jenkins, "A Year of Reckoning: Police Fatally Shoot Nearly 1,000," *The Washington Post*. December 24, 2015, p. 1, http://www.washingtonpost.com/sf/investigative/2015/12/26/a-year-of-reckoning-police-fatally-shoot-nearly-1000, accessed March 19, 2015. The statistics appear near the top of the screen, but do not appear when printed.

[101]No Author, "When Can Police Use Force and What Happens When They Do? Police Foundation, http://www.policefoundation.org/general-resources/use-of-force-infographic, accessed March 19, 2016.

[102]See No author, "Use of Force: Taking Policing to a Higher Standard," Washington, DC, Police Executive Research Forum, January 16, 2016, http://www.policeforum.org/assets/30%20guiding%20principles.pdf, accessed March 16, 2016.

[103]No author, "How PERF"s Use-of-Force Guiding Principles Were Developed," Washington, DC, Police Executive Research Forum, January 29, 2016, p. 1, accessed March 16, 2016.

[104]"Use of Force: Taking Policing to a Higher Standard," p. 1.

[105]No author, "Police Use of Excessive Force," Community Relations Service, Washington, DC: U.S. Department of Justice, 1999, revised 2002, https://www.justice.gov/archive/crs/pubs/pdexcess.htm#41, accessed March 19, 2016.

[106]No author, "Use of Force: Taking Policing to a Higher Standard," p. 1.

[107]David A. Graham, "The FBI Director's Troubling Comments on the 'Furgueson Effect," *The Atlantic*, October 26, 2015, p. 2, www.google.com/webhp?sourceid=chrome-instant&ion=1&espv=2&ie=UTF-8#q=The+FBI+Director%E2%80%99s+Troubling+Comments+on+the+%E2%80%98

Furgueson+Effect%2C%E2%80%9D+The+Atlantic%2C, accessed March 27, 2016.

[108] Jennifer Lunden, "In Baltimore Violent Crime is Up and, Residents say Police Presence is Down, National Public Radio, June 4, 2015, http://www.npr.org/2015/06/04/411917414/since-freddie-gray-s-death-violent-crime-is-up-in-west-baltimore, accessed March 20, 2016, David Clarke, "Clark on Baltimore Murder Spike: Cops Have Quit on the Commish," http://insider.foxnews.com/2015/05/22/sheriff-clarke-baltimore-murder-spike-cops-quit-police-commissioner-batts, accessed March 20, 2016, and Josh Sanburn, "What's Behind Baltimore's Record Setting Rise in Homicides?" *Time*, June 2, 2015, http://time.com/3905876/baltimore-murders-homicide-rate-record, accessed March 20, 2016.

[109] Jessica Chasmar, "Two Los Angles Police Officers were Shot at in Unprovoked Attack," *The Washington Times*, December 29, 2016, http://www.washingtontimes.com/news/2014/dec/29/two-los-angeles-police-officers-shot-at-in-unprovo/, accessed March 20, 2016.

[110] Josh Solomon, "Two Pasco County Sheriff's Deputies Shot at in Dade City," December 28. 2014, http://www.tampabay.com/news/publicsafety/crime/two-pasco-deputies-fired-upon-early-sunday-in-dade-city/2211669, accessed March 20, 2016.

[111] Melanie Eversley, Katharine Lackey, and Trevor Hughes, "2 NYPD Officers Killed in an Ambush-Style Shooting," *USA Today*, December 21, 2014, http://www.usatoday.com/story/news/nation/2014/12/20/new-york-city-police-officers-shot/20698679/, accessed March 20, 2016.

[112] Nick Valencia, "Pistol-Whipped Detective Says He Didin't Shoot Attacker Because of Headlines," CNN News, August 14,2015, http://www.cnn.com/2015/08/13/us/alabama-birmingham-police-detective-pistol-whipped/, accessed March 20, 2016.

[113] Juan A. Lozano, "Deputy Killed in Houston Ambush, Shot 15 Times," *The Dallas Morning News*, August 31, 2015, http://www.dallasnews.com/news/state/headlines/20150831-deputy-killed-in-houston-ambush-shot-15-times-suspect-held-without-bond.ece, accessed March 20, 2016.

[114] No author, "Pistol-Whipped Detective Says He Didn't Shoot Attacker Because of Headlines, CNN News, August 21, 2015, http://www.cnn.com/2015/08/13/us/alabama-birmingham-police-detective-pistol-whipped/, accessed March 19, 2016.

[115] For more on this subject visit https://www.uscis.gov/news/fact-sheets/naturalization-through-military-service-fact-sheet.

[116] These comments are drawn with restatement from President's Task Force on 21st Century Policing, Final Report of the President's Task Force on 21st Century Policing, May 2015, Washington, DC: Office of Community Oriented Policing Services, U.S. Department of Justice.

[117] The original version of this was by noted leadership authority Peter Drucker, "Organizational culture east policy for lunch."

CHAPTER TWO

POLICING TODAY

Learning Objectives

1. Define Community Policing.
2. Describe the four-step problem-solving model called SARA.
3. Describe CompStat.
4. Discuss new police strategies, including evidence-based policing, hot-spots policing, intelligence-led policing, and predictive policing.
5. List and briefly describe some of the more common crime analysis techniques.
6. Describe geographic information systems and explain how such a system would enhance police service.
7. Explain the impact of information technology on policing.
8. Describe how distrust between police and citizens can affect police strategies.

INTRODUCTION

IN THE PAST DECADE, *our society has changed measurably. Economic downturns have, arguably, widened income disparities; politics have become increasingly divisive; and issues of race and equality are at the forefront of the national consciousness in a way that hasn't been seen since the 1960s. Throughout it all, crime levels have largely been on the decline—police departments across the country have enjoyed the lowest crime rates in decades. Inevitably, these rates will increase and we have started to see this in the early months of 2016. Many urban areas are beginning to see huge increases in both violent crime and property offenses, causing law enforcement agencies to reexamine their strategies and reallocate resources. In some cases, departments have shifted from targeted enforcement models back to community policing blends—in other cases, departments have utilized technology in new and different ways.*

Furthermore, the landscape of policing itself looks much different than it did just a few years ago: Various social movements have begun to call on law enforcement agencies to increase transparency and respond to perceptions of biased policing; the trend of police militarization, an outgrowth of SWAT-style techniques and armaments, is being challenged; and the use of technology has transformed many police functions.

This is an interesting era for crime-fighting methodologies—making understanding their evolution even more important. Tracing the genesis of these methods from the reactive and ineffective traditional model of policing common previous to the 1980s, one sees how the shift in focus on social problems and attempts to engage the wider community to assist in curbing crime and disorder emerged into what is now commonly called "community policing." Community policing, still provides a strong philosophical model among police agencies in the United States today. In the early 1990s, community policing was greatly enhanced through a management accountability process known as CompStat (Computer Statistics), originally started under the leadership of the then Commissioner Bill Bratton in New York City. The variety of tactics and strategies being used to address today's unique problems draw greatly from both of these models, as well as utilizing technology and research-bolstered techniques to maximize their effectiveness.

COMMUNITY POLICING

As explained in Chapter 1, the failure of traditional law enforcement methods to curb rising crime rates during the 1970s and 1980s and to reintegrate the police with society gave rise to a new movement, generally referred to as **community-oriented policing(COP)** or **community policing**. One of the first major critics of the traditional policing model was Herman Goldstein.[1] In his classic work *Policing a Free Society*, Goldstein questioned the effectiveness of traditional police methods in safeguarding the constitutional rights and privileges celebrated in American society (e.g., freedom of speech and expression, due process, and the right to privacy) versus the control of crime and the decay of social order. Goldstein pointed out that these two goals may be incompatible under the traditional police model and called for a closer link between the police and the community.

During the same time period, Wilson and Kelling's "broken windows" thesis emerged as a dominant theme in American policing debate.[2] Arguing that crime seemed to increase dramatically in neighborhoods where visible signs of social decay and disorder were present (e.g., graffiti on bridge structures, unkept lots with overgrown weeds, visible drug and prostitution activities, and warehouses with broken windows). Wilson and Kelling argued that areas with these types of crimes are signs of decaying neighborhoods and therefore a breeding ground for more serious crimes. The philosophy of **zero-tolerance policing (ZTP)** focuses on targeting police responses to less serious crimes in these areas, addressing the counter-intuitive argument that disorder may elicit more fear than actual crime.[3] Where adopted, officers are not given any discretion in dealing with minor crimes of disorder; an arrest has to be made. In more recent times, ZTP has been re-labeled as "disorder policing" in some circles.

Although ZTP has been given credit for reducing crime in some jurisdictions, most notably New York City, the empirical evidence of its effectiveness raises some questions,[4] as does the assumed progression from disorder to serious crimes.[5] Moreover, the strategy may have some unintended consequences: In New York City, the implementation of ZTP was accompanied by an increase in citizen complainants and lawsuits alleging police misconduct and abuse of force.[6] Still, some policy makers continue to adopt ZTP, which can be used as the dominant strategy in an agency or within the framework of other policing strategies such as community-oriented policing. Others maintain the two strategies are incompatible and that working closely with the community can achieve ZTP results without generating increases in complainants and lawsuits.[7]

Kelling and Coles went on to argue that "broken windows needed fixing" and that the police must be directed to do more than just "crime control."[8] Indeed, they argued that other functions of the police were as important and maybe more important, than strictly enforcing the law and maintaining order. In this context, police should focus more on a service orientation, building key partnerships with churches, youth centers, and other neighborhood groups in an effort to forge new alliances with the community. Crime was seen not as the sole purview of the police but rather as an entire community responsibility. Police administrators began to look for new techniques and operational strategies that emphasized more service than arrest. Decentralization of services, characterized by storefront operations and neighborhood centers, began to be commonplace in police organizations. Old programs, such as the horse patrol, bike patrol, and the "walking beat" officer, were reintroduced to American policing as ways to bring the police and the community closer together.

Although Braiden[9] argues that community policing was "nothing new under the sun" because it only echoed the ideas expressed by Sir Robert Peel in the early 1800s, community policing did represent a refreshing approach to earlier problems. Community policing embraced the Peelian principle of police as members of the public giving full-time attention to community welfare and existence. Therefore, policing was linked to a myriad of social issues other than simply crime, including poverty, illiteracy, racism, teenage pregnancy, and the like.[10]

Although precise definitions of community policing are hard to find and also vary, it is generally an operational and management philosophy that can be quickly identified. Community policing is characterized by ongoing attempts to promote greater community involvement in the police function. For the most part, the movement focused on programs that fostered five elements: (1) a commitment to crime prevention, (2) public scrutiny of the police, (3) accountability of police actions to the public, (4) customized police service, and (5) community organization.[11]

Community policing advocates argue that **traditional policing** is a system of response; that is, the police respond to calls for services *after* the activity occurs. Police response is then reactive and incident driven (calls for assistance and people reporting crimes) rather than proactive and preventive. Further, a randomized motor patrol neither lowers crime nor increases the chances of catching suspects. Simply, increasing the number of police, then, has limited impact on the crime rate because improving response time on calls for service has little relevance to preventing the original incident.[12] In addition, the role of the individual police officer is largely limited within the confines of

random patrol and response to incidents. In some jurisdictions the calls for service are so high that the amount of time available to random, preventative patrol is negligible.

In present practice, COP is a proactive approach to crime control with three complimentary elements: (1) community partnerships; (2) problem solving, using the Scanning, Analysis, Response, and Assessment (SARA) model; and (3) organizational transformation (see Figure 2.1). The most common types of restructuring associated with community policing include:

- A decentralization of authority, allowing all levels of a department to have an increased level of independence and decision making.
- A flattened hierarchy, which collapses bureaucratic layers and allows for increased efficiency and better communication.
- A reduced number of specialized units, with resources instead being devoted to the direct delivery of police services to the public.
- An emphasis on teamwork, which promotes problem solving and the provision of services by groups of employees.
- Increasing non-sworn personnel, which provides a cost savings because their salaries are typically less than sworn officers and which also allows sworn officers to be used more effectively.[13]

EVALUATION RESEARCH ON COMMUNITY POLICING

Since the 1980s, considerable empirical data has been generated regarding the effectiveness of community policing. Few, however, actually show positive effectiveness of the policing paradigm as a successful methodology to reduce crime and disorder. The evidence, is at best, largely mixed evidence as it relates to positive outcomes. While a portion of the evidence shows some indication that community policing may be related to decreases in crime—as is often the case in social science research—design limitations make it difficult to generalize to other places and time. Findings are also limited when it comes to perceptions and fear of crime. While it is generally accepted that community policing helps community members feel safer and reduces the levels of fear of crime, in reality, actual crime incidents in several test communities reveals no significant changes.[14] In some research findings, favorable decreases in disorder offenses as a result of community policing are clear and consistent evidence that COP improves community relations. And, it appears that community policing models benefit individual police officer attitudes toward both their work and the community. It's not as certain, however, whether community policing actually reduces calls for service or whether it significantly changes police officer behavior. Hence, definitive statements on the impact of community policing are difficult because the concept itself looks very different from agency to

The Primary Elements of Community Policing

Other Government Agencies

Community Members/Groups

Nonprofits / Service Providers

Private Businesses

Media

Agency Management

Organizational Structure

Personnel

Information System (Technology)

Community Partnerships

Organizational Transformation

Problem Solving

S Scanning

A Analysis

R Response

A Assessment

Using the Crime Triangle

FIGURE 2.1 ► Primary Elements of Community Policing *Source:* Community Oriented Policing Services, "Community Policing Defined," p. 2 (2014). www.cops.usdoj.gov/pdf/vets-to-cops/e030917193-CP-Defined.pdf

agency. Some departments emphasize community outreach and programming that directly affect quality of life, while others favor increased patrols and increased reliance on CompStat. There's no standard definition of what a community policing model should look like, and implementation varies wildly across agencies compounding problems relating to evaluation of the community policing model.[15]

COMMUNITY POLICING AND COMPSTAT

Although community policing has *not* had the drastic effects its supporters had hoped, the premise behind the philosophy has in turn led to the quality movement within policing: making

Box 2.1 Harm-Focused Policing

When we attempt to quantify the success of a policing program, we often talk about things that *didn't* happen: Certain crimes *didn't* occur at certain rates or we *prevented* these things from happening. This is a very one-dimensional perspective to look at policing—the technique may be adequate to compare crime rates from year to year, but it does not give a full picture of the role of the police within a specific community, nor does it recognize that all crimes are not equal across the spectrum. According to at least one police scholar (Dr. Jerry Ratcliffe), the field of policing is missing an opportunity to better capture the complex nexus between crime and the criminal justice system by not developing a harm-based evaluation system that explores all of these intricacies. Not only does harm-focused policing take a look at crime numbers and the harm that crime itself causes, but it also explores the inherent harms in different types of police activities. Ratcliffe explains that, for example, in hot-spots policing, increased "stop and frisk" scenarios might drive

down narcotics crime in the area. But as increased patrols tend to unfairly target minorities, the social implications of arresting and sending non-violent offenders through the criminal justice system might have a ripple effect: It might inflame racial tensions, decrease police legitimacy, and increase social problems like poverty among families whose loved ones were arrested. In that case, a slightly decreased number of drug-related crimes as a result of hot-spots policing may not be offset by the social harms it has simultaneously inflicted on the community.

Ratcliffe believes that his harm-focused model is an ideal complement to both intelligence-led policing and evidence-based policing; the model would provide statistics and information on which to focus intelligence-led practices and would provide much in the way of scientific data for evidence-based policies and strategies. This new and innovative policing model, though complex, provides a rich perspective to view the ways that crime and law enforcement actions impact a community.

---

the police be more efficient and effective. Today, most ambitious police methodology focuses on precisely that concept—CompStat. The word CompStat is derived from "comp," stemming from the word "computer," and "stat," which originates from "statistics." The process was originally developed in New York City by the then Commissioner William Bratton in the mid-1990s,[16] and continues in some form today in most major cities. CompStat is a process that looks at the individual needs of the community and then designs proactive strategies to stop or prevent crime. To accomplish this goal, Bratton required his department (New York in the 1990s and Los Angeles in the 2000s) to analyze crime data weekly and required police administrators to meet regularly to share information between divisions and precincts. A key component of CompStat is to force police commanders to address crime and social problems in their areas of responsibility and to address them immediately. Police commanders are then held accountable for the success or failure of their plans and decisions. Combining the two strategies of in-depth analysis with management accountability is the heart of the process.

Essentially, CompStat is a collection of modern management practices, military-like deployment efforts, and strong enforcement strategies all based on the availability of accurate and timely statistical crime data. Four core principles highlight a police department's model of CompStat:

1. *Accurate and timely intelligence and statistical crime information based on geographical settings and/or areas.* High-tech computer systems and geographical mapping programs are most helpful in providing the aggregate and individual data often

required for effective CompStat efforts. However, more rudimentary aspects of visual crime analysis can be accomplished through daily pin mapping and bulletins.

2. *Rapid deployment of resources, particularly combining the immediate presence of uniform patrol working in concert with directed undercover operations.* Rapid deployment of other city and governmental resources, such as nuisance and abatement personnel, sanitation workers, and alcoholic beverage and licensing enforcement, is an additional aspect of this principle.

3. *Effective tactics and strategies of enforcement that focus on visible street crimes or "quality-of-life" crimes,* such as loitering, drinking in public, street prostitution, or even jumping subway turnstiles.

4. *Relentless follow-up and assessment,* which include placing accountability and responsibility not only on the individual police officer on the beat but also on individual police managers of traditionally defined areas, such as division heads, precinct captains, or shift commanders.[17]

CompStat focuses on using the most accurate and timely information and data available to the police, opening lines of communication both horizontally and vertically within the organization, activating the community at large, and improving the overall efficiency and effectiveness of the police. CompStat is problem-oriented and preventive and stresses the need to focus on current problems rather than on past incidents. In this

Box 2.2 Traditional vs. Community Policing: Questions and Answers

	Traditional	Community policing
Question: *Who are the police?*	A government agency principally responsible for law enforcement.	Police are the public and the public are the police: The police officers are those who are paid to give full-time attention to the duties of every citizen.
Question: *What is the relationship of the police force to other public service departments?*	Priorities often conflict.	The police are one department among many responsible for improving the quality of life.
Question: *What is the role of the police?*	Focusing on solving crimes.	A broader problem-solving approach.
Question: *How is police efficiency measured?*	By detection and arrest rates.	By the absence of crime and disorder.
Question: *What are the highest priorities?*	Crimes that are high value (e.g., bank robberies) and those involving violence.	Whatever problems disturb the community most.
Question: *What, specifically, do police deal with?*	Incidents.	Citizens' problems and concerns.
Question: *What determines the effectiveness of police?*	Response times.	Public co-operation.
Question: *What view do police take of service calls?*	Deal with them only if there is no real police work to do.	Vital function and great opportunity.
Question: *What is police professionalism?*	Swift effective response to serious crime.	Keeping close to the community.
Question: *What kind of intelligence is most important?*	Crime intelligence (study of particular crimes or series of crimes).	Criminal intelligence (information about the activities of individuals or groups).
Question: *What is the essential nature of police accountability?*	Highly centralized; governed by rules, regulations, and policy directives; accountable to the law.	Emphasis on local accountability to community needs.
Question: *What is the role of headquarters?*	To provide the necessary rules and policy directives.	To preach organizational values.
Question: *What is the role of the press liaison department?*	To keep the "heat" off operational officers so they can get on with the job.	To coordinate an essential channel of communication with the community.
Question: *How do the police regard prosecutions?*	As an important goal.	As one tool among many.

Source: Malcolm K. Sparrow, "Implementing Community Policing, *Perspectives on Policing* (Washington, DC: U.S. Department of Justice, National Institute of Justice, November 1988). See: https://www.ncjrs.gov/pdffiles1/nij/114217.pdf

manner, CompStat significantly departs from the traditional police model by taking a preventive/proactive approach rather than a reactive, incident-driven approach. CompStat meetings tend to focus on an individual area or a community's problems with an eye toward remedying the situation or variables/people that encourage, cause, or commit crime, thereby preventing continuing problems and crime.

The CompStat process is not limited to large, metropolitan agencies. Indeed, CompStat can be implemented in cities of all sizes with diverse populations and varying crime rates. The process helps police executives clarify their agency's mission and focus its efforts on the most important issues first, identifying problems early and developing effective strategies for remediation and prevention. Most importantly, the CompStat process allows the organization to quickly learn what works and what does not, while providing a flexible methodology to try innovative programs and promising strategies.[18]

CompStat doesn't look the same in every agency, nor should it. When it was first widely implemented, many police chiefs thought that CompStat meetings should be high stakes, discipline-oriented meetings that involved a lot of yelling and finger-pointing, which only served to marginalize the process and make meeting highly unpopular and intimidating to mid-level and even command staff. Today's CompStat meetings are much lighter in tone than in Bratton's version—and many agencies now include outside stakeholders who contribute alongside of commanders, patrol officers, and crime analysts. Depending on the problem, outside stakeholders might include key representatives from a variety of institutions, including public health, the chamber of commerce, public housing, and even private security agencies. For instance, in one city economically oriented to tourism, criminals could easily identify rental cars. When the rentals were stopped by traffic or at lights, the criminals would slash the tires and rob the immobile car occupants. They didn't fear prosecution if apprehended because the visitors were unlikely to return to that city in order to testify. By including a group of stakeholders that included the tourism bureau and the car rental industry, multiple strategies were devised that substantially obviated the problem.

CompStat meetings consistently generate clear performance measurements that emphasize metrics related to crime reduction and quality of life, as opposed to police activity indicators like arrests made and tickets issued.[19] Many policing experts point to CompStat as the single most important advance in police administration in the past century. Whether that will continue to be the case in the future lies within CompStat's ability to incorporate technological advances, disseminate tactical information, and balance its focus on crime with other values critical to law enforcement, such as fair and impartial policing, officer behavior, and community relations.

COMMUNITY POLICING MODELS

Community policing has evolved greatly in the years since its implementation, and as mentioned previously, it takes many different forms across agencies. And though some of the benchmark case studies in policing literature tend to focus on programs that were created decades ago, it remains important to see the genesis of community policing in order to understand how the concept is relevant to today's police organizations. Three cases that still have a major impact on today's community policing philosophies include Newport News, Virginia; Chicago, Illinois; and Minneapolis, Minnesota.

Newport News, Virginia

In 1983, under the direction of a new chief, Darrel Stephens, the Newport News Police Department developed a "problem-oriented" approach to policing. Known as **problem-oriented policing**, this innovative style of community policy focused on the department's traditional response to major, recurring problems. Its goal was to reassess the traditional, incident-driven aspects of police work, and fundamentally change the way the Newport News Police Department viewed its mission. The resulting self-analysis yielded an important four-step, problem-solving methodology (commonly referred to as **SARA**) that has become an integral part of current community policing operations (see Figure 2.2).

Scanning—Instead of relying on broad, law-related concepts, such as robbery, burglary, and auto theft, officers are encouraged to group individual, related incidents that come to their attention as "problems" and define these problems in more precise and useful terms. For example, an incident that typically would be classified simply as a "robbery" might be seen as part of a pattern of prostitution-related robberies committed in center-city hotels. In essence, officers are expected to look for possible problems and accurately define them as part of their daily responsibility.

Analysis—Officers working on a well-defined problem then collect information from a variety of public and private sources, not just traditional police data, such as criminal records and past offense reports. Officers rely on problem analysis guides that direct officers to examine offenders, victims, the social, economic, and

FIGURE 2.2 ▶ The problem-solving system used in Newport News, Virginia, Police Department. *Source:* William Speiman and John E. Eck. "Problem Oriented Policing," in *Research in Brief* (Washington, DC: National Institute of Justice, October 1988), p. 4.

physical environment, and previous responses to the problem. The goal is to understand the scope, nature, and causes of the problem and formulate a variety of options for its resolution.

Response—The knowledge gained in the analysis stage is then used to develop and implement solutions. Officers seek the assistance of citizens, businesses, other police units, other public and private organizations, and anyone else who can help develop a program of action. Solutions may go well beyond traditional police responses to include other community agencies and/or municipal organizations.

Assessment—Finally, officers evaluate the impact and the effectiveness of their responses. Were the original problems actually solved or alleviated? What went right and just as importantly, what didn't work and why. Officers then can use the results to revise a response, to collect more data, or even to redefine the problem.[20]

Goldstein[21] further explains this systematic process in his book *Problem-Oriented Policing,* which has become a classic in the field. Goldstein's work attempts to give greater meaning to each of the four SARA steps. For instance, a *problem* is expanded to mean a cluster of similar, related, or recurring incidents rather than a single incident. The assumption is that few incidents are isolated; instead, they are part of a wider set of urban social phenomena. Examples of such community problems are the following:

- Disorderly youth who regularly congregate in the parking lot of a specific convenience store
- Street prostitutes and associated "jack roll" robberies of patrons that continually occur in the same area

- Drunk and drinking drivers around the skid-row area of the city
- Panhandlers, vagrants, and other displaced people living on the sidewalk in a business district
- Juvenile runaways, prostitutes, and drug dealers congregating at the downtown bus depot
- Robberies of commercial establishments at major intersections of a main thoroughfare of a suburban area that is a corridor leading out of a large central city[22]

Note that each of these problems incorporates not only a potential or real crime but also a wider community/social issue. Further, each problem has been identified with a specific location. Goldstein[23] emphasizes that the traditional functions of crime analysis under the problem-solving methodology can be expanded to have a much wider and deeper importance. The pooling of data and subsequent analysis provide the basis for problem identification and response strategies. Therefore, the accuracy and timeliness of such information becomes a necessity for the department. However, the ultimate challenge in problem-oriented policing is not the identification of problems but rather the integration of the community with the police in developing effective ways of dealing with them (see Figure 2.3).

Chicago, Illinois

In January 1993, Mayor Richard Daley and the then Police Superintendent Matt L. Rodriguez announced the first major operational changes to use community policing in the city of Chicago. The new program, the **Chicago Alternative Policing Strategy (CAPS)**, was designed to move the department from a traditional, reactive, incident-driven agency to a more proactive

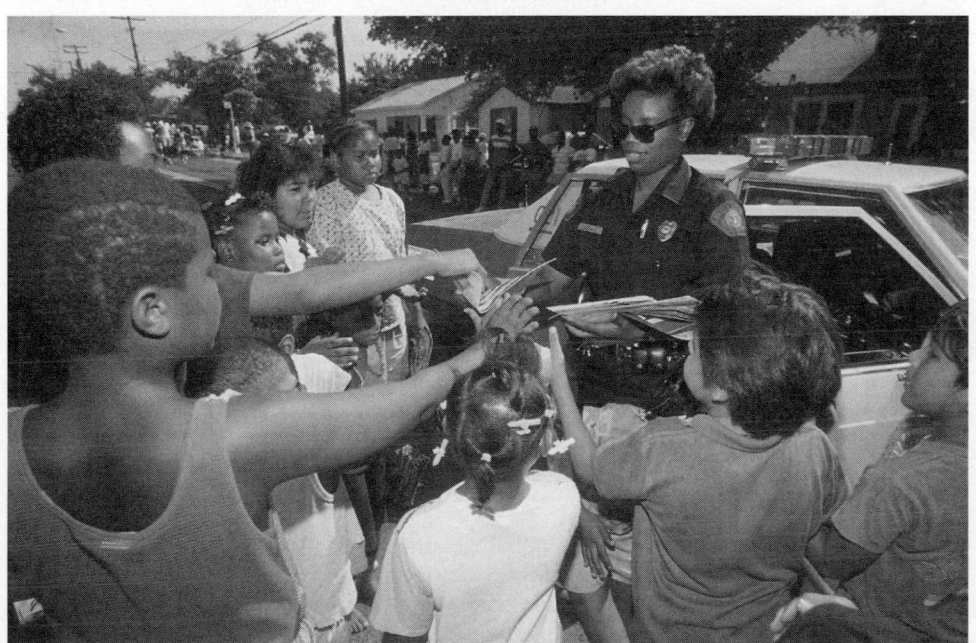

FIGURE 2.3 ▶ Officers focus on problem solving in traditionally high-crime areas, such as low-income, densely populated urban settings. Providing quality policing and an improved image are important parts of the community policing movement. (Larry Kolvoord/The Image Works)

and community-oriented department. At first, CAPS was hailed as a method to combat crime, drugs, and gang activity in the inner city. However, as the implementation plan unfolded, a much broader mission statement evolved that focused on a combined effort with the community to "identify and solve problems of crime and disorder and to improve the quality of life in all of Chicago's neighborhoods."[24]

As in many large cities implementing community policing, Chicago developed five prototype districts to serve as "laboratories" for testing new police ideas, innovations, and strategies (see Figure 2.4).

These districts could then refine the successful new programs and hence improve the overall CAPS model. Essentially, the new CAPS program echoed the methodology for implementing community policing in several other large metropolitan cities at the time. For instance, in Houston, Texas, and New York City, under the direction of the then Commissioner Lee P. Brown, the transition to community policing occurred only in select neighborhoods or districts and was known as **neighborhood-oriented policing**. Similar programs evolved in Phoenix, Arizona; Miami, Florida; Philadelphia, Pennsylvania; and Newark, New Jersey. Only a few cities attempted to implement community policing strategies on a department-wide basis (Portland, Oregon and Baltimore, Maryland). Most cities, and particularly large metropolitan communities, realized that the implementation of community policing demanded dramatic

modification in the existing philosophy, structure, operation, and deployment of police.[25] The gradual evolution toward full-scale adoption essentially continued to redefine both the means and ends of community policing.[26]

CAPS had a number of key features aimed at improving and expanding the overall quality of police services in the city of Chicago, as well as reducing crime.[27] These key features included the following:

- *Crime control and prevention*—CAPS emphasizes both crime control and crime prevention. Vigorous and impartial enforcement of the law, rapid response to serious crimes and life-threatening emergencies, and proactive problem solving with the community are the foundations of the city's policing strategy.

- *Neighborhood orientation*—CAPS gives special attention to the residents and problems of specific neighborhoods, which demands that officers know their beats (i.e., crime trends, hot-spots, and community organizations and resources that are within the geographical areas in which they are assigned) and develop partnerships with the community to solve problems. Beat officers work the same beat on the same watch every day, so they can more intimately know the beat's residents, its chronic crime problems, and the best strategies for solving those problems.

- *Increased geographic responsibility*—CAPS involves organizing police services so that officers are responsible for crime control in a specific area or beat. A new district organizational structure using rapid-response cars to handle emergency calls allows newly created beat teams to engage in community policing activities. The beat teams share responsibility for specific areas under the leadership of a supervising beat sergeant.

- *Structured response to calls for police service*—CAPS system of differential responses to citizen calls frees beat team officers from the continuous demands of 911 calls. Emergency calls are handled primarily by rapid-response sector cars, whereas nonemergency and routine calls are handled by beat officers or by telephone callback contacts. Sector officers also attend to community matters, and sector and beat teams rotate, so that all officers participate in community policing.

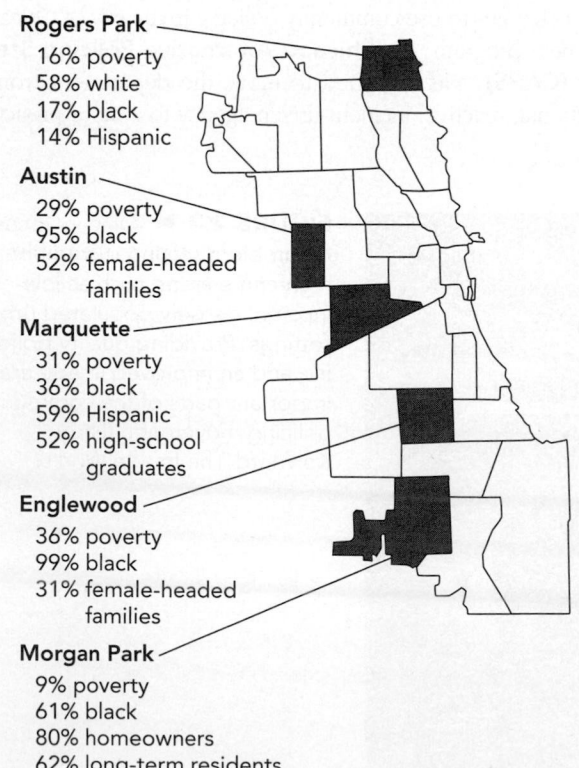

Rogers Park
16% poverty
58% white
17% black
14% Hispanic

Austin
29% poverty
95% black
52% female-headed families

Marquette
31% poverty
36% black
59% Hispanic
52% high-school graduates

Englewood
36% poverty
99% black
31% female-headed families

Morgan Park
9% poverty
61% black
80% homeowners
62% long-term residents

FIGURE 2.4 ▶ Chicago's five experimental districts.
Source: Susan M. Harnett and Wesley G. Skogan, "Community Policing: Chicago's Experience," *NIJ Journal* (April 1999): 3.

Quick Fact: Chicago's CAPS Design

The Chicago Police Department's Current CAPS Organization divides the city into 25 districts. Each district has three sectors and each sector has 3–5 beats, where officers are assigned to work.

- *Proactive, problem-solving approach*—CAPS focuses on the causes of neighborhood problems rather than on discrete/individual incidents of crime or disturbances. Attention is given to the long-term prevention of these problems and to the signs of community disorder and decay that are associated with crime (e.g., "hot-spots" such as drug houses, loitering youth, and graffiti).

- *Combined community and city resources for crime prevention and control*—CAPS assumes that police alone cannot solve the crime problem and that they depend on the community and other city agencies to achieve success. Hence, part of the beat officer's new role is to broker community resources and to draw on other city agencies to identify and respond to local problems. Former Mayor Daley made CAPS a priority of all city agencies. Hence, the mayor's office ensures that municipal agencies are responsive to requests for assistance from beat officers.

- *Emphasis on crime and problem analysis through the CompStat process*—CAPS requires more efficient data collection and analysis to identify crime patterns and target areas that demand police attention. Emphasis is placed on crime analysis at the district level, and beat information is recorded and shared among officers and across watches or shifts. To accomplish this task, each district has implemented a local area network of advanced computer workstations employing a crime analysis system called ICAM (Information Collection for Automated Mapping). This new technology allows beat officers and other police personnel to analyze and map crime hot-spots, track other neighborhood problems, and share this information with the community. The CAPS project also instituted a rigorous CompStat process designed to take CAPS to the next level through management accountability.[28]

- *Training*—The Chicago Police Department has made a significant commitment to training police personnel and the community in the CAPS philosophy and program. Intensive training on problem solving and community partnerships is being provided to district patrol officers and their supervisors. Innovative classroom instruction for the community and a program of joint police–community training have also been developed.

- *Communication and marketing*—The Chicago Police Department is dedicated to communicating the CAPS philosophy to all members of the department and the community. This is a fundamental strategy of the CAPS program. To ensure such communication, an intensive marketing program has been adopted that includes a newsletter, roll-call training, a regular cable television program, information exchanges via computer technology (Internet and fax machines), and various brochures and videos. Feedback is collected through personal interviews, focus groups,

community surveys, a CAPS hotline, and several suggestion boxes. The information collected through this marketing program assists in the refinement and development of the CAPS program.

- *Evaluation, strategic planning, and organizational change*—The CAPS program is undergoing one of the most thorough evaluations of any community policing initiative in the United States. A consortium of four major Chicago-area universities (Northwestern, DePaul, Loyola, and the University of Illinois at Chicago) is conducting an evaluation of the process and results in the prototype districts.

CAPS represents one of the largest and most comprehensive community policing initiatives in the country. During its first 10 years of operation, evaluation findings indicated that major crime and neighborhood problems were reduced, drug and gang problems were reduced, and public perception of the quality of police services was improved[29] (see Table 2.1). Under this orientation, the community is viewed as a valuable resource from which powerful information and ties can be gathered. It aims "to increase the interaction and co-operation between local police and the people and neighborhoods they serve" to combat crime.[30] Hence, the major goals of community policing are not only to reduce crime but also, more significantly, to increase feelings of safety among residents.[31] These two goals appear to be separate but are actually very closely linked in the community policing process. This approach attempts to increase the visibility and accessibility of police to the community. Through this process, police officers are no longer patrol officers enforcing the laws of the state but rather neighborhood officers. These officers infiltrate local neighborhoods, targeting specific areas in need of improvement. By involving themselves within the community, the officers are more available to meet and discuss the specific problems and concerns of each neighborhood and work to develop long-term solutions.[32] These solutions are the root of the proactive approach to policing. By listening to the public, the police will be better informed of the specific problems in each area. As co-operation between police and citizens in solving neighborhood problems increases, residents feel more secure.[33]

CAPS still represents one of the most researched and referred-to community policing initiatives in history, but in 2012, it was at risk of being dismantled altogether. Politics within the city and increasing violent crime shifted focus locally more toward CompStat and reactive policing strategies. Superintendent Garry McCarthy (appointed in 2011) seemed to suggest that he would dismantle the program at one point, but instead announced in 2013 that—in conjunction with Mayor Rahm Emanuel's office—he was revitalizing the program. The superintendent and mayor introduced the changes to CAPS by attempting to change the model from just another bureaucracy to a new and vibrant mindset and approach to policing. As such, CAPS became a new management philosophy that was now centralized directly out of headquarters, and updates to the program were then decentralized, giving district commanders the flexibility to customize programming to the needs of their specific areas. Each district

TABLE 2.1 CHICAGO COMMUNITY POLICING AT A GLANCE	
Chicago's community policing effort is more extensive and more organized than programs in most other jurisdictions, and it permeates the city to a greater extent than in most others. Below is an "at a glance" description of a typical, more limited program compared to Chicago's program.	
Chicago's Community Policing Model	**More Limited Community Policing Model**
Police	*Police*
• The entire patrol division is involved. • The program is fully staffed with permanent officers on regular shifts. • Extensive training is given to both officers and supervisors. • All districts and all shifts are involved. • Program activities are supervised through the regular chain of command and through standard patrol operations.	• Small units are staffed by officers who have volunteered for a community policing assignment. • Officers work overtime and are usually paid with temporary federal funding. • Officers work on evening shift only. • Little training is provided; officers' personal motivation propels the program. • Officers are assigned only to selected areas. • Program activities are supervised by the chief's office or from outside the routine command structure.
Residents	*Residents*
• Residents are expected to take an active role in solving problems. • Residents are encouraged to meet with police regularly to exchange information and report on actions taken. • Public priorities play an important role in setting beat team priorities. • Residents receive training in Chicago's problem-solving model.	• Residents are asked to be the police department's "eyes and ears." • Surveys or postcards are distributed to residents as a way of gathering information. • Residents are called to meet occasionally, to publicize the program. • Residents have no role in setting police priorities or operations.
Municipal Services	*Municipal Services*
• Management systems are in place to trigger a rapid response to service requests. • Agencies are held accountable by the mayor for the effectiveness of their response. • Community policing is the entire city's program, not the police department's program.	• Service agencies have no special responsibility to police or citizen groups. • Service agencies believe community policing is the police department's program and should be funded by the police department's budget.

Source: http://mayor.cityofchicago.org/mayor/en/photo_galleries/press_room_photo_galleries/201 (retrieved on July 16, 2010).

was also assigned a sergeant and two CAPS police officers, as well.[34] Longitudinal research efforts centered on the effectiveness of CAPS were initiated and findings focused on the impact of these programmatic shifts are underway, pressured by a sharp increase (of nearly 15 percent) in homicides in the city during the first half of 2015 (a total of 216 people have been reported killed from January 1 through June 30, 2015).[35] Further, in December 2015, Superintendent Garry McCarthy was terminated from his position by Chicago Mayor Rahm Emanuel as a result of a departmental "crisis of confidence" stemming from the investigation of questionable police involved shootings.[36] The action was highly controversial and threatens to hinder the future of the CAPS project until new leadership assumes control of the Chicago Police Department.

Minneapolis, Minnesota

Comparing the core principles of CompStat with the problem-solving model of Newport News, presented earlier, reveals a significant amount of similarity. Indeed, CompStat may well be the natural evolution of the problem-solving model in today's more sophisticated cities. It is important that Chicago's CAPS program incorporated CompStat as a vehicle to enhance crime fighting and management accountability. While a number of jurisdictions, including Los Angeles, Philadelphia, New Orleans, Albuquerque, Sacramento, Boston, and Dallas, continue to refine the CompStat principles, none has been more successful in implementing the process than the Minneapolis Police Department.

In Minneapolis, the CompStat program was referred to as **CODEFOR** (**C**omputer **O**ptimized **DE**ployment—**F**ocus **O**n **R**esults). This strategy was designed specifically to reduce crime and involves every geographical and structural unit within the Minneapolis Police Department. CODEFOR combined the latest technology in computer applications and geographical mapping with field-proven police techniques. Computer-generated maps identify high-intensity crime areas, and police resources are coordinated to such locations in a timely manner. Each week, police managers gather together and ask directed questions regarding the crime rates in each of their areas (see Figure 2.5).

In CODEFOR's heyday, departmental executives and commanders grilled precinct captains on the crimes in their areas. Precinct captains, while not expected to be able to eliminate crime entirely, were expected to articulate a sensible strategy for reversing a trend or eliminating a hot-spot. In many cases, those leaders who repeatedly failed to rise to the occasion—not unlike what might happen to the manager of a struggling department in a corporation—found themselves promptly reassigned. Police managers were held accountable for reducing crime in their areas. A more enlightened understanding of why the process worked was that it got the top police managers involved with crime once again. In addition to the solution of internal problems, attendance at community meetings, scheduling, and a myriad of other administrative tasks, managers were forced to direct their efforts to addressing crime in their geographical districts of responsibility. This emphasis on crime awareness and crime fighting sparked renewed feelings of self-worth among managers as well as an increase in communication between the beat officer and the precinct captain. Obviously, a more team-oriented spirit naturally arises which increases morale and supports the primary goals of CompStat under the CODEFOR program.[37]

The Minneapolis Police Department was one of the first departments not only to generate specific crime statistics each week by geographical area but also to use a much more refined process of tabulating success or failure. Interestingly, the reports were also provided over the Internet on a monthly basis for public consumption and evaluation.[38]

The major case studies presented (Newport News, Chicago, and Minneapolis) represent only three attempts to develop community policing and CompStat initiatives in the United States. Policing continues to develop and change; it is organic. As such, cities large and small are experimenting with best practices in attempts to significantly reduce crime and improve the quality of life within their communities.

POLICING STRATEGIES TODAY

Discussions of policing strategies today employ a number of catchphrases and acronyms—it seems that every major jurisdiction employs a strategy that they credit with decreasing crime

rates. As previously discussed, though, community policing programs and other contemporary policing initiatives have also revealed similar levels of inefficiency.

In particular, research has provided little in terms of support for problem-oriented policing as presented through broken windows and zero-tolerance philosophies.[39] Furthermore, despite the widespread popularity of community policing strategies, most studies evaluating this type of policing have not found that it greatly impacts crime or disorder; at best, community policing reduces citizens' fear of crime[40] and produces core challenges to police organizations as they attempts to restructure and change to adapt to community policing ideologies.[41]

Nevertheless, there are some new approaches and tactics being used with promising results. **Evidence-based policing** is becoming a major player, with more and more departments across the country engaging with police science and research to determine effective strategy.

Geographic-based and focused policing approaches, such as **hot-spots policing** and directed patrols, represent the most strongly supported policing practices in the United States,[42] aided by the use of geographical information systems (GIS), crime analysis, and artificial intelligence. Similarly, **intelligence-led policing (ILP)** and proactive policing models are also gaining attention as police departments look for ways to do more with fewer resources. Although currently under-researched and new, the geographic-based policing approaches have emerged as innovative strategies for reducing crime and increasing citizen satisfaction with police services. Unfortunately, the sheer number of new and innovative paradigms to combat crime appears to be escalating by the year. Students and scholars alike often have problems segregating and differentiating the various types of policing strategy that may be employed in one city, or for that matter, in one sector of a city. Many of the police strategies employed today are similar, particularly those that are geographically based, with only minor additions or tactical differences. Indeed, many of the "strategies" could be much more easily classified as a police tactic aimed at reducing crime in a specific neighborhood over a specific period of time. The myriad of new names and models has given rise to the thought that the real differences between policing strategies may be more "rhetoric than reality."

Evidence-Based Policing

In recent years, researchers have focused on building a knowledge base as it pertains to what is known about the effectiveness of criminal justice strategies. The ultimate goal is to provide practitioners with sound empirical evidence to help them make informed decisions regarding related policies and programs. Evidence-based policing is a reflection of this philosophy. According to Sherman, "evidence-based policing is the use of the best available research on the outcomes of police work to implement guidelines and evaluate agencies, units, and officers."[43] Rather than focusing on "how" to do police work, as in community policing, or utilizing a generalized problem-solving approach to crime, as in problem-oriented policing, evidence-based policing is a paradigm that utilizes the scientific method

Minneapolis Calls for Service
Shooting - Sound of Shots Fired - Shotspotter Activations
July 6 - July 12, 2016

Legend

★ Shooting

◉ ShotSpotter Activation

● Sound of Shots Fired

Miles
0   1   2   3   4   5

Minneapolis Police Department
Crime Analysis Unit
350 S. 5th St - Room 100
Minneapolis, MN 55415
612-673-2470

Information obtained from 911 CAD System.
NOTE: One incident may be represented by multiple Icons in the map, depending upon the number of callers and location of incoming calls.
**Officers are dispatched to the location where the shooting victim is currently at, which may include the hospital, or location different from the actual shooting incident.

FIGURE 2.5 ▶ Minneapolis' CODEFOR program merges community policing with CompStat. Police executives are held accountable for their strategic response to calls for service and crime. Minneapolis is one of the few departments that shares its crime bulletins and analysis maps with the public on a weekly basis via their website.
Source: http://www.ci.minneapolis.mn.us/police/crime-statistics/codefor/650_MinneapolisShotsFired.pdf, retrieved on July 16, 2016.

to identify, implement, evaluate, and modify the methods that are most effective in reducing crime.[44]

Sherman's model focuses on the *"Triple-T Strategy"*: Targeting, Testing, and Tracking. *Targeting* involves assessing relative levels of harm and allocating police resources based on this measure; in other words, focusing on those issues that the police can lawfully address that will have the most impact. *Testing* looks at examining research for evidence of success (or failure) to determine how a strategy is working. And *tracking* is an effort to continually check performance and implementation, through programs that might include CompStat and even review of body-worn camera data.[45]

Essentially, evidence-based policing means that police agencies should assess research related to "what works and what doesn't work"—and adjust their organizational strategies appropriately. This seems intuitive; however, law enforcement agencies have been historically slow and even resistant to discontinue programs that have been clearly shown through effective evaluation research that they do not work (e.g., Drug Abuse Resistance and Education (DARE) programs, gun buyback programs, and the random moving patrol car). And, in the case of programs that *do* work, like hot-spots policing, departments implement bits and pieces of the philosophy while still maintaining more traditional policing methods overall.[46]

Adopting an evidence-based policing model would have many benefits to willing law enforcement agencies. Using scientifically backed principles to decide on tactics and strategies is more ethically sound than simply choosing whatever is new, popular, and preferred. Furthermore, using programs and strategies that are proven to work will reduce crime and increase quality of life, thereby inherently enhancing police legitimacy. Evidence-based policing also reinforces the concept of police transparency—it's much easier to explain motives, goals, objectives, and plans to the public when there is solid evaluation research to support the effort. Research also plays a very important role in police professionalism: Using evidence-based strategies for hiring, training, and developing/implementing policies and procedures may strengthen the personnel base, decrease inappropriate use of force, and advance the notion of fair and impartial policing. As echoed by the National Research Council (in 2004), current policing strategies in the United States are problematic at best, and future efforts must focus on more effective, evidence-based models:

1. Standard models of policing emphasizing random patrols and unfocused enforcement is *not* effective in reducing crime

2. Community policing strategies aimed at reducing crime, fear of crime, and disorder have had mixed results.

3. Police strategies focused and tailored on specific types of crime, criminals, and geographic locations are more effective.

4. Problem-oriented policing is effective.

5. Future models of policing should be supported by strong and independent evaluation research.[47]

A law enforcement agency that seeks to operate under the philosophy of evidence-based policing probably, at a bare minimum, looks at the latest research for basic knowledge regarding its organizational directives and strategies and incorporates it into their operation on multiple levels from training to crime analysis. Agencies truly committed to the evidence-based model would further emphasize crime analysis and proactive versus reactive policing policies; would base policies and procedures on proven strategies; and work with at least one major academic partner with whom it shares statistics, policies, and plans for the purposes of ongoing and unbiased evaluation.

Shifting to an evidence-based culture in law enforcement will be a slow change; police agencies are notoriously resistant to major transformative change, particularly ones that force them to reassess the way things have been done for years. Institutionalizing research means that police agencies have to work outside their area of comfort, with expert researchers often from academic and research institutions that do not have a political position in the outcome. The relationship between academics and police agencies has been one fraught with historical conflict and mistrust. Today, however, there are a number of relatively isolated but growing collaborations that highlight partnerships between researchers and police. In New York City, the relationship between NYPD and the John Jay School of Criminal Justice flourishes. The Chicago Police Department continues its evaluation research project of CAPS with Northwestern University and the Providence, Rhode Island Police Department continues to collaborate with Roger Williams University for the improvement of their programs. However, there are a number of important and new collaborations in Texas. Sam Houston State University has historically assisted the Houston Police Department in a variety of evaluation projects over the past 30 years; and the Arlington Police Department has emphasized evidence-based practices for several years and is seen as a national model for practical research and evaluation. Under former chief Theron Bowman and continued leadership by Chief Will Johnson, the agency participated in a complex and rigorous study of compressed work weeks in policing, employing randomized controlled trials to aid in the understanding of how different types of shifts affect officer performance, safety, and health. The six-month study required significant resources from the department, but APD remained committed to seeing the outcomes through and adapting its agency policies accordingly. It also participated in programs that highlighted risk-terrain modeling for robbery reductions, national traffic safety studies, and patrol deployment algorithms.[48] Continued research into unmanned aircraft systems, best practices from social media in law enforcement, and body-worn camera deployment again highlight evidence-based policing projects team with local universities for research and evaluation. However, one of the most noted national collaborations was highlighted in Dallas, Texas, in 2008 with the development of the Caruth Police Institute; a collaboration between the Dallas Police Department and the University of North Texas at Dallas and the University of Texas at Dallas. Under the leadership of the then chief David M. Kunkle, a transformative gift of nearly $10 million was presented for the development of the institute among private foundations, local universities, and the Dallas Police Department. The institute is physically located inside the Dallas Police Department and staffed primarily by faculty at the new University of North Texas at Dallas, with an affiliated relationship with the University of Texas at Dallas, which offers a doctoral program in criminology as well as major assistance with research and evaluation projects. The Caruth Police Institute focuses on fulfilling the complex research, career advancement, and leadership development needs of the Dallas Police Department. This places the Dallas Police Department in the unique position of being a national resource for innovative strategies in policing. The venture signifies a bold new relationship between academia and major police departments characterized by cutting-edge research, education, and professional development services.[49]

Tools for agencies seeking to bolster their evidence-based credentials are not in short supply. Academic institutions are forever seeking crime data and access to law enforcement agencies, as well as internships and research opportunities for students. And the Center for Evidence-Based Crime Policy offers a number of resources, including the Evidence-Based Policing Matrix developed by Dr. Cynthia Lum and colleagues (see Figure 2.6). This visual guide classifies police interventions based on the nature and type of target (individuals, groups, neighborhoods, etc.), whether it's proactive or reactive, and the level of focus within each strategy (i.e., general prevention versus focused tactics); included studies must be at least moderately scientifically rigorous. The result of this ongoing collation of data is that practitioners can see at a glance where successful programs cluster—and generally, the data indicates that successful interventions cluster in micro-places or neighborhoods, and are highly focused on specific issues.[50]

Hot-Spots Policing

Much like evidence-based policing, hot-spots policing reflects the direct application of empirical data (through various crime analysis and information technologies) that show that crime is *not* randomly dispersed but rather is concentrated in isolated areas.[51] In their seminal work, Sherman and colleagues found that only a few locations were responsible for a majority of police calls for service and reported crime—particularly predatory crimes such as muggings, vehicle thefts, burglary, robbery, and rape.[52] In addition, they found that all robberies occurred at 2.2 percent of places, all rapes occurred at 1.2 percent of places, and all auto thefts occurred at 2.7 percent of places.[53] These areas or "places" with a higher than average number of crimes are "hot-spots" and represent areas that reflect not only higher than normal crime rates but also are often inhabited by lower-income and high-density populations.[54] Similar to these findings, drug distribution also appears to cluster. In Jersey City, New Jersey drug "hot-spots" were responsible for a

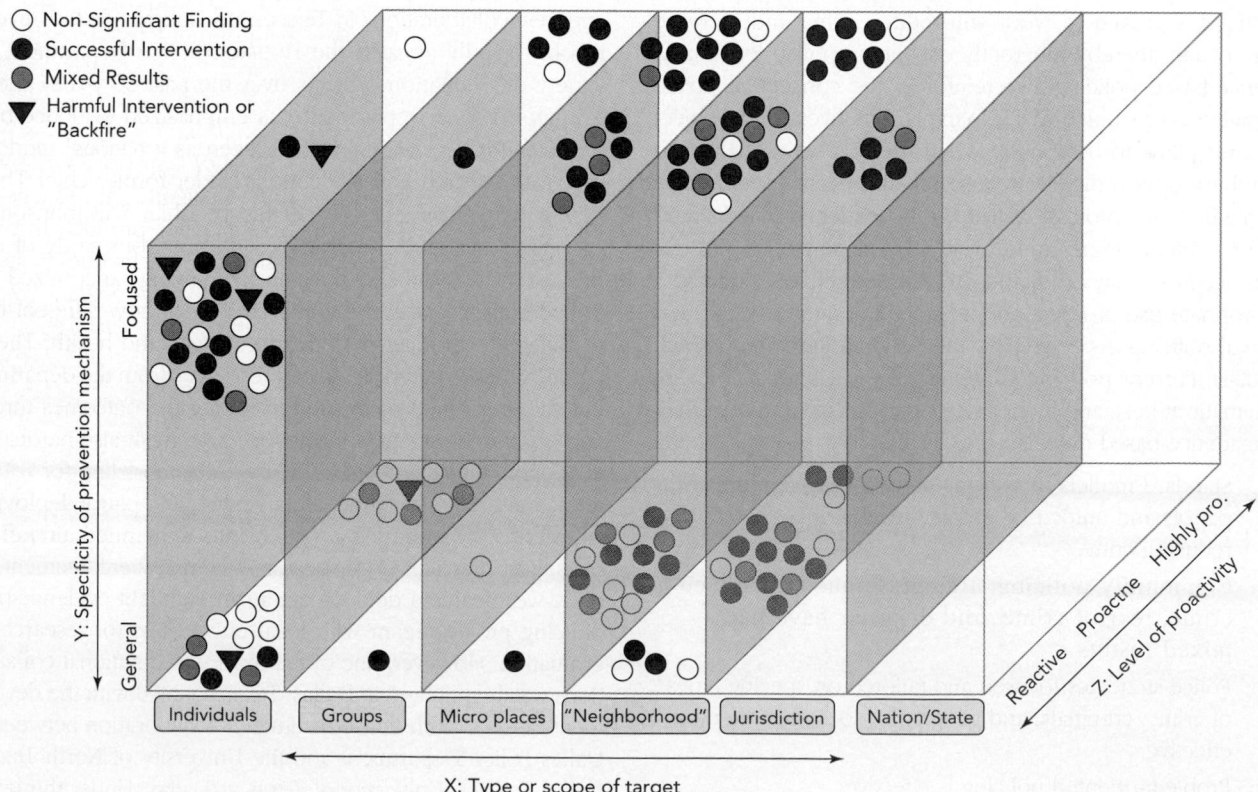

FIGURE 2.6 ▶ The matrix key. *Source:* Cynthia Lum, Christopher Koper, and Cody Telep, Center for Evidence-Based Crime Policy, http://cebcp.org/evidence-based-policing/the-matrix/

disproportionate number of arrests and calls for service to the police. Furthermore, these areas also experienced a greater amount of issues related to crime and disorder compared to other areas; that is, serious crime, disorder, and street-level drug problems cluster in certain areas within the city. Deploying more police resources to these areas reduces the clustering effect.[55]

Although the concept of crime hot-spots has been documented for many years, hot-spots policing is a relatively innovative approach to crime. This type of policing forces the police to identify specific areas with undue concentrations of crime and then direct their resources at those places. This is certainly not a novel idea, and the traditional patrol sergeants of the 1960s could have argued that a map, a few colored pins, and a series of crime reports could have told us "where to send officers" on routine patrol. Again, this appears to be a very important police strategy, particularly in reducing more predatory crimes, recently reinforced by a study in Charlotte, North Carolina. The deployment of street crime units in hot-spot robbery areas not only significantly reduced crime but also reduced the level of fear expressed by citizens.[56] However, the strongest support for "hot-spots" policing comes from the National Academy of Sciences:

> Studies that focused police resources on crime hot-spots provide the strongest collective evidence of police effectiveness that is now available. On the basis of a series of randomized experimental studies, we conclude that the practice described as hot-spots policing is effective in reducing crime and disorder and can achieve these reductions without significant displacement of crime control benefits. Indeed, the research evidence suggests that the diffusion of crime control benefits to areas surrounding treated hot-spots is stronger than any displacement outcome.[57]

Despite the evidence in support of hot-spots policing, it is uncertain as to what specific tactics have the most influence in problem areas, given the wide array of intervention tactics that are used within the model.[58] For example, hot-spots policing tactics include directed patrols, saturation patrol, aggressive traffic enforcement, zero-tolerance, and disorder enforcement, as well as specific drug "buy and bust" programs, even focused problem-oriented policing techniques. In addition, some scholars argue that hot-spots do not actually exist in the real world; that is, hot-spots are an "amalgam" of different types of locations that simply cluster on a map; they are a product of data construction.[59] These data points could be addresses, buildings, apartment complexes, block faces, census tracks, or individual police sectors; however, they are a temporary product of the data world, a logical fallacy that is impossible to operationally identify using agreed-upon, replicable, and scientific criteria.[60]

Today, many police departments are utilizing a hot-spots strategy banking on those studies that show that it reduces and prevents crime; however, they are also utilizing a plethora of patrol and arrest techniques that most likely have varying effects on crime in specific places. Future research in this area should focus on parceling-out the various techniques and tactics used in each type of hot-spot and measuring the impact of each. Hypothetically, we may well find that it is not one approach but rather the cumulative impact of visible police patrol and the employment of various arrest tactics that most likely impacts crime the most in a specific area.

Directed and Saturation Patrols

Directed and saturation patrols are tactics commonly used in policing. Although these strategies are considered low on the scale of diverse approaches, they are often used in conjunction with hot-spots policing. While directed patrol usually involves the "directing" of patrol officers to specific locations during their patrol shift, saturation patrol concentrates *additional* officers on specific locations at specific times. The idea is to maximize visible patrol efforts in a specific area. Both types of patrol involve the assignment of officers to problematic areas for proactive enforcement at high-risk times.[61] In theory, increased police presence through directed and saturation patrols in these areas and times is expected to arrest offenders responsible for a great majority of these crimes and generate reductions in crime. It is, however, unknown as to whether crime is actually reduced or simply moved to another location (displaced); when police visibility is increased, offenders often move to other areas of the city.

There is also conflicting evidence that calls into question the effectiveness of directed and saturation patrols as an effective crime control strategy versus more aggressive arrest tactics. Fritsch, Caeti, and Taylor evaluated police strategies aimed at reducing gang violence in Dallas, Texas.[62] Their initiative targeted five areas that housed seven of the most violent gangs in the city. Officers spent a majority of their time utilizing three suppression tactics, including aggressive curfew enforcement, aggressive truancy enforcement, and saturation patrol, making patrols highly visible in the targeted areas. Although aggressive curfew and truancy enforcement were related to significant reductions in gang violence, saturation patrols did not produce the same effects. Once again, more aggressive arrest techniques in specific areas during specific times aimed at specific predatory crimes may be the most effective tactic in reducing crime.

Intelligence-Led Policing

Unlike directed and saturation patrols, intelligence-led policing (ILP) is not a tactic, nor is it a crime-reduction strategy, but rather a business model for policing. It is "an information-organizing process that allows police agencies to better understand their crime problems and take a measure of the resources available to be able to decide on an enforcement tactic or prevention strategy best designed to control crime."[63] More specifically, intelligence-led policing utilizes criminal intelligence analysis as a means to accomplish crime prevention and reduction through best practices and partnerships with other entities.

There are a number of reasons as to why intelligence-led policing has become popular in recent years. First, widespread recognition of the ineffectiveness of the standard policing model and the difficulty in implementing problem-oriented policing has caused police departments to look for alternatives. Second, departments are increasingly faced with financial constraints though demands remain high and the opportunities to employ additional resources and personnel are limited. Third, more sophisticated technologies in information retrieval and analysis of police information have generated interest in systematic approaches to crime.[64]

Although intelligence-led policing emerged in the United States after the September 11, 2001, terrorist attacks, the movement toward this approach actually began prior to the 1990s and originated in the United Kingdom.[65] At that time, it was recommended by the Audit Commission that police services should *focus on the offender* rather than reported crime. The British government subsequently passed legislation requiring police departments to adopt the National Intelligence Model, which promoted intelligence-led policing.

It is important to note that intelligence is more than simply data; it also involves information. While data are "identifiable, objective facts about events," information is the addition of context and analysis that puts data into comprehensible forms.[66] Data and information do not become intelligence until they are interpreted, evaluated, and used as a means to inform crime prevention and reduction strategies. In ILP, these objectives are believed to be obtainable primarily through the proactive and objective identification and targeting of the criminal subpopulation.[67]

A recent example of intelligence-led policing in practice is Operation Nine Connect. Ratcliffe and Guidetti report that the New Jersey State Police implemented a gang crackdown in 2008 targeting Nine Trey—a subset of the much larger and well-known "Bloods" gang.[68] Together, officers involved in the crackdown conducted over 8,000 hours of electronic surveillance and more than 2,300 hours of physical surveillance, as well as spent over 1,200 hours transcribing wiretaps and approximately 300 hours developing and maintaining confidential sources. The result was the initial arrest of 60 gang members and the subsequent arrest of at least 30 others.

Despite the popularity and the successes of intelligence-led policing, there are a number of limitations associated with this type of approach, including data entry problems and lack of training in advanced analytic techniques within the police. In addition, Ratcliffe notes the organizational problems of intelligence-led policing, such as the lack of continuity in structure across intelligence units and the confusion over the principles of intelligence-led crime reduction.[69] In addition, as discussed later in Chapter 3, some argue that ILP may well be in conflict with civil and constitutional safeguards that ensure that individuals are "innocent until proven guilty." Focusing on specific individuals as offenders tests this important principle of our democracy.

Predictive Policing

Similar to intelligence-led policing, **predictive policing** is a proactive approach to crime and disorder that uses information and analytical tools to achieve the goal of crime prevention while requiring fewer resources.[70] Not only does predictive policing improve upon intelligence-led policing, it also reflects

the principles of problem-oriented, community, and evidence-based policing.[71] According to Beck and McCue, "With new technology, new business processes, and new algorithms, predictive policing is based on directed, information-based patrol; rapid response supported by fact-based prepositioning of assets; and proactive, intelligence-based tactics, strategy, and policy."[72] Consequently, one of the key components of predictive policing is the use of advanced analytics that evaluate and examine data and information through advanced statistics and artificial intelligence. In other words, predictive policing utilizes numerous technologies and techniques such as data mining, crime mapping, and geospatial prediction to plan for and respond to future crime.

Advanced analytics have been used in a variety of capacities from preventing violent crimes to improving deployment, response planning, and policy decision making. For example, police in Richmond, Virginia, used advanced analytics and predictive policing to reduce random gunfire on New Year's Eve. Based on information collected from previous years, police were able to predict the time, location, and type of incident most likely to occur on that particular night. In preparation, officers were placed at those locations to prevent and quickly respond to such crimes. The end result was a 47 percent reduction in random gunfire and a significant increase in the number of seized weapons.[73]

Although predictive policing is a new and promising approach, it too has generated a number of questions and concerns. A major criticism is the novelty of predictive policing given its semblance to other policing models, particularly ILP. Moreover, the central tenets of predictive policing closely resemble what crime analysts have been doing for years. Still, others argue that the outcomes of the model are vague and unclear.[74]

INFORMATION TECHNOLOGIES IN POLICING

The evolution of policing strategies has included the development and use of sophisticated information technologies. Today, information technologies assume a new and more vital role. For instance, police operations are incredibly data and information intensive. Rather than utilizing computers for data storage, police departments are now using them as information and knowledge-based systems.[75] This is especially important as police agencies rely more heavily on intelligence as well as the identification and targeting of crime hot-spots and repeat offenders. Crime analysis, geographic information systems (GIS), and artificial intelligence represent the most widely used information technologies in policing today.

Crime Analysis

As the dynamics of policing move toward an information-driven and evidence-based agenda, the need for accurate analyses is becoming increasingly important. Consequently, crime analysis has emerged as a means to satisfy this requirement. **Crime**

Quick Facts: Crime Rates Fall in the First Half of 2014; Rise Sharply in the First Half of 2015

Crime rates fell for the second year in a row (after slight increases in 2011/2012) in the United States, with figures indicating an overall decrease of 4.6 percent in the number of violent crimes for the first 6 months of 2014 when compared with figures reported for the same time in 2013. The violent crime category includes murder, rape, robbery, and aggravated assault. However, violence crime appears to have risen sharply by 1.7 percent for the first six months of 2015. FBI statistics reveal that most major cities reported dramatic increase in the number of homicides in their community reflecting a 6.2 percent jump in murder alone. FBI Director James Comey raised the possibility that there may be a

connection between violent crime rate increases during this period with changing police behavior. He asserted that officers had stopped more proactive policing tactics and philosophies as a result of fear of being captured by cell phone videos that go viral on the Internet and attract public condemnation.

Source: https://www.fbi.gov/about-us/cjis/ucr/crime-in-the-u.s/2014/preliminary-semiannual-uniform-crime-report-january-june-2014 and Eric Tucker, "FBI: Violent Crime Rose in First 6 Months of 2015 over 2014," *Associated Press*, January 19, 2016. See: http://hosted.ap.org/dynamic/stories/U/US_FBI_VIOLENT_CRIME?SITE=AP&SECTION=HOME&TEMPLATE=DEFAULT&CTIME=2016-01-19-15-57-53

analysis is the process of identifying patterns and relationships between crime data and other relevant data sources to prioritize and target police activity.[76] The uneven distribution of crime in terms of space and place, type of offenders, and victimization theoretically allows analysts to draw inferences from patterns of crime, which can be used as a foundation for allocating police resources. In other words, crime analysis generates associations and relationships between variables (such as space, time, offenders, and victims) that are related to crime. The purpose of crime analysis is to organize massive quantities of raw information from databases used in automated records systems and to forecast specific, future events from the statistical manipulation of these data. In theory, crime analysis provides a thorough and systematic analysis of data on which to make rational decisions regarding past, present, and future actions.[77] Crime analysis is critical when deploying resources based on new policing strategies such as "hot-spots" policing, directed and saturation patrols, and predictive policing (see Figure 2.7).

Crime analysis is not limited solely to reported crime information. Attention has also been given to the statistical analysis of intelligence information. Kinney[78] reports that criminal intelligence analysis supports investigators, decision makers, and policymakers in their attempts to prevent and control crime. The following are some of the more common crime analysis techniques:

- *Tactical crime analysis or crime-specific analysis*—a tabular or graphic display of reported crimes with a given pattern of time and/or location. It is often used to detect patterns of crime (e.g., robberies, burglaries, and auto thefts) that cluster in specific locations during various time periods. The focus of tactical crime analysis is on recent criminal incidents through the examination of characteristics such as how, when, and where the activity has occurred in order to aid suspect identification and case clearance.[79]

FIGURE 2.7 ▶ A series of "hot-spots" indicating vehicle crimes mapped by census track to varying hot-spot thresholds. Note that "hot-spots" become much more apparent as the data used to create the maps are refined. *Source:* John E. Eck, Spencer Chaney, James G. Cameron, Michael Leitner, and Ronald E. Wilson, *NIJ Special Report: Mapping Crime: Understanding Hot-Spots* (Washington, DC: National Institute of Justice, August 2005). See: http://www.ncjrs.gov/pdffiles1/nij/209393.pdf

- *Strategic crime analysis*—the study of crime and/or social problems in a specific area in an effort to determine long-term patterns of activity as well as to evaluate police responses and organizational procedures.[80] Strategic crime analysis is often used to determine the effectiveness of police over a given period of time, or in the evaluation of specific policing strategies as discussed earlier.

- *Link analysis*—a graphic portrayal of associations and relationships among people, organizations, events, activities, and locations from a given point in time. This technique is a powerful analytic tool used to reveal the hidden connections among criminals and the structure of clandestine, organized criminal entities often found in street gangs, La Cosa Nostra families, white-collar crime syndicates, large drug trafficking cartels, and terrorist organizations. Link analysis is invaluable in complex investigations, particularly those that have a "conspiracy" aspect, as is often found in racketeering and continuing criminal enterprise cases. Link analysis is also a powerful tool used extensively in ILP.

- *Telephone toll analysis*—computerized reports derived from court-ordered long-distance telephone billings of suspects in illegal narcotics trafficking. Reports indicate the number and frequency of calls displayed in numerical, chronological, and geographical order. Link analysis can be used to show the relationship between billing numbers and the numbers called.[81]

- *Visual investigative analysis (VIA)*—charting that depicts key events of criminal activity in chronological order. VIA is used to show the degree of involvement of subjects. This method is especially convincing in conspiracy cases and can also be used as a planning tool to focus the resources of an investigative effort.[82] At a conference focusing on school shootings, a graphical VIA was presented on the Virginia Tech University shooting incident.[83] Interestingly, the VIA effort displayed a horizontal graph, over 60 feet long, with over 1,200 entries.

- *Case analysis and management system (CAMS)*—computerized case management in which large amounts of data are compiled and indexed for each retrieval of specific items. This system is used to clarify relationships and calculate the probability of associations.[84]

- *Intelligence analysis*—the identification of networks of offenders and criminal activity, often associated with organized crime, gangs, drug traffickers, prostitution rings, and terrorist organizations. Recent interest in intelligence analysis has given rise to the development of large, centralized intelligence processing hubs, referred to as fusion centers (discussed later in Chapter 3, Intelligence, Terrorism, and Homeland Security). Intelligence analysis also becomes the basis for intelligence-led policing.

Crime analysis is a flexible and dynamic process designed primarily to identify trends and patterns associated with crime and social problems. It is designed to be a perpetual and continuous process and to assist law enforcement executives in making more informed decisions in their response to crime. The technology of crime analysis takes advantage of research and statistical methodologies, often in an automated process. It does not necessarily have to be relegated to advanced statistical techniques, but it can be accomplished quite well with a basic understanding of Microsoft Office programs, such as Word and Excel. Indeed, Mark Stallo's inviting work focuses on developing a relatively sophisticated crime analysis model based solely on the application of Microsoft Office products to reported police data.[85]

Geographic Information Systems (GIS)

The use of **geographic information systems(GIS)** in law enforcement to map criminal events coincided with the results of several environmental criminology studies that illustrated crime patterns. Prior to computerized mapping systems, police commonly used pin maps as a means of tracking crime. Unfortunately, this practice has many limitations due to the difficulties in determining clusters and general trends using point data.[86] However, with the advent of sophisticated computerized mapping, researchers have found a widespread adoption of GIS tools across police departments, particularly larger agencies[87] (see Figure 2.8).

There are two types of crime mapping: statistical spatial analysis and spatial modeling. While statistical spatial analysis focuses on the spatial relationship between crime points in a particular area, spatial modeling is concerned with the technology and application of data.[88] As previously mentioned, GIS has made these two components of crime mapping easy to use in the realm of policing. Given its functionality, it has become an influential mechanism in hot-spots policing as well as Crime Prevention Through Environmental Design (CPTED), situational policing, directed patrols, and crime analysis.

Of course, GIS has a myriad of other uses in policing. Police agencies can use GIS in dispatching police units by providing directions to locations; address histories; and locations of nearby fire and waste hazards, fire hydrants, alarm boxes, high-power lines, water lines, and the like. Police managers can not only use GIS to provide graphic analysis of specific crime patterns and to evaluate new policing strategies but also to track individual officer performance by area.[89] Not surprisingly, GIS has emerged as a powerful tool that helps police executives make better-informed decisions. Due to its wide range of uses, it is likely that crime mapping and geographic information systems will remain key tools in police operations and in the evaluation of police strategies.

The Internet

Clearly, one of the most important technological advantages of the information age is the Internet. The Internet is a worldwide network of computer systems and other computer networks that offers the opportunity for sending information to and receiving information from a vast audience from around the world.

FIGURE 2.8 ▶ Geographic information systems (GIS) provide a wide array of maps and diagrams useful for crime analysis and decision making. (Courtesy of the Dallas Police Department, 2016)

The unique benefits of the Internet are speed and efficiency combined with global reach. There are essentially no barriers to sending information and receiving information from as close as next door to around the world. Of particular importance to police agencies is the ease and speed with which information can be kept current. With the introduction of the World Wide Web, finding information on the Internet is very easy and user friendly.

Local police agencies have capitalized on the use of the Internet, with most major departments establishing their own home pages (see Figure 2.9). In addition, most departments have encouraged their communities to keep abreast of police activities through the Internet. A list of emergency services and phone numbers, names and descriptions of the most "wanted" fugitives in the community, periodic updates on a specific (usually high-profile) case, employment announcements and opportunities within the department, residential and commercial crime alerts, and even online crime reporting are now available through various departments on the Internet.

As worldwide communication and global reach via the Internet expand, policing will likely experience dramatic changes. For instance, the United Nations recently linked various criminal justice research institutes from different countries, allowing for the first time a free exchange of information among countries on issues impacting the world community (e.g., international terrorism, environmental crime, gangs, and computer fraud). New and combined training sessions, various telecommunication partnerships, and interactive information exchanges (podcasts and webinars) are now commonplace on the Internet. The greater access to information provided by the Internet has made a major difference in the future, not only for police agencies and researchers but also for individual communities addressing wider criminal justice issues. Certainly, the Internet has been one of the strongest catalysts for social, economic, and political change in the world.

Social Media and Policing

One of the most surprising technological advances in law enforcement from the past decade can be found in the realm of **social media**, taking police agencies into a whole new world of "likes," "shares," and "re-Tweets." Facebook and Twitter, particularly, have been a boon to police departments across the country, allowing for instantaneous outreach to the community. In one of the best examples of the possibilities that lie within this integrated technology, the Boston Police Department utilized Twitter and Facebook in the immediate aftermath of the Boston

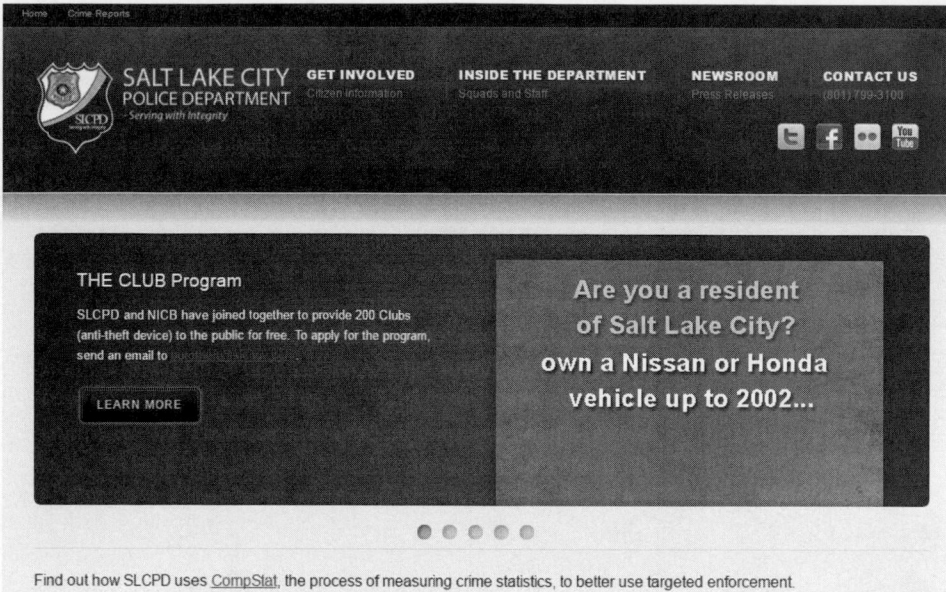

Find out how SLCPD uses CompStat, the process of measuring crime statistics, to better use targeted enforcement.

FIGURE 2.9 ▶ Most police departments use the Internet to share important information with their communities, including crime statistics, most wanted, local and homeland security news, recruitment efforts, and chief's messages. Note the linkages to other web portals (Facebook, YouTube, Twitter, and Flickr) prominently displayed on the Salt Lake City Police Department website. *Source:* http://www.slcpd.com/ (retrieved on July 22, 2015).

Marathon Bombings in 2013. These social media platforms were crucial to distributing public information, coordinating media briefings, giving traffic information related to street closures, coordinating volunteers, and soliciting videos and pictures from the event that, in some cases, contained evidence of the crime.[90]

Boston is not alone in their successful use of social media; it has now become standard for police agencies to use Facebook and Twitter, NextDoor, Tumblr, Instagram, and other social networks to connect with citizens, personnel, other police agencies, and the media. The following examples highlight the use of social media as employed by law enforcement organizations:

- *Communication in emergency situations:* informing the public of a situation; releasing new information as it is available; describing areas to avoid; communicating risks and giving suggestions to avoid those risks; missing persons; and Amber alerts.
- *Agency transparency:* informing the public of use of force complaints brought against the department; releasing officer disciplinary information; explaining the actions of the police agency in a crisis situation; providing insight into day-to-day policing; and announcing new initiatives and strategies.
- *Community outreach:* publicizing community policing events; announcing community events; publicizing policing successes; and humanizing policing through anecdotes, humor, and the like.
- *Networking with other police agencies*: sharing best practices; making investigative contacts.
- *Investigation*: suspect identification; request submission of crime tips or photographic/video evidence; examination of social media sites for criminal activity; and use of social media in undercover operations and stings.
- *Personnel selection*: social media background checks to assess candidates; recruiting outreach.

- *Public relations:* social media allows law enforcement agencies to craft news releases long before the media gets information.

For proponents of evidence-based policing, using social media policing is difficult to evaluate. How do you measure success via social media? Is it the number of followers you have? The number of missing persons found as a result of shared Facebook posts? The number of suspects arrested through YouTube posts? Does it increase police legitimacy, and if so, where is the evidence to suggest such a claim? Few scientifically validated studies have been undertaken to pinpoint the value of police use of social media, but nonetheless, agencies continue to adopt and evolve social media strategies at a breaking speed.

Social media demands significant resources from law enforcement agencies. For instance, accounts need to be monitored constantly to prevent abusive, inflammatory, and/or discriminatory posts. Agencies must constantly reinforce that emergencies should not be reported via social media. Grammatical errors can become news headlines and the threat from hacking is always a real possibility. These types of events can open police departments to potentially devastating public relations nightmares and potential liability, especially when police departments rush to update an incident on social media before all the facts are known, implicating innocent people in criminal activity. Training for officers and police executives entrusted with official social media communications should be rigorous, and departments should have specific policies and procedures that govern their use of social media. Finally, police tout social media as a way to increase transparency and legitimacy, but it is increasingly being used to allow agencies to "manage the message"—or release a story in order to pre-empt the media and control the message. In some cases, monopolizing the message may backfire on perceptions of legitimacy and openness.

Obviously, social media in law enforcement is a phenomenon that has permeated the operations of police agencies at every

Quick Facts: Social Media Adoption in Law Enforcement

According to the 2014 International Association of Chiefs of Police Social Media Survey:

- 95 percent of agencies surveyed reported social media use in some capacity.

- The most common use of social media is for investigative purposes at 82.3 percent.

- The most frequently used social media platforms are Facebook (95.4 percent), Twitter (66.4 percent), and YouTube (38.5 percent).

- 71.7 percent of agencies surveyed have a social media policy and another 12.2 percent are in the process of crafting a policy.

- 78.8 percent of agencies reported that social media has helped solve crimes in their jurisdiction.

- 77.5 percent say that social media has improved police–community relations in their jurisdiction.

Source: http://www.iacpsocialmedia.org/Portals/1/documents/2014SurveyResults.pdf

---

level. As a means to generate goodwill between the police and the public, its value is indispensable—it allows agencies to connect with the people they serve in a creative and instantaneous manner. In the future, social media will continue to shape the way that communities and the police interact.

The Impact of Information Technologies

Clearly, information technologies in policing have assumed a new and more vital role. They have taken on a new dimension, one that is central to the support of new policing strategies. The new task for information technologies is *analysis,* in addition to the storage and maintenance of information as in the past. The analytic support for various police strategies, however, must permeate the entire organizational structure and not be just a function of the crime analysis division. Information technology functionality must be much more flexible—ranging from support for quick, officer-level field inquiries to longitudinal mapping of a specific neighborhood to specific managerial performance measurements. Information technologies can no longer be separated from the integral parts of police management and decision making. They can no longer be relegated solely to the storage, maintenance, and retrieval of vast amounts of police data. Most new policing strategies (e.g., community policing, evidence-based policing, and predictive policing) are information-based and information-intensive and require the ability to identify problems, suggest specific police responses, and evaluate their effectiveness. This function cannot follow the same information-processing path as before.

Today's police officers must be equipped with information and training. The job still requires the ability to relate to various people under stressful conditions in often hostile environments. New policing strategies involve new tactics that call for individual judgment and skill in relating to problems that are both criminal and noncriminal. The police officer of the future must be able to relate to diverse groups of people in ways that stretch the imagination. To meet this challenge, police executives must ensure that three conditions exist. First, information technology development and design must support the emerging strategies in policing, particularly meeting the analytic demands embraced within such strategies. Second, police officers and executives must manage technology rather than allow themselves to be managed by it. Finally, individual police officers must understand their role in the community as aided by, but not controlled by, information technologies.

A CHANGING PARADIGM: FROM WARRIOR TO GUARDIAN

Policing is in a state of flux. A spate of high-profile use-of-force incidents in 2014 and 2015 resulted in the deaths of several unarmed African-Americans. These events have fueled criticisms of, and anger toward, law enforcement agencies across the country. The result was a series of protests, increased anti-policing sentiment, calls for police reforms, and is correlated with a series of ambushes and murders of police officers. It is essential to recognize that the best policing strategy means nothing if the community does not have confidence in the police. Indeed, the events of 2014–2015 provided further evidence that at least part of our communities—particularly parts of the minority community—has lost faith in police organizations.[91] There is an increasing number of people who believe that the militarization of U.S. policing is inconsistent with the community policing philosophy and a threat to it. In 1829 Robert Peel developed plans for the London Metropolitan concepts from the British military. However, he wanted there to be a distinction between the police and the military. Peel viewed the police as having a protective role toward the public versus the British military fighting an armed enemy in a distant land.[92] To make that distinction abundantly clear, Peel's officers wore blue uniforms, a marked contrast to the bright red British army coats and he did not allow them to carry guns.[93] While a military's mission is predicated on the use of force, Peel's principles of policing emphasize crime prevention, the need for public approval, the willing co-operation of the public, and the minimal use of physical force by the police in the performance of their duties. These philosophical statements are echoed in the tenets of today's community and evidence based policing models. Peel's efforts to separate the role of the police from the military essentially distinguishes between the guardian and warrior roles. Although there was some earlier use of police uniforms in America, the adoption of blue uniforms was to some degree a by-product of the availability of surplus union army uniforms after the Civil War and thus essentially not a major movement until after 1865. Traditional law enforcement uniforms serve as a symbol of police authority and provide the public with a quick way to locate an officer if one is nearby, e.g., to help find a wandering child at a school fair. Presently, the wearing of black military-style Battle Dress uniforms (BDUs) by some officers is troubling to militarization critics because: 1) those uniforms blur the line between police and the military, which have distinctly different roles; 2) the BDUs worn by officers are often black, a color often associated with the "bad guys," such as ninja assassins, and 3) the BDUs may re-enforce the police warrior culture.

A 1988 study covering 16-years of National Football League penalties revealed teams wearing black drew more penalties than their opponents, suggesting black uniforms made players more aggressive.[94] Studies of dark uniforms and aggression were conducted in the National Hockey League in 2011, which found a relationship between uniform color and aggression, and 2012, which reached the opposite conclusion.[95] A 2013 study found no significant differences in aggressive measures between departments whose officers wore dark versus departments whose personnel wore light-colored uniforms and a 2008 study concluded black police uniforms elicited more favorable public impressions than light-colored uniforms.[96] Still, there is a view that black BDU-wearing officers appear more formidable, are more aggressive, and less approachable, undercutting public support for policing. An unanswered question is whether a yet-to-be-done study in the post-Ferguson environment would provide a clear answer about any relationship between police behavior and uniform color, as well as public perceptions of the topic.

The Historical Drift Toward Militarization

The historical drift toward militarization is rooted in the social unrest, soaring crime, massive demonstrations, social changes, and political rhetoric that swept America in the 1960s and 1970s. Initially, SWAT teams were created primarily as a mechanism to deal with riots. Over time, there was mission creep as SWATs effectively took on high risk responsibilities, e.g., drug raids and barricaded subjects. These responsibilities required adoption of new tactics and equipment with greater capabilities, some of which were adapted from military models and provided from surplus military inventories. This was an on-going process that moved SWATs to be come increasingly militarized, e.g., using explosives to breach reinforced doors on drug raids and flash-bangs/stun grenades when serving some warrants. Militarization critics, including some Chiefs of Police and Sheriffs, are concerned that militarization re-enforces the warrior role of law enforcement at the expense of serving and protecting the public, unlike the military's role of engaging and destroying the enemy.

In 1997, bank robbers In North Hollywood, California, armed with fully automatic weapons and body armor had police officers equipped with pistols and shotguns at a significant disadvantage and the movement toward arming patrol officers with military AR-15s as "patrol rifles" was energized, spilling military goods into mainstream policing, a process that has continued for decades.[97]

The President's Commission on Law Enforcement and Criminal Justice (1967) issued an overall report as well as ones on the components of the criminal justice system. It had the effect of focusing attention on crime and into our national conversations, policies, and laws. In 1965, President Johnson declared a war on crime and seven years later President Nixon confirmed that "war" was an appropriate term to use with respect to fighting crime.[98]

In 1982, President Reagan maintained illicit drugs a threat to national security.[99] William Bennett, became the first Director of the White House National Drug Control Policy in 1989 and was known as the "drug czar."[100] He is on record as favoring "limiting Constitutional liberties if there was a compelling reason to do so" in the war on drugs.[101] Years later, he observed "it's a funny war when your enemy is entitled to due process and a fair trial."[102]

Until the 1980s, the use of SWAT teams was unexceptional in terms of number of deployments or "callouts." However, during that decade callouts began an explosive expansion. Arguably, this expansion also had the effect of reinforcing the criticism that police officers were too quick to become confrontational, what today is called the warrior mindset. BDUs were first adopted in policing by SWAT teams because they were practical. They also visually communicated the police officers wearing them were highly trained and not to be taken lightly. SWAT members have historically responded to incidents that were beyond the capability of patrol officers and which they were not trained to handle. These incidents often resulted in highly skilled use of force that both took and saved lives. While the mission of SWAT teams vary by agency, among the missions for which they train are building searches, hostage incident/rescue, barricaded suspects, serving high risk warrants, assaults on bus/train/aircraft, and rescue of persons downed. Although SWAT is the most common designation, such units carry different "labels" in law enforcement agencies, such as Emergency Response Team or Special Response Team. The International Association of Chiefs of Police (IACP) studied SWAT operations nationally for 2009–2013. Among its findings: 1) the U.S. military was a source of training for only 7.1 percent of respondents; 2) armored vehicles were deployed with SWAT teams an average of 10 times annually, 3) the most common complaint about SWAT teams was property damage (38 percent) and the least common was unlawful tactics (2 percent) with excessive force constituting 14 percent of all complaints.[103] The results of the IACP study suggest that concerns about police militarization are less about SWAT teams specifically and more about policing generally.

In addition to highly publicized wars on crime and drugs, some police rhetoric over past decades also reinforced the warrior model. Daryl Gates was the Los Angeles Police Chief from 1978 until 1992. Two years before leaving that post he suggested drug offenders should be shot for treason.[104] William Bennett echoed Gates by asserting he had no moral objection to convicted drug dealers being beheaded, although it would be legally difficult.[105]

He also advocated evicting people from public housing on mere suspicion of using drugs.[106] The war on crime perspective threads through the administrations of Presidents George H. Bush, Bill Clinton, and George W. Bush. The last of these famously said if you quit drugs, you join the fight on terrorism.[107] His administration also ran ads that claimed drug use supported terroristic acts. While this is true to a degree, a connection to specific terrorist groups was never made. Still, the rhetoric fanned the some flames against crime, drugs, and terrorism simultaneously.

An unscientific peek into the police culture suggests a warrior, "hard-liner" orientation by some officers. The messages on their occasionally worn T-shirts occasionally provide a basis for that observation. A former chief of police reports that at a SWAT team conference he saw a shirt with the message "We don't do drive-by shootings" on one side and on the other there was a demolished house and under it "We stop."[108] The message is eerily similar to a quote from the Vietnam War "To save this village we had to destroy it." Tshirts worn by officers or sold as fund raisers elsewhere reflect an insensitivity to those they serve: "Baby Daddy Removal Team," "You huff and you puff and we'll blow your house down," and "We get up early just to beat the crowds." More distantly, Just before the 1996 Democratic National Convention in Chicago, an enterprising local printer made shirts that quickly became popular with police "We kicked your father's ass in 1968 . . . wait 'til you see what we do to you." The police shirt that reads "We trust in God, but all others get searched" arguably gets a pass as merely clever.

Perhaps nothing reinforces the perceived need for the "warrior" mentality more than the murders of officer. On September 11, 2001 the loss of 343 firefighters, 8 paramedics, and 60 police officers was a horrific example of just how dangerous public safety and emergency service jobs can be. Collectively, they rushed into incredible danger and an unknown number surely stayed to lead people out at the cost of their own lives. Hero is sometimes an overused word. However, there are no words sufficient to honor those 411 people.

A total of 1,466 police officers have died in the line of duty in tahe past decade, that is an average of one death every 60 hours or 146 officers died in the line of duty per year from 2004 to 2015.[109] There were 117 law enforcement officers killed in the line of duty in 2014.[110] On December 20, 2014, Officers Liu and Ramos were mudered as they simply sat in their patrol car. Afterwards, the gunman, Ismaaiyl Brinsley, ran into a subway station and killed himself.[111] Police academies may also contribute to the warrior mindset. Fifteen percent of all law enforcement academies are primarily stress based and another 38 percent more stress than non-stress. Together, 53 percent of all academies are primarily stress oriented and the stress is not classroom instruction about dealing with it, so much as it is learning to "bear up" under it.[112] Stress training in police academies may well generate an "us versus them" mind-set in rookie officers, which has the potential of creating barriers between the police and the community. Even when community policing is part of an academy curriculum, the stress training may create latent psychological obstacles to the kind of police–citizen relationships necessary to fully operationalize a community policing philosophy.[113]

Current Unrest with the Police

A federal program also has contributed to growing concerns about police militarization The National Defense Authorization Act (1997) allows the Secretary of Defense to provide weapons, vehicles, and other materials to federal and state law enforcement agencies for counter-drug and counter-terrorism activities. These are drawn from surplus stock Department of Defense. Perhaps a majority of this equipment is much needed and used well. As an example, police acquisition of large tents provides shelter and rest areas for volunteers searching for lost children, hunters, hikers, and others in wilderness areas. Figure 2.10. Armored vehicles are legitimately needed by the police to rescue hostages, the public and officers under fire, those who are wounded and lying in the open and may be fired upon at again, and the presence of such vehicles at a barricaded subject situation sometimes causes the peaceful surrender of the subject. In 2016, a lone terrorist murdered 49 people at an Orlando, Florida,

FIGURE 2.10 ▶ The Ferguson, Missouri, Police Department responds to rioting after one of its on-duty officers fatally wounded an unarmed African American teenager who reportedly was trying to take the officer's gun. The clouds appear to be from the deployment of tear gas. Demonstrators later won an injunction to prevent the police from using it. The events in Ferguson became a focal point for critics concerned with police militarization. (Larry W. Smith/epa european pressphoto agency b.v./ Alamy Stock Photo)

Quick Facts: How Much Military Equipment Has Been Transferred to State and Local Law Enforcement Agencies?

Between Fiscal Years 2009 and 2014, the federal government provided nearly $18 billion dollars in funds and resources to support state and local law enforcement agencies. These resources are transferred by various federal programs operated by the Departments of Homeland Security, Justice, Defense and Treasury, as well as the Office of National Drug Control Policy.

Some of the equipment is routine, such as office furniture and computers, personal protective equipment, basic firearms, tents, generators, tarps, tool kits, first aid kits, blankets, safety glasses, storage lockers, shelving, and forklifts. The White House asserts that in the 12-month period ending August 2014, such items made up 96 percent or 1.8 million items transferred, which are non-controlled, meaning that they are not returned to the federal government at the end of their useful life.

Some 460,000 pieces of returnable controlled items have been transferred to state and local police agencies, including 92,442 small arms, 44,275 night vision devices, 5,235 high mobility, multi-purpose vehicles, 617 mine resistant, ambush-protected vehicles, and 616 aircraft.

Source: Executive Office of the President, Review: Federal Support for Local Law Enforcement Equipment Acquisition, December 2014, pp. 1, 7, and 8.

---

nightclub and some of the wounded are in critical condition and the toll could increase. Using an armored vehicle, the police were able to rescue some 30 people trapped in various rooms in the nightclub. Critics of the police don't have a blind eye to a genuine police need for such equipment. However, when the police use the equipment inappropriately or in a way that seems to menace the exercise of Constitutional rights criticisms are rightfully expressed.

Militarization critics recognize that the police need to monitor demonstrations by citizens exercising their First Amendment rights because those events have the potential to spiral out of control quickly and create losses of life and property. Their concern is that an early and unnecessary show of armored vehicles and other military capabilities could be viewed as an intolerance of dissent by government, which could produce an unintended result, rioting. In Ferguson, Missouri, the police response to the 2014 largescale demonstrations following the shooting death of Michael Brown by a police officer has been subject to much criticism. Some of that criticism is due to the presence of 50 police agencies, many small, who had not trained together. Nonetheless, it has set off a national discussion of how the police responded.

A central criticism of the response by police in Ferguson is that it was heavily militarized. That appearance stirred the emotions of citizens, creating fear and anger, and interfering with press documentation of events. Armored vehicles drove on the streets and the community called the "tanks" "an act of aggression." One person said "It looked like the police were invading." Loc. cit. The "overwatch" tactic borrowed from the military provided sniper cover for the protection of officers. It too was heavy-handed. Sometimes the sniper rode on top of an armored vehicle, scanning the crowd through his rifle scope to monitor the crowd. Overwatch is not considered a crowd control tactic. Loc cit. Some officers wore camouflage BDUs that further set a militarized response.

Militarization is negatively effecting public perceptions of the police. A 2015 Gallup survey revealed support for the police is at a 22- year low, only 52 percent, and another poll showed that 40 percent of those surveyed weren't the police confident could use military-grade weapons and equipment appropriately.

In *Militarizing the Criminal Justice System*, Kraska observes as the police and the public view each other over militarization, the police stand to lose legitimacy in the eye of the public. 100 If "we versus them" continues unabated in law enforcement, the public may increasingly view the police as an army of occupation. If the police lose the public, the Republic may well be endangered. Militarization represents traditional policing in all of its negative manifestations—aggressive, reactive, and based on force. There is very little that represents the tenets of proactive de-escalation, conflict resolution, the prevention of harm, and the protection of civil and human rights so passionately expressed in modern tenets of policing.

IMPROVING POLICE–COMMUNITY RELATIONS

In 2014, President Barak Obama called together a task force to address community–police relations and offer guidelines for reforms in the wake of the unrest in Ferguson, New York, and Baltimore. Their recommendations, organized as "pillars," are linked closely to policing strategies discussed in this chapter, and provide opportunities for departments to strengthen and shift their current crime reduction and prevention initiatives:[114]

1. ***Building Trust and Legitimacy:*** This is the foundation on which all police/community interactions rely. Evidence shows that when people perceive authorities to be acting in procedurally just

Box 2.3 Youth Outreach Programs

The recommendations from the President's Task Force on 21st Century Policing make it clear that engaging with youth should be a priority both to increase police legitimacy, tackle systemic quality of life issues, and to reinvigorate community/police dialogue. One agency that has really embraced that model is the Dallas Police Department, which runs a variety of programs aimed at disadvantaged youth of all ages, particularly those from areas identified as policing hot-spots throughout the city.

Though evaluations of these programmatic effects on crime will be longitudinal—and therefore data is not readily available—participation is robust, and activities are highly rated by participants and observers alike. DPD takes a holistic approach to youth engagement, exposing kids to career options, educational activities, athletics, and the arts in the following programs:

Junior Police Academy—includes: Basic Academy, aimed at 4th–7th grades and Advanced Academy, 8th–10th grades. Participants discuss life skills, learn about positive behavioral choices, and have hands-on interactions with police officers from a variety of units within DPD.

Explorer Program—aimed at ages 14–21, this program is held in conjunction with the Boy Scouts of America and emphasizes leadership, service activities, and interest in law enforcement careers.

Junior Explorer Program—aimed at ages 10–13, emphasizes good citizenship, community service, personal responsibility, and leadership skills.

Blue In The School—character education for 4th graders taught by police officers, and emphasizing communication skills and healthy, positive lifestyle choices.

Police Athletic/Activities League (PAL)—includes Midnight Basketball, Soccer Camp, Boxing Club, Community Biking Program, Fitness Adventure, Tennis Camps, Free Play, PAL Gardening, Robotics, Guitar Lessons, PAL Singers (youth choir), "Movin' In The Right Direction" musical, Male Mentoring, Girl Empowerment/DIVA Mentoring, Chess Club, Stuff The Squad Car (school supply & Christmas toy collection drives), Anti-Bullying Presentations, Career Day Presentations, Summer Internship Programs, and a College Prep Program (beginning Fall 2015), held on a local university campus, which will include financial education, etiquette, interview skills, college planning, and additional classes.

UA 2.1 ▶ The Dallas Police Department's Police Athletic League trained participants for a 12-mile bike ride. (Courtesy of the Dallas Police Department)

ways, they are more likely to obey the law. Procedurally just behavior is described as being based on four principles: treating people with dignity and respect; giving individuals a "voice" during encounters; being neutral and transparent in decision making; and conveying trustworthy motives. Specific recommendations include embracing a guardian versus a warrior mind-set acknowledging past injustices; and increasing transparent and proactive communication with the public.

2. *Policy and Oversight:* Simply stated, policies in police agencies must reflect community values. Clear and concise policies must be developed that regulate the use of force, police control of mass demonstrations (particularly in regards to equipment used, such as armored personnel carriers or other "military grade" weaponry), consent to search, racial profiling, internal investigations of improper use of force, in-custody deaths, and officer-involved shootings.

3. *Technology and Social Media:* The implementation, use, and evaluation of technology and social media is acknowledged as a valuable tool for policing, emphasizing that these areas contain valuable opportunities to engage the public and increase police transparency. Technology, such as visual and audio recording devices, biometric devices, and less than lethal technology, should be implemented with community input and should be held to national standards that maintain civil and human rights protections.

4. *Community Policing and Crime Reduction:* The taskforce heralded the potential of community policing to build trust and collaboration, while also reinforcing that communities will only support policing models that reflect their own values. The Task Force also placed significant emphasis on programming that enhances positive youth/police interactions.

5. *Training and Education:* Improving training in police agencies to address a wide range of challenges, particularly those involving minority communities, must include wider community input.

6. *Officer Wellness and Safety:* Recognizing and promoting the importance of officer safety at all levels of a police organization increases officer awareness. Task force recommendations focused on increased funding and national support for initiatives supporting the safety of officers, as well as institutional support for their physical and emotional needs throughout their careers.

Ultimately, there is no means by which police agencies can be forced to adopt these recommendations, unless they are under a consent decree in which the Department of Justice is monitoring their operations. That has been the case in a number of jurisdictions, including Ferguson, MO, Detroit, MI, Los Angeles, CA, Portland, OR, and Cleveland, OH, in which the federal government threatens to sue the agency under civil rights clauses of the Constitution unless significant reforms are enacted. Short of that, however, agencies are left to implement these types of future changes on their own, considering community political pressures and the myriad of evidence-based strategies available today.

What's clear is that change will have to fundamentally occur within not only police organizations but within the police culture as well. Change, too, must occur within our communities. Citizens who do not accept the legitimacy of police are more likely to escalate simple traffic stops to angry confrontations—and unfortunately, as witnessed in the past, police officers with their own biases and entrenched notions of police identity are frequently engaging such incidents with increased violence rather than attempting to de-escalate such instances. American policing must re-invent itself, emphasizing crime prevention (as opposed to arrests), and incorporating citizen response and input. In a similar manner, communities (particularly minority communities) must realize that policing is an inherently dangerous profession and that individual officers serve everyday at the peril of their own lives. New threats from foreign terrorists, mad bombers, and spree killers simply escalate this situation.

This chapter documents the significant movement of major paradigm shifts in the evolution of policing, from traditional patrol and Broken Windows models to community policing, CompStat, and various hybrid blends of evidence-based police practices. The remarkable strides made as part of those seismic shifts give hope that policing organizations and communities within our country can rise to meet the current challenges facing our society.

Chapter Summary

Summary by Learning Objective

1. Define Community Policing.

A policing philosophy that focuses on general neighborhood problems as a source of crime; community policing is preventive, proactive, and information-based.

2. Describe the four-step problem-solving model called SARA.

The problem-solving model called SARA is composed of four specific steps: (1) *Scanning*—Instead of relying on broad, law-related concepts, such as robbery, burglary, and auto theft, officers are encouraged to group individual, related incidents that come to their attention as "problems" and define these problems in more precise and useful terms. For example, an incident that typically would be classified simply as a "robbery" might be seen as part of a pattern of prostitution-related robberies committed by transvestites in center-city hotels. In essence, officers are expected to look for possible problems and accurately define them as part of their daily routine. (2) *Analysis*—Officers working on a well-defined problem then collect information from a variety of public and private sources, not just traditional police data, such as criminal records and past offense reports. Officers rely on problem analysis guides that direct officers to examine offenders, victims, the social and physical environment, and previous responses to the problem. The goal is to understand the scope, nature, and causes of the problem and formulate a variety of options for its resolution. (3) *Response*—The knowledge gained in the analysis stage is then used to develop and implement solutions. Officers seek the assistance of citizens, businesses, other police units, other public and private organizations, and anyone else who can help develop a program of action. Solutions may go well beyond traditional police responses to include other community agencies and/or municipal organizations. (4) *Assessment*—Finally, officers evaluate the impact and the effectiveness of their responses. Were the original problems actually solved or alleviated? They may use the results to revise a response, to collect more data, or even to redefine the problem.

3. **Describe CompStat.**
Essentially, CompStat is a collection of modern management practices, military-like deployment efforts, and strong enforcement strategies all based on the availability of accurate and timely statistical crime data. Four core principles highlight a police department's model of CompStat:

- *Accurate and timely intelligence and statistical crime information based on geographical settings and/or areas.* High-tech computer systems and geographical mapping programs are most helpful in providing the aggregate and individual data often required for effective CompStat efforts. However, more rudimentary aspects of visual crime analysis can be accomplished through daily pin mapping and bulletins.

- *Rapid deployment of resources, particularly combining the immediate presence of uniform patrol working in concert with directed undercover operations.* Rapid deployment of other city and governmental resources, such as nuisance and abatement personnel, sanitation workers, and alcoholic beverage and licensing enforcement, is an additional aspect of this principle.

- *Effective tactics and strategies of enforcement that focus on visible street crimes or "quality-of-life" crimes,* such as loitering, drinking in public, street prostitution, or even jumping subway turnstiles.

- *Relentless follow-up and assessment,* which include placing accountability and responsibility not only on the individual police officer on the beat but also on individual police managers of traditionally defined areas, such as division heads or precinct captains.

CompStat focuses on using the most accurate and timely information and data available to the police, opening lines of communication both horizontally and vertically within the organization, activating the community at large, and improving the overall efficiency and effectiveness of the police. CompStat is problem-oriented and preventive and stresses the need to focus on problems rather than on past incidents.

4. **Discuss newer police strategies, including evidence-based policing, hot-spots policing, intelligence-led policing, and predictive policing.**
Evidence-based policing is a style of policing using the best available research to guide, manage, and evaluate police operations within a community; hot-spots policing is a geographically based approach to crime-fighting focused on in-depth analysis of "places" and times, and deploying police officers to those locations that account for the majority of calls for service and crime in a community. *Intelligence-led policing* (ILP): arose from the 9/11 terrorist attacks, and is focused on offenders, not crime incidents, using intelligence analysis to prevent crime. *Predictive policing* is a proactive policing style that uses information and analytical tools to prevent crime while using the fewest police resources possible.

5. **List and briefly describe some of the more common crime analysis techniques.**
Some of the more common crime analysis techniques are as follows:

- *Tactical crime analysis or crime-specific analysis*— a tabular or graphic display of reported crimes with a given pattern of time and/or location, often used to detect patterns of crime (e.g., robberies, burglaries, and auto thefts) that cluster in specific locations during various time periods.

- *Strategic crime analysis*—the study of crime and/ or social problems in a specific area in an effort to determine long-term patterns of activity as well as to evaluate police responses and organizational procedures. Strategic crime analysis is often used to determine the effectiveness of police over a given period of time or in the evaluation of specific policing strategies.

- *Link analysis*—a graphic portrayal of associations and relationships among people, organizations, events, activities, and locations from a given point in time.

- *Telephone toll analysis*—computerized reports derived from court-ordered long-distance telephone billings of suspects in illegal narcotics trafficking. Reports indicate the number and frequency of calls displayed in numerical, chronological, and geographical order. Link analysis can be used to show the relationship between billing numbers and the numbers called.

- *Visual investigative analysis (VIA)*—charting that depicts key events of criminal activity in chronological order. VIA is used to show the degree of involvement of subjects.

- *Case analysis and management system (CAMS)*—computerized case management in which large amounts of data are compiled and indexed for each retrieval of specific items. This system is used to clarify relationships and calculate the probability of associations.

- *Intelligence analysis*—the identification of networks of offenders and criminal activity, often associated with organized crime, gangs, drug traffickers, prostitution rings, and terrorist organizations.

6. **Describe geographic information systems and explain how such a system would enhance police service.**
   GIS has become an influential mechanism in hot-spots policing as well as Crime Prevention Through Environmental Design (CPTED), situational policing, directed patrols, and crime analysis. GIS has a myriad of other uses in policing. Police agencies can use GIS in dispatching police units by providing directions to locations; address histories; and locations of nearby fire and waste hazards, fire hydrants, alarm boxes, high-power lines, water lines, and the like. Police managers can not only use GIS to provide graphic analysis of specific crime patterns and to evaluate new policing strategies but also to track individual officer performance by area.

   There are two types of GIS crime mapping: statistical spatial analysis and spatial modeling. While statistical spatial analysis focuses on the spatial relationship between crime points in a particular area, spatial modeling is concerned with the technology and application of data.

7. **Explain the impact of information technology on policing.**
   The impact of information technologies on policing cannot be overstated; they take a central support role for policing strategies, allow for community interaction, and provide better analysis and problem-solving capabilities.

8. **Describe how distrust between police and citizens can affect police strategies.**
   Police/community co-operation is the cornerstone of many new police strategies; without police legitimacy and community trust, many of these strategies simply will not work.

Chapter Review Questions

1. Define *community policing*.
2. Describe the four-step problem-solving model commonly referred to as SARA.
3. Identify the problems commonly associated with traditional policing.
4. What is the CAPS program? Discuss some of the key features aimed at improving and expanding the overall quality of police services in the City of Chicago, as well as reducing crime.
5. Define *CompStat* and identify the core principles of CompStat as presented in the New York Police Department model.
6. Define some of today's new police strategies, such as hot-spots policing, intelligence-led policing (ILP), and harm-focused policing.
7. What is evidence-based policing? Describe the *Triple T Strategy* proposed by Larry Sherman as a part of the evidence-based policing philosophy.
8. List and briefly describe some of the more common crime analysis techniques.
9. Describe a geographic information system and explain how such a system enhances police service.
10. What are the benefits and issues that surround the use of social media by police agencies?
11. What factors have contributed to the militarization of the police over the past two decades?
12. How can we improve police–community relations in the United States?

Critical Thinking Exercises

1. Visit your town or city's law enforcement website. Can you tell by the information published what type of policing strategies they employ? Do you think this is an appropriate strategy for your city? Why or why not?

2. Why is police legitimacy so closely tied to community policing? Can you have a good community policing program without police legitimacy? Why or why not?

3. Find a law enforcement agency's Twitter or Facebook page. What examples of policing strategies can you see throughout their posts?

Key Terms

CAPS	evidence-based policing	problem-oriented policing
CODEFOR	geographic information systems (GIS)	SARA
community policing	hot-spots policing	social media
CompStat	intelligence-led policing (ILP)	traditional policing
crime analysis	neighborhood-oriented policing	zero-tolerance policing (ZTP)
directed and saturation patrols	predictive policing	

Endnotes

[1]See Herman Goldstein, *Policing in a Free Society* (Cambridge, MA: Ballinger, 1977).

[2]See James Q. Wilson and George L. Kelling, "The Police and Neighborhood Safety: Broken Windows," *Atlantic Monthly*, No. 249 (1982), pp. 29–38.

[3]See Y. Xu, M.L. Fiedler, and K.H. Flaming, "Discovering the Impact of Community Policing," *Journal of Research in Crime and Delinquency*, Vol. 42, No. 2 (2005), pp. 147–186.

[4]Hyunseok Jang, Larry T. Hoover, and Brian A. Lawton, "Effectiveness of Broken Windows Enforcement on Clearance Rates," *Journal of Criminal Justice*, Vol. 36, Issue 6, (November/December 2008), p. 529. See also, National Research Council of the National Academies, *Fairness and Effectiveness in Policing: The Evidence* (Washington, DC: The National Academies Press, 2001), pp. 228–230.

[5]B.E. Harcourt and J. Ludwig, "Broken Windows: New Evidence from New York City and a Five City Social Experiment," *University of Chicago Law Review*, Vol. 73, Issue 1, (Winter 2006), pp. 271–320. The questioning of this link also appears in the news media; illustratively, see Daniel Brook, "The Cracks in Broken Windows," *The Boston Globe*, on-line, February 19, 2006.

[6]Judith A. Greene, "Zero Tolerance: A Case Study of Police Policies and Practices in New York City," *Crime and Delinquency*, Vol. 45, No. 2 (1999), p. 171–210.

[7]Ibid., p. 171.

[8]George L. Kelling and Catherine M. Coles, *Fixing Broken Windows: Restoring Order and Reducing Crime in Our Communities* (New York: Touchstone Publishing, 1996).

[9]Chris Braiden, "Community Policing: Nothing New under the Sun" (Edmonton, Alberta: Edmonton Police Department, 1987).

[10]Ibid. See Peel's Principle 7, as expressed on p. 2.

[11]Jerome H. Skolnick and David H. Bayley, *Community Policing: Issues and Practices around the World* (Washington, DC: U.S. Department of Justice, 1988), pp. 67–70.

[12]A number of researchers have documented the failures of traditional policing methods. Most notably, see A. J. Reiss, *The Police and the Public* (New Haven, Conn.: Yale University Press, 1971); G. L. Kelling, T. Pate, D. Dickman, and C. Brown, *Kansas City Preventive Patrol Experiment* (Washington, DC: Police Foundation, 1975); M. T. Farmer, ed., *Differential Police Response Strategies* (Washington, DC: Police Executive Research Forum, 1981); L. W. Sherman, P. R. Gartin, and M. E. Buerger, "Hot-Spot of Predatory Crime: Routine Activities and the Criminology of Place," *Criminology* 27 (1989): 27–55; and W. H. Bieck, W.

Spelman, and T. J. Sweeney, "The Patrol Function," in *Local Government Police Management*, ed. William A. Geller (Washington, DC: International City Management Association), pp. 59–95.

[13]Gary W. Cordner. "Community Policing," in *Critical Issues in Policing, Seventh Edition*, eds. Geoffrey Alpert and Roger Dunham, (Long Grove, IL: Waveland Press, 2015), pp 481–498.

[14]Journal of Experimental Criminology, "Community-Oriented Policing to Reduce Crime, Disorder and Fear and Increase Satisfaction and Legitimacy among Citizens: A Systematic Review," - See more at: http://journalistsresource.org/studies/government/criminal-justice/the-impact-of-community-policing-meta-analysis-of-its-effects-in-u-s-cities#sthash.ksuElqOq.dpuf

[15]Early discussions relating to the problems associated with evaluating community policing were highlighted in the following article: Robert W. Taylor, Eric J. Fritsch, and Tory Caeti, "Core Challenges Facing Community Policing: The Emperor Still Has No Clothes." *ACJS Today* 17, No. 1 (May/June 1998).

[16]For a discussion of CompStat as a new police strategy to reduce crime, see William Bratton and Peter Knobler, *Turnaround: How America's Top Cop Reversed the Crime Epidemic* (New York: Random House, 1998); William Bratton and William Edwards, "What We Have Learned about Policing," *City Journal* (spring 1999): William F. Walsh, "CompStat: An Analysis of an Emerging Police Managerial Paradigm," *Policing: An International Journal of Police Strategies and Management* 24, no. 3, (2001): 347–362; William F. Walsh and Gennaro F. Vito, "The Meaning of CompStat," *Journal of Contemporary Criminal Justice* 20, No. 1 (2004), pp. 51–69; John E. Conklin, *Why Crime Rates Fell* (Boston, MA: Pearson Education, 2003).

[17]Much of this section has been adapted from Raymond Dussault, "Maps and Management: Compstat Evolves," *Government Technology* (April 2000), pp. 1–2.

[18]William F. Walsh and Gennero F. Vito, "The Meaning of CompStat," *Journal of Contemporary Criminal Justice* 20, No. 1 (2004), pp. 51–69.

[19]Police Executive Research Forum, "COMPSTAT: Its Origins, Evolution, and Future in Law Enforcement Agencies" (2013), http://www.policeforum.org/assets/docs/Free_Online_Documents/Compstat/compstat%20-%20its%20origins%20evolution%20and%20future%20in%20law%20enforcement%20agencies%202013.pdf (accessed June 23, 2015).

[20]The SARA methodology was adapted from William Spelman and John E. Eck, *Newport News Tests Problem-Oriented Policing* (Washington, DC: National Institute of Justice, SNI 201, January/February 1987), pp. 2–3, and Spelman and Eck, "Police and Delivery," p. 61.

[21]Herman Goldstein, *Problem-Oriented Policing* (New York: McGraw-Hill, 1990).

[22]This list was adapted, in part, from Goldstein, *Problem-Oriented Policing,* pp. 66–67.

[23]Ibid., pp. 36–37.

[24]City of Chicago, Department of Police, "Fact Sheet—the Chicago Alternative Policing Strategy (CAPS)" (July 1995).

[25]Arthur J. Lurigio and Wesley G. Skogan, "Winning the Hearts and Minds of Police Officers: An Assessment of Staff Perceptions of Community Policing in Chicago," *Crime and Delinquency* 40, no. 3 (July 1994): 319.

[26]Mark Moore, "Problem-Solving and Community Policing," in *Modern Policing,* eds. M. Tonry and N. Morris (Chicago: University of Chicago Press, 1992), pp. 99–158.

[27]The key features of the CAPS program presented in this text are adapted from Lurigio and Skogan, "Winning the Hearts and Minds of Police Officers," p. 318, and Chicago Police Department, "Fact Sheet," pp. 1–2.

[28]Ibid.

[29]Ibid.

[30]Stephen Mastrofski, Roger Parks, and Robert E. Worden, "Community Policing in Action: Lessons from an Observational Study," *Research Preview* (Washington, DC: National Institute of Justice, June 1998).

[31]Ibid.

[32]Quint C. Thurman and Jihong Zhao, "Community Policing: Where Are We Now?" *Crime and Delinquency* 43, No. 3 (July 1997), pp. 554–564.

[33]Mastrofski et al., "Community Policing in Action," p. 7.

[34]http://www.myfoxchicago.com/story/20533965/emanuel-mccarthy-plan-to-revitalize-caps-program

[35]Megan Crepeau, "Tracking Homicides in Chicago," *Redeye Chicago News* (July 1, 2015). See: http://homicides.redeyechicago.com/

[36]Chuck Goudie and Barb Markoff, "Chicago Police Superintendent Garry McCarthy Wouldn't Resign, So He was Fired," ABC7 I-Team Investigation, 2016 WLS-TV. See: http://abc7chicago.com/news/cpd-supt-mccarthy-wouldnt-resign-so-he-was-fired/1127182/

[37]Interview with Chief Robert K. Olsen, October 7, 2002.

[38]Refer to www.ci.minneapolis.mn.us/citywork/police/index.html

[39]D. Weisburd and J. E. Eck, "What Can Police Do to Reduce Crime, Disorder, and Fear?" *The Annals of the American Academy of Political and Social Science* 593 (2004), pp. 42–65.

[40]Ibid., and Lawrence W. Sherman, "Policing Communities: What Works?" *Crime and Justice* 8 (1986), pp. 343–386.

[41]See Robert W. Taylor, Eric J. Fritsch, and Tory J. Caeti, "Core Challenges Facing Community Policing: The Emperor *Still* Has No Clothes," *ACJS Today,* No. 1 (May-June, 1998), Volume XVII: 1, pp. 1–5.

[42]See Larry W. Sherman, "Policing for Crime Prevention," in *Preventing Crime: What Works, What Doesn't, What's Promising—A Report to the Attorney General of the United States* eds. L.W. Sherman, D. Gottfredson, D.L. MacKenzie, J.E. Eck, P. Reuter, & S. Bushway (Washington, DC: United States Department of Justice, Office of Justice Programs, 1997).

[43]Larry W. Sherman, "Evidence-Based Policing," *Ideas in American Policing* (Washington, DC: U.S. Department of Justice, Police Foundation, July 1998), pp. 3–4.

[44]Ibid.

[45]Lawrence W. Sherman. "The Rise of Evidence-Based Policing: Targeting, Testing, and Tracking." The Rise of Evidence-Based Policing, Crime and Justice, Volume 42: *Crime and Justice in America: 1975–2015.*

[46]Cynthia Lum and Christopher S. Koper. "Evidence-Based Policing". *Critical Issues in Policing, Seventh Edition,* eds. Geoffrey Alpert and Roger Dunham (Long Grove, IL: Waveland Press, 2015), pp. 260–273.

[47]Cynthia Lum and Christopher S. Koper. "Evidence-Based Policing." *Critical Issues in Policing, Seventh Edition. Geoffrey Alpert and Roger Dunham, eds.* Waveland Press, Long Grove IL. 2015. pp. 260–273

[48]"Evidence Based Policing Hall of Fame: Dr. Theron Bowman." Center for Evidence Based Crime Policy. Retrieved from http://cebcp.org/hall-of-fame/ on July 18, 2015.

[49]See the Caruth Police Institute website at: http://www.untdallas.edu/cpi

[50]"The Matrix." Center for Evidence-Based Crime Policy. Retrieved from http://cebcp.org/evidence-based-policing/the-matrix/ on July 15, 2015.

[51]David Weisburd, "Hot-Spots Policing Experiments and Criminal Justice Research: Lessons from the Field," *Annals of the American Academy of Political and Social Science* 599 (2005), pp. 220–245.

[52]Lawrence W. Sherman, P. R. Gartin, and M. Buerger, "Hot-Spots of Predatory Crime: Routine Activities and the Criminology of Place," *Criminology* 27 (1986) pp. 27–55.

[53]Ibid.

[54]John E. Eck, S. Chainey, and J. Cameron, *Mapping Crime: Understanding Hot-Spots* (Washington, DC: National Institute of Justice, 2005).

[55]David Weisburd and Lorraine G. Mazerolle, "Crime and Disorder in Drug Hot-Spots: Implications for Theory and Practice in Policing," *Police Quarterly* 3 (2000), pp. 331–349.

[56]S. L. Rutherford, K. R. Blevins and V. B. Lord, "An Evaluation of the Effects of a Street Crime Unit on Citizens' Fear of Crime," *Professional Issues in Criminal Justice* 3(2008), pp. 21–36.

[57]Wesley Skogan and Kathleen Frydl (eds), *Fairness and Effectiveness in Policing: The Evidence* (Washington, DC: National Academy of Sciences, Committee to Review Research on Police Policy and Practice, 2004), p. 250. See also, Anthony A. Braga, *U.S. COPS Office Crime Prevention Research Review: Police Enforcement Strategies to*

[57]*Prevent Crime in Hot-Spot Areas* (Washington, DC: U.S. Department of Justice, 2008).

[58]Anthony A. Braga, "The Effects of Hot-Spots Policing on Crime," *Annals of the American Academy of Political and Social Sciences* 578 (2001), pp. 104–125.

[59]Ralph B. Taylor, "Hot-Spots Do Not Exist and Four Other Fundamental Concerns About Hot-Spots Policing," in Natasha A. Frost, J. D. Freilich, and T. R. Clear, *Contemporary Issues in Criminal Justice Policy* (Belmont, CA: Wadsworth Cengage Learning, 2010).

[60]Ibid., p. 272.

[61]C. S. Koper and E. Mayo-Wilson, "Police Crackdowns on Illegal Gun Carrying: A Systematic Review of Their Impact on Gun Crime," *Journal of Experimental Criminology* 2 (2006), pp. 227–261.

[62]Eric J. Fritsch, Tory J. Caeti, and Robert W. Taylor, "Gang Suppression through Saturation Patrol, Aggressive Curfew, and Truancy Enforcement: A Quasi-experimental Test of the Dallas Anti-gang Initiative," *Crime & Delinquency* 45 (2000), pp. 122–139.

[63]Jerry H. Ratcliffe and Robert Guidetti, "State Police Investigative Structure and the Adoption of Intelligence-led Policing. *Policing: An International Journal of Police Strategies and Management* 31 (2008), pp. 111.

[64]Ibid.

[65]Jerry H. Ratcliffe, *Intelligence-Led Policing* (Portland, OR: Willan Publishing, 2008).

[66]C. Clarke, "Proactive Policing: Standing on the Shoulders of Community-Based Policing," *Police Practice and Research,* 7 (2006), pp. 3–17.

[67]Jerry H. Ratcliffe and Robert Guidetti, "State Police Investigative Structure and the Adoption of Intelligence-led Policing."

[68]Ibid.

[69]Jerry H. Ratcliffe, "The effectiveness of police intelligence management: A New Zealand case study." *Police Practice and Research* (In Press).

[70]Craig D. Uchida, *A National Discussion on Predictive Policing: Defining our Terms and Mapping Successful Implementation Strategies* (Washington, DC: National Institute of Justice, 2010).

[71]Beth Pearsall, "Predictive Policing: The Future of Law Enforcement?" *NIJ Journal* 266 (2010), pp. 16–19.

[72]Charlie Beck and Colleen McCue, "Predictive Policing: What Can We Learn from Wal-Mart and Amazon about Fighting Crime in a Recession?" *The Police Chief* 76 (November 2009). Retrieved from http://policechiefmagazine.org/magazine/ on July 20, 2010.

[73]Beth Pearsall, "Predictive Policing: The Future of Law Enforcement?"

[74]Craig D. Uchida, *A National Discussion on Predictive Policing: Defining our Terms and Mapping Successful Implementation Strategies.*

[75]J. W. Brahan, K. P. Lam, H. Chan, and W. Leung, "AICAMS: Artificial Intelligence Crime Analysis and Management Systems," *Knowledge-Based Systems* 11 (2009), pp. 355–361.

[76]N. Cope, "Intelligence Led Policing or Policing Led Intelligence?" *British Journal of Criminology* 44 (2004), pp. 188–203.

[77]Several scholars have provided definitions of crime analysis. See J. B. Howlett, "Analytical Investigative Techniques," *Police Chief* 47 (December 1980), p. 42; Rachel Boba, *Crime Analysis and Crime Mapping* (Thousand Oaks, CA: Sage, 2005), p. 5; S. Gottlieb, S. Arenberg, and R. Singh, *Crime Analysis: From First Report to Final Arrest* (Monclair, CA: alpha, 1994); Mark A. Stallo, *Using Microsoft Office to Improve Law Enforcement Operations: Crime Analysis, Community Policing, and Investigations* (Dallas, TX: Act, Now, 2010).

[78]J. A. Kinney, "Criminal Intelligence Analysis: A Powerful Weapon," *International Cargo Crime Prevention* (April 1984), p. 4.

[79]Boba, *Crime Analysis and Crime Mapping,* p. 14.

[80]Ibid., pp. 15–16.

[81]D. M. Ross, "Criminal Intelligence Analysis," *Police Product News* (June 1983), p. 45.

[82]Ibid.

[83]Incident occurring on Virginia Tech University, April 16, 2007 resulting in over 30 deaths from gunman, Seung-Hui Cho.

[84]Ross, "Criminal Intelligence Analysis," p. 49.

[85]Mark A. Stallo, *Using Microsoft Office to Improve Law Enforcement Operations.* See http://www.actnowinc.org/books.html (July 20, 2010).

[86]Jerry H. Ratcliffe, "Crime Mapping and the Training Needs of Law Enforcement," *European Journal on Criminal Policy and Research* 10 (2004), pp. 65–83.

[87]David Weisburd and C. Lum, "The Diffusion of Computerized Crime Mapping in Policing: Linking Research and Practice," *Police Practice and Research* 6 (2005), pp. 419–434.

[88]J. R. Battin, "Is Hot-Spot Policing Effective Empirically?" *Professional Issues in Criminal Justice* 4 (2009), pp. 35–50.

[89]For more information relating to the applications of GIS technology to policing, see Nancy G. La Vigne and Julie Wartell, *Mapping across Boundaries: Regional Crime Analysis* (Washington, DC: Police Executive Research Forum, 2001).

[90]https://www.ncjrs.gov/pdffiles1/nij/244760.pdf

[91]Justin McCarthy. "Nonwhites Less Likely to Feel Police Protect and Serve Them." *Gallup: Politics,* November 17, 2014.

[92]The concept of the "warrior" versus "guardian" role and mindset has been developed over the last decade. For further information regarding these concepts, please see the works of Radley Balko, "Overkill: The Rise of Paramilitary Raids in America" Unpublished white paper (July 17, 2006); "Rise of the Warrior Cop: Is it Time to Reconsider the militarization of American Policing?" *The Saturday Essay* (August 7, 2013); and *Rise of the Warrior Cop: The Militarization of America's Police Forces* (Jackson, TN: Public Affairs, 2013).

[93]"Will the Growing Militarization of Our Police Doom Community Policing?" *The e-Newsletter of the COPS*

Office 6, no. 12 (December 2013), pp. 1–2; http:// cops. usdoj.gov/html/dispatch/ 12/20/13.

[94] "See Mark G. Frank and Thomas Gilovich, "The Dark Side of Self- and Social Perception: Black Uniforms and Aggression in Professional Sports," Journal of Personality and Social Psychology, Vol. 54, No. 1, 1988, pp. 74–85.

[95] See George D. Webster, Geoffrey R. Erland, and Joshua Correll, "Can Uniform Color Color Aggression? Quasi-Experimental Evidence from Professional Ice Hockey," Social Psychology and Personality Science, Vol. 2, No. 3, May 2011, pp. 306–310 and David F. Caldwell and Jerry M. Burger, "On Thin Ice: Does Uniform Color Really Affect Aggression in Professional Hockey?" Social Psychology and Personality Science, Vol. 3, May 1, 2012, pp. 274–28

[96] Richard R. Johnson, "An Examination of Police Uniform Color and Police-Citizen Aggression," Criminal Justice and Behavior, Vol. 40, No. 2, 2013, pp. 228–244 and Ernest Nickles, "Good Guys Wear Black: Uniform Color and Citizen Impressions of the Police," Policing: An International Journal of Police Strategies and Management, Vol. 31, No. 1, March 2008, pp. 77–92.

[97] See Radley Balko, *Rise of the Warrior Cop: The Militarization of America's Police Forces* (Jackson, TN: Public Affairs, 2013) and Radley Balko, *Our Militarized*

Police Departments: Hearing Before the Subcommittee on Crime, House of Representatives, 110th Cong. (2007) (Testimony of Radley Balko). http://reason.com/archives/2007/07/02/our-militarized-police.

[98] Michael S. Sherry, In the Shadow of War (New Haven, CT: Yale University Press, 1997), p. 309.

[99] President Reagan, June 24, 1982, "Remarks on Signing Executive Order 12368, Concerning Federal Drug Abuse Policy Functions," The American Presidency Project, http://www.presidency.ucsb.edu/ws/index.php?pid=42671%23axzz1P5p1SNqO.

[100] Steve Daley, "Bennett Overwhelmingly Confirmed as Drug Czar," Chicago Tribune, March 10, 1989, http://articles.chicagotribune.com/keyword/william-bennett/featured/3.

[101] Douglas Jehl, "Bennett Would Limit Rights in War on Drugs: Says 'Compelling Reasons' Would be Needed; Military Might Be Given a Wider Role in Arrests," Los Angeles Times, March 3, 1989, http://articles.latimes.com/1989-03-03/news/mn-238_1_compelling-reason.

[102] Norm Sampler, "Losing the Hearts and Minds in the Drug War." The Huffington Post, November 14, 2011, http://www.huffingtonpost.com/norm-stamper/war-on-drugs_b_1088931.html.

[103]International Association of Chiefs of Police and the National Tactical Officers Association, National Special Weapons and Tactics (SWAT) Study: A National Assessment of Critical Trends and Issues from 2009 to 2014 (Alexandria, VA: International Association of Chiefs of Police, 2016), pp. 11 and 18.

[104]Ronald J. Ostrow, "Casual Drug Users Should be Shot, Gates Says," Los Angeles Times, September 6, 1990, http://articles.latimes.com/1990-09-06/news/mn-983_1_casual-drug-users.

[105]No author, "Drug Czar Says Beheading Dealers 'Morally Plausible," Chicago Tribune, June 16,1989, http://archives.chicagotribune.com/1989/06/16/page/25/article/drug-czar-says-beheading-dealers-morally-plausible.

[106]Howard Kohn, "Cowboy in the Capital: Drug Czar Bill Bennett," Rolling Stone, November 2, 1989, http://www.rollingstone.com/culture/features/cowboy-in-the-capital-drug-czar-bill-bennett-19891102.

[107]Duncan Campbell, "Bush Tars Drug Takers with Aiding Terrorists," The Guardian, August 7, 2002, https://www.theguardian.com/world/2002/aug/08/usa.duncancampbell.

[108]Radley Balko, "What Cop T-Shirts Tell Us About Police Culture," Huffington Post, June 22, 2013, http://www.huffingtonpost.com/2013/06/21/what-cop-tshirts-tell-us-_n_3479017.html. The information about T-shirts is drawn with restatement from this source and some additions.

[109]National Law Enforcement Officers Memorial Fund. See: http://www.nleomf.org/facts/officer-fatalities-data/year.html?referrer=https://www.google.com.

[110]Ibid.

[111]Dennis A. Clark, "Number of Cops Killed up 56% in 2014," New York Post, December 30, 2014, http://nypost.com/2014/12/30/number-of-cops-killed-by-guns-up-56-in-2014.

[112]Cynthia Lum and Daniel S. Nagin, "Reinventing American Policing," The Crime Report, June 24, 2015, http://thecrimereport.org/2015/06/24/2015-06-reinventing-american-policing-a-seven-point-blueprin, accessed July 5, 2016.

[113]No author, Recruit Training: "Are We Preparing Officers for a Community Policing Department?" Community Policing Dispatch (The e-newsletter of the Cops Office), Vol. 6, Issue, 6, June 2013, p. 2, http://cops.usdoj.gov/html/dispatch/06-2013/preparing_officers_for_a_community_oriented_department.asp, accessed July 5, 2016.

[114]No author, Final Report of the President's Task Force on 21st Century Policing, May 2015, http://www.cops.usdoj.gov/pdf/taskforce/taskforce_finalreport.pdf, accessed July 5, 2016.

INTELLIGENCE, TERRORISM, AND HOMELAND SECURITY

Learning Objectives

1. Define *intelligence.*
2. Describe the Intelligence Cycle as presented in the *National Criminal Intelligence Sharing Plan (NCISP).*
3. Define a fusion center and briefly list its four primary goals.
4. Describe some of the major criticisms aimed at fusion centers and other law enforcement responses to terrorism.
5. List the four primary areas of responsibility within the Department of Homeland Security.
6. Define *terrorism.*
7. Briefly describe the concept of jihad and name some of the more radical Islamic groups active throughout the world.
8. Describe the concept of a "homegrown terrorist."
9. Discuss why Outlaw Motorcycle Gangs (OMGs) are considered an international threat to the United States. Identify the "Big Four" OMGs that are active in the United States.
10. Define a *hate crime.*
11. Define and identify groups that are commonly called *ecoterrorists.*

INTRODUCTION

ON SEPTEMBER 11, 2001, *our world changed forever. For the first time in the past 60 years, America came under attack by an outside and foreign enemy (see Figure 3.1). Our security weaknesses were exploited, our vulnerability was exposed, and our fear became real. For law enforcement and police officers throughout the United States, the attacks on the World Trade Center and the Pentagon posed yet another new challenge to the already difficult task of reducing crime and maintaining order in our communities (see Chapters 1 and 2 for a discussion of the changing role of police in America).*

The 9/11 attacks and the ongoing war on terror have demonstrated that terrorism respects no jurisdictional boundaries, whether these attacks take the form of aircraft hijackings, the use of biological agents, or more sophisticated attempts to infiltrate crucial infrastructures. This realization has forced local police administrators to focus considerable attention on the need to improve law enforcement intelligence operations. The notion that state and local law enforcement agencies must enhance their intelligence gathering and analysis capabilities represents a fundamental shift in the strategic dimension of local policing that involves making these agencies "intelligence-led" organizations reminiscent of the military model used for gathering, assessing, and distributing critical information.[1]

While much of the effort to reform intelligence operations after 9/11 focused on the need to restructure and better coordinate the intelligence infrastructure and model at the federal level, there has also been a significant effort to define the role state and local law enforcement agencies play in homeland security.

FIGURE 3.1 ▶ The events of 9/11 changed our world forever . . . characterized as one of the defining moments of the 21st century: 2,752 men, women, and children lost their lives in this horrific terrorist attack. According to former Attorney General John Ashcroft, there is no priority higher than the prevention of terrorism; a role now placed squarely on the shoulders of American police and law enforcement officers. (Seth McAllister/Newscom)

INTELLIGENCE AND TERRORISM

Historically, the missing dimension in quality intelligence has been analysis.[2] The transformation of raw data, whether acquired through human, technical, or open sources, must be collated, scrutinized, and processed accurately and quickly. The ultimate goal of this analytical process is a finished product more intelligible, accurate, and usable than the data and information drawn on to prepare it. Herein is the definition of **intelligence**—data and information that have been evaluated, analyzed, and produced with careful conclusions and recommendations. Intelligence, then, is a *product* created from systematic and thoughtful examination, placed in context, and provided to law enforcement executives, with facts and alternatives that can inform critical decisions.[3]

There are three major perspectives on the purpose of intelligence and analysis. Each voices a different focus on the ability of intelligence officers and agents to provide sound information on which responsible decision making can be based. The first perspective is associated with the writings of Sherman Kent; it holds that the role of intelligence is to limit surprise from national security policymaking.[4] In other words, the analysis of data (or the making of intelligence) should render facts and figures, identify trends and patterns, and provide statistical support on *past* events. There are no follow-up investigations, post-audits, or continued evaluations concerning the policy implemented in response to the data provided. In essence, this type of analysis provides the facts and leaves the decisions to decision makers.

In the second perspective, analysts not only should be responsible for providing historical data but also should force policymakers and decision makers to confront alternative views of specific events, potential threats, and/or foreign situations. The emphasis is on connecting the political ends with the course of events. Analysts cannot limit themselves simply to giving situational reports and briefings; they must inherently focus on the dynamics of the political arena in order to give meaning to data. This can be particularly true regarding threats (such as terrorism) from foreign sources, in which state and local police executives may be relatively naïve to the geo-global dimensions of a specific region outside the United States. Most important, analysts need to place intelligence into the relevance and perspective of state and local governments. For instance, increased violence in the West Bank may be of little consequence to rural areas in the United States but much more meaningful to areas outside Detroit, Michigan, where nearly 300,000 Palestinians reside.

The final and sharply contrasting perspective concerning the purpose of analysis is somewhat latent. Its emphasis is not on providing past data on which to base decisions or policy; rather, the focus is squarely on the *prediction* of future events. This shift in emphasis can be viewed as an outgrowth of the second perspective as more technological advances have come to pass. With the advent of advanced analytical software and artificial intelligence systems, more robust records management systems, and relatively easy access to huge data banks (see Chapter 2, Policing Today), it should now be possible to provide accurate and reliable predictions concerning specific events.[5] The ultimate goal is twofold: (1) provide accurate information concerning the future in order to avoid decision and policy pitfalls and bureaucratic blunderings and (2) chart out courses of action directly aimed at achieving specific objectives. This, of course, requires a new way of thinking about policing—one that emphasizes prediction and prevention rather than detection and apprehension.

The Intelligence Process and Cycle

The *National Criminal Intelligence Sharing Plan (NCISP)*, originally released in 2003 and slightly revised in 2005 and 2008, contained 28 specific recommendations for major changes in local policing.[6] However, the key concept from the document emphasized the strategic integration of intelligence into the overall mission of the police organization—intelligence-led policing (refer to Chapter 2). Rather than react and respond to past calls for service, the NCISP placed much more emphasis on predictive analysis derived from the discovery of hard facts, information, patterns, intelligence, and good crime analysis. By concentrating on key criminal activities, problems, and individuals targeted through analysis, significant attention could be directed to alleviate the crime problem. In order to protect the civil liberties of all individuals, the intelligence process was developed with key evaluation points aimed at verifying source reliability and validity at the beginning of the collection cycle. The goal was to develop a universal process that would integrate both law enforcement and national security intelligence agendas, while providing mechanisms for securing individual freedoms and allowing law enforcement agencies to be proactive in preventing and deterring crime and terrorism. The end result was the "Intelligence Cycle," presented by the FBI in an effort to bring varied pieces of information together in an effort to draw logical conclusions from a thorough and systematic process (see Figure 3.2). As important, the Intelligence Cycle also provides a means of communicating and sharing intelligence among individuals and agencies through the dissemination process.

Fusion Centers

The transformation of local police agencies into intelligence-led organizations involves four key objectives: (1) the creation of a task and coordination process, (2) the development of core intelligence products to lead the operation, (3) the establishment of standardized training practices, and (4) the development of protocols to facilitate intelligence capabilities. This approach is intended to improve the capability of local law enforcement in regard to responding to terror threats and traditional anti-crime efforts. Intelligence-led policing blends community partnerships with crime fighting and police accountability in an effort to maximize police efficiency and effectiveness in terrorism prevention and crime reduction. There is evidence to suggest that this initiative has started to alter the face of traditional policing in the United States.

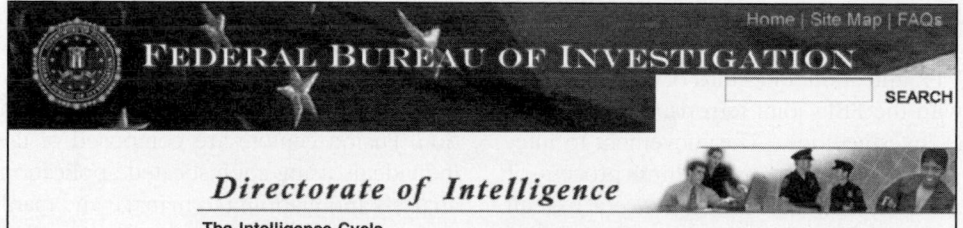

Directorate of Intelligence

The Intelligence Cycle

The intelligence cycle is the process of developing unrefined data into polished intelligence for the use of policymakers. The intelligence cycle consists of six steps, described below. The graphic below shows the circular nature of this process, although movement between the steps is fluid. Intelligence uncovered at one step may require going back to an earlier step before moving forward.

Requirements are identified information needs—what we must know to safeguard the nation. Intelligence requirements are established by the Director of National Intelligence according to guidance received from the President and the National and Homeland Security Advisors. Requirements are developed based on critical information required to protect the United States from National Security and criminal threats. The Attorney General and the Director of the FBI participate in the formulation of national intelligence requirements.

Planning and Direction is management of the entire effort, from identifying the need for information to delivering an intelligence product to a consumer. It involves implementation plans to satisfy requirements levied on the FBI, as well as identifying specific collection requirements based on FBI needs. Planning and direction also is responsive to the end of the cycle, because current and finished intelligence, which supports decision-making, generates new requirements. The Executive Assistant Director for the National Security Branch leads intelligence planning and direction for the FBI.

Collection is the gathering of raw information based on requirements. Activities such as interviews, technical and physical surveillances, human source operation, searches, and liaison relationships result in the collection of intelligence.

Processing and Exploitation involves converting the vast amount of information collected into a form usable by analysts. This is done through a variety of methods including decryption, language translations, and data reduction. Processing includes the entering of raw data into databases where it can be exploited for use in the analysis process.

Analysis and Production is the conversion of raw information into intelligence. It includes integrating, evaluating, and analyzing available data, and preparing intelligence products. The information's reliability, validity, and relevance is evaluated and weighed. The information is logically integrated, put in context, and used to produce intelligence. This includes both "raw" and finished intelligence. Raw intelligence is often referred to as "the dots"—individual pieces of information disseminated individually. Finished intelligence reports "connect the dots" by putting information in context and drawing conclusions about its implications.

Dissemination—the last step—is the distribution of raw or finished intelligence to the consumers whose needs initiated the intelligence requirements. The FBI disseminates information in three standard formats: Intelligence Information Reports (IIRs), FBI Intelligence Bulletins, and FBI Intelligence Assessments. FBI intelligence products are provided daily to the Attorney General, the President, and to customers throughout the FBI and in other agencies. These FBI intelligence customers make decisions—operational, strategic, and policy—based on the information. These decisions may lead to the levying of more requirements, thus continuing the FBI intelligence cycle.

FIGURE 3.2 ▶ The Intelligence Cycle. (Courtesy of Federal Bureau of Investigation).

A national survey found that a majority of responding local and state police agencies have conducted terrorism threat assessments since 9/11, and about one-third of these agencies have collaborated with the FBI's joint terrorism task force to assist in local crime investigations.[7] The movement to integrate information and develop an overarching process of managing the flow of information and intelligence across all levels and sectors of government and private security has been the impetus to create **fusion centers** (see Figure 3.3) inside local and state police agencies. Fusion centers act as effective and efficient mechanisms for exchanging information and intelligence, maximizing police resources, streamlining public safety operations, and improving the ability to fight crime and terrorism by merging data from a variety of sources.[8] Fusion centers serve as clearinghouses for all potentially relevant homeland security information that can be used to assess local terror threats and aid in the apprehension of more traditional criminal suspects.

Originally launched in New York City under the direction of then police commissioner Raymond Kelly in 2002, the concept of a fusion center blended the power of information technology with terrorism prevention and crime fighting. With a price tag exceeding $11 million, the Real Time Crime Center (RTCC) in New York City combs through tens of millions of criminal complaints, arrest and parole records, and 911 call records dating back a decade in an effort to provide NYPD officers with the information tools necessary to stop a terrorist event or investigate a crime.[9] Fusion centers distribute relevant, actionable, and timely information and intelligence, incorporating a simultaneously vertical (i.e., federal, state, and local) and horizontal (i.e., within the agency, with other local agencies, and across disciplines such as fire, EMS, public works, and private partners) approach within a given jurisdiction. Fusion centers are composed of talented and trained individuals using sophisticated application software in crime analysis and mapping to manage and manipulate information and intelligence into a usable product. The resulting analysis acts as a basis for the deployment of police resources and directed operations in a real-time format—that is, almost immediately. The fusion center not only acts as a centralized host for intelligence information and analysis but also serves as a conduit for disseminating critical information to other regional, state, and national authorities. This is a particularly important point that fulfills the NCISP in protecting the homeland. Both large and small, as well as local, state, tribal, and federal law enforcement agencies are encouraged to work toward the systematic sharing of intelligence information relating to criminal and terrorist threats. See Figure 3.4.

Almost every state and several large metropolitan cities have undertaken the development of fusion centers with significant funding assistance from the Department of Homeland Security. For instance, the Chicago Police Department Deployment Operations Center (DOC) was one of the first centers to combine real-time intelligence analysis with the deployment process. In Los Angeles, both the city and the county have well-developed fusion centers, and in Dallas, Texas, the Metropolitan Operations and Analytical Intelligence Center (MOSAIC) provides real-time tactical information to officers on the street 24/7.

FIGURE 3.3 ▶ Fusion centers are high-tech, information-intensive operational centers that analyze and disseminate intelligence relating to terrorism and crime to police officers on the street. (Jason Decrow/AP Images)

1. **Recognize your responsibilities and lead by example**
   Recognize the value of sharing intelligence information within your own agency, and encourage the practice of sharing information with other law enforcement and public safety agencies. Use the guidelines and action steps outlined in the National Criminal Intelligence Sharing Plan ("Plan") to implement or enhance your organization's intelligence function.

2. **Establish a mission statement and a policy to address developing and sharing information and intelligence data within your agency**
   The Plan provides model policies and guidelines for implementing or reviewing an agency's intelligence function. Examples include Criminal Intelligence Systems Operating Policies federal regulation 28 CFR Part 23, the International Association of Chiefs of Police's Criminal Intelligence Model Policy, and the Law Enforcement Intelligence Unit's (LEIU) Criminal Intelligence File Guidelines.

3. **Connect to your state criminal justice network and regional intelligence databases, and participate in information sharing initiatives**
   Many states provide access to other government databases, including motor vehicles, corrections, and others. Regional intelligence databases and sharing initiatives promote communication and collaboration by providing access to other agencies' and organizations' investigative and intelligence data.

4. **Ensure privacy issues are protected in policy and practice**
   The protection of individuals' privacy and constitutional rights is an obligation of government officials and is crucial to the long-term success of criminal intelligence sharing. The Plan provides guidelines that support policies which will protect privacy and constitutional rights while not hindering the intelligence process. Implementing and supporting privacy policies and practices within your agency will also reduce your organization's liability concerns.

5. **Access law enforcement Web sites, subscribe to law enforcement listservs, and use the Internet as an information resource**
   Many Web sites on the Internet and others on closed networks provide valuable intelligence assessments and news. Listservs provide instant and widespread communication for investigators.
   Listservs allow both the receipt and distribution of intelligence information. The Internet provides a wealth of open-source information, including government information and access to private agencies that share with law enforcement.

6. **Provide your agency members with appropriate training on the criminal intelligence process**
   Some training models or modules are already found in Internet-based and interactive CDs, such as the International Association of Law Enforcement Intelligence Analysts (IALEIA), National White Collar Crime Center, and LEIU "Turn Key Intelligence." A listing of available intelligence training sources and specifically scheduled classes is found on the IALEIA website: www.ialeia.org. This listing allows individuals to directly contact training source agencies and organizations for more information on classes and schedules.

7. **Become a member of your in-region Regional Information Sharing Systems® (RISS) center**
   RISS operates the only secure Web-based nationwide network for communication and exchange of criminal intelligence information by local, state, federal, and tribal participating law enforcement member agencies. RISS partners with other law enforcement systems to electronically connect them to RISSNETTM, including High Intensity Drug Trafficking Areas (HIDTA) Investigative Support centers and other federal and state agency systems.

8. **Become a member of the Federal Bureau of Investigation's (FBI) Law Enforcement Online (LEO) system**
   The FBI's LEO system is a sensitive but unclassified, real-time information sharing communications system for all levels of the law enforcement community and is available at no cost to its users. LEO provides secure e-mail capability, a national alert mechanism, and access to over 125 special-interest groups for sharing information by providing access to other networks, systems, databases, and other services.

9. **Partner with public and private infrastructure sectors**
   Regular communication with the entities that control America's critical infrastructures, such as energy, agriculture, transportation, and shipping, is critically important to ensuring the safety and security of the citizens in your community.

10. **Participate in local, state, and national intelligence organizations**
    In most areas of the country, there are locally based intelligence organizations that welcome participation from all agencies and are often affiliated with state and national organizations.

FIGURE 3.4 ▶ Ten simple steps that assist individual police agencies become part of the National Criminal Intelligence Sharing Plan. (Source: https://it.ojp.gov/gist/100/10-Simple-Steps-to-Help-Your-Agency-Become-a-Part-of-the-National-Criminal-Intelligence-Sharing-Plan, Criminal Intelligence Coordinating Council, updated 2015).

The goals of a fusion center are fourfold:

1. Fusion centers support the broad range of activities undertaken by a police department relating to the detection, examination, and investigation of a potential terrorist and/or criminal activity. Ideally, the center serves as a hub of anti-terrorist and anti-crime operations in a specific region, focusing on the recognition of patterns, indications and warnings, source development, interdiction, and the coordination of critical criminal justice resources. These are critical activities for any police agency attempting to be proactive and intelligence-led to be successful in deterring, detecting, disrupting, investigating, and apprehending suspects involved in terrorist and criminal activity directly related to homeland security. Figure 3.5 represents one of several information technology solutions that are commonly used in fusion centers to help identify patterns and indicators associated with terrorism and/or crime.

2. Fusion centers support operations that protect **critical infrastructure and key resources (CI/KRs)** in a given region, support major incident operations, support specialized units charged with interdiction and investigative operations, and assist in emergency operations and planning. The aim of a fusion center is to reduce the vulnerability of the high-value and high-risk targets identified within a jurisdiction. For example, in any major city, there are several important CI/KRs—bank buildings, corporate headquarters, bridges and overpasses, water supply tanks and systems, electronic switching hubs, rail and subway stations, and a myriad of other important infrastructure entities. Fusion centers maintain huge databases that are immediately retrievable for use in thwarting an attack or dealing with an emergency. For instance, the Los Angeles Police Department has implemented the "Archangel Project," aimed at developing a large database for all CI/KRs in the region. Its primary purpose is to maintain as much accessible and critical data as possible on any one given piece of critical infrastructure, so that during an emergency or a potentially threatening event, police resources can be directed appropriately. Hence, building schematics and event histories, alternative road and highway routes, and maps of water supply mains, electrical grids, switching stations, and the like are maintained and accessible within the fusion center. Fusion centers are **all-hazard** in scope—that is, they are developed to support operations during an emergency that is either human-made, such as a

FIGURE 3.5 ▶ *IBM i2 iBase IntelliShare Software* enables multiple web-based users to analyze data in a central repository. Further, individual dashboards can be created to reveal a number of widgets and windows that provide single and unified views of intelligence data. Such intelligence tools can be used in a wide range of investigations, including the following:

- Counterterrorism
- Drug Trafficking
- Money Laundering
- Securities Fraud
- Insurance Fraud
- Forensic Accounting
- Major Incident Management
- Immigration Violations and Human Trafficking
- Identity Theft
- Threat Assessment and Emergency Management

Application Programs

Since 1990, i2 Corporation has been a worldwide leader of visual investigative analysis software for law enforcement, intelligence, military, and Fortune 500 organizations. The application software performs an array of sophisticated analytical techniques, including social network analysis, commodity flow, telephone record analysis, link analysis, and the like, often used in real-time fusion centers to convey analytical findings in intuitive charts that organize support data. i2 is now part of IBM and has developed a number of new analytic tools for intelligence analysis and sharing, such as the IntelliShare dashboard described here. (Courtesy of the IBM Corporation, visit http://www-01.ibm.com/software/info/i2software).

terrorist event, or natural, such as a hurricane, flood, or tornado.

3. Fusion centers often maintain public "tip lines," which give them the capability to promote more public involvement in and awareness of terrorist threats. The goal is to identify and recognize warning signs and potential threats in a timely manner in order to pre-empt potential terrorist attacks and reduce the vulnerability of the CI/KRs in a given region. Fusion centers accomplish this task on a daily basis, focusing on the analysis of crimes that are often linked to terrorist cells and activity for funding, such as narcotics trafficking, credit card abuse, armament and gun theft, prostitution, and human trafficking, by distributing information relating to these linkages to all agencies within a given region. The timeliness of gathering, analyzing, and disseminating information is vital to successfully preventing acts of violence and threats to homeland security.

4. Fusion centers assist police executives in making better-informed decisions, especially during emergencies or critical incidents. Fusion centers are ongoing deployment operations centers with the real-time ability to monitor critical resources. This includes real-time status monitoring of major events, communicating with area medical facilities and trauma units, coordinating the allocation and deployment of multi-agency personnel resources (including military reserve units), monitoring changing weather conditions, and directing all support services through a centralized operations center.

Fusion centers embody the core of collaboration between agencies in law enforcement, as well as members of private security and the general public. The National Governors Associated Center for Best Practices revealed that states ranked the development of intelligence fusion centers as one of their highest priorities in reducing crime and preventing terrorism in the homeland.[10]

The National Fusion Center Association (NFCA) and the National Counterterrorism Center (NCTC)

As of 2015, there were 82 state and major urban fusion centers within the United States.[11] Almost every state has a statewide fusion center, as well as most major urban areas. The National Fusion Center Association (NFCA) is a formal group that represents the interest of state and local urban area fusion centers nationally. In addition, the NFCA promotes the development and sustainment of fusion centers to enhance public safety, the ethical and lawful collection of intelligence gathering, analysis, and dissemination.[12] The goal of the NFCA is to prevent the next terrorist attack on the homeland. To this end, the **Homeland Security Data Network (HSDN)** allows the federal

government to move information and intelligence to the states at the "secret" level, thereby allowing the quick exchange of critical data and information pertaining to an immediate terrorist threat within any jurisdiction of the United States. Through HSDN, fusion center staff can access the **National Counterterrorism Center (NCTC)** via a secure and classified portal to the most current terrorism-related information. The NCTC acts as the nations "hub" for intelligence activity both domestically and internationally, coordinating intelligence information derived by individual members of the intelligence community. It also serves as the single point for the strategic and operational planning of counterterrorism activity. This is often accomplished through interagency meetings and secure teleconferences about terrorist groups, capabilities, plans and intentions, and emerging threats to U.S. interests. The NCTC is located in Washington, DC, and is part of the Office of the Director of National Intelligence. One of the most important duties of the center is to maintain the national repository of known and suspected terrorists and provide assessments to potential threats by these individuals.[13]

Clearly, the 9/11 attacks and the impact of terrorism on our country has transformed the role of the police in our communities. We have witnessed an unprecedented movement on the part of the federal government to employ local, tribal, and state police agencies into the counterterrorism mission. Police executives need to recognize that this trend will not wane in the future, but that the public as well as federal officials, will increasingly expect local police to take a broader and more important role in safeguarding their communities against terrorists.[14]

Policing Terrorism

According to policing scholar George Kelling and current NYPD Commissioner Bill Bratton, cities must create a hostile environment for terrorists by instilling effective intelligence gathering and analysis into the everyday workings of local police departments.[15] More recently, Mathieu Deflem's work on the policing of terrorism emphasized the prevention and response to terrorism as an issue of crime control for every police department and suggests the development of professional standards for investigating terrorist incidents as a crime methodology, rather than singularly a counterterrorism effort.[16] This theme is certainly reinforced by federal authorities as presented in the late 2008 report presented by the U.S. Department of Justice, Office of Community Oriented Policing Services, acting as a police chief's guide to policing terrorism.[17] Central to this document and the mission of policing in preventing terrorism and reducing crime must be the systematic collection, analysis, and sharing of intelligence information between agencies. Several important steps for any local police department to consider in developing its intelligence collection methodology and enhancing its role to prevent terrorism are echoed earlier in Figure 3.4 and include the following:

- Create an intelligence unit that focuses on counterterrorism and/or appoint a terrorist liaison officer.
- Send officers for training in intelligence gathering, analysis, and sharing. Know the legal and privacy issues surrounding police use of intelligence information.

- Join the local Joint Terrorism Task Force (JTTF) sponsored by the FBI field office in the local jurisdiction. Depending on the size of the department, this may not always be feasible or cost-effective since the FBI provides pay for only overtime and equipment; officer salaries are continued by the home department. Therefore, smaller agencies may wish to only designate an officer to coordinate information between the department and the nearest task force.

- Develop an information-sharing environment between agencies of law enforcement within and across jurisdictions. Implement fusion centers when appropriate to analyze and funnel terrorist information to appropriate authorities.

- Participate in the National SAR Initiative (NSI),which is focused on developing and using the Suspicious Activity Reporting System (SARS). In accordance with the National Criminal Intelligence Sharing Plan and the National Strategy for Information Sharing (NSIS), developed within the U.S. Department of Justice, this system promotes an Information Sharing Environment (ISE) important to establishing the timely sharing of SAR information with law enforcement agencies, fusion centers, and theJTTF[18] (see Figure 3.6).

- Promote intelligence-led policing and implement community policing efforts with immigrant communities, especially immigrant Muslim communities.

Criticisms Aimed at Fusion Centers and Other Law Enforcement Responses to Terrorism

As with any new direction, there have certainly been setbacks and problems that have plagued not only the development and transition of the Department of Homeland Security but also befuddled the government's response to terrorism. For instance, there continue to be problems relating to the sharing of information between local law enforcement and the FBI. A 2010 assessment of state and local fusion centers conducted by the U.S. Department of Homeland Security revealed widespread deficiencies in the centers' basic counterterrorism information-sharing capabilities.[19] Especially noted in the study was the need to improve the coordination of federal communication and collaboration within and between fusion centers. One local fusion center director noted that information flow appears to be one way—from the local agency to the FBI.[20]

Fusion centers have also not been without their detractors. Monahan and Palmer note, after an exhausting and comprehensive analysis from 2002 to 2008, that three primary concerns continue to plague these information and intelligence hubs.[21] First, fusion centers are expensive and almost any cost-benefit analysis will reveal significant money spent for very little, tangible evidence of success. The effectiveness of fusion centers, particularly given their financial outlay, is seriously questioned. Few terrorist incidents have actually been prevented due to the

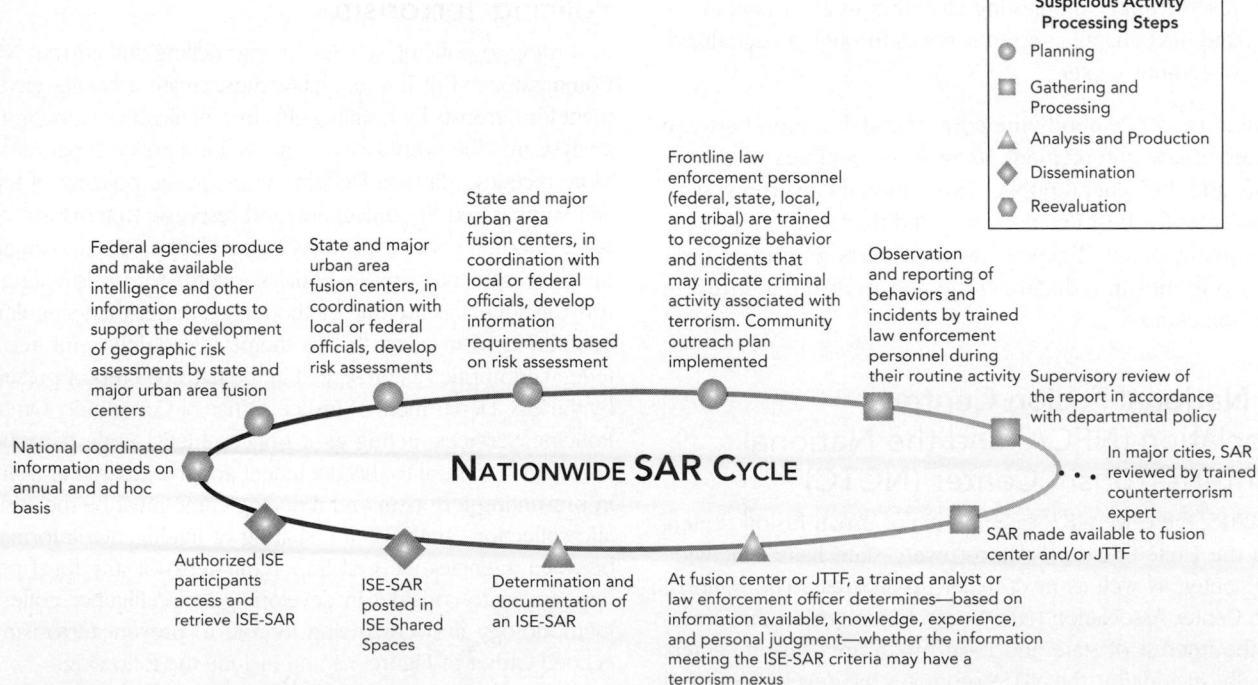

FIGURE 3.6 ▶ The SAR Cycle Chart. This diagram focuses on activities of local, state, and tribal agencies. By following these steps, agencies can be assured that their SAR activities are in alignment with and can support crucial information sharing. This diagram will also help identify gaps in an agency's current process that may need to be addressed and/or corrected. (Suspicious Activity Reporting: Process Implementation Checklist, p. 4. See http://it.ojp.gov/docdownloader. aspx?ddid=1147).

work of fusion centers. Second, many fusion centers appear to suffer from "mission creep"; that is, because there are few cases focused on terrorism, many centers have expanded their role to include crime fighting and reduction. According to Monahan and Palmer, the expansion of fusion centers into this mission is well beyond the initial intention of funding "all-hazard" centers for the coordination of intelligence and information to prevent terrorism. And finally, fusion centers come desperately close to violating the civil liberties of people, especially relating to racial and ethnic profiling and breaches of privacy. The American Civil Liberties Union (ACLU) has also highlighted possible privacy and individual infringements stemming from fusion centers.[22]

Fusion centers have access to an enormous amount of personal information regarding individuals. Data banks involving criminal and arrest records, financial records, civil litigation, credit reports, water bills, and even Internet sites such as Facebook and MySpace are now available to police personnel. Quoting a spotty historical past by police relating to intelligence gathering and analysis, the ACLU suggests a number of important potential improvements:

Eliminate ambiguous lines of authority—In many cases, there appears to be a blurred line between the federal government and individual states or local agencies housing fusion centers. There simply is not a clear portrait of who is actually in charge of fusion centers. Although individual fusion centers were developed by state and local governments, the federal government provided much of the original funding and dispatches its own intelligence officers to work alongside state/local officials. Most state/local agencies cannot access classified information, and, hence, must rely on the DHS employee or the FBI to provide this intelligence.

Eliminate private sector involvement in the fusion process—Private sector participation in fusion centers is designed to encourage a number of public safety, transportation, social service, and private sector entities to join together in the fusion process. Because one of the goals of fusion centers is to protect the nation's critical infrastructure—85 percent of which is owned by private interests—fusion centers are strongly encouraged to seek information from "nontraditional sources" (e.g., private corporations, hospitals, and transportation companies). Allowing private sector corporations access to classified materials and other sensitive law enforcement information may violate individual Constitutional and personal rights. Police and law enforcement entities undergo rigorous training, are sworn to objectively serve their community, and are paid through public salaries, whereas private companies and their employees are motivated to maximize profits. In short, the availability for personal information to be shared between public and private officials, for the sake of forging public and private partnerships, may be a violation of individual rights to privacy guaranteed by our Constitution.

Eliminate military participation in the fusion process—The Posse Comitatus Act of 1878 clearly prohibits the U.S. military from acting in a law enforcement capacity on American soil, except under express authority from Congress. Hence, fusion centers should be prohibited from using active-duty military personnel. However, many fusion centers incorporate the National Guard and the Coast Guard and are a bridge between military and civilian intelligence centers. At least one center in North Dakota is actually located within National Guard facilities. The ACLU argues that military personnel operating in a law enforcement capacity (fusion centers) would erode not only the Posse Comitatus Act but also reduce the Constitutional barriers between the military and American citizenry.

Eliminate illegal data mining in the fusion process—Data fusion can lead to illegal data mining; that is, accessing private sector databases that are not controlled or authenticated. This action clearly jeopardizes an individual's Constitutional right to privacy, as well as subjects the individual to unwarranted scrutiny by the police *without* probable cause. Intelligence gathering and fusion center processes include anticipating, identifying, monitoring, and preventing future criminal and terrorist activities without probable cause. How police agencies focus on one group versus another, and who becomes the target of an investigation, are key questions concerning this issue.

Eliminate excessive secrecy—A fusion center's ability to gather vast amounts of personal information on individuals, with very little oversight, not only undercuts the function and purpose of the intelligence process, but also increases the danger that incompetence and malfeasance will flourish. Fusion centers must be held accountable and transparent to public scrutiny.

Clearly, the power struggle between federal and state/local agencies continues today. Despite the lessons learned from 9/11, there are still major issues in this area. Further, while over a half a billion dollars have been spent to improve the nation's ability to thwart terrorist attacks, the Congressional Research Service (CRS) Reports for Congress indicates that fusion centers are ineffective and continue to suffer from lack of interoperability and a host of political power issues between government levels.[23] The CRS reports that while fusion centers were primarily designed to "fuse" federal, state, and local intelligence regarding potential terrorist attacks, they have gravitated more toward collecting and analyzing information on criminals and offenders in local regions—precisely the concern of the ACLU. The CRS document supports the ACLU stance that fusion centers pose significant risks of civil liberty and privacy incursion. Most revealing of the criticism against fusion centers was a 2012 report by the U.S. Senate Permanent Subcommittee on Investigations.[24] The subcommittee found that the quality of intelligence information forwarded by many fusion centers was "oftentimes shoddy, rarely timely, sometimes endangering citizens' civil liberties and Privacy Act protections" and often taken from previously published public sources.[25] Most damaging was the finding that many times, the "intelligence" was not even related

Box 3.1: USA Freedom Act: High Tech Companies vs the US Government

After 9/11, Congress quickly passed the USA PATRIOT Act that provided new tools to assist law enforcement in securing the country against terrorist attacks. The PATRIOT Act expanded the traditional methodologies of surveillance used by law enforcement and intelligence agencies with significantly reduced checks and balances relating to record searches, wiretaps, search warrants, pen trap and trace orders, and court orders. However, in 2015, a major shift signalling a significant change in American attitudes toward safeguarding civil liberty versus the nation was marked by the expiration of parts of the PATRIOT Act, and the development of new laws curtailing international and domestic intelligence agencies like the Central Intelligence Agency (CIA), the National Security Agency (NSA), and the Federal Bureau of Investigation (FBI). Sparked by a former NSA contractor in 2014, Edward Snowden revealed the presence of a powerful national intelligence apparatus involving the collection of phone and computer records (metadata) from almost every large communications provider in the country. Worse yet, federal bureaucrats denied the existence of the apparatus in Congressional Hearings in 2014–2015.

A new bill, known as the USA Freedom Act, was signed by President Obama on June 2, 2015, that strengthen civil liberty safeguards and allowed three key provisions of the PATRIOT Act to expire: (1) The NSA (or any other agency) will no longer be able to collect newly created logs of Americans' phone calls in bulk; (2) The FBI will no longer be able to invoke the PATRIOT Act to obtain new investigations or new wiretaps on potential suspects without affiliation or linkage to a known terrorist group; and (3) the FBI will be required to obtain a court order to obtain business records relevant to a terrorist organization. The new law represented some of the most significant surveillance reform in decades in the United States, and comes on the heels of information technology companies like Apple and Microsoft, that provided new personal security tools for customers that can prevent "snooping" from both the government and the Internet Service Provider itself.

The conflict between big high-tech companies and the government continued into early 2016, as a U.S. magistrate ordered Apple to produce software that would give FBI agents the ability to access data stored within the new iPhone. Specifically, agents wished to access the data on Syed Rizwan Farook's iPhone, a U.S. citizen accused of killing 14 people at a holiday party in San Bernardino, California on December 2, 2015. Agents were interested in viewing potential emails from members of terrorist organizations (e.g., ISIS, al-Qaeda) in the Middle East with Farook, as well as Farook's conversations on an online dating site in which Farook met his wife, Tashfeen Malik, an accomplice in the San Bernardino massacre. Farook and Malik were both killed in a shoot-out with police after the attack.

to terrorism and that DHS was unable to provide an accurate amount as to how much it had granted to states and cities in support of fusion center efforts. Instead, it provided a range from $289 million to $1.4 billion, without any details regarding a cost-benefit analysis or study on efficiency and effectiveness.[26] Fusion centers can serve a significant purpose in detecting and investigating terrorists, but their current practices are in need of constant monitoring and supervision. And, the public is certainly entitled to an accounting of federal dollars spent on the development of fusion centers with an honest evaluation of the effectiveness of such entities.

HOMELAND SECURITY

In November 2002, President George W. Bush ushered in the largest federal bureaucratic reorganization in 55 years to create the cabinet-level Department of Homeland Security (DHS). Headed by the former governor of Pennsylvania, Tom Ridge, the new department focused the anti-terrorism effort in the United States, absorbing many of the enforcement agencies within the Departments of Treasury and Transportation (Transportation Security Administration; U.S. Coast Guard; U.S. Customs; Bureau of Alcohol, Tobacco, and Firearms; U.S. Secret Service; and

Federal Emergency Management Administration [FEMA]). In addition, the department created a division to analyze intelligence gathered by the FBI, CIA, and other police and military agencies. There are four primary areas of responsibility within the Department of Homeland Security:

- Border security and transportation
- Emergency preparedness and response
- Chemical, biological, radiological, and nuclear countermeasures
- Intelligence analysis and infrastructure protection

The building of the department has been slow, with a variety of changes and setbacks coming from changes in leadership, violations of ethical behavior, and severe criticism stemming from poor agency responses to several national emergencies. For instance, FEMA's lackluster response to the city of New Orleans during Hurricane Katrina in 2005 was eclipsed in 2010 with, again, a very slow and poor response to the largest oil leak in U.S. history crippling the Gulf Coast of Louisiana (British Petroleum's Deep Horizon oil rig explosion and resulting oil spill). And, in 2012 and 2015, the U.S. Secret Service was rocked by scandals involving agents that were drinking heavily and engaging with prostitutes and strippers overseas prior to official duty in safeguarding the President.[27]

Homeland Security and President Barack Obama

On January 20, 2009, Senator Barack Obama from the state of Illinois was sworn in as the 44th President of the United States. One of his first duties was to appoint then Governor of Arizona, Janet Napolitano, as the third Secretary of the Department of Homeland Security. Napolitano had received praise in her role as governor in the areas of terrorism and immigration reform.[28] As Secretary of the Department of Homeland Security, Napolitano played an integral role in bolstering border security by increasing forces along the border, and, in addition, increasing resources and technology to aid in the fight against terrorism.

The Department of Homeland Security, directed by Jeh Johnson since 2013, is the third-largest department and has the ninth-largest budget in the federal government, boasting over 220,000 employees and a total budget authority that exceeds $60 billion (FY 2015), with an additional $12 billion earmarked for grants aimed at funding anti-terror and border security initiatives at the state and local levels (see Figure 3.7). Much of this money will be provided to local and state law enforcement agencies for the development of programs that address one of the four primary responsibilities of DHS.

Beyond the ultimate mission of ensuring the nation's safety and preventing terrorism, DHS is responsible for immigration policy, airport security, and the protection of the president.

POLITICAL VIOLENCE AND TERRORISM

The events of 9/11 and continuing incidents of mass violence in America have had a profound impact on federal, state, and local law enforcement agencies, as police administrators are confronted with the most pressing and significant external issue of their careers: how to investigate, interdict, and prevent terrorism. Police departments around the country have had to address new threats of violence that are sometimes the result of federal actions or international foreign policy actions in which they have no authority. For instance, since 9/11, virtually every large metropolitan police department has been placed on the highest alert. Operational demands required police agencies to perform new activities, including increasing infrastructure security around critical buildings and airports, building anti-terrorism barriers, beefing up intelligence gathering and analysis functions, monitoring activity in Middle Eastern communities, and participating in joint terrorism task forces. Even though an extensive federal structure has been developed to counter the terrorist threat, the first level of prevention (and response) remains with uniformed police officers on the street.

Defining Terrorism

In the popular mind, terrorism is viewed as the illegitimate and violent actions of specific groups that violate the authority of rightfully established governments. **Terrorism** encompasses the threat of and/or use of violence to achieve a specific set of political objectives or goals.[29] Historically, defining terrorism has been a very difficult venture, shaped and altered by a number of factors, including our own national interests, government interpretations, the news media, hidden political agendas, and emotional human rights rhetoric.[30] Such phrases as "guerrilla warfare," "revolutionary movement," "communist-supported terrorism," and "radical Islamic fundamentalist" only heighten ideological sentiment and play to emotion rather than intellect. Hence, we find the cliché that one person's terrorist is another person's freedom fighter to be truly an observation based on perspective and perception.[31] This is certainly the case in the United States, as some actions, such as the first attack on the World Trade Center (1993), the bombing of the Alfred P. Murrah Federal Building in Oklahoma City (1995), the downing of TWA flight 800 (1996), the attacks on 9/11 (2001), the killing of 13 soldiers at Fort Hood, Texas (2009), the Boston Marathon Bombing (2013), the attack on the Dallas Police Department using homemade bombs, automatic weapons, and an armored truck (2015), and the killing of 14 people in San Bernadino, California (2015), are "terrorist," whereas the sporadic bombings at abortion centers or mosques across the country are not.

Large, high-profile terrorist events greatly impact how members of society interact. Random acts of terrorism upset the framework of society, leaving only futile questions without rational answers. Essentially, terrorism tests the basic social structure of dependence and trust. If random bombings and acts of violence occur on a frequent basis at the most secure institutions of a society (e.g., federal buildings, police departments, churches, synagogues, and hospitals), then people tend to lose faith in the existing social and government structure. Safety and security are severely compromised and questioned. Terrorism destroys the solidarity, co-operation, and interdependence on which social functioning is based and substitutes insecurity and distrust.

Terrorism, then, plays to emotion, not intellect.[32] It strikes at the very heart of who we are as Americans. For the first time in modern history (9/11), the United States was rocked by an attack on its own land. People were afraid as their daily lives were impacted and changed forever. The privileges and lifestyle that we so enjoyed in this country appeared to be jeopardized. The ability to travel freely was restricted. Few of us can recall where we were on September 2, 2001, but almost all of us can give vivid details of where we were and what we were doing in the morning hours of September 11, 2001. Even if we were in junior high or grade school, this event was so powerful and impactful on the United States as to be called a modern day "Pearl Harbor," referencing a sneak attack by the Japanese in 1941 that heralded U.S. involvement in World War II.

The overwhelming question plaguing so many of us was, why? We are a great nation that has helped almost every other nation in need. We give billions of dollars away each year in foreign aid. And we consistently stand for the human rights of all people, emphasizing the dignity of the human spirit and integrity of all people to live free, so why were we the victims of such rage on September 11, 2001, and continuing today, from a group of people that few of us even knew?

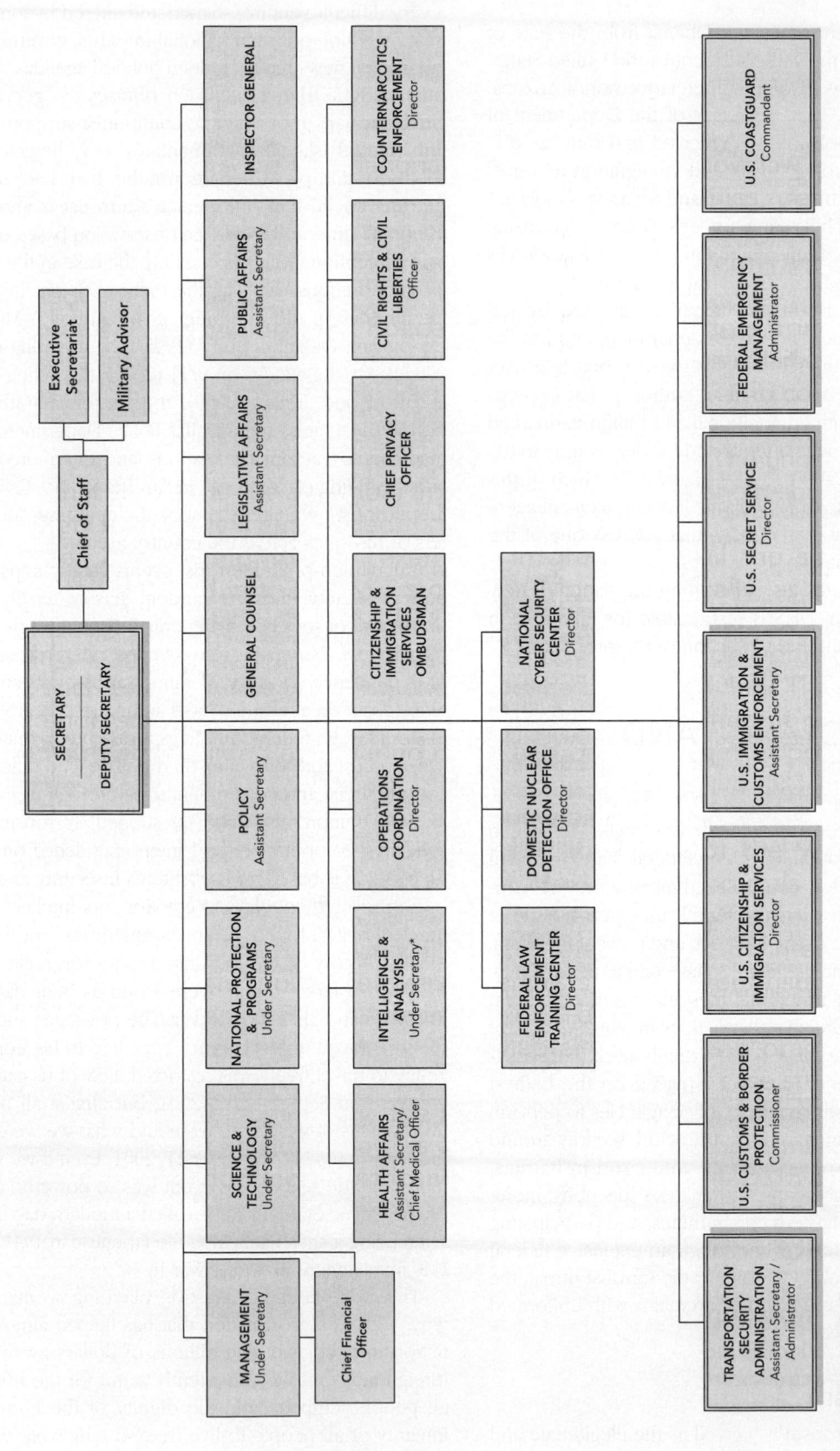

FIGURE 3.7 ▶ U.S. Department of Homeland Security. (U.S. Department of Homeland Security. *Effective April 10, 2015* http://www.dhs.gov/xlibrary/assets/dhs-orgchart.pdf).

Interestingly, the answer may be found in the question. Historically, we have known little about the Middle East. This view is confirmed by the late Osama bin Laden and the al-Qaeda group announcements to the world that one of the primary reasons for the attack was our lack of knowledge about the true political and economic conditions of the Middle East. Indeed, bin Laden made it very clear that they believed our goals in the Middle East were much more motivated by our own self-interest and quest for oil than in safeguarding the human rights of the people in that land. These may be particularly stinging remarks, considering the wars in Iraq and Afghanistan. He maintained that the stationing of American troops in the Middle East—in particular, near the holy city of Mecca (in Saudi Arabia)—was an egregious affront to his religion. He maintained that the people of the Middle East suffer under puppet governments supported by the United States and that these governments practice state terrorism against their own people. Today, we hear similar reasons given for attacks against the United States, only the focus is much more anti-American regarding our involvement in Iraq, Afghanistan, Syria, and other parts of the Middle East.

Here, we see quite profoundly the perspective that terrorism can be different things to different people. Theoretically, scholars have been debating the definition of terrorism for the past 50 years.[33] The goal here is to provide a conceptual framework on which to classify and understand terrorism, particularly in the Middle East. The work of Edward Mickolus provides such a framework.[34]

Terrorism is situationally defined—that is, a number of factors play on the difficulty of defining terrorism, including competing political agendas, national interests, economic security, the news media, fundamental cultural and religious beliefs, and the use of misinformation. By exploiting any one of these, it is possible to distort the facts. Even more disturbing and most compromising is the moral judgment passed on those who are labeled terrorists, for we in America assume that terrorism is "what the bad guys do." Hence, what better way is there to distort the sovereign interest of people than to associate them with illegitimate action or sources? In the Middle East, all of these factors are at play, making for a very complicated and difficult analysis. Those perpetrating terrorism against the United States do not view themselves as criminals. Indeed, many are at war and may well be agents provocateur and within the employ of a foreign government. This is an audience that American law enforcement has had little experience with, and these groups pose special challenges to the everyday police officer now charged with thwarting attacks against our homeland and with securing our infrastructure. Conceptualizing terrorism from a different perspective provides us with an opportunity to learn about our adversaries and hopefully exploit their weaknesses. Mickolus conceptualizes terrorism in four distinct typologies, based on actors:

- **International terrorism**—Actions conducted in the international arena by individuals that are members of a nation state. This usually includes members of intelligence and secret services employed by governments, such as the Cuban DGI, the old Soviet KGB, the Syrian Secret Police, the British M-9, the Israeli Mossad, and even the CIA.

- **Transnational terrorism**—Actions conducted in the international arena by individuals that have no nation-state. The predominate groups for the past 60 years are associated with the Palestinian cause (e.g., Popular Front for the Liberation of Palestine [PFLP], al-Fatah, Black June, Black September Organization, and Abu Nidal). However, other groups have also been active in the Middle East, such as the Kurdish Workers Party (PKK), the Armenians, and various groups from the breakaway lands of the former Soviet Union. The radical Islamic groups, such as al-Qaeda, HAMAS, and Hezbollah, are also classified in this typology. The new **Islamic State (ISIS)** is also a very good example of a transnational terrorist group.

- **Domestic terrorism**—Actions conducted by groups within a nation, usually against the government or specific groups within the nation-state. This may be one of the most difficult aspects of attempting to define the concept of terrorism. When do the rights of a government to control splinter elements within its own country end and the rights of the people to rebel become legitimate? This is a difficult question and one most often "flavored" by the myriad of factors already discussed. In any event, within the United States, groups associated with an extremist perspective (whether from the far left, the far right, or single issue) often fall within this typology. Examples of such groups include the Weather Underground, the Earth Liberation Front, the Animal Liberation Front, the Ku Klux Klan, the Neo-Nazis, the National Alliance, many of the radical militias (e.g., the Republic of Texas Militia and the Hutaree Militia of Eastern Michigan), and a myriad of anarchist groups sprouting up across the country. Most recently in 2016, armed aggressors affiliated with the militia movement calling themselves "Citizens for Constitutional Freedom" occupied the Malheur National Wildlife Refuge in rural Harney County, Oregon. While the occupation ended with the death of one of the leaders of the group during a police confrontation, the incident sparked national debate over the word "terrorist," as the Harney County Sheriff's Office characterized the group as "criminals engaged in trespassing" while the Oregon Governor, Kate Brown, referred to them as "terrorist."[35] The incident was compared to the Ruby Ridge shooting in northern Idaho (1992), the Mount Carmel siege with David Koresh in Waco, Texas (1993), and the Montana Freemen-Christian Patriot standoff in Jordon, Montana (1996) wherein suspects were consistently labeled "terrorist" by the FBI.

- **State terrorism**—Actions conducted by governments against their own population. Unfortunately, history is replete with suppressive governments that victimize their own populations. Certainly, the regimes of Adolph Hitler, Joseph Stalin, and Pol Pot represent these types of regimes, often characterized by ethnic and political cleansing. More recently, we have seen these types of activities in smaller countries throughout the Far East and Latin America. In the Middle East, Saddam Hussein in Iraq and Haffez al-assad and now his son, Bashar al-Assad in Syria, represent these types of entities. Interestingly, many (including the leadership of ISIS and the deceased Osama bin Laden) in the Middle East refer to the governments of Israel, Jordan, Kuwait, Egypt, and Saudi Arabia as suppressive regimes controlled by rich elites that suppress the legitimate rights of their people through the use of kidnapping, death squads, and brutal police tactics. By proxy, the same people also argue that the United States is guilty of state terrorism because it financially and militarily supports these governments. They are quick to point to the military use of power against the Palestinian people in the West Bank and Gaza by the Israelis, the use of armed soldiers in Jordan and Egypt to quell mass demonstrations, and the huge differential between classes in Saudi Arabia. Again, and to re-emphasize, the Middle East is a hodge-podge of cultural, religious, and ethnic groups, all struggling for power and recognition. Precisely defining the terrorist and placing moral judgment is a very difficult task, at best.[36]

From a law enforcement perspective, it is important to understand this conceptualization of terrorism. It provides a framework on which to understand the motivations behind people's actions, particularly in the Middle East and for those expressing a radical Islamic philosophy. Further, it provides a basis on which to develop a conversation or an interview with members of Middle Eastern communities living within the United States, some of whom may be sympathetic to the causes of specific Middle Eastern or radical Islamic groups.

RADICAL ISLAMIC TERRORISM

The list of potential international terrorist threats against the United States is almost unlimited, considering the numerous political conflicts continuing in the international arena. Many of these threats are fueled by political, religious, and/or ideologically motivated causes. Certainly, terrorism from various Middle Eastern groups has posed significant problems to American law enforcement. Historically, the root of conflict in the Middle East was the establishment of Israel in 1948 and the subsequent U.S. support provided to that country. While peace between the two major groups (Israelis and Palestinians) was formally established in 1995, both sides still have major radical movements opposing the process that often act out in the international arena, including the United States.

The most significant activities against the United States in the past 25 years have been led by fundamental Islamic groups acting from clandestine areas in Afghanistan, Iraq, Lebanon, Yemen, and Iran. The first major incident witnessed in the United States connected to fundamental Islam was the bombing of the World Trade Center on February 26, 1993, which killed six people. FBI experts contend that, if the bomb had been just slightly larger and more skillfully placed, the entire building may have collapsed, causing untold devastation and death. Unfortunately, this was just a preview of the horrible events to come just 8 years later. Linkages to Islamic fundamentalist groups in Egypt were developed, resulting in several indictments of Arab nationals living in the United States. One of those convicted was the blind cleric Sheik Abdul Omar Rahman, a spiritual leader and scholar who helped spawn a number of other groups.

al-Qaeda (AQ)

The most infamous of these groups is the **al-Qaeda** (AQ) organization formally led by Osama bin Laden and now, Ayman al-Zawahiri. It is actually a network of many different fundamental Islamic groups in diverse countries. Their ideology is based primarily on the writings of Muhammad Ibn al-Wahhab (1703–1792), Hassan al-Banna (1906–1949), and Sayyid Muhammad Qubt (1906–1966), three early Islamic scholars calling for a violent purification movement throughout the Middle East and the greater Islamic world. This religious movement is commonly called "Wahhabism" and later "Salafism" and can be traced back to the late 1700s in what is now Saudi Arabia and Egypt. According to these radical philosophers, the Middle East must be purged of Western influence. To this end, leaders call for a "holy war," or **jihad**, calling on everyday Muslims to join in their fight against the West. Bin Laden and other members of the al-Qaeda network perverted parts of the Qur'an to justify their philosophy and do not represent mainstream Islam. It is important to understand that Islam is the world's second-largest religion, with over 1 billion peaceful

Quick Facts: Terrorism In The United States

Although terrorism is something of an ever present specter in the American consciousness, the United States is actually a relatively safe haven from terrorist attacks compared to its global counterparts. The U.S. ranks 41st in the world when considered on a scale that measure property damage, loss of life, injury, and other socioeconomic indicators. The top five terror targets are (in order): Iraq, Pakistan, Afghanistan, India, and Yemen. The United States also ranks as a safer place than Great Britain, which is twenty-eighth on the list. More recent attacks (2015–2016) in Paris, Brussels and other parts of Europe continue to highlight the relative safety of the United States.[37]

followers, living primarily in Africa, Asia, and Europe. The actions of radical Islamic fundamentalists represent only a small but growing percentage of all of Islam. Unfortunately, the movement has flourished in Egypt and Saudi Arabia for the past 100 years, countries where American influence is easily observed. Members of the al-Qaeda organization are politically motivated to overthrow the "heretic governments" that they see as puppets of Western influence and replace them with Islamic governments based on the rule of the Shariah (the first book of the Qur'an, strictly regulating all aspects of life).

Osama bin Laden (1957–2011), the son of a wealthy building contractor in Saudi Arabia, rose to power within the fundamental Islamic movement as a student of Ayman al-Zawahiri (see Figure 3.8). However, it was not until the 1979–1989 Soviet–Afghan War that bin Laden actually took a recognized leadership role in the organization. Triumphant over the Soviets and enlisting the aid of American interests in Afghanistan, bin Laden amassed a number of hardened mujahideen (holy warriors) fighters. He became obsessed with Western influence in the Middle East and declared a holy war on the United States in 1996.[38] Fueled by Middle Eastern oil wealth and an increasing radicalization of Islam, bin Laden set out to destroy those entities that he believes have adulterated his homeland. The activities of al-Qaeda have been significant and numerous,

culminating on September 11, 2001, with the attacks on the World Trade Center and the Pentagon.

Since Operation Enduring Freedom, which first sent troops to Afghanistan in 2001, and the recent wars in Iraq and Afghanistan (2003–2015), most scholars and government officials have believed that the stability and operational capability of al-Qaeda have been diminished in the international arena. Certainly, the leadership has been dismantled and most have either been killed or are on the run. According to the U.S. Department of State, much of the 2014 spike in global terror attacks could be attributed to civil conflict in Iraq, Syria, Pakistan, and Afghanistan; areas where AQ played a prominent role.[39] However, today, much of the operational capability of al-Qaeda as a single group has been destroyed, especially with the advent of a much larger and much more violent radical Islamic movement in the Middle East.

The Islamic State (ISIS)

Many of the radical Sunni fighters loyal to al-Qaeda suffered dramatic losses to U.S. forces during the Iraq War. Coupled with the loss of political power and the establishment of a majority Shiite-led government in Iraq, many fled to neighboring countries, and in particular Syria, where violent revolution already in progress was pitting Sunnis against a Shiite-backed al-Assad

FIGURE 3.8 ▶ After the death of Osama bin Laden in 2011, the leadership of al-Qaeda transitioned to Ayman al-Zawahiri, a physician by training and the personal cleric to bid Laden. Al-Zawahiri continues the legacy of a very hardline approach to removing the West, and particularly the United States from social, economic and political involvement in the Middle East. (SIPA/Newscom)

government. The early name of this group became widely known as ISIS (or the Islamic State in Iraq and Syria). Syrian rebel groups quickly welcomed these hardened fighters; however, they soon realized that the Iraqi group had a much larger goal than toppling the al-Assad regime—their goal was to establish a new "Islamic State."

ISIS has been successful in carving out a portion of land in the heart of the Middle East (from Syria across Iraq to Iran) in which to build a new country and recruit other like-minded Sunnis worldwide. The rise of the ISIS was quick and historical, occurring along the banks of the Tigris and Euphrates Rivers, a region commonly known as the cradle of civilization.

In July 2014, the leader of the ISIS, Abu Bakr al-Baghdadi, declared himself "caliph" over the area he controlled and announced the establishment of the new "**caliphate**." He then changed the name of the group to the Islamic State, and within a month (August 2014), he led attacks on Kurdish territories in northern Iraq, prompting an immediate response by the United States—retaliatory air strikes and bombing of IS-held areas. He called upon all Muslims around the world to pledge support and allegiance to him and his country. These were powerful words in the Muslim world, and ones that positioned al-Baghdadi and the Islamic State as a unique challenge to Western nations and a direct threat to the stability of the entire Middle East. This is particularly true as other radical Islamic groups align with the Islamic State. Boko Harem (Nigeria – discussed later in this chapter, Abu Sayyaf (The Philippines), Ansar al-Tawhid (Pakistan/Afghanistan), al-Qaeda on the Arabian Peninsula (AQAP) (Yemen), Answar al-Sahria (Libya), and other have already recognized and become affiliates to al-Baghdadi's proclamation (see Box 3.2, Box 3.1). The Islamic State is not just another radical Islamic group; rather it is a significant movement across the world (some scholars estimate the movement includes over 8 million people) that sees itself as the provocateurs of the coming apocalypse, paving the way for the final Islamic rule in the Middle East and the rest of the world.[40]

Box 3.2: Radical Islamic Groups Active Throughout the World[41]

Radical Islamic ideologies represent a significant threat to Israel, Europe, and the United States. The philosophy represents the most virulent of radical Islamic fundamentalism and has been the base foundation for several active terrorist groups throughout the world. These groups remain active and continue to pose a significant threat of attack in the United States and against American interest abroad.

Abu Sayyaf Group (ASG). ASG is a violent Islamic separatist group operating in the southern Philippine island of Mindanao. Split from the Moro National Liberation Front, the group has been active in narcotics, arms, and human trafficking as well as kidnapping as a means to fund their operations in Southeast Asia.

Al-Qaeda. Established in 1988 by Usama bin Laden in Afghanistan as a resistance movement against the invasion by the Soviet Union, al-Qaeda remains a viable terrorist group aimed at destroying Western influence (particularly the United States) and establishing a worldwide Islamic state. The group has been significantly reduced in number and resources due to military involvement in Iraq and Afghanistan. Al-Qaeda is currently headed by its long-time spiritual leader, Ayman al-Zawahiri and remnants are still committed to their Jihadist cause.

Al-Qaeda in the Arabian Peninsula (AQAP). AQAP is a militant group following the ideological philosophies of the larger al-Qaeda. AQAP is based primarily in Yemen and has been linked with other radical Islamic groups in that country, such as the Yemeni Islamic Jihad and the Aden-abyan Islamic Army. It has been strongly opposed to the House of Saud in Saudi Arabia and has been involved in several terrorist attacks in Saudi Arabia and Yemen. Interestingly, AQAP claimed responsibility for the Christmas Day attempted bombing of Northwest Airlines Flight 253 on December 25, 2009 by Umar Farouk Abdulmutallab. In that incident, Adbulmtallab attempt to set off plastic explosives sewed into his underwear. The explosives failed to detonate and Abdulmutallab was arrested.

Al-Qaeda in Iraq (AQI). AQI is also known as the Islamic State of Iraq and more recently as the Islamic State of Iraq and the Levant (ASIL) was established in 2004 by Abu Musab al-Zarqawi, a long and strong-time supporter of Usama bin Laden. AQI was a primary force against the U.S. military in Iraq, even after al-Zarqawi and other leaders were killed; remnants in Iraq continue to perform acts of terrorism against the established government of Iraq and threaten U.S. interests in the area. Much of the membership of AQI is now associated with the **Islamic State**.

Al-Qaeda in Islamic Maghreb (AQIM). The Maghreb is a geographical region of northwest Africa, comprising the Atlas Mountains and the modern day countries of Mauritania, Morocco, Algeria, Tunisia, Western Sahara, and Libya. AQIM has declared itself as an affiliate of the original al-Qaeda and carries out operations in an attempt to overthrow the Algerian government and institute an Islamic state throughout the Maghreb.

HAMAS. The Palestinian Islamic Resistance Movement or Harakat al-Muqawamah al Islamiyyah (Arabic) is the largest and most politically powerful group expressing radical Islamic ideologies to justify the liberation of Palestine and the destruction of Israel. The group was originally led by the now-deceased Sheik Ahmed Hassan Yassin and conducted a campaign of suicide bombing throughout the Gaza Strip and the West Bank in Israel during the late 1990s to mid-2000s. Significant linkages between HAMAS and groups within the United States have been confirmed over the past decade.

Hezbollah. Arabic for "Party of God," Hezbollah is primarily focused in Lebanon and Syria. The group represents the radical Shiite fundamentalist perspective as opposed to the other radical Sunni Islamic perspective. The group is led by Hassan Nasrallah and was linked directly to the bombing of the barracks in Beirut in 1983, killing 241 U.S. Marines. The group is philosophically, politically, and economically backed by Iran.

Harakat ul-Mujahidin (HUM). Formerly part of the larger radical Islamic movement in Pakistan and Afghanistan called Harakat al-Ansar, HUM operates primarily in Kashmir and can link direct associations with bin Laden and original al-Qaeda fighters in Afghanistan and Pakistan. The group maintains close ties to Jaish e-Mohammad (JEM) or the "Army of Muhammad" in Afghanistan. These groups have maintained significant training camps in Pakistan and represent the primary groups that fight against U.S forces in Afghanistan.

Islamic State in Iraq and Syria (ISIS), Islamic State (IS). Much of the original membership came from al-Qaeda in Iraq (AQI); however, the group now represents a major radical Islamic movement across Iraq and Syria. Led by Abu Bakr al-Baghdadi, the movement claims to be the new "caliphate" and now poses the most significant and violent movement facing Western interests in the Middle East.

Jemaah Islamiya (JA). JA is an Indonesia-based terrorist group active throughout Southeast Asia. JI is headed by Abu Baker Bashir, an Indonesian of Yemini descent, and a highly charismatic cleric and leader. The group has active cells in Thailand, Singapore, Malaysia, and Indonesia and has been linked to the Moro Islamic Liberation Front in the Philippines. The group has been responsible for several high-profile terrorist incidents in Southeast Asia including the 2002 bombing of a nightclub in Bali killing 202 people and the 2003 car bombing of the J.W. Marriott Hotel in Jakarta, Indonesia that killed 12 people.

Lashkar-i-Tayyiba (LT). The Lashkar-i-Tayyiba or "Army of the Righteous" is one of the largest and best trained fighting groups in the Pakistan-Afghan region. It is headed by Hafiz Mohamed Saeed and has conducted a number of terrorist attacks against India (Mumbai).

Muslim Brotherhood (MB). An Islamic fundamental group stemming from the writings of Hassan al-Banna and Sayyid Qutb in 20th century Egypt. The group has been very successful in recent Middle East politics, winning the majority of parliamentary seats in the government of Egypt and moving vigorously in other North African countries. Considered by the FBI as the "father of all militant Islamic groups," the Muslim Brotherhood has established cells in the American Islamic community within the United States.

However, there have been some recent cracks in the movement.[42] For instance, the new Islamic State has been so violent, characterized by videotaped beheadings, executions by burning, and rampant carnage during combat that some former groups have "disowned" them, including the current leadership of al-Qaeda.[43] The Islamic State rules by fear and demands obedience to conservative Islamic law by citizens within its control. The group has become so powerful and so violent in its application of the law that many of the individuals formally associated with the leadership of al-Qaeda, such as Ayman al-Zawahiri, have disavowed any associations with ISIS.

Although this wholesale violence has driven small wedges in the proliferation of the overall Islamic State, it continues to flourish as a movement. See Figure 3.9. American soldiers are the continual targets of ISIS; as well as reported bombings of government buildings, security positions, and non-Islamic schools throughout the Middle East. ISIS bombers and soldiers continue to strike at locations both in the Middle East (Saudi Arabia, Yemen, Tunisia, Brussels, and Turkey) as well as in Europe (Madrid, London, Brussels and Paris), (see Figure 3.10) and the United States (Garland, Texas and San Bernadino, California 2015). From website announcements and flyers to the recruitment of new fighters in the Middle East, ISIS continues to grow in sustained acts of violence against Western interests. Most alarming are the number of attacks being planned or those implemented over the past 2 years from U.S.-born, radical Islamic terrorists.

"Homegrown" Islamic Terrorists

A recent trend observed in the radical Islamic terrorist movement is the development of **"homegrown" terrorists**. The term refers to extremists who are legal U.S. residents or even citizens, and who are linked to or inspired by a specific, often intolerant ideology. This ideology may be motivated by political or religious sources and may be centered in domestic or foreign movements. Indeed, some of them have made connections with well-known, international terror groups, such as ISIS and al-Qaeda.[44] These individuals may receive ideological encouragement, but not financial or material support, making them ancillary to the primary group and very difficult to detect by intelligence and law enforcement services.

For instance, Major Nidal Hasan, perpetrator of the 2009 Fort Hood shootings that killed 13 people and wounded more than 30 others, is a prime example of this type of terrorist—a man who was radicalized due to a belief that American wars

Areas of Influence
- ISIL dominant as of April 2015
- ISIL's territorial losses since August 2014
- Populated area
- Sparsely populated or unpopulated
- --- Administrative boundary

Dominant Group
- ISIL
- Syrian Kurd
- Iraqi Kurdish security forces
- Iraqi Government
- Syrian Government
- Contested city

Note: Our judgment as to which group has dominant influence over a particular city is based on a body of sources that we deem reliable.

FIGURE 3.9 ► Iraq and Syria: ISIL's Reduced Operating Areas as of April 2015.
Source: U.S. Department of Defense, Operation Inherent Resolve, Iraq and Syria: ISIL's Reduced Operating Areas, April 2015, p. 1, http://www.defense.gov/News/Special-Reports/0814_Inherent-Resolve, accessed October 21, 2015.

in Iraq and Afghanistan were wars against the Muslim faith. Hasan had expressed his opposition to these wars, despite his position as a psychiatrist in the U.S. Army, and carried out his attack about a month before he was to be deployed to Afghanistan. Hasan had been in contact with radical Muslim cleric and suspected al-Qaeda propaganda officer Anwar al-Awlaki via a series of e-mails before his attack.[45]

In other cases, terrorist groups target first-generation foreign nationals living in the United States to join their ranks. The perpetrators of the Boston Marathon bombings in 2013 are good examples of this activity and are considered homegrown terrorists. Tamerlan Tsarnaev, who apparently masterminded the attack with the help of his younger brother Dzhokhar, was another young Muslim who had been radicalized by his anger over perceived injustices against the Muslim faith by the United States. Though no direct connections between the two Chechens

and any specific terrorist group have been identified in the year after the bombing, the two did view al-Qaeda training videos on the Internet, and espoused doctrine that was common among al-Qaeda sympathizers.[46] See Figure 3.11.

Similarly, first-generation "homegrown" terrorists were actually known by intelligence and law enforcement services; however, no previous illegal actions had been taken by the suspect. Such was the case in 2015 when Elton Simpson and Nadir Soofi (a first-generation Pakistani) entered the Curtis Culwell Center in Garland, Texas, armed with assault rifles threatening participants in a controversial event designed to show cartoons of the Muslim Prophet Muhammad. Simpson had been convicted of a terror-related charge in 2011 after discussing plans to travel to Somalia to engage in "violent jihad" or a "holy war" and Soofi had expressed similar convictions but not threatened actual violence.[47] Both suspects had

FIGURE 3.10 ▶ Chilling photo of two gunmen just prior to entering the Paris, France offices of satirical magazine Charlie Hebdo and killing 12 people in 2015. The gunmen were later linked to members of the Islamic State (ISIS). (ABACA/Newscom)

been a concern for their radical Islamic beliefs and both had been living together in a Phoenix, Arizona, apartment prior to the shooting incident. Both Simpson and Soofi linked themselves to ISIS which was indeed confirmed by ISIS supporters via various website outlets.[48]

In the United States, such homegrown terrorists have largely flown beneath the radar—many have no criminal records (unlike Simpson), and while their European counterparts tend to be more socially marginalized, it's more likely that American-grown extremists come from a broad variety of educational and socioeconomic statuses. Consider that Major Nidal Hasan had completed medical school; Tamerlan Tsarnaev had gone to college for a time to pursue engineering; and his brother, Dzokhar, was enrolled in American university at the time of the

attacks. Even Nadir Soofi had been a pre-med student at the University of Utah and was described by neighbors and friends as being outgoing, loved cars, was intelligent, and "had a normal American upbringing."[49]

December 2015—A 28-year-old U.S. citizen, Syed Rizwan Farook and his wife, Tashfeen Malik (age 29), a legal immigrant to the United States, walked into a morning holiday party for disabled persons at the Inland Regional Center in San Bernardino, California, and opened fire with semi-automatic weapons and pistols. The attack left 14 individuals dead and another 17 wounded. Farook and Malik were later killed in a shoot-out with police later that evening. Interestingly, Farook was recently married, a graduate student at California State University-Fullerton, and worked for the county as an environmental health specialist.

FIGURE 3.11 ▶ The Boston Marathon Bombing in 2013 shocked the American public as two first-generation foreign nationals and brothers from Chechnia, Tamerlan and Dzhokhar Tsarnaev, carried out the crude attack killing 3 and injuring another 264 people. Tamerlan Tsarnaev was killed by police at the time of his arrest and Dzhokhar was convicted of 30 charges relating to terrorism and sentenced to death in 2015. He is currently awaiting execution in a Federal maximum-security prison in Colorado.
Source: (a) FEMA (b) FBI

Box 3.3: Recent Homegrown Terrorist Incidents

Recent instances that made national news involving U.S. citizens and residents that convert to radical Islamic extremism, plot and commit terrorist acts, or fight for the jihadist movement both inside the United States and in foreign counties:

July 2009—A North Carolina man, Daniel Boyd, along with six other individuals were arrested for operating a terrorist training camp in North Carolina.[50] Daniel Boyd, a U.S. citizen, his two sons, and four others had allegedly been training in their rural lakeside home for "violent jihad." Boyd and his brother had lengthy ties to radical Islamic groups, having been arrested in 1991 in Pakistan on bank robbery charges, and were found with identification indicating they were members of the Islamic terrorist group Hezbollah.[51] Further, Boyd had traveled to the Middle East nearly 20 years prior to train at terrorist camps in Pakistan and Afghanistan, and fought the Soviets (in the Soviet–Afghan War) for 3 years before returning to the United States.[52] Members of his group also traveled to Israel in 2007 with the intent of joining the Palestinian Islamic jihad movement in that country but later returned without incident. The seven men were charged and convicted with providing material support to terrorists.

September 2009—A 19-year old Jordanian citizen, Hosam Maher Husein (Sam) Smadi, was arrested by the Federal Bureau of Investigation in downtown Dallas, Texas, for attempting to detonate an inert/inactive device. The Jordanian had been living and working in Italy, Texas, illegally on an expired tourist visa.[53] He had been under constant surveillance by the FBI and had placed what he believed to be an active car bomb under the Fountain Building in downtown Dallas, a 60-story, glass skyscraper.[54] The decoy device and all materials had been supplied to him by the FBI, who kept him under constant surveillance after discovering him as a potential terrorist in an on-line chat room with a group of extremists. Smadi was subsequently charged with attempting to use a weapon of mass destruction and pleaded guilty to this charge in June 2010.[55]

September 2009—Najibullah Zazi, an Afghan citizen and U.S. legal resident living in Colorado, was arrested on charges of conspiring to use weapons of mass destruction with others against the United States.[56] It was later reported that Zazi had traveled to Pakistan to receive weapons and explosives, and for training in their use and tactics. Zazi pleaded guilty to terrorism charges including conspiracy to use weapons of mass destruction, conspiracy to commit murder overseas, and providing material support for a terrorist organization.[57] He admitted to planning to use explosives when he arrived in New York in September 2009 to make a political statement about civilian killings in Afghanistan.[58] Law enforcement authorities were alerted to Zazi while monitoring various on-line chat rooms. Zazi actually planned his attack on the web and communicated it with others online.

October 2009—David Coleman Headley, a U.S. citizen of Pakistani descent, was arrested for plotting the attacks in Mumbai, India, that killed 170 people, including 6 Americans. Headley, whose original name is Daood Gilani, had his name changed in order to make his overseas traveling easier.[59] Headley actively scouted targets in Mumbai before the attacks and has admitted to planning and scouting targets against a Danish newspaper that printed images of Muhammad in 2005, an attack that was never carried out.[60] The Chicago native pled guilty to conspiring to bomb public places in India, murder people in India and Denmark, and to providing material support to terrorist groups.[61]

November 2009—Five young men from Virginia (all born in the United States) were arrested in Pakistan for attempting to join Jihadist terrorist groups, specifically Al Qaeda.[62] They had been reported missing by their parents in Virginia on the advice of the local Muslim community after the men had traveled to the Middle East without informing their parents.[63] The "Virginia 5" were reported to have been arrested in a safe house of an anti-India terrorist group in possession of Jihadist literature. They were also reported to be building schematics and maps of local areas. Officials believe that they were in the planning stages of a major attack in Pakistan.

November 2009—Major Nidal Malik Hassan, a psychiatrist for the U.S. Army, killed 13 people and wounded 30 others at Ft. Hood, Texas, in a Soldier Processing Center. Major Hassan was reportedly unhappy about the continuing wars in the Middle East and feared an approaching deployment to Afghanistan to assist in the war against his fellow Muslims.[64] Major Hassan had showed signs through his career of resistance to the war effort in the Middle East, as well as many disagreements about U.S. foreign policy. Hassan had even been in contact with the radical Muslim cleric Anwar al-Awlaki.[65] Army officials cited numerous failures in supervision and information sharing to recognize these signs and connect the dots that should have produced increased vigilance on Hassan's mental state and potential terrorist activities[66]

Major Nidal Malik Hassan (Handout/MCT/Newscom)

March 2010—Colleen LaRose, more commonly known as "Jihad Jane," was a U.S. citizen born in 1963 and living in Philadelphia. She was apprehended for conspiracy to provide material support to terrorists, conspiracy to kill in a foreign country, attempted identity theft, and making false statements to a government official.[67] Ms. LaRose had been exchanging e-mails for years in an attempt to recruit fighters for "violent jihad" in South Asia and Europe. Her U.S. citizenship and Caucasian appearance made her appealing to Islamic extremists who used her within the United States.[68] She had also made posts on various online message boards and blogs expressing sympathy with various terrorist groups and movements, and a desire to help in any way possible, including fighting and killing, to help ease the suffering of the Muslim people during their jihad or "holy war." LaRose even traveled to South Asia to marry a known and active jihadist in that area. She supplied her American boyfriend's passport to her new "husband" in an attempt to avoid travel restrictions in the United States and Europe.[69] She planned to use her European looks to blend into the Swedish population and to kill a Swedish artist who depicted the face of Muhammed on a dog in 2007.[70]

April 2013—Two bombs exploded during the Boston Marathon, killing three people and wounding another 250 spectators and runners. The bombs were crudely constructed using ordinary pressure cookers as an improvised explosive device (IED) stuffed with explosive material (black powder) and scrape metal (e.g., BBs, nuts, and bolts). A blasting cap was then placed through the cooker cover and attached to a simple timing device or cell phone. Within 2 hours after the bombing, a police officer for Massachusetts Institute of Technology (MIT) was killed while confronting two potential suspects, and an ensuing gun battle with police in Watertown, Massachusetts, ensued. One suspect, 27-year-old Tamerlan Tsarnaev was shot and killed during the incident. The other suspect (Tamerlan's brother), 20-year-old Dzhokhar Tsarnaev was arrested hiding in a boat parked in the backyard of a Watertown resident later that same night. During the initial investigation, Dzhokhar alleged that Tamerlan was the mastermind of the entire bombing and that they had learned how to build the bombs from online instructions hosted by an al-Qaeda affiliate in Yemen. Both Tsarnaev brothers were born in remote areas of the former Soviet Union, near Chechnya, and grew up in Kyrgyzstan. Both were Muslims who became increasingly radicalized by watching jihadist speakers on the Internet. Dzhokhar Tsarnaev was convicted of 30 charges relating to homegrown terrorism, including use

of weapon of mass destruction and the malicious destruction of property resulting in death. He was found guilty of all 30 charges on April 8, 2015, and sentenced to death.

October 2014—Zale Thompson attacked four NYPD police officers posing for a photograph. He critically injured two officers as he swung a hatchet at them. Thompson, an African-American male, had previously converted to Islam and adopted radical jihadi beliefs having posted numerous threats against police officers online. He was killed during the melee.

June 2015—Two gunmen, Elton Simpson and Nadir Soofi, opened fire outside the Curtis Culwell Center in Garland, Texas. The attackers were motivated by the Charlie Hebdo Shooting in Paris, France, and the Copenhagen Shooting in Denmark earlier in the year. All three attacks involved heavily armed suspect (assault rifles and pistols) sparked by the insensitivity of developing cartoon depictions of the Islamic Prophet Muhammad. Two days after the incident, members of the Islamic State claimed responsibility for the attack through a Twitter post.[71]

July 2015—A lone gunman, Mohammad Youssuf Abdulazeez (24 years old), armed with an assault rifle with a 30-round magazine, opened fire outside a military recruiting office in Chattanooga, Tennessee, killing five soldiers and severely wounding three others. Abdulazeez, born in Kuwait, was a naturalized citizen of the United States for the past 17 years. He had traveled back to the Middle East in the past two years, however, was not a member of any known terrorist organization, nor mentioned on any governmental terrorist watch list. According to numerous friends in the Chattanooga community, Abdulazeez was "very intelligent" and a "good kid." He was killed by police responding to the shooting incident.[72]

December 2015—A 28 year old U.S. citizen, Syed Rizwan Farook and his wife, Tashfeen Malik (age 29), a legal immigrant to the United States, walked into a morning holiday party for disabled persons at the Inland Regional Center in San Bernardino, California and opened fire with semi-automatic weapons and pistols. The attack left 14 individuals dead and another 17 wounded. Farook and Malik were later killed in a shoot-out with police later that evening. Interestingly, Farook was recently married, a graduate student at California State University-Fullerton, and worked for the county as an environmental health specialist. Neighbors and friends refereed to Farook as a "normal guy;" however, both Farook and Malik had expressed allegiance to ISIS leader Abu Bakir Bashir in recent Facebook posts.

Neighbors and friends referred to Farook as a "normal guy;" however, both Farook and Malik had expressed allegiance to ISIS leader Abu Bakir Bashir in recent Facebook posts.[73]

The future of homegrown terrorism is one that will see shifts in the composition of participants, as well as in the networking that they engage in with ISIS, al-Qaeda, and other affiliated movements. As the United States continues to see successes in dismantling the major arteries of these terrorist organizations, homegrown terrorists will seek new ways to interact with them. In the past, some had physically attended training camps or, as in the cases of Hasan and Simpson, communicated directly with terror operatives. As surveillance has intensified and travel has become more scrutinized, those who seek out these radically inclined connections will retreat further into the Internet, particularly the "**deep web**," utilizing gaming sites that appear innocuous on the outside but allow encrypted conversations using their platforms, social media sites, and chat rooms to communicate.[74] The deep web is a vast part of the World Wide Web, not accessible through regular Internet browsing or search engines. Most of the information in the deep web is hidden, accessible from dynamic websites requiring the use of an application called *Tor*. The **Tor network** is synonymous for the deep web. This secretive online world remains mostly untraceable and difficult to access for the regular Internet user and even law enforcement and intelligence operatives. This subsequently allows a large illegal domain to thrive and a hidden venue for secret communications between terrorists, particularly astute worldwide terrorists sharing a common radical Islamic philosophy.[75]

Crude Devices and Non-Sophisticated Weapons aimed at Mass Casualty

Another important trend among homegrown terrorists is the use of crude devices or easily obtained weapons (such as assault rifles and other firearms) to carry out their attacks. The bombs used in the Boston Marathon attacks were basically pressure cookers, found in any large retailer, filled with nails and ball bearings. They were reportedly made using instructions found online. Major Nidal Hasan used legally obtained firearms. Simpson and Soofi were armed with pistols and assault rifles commonly found at local gun stores. Other terror attacks in the past few years have utilized vehicles as weapons, as well as a litany of homemade explosives. Purchasing materials to make more complex weaponry is made more difficult by policy changes restricting certain hazardous or biologic materials—or, if not restricting them outright, triggering a level of scrutiny that would-be terrorists might avoid.[76]

It's for these reasons that then-Attorney General Eric Holder stated that these were the types of potential attacks that keep him up at night; he singled out the homegrown, lone wolf terrorist, stating that he was "very concerned about individuals who get radicalized in a variety of ways . . . sometimes self-radicalized."[77] **Lone wolves** include homegrown

terrorists, but the term also encompasses those who identify with ideologies other than radical Islam; lone wolves can be right-wing extremists, anti-abortion radicals, and leftist environmentalists. They typically operate the same way that homegrown terrorists do—by networking online, seeking out their own information, and utilizing easily made or easily obtained weaponry for their attacks, though they may have more of a tendency than their radical Muslim counterparts to broadcast their intentions in some way.[78] They generally act on their own accord, in the name of some deeply held ideological belief system.

OTHER INTERNATIONAL THREATS

Certainly, the Middle East is not the only area ripe with terrorist activity aimed at the United States. Indeed, the huge growth of Islam in Southeast Asia (e.g., Thailand, Indonesia, Malaysia, and the Philippines) continues to also spawn radical movements aimed at destroying Western interests in the area. Jemaah Islamiya (JI) continues to be an active radical Islamic group in Southeast Asia under the leadership of Abu Bakar Bashir (recently released from his Indonesian prison for participation in bombings in Jakarta [2003] and Bali [2002]). In July 2014, Abu Bakar Bashir pledged allegiance to ISIS, as did several other leaders of radical Islamic groups throughout Southeast Asia. Abu Sayyaf, another Islamic group based in the Philippines followed suit, and released a video swearing allegiance to ISIS as well.[79] And terrorism on the left appears to be escalating throughout Western Europe, fueled in part by the current downturn in the global economy, causing high unemployment and a reduction of government benefits to various populations. Incidents in Germany, Italy, and France have indicated a "reawakening" of the Red Brigades, the Greens, and other cell groups expressing a left-wing, Marxist orientation.[80]

Then, too, a relatively new phenomenon called "**narco-terrorism**" continues to plague American police agencies as well as the international community. The most illustrative cases are seen in South America and Mexico surrounding the highly lucrative cocaine business. Drug lords in the Medellin and Cali cartels continue to be allied with the M-19 group in Colombia and Sendero Luminoso (Shining Path) in Peru for protection in cultivating and trafficking cocaine to the United States. Similar arrangements between drug dealers and anti-Western political groups (or states) have been observed in Cuba, Nicaragua, Panama, Bulgaria, and Burma.[81] One of the most successful of these collaborations is the development of the notorious street gang Mara Salvatrucha (MS-13). Originally composed of former soldiers and fighters from civil wars in El Salvador and Honduras during the 1970s and 1980s, MS-13 has become a violent and sophisticated gang associated with drug and human trafficking from Latin America. More problematic to local police agencies is the connection between ethnic drug dealers (Haitians, Jamaicans, and Cubans) and foreign governments, which results in significant financing and armament supplying in support of drug trafficking to the United States.[82]

Boko Haram

Although having existed for over a decade (since 2002), the Nigerian group Boko Haram gained international notoriety when the group kidnapped 276 schoolgirls in Chibok, Nigeria, in April 2014. The incident brought international condemnation as well as a cooperative venture by Western countries (primarily the United States, Great Britain, and France) aimed at reducing the impact of Boko Haram in northeastern Nigeria. Aside from this infamous kidnapping, the group has also been responsible for a number of other kidnappings for ransom, the wholesale slaughter of hostages taken from Borno, Nigeria, in June 2015, and several bombings using **improvised explosive devices (IEDs)**. Boko Haram means "Western education is forbidden." Its primary goal at inception was the destruction and overthrow of the current Nigerian Government. However, under the leadership of Abubakar Shekau, the group now represents the radical Islamic movement in Nigeria. It has become increasingly more violent and radicalized in the past few years, aligning itself operationally and philosophically with the greater Islamic State in the Middle East.[83] An estimated 13,000 innocent civilians have been killed by Boko Haram in the past 5 years, with the vast majority occurring in 2014 and 2015.[84] Members of Boko Haram have declared the areas in Nigeria that they control to be part of the Islamic State "Caliphate" in greater Africa. See Figure 3.12.

The Mexican Cartels

Violence along the U.S.–Mexican border has dramatically decreased in the past 5 years, so much so, that many refer to places like Ciudad Jaurez and Nogales as "back to normal."[85] For instance, in Ciudad Juarez, once considered the most dangerous city in the world (across the Rio Grande River from El Paso, Texas), over 2,660 people were killed in criminal violence in 2009; that's an average of over seven people killed every day![86] Most of these murders could be attributed to narco-terrorism and violence between cartels vying for control of the primary transportation routes for billions of dollars worth of illegal drugs entering the United States from Mexico annually. The primary groups operating on the border were the Tijuana Cartel; the Vicente Carrillo Fuentes Organization, also known as the Juarez Cartel; the Gulf Cartel; and the Sinaloa Cartel, composed of several smaller groups including the Guzman-Loera Cartel and the Pacific Cartel.

These primary narco-trafficking cartels had direct linkages to Hispanic street gangs operating within the United States (such as the Mexican Mafia, La Familia, and the MS-13 gang), used for street trafficking and enforcement. A rival group operating on the border, Los Zetas, were also very active. Members acted as highly select assassins after deserting from the Mexican Army after extensive training. While originally hired as "enforcers" for the Gulf Cartel, Los Zetas were also violent leaders in the narco-trafficking

FIGURE 3.12 ▶ A member of Boko Haram states demands for the exchange of new girls kidnapped in Nigeria in 2015. The group has expressed its allegiance to the greater caliphate called the Islamic State, and has become a significant threat in Africa. (AP Images)

Box 3.4: The Legend of Joaquin Guzman Loera—"El Chapo"

One of the most notorious Mexican cartel leaders in the world today is Joaquin Guzman Loera, more commonly known as "*El Chapo*." Guzman was born in Culiacan, the capital of the state of Sinaloa, Mexico, into a poor, working class family. He quickly rose through the ranks of the Mexican drug cartels to become of the world's largest and most successful drug traffickers in history.[87] According to some DEA reports, El Chapo was responsible for the death and destruction of millions of people across the globe though drug addiction, violence, and corruption.[88] However to many Mexicans, he is a modern-day folk hero; a person who successfully rose from poverty to fight the deeply unpopular Mexican government, and a person that mythically, cannot be imprisoned having escaped his captors countless times in Mexico. Many people, especially those from poor agrarian backgrounds inside Mexico look to their government as a highly corrupt and aloof elite class. Like his American counterparts, El Chapo represents the hero outlaw, the Al Capone, the Lucky Luciano, the Don Corleone or the Tony Soprano of Mexico . . . the persons who rose from nothing to outsmart the rich and powerful government to run an effective international drug trafficking and crime syndicate.[89]

El Chapo represents the new state of order in some developing countries, a person not afraid to use his massive wealth and influence, (albeit from criminal enterprise) to help the lower classes achieve some status in an otherwise ruthless and corrupt governmental condition. Consequently, he is viewed as the "Robin Hood" of the modern era.[90] The concept is not new to the South American drug world, as Pablo Escobar and Carlos Lehder held similar positions of respect in Colombia during the 1980–early 1990s "cocaine cowboy" era. El Chapo maintains his mythical position as he once again, escaped from Mexico's most secure prison via an elaborate tunnel on July 11, 2015, however was recaptured in early 2016 by Mexican Navy Special Commandos in western Mexico. He is currently fighting extradition to the United States.

Source: (Polaris/Newscom; PGR/NOTIMEX/Newscom; PGR GDA Photo Service/Newscom)

business along the U.S.–Mexico border.[91] This gang's brand of narco-terrorism was particularly vicious, often marked by mass murders and mutilated bodies set for display in an effort to frighten rival groups. However, today, the number of homicides in Mexico is significantly down. In 2014, there were 424 homicides, down over 80 percent from the highs in 2009 and 2010. These are remarkable drops but do not signal that Juarez and the Mexican border is safe, by any means. Comparatively, the number of homicides in Chicago was 407 and in New York 328 in 2014, and only 20 in El Paso (the U.S. city directly across from Ciudad Juarez). Interestingly, El Paso received the "Safest City in America" designation in 2014 for the fourth year in a row according to the City Crime Ranking by CQ Press for cities with a population of over 750,000 people.[92] Across the Rio Grande River, 40 percent of the population in Ciudad Juarez lives below the poverty level, and cartel violence and the resulting crime is still a major problem.

Clearly, the violence in Mexico and particularly along the border will remain a top priority for intelligence agencies and American law enforcement. The violence does not appear to be spilling over into major U.S. cities. During 2015, El Paso was once again designated the "safest city in America," and significant drops in murder rates were also reported in Dallas, San Diego, Tucson, and Phoenix during this same period of time.

Outlaw Motorcycle Gangs (OMGs)

The history of outlaw motorcycle gangs in the United States and the rest of the world is a history of violent confrontations between rival gangs themselves and the police. According to the FBI's *2013 National Gang Intelligence Report*, there may be as many as 50,000 members in the United States alone, with affiliations to approximately 3,000 active outlaw motorcycle clubs.[93] Although, outlaw motorcycle gangs represent only a small percentage against traditional street gangs, they still pose a significant threat.

Calling themselves "1 percenters," representing 1 percent of all the people that are members of the American Motorcycle

Association, outlaw motorcycle clubs gained in popularity after World War II as young combat soldiers, often disenfranchised by the war and unemployed, sought the thrill-seeking, crime-ridden subculture focused around riding a motorcycle. The 1947 Fourth of July week-end that occurred in the small town of Hollister, California, has become part of OMC folklore as well as the subject of many Hollywood movies. The incident was not nearly as infamous as Hollywood made it out to be; however, the reported havoc caused by some 4,000 outlaw motorcycle members descending on a small rural city did nothing more that recruit new members to the lifestyle. The ranks of OMGs have filled through the years with returning veterans from the Korean, Vietnam, and Iraq/Afghanistan Wars.

Today, there are four primary outlaw motorcycle clubs in the United States, with all having chapters in foreign countries: The Hell's Angels (the largest group focused in California with 425 chapters in 50 different countries), the Pagans (located primarily on the east coast of the United States and throughout Canada), the Outlaws (focused in Chicago with 275 chapters in 23 countries), and the Bandidos (focused in Texas with 210 chapters in 22 countries). Each club has their own insignia often proudly displayed on members' leather vests and jackets, commonly called the club's "**colors.**" Most people in the United States would not immediately think of outlaw motorcycle gangs as "an international threat." However, during the past 25 years, almost all of the major outlaw motorcycle gangs have been classified by authorities as international criminal enterprises.

Indeed, there have been several gang battles overseas. For instance in 1984, a shoot-out between the Bandidos and a rival gang called the Comancheros killed seven people and wounded another 28 in Milperra, Australia, and between 1994 through 1997, in what is commonly called, "The Great Nordic Biker War," long-time enemies belonging to the Hell's Angels and the Bandidos shook the Scandinavian countries of Denmark, Finland, Sweden, and Norway. At least 12 people died and over 100 were injured in the 4-year war. On the domestic side, in 2015, in Waco, Texas, over 170 rival OMG members were arrested and charged in a shoot-out at a popular *Twin Peaks* restaurant. Nine bikers were killed and another eighteen were wounded in the gun battle that at one time had over 30 gang members shooting at one another. Over 100 weapons, including various pistols and assault rifles were confiscated by police at the scene, as well as nearly 500 spent shell casings.[94] The incident marked one of the bloodiest confrontations in OMG history. See Figure 3.13.

Outlaw motorcycle gangs are engaged in variety of organized crime activities, including international drug, gun, stolen property, and human trafficking. They also have a long history associated with hate. Many of their symbols mimic Nazi-era insignias such as lightning bolt tattoos, *Waffen SS* initials, the number "88" signifying the 8th letter of the alphabet—"H" or "HH" for Heil Hitler. The role of women in OMG is also quite dubious. Many are referred to as "sheep" and are "owned by the club." It is not unusual to see a women tattooed with "Property of . . ." somewhere on her body as she dances in a biker owned bar.

FIGURE 3.13 ▶ Members of an outlaw motorcycle gang were arrested after a devastating shooting in Waco, Texas, in May 2015. Nine people were killed and another 18 were wounded outside a local restaurant as members from rival gangs (The Bandidos and the Cossacks) engaged in a bloody shoot-out between themselves and then police as they arrived on the scene. (Rod Aydelotte/Waco Tribune-Herald via AP Images)

There are no known African-American or Mexican-American outlaw motorcycle gang members in any of the "Big Four" clubs, and OMGs are often associated with right-wing extremist groups around the world, such as the Aryan Nation, Aryan Brotherhood, the Order and various Neo-Nazi factions.

RIGHT-WING EXTREMISM

The resurgence of right-wing, white supremacist groups across the country, was highlighted in the bombing of the Alfred P. Murrah Federal Building in Oklahoma City on April 19, 1995. The blast killed 169 people, including 19 children, and injured more than 500 others. Convicted and sentenced to death, Timothy James McVeigh held "extreme right-wing views and hated the federal government."[95] According to the FBI, the former army sergeant often wore military fatigues, sold weapons at gun shows, and attended militia meetings.[96] Although the incident recently marked its 20-year anniversary, the bombing of the Murrah Building remains a cold reminder of the potential of hate in America.

The bombing focused attention on a number of right-wing groups and state militias that have traditionally expressed strong anti-government and White-supremacist propaganda. These groups have also supported violence against minorities (African-Americans, Asians, and Jews), homosexuals, and members of the U.S. government (Bureau of Alcohol, Tobacco, Firearms, and Explosives). While the number of members of each of these groups is relatively small, they pose a significant threat because of their ability to communicate and coordinate activities. The groups have multiple names and members, publish regular newsletters, maintain websites, and operate automated bulletin board systems. In some cases, documented collusion between these groups and local law enforcement officials has posed a significant threat. Many people are attracted to these groups because they identify themselves with fundamentalist Christianity. Much of their rhetoric focuses on patriotism as interpreted by their leaders, usually using a perversion of the Constitution or the Bible. These groups consist of well-armed ideologues who possess the potential for increased terrorism, at least in geographical pockets throughout the United States.[97]

Quick Facts: The Threat from Right-Wing Terrorism

Since the 9/11 attacks, nearly twice as many people have been killed by white supremacists and antigovernment fanatics than by radical Islamic terrorists in the United States.

Clearly, public perception does not match the facts: The terrorist threat inside the county is much greater from right-wing hate groups than radical Muslim extremists.[98]

Box 3.5: Major Right-Wing Militant Groups in the United States

Aryan Nation—This is a White-supremacist organization with strong separatist ideology, founded by Richard Butler of Hayden Lake, Idaho, a major figure in the Christian Identity Church, a pseudoreligious justification for White supremacy. The Nation recruits members from White prison gangs. Their goal is to develop an all-White homeland, to be called the "Northwest Mountain Republic," in Washington, Oregon, Idaho, Montana, and Wyoming. In September 2000, a jury awarded $6.3 million to a mother and son who were assaulted by Aryan Nations guards outside their Idaho compound.[99] The Aryan Nations were forced to sell the land on which the compound was built. With the death of Richard Butler in 2004, the group and its philosophical position continue; however, its numbers have dwindled and the group's future is filled with uncertainty.

Covenant, Sword, and Arm of the Lord—This paramilitary group operated primarily in Texas, Arkansas,

and Missouri. Eight members were arrested with illegal weapons, explosives, land mines, and an anti-tank rocket launcher in 1985. They were extreme Christian fundamentalists with survivalist mentalities.

Ku Klux Klan (KKK)—This is primarily a southern states organization, with the largest memberships in Alabama, Georgia, Kentucky, South and North Carolina, and Mississippi. Several of the chapters have forgone the traditional cross burning and hooded robes in favor of automatic weapons, paramilitary training camps, and camouflage uniforms. In 2008, a jury awarded $1.5 million in compensatory damages and $1 million in punitive damages to plaintiff Jordan Gruever, represented by the Southern Poverty Law Center against the KKK.[100] The jury found that five KKK members had brutally beaten Gruver, then a 16-year-old of American Indian descent, at a Kentucky county fair. The case, similar to the one against the Aryan Nations in 2000, had a significant impact on the Klan, as its numbers and donations fell dramatically. Current estimates of KKK membership hover around 5,000; however, increases in splinter groups appear to be growing since the election of President Barack Obama in 2008. The group still maintains the White-supremacist and anti-Semitic beliefs prominently characterizing the KKK historically.

Minutemen—This paramilitary organization was strongest during the 1960s. Small enclaves still exist that express strong anti-communist rhetoric and violence against liberals. Their insignia of the crosshairs of a rifle scope usually earmarks this group from other right-wing extremists.

National Alliance—This is a Neo-Nazi group founded by William L. Pierce, who started a new White enclave in rural West Virginia. Pierce was the author of *The Turner Diaries,* the saga of a family that survives the impending race war against African-Americans and retreats to the mountains for safety. Pierce's death in 2002 heralded the rise of Erich Gliebe as national chairman. His primary goal has been to foster international membership expressing the White supremacy doctrines of the past, particularly those stemming from Nazi Germany. Significant in-fighting for top leadership positions within the group has greatly diminished membership and finances.

Posse Comitatus—This is a loose-knit group attracting rural farmers. Strong anti-government sentiment claims that the Federal Reserve System and income tax are unconstitutional. Posse leaders have fused tax-protest doctrine with virulent anti-Semitism. Leader Gordon Kahl murdered two U.S. marshals in North Dakota and was subsequently killed in a shoot-out in 1983.

Skinheads—This is a violence-prone, Neo-Nazi youth gang whose members are noted for their shaved heads. They express a strong White-supremacist, racist, and anti-Semitic ideology and have close linkages to the Ku Klux Klan.

The Order—This is the most violent of the Neo-Nazi groups, with several ties to the Aryan Nations. It is responsible for the murder of a Jewish radio personality in Denver in 1984; at least two armored car robberies totaling $4 million in Seattle, Washington, and Ukiah, California; and a large bombing attempt in Coeur d'Alene, Idaho. The Order has been very quiet during the past decade.

White Aryan Resistance (WAR)—This is the main White-supremacist group in California, headed by Tom Metzger, former Grand Dragon of the California Ku Klux Klan. It currently produces *Race and Reason,* a White-supremacist program shown on public access cable television.

White Revolution—This group was founded in September 2002 by Billy Roper after he was expelled from the National Alliance during a power struggle with Erich Gliebe. The Arkansas-based White Revolution is a racist organization that promotes co-operation between White supremacist groups in the United States and in Europe.

State militias—Active paramilitary organizations exist in almost every state (e.g., the Michigan Militia, the Republic of Texas Militia, and the Arizona Vipers), expressing a strong white, Protestant, local constitutionalist perspective of government. They conduct a variety of paramilitary camps and are preparing for an "impending race war." Many groups have legitimate firearms licenses allowing automatic weapons and explosives. One group in Arizona is known to have purchased a World War II–era tank. Strong linkages to local police agencies have been documented. Members are strong gun owner advocates with a superpatriotism and anti-federal government sentiment. Since 2009, their financial strength and membership rolls have grown apparently due to deep-seeded conflict over immigration reform and the election of the first Black President, Barak Obama, in 2008. The Southern Poverty Law Center estimates that there are close to 800 militia groups active in the United States. None are more potentially violent than the *Hutaree or Christian Warrior Militia* based in eastern Michigan's Lenawee County. Established in 2008, the group was heavily paramilitary, participating in extensive training for a future war "preparing for the end time battles" with forces of the anti-Christ.[101]

Nine members of the group (located in Michigan, Ohio, and Indiana) were indicted by a grand jury in Detroit for conspiring to murder police officers and civilians using explosives and firearms.[102] Their intent was apparently to "replace" all factions of the government, starting with police officers.

Hate Crimes

Right-wing extremist groups represent a movement that promotes Whites, especially northern Europeans and their descendants, as intellectually and morally superior to other races.[103] It is not coincidental that as these groups have grown in strength, so have the number of reported hate crimes. **Hate crimes** are harms inflicted on a victim by an offender whose motivation derives primarily from hatred directed at a perceived characteristic of the victim (e.g., the person's race, religion, ethnicity, gender, and/or sexual orientation). These crimes are particularly heinous because of their unique impact on victims as well as on the community. Victims often suffer from the suspect's underlying criminal behavior, such as the physical injury caused by violence or the property damage associated with vandalism. In addition, they are victims by the thought that such acts were *not* random, that at least some people in our society detest them because of who they are: African-American, Jewish, Islamic, gay-lesbian-transgender, and so on. Hate crimes are often brutal and injurious, and victims are not only physically hurt but also emotionally traumatized and terrified. Others in the community who

Box 3.6: Charleston, South Carolina Church Massacre

Around 8:00 pm on Wednesday, June 17, 2015, a young white man, Dylann Storm Roof entered the Emanuel A.M.E. Church in Charleston, South Carolina, and began shooting African-Americans in a Bible study group, resulting in nine deaths. He then fled the scene in a black four-door sedan.[104] Roof was armed with a handgun that the FBI reports should not have been able to purchase.[105]

Roof was quickly arrested and subsequently confessed to the grotesque massacre of church members. Roof's motive was to start a race war and in that context he saw himself as a heroic figure, doing what others did not dare to do. His website was filled with comments about Nazis and rants about African-Americans, Jews, Hispanics, and east Asians. A survey taken 10 days after the massacre revealed that 87 percent of Americans saw the murders as a hate-based crime.[106] Roof's murderous rampage did not give rise to hatred, but public forgiveness by the church members, including relatives of slain members, a demonstration of unshakeable Christian belief.

Roof's actions are characteristic of the lone wolf attack, which seemingly comes out of nowhere, with no warning. Even his website did not provide an indication that an actual attack would be carried out. Lone wolves do not have to coordinate with anyone; there is no group decision-making or supporters who might mediate the wolf's deadly intent.[107]

As an indication of the harm that can be wrought by a lone wolf, the first midair plane bombing, airplane hijacking, anthrax attack, and product contamination were all executed by lone persons.[108]

SEEKING INFORMATION

Wanted for Questioning
Murder Investigation

DYLANN STORM ROOF

Multimedia: Images

Remarks: Storm may be travelling in a 2000 Hyundai Elantra GS with South Carolina license plates LGF330.

DETAILS

Dylann Storm Roof is wanted for questioning in connection with several murders in Charleston, South Carolina. On Wednesday, June 17, 2015, at approximately 8:00 p.m., several members of the Emanuel African Methodist Episcopal (AME) church located at 110 Calhoun Street were murdered during their Bible study.

SHOULD BE CONSIDERED ARMED AND DANGEROUS

If you have any information regarding this case, please contact the FBI's toll-free tip line at 1-800-CALL-FBI (225-5324); your local FBI office; or the nearest American Embassy or Consulate. You can also submit a tip on the FBI's website by visiting tips.fbi.gov.

Field Office: Columbia

Source: (Splash News/Newscom)

---

share the victim's characteristic may also feel vulnerable, and this may escalate the conflict as they attempt to retaliate for the original offense.

In the past, police officers have not been adequately trained to handle such incidents, treating them as routine assaults or vandalism. However, enacted federal legislation has resulted in the development of the National Institutes Against Hate Crimes and Terrorism, located at the Simon Wiesenthal Center in Los Angeles, California. The institute provides training for teams of criminal justice professionals from the same jurisdiction to combat hate crimes. Its goal is to provide new strategic approaches to combating hate crimes based on an understanding of the unique elements that differentiate such crimes from other acts. The center has been highly successful in training over 500 participants and providing an ongoing support center for follow-up communication, program evaluation, and professional development via website updates and videoconferences.[109]

Legal definitions of hate crimes vary. The federal definition addresses civil rights violations under 18 U.S.C. Section 245. A hate crime is a criminal offense committed against persons, property, or society that is motivated, in whole or in part, by an offender's bias against an individual's or a group's perceived race, religion, ethnic/national origin, gender, age, disability, or sexual orientation.[110] Most states have a hate crime statute that provides enhanced penalties for crimes in which victims are selected because of the perpetrator's bias against the victims' perceived race, religion, or ethnicity. Some states also classify as hate crimes those in which a victim is selected on the basis of a perception of his or her sexual orientation, gender, or disability. In some states, the passage of hate crime statutes has been controversial as politicians have debated the constitutionality of enhanced penalties based on a suspect's association with an extremist group or the inclusion of homosexuality as a protected class.

Digital Hate

Many White-supremacist groups have used the Internet to recruit potential members and spread their message of hate. See Figure 3.14. Over 1,500 websites can be identified and attributed to extremist organizations that incite racial hatred and religious intolerance as well as terrorism and bomb making. More disturbing is the directed effort by many of these groups to attract young people into their ranks. Based in part on links to other social youth movements involving music and dress

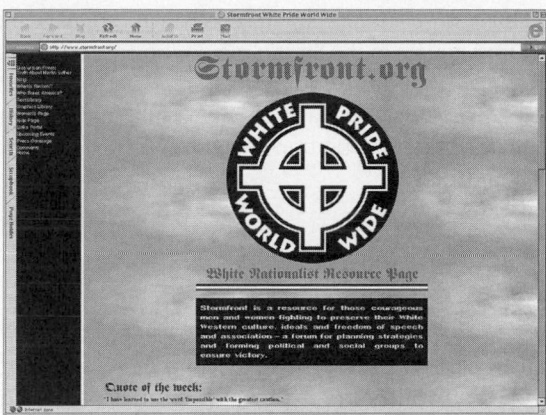

FIGURE 3.14 ▶ Selected Hate Sites on the Internet.
Source: The New Lexicon of Hate: The Changing Tactics, Language and Symbols of America's Extremists (Los Angeles: Simon Wiesenthal Center, 1999), www.wiesenthal.com. See also Robert W. Taylor, Eric J. Fritsch, and John Liederbach, *Digital Crime and Digital Terrorism*, 3rd edition (Upper Saddle River, N.J.: Pearson, 2015).

(e.g., Skinheads, Black cults, and heavy-metal music), aggressive recruitment on college campuses and the development of web pages designed to attract young people are now quite common. In addition, White-power rock concerts are often sponsored by extremist groups, such as the National Alliance and the World Church of the Creator. These concerts provide face-to-face opportunities for meeting and recruitment.

White-supremacist groups have also created sophisticated computer games aimed at attracting teenagers. *Ethnic Cleansing*, the most high-tech game of its kind, encourages players to kill Blacks, Jews, and Hispanics as they run through urban ghettos and subway environments. In the game, players can dress in Ku Klux Klan robes and carry a noose. Every time a Black enemy is shot, he emits a monkeylike squeal, while Jewish characters shout, "Oy vey!" when they are killed.[111] Quite predictably, the game has spurred significant controversy between game developers and censor advocates. However, very little can be done to ban the game, since many other video games are designed to allow enthusiasts to create new levels and characters, while free software tools enable programmers to build new platforms easily.

These types of games and directed recruitment efforts have been effective tools in swelling the ranks of some extremist organizations.[112] According to one Skinhead source, young people represent the future—"they are the frontline warriors in the battle for white supremacy."[113]

ECOTERRORISTS AND ANIMAL RIGHTS GROUPS

Many of the single-issue terrorist groups, such as the **Earth Liberation Front (ELF)** and the **Animal Liberation Front (ALF)**, arose from relatively peaceful movements and call for a renewal of the planet's geophysical and biological environment.

These groups are commonly called "ecoterrorists" since their primary motivation focuses on improving the ecology of the world. The notable difference between the terrorist group and the more passive movements (e.g., Earth First and People for the Ethical Treatment of Animals [PETA]) is in the advocacy of violence and destruction to accomplish their ends. Single-issue groups, such as ELF and ALF, pose one of the most significant new threats in domestic terrorism. Both organizations work in small groups with no central hierarchy. They have no formal membership lists, and they work independently in a cell-structured manner similar to other violent groups. The ELF and ALF declared solidarity in 1993 and members of either group usually carry out acts on behalf of both groups. To date, most of their activities have been aimed at the destruction of property and vandalism.

Both groups began in England and migrated to the United States during the 1980s. Like so many other groups, ELF was inspired by the fictional writings of one author, Edward Abbey, whose 1975 novel, *The Monkey Wrench Gang,* told the story of a group of ecologists who were fed up with industrial development in the West. In the novel, environmental activists travel through the western U.S. spiking trees, burning billboards, sabotaging bulldozers, and damaging the property of people they deem to be destroying the environment. This type of low-level activity has become so popular that, among activists, the term "monkey wrenching" has become a key touchstone for ecoterrorism.[114] The FBI designated ELF a terrorist organization in January 2001. This action was based primarily on the arson attack of a ski resort under construction near Vail, Colorado, in 2001. ELF burned three buildings and caused the destruction of four ski lifts. The group quickly claimed responsibility for the attack, which caused an estimated $12 million in damages. Ironically, the fire almost swept through the adjoining forest and would have destroyed the very habitat ELF was attempting to "save" for the preservation of wildlife. Of course, this was not the only attack from ELF, but it does represent one of the most financially destructive incidents directly attributed to the group. More recently, ELF has had a resurgence in England, fire-bombing several cars in London (2014) in response to the death of Remi Fraisse, an environmental activist, and a major arson attack of a U.S. Forest Service Research Station in Pennsylvania causing over $700,000 in damages and destroying 70 years of research in 2012.[115]

ALF grew substantially during the 1990s and took on a much more destructive perspective. Instead of just tossing blood or spray-painting individuals wearing furs, the group began a campaign to "free" animals from cages and destroy animal-linked farms, business, and laboratories. Breeding companies were attacked when the animals were released from their cages and the surrounding areas destroyed by fire and/or vandalism. Several of the targets were major research universities in Michigan and California, which not only suffered significant physical damage to buildings but also lost years of research findings and records.[116] However, in January 2006, after a 9-year investigation, the FBI indicted 11 people in connection with a 5-year wave of arson and sabotage claimed by the Earth Liberation Front and the Animal Liberation Front. Detailing nearly 20 attacks from 1996 to 2001, causing no deaths but nearly

$25 million in damage to lumber companies, a Vail ski resort, meat plants, and electric towers throughout the Pacific Northwest, the "vast ecoterrorism conspiracy" was dealt a very severe blow, one that placed a significant dent in the movement.[117] In the last few years, ALF activities have been limited to a few isolated events involving, again, the firebombing of a UCLA researcher's house in 2006 for research with animals and the arson of four houses in the Seattle region, causing nearly $7 million in damages because the houses were not deemed to be "built green" (2009),[118] and a 2011 arson of the Rocky Mountain Fir and Fireworks Corporation in Boise, Idaho causing over $100,000 in damages.[119]

Chapter Summary

Summary by Learning Objective

1. **Define _intelligence_.**

    Intelligence is data and information that have been evaluated, analyzed, and produced with careful conclusions and recommendations. Intelligence, then, is a _product_ created from systematic and thoughtful examination, placed in context, and provided to law enforcement executives, with facts and alternatives that can inform critical decisions.

2. **Describe the Intelligence Cycle as presented in the _National Criminal Intelligence Sharing Plan (NCISP)_.**

    The _National Criminal Intelligence Sharing Plan (NCISP)_ contains 28 specific recommendations for major changes in local policing. The key concept from the document emphasized the strategic integration of intelligence into the overall mission of the police organization—intelligence-led policing. Rather than react and respond to past calls for service, the NCISP places much more emphasis on predictive analysis derived from the discovery of hard facts, information, patterns, intelligence, and good crime analysis. By concentrating on key criminal activities, problems, and individuals targeted through analysis, significant attention can be directed to alleviate the crime problem. In order to protect the civil liberties of all individuals, the intelligence process was developed with key evaluation points aimed at verifying source reliability and validity at the beginning of the collection cycle. The goal was to develop a universal process that would integrate both law enforcement and national security intelligence agendas, while providing mechanisms for securing individual freedoms and allowing law enforcement agencies to be proactive in preventing and deterring crime and terrorism. The end result was the "Intelligence Cycle," presented by the FBI as a means of developing data into refined and polished intelligence and communicating or sharing that intelligence among individuals and agencies through the dissemination process.

3. **Define a _fusion center_ and briefly list its four primary goals.**

    Fusion centers act as a hub for exchanging information and intelligence, maximizing police resources, streamlining public safety operations, and improving the ability to fight crime and terrorism by merging data from a variety of sources. Fusion centers serve as clearinghouses for all potentially relevant homeland security information that can be used to assess local terror threats and aid in the apprehension of more traditional criminal suspects. The four primary goals of a fusion center are as follows: (1) Fusion centers support the broad range of activities undertaken by a police department relating to the detection, examination, and investigation of a potential terrorist and/or criminal activity; (2) Fusion centers support operations that protect critical infrastructure and key resources (CI/KRs) in a given region, support major incident operations, support specialized units charged with interdiction and investigative operations, and assist in emergency operations and planning. The aim of a fusion center is to reduce the vulnerability of the high-value and high-risk targets identified within a jurisdiction; (3) Fusion centers often maintain public "tip lines," which give them the capability to promote more public involvement in and awareness of terrorist threats. The goal is to identify and recognize warning signs and potential threats in a timely manner in order to pre-empt potential terrorist attacks and reduce the vulnerability of the CI/KRs in a given region; and (4) Fusion centers assist police executives in making better-informed decisions, especially during emergencies or critical incidents.

4. **Describe some of the major criticisms aimed at fusion centers and other law enforcement responses to terrorism.**

    The major criticisms aimed at fusion centers and other law enforcement responses to terrorism include the following: (1) Problems relating to the sharing of information between local law enforcement and the FBI. The sharing of information appears to be one way, from local police agencies to the FBI; (2) Fusion centers are expensive and almost any cost-benefit analysis (including a 2012 U.S. Senate Permanent Subcommittee investigation) revealed significant money spent for very little, tangible evidence of success. The effectiveness of fusion centers, particularly given their financial outlay, has seriously been questioned; (3) Many fusion centers appear to suffer from "mission creep"; that is, because there are few cases focused on terrorism, many centers have expanded their role to include crime fighting and reduction; and (4) Many fusion centers come desperately close to violating the civil liberties of people, especially relating to racial and ethnic profiling and breaches of privacy.

5. **List the four primary areas of responsibility within the Department of Homeland Security (DHS).**

   There are four primary areas of responsibility within the Department of Homeland Security: (DHS): (1) border security and transportation; (2) emergency preparedness and response; (3) chemical, biological, radiological, and nuclear countermeasures; and (4) intelligence analysis and infrastructure protection.

6. **Define** *terrorism.*

   In the popular mind, terrorism is viewed as the illegitimate and violent actions of specific groups that violate the authority of rightfully established governments. Terrorism encompasses the threat of and/or use of violence to achieve a specific set of political objectives or goals. Historically, defining terrorism has been a very difficult venture, shaped and altered by a number of factors, including our own national interests, government interpretations, the news media, hidden political agendas, and emotional human rights rhetoric. Terrorism is situationally defined—that is, a number of factors play on the difficulty of defining terrorism, including competing political agendas, national interests, economic security, the news media, fundamental cultural and religious beliefs, and the use of misinformation. For this reason, scholars have conceptualized terrorism in four distinct typologies, based on the actors: (1) *International terrorism*—Actions conducted in the international arena by individuals that are members of a nation state; (2) *Transnational terrorism*—Actions conducted in the international arena by individuals that have no nation-state; (3) *Domestic terrorism*—Actions conducted by groups within a nation, usually against the government or specific groups within the nation-state; and (4) *State terrorism*—Actions conducted by governments against their own population.

7. **Briefly describe the concept of "jihad" and name some of the more radical Islamic groups active throughout the world.**

   The concept of "jihad" or "holy war" is rooted in an early religious movement commonly called "Wahhabism" and later "Salafism" and can be traced back to the late 1700s in what is now Saudi Arabia and Egypt. The ideology is based primarily on the writing of radical Islamic philosophers, Muhammad Ibn al-Wahhab, Hassan al-Banna, and Sayiid Muhammad Qubt and calls for the purging of Western influence throughout the entire Middle East. The concept is justified throughout passages in the Qur'an that are perverted and misinterpreted to justify a "holy war" against the West. It is important to note that radical Islamic fundamentalists represent only a small but growing percentage of all Islam. Some of the groups that espoused "jihad" throughout the world are al-Qaeda, the Islamic State, Abu Sayyaf Group, HAMAS, Jemaah Islamiya, Lashkar-i-Tayyiba, and the Muslim Brotherhood,

8. **Describe the concept of a "homegrown terrorist."**

   The term "**homegrown terrorist**" refers to extremists who are legal U.S. residents or even citizens, and who are linked to or inspired by a specific, often intolerant ideology. This ideology may be motivated by political or religious sources and may be centered in domestic or foreign movements. Indeed, some of them have made connections with well-known, international terror groups, such as ISIS and al-Qaeda. These individuals may receive ideological encouragement, but not financial or material support, making them ancillary to the primary group and very difficult to detect by intelligence and law enforcement services.

9. **Discuss why Outlaw Motorcycle Gangs (OMGs) are considered an international threat to the United States. Identify the "Big Four" OMGs that are active in the United States.**

   Most people in the United States would not immediately think of outlaw motorcycle gangs as "an international threat." However, during the last 25 years, almost all of the major outlaw motorcycle gangs have been classified by authorities as international criminal enterprises. Indeed, there have been several gang battles overseas. For instance in 1984, a shoot-out between the Bandidos and a rival gang called the Comancheros killed seven people and wounded another 28 in Milperra, Australia, and between 1994 and 1997, in what is commonly called, "The Great Nordic Biker War," long-time enemies belonging to the Hell's Angels and the Bandidos shook the Scandinavian countries of Denmark, Finland, Sweden, and Norway. At least 12 people died and over 100 were injured in the 4-year war. On the domestic side, in 2015, in Waco, Texas, over 170 rival OMG members were arrested and charged in a shoot-out at a popular *Twin Peaks* restaurant. Nine bikers were killed and another eighteen were wounded in the gun battle that at one time had over 30 gang members shooting at one another. There are four primary outlaw motorcycle gangs in the United States, with all having chapters in foreign countries: The Hell's Angels (the largest group focused in California with 425 chapters in 50 different countries), the Pagans (located primarily on the east coast of the United States and throughout Canada), the Outlaws (focused in Chicago with 275 chapters in 23 countries), and the Bandidos (focused in Texas with 210 chapters in 22 countries). Clearly, OMGs pose an international as well as a domestic threat.

10. **Define a *hate crime*.**

    A hate crime is a criminal offense committed against persons, property, or society that is motivated, in whole or in part, by an offender's bias against an individual's or a group's perceived race, religion, ethnic/national origin, gender, age, disability, or sexual orientation. Most states have a hate crime statute that provides enhanced penalties for crimes in which victims are selected because of the perpetrator's bias against the victims' perceived race, religion, or ethnicity. Some states also classify as hate crimes those in which a victim is selected on the basis of a perception of his or her sexual orientation,

gender, or disability. In some states, the passage of hate crime statutes has been controversial as politicians have debated the constitutionality of enhanced penalties based on a suspect's association with an extremist group or the inclusion of homosexuality as a protected class. There is also a federal statute that addresses civil rights violations under 18 U.S.C. Section 245.

11. **Define and identify groups that are commonly called *ecoterrorists*.**

    Groups commonly called "ecoterrorists" are primarily motivated on improving the ecology of the world. Many of these single-issue terrorist groups arose from relatively peaceful movements and the call for a renewal of the planet's geophysical and biological environment. The two most notable "ecoterrorist" groups are the Earth Liberation Front (ELF) and the Animal Liberation Front (ALF). Despite recent and significant law enforcement and prosecution successes against these groups, both are still active today, with most of their activities aimed at the destruction of property and vandalism.

Chapter Review Questions

1. Define *intelligence*, and identify the two ultimate goals of intelligence.

2. List and briefly explain the six steps of the Intelligence Cycle as presented in the *National Criminal Intelligence Sharing Plan (NCISP)*.

3. What is a fusion center and briefly list their four primary goals?

4. What are the 10 simple steps that assist individual police agencies become part of the National Criminal Intelligence Sharing Plan?

5. What are critical infrastructure and key resources (CI/KRs)? Give some examples.

6. What is the National Counterterrorism Center (NCTC)?

7. What are the four primary areas of responsibility within the Department of Homeland Security?

8. Briefly discuss some of the issues and criticisms relating to police and intelligence generally, and with fusion centers specifically.

9. Define *terrorism*.

10. Briefly describe the concept of jihad and name some of the more radical Islamic terrorist groups active throughout the world.

11. What is ISIS and who is Abu Bakr al-Baghdadi?

12. What is a "homegrown" terrorist? Give some examples and recent incidents involving homegrown terrorists.

13. What is Boko Haram?

14. Who is "el Chapo" and what is his importance to the Mexican Cartels?

15. Why are Outlaw Motorcycle Gangs (OMGs) considered an international threat to the United States. Identify the "Big Four" OMGs that are active in the United States.

16. What is a *hate crime*? In your answer be sure to identify some of the major right-wing groups active in the United States.

17. What is an *ecoterrorist*? Identify some of the major groups called ecoterrorists.

Critical Thinking Exercises

1. **Historical Problems in the Levant.** Research the Middle Eastern area known as the Levant—An area of land between Egypt, Anatolia, Mesopotamia, and the Arabian Desert. The Levant is an ancient

land of great historical civilizations—from the center of the Ur civilization (2100 BC) to the kingdom of Babylonia (1700 BC), to the ancient Greek and Roman Empires (300 BC to 400 AD), to the great Ottoman Empire of the 20th century—the Levant has been the crossroad for communication, trade, and commerce between the Middle East and the rest of the world (Europe). The Levant is a geographical area composed of the modern day countries of Israel, the Palestinian territories of the Gaza and West Bank, Syria, Jordan, and Lebanon. It is a fertile area located on the southeastern shores of the Mediterranean Sea. Great spiritual meaning has also been given to the area of the Levant as it represents the lands of Abraham, Moses, Jesus, and Muhammad. It is also an area that has witnessed significant historical conflict. Study the countries of the Levant and focus on the current conflict in Syria. Try to identify which groups discussed in this chapter are actively fighting or supporting a specific side in Syria. Now research the history of the al-Assad family in Syria. Who is Bashar al-Assad and do you think he will abdicate his monarchy in the near future? Why or why not?

2. **Mass Shooters and Lone Wolves.** Scour the Internet for mass shooters and lone wolf attacks in the United States. Are there any common denominators between the shooters and their horrific events of the past decade? Review the CNN story and videos entitled, "The 25 Deadliest Mass Shootings in U.S. History Fast Facts" at: http://www.cnn.com/2013/09/16/us/20-deadliest-mass-shootings-in-u-s-history-fast-facts/. Now review the article entitled, "A Guide to Mass Shootings in America," at: http://www.motherjones.com/politics/20/07/mass-shootings-map. Note that both articles make a difference between Mass murders (single incident) and Spree killing (Multiple incidents). View the map presented in the second story, and try to identify any patterns that can be made geographically about these events. Also note the stories are dated October 26, 2013, and April 2, 2014, respectively. Can other events be added to the story since those dates, like the Emanuel AME Church massacre in Charleston, South Carolina, in 2015? Discuss the problem of mass shootings and spree killings in class. What do you think can be done to prevent such horrific problems in the future?

3. **Research Intelligence on Terrorist Organizations and Groups Globally.** Visit and preview the Terrorism Research and Analysis Consortium (TRAC), created by the Beacham Group, LLC on the Internet at: www.terrorismresearch.org. Watch the preview and explore the site. TRAC is one of the most comprehensive terrorism research sites on the Internet and provides an efficient series of filters in which to study various types of terrorist targets, tactics, and groups. Play with the filters, watch some of the posted videos, read some of the articles on ideology, and read the intelligence reports about the latest information on active groups in any area of your choosing. Consider subscribing, or having your university or college subscribe to the site. TRAC was specifically designed to fulfill the research and intelligence needs of faculty, scholars, students, government, and defense professionals studying terrorism.

4. **The National Counter Terrorism Center (NCTC).** The Office of the Director of National Intelligence houses the National Counter Terrorism Center (NCTC). The two core missions of the NCTC are to serve the primary organization in the United States for the analysis and integration of terrorism intelligence, and the second mission is to conduct strategic operational planning for counter terrorism activities. Visit the NCTC website at: www.nctc.gov. Name the key partners associated with the NCTC and view the Counter Terrorism Calendar. Now explore career possibilities within the intelligence field. What types of career opportunities exist within the Intelligence Community at the federal level? As important, what knowledge, skills, and abilities are required to fulfill these types of positions and are you qualified? Develop an action plan for yourself to accomplish education and training goals that would qualify you for an intelligence analyst position within the NCTC.

Key Terms

al-Qaeda
all-hazard
caliphate
colors
critical infrastructure and key resources (CI/KRs)
deep web

Earth Liberation Front (ELF), Animal Liberation Front (ALF)
fusion centers
hate crimes
homegrown terrorism
improvised explosive devices (IEDs)
intelligence

Islamic State (ISIS)
jihad
lone wolf (wolves)
narco-terrorism
terrorism
Tor network

Endnotes

[1]Marilyn Peterson, *Intelligence-Led Policing: The New Intelligence Architecture* (Washington, DC: U.S. Department of Justice, BJA, September 2005) NCJ 210681, and K. Riley, G. Terverton, J. Wilson, and L. Davis, *State and Local Intelligence in the War on Terror* (Washington, DC: The RAND Corporation, 2005).

[2]For a more thorough discussion of the role of intelligence in combating terrorism, see Robert W. Taylor, "Terrorism and Intelligence," *Defense Analysis* 3, No. 2 (1987), pp. 165–175.

[3]Peterson, *Intelligence-Led Policing: The New Intelligence Architecture*, p. 3.

[4]For a more thorough discussion of the first two schools of thought, refer to R. Godson, ed., *Intelligence Requirements for the 1980s: Analysis and Estimates* (Washington, DC: National Strategy Information Center, 1983).

[5]Early models of predictive intelligence are discussed in R. Hever, *Quantitative Approaches to Political Intelligence* (Boulder, Colo.: Westview Press, 1978).

[6]*National Criminal Intelligence Sharing Plan* (Washington, DC: U.S. Department of Justice, 2003, and revised in July 2005).

[7]K. Riley, G. Treverton, and L. Davis, *State and Local Intelligence in the War on Terror*.

[8]*Fusion Center Guidelines: Developing and Sharing Information and Intelligence in a New Era* (Washington, DC: U.S. Department of Justice, 2006).

[9]Joseph D' Amico, "Stopping Crime in Real Time," *Police Chief*, (September 2006): pp. 20–24.

[10]*Fusion Center Guidelines: Developing and Sharing Information and Intelligence in a New Era.*

[11]U.S. Department of Homeland Security, "Fusion Center Locations and Contact Information." See http://www.dhs.gov/fusion-center-locations-amd-contact-information.

[12]See https://nfcausa.org/.

[13]For a complete description of the National Counterterrorism Center, visit: www.nctc.gov.

[14]Samuel Walker and Charles M. Katz, *The Police in America*, 5th ed. (Boston: McGraw-Hill, 2005).

[15]George L. Kelling and William K. Bratton, "Policing Terrorism," *Civi Bulletin* 43, New York: Manhattan Institute for Policy Research (September 2006), p. 2.

[16]Mathieu Deflem, *The Policing of Terrorism: Organizational and Global Perspectives* (New York: Routledge Publishing, 2012).

[17]See Graeme R. Newman and Ronald V. Clarke, *Policing Terrorism: An Executive's Guide* (Washington, DC: U.S. Department of Justice, October, 2008).

[18]See Nationwide SAR Initiative (NSI), *http://nsi.ncirc.gov/default.aspx* (June 2010).

[19]U.S. Department of Homeland Security, *2010 Baseline Capabilities Assessment of Fusion Centers*. See: http://www.dhs.gov/2010-baseline-capabilities-assessment-fusion-centers-and-critical-operational-capabilities-gap.

[20]Information received during conversations with various fusion directors at the Fourth National Fusion Center Conference, New Orleans, LA (February 23–25, 2010).

[21]For a thorough critique focusing on fusion centers, see Torin Monahan and Neal A. Palmer, "The Emerging Politics of DHS Fusion Centers," *Security Dialogue* 40, No. 6 (December, 2009), pp. 617–636.

[22]Michael German and Jay Stanley, "What's Wrong with Fusion Centers? Retrieved June 8, 2008 from http://www.aclu.org/pdfs/privacy/fusioncenters_20071212.pdf.

[23]John Rollins, *Fusion Centers: Issues and Options for Congress* (Washington, DC: Congressional Research Services, January 2008).

[24]U.S. Senate Permanent Subcommittee on Investigations, *Federal Support For and Involvement in State and Local Fusion Centers*. See: http://www.hsgac.senate.gov/search/?q=federal+support+for+and+involvement+in+state+and+local+fusion+centers.

[25]Ibid., p. 1.

[26]Ibid., p. 5.

[27]See "Norah O'Donnell and Jillian Hughes, "New Code of Conduct Issued for Secret Service Agents," *CBS News*, April 27, 2017 and Alicia Caldwell, "REPORT:Secret Service Agents 'Likely' Impaired by Alcohol, *The Huffington Post*, May 14, 2015. See: http://www.huffingtonpost.com/2015/05/14/secret-service-agents-wer_n_7281024.html.

[28]See: http://change.gov/newsroom/entry/key_members_of_obama_biden_national_security_team_announced/ (May 31, 2010).

[29]Richard Schultz, "Conceptualizing Political Terrorism: A Typology," *Journal of International Affairs* 4, no. 8 (spring/summer 1978): p. 8.

[30]Robert W. Taylor and Harry E. Vanden, "Defining Terrorism in El Salvador: La Matanza," *Annals of the American Academy of Political and Social Science* (September 1982): pp. 106–117.

[31]Ibid., p. 109.

[32]Ibid.

[33]For a discussion on the various definitions of terrorism, see Richard Schultz, "Conceptualizing Political Terrorism: A Typology," *Journal of International Affairs* 4, No. 8 (spring 1978); Martha Crenshaw Hutchinson, *Revolutionary Terrorism* (Stanford, CA.: Hoover Institute Press, 1978); Brian Jenkins, *The Study of Terrorism: Definitional Problems* (Santa Monica, CA.: The RAND Corporation, 1980); James M. Poland, *Understanding Terrorism: Groups, Strategies, and Responses* (Upper Saddle River, NJ: Prentice Hall, 1988); Paul Wilkinson, *Political Terrorism* (New York: Wiley Press, 1974); Bruce Hoffman, *Inside Terrorism* (New York: Columbia University Press, 1998); and Jonathan R. White, *Terrorism: An Introduction* (Belmont, CA: West/Wadsworth, 2003).

[34]The conceptualization of terrorism is presented in a number of works. See Edward Mickolus, "Statistical Approaches to the Study of Terrorism," in *Terrorism: Interdisciplinary Perspectives*, Yonah Alexander and Maxwell Finger, eds. (New York: McGraw-Hill, 1977), pp. 209–269. For additional reading on this subject, see David Milbank, *International and Transnational Terrorism: Diagnosis and Prognosis* (Washington, DC: CIA, 1976), and Richard Schultz, Jr., and Stephen Sloan, *Responding to the Terrorist Threat: Security and Crisis Management* (New York: Pergamon Press, 1980).

[35]See: CBS News, "Armed militia takeover in Oregon Sparks Debate on Meaning of Terrorist." (New York: CBS, January 3, 2016) and Rob Manning, "Oregon Governor Brown on

Burns: "Spectacle Must End," (Portland, OR: Oregon Public Broadcasting, January 20, 2016).

[36]Ibid.

[37]See Robert W. Taylor and Charles R. Swanson, *Terrorism, Intelligence and Homeland Security* (Upper Saddle River, NJ: Pearson, 2016), and Jennifer Harper, "As a Target for Terrorists, U.S. Ranks 41st in the World," The Washington Post, December 4, 2012.

[38]For detailed information on the life of Osama bin Laden, see Yossef Bodansky, *Bin Laden: The Man Who Declared War on America* (Rocklin, CA: Prima, 1999).

[39]U.S. Department of State, *Country Report on Terrorism, 2014*, released June 19, 2015.

[40]Graeme Wood, "What ISIS Really Wants," *The Atlantic,* March 2015. See: https://www.theatlantic.com/features/archive/2015/02/what-isis-really-wants/384980/?fb_ref=Default.

[41]Robert W. Taylor and Charles R. Swanson, *Terrorism, Intelligence and Homeland Security* (Upper Saddle River, NJ: Pearson, 2016) and the National Counter Terrorism Center (NCTC) website. See: http://www.nctc.gov/site/index.html.

[42]See Robert W. Taylor and Charles R. Swanson, *Terrorism, Intelligence and Homeland Security* (Upper Saddle River, NJ: Pearson, 2016).

[43]Zelna Karam, Vivian Salama, Bram Janssen, and Lee Keath, "Inside Islamic State Group's Rule: A Nation of Fear," *Associated Press,* June 17, 2015.

[44]Ally Pregulman and Emily Burke, "Homegrown Terrorism," *AQAM Futures Project Case Studies Series,* April 2012, http://csis.org/files/publication/120425_Pregulman_AQAMCaseStudy7_web.pdf.

[45]Rick "Ozzie" Nelson and Ben Bodurian, "A Growing Terrorist Threat? Assessing 'Home-grown Extremism' in the United States." *Center for International and Strategic Studies,* March 8, 2010, retrieved from www.csis.org/files/publication/100304_nelson_growingterroristthreat_web.pdf on July 15, 2015.

[46]Katherine Q. Seelye, "Bombing Suspect Cites Islamic Extremist Beliefs as Motive," *The New York Times,* April 23, 2013, www.nytimes.com/2013/04/24/us/boston-marathon-bombing-developments.html?hp&pagewanted=all&_r=1&.

[47]Holly Yan, "Texas Attack: What we know about Elton Simpson and Nadir Soofi," *CNN Video AP,* May 5, 2015.

[48]Catherin Schoichet and Michael Pearson, "Garland, Texas: Shooting Suspect Linked Himself to ISIS in Tweets," CNN Video AP (May 4, 2015).

[49]Matt Pearce and Nigel Duara, "Texas gunman's mother: "He had a normal American upbringing." *Los Angeles Times,* May 5, 2005. See: http://www.latimes.com/nation/la-na-texas-gunman-20150505-story.html#page=1.

[50]Alejandro J. Beutel, "Data on Post-9/11 Terrorism in the United States," *Muslim Public Affairs Council: Policy Memo Backgrounder* (April 1, 2010), pp. 1–16.

[51]See M. J. Stephey, "Daniel Boyd: A Homegrown Terrorist?" *Time Online,* July 30, 2009, retrieved online from www.time.com/time/nationa/article/0,8599,1913602,00.html on April 23, 2010.

[52]See M. Baker, "Daniel Boyd, Six Others in North Carolina, Charged with Terror Conspiracy," *The Huffington Post,* July 27, 2009, retrieved online from www.huffingtonpost.com/2009/07/27/daniel-boyd-six-others-in_n_245792.html on April 23, 2010.

[53]See A. Gary, "Hosam Maher Husein Smadi Arrested for Dallas Bomb Plot," *The Huffington Post,* September 24, 2009, retrieved online from www.huffingtonpost.com/2009/09/24/hosam-maher-husein-smadi-_n_299340.html on April 25, 2010.

[54]See J. Trahan, T. J. Gillman, and S. Goldstein, "Dallas bomb plot suspect told landlord he was moving out," *The Dallas Morning News,* September 26, 2009, retrieved from www.dallasnews.com/sharedcontent/dws/dn/latestnews/stories/092409dnmetbombarrest.1b177db8b.html on April 25, 2010.

[55]Ibid.

[56]Rick "Ozzie" Nelson and Ben Bodurian, "A Growing Terrorist Threat? Assessing 'Home-grown Extremism' in the United States." *Center for International and Strategic Studies,* March 8, 2010, retrieved from www.csis.org/files/publication/100304_nelson_growingterroristthreat_web.pdf on April 22, 2010.

[57]"Najibullah Zazi," *The New York Times,* updated February 22, 2010, retrieved online from http://topics.nytimes.com/topics/reference/timestopics/people/z/najibulla_zazi/index.html on April 18, 2010.

[58]Michael Leiter, Director of National Counterterrorism Center, "*Hearing Before the Senate Homeland Security and Governmental Affairs Committee: Eight Years After 9/11: Confronting the Terrorist Threat to the Homeland,*" September 30, 2009. Transcript online at www.nctc.gov/press_room/speeches/hbshsgac_8years_9-3—29.pdf, retrieved April 22, 2010.

[59]See G. Miller, "Al Qaeda's new tactic is to seize shortcuts," *Chicago Tribune,* March 19, 2010, retrieved online from www.chicagotribune.com/news/nationworld/la-fg-qaeda19-2010mar19,0,3312538.story on April 18, 2010.

[60]See P. Belien, "Jihad against Danish Newspaper," *The Brussels Journal,* October 22, 2005, retrieved online from http://www.brusselsjournal.com/node/382 on April 16, 2010.

[61]Rick "Ozzie" Nelson and Ben Bodurian, "A Growing Terrorist Threat? Assessing 'Home-grown Extremism' in the United States."

[62]Spencer Ackerman, Pakistani Court Indicts "Virginia Five," *The Washington Independent,* March 17, 2010, retrieved online from http://washingtonindependent.com/79466/pakistani-court-indicts-virginia-five on April 10, 2011.

[63]See S. Ackerman, "A Mixed Picture on Domestic Radicalization?" *The Washington Independent,* December 10, 2009, retrieved online from http://washingtonindependent.com/70388/a-mixed-picture-on-domestic-radicalization on April 24, 2010.

[64]See G. Whittell, "Profile: Major Nidal Malik Hassan was trained to treat post-traumatic stress," *The Times,* November 6, 2009, retrieved online from www.thetimes.co.uk/tto/news/world/americas/article2001549.ece on April 20, 2010.

[65]Rick Nelson and Ben Bodurian, "A Growing Terrorist Threat? Assessing 'Home-grown Extremism' in the United States."

[66]See, "Major Hassan's Smooth Ascension," *The New York Times,* January 15, 2010, retrieved online at www.nytimes.com/2010/01/16/opinion/16sat2.html on April 23, 2010. Appeared in print (January 16, 2010), p. A-20.

[67]Department of Justice, "Pennsylvania Woman Indicted in Plot to Recruit Violent Jihadist Fighters and to Commit Murder Overseas," Federal Bureau of Investigation Philadelphia Office Press Release, March 9, 2010, retrieved online at http://philadelphia.fbi.gov/dojpressrel/pressrel10/ph030910a.htm on April 24, 2010.

[68]See H. Khan, E. Friedman, and J. Ryan, "'Jihad Jane's' Arrest Raises Fears about Homegrown Terrorists," *ABC News*, March 10, 2010, retrieved online at http://abcnews.go.com/GMA/politics/jihad-jane-arrest-colleen-larose-raises-fears-homegrown/story?id=10056187 on April 22, 2010.

[69]Department of Justice, "Pennsylvania Woman Indicted in Plot to Recruit Violent Jihadist Fighters and to Commit Murder Overseas."

[70]See "Profile: 'Jihad Jane' from Main Street," *BBC News,* last updated March 11, 2010, retrieved online at http://news.bbc.co.uk/2/hi/americas/8561888.stm on April 26, 2010.

[71]See http://dfw.cbslocal.com/2015/05/03/breaking-shooting-in-garland.

[72]Catherine E. Shoichet and Gary Tuchman, "Chattanooga Shooting: 4 Marines Killed, a Dead Suspect and Questions of Motive," CNN News (July 17, 2015). See: http://www.cnn.com/2015/07/16/us/tennessee-naval-reserve-shooting/.

[73]Saeed Ahmed, "Who were Syed Rizwan Farook and Tashfeen Malik?" CNN Reports (December 4, 2015). See: http://www.cnn.com/2015/12/03/us/syed-farook-tashfeen-malik-mass-shooting-profile/.

[74]Frank Gardner, "How Do Terrorists Communicate?" *British Broadcasting Company*, November 2, 2013, www.bbc.com/news/world-24784756.

[75]Robert W. Taylor, Eric J. Fritsch, and John Liederbach, *Digital Crime and Digital Terrorism* (Upper Saddle River, NJ: Pearson, 2014).

[76]Pregulman and Burke, "Homegrown Terrorism."

[77]Evan Perez and LeeAnn Caldwell, "Holder Fears 'Lone Wolf' Terrorist Attack, Doesn't Want TSA Armed," *CNN*, November 5, 2014. See: www.cnn.com/2013/11/05/politics/holder-terror-snowden-interview/.

[78]Sarah Teich, "Trends and Developments in Lone Wolf Terrorism in the Western World: An Analysis of Terrorist Attacks and Attempted Attacks by Islamic Extremists," *International Institute for Counterterrorism*, October 2013. See: www.ict.org.il/LinkClick.aspx?fileticket=qAv1zIPJIGE%3D&tabid=66.

[79]The ISIS Study Group, "People are Waking-up to the Southeast Asia ISIS Threat – But things are still being Missed," (November 30, 2014). See http://isisstudygroup.com/?p=3314.

[80]See Robert Kupperman and Jeff Kamen, "A New Outbreak of Terror Is Likely," *New York Times,* (April 19, 1988): p. 6, and Alan Riding, "Rifts Threaten Plan to Remove Borders," *CJ International* 6, no. 5 (September/October 1990): p. 3.

[81]David W. Balsiger, "Narco-Terrorism 'Shooting Up' America," in *Annual Edition: Violence and Terrorism 1990/91* (Guilford, CT: Dushkin, 1990), pp. 164–166.

[82]Ibid.

[83]*Al Arabiya*, "Boko Haram Voices Support for ISIS' al-Baghdadi" (July 13, 2014).

[84]Jack Moore, "Nigerian Military Enters Final Stages of Boko Haram Offensive," *Newsweek* (April 23, 2015).

[85]Nick Valencia, "After Years of Violence and Death, "Life is Back" in Juarez," *CNN* (April 21, 2015).

[86]Nick Allen "Mexican city is 'murder capital of the world'" – *The Telegraph* (October 22, 2009).

[87]Pamela Engel, "The Astonishing Rise of the World's Most Notorious Drug Lord," *Business Insider* (July 18, 2015).

[88]William Neuman and Azam Ahmed, "Public Enemy? Escaped 'El Chapo' is Folk Hero No. 1" *New York Times* (July 18, 2015).

[89]Ibid.

[90]Catherine E. Shoichet, Don Melvin and Mariano Castillo, "The Legend of 'El Chapo': Cartel Chief Cultivated Robin Hood Image," *CNN* (July 14, 2015). See: http://edition.cnn.com/2014/02/22/world/americas/mexico-el-chapo-profile/.

[91]See George Grayson, "Los Zetas: the Ruthless Army Spawned by a Mexican Drug Cartel". U.S. Foreign Policy Research Institute. http://www.fpri.org/enotes/200805.grayson.loszetas.html, and Michael Ware, "Los Zetas called Mexico's most dangerous drug cartel". *CNN News* (August 6, 2009) http://www.cnn.com/2009/WORLD/americas/08/06/mexico.drug.cartels/index.html.

[92]Daniel Borunda, "El Paso Rankings: Safest, Best Places for Families, Least Hipster," *El Paso Times* (January 6, 2015).

[93]Federal Bureau of Investigation, *National Gang Intelligence Report, 2013*. See: https://www.fbi.gov/stats-services/publications/national-gang-report-2013/view.

[94]Ibid.

[95]"Families Scoff at Suspect's New Images," *Sunday Oklahoman,* (July 2, 1995): p. 24.

[96]Ibid.

[97]Louis A. Radelet and David Carter, *Police and the Community*, 5th ed. (New York: Macmillan, 1994), p. 248.

[98]Scott Shane, "Homegrown Extremists Tied to Deadlier Toll than Jihadists in U.S. Since 9/11," *The New York Times*, June 24, 2015. See: http://www.nytimes.com/2015/06/25/us/tally-of-attacks-in-us-challenges-perceptions-of-top-terror-threat.html.

[99]*Keenan v. Aryan Nations,* CV 99-441 (September 8, 2000).

[100]See *Gruver v. Imperial Klans of America,* Civil Action Number 07-CI-00082 (November 14, 2008).

[101]See http://hutaree.com/.

[102]See *United States v. Hutaree Members,* copy of federal indictment. See: http://commons.wikimedia.org/wiki/File:Federal-hutaree-indictment-mar-2010.pdf) (June 10, 2010).

[103]*The New Lexicon of Hate: The Changing Tactics, Language and Symbols of America's Extremists* (Los Angeles: Simon Wiesenthal Center, 1999).

[104]Federal Bureau of Investigation, "Seeking Suspect in Church Shootings in Charleston, South Carolina, June 18, 2015, p. 1, https://www.fbi.gov/news/news_blog/seeking-suspect-in-church-shootings-in-charleston-south-carolina (accessed October 20, 2015).

[105]Statement by FBI Director James Comey Regarding Dylann Roof Gun Purchase, July 10, 2015, https://www.fbi.gov/news/pressrel/press-releases/statement-by-fbi-director-james-comey-regarding-dylann-roof-gun-purchase (accessed October 20, 2015).

[106]Janell Ross, Why Blacks See Dylann Roof As a Terrorist and Whites Don't," The Washington Post, July 3, 2015, p. 1, https://www.washingtonpost.com/news/the-fix/wp/2015/07/03/why-blacks-see-dylann-roof-as-a-terrorist-and-whites-don't (accessed October 20, 2015).

[107]Robert Taylor and Charles Swanson, Terrorism, Intelligence, and Homeland Security (Boston, Pearson, 2015, p. 112.)

[108]See: Jeffrey D. Simon, *Lone Wolf Terrorism: Understanding the Growing Threat* (Amherst, NY: Prometheus Books, 2013) and Mark Thompson, "The Danger of the Lone-Wolf Terrorist," February 27, 2013, www.nation.time.com/2013/02/27/the-danger-of-the-lone-wolf-terrorist (accessed October 20, 2015).

[109]For more information, see the National Institutes Against Hate Crimes and Terrorism, visit their website: http://www.museumoftolerance.com/site/c.tmL6KfNVLtH/b.5052739/.

[110]*Responding to Hate Crimes: A Police Officer's Guide to Investigation and Prevention* (Washington, DC: U.S. Department of Justice and International Association of Chiefs of Police, 1999).

[111]Victor Godinez, "Hate Group Wooing Teens by Making a Game Out of Racism," *Dallas Morning News*, (March 14, 2002): p. A2.

[112]Robert W. Taylor and Eric. J. Fritsch, *Juvenile Justice: Policies, Programs, and Practices*, 4th edition (New York:

McGraw-Hill, 2015). See also Robert W. Taylor, Eric J. Fritsch, and John Liederbach, *Digital Crime and Digital Terrorism*, 3rd edition, (Upper Saddle River, NJ: Pearson Prentice Hall, 2015).

[113]An interview with leader of the Texas Militia in Dallas (December, 2014), reflecting much of the sentiments expressed by Tom Metzger, a leader of the White Aryan Resistance (WAR).

[114]Jonathan R. White, *Terrorism and Homeland Security*, 6th ed. (Belmont, CA: Wadsworth Cengage Learning, 2009), p. 233.

[115]University of Maryland, *Global Terrorism Data Base*, Incident Summary Number 201411250074 and 2012201208110011. See: www.Start.umd.edu/gtd/Search.

[116]Cindy C. Combs, *Terrorism in the Twenty-First Century*, 3rd ed. (Upper Saddle River, NJ: Prentice Hall, 2003), pp. 164–166.

[117]See Blaine Harden, "11 Indicted in 'Eco-Terrorism' Case," *Washington Post* (January 21, 2006): p. A-3.

[118]See "Terror at UCLA," *Critical Mass* (August 22, 2006) and "Luxury Homes Burn in Apparent Eco-Attack," *Associated Press* (March 3, 2008).

[119]University of Maryland, *Global Terrorism Data Base*, Incident Summary Number 201109260012. See: www.Start.umd.edu/gtd/Search.

CHAPTER FOUR

POLITICS AND POLICE ADMINISTRATION

Learning Objectives

1. Explain the significance of the U.S. Supreme Court decisions in each of the following cases: *Mapp v. Ohio* (1961), *Gideon v. Wainwright* (1963), *Escobedo v. Illinois* (1964), and *Miranda v. Arizona* (1966).

2. Identify three distinctly different styles of law enforcement discussed by James Q. Wilson.

3. Explain the legally defined roles of city councils.

4. Discuss the ways in which the tasks and roles of sheriff's department and police departments were historically different but have become similar in recent years.

5. Explain how the state prosecutor's policies and procedures can have an observable effect on police practices and procedures.

6. Discuss the ways in which the judiciary impacts police practices.

7. Understand the differences between the four existing forms of citizen oversight agencies.

8. Identify and briefly discuss the reasons for friction between the news media and law enforcement.

9. Discuss the advantages for police officers wearing body cameras that are cited by police administrators.

10. Define racial profiling.

11. Discuss two major concerns that state and local law enforcement administrators have in becoming involved in immigration enforcement.

INTRODUCTION

IN DISCUSSING THE RELATIONSHIP *between politics and police administration, it is important to distinguish between "Politics" and "politics."* **Politics***, when used negatively, refers to attempts to impose external, partisan political influence on the operation of a department.*

However, **politics***, used in the positive sense, means governance of a city. Aristotle's original understanding of the word politics was "science of the polis," seeking the good of both citizen and city-state.*[1]

In order to successfully maneuver through the minefields of politics in any community, a police administrator should possess the following information: (1) how politics at the federal and state level can impact local law enforcement; (2) how the dominant political culture of a local community can affect the quality and style of law enforcement services provided; (3) why the politics and organizational structures of police departments and sheriffs' departments have traditionally been so different but in recent years the functions they perform have become increasingly similar; (4) the ways in which judges and prosecutors can impact on enforcement practices; (5) why some communities have the need for and demand the creation of **citizen oversight** *committees; (6) the important roles played by chambers of commerce, churches, and the media; (7) the political fallout from allegations and actual incidents of police brutality and the ways in which body cameras can be a useful tool to protect officers from false allegations as well as preventing officers from engaging in misconduct; (8) being aware of the intentional or unintentional racial profiling of enforcement practices; and (9) the role of the local and state police in immigration enforcement.*

FEDERAL INFLUENCE IN LAW ENFORCEMENT

Some authorities believe that trends occurring from the 1960s to the present have resulted in the partial nationalization of criminal justice. Up to the 1960s, it was safely said that criminal justice was almost completely the responsibility of state and local governments. Federal criminal statutes were limited in their coverage, federal assistance to local law enforcement was generally in the areas of training and the processing of evidence, and the U.S. Supreme Court concerned itself with only the most notorious violations of Constitutional rights by state and local authorities.[2] This trend was reversed in no small measure by a series of opinions, rendered by the Supreme Court under the strong leadership of Chief Justice Earl Warren that greatly strengthened the rights of accused persons in criminal cases (see Figure 4.1). However, as the Supreme Court has become more conservative in the past two decades, an "erosion" of many of the landmark cases of the Warren era can be observed.[3]

Supreme Court Decisions Affecting Law Enforcement: 1961 to 1966

Significant judicial review of local police actions has been a somewhat recent practice.[4] From 1961 through 1966—a period frequently referred to as the "due process revolution"—the Supreme Court took an activist role, becoming quite literally givers of the law rather than interpreters of it. The Warren Court's activist role in the piecemeal extension of the provisions of the Bill of Rights, via the due process clause of the Fourteenth Amendment, to criminal proceedings in the respective states appears to have been a policy decision.[5] Normally, the Supreme Court writes opinions in about 115 cases during any particular term. During the 1938–1939 term, only five cases appeared under the heading of criminal law; a scant three decades later,

FIGURE 4.1 ▶ The U.S. Supreme Court led by Chief Justice Earl Warren was responsible for some of the most important decisions affecting law enforcement in the 1960s. (Library of Congress Prints and Photographs Division [LC-USZ62-41653])

during the height of the due process revolution, about one-quarter of each term's decisions related to criminal law.[6] The Supreme Court could scarcely have picked a worse period in which to undertake the unpopular role of policing the police; a burgeoning crime rate far outstripped population increases, and many politicians were campaigning on "law and order" platforms that all too often dissolved into hyperbolic rhetoric in their election campaigns. The problem of crime increasingly came to the public's eye through the media. In sum, the high court extended procedural safeguards to defendants in criminal cases precisely when the public's fear of crime was high and there was great social pressure to do something about crime.

Fundamentally, the Supreme Court's role in the due process revolution was a response to a vacuum in which the police themselves had failed to provide the necessary leadership. The era of strong social activism by various special-interest groups was not yet at hand, and neither the state courts nor the legislatures had displayed any broad interest in reforming the criminal law. What institution was better positioned to undertake this responsibility? The Court may even have felt obligated by the inaction of others to do so. Therefore, it became the Warren Court's lot to provide the reforms so genuinely needed but so unpopularly received. The high court did not move into this arena until after it had issued warnings that, to responsive and responsible leaders, would have been a mandate for reform.

Several key decisions were made by a split vote of the Court and drew heavy criticism from law enforcement officers and others as handcuffing police in their struggle with lawlessness. These decisions included:

- *Mapp v. Ohio* (1961), which banned the use of illegally seized evidence in criminal cases in the states by applying the Fourth Amendment guarantee against unreasonable searches and seizures
- *Gideon v. Wainwright* (1963), which affirmed that equal protection under the Fourteenth Amendment requires that legal counsel be appointed for all indigent defendants in all criminal cases
- *Escobedo v. Illinois* (1964), which affirmed that a suspect is entitled to confer with an attorney as soon as the focus of a police investigation of the suspect shifts from investigatory to accusatory
- *Miranda v. Arizona* (1966), which required police officers, before questioning suspects, to inform them of their constitutional right to remain silent, their right to an attorney, and their right to have an attorney appointed if they cannot afford to hire one. Although the suspect may knowingly waive these rights, the police cannot question anyone who, at any point, asks for a lawyer or indicates "in any manner" that he or she does not wish to be questioned.[7]

The impact of these decisions on police work was staggering. In an effort to curb questionable and improper tactics, the Supreme Court essentially barred the use of illegally obtained evidence in a criminal prosecution to prove guilt. This action,

known as the *exclusionary rule,* rested primarily on the judgment that deterring police conduct that violates the Constitutional rights of an individual outweighs the importance of securing a conviction of the specific defendant on trial. A need for new procedures in such areas as interrogations, lineups, and seizures of physical evidence was created.

Although the decisions of the due process revolution initially were criticized by many law enforcement officers, over the years that view has changed as new generations of law enforcement officers joined the profession and for whom those decisions were simply the correct way to do things. Also, officers from the due process revolution have retired or left the profession because they could not abide or adapt to the new procedures mandated by the Supreme Court.

Finally, there was a growing willingness among law enforcement leaders to acknowledge not only that some of their tactics needed changing but also that *Miranda* and other decisions had accomplished it. There is a sense in which the due process revolution furthered police professionalization.

THE ROLES OF STATE AND LOCAL GOVERNMENTS IN LAW ENFORCEMENT

From the outset, most Americans had a firm belief that the police should be controlled by local officials organized along municipal lines. For them, a national police, such as the Italian *carabinieri,* was inconceivable, and a state police, such as the German *polizei,* was undesirable.[8] However, the history of state and local relations in the United States in the area of law enforcement, especially in the last half of the 1800s, was often rocky and tumultuous with the states taking over the operation of many local law enforcement agencies.[9] These takeovers were motivated to a great extent by power struggles between the Democratically controlled cities and Republican-controlled state legislatures. This type of direct takeover of local law enforcement by the states will very likely not occur again, or at least not on the grand scale of the late 1800s, but there have been some isolated cases in recent years where similar action has been contemplated. For example, several years ago some public officials in Georgia were urging the state to take over the administration of the Atlanta Police Department because of dramatic political upheavals that were affecting the morale and effectiveness of that department. A takeover by the state did not occur, but the political atmosphere was conducive to such a move.

In a positive vein, the impact of the state on the affairs of local law enforcement is continuing via the imposition of pre-employment and training standards, as well as through various funding formulas tied to these standards. The first state to impose minimum standards of training for police officers was California, in 1959. This move was soon followed by the states of New York, Oklahoma, and Oregon. In 1970, the Law Enforcement Assistance Administration (LEAA) did make available discretionary grants to those states that wanted to implement minimum standards programs. Today all 50 states have mandated training for law enforcement officers. It must be noted, however, that much of the impetus for the implementation of minimum standards on a statewide basis comes from the local law enforcement community. Requirements related to the minimum standards for employment for police officers are administered through state organizations, often termed Police Officers Standards and Training Commissions (POSTs), which generally operate under four broad mandates: (1) to establish minimum standards for employment in a state, county, or local law enforcement agency; (2) to articulate academy and annual training requirements for police officers; (3) to conduct and encourage research designed to improve all aspects of law enforcement;[10] and (4) to remove the certification of police officers for certain disciplinary or criminal violations, effectively revoking their "licenses" to be a sworn officer.

In its assessment of the role of the states in criminal justice planning, in general, the National Advisory Commission on Criminal Justice Standards and Goals suggested that the State Planning Agencies (SPAs), which were created by the Omnibus Crime Control and Safe Streets Act of 1968 as the state-level organizations through which federal funds were funneled from the LEAA, bear a special responsibility for the formation of minimum statewide standards.[11] However, with the demise of LEAA in 1982, there has been a reduction in or total dismantling of large state planning agencies.

LOCAL POLITICAL FORCES

The special dimension of police politics varies from community to community, but law enforcement activities are governed for the most part by the dominant values of the local political culture. James Q. Wilson, in his now classic study of the police in eight communities, identified three distinctly different styles of law enforcement, all of which were reflective of the political culture of the communities they served: (1) the "watchman" style of law enforcement emphasizes maintenance of order and is found in economically declining cities with traditional political machines; (2) the "legalistic" style of law enforcement is found in cities with heterogeneous populations and reform-oriented, professional governments (law enforcement of both a reactive and proactive nature characterizes this style); and (3) in the homogeneous suburban communities, the "service" style of law enforcement is oriented toward the needs of citizens.[12] As a small town police chief once told a consultant, "We're rich as all get-out and not interested in consolidating with some larger department. We know who needs to get that traffic ticket and who just needs a quick reminder."

In Wilson's studies, these variations in the community political culture manifested themselves in a number of ways that subsequently affected both the qualitative and the quantitative enforcement action taken by the police. Significant enforcement variations emerged in the areas of vice, juvenile offenses, order

maintenance, and traffic enforcement. Numerous variations, linked to the community's political culture, also emerged in the police department's personnel entry standards, promotional policies, extent of specialization, and level of managerial skills. These, in turn, affected the overall operations of the department, which in turn impacted the citizens' perception and confidence in the police department.

There is an unfailing, consistent, and close relationship between the type of law enforcement a community has and its dominant political culture. This is not to suggest, however, that any community's political culture is unalterably fixed. In fact, the reform movements that have been a part of the American political scene throughout much of its history have corresponded with the emergence of new political cultures. Each new dominant political culture in time leaves its own unique mark on the unit of government within its sphere of control.

Strong Mayor

To some extent, the type of local government that a community has impacts the way police chiefs are selected, the freedom they enjoy in the performance of their status, and their **tenure**. For example, with a **strong mayor** form of government, the mayor is elected to office and serves as the chief executive of the city. The city council constitutes the chief legislative and policymaking body. The mayor nominates a candidate to serve as police chief, and sometimes, but not always, majority approval is needed from the city council. Once approved, the candidate assumes the position of police chief and serves at the discretion of the mayor (see Figure 4.2).

Ideally, the person the mayor selects as police chief should possess the full range of skills necessary to operate the police department. However, to a great extent, the kind of person selected to serve as police chief is determined by the mayor's professional qualifications, philosophy about the role of law enforcement, and political commitments. If the mayor is

FIGURE 4.2 ▶ New York City, which has a strong mayor form of government, recently elected William de Blasio who in turn appointed as his new police commissioner William J. Bratton. (Spencer Platt/Getty Images)

endowed with sound business or public administration skills and has a "good government" philosophy, then the chief of police will very likely be selected on the basis of professional abilities rather than on extraneous political factors. Unfortunately, on too many occasions in the past, this appointment has been a method of repaying political favors. A classical case of the misuse of this appointing authority was illustrated by the Wickersham Commission in 1931:

> A few years ago the newly elected mayor of Indianapolis was called upon to introduce his appointee as police chief to an assemblage of police chiefs during one of their conferences. In the course of his introductory remarks, the mayor said, "I know that my man is going to be a good chief because he has been my tailor for 20 years. He knows how to make good clothes; he ought to be a good chief."[13]

No big-city mayor would make the same choice today, but the choice will nevertheless be a reflection of the mayor's personal value system and abilities and the political environment of the community.

In the strong mayor form of local government, the tenure of the chief of police is often linked directly to the mayor, and the nature of the relationship is such that the chief is quite dependent on the mayor for support and guidance on budgetary matters, enforcement practices, and a multitude of other areas essential to the overall success of the police department. If there is mutual respect between the police chief and the mayor, a strong professional and political bond will be formed. If the reverse holds true, however, significant antagonisms are almost certain to emerge. There are too many situations to enumerate positively or negatively that can affect the working relationship between a mayor and a police chief. The important differences that do emerge are frequently those that evolve out of philosophical and ethical differences rather than questions of legality. These are differences that can occur in any form of government (see Figure 4.3).

City Manager

Every form of local government found in the United States has its supporters and detractors. The proponents of the city manager form claim that it provides the most conducive atmosphere in which professional law enforcement can operate and minimize

external interference. One of the reasons for this assessment is the balancing mechanisms developed over the years that are typically inherent in the city manager form of government: (1) the city manager is accountable to the elected members of the city council as a body rather than to any individual council member; (2) individual council members are prevented (by law or council rules) from giving administrative, operational, or policy direction to the city manager; (3) the council as a body may not give specific administrative direction to the city manager, who generally has exclusive executive authority over city employees; (4) the city manager, consistent with civil service statutes and subject to employee appeals, has full authority to hire, promote, and discipline city personnel; (5) the city manager has broad authority within state municipal financial statutes to manage the budget and to depart from line item appropriations to meet unanticipated needs; and (6) the council as a body hires the city manager and may dismiss the city manager at its discretion without stating its cause. The city manager model is significant because it has been clearly successful in the American local political milieu and because its separation of the political policymaking body and the independent chief executive is realistically defined.[14]

The **city manager**, more often than not, is a professional administrator who is recruited for certain skills and training and is appointed by the city council. A person with this background tends to make sincere efforts to select a competent individual to serve as police chief because the manager's professional reputation is tied inextricably to the effective management of the city departments.

It is significant that city managers have sought qualified police chiefs and have, in most instances, based their selection on the professional qualifications of the candidate rather than on political or other extraneous considerations that too often have governed appointments to this position in the past.[15] This does not mean that the city manager form of government removes the chief from local politics, but it does create more distance and insulation than the one-to-one political relationship commonly found in the strong mayor form of government (see Figure 4.4).

City Councils

The legally defined roles of a **city council** are fairly consistent throughout the United States; namely, it acts as the chief legislative and policymaking body. Through its ordinance power,

FIGURE 4.3 ▶ The strong mayor form of government. The mayor serves as the chief executive and appoints all department heads. The department heads serve at the pleasure of the mayor.

FIGURE 4.4 ► The city manager form of government. The city manager is appointed by the council (typically the majority), and the manager serves at the pleasure of the city council. The city manager in turn appoints all department heads, and they serve at the pleasure of the manager.

subject to constitutional and statutory provisions, including the city charter, the council carries out its legislative function. When within the council's authority, its enactments have the force of law and are binding on both administration and electorate. In addition to legislative and policymaking functions, the council, in common with most legislative bodies, holds the purse strings and exercises control over appropriations.[16] Thus, the immediate impact of a council's actions on the operation of a law enforcement agency is considerable.

The record of involvement by council members and other elected officials in police operations to the detriment of both the efficiency and the effectiveness of the police establishment is a well-established fact. One observer of this problem has noted:

> Local political leaders frequently promote more abuses of police power than they deter. In seeking favored treatment for a violator of the law or in exerting pressure for police assistance in the sale of tickets to a fund-raising dinner, the politician only encourages the type of behavior he/she is supposed to prevent. Although such political interference into police work is not as extensive as it once was, it still exists.[17]

The record of involvement by council members and other elected officials in police operations to the detriment of both the efficiency and the effectiveness of the police establishment is historically accurate. One observer of this problem described this issue in the following way:

> A few local political leaders episodically engage in abuses of police power instead of deterring such behavior, e.g., they ask to have traffic tickets given to their friends or family members voided or reduced to warnings. Although such unhealthy political interference in police work is no longer pervasive, some still exists.[18]

The removal of negative politics has substantially been achieved, but eliminating positive politics has not, nor should it be because it is the process in our system of government by which people hope to gain and maintain influence over governmental policy and decision making. It remains true in many police departments even today that promotions to senior leadership positions are sometimes influenced by political figures. In a handful of states with which the authors are familiar, until roughly the early to mid-1960s, being hired by the state patrol required the endorsement of the county chairperson of the political party in power for the county in which the applicant resided. Similar arrangements existed during that time period in many small and large cities. While James Ahern was Chief of Police in New Haven, Connecticut (1968–1970), he had to deal with internal and external forces as he moved to gain control over personnel matters in his department:

> New Haven Mayor Dick Lee (1917–2003) possessed a substantial national reputation for championing urban renewal and low cost public housing. On occasion, he intervened in police promotions, but it was to further the advancement of officers who were deemed to have two qualities in abundance: honesty and effectiveness. Although it reduced his own power, Mayor Lee supported Chief Ahern's reforms, who quickly took a series of actions.

> The day after he became Chief, Ahern closed the door that led from the police department to Mayor Lee's Office and re-issued an existing order which theretofore was most often not followed: No officer could visit the Mayor without the Chief's prior approval. This action communicated that if Ahern wouldn't let the Mayor who had selected him effect personnel matters, then neither would he allow other powerful figures to do so.

> Ahern also established the principle that if approached by political figures or other power brokers seeking that Ahern promote an officer or transfer the officer to easy duties that

the officer for whom the favor was sought would be barred permanently from them. Having a "hook" or "rabbi" intervene for them was so ingrained in officers that Ahern concluded that many couldn't imagine another way of getting ahead. However, Ahern successfully halted interventions by power brokers.[19]

To suggest that the experience of New Haven is typical of most communities would be an inaccurate generalization, but there is little doubt that the council's fiscal control over the police department's budget and its legislative powers make it a political force that is never taken lightly by chiefs of police. As a matter of fact, most police chiefs will go to great lengths to maintain the goodwill and support of their council members.

POLITICS AND THE POLICE CHIEF

A study conducted in California showed that the average tenure of a police chief in that state was less than 3 years before the chief was fired or resigned.[20] Even though the tenure of police chiefs across the nation has somewhat improved since this study was conducted, the national average is still only about 5 years[21] with most chiefs still having no contract or agreement. Of course, the reasons for police chiefs leaving their positions are numerous, including the opportunity to move to another (often larger) police department with better pay and improved benefits, politics, health issues, stress, personal issues, retirement, and, of course, dismissal. Much has been written about the need for some type of protection for police chiefs against the arbitrary and unjustified removal from office by an elected or political officeholder.[22] In some states, such as Illinois, statutory protections have been implemented to protect police chiefs against such actions. Special boards or commissions have been created for the sole purpose of establishing recruitment, selection, and retention policies for chiefs of police. In Illinois, the law prohibits the removal or discharge of a member of the fire or police department (including the chief) without cause; the individual must also be given written charges and an opportunity to be heard in his or her defense. While this is a state mandate, these protections are available only when there is no local ordinance prescribing a different procedure. If such an ordinance exists, the statute requires the municipal appointing authority to file the reasons for the chief's removal but does not require a showing of cause or a hearing.

New Hampshire affords significant protection to police chiefs. It requires written notice of the basis for the proposed termination, a hearing on the charges, and a finding of cause before the dismissal can be effected. Minnesota, on the other hand, provides no mandatory protections for police chiefs but does require they be included in any civil service system adopted by a municipality.

A few other states have attempted to provide police chiefs with at least some job security whenever they have been promoted from within the ranks of the police department. Both Illinois and Ohio allow chiefs who resign or who are removed from their positions to return to the ranks they held within their departments before being appointed chiefs. Most states, however, offer very little protection. Chiefs across the country are therefore forced to look for job protections in local civil service codes, local municipal ordinances, and such individual employment contracts as they are able to negotiate.[23]

However, for the most part, the ability to endure the realities of the position of chief of police requires a unique blend of talent, skill, and knowledge that is often not "guaranteed" in statute or law. The reality is that few protections exist for persons occupying the highest position of a police agency except for those developed in the person themselves. That is to say, the characteristics and qualities of excellent management and leadership imbued in the person are generally the reasons a chief remains in office.

TENURE AND CONTRACTS FOR POLICE CHIEFS

Police chiefs who lack protection from arbitrary and unjustified termination cannot objectively and independently fulfill their responsibilities. They will also likely be less willing to implement innovative programs that are controversial. This is so because a failure could jeopardize their position.

The conservative nature of many police chiefs and their risk-aversive tendencies are not surprising when one considers where police chiefs come from. Most top police executives today, as in the past, reach their position as police chief in the twilight of their policing careers. Charles Gain, former chief of the Oakland, California, Police Department, argued that police chiefs in this twilight period tend to resist organizational change because they fear the loss of the position for which they have so long waited, and as they are in the final stages of their career, they engage in a "holding action."[24] Gain further commented that, when chiefs make it to the top, they are not going to jeopardize their position by setting new goals and moving ahead.[25]

Researchers of the Police Executive Development Project at Pennsylvania State University found that top police executives showed greater devotion to their own job security than for the citizens they served. Their findings also indicated that top police executives showed greater submission to authority than did the general public. This subservient attitude is formed as a result of working in a rigid organizational structure that demands and rewards obedience to authority.[26] The results of the project indicated that the average police executive failed to possess initiative, self-reliance, and confidence because of a lifelong habit of submission and social conformity. The study concluded that these findings correlate to some extent with the suggestion that police chiefs tend to treat their job as a sinecure and are incapable of innovation at this late stage in their police careers.[27] Without some form of contract protection, it is difficult to expect any police chief to jeopardize his or her job by implementing a vision or a program that has any chance of failure.

POLITICS AND THE COUNTY SHERIFF

There are approximately 3,100 county sheriff's departments in the United States.[28] The county sheriff's department is unique among American law enforcement agencies in terms of both its role and its legal status.[29] However, in discussions about police administration, sheriff's departments have too often been overlooked. Historically, the tasks and roles of sheriff's departments and police departments have been fundamentally different.[30] Sheriff's law enforcement functions have often been relegated to jurisdictions of sparse populations that cannot support municipal police agencies. **Sheriffs** are typically elected, as opposed to their appointed counterpart police chiefs. In addition, sheriffs routinely have a custodial role in the detention of prisoners not common to municipal police functions. This all changed somewhat after World War II, when populations expanded into rural areas that eventually became the suburbs. This eliminated part of the distinction between sheriffs and chiefs when big-city problems came to these areas.[31]

The 20th century brought a marked decline in the political strength of sheriff's departments in many parts of the country. As law enforcement became more abundant, a curious academic neglect of the office of the sheriff resulted in serious breaks of understanding regarding the role of sheriff in the criminal justice system. The early 20th century literature about policing and law enforcement analyzed the office as a jailer, court bailiff, process server, and county tax collector. However little, if any, emphasis was placed on the office in police literature, and if there was reference to the position, it was generally unfavorable. In 1925, Bruce Smith's book *The State Police* referred to the sheriff's office as a "dying medieval" throwback. A later book by the same author, *Rural Crime Control,* alluded to county government in general as the "dark continent of American politics." A 1935 book by A. E. Parker and A. Vollmer, *Crime and the State Police,* stated that the sheriff was an outdated law enforcement institution.[32]

Patterns of academic neglect continued after mid-century, even as the nation's police interest was escalating. O. W. Wilson neglected to mention sheriffs in his 1950 book *Police Administration.* R. E. Clift neglected reference to the position in the 1956 edition of *A Guide to Modern Police Thinking* but did make small reference to the office in his third edition in 1970. George Felkenes devoted considerable discussion to the decrease and scope of the office in an inverse relationship with urbanization in his 1973 *The Criminal Justice System: Its Functions and Personnel.* He further observed that sheriffs were banished to only four modes of operation: (1) contract law enforcement for small or rural communities, (2) supervision of metropolitan police agencies along the East Coast only, (3) civil process functions, and (4) custodial functions as prescribed by law.[33] Some law enforcement journals have noted that the sheriff's law enforcement functions lacked the professional standards of larger police departments.

A strong criticism of the position came from Brammer and Hurley, who wrote *A Study of the Office of Sheriff in the United States Southern Region* in 1968.[34] After they alluded to the sheriff as often the most important, if not the sole, law enforcement agency in many unincorporated areas of the South, they added:

> The elected nature of the office has been cause for the most serious indictments of the office. Allegations regarding a sheriff being required to participate in partisan politics in order to hold his office are the most prevalent criticism. Yet in reality, all law enforcement executives are politicians in one form or another. Some may refute this assertion, but only out of misguided notions that politicians are evil or that an administrator cannot be a politician and a professional manager at the same time. Realistically, a politician is nothing more than a person accountable to the public for decisions made in the performance of duty. Certainly a police chief or police commissioner could fall into this category as easily as a sheriff.[35]

Unique Legal Status of Sheriffs

The county sheriff's legal status is unique in two ways. First, in 37 states, it is specified by the state constitution. As a result, major changes in the office of sheriff require a constitutional amendment which is not always easily accomplished.

In terms of size, with some notable exceptions such as the Los Angeles County Sheriff's Department (see Figure 4.5), most sheriff's departments are small. Nearly two-thirds of them employ fewer than 25 sworn officers, and a third employ fewer than 10. About half serve a population of less than 25,000.[36]

As elected officials, sheriffs are important political figures. In many rural areas, the sheriff is the most powerful political force in the county. As a result, sheriffs are far more independent than appointed law enforcement executives because, as discussed earlier, police chiefs can be removed by the mayors or city managers who appoint them. However, this is not to suggest that because sheriffs enjoy greater independence than police chiefs they are not subject to powerful political forces within their communities. Indeed, because the office is usually an elected position, there is considerable media scrutiny and state accountability. Individuals seeking the position of sheriff must run for public office the same as any other public official. In fact, the office of sheriff is the only local law enforcement position recognized and decreed by many state constitutions, a holdover from the days when local sheriffs were the only law of the land.

The extent to which politics, in the negative sense, enters into the sheriff's race and subsequently into the operations of the sheriff's department varies radically from community to community and even among sheriff's races. For example, in states in which sheriffs—because they are constitutional officers—are not bound by normal purchasing restrictions, some potential for abuse exists. If a candidate running for the office of sheriff has accepted a large donation from a certain business, there would likely be an expectation of reciprocity in return for such "support." This could result in purchases of cars from

FIGURE 4.5 ▶ Recent graduates of the Los Angeles County Sheriff's Department police academy. This organization is one of the largest of its kind in the United States with nearly 18,000 sworn and professional staff. (Courtesy of Los Angeles County Sheriff's Department)

Quick Facts: Length of Terms the Sheriffs Will Serve Vary

In 43 states, sheriffs are elected to 4-year terms. In two states, Arkansas and New Hampshire, their terms are 2 years in length. In New Jersey, a sheriff's term is 3 years in length and in Massachusetts it is 6 years in length. Alaska has no county government; thus they do not have any Sheriff's Offices. In Connecticut, sheriffs have been replaced with a State Marshall system, and in Hawaii, there are no sheriffs but deputy sheriffs serve in the Sheriff's Division of the Hawaii Department of Public Safety.[37]

"loyal" car dealers, food for jail inmates from certain distributors, uniforms from a specific uniform company, and so forth. However, a sheriff who becomes too partisan in his or her purchasing risks disappointing other vendors. As such, a marshaling of support for a different candidate in the next election usually occurs. The "real politics" of such a situation is that, while more purchases will be made from key supporting organizations, the incumbent must "spread around" enough purchasing to appease other vendors.

Then, too, there are potentials in any political environment for dirty campaigns, and sheriff's races are no exception. For example, several years ago, an incumbent sheriff who realized he might not be reelected because of strong opposition from a highly qualified opponent contacted one of his vice squad officers to see if he could create a situation that would be embarrassing to his opponent. The vice squad officer made contact with a young and exceptionally attractive prostitute, who also served as his informant. He asked her to approach the man running against the incumbent sheriff at his place of business and try to entice him into joining her in a nearby hotel to have sex. The preselected hotel room had been set up with audiovisual equipment, so that the entire event could be recorded. Once the planned act was consummated and recorded, the videotape would be sent to the candidate's wife, along with copies to his minister and other key people in his life. It was felt that such a tape in the hands of these people would be sufficiently disruptive to the candidate's personal life to make him ineffectual as a campaigner. The prostitute, as instructed, did go to the business of the candidate and attempted to entice him to join her. The candidate, who was a politically astute individual, saw through this transparent farce and told the woman to leave his business. However, as soon as she left, he very discreetly followed her for a couple of blocks and saw her getting into an unmarked sheriff's department vehicle, which was being driven by the vice squad officer, whom he recognized. When the election was held, the incumbent sheriff lost. Since this was only one of many "dirty tricks" attempted by a number of employees of the sheriff's department, the newly elected sheriff immediately "cleaned house" and fired everyone who he could prove (or suspected) was involved in the efforts to embarrass him.

Inside the sheriff's department, politics can also be a decisive factor in the operational effectiveness of the organization. It is no accident that increased enforcement activity by the local sheriff's department usually precedes an election. The activity usually focuses on highly visible suspects or signs of disorder. Characteristic events include the roundup of local prostitutes, the crackdown on street corner vagrants, and the closing of "X-rated" video stores, all of which just happen to ensure considerable positive media attention. The interpretation is obvious—that the incumbent sheriff is "tough" on crime. Sheriffs serving in smaller counties may even instruct their deputies to decrease the number of traffic citations that are given, except for the most serious violations such as DUI and reckless driving, and to start issuing more warning traffic citations, especially to those motorists who live in the county. This, of course, is based upon the assumption that unhappy citizens could translate this dissatisfaction in a vote against the incumbent sheriff.

One of the most important political processes that impact the internal organization is the absence of local or state civil service boards. In many states, employees of the county sheriff's department serve at the pleasure of the current sheriff. Therefore, if the incumbent sheriff either decides not to run for office or is defeated in the next election, the newly elected sheriff may decide to fire a high percentage of the employees currently working at the sheriff's department. However, if wholesale dismissals do occur, this will result in a lack of continuity in the skill level of employees and affect the quality of service being delivered to the public. It also creates enormous job insecurity and provides a mechanism whereby unqualified persons may be elected to one of the highest positions of law enforcement in the community. Thus, the very nature of the electoral process and the enormous power inherent in the office can foster an environment in which politics prevails.

STATE PROSECUTOR

The **prosecutor**, also called the state's attorney, district attorney, or commonwealth attorney, is the chief law enforcement officer under the statutes of some states, but in most states, it is the sheriff. However, despite this designation, the state prosecutor does not have overall responsibility for the supervision of the police.[38] Even so, the prosecutor's enforcement policies, procedures for review of all arrests before their presentation in court, and overall supervision of the cases prepared by the police do have an observable effect on police practices and enforcement policies. The initial contact of police officers with prosecutors occurs when the former brings a complaint to be charged. This encounter may be critical because it is an important point for making decisions about the disposition of the case and whether the complaint will be dismissed or reduced to a lesser offense. This discretionary power given to the prosecuting attorney has tremendous influence on the ways and the extent to which certain laws are enforced or ignored. Police chiefs who perceive that the prosecutor consistently reduces or fails to vigorously enforce certain types of violations may very likely divert their enforcement efforts and resources elsewhere.

Then again, some chiefs may decide to "go public" and try to mobilize community support for enforcing the ignored violations. However, few police chiefs take this course of action because it could result in a serious deterioration in the working relationship with the local prosecutor, a situation most would prefer to avoid.

From the prosecutor's perspective, a cordial relationship with the police is also a desired condition. This is not, however, always possible. For example, the prosecutor cannot ignore suspicions of corruption or other illegal activity by local police officers. When prosecutor-led investigations become public knowledge or lead to indictments, a prosecutor's rapport with the police can be severely strained and may require sustained effort to recultivate. The resulting tension may become high if officers believe that the prosecutor is "sticking it to the police department by dragging the thing out," or by not allowing affected officers to plea bargain to lesser charges, or if the prosecutor is suspected of furthering his or her career at the officers' expense.

THE JUDICIARY

Once the police have made an arrest and brought the arrestee before a judge, from pretrial release onward the case is within the domain of the **judiciary**. In its assessment of the relationships of the judiciary and the police, one government report noted that trial judges have acted as chief administrative officers of the criminal justice system, using their power to dismiss cases as a method of controlling the use of the criminal process. However, except in those rulings involving the admissibility of evidence, this has been done largely on an informal basis and has tended to be haphazard, often reflecting primarily the personal values of the individual trial judge.[39]

In contrast, the function of trial judges in excluding evidence that they determine has been obtained illegally places them very explicitly in the role of controlling police practices. Trial judges have not viewed this role as making them responsible for developing appropriate police practices. However, many trial judges, when asked to explain their decisions, indicate that they have no more responsibility for explaining decisions to police than they have to private litigants.[40]

Occasionally, judges grant motions to suppress evidence to dismiss cases they feel should not be prosecuted because the violation is too minor or for some other reason. The use of a motion to suppress evidence in this manner confuses the standards that are supposed to guide the police and has a disturbing, if not demoralizing, effect on them.[41]

If judges consistently interject their personal biases into the judicial process and make it very clear to the police they will dismiss certain categories of violations, the police may discontinue enforcing that law.

For example, one of the co-authors of this book had previously been a motorcycle officer whose primary functions were traffic law enforcement and accident investigation. It became apparent during the course of investigating traffic accidents that one of the major causes of rear-end collisions was drivers who were following too close. However, it was the practice of his agency not to issue traffic citations for following too close unless an accident had occurred. In an effort to be proactive, he decided to start issuing traffic citations to motorists who were clearly following too close but to do so before accidents actually occurred. At the end of his shift, like he routinely did, he submitted his traffic citations for the following too close violations to his supervisor, who wanted to know where the accident reports were. He explained that there were no traffic accidents and that this was his effort to be proactive and prevent rear-end collisions from occurring by enforcing the traffic violations against following too close before the accidents occurred. The sergeant just smiled and accepted the tickets without saying a word. When the court date came to appear before the judge, along with the unhappy citizens who had received the traffic citations, he started to testify about the following too close violations he had witnessed and the rationale for issuing the tickets. When the judge realized that the traffic citations were issued without any accidents having occurred, he summarily dismissed all of the cases. The judge never told him to stop writing traffic citations for this particular traffic violation, but suffice it to say, no more traffic citations were written for following too close unless there were rear-end collisions.

CITIZEN OVERSIGHT OF THE POLICE

Since the 1960s, civil rights groups have argued that police departments fail to investigate citizen complaints thoroughly or fairly. As an alternative, they have demanded the creation of **citizen oversight** of the police. Citizen oversight is defined as a process by which people who are not sworn officers are involved in some way in the review of citizen complaints against police officers. Citizen oversight rests on the assumption that because of the police subculture, police officers cannot objectively investigate complaints against fellow officers,[42] and therefore, citizen oversight has grown tremendously in the last 30 years.

Quick Facts: Current Status of Police Oversight

In almost all big cities, there is now some form of oversight agency. The most recent report by the National Association of Civilian Oversight of Law Enforcement (NACOLE) reports that over 100 law enforcement agencies have reported they have some form of oversight.[43]

TYPES OF CITIZEN OVERSIGHT SYSTEMS

There is no single model of citizen oversight. However, most procedures have features that fall into one of four types of oversight systems:

- Type 1: *Citizens investigate allegations* of misconduct and *recommend findings* to the chief or sheriff.
- Type 2: Police officers investigate allegations and develop findings; *citizens review and recommend* that the chief or sheriff approve or reject their findings.
- Type 3: Complainants may *appeal findings* established by the police or sheriff's department *to citizens*, who review them and then recommend their own findings to the chief or sheriff.
- Type 4: An auditor *investigates the process* by which the police or sheriff's department accepts and investigates the complaints and reports on the thoroughness and fairness of the process to the department and the public.

Advantages and Drawbacks of Citizen Oversight

Each type of system has advantages and drawbacks. For example, oversight systems that involve investigating citizen complaints (Type 1) can help reassure the public that investigations of citizen complaints are thorough and fair. However, hiring professional investigators can be expensive, and the investigation models typically have no mechanism for soliciting the public's general concerns about police conduct.

Concerns Expressed by Law Enforcement and Unions

It is important to note that many police and sheriffs' departments are not pleased with trends involving citizen oversight of their agencies and have expressed some concerns (see Table 4.1). These negative reactions also apply to some union leaders. One spokesman for a local police association even predicted strong negative consequences from rank and file officers should a city decide to create an oversight board.

PUBLIC INTEREST ORGANIZATIONS

Several years ago, the local chapter of the American Civil Liberties Union (ACLU) in Oakland, California, had volunteers systematically call different units of the Oakland Police Department and ask how to file a citizen complaint. The callers found that few Oakland officers handling their calls gave out correct information. Many, apparently, were simply uninformed about the department's complaint process. Some others may have deliberately not given out the right information. The ACLU

Quick Facts: St. Louis Police Threaten to Quit or Slowdown if Civilian Oversight Passes

A bill to create a seven-member civilian oversight board for the St. Louis, Missouri Police Department, is looking like a sure bet to pass. The majority of the Board of Aldermen and even Mayor Francis are attaching their names to it. Jeff Roorda, a spokesperson for the St. Louis Police Officers' Association announced that St. Louis police officers will quit the department or do only the bare minimum on patrol if the city creates the proposed civilian oversight board.[44]

TABLE 4.1 CONCERNS MANY POLICE AND SHERIFF'S DEPARTMENTS—AND UNION LEADERS—EXPRESS ABOUT CITIZEN OVERSIGHT—AND POSSIBLE RESPONSES

Assertion: Citizens Should Not Interfere in Police Work	
Concerns	**Responses**
• The chief must be held accountable for discipline to prevent misconduct.	• Most oversight bodies are only advisory,
• Internal affairs already does a good job.	• Even when the department already imposes appropriate discipline without citizen review, an oversight procedure can reassure skeptical citizens that the agency is doing its job in this respect.
	• The next chief or sheriff may not be as conscientious about ensuring that the department investigates complaints fairly and thoroughly.

Assertion: Citizens Do Not Understand Police Work	
Concerns	**Responses**
• Oversight staff lack experience in police work.	• Board members typically have pertinent materials available for review, and ranking officers are usually present during hearings to explain department procedures.
	• Oversight administators need to describe the often extensive training they and their staff receive.
	• Citizen review is just that—*citizens* reviewing police behavior as private citizens.
• Only physicians review doctors, and only attorneys review lawyers.	• Doctors and lawyers have been criticized for doing a poor job of monitoring *their* colleagues' behavior.

Assertion: The Process Is Unfair	
Concerns	**Responses**
• Oversight staff may have an "agenda"—they are biased against the police.	• Oversight staff need to inform the department when they decide in officers' favor.
	• Oversight staff and police need to meet to iron out misconceptions and conflict.
• Not sustained findings remain in officers' files.	• Indecisive findings are unfair to both parties and should therefore be reduced in favor of unfounded, exonerated, or sustained findings.
• Adding allegations unrelated to the citizens' complaint is unfair.	• Internal affairs units themselves add allegations in some departments.
• Some citizens use the system to prepare for civil suits.	• Board findings can sometimes help officers and departments defend against civil suits.

Source: Citizen Review of Police: Approaches and Implementation, NIJ Issues and Practices, U.S. Department of Justice, Washington, DC, March 2001, p. 110.

report blasting the Oakland Police Department for this failure was only one in a long series of investigations and reports on police misconduct by that organization.

The ACLU is a private, nonprofit **public interest organization**. Private groups play an important role in police accountability. For the most part, they have been involved in attacking police misconduct. The National Association for the Advancement of Colored People (NAACP) has a long record of fighting police use of excessive force against African-Americans. The ACLU was responsible for some of the most important Supreme Court cases involving the police. For example, ACLU briefs were the basis for the Court's decisions in the landmark *Mapp* and *Miranda* cases discussed earlier in this chapter. The ACLU has been the leading advocate of citizen review of the police in New York City, Los Angeles, and many other cities. At the same time, the ACLU has defended the rights of police officers in cases involving, for example, grooming standards and department investigations of alleged police misconduct. The ACLU even published a handbook on *The Rights of Police Officers*.[45]

CHAMBERS OF COMMERCE AND SERVICE CLUBS

Local chambers of commerce and service clubs typically are supportive of efforts that lead toward efficient and clean government. Although such groups are characterized as being apolitical, they do exercise considerable influence. Their support for improving the quality of law enforcement in the community is frequently heard in the chambers of city hall and is demonstrated through various community projects intended to assist local law enforcement. Attuned police chiefs realize the benefit to be gained from the support of such groups, encourage personnel to become active members in these clubs, and frequently join one or two themselves. Support from these groups is not surprising when one considers that many are composed of men and women who are well educated and deeply involved in many aspects of community leadership. Such groups often have mobilized behind a police chief to get much-needed budget increases for salaries, additional personnel, and equipment.

CHURCHES

The religious leaders and congregations of the churches in a community represent one of the most potentially powerful political pressure groups in the community. Their influence can, and frequently does, extend into the voting booth, which assures a high degree of responsiveness from local elected officials. Church leaders and their congregations almost always find an open door and a receptive ear at the office of their local police chief when they present their concerns. The problems that are frequently of greatest concern to such groups are vice-related, such as prostitution, massage parlors, X-rated theaters, and adult bookstores. It is true that individual communities impose different standards and have varying levels of tolerance, but if the church leaders of a community mobilize and call on their police chief to eradicate or reduce what they perceive to be a serious problem, there is a high probability that they will receive some positive response. And if the police chief suggests that the police department cannot cope realistically with the problem because of limited personnel and resources, those church groups will likely begin applying pressure on the city officials to give the police chief the needed resources. Thus, the religious leaders of the community can be powerful allies of the police chief in certain types of enforcement efforts. On the other hand, this pressure group may force the chief to redirect resources away from areas that may have a higher priority.

NEWS MEDIA

It is the responsibility of the police department, and especially its top leadership, to establish and maintain a cordial association with all media representatives.[46] Both the electronic and print news media can be powerful friends or devastating antagonists of a local police department and, to a great extent, this is determined by the attitudes, policies, and working relationships among editors, news directors, and the police chief. When friction does occur between the police and the news media, as it invariably does in every community, it frequently emanates from the events surrounding a major crime or an unusual occurrence.

Often in the case of major crimes or incidents, police departments do not want to release information that will jeopardize the safety of the public or its officers, impair the right of a suspect to a fair and impartial trial, or impede the progress of an investigation. On the other hand, the news media have a different orientation and duty: to inform the public. Although their goals are often compatible, the police and the news media can sometimes disagree irreconcilably. The following case illustrates this point.

One of the authors was involved in the investigation of the murders committed by Theodore Robert (Ted) Bundy in Tallahassee, Florida, and learned firsthand how differences in philosophy can play out to the detriment of a criminal investigation and cause conflict between the media and law enforcement. The facts are as follows:

At approximately 2 a.m. on a Sunday morning, Bundy entered an unlocked door to the Chi Omega sorority house, located near the campus of Florida State University. Prior to entering, he had armed himself with a tree limb from a pile of firewood that was in close proximity to the sorority house. After entering the sorority house, he went to the second floor, which was the bedroom area. In the first room, he encountered a lone woman was asleep in her bed. He entered the room and clubbed her with the tree limb, rendering her immediately unconscious. He then strangled her with the pantyhose he had brought to the scene with him. He left her room and went to a second room and proceeded to batter a second sleeping woman with the tree limb. Like the previous victim, he rendered her unconscious and then proceeded to strangle her manually. He also bit off the nipple of her right breast, bit her twice on the left buttocks, and sodomized her with a hairspray bottle. He left her room, went down the hall and entered a third room where he encountered two more sleeping women and proceeded to batter each of them. Neither of them was killed. Still armed with the tree limb, he started walking down the flight of stairs leading to the front door of the sorority house when he was observed by one of the sorority women returning from a date. She had no knowledge at that time that anything had occurred and the presence of a man in the sorority house, even at that time of the morning, was not that unusual. Bundy then left the premises, but shortly after leaving, one of the injured women started screaming for help and at that point the police and medical personnel were called.

The investigation involved three different law enforcement agencies: the local sheriff's office, the municipal police department, and the campus police. At the end of the first day, it was agreed that all 35 criminal investigators who had worked independently of each other on the case would meet at the municipal police department headquarters to discuss facts they had gathered. It was made clear to all those present that highly specific information such as the name of the only eyewitness and the ways in which the victims were killed and assaulted should not be released to the media because this information would jeopardize the safety of the eyewitness, who said she would be able to identify the man if she ever saw him again. It could also result in the possible destruction of physical evidence by the suspect or perhaps encourage him to flee the area. In spite of this admonition, the following day the local newspaper printed every detail of the crime, including the name of the young woman who had observed the suspect leaving the Chi Omega sorority house. Once she read the headlines, which identified her by name and location, she packed her bags and went home. Her reaction was perfectly understandable considering her personal safety concerns. The sheriff who was heading this investigation was very upset by the release of this information, which very likely had been provided to the newspaper by one or more of the investigators at the meeting the day before. He went to the local newspaper to talk to the editor to find out why it was necessary to divulge all of this highly specific information, which endangered the victim's life, and also raising the possibility the suspect might now destroy important physical evidence. The editor's comment was that the public had the right to know all of the facts available on the case and he would continue to publish any information provided from any source as long as it was reliable.

Also, there is little question, from a purely business perspective, that the more sensational and salacious the information printed about the crime, the more papers that would be sold. An old axiom in the media is "If it bleeds it leads" and this is true for both the print and electronic media. Bundy was eventually arrested, convicted, sentenced to death, and subsequently executed in the electric chair. Prior to his death he confessed to murdering 35 young women in three states.

Other circumstances for potential tension or conflict in police–news media relationships include "off-the-record" police information appearing in the news media, the occasional claim by a police administrator that he or she was misquoted, and the involvement of press at the scenes of bank robberies, gangland killings, and hostage situations or in the sensitive investigations of kidnapings and drug rings.

From a legal standpoint, the police may release relevant information about a defendant if it is not prejudicial to the defendant's right to a fair trial. Many police departments have policies that protect the defendant's rights, but those policies may obstruct the needs of reporters to gather images and information for the public.

ALLEGED POLICE MISCONDUCT IN BALTIMORE, MARYLAND, AND THE POLITICAL FALLOUT

On April 12, 2015, a 25-year-old African-American male, Freddie Gray was arrested by Baltimore police officers after he ran from them. As a result of a fatal spinal cord injury he received while in police custody, he died. Shortly after his funeral rioting broke out in the City of Baltimore. The following are the facts of the case as set forth by the District Court of Maryland, Baltimore City.[47]

Statement of the Charges

On April 12, 2015, between 8:45 and 9:15 a.m., near the corner of North Avenue and Mount Street, Lieutenant Brian Rice of the Baltimore Police Department (BPD), while on bike patrol with Officers Garrett Miller and Edward Nero, made eye contact with Mr. Freddie Carlos Gray, Jr. (DOB 8-16-1989). Having made eye contact, Mr. Gray subsequently ran from Lt. Rice. Lt. Rice then dispatched over a departmental radio that he was involved in a foot pursuit, at which time bike patrol Officers Miller and Nero also began to pursue Mr. Gray. Having come in contact with the pursuing officers, Mr. Gray surrendered to Officers Miller and Nero in the vicinity of the 1700 block of Presbury Street. Officers Miller and Nero handcuffed Mr. Gray's arms behind his back and moved him to a location a few feet away from his surrendering location. He was then placed in a prone position. It was at this time that Mr. Gray indicated that he could not breathe and requested an inhaler to no avail. Officers Miller and Nero then placed Mr. Gray in a seated position and subsequently found a knife clipped to the inside of his pants pocket. The blade of the knife was folded into the handle. The knife was not a switchblade knife and is lawful under Maryland law. Those officers subsequently removed the knife and placed it on the sidewalk. Mr. Gray was then placed back down on his stomach at which time Mr. Gray began to flail his legs and scream as Officer Miller placed Mr. Gray in a restraining technique known as a "leg lace" while Officer Nero physically held him down against his will until a BPD wagon arrived to transport Mr. Gray. Lt. Rice, Officer Miller, and Officer Nero failed to establish probable cause for Mr. Gray's arrest as no crime had been committed by Mr. Gray. Accordingly, Lt. Rice, Officer Miller, and Officer Nero illegally arrested Mr. Gray. Upon arrival of the transport wagon, driven by Officer Casear Goodson Jr., Lt. Rice, Officer Nero, and Officer Miller loaded Mr. Gray into the wagon and at no point was he secured by a seat belt while in the wagon, contrary to BPD General Order. Lt. Rice then directed the BPD wagon to stop at Baker Street. At Baker Street, Lt. Rice, Officer Nero, and Officer Miller removed Mr. Gray from the wagon, placed flex cuffs on his wrists, placed leg shackles on his ankles, and completed required paperwork. Officer Miller, Officer Nero, and Lt. Rice then loaded Mr. Gray back into the wagon, placing him on his stomach, head first onto the floor of the wagon. Once again, Mr. Gray was not secured by a seat belt in the wagon, contrary to BPD General Order. Lt. Rice then directed Officer Goodson to transport Mr. Gray to the Central Booking and Intake Facility. Following transport from Baker Street, Mr. Gray suffered a severe and critical neck injury as a result of being handcuffed, shackled by his feet, and unrestrained inside the BPD wagon. From Baker Street, Officer Goodson proceeded to the vicinity of Mosher Street and Fremont Avenue, where he subsequently parked the wagon and proceeded to the back of the wagon in order to observe Mr. Gray. Despite stopping for the purpose of checking on Mr. Gray's condition, at no point did he seek, nor did he render, any medical assistance for Mr. Gray. Officer Goodson returned to his driver's seat and proceeded toward the Central Booking and Intake Facility, with Mr. Gray still unsecured by a seat belt, contrary to BPD General Order.

Several blocks later, Officer Goodson called into dispatch that he needed to check on the status of this prisoner and requested additional units at Dolphin Street and Druid Hill Avenue. Officer William Porter arrived on the scene near Dolphin Street and Druid Hill Avenue. Both Officer Goodson and Officer Porter proceeded to the back of the wagon to check on the status of Mr. Gray's condition. Mr. Gray requested "help" and indicated that he could not breathe. Officer Porter asked Mr. Gray if he needed a medic, at which time, Mr. Gray indicated at least twice that he was in need of a medic. Officer Porter then physically assisted Mr. Gray from the floor of the van to the bench. However, despite Mr. Gray's appeal for a medic, both officers assessed Mr. Gray's condition and at no point did either of them restrain Mr. Gray, per BPD General Order, nor did they render or request medical assistance. While discussing the transportation of Mr. Gray for medical attention, a request for additional units was made for an arrest at 1600 W. North Avenue. Officer Porter left the vicinity of Dolphin Street and Druid Hill Avenue to assist in the arrest of another prisoner at North Avenue. Despite Mr. Gray's obvious and

recognized need for medical assistance, Officer Goodson, in a grossly negligent manner, chose to respond to the 1600 block of W. North Avenue, with Mr. Gray still unsecured by a seat belt in the wagon, without rendering to or summoning medical assistance for Mr. Gray.

Officer Goodson arrived at North Avenue to transport the individual arrested at the location of North and Pennsylvania Avenues, at which time he was again met by Officers Nero, Miller, Porter, and Lt. Rice. Once the wagon arrived, Officer Goodson walked to the back of the wagon and again opened the doors to the wagon to make observations of Mr. Gray. Sgt. Alice White, Officer Porter, and Officer Goodson observed Mr. Gray unresponsive on the floor of the wagon. Sgt. White, who was responsible for investigating two citizen complaints pertaining to Mr. Gray's illegal arrest, spoke to the back of Mr. Gray's head. When he did not respond, she did nothing further despite the fact that she was advised that he needed a medic. She made no effort to look, assess, or determine his condition. Despite Mr. Gray's seriously deteriorating medical condition, no medical assistance was rendered to or summoned for Mr. Gray at that time by any officer.

After completing the North Avenue arrest and loading the additional prisoner into the opposite side of the wagon containing Mr. Gray, Officer Goodson then proceeded to the Western District Police Station, where contrary to the BPD General Order, he again failed to restrain Mr. Gray in the wagon for at least the fifth time.

At the Western District Police Station, the defendant arrested at North Avenue was unloaded, escorted, and secured inside of the police station prior to attending to Mr. Gray. By the time Officer Zachary Novak, Sgt. White, and an unknown officer attempted to remove Mr. Gray from the wagon, Mr. Gray was no longer breathing at all. A medic was finally called to the scene, where upon arrival the medic determined that Mr. Gray was now in cardiac arrest and was critically and severely injured.

Mr. Gray was rushed to the University of Maryland Shock Treatment Unit, where he underwent surgery. On April 19, 2015, Mr. Gray succumbed to his injuries and was pronounced dead. The manner of death, deemed a homicide by the Maryland State Medical Examiner, is believed to be the result of a fatal injury that occurred while Mr. Gray was unrestrained by a seat belt in the custody of the BPD wagon. All events occurred in Baltimore City, Maryland.

The Rioting Starts

On April 27, 2015, the funeral services were held for Freddie Gray. That same afternoon rioting started in the same part of Baltimore where he had been arrested. The riots resulted in extensive burning and looting of hundreds of businesses in the area as well as dozens of police officers being injured primarily by bricks, stones, and other objects being thrown at them. In the next couple of days an additional 5,000 thousand police officers were brought to Baltimore from other Maryland cities and counties, as well as officers from New Jersey and Pennsylvania. Also called in for assistance was the Maryland

National Guard. A curfew was imposed from 10:00 p.m. to 5:00 a.m. for 5 days and eventually the rioting was brought under control (see Figure 4.6).

The Decision to Prosecute

Upon receiving the medical examiner's report ruling that Freddie Gray had died as a result of a homicide, the decision was made by Baltimore State's Attorney Marilyn Mosby to charge the six officers criminally. She concluded that Mr. Gray should never have been arrested on the morning of April 12th. She also said police officers lacked probable cause to chase him when he ran after making eye contact with the lieutenant and it wasn't against the law for him to have the knife that he was charged with illegally possessing.

Ms. Mosby alleges that during the 45 min between the time of Mr. Gray's arrest and his emergence from the back of a police van with a fatal spinal cord injury, all six officers at various points saw him in need of medical help but offered no aid while he was handcuffed and shackled in the back of the van[48] (see Figure 4.7).

Charges Filed Against the Six Officers

- Officer Caesar Goodson Jr.—second-degree murder, manslaughter, second-degree assault, two vehicular manslaughter charges, and misconduct in office.
- Officer Garrett Miller—second-degree assault, misconduct in office, and false imprisonment.
- Officer Edward Nero—second-degree assault, misconduct in office, and false imprisonment.
- Sgt. Alicia White—involuntary manslaughter, second-degree assault, and misconduct in office.
- Lt. Brian Rice—involuntary manslaughter, second-degree assault, and misconduct in office.
- Officer William Porter—involuntary manslaughter, second-degree assault, and misconduct in office.

FIGURE 4.6 ▶ Rioting breaks out in Baltimore, Maryland, after the funeral of Freddie Gray. (Andrew Burton/Getty Images)

FIGURE 4.7 ▶ Baltimore, Maryland, State's Attorney, Marilyn Mosby, announcing the criminal charges being placed against the six Baltimore, Maryland, police officers on the death of Freddie Gray. (Alex Brandon/AP/Corbis)

All six officers bonded out after being arrested and booked for these charges but were subsequently indicted by a Baltimore County, Maryland, grand jury. However, the false imprisonment charges were dismissed by the grand jury.

The Political Divide

As a result of the death of Freddie Gray, there has emerged a considerable political divide among the local prosecutors, members of the minority community, and the police union representing these officers. For example, the Baltimore Chapter of the Fraternal Order of Police called the speed at which the prosecutor moved on the case politically motivated. "The actions taken today by the State's Attorney are an egregious rush to justice," said Michael E. Davey, the Union's lawyer. "We believe that these officers will be vindicated as they have done nothing wrong."[49] There is also a strong feeling among some pro-police advocates that the prosecutor's decision was a political one as well as an effort to appease those who were rioting and looting in the hopes that they would discontinue their actions.

On the other hand, there are those in the community who believe that the criminal charges placed against these six officers were justified and would like to see these officers punished and imprisoned. There have also been some anonymous threats that if these officers are not convicted and sent to prison the rioting would start again.

The U.S. Department of Justice has also started a civil rights investigation. Its focus will be to assess if any civil rights have been violated as well as to determine if the Baltimore Police Department has a custom of employing discriminatory policies and practices in dealing with the local African-American community, especially as it relates to the use of excessive force and making unconstitutional searches and arrests. At the time this book was being revised Officer William Porter had already been tried but the case was declared a mistrial and Officer Edward Nero had also been tried and was found not guilty.

Only time will tell what the final outcome of this case will be, but hopefully in the end it will be based upon the legal facts of the case and not upon emotions or political considerations.

THE USE OF POLICE BODY-WORN CAMERAS AND POLITICS

The question that is consistently raised in police–citizen interactions is what can be done to prevent officers from using excessive force in the first place and equally important what can be done to determine, with a high degree of certainty, what actually transpired in an interaction between a police officer and a citizen when there is an allegation of excessive force or other misconduct is alleged.

One of the technological innovations that can assist both law enforcement agencies as well as citizens in coming to a reasonably definitive conclusion as to just exactly what did transpire is through the use of body-worn cameras (BWCs) worn by police officers (see Figure 4.8). Police administrators who are in favor of the use of these devices argue that they can provide valuable evidence in court and provide a clear and objective image of

FIGURE 4.8 ▶ Near the right ear note that the camera is attached to the frame of the sunglasses. The camera can easily be moved from one type of glasses to another. The model also wears a body camera on his chest. It could easily be attached to an epaulette on a shirt or coat. (Courtesy WOLFCOM®, a Los Angeles-based company that is a leader in body-camera applications)

exactly what actions transpired between their officers and individuals who may be taken into custody. There is also the implied suggestion that such devices will deter those officers who might be inclined to engage in misconduct from doing so, as well as discouraging citizens inclined to make false allegations when they know the entire interaction is being recorded.

The body cameras that are presently being employed by law enforcement agencies are small in size and can be hooked onto collars, caps, shirt labels, sunglasses, and even worn on the ear.

Even the ACLU, which generally is wary of surveillance, recently expressed support for the use of such cameras. However, they do acknowledge that privacy concerns of the police and public and its import comes with conditions. "I absolutely know this tool will transform policing," Scott Greenwood, a police accountability attorney and general counsel for the ACLU, said in an interview. "It's an unalloyed good, provided that there are policies in place that mandate the use of devices rather than leaving it up to the discretion of the officers."[50]

Because increasing numbers of police departments are presently using the cameras both objective and anecdotal information seems to be accumulating pointing to the benefits of cameras. For example, the Institute of Criminology at the University of Cambridge recently conducted a body camera study with the Rialto Police Department, California, and the results were that complaints against officers dropped by 88 percent and officers wearing cameras used force almost 60 percent less.[51,52]

The Catalyst for Accelerated Change

There was previously a slow but steady trend toward police departments utilizing BWCs for their police officers. However, this trend dramatically accelerated starting in August 2014 after a Ferguson, Missouri, white police officer Darren Wilson shot and killed 18-year-old Michael Brown, a black teenager.

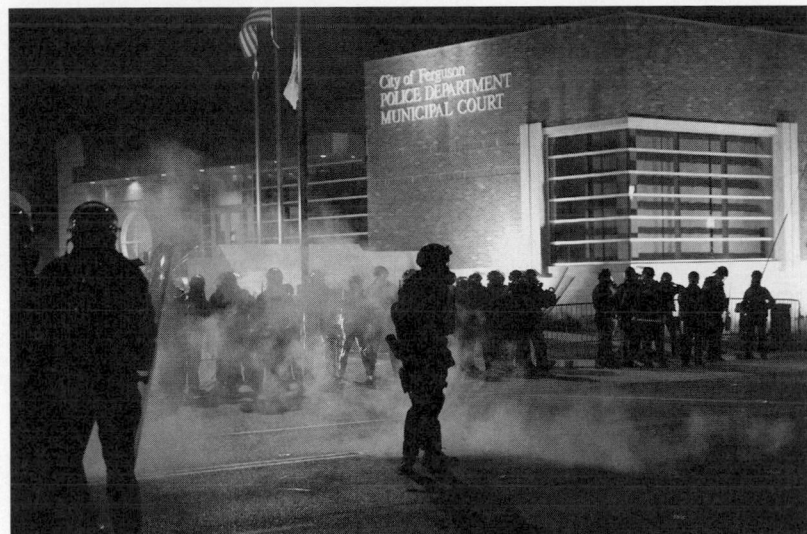

FIGURE 4.9 ▶ Police guard the Ferguson, Missouri Police Department and Municipal Court building as rioting erupts following the grand jury announcement exonerating Officer Darren Wilson in the shooting of Michael Brown. (Scott Olson/Getty Images)

Not surprisingly, there was considerable conflicting testimony between Officer Wilson and some of the eyewitnesses. Because there was no video recording from either a dash camera or a BWC the grand jury had to rely upon physical, ballistics, forensic, and crime scene evidence, medical reports, autopsy reports as well as hearing the testimony of dozens of witnesses. In the end, the grand jury concluded that Officer Wilson was justified in using deadly force in defense of his life. The U.S. Department of Justice, Civil Rights Division, which conducted its own investigation, came to the same conclusion.[53] However, in spite of the overwhelming evidence to support these findings, there were many in the community who disputed the grand jury findings; thus, this is precisely the kind of case where a video recording of the events would have been very useful to reconcile some of the conflicting accounts by eyewitnesses.[54]

Following the grand jury's decision to exonerate Officer Wilson from any wrongdoing a riot erupted in Ferguson, Missouri, followed by major demonstrations in numerous cities throughout the United States (see Figure 4.9).

Body-Worn Cameras (BWCs) and Privacy Issues

Police officers routinely patrol their communities on a daily basis, responding to calls for assistance as well as initiating citizen contacts. Completing their duties often takes police inside people's homes and businesses, as well into alleys, fields, cars, and a wide variety of other locations. Additionally, what officers actually see and hear on some of these calls can be very graphic and personal. With these thoughts in mind, agencies implementing the use of BWCs should consult closely with their legal advisor to ensure the operational protocol properly addresses privacy concerns.[55]

A second aspect of the privacy issue is states' laws governing audio or video recording of parties involved in the communication. States can be described as a one-party consent state or a two-party consent state. In one party state, only one party to the communication has to consent for the recording to be legal.[56] In a two-party consent state, all parties to the communication must consent for the recording to be legal. In those states, it stands to reason that the police would have to obtain consent from the citizen before recording the encounter.

It is imperative that the privacy issue be thoroughly reviewed with legal counsel and legal advice strictly followed. The reasonable expectation of privacy doctrine will certainly be at the forefront of this issue, but it is not always crystal clear for operational purposes.[57]

Redaction Capabilities

Any camera system selected must have easy-to-use redaction software for both the video and the audio or be compatible for redaction with other software. It is very likely that many recordings will be released to the public, for example, via each state's open record law. At the same time, there may be certain sections of the released video or audio that the law requires to be redacted or blocked out. Absent user-friendly software for redaction purposes, the agency could experience significant complications. Demonstration visits from the vendors should include a thorough demonstration of the software's redaction capability.[58]

Storage of Recordings

Digital recordings can consume a lot of space. An in-house analysis by one agency with 200 sworn officers indicated that 33 terabytes of storage would be needed each year, based on a conservative estimate of 1 hour of recording per officer work shift.[59] The amount of space needed will be contingent on three primary variables: (1) the number of officers using the BWCs, (2) the policy requirement for recording, and (3) the retention requirements for the recordings. Smaller agencies will likely need less storage capacity than medium and large agencies. Continuous recording will result in a massive amount of stored data, but recording only during citizen contacts will significantly reduce the storage space required. How long the recordings must be saved will probably be determined by state laws governing the retention of official records.[60]

In-house storage of video data requires significant expenditure of resources, including servers, redundancy, proper physical space, and IT personnel. Using cloud storage can reduce the cost by as much as 30–50 percent and give the agency access to cutting-edge technology and the best security available.[61] Considerable preplanning for storage is critical for proper maintenance of the data.[62]

Costs

Agencies contemplating the use of BWCs should calculate the total costs of the implementation, including start-up costs and maintenance costs. Start-up expenses, at a minimum, include the cameras, any accessories, policy development, data storage, training, and related infrastructure or technical costs, such as space requirements for equipment and technical training of appropriate employee(s) to oversee the system. Maintenance costs, at a minimum, will include manpower associated with managing and maintaining the equipment. Additionally, camera replacement due to breakage (physical altercations with suspects) and technical malfunctions will need to be considered. The ongoing cost associated with storage of the data must be calculated, and the potential increase in open records requests and the resultant workload increase must be considered. The personnel cost could increase substantially after factoring in redaction requirements.[63]

RACIAL AND ETHNIC PROFILING

Nothing has fueled the political fire between police and minorities more than the use of race and ethnicity as criteria in police decision making during discretionary traffic and field interrogation stops, often described as "racial and ethnic profiling."[64] Weitzer and Tuch define **racial profiling** as "the use of race as a key factor in police decisions to stop and interrogate citizens."[65] The term has several meanings, most of which are associated with law enforcement officers making the decision to stop an individual because of race or ethnicity.

Officers often use the "pretext" or "suspicious vehicle stop" argument to justify their actions as legal (e.g., using a legal pretext, such as an illegal lane change or broken license plate light, to stop the vehicle and then gain a basis to search for illegal drugs).[66] However, if a specific crime occurs (e.g., a rape, robbery, or a murder) and the suspect description by a witness includes race, gender, or ethnicity, it is lawful for the police to stop a citizen on the basis of how closely the individual resembles the characteristics or description within the "profile" (see Figure 4.10).

Media Accounts of Profiling on Local and National Politics

Starting in the late 1990s, racial profiling became a major race relations issue in U.S. politics, and the media played a prominent role in bringing it to national attention. The media's account of illegal treatment of minority citizens led many state governments to enact legislation that would ban racial profiling and hold police organizations accountable for systematically targeting minority citizens. In addition to the legislation, in 1999, Attorney General Janet Reno convened the Strengthening Police-Community Relations Conference held in Washington, DC, with the purpose of assisting police organizations in collecting data on this issue. By 2000, more than 4,000 law enforcement agencies across the United States were involved in data collection efforts. As early as 1999, several states—including North Carolina—adopted legislation that required data collection on every police-initiated stop. In North Carolina, Senate Bill 76 required all state law enforcement agencies to track the race and ethnic backgrounds of motorists stopped to monitor officers who might be targeting minority drivers. Prior to Senate Bill 76, officers recorded the race/ethnicity of motorists who were formally cited for a violation (e.g., citations and written warnings). By 2015, the majority of states had passed similar legislation.[67]

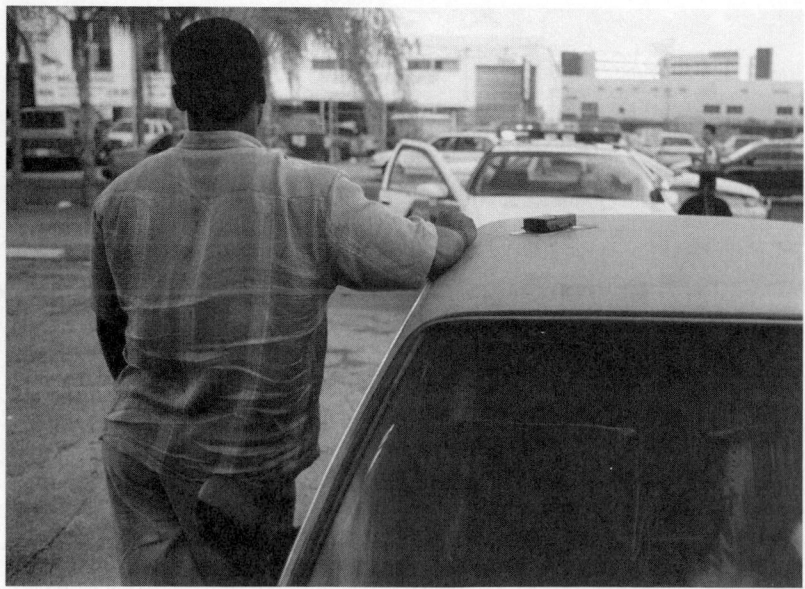

FIGURE 4.10 ▶ Racial profiling in traffic stops have become an increasingly controversial issue in police procedure. (Steve Lehman/Corbis Saba)

The Role of the U.S. Department of Justice in Investigating Allegations of Police Profiling

Earlier in this chapter, we briefly discussed the investigation conducted by the U.S. Department of Justice (DOJ), Civil Rights Division of the shooting involving Officer Darren Wilson of the Ferguson, Missouri, Police Department (FPD) and Michael Brown, an unarmed African-American teenager. The investigation by the DOJ was to determine if the shooting was justified. However, the DOJ investigators expanded their investigation to examine the operations and practices of the FPD after serious allegations were raised by members of the African-American community that racial profiling was being employed by this agency. The DOJ released their very comprehensive report on March 4, 2015, and investigators determined that there were at least five problem areas as it relates to the potential profiling of African-Americans residing in the city of Ferguson. These categories were:

- The Use of Enforcement for the Purpose of Generating Revenue
- Police Practices
- Municipal Court Practices
- Racial Bias
- Community Distrust[68]

The Use of Enforcement for the Purpose of Generating Revenue

The DOJ report said that Ferguson's law enforcement practices were shaped by the City's focus on revenue rather than by public safety needs and that this emphasis on revenue has compromised the institutional character of Ferguson's police department, thus, contributing to a pattern of unconstitutional policing. This has also shaped its municipal court and has led to procedures that have raised due process concerns and inflicted unnecessary harm on members of the Ferguson community. Further, Ferguson's police and municipal court practices both reflect and exacerbate existing racial bias, including racial stereotypes. Ferguson's own data establish clear racial disparities that adversely impact African-Americans. This evidence also showed that discriminatory intent is part of the reason for these disparities. Over time, Ferguson's police and municipal court practices have sown deep mistrust between parts of the community and the police department, undermining law enforcement legitimacy among African-Americans in particular.[69]

Police Practices

The City's emphasis on revenue generation has had a profound effect on FPD's approach to law enforcement. Patrol assignments and schedules are geared toward aggressive

enforcement of Ferguson's municipal code, with insufficient thought being given to whether enforcement strategies promote public safety or unnecessarily undermine community trust and co-operation. Officer evaluations and promotions depend to an inordinate degree on "productivity," meaning the number of citations issued. Partly as a consequence of City and FPD priorities, many officers appear to see some residents, especially those who live in Ferguson's predominantly African-American neighborhoods, less as constituents to be protected than as potential offenders and sources of revenue.

This culture within FPD influences officer activities in all areas of policing, beyond just ticketing. Officers expect and demand compliance even when they lack legal authority. They are inclined to interpret the exercise of free-speech rights as unlawful disobedience, innocent movements as physical threats, and indications of mental or physical illness as belligerence. Police supervisors and leadership do too little to ensure that officers act in accordance with law and policy and rarely respond meaningfully to civilian complaints of officer misconduct. The result is a pattern of stops without reasonable suspicion and arrests without probable cause in violation of the Fourth Amendment; infringement on free expression, as well as retaliation for protected expression, in violation of the First Amendment; and excessive force in violation of the Fourth Amendment.

Municipal Court Practices

Ferguson has allowed its focus on revenue generation to fundamentally compromise the role of Ferguson's municipal court. The municipal court does not act as a neutral arbiter of the law or a check on unlawful police conduct. Instead, the court primarily uses its judicial authority as the means to compel the payment of fines and fees that advance the City's financial interests. This has led to court practices that violate the Fourteenth Amendment's due process and equal protection requirements. The court's practices also impose unnecessary harm, overwhelmingly on African-American individuals, and run counter to public safety.

Most strikingly, the court issues municipal arrest warrants not on the basis of public safety needs, but rather as a routine response to missed court appearances and required fine payments. In 2013 alone, the court issued over 9,000 warrants on cases stemming in large part from minor violations such as parking infractions, traffic tickets, or housing code violations. Jail time would be considered far too harsh a penalty for the great majority of these code violations, yet Ferguson's municipal court routinely issues warrants for people to be arrested and incarcerated for failing to timely pay related fines and fees. Under state law, a failure to appear in municipal court on a traffic

(continued)

charge involving a moving violation also results in a license suspension. Ferguson has made this penalty even more onerous by only allowing the suspension to be lifted after payment of an owed fine is made in full. Further, until recently, Ferguson also added charges, fines, and fees for each missed appearance and payment. Many pending cases still include such charges that were imposed before the court recently eliminated them, making it as difficult as before for people to resolve these cases.

The court imposes these severe penalties for missed appearances and payments even as several of the court's practices create unnecessary barriers to resolving a municipal violation. The court often fails to provide clear and accurate information regarding a person's charges or court obligations. And the court's fine assessment procedures do not adequately provide for a defendant to seek a fine reduction on account of financial incapacity or to seek alternatives to payment such as community service. City and court officials have adhered to these court practices despite acknowledging their needlessly harmful consequences.

Racial Bias

Ferguson's law enforcement practices overwhelmingly impact African-Americans. Data collected by the FPD from 2012 to 2014 shows that African-Americans account for 85 percent of vehicle stops, 90 percent of citations, and 93 percent of arrests made by FPD officers, despite comprising only 67 percent of Ferguson's population. African-Americans are more than twice as likely as white drivers to be searched during vehicle stops even after controlling for non-race-based variables such as the reason the vehicle stop was initiated but are found in possession of contraband 26 percent less often than white drivers, suggesting that officers are impermissibly considering race as a factor when determining whether to search. African-Americans are more likely to be cited and arrested following a stop regardless of why the stop was initiated and are more likely to receive multiple citations during a single incident. From 2012 to 2014, FPD issued four or more citations to African-Americans on 73 occasions but issued four or more citations to non-African-Americans only twice. FPD appears to bring certain offenses almost exclusively against African-Americans. For example, from 2011 to 2013, African-Americans accounted for 95 percent of Manner of Walking in Roadway charges and 94 percent of all Failure to Comply charges. Notably, with respect to speeding charges brought by FPD, the evidence shows not only that African-Americans are represented at disproportionately high rates overall but also that the disparate impact of FPD's enforcement practices on African-Americans is 48 percent larger when citations are issued not on the basis of radar or laser, but by some other method, such as the officer's own visual assessment.

These disparities are also present in FPD's use of force. Nearly 90 percent of documented force used by FPD officers was used against African-Americans. In every canine bite incident for which racial information is available, the person bitten was African-American.

Municipal court practices likewise cause disproportionate harm to African-Americans. African-Americans are 68 percent less likely than others to have their cases dismissed by the court, and are more likely to have their cases last longer and result in more required court encounters. African-Americans are at least 50 percent more likely to have their cases lead to an arrest warrant and accounted for 92 percent of cases in which an arrest warrant was issued by the Ferguson Municipal Court in 2013. Available data show that, of those actually arrested by FPD only because of an outstanding municipal warrant, 96 percent are African-American.

The DOJ investigation indicated that this disproportionate burden on African-Americans cannot be explained by any difference in the rate at which people of different races violate the law. Rather, the investigation revealed that these disparities occur, at least in part, because of unlawful bias against and stereotypes about African-Americans. It found substantial evidence of racial bias among police and court staff in Ferguson. For example, the DOJ investigators discovered emails circulated by police supervisors and court staff that stereotype racial minorities as criminals, including one email that joked about an abortion by an African-American woman being a means of crime control.

City officials have frequently asserted that the harsh and disparate results of Ferguson's law enforcement system do not indicate problems with police or court practices, but instead reflect a pervasive lack of "personal responsibility" among "certain segments" of the community. The DOJ investigation found that the practices about which area residents have complained are in fact unconstitutional and unduly harsh. But the City's personal-responsibility refrain is telling: It reflects many of the same racial stereotypes found in the emails between police and court supervisors. This evidence of bias and stereotyping, together with evidence that Ferguson has long recognized but failed to correct the consistent racial disparities caused by its police and court practices, demonstrates that the discriminatory effects of Ferguson's conduct are driven at least in part by discriminatory intent in violation of the Fourteenth Amendment.

Community Distrust

Since the August 2014 shooting death of Michael Brown, the lack of trust between the FPD and a significant portion of Ferguson's residents, especially African-Americans, has become undeniable. The causes of this distrust and division, however, have been the subject of debate. Police and other City officials, as well as some Ferguson residents, have insisted that the public outcry is attributable to "outside agitators" who do not reflect the opinions of "real Ferguson residents." That view is at odds with the facts gathered during the investigation. The investigation has shown that distrust of the FPD is longstanding and largely attributable to Ferguson's approach to law enforcement. This approach results in patterns of unnecessarily aggressive and at times unlawful policing; reinforces the harm of discriminatory stereotypes; discourages a culture of accountability; and neglects community engagement. In recent years, FPD has moved away from the modest community policing efforts it previously had implemented, reducing opportunities for positive police–community interactions, and losing the little familiarity it had with some African-American neighborhoods. The confluence of policing to raise revenue and racial bias thus has resulted in practices that not only violate the Constitution and cause direct harm to the individuals whose rights are violated but also undermines community trust, especially among many African-Americans. As a consequence of these practices, law enforcement is seen as illegitimate, and the partnerships necessary for public safety are, in some areas, entirely absent.

DOJ Conclusion

This investigation revealed a pattern or practice of unlawful conduct within the FPD that violated the First,[70] Fourth,[71] and Fourteenth Amendments[72] to the U.S. Constitution, and federal statutory law.

Political Fallout and Changes as a Result of the Ferguson, Missouri Police Department Shooting Incident

- The Ferguson Police Department has agreed to overhaul its policies, training, and practices as a sweeping deal with the Justice Department.
- Thus far, three city officials have resigned. This includes the city manager, a municipal court judge and the police chief who was replaced by an African-American, Delrish Moss.
- The FPD has dramatically increased its efforts to recruit African-American males and females into the agency so that composition of its personnel more closely reflects the percentage of African-Americans living within the city of Ferguson, Missouri.

- The enforcement of minor traffic violations and non-traffic city ordinance violations has been dramatically reduced, with the hopes that it will result in fewer negative contacts between FPD officers and African-American citizens in the community.
- Ferguson officials have agreed to rewrite their municipal code to limit the use of fines and jail time for petty violations.
- There is now a strong movement to emphasize a community policing philosophy within the FPD.
- The FPD has purchased BWCs with microphones for all patrol officers, supervisors, and jail personnel.[73]

Quick Facts: Minority Recruiting: An Uneven Trend

Nationwide, the total number of minority police officers has risen, but they remain heavily concentrated in larger cities, with the numbers falling off sharply in smaller ones. Data from a recent federal survey of police departments found that nearly 400 police departments, most with fewer than a hundred officers, were substantially whiter than the populations they served. In these departments, the share of white officers was greater than the share of white residents by more than 50 percentage points.[74]

OTHER RECENT SIGNIFICANT DEADLY ENCOUNTERS BETWEEN THE POLICE AND AFRICAN-AMERICAN MALES

A series of recent citizen-generated cellphone video recordings of deadly encounters between police officers and unarmed African-American males which has been covered extensively by social media and the news media has resulted in unprecedented scrutiny of law enforcement. Although each of the facts of these situations has been quite different the political fallout has been similar in that it has negatively impacted police–community relations. It remains to be seen whether these events represent a watershed moment in policing or a momentary disturbance, although the former seems more likely. Among the most highly publicized string of police shootings are the following:

1. On July 17, 2014, Mr. Eric Garner a 350 pound African-American man was on a street corner in New York City selling "loosies," which is the term used for selling one

cigarette at a time. While he was engaging in this act the price of a pack of cigarettes in New York City was approximately $13.00 a pack because of substantial city taxes. A single "loosie" costs 75 cents, but two could be purchased for a dollar. On the face of it, selling loosies would appear to be a minor crime, except for the fact that it deprives shop owners of the income from selling them and more importantly, the city loses substantial tax revenue from the practice. State-wide, loosies sales deprive New York governments of $1.7 billion dollars in revenue, 6,700 jobs, and it is estimated that 60 percent of the cigarettes smoked in the State of New York are illegally sold. Arguably, it was the motivation to fully collect all legal tax dollars that contributed to Mr. Garner's death and the police were the instrumentality to do so in this July 17, 2014 encounter.

A police officer observing Mr. Garner engaged in selling these loosies approached him, determined he was violating the law and advised him he was under arrest. When the officers tried to physically take him into custody he resisted. This officer, along with several other officers at the scene, took him to the ground and placed him in handcuffs. One of the officers who wrestled Mr. Garner to the ground while holding him around the neck claimed he was using an approved "take down" maneuver taught in the police academy. Others in the community claimed it was an illegal chokehold. While being held down on the pavement Mr. Garner complained several times that he could not breathe and subsequently died.

All the officers, except the one holding Mr. Garner around the neck, were given immunity for their testimony. However, the grand jury declined to indict the officer who was holding him around the neck on the pavement. This was also the same officer who had made the initial contact with Mr. Garner and told him he was under arrest. As a result of the grand jury absolving this officer, several large demonstrations and marches were held in NYC and around the country to demand justice for Mr. Garner.[75]

2. At approximately 3:22 p.m. on November 22, 2014, Cleveland (Ohio) Police Officers were responding to a 911 call that someone had been taking a gun out of his waistband and pointing it at people in a local park. The dispatcher apparently did not pass on critical information that had been given by the person telephoning in the information that the "guy" was likely a juvenile and the gun was "probably fake." As the officers came to a stop and exited the car, an African-American juvenile later identified as 12-year-old Tamir Rice reached for, or pulled out a gun, which would later be determined to be an air-soft pellet gun. The orange tip on the gun, that would have alerted the officer it was not an actual weapon, was missing. The police officers reported that they told Tamir to "Show your hands" three times before a shot was fired.

Witnesses who were at the scene say they did not hear the officers issue a warning.[76] Seconds after the encounter, one officer shot and fatally wounded Rice, who died the next day. Tamir Rice could have been mistaken for an adult, he was 5 feet 7 inches tall and weighed approximately 195 lbs and looks like he was in his late teens or early 20s. An unidentified witness in the police report is quoted as saying that he gave the gun to Tamir and warned him someone might think it was a real gun.[77]

The Cuyahoga County Sheriff's Office conducted the investigation, producing a report of several hundred pages. A Cleveland Police Union Official said the officers' actions were "justified." The Prosecutor presented all the evidence gathered from the shooting to a grand jury to consider whether rookie Officer Timothy Loehmann, who shot Tamir should face criminal prosecution along with his training partner, Officer Frank Garmback.[78] The grand jury concluded the shooting was justified and as a result the prosecutor decided not to file charges against either officer. However, recently the City of Cleveland settled the case with Rice family for $6 million.

3. In Oklahoma on April 2, 2015, a White 73-year-old Tulsa County Reserve Deputy Sheriff assigned to the Violent Crimes Task Force pulled a gun and shot an unarmed African-American man. The suspect, Eric Harris, reportedly was on the ground struggling with deputies trying to effect his arrest on charges related to the alleged sale of a 9 mm semiautomatic pistol and 300 rounds of ammunition. The Reserve Deputy shot Mr. Harris, mistakenly thinking he had pulled his Taser but in reality had pulled out his firearm.

Because the Reserve Deputy had 7 years' experience and a strong training record, the mistake seemed baffling. Some media outlets raised questions as to whether a 73-year-old man should even be a reserve deputy and questions arose whether his training record was accurate. Questions were also raised about his contribution of equipment to the Sheriff's Office, suggesting that this was at least part of the reason he was granted special treatment. Following an investigation, the Reserve Deputy was charged with second-degree Manslaughter.

4. On April 4, 2015, A North Charleston, South Carolina, White Police Officer made a traffic stop of a vehicle with a broken tail light. The driver, African-American Mr. Walter Scott, ran from the Officer after a brief conversation. The two men ran into a park-like setting, and Mr. Scott continued to run when he was reportedly ordered to stop by the Officer. A civilian passing by used a cellphone to videotape the two men struggling and then Mr. Scott running away. The Officer fired eight times at the fleeing Mr. Scott, causing his death. The autopsy report revealed that Mr. Scott had sustained multiple gunshot wounds to his back. The video also depicts what appears to be the Officer moving one or

more items at the scene closer to the body.

It is unclear why this was done but serious questions can be raised whenever a crime scene is altered. The officer claimed that during his initial encounter with Mr. Scott he had to use a Taser and that Mr. Scott had initially tried to take his gun. The Officer was fired and charged with murder. In addition to the pending trial, a federal civil rights investigation is on-going. Large demonstrations protested the shooting of Scott were held across the nation, including in New York City where people marched to Times Square.[79]

THE POLICE OPERATIONAL BACKLASH

As one can see from the cases examined thus far, the past couple of years have garnered considerable negative publicity for law enforcement. There is both anecdotal and objective evidence to suggest that some police officers have made an informal decision to avoid becoming involved in situations in those parts of their community which have the potential to result in serious clashes. This is being done in some cases by simply by-passing individuals on the streets who are not committing crimes but whose actions may be suspicious and who previously would have been stopped and frisked. In other instances, some police officers have made a decision to reduce their patrol time in these areas in order to diminish the potential for conflict. These reduced enforcement efforts by police officers are not resulting from fear for their personal safety but rather from the fear of becoming involved in those situations that could potentially result in their being fired, indicted, arrested, and imprisoned.

There is also some evidence from recent local crime statistics to suggest that this reduction in proactive patrolling has resulted in an increase in violent crimes in the cities of New York and Baltimore.[80]

ILLEGAL IMMIGRATION: THE POLICE AND LOCAL POLITICS

In recent years, local police have become increasingly involved in the identification and arrest of undocumented immigrants. The term "**undocumented immigrant**" generally includes several categories of individuals who are subject to removal from the United States for a variety of reasons defined by the federal Immigration and Nationality Act. In general, an individual may be considered "removable" because he or she does not qualify for admission in to the United States, has entered the country illegally by crossing the border without formal inspection or has violated the terms of a legal admission, for example, by entering the country on a student visa and then dropping out of school.[81]

Enforcement action taken against this category of immigrants is normally the province of federal agents of the Immigration and Customs Enforcement (ICE), a unit of the Department of Homeland Security. However, a federal program to train local police officers in such duties has existed since 1996. Florida, the first state to join the federal program in the wake of the September 11, 2001 terrorist attacks, tailored its version to help block possible terrorist infiltrators. Interest in the program has taken off recently as the national debate over illegal immigration has heated up. Federal funds have been available to create a program to train local and state police officers in immigration duties (see Figure 4.11).

For example, Alabama decided to join the program because local officials believed ICE's small staff in the state was unable to cope with the swelling numbers of undocumented immigrants. The Governor pledged to double the number of state troopers trained to deal with undocumented immigrants, saying: "Alabama welcomes those who enter the country legally, but we won't stand idly by when we catch illegal immigrants in our state."

Forty-four of the 650 Alabama state troopers in the state, a figure that includes administrative and field officers, have taken the 5-week training course and are now authorized to enforce

FIGURE 4.11 ▶ An undocumented immigrant being taken into custody by Immigration and Customs Enforcement (ICE) special agents. (Photo courtesy ICE)

federal immigration law. That training involves detecting false identification, understanding the details of federal immigration law as well as the pitfalls of racial profiling and other possible civil rights violations.

The ICE partnership empowers local officers to temporarily detain someone who has violated federal immigration law—something they are typically not allowed to do. That is a valuable tool in states where there are few ICE agents. The trained officers usually do not participate in sweeps or actively search for undocumented immigrants; the emphasis is on human smugglers and convicted felons that officers come across during the course of their duties.

Quick Facts: The Number of Undocumented Immigrants in the United States by Ethnicity

As of 2012, the population of undocumented immigrants in the United States illegally is estimated to be approximately 11.43 million, or roughly 3.7% of the entire US population, 59% of the undocumented immigrants in the country illegally are from Mexico, and 25% of all undocumented immigrants in the country illegally reside in California. 53% of the undocumented immigrants in the United States illegally are male. In 2008, approximately 31% of workers in the roofing industry and 27% of maids/housekeepers were undocumented immigrants living in the country illegally.[82]

Chapter Summary

Summary by Learning Objective

1. **Explain the significance of the U.S. Supreme Court decisions in each of the following cases: *Mapp v. Ohio* (1961), *Gideon v. Wainwright* (1963), *Escobedo v. Illinois* (1964), and *Miranda v. Arizona* (1966).**

   Mapp v. Ohio (1961) banned the use of illegally seized evidence in criminal cases in the states by applying the Fourth Amendment guarantee against unreasonable searches and seizures. *Escobedo v. Illinois* (1964) affirmed that a suspect is entitled to confer with an attorney as soon as the focus of the police investigation of the suspect shifts from investigatory to accusatory. *Gideon v. Wainwright* (1963) affirmed that equal protection under the Fourteenth Amendment requires that legal counsel be appointed for all indigent defendants in all criminal cases. *Miranda v. Arizona* (1966) required police officers, before questioning suspects, to inform them of their constitutional right to remain silent, their right to an attorney, and their right to have an attorney appointed if they cannot afford to hire one.

2. **Identify the three distinctly different styles of law enforcement discussed by James Q. Wilson.**

   (1) The "watchman" style of law enforcement emphasizes maintenance of order and is found in economically declining cities with traditional political machines; (2) the "legalistic" style of law enforcement is found in cities with heterogeneous populations and reform-oriented, professional governments (law enforcement of both a reactive and proactive nature characterizes this style); and (3) in the homogeneous suburban communities, the "service" style of law enforcement is oriented toward the needs of the citizens.

3. **Explain the legally defined roles of city councils.**

   It acts as the chief legislative and policymaking body. Through its ordinance power, subject to constitutional and statutory provisions, including the city charter, the council carries out its legislative function.

4. **Discuss the ways in which the tasks and roles of sheriff's departments and police departments were historically different but have become similar in recent years.**

   In the past, sheriff's law enforcement functions have often been relegated to jurisdictions of sparse populations that cannot support municipal police agencies. Sheriffs are typically elected, as opposed to their appointed counterpart police chiefs. In addition, sheriffs routinely have a custodial role in the detention of prisoners not common to municipal police functions. This all changed somewhat after World War II, when populations expanded into rural areas that eventually became the suburbs. This eliminated part of the distinction between sheriffs and chiefs when big-city problems came to these areas.

5. **Explain how the state prosecutor's policies and procedures can have an observable effect on police practices and procedures.**

   Police chiefs who perceive that the prosecutor consistently reduces or fails to vigorously enforce certain types of violations may very likely divert their enforcement efforts and resources elsewhere.

6. **Discuss the ways in which the judiciary impacts police practices.**
   If judges consistently interject their personal biases into the judicial process and make it very clear to the police they will dismiss certain categories of violations, the police may discontinue enforcing that law.

7. **Understand the differences between the four existing forms of citizen oversight agencies.**
   Type 1: *Citizens investigate allegations* of misconduct and *recommend findings* to the chief or sheriff.
   Type 2: Police officers investigate allegations and develop findings; *citizens review and recommend* that the chief or sheriff approve or reject their findings.
   Type 3: Complainants may *appeal findings* established by the police or sheriff's department *to citizens*, who review them and then recommend their own findings to the chief or sheriff.
   Type 4: An auditor *investigates the process* by which the police or sheriff's department accepts and investigates the complaints and reports on the thoroughness and fairness of the process to the department and the public.

8. **Identify and briefly discuss reasons for friction between the news media and law enforcement.**
   It frequently emanates from the events surrounding a major crime or an unusual occurrence. Often in the case of major crimes or incidents, police departments do not want to release information that will jeopardize the safety of the public or its officers, impair the right of a suspect to a fair and impartial trial, or impede the progress of an investigation. On the other hand, the news media have a different orientation and duty: to inform the public. Although their goals are often compatible, the police and the news media can sometimes disagree irreconcilably.

9. **What are the advantages for police officers wearing body cameras that are cited by police administrators?**
   They can provide valuable evidence in court and provide a clear and objective image of exactly what actions transpired between their officers and individuals who may be taken into custody. There is also the implied suggestion that such devices will deter those officers who might be inclined to engage in misconduct from doing so, as well as discouraging citizens inclined to make false allegations when they know the entire interaction is being recorded.

10. **Define racial profiling.**
    The term has several meanings, most of which are associated with law enforcement officers making the decision to stop an individual because of race or ethnicity. Officers often use the "pretext" or "suspicious vehicle stop" argument to justify their actions as legal (e.g., using a legal pretext, such as an illegal lane change or broken license plate light, to stop the vehicle and then gain a basis to search for illegal drugs).

11. **Discuss the two major concerns state and local law enforcement administrators have in becoming involved in immigration enforcement.**
    A key concern is that state and local enforcement involvement in immigration can have a chilling effect on the relationship with the immigrant community in their jurisdiction and could lead immigrants to become reluctant to report crimes or cooperate with officers in investigating incident. In addition, many police chiefs and sheriffs have also expressed concerns about the additional numbers of personnel it would take for these federal immigration laws to be enforced in their local communities.

Chapter Review Questions

1. What four local broad mandates do Police Standards and Training Commissions (POSTs) have?

2. What are the major differences between the strong mayor form of government and the city manager form of government as they relate to the appointment of the police chief?

3. Why can police chiefs not objectively and independently fulfill their responsibilities if they lack job protection?

4. Describe the differences in the status between an elected county sheriff and an appointed police chief.

5. What role do public interest organizations play in police accountability?

6. Why do religious leaders and congregations of churches in a community represent one of the most potentially powerful pressure groups?

7. What was the catalyst for the accelerated change in the decision by law enforcement administrators to purchase body-BWCs for many of their officers working on the street?

8. What conclusions did the US Department of Justice reach in its investigation of the patterns and practices of the Ferguson, Missouri Police Department?

9. The term "undocumented immigrant" includes several categories of individuals. What are these categories?

Critical Thinking Exercises

1. **The Use of Deadly Force.** Within the past 3 years, there has been a dramatic increase in the number of deadly force encounters between white police officers and young African-American males in your community.

   a. You know from personal experience that the police academy street survival unit of instruction has been radically modified in recent years and has increasingly focused on the street violence being directed toward police officers. You strongly suspect that some of this has resulted in police officers becoming "hyper-vigilant" to potential dangers to their personal safety on the street and this could possibly be leading them to over-react to situations they encounter, especially with those involving young African-American males.

   b. Serious allegations have been raised that your officers are profiling young African-American males and stopping them on the streets without reasonable suspicion or probable cause that they have been involved in any type of criminal activity.

   c. There are serious allegations being raised by members of the minority community that the police department is incapable of investigating itself, especially as it relates police officers' use of deadly force and have recommended the creation of a citizen oversight committee to evaluate police officer shootings.

   How would you go about addressing each of these problems?

2. **Undocumented Immigrants.** Recently, there has been a dramatic increase in the number of undocumented immigrants moving into your community. Some powerful local politicians and local citizens of the city have been very critical of the police department's decision not to aggressively enforce immigration laws as it relates to undocumented immigrants unless they are actively involved in the commission of crimes not related to immigration issues.

   a. The objective evidence available indicates that the vast majority of undocumented immigrants are law abiding and supporting themselves by engaging in farm work, construction labor, and domestic work. However, the few who have committed serious crimes have gotten a disproportionate amount of attention from both local and national media

   b. You also know that undocumented immigrants are disproportionately targeted by criminals within their groups for financial exploitation but they are reluctant to report this to the police because they believe it might reveal their illegal status and result in their deportation.

   Since you have made a conscious effort not to become involved in enforcing immigration laws, you must provide local politicians, and local citizens expressing concern with the rationale for your decision to not enforce these laws.

Key Terms

citizen oversight
city council
city manager
judiciary
politics

Politics
prosecutor
public interest organizations
racial profiling
sheriffs

strong mayor
tenure
undocumented immigrant

Endnotes

[1] W. H. Hudnut III, "The Police and the Polis: A Mayor's Perspective," in *Police Leadership in America: Crisis and Opportunity*, ed. William A. Geller (Westport, CT: Praeger, 1985), p. 20.

[2] N. G. Holten and M. E. Jones, *The Systems of Criminal Justice* (Boston: Little, Brown, 1978), p. 416.

[3] For a more detailed discussion on this topic see C.R. Swanson, N.C. Chamelin, L. Territo and R.W. Taylor, *Criminal Investigation*, 11th edition (New York, NY: The McGraw-Hill Companies, Inc., 2012), pp. 143–144.

[4] Treatment of the Supreme Court's influence has been drawn from Thomas Phelps, Charles Swanson, and Kenneth Evans, *Introduction to Criminal Justice* (Santa Monica, CA: Goodyear, 1979), pp. 128–131.

[5] In a legal sense, the Supreme Court opted for a piecemeal application when it rejected the "shorthand doctrine" (i.e., making a blanket application of the federal Bill of Rights provisions binding on the states) in its consideration of *Hurtado v. California*, 110 U.S. 516 (1884); therefore, the statement should be read in the context that the activist role was a policy decision.

[6] Fred P. Graham, *The Self-Inflicted Wound* (New York: Macmillan, 1970), p. 37. For a look at the police and due process, see A. T. Quick, "Attitudinal Aspects of Police

Compliance with Procedural Due Process," *American Journal of Criminal Law* 6 (1978), pp. 25–56.

[7]T. R. Dye, *Politics in States and Communities* (Englewood Cliffs, N.J.: Prentice Hall, 1973), p. 214.

[8]Robert M. Fogelson, *Big-City Police* (Cambridge, MA: Harvard University Press, 1975), pp. 14–15.

[9]For a more detailed discussion of the cities that were taken over by the states in the 1800s, see Robert M. Fogelson, *Big-City Police* (Cambridge, MA: Harvard University Press, 1975), p. 14.

[10]Information provided by the National Association of State Directors of Law Enforcement Training.

[11]The National Advisory Commission on Criminal Justice Standards and Goals, *A National Strategy to Reduce Crime* (Washington, DC: U.S. Government Printing Office, 1972), p. 149.

[12]James Q. Wilson, *Varieties of Police Behavior* (New York: Atheneum, 1973).

[13]The President's Commission on Law Enforcement and Administration of Justice, *Task Force Report: The Police* (Washington, DC: U.S. Government Printing Office, 1967), p. 127.

[14]A. H. Andrews, Jr., "Structuring the Political Independence of the Police Chief," in *Police Leadership in America: Crisis and Opportunity*, ed. William Geller (New York: Praeger, 1985), pp. 9, 10.

[15]V. A. Leonard and H. W. Moore, *Police Organization and Management* (Mineola, NY: Foundation Press, 1971), p. 21.

[16]G. E. Berkeley et al., *Introduction to Criminal Justice* (Boston: Holbrook Press, 1976), p. 216.

[17]Leonard and Moore, *Police Organization and Management*, p. 15.

[18]Leonard and Moore, *Police Organization and Management*, p. 15.

[19]J. F. Ahern, *Police in Trouble* (New York: Hawthorn Books, 1972), pp. 96–98.

[20]J. J. Norton and G. G. Cowart, "Assaulting the Politics/Administration Dichotomy," *Police Chief* 45, no. 11 (1978): 26.

[21]Interview with staff assistants at the International Association of Chiefs of Police, Washington, DC. (December 8, 1995).

[22]One of the most comprehensive collections of articles and essays focusing on the role of the chief of police is found in Geller, *Police Leadership in America*.

[23]Janet Ferris et al., "Present and Potential Legal Job Protections Available to Heads of Agencies," *Florida Police Chief* 14, no. 5 (1994), pp. 43–45.

[24]J. Ruiz, "The Return of the Ultimate Outsider: A Civilian Administrator as the Top Cop" (unpublished paper, 1997).

[25]Ibid.

[26]Ibid.

[27]Ibid.

[28]See S. Walker, *The Police in America* (New York: McGraw-Hill, 1992), 44, and B. A. Reaves, *Sheriff's Departments 1990* (Washington, DC: U.S. Department of Justice, Bureau of Justice Statistics), p. 1.

[29]National Sheriff's Association, *County Law Enforcement: Assessment of Capabilities and Needs* (Washington, DC: National Sheriff's Association, 1995), p. 1.

[30]Most of the following material has been excerpted from Harry C. Guffardi, "History of the Office of Sheriff," www.hostpc.com/Buffardi/htm.

[31]B. L. Garmire, ed., *Local Police Management* (Washington, DC: Institute for Training in Municipal Administration, 1982, 2001).

[32]D. R. Struckoff, *The American Sheriff* (Joliet, IL: Justice Research Institute, 1994), 43.

[33]Ibid., pp. 44–45.

[34]D. B. Brammer and J. E. Hurley, *A Study of the Office of Sheriff in the United States Southern Region* (Oxford, MS: University of Mississippi Bureau of Government Research, 1968),pp. 1–2.

[35]R. N. Holden, *Modern Police Management* (Englewood Cliffs, NJ: Prentice Hall Career and Technology, 1994), p. 13.

[36]Brian A. Reaves, "Census of State and Local Law Enforcement Agencies, 2008," U. S. Department of Justice, Office of Justice Programs, Bureau of Justice Statistics, July 2011; http://www.bjs.gov/content/pub/pdf/csllea08.pdf; (accessed June 22, 2015).

[37]One Voice for the Office of Sheriff, National Sheriffs' Association; http://www.sheriffs.org/content/faq; (accessed June 22, 2015).

[38]The President's Commission, *Task Force Report*, p. 30.

[39]Ibid., p. 31.

[40]Ibid.

[41]Ibid.

[42]Samuel Walker and Charles M. Katz, *The Police in America*, 7th ed. (New York: McGraw-Hill Companies, 2008), pp. 486–490.

[43]National Association for Civilian Oversight of Law Enforcement (NACOLE); https://nacole.org/about-us/; (accessed June 21, 2015).

[44]Cassandra Fairbanks, "St. Louis Police Threaten to Quit or Slowdown If Civilian Oversight Passes," *The Free Thought Project.com*, January 31, 2015; http://thefreethoughtproject.com; (accessed June 28, 2015).

[45]National Association for Civilian Oversight of Law Enforcement.

[46]E. M. Davis, "Press Relations Guide for Peace Officers," *Police Chief* 39, no. 3 (1972), p. 67.

[47]Application for Statement of Charges, District Court of Maryland for Baltimore City, 5800 Wabash Ave, Baltimore, MD 21215, DC Case No. 0B02294453.

[48]Scott Calvert, "What Baltimore Prosecutors Say Happened to Freddie Gray on Van Ride," *The Wall Street Journal*, May 1, 2015; available at: http://www.wsj.com/articles/what-baltimore-prosecutors-say-happened-to-freddie-gray-on-van-ride-1430515289.

[49]Alan Blinder and Richard Perez-Pena, "6 Baltimore Police Officers Charged in Freddie Gray Death," *The New York Times* (May 1, 2015).

[50]Rachel Weiner, "Police Body Cameras Spur Privacy Debate," *Washington Post*, November 10, 2013; retrieved from: *http://www.washingtonpost.com/local/crime/police-body-cameras-spur-privacy-debate/2013/11/10/7e9ee504-2549-11e3-b75d-5b7f66349852_story.html*; (accessed February 17, 2014).

[51]Stephanie Hayes, "USF to Study Police Officers Wearing Body Cameras," *Tampa Bay Times*, January 11, 2014; retrieved from: *http://www.tampabay.com/news/education/college/usf-to-study-police-officers-wearing-body-cameras/2160669*; (accessed February 17, 2014).

[52]For a more detailed discussion of the Rialto Police Department's use of body-worn cameras see William

Farrar, "Operation Candid Camera: The Rialto Police Department's Body-Worn Camera Experiment," *The Police Chief* (January 2014), pp. 20–25.

[53]Department of Justice Report Regarding the Criminal Investigation into the Shooting Death of Michael Brown by Ferguson, Missouri Police Officer Darren Wilson, March 4, 2015; retrieved from: http://apps.washingtonpost.com/g/documents/national/department-of-justice-report-on-the-michael-brown-shooting/1436/.

[54]For a more detailed discussion of the facts of this case see the *State of Missouri v. Darren Wilson, Grand Jury,* Vol. 5, (September 15, 2014).

[55]Larry E. Capps, "Police Body-Worn Cameras: An Overview," *Police Chief Magazine* (February, 2015), pp. 53–54.

[56]Eugene P. Ramirez, *A Report on Body Worn Cameras* (Los Angeles, CA: Manning & Kass, Ellrod, Ramirez, Trester LLP), 14, http://www.parsac.org/parsac-www/pdf/Bulletins/14-005_Report_BODY_WORN_CAMERAS.pdf; (accessed September 8, 2014).

[57]Capps, "Police Body-Worn Cameras," p. 53.

[58]Capps, "Police Body-Worn Cameras," p. 53.

[59]Vern Sallee, "Outsourcing the Evidence Room: Moving Digital Evidence to the Cloud," *The Police Chief* 81, no. 4 (April 2014): 44, http://www.policechiefmagazine.org/magazine/index.cfm?Fuseaction=display&article_id=3319&issue_id=42014; (accessed September 8, 2014).

[60]Capps, "Police Body-Worn Cameras," p. 53.

[61]Ibid.

[62]Ibid.

[63]Ibid., p. 54.

[64]Special thanks to Brooke Nodeland for her assistance in developing this section on racial and ethnic profiling. See also Robin Engle, Jennifer Calnon, and Thomas Bernard, "Racial Profiling: Shortcomings and Future Directions in Research," *Justice Quarterly* 19, no. 2 (June 2002), pp. 249–273.

[65]Ronald Weitzer and Steven Tuch, "Perceptions of Racial Profiling: Race, Class, and Personal Experience," *Criminology* 40, no. 2 (2002).

[66]See *Whren v. United States,* 517 U.S. 06 (1996).

[67]Warren and Tomaskovi-Devey, "Racial Profiling and Searches," p. 349.

[68]U.S. Department of Justice, Civil Rights Division, Investigation of the Ferguson Police Department, March 4, 2015, 1–6; retrieved from: http://www.justice.gov/sites/default/files/opa/press-releases/attachments/2015/03/04/ferguson_police_department_report.pdf.

[69]Ibid., p. 2.

[70]The First Amendment guarantees freedoms concerning religion, expression, assembly, and the right to petition. It forbids Congress from both promoting one religion over others and also restricting an individual's religious practices. It guarantees freedom of expression by prohibiting Congress from restricting the press or the rights of individuals to speak freely. It also guarantees the right of citizens to assemble peaceably and to petition their government.

[71]The Fourth Amendment prohibits the government from conducting unreasonable searches (intrusions on a person's privacy) and seizures (control of the government over a person or a thing). Reasonableness here requires that the warrant be obtained before a search can be commenced.

[72]Four principles were asserted in the text of the 14th amendment. They were: (1) State and federal citizenship for all persons regardless of race both born or naturalized in the United States was reaffirmed; (2) no state would be allowed to abridge the "privileges and immunities" of citizens; (3) no person was allowed to be deprived of life, liberty, or property without "due process of law"; (4) no person could be denied "equal protection of the laws."

[73]Associated Press, "Ferguson, US Reach Tentative Agreement," *Tampa Bay Times,* (January, 28, 2016), 5A.

[74]Shaila Dewan, "In Many Cities, Police Struggle for Diversity," *The New York Times* (September 10, 2014), p. A1.

[75]J. David Goodman and Al Baker, "Wave of Protests After Grand Jury Doesn't Indict Officer in Eric Garner Chokehold Case," *New York Times* (December 3, 2014); http://www.nytimes.com/2014/12/04/nyregion/grand-jury-said-to-bring-no-charges-in-staten-island-chokehold-death-of-eric-garner.html?_r=0; (accessed June 27, 2015).

[76]Ida Lieszkovsky, "Tamir Rice Investigation Released: The Big Story," *Cleveland.com* (June 13, 2015); http://www.cleveland.com/metro/index.ssf/2015/06/tamir_rice_investigation_relea.html; (accessed June 23, 2015).

[77]Matthew Dolan, "Cleveland Police Officer Who Shot Tamir Rice Said He Had 'No Choice,' Probe Finds," *Wall Street Journal,* June 13, 2015; http://www.wsj.com/articles/sherrifs-report-doesnt-say-whether-cleveland-boys-death-warrants-charges-against-police-1434224512; (accessed June 27, 2015).

[78]Lieszkovsky, "Tamir Rice Investigation Released."

[79]Denis Slattery, Edgar Sandoval, Laura Bult, and Tina Moore, "More than 400 Anti-Police Brutality Demonstrators March on Union Square to Protest Walter Scott Shooting," *New York Daily News,* Tuesday April 14, 2015; http://www.nydailynews.com/new-york/nyc-crime/400-anti-police-brutality-protestors-march-union-square-article-1.2185101; (accessed June 23, 2015).

[80]For more information on the issues addressed in this discussion of the police political backlash see the following news articles: The Editorial Board, "Crime and Confusion in a Safer New York City," *The New York Times,* June 5, 2015 ; http://www.nytimes.com/2015/06/06/opinion/crime-and-confusion-in-a-safer-new-york-city.html?_r=0; Dave Evans; (accessed June 9, 2015); "Activists Bring Coffin to City Hall to Protest Rise in NYC Violent Crime," *Eyewitness News ABC7-WABC-TV,* New York, June 3, 2015; Adam Marton and Greg Kohn, "Graphic: Homicides and Shootings Spike While Arrests Decline in Baltimore City," *Baltimore Sun,* May 31, 2015; http://www.baltimoresun.com/news/maryland/baltimore-crime-beat/bal-homicides-and-shootings-hit-record-highs-while-arrests-decline-in-baltimore-city-20150528-htmlstory.html; (accessed June 9, 2015); Yvonne Wenger, "Baltimore's Mayor: Spike in Crime 'Disheartening,'" *Baltimore Sun,* May 21, 2015; s/maryland/baltimore-crime-beat/bal-homicides-and-shootings-hit-record-highs-while-arrests-decline-in-baltimore-city-20150528-htmlstory.html; (accessed June 9, 2015); Justin George, "Mayor Believes City Will Rebound After Record Month of Violence," *Baltimore Sun,* June 1, 2015;

http://www.baltimoresun.com/news/maryland/crime/
blog/bs-md-ci-safe-streets-20150601-story.html#page=1;
(accessed June 9, 2015); Josh Sanburn, "Rising Violence:
After Decades of Decline, Crime Ticks Back Up," *Time
Magazine*, June 15, 2015 ; http://time.com/3908626/
rising-violence/; (accessed June 9, 2015).
[81]Critical Issues in Policing Series: *Police Chiefs and
Sheriffs Speak Out on Local Immigration Enforcement*
(Washington, DC: Police Executive Research Forum,
2008), p. 3.

[82]Bryan Baker and Nancy Rytina, "Estimates of the Unauthorized
Immigrant Population Residing in the United States: January
2012"; Michael Hoefer, Nancy Rytina, and Bryan C. Baker,
"Estimates of the Unauthorized Immigrant Population Resid-
ing in the United States: January 2008"; Michael Hoefer,
Nancy Rytina, and Christopher Campbell, "Estimates of the
Unauthorized Immigrant Population Residing in the United
States: January 2005", August 2006; retrieved from http://
immigration.procon.org/sourcefiles/illegal-immigration-
population-2012.pdf.

PART 2 The Organization and the Leader

The five chapters in this section deal with broad aspects of law enforcement agencies, including how to organize them from theoretical and practical perspectives, different approaches to leading departments and what research tells us about these approaches, planning and decision-making models, and the legal and "hands-on" aspects of human resource management in a law enforcement agency.

Chapter 5, "Organizational Theory," is a longer chapter on a difficult and under-appreciated subject. All organization structures reflect assumptions, one way or another, about the people that work in them and reveal the leader's preferences for one form over another. This chapter provides the basis on which leaders can thoughtfully examine what they implicitly or explicitly believe in with respect to how work is organized and authority is distributed. Roughly over the past 35 years policing and governments have produced reformatted/neo bureaucracies. While they retain some features of the bureaucratic model, such as the hierarchical structure and chain of command, they have also implemented newer philosophies, such as intelligence led policing, greater empowerment of employees, and reassessing their relationships with other entities. This reassessment is also reflected in the city/county sanctuary movement, which has led to conflict between cities/counties and the federal government.

Chapter 6, "Organizational Design," examines the practical choices faced by law enforcement administrators when they are modifying their organizations, e.g., to achieve their missions. Such choices include determining to what degree they will be "flat" or "tall," what types of units will be grouped together or separated, and the extent of specialization that will exist. Local law enforcement agencies share many of the same characteristics in their organizational structures, such as placing line and staff functions in different groupings. Beyond these basic commonalities, subtle variations are seen. Some law enforcement executives may want the Intelligence and Professional Standards units reporting directly to their office so they "can keep their finger on the department's pulse," while others may want to place more distance between their office and these functions so "they can keep their eye on the big picture." Thus, some aspects of organizational structures reflect the idiosyncratic personal preferences of the law enforcement executive and may not be inherently "right" or "wrong."

Chapter 7, "Leadership," is a critical examination of that subject in law enforcement agencies. It examines what leadership is and does, probes the leader-manager dichotomy, scrutinizes why some police leaders are effective and others fail, and provides comprehensive coverage of leadership theories and the research findings on them. The theories discussed span the distance from "Great Man" explanations to the more recent work on transactional, transformational, ethical, charismatic, servant, spiritual, and authentic leaders.

Chapter 8, "Planning and Decision Making," joins these two topics because planning is decision making for the future and these two subjects have some similarities. It covers the importance of these topics, including types of plans, characteristics of effective plans, Synoptic, Incremental, Transactive, and Radical (SITAR) plans, decision-making tools such as

Strengths, Weaknesses, Opportunities, and Threats (SWOT) Analysis and the Pugh Decision Matrix. Also including are illuminating case studies of police planning and decision making during the 2014 active shooter at the Navy Shipyard in Washington, DC, and the hosting of the 2012 National Republican Convention in Tampa, Florida.

Mastery of Chapter 9, "Human Resource Management," is a necessity. The larger a law enforcement agency is, the more likely it has taken on some of the functions performed by the unit of government's central personnel office. An important aspect of human resource (HR) management is is understanding the applicable laws and regulations. Many local, state, and federal laws create legal rights for officers and other employees and violations of these can create unnecessary conflict and cause lingering labor relations problems. This chapter examines the applicable federal laws prohibiting discrimination and provides summaries of relevant legal decisions. It is generally thought that the preponderance of personnel problems is created through a faulty selection process; Chapter 9 examines this process in detail. Successive waves of generations hired into policing reveal important differences in their expectations, and law enforcement agencies must successfully craft messages to attract and retain them,. Other areas covered by this wide-ranging chapter include military call-ups of reservist officers, discipline, performance appraisal, and retirement counseling. Promotional systems and testing also receive significant treatment.

CHAPTER FIVE

ORGANIZATIONAL THEORY

Learning Objectives

1. Identify and define four types of organizations based on who benefits from each type.
2. Describe two sources of pressures for police departments.
3. Identify the three stems of traditional organization theory.
4. State the focus of scientific management.
5. Define functional supervision and the exception principle.
6. List the characteristics of Weber's bureaucratic model.
7. Define street-level bureaucrats and the two modes out of which they operate.
8. Define administrative theory and its benchmark.
9. Explain why the human relations school developed.
10. Describe organizational humanism and how it differs from traditional organizational theory and the human relations school.
11. List the levels of Maslow's needs hierarchy.
12. Contrast McGregor's Theory X and Theory Y assumptions at a broad level.
13. Differentiate between Herzberg's motivation and hygiene factors.
14. Explain how force-field analysis works.
15. Describe the entropic process.
16. Critique open systems theory.
17. Give a generalized comparison of networked and virtual organizations.
18. Explain sense making.
19. Summarize chaos theory.
20. Describe self-organizing and the butterfly effect.

INTRODUCTION

ORGANIZATIONAL THEORY, WHICH DRAWS

on many disciplines, is a tough subject. It is reasonable to ask why it is important to take time to become familiar with it. Knowledge of organizational theory is important because it (1) makes organizations more understandable; (2) reveals how authority is distributed across the organization; (3) explains why some police departments are less or more open to change and innovation; (4) makes assumptions, one way or another, about followers; (5) incorporates notions about the environments that the police department faces (e.g., political and legal) and how these can impinge on the department; and (6) provides an essential tool for leaders to decide where and how work will be done and the structure and relationship of the work units needed to do it.

FORMAL ORGANIZATIONS

Formal organizations are not a recent innovation.[1] Alexander the Great and Julius Caesar used them to conquer, the pharaohs employed them to build pyramids, the emperors of China constructed great irrigation systems with them, and the first popes created an organization to deliver religion on a worldwide basis.[2] The extent to which contemporary America is an organizational society is such that:

> We are born in organizations, educated by organizations, and spend most of our lives working for organizations. We spend much of our time . . . playing and praying in organizations. Most of us will die in an organization and when the time comes for burial, the largest organization of all—the state—must grant official permission.[3]

The basic rationale for the existence of organizations is that they do those things that people are unwilling or unable to do alone. Parsons notes that organizations are distinguished from other human groupings or social units in that, to a much greater degree, they are constructed and reconstructed to achieve specific goals; corporations, armies, hospitals, and police departments are included within this meaning, whereas families and friendship groups are not.[4] Schein defines an organization as the rational coordination of the activities of a number of people for the achievement of some common explicit purpose or goal, through division of labor and function and a hierarchy of authority and responsibility.[5]

Burns and Stalker break organizations into a dichotomy: **mechanistic** and **organic**[6]:

1. Mechanistic organizational structures are set up to run like a machine, tightly controlled, error free and producing a sustained, unflawed output. They incorporate many of the features of the bureaucratic structure, for example, a hierarchy, chain of command, and specialization. Much of the communication is top-down. Mechanistic organizations are also called "closed systems" because their boundaries are regarded as being fairly impermeable to outside influences.

   Mechanistic organizations function well when faced with a stable environment where there is no need to change and employees perform routine tasks. Tightly controlling their employees, mechanistic organizations are low on creativity and innovation. As a consequence, they are slow to adapt to new conditions. Many theorists use mechanistic, closed system, and bureaucracies synonymously.

2. Organic organizations recognize that they have permeable boundaries and are therefore co-dependent with the larger environment in which they are embedded. Knowing they face an unstable environment, organic organizations are adaptable and "nimble on their feet." Organic and open systems are used synonymously. Mechanistic and organic organizations can be thought of as opposite ends of a continuum.

Blau and Scott identified four types of formal organizations by asking the question of *cui bono,* or who benefits: (1) **mutual benefit associations**, such as police labor unions, where the primary beneficiary is the membership; (2) **business concerns**, such as Lynn Peavey, which sells crime scene equipment and supplies, where the owner is the prime beneficiary; (3) **service organizations**, such as homeless shelters and community mental health centers, where a specific client group is the prime beneficiary; and (4) **commonweal organizations**, such as the Department of Defense and law enforcement agencies, where the beneficiary is the public at large.[7]

Each of these four types of formal organizations has its own unique issues.[8] Mutual benefit associations, such as police unions, face the crucial problem of maintaining the internal democratic processes—providing for participation and control by their membership (see Box 5.1). For businesses, the central issue is maximizing profits in a competitive environment. Service organizations are faced with the conflict between restrictions imposed by administrative regulations versus providing the services judged by the professional to be most appropriate. In the case of a community mental health center, an illustration is that, following a reduction in funding, a regulation is placed into effect that requires all clients to be treated in group sessions when the psychiatric social worker believes the only effective treatment for a particular client is to be seen individually.

The key issue for law enforcement agencies and other types of commonweal organizations is finding a way to accommodate

---

Box 5.1 The Bridgeport, Connecticut, Police Union as a Mutual Benefit Association

Bridgeport Police Union Local 1159 bargains for some 400 officers. In 2015, members voted 260–79 to accept a four-year contract. As one officer put it, "It's the best we're gonna get." Three of the four years of the contract were retroactive, so by mid-2016, management and labor were back at the bargaining table. Under the deal made, officers get a 2.5 percent raise for each of the four years, but agreed to lose five days pay in each year of the contract, which also ended medical coverage for retirees. The Chief lost his authority to fire officers and his maximum disciplinary authority is a 30-day suspension, beyond that a hearing before the Police Commission is required. At the same time, the Chief got broader authority to change work assignments and create or eliminate units. It may have been the best the union could get, but there was some sentiment among union members that it was a poor contract at a time when their job is getting harder.[9]

---

pressures from two sources: (1) external democratic control and (2) internal control. The public expects to have external democratic control of its police department through its elected and appointed representatives. This external democratic control feature also has the expectation that the internal workings of the police department will be effective and efficient, but not also democratic. This is because democratic control by the members of a police department would inevitably lead to the department being in conflict at various times with the will of the community (e.g., one favoring a hard-line approach to crime control versus the other being in favor of a more moderate approach). Internally, large numbers of officers at the lower levels of the police department do not want to be treated like "cogs in a machine" and desire some voice in how the department operates. Thus, the challenge for police managers is how to maintain an organization that meets society's needs and the needs of the officers who work in it. This requires an understanding of such things as the different ways of organizing and the contrasting assumptions that various organizational forms make about the nature of people. Such knowledge is found within organizational theory.

TRADITIONAL ORGANIZATIONAL THEORY

Traditional theory is associated with organizations described as classical, mechanistic, and closed systems, which assume little influence from outside of the organization. Its underlying assumption is that there is one best way to structure and operate an organization. This body of knowledge evolved over centuries and crystallized between 1900 and the 1950s. The three branches or stems of traditional organizational theory are: (1) scientific management, (2) the bureaucratic model, and (3) administrative or management, theory.

Taylor: Scientific Management

The father of scientific management is Frederick W. Taylor (1856–1915), and the thrust of his thinking was to find the "one best way" to do work (see Figure 5.1). In addition to its status as

---

Quick Facts: Taylor's "One Best Way" Permeated His life

A Pennsylvanian born of Quaker–Puritan parents, Taylor was so discontented with the "evils" of waste and slothfulness that he applied careful analysis to finding the best way of playing croquet and of taking a cross-country walk with the least fatigue that was to be the hallmark of his later work in factories.[10]

---

a theory of work organization, Taylor's scientific management is also a theory of motivation in its belief that employees will be guided in their actions by what is in their economic self-interest.

From 1878 to 1890, Taylor worked at the Midvale Steel Company in Philadelphia, rising from the ranks of the laborers to chief engineer in just 6 years.[11] Taylor's experience at Midvale gave him insight into the twin problems of productivity and worker motivation. He saw workers as deliberately restricting productivity by "natural soldiering" and "systematic soldiering."

Natural soldiering came from the natural inclination of employees not to push themselves; **systematic soldiering** came from workers not wanting to produce so much as to see their quotas raised or other workers thrown out of their jobs.[12] To correct these deficiencies, Taylor called for a "complete mental revolution"[13] on the part of both workers and managers, although it is certain that he faulted management more for its failure to design jobs properly and to give workers the proper economic incentives to overcome soldiering than he did workers for not producing.[14]

Taylor's scientific management is only loosely a theory of organization because its focus was largely on work at the bottom part of the organization rather than being a general model. Scientific management's method was to find the most physically and time-efficient way to sequence tasks and then to use rigorous and extensive controls to enforce the standards. Taylor's conversation with "Schmidt" illustrates this:

FIGURE 5.1 ▶ Frederick W. Taylor's meticulously combed hair and well-groomed appearance hint at his obsession with details. (Library of Congress Prints and Photographs Division [LC-USZ62-79079])

"Schmidt, you can keep making $1.15 a day like the rest of these workers or you can be a high-price man and make $1.85 each and every day. Do you want to be a high-price man?"

"Vell yes, I vant to be a high-price man."

"Good. When this man tells you to load pig iron on the car, you walk, pick up the pig and load it exactly like he tells you. Rest when he tells you to and never give him any back-talk. That's what a high-price man does."

"I vant to be a high-price man and vill do what this man tells me."[15]

For Taylor, authority was based not on position in a hierarchy but rather on knowledge; **functional supervision** meant that people were responsible for directing certain tasks, despite the fact that this meant the authority of the supervisor might cut across organizational lines.[16] The **exception principle** meant that routine matters should be handled by lower-level managers or by supervisors and that higher-level managers should only receive reports of deviations above or below standard performances.[17] The integration of cost accounting into the planning process became part of some budgeting practices discussed in Chapter 12, Financial Management.

Despite the success of scientific management in raising productivity and cutting costs, "Taylorism" was attacked from several directions. Union leaders saw it as a threat to their movement because it seemed to reduce, if not eliminate, the importance

Box 5.2 Traffic Ticket Quotas or Performance Standards: The New Scientific Management?

A recurring theme in law enforcement is traffic ticket quotas. Historically, pressure to "improve ticket productivity," comes from city hall, labeled as "performance standards." Ostensibly, the quotas are established to ensure the safety of pedestrians and the motoring public. As matter of reality, the fines levied are sometimes an important part of small-town budgets. In some states (e.g., Georgia), there is a presumption that if an agency writes speeding tickets for which the fines are more than 40 percent of the agency's annual operating budget, the detection devices are being used for something other than public safety. If it is determined that traffic enforcement is being used as a funding mechanism by local units of government, the Georgia State Patrol may assume those duties until the issue is resolved.

With regard to traffic citations, the situation in Beverly Hills (Missouri) Police Department deserves thoughtful attention. The town's population is 574, geographically it encompasses .09 square miles, and has traffic enforcement cameras. It also has 14 officers who wrote 3,250 traffic citations in 2013. The Chief maintains the officers are crucial to the community-oriented policing approach they use and that the department also provides police services to neighboring Velda Village Hills. Without actually being in

Beverly Hills, observing, interviewing, and collecting data, it's not possible to reach a definitive conclusion regarding the possibility of traffic enforcement being a pretext for raising revenue for the city. However, there is an inescapable fact: 3,250 traffic citations[18]

Quotas are often resisted by officers, who maintain that no one really knows how many good cases they will see on a daily or monthly basis. They argue that the number and types of offenses vary by geographical area and demographic characteristics; for example, older people commit fewer driving violations than do younger operators. Moreover, officers are also quick to point out that quotas force them to make marginal cases in order to get good evaluations, thereby decreasing public goodwill and support.

The recession of 2007–2009 hit city and county budgets hard in many places. In a few cities, writing a certain number of traffic citations was a performance measure within the budget request. In Michigan and Illinois, it is a violation of state law to have ticket quotas for law enforcement officers. Whether called quotas or performance standards, the fact remains that both terms refer to a mandated system of production. Moreover, in some jurisdictions officers are being disciplined for not meeting the "numbers" required.

of unions. The management of Bethlehem Steel ultimately abandoned task management, as Taylor liked to refer to his system because managers were uncomfortable with such an accurate appraisal of their performance[19] and some liberals saw it as an exploitation of workers. Upton Sinclair, one of the muckrakers (see Chapter 1, Evolution of Police Administration), charged that Taylor had given workers a 61 percent increase in wages while getting a 362 percent increase in productivity.[20] Taylor replied to this charge by saying that employees worked no harder, only more efficiently. In hearings before the U.S. House of Representatives in 1912, Taylor's methods were attacked thoroughly, and he died 3 years later a discouraged man. Nonetheless, Henry Ford recast scientific management and used it to increase production and lower costs for the mass-produced model T Ford (1909–1927).

Scientific management did not disappear with Taylor, however. There remained a core of people devoted to its practice, including Henry L. Gantt (1861–1919); Watlington Emerson (1853–1931), also a promoter of the staff concept; Frank (1868–1924) and Lillian (1878–1972) Gilbreth; and Morris Cooke (1872–1960), who in *Our Cities Awake* (1918) called for the application of scientific management in municipal government. Gantt gained a measure of immortality by developing a basic planning chart, illustrated in Figure 5.2, which remains in wide use today and still bears his name. Developed during the summer of 1917 while Gantt worked at the Frankford Arsenal, the Gantt chart contained the then-revolutionary idea that the key factor in planning production was not quantity but time.[21]

Some international interest in scientific management also remained after Taylor's death; in 1918, France's Ministry of War called for its use, as did Russia's Lenin in an article in *Pravda*.[22] It is ironic that a communist society should call for the use of a management system based on the principle that economic self-interest guides the behavior of workers.

Although scientific management has long since ceased to be a dominant force, it does not mean that it is now just history. In addition to Gantt charts, many of the techniques associated with scientific management remain in use. Time and motion studies have been used to analyze how detectives use their time, identifying wasteful activities such as waiting for a vehicle to become available at the motor pool. Workflow analysis (depicted in Figure 5.3) remains used in industrial engineering. Other modern successors to scientific management were developed during World War II to support the war effort, and the refinement and more general application of these techniques is a post-1945 movement. The new techniques have alternatively been referred to as management science and operations research (OR), and their central orientation has been the application of quantitative and technical analysis to decision making.[23] Thus, the most enduring contribution of Taylor is as a promoter of both rationalization in organizations and management control systems.[24]

In 1997, Taylor's *The Principles of Scientific Management* (1911) was re-released due to continuing interest in his methods and Kanigel wrote a balanced criticism of Taylor's work,[25] as did Caldari in 2007.[26] Read together, they serve to essentially rehabilitate both Taylor's work and his reputation.

State Police Testing Project								
Task Name	Duration	Start	End	2017				
				12/Sep	19/Sep	26/Sep	03/Oct	1
Order Project Equipment	18.0 d	13/Sep/17	06/Oct/17	███				
Write Request for Computer Printer, and Software	2.0 d	13/Sep/17	14/Sep/17	▭				
Obtain Administrative Approval for Equipment Request	3.0 d	15/Sep/17	17/Sep/17	▭				
Order Equipment & Software through Procurement	3.0 d	20/Sep/17	22/Sep/17		▭			
Equipment and Software on Order	8.0 d	23/Sep/17	04/Oct/17			▭		
Receive and Configure Equipment	2.0 d	05/Oct/17	06/Oct/17				▭	
Staff Project	14.0 d	13/Sep/17	30/Sep/17	███				
Develop Job Descriptions	2.0 d	13/Sep/17	14/Sep/17	▭				
Announce Positions	3.0 d	15/Sep/17	17/Sep/17	▭				
Screen Applicants	3.0 d	20/Sep/17	22/Sep/17		▭			
Interview Finalists	2.0 d	23/Sep/17	24/Sep/17		▭			
Make Hiring Decisions	1.0 d	27/Sep/17	27/Sep/17			▭		
Train Staff	3.0 d	28/Sep/17	30/Sep/17			▭		

FIGURE 5.2 ▶ A Portion of a Gantt Chart for a State Police Promotional testing project. Weekends are not included in the count of days from "Start" to "End."

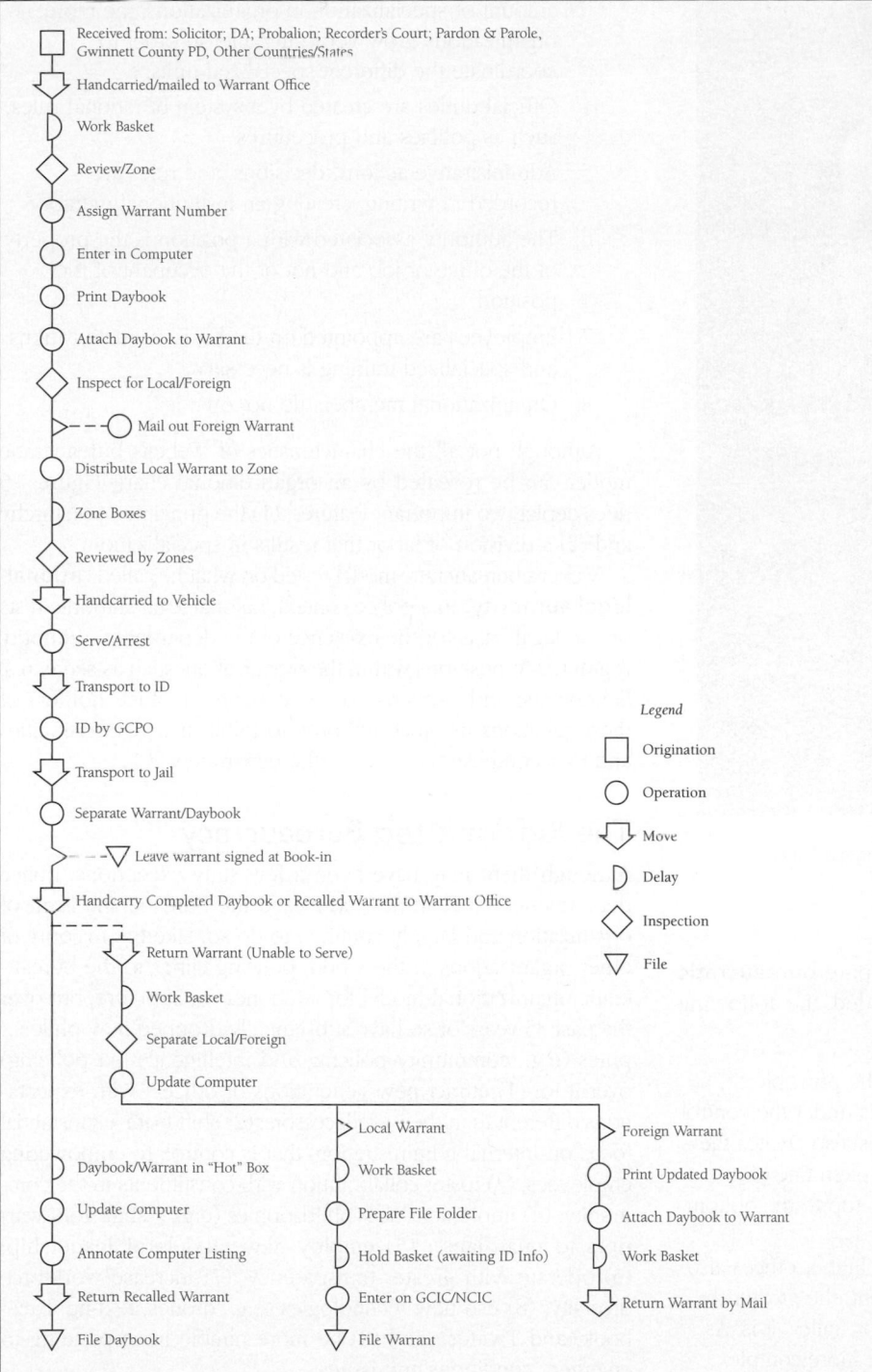

FIGURE 5.3 ► Workflow analysis of criminal warrants in a sheriff's office.

Weber: The Bureaucratic Model

In popular use, *bureaucracy* has come to mean slow-performing organizations using unnecessarily complicated procedures with answers that don't seem to quite meet our needs.[27] This meaning is far from the image of the ideal or pure bureaucracy developed by the towering German intellect **Max Weber** (1864–1920),

the founder of modern sociology (see Figure 5.4). For Weber, the choice was "only between bureaucracy and dilettantism in the field of administration."[28] In this regard, Weber claimed that the pure bureaucratic model was superior to all other methods of organizing with respect to efficiency, control, and stability.[29]

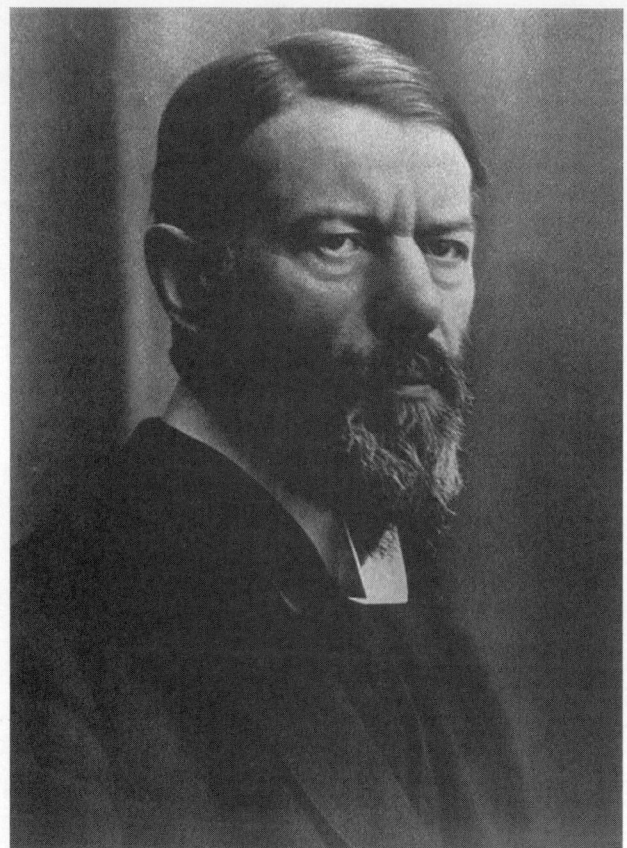

FIGURE 5.4 ▶ Max Weber. (Library of Congress Prints and Photographs Division [LC-USZ62-74580])

With some added commentary, Weber's pure **bureaucratic model** of organizational structure included the following characteristics:

1. The organization of offices follows the principle of hierarchy; that is, each lower office is under the control and supervision of a higher one. This also creates the chain of command, creating an unbroken line of authority and responsibility from the top to the bottom of an organization.

   This arrangement of successively higher offices also creates "layers" in a police department; the greater the number of layers, the more vertical or "taller" it is. As organizations get taller, they become more complex because there are more layers. Hierarchy also provides the "vertical highways" that establish reporting and communication channels.

2. There is a right of appeal and of statement of grievances from the lower to the higher offices.

3. Specified areas of competence, meaning a division of labor, exist. This division of labor or specialization increases the width and horizontal complexity of law enforcement agencies because different units are created, such as investigations, public relations, records, training and traffic enforcement. The greater the amount of specialization in organizations, the more organizations grow vertically/taller in order to coordinate the different specialized units.

4. Official duties are created by a system of rational rules, such as policies and procedures.

5. Administrative actions, decisions, and rules are recorded in writing, creating an institutional memory.

6. The authority associated with a position is the property of the office or job and not of the occupant of the position.

7. Employees are appointed on the basis of qualifications, and specialized training is necessary.

8. Organizational members do not own it.[30]

Although not all the characteristics of Weber's bureaucratic model can be revealed by an organizational chart, Figure 5.5 does depict two important features: (1) the principle of hierarchy and (2) a division of labor that results in specialization.

Weber's bureaucratic model rested on what he called **rational-legal authority.** In a police context, rational legal authority rests on the legal basis for the existence of the department. Authority is granted to positions within the organization, such as sergeants, lieutenants, and captains. The occupants or office holders of those positions use that authority to fulfill their responsibilities and to accomplish the goals of the department.[31]

The Reformatted Bureaucracy

Although there may have been a few stray exceptions, police departments for centuries have used the bureaucratic form of organization and largely continue to do so. Like the majority of other organizations in the world, policing clings to the bureaucratic organizational model for its "bones" or structure, but over the past 35 years or so have substantially dropped new philosophies (e.g., community policing and intelligence-led policing) over it to: (1) attract new generations of officers with expectations different than their predecessors; (2) shift from a substantial focus on internal administration, that is control, to empowering employees; (3) foster collaboration with constituents in the community; (4) implement new philosophies (e.g., a shift from warriors to guardians); (5) employ new models of leadership; (6) operate with greater transparency; (7) increase workforce diversity; (8) use new technologies (e.g., drones, texting, Facebook, and Twitter); and (9) be more nimble in responding to emergent conditions and issues.

Many law enforcement agencies have also rapidly moved into **e-government**,[32] facilitating the use of government services online. The Springfield (Missouri) Police Department's website allows citizens to obtain crime maps of their neighborhoods, search police reports, request copies of traffic accident and incident reports, locate the residence of sexual offenders, and file a complaint against or extend recognition to officers.

The preceding two paragraphs illustrate a "**reformatted bureaucracy**" that is a shift from close adherence to traditional organizational theory/closed system views to a neoclassical or neo-Weberian view that incorporates open systems precepts.[33]

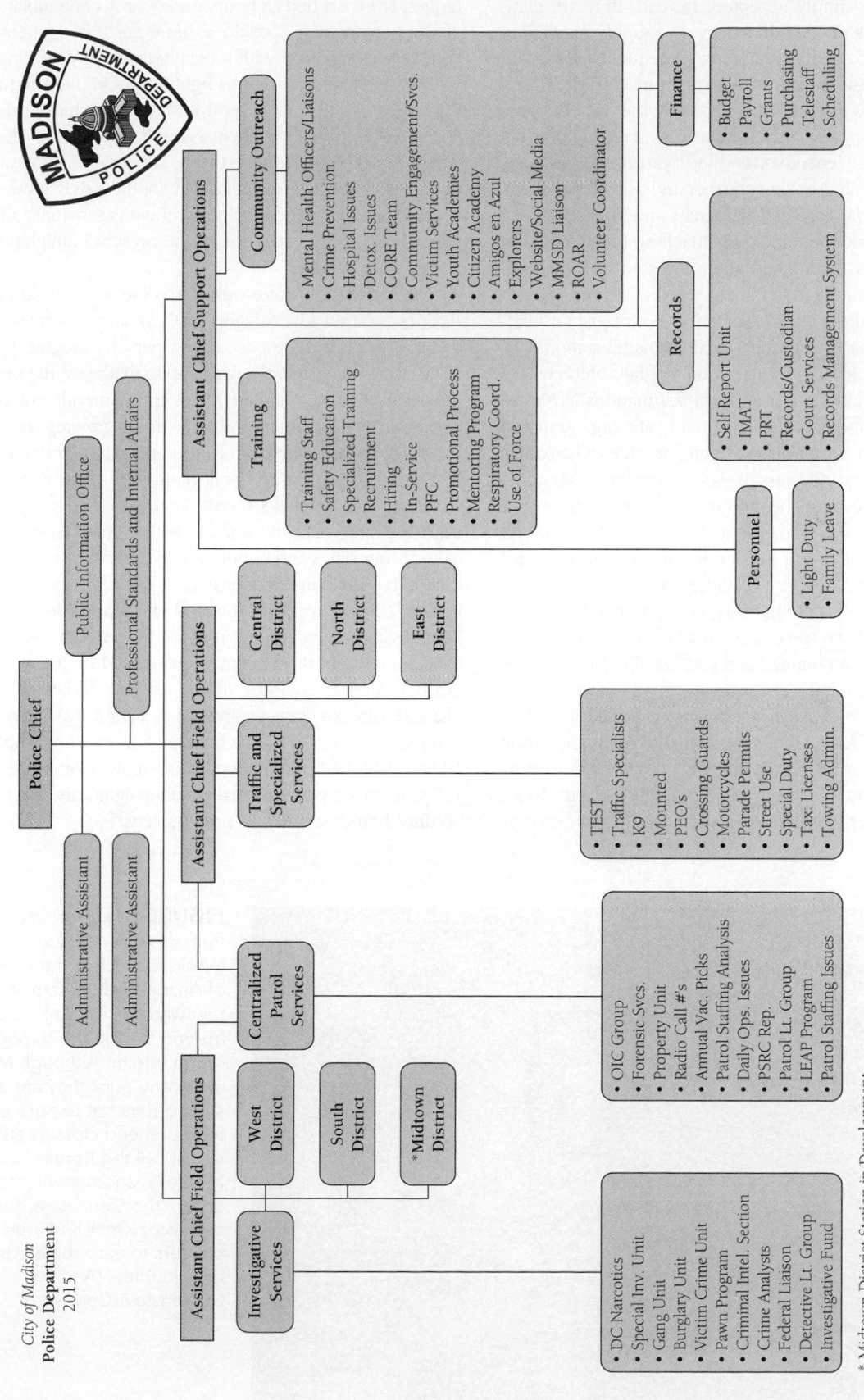

City of Madison
Police Department
2015

FIGURE 5.5 ▲ Madison (Wisconsin) Police Department organizational chart (Courtesy Madison, Wisconsin, Police Department, http://www.cityofmadison.com/police/documents/orgChart.pdf)

* Midtown District Station in Development

The practical meaning of this is that traditional practices and views no longer are simply accepted; instead, they are challenged and altered as needed. Illustratively, roughly paralleling this development and seemingly adding some fuel to it was the articulation of the **new public management (NPM)**, which began in the 1980s. At its core, NPM called for the use of private sector approaches in public organizations (e.g., creating productivity gains, getting citizens involved, and outsourcing services, including police, if it can be done cheaper and as well or better). In tandem, the neoclassical/neo-Weberian and NPM developments taught states, counties, and cities that long-held tenets and assumptions about governmental affairs needed to be closely examined to determine their validity.

This focus on challenging past practices is not just an intellectual exercise; it had profound practical manifestations. To illustrate, a study of 304 California municipal law enforcement agencies in cities identified as immigrant destinations illustrates the pervasiveness of the neoclassical bureaucratic organizational model.[34] Immigration, a "hot button" issue, provides a backdrop to contrast classical and neoclassical law enforcement agencies. American nativists are staunchly anti-immigration on any basis. In Arizona and other states sharing a border with Mexico, volunteers watch portions of the border and report illegal entries to the Border Patrol (see Figure 5.6). Others support immigration reform as long as there is no amnesty, while a liberal immigration reform law will have some support as well.

In past practice, when Immigration and Customs Enforcement (ICE) learned undocumented aliens they wanted to take custody of were being held by a local agency, they issued a written **detainer** for them. A detainer is essentially an "immigration hold" request.[35] Honoring the detainer is voluntary, not mandatory, although past practice has overwhelmingly been to do so. Included in a detainer is information about the person, such as any past criminal behavior, why he/she will be deported, and a request to be notified 48 hours prior to any contemplated release of the person so ICE could assume custody. In many places, voluntary compliance with a detainer officially no longer exists.

People fleeing the vicious fighting in Central America during the 1980s escaped to several countries, including the United States. Some number of them entered this country illegally and some churches granted them sanctuary to avoid being deported.[36] That modest development ultimately grew into what is presently a large political and religious sanctuary movement, which takes sharp exception to the present immigration system and splitting families.

The **sanctuary movement** also objected to what many jurisdictions were already struggling with: Detainers were issued by an administrative decision based on a person's judgment and were not a court-issued order or warrant. In that view, the process was inherently flawed, violated the Fourth Amendment protection against unlawful seizures, and came under growing criticisms from pastors, activists, members of the immigration community, some immigration attorneys and politicians, local governments, demonstrations, and the news media. In reaction to voices from the sanctuary movement and some in the law enforcement community as well, four states and hundreds of jurisdictions have responded. California and Connecticut enacted Trust Acts[37] and the Governors of Rhode Island and Illinois issued executive orders, all of which limited state and local support of the federal Secure Communities Program (S-Comm). S-Comm was operated by ICE during 2008–2014. A detainer could be issued if (1) an individual had been charged with, but not yet convicted of a crime, (2) individuals with no criminal history, but for whom final orders of removal from the United States had been issued by an immigration judge, and (3) if ICE determined an individual posed a significant risk to national security, border security, or public safety.[38]

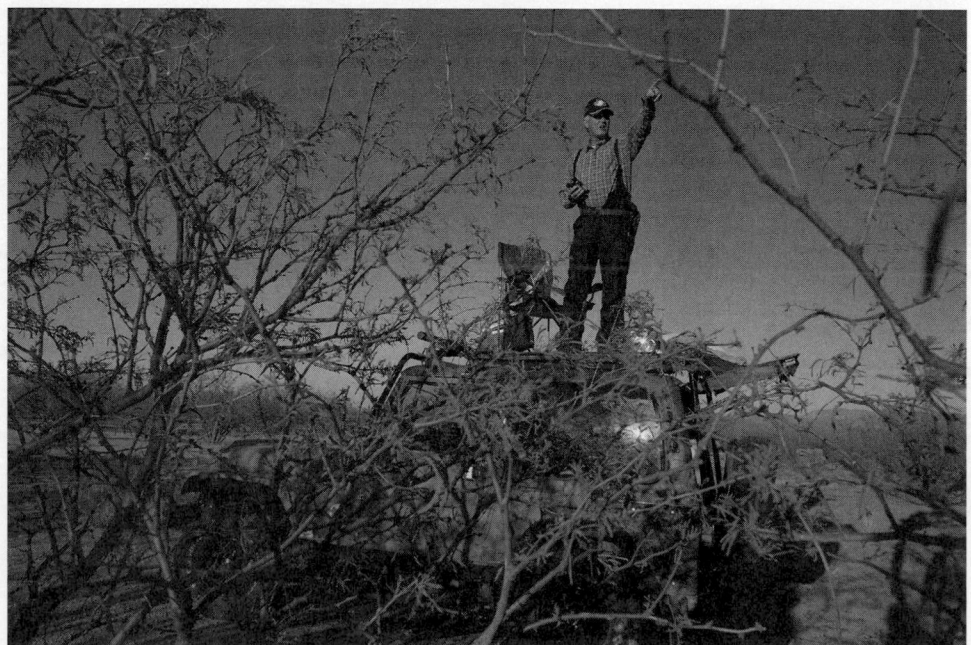

FIGURE 5.6 ▶ Thirty miles from the U.S.-Mexican border on a private ranch in the Altar Valley of Arizona, a Minuteman volunteer watches for illegal crossers making their North through the rough terrain. Although Minutemen carry guns they are under strict orders not to pursue or try to apprehend crossers and to just call the Border Patrol. Ironically, another volunteer group, the Samaritans, place caches of water and food for crossers to ease the hardship of their journey. (Andrew Lichtenstein/Corbis).

The actions taken in the four previously named states, along with similar actions taken by the governing bodies in more than 270 local jurisdictions, obstructed S-Comm to the degree that in 2015 it was abandoned and replaced with ICE's Priority Enforcement Program (PEP).[39] Under PEP, detainers will no longer be issued for individuals with a civil immigration offense alone or those charged, but not convicted, of criminal offenses. As provided for by PEP, ICE will seek to gain custody of those convicted of certain specific serious offenses, have intentionally participated in gang activity, or pose a threat to national security. The new detainer form requires that a basis of "probable cause" be recorded on it, such as: (1) there is a final order of removal, (2) removal proceedings are pending against the individual, or (3) statements to the immigration officer and/or other reliable evidence.[40]

However, there is a cost to the sanctuary movement that protects undocumented aliens. In just the first eight months of 2014, 8,811 ICE-issued detainers were not honored and after satisfying the conditions of their local confinement the undocumented aliens were released from custody.[41] Twenty-seven percent of the targets of declined detainers (1,867 undocumented aliens) were later arrested 4,298 times on 7,491 new charges.[42]

The crimes committed by undocumented aliens released because of declined detainers, and in particular the death of Kate Steinle, are immediately incomprehensible to us and have caused great suffering. At its heart are questions such as: "What is the role of local government in immigration control?" Should a local government detain undocumented aliens without legal cause to do so? Will detainer request under the new PEP program be recognized as sufficient authority? What duty is owed to whom? A few members of Congress have suggested cutting off federal funds to state and local governments that don't honor

Quick Facts: Declined Detainer Leads to Woman's Death

"Joseph" is a foreign national who as an undocumented alien has been deported five times. He also has seven felony convictions on his record. Joseph was in the custody of the San Francisco Sheriff's Department in 2015 and ICE made a detainer request for him. The Sheriff's Department doesn't recognize detainers as a legal cause to hold someone and he was released. The federal view is that the Sheriff's Department didn't have to hold Joseph past his scheduled release time; they could have just notified ICE that it was coming up. Subsequently, a gun was apparently stolen from a federal agent's car. Joseph allegedly said he found it wrapped in a rag on the ground. Joseph maintains while he was handling the gun it accidently went off. A bullet struck Kate Steinle, 31, in the chest as she walked with her father on San Francisco's Pier 14, a tourist attraction, and she died shortly thereafter.[43]

detainers, which seems unlikely at this point. Democracy is a magnificent way to govern, but its meaning is always in the details. Under the First Amendment, hate groups have the right to say vile things in public and the Second Amendment continues to frustrate gun control advocates who point to the Sandy Hook massacre in 2012 and the more recent murders in 2015 of reporter Alson Parker and cameraman Adam Ward of Roanoke, Virginia, WDBJ-TV as they were doing an on-the-air interview as another example of the need for universal background checks before weapons can be purchased. Detainers are another hard, unpleasant issue that will not be quietly or quickly resolved and bears watching.

Although there is already a substantial number of jurisdictions which provide sanctuary, they are many more which have done nothing. Thus, in many units of local government, what to do about undocumented aliens is an open question. Ideally, locally elected officials would develop a policy statement in conjunction with their department heads and order its implementation. However, a study found a low understanding of undocumented immigrant issues among elected officials and a lack or guidance from them to department heads. As an example, 72 percent of local elected officials did not know if their law enforcement agencies contacted federal authorities when undocumented immigrants were encountered.[44] This results in some discretionary space for law enforcement agencies, which then have the freedom to forge their own policies. For example, do we accept the matricula consular identification card issued by the Mexican government to its citizens? Do we contact federal Immigration and Customs Enforcement when such cards are presented?[45]

In a pure bureaucratic model, there would be little or no discretion on immigration matters and they would handled by "going by the book" strict enforcement. Undocumented aliens would be arrested and all detainers would be honored, absent any oversight from the city council or county commission. If requested by ICE to help take undocumented aliens into custody, the bureaucratic model police department might do so, perhaps almost as a reflex while a neoclassical police agency would consider what if anything, the activity contributed to accomplishing the agency's mission.

However, the new strategic law enforcement leadership thinks in terms of the resources available, what should and should not be done in furtherance of a department's mission.[46] Many law enforcement agencies surveyed have formulated policies that may make undocumented immigrants' encounters with police officers less stressful; 81 percent of the agencies considered bilingualism as a favorable part of a police applicant's background and 87 percent provided additional pay for language skills.[47] The largest number of agencies studied accepted the matricula consular identification card, did not inquire about immigration status when it was presented, and did not contact ICE when, during the course of a contact, immigration status was uncertain or undocumented.[48] However, if a violent crime is involved, law enforcement agencies checked immigration status and/or contacted ICE nearly 90 percent of the time.[49]

A national study confirmed that police departments often act without guidance on undocumented immigrants from elected officials. Fifty-one percent of the agencies surveyed had no guidance, 9 percent had informal direction, and 4 percent of the communities chose to create a sanctuary for undocumented immigrants, so long as they were law abiding.[50]

In developing their agencies' immigration policies and practices, some chiefs are faced with a rough calculation of what is the greater good for their communities and have decided that strict enforcement is likely to alienate relationships with documented and undocumented immigrants, who are often mixed together as families, reducing their willingness to report crimes and to provide assistance to investigators. To some degree, these policies reflect that 72 percent of chiefs believed immigration was a federal enforcement responsibility.[51] Unlike pure bureaucracies, neoclassical reformatted law enforcement agencies are strategic, nimble, and practical-minded.

The Police as Street-Level Bureaucrats

Street-level bureaucrats, such as police officers working in the field, are the face of government, meeting with members of the public and using their discretion on how to implement public policy.[52] In doing so, officers operate out of two modes: (1) "state agents," who believe in following the law and policies and (2) "citizen agents," who will bend or ignore them.[53] Although some officers may operate largely out of one mode or the other, most use both of them. People enter their law enforcement careers with different genders, sexual preferences, educational levels, races, economic backgrounds, and life experiences.[54] By doctrine, police departments expect that through training and supervision, officers will end up handling each similar call in the same manner, as a state agent, which clearly doesn't happen. After the academy and by the completion of 2 years of service, the sole or predominate orientation toward being a state agent fades under the weight of new experiences, the views of veteran officers, and the policing street culture, which is often antithetical to the values espoused in the academy.[55] In short, officers go from "nobody who breaks the law deserves a break" to "you have to approach things realistically, few situations are exactly the same, sometimes you need to cut somebody some slack."

Several important observations flow from the balancing act officers do with state and citizen agent modes: (1) however official-sounding the law and public policy are, their implementation is to some extent idiosyncratic; (2) the latent power of personal experience on the street is somewhat of an antidote to the expectations of doctrine; and (3) unaccounted for by advocates for the uniform, and therefore theoretically equitable, implementation of public policy is the personal circumstances of street officers. For example, some officers who don't have any court cases scheduled, but are forced to make an arrest, will say, "Well, if I have to go to court now, nobody catches a break."

Two dimensions to Weber's work are often not considered. First, he feared that the bureaucratic model's efficiency constituted a threat to individual freedom by its impersonal nature and oppressive routine.[56] Second, Weber deplored the career professional of moderate ambitions who craved security; Weber saw this type of person as lacking spontaneity and inventiveness, the modern-day "petty bureaucrat."[57]

Weber did not invent the bureaucratic model; it had existed for centuries; he only described it and didn't like all that he saw.[58] Thus, whereas Weber spawned the formal study of organizations, it scarcely seems fair to lay at his feet any real or fancied inadequacies of the model or its operation. Moreover, although it would be difficult to overstate Weber's contributions, it must be borne in mind that, although some people read him in the original German,[59] his work was not translated into English and therefore not generally available until 1947, long after the bureaucratic model was well entrenched.

Administrative Theory

Administrative theory, also referred to as management theory and the principles approach, sought to identify generic or universal methods of administration. Its benchmark is the 1937 publication of **Luther Gulick** (1892–1993) and Lyndall Urwick's (1891–1983) edited *Papers on the Science of Administration*. In content, administrative theory is more compatible with the bureaucratic model than with scientific management because it concentrates on broader principles (see Table 5.1). Administrative theory is distinguished from the bureaucratic model by its "how-to" emphasis. At some risk of oversimplification, the principles both operationalize and reinforce features of the bureaucratic model. Consequently, because of the continuing pervasiveness of the bureaucratic model, the principles either explicitly or implicitly continue to play an important role in organizations, including police departments. Other key contributors to this school are Henri Fayol (1841–1925), James Mooney (1884–1957), and Alan Reiley (1869–1947).

Henri Fayol graduated as an engineer at the age of 19 from France's National School of Mines at St. Etienne and began a 40-year career with the Commentary-Fourchambault Company.[60] His contributions are based on writings that were an outgrowth of his experiences as a manager. Fayol's fame rests chiefly on his *General and Industrial Management* (1916). The first English edition of this appeared in Great Britain in 1923, and although his "Administrative Theory of the State" appeared in *Papers on the Science of Administration (1937)*, his main work, *General and Industrial Management,* was not widely available in this country until 1949. Fayol's principles included the following: (1) a division of work or specialization; (2) authority, the right to give orders and expect compliance; whoever issues an

Quick Facts: Luther Gulick

Born in Osaka, Japan, to missionary parents, Gulick later taught at Columbia University where he founded the Institute for Public Administration. He was an important adviser to President Franklin Delano Roosevelt (1882–1945) during World War II. During his remarkable career, he would periodically leave the university to take a practitioners job, distinguishing himself as a first-rate scholar/practitioner.

TABLE 5.1 GULICK'S POSDCORB	
Activity	**Description**
Planning	Identifying the things that need to be done and the methods for doing them to accomplish the goals of the agency.
Organizing	The establishment of a formal structure of authority through which work subdivisions are arranged, defined, and coordinated.
Staffing	Recruiting, screening, hiring, training, and evaluating officers.
Directing	The continuous effort of making decisions, communicating them, and seeing that they are properly implemented.
COordinating	The all-important duty of interrelating the various parts of the work.
Reporting	Keeping those to whom the leader is responsible informed as to what is going on and ensuring subordinates also stay informed.
Budgeting	The process of developing a plan stated in financial terms.

order or delegates a task is still personally responsible for its execution; (3) discipline, obedience to laws, policies, procedures, and orders to further the accomplishment of the department's mission; (4) unity of command, on any assignment a subordinate shall only be directed by a single supervisor; (5) unity of direction—leaders must establish a direction for the department; unity of command is meaningless without unity of direction; (6) subordination of personal interest to the interest of the department; (7) compensation must be fair and uniform to people with the same jobs, qualifications, and experience; (8) centralization, which allows the active steering of the department in the direction intended; (9) the scalar chain—authority and responsibility must flow in a clear and unbroken line from the top to the bottom of the department through the various ranks, often referred to as the chain of command; (10) order is another manifestation of discipline; the building, equipment, records, and related matters must be properly maintained and accounted for; (11) equity, that quality of leadership and processes that combine kindness and justice; (12) stability of personnel, which allows employees to become familiar with their jobs; (13) initiative at all levels of the organization is a source of productivity; and (14) esprit de corps, harmony, and union of personnel—these constitute a great strength, and efforts should be made to establish them.[61]

Fayol recognized that his scalar principle could produce disastrous consequences if it were followed strictly because it would hamper swift action.[62] He therefore developed Fayol's "gangplank," or horizontal bridge, as a means of addressing this problem. First-line supervisors and middle managers in different units who interact regularly "cut across" the organization on the gangplank, eliminating the time-consuming process of going up one hierarchy and down another. Inside of and between law enforcement agencies e-mail and texting have become modern gangplanks (also see Chapter 10, Organizational and Interpersonal Communication). In 2002, Wren, Bedian, and Breeze concluded that the richness of Fayol's contributions can best be understood by reading the "small, stepping stone" publications that led to his theory.[63]

Mooney and Reiley's *Onward Industry* (1931) was generally consistent with the work of Fayol, as were the subsequent revisions of this publication, which appeared in 1939 and 1947 under the title *The Principles of Organization*.[64] In "Notes on the Theory of Organization," which was included in *Papers on the Science of Administration,* Gulick coined the most familiar and enduring acronym of administration, **POSDCORB** (see Table 5.1).[65] Gulick acknowledged that his POSDCORB was adapted from Fayol's principles. Likewise, Urwick drew on the work of another Frenchman, A. V. Graicunas, for his view on the span of control. Urwick asserted that no one should directly supervise five or at the most six subordinates whose work was unrelated.

Subsequent research on the maximum number of persons someone can supervise showed the figure of six is arbitrary and the actual number depends on such factors as the qualification and experience of those supervised and their supervisor, the nature of the work, and it's level of difficulty.

Critique of Traditional Theory

Scientific management is decried because of its "man as machine" orientation, and ample life is given to that argument by even a casual reading of the conversation between Taylor and the legendary "Schmidt." On balance, although Taylor's emphasis was on task, he was not totally indifferent to the human element, arguing that no system of management can be woodenly applied and all opinions of workers should be considered.[66]

The pure bureaucratic model has no shortage of critics, although their arguments, when read in the context of today's neo-Weberian bureaucracies, are largely outdated. Nonetheless, they are covered here to provide an understanding of how the bureaucratic model has evolved. The reformatted or neoclassical bureaucracy has taken us well beyond the Weber's pure model.

Organizational humanism called for a softening or elimination of many features of the pure bureaucractic model; perhaps initially foremost among the humanists was Warren Bennis, who leveled the following specific criticisms of it (1966): (1) bureaucracy does not adequately allow for the personal growth and development of mature personalities; (2) it develops conformity and "group think"; (3) it does not take into account the "informal organization" and emerging and unanticipated problems; (4) its systems of control and authority are hopelessly outdated; (5) it has no adequate judicial process; (6) it does not possess adequate means for resolving differences and conflicts between ranks and, most particularly, between functional groups; (7) communication and innovative ideas are thwarted or distorted due to a tall hierarchy; (8) the full human resources are not utilized due to mistrust, fear of reprisals, and so on; (9) it cannot assimilate the influx of new technology entering the organization; and (10) it modifies the personality structure such that each person becomes and reflects the full, gray, conditioned "organization person."[67] These criticisms started an important conversation, but for the most part lack potency with the reformatted bureaucracy.

In 1957, Robert Merton (1910–2003) noted that rigid enforcement of rules can become dysfunctional. Originally intended to promote efficiency and equity in dealing with clients, the intention of the rules can become lost and what is left is a slavish devotion to enforcing them. Merton saw this as creating a "bureaucratic virtuoso," who never forgets a single rule, but may not know what value or pupose it seves.

Herbert Simon (1916–2001) took issue with administrative theory. In 1945, he noted that if you narrow the span of control to five or six employees, you make the organization "taller," creating

more layers and greater vertical complexity, and that decreases efficiency because a matter going up the chain of command is more time-consuming as each layer considers how to handle it.[68]

Less critical than both Bennis and Simon, Hage describes bureaucracy in the mixed terms shown in Table 5.2.[69] In *Complex Organizations* (1972), Perrow argues that the preoccupation with reforming, humanizing, and decentralizing bureaucracies diverts attention from acknowledging how superior they are to other forms of organization. Goodsell, in *The Case for Bureaucracy* (1985), concludes that denunciations of bureaucracy may be fashionable, but not necessarily solid.[70] He asks the question: "How can we believe that all public bureaucracies, all of the time, are inefficient, dysfunctional, rigid, obstructionist, secretive, oligarchic, conservative, undemocratic, imperialist, oppressive, alienating, and discriminatory?"[71] Gouldner is more blunt, declaring the unending criticisms as being qualitative arguments devoid of any "empirical trimmings."[72]

HUMAN RELATIONS SCHOOL

The **human relations school** was developed in reaction to the mechanistic orientation of traditional organizational theory, which was viewed as neglecting or ignoring the human element and helped set the stage for organizational humanism. This school rests on the research of Elton Mayo (1880–1949) and Fritz Roethlisberger (1898–1974). Originally started to study worker fatigue, the research (1927–1932) was expanded several times and was carried out near Chicago at the Western Electric Company's Hawthorne Plant.[73] The major contribution of the Hawthorne Studies is the view that organizations are social systems. Two key studies were conducted: (1) the telephone relay assembly study and (2) the telephone switchboard wiring study.[74]

In the first study, five women assembling telephone relays were put into a room and subjected to varying physical work conditions.[75] Even when the conditions changed unfavorably, production increased. Mayo and his associates were puzzled by these results. Ultimately, they decided that (1) when the experimenters took over many of the supervisory functions, the work environment became less strict and less formal; (2) the women behaved differently from what was expected because they were receiving attention, creating the **Hawthorne effect**; and (3) by placing the women together in the relay assembling test room, the researchers had provided the opportunity for them to become a closely knit group.[76] On the basis of these

---

Quick Facts: Warren Bennis, Infantry Leader

In 1944, Warren Bennis arrived in Europe as a 19-year-old Lieutenant, commanding a platoon, as the Battle of the Bulge was ending. For subsequent action, Bennis received a Purple Heart for a combat wound and a Bronze Star for Valor. His difficult early years did not diminish a fervor for organizational humanism or perhaps those years helped to produce it.

TABLE 5.2 HAGE'S SUMMARY OF THE MIXED CHARACTERISTICS OF THE BUREAUCRATIC MODEL

High	Low
Centralization	Adaptability
Formality	Job Satisfaction
Stratification	Complexity
Production	
Efficiency	

observations, the researchers concluded that an important influence on productivity is the interpersonal relations and spirit of co-operation that had developed among the women and between the women and their supervisors. The influence of these "human relations" was believed to be every bit as important as physical work conditions and financial incentives.[77]

In the telephone switchboard wiring study, 14 men were put on a reasonable piece rate; that is, without physically straining themselves, they could earn more if they produced more. The assumption was that the workers would behave as rational economic actors and produce more, because it was in their own best interest. To insulate these men from the "systematic soldiering" they knew to exist among the plant's employees, the researchers also placed these workers in a special room. The workers' output did not increase, which contradicted scientific management's view that given the opportunity to earn more, workers will be more productive. The values of the informal group appeared to be more powerful than the allure of financial betterment: (1) don't be a "rate buster" and produce too much; (2) if you turn out too little work, you are a "chiseler"; (3) don't be a "squealer" to supervisors; and (4) don't be officious; if you are an inspector, don't act like one.[78]

As a result of the Hawthorne Studies, it was concluded that (1) the level of production is set by social norms, not by physiological capacities; (2) often workers react not as individuals but as members of a group; (3) the rewards and sanctions of the group significantly affect the behavior of workers and limit the impact of economic incentive plans; and (4) leadership has an important role in setting and enforcing group norms, and there is a difference between formal and informal leadership.[79]

When workers react as members of an informal group, they become susceptible to the values of that group. Thus, the informal group can be a powerful force in organizations. Illustratively, a number of police unions started as an unorganized, small informal group of dissatisfied officers. Although many factors contribute to the enduring problem of police corruption, such as disillusionment and temptation, an informal group that supports taking payoffs makes it more difficult to identify and prosecute "bad cops." In 1972, the **Knapp Commission**, investigating corruption in the New York City Police Department, distinguished between "meat-eaters" (those who overtly pursued opportunities to profit personally from their police power) and "grass-eaters" (those who simply accepted the payoffs that the happenstances of police work brought their way).[80] The behavior of the grass-eaters can be interpreted within the framework of the power that informal groups have. In its investigation of corruption in the New York City Police Department, the Knapp Commission learned that the motive for grass-eaters taking petty graft was to be seen as "one of the boys" and therefore trusted by the **meat-eaters.**

The foregoing discussion should not be interpreted to mean that informal groups always, or even frequently, engage in troublesome or unethical behavior but rather is an illustration of the potency that such groups have. Astute law enforcement administrators are always alert for opportunities to tap the energy of informal groups to support departmental goals and programs.

Critique of the Human Relations School

Mayo's human relations school has been challenged on a number of grounds:

1. The research methods were not rigorous and such lapses may have tainted the findings.[81]
2. The human relations school claims conflicts between management and workers can be resolved by "harmony" between them. This attributes too much potency to "harmony." Moreover, it ignores the possibility that properly handles conflict can be a source of creativity and innovation.

Box 5.3 Francesco "Frank" Serpico

Born in 1936, Frank Serpico joined the NYPD in 1959. A "straight-arrow" officer, he gradually learned of significant corruption within the department. Illustratively, while some officers would accept occasional, petty bribes not to issue summons, the most serious corruption involved officers who were "on the pad," getting regular payments to protect activities like prostitution, gambling, the numbers racket, and narcotics.

In 1970, Serpico reported it, but it appeared nothing was being done. He subsequently did a newspaper interview, which appears to have been a contributing factor to Mayor Lindsay appointing the Knapp Commission.

In 1971, Serpico was on a narcotics raid, got his head slammed in the door and was shot in the face. His two backups reportedly left the scene without calling for an ambulance, perhaps because he was already detested on the department for breaking the "blue curtain of silence." Serpico was belatedly promoted to detective and awarded the NYPD's Medal of Honor. Retired in 1972, he went to Europe for a decade and traveled widely before returning to the United States, living a semi-reclusive life in a cabin he built. Serpico still occasionally speaks out on police issues, like excessive use of force.

In 1992, the Mollen Commission began looking into corruption in the NYPD and produced its report in 1994. It did not find the systemic selling and buying of protection corruption of the Knapp Commission but did uncover pockets of "crew-based" corruption. However, substantial use of undetected excessive force was identified, which the Mollen report characterized as being justified by officers as morally correct when a "guilty" person who would otherwise go unpunished was the recipient.

3. The single-mindedness with which advocates insisted on the importance of human relations was evangelistic.

4. Entirely too much emphasis was placed on the informal side of organization to the neglect of the organization as a whole.[82]

Human relations is also criticized as having a pro-management bias from several perspectives. First, it saw unions as promoting conflict between management and labor, a condition antithetical to the values of human relations. Second, by focusing on workers, the Hawthorne studies provided management with more sophisticated means of manipulating employees. Finally, the goal of human relations is indistinguishable from that of scientific management in that both aim for a more efficient organization:

> Scientific management assumed that the most efficient organization would also be the most satisfying one, since it would maximize both productivity and workers' pay . . . the Human Relations approach was that the most personally satisfying organization would be the most efficient.[83]

In 2010, job satisfaction in the United States hit a 20-year low.[84] Although the Hawthorne Studies never showed a clear-cut relationship between satisfaction and job performance,[85] the human relations "chant" that satisfied people are more productive has become a widely held and cherished belief. It is a logically appealing and commonsense position whose endless repetition has accorded it the status of "fact." There is, however, no consistent research evidence to support that job satisfactions causes or is correlated with productivity.

A 2008 study reviewed 70 years of research and concluded that uncertainty remains as to whether happier workers are more productive.[86] The study essentially confirms the most scornful dismissal of the human relations school as "contented cows give more milk" theory. In 2009, researchers found that in nonenforcement situations with the public, officers had greater job satisfaction when they perceived higher levels of public support.[87] In a smaller study (2009), the best predictors of job satisfaction among police officers was job autonomy and regular feedback.[88] Job satisfaction can be decreased or increased by the velocity or speed at which a person is able to make progress toward important goals (2010).[89] There is also some evidence (2008) that employer-provided support services, such as child care and exercise opportunities, are a shield to job dissatisfaction and may decrease turnover.[90]

ORGANIZATIONAL HUMANISM

Organizational humanism (OH) shares the human relations school's distaste for traditional organizational theory. OH differs from traditional organizational theory and the human relations school in three fundamental ways: (1) the work intrinsically, in and of itself, should be satisfying and help to motivate workers; (2) organizations must pay attention to the on- and off-the-job needs of workers; and (3) work shouldn't be just something that

people endure to make a living.[91] Covered in this section are Maslow's needs hierarchy; Argyris's immaturity/maturity changes; McGregor's Theory X–Theory Y; and Herzberg's motivation-hygiene theory. Likert's management systems, a four-step continuum from authoritarian to participative work environments, could also fit here, although it is covered in Chapter 7, Leadership. These organizational humanists must be read in the context of their times; their views were written from 1943 (Maslow, the needs hierarchy) until 1966 (Herzberg, motivation-hygiene theory). Presently, some of their views are archaic; in fairness, they could not foresee the rise of neoclassical organizational theory and the neo-Weberian organizational processes. Nonetheless, organizational humanism is an important milestone in helping to move thinking beyond traditional organizational theory and the human relations school and helped to set the stage for new styles of leadership and organizational processes (see Chapter 7, Leadership).

Maslow: The Needs Hierarchy

Abraham Maslow (1908–1970) was a psychologist who developed the **needs hierarchy** to explain individual motivation. The model appeared first in a 1943 article[92] and later received extended coverage in Maslow's *Motivation and Personality* (1954); it is summarized in Figure 5.7.[93]

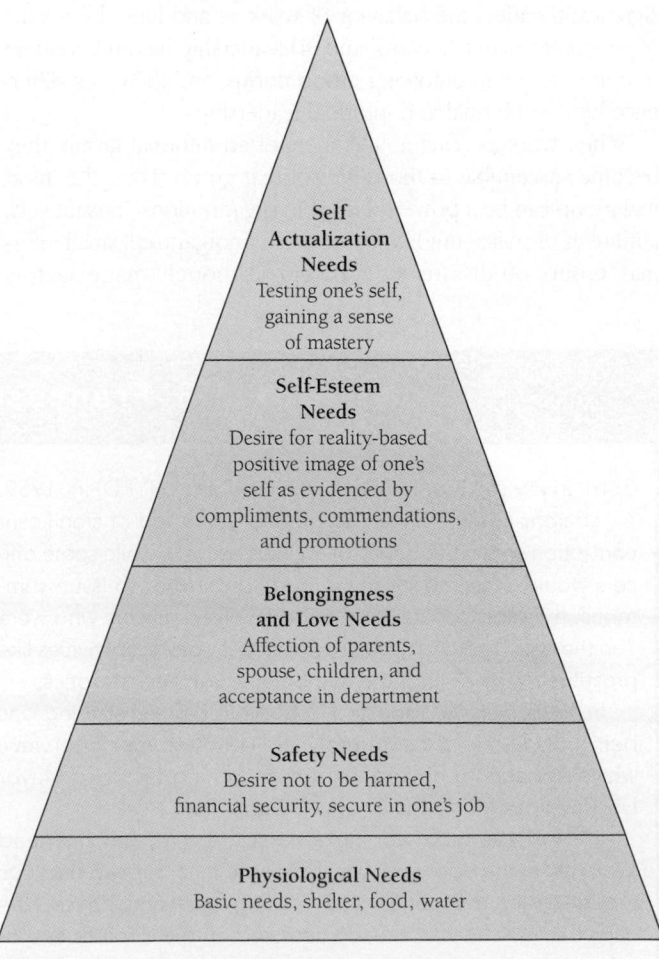

Self Actualization Needs
Testing one's self, gaining a sense of mastery

Self-Esteem Needs
Desire for reality-based positive image of one's self as evidenced by compliments, commendations, and promotions

Belongingness and Love Needs
Affection of parents, spouse, children, and acceptance in department

Safety Needs
Desire not to be harmed, financial security, secure in one's job

Physiological Needs
Basic needs, shelter, food, water

FIGURE 5.7 ▶ Maslow's needs hierarchy.

The needs hierarchy is arranged, like the rungs on a ladder, from the lower-order to the higher-order needs. A person does not move from one level to the next-higher one until the majority of the prior level's needs are met. Once those needs are met, they cease to motivate a person, and the needs at the next level of the hierarchy predominate. For example, one does not attempt to self-actualize until one has feelings of self-confidence, worth, strength, capability, adequacy, and mastery;[94] these feelings are generated only with the meeting of the self-esteem needs. It is important to understanding the needs hierarchy that the character of something does not necessarily determine what need is met but rather to what use it is put; money can be used to buy food and satisfy a basic need, or it can be put in a savings account to satisfy safety needs. Also, any progress up the hierarchy can be reversed; a police officer who is fired or is given a lengthy suspension may be thrust into a financial situation in which the physiological needs will predominate.

Police agencies that are managed professionally attempt to make appropriate use of theoretical constructs. For example, the fourth level of Maslow's needs hierarchy is self-esteem, which includes the need for recognition as evidenced by compliments and commendations. The Ohio State Highway Patrol used this need level to combat vehicle theft by creating the Blue Max Award. Each time a state trooper arrests a suspect in a stolen car, he or she receives a lightning bolt decal to place on the side of his or her patrol car. For five such arrests, a trooper receives a license plate that reads "ACE" with a single lightening bolt next to it. Each additional five arrests results in an additional lightening bolt on the license plate. The trooper with the most stolen car arrests at the end of the year receives a citation of merit, a uniform ribbon, and exclusive use of a new patrol car for a year. In 2014, the top trooper recovered 18 vehicles worth $68,288 and resulted in the apprehension of 18 subjects.[95]

Argyris: Immaturity-Maturity Theory

Chris Argyris (1923–2013) is a leading proponent of more open and participative organizations. In *Personality and Organization: The Conflict between System and the Individual* (1957), he states a theory of **immaturity versus maturity**. Argyris believes that as one moves from infancy toward adulthood in years of age, the healthy individual also advances from immaturity to maturity. Simultaneously, Argyris views formal organizations as having certain properties that are barriers to the development of maturity: (1) specialization reduces worker initiative because employees repeatedly perform unchallenging tasks and (2) the chain of command and narrow span of control make workers submissive, passive, and dependent.[96]

Argyris believed that when the needs of a healthy, mature worker collided with the properties of the formal organization, dysfunctional things could happen, including the worker becoming frustrated, choosing to produce less, developing psychosomatic illnesses, and choosing to seek employment elsewhere.[97] He doubted that it was possible to have a relationship between the individual and the organization that allowed the simultaneous maximizing of the values of both.[98] Argyris modified his theory in

1966 with a mix model, asserting that organizations could reduce some of their unintended, nonproductive employee practices to free up more productive uses of their energy.[99] He also noted that having some unchallenging work was an asset because it allowed recovery time for workers and routine tasks could get done.[100]

McGregor: Theory X–Theory Y

Douglas McGregor (1904–1964) believed that many managerial acts rested on conscious or subconscious assumptions and beliefs about how workers behave.[101] In *The Human Side of Enterprise* (1960), McGregor stated two different sets of assumptions that managers make about people;[102] his **Theory X–Theory Y** reflects two polar opposite characterizations of these assumptions and beliefs (see Table 5.3).[103]

American police departments have historically been dominated by Theory X assumptions. Even police departments with progressive national images can be experienced as tightly controlling environments by the people who actually work in them:

> The person leading a training session with about 35 managers of a West Coast police department observed that we often react to organizations as though they were living, breathing things. The managers agreed with this and noted the use of such phrases as "the department promoted me this year" and "the department hired me in 2000." They also understood that in fact someone, not the police department, had made those decisions. The managers were then divided into five groups and asked to make a list of what they thought the police department would say about them if it could actually talk. When the groups reported back, they identified a total of 42 statements, some of which were duplicates of each other. These managers, all of whom were college graduates and many of whom held advanced degrees, indicated the police department would make some positive statements, but would also say "They are idiots," "They don't have any sense," "Watch them or they'll screw up royally."

Theory X assumptions are readily recognized as being those that underpin traditional organizational theory. For example, we can relate a narrow span of control to Theory X's first two propositions. In contrast, Theory Y is formed by a set of views that are supportive of Argyris's mix model; they postulate that the interests of the individual and the organization need not be conflictual but can be integrated for mutual benefit. The principal task of management in a Theory X police department is control. In a Theory Y department, it is supporting subordinates by giving them the resources to do their jobs and creating an environment where they can be self-controlling, mature, contributing, and self-actualizing—within the context of the agency's mission and goals.

Herzberg: Motivation-Hygiene Theory

Motivation-hygiene theory was developed from research conducted by **Frederick Herzberg** (1923–2000), Bernard Mausner, and Barbara Snyderman on job attitudes at 11 work sites in the Pittsburgh area and reported in *The Motivation to Work* (1959). The major statement of the theory, which evolved

TABLE 5.3 MCGREGOR'S THEORY X–THEORY Y ASSUMPTIONS ABOUT WORKERS

Theory X	Theory Y
1. The average human has an inherent dislike of work and will avoid it if possible. 2. Most people must be coerced, controlled, directed, and threatened with punishment to get them to put forth adequate effort toward the achievement of organizational objectives. 3. The average human prefers to be directed, wishes to avoid responsibility, has relatively little ambition, and wants security above all.	1. The expenditure of physical and mental effort in work is as natural as play or rest. 2. External control and the threat of punishment are not the only means for bringing about effort toward organizational objectives. People will exercise self-direction and self-control in the service of objectives to which they are committed. 3. Commitment to objectives is a function of the rewards associated with their achievement. 4. The average human learns, under proper conditions, not only to accept but also to seek responsibility. 5. The capacity to exercise a relatively high degree of imagination, ingenuity, and creativity in the solution of organizational problems is widely, not narrowly, distributed in organizations. 6. Organizations only partially utilize the abilities of their employees; unleashing that energy leads to greater organizational achievements and more fulfilled employees.

out of this earlier research, is found in Herzberg's *Work and the Nature of Man* (1966).

Herzberg saw two sets of variables operating in the work setting: (1) hygiene factors, which he later came to call maintenance factors, and (2) motivators. Table 5.4 identifies Herzberg's hygiene factors and motivators. The hygiene factors relate to the work environment; the motivators relate to the work itself. Herzberg borrowed the term *hygiene* from the health-care field and used it to refer to factors that, if not treated properly, could lead to a deterioration in performance, creating an "unhealthy" organization.

Hygiene factors that are not treated properly are a source of dissatisfaction. However, even if all of them are provided, a police department does not have motivated officers, just ones who are not dissatisfied. Hygiene factors and motivators operate independently of each other; the police manager can motivate subordinates if they are somewhat dissatisfied with their salaries. However, the greater the level of dissatisfaction, the more difficult it becomes to employ the motivators successfully.

Note that law enforcement leaders have more control over motivators than they do over basic hygiene factors. When leaders

TABLE 5.4 HERZBERG'S MOTIVATION-HYGIENE THEORY

Hygiene/Maintenance Factors	Motivators
Supervisory practices	Achievement
Policies and administration	Recognition for accomplishments
Working conditions	Challenging work
Interpersonal relationships with subordinates, peers, and superiors	Increased responsibility
Status	Advancement possibilities
Effect of the job on personal life	Opportunity for personal growth and development
Job security	
Money	

Source: "Herzberg's motivation-hygiene theory" from *Work and the Nature of Man* by Frederick Herzberg (Cleveland: World Publishing, 1966), pp. 95–96.

exercise control over hygiene factors, they can do a considerable amount of good in reducing dissatisfaction and facilitating the use of the motivators, or they can cause considerable unhappiness:

> The commander in charge of the uniformed division of a 100-officer department suddenly announced that officers were going to be placed on permanent shifts. Surprised and angered by this move, the officers and their wives mobilized to oppose the plan, and after a mass meeting with the commander, the plan was abandoned. The legacy of this incident was a period of barely subdued hostility, distrust, and low morale.

The nature of police work is challenging, and some motivational effect is thus naturally occurring. Police managers can build on this by varying assignments appropriately. Measures that employ various other motivators include an active awards system, the creation of a master patrol officer designation, an annual police awards banquet, an active staff development program, and a career system with various specialization tracks.

Maslow's needs hierarchy and Herzberg's motivation-hygiene theory can be interrelated; the physiological, safety, and love and belongingness needs of Maslow correspond to Herzberg's hygiene factors; the top two levels of the needs hierarchy—esteem and self-actualization—correlate with Herzberg's motivators.

Critique of Organizational Humanism

In one way or another, organizational humanism (OH) theories depend to some degree on open and honest communication between organizational members who respect and trust each other. An attractive theme, it gives insufficient weight to the consequences that can occur when authenticity meets power. Illustratively, movie maker Samuel Goldwyn told his staff, "I want you all to tell me what's wrong with our operation even if it means losing your job."[104]

An underlying assumption of OH is that people want more rewards than just money from doing their work. Ignored is the reality that some proportion of workers have a utilitarian involvement with the job. It simply provides the money necessary to live; they save their energies and obtain their rewards from their families, operating their own on-line businesses, or other non-job-related sources, such as hobbies.

Despite the lack of research and the fact that the few existing studies do not support Maslow, there remains an almost metaphysical attraction to the needs hierarchy,[105] a condition made even more perplexing by noting that Maslow's work on motivation came from a small clinical study of neurotic people.[106] In turn, Maslow points at Theory X–Theory Y and notes that a good deal of what McGregor bases his conclusions on comes from my research ". . . and above all people I know just how shaky that foundation is . . . I am concerned that enthusiastic people will swallow it whole."[107]

In contrast to the lack of research on the needs hierarchy, there has been considerable research on Herzberg's motivation-hygiene theory; after reviewing this evidence, Gibson and Teasley concluded the range of findings run from general support to a vigorous condemnation of Herzberg's methodology.[108]

The research support for Argyris's immaturity-maturity theory is generally weak. Heavily influenced by Maslow, Argyris's own research only used semi-structured interviews and the theory assumes that workers' needs are uniform[109] A major test of the theory, which included 800 respondents, did not find sufficient evidence to support it.[110]

BEHAVIORAL SYSTEMS THEORY

The successor to organizational humanism was **behavioral systems theory** (BST), founded by **Kurt Lewin** (1890–1947), a psychologist who fled from Germany in the early 1930s.[111] The theorists in this school saw organizations as being composed of the behavior of individuals and groups and were interested in making organizations more democratic and participative. The work of some organizational humanists is sometimes included in BST.

Lewin was interested in group dynamics—how groups form and how their members relate to each other—and he also developed a decision-making tool, **force-field analysis** (see Table 5.5).

In force-field analysis, driving forces push for a new condition and restraining forces resist the change. If there are exactly opposing driving and restraining forces, the arrows of these opposing forces meet at the vertical zero, or balance, line. In some instances, there might not be an exactly opposite force, in which case an arrow is simply drawn, as in Table 5.5, to the balance line. After all entries are made and the situation is summarized, the relative power of the driving and restraining forces must be subjectively evaluated. In this regard, the balance line should be regarded as a spring that will be moved in one direction, suggesting the action that needs to be taken or the decision that needs to be made.

In the *Human Group* (1950), George Homans (1910–1989) advanced the idea that groups have both an internal and an external system.[112] The internal system comprises factors that arise within the group itself, such as the feelings that members of a group develop about each other during the life of the group. In contrast, the external system consists of variables in the larger environment in which the group exists. Members of the same patrol shift may form one or more groups and these groups exist within the context of the law enforcement agency employing them. To illustrate, a chief suspends an officer for three days following a high-speed pursuit in which the officer had an at-fault accident. The officers who work on the same shift as the suspended officer viewed the discipline as unjust and agreed among themselves not to write any traffic citations during the three-day suspension.

Much of Warren Bennis's (1925–2014) effort was in **organizational development** (OD), a change management process. OD is used to "recalibrate" the work attitudes and values of employees with respect to the changes the organization wishes to make and often involves surveying and training employees. It is intended to take the chaos and uncertainty out of organizational changes. When police departments plan and implement community or intelligence-led policing or servant leadership (see Chapter 7, Leadership), they are engaged in organizational development change (see Chapter 15, Organizational Change).

TABLE 5.5 FORCE-FIELD ANALYSIS OF CONFLICT INVOLVING A POLICE PROMOTIONAL SYSTEM

Driving Forces	Restraining Forces
Minority officers discontent with lack of minority promotions	Majority and some minority officers support present promotional system
Several discrimination complaints filed by minority officers	Elected and appointed officials willing to initiate change, but wanted the fullest and fairest competition to ensure public confidence in those selected for leadership positions
Minority employees association formed and their attorney had presented plan that would grant preferential treatment to minorities temporarily	Majority officers association took no official policy stand but association's President appeared before Council to oppose changing the current promotional process
Elected and appointed community officials want to respond to legitimate employee and community concerns	Ill-considered change could splinter the department badly along racial lines
Possibility of litigation and court intervention	Fifty majority employees allegedly prepared to get $5,000 second mortgages on their homes to raise $250,000 for filing a cross suit
	Officers with seniority and/or higher education opposed to reducing the importance of these factors in any new police promotional ordinance
Litigation could result in adverse publicity, damaging the city's progressive reputation and economic development	

Critique of Behavioral Systems Theory

Although behavioral systems theory (BST) was relatively short-lived, its theorists helped sustain the movement away from mechanistic views of organizations and toward the people in them. Homans's work on internal and external systems served to set the stage for open systems theory.

ORGANIZATIONS AS OPEN SYSTEMS

Ludwig von Bertalanffy (1901–1972), a biologist, articulated general systems theory (GST) in 1940. However, the application of GST principles to organizational theory did not begin to gain prominence until the 1960s when it was recast as open systems

theory (OST) by Katz and Khan in their *The Social Psychology of Organization* (1966).

A system is a grouping of separate but interrelated components working together toward the achievement of a common objective (see Figure 5.8). Organizations can be characterized as closed or open systems. In actuality, there are no entirely closed or entirely open organizations; these are terms used only to describe the extent to which an organization approximates one or the other. Closed systems operate under assumptions that they are rational, effective, efficient, substantially self-sufficient, can reasonably predict what is going to happen, and "know what's best." This line of thinking is accompanied by, or breeds, an insensitivity to influences from the larger environment, which reinforces the isolation of a closed system organization.

Open systems theory views hierarchical organizations, such as law enforcement agencies, as being comprised of multiple

FIGURE 5.8 ▶ A basic open system view of a law enforcement agency with illustrated processes.

subsystems interfacing with the larger environment. It both accommodates the hierarchical feature of traditional organizational theory and describes the organization's functioning in an open systems context. By doing so, the effect of factors in an organization's environment can systematically be taken into account in explanations of its performance.

Both traditional organizational theory and the early police professionalism movement (see Chapter 1, The Evolution of Police Administration) reinforced a closed system view, which

regards whatever is "outside of it" as being inconsequential. In contrast, open systems:

1. Recognize that everything beyond their boundary/ structure is part of their environment;[113]
2. Know they have regular on-going relationships in the larger environment in which they are embedded; this is the quality of being interdependent; numerous factors impinge on law enforcement agencies (see Table 5.6);

TABLE 5.6 ILLUSTRATIVE ENVIRONMENTAL FACTORS POTENTIALLY IMPACTING LAW ENFORCEMENT AGENCIES

Illustrative Environmental Factors	Potential Impacts
Police Unions	Oppose increased cost of health and pension benefits to their members; furloughs and layoffs; wage concessions; freezing cost of living increases for their retirees; early release of violent offenders; parole of "Cop Killers"; increases in hiring standards and some disciplinary actions; support specific political candidates; usually gun control; some tax increases; and legislation requiring the death penalty for those killing officers in the performance of their duties.
Partners	Multiagency single purpose and standing task forces may create friction about budgetary support, credit for successes, and blame for failures; mutual aide compacts allow agencies to share the use of special resources, aircraft, SWAT teams, and bomb disposal units.
Events	Agency resources may be overrun by natural disasters, protests and riots, catastrophic industrial accidents, terrorist attacks, and searching for children lost in wilderness areas. Events may also be positive, e.g., gifts and grants.
Legal Framework	New court rulings, federal, and state laws may require new expenses and procedures and/or provide agencies with new authority. Some federal laws, e.g., Americans with Disability Act (ADA) and Occupational Health and Safety Act (OSHA) provide protection to officers (See Chapter 9, Human Resources).
Governing Body	May slash budgets, impacting agency operations and keeping high-mileage cars in the fleet; declare city a sanctuary for undocumented immigrants putting the agency between official policy and public demands for strict enforcement; and approve take-home cars.
Special Interest Groups/Stakeholders	May call for special unit to deal with the gay, lesbian, bisexual, and transgendered communites; Washington DC has a GLBT Police Unit for this purpose; advocate for more officers walking beats in business areas; and demand strict enforcement of loitering, panhandling and noise ordinances.
Technology	Can be used to make agency more transparent, as a recruiting tool, and to provide e-government services.
Other Departments	May see offers to engage in collaborative projects as an attempt by police to "build empire" or use their resources; equipment and supplies selected by purchasing may be seen by rank and file as substandard/inadequate.

3. Have walls or boundaries that are permeable, allowing things, for example, information and information, in and out. Too many inputs will overwhelm an open system and threaten its **homeostasis** or balance; from the Greek, *homeostasis* literally means "standing still";

4. Use **coding** to prevent being overwhelmed, which functions like a priority system; important inputs get through quickly: calls from a city manager will usually be received by the chief, but citizens asking to talk to the chief often find themselves redirected and speaking to someone else;

5. Have the tendency to become more complex and specialized; as specialization proceeds, its fragmenting effect on the department is countered by the unifying elements of its **internal subsystems** (see Table 5.7);

6. Face the prospect of moving toward decline, disorganization, and death—the **entropic process**. Only 13 of the businesses existing at the time of the American Revolution remain as autonomous entities, and during a 20-year period, 46 percent of the companies on the Fortune 500 list of America's largest and most powerful businesses disappeared from that list.[114] Law enforcement agencies have no exemption from the entropic process. In the current financial environment, thousands of agencies have experienced hiring freezes, furloughs, layoffs, and being shut down (see Chapter 12, Financial Management). To fight entropy, departments continuously import more inputs than they can use (e.g., gasoline), and store it to allow operations to continue if supplies are interrupted. "Buffering" describes this processing of storing some inputs and it allows the department to develop negative entropy, or the capacity to resist decline.

7. Must evolve, in order to avoid decline, the quality of adaptability;

8. Become double-loop learning organizations in order to be adaptive: (1) **single-loop learning** allows organizations to make corrections and carry out their present efforts toward achieving objectives and (2) **double-loop learning,** articulated by Chris Argyris, goes deeper, enabling organizations to judge whether they are pursuing the right objectives, programs, and policies.[115] Law enforcement practices associated with double-loop learning include after action reports, staff inspections, and program evaluation;

9. Follow the principle of **equafinality**, which means there are multiple ways to achieve goals; and

10. Can never be more varied than the larger environment.[116] **Isomorphism**, from the Greek meaning equal shape, dictates that the resource-dependent agencies tend to mirror the complexity and demands of their environment and develop policies, programs, and units that are signaled to be important by the environment.

Critique of Open Systems Theory

Some critics question whether GST, which originated in biology and was applied to organizations as OST, can unequivocally be used to explain contrived man-made organizations.[117] The essence of this criticism is that using explanations of living systems to describe the behavior of artificially created, non-organic organizations poses the danger of a misapplication of knowledge and the creation of false, but persuasive, analogies. These critics argue that the extension of GST into organizations as open systems may fail to account for or understate crucial aspects of organizations. Finally, these critics maintain that organizations may be systems, but they are not natural systems that are subject to immutable laws[118] and do not invariably follow the birth, growth, maturity, and death cycle of biological systems.

In more positive terms, open systems theory provides a framework and language for understanding how law enforcement is

TABLE 5.7 THE INTERNAL SUBSYSTEMS OF A LAW ENFORCEMENT AGENCY	
Subsystems	**Illustrative Functions**
Managerial	Sets direction for agency, controls, directs, coordinates, evaluates, takes corrective action, empowers employees, sets budget priorities and presents and defends operating budget
Supportive	Acquires resources from larger environment and distributes them; budget and grant preparation, recruits, obtains surplus government property, promotes positive image of agency
Production	Components that transform inputs into outputs, patrol, investigation, crime prevention, DUI checkpoints, e-government services
Maintenance	Building, grounds, equipment, special emphasis on employees, fair compensation and benefits, favorable work environment
Adaptive	Scans environment, identifies problems, opportunities, and challenges; develops response strategies and tactics

Source: These subsystems were identified in Danial Katz and Robert L. Kahn, *The Social Psychology of Organizations.* New York: Wiley, 2nd Edition, 1978.

loosely connected to and interacts with elected and appointed governmental leaders, prosecutors, the judiciary, federal departments, grant awarding agencies, clients, consultants, and other entities, as well as how they handle inputs such as information.

OTHER PARADIGMS OF ADMINISTRATION

A paradigm is a coherent, internally consistent, and integrated approach to making sense of whatever is being studied. In essence, it is a model. If you are defining a problem in a conventional, habitual, or customary way, you are "thinking inside the box," a condition created by "paradigm paralysis." If trying to solve the problem by thinking "outside of the box," you will have some quirky, unconventional thoughts that may lead you to important innovations or paradigm shifts. This section covers some theories that are not mainstream but are interesting ways of looking at organizations.

Environmental Theories

This group of theories relates organizations to the broader environments in which they are embedded: (1) environmental contingency theory, (2) resource dependency theory, (3) population ecology, (4) old institutional theory; and (5) neo institutional theory.

Environmental Contingency Theory Burns and Stalker (1961, 1968) maintain that there is no one best way to structure an organization.[119] Instead, leaders must "read the environment" and decide what type of structure is the best "fit" with the environment being faced. For example, if the environment is stable and the tasks to be performed are routine, than a mechanistic form of organization might be the best choice. Very successful organizations are able to find the best "fit."

Organizations may still survive, with varying degrees of success, with "adequate" or "good" fits, but they are unlikely to excel and may even have to abandon a fit they have chosen. Around 1980, a few police departments tried to "flatten" the seven or eight layers of their hierarchy, which made their structure grow horizontally and shrink in height. These experiments were quickly abandoned because others in the environment (e.g., local, state, and federal agencies) didn't know what unit or person they should contact about any matter. "Fit" is also being used to determine whether a person can be a productive part of an organization or a work team; although ability is a key factor, emotional stability is proving to be even more important.[120]

Resource Dependency Theory The fullest expression of resource dependency theory (RDT) was produced by Pfeffer and Salancik (1978).[121] The basic thrust of RDT is that all agencies must get the resources they need to operate from the larger environment, creating resource dependency. The control of resource distribution by the larger environment is a source of power over agencies and makes them dependent. Failure to capture resources makes an agency more vulnerable and moves it toward entropy. RDT helps agency leaders identify the standing of other agencies competing for resources and who has power in the environment. RDT views organizational success as organizations maximizing their power. Organizations can do so by forming co-operative ventures with other organizations and by making resource providers view their contributions as crucial.

Population Ecology RDT and population ecology (PE) share the same views on organization resource dependence and the power of the larger environment. However, they use different levels of analysis; RDT focuses on agencies and PE focuses on the larger environment.[122] PE, which fundamentally had a mid- to late-1970s start, seeks to discover why organizations competing in the same resource pool or ecological niche are more, and others less, successful. Hannan and Freeman's *The Population Ecology of Organizations* (1977) was a major development in this line of thinking.

Old Institutional Theory "Old" institutional theory (OIT) is associated with traditional organizational theory. In explaining organizations, it tended to rely on historical justifications for structures and processes, OIT was the legal foundation for the existence of public organizations, holding that the structure of an organization dictated the behavior of its members. Therefore, OIT was relatively uninterested on how organizations impacted individuals.[123] The old institutional writings were descriptive and value laden, substantially lacking an empirical base. Nonetheless, along with traditional organizational theory, the old institutionalism was part of the progressive era/good government movement that lasted from roughly 1890 into the 1920s (see Chapter 1, The Evolution of Police Administration).

Neo Institutional Theory Neo-institutionalism was named by March and Olsen (1984)[124] and its beginning dates from the late 1970s until the mid-1980s. There are a half-dozen or more varieties of neo-institutionalism; the political institutional framework (PIF) is briefly described here.[125] PIF's view is that organizations are not simply acted upon by the larger/external political system (e.g., inevitably pressured into the mandatory adoption of strategies, programs, and policies). Instead, organizations are often themselves potent political forces that can resist pressures and shape part of their external political landscape.[126] PIF recognized that politics is "done" both to, and by, organizations.

Networked and Virtual Organizations

Networked and virtual organizations are goal directed and share many characteristics. Advanced information technology is the glue that allows them to function; geographic proximity may not be an issue; dispersion may provide some advantages; and horizontal communication accounts for most message traffic. As a generalization, **networked organizations** (NOs) have relationships that are planned and stable, whereas **virtual organizations** (VOs) have relationships that often arise spontaneously out of special needs and may be temporary.[127]

Networked organizations (NOs) date from the early 1980s when tall, hierarchical organizations faced a tough economy. They realized that there were some things other organizations or individuals could do cheaper, faster, and better. The result was a period of corporate downsizing as individual jobs and functions were subcontracted out. The separate members of a networked organization are termed *nodes* and are simultaneously autonomous and collaborative, pooling their resources, and geographically dispersed to one degree or another. The relationships of the nodes are spelled out in contracts. To illustrate, Firm A designs a car; Firm B does the engineering; Firm C builds it with parts provided by supplier nodes; and Firm D markets the vehicle. NOs flatten the organizational hierarchy and broaden the organizational structure horizontally. This requires continuing horizontal communication, which results in personal relationship developing between people in different nodes. These relationships are added value; people go out of the way to help those they know. NOs may use some overarching or meta-management to coordinate functions (e.g., a board of directors). Although NOs can be used for a single project, they tend to be ongoing enterprises with some node members being replaced from time to time to achieve greater efficiency or for other reasons.

Although NOs and VOs are sometimes used synonymously, others describe VOs as being created more spontaneously, not regulated by formal agreements, more informal, and driven by the need to accomplish a single task. Node members, who can withdraw at any point, participate voluntarily and leadership may not be formally designated; the nodes can be self-directed because of their mutuality of needs.

In 2002, a sniper went on a rampage in the Washington, DC, area; victims were shot with a high-power rifle from a distance, leaving no witnesses and few investigative leads for law enforcement agencies (see Figure 5.9).[128] By the time an arrest was made, there were 14 shootings, 10 deaths, and thousands of local, state, and federal law enforcement officers involved.[129] A total of five different task forces from different involved jurisdictions were in operation and one had three co-equal leaders.[130] The task forces were built "on the fly" and nobody had a chance to step back and critically assess what was being done.[131] Task force leaders said that they didn't need more control over the other task forces; they needed more coordination.[132] There was no central hub to coordinate investigative priorities, use of resources, and information sharing.

The sniper case reflects the following elements, many of which reflect virtual organizational theory: (1) there was a spontaneous need; (2) although some agency and personal relationships preexisted, other relationships were unplanned; (3) the law enforcement agencies were geographically dispersed; (4) in the absence of a central command and control hub, greater horizontal communication was needed; (5) co-operating agencies could withdraw investigators at any point; (6) the enterprise was driven by a single purpose: apprehension; and (8) it is not clear to what extent any of the task forces operated under memorandums of understanding and those that did exist lacked written clarity and had obscure lines of authority and information—handling procedures.

Task forces can be established for a single purpose, such as the apprehension of a serial offender, or they can operate continuously, as in the case of the FBI's multijurisdictional Joint Terrorism Task Forces (JTTF) that were developed in the wake of 9/11. Mechanism of these types allows for a reasonable time horizon to plan, organize, and implement them under well-considered written guidance.

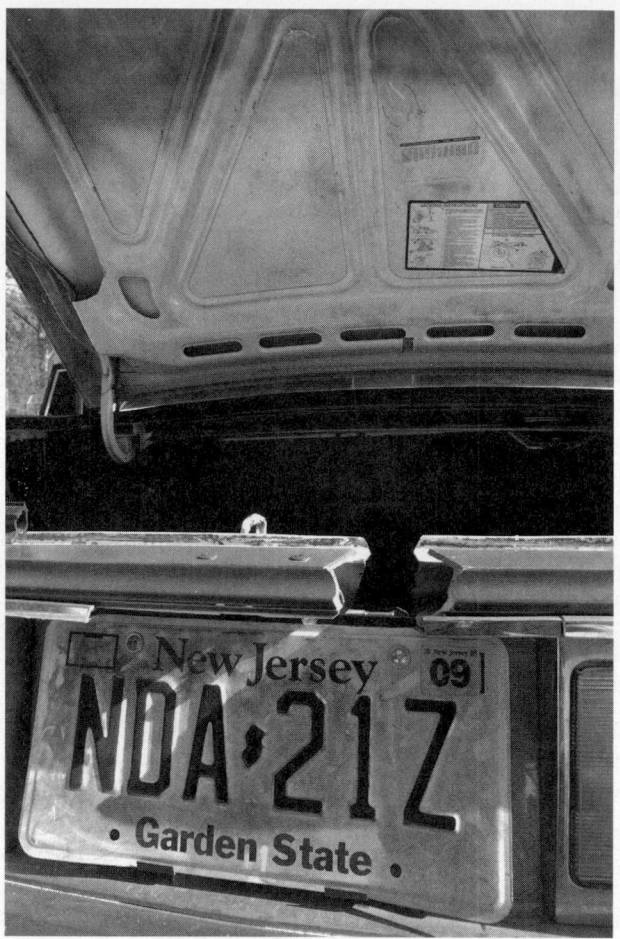

FIGURE 5.9 ▶ The sniper who terrorized the Washington, DC, area for 3 weeks in 2002 shot from inside of his car's closed trunk using a Bushmaster .223 rifle with a scope for accuracy and a tripod for stability. Note the cut-out in the body of his car so he could take position and shoot without anyone seeing him. (Mary Altaffer/AP Images)

One of the situations requiring multiple jurisdiction involvement is serial murder investigations because such crimes may be committed across several counties and states. To illustrate, Ted Bundy killed a number of young women during the 1970s. His method of operation was to kidnap a victim in one county and leave the body in another one to complicate investigations by involving several agencies, which he did in multiple states before being apprehended, convicted, and executed in Florida (1989).

Law enforcement agencies should give some consideration to evaluating the features of networked and virtual organizations, modifying them for off-the-shelf immediate use to meet spontaneous demands.

Sense Making

Sense making in organizations is how we process our experiences and what we do with them. In addition to his other publications, Weicke's *Sense Making in Organizations* (1995) and *Making Sense of Organizations* (2001) mark him as an influential theorist on this topic.

When something happens in a law enforcement executive's "world," the meaning may not be clear. Failure to resolve this uncertainty keeps the executive in an unhealthy state of tension. To resolve it, sense has to be made of the experience. Even if no additional information can be gathered, the event still has to be "processed." The experience is relived, reflected on, interpreted, analyzed, and meaning is assigned to it. From an internal perspective, the meaning just has to be plausible; it doesn't have to rise to the level of objective "truth." Sense making can occur within a single person or a group. These constructions often become shared and some ultimately achieve the status of organizational lore. This process of sense making is not episodic, but continuous, as experiences pile up. Like digital information, our interpreted experiences can be stored and retrieved.

Accumulated sense making produces **cognitive maps** or "mental understandings." The term may have been coined by Tolman (1948).[133] These maps help us understand our "landscape" and navigate our "world" so we can do such things as (1) understand the actions of commanding officers, (2) predict what others may do in different situations, (3) know who to take things to for swift handling, (4) decide who is like us, (5) identify potential mentors, and (6) select career paths in the department that match our interest and abilities.

Chaos Theory

Kiel's *Managing Chaos and Complexity in Government* (1994) was an early effort to apply **chaos theory** to the public sector.[134] In organizational theory, chaos is a state of non-equilibrium. It is precipitated by a crisis event(s) during which the everyday predictability and the usual order of things are disrupted, replaced at some level by a mix of factors, such as (1) widespread uncertainty and fear; (2) the delivery of normal services is not possible; (3) an initial lack of basic information about the event; (4) informational overload caused by inputs from political figures, inquiries from federal agencies or the news media, offers of assistance, and urgent citizen appeals; (5) the realization that plans are inadequate or nonexistent for the event; (6) recognition that available resources and modes of operation are insufficient or ineffective; and (7) the need to solve unfamiliar problems whose magnitude, complexity, and durability exceed anything we could imagine, a condition referred to as **cosmology**.[135] Under these circumstances, maladaptive decisions may increase the level of chaos, producing unintended consequences. **Bifurcation** is the flash-point when chaos overwhelms normal conditions in an agency[136] and compels the use of innovative efforts and alliances to restore stability in the community. The 9/11 attacks and Hurricane Katrina possessed the qualities of cosmology and bifurcation (see Figure 5.10).

Contrary to popular view, chaos theory does more than describe under what conditions events spin out of control, and total collapse seems both possible and imminent.[137] Its ultimate value is in how order is restored against seemingly insurmountable adversity. The way off the slippery slope of a chaos event is through self-organization. Police and other agencies don't have to do everything; individuals, neighbors, ad hoc groups, and

FIGURE 5.10 ▶ Hurricane Katrina devastated New Orleans on an unimaginable scale in 2005. Many residents were rescued from their rooftops by boats and others were able to wade to safety through the floodwaters. (FEMA/Win Henderson)

volunteers from other communities pitch in with helpful acts; they rescue people and pets from debris, open their homes to others, deliver food and water, set up temporary shelters and rudimentary first aid clinics, stand guard, reunite family members, and allow others to use their cell phones. These steps produce the butterfly effect, which ripples across the community, energizing people to help themselves and others. At the organization level, self-organization, or perhaps more precisely, self-reorganization occurs on a continuous basis during a chaos event. Organizations use sense making and, from their understanding of their experiences, use the quality of adaptability, developing new priorities, standards, services, procedures, and alliances. In the wake of a chaos event, organizations evolve into something more complex, with new goals, partnerships, structures, equipment, and communication channels to accommodate what they have learned.

Critique of Other Paradigms of Administration

Environmental contingency theory assumes organizations that are a "misfit" with their operating environment will "shift gears" and move to a "good fit" but fails to provide details on how this occurs and at what velocity. One way to look at a misfit is when the number of risk factors in a community "overpower" the ability of law enforcement agency to provide the desired level of public safety. A 2008 study of 133 local law enforcement risk factors (e.g., unemployment, the percent of housing that is renter-occupied, and percent of resident population ages 15–24, and 25 or more) had a significant impact on resource allocation and performance.[138]

Unsurprisingly, agencies, with higher per capita earning had lower levels of "risk factors," were less crime prone, and also better resourced.[139] Such agencies were less cost-efficient than lower resourced agencies because they had lower demands for service and thus fewer outputs.

Donaldson, an advocate of environmental contingency theory, is highly critical of resource dependency theory, population ecology, and neo-institutionalism. He dismisses them as part of the proliferation of theories by academics seeking momentary fame and diverting attention from studying more "worthy" theories (i.e., contingency theory).[140] Some theorists find Donaldson's criticisms too severe and unrelenting.

There are numerous praises of networked and virtual organizations, but they may be overstated with respect to how well NOs and VOs actually function and their efficiency. The literature is sparse about their failure rates and dysfunctionalities (e.g., the consequences of lingering personality conflicts between node members who have continuing contacts).

Chaos theory teaches us that crisis events that produce cosmology and bifurcation are not situations to be endured and resolved as much as they are the important aspects of organizational life whereby a law enforcement agency can adapt to its environment, maintain and renew itself, and ultimately adapt through self-organization and emerge stronger.

Chapter Summary

Summary by Learning Objective

1. **Identify and define four types of organizations based on who benefits from each type.**

   (1) Mutual benefit associations, such as police labor unions, where the primary beneficiary is the membership; (2) business concerns, such as Lynn Peavey, which sells crime scene equipment and supplies, where the owner is the prime beneficiary; (3) service organizations, such as homeless shelters and community mental health centers, where a specific client group is the prime beneficiary; and (4) commonweal organizations, such as the Department of Defense and law enforcement agencies, where the beneficiary is the public at large.

2. **Describe two sources of pressures for police departments.**

   (1) External democratic control: The public expects to have external democratic control of its police department through its elected and appointed representatives. This external democratic control feature also has the expectation that the internal workings of the police department will be effective and efficient, but not also democratic. This is because democratic control by the members of a police department would inevitably lead to the department being in conflict at various times with the will of the community (e.g., one favoring a hard-line approach to crime control versus the other being in favor of a more moderate approach) and (2) Internal Control: Internally, large numbers of officers at the lower levels of the police department do not want to be treated like "cogs in a machine" and desire some voice in how the department operates. Thus, the challenge for police managers is how to maintain an organization that meets society's needs and the needs of the officers who work in it.

3. **Identify the three stems of traditional organization theory.**

   The three branches or stems of traditional organizational theory are (1) scientific management, (2) the bureaucratic model, and (3) administrative, or management, theory.

4. **State the focus of scientific management.**

   It is to find the "one best way" to do work.

5. **Define *functional supervision* and the *exception principle*.**

   Functional supervision meant that people were responsible for directing certain tasks, despite the fact that this meant the authority of the supervisor might cut across organizational lines. The exception principle meant that routine matters should be handled by lower-level managers or by supervisors and that higher-level managers should only receive reports of deviations above or below standard performances.

6. **List the characteristics of Weber's bureaucratic model.**

   i. The organization of offices follows the principle of hierarchy; that is, each lower office is under the control and supervision of a higher one. This also creates the chain of command. This arrangement of successively higher offices also creates "layers" in a police department; the greater the number of layers, the more vertical complexity a department has. Hierarchy also provides the "vertical highways" that establish reporting relationships, as well as formal communication channels.

ii. There is a right of appeal and of statement of grievances from the lower to the higher offices.

iii. Specified areas of competence, meaning a division of labor, exist. This division of labor or specialization increases the width and horizontal complexity of law enforcement agencies. The greater the amount of specialization in organizations, the more organizations grow vertically to have the ability to coordinate the different units.

iv. Official duties are bound by a system of rational rules, such as policies and procedures.

v. Administrative acts, decisions, and rules are recorded in writing, creating an institutional memory.

vi. The authority associated with a position is the property of the office or job and not of the occupant of the position.

vii. Employees are appointed on the basis of qualifications, and specialized training is necessary.

viii. Organizational members do not own it.

7. Define street-level bureaucrats and the two modes out of which they operate.

Police officers working in the field are the face of government. They meet with members of the public and decide how to implement public policy. In doing so, officers operate out of two modes of street-level bureaucrats: (1) "state agents," who believe in following the law and policies and (2) "citizen agents," who will bend or ignore them.

8. Define administrative theory and its benchmark.

Administrative theory, also referred to as management theory and the principles approach, sought to identify generic or universal methods of administration. Its benchmark is the 1937 publication of Luther Gulick (1892–1993) and Lyndall Urwick's (1891–1983) edited Papers on the Science of Administration.

9. Explain why the human relations school developed.

The human relations school developed in reaction to the mechanistic orientation of traditional organizational theory, which was viewed as neglecting or ignoring the human element.

10. Describe organizational humanism and how it differs from traditional organizational theory and the human relations school.

Organizational humanism (OH) shares the human relations school's distaste for traditional organizational theory. OH differs from traditional organizational theory and the human relations school in three fundamental ways: (1) the work intrinsically, in and of itself, should be satisfying and help to motivate workers; (2) organizations must pay attention to the on- and off-the-job needs of workers; and

(3) work shouldn't be just something that people endure to make a living.

11. List the levels of Maslow's needs hierarchy.

Going from the bottom toward the top, the levels are (1) physiological, (2) safety, (3) belongingness and love needs, (4) self-esteem needs, and (5) self-actualization.

12. Contrast McGregor's Theory X and Theory Y assumptions at a broad level.

McGregor believed that many management acts rested on their assumptions and beliefs about how workers behave. Theory X and Theory Y are polar opposite characterizations of those assumptions and beliefs. Theory X characterizations underpin traditional organization theory while Theory Y characterizations are more positive: The interests of the organization and the individual need not conflict but can be integrated for their mutual benefit.

13. Differentiate between Herzberg's motivation and hygiene factors.

Herzberg saw two sets of variables operating independently in the work setting: (1) hygiene factors (which he later called maintenance factors) and motivators. Hygiene factors relate to the work environment and motivators to the work itself. If not properly attended to, hygiene factors could lead to a deterioration of the department's performance by creating an unhealthy environment. Even if all hygiene factors are satisfied you do not have a motivated officers, just ones that are not dissatisfied. In contrast, with fulfilled motivators, you have a workforce that is motivated. Even if hygiene factors are creating some dissatisfaction, police leaders can still motivate their officers. However, the higher the level of dissatisfaction, the more difficult it is to effectively use motivators.

14. Explain how force-field analysis works.

In force-field analysis, driving forces push for a new condition and restraining forces resist the change. If there are exactly opposing driving and restraining forces, the arrows of these opposing forces meet at the vertical zero, or balance, line. In some instances, there might not be an exactly opposite force, in which case an arrow is simply drawn to the balance line. After all entries are made and the situation is summarized, the relative power of the driving and restraining forces must be subjectively evaluated. In this regard, the balance line should be regarded as a spring that will be moved in one direction, suggesting the action that needs to be taken or the decision that needs to be made.

15. Describe the entropic process.

All organizations face the entropic process, moving toward decline. To fight entropy, departments continuously import more inputs than they can use (e.g., gasoline), and store it to allow operations to continue if supplies are interrupted. Buffering describes this processing of storing, and it allows the department to develop negative entropy, the capacity to resist decline.

16. Critique open systems theory.

Some critics wonder if open systems theory, which originated in biology, can unequivocally be used to explain contrived man-made organizations. Open systems theory may fail to account for or understate crucial aspects of organizations. Organizations can be systems, but they are not natural systems that are subject to immutable laws. Organizations do not invariably follow the birth, growth, maturity, and death cycle of biological systems. The definition of what is included in system theory is vague, does not account for variations in organizational complexity, and fails to provide guidance about handling conflict between components.

17. Give a generalized comparison of networked and virtual organizations.

As a generalization, networked organizations have relationships that are planned and stable, whereas virtual organizations have relationships that often arise spontaneously out of special needs and may be temporary.

18. Explain sense making.

When something happens in a law enforcement executive's "world," the meaning may not be clear. Failure to resolve this uncertainty keeps the executive in an unhealthy state of tension. To resolve it, sense has to be made of the experience. Even if no additional information can be gathered, the event still has to be "processed." The experience is relived, reflected on, interpreted, analyzed, and meaning is assigned to it. From an internal perspective, the meaning just has to be plausible; it doesn't have to rise to the level of objective "truth." Sense making occurs with a single person or in a group. These constructions often become shared and some ultimately achieve the status of organizational lore. This process of sense making is not episodic, but continuous, as experiences pile up. Like digital information, our interpreted experiences can be stored and retrieved.

19. Summarize chaos theory.

In organizational theory, chaos is a state of nonequilibrium. It is precipitated by a crisis event(s) during which the everyday predictability and the usual order of things are disrupted, replaced at some level by a mix of factors, such as: (1) widespread uncertainty and fear; (2) the delivery of normal services is not possible; (3) an initial lack of basic information about the event; (4) informational overload caused by inputs from political figures, inquiries from federal agencies or the news media, offers of assistance, and urgent citizen appeals; (5) the realization that plans are inadequate or nonexistent for the event; (6) recognition that available resources and modes of operation are insufficient or ineffective; and (7) the need to solve unfamiliar problems whose magnitude, complexity, and durability exceed anything we could imagine, a condition referred to as cosmology.

Under these circumstances, maladaptive decisions may increase the level of chaos, producing unintended consequences. Bifurcation is the flashpoint when chaos overwhelms normal conditions in an agency and compels the use of innovative efforts and alliances to restore stability in the community. The 9/11 attacks and Hurricane Katrina possessed the qualities of cosmology and bifurcation.

20. Describe self-organizing and the butterfly effect.

Contrary to popular view, chaos theory does more than describe under what conditions events spin out of control and total collapse seems both possible and imminent. Its ultimate value is in how order is restored against seemingly insurmountable adversity. The way off the slippery slope of a chaos event is through self-organization. Police and other agencies don't have to do everything; individuals, neighbors, ad hoc groups, and volunteers from other communities pitch in with helpful acts; they rescue people and pets from debris, open their homes to others, deliver food and water, set up temporary shelters and rudimentary first aid clinics, stand guard, reunite family members, and allow others to use their cell phones.

These steps produce the butterfly effect, which ripples across the community, energizing people to help themselves and others. At the organization level, self-organization, or perhaps more precisely, self-reorganization occurs on a continuous basis during a chaos event. Organizations use sense making and, from their understanding of their experiences, use the quality of adaptability, developing new priorities, standards, services, procedures, and alliances. In the wake of a chaos event, organizations evolve into something more complex, with new goals, partnerships, structures, equipment, and communication channels to accommodate what they have learned.

Chapter Review Questions

1. Why do organizations exist?
2. At a general level, how are mechanistic and organic organizations different?
3. What are natural soldiering and systematic soldiering?
4. What is the most enduring image of F. W. Taylor?
5. What does "Reformatted bureaucracy" mean in policing?
6. What did Merton mean by "bureaucratic virtuoso?"
7. What key question did Goodsell ask about the numerous denunciations of the bureaucratic model?
8. The "Hawthorne effect" means what?
9. To what belief does "Contented cows give more milk" refer? Is that belief true?
10. What is organizational development?

Critical Thinking Exercises

1. Are sanctuaries and declined detainers a threat to public safety? If so, why? What, if anything, should be done about it specifically?
2. Is the power of an officer's accumulated street experience somewhat of an antidote to a police department's doctrine, that is, its operating philosophy, rules, and regulations? If yes, what, if anything, can and should be done about it? If no, state your reasons for believing it is not an antidote.

Key Terms

administrative theory
Argyris, Chris
behavioral systems theory
bifurcation
buffering
bureaucratic model
business concerns
butterfly effect
chaos theory
coding
cognitive maps
commonweal organizations
cosmology
detainer
double-loop learning
e-government
entropic process
equafinality
exception principle
force-field analysis

functional supervision
Gulick, Luther
Hawthorne effect
Herzberg, Frederick
homeostasis
human relations school
immaturity versus maturity
internal subsystems
isomorphism
Knapp Commission
Lewin, Kurt
Maslow, Abraham
McGregor, Douglas
mechanistic organizational structure
motivation-hygiene theory
mutual benefit association
natural soldiering
needs hierarchy
negative entropy
networked organizations

new public management (NPM)
open systems theory
organizational development (OD)
organizational humanism
organic organizations
POSDCORB
rational-legal authority
reformatted bureaucracy
sanctuary movement
scientific management
sense making
service organizations
single-loop learning
street-level bureaucrats
systematic soldiering
Taylor, F. W.
Theory X–Theory Y
traditional organizational theory
virtual organizations
Weber, Max

Endnotes

[1] Amitai Etzioni, *Modern Organizations* (Englewood Cliffs, NJ: Prentice Hall, 1964), p. 1.
[2] Ibid., with some additions.
[3] Ibid.
[4] Talcott Parsons, *Structure and Process in Modern Societies* (Glencoe, IL: Free Press, 1960), p.17.
[5] Edgar H. Schein, *Organizational Psychology* (Englewood Cliffs, NJ: Prentice Hall, 1965), p. 9.
[6] See T. Burns and G. Stalker, *The Management of Innovation* (London: Tavistock, 1961), Chapter 6, Mechanistic and Organic Systems of Management, pp. 96–125.
[7] Peter W. Blau and W. Richard Scott, *Formal Organizations* (Scranton, PA: Chandler, 1962), p.43, with some changes.
[8] The treatment of the central issues of the four types of formal organizations is taken from Blau and Scott, *Formal Organizations*, pp. 43, 55, with some changes.

[9]Brian Lockhart, "Bridgeport Police Approve New Contract," Connecticut Post, March 25, 2015, 2 pp, http://www.ctpost.com/local/article/Bridgeport-police-approve-new-contract-6159297.php, accessed August 21, 2015.

[10]Daniel A. Wren, *The Evolution of Management Thought* (New York: Ronald Press, 1972), p. 112.

[11]Ibid., p. 114.

[12]Ibid., pp. 114–115.

[13]See the testimony of F. W. Taylor before the Special Committee of the House of Representatives Hearings to Investigate Taylor and Other Systems of Shop Management, January 25, 1912, p. 1387.

[14]Wren, *Evolution of Management Thought,* p. 115.

[15]Frederick W. Taylor, *Principles of Scientific Management* (New York: Harper & Row, 1911), pp. 44–47, with minor restatement.

[16]See Frederick W. Taylor, *Shop Management* (New York: Harper & Brothers, 1911), for a discussion of this concept.

[17]Ibid., p. 126.

[18]Lisa Riordan Seville, "Why Does A City with 600 Residents Need 14 Cops?" *NBC News* (September 7, 2014), pp. 1–2, http://www.nbcnews.com/storyline/michael-brown-shooting/why-does-city-600-residents-need-14-cops-n197676 (accessed August 22, 2015).

[19]Wren, *Evolution of Management Thought,* p. 132. Not only did Bethlehem Steel abandon the system, but it also fired Taylor.

[20]Ibid., p. 131.

[21]L. P. Alford, *Henry Lawrence Gantt* (Easton-Hive Management Series: No. 6, 1972; facsimile reprint of a 1934 edition by Harper and Brothers), pp. 207, 209.

[22]Sudhir Kakar, *Frederick Taylor: A Study in Personality and Innovation* (Cambridge, Mass.: MIT Press, 1973), p. 2.

[23]Fremont E. Kast and James E. Rosenzweig, *Contingency Views of Organization and Management* (Chicago: Science Research Associates, 1973), p. 7.

[24]Mary Jo Hatch with Ann L. Cunliffe, Organization Theory (New York: Oxford University Press, Second Edition, 2006), p. 33.

[25]Robert Kanigel, *The One Best Way: Frederick Winslow Taylor and the Enigma of Efficiency* (New York: Viking Press, 1997).

[26]Katia Caldari, "Alfred Marshall's Critical Analysis of Scientific Management," *European Journal of the History of Economic Thought,* Vol. 14, Issue 1, (March 2007), pp. 55–78.

[27]Michael Crozier, *The Bureaucratic Phenomenon* (Chicago: University of Chicago Press, 1964), p. 3.

[28]Max Weber, *The Theory of Social and Economic Organization,* trans. A. M. Henderson and Talcott Parsons (New York: Free Press, 1947), p. 337.

[29]Ibid.

[30]Ibid., pp. 330–332, with limited restatement for clarity.

[31]Ibid., p. 328.

[32]On this point see Paul Henman, *Governing Electronically: E-Government and The Reconfiguration of Public Administration, Policy, and Power* (New York: Palgrave Macmillan, 2010).

[33]For example, see John P. Crank and Andrew Ciacomazzi, "A Sheriff 's Office as a Learning Organization," *Police Quarterly,* Vol. 12, Issue 4, December 2009, pp. 351–369 and

Phil Johnson, et.al., "The Rise of Post-Bureaucracy," *International Sociology,* Vol. 24, No. 1, January 2009, pp. 37–61.

[34]Paul G. Lewis and S. Karthick Ramakrishnan, "Police Practices in Immigrant Destination Cities," *Urban Affairs Review,* Vol. 42 (2007), pp. 874–900.

[35]No author, "Immigrant Detainers," American Civil Liberties Union, August 25, 2015, p. 1, https://www.aclu.org/issues/immigrants-rights/ice-and-border-patrol-abuses/immigration-detainers (accessed August 26, 2015).

[36]On this point see Miriam Jordan, "Churches Offer Immigrants Sanctuary," *Wall Street Journal*, September 11, 2014 and Puck Lo, "Inside the New Sanctuary Movement That's Protecting Immigrants from ICE," The Nation, May 6, 2015, http://www.thenation.com/article/inside-new-sanctuary-movement-thats-protecting-immigrants-ice, accessed August 25, 2015.

[37]No author, Declined Detainer Outcome Report, Law Enforcement Systems and Analysis, Department of Homeland Security, October 8, 2014, p. 1.

[38]No author, "Comparison of Secure Communities and Priority Enforcement Program, U.S. Immigration and Customs Enforcement, 2015, p. 1, https://www.ice.gov/sites/default/files/documents/Fact%20sheet/2015/pep_brochure.pdf, accessed August 28, 2015.

[39]Declined Detainer Outcome Report, p. 1.

[40]Comparison of Secure Communities and Priority Enforcement Program, p. 1.

[41]Declined Detainer Outcome Report, p. 7.

[42]Loc. cit.

[43]This information is drawn with restatement from Dan Simon, Sara Sidner, and Ed Payne, "Gun in San Francisco Killing Stolen from Federal Agent's Vehicle, Source Says," CNN.com, July 8, 2015, http://cnnnewsource.com/gun-in-san-francisco-killing-stolen-from-federal-agents-vehicle-source-says (accessed August 27, 2015), Michael Pearson, "Suspect Tells TV Station He Killed San Francisco Woman," CNN.con, July 7, 2015, http://www.cnn.com/2015/07/06/us/san-francisco-killing (accessed August 28, 2015), and Steve AlmasayPamela Brown, and Augie Martin, "Suspect in Killing of San Francisco Woman Had Been Deported Five Times," CNN.com, July 4, 2015, http://www.cnn.com/2015/07/03/us/san-francisco-killing-suspect-immigrant-deported, (accessed August 27, 2015).

[44]Ibid., Table 3, p. 888.

[45]Ibid., pp. 886–887.

[46]Ibid., p. 881.

[47]Ibid., p. 885.

[48]Ibid., pp. 886–887.

[49]Scott Decker, Paul Lewis, Doris Provine, and Monica Varsanyi, "Immigration and Local Policing: Results From a National Survey of Law Enforcement Executives," in *The Role of Local Police: Striking a Balance Between Enforcement and Civil Liberties* (Washington, DC: Police Executive Research Forum, 2009), p. 177.

[50]Ibid., p. 176.

[51]Ibid., pp. 175–176.

[52]Zachary W. Oberfield, "Shaping the State: The Development of Street-Level Bureaucrats," Midwestern Political Science Association Annual Meeting, Washington, DC, 2008, p. 1.

[53]Ibid., pp. 3–4.

[54]Ibid., p. 6.

[55]Ibid., pp. 6, 16.

[56]On this point, see Nicos P. Mouzelis, *Organization and Bureaucracy* (Chicago: Aldine, 1967), pp. 20–21 and footnote 29 of that work.

[57]H. H. Gerth and C. Wright Mills, *From Max Weber: Essays in Sociology* (New York: Oxford University Press, 1946), p. 50.

[58]Christopher Hood, "The 'New Public Management' in the 1980s: variations on a theme," *Accounting, Organization, and Society*, Vol. 20, No. 2/3 (1995), p. 94.

[59]Wren, *Evolution of Management Thought*, p. 230.

[60]Henri Fayol, *General and Industrial Management,* trans. Constance Storrs (London: Sir Isaac Pitman, 1949), p. vi.

[61]Ibid., pp. 19–41.

[62]Ibid., p. 34.

[63]Danial A. Wren, Arthur G. Bedian, and John D. Breeze, "The Foundations of Henri Fayol's Administrative Theory," *Management Decision*, Vol. 40, No. 9 (2002), p. 917.

[64]The 1939 edition was coauthored, but the 1947 edition appeared under Mooney's name.

[65]Luther Gulick, "Notes on the Theory of Organization," in *Papers on the Science of Administration,* eds. Luther Gulick and L. Urwick (New York: August M. Kelley, a 1969 reprint of the 1937 edition), p. 13.

[66]Taylor, *Shop Management,* p. 184.

[67]Warren Bennis, "Organizational Developments and the Fate of Bureaucracy," *Industrial Management Review* 7, no. 2 (spring 1966), pp. 41–55.

[68]Herbert A. Simon, *Administrative Behavior* (New York: Free Press, 1945), p. 20. For additional criticism of the principles approach, see Dwight Waldo, *The Administrative State* (New York: Ronald Press, 1948).

[69]J. Hage, "An Axiomatic Theory of Organizations," *Administrative Science Quarterly* 10 (1965–1966), p. 305, Table 4.

[70]Charles Perrow, *Complex Organizations* (Glenview, IL: Scott, Foresman, 1972), pp. 6–7.

[71]Ibid., pp. 11–12.

[72]Alvin W. Gouldner, "Metaphysical Pathos and the Theory of Bureaucracy," *American Political Science Review* 49 (June 1955), 501, as quoted by Goodsell, *The Case for Bureaucracy,* p. 12.

[73]As early as 1924, researchers from the National Academy of Sciences had experiments underway; for present purposes, the work at the Hawthorne plant is described following the arrival of Mayo.

[74]The designation of this study as the bank wiring study is also found in the literature; banks were telephone switchboards.

[75]There were actually two relay assembly test room studies, one following the other. The second involved a change in the wage incentive and confirmed the importance of the social group.

[76]Roethlisberger and Dickson, *Management and the Worker,* pp. 58–59, 180–183.

[77]Bertram M. Gross, *The Managing of Organizations,* Vol. 1 (New York: Free Press, 1964), p. 163.

[78]Roethlisberger and Dickson, *Management and the Worker,* p. 522.

[79]Etzioni, *Modern Organizations,* pp. 34–37.

[80]Whitman Knapp, Chairman, "Commission to Investigate Allegations of Police Corruption and the City's Anti-Corruption Procedures," *Commission Report* (New York, 1972), pp. 4, 65; see also Herman Goldstein, *Police Corruption* (Washington, DC: Police Foundation, 1975).

[81]Also see H. W. Parsons, "What Caused the Hawthorne Effect?" *Administration and Society* 10 (November 1978), pp. 259–283, and Henry Lansberger, *Hawthorne Revisited* (Ithaca, NY: Cornell University Press, 1958).

[82]These points are drawn, with change, from William H. Knowles, "Human Relations in Industry: Research and Concepts," *California Management Review* 2, no. 2 (fall 1958), pp. 87–105.

[83]Etzioni, *Modern Organizations,* p. 39.

[84]No author, "U.S. Job Satisfaction Rates Hit 20-Year Low," *Quality Progress,* Vol. 43, Issue 2, (February 2010), p. 13.

[85]Edward E. Lawler, *Motivation in Work Organizations* (Monterey, CA: Brooks/Cole, 1973), p. 62.

[86]John M. Zelenski, Steven A. Murphy, and David A. Jenkins, "The Happy-Productive Worker Thesis Revisited," *Journal of Happiness Studies,* Vol. 9, (2008), p. 521.

[87]Youngyol Yim and Bryan D. Schafer, "Police and Their Perceived Image: How Community Influences Officers' Job Satisfaction," *Police Practice and Research,* Vol. 10, Issue 1, (February 2009), pp. 17–29.

[88]Holly A. Miller, Scott Mire, and Bitna Kim, "Predictors of Job Satisfaction Among Police Officers; Does Personality Matter?" *Journal of Criminal Justice,* Vol. 37, Issue 5, September 2009, pp. 419–426.

[89]Daisy Chu-Hsiiang Chang, Russell E. Johnson, and Robert G. Lord, "Moving Beyond Discrepancies: The Importance of Velocity as a Predictor of Satisfaction and Motivation," *Human Performance,* Vol. 23, Issue 1, January/March 2010, pp. 58–80.

[90]Kathryn Wilkins and Magot Shields, "Employer-Provided Support Services and Job Dissatisfaction in Canadian Registered Nurses," *Nursing Research,* Vol. 58, Issue 4, July/August 2009, pp. 255–263.

[91]Michael E. Milakovich and George J. Gordon, *Public Administration in America* (Belmont, CA: Wadsworth/Thomson, 2004), p. 165.

[92]A. H. Maslow, "A Theory of Human Motivation," *Psychological Review* 50 (July 1943), pp. 370–396.

[93]These five elements are identified in A. H. Maslow, *Motivation and Personality* (New York: Harper and Brothers, 1954), pp. 80–92. Maslow later added a sixth category, "metamotivation," but it never received substantial interest. See "A Theory of Metamotivation," *Humanitas* 4 (1969), pp. 301–343.

[94]Ibid., p. 91.

[95]No author, "Patrol Announces 2014 Leadership Awards"; Ohio State Patrol Media Release, February 13, 2015, http://statepatrol.ohio.gov/media/2015/15-019.html, accessed August 21, 2015.

[96]Chris Argyris, *Personality and Organization: The Conflict between System and the Individual* (New York: Harper and Brothers, 1957), pp. 58–66.

[97]Ibid., pp. 76–122.

[98]Chris Argyris, *Integrating the Individual and the Organization* (New York: John Wiley & Sons, 1964), p. 3.

[99]For extended treatment of this subject, see Ibid., pp. 146–191.

[100]Ibid., p. 147.

[101] Douglas McGregor, *The Human Side of Enterprise* (New York: McGraw-Hill, 1960), p. 6. See also Louis A. Allen, "M for Management: Theory Y Updated," *Personnel Journal* 52, no. 12 (1973), pp. 1061–1067.

[102] Ibid., p. 7.

[103] Ibid., pp. 33–57.

[104] Bennis, *Changing Organizations,* p. 77.

[105] Walter Nord, "Beyond the Teaching Machine: The Neglected Area of Operant Conditioning in the Theory and Practice of Management," *Organizational Behavior and Human Performance* 4 (November 1969): 375–401; see also Lyman Porter, "Job Attitudes in Management," *Journal of Applied Psychology* 46 (December 1962): 375–384; and Douglas Hall and Khalil Nougaim, "An Examination of Maslow's Need Hierarchy in an Organizational Setting," *Organizational Behavior and Human Performance* 3 (February 1968), pp. 12–35.

[106] Maslow, *Motivation and Personality,* pp. 79–80. Also see, David L. Rennie, "Two Thoughts on Abraham Maslow," *Journal of Humanistic Psychology,* Vol. 48, Issue, 4, (October 2008), pp. 445–448.

[107] Abraham Maslow, *Eupsychian Management: A Journal* (Homewood, IL: Dorsey Press, 1965), pp. 55–56.

[108] Gibson and Teasley, "The Humanistic Model," p. 92.

[109] Ansfried B. Weinert, "Testing Argyris' Theory of Organizational Behavior," *Scandinavian Journal of Management Studies,* Vol. 3, Issue 1, (1986), 26–27.

[110] Ibid., p. 41.

[111] Wren, *Evolution of Management Thought,* p. 324. Lewin lived in this country for the 15 years preceding his death in 1947.

[112] George C. Homans, *The Human Group* (New York: Harcourt Brace, 1950), pp. 81–130.

[113] Clint Fuhs, "Toward an Integral Approach to Organization Theory," unpublished paper, p. 6, by permission. Also see ClintFuhs.com.

[114] Michael T. Hannan and John Freeman, "The Population Ecology of Organizations," *American Sociological Review,* Vol. 82, No. 5, (March 1977), p.: 960. Some of the disappearances were from mergers and name changes.

[115] Chris Argyris, "Double Loop Learning in Organizations," *Harvard Business Review,* (September/October 1977), p. 116. Also see Crank and Giacomazzi, "A Sheriff's Office as a Learning Organization."

[116] Daniel Katz and Robert Kahn, *The Social Psychology of Organization,* 2nd ed. (New York: John Wiley & Sons, 1978), pp. 23–30, with some change.

[117] The thoughts in this paragraph are taken with restatement from Francis Amagoh, "Perspectives on Organizational Change: Systems and Complexity Theories," *The Public Sector Innovation Journal,* Vol. 13, No. 3 (2008), pp. 1–7, an on-line peer-reviewed journal.

[118] Timothy L. Snellnow, Matthew W. Seeger, and Robert R. Ulmer, "Chaos Theory, Informational Needs, and Natural Disasters," *Journal of Applied Communication Research,* Vol. 30, No. 4, (November 2002), p. 276.

[119]T. Burns and G. M. Stalker, *The Management of Innovation* (London: Tavistock, 1968).

[120]John R. Hollenback, et al., "Structural Contingency Theory and Individual Differences," *Journal of Applied Psychology*, Vol. 87, No. 3, (2002), p. 599.

[121]J. Pfeffer and G. Salancik, *The External Control of Organizations* (New York: Harper & Row, 1978).

[122]Hatch with Cunliffe, *Organization Theory*, p. 83.

[123]Guy Peters, *Institutional Theory in Political Science: The New Institutionalism*, 2nd ed (New York: Continuum, 2nd Edition, 2005), pp. 6–10.

[124]James G. March and Johan P. Olsen, "The New Institutionalism: Organizational Factors in Political Life," *American Political Science Review*, Vol. 78, No. 3, (September 1984), p. 734.

[125]James F. Wolf, "Public Administration's Multiple Institutionalized Framework," *Public Organization Review: A Global Journal*, No. 5 (2005), p. 183.

[126]On this point see Seth Abrutyn, "Toward a General Theory of Institutional Authority," *Sociological Theory*, Vol. 27, Issue 4, (December 2009), pp. 449–465.

[127]Hans Jagers, Wendy Jansen, and Wichard Steebakkers, "Characteristics of Virtual Organizations," in Pascal Sieber and Joachim Griese, Editors, *Organizational Virtualness* (Bern, Switzerland: Institute of Informational Systems, 1998), p. 65.

[128]Gerard R. Murphy and Chuck Wexler, with Heather J. Davies and Martha Plotkin, "Managing a Multijurisdictional Case," Identifying the Lessons Learned from the Sniper Investigation (Washington, DC: Police Executive Research Forum, 2006), p. V.

[129]Ibid., p. 113.

[130]Ibid., pp. 20–21.

[131]Ibid., p. 23.

[132]Ibid., p. 22.

[133]E. C. Tolman, "Cognitive Maps in Rats and Men," *Psychological Review*, Vol. 55, No. 4, (1948), pp. 189–208.

[134]L. Douglas Kiel, *Managing Chaos and Complexity in Government* (San Francisco: Jossey-Bass, 1994).

[135]Snellnow, Seeger, and Ulmer, "Chaos Theory, Informational Needs, and Natural Disasters," p. 271.

[136]Ibid.

[137]Overman, "The New Science of Administration," p. 487.

[138]Jeffrey W. Goltz, "Determinants of Performance of Police Organizations in the State of Florida: An Evidence Based Confirmatory Approach," *International Journal of Public Policy*, Vol. 3, No. 5/6, (2008), Table 2, pp. 423 and 428.

[139]Ibid.

[140]Lex Donaldson, *American Anti-Management Theories of Organization: A Critique of Paradigm Proliferation* (New York: Cambridge University Press, 1995).

CHAPTER SIX

ORGANIZATIONAL DESIGN

Learning Objectives

1. Explain the principle of hierarchy as it relates to organizational design.
2. Describe the concept of span of management.
3. Distinguish between vertical and horizontal differentiation.
4. Discuss the differences between tall organizational structures and flat organizational structures.
5. List and describe four basic types of police organizational design.
6. Discuss the major crime factors that impact investigative function; list the various models of investigative style.
7. Identify the basic causes for tension between line and staff and suggest strategies to be used as solutions.
8. Describe the characteristics of an informal organization.

INTRODUCTION

IN CHAPTER 5, ORGANIZATIONAL THEORY,
*we discussed the major theoretical concepts
associated with organizations and the ways in
which they function. In this chapter, we will see how
these theories are applied in police organizations.
The topics we will be specifically discussing are
(1) the ways in which police administrators can
modify or design their organizations in order to
fulfill their missions; (2) the principle of hierarchy,
which requires each lower level within the
organization to be supervised by a higher level;
(3) the differences between the span of control and
span of management; (4) some of the more
common ways in which activities and personnel are
grouped within a police department; (5) the impact
of community policing and intelligence-led
policing (ILP) philosophies on organizational
structure; (6) the placement of the investigative
function within the organizational design; (7) the
organizational differences between municipal
departments and sheriff's departments;
(8) understanding the importance of line and staff
relationships; why there are sometimes problems
and how they can be resolved; and (9) the
importance of understanding the informal
organization and its potential impact on the formal
organization.*

ORGANIZING: AN OVERVIEW

Police administrators modify or design the structure of their organization in order to fulfill the mission that has been assigned to the police. An organizational chart reflects the formal structure of task and authority relationships determined to be most suited to accomplishing the police mission. However, within the need to accomplish the mission there can also be accommodations of a law enforcement executive's preferences for the arrangements of units in a particular way.

This reality explains both the similarities across law enforcement organizations of a similar type and their diversity. Stated more simply, while there are some underlying concepts, there is also "more than one way to skin a cat."

The process of determining this formal structure of task and authority relationships is termed **organizing**. The major concerns in organizing are (1) identifying what jobs need to be done, such as conducting the initial investigation, performing the latent or follow-up investigation, or providing for the custody of physical evidence seized at the scene of a crime; (2) determining how to group the jobs, such as those responsible for patrol, investigation, and the operation of the property room; (3) forming grades of authority, such as officer, detective, corporal, sergeant, lieutenant, and captain; and (4) equalizing responsibility and authority, illustrated by the example that if a sergeant has the responsibility to supervise a team of detectives, that sergeant must have sufficient authority to discharge that responsibility properly or he or she cannot be held accountable for results[1] (see Figure 6.1).

SPECIALIZATION IN POLICE AGENCIES

Central to this process of organizing is determining the nature and extent of specialization. Some 2,300 years ago, Plato observed that "each thing becomes . . . easier when one man, exempt from other tasks, does one thing."[2] **Specialization**, or the division of labor, is also one of the basic features of traditional organizational theory.[3] As discussed more fully later in this chapter, specialization produces different groups of functional responsibilities, and the jobs allocated to meet those different responsibilities are staffed with people who are believed to be especially qualified to perform those jobs, for example, by experience and training. Thus, specialization is crucial to effectiveness and efficiency in large organizations. However, specialization makes the organizational environment more complex by complicating communication, by increasing the number of units from which co-operation must be obtained, and by creating conflict among differing interests and loyalties. Also, specialization creates greater need for coordination and, therefore, additional hierarchy and can lead to the creation of narrow jobs that stifle the willingness or capacity of personnel to work energetically in support of broader goals. Police departments are not insensitive to the problems of specialization and attempt through various actions to keep the interest and motivation of employees at a high level. Personnel can be rotated to different jobs, they can be given additional responsibilities that challenge them, they can be involved in organizational problem solving, and police departments can experiment with different forms of organizational structures. Although specialization is an essential feature of large-scale organizations, maintaining its positive impact requires thoughtful action.

One of the first police executives to explore systematically the relationship between specialization and the organizational structure was O. W. Wilson.[4] He noted that most small departments do not need to be concerned with widely developed specialization because their patrol officer is a jack-of-all-trades. Moreover, specialized assistance can be obtained from a neighboring large department or a state investigative agency. Conversely, in large departments, the volume of particular tasks, for

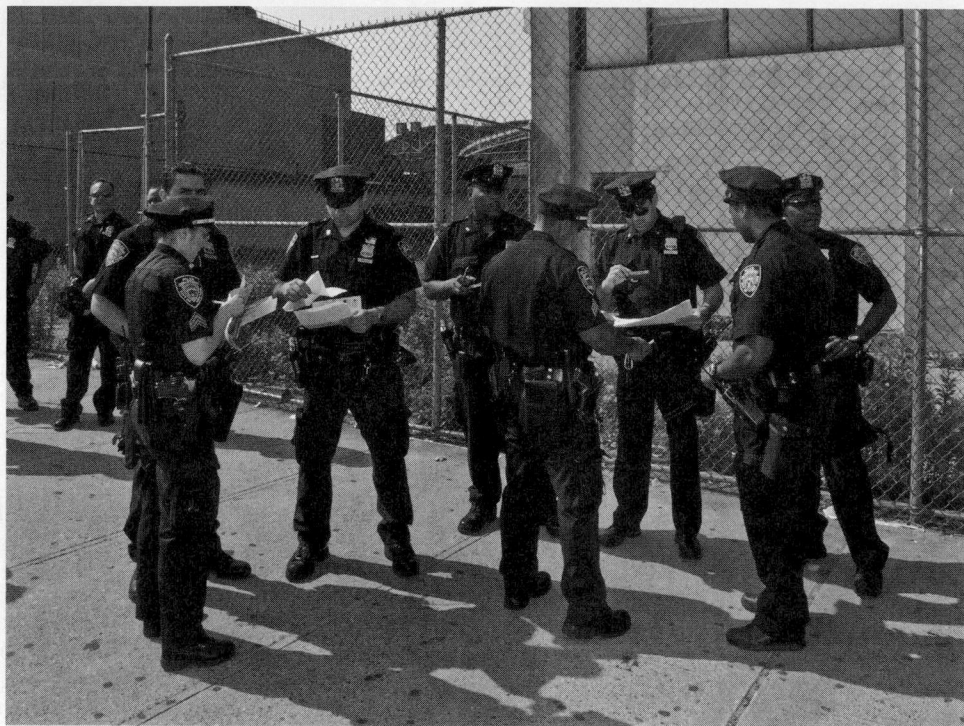

FIGURE 6.1 ▶ Grades of authority are designated by rank, starting with the police officer and following the chain of command up to Chief of Police. (Marmaduke St. John/ Alamy Stock Photo)

example, homicide investigation, virtually require specialized units. Specialization presents a number of advantages for large departments:

Placement of responsibility—The responsibility for the performance of a given task can be placed on specific units or individuals. For instance, a traffic division is responsible for the investigation of all traffic accidents, and a patrol division is responsible for all requests for general police assistance.

Development of expertise—A narrow field of interest, attention, or skill can be the subject of a specialized unit. For instance, many police agencies have highly skilled special weapons and tactics (SWAT) teams that train regularly to respond to critical incidents, such as terrorist activities, hostage situations, or serving high-risk search/ arrest warrants (see Figure 6.2). Advanced training in this area yields increased officer safety and produces a high degree of expertise. Specialization is also helpful during the investigation of narrowly defined, technical crimes, such as computer fraud, arson, and bombings.

Promotion of group esprit de corps—Any group of specially trained individuals sharing similar job tasks and, to some degree, depend on each other for success tends to form a highly cohesive unit with high morale.

Increased efficiency and effectiveness—Specialized units show a higher degree of proficiency in job task responsibility. For instance, a white-collar fraud unit will ordinarily be more successful in investigating complex computer fraud than a general detective division.[5]

Specialization appears to be a sure path to operational effectiveness. It allows each employee to acquire expertise in one area, so as to maximize his or her contribution to the overall department. However, as noted earlier, specialization has also been associated with increased friction and conflict within police departments. As units such as traffic, detective, and SWAT teams develop, an increase in job factionalism and competition also develops. The result may be a decrease in a department's overall job performance as individuals within each group show loyalty primarily or only to their unit. This traditional problem can be observed in the relationship between patrol officers and detectives. Patrol officers are sometimes reluctant to give information to detectives because they feel detectives will take credit for their work. Specialization also increases the number of administrative and command relationships, complicating the overall organizational structure. Additionally, each unit requires a competent leader. In some instances, this competent leader must also be a qualified specialist. A thorny problem here is when the specialist does not qualify for the rank usually needed to head a major unit. An example of such a problem is observed in the staffing of an air patrol unit in which the commanding officer may be a lieutenant or a sergeant because that individual is the highest-ranking officer with a pilot's license. In this case, the level of expertise (high) does not coincide with the level of rank (lower), which may cause difficulties when the individual tries to deal with other commanding officers of units who hold the rank of captain or major.

Finally, specialization may hamper the development of a well-rounded police program. As specialization increases, the resources available for general uniformed patrol invariably

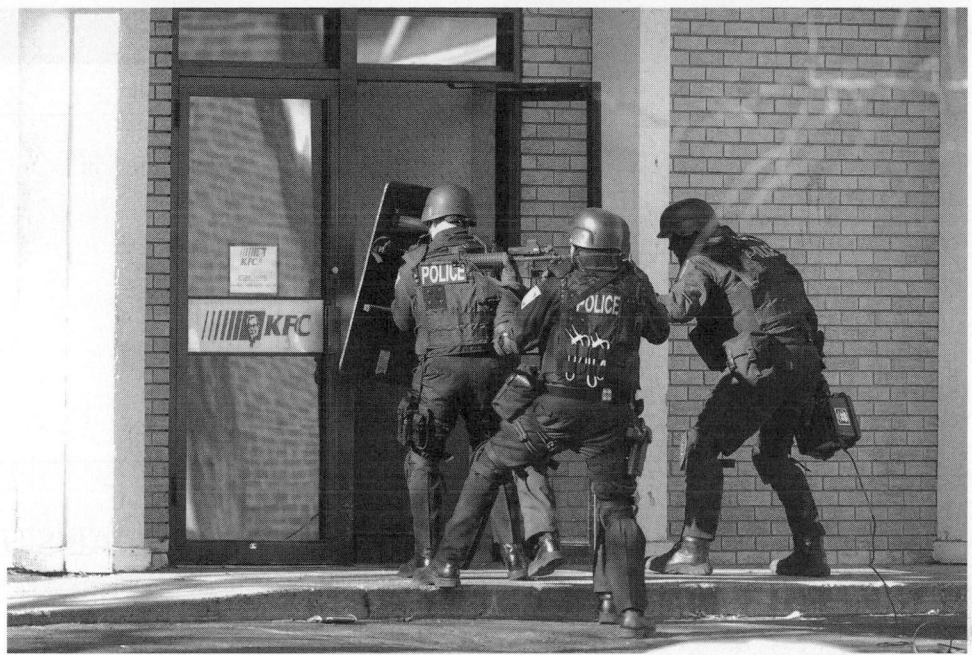

FIGURE 6.2 ▶ Specialization occurs when unique tasks require extensive and detailed training, such as helicopter units, search and rescue units, and SWAT operations. (Peter Casolino/Alamy Stock Photo)

decrease, often causing a lopsided structure wherein the need for general police services becomes second to the staffing of specialized programs and units.[6] When this happens, the great danger is that so many positions are siphoned off from patrol, which is the primary line unit, that its ability to provide services is crippled, and response times on calls and public dissatisfaction with the police increase.

THE PRINCIPLE OF HIERARCHY

This discussion of the principle of hierarchy builds on its coverage in Chapter 5, Organizational Theory. The **principle of hierarchy** requirement that each lower level of organization be supervised by a higher level results not only in the use of multiple spans of control but also in different grades of authority that increase at each successively higher level of the organization. This authority flows downward in the organization as a formal grant of power from the chief of police to those selected for leadership positions. These different grades of authority produce the chain of command.[7] Although there are many similarities from one department to another, the American police service does not have a uniform terminology for grades of authority and job titles.[8] In recent years, some police departments have moved away from using traditional military-style ranks and have adopted, instead, alternative titles as summarized in Table 6.1. However, in many departments, there remains a distinction between rank and title.[9] In these, *rank* denotes one's place in terms of grade of authority or the rank hierarchy, whereas *title* indicates an assignment. Where this distinction is made, a person holding the title of

division commander or director, for example, may be a captain, major, or colonel in terms of the rank hierarchy. Although some smaller departments have flattened or made the organizational structure less tall be eliminating one or two ranks, the complexity of large police agencies seemingly requires a taller hierarchy to coordinate its many parts. For instance, several departments have eliminated the rank of "captain" and placed more responsibility on deputy chiefs and lieutenants. This is particularly true in departments that have adopted a more "community-based" approach to policing.[10] Then too, over the last two decades, several large police departments have merged with the surrounding county to become **city-county consolidated governments**. Policing in these types of governmental structures reflects various ranks and structures. For instance, the county sheriff's rank and title names continue in the Las Vegas, Nevada Metropolitan Police Department, whereas the chief executive of the police in the Louisville, Kentucky Metropolitan Police Department is referred to as the Chief and Director of Police Services. In Kansas City, Missouri, the consolidated police department maintained the more traditional rank and titles of a city department with the Chief of Police at the helm of that agency[11] (refer to Table 6.1).

SPAN OF CONTROL VS. SPAN OF MANAGEMENT

The term **span of management** instead of "span of control" is used to describe the number of personnel a supervisor can personally manage effectively. The term "span of management" is

TABLE 6.1 TRADITIONAL POLICE RANKS VS. ALTERNATIVE TITLES	
Traditional Ranks	**Alternative Titles (Including County Agencies)**
Chief of police	Commissioner/Director/Superintendent/Sheriff
Deputy chief	Assistant director/Undersheriff/Chief Deputy Sheriff
Colonel	Division director/Inspector/Commander
Major	Inspector/Commander
Captain	Commander
Lieutenant	Manager
Sergeant	Supervisor
Detective	Investigator/Inspector
Corporal	Senior officer/Master patrol officer
Officer	Public safety officer/Agent/Deputy Sheriff

broader than "span of control" and encompasses factors relating to an individual's capacity to oversee the activities of others directly, such as the police manager's ability, experience, and level of energy.

"Span of management" more suitably describes the process of the number of personnel a supervisor can manage than does the term "span of control." Control is only one aspect of the management process. The term "span of management" encompasses more of the factors relating to the problem of an individual's capacity to oversee the activities of others.

How wide a span of management is depends on many factors. Some state that the ideal number of subordinates reporting to a supervisor is 8 to 12, but the number varies widely depending upon a number of factors[12] (see Table 6.2).

Although many law enforcement agencies prefer lower spans of management, with multiple layers of hierarchy, as indicated earlier, there is some movement toward flatter organizational structures with wider spans of management. Organizational humanists argue that this type of structure can produce better communication within the organization, increase the sense of fiscal and personal responsibility, provide greater organizational flexibility, and increase delegation by supervisors. Humanists also hold that employees also favor flatter structures with higher spans of management because they receive less detailed and micromanaged supervision. Arguably, when this occurs (1) personnel have more authority and responsibility, (2) feel trusted by their supervisors, and (3) employees have a good environment in which to grow, and therefore become more fulfilled and satisfied with their work.[13]

ORGANIZATIONAL STRUCTURE AND DESIGN

Tansik and Elliot suggest that, when we consider the formal **structure** (or pattern of relationships) of an organization, we typically focus on two areas:

1. The formal relationship and duties of personnel in the organization, which include the organizational chart and job descriptions; and

2. The set of formal rules, policies, procedures, and controls that guide the behavior of organizational members within the framework of the formal relationships and duties.[14]

Organizational design focuses on two spatial levels of differentiation—vertical and horizontal—depicted in Figure 6.3. **Vertical differentiation** is based on levels of authority, or positions holding formal power within the organization; Table 6.3 reflects one range of vertical differentiation found in police agencies. Persons with vertical authority have the power to assign work and exercise control to ensure job performance.[15] In Figure 6.3, the deputy chief has a span of management of three, all of whom are captains and to whom he or she can give assignments and expect performance.

Horizontal differentiation, on the other hand, is usually based on activity. However, in some cases, horizontal differentiation is based on specific projects or even geographical distribution. For instance, many state police departments are responsible

Quick Facts: Organizational Structure Impacts Police Misconduct

A 2014 study of nearly 500 police departments nationwide revealed that the existence of a full-time professional standards/internal affairs unit, and relevant in-service training tends to reduce both the number of complaints against officers and the number of sustained complaints against them. An organizational structure that provides closer supervision of officers may also produce similar results.

TABLE 6.2 FACTORS IMPACTING THE SPAN OF MANAGEMENT

Factors Enabling an Increased Span of Management

Factor 1: The simplicity of the work
The simpler the task, the less need there is for supervision. The more diversified, complex tasks require more supervision. Traditionally, the patrol function has a larger span of control since the work is similar on each beat, and one supervisor can oversee the work conducted on several beats.

Factor 2: Efficient use of information technology
Readily available information technologies can obtain needed information to do the job as well as receive direction from supervisor increases the span of control. In-car computers, cameras, and individual communication systems enable officers to be in constant touch with supervisors.

Factor 3: The quality, skills, and capabilities of subordinates
Recruiting quality employees having the necessary education, training, and experience to be able to learn and do the assigned work requires providing less supervision by the department. In contrast, hiring the less educated and unskilled subordinates will require extensive coaching by the supervisors to teach these employees the job.

Factor 4: The skills and capabilities of the supervisor
Departments that invest in developing supervisors and managers find that the more knowledgeable and skillful the supervisor—along with the ability to clearly communicate the work—the more people he or she can supervise.

Factor 5: The quality of the department's training program
Subordinates fully knowledgeable of the laws, procedures, and administrative processes require less supervision.

Factor 6: The harmony of the workforce
When the subordinates are of like minds and working toward the same objectives in harmony, fewer incidents require supervision intervention.

Factors Narrowing the Span of Management

Factor 1: Change taking place in the work environment
When the work is forever changing, and new procedures and processes are introduced into the work, the greater the need for narrow supervision.

Factor 2: Dispersed workforce, either by time or geographically
The greater the geographic distances and the difference in time that the force works, the smaller the supervision ratio. This is often observed in the investigative division, which frequently requires more supervisors in relation to the number of investigators.

Factor 3: New and inexperienced workforce
Law enforcement in the next few years is experiencing significant retirement numbers in the supervisory and management ranks. This requires promoting younger persons with lesser experience directing the work of others.

Factor 4: Administrative requirements
The greater the administrative burden on each level of management, the greater the need for a narrow span of control. Jobs free of bureaucratic requirements can focus on the work.

Factor 5: The extent of coordination
When employees' work must be coordinated and the subordinates depend upon each other to accomplish the work, the narrower the supervision requirements. This relationship exists in many of the tactical and technical positions in a police department.

Factor 6: Employees' expectations
The higher the employees' expectations for feedback, career and development coaching, and management interaction, the narrower the requirement for supervision. Many observe that the new workforce entering policing today looks for immediate feedback from management on their progress.

Source: Adapted from Troy Lane, "Span of Control for Law Enforcement Agencies," *The Police Chief*, Volume 73, number 10 (October 2006). Retrieved on July 15, 2015: http://policechiefmagazine.org/magazine/index.cfm?fuseaction=display&article_id=1022&issue_id=102006.

for large geographical areas. Their organizational structure often reflects horizontal differentiation based on location rather than function. Some of the more common ways in which activities of personnel are grouped within a police organization (on a horizontal dimension) are as follows:

Grouping by clientele—The simplest method of grouping within a police department is by clientele. Personnel are assigned by the type of client served, such as juvenile division, senior citizen crime detail, mayor's security unit, gang squad, and human trafficking unit. Each group focuses on the needs of a special clientele, which can be either temporary or permanent. In this manner, officers become familiar with the specific enforcement problems and patterns associated with different client populations.

Grouping by style of service—A police department usually has a patrol bureau and a detective bureau. The grouping of uniformed patrol officers on the one hand and of plainclothes investigators on the other illustrates how the

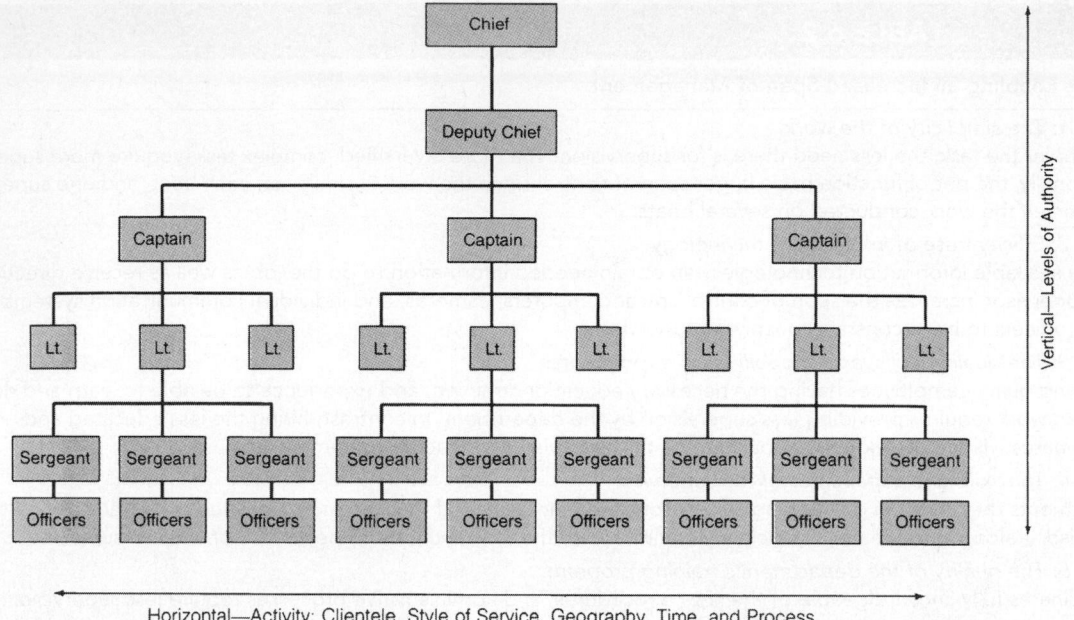

FIGURE 6.3 ▶ Organizational chart showing vertical and horizontal levels of differentiation. In some departments, especially large ones, a number of other ranks may be present within the chart.

former are grouped by the nature of their services (conspicuous, preventive patrol, and preliminary investigations) and how the latter are grouped also by this same principle (follow-up investigations). This form of grouping also takes advantage of specialization of knowledge and skill and permits the pinpointing of responsibility for results.

Grouping by geography—Where activities are widespread over any given area, it may be beneficial or even necessary to provide local command. Instances of this type of operation are large-city precincts or district-type operations and state police/patrol posts that are located throughout a state. An example of this appears in Figures 6.4A and 6.4B. Even in the headquarters building, activities that are related usually share the same floor. Instances of this arrangement are records, communications, and crime analysis in close proximity to each other. This permits supervisors to become familiar with

operating problems of related units and to coordinate the various efforts by more direct and immediate control.

Grouping by time—This grouping occurs when the need to perform a certain function or service is greater than one normal work period for a single shift, for example, the difference between one 8-hour shift of services versus grouping several shifts together to provide 24-hour patrol services. Grouping by time tends to create problems of coordination and unity of direction because top administrators work normal day hours, whereas many of their officers perform their functions on the evening and midnight shifts. The need to delegate sufficient authority becomes critical under these circumstances. For example, police policy manuals often or usually require the approval of a Lieutenant or Captain before a Sergeant can suspend an officer. In some exigencies, such as an officer getting drunk on duty and becoming a danger to himself and others, a policy manual

TABLE 6.3 LINE, AUXILIARY/SUPPORT, AND ADMINISTRATIVE STAFF FUNCTIONS		
	Staff	
Line	**Auxiliary/Support**	**Administrative**
• Uniformed patrol	Crime laboratory	Personnel
• Investigations	Detention and jail	Training
• Vice and narcotics	Records	Planning and research
• Traffic enforcement	Identification	Fiscal/budgeting
• Juvenile service	Communications	Legal services
	Property maintenance, transportation, and vehicle maintenance	Media relations

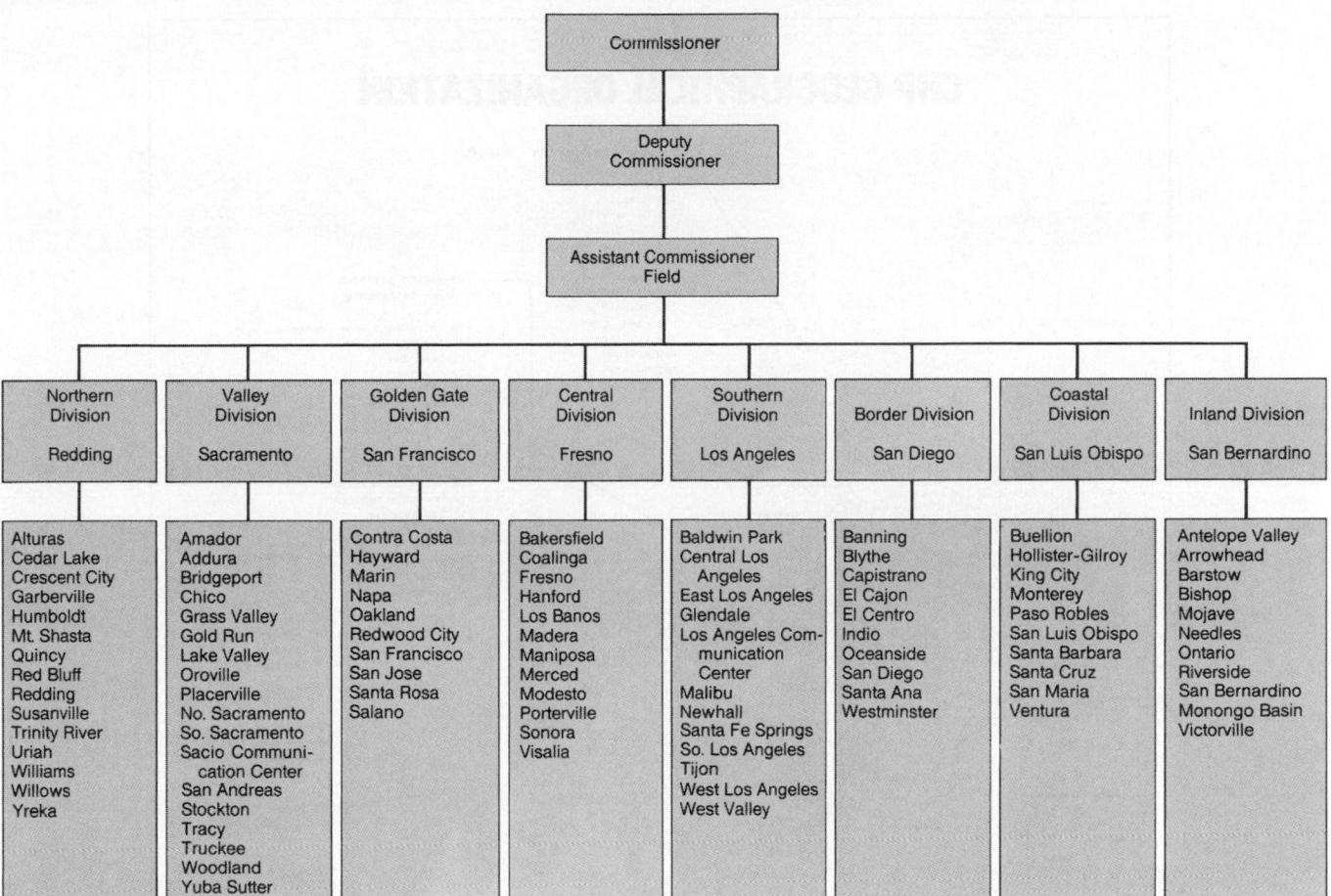

FIGURE 6.4A ▶ Organizational chart for the California Highway Patrol (Field) with modification, showing five levels of control. *Source:* Courtesy of the California Highway Patrol, Sacramento, California.

may authorize a Sergeant to immediately suspend the officer and then notify their appropriate senior official.

Grouping by process—This involves the placing of all personnel who use a given type of equipment in one function. Examples include a word processing center, crime laboratory personnel placed in a section to handle certain types of scientific equipment, and automotive maintenance units. This type of grouping lends itself to expertise involving a single process and makes the most efficient use of costly equipment.[16]

Top-Down vs. Bottom-Up Approaches

The level of complexity within a police organization is largely determined by the amount of horizontal and vertical differentiation that exists.[17] Size is often, but not necessarily, related to complexity. Some organizations, even relatively small police departments, can be highly differentiated and quite complex in organizational design.

According to Hodge and Anthony,[18] the differentiation process can occur in two basic ways in police agencies: (1) bottom-up or (2) top-down.

The bottom-up, or synthesis, approach focuses on combining tasks into larger and larger sets of tasks (see Figure 6.5A). To illustrate, an officer's task set may primarily be in the relatively small geographical zone he or she patrols. The task set of Sergeants is to supervise squads of patrol officers. Patrol Lieutenants may supervise a number of Patrol Sergeants, while a Captain often commands an entire shift city-wide. In turn, the Major in charge of the Patrol Division leads all three Captains and is responsible for all patrol services, 24 hours a day.

The top-down, or analysis, approach looks at the overall work of the organization at the top and splits this into increasingly more specialized tasks as one moves from the top to the bottom of the organization (see Figure 6.5B). The top-down approach considers the overall police mission—to protect and to serve the public.

At the top level of a police agency, this can be defined into various administrative tasks, such as representing the department to the larger environment (e.g., elected and appointed officials and the public), envisioning goals, setting priorities, and presenting the department's budget request. Middle management/leaders perform activities such as setting goals with subordinates, conducting studies that improve the police department, writing

FIGURE 6.4B ▶ Geographical organization of area offices for the California Highway Patrol.
Source: Courtesy of the California Highway Patrol, Sacramento, California.

policies for the approval of the command staff, preparing unit reports, implementing improvements within their domain, and writing performance appraisals. At the very bottom of a large police department, tasks sets are illustrated by crime scene processing, evidence intake and storage, examining tool marks in the crime lab, follow-up investigation on burglaries, surveillance

of open air drug markets, analysis of crime patterns, patrol, investigate traffic and pedestrian accidents, and serve as field training officers.

Both approaches are commonly found in police organizations. The top-down analysis is often used in growing organizations because it is easy to visualize the set of tasks to be

Quick Facts: Bottom-Up Approaches Improve Performance and Officer Morale

The organization of police departments along hierarchical, classical management lines makes it difficult to solve common internal problems in policing, such as performance improvement, complaints against officers, and low morale. The main reason for this fact is that top-down reform invites resistance from rank-and-file officers who feel that their ideas are disregarded and not valuable to leadership. By contrast, individual approaches to officers from supervisors that reflected a more bottom-up perspective was much more successful to organizational effectiveness and efficiency. Bottom-up approaches tend to harness the experience of individual officers, produce an often-needed team-oriented environment with officer squads, reduce opposition to innovation in police strategies and operations, generally increase overall officer morale, and most surprisingly, reduce the number of incidence of use of excessive force in metropolitan police departments.[19]

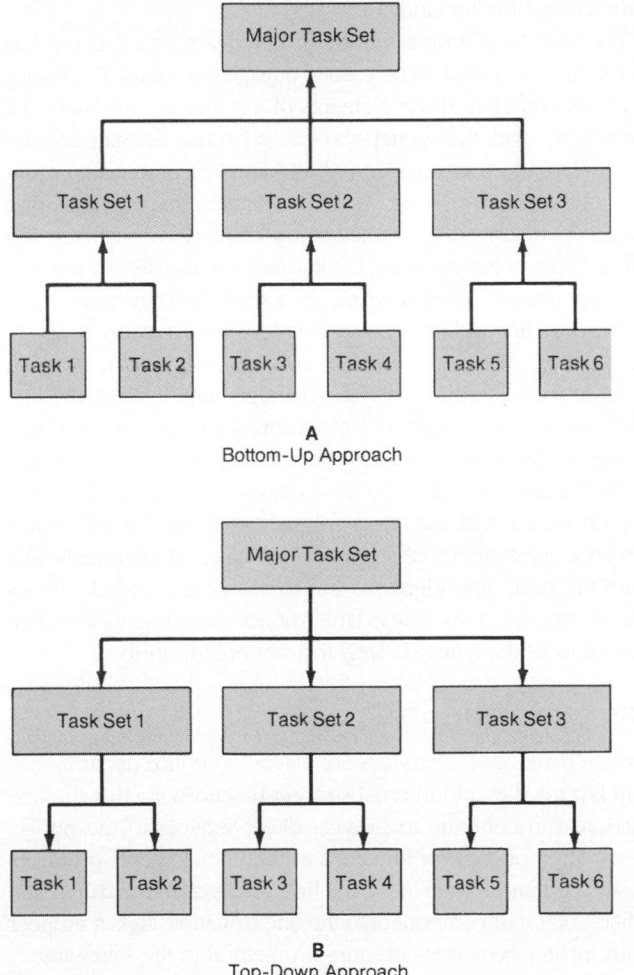

A
Bottom-Up Approach

B
Top-Down Approach

FIGURE 6.5 ▶ The bottom-up and top-down approaches to building structure around differentiation. *Source: Organization Theory: A Strategic Approach, 6/e by Hodge/Anthony/ Gales. Reprinted by permission of Pearson Education Inc., Upper Saddle River, NJ.*

The policing style or philosophy can also impact top-down or bottom-up approaches. This is exemplified in philosophical changes from community and problem-oriented policing to ILP over the past decade. Whereas community and problem-oriented policing is a bottom-up philosophy that places street officers at the forefront of problem identification and subsequent solution, Compstat and ILP are much more hierarchical and emphasize the top-down approach. Increasing accountability at supervisory and command levels is an important element of Compstat, often characterized by strong role definitions, tighter lines of control, and smaller spans of management. And in ILP, criminal intelligence flows up the organizational pyramid to executives who set priorities and develop strategies aimed at prevention and enforcement and then communicate these priorities back down the organizational chain for operational tasking.[20]

Some organizations have narrow spans of management with tall structures and many levels, whereas others reduce the number of levels by widening the span of management at each level. Many narrower spans of control make a police department "taller." The California Highway Patrol (CHP) appears to have five levels, as shown in Figure 6.4A. These levels are commissioner, deputy commissioner, assistant commissioner, field division chief, and area office commander. From a more functional perspective, each area office also has a chain of command consisting of four layers—captain, lieutenant, sergeant, and officer. Thus, when the rank layers in the area offices are considered, the CHP is a tall organization with a number of different levels of authority. Seven to nine levels of rank are fairly typical of large police organizations. Figure 6.4B displays each CHP area office by geographical grouping, as described earlier in this chapter.

The complexity of a police department is increased by the proliferation of levels because they can negatively affect communication up and down the chain of command. For example, during urban riots, police departments found that an initially small incident grew rapidly beyond the ability of a small group of officers to control it. The process of getting approval from senior police officials to send additional officers took so long that, by the time the officers arrived at the scene, the once-small incident had grown into an uncontrollable riot. Thus, most departments shifted the authority to deploy large numbers of police officers downward, in some cases all the way to the

accomplished and then to break these sets down into specific tasks and subtasks. The bottom-up approach is often used during periods of retrenchment when organizational growth has declined because combining tasks such as those found in patrol and traffic bureaus can consolidate jobs or even units.

individual police officer at the scene. This example illustrates several important principles:

1. Narrow spans of control make police departments taller.

2. Taller organizations are complex and may react slowly during crisis situations, as effective communication is hampered by the number of different levels present within the chain of command.

3. Successful tall departments must develop policies and procedures that overcome problems created by increased complexity.

Many police agencies, such as the Phoenix, Arizona Police Department, have redesigned their organizations to reflect larger spans of control or management and, hence, flatter organizational structures. Figure 6.6 shows only three major organizational levels—chief, division, and bureau. Although this structure is flatter than that of the CHP, traditional grades of authority, such as commander, lieutenant, sergeant, and officer ranks, continue to exist in the Phoenix Police Department. With higher educational standards for entry-level police officers and efforts toward professionalism, police organizational structures may reflect additional changes of this nature. Ultimately, however, the capacity to flatten out police organizational structures depends to no small degree on reducing the number of traditional ranks, a movement sure to be met with resistance from the rank and file and unions because it means less opportunity for upward mobility.

McFarland[21] argues that flat structures associated with wider spans of control offer numerous advantages over the more traditional tall structures. First, they shorten lines of communication between the bottom and top levels. Communication in both directions is more likely to be faster and more timely. Second, the route of communication is more simple, direct, and clear than it is in tall organizations. Third, distortion in communication is minimized by a reduced number of people being involved. Fourth, and probably most important, flat structures are generally associated with employees with higher morale and job satisfaction as compared to employees in tall, structured organizations.

Flat structures do, however, place demanding pressures on supervisors, require high-caliber managers, and work best in organizations in which employees are held strictly accountable for measurable and objective results. Considering the role of the police and the continuing problems associated with evaluating police services, such a structure may cause inordinate stress on personnel. Top executives can attempt to direct the development of police agencies in such a way as to maintain structural balance. Some amount of hierarchy is needed for coordination, but the extremely tall police organization should be carefully scrutinized. In balance, no major city has successfully flattened out both the numbers of organizational layers or units and the traditional rank structure to any significant and continuing degree. Thus, any substantial flattening of a police organization is likely to be an experiment in organizational design rather than an institutionalized reform.

BASIC TYPES OF POLICE ORGANIZATIONAL DESIGN

Four basic structural types of design can be found within police organizations. They are line, line and staff, functional, and matrix. These types exist separately or in combination.

Line Structure

The **line structure** is the oldest, simplest, and clearest form of organizational design. As illustrated in Figure 6.7, authority flows from the top to the bottom of the organization in a clear and unbroken line, creating a set of superior–subordinate relations in a hierarchy commonly called the *chain of command*. A primary emphasis is placed on accountability by close adherence to the chain of command.

The term "line" originated with the military and was used to refer to units that were to be used to engage the enemy in combat. "Line" also refers to those elements of a police organization that perform the work the agency was created to handle. Stated somewhat differently, line units contribute directly to the accomplishment of the police mission. Thus, the primary line elements of a police department are uniformed patrol, criminal investigation, and traffic. Within police agencies, the line function can also be referred to as "operations," "field services," or a similar designation.

The pure line police organization does not have any supporting elements that are internal or part of it, such as personnel, media relations, training, or fiscal management. Instead, the line police organization uses its total resources to provide services directly to the public. Typically found only in small towns and small counties, the line is the most common type of police organization because of the sheer frequency of small jurisdictions. However, most police officers work in larger departments that retain the basic line elements but to which are added various types of support units. These larger police departments are often referred to as the *line and staff* form of organization.

Line and Staff Structure

As more demands for services are placed on police departments, there is a need to add internal support functions, so that the line functions can continue to provide direct services to the public. The addition of support functions to the line elements produces a distinct organizational form: the **line and staff structure**. The addition of a staff component to the line structure offers a number of advantages because such units are helpful in the following:

1. Providing expert advice to line units in special knowledge areas as demonstrated by the opinions of legal advisors;

2. Relieving line managers from performing tasks they least prefer to do or are least qualified to do, such as financial management and providing legal guidance;

3. Achieving departmentwide conformity in activities that affect the entire organization, such as disciplinary procedures; and

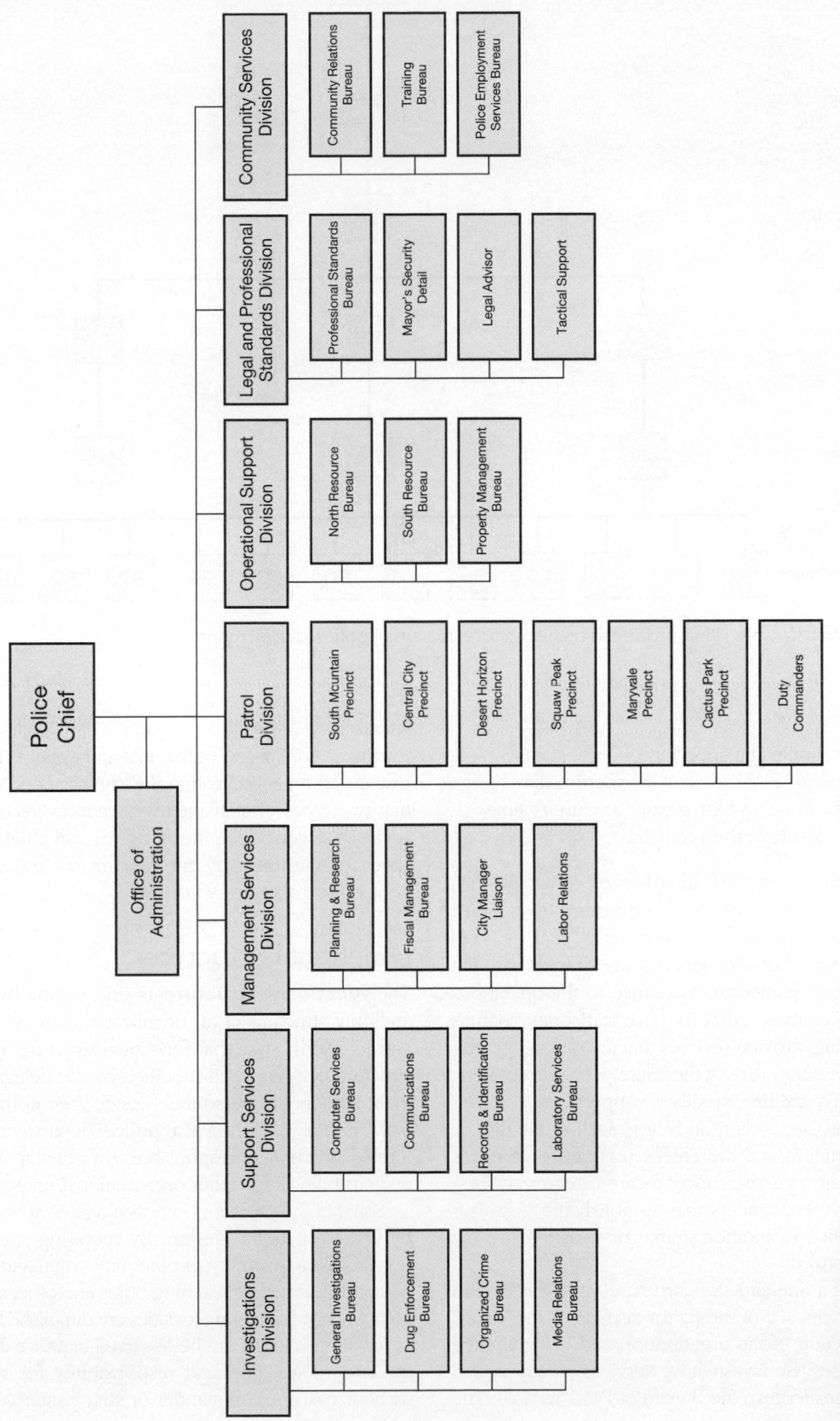

FIGURE 6.6 ▶ Flat organizational structure. *Source:* Courtesy of the Phoenix Police Department, Phoenix, Arizona.

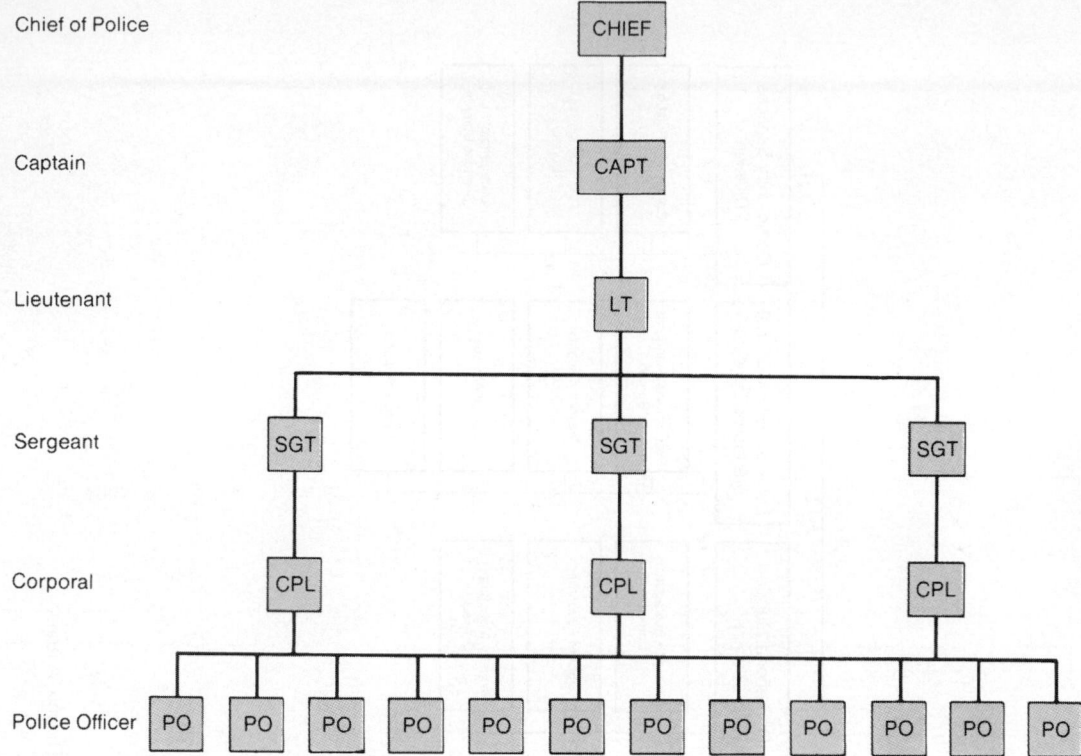

Chief of Police — CHIEF

Captain — CAPT

Lieutenant — LT

Sergeant — SGT SGT SGT

Corporal — CPL CPL CPL

Police Officer — PO PO PO PO PO PO PO PO PO PO PO PO

FIGURE 6.7 ▶ Line organizational structure in a small police department.

4. Reducing or eliminating special problems, such as corruption, because of the greater expertise they bring to bear on the issue and the greater amount of time they have to devote to the problem.[22]

Staff functions are sometimes further broken down into two types: auxiliary or support and administrative staff. Under this arrangement, auxiliary/support units, such as communications and crime laboratory services, are charged with the responsibility of giving immediate assistance to the operations of line elements. In contrast, administrative staff units, such as personnel and training, provide services that are of less immediate assistance and are supportive of the entire police department. Table 6.3 identifies typical line, auxiliary/support, and administrative staff functions. Depending on factors such as the history of the police department and the chief's preferences, there is some variation as to how these functions are categorized. Less frequently, legislative enactments may establish the organizational structure, which is another source of variation in how functions are categorized.

Figure 6.8 shows a line and staff structure. In it, the Bureau of Field Services (composed of the patrol districts) is the "heart" or primary line function of the organization and is highlighted to show that purpose. The investigative services bureau is also a line function but smaller than the Bureau of Field Services. The Bureau of Administrative Services and upper-echelon offices represent staff functions within the organization. Note in Figure 6.8 that two types of staff members report directly to the chief of police: the generalist, illustrated by the chief of staff, and the specialist, illustrated by the legal advisor and internal investigations office.

Functional Structure

The **functional structure** is one means by which the line authority structure of an organization can be modified. Hodge and Johnson[23] state that functional structure "is a line and staff structure that has been modified by the delegation of management authority to personnel outside their normal spans of control." Figure 6.9 shows a police department in which the intelligence unit is responsible to three captains whose main responsibility is for other organizational units.

Some of the problems in police organizations can be reduced by using functional design. By requiring specific units to be responsible to a variety of other unit commanders, critical information is assured of reaching other line officers. Sharing is promoted, while competing loyalties are diminished. Good examples of functional design can be observed in police departments moving toward geographical responsibility for supervisors on a 24-hour basis. A commander or shift (watch) supervisor (often

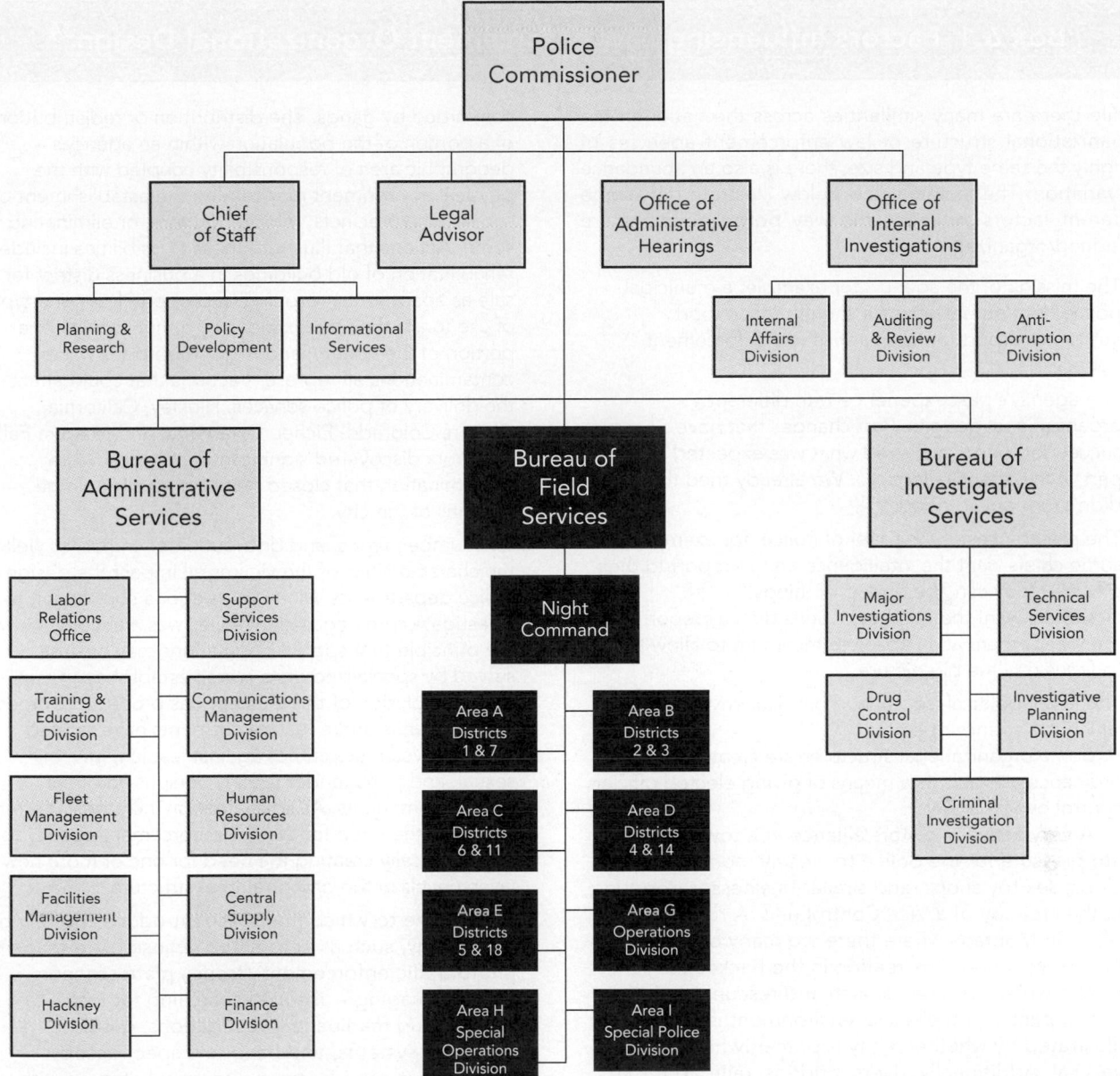

FIGURE 6.8 ▶ Line and staff structure in a police department. Note that line functions are grouped in the middle of the structure highlighted as "Bureau of Field Services." *Source:* Courtesy of the Boston, Massachusetts, Police Department.

a lieutenant or Captain) assigned to the day watch may be responsible for solving violent street crimes (e.g., robberies) that occur in a specific area on all three shifts. However, officers on at the evening and night shifts get their overall supervision from the Lieutenant or Captain assigned to their shifts, creating the potential for conflict between the orders from the day shift Captain on what strategies to use in combating violent crimes versus the orders that officers on the evening and night shifts get on the same subject from their own shift leaders. This creates more

than a conflict between shift leaders because it causes confusion and some stress with officers as to whose orders they should follow.

Dallas and Fort Worth, Texas, as well as San Diego, California, are just a few departments that have noted these types of problems stemming from the implementation of geographical responsibility for managers, resulting in a functional design. In some areas, this type of formalized geographically based, or "geo" policing is referred to as **sector policing**. While the name might

Box 6.1 Factors Influencing Law Enforcement Organizational Design[24]

While there are many similarities across the nation in the organizational structure of law enforcement agencies of roughly the same type and size, there is also an abundance of variation. The factors listed below illustrate how some different factors influence the way police agencies are designed/organized.

1. The mission of the agency, for example, a municipal police department versus a sheriff's office, port authority, airport, or mass transit law enforcement agency.

2. The agency's past experience with different organizational designs. Past changes that have succeeded or not achieved what was expected become part of the agency's legacy. "We already tried that and it didn't turn out so good."

3. The preferences of the Chief of Police, for example, some chiefs want the intelligence unit to report to their office so they can "be on top of things."

   Others want the number of units directly reporting to them kept them at an absolute minimum to allow them to focus on "the big picture."

4. The legal, political, social, and physical environment in which the agency operates.

   Some organizational structures are created by local ordinances, largely as a means of giving elected officials control over changes.

   A very active ministers alliance in a town may create pressure for the police to closely monitor strip clubs, sex toy shops, and similar businesses, resulting in the creation of a Vice Control unit. A rural sheriff's office in Montana where there are many opportunities for year-round recreation in the backcountry must have a well-developed search and rescue capability. The impact of the physical environment is also illustrated by whether a city is primarily horizontal or vertical. Additionally, rivers, bridges, railroad tracks, and other environment characteristics dictate the boundaries of patrol zones.

5. The size of the population served and its demographics, for example, policing a retirement community is different than a city with a strong young demographic from which many crimes spring, such as those committed by gangs. The distribution or redistribution of a portion of the population within an agency's geographic area of responsibility coupled with the physical environment may require the establishment of substations/precincts, relocating them, or eliminating some. Actions that illustrate these possibilities include, rehabilitation of old buildings in a business district for sale as apartments, rezoning of property from one type of use to another, annexations by a municipality of a portion of the county, and major hazardous waste contaminations all represent actions that could affect the delivery of police services. Hinkley, California, Gilman, Colorado, Picher, Oklahoma, and Niagara Falls, New York discovered significant hazardous waste contamination that closed neighborhoods or large portions of the city.

6. The number, types, and distribution of crimes, as well as the characteristics of the victims all impact the design of police departments. Many years ago, a special unit to investigate crime against juveniles was a novelty. Now, the principle that special populations may best be served by specialized units is well established.

   The evolution of this concept has produced Domestic Violence Units and a few departments have formed units to investigate crimes against lesbian, gay, bisexual, and transgender (LGBT) persons and their allied communities. As specialization increases, it often produces the need for the law enforcement agency to grow vertically creating the need for one or more new layers/levels in the organizational structure.

7. The degree to which the police introduce and rely on technology, such as automated license plate readers, photo traffic enforcement, license plate scanners, thermal imaging—useful in searching for lost persons and marijuana investigations, gunshot detection systems, and handheld spectroscopy devices that can identify powdery substances with great accuracy.

   A technology that is on the near horizon for actual use is RF Safe-Stop, which can electronically "confuse" the operating system of a fleeing car and cause it to stop. In tests, it has been effective at 50 meters/164 feet.

be different, the approach is still focused on providing a proactive and geographically based structure for police strategies, personnel deployment, and accountability.[25]

In conclusion, the major disadvantage of the functional design is that it increases organizational complexity. In Figure 6.9, members of the intelligence division receive instructions from several superiors. This can result in conflicting directions, and thus extensive functionalized structures are seldom found in police agencies. Law enforcement executives should explore the use of the functional design but be ever cautious of the confusion that can result if the process is not properly monitored and controlled.

Matrix Structure

One interesting form of organizational design is variously referred to as the **matrix (or grid) structure**. In some cases, the style has been inclusively part of "project" or "product"

FIGURE 6.9 ▶ Functional structure in a police organization.

management. The essence of matrix structure is in the assignment of members from different functional areas (e.g., patrol, detective, and support services) to specific projects (e.g., task forces and crime-specific programs). The most typical situation in which the matrix approach is used is when a community has had a series of sensationalized crimes and the local police department announces it has formed a task force to apprehend the violator. One notable example of this occurred in East Los Angeles in 2014, where a task force comprising over 800 federal, state, and local law enforcement officers arrested 25 members and indicted another 38 individuals of a multigenerational street gang name "Big Hazard" on charges of federal racketeering and maintaining a criminal enterprise. The violent street gang was linked to multiple murders, extortions, robberies, drug trafficking, prostitution, and many other crimes in the Boyle Heights area of Los Angeles over the last 70 years.[26] The advantage of this type of organizational design is in the formation of specific groups of individuals, combining varied talents and levels of expertise in order to fulfill a designated mission or goal. Quite often, the matrix structure is used for relatively short periods of time when specific programs are conducted. After the assignment is completed, individuals return to their respective units.

Figure 6.10 displays the matrix design applied to a police organization. This chart reflects the basic line and staff elements found in most police agencies. However, four specific projects have been initiated that require the use of personnel from five different units, which further requires each project to organize along the lines suggested by Figure 6.11.

Because the matrix structure greatly increases organizational complexity, it has been successful only in the short-term delivery of police services.

ORGANIZATIONAL STRUCTURE TODAY

The impact of community policing during the late 1990s had a dramatic impact on organizational structure. It was most apparent in agencies that adopted **decentralization** strategies. The purpose behind such strategies was that police departments could more effectively serve their communities through an organizational design focused on individual areas and neighborhoods rather than the entire city. Further, decentralization in organizational structure was seen as being much more flexible and having a fluid design in which to provide essential public and human services.[27]

Electing to compartmentalize the activities of the community policing concept, some departments opted to provide such services solely through one unit or bureau. For instance, the Anaheim Police Department in Anaheim, California, had a single bureau devoted to community policing. Through this one unit, the Community Policing Team developed strategies that employed a total community effort involving the police department, city and county government, schools, churches, and businesses. These alliances formed neighborhood partnerships. The mission of the Community Policing Team was to develop, promote, and implement community-based partnerships aimed at addressing various criminal and social problems confronting the city of Anaheim.[28] The important note here is that the entire community policing effort was relatively confined to the one unit—the Community Policing Team.

In contrast, other departments (e.g., those in Portland, Oregon; Madison, Wisconsin; Charlotte-Mecklenburg, North Carolina; and Minneapolis, Minnesota) opted to implement the

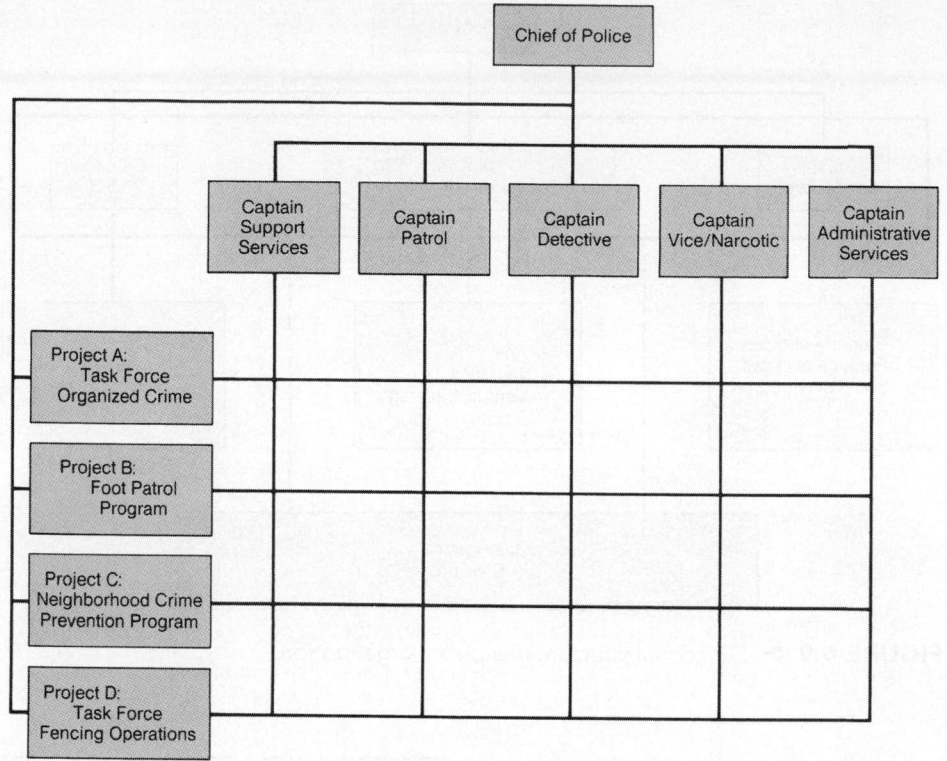

FIGURE 6.10 ▶ Matrix structure in a police organization.

community policing concept holistically; that is, community policing was reflected in all aspects of the organization, and, therefore the organizational structure did not reflect a single unit devoted to community policing. Instead, the community policing philosophy was simply pervasive throughout the organization. In these cases, the organizational chart was reflective of the philosophical changes imbued in community policing.

Traditional Design vs. Structural Change

Although a number of community policing methods have been adopted across the country, several structural problems have been identified.[29] To illustrate, community policing depends on granting officers' greater authority and latitude in decision making, particularly with respect to developing police strategies to impact on problems of concern to people in the area in which officers

FIGURE 6.11 ▶ The detailed organization of projects.

Box 6.2: Organizational Structure Impacted by Policing Philosophy

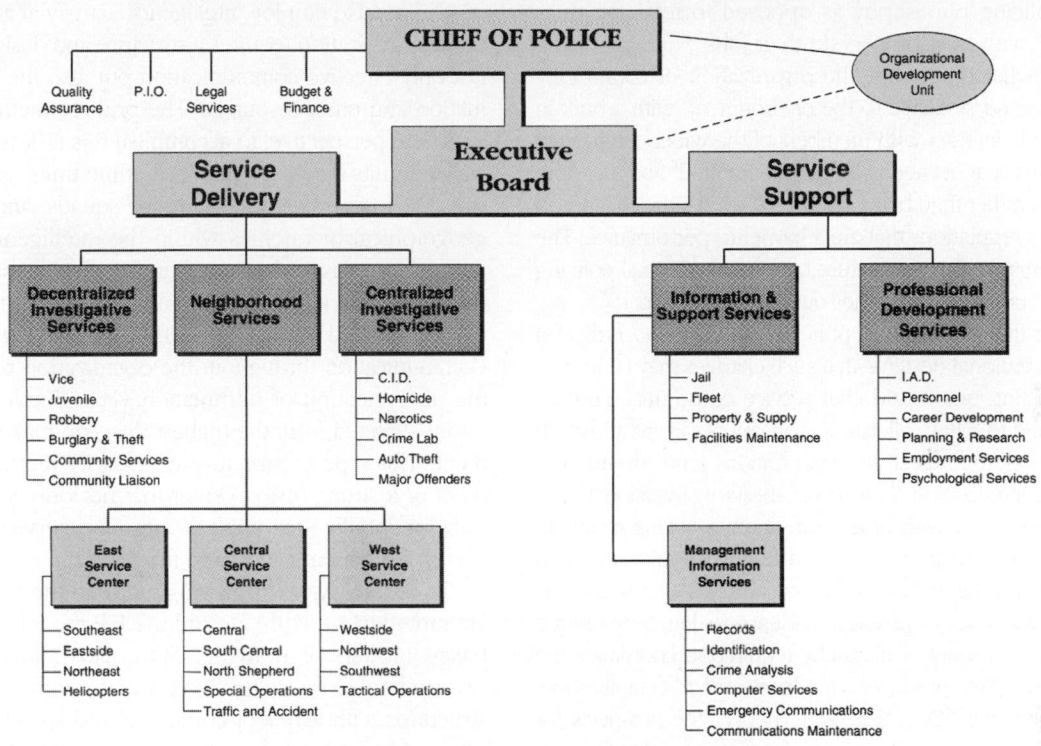

Houston Police Department

Organizational chart of the Houston Police Department reflecting an emphasis on service delivery and support through a community-represented "executive board." *Source:* Courtesy of the Houston, Texas, Police Department.

Under the leadership of then-Chief Lee P. Brown (1990), the Houston Police Department acted as a model for community policing departments. Reflective of these philosophical changes, the organizational chart of the department provided a new and dynamic look. Note that the focus of the department was on service delivery and support rather than the traditional modes of assignment, such as patrol and investigations. The police department was viewed more as a community organization than as a control agency. As such, the organization was operated similarly to a service corporation that is fully responsible to an executive board comprising police and community leaders. In this manner, community policing made individual police officers accountable directly to the people of Houston. The chief of police acts more as a chairman of the board or a chief executive officer for a major corporation than as a traditional police manager. Innovation in organizational structure has somewhat waned in the last several years, as many departments have continued to use, or returned to some degree to a more traditional, bureaucratic structure to cope with problems such as deep personnel cuts, local responsibilities for combating terrorism, and other factors.

patrol. This practice conflicts with traditional bureaucratic theory's desire to have close supervision of officers through narrow spans of control/management, which in turn produces taller, multi-layered, organizational structures. In contrast, community policing requires a shorter and flatter organizational design. Services are decentralized and community-based. Necessarily, such a design will be less formalized, less specialized, and with less emphasis on bureaucratic rules. Cordner[30] suggests that police agencies shift from substantial reliance on traditional written rules and regulations to a straightforward situation-oriented approach. Some portion of traditional rules and regulations, with their strong control orientation, actually get in the way of community policing.

Community policing advocates empowering the individual officer with greater authority, responsibility, and discretion and responsibility than does traditional policing. As a consequence, direction from the organization must emphasize shared values, participatory decision making, and a collegial atmosphere. For written rules and regulations to be fully useful in a community policing context some number of them must be rewritten to further that policing philosophy as opposed to retaining ones which interfere with how officers do their jobs.

Stated somewhat differently, the organization of community policing is open and sensitive to the environment, with a built-in need to frequently interact with members of the wider community and to be responsive to its needs or "results-oriented" and therefore accountable to it rather than being hampered by insufficient authority and rules and regulations that are a barrier to performance. The differences in organizational structure between traditional policing and community policing are further outlined in Table 6.4.

Some argue that community policing calls for too radical a change in organizational design—that such changes may be impossible under existing union and civil service constraints. Further, organizations tend to follow Michael's "iron law of oligarchy," which indicates that modern, large-scale organizations tend toward specialization and centralization.[31] However, these organizational traits appear to be in conflict with other community policing or intelligence-led structures. Large police departments require a certain amount of specialization to handle diverse tasks efficiently, such as examining various types of physical evidence or handling unique situations, and the amount of hierarchy required to coordinate the various specialized parts produces a tendency toward centralization. As stated in Chapter 5, "Organizational Theory," the prospects for police agencies totally abandoning the bureaucratic structure are not strong. What is now being done is preserving the best features of bureaucracy, such as having an organization that is responsive to lawful orders, and supplementing or "dropping over" its processes, policies, procedures, rules, and regulations that blunt the worse features and support initiatives, such as community policing.

Intelligence-Led Policing (ILP) and Organizational Structure

The Compstat movement during the early 2000s was credited with significantly reducing crime in major cities across the United States, but it had very little impact on the organizational structure or design of police agencies. However, the movement toward ILP has placed much more emphasis on the "functional structure" of organizations as previously described (see Figure 6.9). Requiring police agencies to be much more proactive and preventative based, the focus is on integrating the intelligence function throughout the organization. ILP requires accurate and timely information, the source of which is often through the development of partnerships and problem-solving methodologies employed with other departments and agencies. ILP also requires energetic and competent analysts to communicate their findings to decision makers, and much more importantly, that decision makers then communicate their strategies to lower levels of the organization, again, much more "top-down" in style.[32]

In contrast to community policing, Ratliff asserts that decentralized structures (often stemming from community policing philosophies) reflect a purpose rather than a geographic focus. This tends to produce stovepipes within the organization, separating police specialties from one another, and decreasing communication and information flow between units, a condition critically important for the success of ILP.[33]

The need to employ intelligence activity at almost every level of the organization requires a structure and design that highlights not only effective communication but also the sharing of information and other resources. The primary methodology, from a structural perspective, to accomplish this task is to organize specialized units (such as organized crime units, gang units, terrorism task forces, narcotics and vice squads, and the like) along geographical hierarchies within the intelligence division—the theme being to highlight intelligence operations within a police department as the central element to planned activities rather than haphazard reactions to crime and potential terrorist strikes. Communication throughout the organization rests primarily on the dissemination of information via technology and planned efforts directed from the highest decision makers in the department. This type of structure necessarily requires the development of a strong fusion center that not only acts as the central hub for intelligence analysis but also serves as the primary "brain" for dissemination and feedback.

Quite frankly, few police agencies in the United States have attempted to structure around the ILP model (or the evidence-based model) of policing. Moreover, many agencies have reverted to more centralized and traditional organizational structures with levels of command and spans of management often observed prior to the community policing movement. This may well be a movement away from community-based approaches as well as a natural result of the Compstat movement and the new demands on policing posed by the threat of terrorism. While the structures may be somewhat flatter, communication within and between organizations continues to be problematic, and the strategies aimed at relatively quick solutions to very complex problems. Even Ratcliffe admits that the criteria for success of ILP is on the immediate detection, reduction, and disruption of criminal and potential terrorist activities, and not on the long-term improvement of social conditions that often encourage crime and disorder. As a result of such difficulties, the continued implementation of ILP should provide a dynamic arena for police organizational structure in the future.

ORGANIZATIONAL DESIGN AND THE INVESTIGATIVE FUNCTION

Police agencies across the country have been reeling from budget cuts in an effort to be more streamlined, more efficient, and more cost-effective.[34] Many of these cuts have been targeted at staff and support functions, particularly in investigative units in an effort to increase the number of uniform officers on the street and available for calls for service. Some departments, like

TABLE 6.4 DIFFERENCES BETWEEN TRADITIONAL AND COMMUNITY POLICING

Traditional Policing	Community Policing
1. *Bureaucratic and control based:* characterized by detailed standard operating procedures and rigid written policies; high formalization of the organizational pyramid	1. *Nonbureaucratic:* based on the corporate model; more flexible and adaptive than traditional paramilitary structure; focus on building teams within a more collegial environment
2. *Centralized and hierarchical organizational structure:* highly centralized with authority flowing from top to bottom, particularly in operations; characterized by tall organizations with multiple ranks and levels; communication is slow and almost always downward	2. *Decentralization, shorter and flatter organizational structure:* authority and function is derived from community-based demands; characterized by decentralized services with multiple neighborhood storefronts and more service-oriented environments; communication is open and free-flowing between ranks both vertical and horizontal in the organization
3. *Autocratic management style:* leadership is based on rank with rights associated with the office; emphasis on control-based methodologies in managing people within the organization; loss of individual leadership capabilities within the organization	3. *Democratic and participatory management style:* leadership is encouraged at all ranks with focus on challenging the status quo, enabling and inspiring others; ennobling shared visions and possibilities, modeling ethical and collaborative behavior, rewarding others, and reflecting on self and individual service
4. *High specialization and task orientation:* police functions performed by smaller units of highly trained and specialized personnel, often characterized by high esprit-de-corps and unique unit identification; personnel loyalty is often observed to the unit versus the larger department (e.g., SWAT-tactical teams, homicide units, motor patrol, gang units)	4. *Generalization:* police officers act as generalists with specialized training in multiple areas; patrol often becomes the primary and emphasized police function with all other units and divisions supporting the patrol function; officers embrace patrol as the primary mechanism for neighborhood and community engagement
5. *Emphasis on random patrol:* the organization employs traditional policing methodologies focused on random-moving patrol vehicles; little use of technology in the patrol function and crime analysis is limited to plotting crime and activities after the fact	5. *Directed patrol based on crime and intelligence analysis:* the patrol function is directed for high impact, preventative-based activities as defined by detailed and real-time crime and intelligence analysis; wide use of technology and highly trained analysts often observed in crime analysis and fusion centers
6. *Large goal oriented:* preoccupation with crime rates and numbers; arrest orientation with focus on paramilitary structure and function of police to combat crime; individual tasks are quantity oriented	6. *Embraces multiple objectives, problem-solving and individual successes:* celebration of innovative strategies that have a positive impact on the community; goals and objectives are community/client driven; individual tasks are quality oriented
7. *Crime-fighting officer perspective within reactive organization, emphasis on mediocrity:* focus is primarily on crime detection, investigation, and arrest *after* the fact; orientation for the organization is based on the traditional "crime-fighting and order maintenance" model; organizations focus on arrest, cases cleared, and similar measures of success in traditional policing	7. *Preventive-based approach to crime within a proactive organization, emphasis on quality:* focus is on the prevention of crime *before* the activity occurs, with emphasis on broader social issues as well as neighborhood problems; crime prevention through environmental design; success is measured in numbers of interactions with the community and the building of new relations and partnerships
8. *Closed organization orientation:* distinct from environment, resistant to environmental influence and change, internally defined agenda, justification of means over ends; stifling of innovation and creativity; loss of individual worth for group think	8. *Open organization model:* organization attempts to effectively interact with the community, open to change, sensitive to environment; focused on long-term and results-oriented goals; emphasis placed on individual and organizational creativity
9. *"Fear of crime" justifies existence and tactics:* police are responsible for fighting the "war" on crime; symbols focused on the power of the police and control of the community	9. *Uses evidence-based approaches to justify police functions:* embraces on-going research to developed cost effective "best practices" in police strategies and tactics; emphasis on knowing contemporary research in policing
10. *High individual and managerial accountability:* organizational demand on accountability focused on numbers; reaction to increased crime rates result in increased traditional solutions such as more patrol, visible arrests, higher profile policing in specific neighborhoods; CompStat becomes a means to an end	10. *Accountability and police focus is a reflection of community demand:* police functions and foci are developed with the community at the neighborhood level; the community is actively engaged in measuring police performance through shared meetings; emphasis is on community engagement and partnerships

Source: Adapted by Robert W. Taylor (July 2015) from R. W. Taylor, E. J. Fritsch, and T. J. Caeti, "Core Challenges Facing Community Policing," *ACJS Today*, volume XVII, issue 1, May/June 1998 and C. Murphy, Contemporary Models of Urban Policing: Shaping the Future (Ontario: Ministry of the Solicitor General, 1991), p. 2.

Oakland, California have conducted massive overhauls of their organizational structure to include the disbanding of the entire Criminal Investigations Division and traditional subunits such as homicide, assault, robbery, burglary, sex crimes, vice, narcotics.[35] Other agencies, particularly during the community policing era (NYPD, Dallas Police Department, LAPD) moved to a more decentralized investigative structure, moving traditional detectives to neighborhood precincts and divisions. Interestingly, many agencies are now realizing that decentralization, especially popular during the community policing era, was inefficient and ineffective. Recent research reveals that traditional persons-crimes such as homicide, robbery, and sex crime that are centralized promoted an increased clearance rate by arrest and decreased reported violent crime in most major cities.[36] This new research has caused many departments to "re-think" the concept of decentralization of police services.

There are only a few studies that have focused on organizational design and the criminal investigative function.[37] Plain-clothes investigators, or detectives, in most city police department, primarily perform the following tasks:

1. Determine that a crime has been committed;
2. Identify the individual who committed it;
3. Locate and apprehend the individual;
4. Collect evidence of guilt (or innocence) for courtroom use; and
5. Recover wrongfully held persons and property.

The amount of effort that any individual investigator expends on each of the five tasks is a function of the complexity of the investigation and the specific assignment of the investigator. For example, in a burglary investigation, establishing that a crime has actually been committed consumes far less investigative effort than identifying the offender. On the other hand, an investigator visiting a pawnshop may recover a large amount of stolen property without ever determining the identity of the victim or offender. Then too, determining if a person met with an accident, committed suicide, or was murdered is often a very time-consuming and arduous task.

This combination of diversity of assignment and complexity of investigation prevents several problems for determining the organizational role, staffing and structure of investigators within a police department. Unlike the patrol function where calls for service are largely evenly distributed and where essentially the same type of service is provided to the public regardless of geographic deployment, investigative functions are diverse relative to assignment and responsibility.

While significant research has been conducted on the line function of uniform patrol (see Chapter 2), very little work has correspondingly studied the role and assignments of plainclothes personnel in a police department. Most research on the investigative function has examined either the nature of the investigative function in the abstract or the identification of "solvability factors" to assist in the efficient use of investigative personnel. Three of the better known, albeit now relatively old, studies on the nature of the investigative function relevant to

organizational design were conducted by (1) President's Commission on Crime and Administration of Justice in 1967[38]; (2) RAND Corporation in 1976[39]; and (3) National Institute of Justice in 2001.[40]

The President's Commission examined the investigative practices of the Los Angeles Police Department. The report, *The Challenge of Crime in a Free Society: Science and Technology* identified several factors that must be considered when creating or changing an organizational structure. The study found that the patrol force made a large portion (90 percent) of the arrests. About 25 percent of these were based on detective follow-ups (warrants). Thus, detectives were directly or indirectly responsible for about 35 percent of all arrests. About one-third of all arrests were made within 30 min of the commission of the offense while nearly one-half of all arrests were made within 2 hours of the commission of the offense; presumably, uniformed patrol officers were primarily responsible for these arrests. The research also found two-thirds (66 percent) of all arrests being made within one week of the commission of the offense; 94 percent of all arrests occurred within one month of the commission of the offense. Investigative efforts expended over the next 11 months raised that percentage by only 4.5. Thus, 98.5 percent of all offenders who would be arrested had been arrested within one year of the crime coming to the attention of the police. Within this group, about half were arrested by patrol officers without extensive follow-up investigation. The study further reports that 2.8 cases were cleared for each arrest made, indicating that single perpetrators are responsible for multiple offenses. As to the work of the detectives, two-thirds of the cases they cleared involved suspects whose identity was initially determined by responding patrol officers. The LAPD study leads to several conclusions. First, in half of the arrests, the plainclothes investigator's role was largely case preparation not related to the identification of the suspect. Further, the study reveals that investigative effort beyond one month after the commission of the offense, on average, produces only an incremental difference in arrest rates. Finally, reactive investigation of criminal incidents is most successful when the identity of the offender is already known.

The RAND study examined the investigative practices of 153 cities. Once again, the question of investigative division staffing and placement was not directly addressed. However, the study concluded that differences in staffing levels appeared to have no appreciable effect on crime, arrest, or clearance rates. "In other words, if the total number of officers in a department is kept fixed, switching some of them into or out of investigative units is not likely to have a substantial effect on arrest or clearance rates."[41] As to investigative activity, the RAND study found that, on average, investigators spent 45 percent of their time on non-case work, such as travel and administrative matters. More importantly, of the 55 percent of the time actually spent investigating, 40 percent of the time (22 percent overall) was expended on investigating matters that are never solved. Only 12 percent of the time (7 percent overall) was expended on investigating matters that were solved. Another 48 percent of the time (26 percent overall) was spent on cleared cases after arrest.

Twenty-five years after the RAND study, the National Institute of Justice sponsored a study to examine police practice, policies, goals, and perspectives of the criminal investigation process. The grant was given to Michigan State University. The study marked the first nationally representative research endeavor of police criminal investigation practice in the United States. Generally, the study revealed that the criminal investigation process has remained relatively unchanged over the past 30 years, despite significant paradigm shift in policing. For instance, during this same period of time, policing strategies and philosophies significantly changed with the advent of new technology, team policing, community policing, COMPSTAT, ILP, and evidence-based policing. Further, the study somewhat echoed the finding of previous research in that the role of the individual police officer in solving a crime was highlighted versus the role and function of plainclothes detectives. These findings were supported in 2011, by a study that attempted to reason "why" the function of detectives remained relatively unchanged:

- Detectives spend an inordinate portion of time on clerical and administrative duties; and this remains a significant portion of their job task;

- Activities that have been associated with the major paradigm shifts in policing such as in community policing (attending neighborhood meetings, school policing, crime analysis, etc.) are largely performed by officers and civilian support staff but not investigators or detectives; and

- Detective work varies across investigative units that are functionally differentiated.[42]

One other bit of research on the investigative function bears mention. The Bureau of Justice Statistics' Law Enforcement Management and Administrative Statistics (LEMAS) reports that nationwide, on average, 16 percent of the sworn personnel in police departments are assigned to investigative functions. The LEMAS study[43] does not further disaggregate the data. Thus, national averages for the number of homicide detectives versus the number of undercover narcotics investigators in agencies of varying size are not available. Correspondingly, the previously mentioned RAND study found that over all respondents, 17.3 percent of their sworn force was assigned to investigative units. Over one-half of the participating departments reported 14 to 20 percent of personnel assigned as investigators. Within this group of investigative personnel, 78 percent worked "reported crime" while 22 percent worked in vice, narcotics, internal affairs, and other proactive investigative units.[44]

Detailed research to compare one department to another in terms of investigator staffing and placement of the investigative function within the organization has simply not been undertaken at the national level. This type of comparison would probably not be valuable since the definition of investigator is speculative and widely varies with the internal policies defined by each department. In addition, the concept of investigator as an officer or detective also varies greatly. In most departments, investigative functionality is relegated primarily to detectives; however in some agencies, investigative work is a functional assignment of officers. The problem becomes even more acute when attempting to compare unionized departments with contractual documents that treat investigative functions and assignment with a promotional rank (e.g., New York Police Department, Portland, OR., Phoenix, AZ., San Diego, CA., Seattle, WA.), or with those agencies that are not unionized under collective bargaining, as is the case with most police departments.

In the past 10 years, the ratio of investigators to total sworn personnel has slightly increased to a national average of 20 percent, largely a reflection of federal grant money available to combat drug trafficking and terrorism.[45]

Crime Factors Impacting Investigation

James Q. Wilson in his highly acclaimed book *Varieties of Police Behavior* noted that uniformed patrol officers could deliver police services in one of several possible styles: law enforcement, order maintenance (watchman), or service.[46] Similarly, it may be hypothesized that investigative units in a police department carry out their respective responsibilities utilizing a variety of analogous responses. How police investigators respond to the incidence of crime is a function of several factors. Depending on the nature of the incident, any particular factor may receive greater or lesser emphasis in the decision to investigate and, more importantly, the level of investigative energy devoted to the matter. The factors to be considered are as follows:

- **The manner in which the crime comes to the attention of the police**—Is the crime reported by the citizen-victim, such as a sexual assault or robbery? Is the response a result of a generic complaint of illegal activity, for example, public drug market, solicitation of prostitution? Is the crime detected by proactive efforts of the police, such as undercover drug sales or stolen property stings? Is the crime detected by police administrative inspections, for example, review of pawnshop tickets or automobile salvage yards?

- **The severity of the crime**—While, in theory, all victims deserve a complete investigation of their criminal complaints, scarce resources necessitate that priorities be established. Many departments employ differential response policies to address priority handling and time allocation to more serious or aggravated crimes, while others are simply addressed by telephone. Consequently, felony offenses tend to take precedence over misdemeanors, crimes involving personal injury may take precedence over property offenses, and offenses involving large monetary amounts of loss receive greater attention than events resulting in little monetary loss.

- **The historical experience in solving similar crimes**—Clearance rates of Part I offenses nationwide give insight to this factor. While the clearance rate for murder is relatively high (64.1 percent in 2013), the solution rate for automobile theft is less than one in ten.[47] Thus, certain types of offenses are by their very nature difficult to clear by arrest. Even within certain crime classifications, such as burglary, investigators soon develop an ability to discern between cases for which expending investigative effort might prove worthwhile and futile. Consider a residential burglary with no witnesses, no latent fingerprints, and the owner cannot provide a detailed description of the property taken. Such a case borders on unsolvable regardless of the amount of investigative effort that might be expended. An experienced investigator will simply process the paperwork on this case and conduct little to no investigation. Clearly, this is part of the reason that burglary is one of the least solved crimes in America with less than 10 percent of the cases ever being cleared.[48]

- **Legal considerations**—As a matter of law, unattended deaths require reporting and a response by designated public officials, generally the police and/or medical examiner. An investigation—sometimes simple, sometimes complex—is initiated to determine if the death was a suicide, an accident, the result of natural causes, or a criminal homicide. Similarly, child abuse reports necessitate a police response. Further, the local prosecutor may choose not to prosecute certain cases or not to take the case unless certain witnesses or evidence is available. These law-related issues affect the police investigative effort, and their position within the organizational design of the department.

- **Department policies**—The chief of a police agency may adopt procedural rules that affect the investigative process. For example, commonly, by policy, unsolved murder cases are never placed in a closed status. Also, a policy of mandatory arrest at domestic disturbances generates cases for investigative follow-up. Perhaps most importantly, the degree to which the responding uniformed officer follows up initial leads affects the amount of work the investigative officer will perform on an individual case. Departmental policy is even more apparent in proactive investigative functions such as intelligence, gang, vice, narcotics, and terrorist investigations where cases are not the result of calls for service, but rather officer initiation or intelligence reports presented fusion centers. How many officers are assigned to these units are often the result of federal task force grants and a rather obscure number derived from history and perceived problems associated with these specific areas of enforcement. For instance, if the number of gang-related or narcotics-related aggravated assaults, robberies, and murders increase in a specific area or over a specific time period, investigative allocation relating to these areas often increases. The same can be true when federal grants are available to combat these same types of crime, or issues. This is certainly the case with the New York Police Department after 9/11, when significant manpower and hence, an entirely new division focused on terrorism was added to the organizational chart.

These factors, when considered together, produce several possible models of investigative style. Each style necessitates a different staffing strategy, that is, a different way of computing workload, and more importantly, a new way of placing the unit(s) within the organizational framework of the police department.

- **Style I—Reinforcing Patrol.** Incident driven; staffing determined by number of incidents independent of complexity. A citizen complains, patrol initially responds, but an investigator is subsequently assigned to the matter. Domestic assaults are an illustration. Time spent on each incident is approximately the same. Cases are quickly resolved and closed. Since the time spent on each incident is roughly the same, the number of incidents, not time spent, is the most important factor in determining staffing levels. Where relevant, response time to the scene is examined for some categories of incidents. In some cases response time may not be relevant, for example, patrol makes a domestic assault arrest and refers the case to CID. While response time levels would not be expected to fall within the same range as initial patrol response time, since these units supplement patrol, response times should be reasonably prompt. The slower the response time of the CID unit, the longer the patrol officer is tied to the scene.

- **Style II—Standard Reactive.** Incident and complexity driven. Requires response and follow-up a little or a lot depending on the particular case. Case may or may not ever be solved. Cases may be closed or placed in inactive status when all logical investigative leads have been exhausted. Robbery and burglary are illustrations.

- **Style III—Major Cases.** All incidents are thoroughly investigated and cases are not closed although reasonable investigative leads may diminish over time. Homicides and unknown assailant sexual assaults are illustrations. Staffing of these units is determined similarly to Standard Reactive units. However, allowance may need to be made for two forms of cases in the primary caseload—active and inactive matters. The latter would be those cases where leads no longer exist but are kept open because of policy. Likewise, because of the severity of the types of cases handled and the likelihood that solved cases may result in a trial, the secondary caseload may demand more attention than with other investigative styles. Actual caseload numbers in this unit will likely be low. Units that investigate homicide and rape are traditionally Style III Units.

- **Style IV—Regulatory Inspection.** Primarily inspection/regulatory work that uncovers the existence of a crime. Actual follow-up investigation may be assigned to others. Pawn shop and auto salvage yard inspections fall into this category. Caseload is determined on the number of locations needed to be inspected. This is one area where average time spent at each site may provide insight into the number of personnel needed. As the number of bars and adult entertainment centers, pawnshops, salvage yards, and the like change, it would be expected that the number of persons assigned to these units would need to be altered. Interestingly, many departments are shifting the inspections and investigations of these businesses to civilian personnel. These are excellent civilianization steps for cost savings within a department.

- **Style V—Passive Notation.** Primarily report-taking/ support functions with only selective investigative effort. Routine stolen property reports and bad check cases are illustrations. Since little follow-up exists to these reports, the number of complaints determine workload. Investigators are expected to carry a large secondary caseload and a relatively small primary caseload. Many of the traditional investigative roles in this style, such as those observed and associated with Sex Offender Registration and Tracking, are also commonly staffed by civilians.

- **Style VI—Discovery Enforcement.** Largely proactive investigations where covert police officers detect the occurrence of crime and identify suspects, usually at about the same time. Individual officer effort largely determines the size of the caseload. The number of investigators assigned to these units is primarily a policy decision. Since investigations are largely proactive in nature, additional officers or investigators will likely be able to make cases at a rate similar to existing staff. In theory, staffing could exceed its marginal utility—an additional officer or detective adds only incrementally to the number of crimes detected. This is particularly true in geographical areas of high vice and drug activity.

Three key elements exist in the above models. First, is the recognition that investigative units vary in the manner in which they operate; thus, organizational models likewise need to differ. Unlike patrol, which is the primary line function of all police departments, there is no universal mathematical model that can be constructed to determine appropriate staffing levels, or exactly "where" the investigative unit should be placed. Second, historical data should be used to determine baseline staffing, and organizational placement of the investigative function. And third, for all but the specialized investigations units within a criminal investigative, representing Style VI-Discovery Enforcement Units (e.g., terrorist investigations, intelligence, gang officers, narcotics,

and vice enforcement), caseload should be calculated as the number of new cases per month. In this manner, conflicts between patrol officer investigations versus specialized investigations are minimized.

SOME UNIQUE ORGANIZATIONAL FEATURES OF SHERIFF'S OFFICES

A detailed discussion of "politics and the county sheriff" was addressed in Chapter 4, Politics and Police Administration. However, in addition to some of the unique political features discussed therein, there are also some organizational differences that typically exist between municipal police departments and sheriff's offices. For example, most police departments do not have a single commanding officer positioned between the police chief and all of the operating and administrative bureaus. However, this is not true of sheriff's offices. Most sheriff's offices have a chief deputy/undersheriff and, with the blessing of the sheriff, this person typically assumes considerable operational command over the entire organization (see Figure 6.12). The position exists because, although the elected sheriff is the chief law enforcement officer of the agency, the sheriff must devote a considerable amount of time addressing the political needs of the sheriff's office within the community to assure that a positive image is created and maintained and public support is maximized. In addition, if the sheriff should decide to run for re-election, he or she must devote considerable time and effort to this endeavor.

In many respects, the role of the chief deputy/undersheriff is very similar to that of the police chief in a municipal police department, in that the person occupying this position assumes direct operational command over the entire organization. However, it is also important to note that, because sheriff's offices typically are responsible for supervising the operation of county jails, the chief deputy/undersheriff should also ideally have a good background in jail administration (see Figure 6.13). This is so because jails consume a substantial portion of the agency's resources for both personnel and operating expenses. Although the position of sheriff, like that of police chief, has traditionally been held by men, this has changed and now women are increasingly being elected as sheriff.

Quick Facts: Sheriffs in the United States

There are 3,080 sheriff's departments in the United States. A Sheriff is generally (but not always) elected to office and represents the highest law enforcement officer of a county. In contrast, a Chief of Police is usually appointed and serves as the head of a municipal or city department. Interestingly, three states do not have sheriffs. They include:

1. Alaska. There are no county governments in the state;

2. Connecticut. Sheriff's departments have been replaced by a State Marshal System; and

3. Hawaii. While there are no sheriffs in Hawaii, there are "deputy sheriffs" that serve as part of the Sheriff's Division of the Hawaii Department of Public Safety, a unique merging of traditional county functionality with state police.[50]

HILLSBOROUGH COUNTY SHERIFF'S OFFICE

ORGANIZATIONAL CHART

```
                              ┌─────────────┐
                              │   Sheriff   │
                              └─────────────┘

┌──────────────┐         ┌───────────────────────┐         ┌──────────────┐
│    Public    │─────────│                       │─────────│ Legal Office │
│ Information  │         │ Office of the Chief   │         └──────────────┘
│    Office    │         │       Deputy          │         ┌──────────────┐
└──────────────┘         │                       │         │ Information  │
┌──────────────┐         └───────────────────────┘─────────│   Services   │
│  Community   │─────────                                   │   Division   │
│    Affairs   │                                            │Chief Information Officer│
│    Office    │                                            └──────────────┘
└──────────────┘
```

Department of Patrol Services Colonel	Department of Investigative Services Colonel	Department of Administrative Services Colonel	Department of Detention Services Colonel
Uniform Patrol District I Major	Criminal Investigations Division Major	Support Services Division Civilian Director	Jail Division I Major
Uniform Patrol District II Major	Homeland Security Division Major	Training Division Major	Jail Division II Major
Uniform Patrol District III Major	Child Protective Investigations Division Major	Office of the Comptroller Comptroller	Jail Division III Major
Uniform Patrol District IV Major	Special Investigations Division Major		
Communications Bureau Lieutenant			

03/02/07

FIGURE 6.12 ▶ Hillsborough County Sheriff's Office (organizational chart showing the office of the chief deputy in charge of the entire organization, but subordinated to the Sheriff). *Source:* Courtesy of the Hillsborough County Sheriff's Office, Tampa, Florida.

LINE AND STAFF RELATIONSHIPS IN POLICE AGENCIES

The rapid growth in size of many police agencies has been accompanied by a corresponding rapid growth in specialization and a need for the expansion of staff services to provide support for operating units. This expansion and division of responsibility, which occurs in all police departments except those that are a pure line form of organization, is sometimes fraught with difficulty and dissension. If left uncorrected, these conditions will have a serious negative effect on both the quality and the quantity of service a police agency is able to deliver to its citizens. The following represent some of the major causes of conflict between line and staff.

FIGURE 6.13 ▶ Sheriff's departments are often responsible for the county jail, as well as more traditional law enforcement duties. (Image Source/Getty Images)

The Line Point of View

One of the basic causes of organizational difficulties, as line operations view them, is that staff personnel attempt to assume authority over line elements instead of supporting and advising them.[49] Line commanders feel that the chief looks to them for accountability of the operation; therefore, staff personnel should not try to control their operation because they are not ultimately responsible for handling line problems. Another commonly heard complaint is that staff personnel sometimes fail to give sound advice because their ideas are not fully thought out, not tested, or "too academic." This attitude is easy for line commanders to develop because of the belief that staff personnel are not responsible for the ultimate results of their product and therefore propose new ideas too quickly.

Communications problems sometimes emerge between the staff specialist and line commanders. Staff personnel on occasion fail to explain new plans or procedures and do not give line commanders sufficient time to propose changes. For example, a major staff project with an ambitious time line for completion was initiated in a patrol division after only a very brief period of time had passed from its announcement until the starting date. Some attempts were made to prepare the personnel for the project by the use of memos, but this task was largely left to line supervisors to do, and they did not have enough information to fully explain the new program. This resulted in confusion. Individual officers were unsure of what they were to do, so they did little. It took several weeks to recognize the problem and several more weeks to explain, train, and guide the personnel to operate under the new plan. After a three-month delay, the plan began to show results. However, the crime picture for this period was the worst in four years. The chief placed the blame at his precinct commanders' doors. They, in turn, blamed staff for poor preparation and lack of coordination.

Line commanders frequently claim that staff personnel take credit for successful operations and point the finger of blame at the line commander when programs fail, reflecting the adage that failure is an orphan and success has many fathers. In one department, a new report-writing program was installed under staff auspices. This program was designed to improve the statistical data that the staff group would use in preparing the various departmental reports and to help the patrol commander to evaluate patrol personnel. During the first year of the program, several flaws showed up that prompted staff to write a report that stated the patrol supervisors were not checking the reports carefully, and as a result erroneous information was appearing that made evaluation impossible. A retraining program was instituted, and the defects were ironed out. The personnel assigned to do the training then wrote a report taking full credit for the improvement. The commander of the patrol division took a rather dim view of this self-congratulatory report because he, along with some of his subordinates, worked very closely with the training section in formulating the retraining program.

Operational commanders sometimes express the concern that staff personnel do not see the "big picture" because they have only limited objectives that reflect their own nonoperational specialties. For example, the personnel unit of one police department developed a test for the rank of lieutenant. Most of the sergeants who took the examination did poorly. Many became frustrated and angry because they had built up fine work records and believed that the examination procedure failed to measure their potential ability for the rank of lieutenant accurately. The members of the personnel unit who developed the examination procedure were not sympathetic and suggested that the department just did not have the caliber of personnel who could pass a valid examination. The line commanders claimed that the personnel unit did not know enough about the department's needs, and if they would put more effort into helping instead of "figuring out reasons why we're no good, then we'd be better off."

The Staff Point of View

Staff personnel contend that line commanders do not know how to use staff. Instead of using their analytic skills, staff personnel feel that line commanders simply want to use them as researchers and writers. As an example, in one medium-sized department, the robbery caseload for detectives was increasing at an alarming rate. When staff were approached to work on the problem, the chief of detectives told them how he saw the problem, asked them to prepare an order for his signature setting out the changes as he saw them, and refused any staff personnel the opportunity to contact the operating field units to determine what the problems were as they saw them.

Many staff personnel also feel that line officers are shortsighted and resist new ideas. As an example, a department had expanded, and numerous personnel were promoted, but some of the personnel promoted to administrative and executive positions could not function effectively because they had not been properly trained to assume their new roles and responsibilities. The results were inefficiency and personal conflict. The planning and research officer had much earlier wanted to install a training program for career development for the ranks of lieutenant and above, so that there would be a trained group to choose from when needed. The planning and research officer blamed the line commanders for being shortsighted and not cooperating earlier to develop career development programs.

Solutions

The problems of line and staff relationships can be corrected. What is needed is a thorough indoctrination and training program and clear definitions as to the tasks of each.

The line is principally responsible for successful operations of the department, and therefore, line employees must be responsible for operational decisions affecting them. Staff, on the other hand, exists to assist the line in reaching objectives by providing advice and information when requested to do so. This does not, however, prohibit staff from volunteering advice they believe is needed.

The use of staff assistance is usually at the option of line commanders, but they must recognize that the chief can decide to use staff services to review any operation and that this decision is binding. As an example, the chief may order a planning and research officer to determine if patrol officers are being properly used. The patrol commander is responsible for making effective use of advice received under such circumstances.

If the patrol commander disagrees with staff findings, then an opportunity for reply and review by a higher authority should be available.

Staff exist to help line elements accomplish the objectives of the department. To do this effectively, staff must know what the line elements are doing. Illustratively, the personnel officer who does not know what tasks police officers must perform cannot effectively prepare selection standards for the hiring of personnel. Both staff and line must exert effort to ensure that staff stay in contact with what is going on in line units.

Line personnel are concerned primarily with day-to-day operating objectives within the framework of departmental goals. Staff can perform a valuable task for them by thinking ahead toward future problems and operations before they arise. The possibility of a plane crash in a community that has an airport is a subject that staff, in co-operation with line commanders, can anticipate. Thus, staff can accomplish time-consuming planning and the development of orders and procedures well before they are needed.

Line commanders should know what the various staff functions are and what they can contribute to the improvement of the line units. In some departments, this can be done at meetings by allowing the staff heads to explain what they can do for the line commanders. At the same time, line commanders can make known their expectations about staff support. Such discussions lead to closer coordination and improved personal relationships that are essential for effectiveness. Staff's ideas will be more readily accepted if they demonstrate an understanding of line operations.

Staff activity deals primarily with change. However, people tend to resist change and ideas that threaten the status quo. Change by itself indicates the possibility that the old way is no longer acceptable. Staff should anticipate and dispel resistance to change by doing the following:

1. Determining to what extent the change proposed will affect the personal relationships of the people involved. Is the change a major one that will affect the social patterns established in the formal and informal organizations discussed later in this chapter? Can the change be broken down into a series of small moves that will have less negative impact than a single, large change? The single big change versus a succession of smaller steps toward completing the change should be carefully considered: A boy had a dog with a long tail, but wanted him to have a short one. The boy didn't want to hurt the dog by chopping the tail all off at once, so he cut it off in sections. Massive change all at once can be detrimental to morale and operations. However, we should not underestimate the importance of fully preparing the police department for change— whether it's large or small—by giving officers a chance for input throughout the process.

2. It is at least arrogant, if not reckless, to impose change without meaningful involvement of those who will be most affected by it. "Meaningful involvement" means

Box 6.3: Front-End Engagement of the State Patrol Troopers

A State Patrol hired a consultant to develop a new promotional system. After making the necessary appointments and sharing all of the available information, the consultant went around the state meeting with a group of officers from each of the Patrol's 50 posts. Some important ideas were contributed, such as closing off making promotions for favored troopers by making exceptions to the competitive examination promotional roster.

The consultant told the groups two things which proved to be important: (1) Occasionally he would react to a trooper's suggestion by saying something like, "I won't recommend that because it would be in conflict with Equal Opportunity Commission guidelines" and (2) "Whatever I tell you today, I believe it to be factually correct. If that changes or turns out not to be the case, I'll send message of correction to all Posts." In the end, a system was developed and implemented in 1998 without opposition from troopers or their association and is still in place. The consultant believes this was due to the high involvement of the rank and file in the actual development of the promotional policy as opposed to giving the troopers a policy and asking them for their input.

---

the genuine opportunity to shape decisions effecting the change being contemplated. While some changes may be mandated by law, changes in FBI Uniform Crime Reporting guidelines, Supreme Court decisions, or other entities, even under such mandates, the details about the change should involve those most affected. Excluding them communicates the belief that they could not possibly have important insights and recommendations to contribute. Also, it implicitly suggests that only staff members and senior commanders are capable of having cogent thoughts. Although it may not be possible for everyone to participate, the use of representative groups of employees is often effective in helping to facilitate change (see Box 6.3).

3. Communicating throughout the entire planning stage. The personnel who will be affected by the change will accept it better if (a) they believe it will benefit them personally—that it will make their work easier, faster, or safer (the change should be tied in as closely as possible with the individual's personal goals and interests—job, family, future); (b) the personnel have an opportunity to offer suggestions, ideas, and comments concerning the change as it affects them— provided these suggestions are sincerely wanted and are given serious consideration; and (c) they are kept informed of the results of the change (see Chapter 15, Organizational Change).

To achieve organizational objectives, a line commander should know how to use staff assistance. The specialized skills of staff people can be used to help achieve these goals more efficiently and economically. By involving staff in the problems of the line, staff personnel can become more effective by learning the line commanders' way of thinking. Line commanders must be able to identify their problems precisely before seeking assistance. They must not vaguely define a problem and then expect the staff unit to do all the work. It is also important for staff to keep other staff informed of decisions that will affect them. Keeping others involved and informed before taking action also applies to chiefs (see Box 6.4).

Box 6.4: A Lack of Coordination on a Command Staff

A police department received budget authority to hire and train 160 new officers. This represented about four normal-sized recruit classes. The Chief issued a memo calling for two "super-sized" recruit classes and set their dates. Although the Majors commanding the personnel and training divisions had previously discussed the new hirings in general with the Chief several times, they were surprised that he had acted without hearing their specific recommendations. When the Chief refused to alter the academy dates, the personnel and training division commanders tried hard to make them work. However, there were too many people marginally qualified and a few who had a more thorough background check would have excluded.

The result was a higher than usual attrition for students in the academy and during the six-month probationary period that followed their graduation: (1) In the third week of the academy, a recruit was fired for pulling a few books off of the shelf at a public library and fondling himself as he watched young girls and (2) A probationary officer was dismissed because he forged a doctor's note to cover his use of a sick day to go play blackjack at a casino. Other problems were also encountered during the first academy, the most serious of which was that some of the best outside instructors had other commitments or family plans and could not participate. While similar problems were also encountered in the second academy, the overall attrition was marginally less.

Quick Facts: Transition Training Is Crucial

A roughly 100-officer police department near Atlanta had finished the transition training to Glocks. An officer from that department had an off-duty job providing security in uniform at a popular local restaurant. Several days after finishing the transition training, he reported to his extra job through the restaurant's rear door, which led to the large cooking area. At the same time, two robbers came into it from the main restaurant area, seeking to flee out the back. They both fired shots at the officer and ducked behind a steel encased table. The officer also found cover and the three men exchanged multiple shots. Confused about how many shots he had fired, the officer followed his transition training, released the magazine from his pistol and seated a new one, just in time to hear one of the robbers yell, "He's fired six shots. No more rounds. Let's rush him." The flaw in their thinking was the officer had a revolver and to the officer's credit he had followed his transition training. Both robbers leaped from behind the steel encased table and charged the officer, who wounded both of them in an exchange of gunfire. However, the officer was not injured.

One thing that people working staff functions typically have is necessary time and research skills to delve into operational problems. As an example, when many police departments were transitioning from revolvers to semi-automatics, a common staff function was to make and support a recommendation to the Chief about which semi-automatic to select. Factors normally considered included the caliber, acquisition cost, reliability, experiences of test shooters from the department, any gender shooting disparities, and the amount and cost of transition training to the firearm selected.

The steps taken by a staff when asked to recommend other equipment would parallel those used to develop a recommendation for the semi-automatic. Researching such potential changes is more complex than immediately meets the eye. Gathering the information includes such activities as (1) gathering any research findings, (2) requesting the applicable policies from departments already using the equipment, (3) tabulating surveys of other agencies' practices, (4) making telephone calls to obtain information, (4) sending e-mails to agencies asking them to complete the survey, and other detailed work.

THE INFORMAL ORGANIZATION

The **informal organization** does not appear on organizational charts, but it does exist in every organization because people are not simply objects in boxes connected by lines. Officers have needs, attitudes, and emotions and informal organizations are built on the friendships that spring up around them. Informal organization members have views and goals that may or may not coincide or support those of the police department. The informal organization has its own communications and behavior patterns, as well as a system of rewards and punishments to assure conformity.[51]

An important attribute for police leaders is to recognize the existence of the informal organization and to inculcate its support of the department as opportunities permit. Sometimes, the informal organization is regarded as a threat to the established authority of the department or to one or more leaders, such as the chief or sheriff. If a leader actively opposes the informal organization it strengthens the bond among its members and obviates the opportunity to court its support for departmental activities, for example, new programs. Continuing active opposition to the informal organization sometimes, perhaps often, has an unpleasant ending (see Box 6.5).

Police leaders must communicate clearly to all employees what the department's goals are and how each of them contributes to achieving them. When this is done properly several things are accomplished: (1) employees understand their role in the department, (2) they feel valued, and (3) contributing to the department's achievement of goals becomes attractive, and perhaps reduces the likelihood of the informal organization becoming oppositional.

The informal organization has several important characteristics:

Naturalness—The informal organization is natural and spontaneous; it does not ordinarily take on the characteristics of a social group because a commanding officer ordered it to develop.

Instead, the informal group evolves and develops in response to conditions and needs of people in the organization.

Interactions (or group dynamics)—Group members interact with each other because they want to; they have a natural, spontaneous desire to do so.

Empathy—Members of a social group have a high degree of attraction and empathy for each other, which comes out of shared attitudes and values. They like to be with each other and know they are safe expressing their true feelings about things at work. While some members of a social group are attracted to each other more than others, the general level of mutual attraction is high.

Social distance—Members of a social group do not feel too much social distance. That is, they do not feel that there are status or other types of barriers (e.g., ethnic, gender, and racial) between themselves and other members. Social

Box 6.5 The Sheriff and the "Disloyal" Deputies

"Joe" was a first term Sheriff in a Southern state, an area where Sheriffs have historically been very politically powerful. He made erratic decisions, some of which played havoc with the deputies' assignments and their family life. Eleven months before the next election, Joe began hearing that some unidentified deputies were opposed to his re-election and aligning themselves with the challenger in the next election. He told his command staff those deputies were "disloyal piss-ants" and he would deal with them. Subsequently, Joe went on a "witch hunt" trying to find out who these deputies were. Deputies suspected of "disloyalty" were covertly followed on- and off-duty to see where they went and with whom they might be meeting. On mere suspicion, some deputies were reassigned to less desirable duties and subject to strict discipline for even minor infractions. A handful of deputies were left for other employment because of the sheriff's antics and two "disloyals" were fired for thin reasons. These actions galvanized the remaining deputies, even those whom theretofore been neutral, and support for the challenger increased substantially.

The challenger defeated Joe and went right to work. Among the newly elected sheriff's initial priorities was offering to rehire deputies that had left for other employment. Several of them took the offer, one because he needed a few more years as a deputy to be vested in the pension system. The new sheriff also worked with the Peace Officers Standards and Training Council to clear the records of the two fired "disloyals." One subsequently came back into law enforcement with a municipality and the other continued to work in his family-owned business. The former sheriff started a private security firm that failed in its third year.

distance is the reason that uninhibited interaction often fails to take place in management meetings attended by personnel from several rank levels.

Democratic orientation—The social group has a strongly democratic orientation. The very essence of social group action is the attraction that members have for each other, supplemented by uninhibited communication and self-expression. Naturalness and freedom characterize effective social groups.

Leadership—Leaders tend to emerge naturally from the group. This does not mean, however, that social groups cannot exist where leaders have been designated from the outside. Much depends on the characteristics and behavior of the leader. When an aggregation of people begins to become a social group, some people initiate interaction more than others and they are usually attractive to a large number of people. These are the natural leaders, but they may not necessarily also be designated as hierarchical leaders.

Group pressures—One aspect of the social group is the pressure exerted to get the members to conform to group standards in thought and action. The phenomenon can be used either to thwart the goals of management or to facilitate their achievement.

Cohesiveness and unity—In order to endure, a social group must have a certain amount of cohesiveness. Members must have sufficient desire to belong, to keep the group together and in continued existence. In short, there must be enough attractiveness in group goals and associations to ensure their observance as a means of maintaining the group.[52]

Chapter Summary

Summary by Learning Objectives

1. **Explain the principle of hierarchy as it relates to organizational design.**

   The principle of hierarchy states that each lower level of an organization be supervised by a higher level. This principle results not only in the use of multiple spans of control but also in different grades of authority that increase at each successively higher level of the organization. According to the principle of hierarchy, this authority flows downward in the organization as a formal grant of power from the chief of police to those selected for leadership positions. These different grades of authority produce the chain of command. Although there are many similarities from one department to another, the American police service does not have a uniform terminology for grades of authority and job titles. In recent years, some police departments have moved away from using traditional military-style ranks (such as commander, captain, lieutenant, and sergeant) and have adopted, instead, alternative titles (such as director, manager, and supervisor) reflecting changes in both organizational structure and policing philosophy.

2. **Describe the concept of span of management.**

   The term span of management instead of "span of control" is used to describe the number of personnel a supervisor can personally manage effectively. The term "span of management" is broader than "span of control" and encompasses factors relating to an individual's capacity to oversee the activities of others directly, such as the police manager's ability, experience, and level of energy. The term "span of management" encompasses more of the factors relating to the problem of an individual's capacity to oversee the activities of others. How wide a span of management is depends on many factors. Some scholars argue that the ideal number of subordinates reporting to a supervisor is 8 to 12 but that number varies widely in practice.

3. **Distinguish between vertical and horizontal differentiation.**

   Vertical differentiation is based on levels of authority, or positions holding formal power within the organization. Persons with vertical authority have the power to assign work and to exercise control to ensure job performance. Horizontal differentiation, on the other hand, is usually based on activity. However, in some cases, horizontal differentiation is based on specific projects or even geographical distribution. For instance, many state police departments are responsible for large geographical areas. Their organizational structure often reflects horizontal differentiation based on location rather than function.

4. **Discuss the differences between tall organizational structures and flat organizational structures.**

   The complexity of a police department is increased by the proliferation of levels because they can negatively affect communication up and down the chain of command. Tall organizational structures have many levels with narrow spans of control. Taller organizations are complex and may react slowly during crisis situations, as effective communication is hampered by the number of different levels present within the chain of command. Successful tall departments must develop policies and procedures that overcome problems created by increased complexity. Larger spans of management or control yield flatter organizational structures. However, the capacity to flatten out police organizational structures depends to no small degree on reducing the number of traditional ranks, a movement often met with resistance because it means less opportunity for upward mobility. Thus, flatter structures are associated with wider spans of control that offer numerous advantages over the more traditional tall structures. First, they shorten lines of communication between the bottom and top levels. Communication in both directions is more likely to be faster and more timely. Second, the route of communication is more simple, direct, and clear than it is in tall organizations. Third, distortion in communication is minimized by a reduced number of people being involved. Fourth, and probably most important, flat structures are generally associated with employees with higher morale and job satisfaction as compared to employees in tall-structured organizations.

5. **List and describe four basic types of police organizational design.**

   There are four basic structural types of design that can be found within police organizations. They are as follows:

   Line Structure: This is the oldest, simplest, and clearest form of organizational design. Authority flows from the top to the bottom of the organization in a clear and unbroken line, creating a set of superior–subordinate relations in a hierarchy commonly called the *chain of command.* A primary emphasis is placed on accountability by close adherence to the chain of command.

   Line and Staff Structure: As more demands for services are placed on police departments, there is a need to add internal support functions, so that the line functions can continue to provide direct services to the public. The addition of support functions to the line elements produces a distinct organizational form: the line and staff structure. The addition of a staff component to the line structure offers a number of advantages such as (1) providing expert advice to line units in special knowledge areas as demonstrated by the opinions of legal advisors; (2) relieving line managers from performing tasks they least prefer to do or are least qualified to do, such as training and scientific analysis of physical evidence; (3) achieving departmentwide conformity in activities that affect the entire organization, such as disciplinary procedures; and (4) reducing or eliminating special problems, such as corruption, because of the greater expertise they bring to bear on the issue and the greater amount of time they have to devote to the problem.

   Functional Structure: The functional structure is one means by which the line authority structure of an organization can be modified. The functional structure is a line and staff structure that has been modified by the delegation of management authority to personnel outside their normal spans of control. By requiring specific units to be responsible to a variety of other unit commanders, critical information is assured of reaching other line officers. Sharing is promoted, while competing loyalties are diminished. Good examples of functional design can be observed in police departments moving toward geographical responsibility for supervisors on a 24-hour basis. A commander or shift (watch) supervisor (normally a lieutenant) assigned to the day watch may be responsible for solving violent street crimes (e.g., robberies) that occur in a specific area on all three shifts; however, officers on at least two of the shifts (evenings and nights) are not directly assigned to that supervisor.

Matrix Structure: One interesting form of organizational design is variously referred to as matrix (or grid) structure. In some cases, the style has been inclusively part of "project" or "product" management. The essence of matrix structure is in the assignment of members of functional areas (e.g., patrol, detective, and support services) to specific projects (e.g., task forces and crime-specific programs).

6. **Discuss the major crime factors that impact investigative function; list the various models of investigative style.**

Investigative units in a police department carry out their respective responsibilities utilizing a variety of responses. How police investigators respond to the incidence of crime is a function of several factors. Depending on the nature of the incident, any particular factor may receive greater or lesser emphasis in the decision to investigate and, more importantly, the level of investigative energy devoted to the matter. The factors to be considered are as follows: (1) The manner in which the crime comes to the attention of the police; (2) The severity of the crime; (3) The historical experience in solving similar crimes; (4) Legal considerations; and (5) Department policies. These factors, when considered together, produce several possible models of investigative style:

Style I—Reinforcing Patrol. Incident driven; staffing determined by number of incidents independent of complexity. A citizen complains, patrol initially responds, but an investigator is subsequently assigned to the matter. Domestic assaults are an illustration.

Style II—Standard Reactive. Incident and complexity driven. Requires response and follow-up a little or a lot depending on the particular case. Case may or may not ever be solved. Cases may be closed or placed in inactive status when all logical investigative leads have been exhausted. Robbery and burglary are illustrations.

Style III—Major Cases. All incidents are thoroughly investigated and cases are not closed although reasonable investigative leads may diminish over time. Homicides and unknown assailant sexual assaults are illustrations.

Style IV—Regulatory Inspection. Primarily inspection/regulatory work that uncovers the existence of a crime.

Actual follow-up investigation may be assigned to others. Pawn shop and auto salvage yard inspections fall into this category.

Style V—Passive Notation. Primarily report-taking/support functions with only selective investigative effort. Routine stolen property reports and bad check cases are illustrations.

Style VI—Discovery Enforcement. Largely proactive investigations where covert police officers detect the occurrence of crime and identify suspects, usually at about the same time. Individual officer effort largely determines the size of the caseload. Terrorism, narcotics, and vice operations are examples of discovery enforcement.

7. **Identify the basic causes for tension between line and staff and suggest strategies to be used as solutions.**

The rapid growth in size of many police agencies has been accompanied by a corresponding rapid growth in specialization and a need for the expansion of staff services to provide support for operating units. This expansion and division of responsibility, which occurs in all police departments except those that are a pure line form of organization, is sometimes fraught with difficulty and dissension. If left uncorrected, these conditions will have a serious negative effect on both the quality and the quantity of service a police agency is able to deliver to its citizens. One of the basic causes of organizational difficulties, as line operations view them, is that staff personnel attempt to assume authority over line elements instead of supporting and advising them. Another commonly heard complaint is that staff personnel sometimes fail to give sound advice because their ideas are not fully thought out, not tested, or "too academic." Communications problems sometimes emerge as well between the staff specialist and line commanders. Staff personnel on occasion fail to explain new plans or procedures and do not give line commanders sufficient time to propose changes. Line commanders frequently claim that staff personnel take credit for successful operations and point the finger of blame at the line commander when programs fail. Further, operational commanders sometimes express the concern that staff personnel do not see the "big picture" because they have only limited objectives that reflect their own nonoperational specialties. On the other hand, staff personnel contend that line commanders do not know how to use staff. Instead of using their analytic skills, staff personnel feel that line commanders simply want to use them as researchers and writers. Many staff personnel also feel that line officers are shortsighted and resist new ideas. The problems of line and staff relationships can be corrected. What is needed is a thorough indoctrination and training program and clear definitions as to the tasks of each. The line is principally responsible for successful operations of the department, and therefore line employees must be responsible for operational decisions affecting them. Staff, on the other hand, exist to assist the line in reaching objectives by providing advice and information when requested to do so. This does not, however, prohibit staff from volunteering advice they believe is needed. Staff exist to help line elements accomplish the objectives of the department. To do this effectively, staff must know what the line elements are doing. Both staff and line must exert effort to ensure that staff stay in contact with what is going on in line units. Line personnel are concerned primarily with day-to-day operating objectives within the framework of departmental goals. Staff can perform a valuable task for them by thinking ahead toward future problems and operations before they arise.

8. **Describe the characteristics of an informal organization.**

The informal organization is built on friendships and common desires. It, too, may have goals that may or may not coincide with the formal organization's goals. The informal organization has its own communications and behavior patterns, as well as a system of rewards and punishments to assure conformity. The informal organization has several important characteristics:

Naturalness—The informal organization is natural and spontaneous; it does not ordinarily take on the characteristics of a social group as a result of an order or edict from higher authority. Instead, the informal group evolves and develops in response to conditions and needs of people in the organization.

Interactions (or group dynamics)—Group members interact with each other because they want to; they have a natural, spontaneous desire to do so.

Empathy—Members of a social group have a high degree of attraction and sympathy for each other. They like to be with each other. Their social inhibitions are at a minimum and they feel a lack of the type of restraint that results from expected disapproval of one's associates.

Social distance—Members of a social group do not feel too much social distance. That is, they do not feel that there are status or other types of barriers (ethnic, gender, and racial) between themselves and other members.

Democratic orientation—The social group has a strongly democratic orientation. The very essence of social group action is the attraction that members have for each other, supplemented by uninhibited communication and self-expression. Naturalness and freedom characterize effective social groups.

Leadership—Leaders tend to emerge naturally from the group.

Group pressures—One aspect of the social group is the pressure exerted to get the members to conform to group standards in thought and action. The phenomenon can be used either to thwart the goals of management or to facilitate their achievement.

Cohesiveness and unity—In order to endure, a social group must have a certain amount of cohesiveness. Members must have sufficient desire to belong, to keep the group together and in continued existence. In short, there must be enough attractiveness in group goals and associations to ensure their observance as a means of maintaining the group.

Chapter Review Questions

1. What is the *principle of hierarchy?*
2. What is the distinction between rank and title?
3. What six factors will affect the span of management?
4. Distinguish between vertical and horizontal differentiation.
5. What are some of the more common ways in which activities and personnel are grouped within police organizations?
6. Discuss the differences between tall organizational structures and flat organizational structures.
7. List and discuss four basic types of structural designs within police departments.
8. Why have the functions of detectives remained relatively unchanged over the history of policing?
9. What are the crime factors that impact investigation?
10. Identify and discuss the six models of investigative style commonly observed within the investigative function.
11. Identify major organizational differences between sheriff's offices and municipal police departments.
12. Identify the basic causes of tension between line and staff.
13. Describe the characteristics of the informal organization.

Critical Thinking Exercises

1. Learn from individual police officers. Contact your local police department and if possible, arrange for a ride-along. Interview the officer and inquire about his or her attitudes toward supervision, management, and leadership within the department. What statements can you make about the informal organization within the police department versus the formal structure of the department?

2. Compare and contrast the organizational structure of a major police department versus a major private corporation in the United States. What differences exist between the two types of structure? Can you find any similarities? What do you think are the advantages and/or disadvantages of each organizational structure?

3. Visit the web page of the New York Police Department at: http://www.nyc.gov/html/nypd/html/home/home.shtml.

4. How did the events of 9/11 impact the structure of the NYPD? Who is the head of the Intelligence and Counterterrorism Division of the NYPD? Do research on this person and describe his background and specific qualifications for this position. Do you think he is qualified to hold such a controversial position? Why or why not?

Key Terms

city-county consolidated governments	line and staff structure	sector policing
decentralization	line structure	span of management
functional structure	matrix (or grid) structure	specialization
horizontal differentiation	organizing	structure
informal organization	principle of hierarchy	vertical differentiation

Endnotes

1. S. P. Robbins, *The Administration Process* (Englewood Cliffs, NJ: Prentice Hall, 1976), pp. 17–18.

2. *The Republic of Plato,* trans. A. Bloom (New York: Basic Books, 1968), p. 47.

3. For example, see Luther Gulick and L. Urwick, eds., *Papers on the Science of Administration* (New York: August M. Kelley, a 1969 reprint of the 1937 edition).

4. O. W. Wilson and R. C. Mclaren, *Police Administration,* 3rd ed. (New York: Mcgraw-Hill, 1972), p. 79.

5. Ibid., p. 81.

6. Ibid., p. 83.

7. N. C. Kassoff, *Organizational Concepts* (Washington, DC: International Association of Chiefs of Police, 1967), p. 22.

8. Wilson and McLaren, *Police Administration,* p. 56.

9. Ibid.

10. Gary W. Cordner, "Community Policing: Elements and Effects," in Roger G. Dunham and Geoffrey P. Alpert, *Critical Issues in Policing,* 6th ed. (Long Grove, IL: Waveland Press, 2010), pp. 432–449.

11. "City and County to Unify," The Kansas City Star (November 11, 2007), p. 1.

12. Troy Lane, "Span of Control for Law Enforcement Agencies," *Police Chief Magazine* 73 (October 2006), p. 10. Retrieved from http://policechiefmagazine.org/magazine/index.cfm?fuseaction=print_display&article_id=1 (June 25, 2010).

13. Troy Lane, "Span of Control for Law Enforcement Agencies," *Police Chief Magazine.*

14. D. A. Tansik and J. F. Elliot, *Managing Police Organizations* (Monterey, CA: Duxbury Press, 1981), p. 81.

15. Ibid.

16. B. J. Hodge and W. P. Anthony, *Organizational Theory: An Environmental Approach* (Boston: Allyn & Bacon, 1979), p. 240.

17. Richard Hall, *Organizations: Structure and Process* (Englewood Cliffs, NJ: Prentice Hall, 1972), p. 143.

18. This Section Is a Synopsis of the "Nature and Process of Differentiation" found in Hodge and Anthony, *Organizational Theory,* p. 249.

19. Hans Toch, "Police Officers as Change Agents in Police Reform," *Policing and Society,* Vol. 18, No. 1 (March 2008), pp. 60–71.

20. Ronald Wells, "Intelligence-Led Policing: A New Paradigm in Law Enforcement" *PATC Bulletin* (Indianapolis, IA: PATC Law Enforcement Training Council, September 2009).

21. Darlton E. Mcfarland, *Management: Foundations and Practices,* 5th ed. (New York: Macmillan, 1979), p. 316.

22. Ibid., p. 309.

23. B. J. Hodge and H. J. Johnson, *Management and Organizational Behavior* (New York: John Wiley & Sons, 1970), p. 163.

24. Modified by Robert W. Taylor (July 2015). See: Edward R. Maguire and Craig D. Uchida, "Measurement and Explanation in the Comparative Study of American Police," in *Measurement and Analysis of Crime and Justice,* Criminal Justice 2000, Vol. 4 (2000). See also Edward R. Maguire, *Organizational Structures in American*

Police Agencies: Context, Complexity and Control (Albany, NY: SUNY Press, 2003).

[25]W. Michael Phibbs, "Should Sector Policing Be in Your Organization's Future?" *FBI Law Enforcement Bulletin* (April 2010), pp. 1–2, 7.

[26]U.S. Department of Justice, Press Release, "Multi-Agency Investigation into East LA Gang Results in Federal RICO Indictment that Charges 38 Gangsters,"(December 10, 2014).

[27]Richard Kitaeff, "The Great Debate: Centralized vs. Decentralized Marketing Research Function," *Marketing Research: A Magazine of Management and Applications* 6 (Winter 1993), p. 59.

[28]Anaheim Police Department (Anaheim, CA), "Community Policing Team Annual Report," 1994.

[29]Several critiques of experimental police methods have been noted in the literature. See Robert W. Taylor and Dennis J. Kenney, "The Problems with Problem Oriented Policing" (paper presented at the Academy of Criminal Justice Sciences Annual Meeting, Nashville, Tennessee, March 1991); Kenneth W. Findley and Robert W. Taylor, "Re-Thinking Neighborhood Policing," *Journal of Contemporary Criminal Justice* 6 (May 1990), pp. 70–78; Jerome Skolnick and D. Bayley, *Community Policing: Issues and Practices around the World* (Washington, DC: National Institute of Justice, 1988); Jack Greene and Ralph Taylor, "Community Based Policing and Foot Patrol: Issues of Theory and Evaluation," in Jack Greene and Stephen Mastrofski (eds.), *Community Policing: Rhetoric or Reality?* (New York: Praeger, 1988), pp. 216–219; Stephen Mastrofski, "Police Agency Accreditation: The Prospects of Reform," *American Journal of Police* (May 15, 1986), pp. 45–81.

[30]Gary W. Cordner, "Written Rules and Regulations: Are They Necessary?" *FBI Law Enforcement Bulletin* 58 (July 1989), pp. 17–21.

[31]See Robert Michaels, *Political Parties* (New York: Dover, 1959).

[32]Jerry H. Ratcliffe, "Intelligence-Led Policing," in R. Worley, L. Mazerolle and S. Rombouts (eds.), *Environmental Criminology and Crime Analysis* (Portland, OR: Willan Publishing, 2008).

[33]Jerry H. Ratcliffe and Ray Guidetti, "State Police Investigative Structure and the Adoption of Intelligence-Led Policing," *Policing: An International Journal of Police Strategies and Management*, Vol. 31 (2008), p. 1.

[34]The current fiscal crisis confronting many police departments, especially in California, over the past decade has prompted considerable effort in maximizing the efficiency of police agencies in general, and the investigative function more specifically. Many departments have conducted evaluations of staff and workload studies to meet this demand. Much of this section has been used in evaluation studies conducted by the author, Robert W. Taylor first originated with Dr. Jerry Dowling, Chief Marlin Price, and Dr. Larry Hoover, *An Evaluation of the Fort Worth, Texas Police Department—Staffing of the Investigative Function* (January 2002) *and Final Executive Report* (March 2002) (Huntsville, TX: JUSTEX Systems, Inc.).

[35]Steve Fainaru, "Oakland Police Force Restructuring Could Hinder Murder Investigations and More," *The New York Times* (May 15, 2011).

[36]John D. McCluskey, Jefferey M. Cancino, Marie Skubak Tillyer, and Rob Tillyer, " Does Organizational Structure Matter? Investigation Centralization, Case Clearances and Robberies," *Police Quarterly*, Vol. 17, No. 3 (September 2014).

[37]Much of the early scholarly work on detective staffing, function and relationship within the organizational design of a police agency has been conducted during consulting projects. Foremost in this area of study is the work of our good friend, Dr. Jerry L. Dowling, Sam Houston State University. The only published work presented in this area by Jerry is as follows: "Analysis of Detective Staffing Patterns in Law Enforcement Agencies," paper presented to 41st Annual Meeting of the Academy of Criminal Justice Sciences, Las Vegas, Nevada, March 2004.

[38]President's Commission on Law Enforcement and Administration of Justice, *Challenge of Crime in a Free Society: Science and Technology Report*, (USGPO: 1967). See: https://www.ncjrs.gov/App/Publications/abstract.aspx?ID=42.

[39]Peter W. Greenwood, *The RAND Criminal Investigation Study: Its Findings and Impacts to Date* (Santa Monica, CA: RAND Corporation, 1979). See: http://www.rand.org/pubs/papers/P6352.

[40]Frank Horvath, Robert T. Meesig, and Yung Hyeock Lee, *National Survey of Police Policies and Practices Regarding the Criminal Investigations Process: Twenty-Five Years after RAND* (East Lansing, MI: Michigan State University, 2001). See: https://www.ncjrs.gov/pdffiles1/nij/grants/202902.pdf.

[41]See Peter Greenwood, Jan Chaiken, and Joan Petersilia, *The Criminal Investigation Process* (D.C. Heath & Co., Lexington, MA, 1977), p. 228.

[42]John Liederbach, Eric Fritsch, and Charissa Womack, "Detective Workload and Opportunities for Increased Productivity in Criminal Investigations," *Police Practice and Research: An International Journal*, Vol. 1, No. 1 (December 2011), p. 60.

[43]See U.S. Department of Justice, *Data Collection: Law Enforcement Management and Administrative Statistics (LEMAS) Report: Local Police*, 2013. See: http://www.bjs.gov/index.cfm?ty=tp&tid=71.

[44]Ibid.

[45]Ibid.

[46]James Q. Wilson, *Varieties of Police Behavior: The Management of Law and Order in Eight Communities* (Boston, MA: Harvard University Press, 1968).

[47]Martin Kaste, "Open Cases: Why One-Third of Murders in America Go Unresolved," *National Public Radio*, March 30, 2015. See: http://www.npr.org/2015/03/30/395799413/how-many-crimes-do-your-police-clear-now-you-can-find-out, and http://www.npr.org/2015/03/30/395069137/open-cases-why-one-third-of-murders-in-america-go-unresolved.

[48]Ibid.

[49]Kassoff, *Organizational Concepts*, pp. 31–38.

[50]National Sheriffs' Association. See: http://www.sheriffs.org/content/faq.

[51]Ibid., pp. 22–26.

[52]John M. Pfiffner and Frank P. Sherwood, *Administrative Organization* (Englewood Cliffs, NJ: Prentice Hall, 1965), pp. 43–44.

CHAPTER SEVEN

LEADERSHIP

Learning Objectives

1. Give two definitions of leadership.
2. Explain and elaborate on "leading and managing are co-dependent skill sets."
3. Provide four key characteristics and three key activities of effective senior police leaders.
4. Distinguish between authority and power.
5. Compare socialized and personalized power needs.
6. Identify and describe the three components of the leadership skill mix.
7. State two Great Man theories.
8. Define the Big Five.
9. Briefly describe "organizational citizenship behavior."
10. Distinguish among authoritarian, democratic, and laissez-faire leadership.
11. Describe Downs's four leader styles.
12. Contrast station house sergeants and street sergeants.
13. State the three organizational forces from Tannenbaum and Schmidt's contingency theory.
14. State the "central thought" or the "essence" of House's Path-Goal Theory.
15. Define the "merit" of a police officer in Leader-Member-Exchange Theory.
16. Compare leadership substitutes and neutralizers.
17. Contrast transactional leaders and transformational leaders.
18. Complete the following statement: The common characteristics shared by "new leadership" theories attempt to explain how leaders:

INTRODUCTION

KNOWLEDGE OF LEADERSHIP IS *important because: (1) officers deserve serious and competent leadership; (2) leadership weakness can reduce unit effectiveness and be a precursor to conduct problems by officers due to a lack of corrective action; (3) leadership failures can result in civil liability problems (see Chapter 14, Legal Aspect of Police Administration); (4) personnel costs, including fringe benefits, may account for 80 or more percent of the police budget (see Chapter 12, Financial Management); (5) leadership style communicates what commanders think about the people they lead; (6) while some people might be "born leaders," everyone else has to learn about it and integrate that knowledge with their behavior in small steps; and (7) leadership mistakes can result in injuries and deaths to those who are led, as well as to members of the public.*

POLICE LEADERSHIP

Although effective leadership is desired within police departments and there is an abundance of training programs to help provide it, there is a curious lack of substantial depth in the empirical research on effective police leadership processes.[1] Schafer argues that much of what is known is from small case studies, descriptive accounts, and anecdotal reports from "celebrity chiefs."[2] The police profession is a consumer of leadership theory. The theories relied upon are overwhelmingly developed by academics as general propositions and then researched almost entirely in non-police settings. When the theories are tested in police settings, the studies often involve small sample sizes that are largely unreplicated. Moreover, leadership studies conducted by observation that departments may consist of a cursory analysis lacking rigor and focusing only on the short-term impact.[3]

At least often, leadership theories or portions of them work in law enforcement agencies. From this we can conclude that many aspects of leadership are universal, such as integrity and fostering meaningful participation. However, we are left to wonder if theories generated specifically from studies of law enforcement leadership would merely confirm what we know or identify subtle, but important differences, such as policing uses skills with the same names, but define and enact them differently than in general theories.

Our preoccupation with crime, homeland security, and the need to be seen as "current" by adopting each operational innovation that comes along has diverted attention from developing a passion about leadership excellence. Some of the barriers to such excellence include: (1) *insufficient effort and funding are devoted to leadership development at every level of our agencies*, although our chief resource is people (see Chapter 12, Financial Management); (2) *We need more strong leadership role models in law enforcement agencies*. Perhaps the most potent way to change behavior in organizations is "wear it" consistently; (3) *Law enforcement generally fails to identify potential leaders earlier in their careers*. A modest start would be to give them small projects to showcase their abilities, staying out of their way as they grapple with their assignments, and giving them honest critiques; and (4) *Ineffective police leaders are seldom demoted nor are they thoughtfully retrained*; We manage around their shortcomings or transfer them to minor duties for which they are often over-ranked, wasting valuable resources and allowing the continuation of a poor role model.[4] It is a practice that is simultaneously humane and costly.

Developing police leadership is not a one-time investment; like the maintenance on police vehicles, it should be conceived of as a continuing expenditure. To help keep our eyes on the ball, the cost of leadership should not be aggregated under training. It must be a separate line in the budget supported by an abundance of individual staff development plans. If leadership is really dispersed in our departments, then it must find its reality in the commitment of dollars.

Pearson-Goff and Herrington did a systematic review of the police leadership literature published in journals between 1990 and 2012, which identified 9,624 records.[5] After applying filters such as only including empirical studies with a large sample size and using only reports written in English, they were left with 66 studies. Several of these were eliminated because of low relevance or other reasons, leaving 57 studies to be closely examined.[6]

These studies were mostly published between 2002 and 2012 in the United States and largely are derived from perceptions of senior police leaders by officers.[7] Analysis of seven key characteristics of effective senior police leaders and five key activities in which they engaged (see Table 7.1).[8] Unifying these two factors was the observation that senior police leaders are focused on providing a vision for the future and the mission.[9]

Implicitly, leadership is often thought of being positive—a good thing, uplifting and guiding toward some important accomplishment. That is the major thrust of this chapter, although the "dark side" of leadership is also covered.

LEADER AND MANAGER

There are many definitions of leadership, each reflecting certain perspectives, but all incorporate the notion that the essence of leadership is interacting with and influencing others. For example, **leadership** can be simply defined as the difference between pushing a string and pulling it or being a "difference maker." More completely, leadership has external and internal components; it is the process of (1) relating the police department to the larger environment, such as city council, the news media,

TABLE 7.1 PEARSON-GOFF AND HERRINGTON: KEY CHARACTERISTICS AND ACTIVITIES OF EFFECTIVE SENIOR POLICE LEADERS*	
Seven Key Characteristics of Effective Senior Police Leadership	**Five Key Activities**
1. Ethical behavior, a genuine sense of integrity and honesty that encourages subordinates to do likewise with each other.	1. Creating a shared vision that helps police department members know where they are going.
2. Trustworthy, being viewed within the law enforcement agency, in government, and across the community as a "straight arrow."	2. Engendering organizational commitment by strategies such as providing a system of rewards and power sharing, e.g., giving members a voice in some decisions or creating committees on which they can have input to policies and other matters.
3. Legitimacy, perceived as someone who still knows how to work the street as opposed to being desk bound and out of touch with the daily realities of policing.	3. Caring for subordinates involves a cluster of actions, illustrated by coaching, mentoring, training opportunities, engaging assignments, and participating on committees and projects that both challenge them and provide an opportunity to demonstrate their abilities.
4. Being a role model, serving as an example of the behavior expected from subordinates.	
5. Communication, the capacity to share ideas, explain decisions, create support, and respond to criticism within the police department, across agencies, with stakeholders, and as a voice in government policy making.	4. Driving and managing change without which the status quo is perpetuated. Announcing change doesn't produce it. Change requires champions and senior police leaders are one important source of energy to help propel change from a plan to a reality. As an aside, lower ranking officers are more likely to cling to the status quo than quickly embrace change.[10]
6. Decision making, a competency in making decisions that move the agency forward, e.g., obtaining resources, removing performance barriers, and achieving goals.	
7. Critical, creative/innovative, and strategic thinking ability, which entails looking to the future and determining what conditions need to be met or created to be successful then.	5. Problem solving by senior leaders ordinarily does not involve easily resolved "garden variety problems." The less thorny problems have already been handled by mid-level or lower leaders. The more intractable problems end up on the desks of senior police leaders.[11]

* The present authors have added comments in both columns intended to be consistent with Pearson-Goff and Herrington's and to amplify their views. No reformulation of the original work is intended.

civic organizations, and the general public and (2) influencing officers to use their energies willingly and appropriately to facilitate the achievement of the department's goals. Perhaps more than any other local government department head, police chiefs become very public figures and they and their families lose a great deal of privacy.

Leadership occurs in dyads (e.g., a chief and an assistant chief); small face-to-face groups, such as a command staff meeting; at the entire police department level; and externally as a symbol of the department. Some argue that individual officers can provide leadership to themselves by monitoring their own behavior and learning from their mistakes so they are not subsequently repeated. In this view self-leadership leads to enhanced performance. This line of thinking seems thin: Leaders need one or more followers. However, in a different way, Anderson's *Every Officer Is a Leader* effectively argues that officers must lead business owners, neighborhood associations, planning and zoning employees, and others outside of their agency to make community policing work[12] (see Figure 7.1).

There are diverse definitions of the terms **leader** and **manager**. Those terms are also used imprecisely sometimes.[13] Occasionally, they are erroneously employed to mean the same thing and sometimes synonymously with *leadership* and *managing*. Alimo-Metcalfe and Alimo-Metcalfe argue that many models of leadership are better regarded as management styles; *they maintain management is the content of a job and leadership is how it is carried out*.[14]

Others maintain that a person can be a leader, a manager, both, or neither[15] and the mix of those skill sets and the responsibilities involved can vary over situations and time. Another line of thought maintains effective administrators must be both leaders and managers. In this assessment leading and managing are co-dependent skill sets.

Leader and manager can also be examined using three contrasting lens: (1) placement in hierarchy, (2) organizational theory, and (3) role enactment:

1. In this view, whether you are a leader or a manager depends on where you are placed in the organization's hierarchy senior leaders are clustered at the top of an

Quick Facts: Leadership and Management

Peter Drucker (1909–2005) was among the preeminent thinkers of his generation on these subjects, publishing 41 books. In *Essential Drucker: Management, the Individual, and Society* (2001), he viewed leadership as doing the right thing and management as doing things right.

FIGURE 7.1 ▶ A Citizen Potawatomi Nation (CPN) community policing officer visits with senior citizens to learn of any needs or problems. The CPN is located on their reservation in Oklahoma with some 29,000 Native American members. The federal government has supported the development of community policing for local state, and tribal governments. (Courtesy of Citizen Potawatomi Nation)

organization while managers are in non-line units "further down" the organizational chart and "off to one side" with responsibility for staff functions, fewer people to supervise, and less flexibility and perhaps less discretionary authority than line commanders. Illustrations of staff activities include strategic planning, quality control, crime analysis, professional standards, records, and public information/affairs (see Table 7.2).

2. Drawing from organizational theory, Weber notes that in the bureaucracy model, each subordinate person and unit is under the direction/command of a higher office. It is from this arrangement that an organizational chart can be drawn. At the top of the pyramid is a lone figure, the police chief. By custom, people refer to the occupant of that office not only as "Chief" but also as "The Leader." Can there be other leaders in a police department? How would we know whether the commanders of various units on an organizational chart are leaders or managers? Arbitrarily, are those commanding line units "leaders," and staff commanders "managers"? Should job descriptions be scrutinized to see which ones specify "leads" versus "manages"? Other than identifying "The Leader," the bureaucratic model is not very illuminating on this issue.

TABLE 7.2 USING THE VIEW THAT YOUR PLACEMENT IN THE LAW ENFORCEMENT AGENCY'S HIERARCHY DETERMINES WHETHER YOU ARE A LEADER OR A MANAGER RESULTS IN THESE TYPES OF DISTINCTIONS	
Leaders	**Managers**
1. Are at or near the top	1. Occupy the middle ground between leaders and first-line supervisors
2. Have wide responsibilites.	2. Have narrower responsibilities.
3. Work on a broad stage, both outside and within the organization.	3. Are primarily directed toward those in their units.
4. Have both followers and subordinates.	4. Have subordinates.
5. Elevate how others do their jobs.	5. Make sure subordinates do their jobs.
6. Envision the future and are change oriented.	6. Are oriented toward shorter time frame, create agendas, maintain status quo.
7. Think strategically.	7. Think tactically.

3. Role enactment may be the surest way of determining who is acting out of a leadership skill set and who does so out of a management skill set. However, this delineation of skills is not precise; some skills, such as decision making, overlap. Role enactment is revealed by observing how a person with authority over the performance of others behaves. For example, those who are acting out of their leadership skill set tend to be visionaries who want to improve on the status quo whenever possible and will also unleash energy and creativity by trusting and empowering subordinates to come up with better ideas for doing things. Leaders know that they do not have a lock on good ideas and create the environment in which energy can be released and ideas generated. While those acting out of a management skill set may also do this, but in the main they have a bias toward maintaining the status quo, for example, refining or developing policies and the procedures supporting them and work within the established agency boundaries. One skill set is often restless with the status quo and the other tends to embrace it.

Of necessity, the challenge of leading and managing the activities of the department must be widely distributed.[16] Police departments, except for very small ones, cannot function without distributed authority. The extension of this reality is that law enforcement agencies need individuals who possess both leadership and managerial skill sets. Leadership and management skills are not mutually exclusive, but are usually not co-equal. It is perhaps inevitable that subconsciously or through introspection, officers recognize the mix of aptitudes they have and gravitate toward assignments that are a good match for their strongest skill set.

Police chiefs have multiple roles, such as preserving the trust and confidence of the public in the department, modeling and communicating values, envisioning the future, determining the operational philosophy, being a change agent and a budget gladiator, allocating resources, resolving conflicts, solving problems, recognizing and celebrating the achievements of officers (see Figure 7.2) and civilian staff, and being a spokesperson. In state police, state patrol, larger county, and municipal departments, sheriffs and chiefs have the additional task of leading personnel at district stations/precincts "remotely."[17] These tough roles and other factors lead to an average tenure for police chiefs of about 2.5 to 4.5 years.[18]

Some of this turnover is due to chiefs deciding that leading police departments simply takes too much out of them and their families. The exiting chiefs often dealt with multiple issues, many of which occurred repetitively:

- fiscal constraints
- escalating service demands
- new roles for local and state law enforcement in homeland security programs
- homeless encampments
- political skirmishes
- long hours
- unions
- domestic violence by police officers
- achieving diversity
- monitoring racial profiling
- escalation in human trafficking
- the push for more transparency and community engagement

FIGURE 7.2 ▶ Kitsap County, Washington, Deputy Sheriff Krista McDonald received a Public Safety Officer Medal of Valor from Vice President Joe Biden (R) and Attorney General Eric Holder (L) in 2013. Two deputies had been wounded by a gunman. Responding as a backup, Deputy McDonald directed fire from the cover of her patrol car. Quickly recognizing the danger her downed colleagues were in, she advanced under fire to protect them. She wounded the gunman, who committed suicide shortly afterward. (Charles Dharapak/AP/Corbis)

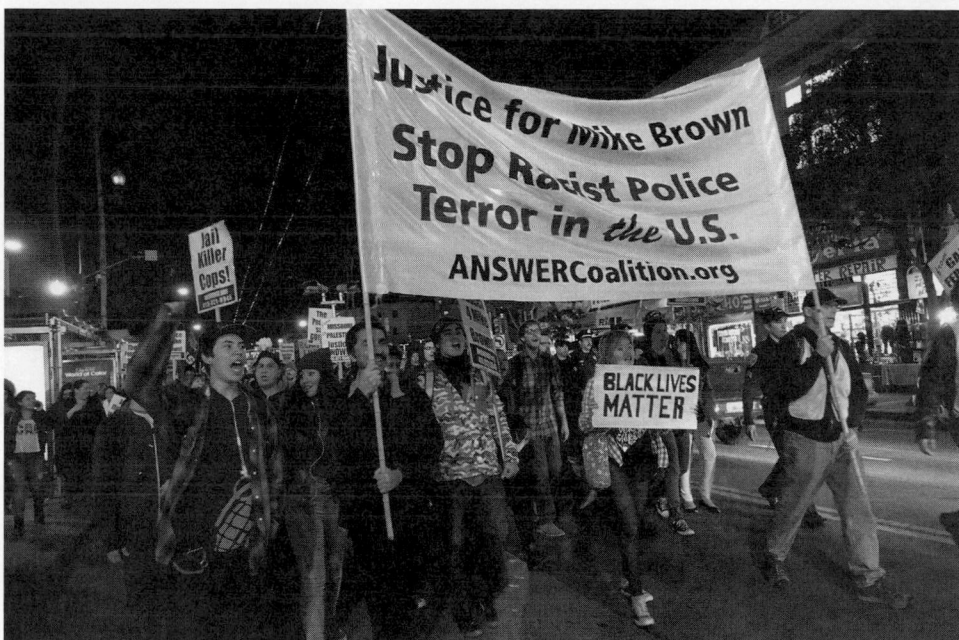

FIGURE 7.3 ▶ After the Grand Jury declined to indict the Ferguson, Missouri police officer who shot and killed unarmed 18-year-old Michael Brown, demonstrations erupted across the country and in Europe as well. This November 25, 2014 San Francisco demonstration marched to a police station as part of their protest against both the shooting and the Grand Jury's decision (Steve Rhodes/Demotix/Corbis).

- demonstrations arising out of officers' use of deadly force (see Figure 7.3)
- being named in lawsuits,
- illegal/undocumented immigrants
- sanctuary cities
- drugs, violent gangs
- transnational crime

To this list New Jersey State Police Superintendent Rick Fuentes adds that in the post-9/11 environment there has been a blurring of hometown and homeland security.[19]

The multiple roles and tough problems also affect recruiting to fill vacant chiefs jobs; in some areas of the country, there are roughly 50 percent fewer candidates seeking them.[20]

THE FALL OF POLICE LEADERS

Police leaders may be compelled to resign or are terminated for reasons beyond their control. Some of these dismissals are unfair because of a politically based, almost compulsive, need to have somebody to blame: Former Los Angeles Police Chief Bill Bratton believes that if you are going to mobilize support, you must innovate, and that involves taking risks. In Bratton's view, that means setting goals that can be measured, which is both a necessity[21] and some chiefs' undoing. Chiefs also act as change agents. When you make changes you make some people mad and a portion of them may become adversarial, that is, "enemies."[22] Sooner or later your enemies become 51 percent, leading to a shortened shelf life for chiefs.[23]

"Leadership is considered a set of positive traits; those lacking them are not true leaders"[24] and they fail because of their own inadequacies.[25] Schafer's survey of 304 leaders attending the FBI's National Academy identified ineffective "leaders"

by their: 1) commission, doing things they shouldn't and 2) omission, the lack of needed skills and/or the inability to recognize or lack of willpower to do what is needed[26]

1. These five points are the acts of commission by police leaders: (a) *focusing on themselves over others*, a "me first mindset"; (b) *displays of ego/arrogance* beyond the realm of healthy confidence and self-assurance; (c) *a closed mindedness* demonstrated by the failure to listen to, and value, the ideas of others; (d) *micromanaging*, reflecting a lack of trust in subordinates. In this regard, a sergeant from a small municipal agency noted that micromanagers failed to delegate when appropriate; and (e) *being arbitrary and capricious*, represented by inconsistent decision making and a lack of a systematic approach. Being able to anticipate likely decisions allows subordinates to take actions and make decisions that support their Chief. Absent that, it makes subordinates use of their discretionary authority tentative and difficult. Capricious leaders also put personal relationships ahead of what is right, just, and consistent with past practices.[27]

2. Ineffective leaders can also be characterized by five points of omission: (a) *a poor work ethic*, revealed by laziness, doing the minimal necessary work, and essentially "retiring in place" (RIP). Police leaders with a poor work ethic are frequently late in their careers and have lost their enthuisasm and commitment. Concurrently, they display a negativity; (b) *failing to take action and make decisions* in a variety of circumstances; (c) *ineffective communicating*, but not because they have weak written and verbal skills. Instead, they are unable or unwilling to have two-way conversations, don't explain their actions or decisions, and don't accept input; (d) *lacking appropriate interpersonal skills*,

Box 7.1 The Police Chief and His Internet Videos

During 2013, the Gilberton, Pennsylvania, Police Chief gained national notoriety for internet videos during which he shot rifles and shouted vulgarities against liberals, Secretary of State John Kerry, and the United Nations, which he dared to come and take his weapons. The Associated Press described the Chief as being active in "gun circles" and who began an armed group critics characterized as a "private militia." The city council sidestepped those issues and concluded that the weapon used in the videos was the property of Gilberton and it was used without authorization. The Chief claimed his videos were protected by free speech and he had been a good Chief, asserting that if he had done something wrong he'd be in handcuffs. Nonetheless, the Chief was suspended and in 2014, Gilberton disbanded the one-person police department.[28] The Chief later claimed he made the videos to attract "sickos" as part of his role as an FBI informant, but neither the FBI nor the Pennsylvania State Police comment on people claiming to be informants.[29]

considered as impoverished basic human relations skills. One survey respondent, an investigations supervisor from a small state agency, summarized this omission as "they fail to realize they are leading people"[30]; and (e) integrity and forthrightness are among the bedrock values of policing; the *lack of integrity* erodes public respect and support. Inside of law enforcement agencies leaders who are seen by subordinates as being weak, lacking, or may have tarnished or lost their reputation for being trustworthy will not be able to lead for very long.[31]

Some police leaders, often unknowingly, set in motion events that will lead to their forced resignation or dismissal, or they may simply fall immediately. They may develop or have personality quirks or defects that result in them wounding or harming those they are supposed to be leading, creating lingering problems, damaging morale, and reducing what they can get others to do willingly. The result is a smaller zone of effectiveness. Occasionally, the public posturing of Chiefs calls their leadership into question and when examined they are dismissed, or their contract is not renewed, or their position is abolished (see Box 7.1 and Figure 7.4).

Misjudgments and character flaws by some police chiefs reveal themselves in a variety of activities. Among these are making personal use of items entered into the evidence room, for example, big-screen televisions and jewelry; sexually harassing or having sex or affairs with subordinates or members of the public (see Box 7.2); becoming aloof and remote, reducing the communications sent to them, which chokes off their effectiveness; their drinking gets out of control; and they irritate subordinates by their maladaptive leadership styles, for example, "seagull chiefs" who don't give guidance on the front end, swoop in and poop on everyone when a problem arises, and fly away without providing any solutions.[32] All of these examples lead to the quick path out of the department.

Box 7.2 A Tale of Two Police Chiefs: One Resigns and the Other Fired

The Casselberry Police Department (CPD) consists of 52 sworn officers and 11 civilians. In 2014, the Police Chief of Casselberry, Florida, resigned from 26 years of service on the department amidst sexual misconduct charges. A 2015 report revealed nearly 800 pages of sworn statements from police officers and employees describing the former Chief as having sexually harassed female workers, repeatedly asking female employees out on dates, made unprofessional comments about their appearance and perfume, and sent them romantic poems. The most sensational allegations involve a female officer to whom the former chief sent something in the order of 100 photographs and 50 videos, some of which showed his sex organ. In other images, he was manipulating it. He also described as having "vulgar temper tantrums" during meetings and degrading people in front of others. At least six people have filed a suit against the city and its former chief for creating a hostile work environment. At some point, a report has or will be submitted to the Florida Criminal Justice Standards and Training Commission to determine if the former chief's certification should be subject to a disciplinary procedure.[33]

The Chief of the four-officer Maypearl, Texas, Police Department (MPD) was fired in 2015 after surrendering on four felony charges involving a sexual relationship with a 14-year-old girl. Over video chat the man asked the victim to perform naked sexual acts and exposed himself to her multiple times. When they met in person, sometimes in the Chief's office, he would insert his hand inside of her underpants. According to the MPD's website, the Chief was a certified sexual assault investigator.[34]

If the Casselberry suit and the four felony charges are substantiated, they would represent aberrant conduct that departs from the high-professional standards held by the men and women who serve law enforcement at the local, state, and federal levels. These case studies are presented as a cautionary tale that humans can be frail and without disciplined conduct a fall could be on the horizon.

FIGURE 7.4 ▶ The former Gilberton police chief who gained national attention with his internet video rants against government and government officials. (Frank Andruscavage/Pottsville Republican Herald/AP Images)

Leaders also fail because they are toxic. They pit followers against each other, lie to subordinates, undermine anyone who is seen as a threat, take credit for the ideas and accomplishments of others, create an image that they are defending the department from outside forces to distract followers, stifle constructive criticism, and make others scapegoats for their own failures.[35] They lack integrity, are incapable of introspection, are blind to their own shortcomings, shrink from hard decisions, and have a reckless disregard of how their actions affect others.[36] In the end, they are found out and lose their jobs, but they leave a legacy that the incoming chief must work hard to overcome (e.g., regaining the trust of the rank-and-file).

Law enforcement leadership doesn't just mean occupying a position; reduced to its simplest, it means being a "difference maker." Leadership success depends on exhibiting positive leadership behaviors and avoiding a catastrophic error[37] (see Box 7.3).

The absence or presence of competent leadership can often be gauged by simply observing:

- Police officers, operating a dirty patrol vehicle, approached a motorist they had stopped for a traffic violation. The officers' interaction with the driver was superficially correct but had a definite underlying tone of arrogance.

- The chief of police of a medium-sized city chronically complained to anyone who would listen that his commanders "aren't worth anything" and that he was "carrying the whole department on his back."

- A visitor to a city approached an officer walking a beat and asked where the nearest car rental agency could be found; he replied, "What the hell do I look like, an information booth?" and walked away.

- A woman asked an officer standing on a street corner where the First National Bank Building was. The officer took the woman's arm, escorted her across the street, and said, "Lady, you see that big building on the corner where

---

Box 7.3 "Chief Herbert's" Career Ending Mistake

A single statement produced a self-inflicted and fatal career wound. Herbert led a 38-officer department. A popular chief, he was asked to meet in closed session with the mayor and city council to discuss a raise for the police department.

Council members initiated the meeting because they wanted to do something extra for the officers. They proposed a 10 percent increase, to which Herbert, for reasons he couldn't later articulate, replied the officers would be well pleased with 6 percent, which is what they got. One council member felt Herbert had sold out the welfare of officers' families to curry favor with the council. The story was leaked

to the newspaper and officers raged at "the betrayal." Officers began making secretive end runs around Herbert to some members of council, giving them inside information on the department. The council gradually sharpened its questioning of Herbert's decisions.

As the Fall election drew closer, two candidates for council made "things in the police department" a campaign issue. The rank-and-file waited until the tide was turning against Herbert before giving him a no-confidence vote. Faced with strong internal opposition and dwindling political support, Herbert retired.

we were just standing? Well, if it had fallen, we'd have both been killed by the First National Bank"

- Based on limited new information, the commander of an investigations bureau reopened the case file on a convicted "no-good" who had already served 14 months for the offense in question. Subsequently, new evidence and a confession resulted in his release and the conviction of the actual perpetrator.

LEADERSHIP, AUTHORITY, AND POWER

Weber identified three sources of **authority**: (1) charismatic, resting on the exceptional heroism, exemplary character, or sanctity of a person, such as Medal of Honor recipients, Mahatma Gandhi, and the Pope; (2) traditional authority, illustrated by kings and queens; and (3) rational-legal, a grant of authority made by the formal organization to a position, the incumbent of which wields it in fulfilling his or her responsibilities (e.g., a chief of police).[38] French and Raven concluded that there were five types of power: (1) legitimate, the belief that someone has the right to make demands on how you do your job; (2) expert, derived from a person's expertise and skill; (3) reward, the ability to compensate others for their compliance; (4) coercive, the expectation that you will be disciplined for your failure to conform to legitimate expectations; and (5) referent, to become liked or respected to such a degree that subordinates willingly follow orders.[40] Whatever the source of a leader's authority, power is a separate concept.

The fact that a formal grant of authority has been made does not mean that the person receiving it is also automatically able to influence others to perform at all, let alone willingly (see Quick Facts: Authority, But Not Power).

This incident illustrates that, while the commissioner had the authority to promote Officer Murphy, he did not have the power to make him accept it. Some power to affect an officer's performance is inherent in positions of formal authority. But to a significant degree, **power**, as suggested by Barnard, is a grant made by the led to the leader.[41] A police leader whose subordinates refuse to follow orders is not without power; subordinate officers may be given verbal or written reprimands, reassigned, suspended, or terminated.[42] The use of this type of power must be considered carefully; failure to invoke it may contribute to a breakdown in discipline and organizational performance; the clumsy use of it may contribute to morale problems or have other negative side effects, including calling into question the abilities of the leader (see Box 7.4).

Box 7.4 The Water Cooler Commando

A uniformed officer riding alone informed the dispatcher that he was stopping a motorist who may have been drinking. His sergeant, who had only been promoted and assigned to the squad two weeks previously, heard the transmission and came to the scene as a backup.

When the sergeant, a nine-year veteran, but who had not served in any "street" assignment for the past six years, arrived a Marine corporal had just gotten into a taxicab. The sergeant talked briefly with the corporal and walked back to the officer. Unseen, the cab eased away. When questioned, the officer told the sergeant that while the Marine had a few drinks, he was not impaired. The sergeant accused him of dereliction of duty for not charging a "fellow Marine" with DUI.

The officer received a mild letter of reprimand; the "slap on the wrist" was widely viewed as the platoon commander reluctantly supporting a green sergeant. The squad saw the sergeant as a "water cooler commando" and didn't trust him. Another misstep several months later resulted in the sergeant being transferred to a minor staff position, where he oversaw several functions, but supervised nobody.

Leadership also arises, as demonstrated by the Hawthorne Studies, out of the informal side of an organization. In police departments, officers "give" power to more-seasoned or decorated colleagues, listening carefully to their opinions and suggestions. In some cases, informal leaders take exception to new policies and procedures and have the potential to disrupt a unit's harmony. A related problem is when younger officers make sergeant, passing veteran officers. Dismissing them as "test takers," the more experienced officers may quietly "compete" with the new supervisor to influence the attitudes and actions of the unit. If, however, informal leaders support the police department's goals, they can be a significant additive and even help compensate for mediocre formal leadership.

THE POWER MOTIVATION OF POLICE LEADERS

Power is an indispensable dimension of police departments; it requires that a person have a desire to play a key role in influencing the outcome of activities. Former Richmond, California, Police Chief Chris Magnus says about power, "I think being a chief is very seductive in terms of power and influence. It's hard not to get caught up in this racket. You sort of lose focus."[43]

As we have seen, power is both a grant from the formal organization to a position, as well as a grant from the led to the leader. Power, however, is not always used for the same purpose;

the term "**power motivation**" refers to the reasons, intentions, and objectives that underlie the use of power.[44]

McClelland and his associates studied the motivations of leaders extensively and concluded there were three types of power: (1) a high achievement or a **socialized power** motivation—the need to have a positive impact on a police department's administration and operations; (2) a high power or **personalized power needs**—the need to be in control for selfish, self-aggrandizing reasons (see Table 7.3); and (3) **affiliation needs**—the desire to be liked and accepted. Affiliation needs and aspirations are not true power needs because they reflect a greater preoccupation with being accepted and liked than with having an impact on events. Affiliation needs can mediate some degree of personalized power needs. The contexts for these motivations may also be important; there is limited evidence that in conflict situations, socialized power leaders may make better decisions than those with personalized power needs.[45]

The difference between personalized power and socialized power has practical implications. A police leader with personalized power needs will tend toward being authoritarian, making most decisions and tightly controlling work. An authoritarian chief believes that officers will not work without close supervision. This style of leadership ultimately leads to problems because the lack of trust becomes apparent, officers chafe at the tight control, morale suffers, and departmental performance declines, often accompanied by a spike in turnover by officers seeking a better work environment. A study of the department may be called for and the report used as the basis for firing the chief.

TABLE 7.3 PERSONALIZED AND SOCIALIZED POWER NEEDS	
Police Leaders with Personalized Power Tend to Be	**Police Leaders with Socialized Power Tend to Be**
• Impulsive and erratic in their use of power	• Inhibited and self-controlled in their use of power
• Rude and overbearing	• Respectful of others' rights
• Exploitative of others	• Concerned with fairness
• Oriented toward strength	• Oriented toward justice
• Committed to the value of efficiency	• Committed to the value of working per se
• Proud	• Egalitarian
• Self-reliant; individualists	• Organization-minded; joiners
• Excited by the certitudes of power	• Ambivalent about power
• Competitive	• Collaborative
• Concerned with exceptionally high goals	• Concerned with realistic goals
• Defensive—protective of own sense of importance	• Non-defensive—willing to seek help
• Inspirational leaders	• Builders of systems and people
• Difficult to replace—leaves behind a group of officers who were dependent on the leader; does little to develop officers	• Replaceable by other managers—leave a system intact and self-sustaining
• Sources of direction, expertise, and control	• Sources of strength for others

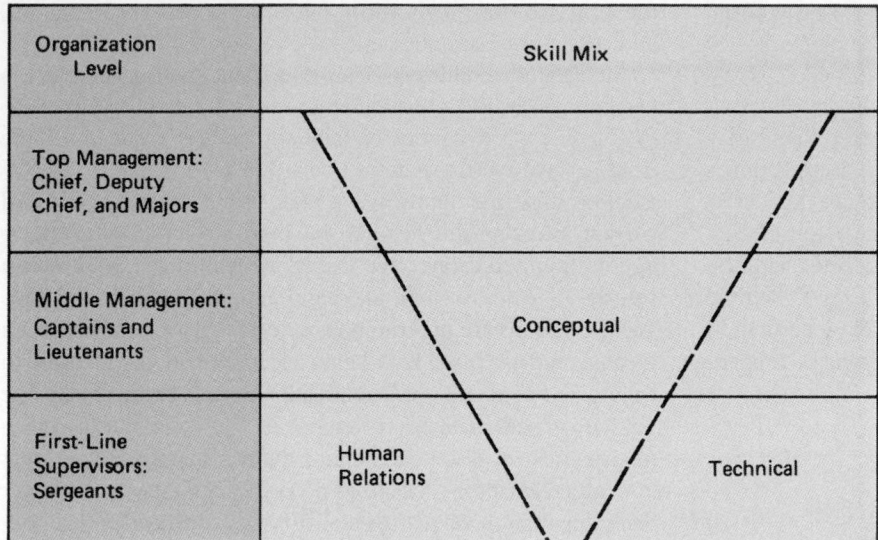

Organization Level	Skill Mix		
Top Management: Chief, Deputy Chief, and Majors			
Middle Management: Captains and Lieutenants		Conceptual	
First-Line Supervisors: Sergeants	Human Relations		Technical

FIGURE 7.5 ▶ The leadership skill mix. The distribution of the skills across organization levels is for illustration. It is not intended to represent a mathematical distribution and may vary across law enforcement agencies.

In contrast, chiefs with socialized power tend to help people around them and have a stabilizing effect, are restrained in their use of power, share some of their power with subordinates, and are restrained and polite, helping people to achieve their potential. Leadership styles are discussed in greater detail later in this chapter.

THE LEADERSHIP SKILL MIX

Skill is how knowledge is translated into action. As depicted in Figure 7.5, a police department can be divided into three levels with various mixes of three broad categories of skills associated with them.[46] The ranks indicated at each of the three levels of the organization identified in the figure are illustrative only and will vary depending on departmental size and other factors. Additionally, in the discussion of these skills that follows, it is possible to include only a few of the many examples available.[47]

Human Relations Skills

Human relations skills involve the capacity to interact positively with other people and are used at all levels of a police department (see Figure 7.6) and also externally. Examples include motivation, conflict resolution, and interpersonal communication skills. The single, most important human relations skill is communication; without it, nothing can be set in motion, and programs underway cannot be guided.

As officers progress up the rank hierarchy of a police department, they typically become responsible for more people but have fewer people reporting directly to them. The human relations

FIGURE 7.6 ▶ At a $4.5 million mansion in Washington DC one or more suspects beat and murdered a family of three and their housekeeper. At this 2015 press conference Mayor Muriel Bowser (L) and Police Commissioner Cathy Lanier (R) appealed to the public to help locate an identified suspect. Cathy Lanier was appointed Commissioner in 2007, in part because of her "people skills." (Win McNamee/Getty Images).

skills of a police department's top managers remain important, however, as they are used to win political support for the agency's programs and to obtain the resources necessary to operate them. In particular, the chief's human relations skills are critical, as this person is the department's key representative to the larger environment. The way in which he or she "comes across" is, to a certain degree, the way in which some significant others—such as the city manager and members of city council—will regard the police department. The question of the fairness of that fact aside, the practical implication is that the chief must be aware of and fulfill the symbolic leadership role.

Within the department, top management must communicate its goals and policies downward and be willing to receive feedback about them. As mid-level managers, lieutenants and captains play an important linking function, passing downward in implementable forms the communications they receive from top management and passing upward certain communications received from first-line supervisors. Because sergeants ordinarily supervise directly the greatest number of people, they use human relations with great frequency, often focusing on issues such as resolving interpersonal problems, communicating the department's vision, and providing guidance.

Conceptual Skills

Conceptual skills include the ability to understand and to interrelate various parcels of information that may seem unrelated, or those for which the meaning or importance is not immediately apparent. Although this skill is used at all levels of the police department, the standards for handling the information become less certain and the level of abstraction necessary to handle the parcels becomes greater as one moves upward. Illustrative is the difference between a sergeant helping a detective evaluate the legal significance of evidence and a chief envisioning a future for the department and how to create and maintain a culture that will support the innovations being considered.

Technical Skills

Technical skills vary by level within a police department. Uniformed sergeants assigned to field duties must be able to help develop and maintain the skills of subordinates in areas such as handling domestic violence calls. As one progresses upward toward middle and top management, the range of technical skills narrows and conceptual skills come to predominate. In that upward progression, the character of the technical skills also changes from being operations oriented to management oriented and gradually includes new elements, such as budgeting, planning, and the kind of decision making that increasingly requires the use of conceptual skills. To elaborate further, one may not be able to tell by the generic label whether a particular skill is, for example, technical or conceptual. To illustrate this point, an understanding of the many aspects of financial management (see Chapter 12, Financial Management) is a conceptual skill, but the actual preparation of the budget is a technical skill required of middle managers and those more senior.

Factors both inside and outside of a police department will impact on the skills that are most important at any particular time.

A survey of the 20 best run companies in America revealed that in 2009, the most important leadership skill was execution; in 2010, it shifted to strategic thinking—envisioning the future of the enterprise in a fiscally constrained, uncertain, and highly competitive environment.[48] In 2020, sense making, the ability to determine the deeper meaning or significance of what is being expressed is expected to be the most important work skill; other top 10 work skills for 2020 include novel and adaptive thinking, finding responses and solutions that are not simply based on routines or resolved by applying rules; cross-cultural literacy, the capacity in a global economy and connected world to work effective across cultures; and being transdisciplinary, understanding and employing concepts from multiple disciplines.[49]

THEORIES OF LEADERSHIP

Theories of leadership attempt to explain the factors associated with the emergence of leadership or the nature of leadership. This chapter examines leadership under the following headings: (1) traditional leadership theory, (2) behavior and leadership styles theory, (3) contingency and situational theory, (4) transactional and transformational theories, (5) comparison of charismatic and transformational leadership, and (6) the "new leadership": servant, spiritual, authentic, and ethical leadership.

Traditional Leadership Theory

There are two branches to traditional leadership theory: (1) great man and (2) the traits approach.

GREAT MAN THEORIES

"Great man" theories were advanced by Thomas Carlyle (1795–1881) and George Hegel (1770–1831).[50] Carlyle (see Figure 7.7) believed that leaders were unusually gifted individuals who made history. He may not have been entirely wrong—there is preliminary evidence that approximately 30 percent of the variation in leadership styles is accounted for by heredity, the balance being environmental influences, including leadership development opportunities and roles.[51] Reversing the direction of causality, Hegel argued that it was events that produced the "great man." As an illustration of this, Dwight Eisenhower (1890–1969) was an obscure Army Colonel in 1941, three years into World War II he was a five star General and later President. The "born leader" concept is associated with Francis Galton (1822–1911), who espoused that leaders were the product of genetics,[52] transmitted from one generation to the next one. If Galton is correct—that leaders are born—then arguably police departments may be wasting money on leadership development (see Table 7.4).

THE TRAITS APPROACH

The traits approach is a natural extension of great man theory. **Traits** are relatively stable predispositions to behave in certain ways; examples include being energetic, emotionally stable, and extroverted.[53] Field Marshal Montgomery, one of England's great World War II commanders,[54] believed that leaders were made, not born; however,

FIGURE 7.7 ▶ Thomas Carlyle: unusually gifted people make history. (Library of Congress Prints and Photographs Division [LC-USZ62-134797])

they had certain traits, such as an infectious optimism, confidence, intellect, and the ability to be a good judge of character.

Beginning around 1910 and continuing through the 1950s, research on traits dominated the thinking about leadership. The research was so substantial that Allport and Odbert (1936),[55] Stogdill (1948),[56] and Goode (1951)[57] attempted to consolidate hundreds of studies and still ended up with lengthy lists of traits. The earlier traits research suffered from several deficiencies: (1) traits such as loyalty, diligence, and perseverance were difficult to define and hard to measure; (2) some traits aren't portable from one setting to another; (3) traits are variable in their importance; and (4) situational factors can diminish the importance of traits or cause others to be needed (e.g., creating a police department for a newly incorporated city).

The traits approach was re-energized beginning in the 1970s as new methodological and statistical techniques were developed and older ones improved. Meta-analysis, first used in 1904 and since greatly enhanced, allows the results from many comparable studies to be analyzed; its use led to the "Big Five" model of traits. The **Big Five** is the result of efforts to find a small number of broad trait categories into which many specific traits can be fitted (Table 7.5); it continues to be an important classification system for traits research.[58] In 2010, Erdle and colleagues confirmed the existence of a **Big Two** within the Big Five: (1) stability, consisting of emotional stability, agreeableness, and conscientiousness; and (2) plasticity, composed of extraversion and being open minded.[59]

Zaccaro, after examining research findings, concluded that there is mounting evidence that some traits are "precursors" of

---

TABLE 7.4 A SAMPLE OF PRIVATE, STATE, AND FEDERAL LEADERSHIP TRAINING OPPORTUNITIES
FBI   • National Academy (NA): improves administration of agencies, nomination process, by invitation.   • National Executive Institute (NEI): agency heads of departments with 500 or more sworn.   • Law Enforcement Executive Development Seminar (LEEDS): mid-sized agency heads.   • Regional Command Colleges: 22 nationally, agency heads, seconds in command, departments with fewer than 25 officers.   **Federal Law Enforcement Training Center (FLETC):** Law Enforcement Leadership Institute (LELI): Seminars   **Harvard University National Preparedness Leadership Initiative (NPLI):** increases the number of leaders who can optimally deal with homeland security preparedness and response activities   **International Association of Chiefs of Police, Center for Police Leadership:** early proponent of Leadership in Police Organizations (LPO), based on the West Point Leadership Program (WPLP) and adapted for the needs of law enforcement. Core concept: leadership is distributed in a police department and qualities of leadership are expected from all officers. Illustrative users include the Delaware and New Mexico State Police, the Los Angeles and Tulsa Police Departments, and the Minnesota State Patrol and Bureau of Criminal Apprehension.   **National Highway Transportation Safety Administration/National Sheriff's Association (NHSTA/NSA) Leadership Program:** develops leaders for state of the art highway safety initiatives   **University of Louisville, Southern Police Institute, Administrative Officers Course:** develops informed, effective, ethically and technically competent police managers

TABLE 7.5 THE CORRESPONDENCE BETWEEN THE "BIG FIVE" AND SPECIFIC TRAITS	
Big Five Personality Traits	**Specific Traits**
Surgency	Extroversion/Outgoing Energy/Activity level Need for power/Assertive
Conscientiousness	Dependability Personal integrity Need for achievement
Agreeableness	Cheerful/Optimistic Nurturing/Sympathetic/Helpful Need for affiliation
Adjustment	Emotional stability Self-esteem Self-control
Intellectance	Curious/Inquisitive Open-minded Learning oriented

Source: Courtesy of Gary Yukl, *Leadership in Organizations*, Upper Saddle River, NJ: Prentice Hall, 7th Edition, 2010.

leadership effectiveness.[60] Emotional intelligence (EI) and social intelligence (SI) appear to be among them. EI and SI have been examined both as single traits and combined. Bar-On used a combined Emotional Social Intelligence (ESI) measure to help the Air Force identify potential recruiters who could be high performers. The use of ESI data resulted in nearly a 300 percent increase in selecting high-performance recruiters.[61]

EI is positively associated with the quality of peer relationships,[62] and may account for a lack of progress among intelligent people in psychotherapy,[63] and helps manage stress. Units with higher levels of EI experience less task and relationship conflict, and when it occurs, it is less intense.[64] A study of EI in Nigerian police officers 2008 revealed that it was not related to gender, marital status, length of service, or age.[65,66] In an earlier study, Barbera et al. (2002) found evidence to the contrary, suggesting that the emotional and social intelligence may develop over time.[67] In 2010, Bar-On called for more research into emotional intelligence, particularly with respect to a sense of well-being; happiness; raising and educating well-adjusted, productive, healthy children; and the search for a more meaningful life.[68] Ultimately, researchers may find that the amounts of EI and SI are less important than what combinations of them are related to effective leadership.

Riggio and Reichard (2008) concluded that another way to approach EI and SI was through the skills related to them. They developed a taxonomy—a classification system—for **emotional skills (ES)** and **social skills (SS)** (Table 7.6). ES as the ability to accurately perceive and appraise your own emotions and those of others, to regulate your own emotions, and to do so while adapting and responding to the needs of others.[69] Social skills are closely related to emotional skills and are defined as the ability to express one's self in social situations; the ability to "read" social situations, recognizing different social roles and expected behavior; and interpersonal problem solving.[70]

ES and SS are associated with being (1) more favorably viewed in social situations; (2) more confident; (3) a better public speaker; (4) more physically attractive; (5) more upwardly mobile in one's career; (6) seen as more effective by followers; and (7) savoir-faire, or seemingly able to know just what to do.[71]

Police officers have also weighed in on leadership traits. While they have some preference for leaders with greater field experience, the characteristics they most prefer in command, middle managers, and first-line supervisors are honesty, dependability, competency, and being broad minded.[72]

Organizational citizenship behavior (OCB) is composed of subtle things that employees do voluntarily and are not required or expected but contribute to overall organizational effectiveness.[73] Examples include police officers officially at the end of their tour of duty volunteering to back up a unit on a traffic stop or giving words of encouragement or suggestions to another detective who is working a tough, high-profile case. Several studies have found that overall, the Big Five personality traits are positively associated with OCB. Although OCB continues to be researched as a separate topic, by 2008, researchers were increasingly interested in a broader concept, **positive organizational behavior (POB)**. In at least some studies, POB included OCB as a component factor. Presently, POB lacks anything approaching a consensus definition, but it has the potential to do for current leadership interests what the Big Five did for traits research.

Counterproductive work behavior (CWB) also commands research interest. CWB is behavior that has a detrimental effect on relationships with other commanders and officers and/or on the efficiency of operations.[74] Examples include being verbally aggressive or rude to coworkers, emotional outbursts, engaging in anger-producing behavior, refusing to help a coworker, using demeaning language, and maintaining interpersonal conflicts with others.[75]

TABLE 7.6 EMOTIONAL AND SOCIAL SKILLS

Skill	Example	Purpose
EI Skills		
Emotional Expressiveness	Chief communicates nonverbally, e.g., command presence, selection of seat at table, facial expression, posture, or gesture	Communicates place in hierarchy; approval and disapproval to subordinate commanders
Emotional Sensitivity	Chief receives and accurately interprets non-verbal (e.g., body language) expressions of members of command staff	Gains understanding of others needs and emotional states, enhances ability to establish rapport
Emotional Control	Chief controls the display of his/her emotions	Eliminates the immediate display of anger or other strong emotional responses, requires a high degree of self-monitoring. A self-indulgent display of anger may impair relationships and impede goal achievement. A premeditated display may be useful in reinforcing the Chief's priorities, policies, and programs.
SI Skills		
Social Expressiveness	Chief has command of language, evoking powerful images through well-crafted articulation	Increases Chief's effectiveness within the department, at external meetings, and before audiences, enhances performance as mentor and coach
Social Sensitivity	Chief accurately interprets verbal communications from others and monitors social situation	Chief tailors comments and interaction to the conversation or situation at hand, is "smooth"
Social Control	Chief manages how he/she presents him/herself to others; is tactful, but doing so doesn't reduce impact of message; conveys ability to "get things done"	Represents him/herself and department well, creates new opportunities, and responses to criticisms are seen as reasonable, thoughtful

Source: Adapted with restatement into a police framework and some re-organization from Ronald E. Riggio and Rebecca J. Reichard, "The Emotional and Social Intelligences of Effective Leadership," *Journal of Managerial Psychology,* Vol. 23, No. 2, 2008, p. 172, Table 1.

Quick Facts: The Perfect Chief Who Couldn't Get an Important Thing Done

Even if chiefs have all of the important traits, their efforts may amount to nothing. "Willow City," with 102 nonunionized officers, hired its first outside chief since the department was established in the early 1800s. Although "Chief Henry" had a strong task orientation, his relational skills were also excellent. He had impeccable education and training credentials and, on the basis of having led his former department to accreditation by the Commission on Accreditation of Law Enforcement Agencies (CALEA), Willow City hired him with the understanding he would do likewise with its department. However, it never happened.

His staff dragged their heels on assignments and otherwise thwarted "Chief Henry's" efforts. Rank-and-file officers were irrational in their opposition to him. For example, one officer told another something the chief had allegedly done.

The second officer replied that he knew the chief didn't do it "but would've if he thought he could get away with it." Even when "innocent," the chief was "guilty." The negligible staff support, rank-and-file carping, and evaporating political support became powerful **leadership neutralizers,**[76] negating "Chief Henry's" efforts. Recognizing he had been rendered ineffectual, the chief resigned; his outstanding background produced nothing because he lacked the most essential trait of all: being an insider.

The assistant chief, a life-long local resident, was promoted to replace him and the department relaxed. As of 2015, 22 years after "Chief Henry" left, "Willow City" had still not been accredited. Speculatively, the process may have become tainted by being deeply associated with the outsider.

Behavior and Leadership Style Theories

Whereas trait theories attempt to explain leadership on the basis of what the leader is, behavioral theories try to do the same thing by concentrating on what the leader does.[77] These behaviors are often described in terms of leadership styles, meaning the continuing patterns of behavior as perceived and experienced by others that they use to characterize the leader. The behavior and leadership style theories were the main focus of researchers during the 1950s and 1960s.

LEWIN, LIPPITT, AND WHITE: AUTHORITARIAN, DEMOCRATIC, AND LAISSEZ-FAIRE

Although the three leadership styles these researchers studied had been previously identified, it was their 1939 study that systematized thinking about them.[78] The **authoritarian/autocratic leader** ("My way or the highway") makes all decisions, closely controls work, and is a micromanager; the **democratic leader** ("Let's talk about it") encourages individual or group participation in matters affecting the organization; and the **laissez-faire leader** (LFL) ("Whatever") takes a passive, "hands-off" posture. Only reluctantly do LFLs use the authority of their position; they do not make necessary decisions and delay taking any kind of action. This has the effect of providing subordinates with substantial autonomy.[79] LFLs provide only episodic leadership and that may be ineffectual. The larger the stakes, the more invisible LFLs become.

Lewin, Lippitt, and White concluded that although the quantity of work was somewhat greater under the autocratic leader, autocracy could generate hostility and aggression. The democratically controlled groups were about as efficient as the autocratically controlled ones, but the continuation of work in the former did not depend on the presence of the leader. Under the laissez-faire leader, less work was produced, the work quality was poorer, and the work was less organized and less satisfying to members of the group.[80] A study of leader styles and follower attitudes in a mid-sized New England police agency confirmed the much earlier findings of Lewin, Lippitt, and White.[81]

LIKERT: MANAGEMENT SYSTEMS

In *New Patterns of Management* (1961) and *The Human Organization* (1967), Rensis Likert (1903–1981) echoed and extended Lewin, Lippitt, and White's work by specifying four different management systems (see Table 7.7). The names of these systems are also used to describe leadership styles and, for that reason, Likert's work is included in this section. Likert believed most people worked in a System 2 organization.

Authoritarian/autocratic police leaders, associated with Likert's Systems 1 and 2, have largely gone the way of the dinosaurs. The demise of the authoritarians is due to the world around them changing, becoming more liberal, as well as the perspectives and experiences associated with each new generation of workers entering law enforcement agencies. The characterization of these generations and their attributes vary somewhat in the research literature and are discussed in Chapter 9, Human Resource Management.

TABLE 7.7 LIKERT'S MANAGEMENT SYSTEMS

Organizational Variable	System 1	System 2	System 3	System 4
Leadership Processes Used				
Extent to which superiors have confidence and trust in subordinates	Have no confidence and trust in subordinates	Have condescending confidence and trust, such as master has to servant	Substantial but not complete confidence and trust; still wishes to keep control of decisions	Complete confidence and trust in all matters
Extent to which superiors behave so that subordinates feel free to discuss important things about their jobs with their immediate superior	Subordinates do not feel at all free to discuss things about the job with their superior	Subordinates do not feel very free to discuss things about the job with their superior	Subordinates feel rather free to discuss things about the job with their superior	Subordinates feel completely free to discuss things about the job with their superior
Extent to which immediate superior in solving job problems generally tries to get subordinates' ideas and opinions and make constructive use of them	Seldom gets ideas and opinions of subordinates in solving job problems	Sometimes gets ideas and opinions of subordinates in solving job problems	Usually gets ideas and opinions and usually tries to make constructive use of them	Always gets ideas and opinions and always tries to make constructive use of them

Source: The Human Organization by Rensis Likert. Copyright © 1967 McGraw-Hill Book Company. Used with permission of McGraw-Hill Book Company.

BLAKE AND MOUTON: THE MANAGERIAL GRID

Developed by Robert Blake and Jane Mouton,[82] the **Managerial Grid** has received a great deal of attention since its appearance in 1962 in the *Journal of the American Society of Training Directors*. The grid is part of the survey research feedback stem of organizational development and draws on earlier work done at Ohio State University and the University of Michigan.[83]

Depicted in Figure 7.8, the grid has two dimensions: concern for production and concern for people. Each axis, or dimension, is numbered from 1, meaning low concern, to 9, indicating high concern. The way in which a person combines these two dimensions establishes a leadership style in terms of one of the five principal styles identified on the grid. The numbers associated with each of the styles reflect the level of concern for each of the two dimensions of the grid. For example, 9,1 indicates a maximum concern for production or the needs of the organization and a minimum orientation toward the needs of people in the organization. The first style number is always read off the production axis.

Some of the leadership styles identified previously can be related readily to the grid. Authoritarian leaders are represented by the 9,1 style; laissez-faire leaders by the 1,1; and democratic leaders by the 5,5. Additionally, the 9,1 and 9,9 styles are consistent, respectively, with the streams of thought summarized in Chapter 5 under the headings of "Traditional Organizational Theory" and "Open Systems Theory."

The leadership style of an individual can be identified by using a questionnaire based on the work of Blake and Mouton.

According to the grid, one moves from the "best" to the "worst" styles as one moves from 9,9 through 5,5; 9,1; 1,9; and 1,1. The most desirable combination of a primary and backup style is the 9,9 with a 5,5 backup.

A difficulty in using the grid questionnaire is that the data produced are no more accurate than the self-perceptions of the person completing the instrument. When consulting with law enforcement agencies, one way to overcome this is to have each commander complete the instrument and then have each of his or her subordinates fill one out on how they experience the commander. Comparing these two sets of data provides useful information. Typically, more weight is given to the subordinate's combined data because they reflect how the leader is "coming across."

DOWNS: LEADERSHIP STYLES IN BUREAUCRATIC STRUCTURES

Downs[84] described four types of leader behavior in bureaucratic structures: (1) climbers, (2) conservers, (3) zealots, and (4) advocates.

Climbers are strongly motivated by power and prestige needs to invent new functions to be performed by their unit, particularly functions not performed elsewhere. If climbers can expand their functions only by moving into areas already controlled by others, they are likely to choose ones in which they expect low resistance. To protect their "turf," climbers tend to economize only when the resultant savings can be used to finance an expansion of their functions.[85] An example of a climber is a newly promoted

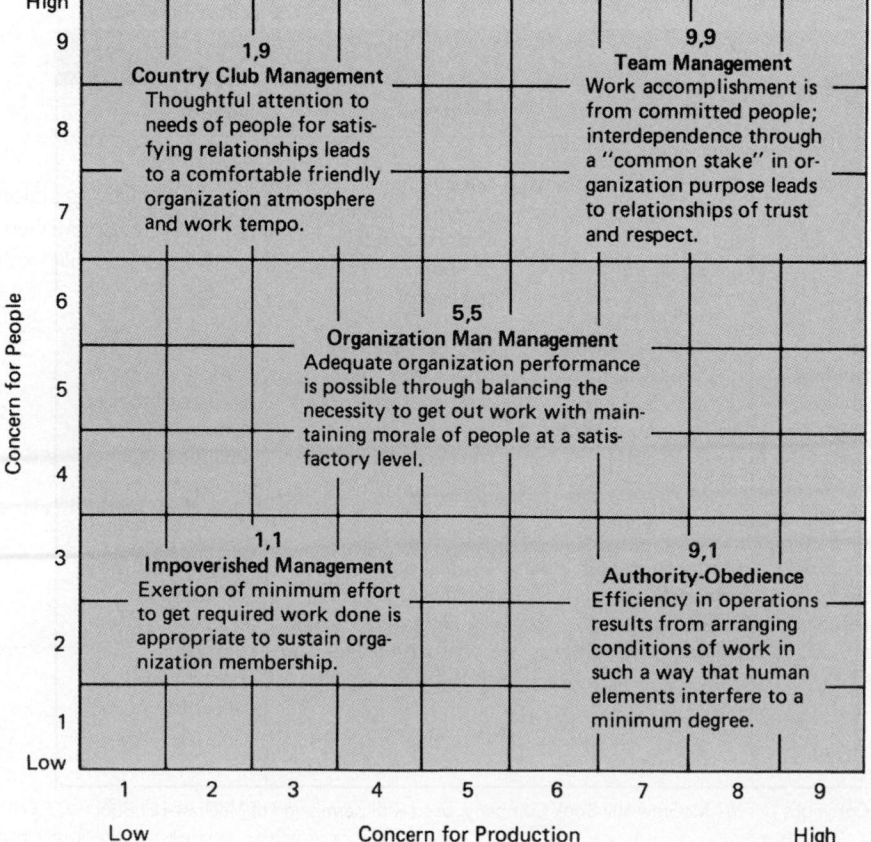

FIGURE 7.8 ▶ The Managerial Grid.

major commanding the Patrol Division who argues that the Traffic Division should be "folded" into the Patrol Division.

The bias of **conservers** is toward maintaining things as they are. The longer a person is in the same job and the older one becomes, the lower one assesses any chances for advancement and the stronger one becomes attached to job security, all of which are associated with the tendency to become a conserver. Climbers can become conservers when they assess their probability for advancement and expansion to be low. Desiring to make their organizational lives comfortable, conservers dislike and resist change.[86] A Lieutenant with 19 years of service and no promotions in the last seven years would tend to be a conserver.

The peculiarities of the behavior of **zealots** stem from two sources: their narrow interest and the missionary-like energy, which they focus almost solely on their special interest. As a consequence, zealots do not attend to all of their duties and often antagonize other administrators by their lack of impartiality and their willingness to trample over all obstacles to further their special interest. Zealots rarely succeed to high-level positions because of their narrowness and are consequently poor administrators. An exception is when their interest comes into favor and they are catapulted into high office.[87] Some Commanders of Special Weapons and Tactics (SWAT) units may fall into the zealot category.

Unlike zealots, **advocates** promote everything under their jurisdiction. To those outside their units, they appear highly partisan, but within their units they are impartial and fair, developing well-rounded programs. Loyal to their organizations, advocates favor innovation. They are also simultaneously more radical and more conservative than climbers. They are more radical in that they are willing to promote programs and views that may antagonize politicians, superiors, and other powerful groups, such as the news media, if doing so helps their departments. They are more conservative because they are willing to oppose changes from which they might benefit but which would not be in the overall interest of their agencies.[88] Advocates may spring up anywhere in a police agency, confident and focused they are sometimes unaware of how others see them or simply don't care.

VAN MAANEN: STATION HOUSE SERGEANTS AND STREET SERGEANTS

In a study of a 1,000-officer police department, Van Maanen[89] identified two contrasting types of police sergeants: "station house" and "street." **Station house sergeants** had been out of the "bag" (uniform) before their promotions to sergeant and preferred to work in an office environment once they won their stripes; this preference was clearly indicated by the nickname of "Edwards, the Olympic Torch who never goes out" given to one such sergeant. Station house sergeants immersed themselves in the management culture of the police department, keeping busy with paperwork, planning, record keeping, press relations, and fine points of law. Their strong orientation to conformity also gave rise to nicknames as suggested by the use of "by-the-book Brubaker."

In contrast, **street sergeants** (see Figure 7.9) were serving in the field when they received their promotions. Consequently,

FIGURE 7.9 ▶ A street sergeant on Staten Island, New York. Note his numerous decorations and five "hash marks" on his lower sleeve, each one denoting the completion of five years of service. (Robert Essel NYC/Corbis)

they had a distaste for office procedures and had a strong action orientation, as suggested by such nicknames as "Shooter McGee" and "Walker the Stalker." Moreover, their concern was not with conformity but with "not letting the assholes take over the city."

In addition to the distinct differences already noted, station house sergeants and street sergeants were thought of differently by those whom they supervised: station house sergeants "stood behind their officers," whereas street sergeants "stood beside their officers." Each of these two different styles of working as a sergeant also has its drawbacks and strengths. Station house sergeants might not have been readily available to officers working in the field; however, they could always be located when a signature was needed and were able to secure more favors for officers than street sergeants were. Although immediately available in the field when needed, street sergeants occasionally interfered with the autonomy of their subordinates; unrequested, they responded to calls for service assigned to subordinates and handled them or, otherwise, at least in the eyes of their officers, "interfered."

A consideration of Van Maanen's work leads to some generalizations about the future careers of station house sergeants versus street sergeants. Station house sergeants are learning routines, policies, procedures, and polishing skills that will improve future promotional opportunities. Their promotional opportunities are further enhanced by contacts with senior police commanders who can give them important assignments and who may, if favorably impressed, influence future promotions. In contrast, street sergeants may gain some favorable publicity and awards for their exploits, but they are also more likely to have citizen complaints filed against them, more likely to be investigated by internal affairs, and more likely to be sued. Consequently, very aggressive street sergeants are regarded by their superiors as "good cops" but difficult people to supervise. In short, the action-oriented street sergeant who does not "mellow out" may not go beyond a middle manager's position in a line unit, such as patrol or investigation.

Contingency and Situational Leadership Theories

Contingency leadership and situational leadership are similar; both postulate that there are no approaches that are always right. Contingency theory is somewhat broader, considering both leader capabilities and other factors in any given circumstance; **situational leadership** focuses more on what leaders should do.

TANNENBAUM AND SCHMIDT: FROM LEADER STYLES TO A CONTINGENCY MODEL

In 1958, **Tannenbaum and Schmidt** published "How to Choose a Leadership Pattern," which was the first situational leadership theory, subsequently revising it in 1973 (see Table 7.8).[90] They asserted that the societal environment and organizational forces interplayed to form situations in which one leadership style would be more effective than other styles and leaders had to find that "good fit." Although we would presently substitute other societal environment examples, Tannenbaum and Schmidt identified: (1) the younger generation's distrust of "establishment" organizations; (2) the civil rights movement with its call for more participation and influence for all people; and (3) a growing desire for workers to have a higher quality of life within the organizations that employ them. The organizational forces, stated here in a police context, are as follows:

1. Forces in the police leader, such as his or her value system, confidence in subordinate officers, leadership inclinations, and need for security in uncertain situations (e.g., "I can afford to be wrong on this one");

2. Forces in subordinate officers, including their knowledge, skills, and experience; more can reasonably be expected from a veteran squad than one that is light on experience; and

3. Forces in the department, formal and informal (e.g., a policy not to participate in federal immigration roundups or the practice of not arresting nonpersistent panhandlers).

The most common criticism of Tannenbaum and Schmidt's theory is that while it discusses variables, including the leader,

the followers, and the situation, the theory stops short of specifying how the variables are combined and translated into leadership behavior.[91]

FIEDLER: LEAST PREFERRED COWORKER (LPC)

Fiedler, a clinical psychologist, was originally interested in the relationship between psychotherapists and patients, later shifting his focus to leader–follower relationships.[92] His *A Theory of Leadership Effectiveness* (1967) attracted wide attention and has been subsequently modified several times. According to Fiedler, group effectiveness is a function of the interaction between the leader's esteem for his least preferred coworker (LPC) and three situational variables: (1) the task structure, (2) leader–follower relations, and (3) the power position of the leader.[93] Fiedler's use of "power" should be read to mean "authority" in the sense that Weber uses rational-legal authority; we have substituted "follower" for his "member." Although Fiedler provides scales to determine the level of each of these three variables, only their short definitions are shown below:

1. **Task structure** refers to the degree a task is or is not clearly spelled out as to goals, methods of handling, and standards of performance. Arresting a motorist for drunk driving has high structure; by policy, there are a series of things that officers must do to properly perform the task. In contrast, the police reaction to a terrorist's detonation of a nuclear device in one of our major ports has low-task structure. There are no or only very general guidelines; there are many ways to approach the task; and there may be more than one acceptable solution. In the most extreme situations, the actual outcome of any solution may not be clearly foreseeable.

2. **Leader–follower relations** are characterized by the extent to which commanders enjoy the confidence and goodwill of the officers they lead and relations are cordial. Good relations make many things both possible and easier; poor relations render all things more difficult and if not corrected can become leadership neutralizers.

3. The **leader's position power** is the degree to which the commander has, or is perceived to possess by officers, the authority to reward or punish them for their performance.[94]

The LPC is a single individual with whom the leader presently works or another individual with whom he or she has worked in a different unit; someone who might be described in terms such as difficult, unpleasant, or uncooperative. Underlining LPC theory is the assumption that how leaders regard the person they least like is an indicator of their leadership preference. To determine whether leaders have a task or relationship orientation, they complete the LPC scale using pairs of descriptors (see Table 7.9).

The LPC score determines whether a leader is task motivated (low LPC) versus being relationship oriented (high LPC).

TABLE 7.8 A CONTINUUM OF POLICE LEADERSHIP STYLES AND IMPACTS ON SUBORDINATES

Chiefs/Supervisors Orientation	Characteristic Leadership Behavior	Impact on Subordinates
Overt Authoritarian/Autocratic	**Authoritarian/Autocratic (AA) Leadership Level 1** AAs are not open minded and value their own thoughts/opinions over those of others. AAs tend to discourage dissenting views and often surround themselves with "Yes People." As a result, AAs forfeit growth opportunities and movement toward greater competency because Yes People don't give genuine feedback. AAs are decisive and make quick decisions, leading some subordinates to regard them as "often wrong, but never in doubt." If AAs make the right decisions in crisis and tactical situations their decisive style is an asset. Although AAs crave total control of their departments, they, like other police leaders, can never achieve it because their control is diluted by: 1) federal and state investigative agencies and laws; 2) grand jury indictments and reports, court decisions, and consent decrees; 3) the actions of elected and appointed governmental officials and their legislative bodies; 4) local government charters and ordinances; and 5) any collective bargaining agreements. Communication between AAs and subordinates are usually one-way, telling them how to do their jobs. Real social interactions are limited and more often are superficial, e.g., "Who do you think is going to win the game?" The overt authoritarian approach may be rooted in a need to be in control for self-aggrandizing reasons. The Chief's motto is "My way or the highway."	**Authoritarian/Autocratic Leadership Level 1** Rank-and-file (RF) participation in the key processes of the department, e.g., planning, policy formulation, and decision making, is negligible to non-existent. Officers are careful with whom they talk about job conditions out of fear of retribution, e.g., "Well, dinosaurs once ruled the world, but they're gone. Maybe soon this chief will be too." Strict discipline contributes to a high turnover as evidenced by comments such as "You rarely get an 'attaboy' around here, but slip-up just a little and they stick it to you." Some officers who remain may not be of high caliber and/or have no or few other options for other careers. Others accept working for AAs because of the salary, fringe benefits, pension, and civil service job security. A third group of officers remain for only as long as it takes to achieve personal goals, such as finishing a degree or completing some family or other important personal obligation. In states where it is authorized, the collective bargaining process is a force that mediates AA leadership. Moreover, team policing, community policing, compstat, intelligence-led and strategic policing require participation by officers, which tends to blunt, but not eliminate, AA behavior.
Softer Authoritarian/Autocratic	**Authoritarian/Autocratic Leadership Level 2** The core dynamics of Level 1 still prevail, but less overtly. Infrequently, to occasionally, AAs will "toss a bone" to the RF and informally or formally solicit its input by appointing a temporary committee and its chairperson to do so. The greater the importance of a topic to AAs, the less likely that RF input will be encouraged or solicited. AAs especially want their way on issues that are important to them. Input could jeopardize AAs preferred solutions.	**Authoritarian/Autocratic Leadership Level 2** Away from participation, but others are curious about it and become engaged with the department in a new way. AAs watch these reactions and the quality of their input closely.

(continued)

	TABLE 7.8 (CONCLUSION)	
Chiefs/Supervisors Orientation	**Characteristic Leadership Behavior**	**Impact on Subordinates**
Democratic Leadership Emerges	**Transitional Leadership Level 1** Agencies are in the initial stage of moving toward democratic leadership (DL), which is a precursor for the emergence of participatory leadership. A shift to DL may occur due to current or new chiefs concluding that input from department members, including the RF, could lead to improved decision making and generate higher levels of organizational commitment. The chief appoints more temporary committees and names the chairperson for each one. By memo, the authority of each committee is carefully limited to making a recommendation and the topic to be evaluated is carefully defined to prevent the committee from exceeding its role. Chiefs unsure what RF input might be and worry that it could create opposition to their own preferred course of action. They are also unsure of how and how far to proceed with the DL model. Sheriffs may be looking for something new to showcase in their re-election campaign and may be open to change they believe they can control.	**Transitional Leadership Level 1** Important decisions are still made at the highest level. Most department members have not yet served on any committee. Still, there are slowly increasing opportunities for wider RF input because leadership recognizes it is getting fresh information and some worthy recommendations. Some leaders in the department don't see any value to getting RF input, but are not overtly resistant to doing so. Still, among trusted friends, they express doubt about the process: "I've been on the job 12 years and some rookie knows more than me what the department needs to do?" The real issue: a handful of leaders are not sure they can or want to change and fear their job will become less important. The jobs of police leaders actually become more important because they make a shift from simply telling others what to do, to coaching them to achieve high performances.
Democratic Leadership Maturing	**Transitional Leadership Level 2** From lessons learned in Transitional Leadership 1, there is a broadening of the issues for which the input of subordinates is solicited. To some extent the movement toward more involvement of officers is driven by new generations of officers who have an expectation they will be involved with the department's important processes. Leadership's acceptance of some recommendations in Transitional Leadership Level 1 from the temporary committees has made a positive impression on the RF. Committee work is no longer considered "busy work" or "show and tell."	**Transitional Leadership Level 2** A paradigm shift in leadership style is underway. Although not yet fully developed, RF participation in organizational processes and decisions is no longer considered novel. The RF is unsure of where participation will lead and how much of it they will be allotted, but the future seems to hold new and interesting possibilities. Existing unions may be suspicious, skeptical, or threatened by the budding changes. They may fear that growing participation could make the union less important. Historically, police unions have been likely to support aggressive enforcement programs.
Participative Leadership Emerges	**Participative Leadership Level 1** From lessons learned at Transitional Leadership Levels 1 and 2, the involvement of subordinates continues to be cautiously expanded. A few standing committees are appointed on "safe" subjects, such as training and equipment. The chief continues to select committee members, who can only make recommendations, but the committees elect their chairpersons.	**Participative Leadership Level 1** First-line supervisors feel they are in a bind. Their department is moving toward participative leadership, but their work in the field often requires quick action that doesn't allow for it. Supervisors are trained to use participatory leadership as a core model and situational leadership as needed.

(continued)

TABLE 7.8 *(CONCLUSION)*		
Chiefs/Supervisors Orientation	**Characteristic Leadership Behavior**	**Impact on Subordinates**
	Involvement of community stakeholders begins or is expanded as the police department moves toward more departmental transparency. Departmental leaders have learned that some policy shifts, such as community engagement, must be treated as an organizational change intervention, and training to provide the new skills needed is provided.	Situational leadership is an adaptive response where supervisors choose an appropriate leadership style for the demands of the situation and in consideration of the capabilities of subordinates and other resources, e.g., unilaterally directing subordinates to contain a just developed hostage situation while waiting for hostage negotiators to arrive.
	Some decisions normally made by mid-level and even senior leaders are being pushed to the lowest level in the department that they can be made effectively.	The new grants of authority and expanded role of first-line supervisors have a positive effect on them. Middle managers do not feel disenfranchised because they have their own new authority and roles.
Participative Leadership Maturing	Participative Leadership Level 2	Participative Leadership Level 2
	The chief seeks further opportunities to engage officers, e.g. establishes an electronic suggestion box on the department's intranet. More standing committees appear, such as awards and decorations, ethics, off-duty work, accident review, and homeland security.	Officers acting jointly develop outreach programs to serve special populations, such as teaching the elderly how to be less vulnerable to victimization and develop alcohol safety programs for bars and restaurants to reduce their liability for drunk drivers and to reduce the frequency of related arrests, accidents, and injuries.
	The departments issues or broadens its committee policy. While some ad hoc committees may still be appointed, the emphasis is on standing committees and their authority. Units elect their own representatives to committees and those members elect their respective chairpersons. The use of committees is now well institutionalized.	Some agencies employ 360 degree evaluations of officers and leaders, where each individual receives feedback from subordinates, peers, and their supervisors.
	Community engagement has evolved into a key focus and is accomplished by interactive websites, town hall meetings, and other mechanisms. Stakeholders participate in key organizational processes, such as serving on promotional boards and strategic planning groups. The use of civilian volunteers expands into increasingly important responsibilities. A volunteer coordinates the recruitment of people with special capabilities, e.g., conducting an annual survey of satisfaction with police services.	Organizational citizenship is widespread with officers taking individual initiatives to help the department forward in small ways that may go unnoticed and larger ways such as volunteering to help with specific projects.

(continued)

	TABLE 7.8 (*CONCLUSION*)	
Chiefs/Supervisors Orientation	**Characteristic Leadership Behavior**	**Impact on Subordinates**
	Ad hoc committees/task forces are appointed in special circumstances. In 2014 and 2015, a series of police use of force cases prompted nation-wide reviews of policies, equipment, and training. Ad hoc committees were appointed and included a cross section of the department, as well as stakeholders, e.g., government officials, community members, mental health professionals, and private sector representatives.	
	Many of these developments are associated with the use of community policing, raising a chicken and egg question: Did community policing produce participative leadership or did that style of leadership foster it?	

Although Table 7.8 was referenced in the discussion of Tannenbaum and Schmidt's work, it was prepared by Charles R. Swanson, Leonard Territo, and Robert Taylor prepared their own similar table to illustrate the concepts using police examples.

A third group, the middle-LPC scorers, do not have a distinct preference for task or relationship approaches to leadership and have been somewhat ignored.[95] Low LPCs get their psychological subsistence from completing their assigned tasks and are less concerned about how their drive to complete assignments impacts their followers. Conversely, high LPCs derive their sense of well-being in the workplace by creating and maintaining satisfying interpersonal relationships. Further differences in these two types of leadership approaches are shown in Table 7.10. Fiedler considered leader behavior fairly stable and difficult to change. The interplay among task structure, leader–follower relations, and the power position of the leader produced situations that were more or less favorable to high- and low-LPC leadership preferences (see Table 7.11.)

LPC has been studied extensively; Vecchio's test of the model (1977) concluded that factors other than those specified in the model or different combinations of them were responsible for group performance.[96] Rice (1978) reviewed 25 years of research on it and found general support for the low-LPC and high-LPC leadership preferences.[97] Peters, Hartke, and Pohlmann (1985)

reached the same conclusion.[98] Middle LPCers are less involved with both tasks and relationships and approach their jobs less emotionally than the other two LPC preferences.[99] In 1982, Kennedy found that the middle-LPCers' leadership performance was higher than the other two leadership preferences within the parameters described by Fiedler's model.[100]

HOUSE: PATH-GOAL THEORY

Although there was an earlier version of **path-goal theory (PGT)** by Evans in 1970, it is more closely associated with House, who built on Evan's work by formulating a more elaborate version that included situational variables (1971); it has been revised several times.[101] The central thought of PGT is that leaders should remove the obstacles that inhibit, make more difficult, or prevent individual followers from doing a good job.[102] Originally, PGT was not about leadership of groups or work units; it was a dyadic supervisor to an individual subordinate theory.[103]

In 1996, House's early work was reformulated as both an individual and work unit performance theory, stated here in law enforcement terms, that incorporates five notions: (1) the behavior

TABLE 7.9	A PORTION OF FIEDLER LPC SCALE	
Descriptor	**Scale**	**Descriptor**
Unfriendly	1 2 3 4 5 6 7 8	Friendly
Considerate	8 7 6 5 4 3 2 1	Inconsiderate
Insincere	1 2 3 4 5 6 7 8	Sincere
Warm	8 7 6 5 4 3 2 1	Cold
Backbiter	1 2 3 4 5 6 7 8	Loyal

Source: Fred E. Fiedler and Joseph E. Garcia, *New Approaches to Effective Leadership* (New York: John Wiley & Sons, 1987), extracted from Figure 7.1, p. 71.

TABLE 7.10 DIFFERENCES BETWEEN FIEDLER'S TASK AND RELATIONSHIP MOTIVATED LEADERS

Task Motivated (Low LPC)	Relationship Motivated (High LPC)
• Accomplishing tasks is paramount and the source of self-esteem	• The leader's self-esteem comes from having satisfying relationships with subordinates.
• Highly critical of subordinates who don't contribute to task completion; may call them "slugs," "worthless" or "despicable"; blinds them to leader's to subordinates good characteristics.	• A pleaser, the leader is reluctant to criticize, overlooks followers deficits and focuses on good attributes
• Leader is courteous and ingratiating when needs co-operation of subordinates.	• The leaders is consistently courteous and friendly
• Primary focus is completing tasks, but when accomplished the leader may turn to repairing relationships.	• The leader's primary focus is people, but may become more directive around assignments they feel competent about
• Subordinate expertise is important concern.	• To the leader, loyalty from subordinates is an important concern.

of commanders is acceptable to subordinates to the extent to which it is seen as an immediate source of gratification or as a pathway to future satisfaction; (2) commanders can enhance subordinates' focus on goals to the extent that the commander's behavior increases motivation, builds task relevant skills, provides useful guidance, reduces obstacles to performance and organizational rewards, and provides the resources that subordinates need to do their job effectively; (3) commanders can increase subordinates' motivation by providing psychological support and linking their subordinates satisfaction of personal needs to job performance; (4) commanders must be role models. A study of 2,130 officers, police leaders modeling ethical behavior was found to be significant in limiting unethical conduct when the modeling occurred in an interpersonal, as opposed to a more distant context;[104] and (5) work unit performance is enhanced by a commander encouraging collaborative support among subordinates, maintaining a good relationship between the work unit and the larger organization in which it is embedded and demonstrating to the larger department the importance of the work performed by the unit.

In his revised work unit model (1996), House specifies eight types of leadership behavior that is acceptable, satisfying, facilitative, and motivational to subordinates. The essence of PGT is that for leaders to be effective, they must engage in leader behaviors (see Table 7.12) that compensate for the deficiencies of subordinates, enhances their performance, and is instrumental to their individual and work unit performance and satisfaction.[105] It is unlikely that any single commander will have the ability to engage in the eight leadership behaviors all or even most of the time; effective leaders are likely to select the behaviors with which they are most comfortable, based on their personality and abilities.[106]

DANSEREAU, GRAEN, AND HAGA: LEADER-MEMBER EXCHANGE (LMX)

Police officers know that their leaders treat subordinates differently, as do practitioners in other settings. Researchers, until LMX (1975),[107] made two wrong assumptions about leader behavior: (1) its effect on followers was homogenous or "averaged out," affecting their behavior "on average equally" or (2) leaders

TABLE 7.11 MIX OF SITUATIONAL VARIABLES AND FAVORABLENESS TO HIGH- AND LOW-LPC PREFERENCES

Task Structure	Leader–Follower Relations	Leader's Position Power	Situation Favorable to Leader Preference
High	Good	Strong	Low LPC
High	Good	Low	Low LPC
Low	Good	Strong	Low LPC
Low	Good	Low	High LPC
High	Weak	Strong	High LPC
High	Weak	Low	High LPC
Low	Weak	Strong	High LPC
Low	Weak	Low	Low LPC

TABLE 7.12 HOUSE'S EIGHT LEADERSHIP BEHAVIORS	
Leader Behavior	**Descriptions**
Path-Goal Clarifying	Clarifies subordinates' performance goals; the means to be used; the standards by which they will be evaluated; discusses the expectations about job performance which others may hold, e.g., merchants for an officer walking a beat, which should and shouldn't be honored; and judiciously uses rewards and discipline to shape performance.
Achievement Oriented	Achievement motivation is an individual's usually non-conscious desire to measure one's self against some standard of excellence or unique achievement. The ability of the leader to foster an achievement-oriented work unit will vary by the individuals assigned to it. Some officers are innately achievement oriented and motivated, "self-starters." Officers with lesser achievement motivation require more effort. In these officers, leaders must identify and arouse the subordinates' needs that will lead to a higher achievement motivation.
Work Facilitation	Consists of planning, scheduling, and organizing work; coordinating the work of subordinates; coaching, guiding, counseling, providing feedback, and mentoring them; reducing obstacles to their performance; eliminating bottlenecks to the resources they need; and authorizing them to take actions requiring the leader's prior approval.
Supportive	Supportive behavior provides psychological support to subordinates, especially when the task or incident is distressing, e.g., investigating child abuse and working the murder of another officer; supportive relationships reduce stress and make the leaders–subordinate relationship more satisfying; conversely, when work is satisfying and not dangerous or stressful, supportive behavior has little or no influence on subordinate's behavior.
Interaction Facilitation	Resolving disputes; facilitating communication; giving those in the minority the opportunity to voice their opinion; interaction facilitation may reduce voluntary absenteeism and attrition.
Group-Oriented Decision Process	Involves the way in which decisions that affect the group are made; group oriented decision making increases both the quality and acceptance of the decision; leader encourages full participation, inhibits domination by one subordinate or a faction, allows full search for alternatives, facilitates discussion of alternatives, and the group makes the decision.
Representation and Networking	Some work units have a high status and an easier time getting the resources they need from other units. Other units do not enjoy such a favorable situation. Leaders must be able to increase their unit's standing and perceived value to the larger organization and therefore their legitimacy to make claims on resources which will be honored.
Value Based	Value-based leaders receive extraordinary commitment from followers, tapping into their cherished beliefs, their identification with the leader, their support of organizational goals, and their self-worth and identities. Value-based leaders articulate the vision of a better future; display self-confidence and self-sacrifice in the interest of the vision; take risks to further the vision; communicate high-performance expectations for subordinates; and express confidence in their ability to meet those expectations.

treated all subordinates in the same manner. The core of LMX is that leaders develop different types of relationships with their subordinates. Exchange relationships can be thought of as the unique quality of the interpersonal relationship between the leader and a follower, which also has practical consequences for the leader, follower, and the department. The "merit" of an officer is contingent on how well he or she fits with the values, attitudes, preferences, and outlook of the leader.

An LMX police leader divides officers into two different groups: in-group and out-group, with a small holding category, "try-out" (see Figure 7.10). Through one-on-one encounters, the

FIGURE 7.10 ▶ The LMX in-group and out-group model.

leader forms opinions about each officer, sometimes in as little as two weeks. Where the leader and an officer are "simpatico," like-minded, congenial, and develop trust and respect in each other, the officer goes to the in-group. Where the "fit" is not good, the officer goes to the out-group. On rare occasions, a leader will move an officer from the out-group to the in-group, but this requires potent new evidence, such as clearing a string of burglaries or apprehending a serial killer. Newly hired officers always go to the try-out category. Experienced officers transferred into the unit usually have a reputation of some sort. Still, unless the leader has had prior personal experience with them, they go to "the try-out bin." The new hires and transfers do not know they are in the try-out bin; in time, they will come to notice the difference between being an in-group and out-group member. Ultimately, they will figure out which group they are in by the way the leader treats them.

In-group members receive more leader attention, have performance appraisals greater than merited, high-job satisfaction,

faster career progression, a high level of organizational citizenship behavior (OCB), reduced turnover, and more diverse work assignments. Out-group members are given accurate performance appraisals and their characteristics are essentially the "flip side" of the in-groupers.[108]

In 1995, Graen and Uhl-Bien moved away from the in- and out-group model, re-conceptualizing it as a continuum of leader and follower **relationships** (see Table 7.13).[109] In it, the purpose of the leaders is to form individual relationships with officers that will help them grow into the Mature Partnership stage to the betterment of leaders, subordinates, and the performance of the organization.

In Table 7.13, the progress from the Stranger stage to the Mature Partnership stage is not assured. Leadership methods may be ineffective and some officers might simply want to do their job and go home, seeking nothing more than doing an honest day's work for a fair wage. Such officers may see policing not as a profession, just where they work to make a living. Their lack

TABLE 7.13 LIFE CYCLE LMX LEADERSHIP

Characteristic	Stages of Relationship		
	1 **Stranger Stage**	**2** **Acquaintance Stage**	**3** **Mature Partnership Stage**
Phase of Relationship Building	Although roles understood and shaped by rules, leader and follower feel each other out; e.g., "How are we going to relate to each other?" At some point, the leader or the follower must create opening to move the relationship forward on a career interest basis	Some sharing of personal and work information; relationship evolving; "putting meat on the bones of their relationship"	Relationship is at mature stage; mutual roles understood and well accepted
Type of Reciprocity	Formal and limited; leader expects follower to do job and follower does it, but no more	Some formalities of the relationship fade as leader and the follower explore reciprocity; e.g., leader offers new challenge in which follower has an interest	Full reciprocity; relationship has been tested and is dependable
Reciprocity Occurs	Immediately, but only within the job context	Some delay involved as the dynamics of reciprocity with the relationship are figured out; e.g., is immediacy of reciprocity most important or is an equivalent reciprocity received later acceptable?	On-going, comfortable; dynamics have been worked out
Leader–Follower Exchange	Leaders provide only resources needed to do job; followers meet basic job requirements	Followers may have access to additional benefits, e.g., being assigned to patrol a particular area, sent to special training classes	Highly developed; emotional component becomes more prominent: mutual respect, trust, loyalty, sense of mutual obligation
Mutual Influence	Mostly one-way, leader directing follower's job performance	Still mostly one-way, but some limited mutual influence	Bi-directional; genuine feedback can be provided without damage to relationship

of a richer involvement might signal that their family is the first priority or that they want to put their energy into a family business, hobbies, or recreational pursuits. Thus, some officers are content to remain in the Stranger stage. Regression is possible also; officers in the Acquaintance stage and the Mature Partnership stage may return to an earlier stage if they become discouraged with their career or have catastrophic losses that adversely affect their job performance.

Beyond the three stages identified in Table 7.13, Graen and Uhl-Bien identify a fourth stage. This involves dropping an overlay of relevant Mature Partnership stage dyads over the task structure of the police department to maximize the use of talent. Developing a research framework to test this fourth stage has proven troublesome and therefore made it resistant to empirical study. Otherwise, the existing research for both the 1975 and 1995 iterations of LMX has generally been favorable. Much of the research on LMX since the 1970s has been on how it correlates with other characteristics, such as OCB, intelligence, gender, and cross-cultural implementation.

KERR AND JERMIER: LEADERSHIP SUBSTITUTES AND NEUTRALIZERS

In 1978, Kerr and Jermier observed that in some situations, hierarchical leadership didn't seem to make much of a difference in what subordinates did, and under other circumstances, it even appeared to be irrelevant. Stopping well short of Miner's 1975 proclamation that the concept of leadership had outlived its usefulness,[110] they asked a startling question: "Are there variables in the work setting that can substitute for, or even neutralize, leader behavior?"[111] Earlier in this chapter the Willow City case study established that leadership can be neutralized. Kerr and Jermier's work gives us a broader understanding of substitutes and neutralizers; it was conducted with reference to two styles of leadership: task oriented and relationship oriented. The model explores how the impact of leadership is contingent upon specific variables in the workplace.

Leadership substitutes are variables or factors that diminish the importance of leadership behavior or take its place entirely. Examples of substitutes include: (1) Officers, who accurately perceive that they require little or no personal supervision by virtue of their training, job experience, knowledge, and job commitment—moreover, they may rankle under it. (2) Officers with a professional orientation may be heavily influenced by an external organization, such as the National Tactical Officers Association (NTOA) and the opinions of qualified peers. (3) Sergeants are unlikely to find success trying to motivate officers who find police work intrinsically satisfying. (4) Close-knit peer groups may provide sufficient approval needs to diminish the efficacy of a sergeant using a relationship approach.

Neutralizers are variables that make task and relationship leadership approaches ineffective or impossible. An officer seriously considering leaving the department to work full-time on a graduate degree, attend law school, start a business, or with multiple external job opportunities is outwardly directed, away from the department. Guidance, support, or threats from a supervisor may have little saliency, no real importance, because the officer mentally has "one foot out the door." However, the department does hold one important card: the letter of recommendations leaders may be requested to write. Even going out the door, most officers do not want to "soil their nests." A few officers leaving an agency will tell one or more supervisors what "assholes" they are. Later, when these officers want a letter of recommendation or are seeking reinstatement to the department, they come to regret indulging themselves that way.

Officers who have a misperception of their own abilities and experience and think they don't need any supervision are neutralizers; they are a bad mix of arrogance and faulty perception. The more consistently a leader and followers are separated by location, the greater the likelihood is that without special leader measures, his or her leadership will be seen as less important over time. Thus, chiefs with precincts need to do more than use technology to communicate with dispersed officers; they must also establish a personal presence by visiting those precincts. Other neutralizers include officers who are indifferent to the award system, a perception that leaders occupy a low status in the "food chain"; inflexible work guidelines that create unnecessary work; and leaders who one way or another inflict "wounds" on themselves, which lowers the regard in which their officers hold them.

Researchers have only found mixed support for this theory.[112] However, it still has practical significance in that it identifies factors leaders should consider when they ask themselves "How am I doing?" Perhaps the most important contribution of this theory is that it spawned interest in learning more about the role of trust in organizations. Lewicki, Wiethoff, and Tomlinson identified two types of trust in organizations: (1) calculus-based trust (CBT), in which the parties to a relationship must determine the costs of maintaining or severing it; and (2) identification-based trust (IBT), based on a mutual understanding of each other's needs and wants.[113]

HERSEY AND BLANCHARD: SITUATIONAL LEADERSHIP THEORY

Although many situational variables are important to leadership—such as the demands of time, the leader, the led, superiors, the organization, and job demands—Hersey and Blanchard (1977) emphasize what they regard as the two key variables: (1) the behavior of the leader in relationship to (2) the maturity of followers.[114] Maturity is defined in situational leadership as the capacity to set high but attainable goals, the willingness to take responsibility, and the education and/or experience of the individual or the group.[115] Age may be a factor, but it is not related directly to maturity as used in situational leadership theory.[116] An individual or group is not mature or immature in a total sense but only in relation to the specific task to be performed.[117] This task-relevant maturity involves two factors: job maturity, or the ability and technical knowledge to do the task, and psychological maturity, or feelings of self-confidence and self-respect about oneself as an individual.[118]

Table 7.14 summarizes the Hersey–Blanchard model, which includes references to task and relationship dimensions in the same manner as the Managerial Grid. Although it is easier said than done, the effective use of Hersey–Blanchard model depends

TABLE 7.14 HERSEY AND BLANCHARD'S SITUATIONAL LEADERSHIP

Subordinates' (S) Capabilities	Hersey and Blanchard's Best Leadership Style	Corresponding Managerial Grid Style
Ss are insecure, may be rookies, and/or have lower levels of experience. Ss are not willing to perform the task and/or resist taking responsibility for it.	**Telling:** Relies on one-way communication with the unstated stance of "I have authority and you will obey." Gives them very specific directions and supervises Ss closely.	**9/1, Authority/Obedience** In authoritarian approach, task has high importance, but there is low concern for people. Work always comes first. Deviations usually result in discipline.
Ss are willing, but unable to accept responsibility for the task.	**Selling:** Need to engage Ss in a constructive conversation. Begin with emphasizing, "We are a team . . . what we do reflects on all of us." Provide step-by-step directions about how to execute the task and the importance of their role to the success of the department. Elicit and respond to questions. Engaging Ss in two-way communication is a key dynamic.	**9/9, Team Management** High concern for both work and people, tries to find ways to create "win" strategies for both tasks and people.
Ss know how the task should be performed, but refuse to accept responsibility for doing it.	**Participating:** Superficially, leadership appears to be democratic with give and take in discussing the task and decision making about the task. However, it is always people first and task second. Makes appeals to their relationship **to** encourage accepting the task.	**1/9 Country Club Management** Wants relaxed atmosphere. Tries to protect Ss from censure by persons superior to supervisor for task not being performed.

on police leaders developing or having a diagnostic ability and the flexibility to adapt their leadership styles to given situations.[119] Research on the model has been mixed; Cairns and colleagues (1998) found it intuitively appealing and empirically contradictory.[120] Perhaps, like several other theorists, Hersey–Blanchard model could be beneficially reformulated, employing emotional intelligence (EI) and social intelligence (SI) concepts.

VROOM, YETTON, AND JAGO: NORMATIVE DECISION-MAKING THEORY

Collaborative work between Vroom and Yetton (1973) and Vroom and Jago (1988) resulted in this theory, which is narrow in its focus—decision making—and not a general leadership model. It is "normative," stipulating under what conditions one leadership approach to decision making is more likely to be successful than another. Table 7.15 summarizes three leadership approaches to decision making: authoritarian, consultative, and group. Table 7.16 identifies eight contingency factors and the corresponding key questions/concerns leaders should consider. Research evidence for the initial model (1973) was adequate, but there were criticisms of it. The reformulation of the model (1988) responded to those criticisms and there was an impressive increase in research evidence supporting it. In one study, effective decisions were made 68 percent of the time using the normative model as compared to 32 percent using other methods.[121] Yukl (2010) concludes that it is "probably the best supported of the contingency theories of leadership."[122]

Transactional and Transformational Leaders

Burns (1978) contrasted transactional and transformational leaders, thinking of them as polar opposites.[123] Most leader–follower relationships are transaction based. **Transactional leaders** give something to get something. They motivate followers by appealing to their self-interest; contingent upon a follower doing a good job, the leader will provide favorable evaluations, raises, and desired assignments. Each party to the transaction, or "bargain," is at least implicitly aware of the resources of the other, and the purposes of both are entwined.[124] To function, both parties to a bargain must have certain values, such as reliability, honesty, fairness, and reciprocity.[125] Commanders using a transactional leadership style clearly state their expectations for what subordinates need to do to fulfill their part of the bargain and monitor the performance of followers.

Essentially, **transformational leadership** emphasizes the upper levels of Maslow's needs hierarchy—esteem and self-actualization—to motivate followers[126] (see Chapter 5, Organizational Theory). These two levels of need include such factors as the need to test yourself against challenging work and standards, the quest for self-esteem and confidence, and autonomy in problem solving. Transformational leadership consists of several factors, referred to as the "Four Is" (see Table 7.17). The use of the "Four Is" was studied in a Royal Canadian Mounted Police (RCMP) detachment. It concluded that transformational leadership increased commitment, work satisfaction, and motivation.[127]

TABLE 7.15 VROOM-YETTON-JAGO NORMATIVE DECISION-MAKING MODEL

Leader Approach	Description	Decision Maker
Authoritarian	**A1**: Chief uses all information immediately available	Chief
	A2: Chief obtains any necessary information from staff members, may not disclose why the information is needed	Chief
Consultative	**C1**: Chief shares problem/situation/opportunity with relevant staff members individually; decision may or may not reflect input received	Chief
	C2: Chief convenes command staff or other group; gets their input, decision may or may not include any signs of influence from group	Chief
Group	**GI:** Chief and one subordinate work to solve a limited problem.	Group
	GII: Chief briefs group on situation without attempting to influence them as to the preferred solution. Chief may act as an equal to group members, careful not to use his/her status to influence the group or Chief may loosely "manage" the process with a light hand. The consensus decision of the group is accepted.	Group

As conceived of by Burns (1978) and Bass (1985),[128] transformational leaders are inspirational; they motivate followers to "elevate their game," to go beyond their own self-interests for the good of the unit or department, making more and larger contributions than they had expected to make (see Table 7.16)[129]; in this process, police transformational leaders help subordinates grow personally and to develop their own capacity for leadership.[130] This help takes the form of individual attention to officers, empowering them, appealing to their ideals and values, and aligning their interests and the goals with the leader, the unit, and the department. This results in the followers' commitment to work "now," a well-articulated vision of the future, and strong organizational citizenship behavior.[131] While accommodating the needs of officers, transformational leaders "send the same message" about their vision and the challenging goals ahead to everyone.[132] "Even when a chief has a vision, implementation is not always easy."[133] In many cases, the chief's vision may clash with that of other entities that do not relate directly with the

TABLE 7.16 CONTINGENCY FACTORS IN THE NORMATIVE DECISION-MAKING MODEL

Contingency Factors	Key Questions/Concerns
Quality of Decision	How important is the quality of this decision, e.g., "just good enough" versus optimum
Leader Information	Does the chief have enough information to make a high-quality decision?
Follower Information	Do others have enough information to make a high-quality decision?
Structure of the Problem	Clear, action needed well known versus structure unclear, ill-defined, unfamiliar, alternatives need to be identified and evaluated
Goal Congruence	Are followers and organizational goals aligned, a "win-win" situation or in conflict, "win-lose"
Follower Conflict	Are followers divided on what the outcome should be? Failure to build consensus may lead to a lack of commitment/support
Commitment Probability	If an authoritarian decision made, will it matter to followers?
Commitment Required	How important is it to the Chief that follower commitment to the decision be substantial?

TABLE 7.17 THE FOUR "IS" OF TRANSFORMATIONAL LEADERSHIP

1. **Idealized Influence (IL):** Transformational leaders serve as role models, generating respect, trust, and admiration. They can be counted on to do the right thing and followers identify with them and emulate them. Chiefs who do not "walk the talk" cannot be transformational because followers quickly discount them.

2. **Inspirational Motivation (IM):** In a genuine manner, Chiefs behave in ways that motivate and inspire those around them. They manage the meaning of events, display optimism and enthusiasm, work hard, and actively demonstrate their own personal commitment to the vision of the future. The ability to communicate ideas nonverbally, verbally, symbolically, and in written form is an essential part of "winning hearts and minds."

3. **Intellectual Stimulation (IS):** Transformational Chiefs supportively probe their followers' progress toward creativity and innovation by questioning their assumptions, line of reasoning, and approach to solving persistent and new problems. This helps followers reframe problems and see new possibilities for their solution. Challenging assignments also stimulate growth. Ideas that are different from the Chief's are not just tolerated; they are encouraged.

4. **Individualized Consideration (IC):** The needs of individual followers for growth and accomplishment are attended to by coaching and mentoring, moving them to successively higher levels. Interactions with followers are personalized, e.g., the transformational Chief recalls past conversations about families and work, sees follower as whole person.

police department's mission,[134] for example, indigent and low-income health-care agencies not only serve local needs but also attract more homeless from afar, creating more order maintenance needs.

Ideals and values are powerful forces; our Declaration of Independence (1776) rings with them: "All men are created equal . . . with unalienable rights . . . life, liberty, and the pursuit of happiness." Although not the sole contributor to gaining our independence from what was then the most powerful nation in the world, the words resonated and took deep root in the minds of our populace, evoking passion about them. Mohandas Gandhi (1869–1948), the Bapu, or Father of India, led his country to independence from England by advocating non-co-operation and mass civil disobedience, tactics used by Dr. Martin Luther King, Jr., in the civil rights movement (see Chapter 1, Evolution of Police Administration). Ironically, both men, who advocated peaceful resistance, were assassinated. However, their lives demonstrate how transformational leaders can use ideals and values to achieve enormous political and social change.

"Charismatic" and "transformational leadership" are used interchangeably by some theorists, largely because the first two of the "Four Is," "idealized influence" and "inspirational motivation" were often combined together in early research as "charismatic leadership."[135] Indeed, some theorists maintain that there can be no transformational leadership without a charismatic leader. However, if the "Four Is" are studied individually, with no combining of the four factors, charismatic leadership becomes *one of the styles* that works with a transformational approach.[136] For example, a leader can be inspirational without being charismatic.[137] Followers can be drawn to the purposes, goals, and vision of an inspirational leader, without being drawn to the person per se as in charismatic leaders,[138] a pivotal and profound difference.

There is ample evidence supporting transactional and transformational leadership. Like transformational leadership, properly executed transactional leadership can result in trusting the leader,

organizational citizenship behavior, and commitment; moreover, it may establish the foundation from which transformational leadership can develop.[139] Transformational leadership increases followers' job satisfaction[140]; its individual support of followers may help protect them from depression,[141] builds committed, cohesive work teams,[142] and produces organizational innovations, such as new approaches to doing the work.[143] Women are slightly more likely than men to use transformational leadership.[144]

A study of Texas police chiefs found there were slightly more transactional than transformational leaders.[145] A study of the "Four Is" in the Royal Canadian Mounted Police (RCMP) found support for them. Officers said that the first and foremost aspect of *idealized influence* (IF) was when commanders knew their "true north," leading their personal and professional lives consistent with the values of the RCMP.[146] The RCMP respondents said that *inspirational motivation* (IM) was not complete with respect to the use of community policing because while there was no active resistance to it, "buy-in" by officers wasn't 100 percent. A RCMP commander reported that one of his approaches to *intellectual stimulation* (IS) was to assign unusual cases to a very experienced investigator and then team that person with someone who would learn and grow from being involved. As to *individualized consideration* (IC), another commander stated that the most effective tool was simply getting the right person in the right job. The largest study of transformational leadership in a police setting was conducted in England by the Home Office (see Table 7.1). Overall, 70 percent of the 1,066 officers surveyed agreed with 10 statements reflecting a transformational approach. The remaining 30 percent raises interesting questions: (1) How many of that portion might change their opinions? (2) Over a period of time will the majority experiencing transformational leadership remain stable? (3) For transformational leadership, as well as other theories, is there a saturation point (e.g., 70 percent) beyond which you simply are not going to get more "converts"? and (4) Is there always some "loyal opposition," albeit it muted?

TABLE 7.18 BRITISH POLICE OFFICERS' (*N* = 1,066) PERCEPTIONS OF THEIR LEADERS

Element	Percent Disagree	Percent Agree	Total Percent
Behaves in a way that increases my motivation to achieve	23	77	100
Manages and leads in a way that I find very satisfying	30	70	100
Behaves in a way that has a positive effect on my job commitment	25	75	100
Behaves in a manner that has a positive effect on my self-confidence	23	77	100
Behaves in a manner that raises my sense of fulfillment for the job	22	78	100
Reduces my stress level by his/her approach to leadership	37	63	100
Leads and behaves in such a way that it increases my job satisfaction	32	68	100
Manages and behaves in a manner that increases my self-esteem	32	68	100
Has a leadership style that increases my organizational commitment	32	67	100
Acts in a manner that enables me to achieve beyond my expectations	35	65	100

Source: John Dobby, Jane Anscombe, and Rachel Tuffin, "Police Leadership: Expectations and Support," (Home Office: London, England, 2004). Table 4.2, p. 25. The six columns of data in Table 4.2's 6-point Likert Scale were collapsed into "Disagree" and "Agree" categories and then converted to percentages.

Comparison of Charismatic and Transformational Leadership

Historically, **charisma** was thought to be a divine gift, bestowed on one who was favored by the "gods," an early characterization of the born leader. Leaders cannot declare that they are charismatic, nor can they be such if they are not successful (Figure 7.11). "Charisma" is a label that can only be authentically applied by followers. Charismatic leaders have certain traits: (1) their vision is a significant shift from the present status quo but still acceptable to followers; (2) they use new, unconventional strategies to implement the vision; (3) they take risks and self-sacrifice to achieve the vision (e.g., possible loss of the chief's position); (4) they are less motivated by self-interest than by concern for followers; (5) they radiate a contagious confidence and enthusiasm; (6) they rely more on emotional appeals to followers than on the use of authority to get performance; and (7) they select a vision that is innovative, relevant to followers, and timely in its implementation.[147]

These traits are the "ideal version" of a charismatic leader; however, charisma also has a "dark side" (e.g., Hitler and Stalin). On a smaller scale, Charles Manson gathered a "family" of followers and in 1969 dispatched them to commit gruesome murders, including fatally stabbing actress Sharon Tate, who was nearly nine months pregnant.

It may not be possible to immediately differentiate whether charisma is positive or good; even charismatics who help their department and followers to substantial achievements may also do some damage to some officers along the way. Without dismissing the matter lightly, it is somewhat like breaking a few eggs to make an omelet, except the stakes are much higher: The impact on the lives of officers negatively affected can be catastrophic. Other aspects of charismatic leadership that are problematic include: (1) the desire of officers to be "in good standing" might inhibit useful criticisms from them; (2) widespread approval by officers can breed a dangerous sense of infallibility in chiefs; (3) excessive confidence by charismatic chiefs can lead them into dangerous mistakes; and (4) charismatic behavior

FIGURE 7.11 ▶ Three of the most successful allied leaders of World War II. England's Prime Minister Churchill (L) was energetic and inspirational. American General Eisenhower (C) was a strong administrator, building the allied coalition; although decisive he often relied on persuasion as opposed to simply giving orders. Field Marshal Montgomery (R) was an effective, but temperamental combat commander who made harsh criticisms of Eisenhower and other allied leaders after WW II.
(Manchester Daily Express/SSPL/Getty Images)

inevitably breeds believers but also determined enemies who prefer to cling to more familiar ways and will opportunistically look for ways to discredit or remove the leader from office.[148]

Charismatic and transformational leadership has been used synonymously, described as overlapping, and sharply differentiated; earlier charismatic leadership theories have been revised, causing some convergence with transformational leadership.[149] Not all charismatic leaders are transformational. While there are some similarities between charismatics and transformationals, there are also some important distinctions: (1) transformationals, by developing followers' abilities and eliminating unnecessary controls, make followers less dependent on them; (2) transformational leaders are more common, whereas charismatics are rare and their emergence depends upon circumstances being favorable for their leadership approach; (3) charismatics, as described earlier, elicit more diverse and extreme reactions; and (4) charismatics are much more attuned to managing their image.[150]

The "New Leadership" Theories: Servant, Spiritual, Authentic, and Ethical

Because these theories share some common characteristics, and for ease of reference, theorists have labeled them "neo-charismatic" or the "new leadership," independent from when they were actually initially formulated. In some fashion, they all attempt to explain how leaders: (1) take organizations on an upward trajectory to outstanding accomplishments; (2) engender extraordinary levels of follower motivation, trust, dedication, and loyalty; (3) use symbolic and emotionally appealing behaviors, such as envisioning, empowering, and supporting, to rally followers to their vision; and (4) employ leadership to increase followers' self-esteem, job satisfaction, and performance.[151] They also fall short of being full leadership theories in that the linkage between leader behavior—the resulting follower behavior—and organizational outcomes are neither fully explained nor demonstrated.

SERVANT LEADERSHIP

Greenleaf (1904–1990) articulated the core notion of **servant leadership** (1977): The servant leader is servant first . . . making sure that other people's highest priority needs are met.[152] The idea is consistent with many of the teachings of the world's religions. Servant leadership (SL) includes the concepts of nurturing, defending, and empowering followers; helping them to be more complete persons, healthier, wiser, and more willing to accept their responsibilities; listening to their aspirations and frustrations; keeping actions consistent with their own values; and preparing people to lead when their opportunity comes.[153] Law enforcement agencies using SL include Boone, North Carolina; Casper, Wyoming, Hartford, Vermont, Coppell, Texas, and Peachtree City, Georgia.

A principal difference between transformational leadership and SL is that ultimately, the former focuses on organizational outcomes, whereas the latter's "wheelhouse" is followers.[154] Spears identifies 10 characteristics of SL:

1. *Listening*—SLers have a deep commitment to listen to others, apprehending both what is said and what is omitted. They are alert to emotional states and nonverbal cues;

2. *Empathy*—Empathy is the ability to vicariously understand and perhaps even experience (e.g., grief) what another person is feeling or a situation. Empathy approximates emotional intelligence and social intelligence, discussed earlier in this chapter;

3. *Healing*—Many relationships become strained or fractured. Uncomfortable, we avoid the other person involved and worry about what will happen. If we feel misunderstood, disappointed, injured, wounded, or betrayed, moving forward can be a difficult task. The longer we remain in that state, the more we reduce the quality of what our personal and organizational lives can be. The healing brought about by a kind gesture, "closing

the distance," a forthright, thoughtful, "air clearing" discussion, forgiveness, or similar action has enormous restorative powers for us and those with whom we are in some sort of a conflict. SLers heal themselves and followers. As a practical matter, many people make a habit of "never letting the sun go down on their anger"; they know lingering anger is destructive. Disciplina was a minor Roman deity; from her identity, we derive *disciplina*, the Latin root word for discipline, meaning to teach and to learn. Properly conducted discipline can also be a healing act, correcting a situation and putting it into the past. The Biblical basis for this is the forgiveness of our sins: As far as the east is from the west so far has He removed our transgressions from us (Psalm 103:12). The "Bibles" of other world religions, such as the Torah and Koran, contain very parallel statements.

4. *Awareness*—This capacity strengthens SLers, helping them to stay in touch with themselves and their values and ethics;

5. *Persuasion*—SLers rely less on authority and more on persuasion and consensus, seeking others to join rather than telling them to perform;

6. *Conceptualization*—Whereas traditional leaders are often captured by the daily "tyranny of events" and focus on short-term operational needs, SLers look beyond day-to-day realities, further into the future, and see new opportunities, delicately balancing both time frames;

7. *Foresight*—Little has been written about the role of foresight in leadership; it is less like tactical and strategic planning and more akin both to awareness and intuitiveness. It allows SLers to draw upon past lessons, factors and situations in the present, and the likely consequences of decisions about the future;

8. *Stewardship*—This characteristic means the responsible care of something entrusted to your care. In SL, the "prime directive" for stewardship is always the commitment to serve others;

9. *Commitment to the growth of people*—SLers are deeply committed to the personal, professional, and spiritual growth of each person in the organization; and

10. *Sense of community*—Our lives are dominated by large-scale organizations (e.g., employers, banks, health care, and school systems). In large part, the movement of families to villages and small towns is an attempt to live life differently, to create a sense of intimate belonging. City dwellers do the same thing without moving, creating their own, typically multiple, "communities" to which they can belong and from which they can derive meaning and psychological sustenance. SLers make organizations viable "communities."[155]

Welsh conceptualized the role of police officers as "Warrior Servants." "Werreieor" was 13th century French word and also an old English word during the second half of that century denoting someone who is skilled in warfare or engaged in it. In modern English, the word is recognized as warrior. The police have been described as "fighting the war on crime" and "crime fighters." In 2014, Welsh proposed the "hybrid" Warrior-Servant-Leader Code (see Box 7.5).[156] Had this existed in the 1960s, 1970s, 1980s and even into the 1990s, it may have been an easier "sell." Community policing took root as a national movement in the 1990s and subsequent ideas have also flourished. However, if the critics of police militarization and the proponents of the Guardian model make inroads in policing, the warrior-servant code may not flourish simply because of the warrior part of its name. American policing seems perched on the edge of a paradigm shift. The current demand for more community engagement by the police may not be quickly achievable in light of budget cuts and some communities wondering if they can really afford the policing they used to have, as well as wondering if they even need it. The deaths of unarmed African-Americans by police during 2014–2015 appalled many Americans and there have been many calls for reforms. The call for body cameras is reasonable, but puts jurisdictions in the role of providing evidence for civil suits when there is police misconduct but also exonerating officers who have been falsely accused. Largely ignored in all of this is an important, but disturbing fact: some officers don't deserve to wear a badge and need to be removed from the profession because they unfortunately shape the public's view of those that remain.

Much of the evidence about SL is from case studies and anecdotal accounts; although researchers are developing reliable

---

Box 7.5 The Warrior-Servant-Leader Code

- I am a Warrior-Servant-Leader.
- It is my duty in all that I do to Protect, Serve and Lead others with all my heart, mind and soul.
- I will Protect with courage.
- I will Serve with humility.
- I will Lead with compassion.
- In all my thoughts, words and actions I will ask myself:
  - Am I doing the right thing?

- At the right time?
- In the right way?
- For the right reasons?
- I will always strive to live up to my duty and not blame others when I fail.
- I will always strive to grow in my knowledge, understanding and skills of being a true Warrior-Servant-Leader.

scales to measure its concepts.[157] The sparse evidence on SL correlates with increased organizational citizen behavior, follower trust in the leader and the organization, job satisfaction, and some organizational effectiveness.[158] Some critics of SL believe that by definition the spiritual leader is so occupied with the needs of followers that legitimate, short-term, organizational needs become secondary in importance. Women, ethnic minorities, and others who have traditionally been held to lesser roles may find the idea of SL unappealing.[159] More critically, Eicher-Catt believes it accentuates gender bias.[160] The theory also fails to take into account how SLers behave when the needs of the organization and the followers are in conflict (e.g., the downsizing seen in police departments during an economic downturn), as well as the possibility that the SLers' emphasis on humility, equality, and empowerment may be seen as weaknesses.[161]

SPIRITUAL LEADERSHIP

There are two major views about spiritual leadership:

1) Firstly, it is based on theology or religion based. This belief may produce an immediate visceral reaction so strong that the concept is quickly dismissed by some without taking the time to examine what it actually entails. Every time this happens, spiritual leadership loses another opportunity to flourish. Books authored by leadership gurus with titles like Jesus, CEO (1996), What Would Buddha Do at Work? (2002), and Prophet Muhammad: The Hallmark of Leadership, (2015) seemingly imply that spiritual leadership is rooted in theological or religious beliefs. This may contribute to some headwind for wider use of spiritual leadership.

Thomas Jefferson (1743–1826) and other finding founding fathers were successful in creating Constitutional barriers that formed a wall between church and state. The Supreme Court has consistently upheld that position. For that reason, there can be no reasonable concern of a theological or religious based leadership existing in public sector organizations.

However, in the private sector, religious beliefs may legally affect business policies and practices. Illustratively, Truett Cathy (1921–2014), founder of Chick-Fil-A (1964), was deeply religious.

Because of his beliefs, that business—whether company owned or operated as a franchise—is always closed on Sundays so people can go to church. Likewise, the Supreme Court exempted a closely held business, Hobby Lobby, from providing employees with certain types of birth control under "Obama Care" because of the company's religious beliefs. In what seems like a contradiction, Hobby Lobby does provide both Viagra and vasectomies.

2) Although spiritual leadership shares some values with theology and religion, those ideals are also found in many lands and times as well, including ancient Egypt, Greece, and Rome. In Western Europe, the Code of Chivalry for Knights and in Japan the Code of Bushido for samurai warriors espoused values such as honesty, hope, diligence, mercy, and politeness. It appears there was not a Code of Chivalry per se, but a set of shared and commonly understood values which are also acknowledged in literature. The Code of Bushido was much like that of chivalry's and evolved over hundreds of years beginning in the 8th century. In the remainder of this section workplace spiritual leadership is examined in its non-theological and non-religious context.

Spirit is drawn from the Latin word for breath (spiritus) and in spiritual leadership refers to an abstract power which keeps people self-aware, invigorated, and connected to their vocational calling, workplace, and others.[162] Fry maintains that workplace spirituality meets an essential need of people, to have meaning in their lives and particularly in the workplace where they spend so much time.[163] More particularly, their calling to a vocation must provide a belief their lives are making a difference. As an illustration of the importance of work in our lives, when people ask us who we are, often our response is to tell people what we do, e.g., "I'm a police officer." Spirituality connects us with higher values that otherwise may not be routinely accessible by us, giving meaning, purpose, and providing inner sustenance to our lives.[164]

Spiritual leadership emerges from the interaction of vision, altruistic love, and hope/faith; Table 7.19 summarizes the qualities of spiritual leadership identified by Fry.[165] "Vision" refers to a future state which appeals to a police department's members in a way that makes them want to achieve it.[166] The short version

TABLE 7.19 QUALITIES OF SPIRITUAL LEADERSHIP		
Vision	**Altruistic Love**	**Hope/Faith**
• Broad Appeal to Key Stakeholders	• Trust/Loyalty	• Endurance
• Defines the Destination and Journey	• Forgiveness/Acceptance/Gratitude	• Perseverance
• Reflects High Ideals	• Integrity	• Do Stretch Goals
• Encourages Hope/Faith	• Honesty	• Excellence
• Establishes Standard of Excellence	• Courage	• Expectation of reward/victory
	• Humility	• Do what it Takes
	• Kindness	
	• Compassion	
	• Patience/Meekness/Endurance	
	• Excellence	
	• Fun/Work should be pleasurable/Not endured	

Source: ©Louis W. Fry, "What is Spiritual Leadership?" International Institute for Spiritual Relations, 2016.

of "altruistic love" is that is produced by a sense of harmony, wholeness, and well-being that springs from care, concern, and appreciation for ourselves and others.[167]

"Hope/Faith" is a belief rooted in values, attitudes, and behaviors that reveal officers are certain of reaching their goals.[168] It allows them to endure doubters, criticisms, setbacks, hardships, and even suffering to do so. Suffering may seem like an unusual word choice. However, officers who have stood in 30" or more of water directing traffic at an intersection flooded by a hurricane for many hours without relief know a degree of suffering. For spiritual leadership to flourish, leaders must model these qualities, officers must respond to them, and they will ultimately define an organization's culture.[169]

There is evidence that spiritual leadership can produce benefits important to officers and organizational performance, including increased senses of satisfaction, self-fulfillment, creativity, morale, and commitment, as well as mutual honesty and trust leading to greater cooperation between organizational members and work becoming an intrinsic motivator: the work itself motivates employees, instead of being something to just be endured.[170]

Police departments have long maintained associations with Chaplins from one or several faiths. The traditional role of Chaplins has been to tend to the needs of officers, e.g., as a pastor or visiting them when hospitalized, accompany officers when they deliver death messages or other unpleasant news if a family's pastor cannot be identified or is unavailable, serve as a member of a crisis response team, be a link to a community's clerics, offer prayers at police functions, such as academy graduations and awards ceremonies, and related activities.

In the wake of controversial shootings during 2014–2015, law enforcement agencies have also been more inclusive of religious leaders to help calm situations or otherwise involved them in departmental activities, such as community walks in support of, or against, various situations.

While there have been articles in the FBI Law Enforcement Bulletin, The Police Chief, and other journals on workplace spiritual leadership and the topic is also included in some leadership courses, including those for police executives at the prestigious FBI National Academy (NA), accounts of law enforcement

agencies adopting spiritual leadership are sparse. However, it seems more likely than not that at least pieces of spiritual leadership have made their way into policing.

AUTHENTIC LEADERSHIP

Partially in response to the mismanagement and "ethical meltdowns" of Fortune 500 companies[172] that wreaked so much havoc on the lives of employees and investors, substantial interest in **authentic leadership** (AL) began by the early 2000s. AL is more than being "real" or "genuine"—you can be a "real bastard" and "genuinely insensitive." AL is defined as: (1) being deeply aware of how you think, behave, and are seen by others; (2) being aware of your own and others' values/moral perspectives, knowledge, and strengths; (3) understanding the context in which you and others operate; and (4) being grounded by confidence, hopefulness, optimism, resiliency, and high-moral character.[173] While aware of the opinions of others, ALers are not driven by their expectations, and moral character separates them from those who are merely "real" or "genuine." Chief Seabrooks is an advocate of authentic leadership, avowing that "I am about the truth and that does not change."

Avolio and Gardner (2005) argue that AL is the "root construct" that underlies transformational, charismatic, servant, spiritual, and ethical theories.[174] ALers can incorporate elements of all of these theories into their behavior. For example, an ALer may use a charismatic approach but may or may not be perceived as such by followers; likewise, when employing a transformational style, little or no emphasis may be placed on the proactive development of followers, although they may have a positive impact by modeling important behaviors.[175]

AL suffers from some of the same deficits that other leadership theories do: (1) there is an absence of a consensus definition; (2) the conceptual distinction between it and other "new" leadership theories is not developed; (3) the claim of being a "root construct" is undemonstrated; (4) how long it will take before the effects of AL can be seen is unknown; (5) whether people can be trained to be authentic is questionable; (6) it fails to explain how authentic leaders should behave when dealing with authentically difficult followers; and (7) it is unknown how

Quick Facts: Antidotes to Destructive Leadership

Servant, Spiritual, and other forms of altruistic leadership have the potential to prevent the development of destructive emotions or mediate their impact on organizational members. Such emotions can also hamper the performance of the organization itself. Destructive emotions may stem from a lack of positive core convictions about yourself, not getting what you want or think you deserve, and the loss of something valued, such as a relationship or job.

The four broad categories of destructive emotions are: 1. *fear*, including anxiety, worry, and apprehension; 2. *anger*, including, hostility, resentment, envy, jealousy, and hatred; 3. *sense of failure*, including such things as discouragement,

depressed moods, and various guilt feelings that lead to self-destruction; and 4. *Pride* which is dysfunctional, including prejudice, selfishness, and conceit.[171]

Altruistic leadership approaches can be an antidote to destructive emotions. It can ferment joy, peace, and serenity. Joy is a sense of gladness, delight, and lively pleasure about a past, present, or anticipated event. Peace is the condition of our minds when they are free of disturbance, agitation, or strife, sometimes described as "feeling balanced" or "in tune with the world." Serenity is that inner sense that all is well, giving rise to calmness, awareness, and clarity.

many "slips" authentic leaders can make before followers dismiss them as "unauthentic."[176] Until these difficulties are resolved, it is hard to imagine that large-scale studies can be usefully undertaken.[177]

ETHICAL LEADERSHIP

Ethical Leadership is the consistent demonstration of moral values through personal actions, in interpersonal relationships, and the communication of those values to followers through two-way communication, reinforcement, and decision making.[178] Researchers have identified two components to ethical leadership: (1) the **moral person**, a fair and principled decision maker, who is altruistic, cares about people and the broader society and (2) the **moral manager**, who proactively strives to reinforce followers' ethical behavior. Moral managers explicitly make ethics part of their leadership agenda by frequently communicating about it, modeling it, and using discipline to hold followers accountable for ethical lapses.[179] Discipline provides important learning to organizational members, who by the actions taken are able to reliably distinguish between what is acceptable behavior and what is not.[180]

At one level or another, transformational, servant, spiritual, authentic, and ethical leadership are concerned with being a good role model, integrity, and altruism or care for others. While ethical leaders keep their eye on modeling, communicating, and reinforcing moral values, the other "new" leadership styles have different preoccupations: (1) ultimately, transformational leaders are concerned about organizational outcomes or results; (2) servant leaders look to the needs of others; (3) spiritual leaders are interested in their own and their followers' spiritual survival; and (4) authentic leaders are keenly aware of how they think, behave, and are seen by others.

Ethical leadership matters because it influences what followers do. Ethical leaders are attractive role models who followers want to emulate—to be like. This increases ethical reasoning and action, even if the leader is not immediately present, stimulates organizational citizenship behavior, increases job satisfaction and trust in the leader, and reduces counterproductive follower behavior[181] (e.g., abuse of sick leave, being quarrelsome, and failing to complete assignments on a timely basis). Despite the interest in ethical leadership, Yukl notes (2010) that much of the research done has been superficial.[182]

Conclusion

Leadership is a slippery concept. It can be the traits exhibited by a leader, the manner or style in which the leader behaves, the way in which subordinates perceive the leader, how the leader affects the behavior and growth of subordinates, and the organizational performance leadership produces and sustains. In almost every situation, one or more leadership approaches will work. Many of the theories discussed produce similar affects; this fact is not surprising because researchers attempt to determine if the theories produce a fairly standard set of impacts on subordinates and organizational outcomes (e.g., increased trust and organizational commitment). This chapter describes "pure" or idealized models that rarely have a counterpart in the "real world." Ultimately, leadership is often a hybrid of things leaders do that are within their comfort zone.

Chapter Summary

Summary by Learning Objectives

1. Give two definitions of leadership.

There are many definitions of leadership, each reflecting certain perspectives, but all incorporate the notion that the essence of leadership is interacting with and influencing others. For example, leadership can be simply defined as the difference between pushing a string and pulling it or being a "difference maker." More completely, leadership has external and internal components; it is the process of: (1) relating the police department to the larger environment, such as city council, the news media, civic organizations, and the general public and (2) influencing officers to use their energies willingly and appropriately to facilitate the achievement of the department's goals.

2. Explain and elaborate on "leading and managing are co-dependent skill sits."

Effective administrators must be both leaders and managers. Leadership and management skills sets are usually not co-equal. Instead they represent a mix. It seems perhaps inevitable that leaders subconsciously or through introspection gravitate toward assignments that are a good match with their skill set.

3. Provide four key characteristics and three key activities of effective senior police leaders.

The four key characteristics can be drawn from any of the following: (1) ethical behavior, (2) trustworthy, (3) legitimacy, (4) being a role model, (5) communication, (6) decision making, and (7) critical, creative/ innovative, and strategic thinking ability. Likewise, the three key activities can be drawn from any of the following: (1) create a shared vision, (2) engendering organizational commitment, (3) caring for subordinates, (4) driving and managing change, and (5) problem solving.

4. **Distinguish between rational-legal authority and power.**
Rational-legal authority is a grant of authority made by an organization to a position, the incumbent of which uses it for fulfilling his/her job responsibilities. Some power accompanies a grant of authority, for example, to give a verbal or written reprimand, but to a large extent power is a grant made by the led to the leader. Authority and power are related but separate concepts.

5. **Compare socialized and personalized power needs.**
Socialized power can be defined as wanting/needing to have a positive impact on a police department's administration and operations. In contrast, personalized power needs include the need to be in control for selfish, self-aggrandizing reasons.

6. **Identify and briefly describe the three components of the leadership skill mix.**
Human relations: the capacity to interrelate positively with other people who are at all levels of the police department. *Conceptual Skills:* include the ability to understand and interrelate various parcels of information that seem unrelated or those for which the meaning or importance is not immediately apparent. *Technical Skills:* These skills vary by level within the police department. A patrol sergeant must be able to help subordinates develop skills in handling domestic violence and other calls. As one progresses up toward middle and top management, the character of technical skills changes also, for example, budgeting skills.

7. **State two Great Man theories.**
Carlyle believed unusually gifted people made history, while Hegel believed that it was events that produced the "great man."

8. **Define the Big Five.**
The Big Five was the result of efforts to find a small number of broad traits into which many specific traits can be placed.

9. **Briefly describe "organizational citizenship behavior."**
OCB consists of subtle things employees do voluntarily and are not required to do or expected but contribute to overall organizational effectiveness.

10. **Distinguish among authoritarian, democratic, and laissez-faire leadership.**
An authoritarian leader (My way or the highway) makes all decisions, closely controls work, and is a micromanager. A democratic leader (Let's talk about it) encourages individual or group participation in matters affecting the organization. The laissez-faire leader (Whatever) takes a passive, hands-off posture. Only reluctantly do LFLs use the authority of their position. They do not make necessary decisions and delay taking any kind of action, allowing subordinates substantial autonomy.

11. **Describe Downs's four leader styles.**
Found in bureaucratic organizational structures, these four leader styles are: (1) climbers, who are strongly motivated by power and prestige needs to invent new functions for their unit, especially if they have not already performed elsewhere; (2) conservers, who have a bias of maintaining things as they are. The longer someone is in a job and the lower one assesses chances for advancement, the stronger one becomes attached to job security, all of which are associated with the tendency to become a conserver; (3) zealots' behavior stems from two sources, their narrow interest and the missionary-like energy they focus almost exclusively on their special interest; and (4) unlike zealots, advocates promote everything under their command. They appear highly partisan to outsiders, but within their units they are fair and impartial, developing well-rounded programs. They are loyal to their organization, favor innovation and are simultaneously more radical and more conservative than climbers. Advocates are more radical in that to promote their program and views they may antagonize politicians, superiors, other powerful groups, and the news media if it helps their department. They are more conservative because they are willing to oppose changes that might help their interests but is not in the best overall interest of their agency.

12. **Contrast station house sergeants and street sergeants.**
Station house sergeants had been out of the "bag" (uniform) before their promotions to sergeant and preferred to work in an office environment once they won their stripes. Station house sergeants immerse themselves in the management culture of the police department, keeping busy with paperwork, planning, record keeping, press relations, and fine points of law. Their strong orientation to conformity also gave rise to nicknames like "by-the-book Brubaker." In contrast, street sergeants were serving in the field when they received their promotions. Consequently, they have a distaste for office procedures and have a strong action orientation, as suggested by such nicknames as "Shooter McGee" and "Walker the Stalker." Moreover, their concern is not with conformity but with "not letting the assholes take over the city." Station house sergeants and street sergeants were thought of differently by those whom they supervised: station house sergeants "stood behind their

officers," whereas street sergeants "stood beside their officers." Each of these two different styles of working as a sergeant also has its drawbacks and strengths. Station house sergeants might not be readily available to officers working in the field; however, they can always be located when a signature is needed and are able to secure more favors for officers than street sergeants are. Although immediately available in the field when needed, street sergeants occasionally interfered with the autonomy of their subordinates; unrequested, they responded to calls for service assigned to subordinates and handled them or, otherwise, at least in the eyes of their officers, "interfered."

A consideration of Van Maanen's work leads to some generalizations about the future careers of station house sergeants versus street sergeants. Station house sergeants are learning routines, policies, procedures, and polishing skills that will improve future promotional opportunities. Their promotional opportunities are further enhanced by contacts with senior police commanders who can give them important assignments and who may, if favorably impressed, influence future promotions. In contrast, street sergeants may gain some favorable publicity and awards for their exploits, but they are also more likely to have citizen complaints filed against them, more likely to be investigated by internal affairs, and more likely to be sued. Consequently, very aggressive street sergeants are regarded by their superiors as "good cops" but difficult people to supervise. In short, the action-oriented street sergeant who does not "mellow out" may not go beyond a middle manager's position in a line unit, such as patrol or investigation.

13. **State the three organizational forces from Tannenbaum and Schmidt's contingency theory.**
   These three forces are: (1) forces in the leader, such as his/her value system; (2) forces in subordinate officers, like their knowledge, skills, and experience; and (3) forces in the department, for example, a practice of not arresting non-persistent panhandlers.

14. **State the "central thought" or the "essence" of House's Path-Goal Theory**
   The central thought and the essence of PGT are statements that basically express the same thought in slightly different terms. They differ in that the former term is associated with the original model and the latter with a revised model in 1996. The *central thought* of PGT is leaders should remove the obstacles that inhibit, make more difficult, or prevent individual followers from doing a good job. In a similar vein, the *essence* of PGT is to be leaders must engage in behaviors that compensate for the deficiencies of subordinates, enhances their

performance, and is instrumental to their individual and work unit performance and satisfaction.

15. **Define the "merit" of a police officer in Leader-Member-Exchange Theory.**
   The merit of an officer is contingent on how well he or she fits with the values, attitudes, preferences, and outlook of the leader.

16. **Compare leadership substitutes and neutralizers.**
   Leadership substitutes are variables or factors that diminish the importance of leadership behavior or take its place entirely. In contrast, Neutralizers are variables that make task and relationship leadership approaches ineffective or impossible.

17. **Contrast transactional leaders and transformational leaders.**
   These two types of leaders are polar opposites. *Transactional leaders* give something to get something. They motivate followers by appealing to their self-interest; contingent upon a follower doing a good job, the leader will provide favorable evaluations, raises, and desired assignments. Each party to the transaction, or "bargain," is at least implicitly aware of the resources of the other, and the purposes of both are entwined. Essentially, *transformational leadership* emphasizes the upper levels of Maslow's needs hierarchy—esteem and self-actualization—to motivate followers. These two levels of need include such factors as the need to test yourself against challenging work and standards, the quest for self-esteem and confidence, and autonomy in problem solving. Transformational leadership consists of several factors called the "Four Is:" idealized influence, inspirational motivation, intellectual stimulation, and individual consideration. Transformational leaders are inspirational; they motivate followers to "elevate their game," to go beyond their own self-interests for the good of the unit or organization, making more and larger contributions than they had expected to make. In this process, transformational leaders help followers to grow personally and to develop their own capacity for leadership.

18. **Complete the following statement, the common characteristics shared by "new leadership" theories attempt to explain: how leaders:**
   These common characteristics attempt to explain how leaders: (1) take organizations on an upward trajectory to outstanding accomplishments; (2) engender extraordinary levels of follower motivation, trust, dedication, and loyalty; (3) use symbolic and emotionally appealing behaviors, such as envisioning, empowering, and supporting, to rally followers to their vision; and (4) employ leadership to increase followers' self-esteem, job satisfaction, and performance.

Chapter Review Questions

1. What are the seven key characteristics of effective senior police leadership?

2. Schafer's study identified five things that ineffective police leaders do. What are they?

3. What are the five things that toxic leaders do that "poisons" the work environment?

4. In a single sentence, what is servant leadership?

5. How is authentic leadership defined?

Critcal Thinking Exercises

1. Reread the Casselberry case study in Box 7.1. For what reasons do you think the City of Casselberry allowed the Police Chief to resign instead of firing him and charging him with any applicable crimes?

2. Assume that an area in a county with a population of about 78,000 was dissatisfied with services by the Sheriff's Office and incorporated as a totally new city of Flower Creek with a deadline to have its own police services within 12 months. You have been hired as the first Chief of Police. The Flower Creek Police Department does not yet exist. You have to design and staff it. For now, your only support is an administrative secretary. You have authorization to hire four people for your command staff. When interviewing applicants for those positions what are the most important things about your leadership beliefs to communicate to those applicants?

Key Terms

advocates
affiliation needs
authentic leadership
authoritarian/autocratic
authority
big five
big two
charismatic leadership
climbers
conceptual skills
conservers
counterproductive work behavior (CWB)
democratic
emotional skills (ES)
ethical leadership
"great man" theories
human relations skills

important thing
laissez-faire
leader
leader member exchange (LMX)
leadership
leadership neutralizers
leadership substitutes
least preferred coworker (LPC)
management systems
manager
managerial grid
moral manager
moral person
normative decision-making theory
organizational citizenship behavior (OCB)
path-goal theory (PGT)
personalized power needs

positive organizational behavior (POB)
power
power motivation
servant leadership
situational leadership
skill
social skills (SS)
socialized power needs
spiritual leadership
spiritual survival
station house sergeants
street sergeants
Tannenbaum and Schmidt
technical skills
traits approach
transactional leadership
transformational leadership
zealots

Endnotes

[1] Joseph A. Schafer, "Developing Effective Leadership in Policing: Perils, Pitfalls, and Paths Forward," *Policing: An International Journal of Police Strategies and Management*, Vol. 32, No. 2 (2009), p. 239.

[2] Ibid., p. 239.

[3] Among the exceptions to this is Joseph A. Devine, An Analysis of the West Point Leadership and Command Program's Impact Upon Law Enforcement Leadership, Dissertation in Partial Fulfillment of the Requirements for the Doctor of Education Degree, Seton Hall University, 2007.

[4] Developing Effective Leadership in Policing, pp. 247–250. The authors have extended some of Schafer's cogent points; any distortion or dilution is unintended.

[5] Mitchell Pearson-Goff and Victoria Herrington, "Police Leadership: A Systematic Review of the Literature," *Policing: A Journal of Policy and Practice*, Vol. 8, No. 1 (2014), pp. 2–3.

[6]Ibid., pp. 3–4.

[7]Loc. Cit and p. 7.

[8]Ibid., pp. 4–5 and pp. 6–7.

[9]Ibid., p. 5.

[10]Loc. Cit.

[11]Ibid., pp. 6–7

[12]Terry D. Anderson et al., *Every Officer Is a Leader* (Boca Raton: St. Lucie Press, 2000), p. viii.

[13]J. Gregory Reynolds and Walter H. Warfield, "Discerning the Differences Between Managers and Leaders," *Educational Digest*, Vol. 75, No. 7 (March 2010), pp. 26–29.

[14]Beverly Alimo Metcalfe and John Alimo-Metcalfe, "The Myths and Morality of Leadership in the NHS," *Clinician in Management*, Vol. 12 (2004), p. 49.

[15]John P. Kotter, "What Leaders Really Do," *Harvard Business Review* (May/June 1990), pp. 103–111.

[16]See Brigitte Steinheider and Todd Wuestewald, "From the Bottom Up: Sharing Leadership in a Police Agency," *Police Practice and Research*, Vol. 9, No. 2, (May 2008), pp. 145–163.

[17]On this point see Derrick J. Neufeld, Zeying Wan, and Yulin Fang, "Remote Leadership, Communication Effectiveness and Leader Performance," *Group Decision and Negotiation*, Vol. 19, No. 3 (May 2010), pp. 227–246. For more extended information see Suzanne Weisband, *Leadership at a Distance* (New York: Lawrence Erlbaum Associates, 2008).

[18]On the low end, see Fred W. Rainguet and Mary Dodge, "The Problems of Police Chiefs: An Examination of the Issues in Tenure and Turnover," *Police Quarterly*, Vol. 4, No. 3 (September 2001), p. 269 and on the high side, Steve Krull, *California Police Chief Demographic Study* (Sacramento: California Police Chiefs Association, 2004), p. 2.

[19]Jim Isenberg, *Police Leadership in a Democracy: Conversations with America's Police Chiefs* (Boca Raton: CRC Press, 2010), p. 28.

[20]Phil Coleman, "New Ideas for Solving the Police Chief Recruitment Crisis" (Sacramento: League of California Cities, October, 2007), p. 1.

[21]Isenberg, *Police Leadership in a Democracy: Conversations with America's Police Chiefs*, p. 42.

[22]Jill Leovy, "Little Job Security in Being a Police Chief," Los Angeles Times, May 5, 2002, p.1, http://articles.latimes.com/2002/may/05/local/me-dance5 (accessed July 27, 2015).

[23]Loc. Cit.

[24]Joseph A. Schafer, "The Ineffective Police Leader: Acts of Commission and Omission," *Journal of Criminal Justice*, Vol. 38, No. 4 (2010), p. 737.

[25]Paul B. Thornton, "While Some Leaders Succeed and Others Fail," *Leader to Leader* 2011, no. 60, pp. 17–21, the police language was added by the authors, http://web.b.ebscohost.com/ehost/pdfviewer/pdfviewer?sid=f78f7e9f-d762-4092-8e57-90b636995817%40sessionmgr112&vid=8&hid=102 (accessed July 27, 2015).

[26]Schafer, "The Ineffective Police Leader: Acts of Commission and Omission," p. 739.

[27]Ibid., pp. 741–742 with restatement.

[28]Restated from Scott Neumann, "Pennsylvania Police Chief Fired Months after Video Rants," NPR (National Public Radio), September 20, 2013, p.1, http://www.npr.org/sections/thetwo-way/2013/09/20/224462040/pennsylvania-police-chief-fired-months-after-video-rants (accessed July 26, 2015).

[29]No author, "Mark Kessler Claims Video Rants Aimed to Snare Militia Members," LeighValleyLive.com, December 22, 2014, pp. 1–2, http://www.lehighvalleylive.com/breaking-news/index.ssf/2014/12/mark_kessler_claims_video_rant.html.

[30]Ibid., p. 743.

[31]Schafer, "The Ineffective Police Leader: Acts of Commission and Omission," pp. 742–743 with restatement.

[32]Kenneth Blanchard, DreaZigarmi, and Patricia Zigarma, *Leadership and the One-Minute Manager: Increasing Effectiveness Through Situational Leadership* (New York: William Morrow, 1999), p. 38.

[33]This account is drawn with restatement from Martin E. Comas, "Employees Tell Investigators That Ex-Casselberry Police Chief McNeil Bullied, Harassed Them for Years," Orlando Sentinel, July 26, 2015, 3 pp., http://www.orlandosentinel.com/news/breaking-news/os-casselberry-police-harassment-documents-20150226-story.html (accessed July 26, 2015) and Steven Lemongello and Gal TzipermanLotan, "Casselberry Police Chief Bill McNeil Resigns Amid Sexual Misconduct Allegations," Orlando Sentinel, October 30, 2014, 2 pp, http://www.orlandosentinel.com/news/seminole/os-casselberry-police-chief-resigns-20141030-story.html (accessed July 26, 2015).

[34]Drawn with restatement from Elise Schmelzer, "Maypearl Police Chief Fired After Surrendering on Four Felony Charges Alleging Sexual Relationship with Teen," The Dallas Morning News, July 22, 2015, 3 pp., http://crime-blog.dallasnews.com/2015/07/maypearl-police-chief-surrenders-on-four-felony-charges-alleging-sexual-relation-with-teen.html (accessed July 26, 2015) and Jason Whitely and Monica Hernandez, "Former Maypearl Police Chief Surrenders on Child Sex Charges," WFAA8 ABC, July 23, 2015, 3 pp, http://www.wfaa.com/story/news/crime/2015/07/22/maypearl-police-chief-surrenders-on-five-felony-charges/30519815 (accessed July 26, 2015).

[35]Jean Lipman-Blumen, *The Allure of Toxic Leaders* (New York: Oxford University Press, 2005), pp. 19–20.

[36]Ibid., pp. 21–22.

[37]Melissa Horner, "Leadership Theory: Past, Present, and Future," *Team Performance Management*, Vol. 3, No. 4, (1997), p. 276.

[38]Max Weber, *The Theory of Social and Economic Organizations*, translated by A. M. Henderson and Talcott Parsons, (New York: Free Press, 1947), p. 328.

[39]Jacques Steinberg, "Police Officer Rejects Promotion," The *New York Times* (June 2, 1991). Although an older example, it is a perfect illustration of the point made in the text.

[40]J. R. French and B. Raven, "The Bases of Social Power," in D. Cartwright (ed.) *Studies in Social Power* (Ann Arbor: University of Michigan, Institute for Social Research, 1959), pp. 150–167.

[41]Chester Barnard also wrote on organizations as an open system. See *The Functions of the Executive* (Cambridge, MA: Harvard University Press, 15th ed., 1962). *Functions* was originally published in 1938. On many points he must be read in the context of his own time. See Steven M. Dunphy and James Hoopes, "Chester Barnard: Member of

the Elite?" *Management Decision*, Vol. 40, No. 10 (2002), pp. 1024–1028.

[42]The flip side of the coin is the question "Under what conditions do organizational members voluntarily elect to leave, stay and protest, or simply stay?" An important book addressing these issues is Albert O. Hirschman, *Exit, Voice, and Loyalty* (Cambridge, MA: Harvard University Press, 1970).

[43]Isenberg, *Police Leadership in a Democracy: Conversations with America's Police Chiefs*, p. 119.

[44]The description of power motivation styles is drawn, with restatement into a police context, from Jay Hall and James Hawker, "Interpreting Your Scores from the Power Management Inventory" (The Woodlands, Texas: Teleometrics International, 2000).

[45]See Joe C. Magee and Carrie A. Langer, "How Personalized and Socialized Power Motivation Facilitate Antisocial and Prosocial Decision Making," *Journal of Research in Personality* 42, No. 6 (December 2008), pp. 1547–1559.

[46]The basic model is drawn from Robert Katz, "Skills of an Effective Administrator," *Harvard Business Review*, Vol. 33, No. 1 (1955), pp. 33–42. It continues to draw attention; see Robert L. Katz, "Skills of an Effective Administrator" (Cambridge, MA: Harvard Business Review, 2005).

[47]There is no shortage of skill models. For example, see Troy V. Mumford, Michael A. Campion, and Frederick P. Morgeson," The Leadership Skills Strataplex: Leadership Skill Requirements Across Organizational Levels, *The Leadership Quarterly*, Vol. 18 (2007), pp. 154–166. The model uses four skills: factors: cognitive, interpersonal, business, and strategic. See p. 156.

[48]No author, "Leadership Trends for 2010," *Business Week Online* (February 17, 2010), p. 1k.

[49]Anna Davies, Devin Fidler, Marina Gorbis, *Future Work Skills 2020* (Palo Alto, California, Institute for the University of Phoenix Research Institute, 2011), pp. 5,6, and 9.

[50]Thomas Carlyle, *Heroes, Hero-Worship and the Heroic in History* (New York: A. L. Burt, 1902) and G. W. F. Hegel, *The Philosophy of History* (Indianapolis: Bobbs-Merrill, 1952).

[51]See R. D. Avery et al., "Developmental and Genetic Determinants of Leadership Role Occupancy among Women," *Journal of Applied Psychology*, Vol. 92, No. 3 (2007), pp. 693–706.

[52]Francis Galton, *Hereditary Genius: An Inquiry into Its Laws and Consequences* (New York: D. Appleton, revised with an American preface, 1887).

[53]Gary Yukl, *Leadership in Organizations* (Upper Saddle River, NJ: Prentice Hall, 2010), p. 190.

[54]Field Marshal Montgomery, *The Path to Leadership* (New York: Putnam, 1961), pp. 10–19. To some extent, Montgomery also holds with Carlyle in that the former asserted that the leader must be able to dominate and master the surrounding events.

[55]W. Allport and H. S. Odbert, "Trait-Names: A Psycholexical Study," *Psychological Monographs*, 47, No. 211 (1936).

[56]Ralph M. Stogdill, *Handbook of Leadership: A Survey of Theory and Research* (New York: Free Press, 1974), p. 81 and "Personality Factors Associated with Leadership: A Survey of the Literature," *Journal of Psychology*, pp. 25–26 (January 1948), pp. 35–71.

[57]Cecil Goode, "Significant Research on Leadership," *Personnel* 25, No. 5 (1951), p. 349.

[58]For example, see Robert J. Allio, "Leadership—The Five Big Ideas," *Strategy and Leadership*, Vol. 37, No. 2 (2009), p. 412.

[59]Stephen Erdle et al., "The General Factor of Personality and Its Relation to Self-Esteem," *Personality and Individual Differences*, Vol. 48 (2010), p. 344.

[60]Stephen J. Zaccaro, "Trait-Based Perspectives of Leadership," *American Psychologist*, Vol. 62, No. 1 (January 2007), p. 14, on-line access.

[61]Reuven Bar-On, "The Bar-On Model of Emotional-Social Intelligence," in P. Berrocal and N. Extremera, Guest Editors, Special Issue on Emotional Intelligence, *Psicothema*, Vol. 17 (2005), p. 15.

[62]Lynda, Jiwen Song et al., "The Differential Effects of General Mental Ability and Emotional Intelligence on Academic Performance and Social Interactions," *Intelligence*, Vol. 38, No. 1 (January 2010), pp. 137–143.

[63]Melanie B. Malterer, Samantha Glass, and Joseph Newman, "Psychotherapy and Trait Emotional Intelligence," *Personality and Individual Differences*, Vol. 44, No. 3 (February 2008), pp. 733–743.

[64]Oluremi Ayoko, Victor Callan, and Charmine Hartel, "The Influence of Emotional Intelligence Climate on Conflict and Team Members' Reactions to Conflict," *Small Group Research*, Vol. 39, No. 2 (April 2008), pp. 121–149.

[65]A. Oyesoji Aremu and T. Oluwayemisi, "Assessment of Emotional Intelligence Among Nigerian Police," *Journal of Social Science*, Vol. 16, No. 3 (2008), p. 275.

[66]OluremiAyoko, Victor Callan, and CharmineHartel, "The Influence of Emotional Intelligence Climate on Conflict and Team Members' Reactions to Conflict," *Small Group Research*, Vol. 39, Issue 2, (April 2008), pp. 121–149.

[67]Kathryn L. Barbera et al., "Relating Emotional and Social Intelligence to Sex and Age," Nevada State Psychological Association Meeting, Las Vegas, May 17, 2003, p. 3.

[68]Reuven Bar-On, "Emotional Intelligence: An Integral Part of Positive Psychology," *South African Journal of Psychology*, Vol. 40, No. 1 (April 2010), p. 46.

[69]Ronald E. Riggio and Rebecca J. Reichard, "The Emotional and Social Intelligences of Effective Leadership," *Journal of Managerial Psychology*, Vol. 23, No. 2 (2008), p. 171.

[70]Ibid., pp. 172–173, 175–176.

[71]John D. Mayer and Peter Salovey, "What Is Emotional Intelligence?" in Peter Salovey and D. Sluyter (eds.), *Emotional Development and Emotional Intelligence* (New York: Basic Books, 1997), p. 10.

[72]FatihTepe, Leadership Characteristics Among Command, Middle, and Line Level Police Department Personnel in the Era of Terrorism, Dissertation Abstracts International, *The Humanities and Social Sciences*, Vol. 69, No. 7 (2002), p. 2564, 2009.

[73]Kuldeep et al. "Linking the Big Five Personality Domains to Organizational Citizenship Behavior," *International Journal of Psychological Studies*, Vol. 1, No. 2 (December 2009), p. 73.

[74]Suzy Fox, Paul E. Spector, and Don Miles, "Counter Productive Work Behavior in Response to Job Stressors and Organizational Justice," *Journal of Vocational Behavior*, Vol. 59 (2001), p. 292.

[75]Ibid., p. 297.

[76]Jennifer M. George and Garth R. Jones, *Organizational Behavior* (Addison-Wesley Publishing Company, 1999), p. 41.

[77]Gary Dessler, *Organization and Management: A Contingency Approach* (Englewood Cliffs, NJ: Prentice Hall, 1976), p. 158.

[78]See K. Lewin, R. Lippitt, and R. White, "Patterns of Aggressive Behavior in Experimentally Created Social Climates," *Journal of Social Psychology* 10 (May 1939), pp. 271–299; R. Lippitt and R. K. White, "The Social Climate of Children's Groups," in R. G. Baker, K. S. Kounin, and H. F. Wright (eds.), *Child Behavior and Development* (New York: McGraw-Hill, 1943), pp. 485–508; Ralph White and Ronald Lippitt, "Leader Behavior and Member Reaction in Three Social Climates," in Dorwin Cartwright and Alvin Zander (eds.), *Group Dynamics: Research and Theory*, 2nd ed. (New York: Harper & Row, 1960), pp. 552–553; and Ronald Lippitt, "An Experimental Study of the Effect of Democratic and Authoritarian Group Atmospheres," *University of Iowa Studies in Child Welfare* 16 (January 1940), pp. 43–195.

[79]Bernard M. Bass and Ronald E. Riggio, *Transformational Leadership* (Mahwah, NJ: Lawrence Erlbaum Associates, 2nd ed., 2006), pp. 8–9.

[80]White and Lippitt, "Leader Behavior," pp. 539–545, 552–553.

[81]Stephen A. Morreale, "Perceived Leader Styles in Law Enforcement," Master's Thesis, Nova Southeastern University, 2002, p. 12, on-line access to abstract.

[82]Robert R. Blake and Jane Mouton, "The Development Revolution in Management Practices," *Journal of the American Society of Training Directors*, Vol. 16, No. 7 (1962), pp. 29–52.

[83]The Ohio State studies date from the mid-1940s and identified the dimensions of consideration and structure; the University of Michigan studies date from the late 1940s and identified employee- and production-centered supervisors.

[84]Anthony Downs, *Inside Bureaucracy* (Boston: Little, Brown, 1967).

[85]Ibid., pp. 92–96.

[86]Ibid., pp. 96–101.

[87]Ibid., pp. 109–110.

[88]Ibid., pp. 107–109.

[89]John Van Maanen, "Making Rank: Becoming an American Police Sergeant," *Urban Life* 13, No. 2–3 (1984), pp. 155–176. The distinction between station and street sergeants is drawn from Van Maanen's work with some restatement and extension of views. The speculation about future career patterns is the work of the present authors.

[90]Robert Tannenbaum and Warren Schmidt, "How to Choose a Leadership Pattern," *Harvard Business Review*, (May/June,1973), pp. 162–180.

[91]Victor H. Vroom and Philip W. Yetton, *Leadership and Decision-Making* (Pittsburgh: University of Pittsburgh Press, 1973), p. 18.

[92]John B. Miner, *Organizational Behavior* (New York: Oxford University Press, 2002), pp. 320–321.

[93]Gary Yukl, "Toward a Behavioral Theory of Leadership," *Organizational Behavior and Human Performance*, Vol. 6, No. 4 (July 1971), p. 434.

[94]Fred E. Fiedler and Joseph E. Garcia, *New Approaches to Effective Leadership* (New York: John Wiley & Sons, 1987), pp. 52–61.

[95]Afsaneh Nahavandi and Ali R. Malekzadeh, *Organizational Behavior* (Upper Saddle River, NJ: Prentice Hall, 1999), pp. 305–306.

[96]Robert P. Vecchio, "An Empirical Examination of the Validity of Fiedler's Model of Leadership Effectiveness," *Organizational Behavior and Human Performance*, Vol. 19, No. 1 (June 1977), p. 203.

[97]R. W. Rice, "Construct Validity of the Least Preferred Coworker Scale," *Psychological Bulletin*, Vol. 85, No. 6 (November 1978), pp. 1199–1237.

[98]Lawrence H. Peters, Darrell D. Hartke, and John T. Pohlmann, "Fiedler's Contingency Model," *Psychological Bulletin*, Vol. 95, No. 2 (March 1985), pp. 274–285.

[99]*New Approaches to Effective Leadership*, pp. 76–77.

[100]John K. Kennedy, Jr., "Middle LPC Leaders and the Contingency Model of Leadership Effectiveness," *Organizational Behavior and Human Performance*, Vol. 30, No. 1 (August 1982), pp. 1–14.

[101]Yukl, *Leadership in Organizations*, p. 228.

[102]R. J. House, "A Path Goal Theory of Leadership Effectiveness," *Administrative Science Quarterly*, Vol. 16 (1971), pp. 321–329.

[103]Robert J. House, "Path-Goal Theory of Leadership: Lessons, Legacy, and a Reformulated Theory," *The Leadership Quarterly*, Vol. 7, No. 3 (Autumn 1996), p. 325.

[104]L. Huberts, M. Kaptein, and K. Lasthuizen, "A Study of the Impact of Three Leadership Styles on Integrity Violations by Police Officers," *Policing*, Vol. 30, No. 4 (November 2007), pp. 587–606. The findings are based on the responses of Netherlands police officers.

[105]"Path-Goal Theory of Leadership: Lessons, Legacy, and a Reformulated Theory," p. 348.

[106]Ibid., p. 347.

[107]Although not using the LMX designation, the first articulation of it was Fred Dansereau, George Graen, and William J. Haga, "A Vertical Dyad Linkage Approach to Leadership within Formal Organizations," *Organizational Behavior and Human Performance*, Vol. 13 (1975), pp. 46–78.

[108]The descriptions of these two groups are drawn from Jun Liu and Xiaogu Liu, "A Critical Review of Leadership Research Development," *International Journal of Business and Management*, Vol. 1, No. 4 (August 2006), pp. 7–8.

[109]George Graen and M. Uhl-Bien, "Relationship Based Approach to Leadership: Development of a Leader-Member Exchange (LMX) Theory of Leadership Over 25 Years," *Leadership Quarterly*, Vol. 6, pp. 219–247. The concepts were not clearly defined and understanding of them was partially derived by the context in which they were used. Our characterization of the authors' work is our best understanding of what they intended.

[110]J. Miner, "The Uncertain Future of the Leadership Concept," in James Hunt and Lars Larson (eds.), *Leadership Frontiers* (Kent, OH: Kent State University Press, 1975).

[111]Steven Kerr and John M. Jermier, "Substitutes of Leadership: Their Meaning and Measurement," *Organizational Behavior and Human Performance*, Vol. 22, No. 3 (1978), pp. 377, 395.

[112]Margaret L. Williams and Philip Podsakoff, "A Preliminary Analysis of the Construct Validity of Kerr and Jermier's Substitutes of Leadership Scales," *Journal of Occupational Psychology*, Vol. 61, No. 4 (1988), pp. 307–333.

[113]R. J. Lewicki, E. C. Wiethoff, and E. Tomlinson, "What Is the Role of Trust in Organizational Justice?" in Jerald Greenberg and Jason Colquitt (eds.), *Handbook of Organizational Justice* (Mahwah, NJ: Lawrence Erlbaum Associates, 2005), pp. 247–270.

[114]Hersey and Blanchard, *Management of Organizational Behavior*, pp. 160–161.

[115]Ibid.

[116]Ibid., p. 163.

[117]bid., p. 161.

[118]Ibid., p. 163.

[119]bid., p. 159.

[120]Thomas D. Cairns et al., "Technical Note: A Study of Hersey and Blanchard's Situational Theory," *Journal of Leadership and Organization Development*, Vol. 19, No. 2 (1998), pp. 113–116.

[121]Bernard M. Bass with Ruth Bass, *The Bass Handbook of Leadership* (New York: Free Press, 2008), p. 493.

[122]Yukl, *Leadership in Organizations*, p. 99.

[123]James McGregor Burns, *Leadership* (New York: Harper & Row, 1978).

[124]Ibid., pp. 4, 19–20.

[125]Yukl, *Leadership in Organizations*, p. 261.

[126]Bass and Bass, *The Bass Handbook of Leadership*, p. 619.

[127]Steven A. Murphy and Edward N. Drodge, "The Four Is of Police Leadership," *International Journal of Police Science and Management*, Vol. 6, No. 1 (March 2004), pp. 1–15.

[128]See B. M. Bass, *Leadership and Performance* (New York: Free Press, 1985).

[129]V. R. Krishan, "Transformational Leadership and Outcomes," *International Journal of Value Based Management*, Vol. 25, No. 5/6 (2005), pp. 19–33.

[130]Bass and Riggio, *Transformational Leadership*, p. 3.

[131]Ronald F. Piccolo and Jason A. Colquitt, "Transformational Leadership and Job Behaviors," *Academy of Management Journal*, Vol. 49, No. 2 (2006), p. 327.

[132]Simon A. Moss and Somon Ngu, *Current Research in Social Psychology*, Vol. 11, No. 6 (2006), p. 71.

[133]Isenberg, *Police Leadership in a Democracy: Conversations with America's Police Chiefs*, p. 115.

[134]Ibid.

[135]Bass and Riggio, *Transformational Leadership*, p. 228.

[136]Ibid., pp. 228–229.

[137]Hersey and Blanchard, *Management of Organizational Behavior*, p. 163.

[138]Pat Welsh, "Are You a Warrior, Servant, and Leader?" Law Enforcement Today, January 3, 2014, 3, http://www.lawenforcementtoday.com/2014/01/03/are-you-a-warrior-servant-and-leader (accessed August 1, 2015).

[139]Lee Whittington et al., "Transactional Leadership Revisited," *Journal of Applied Social Psychology*, Vol. 39, No. 8 (August 2009), pp. 1860–1886.

[140]Yi-Feng Yang, "An Investigation of Group Interaction Functioning Stimulated by Transformational Leadership on Employee Intrinsic and Extrinsic Job Satisfaction," *Social Behavior and Personality*, Vol. 37, No. 9 (2009), pp. 1259–1277.

[141]Fehmidah Munir, Karina Nielsen, and Isabella Gomes, "Transformational Leadership and Depressive Symptoms," *Journal of Affective Disorders*, Vol. 120, No. 1–3 (January 2010), pp. 235–239.

[142]Rajinandini Pillai and Ethlyn Williams, "Transformational Leadership, Self-Efficacy, Group Cohesiveness, Commitment, and Performance," *Journal of Organizational Change Management*, Vol. 17, No. 2 (2004), pp. 144–159.

[143]Rabia Khan, Abaid Ur Rehman, and Afsheen Fatima, "Transformational Leadership and Organizational Commitment," *African Journal of Business Management*, Vol. 3, No. 11 (November 2009), p. 683.

[144]Roya Ayman and Karen Korabik, "Why Gender and Culture Matter," *American Psychologist*, Vol. 65, No. 3 (April 2010), p. 164.

[145]Mary Sarver, Holly Miller, and Jennifer Schulenberg, "Leadership and Effectiveness: An Examination of the Leadership Styles of Texas Police Chiefs," Paper presented at the 2008 Annual Meeting of the American Society of Criminology, St. Louis, on-line access of abstract.

[146]Steven A. Murphy and Edward N. Drodge, "The Four Is of Police Leadership," *International Journal of Police Science and Management*, Vol. 6, No. 1 (2004), p. 10. The description of all Four Is is drawn from this source.

[147]Yukl, *Leadership in Organizations*, p. 262.

[148]Ibid., pp. 272–274.

[149]Ibid., p. 285.

[150]Ibid., pp. 261 and 285–286.

[151]Robert J. House and Ram N. Aditya, "The Social Scientific Study of Leadership: Quo Vadis?" *Journal of Management*, Vol. 23 (May/June 1997), pp. 409–473.

[152]Robert K. Greenleaf, *Servant Leadership* (Mahwah, NJ: The Paulist Press, 1977), p. 13.

[153]Yukl, *Leadership in Organizations*, p. 419.

[154]A. Gregory Stone, Robert Russell, and Kathleen Patterson, "Transformational Leadership: A Difference in Leader Focus," *Leadership and Organization Development*, Vol. 25, No. 4 (2003), pp. 349–361.

[155]Larry Spears, "Practicing Servant-Leadership," *Lead to Leader Journal*, No. 34 (2004), approximately three pp., on-line access. The authors have restated portions of these 10 points and added commentary. No alteration of the author's position is intended.

[156]Pat Welsh, "Are You a Warrior, Servant, or Leader?" Law Enforcement Today, January 3, 2014, http://www.lawenforcementtoday.com/2014/01/03/are-you-a-warrior-servant-and-leader, accessed April 19, 2016.

[157]Yukl, *Leadership in Organizations*, p. 421.

[158]For example, see John E. Barbuto, Jr., "Scale Development and Construct Clarification of Servant Leadership," *Group and Organization Development*, Vol. 31, No. 3 (2006), pp. 300–326.

[159]Mark McKergow, "Host Leadership," *International Journal of Leadership in Public Services*, Vol. 5, No. 1 (March 2009), p. 20.

[160]Deborah Eicher-Catt, "The Myth of Servant-Leadership: A Feminist Perspective," *Women and Language*, Vol. 28, No. 1 (Spring 2005), pp. 17–25.

[161]Yukl, *Leadership in Organizations*, p. 421.

[162]Bruce J. Avolio, Fred O. Walumbwa, and Todd J. Wheeler, "Leadership: Current Theories, Research, and Future Directions," *The Annual Review of Psychology* (2009), p. 438.

[163]Cathy Lynn Grossman, "Survey: 72% of Millennials 'More Spiritual than Religious,'" *USA Today* (April 27, 2010).

[164]Louis W. Fry, "Toward a Theory of Spiritual Leadership," *The Leadership Quarterly*, Vol. 14 (2003), p. 702.

[165]Toward a Theory of Spiritual Leadership,"pp. 703–705,716.

[166]Ibid., pp. 702–705, 711.

[167]Yukl, *Leadership in Organizations*, p. 422.

[168]Laura Reave, "Spiritual Values and Practices Related to Leadership Effectiveness," *The Leadership Quarterly*, Vol. 16, No. 5 (October 2005), pp. 655–687.

[169]Frank Markow and Karin Klenke, "The Effects of Personal Meaning and Calling on Organizational Commitment: An Empirical Investigation of Spiritual Leadership," *International Journal of Organizational Analysis*, Vol. 13, No. 1 (2005), pp. 8–27.

[170]Maragret Benefiel, "The Second Half of the Journey," *The Leadership Quarterly*, Vol. 16, No. 5 (October 2005), p. 727.

[171]Fry, "Toward a Theory of Spiritual Leadership," pp. 715–716.

[172]William L. Gardner et al., "Can You See the Real Me?" *The Leadership Quarterly*, Vol. 16 (2005), p. 344.

[173]Cecily Cooper, Terri Scandura, and Chester Schriesheim, "Looking Forward But Learning from Our Past: Potential Challenges to Developing Authentic Leadership Theory and Authentic Leaders," *The Leadership Quarterly*, Vol. 16, No. 3 (June 2005), p. 478.

[174]Bruce J. Avolio and William A. Gardner, "Authentic Leadership Development: Getting to the Root of Positive Forms of Leadership," *The Leadership Quarterly*, Vol. 16, No. 3 (June 2005), p. 327.

[175]Ibid., p. 328.

[176]Cooper, Scandura, and Schriesheim, "Looking Forward But Learning from Our Past: Potential Challenges to Developing Authentic Leadership Theory and Authentic Leaders," pp. 481–483.

[177]Yukl, *Leadership in Organizations*, p. 427.

[178]M. E. Brown et al., "Ethical Leadership," *Organizational Behavior and Human Decision Processes*, Vol. 97 (2005), p. 120.

[179]Michael E. Brown and Linda K. Trevino, "Ethical Leadership: A Review and Future Directions," *The Leadership Quarterly*, Vol. 17, No. 6 (December 2006), p. 599.

[180]Ibid., p. 600.

[181]Ibid., pp. 610–611.

[182]Yukl, *Leadership in Organizations*, p. 416.

CHAPTER EIGHT

PLANNING AND DECISION MAKING

Learning Objectives

1. Explain what planning is expected to accomplish.

2. Define what a plan is.

3. Discuss synoptic planning.

4. Identify the specific elements of administrative, procedural, operational, tactical, and strategic plans.

5. Discuss what planning can be expected to accomplish.

6. State Simon's concept of "bounded rationality."

7. Explain Lindblom's incremental decision making.

8. Describe Gore's decision-making process.

9. Explain the concept of the thin-slicing theory.

10. State the advantages of group decision making.

11. Discuss the liabilities of group decision making.

12. Explain the concept of brainstorming.

INTRODUCTION

PLANNING AND DECISION MAKING are both critical processes for effective police administration and are inextricably intertwined. These two processes are important steps toward establishing the direction and operation of a police department. Often, planning is precipitated by recognizing that a problem, either small or large, exists that needs to be addressed. That situation is sometimes called problem-oriented planning.

Although natural and man-made disasters may not occur with regularity in a jurisdiction, there is still a need for effective planning and decision making that may save lives and reduce property losses. A well-prepared plan on the shelf is more valuable, even if it is never needed, than an extemporaneous plan created in haste. Planning is seldom a wasted effort although some events may briefly overcome it, such as a series of large organizational changes conducted too rapidly, which can confuse law enforcement officers about their roles and responsibilities and new missions thrust on agencies like homeland security. Even if a specific plan has not been developed to address an unanticipated crisis having experience in dealing with the planning process in general can be very valuable experience. A classic example of this is when Apollo 13 was nearing the moon and was rocked by a series of events that made the survival of the crew very uncertain. It was only through continuous and improvised planning by the National Aeronautic and Space Administration (NASA) over 3 days that got the crew safely home.

In this chapter, we will examine elements of the planning and decision-making process. This will include the following: (1) planning; (2) planning as a process; (3) planning and time orientations; (4) synoptic planning; (5) other categories of plans; (6) the blending of the five types of planning; (7) decision making; (8) the use of computers in the decision-making process; (9) decision making during crisis events; (10) group decision making; (11) ethics and decision making; (12) common errors in decision making; and (13) improving decision making.

PLANNING

The planning landscape is crowded with many approaches to that task, as well as the associated techniques. Together, they range from simple/basic, but effective schemes, to those that are heavily based on statistical analysis. While many organizations know the value of planning and do it well, others discover too late that their planning is woefully inadequate.

For example, the BP oil spill in the Gulf of Mexico in 2010 reflects a lack of in-depth planning. BP had template procedures to address emergency situations, but when an oil rig explosion blew out an underwater well, the company took nearly 12 days to formulate its first plan of attack. The templates failed to consider, or adequately anticipate, an accident of such magnitude. The result was that a catastrophic amount of oil spilled into the Gulf, contaminating coastlines and wildlife around portions of the Gulf Coast. Consider what would happen if police organizations took a similar approach to planning, for example, stopping to formulate a response to a complex and fluid situation like the 2013 active shooter who murdered 12 people at the Navy Yard in Washington, DC (discussed in greater detail later in this chapter). In such cases, there is simply not enough time to stop operations while adjustments are made to a basic template.

Some police administrators may not have a full appreciation of the importance of planning because of their pattern of career development. If they have spent substantial portions of their careers in line divisions, such as patrol and investigative services, they may be field oriented to the degree that staff functions, such as planning, do not receive the executive attention or support that they deserve.

Planning is one of the most critical ingredients for the success of any organizational undertaking.[1] Police leaders must fully embrace the planning process in order to resolve

Quick Facts: The Apollo 13 Mission

On this much-analyzed mission, the problems started when oxygen tank No. 2 blew up, causing the No. 1 tank to also fail. The command module's normal supply of electricity, light, and water was lost, and they were about 200,000 miles from Earth. Visit NASA at https://www.nasa.gov/mission_pages/apollo/missions/apollo13.html#.Vb6f1zBViko to learn what happened.

problems and be prepared for the future. Sound planning and programs can reduce the opportunity for crimes to occur, as well as prevent some other unknown number of crises from occurring or at least to handle them more efficiently when they do occur, for example, hurricanes, earthquakes, forest fires. Arguably, law enforcement agencies that are perpetually in crisis suffer from the absence of good leadership and have either no planning function or an unsupported and overwhelmed one. Such factors foster an environment where crisis is unfortunately predictable and further supported by an orientation that is too past or present oriented and only minimally oriented to the future, the proverbial "short time horizon." In contrast, effective planning can be expected to accomplish the following:

1. Improve/strengthen the analysis of problems.
2. Provide better information and data for decision making.
3. Help to clarify goals, objectives, and priorities.
4. Foster a more effective allocation of resources.
5. Improve inter- and intradepartmental co-operation and coordination.
6. Enhance the performance of programs.
7. Clearly communicate the department's direction to all employees, other agencies, and the public.
8. Generate opportunities for community engagement.
9. Increase the commitment of personnel by involving them.

In short, competent planning is a sure sign of good police administration and enhances the ability of an administrator to make more effective and efficient decisions.[2]

PLANNING AS A PROCESS

The word **planning** achieved prominence in the vocabulary of criminal justice agencies when the federal grant-awarding Omnibus Crime Control and Safe Streets Act of 1968 became law. However, what was missing from that document was an explanation of what planning actually involved or what it meant in the operation of criminal justice organizations. A plan essentially is a decision about a future course of action. The briefest definition of a plan is "How we get from here to there." Weiss[3] asserts that a primary purpose of planning is in evaluation, comparing "what is" with "what should be." Hudzik and Cordner[4] defined planning as "thinking about the future, thinking about what we want the future to be, and thinking about what we need to do now to achieve it." Stated more succinctly, planning involves linking present actions to future conditions. Mottley views planning as

> a management function concerned with visualizing future situations, making estimates concerning them, identifying the issues, needs and potential danger points, analyzing and evaluating the alternative ways and means for reaching desired goals according to a certain schedule, estimating the

necessary funds and resources to do the work, and initiating action in time to prepare what may be needed to cope with changing conditions and contingent events.[5]

The SITAR Approaches to Planning

Planning can also be defined by the approaches used and they are sometimes referred to by the acronym SITAR:

1. **Synoptic**—This is a rational approach and still the dominant planning process in policing and elsewhere. Its roots are in England where rudimentary planning became an essential part of the Industrial Revolution (1760–1850). As society took advantage of manufacturing, people left their farms to find work in rapidly growing cities. Because the synoptic model is the dominant approach, it is also covered in greater detail in a subsequent section of this chapter.

2. **Incremental**—In 1959, Lindblom developed the concept of "muddling through" that challenged the notion of rationality in policymaking. In his view, policy decisions are made on the basis of "muddling through" or a series of limited comparisons of policy options, which reduces rationality. When muddling through is applied to planning in law enforcement agencies and other organizations, the result is small, incremental changes made to existing plans. This perpetuates the status quo by making plans evolutionary but not revolutionary. It is disjointed because there are no larger, more comprehensive considerations and as a consequence incremental planning, which is more "now focused" than future oriented, is used.

3. **Transactive**—This relies on acquiring face-to-face knowledge of people's problems and not those of some anonymous group's. It focuses largely on obtaining data by conversations with members of the target population. To some degree, community policing reflects transactive planning.

4. **Advocacy**—This model rests on the adversarial process of the legal profession and is usually applied to help the weak and disadvantaged against powerful interests, for example, government and business. In doing so, advocacy implicitly incorporates a more political view of planning. Paul Davidoff coined the term advocacy planning in 1965.

5. **Radical**—This rests on the notion that planning is most effective when done by lay people on neighborhood committees that best know their own problems. Ideally, those people feel empowered to collectively address their own problems. At its heart, radical planning incorporates Marxist thinking. Part of radical planning's bias is an almost urgent need to change the status quo.

PLANNING AND TIME ORIENTATIONS

One way or another all plans have a time orientation and we instinctively think of them as being future oriented. A budget is a plan stated in financial terms; most law enforcement agencies have a 1-year operational budget (see Chapter 11, Financial Management). Strategic plans are multi-year plans of usually 3 to 5 years. Tankha identified four types of planning approach based on their time orientations. These approaches are "pure" in nature and in actual practice several of them may be practiced in a single agency.[6]

1. **Inactive Planning.** Law enforcement agencies that do little or no real planning and the process is markedly underemployed or altogether dormant implicitly rely on the **inactive planning** approach. Its underlying assumption is that things will continue to be as they are and it will be "business as usual." Its time orientation is substantially rooted in the present under the assumption that it's better than the past and not as dangerous as the uncertainties of the future. There is no systematic scanning of the environment to detect new opportunities. Such agencies are change resistant, even in the face of community calls for new responses to crime. In trying to sustain things as they are now, while the world around the agency changes, it is more likely than not that their services will degrade over time.

2. **Reactive planning.** As its name suggests, it is in reaction to problems that have recently occurred and are being addressed or are presently happening and require an immediate response. It is both past and present oriented. Reactive departments are not leaders in innovation and are generally slow to change. Characteristically, reactive agencies make incremental changes cautiously, using the back edge of leading thoughts and technology. However, there are two exceptions to this:

   (1) They react as swiftly as possible to strong social/community pressures, such as issuing body-worn cameras to all of their uniformed officers, allowing more citizen participation in crime reduction efforts, or putting more video surveillance cameras in crime hot-spots.

   (2) Also, assuming hypothetically that the federal Occupational Safety and Health Administration (OSHA) issued new guidelines on how certain classes of physical evidence such as body fluids should be collected and stored, the reactive agency would quickly mobilize resources to be in compliance.

3. **Preactive planning.** This is centered on the future, attempting to predict changes in the larger environment. Once armed with this knowledge, preactive police agencies use it to acquire the skills and competencies they need in the future they envision.

4. **Proactive planning.** This model has some similarities with the preactive, for example, interactively engaging government agencies, examining "think tank" publications, assessing demographic analyses, criminal use of recent technological developments or combinations of them, for example, terrorists using drones to launch attacks, labor statistics, and other sources. Where the preactive and proactive agencies part company is when the latter attempts to change anticipated future events that are likely to occur. For example, assume that a city's population of individuals who are between 18 and 24 years of age is expected to increase by 24 percent over the next 3 years because a new technical college opened 17 months ago with several majors geared to skills needed for the two software development companies that have just relocated there. Another major computer industry company is also considering relocating to the city. With all the positive things these developments will bring, there are also some negatives. The population increase among younger adults falls into the 15–24 age range that is highly victimized and also commits a large share of crimes. Just on this one issue the police department is searching for strategies and programs that will mediate those facts and thereby change the future. There are also other types of plans that are identified in the appropriate sections that follow.

SYNOPTIC PLANNING

Synoptic planning, or the rational comprehensive approach, is the dominant tradition in planning. It is also the point of departure for most other planning approaches, which in general are either modifications of synoptic planning or reactions against it. The classic and most basic synoptic model had four steps: (1) goal setting, (2) identification of alternatives, (3) evaluation of the means against the end, and (4) implementation of decision. Figure 8.1 represents a common version of the synoptic model. It is theoretically based on "pure" or "objective" rationality and attempts to ensure optimal achievement of desired goals from a given situation.[7] It can be more or less labor intensive depending how "deep" each component is considered.

This model is especially appropriate for police agencies, as it accommodates a problem-oriented approach to planning. It relies heavily on the problem identification and analysis phase of the planning process and can assist police administrators in formulating goals and priorities in terms that are focused on specific problems and solutions that often confront law enforcement.

Steps in Synoptic Planning

The steps in synoptic planning are designed to provide those involved in the planning process with a logical course of action as the model unfolds.[8] Using Figure 8.1 as a reference, a discussion of those steps follows:

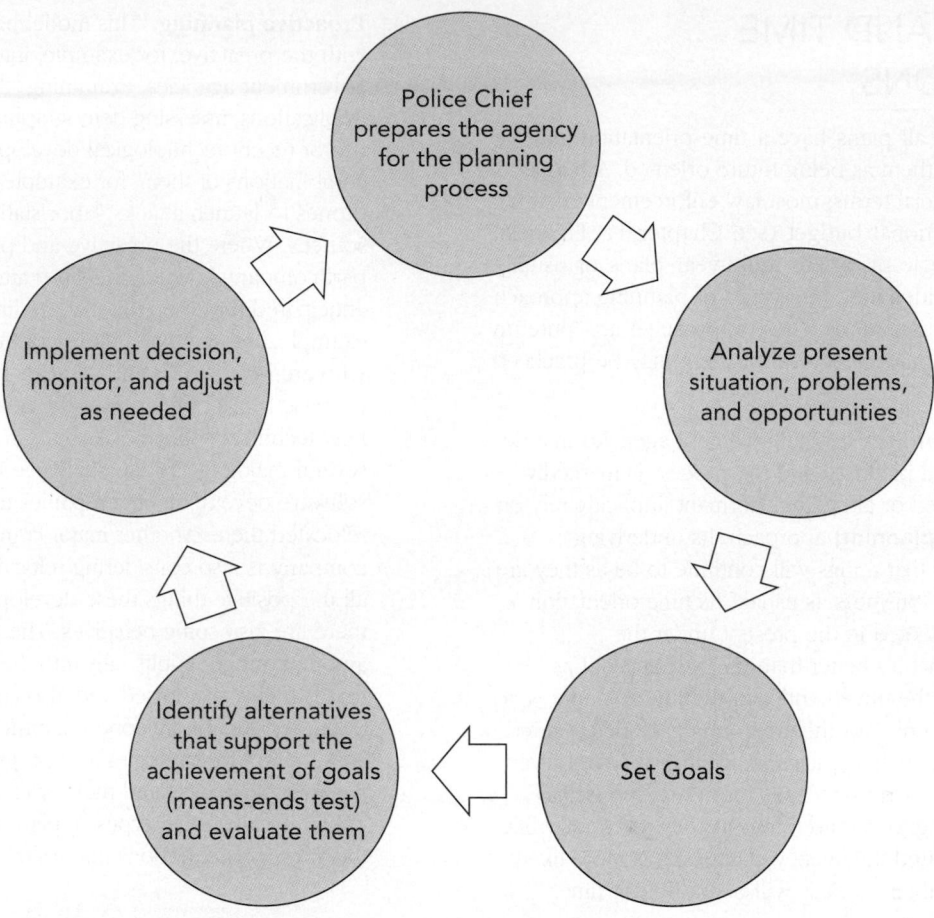

FIGURE 8.1 ▶ The Synoptic Planning Model.

Preparation for Planning. It is during this step that the police chief focuses the planning effort by issuing a memorandum that describes its organization, goals, responsibilities, methods, timeline, and desired results. Unless otherwise determined, for example, planning security for a visiting dignitary, citizen participation in the planning process should be considered essential and in many jurisdictions this is considered a routine matter. It is also fundamental to community policing. Community engagement gives citizens voices about what their police departments do and how they do it, which builds trust. The Chief's memorandum should include mention of any citizen involvement.

Analyze the Present Situation, Problems, and Opportunities. There are multiple sources of information to describe the present situation, problems, and opportunities, for example, citizen surveys of satisfaction with the law enforcement agency's service, program evaluations, auditor reports, staff inspection results, the current history of lawsuits against the department, communications to and from unions, local newspaper coverage of the agency, self-assessment for accreditation or re-accreditation, and the results of the mock assessment prior to the actual visitation by the Commission on Accreditation for Law Enforcement Agencies (CALEA). There are also tools that can be used to assess the broader

environment that are useful in both short-term and strategic planning. One of these tools is the four-quadrant SWOT (strengths, weaknesses, opportunities, and threats) analysis, which was developed by Albert Humphrey at Stanford during the 1960s (see Figure 8.2). Its development is also credited to Edmund Learned, C. Christensen, Kenneth Andrews, and others.

Set Goals. Goals are future conditions or "states" that a police department wants to reach. The rule of thumb is that generally in any year goals may become more attainable by limiting them to roughly five to seven priority ones which can receive concentrated attention and stay firmly in focus. However, that varies by local circumstances. Not all goals are equally important. There is an increased use of "priority goals" in local government to distinguish them from ones that are important but which are not as salient as those designated as priority.

Goals communicate what we hope to become. They lift our vision from the "now" to the future, creating forward motion and driving performance as we strive to reach them. Goals establish a collective sense of responsibility for achieving them, engendering higher performance levels. We like being on winning teams whether it's selling Girl Scout cookies, scavenger hunts, the middle school quiz bowl, or sports. Departmental goals that are achieved provide law enforcement officers with professional satisfaction.

Determining Strengths	Identifying Opportunities
• How does our agency do on UCR Part 1 benchmarks?* • What does the most recent citizen survey tell us about their satisfaction with our services? • Are our previously defined mission-related skills better than average? • Are we properly trained for simultaneous large-scale/multiple shooter events? • What is our present reputation with the administration and political body? • How do our officers place in regional and national athletic, marksmanship, and SWAT competitions?	• What economic, social, technological, or other large-scale external shifts are favorable to us? • What innovations would reduce response time? • How can we meet the community's need for more engagement in crime fighting? • New grants available from the federal Department of Homeland Security that would bolster our capabilities in that area.
Determining Weakness**	**Identifying Threats**
• What programs or activities do not support our mission? • What deficiencies did the most recent financial and program auditors note? • How can we get annual voluntary separations below 9%?	• What economic, social, technological, or other large-scale external shifts are unfavorable to us? • Sworn and civilian salaries are not competitive.
* A benchmark is a comparison against a fixed standard, such as the national average for Uniform Crime Reports (UCR) Part 1 arrests for jurisdictions in our population range or relative to similar sized jurisdictions in our state or region. ** The answers to some questions in determining strengths may fall into this category.	

FIGURE 8.2 ▶ SWOT Analysis for a Law Enforcement Agency.

A goal should be stated in terms that allow progress toward it to be measurable. A goal statement should have three indispensable features: (1) time-phased, (2) quantitative, and (3) target specific. An example of these might be stated as follows: "During the year 2017, the Ocean View Police Department will reduce juvenile violent crimes by 6 percent." A goal may be difficult to achieve but must be realistically attainable. Goals often have subordinate or short-term objectives that represent milestones. For example, a subordinate objective may be stated as follows: In the first 31 days of 2017, the agency will complete the training of 100 percent of its officers who are assigned to field duties in the subject of conflict de-escalation.

Identify Alternatives. A simple truth is that alternative courses of action to reach a goal cannot be identified until a goal is selected. Often, there are several alternatives that are attractive. Generally, alternatives proposed by members of the planning team should be worthy of genuine consideration. However, brainstorming (discussed in detail later in this chapter) is sometimes done with suggestions recorded on a flip chart to get the "creative juices" flowing, including some suggestions that may seem frivolous. In the discussion of the alternatives that follows, some number of them may be quickly discarded, but occasionally a seemingly frivolous alternative may spark conversations that are useful. A more thoughtful session for the generating of alternatives may follow the brain-storming exercise. Some alternatives proposed may be so close together that a discussion may be needed to flesh them out more to see what their fuller version looks like or they may be combinable. When comparing alternatives, there are several easy-to-use tools that can be utilized. For example:

A. The Decision Matrix. This technique was developed by Stuart Pugh (1929–1993) and is both simple and elegant. Its steps are to (1) identify and define the criteria against which all alternatives will be evaluated. Examples of such criteria include cost, sustainability, and compliance with CALEA standards; (2) develop the decision matrix; (3) have each member on the planning team score each alternative on all criteria with the points defined on an accompanying scale; (4) compute the total score for each alternative; and (5) discuss the higher scoring alternatives and make a selection. The scores should be considered carefully but not without some flexibility. This also applies to the results obtained from the second tool discussed in this section. If judiciously used, there is a role for experienced judgment to supplement the results of the decision matrix.

Figure 8.3, the Pugh Decision Matrix worksheet, provides an example. For purpose of illustration, assume that Criterion A is "Increase Receiving Stolen Property Arrests by 15%." The criteria column may be lettered and may have a short definition for each criterion in it. Each criterion and its full definition should be readily viewable on flip charts, handouts, or a PowerPoint to make sure that team members consistently have the definitions before them. A Pugh Decision Matrix worksheet may have another column to the right of the criteria column where importance weights are assigned and which vary according to the perceived value of each criterion. When using weights, the score (see Figure 8.3) assigned to each criterion is multiplied by its associated importance weight. Each member of the planning team would

Date:_____ Rater:_____

Criteria	Scores for Alternative 1	Scores for Alternative 2	Scores for Alternative 3	Scores for Alternative 4
A	+2	+1	+3	+2
B	+2	+2	+3	+2
C	+1	+1	+3	+2
D	+1	+2	+3	+3
E	+2	+1	+1	+2
Total +	+8	+7	+13	+11
Total −	−0	−0	−0	−0
Final Score	+8	+7	+13	+11

The Scoring Scale:
+3 Far more than likely
+2 More than likely
+1 Likely, but no more than that
−1 Likely to fall short
−2 More than likely to fall short
−3 Far more than likely to fall short

FIGURE 8.3 ▶ Example of a Pugh Decision Matrix.

complete the Figure 8.3 worksheet and subsequently all of the scores would be consolidated, displayed, and discussed to reach consensus. During these discussions, some excellent points are made, which may precipitate some rescoring by individuals. If the scores in Figure 8.3 were the averages for all raters, an agency may elect to only do a consensus discussion for Alternatives 3 and 4.

B. The Paired Comparison Method. The earliest writings about paired comparison were those of Witmer and Cohn (1894) and Kitchener (1901).[9] Their technique remains in wide use today with variants ranging from rudimentary to those dependent on statistical analysis.[10] As with the other tools discussed in this section, paired comparisons provide law enforcement decision makers with a systematic way of sorting out which of the alternatives "best" meets their agency's needs. For discussion purposes, there are five raters. A pool/set of criteria must be developed and defined. Hypothetically six of them are generated. The criteria essentially represent the "standards" against which all alternatives are individually evaluated on separate worksheets by decision makers. Figure 8.4 shows an individual worksheet for evaluating the first criterion, "How likely is this alternative to fully meet the goal?"

In Figure 8.4, Alternative A cannot be evaluated against itself, so the first rating involves the judgment whether Alternative A is more likely than Alternative B to meet Criterion 1. Hypothetically, the number on the scale in Figure 8.4 that is consistent with the rater's judgment is entered into

the worksheet; in this illustration it is a "7." Working from left to right across the worksheet, the other two numbers are, in turn, entered, 9 and 9. When the rater completing the worksheet is done entering ratings in the worksheet, the sum of the rows and the standing in the ranks are recorded. Although Alternative C is seemingly in good shape with 27 points, Alternative A has 25 points. There are two things to keep in mind: (1) This is the worksheet for just one of five raters and for this criterion and (2) there are five more criteria to be evaluated for each alternative.

Implement Decision, Monitor, and Adjust the Plan as Needed

The Chief of Police may assign a unit commander or designate a civilian project manager to implement the alternative chosen, depending on the alternative. The purpose of this assignment is to fix responsibility for its monitoring, progress, and success. The planning committee should have laid out an evaluation plan for the alternative selected and made sure the data for it is actually being collected. If some needed evaluation data is not being collected, the evaluation plan must be adjusted on the authority of the person responsible for the implementation of the alternative or by the authorization of any steering committee to which he/she reports and forms devised to capture the data from the very beginning.

Evaluation requires comparing what actually happened with what was planned for—and this may not be a simple undertaking.[11] Feedback must be obtained concerning the results of the implementation of the alternative, as well as the effectiveness and other impacts of it. Hudzik and Cordner[12] point out that evaluation completes one cycle of synoptic

Alternatives	A	B	C	D	Sum of Rows	Rank of Alternative
A		7	9	9	25	2
B	5		7	3	15	3
C	9	9		9	27	1
D	5	5	3		13	4

Scale for Paired Comparison

Scale	Definition	Explanation
1	Less than likely	The evidence does not suggest the possibility
3	Likely	The evidence suggests the possibility
5	More than likely	The evidence suggests a moderate possibility
7	Much more than likely	The evidence suggests a strong possibility
9	Absolutely likely	The evidence suggests a very strong possibility

FIGURE 8.4 ▶ Criterion 1: "How likely is this alternative to fully achieve the goal?"

planning. The need to identify and resolve problems must be considered repetitively.

OTHER CATAGORIES OF PLANS

From an applications perspective, the planning process yields an end product—a plan. These can be categorized by use and are delineated into five groups:[13]

1. Administrative or Management Plans
2. Procedural Plans
3. Operational Plans
4. Tactical Plans
5. Strategic Plans

Administrative or Management Plans

This includes formulation of the department's mission statement, values, goals, and policies and procedures; the organizational structure, the functions, authority, and responsibilities of positions and units; the allocation of resources; sick leave, vacation time, court appearances, and other related topics.

Procedural Plans

This category of plans are ordinarily included as part of a police department's written directive system, a copy of which is assigned to every officer and is updated periodically. Procedural plans are the guidelines for the action to be taken under specific circumstances. For example, this could include the following: proper application of the use of force; responding to bank robberies; evidence handling; when and how to utilize canine teams; responding to domestic violence calls; informant management and dozens of other similar police matters.

Operational Plans

These are often called work plans and describe specific actions to be taken by line units (patrol officers, precinct groups, and/or division teams). Work plans are usually short and terse, giving both direction and time constraints in accomplishing a given task. In community policing ventures, the work plan usually focuses on a defined community need in a specific neighborhood.

Tactical Plans

These involve planning for emergencies of a specific nature at known locations. Some tactical plans are developed in anticipation of such emergencies as the taking of hostages at a prison or a jailbreak and are subject to modification or being discarded altogether in peculiar and totally unanticipated circumstances. Other tactical plans are developed for specific situations as they arise, such as how to relate to a demonstration in the park or a march on city hall as well as hosting political conventions. Although well-operated police agencies invest considerable effort in developing tactical plans, they may seldom or never be used. Nevertheless, their very existence stimulates confidence among field officers and lessens the likelihood of injury to officers, the public, and violators.

However, sometimes even the best laid out tactical plans do not go exactly as planned because not every eventuality can be anticipated. A good example of this occurred in an **active shooter** situation on September 16, 2013, at the Washington, DC, Navy Yard that resulted in 12 individuals being killed and several others being injured.[14] The active shooter, Aaron Alexis, 34, was subsequently shot and killed at the scene by a Metropolitan Police Department officer who had first been fired upon by Alexis but was saved by his protective vest.[15] The following is a summary of the After Action Report resulting from this incident.

CASE 1

AFTER ACTION REPORT
WASHINGTON NAVY YARD SEPTEMBER 16, 2013
INTERNAL REVIEW OF THE METROPOLITAN POLICE DEPARTMENT
WASHINGTON, DC

At the beginning of the incident, the streets were blocked off by the police. (see Figure 8.5) One hundred seventeen law enforcement officers from various agencies entered the building to search for the gunman.[16] Many of the search teams consisted of officers or agents from a variety of different agencies. Despite the mixed composition of the teams, the team members quickly went to work searching for the shooter.

The harsh lessons of Columbine in Colorado,[17] in which the initial responding officers waited for the arrival of the Special Weapons and Tactics (**SWAT**) team, have forced law enforcement to adapt its response protocols and enter as quickly as possible in order to search for the shooter. Waiting for the specially trained SWAT teams or Emergency Response Team (ERT) officers to arrive and lead the tactical response is no longer considered an option during active shooter incidents.

The first officers on scene must form active shooter teams, make entry, and immediately begin searching for the shooter, moving as quickly, but prudently, as possible. They have also been trained to bypass downed victims, when the gunman is still active, in order to find and neutralize the threat as quickly as possible. Those first officers may

Quick Facts: Active Shooter Lessons

For more information on planning and training regarding responding to active shooter incidents, see Greg Ellifritz, "10 Lessons Learned from the new FBI Study on Active Shooters"; http://www.activeresponsetraining.net; Dan Marcou, "5 Phases of the Active Shooter Incident"; http://www.policeone.com/; and Office of Homeland Security, "Active Shooter Preparedness,"; http://www.dhs.gov/active-shooter-preparedness.

FIGURE 8.5 ▶ Upon responding to the active shooter call at the U.S. Navy Yard in Washington, DC, one of the first things the Metropolitan Police Department did was to block off all the intersections in the proximity of this facility. (Demotix sourced/Demotix/Corbis)

be all that stands between the gunman and even more victims.

The rapid entry of the first officers on the scene proved critical in stopping the gunman from taking the lives of even more people in the building. Unlike the shooters in some previous tragedies, this active shooter did not take his own life when the first officers entered, but rather seemed determined to first evade and then engage law enforcement officers. The sheer size and maze-like layout of Building 197 likely contributed to the active shooter being able to evade and then ambush officers he encountered. However, upon entering the officers were able to neutralize the threat without further loss of life.

After prior training scenarios were reviewed, it was noted that law enforcement had conducted extensive active shooter training exercises and scenario-based drills in many types of locations (such as schools, hotels, hospitals, universities, transportation hubs, government buildings, and more), but military bases were often excluded from the training even after 2009 shooting at Fort Hood.[18] Also, civilian police department personnel may hold the mistaken belief that the personnel working within gated military installations in the United States, such as the Navy Yard, are heavily armed and capable of defending against threats. The truth, however, is that the majority of the individuals working on military bases are not armed. Out of the 14,000 workers at the Navy Yard, an extremely small number either possessed or had access to a firearm. In terms of an armed presence, the Navy Yard was really no different than other civilian agencies or private facilities that employ limited numbers of armed security personnel at entrances.

After Action Constructive Suggestions

During the review meetings with internal units and agency partners, there were two suggestions that were made related to the officers who entered the building.

First, some participants in the discussion indicated that the use of ballistic shields may have assisted in increasing the speed of officers' movement. Under the current training standard, officers were instructed to move as quickly and safely as possible to neutralize the threat. The officers' perception or judgment as to the proper balance of speed and safety in those circumstances will likely differ; however, it was agreed that it was an important consideration for future tactical training. It was recommended that the police department should consider procuring ballistic shields as they provide officers with additional protection, which may increase their speed of movement. There are, however, practical considerations and, for some departments, financial considerations that make outfitting every officer

in the department with certain equipment unfeasible. For example, many patrol officers are not in vehicles, but rather are on foot, bikes, motorcycles, or other modes that do not allow for carrying large pieces of equipment or large amounts of equipment.

A second issue that was raised in the after action assessment was that some personnel from other law enforcement agencies did not appear to be willing to take instructions or commands from the Washington, DC, Metropolitan Police Department (MPD) forward operating commander, who was coordinating the entry of the active shooter teams. These law enforcement officers responded into the building on their own. It was reported that at least one law enforcement officer indicated that he and his colleagues were federal officers and the Navy Yard was a federal facility; therefore, they did not need "permission" to respond to the incident and enter the scene. Despite the truth of that statement, the officer is ignoring the much greater implications and increased risk created by an uncoordinated response. Furthermore, it was clear that Incident Command was operating and that MPD was the lead agency. This issue can ultimately be addressed through training and communication.

Recommendations

Neighboring law enforcement agencies, both federal and local, should conduct collaborative, inter-agency training exercises. By training together, officers from different agencies are able to develop trust and mutual understanding prior to responding together to an incident that may require a multi-agency response. The tactical teams for the various regional agencies train together on a regular basis. MPD's Emergency Response Team (ERT) and the other area agencies' tactical operators are extremely familiar with one another's teams, tactics, and response plans. This familiarity should exist on additional levels throughout the agency— including patrol officers, field agents, and deputies—since these will often be the first personnel to arrive on the scene of an active shooter. Active shooter training should include different types of locations, including military bases. It is also important to note that even if a closed campus or gated facility has its own plans and protocols to respond to and manage a crisis, it is vital that the facility's personnel plan for the unexpected and this includes a larger-scale response.

The personnel from different agencies should receive standardized training, which results in a consistent understanding of tactics, communication, and approach. Collaborative training is also an opportunity to highlight the importance of a coordinated response by all involved. Ultimately, all personnel who arrive on scene should report to and be deployed by the incident commander.[19]

Strategic Plans

A strategic plan is one that an organizational management activity can use to set priorities, focus energy and resources, strengthen operations, ensure that employees and other stakeholders are working toward common goals, establish agreement around intended outcomes/results, and assess and adjust the organization's direction in response to a changing environment. It is a disciplined effort that produces fundamental decisions and actions that shape and guide what an organization is, who it serves, what it does, and why it does it. Also strategic plans are longer in duration, typically 3 to 5 years.

Quick Facts: Strategic Planning Example

For more information regarding strategic planning, see: *Madison Police Department's Trust- Based Initiatives and Collaborative Efforts with Madison's Diverse Community;* https://www.cityofmadison.com/police/documents/trustbasedinitiatives.pdf.

BLENDING FIVE TYPES OF PLANS

In 2009, the City of Tampa, Florida, agreed to host the Republican National Conference that was scheduled to be held in 2012. The entire planning process took 3 years and involved administrative, procedural, operational, tactical, and strategic planning. In the earliest planning stages, one of the major security concerns was that some individuals or groups might attempt to disrupt the convention. This did not occur to a great extent because of this agency's careful planning. The steps that were taken in the planning process are summarized in "The Tampa Quick Look Analysis Report."

CASE 2

THE TAMPA QUICK LOOK ANALYSIS REPORT

Introduction

The hosting of a national political convention posed unique planning and operational challenges. Due to their high-profile nature (i.e., political, economic, social, or religious nature) and the large number of attendees, national conventions have the potential to adversely impact public safety and security. Though many conventions have occurred, detailed documentation to guide local law enforcement on planning and operational best practices is sparse.

In order to address this gap in knowledge and to respond to requests from law enforcement leaders, the U.S. Department of Justice's Bureau of Justice Assistance (BJA) worked in partnership with the Center for Naval Analyses (CNA) to provide technical assistance and support to local law enforcement security operations prior to and during the 2012 national conventions. The primary goal of the technical assistance was to develop an after action report (AAR) that documents key findings of the overall security planning and operations. CNA analysts were deployed to Tampa, Florida, to support public safety and security operations for the 2012 Republican National Convention (RNC) from August 26 through August 31, 2012.

In addition to this Tampa Quick Look Analysis Report, the lessons learned and best practices from this event will serve as a blueprint for future law enforcement agencies in charge of maintaining security. The BJA, with the support of CNA, documented key findings from the 2012 Democratic National Convention and the 2012 Republican National Convention in a comprehensive AAR, titled, Managing Large-Scale Security Events: A Planning Primer for Local Law Enforcement Agencies.

The Tampa Police Department (TPD) understood the magnitude of the event and the potential for violent clashes between the police and demonstrators, and the high risk to officer safety. In reviewing the law enforcement response in previous similar large-scale events, it became clear to the Chief and Assistant Chiefs that a different philosophy had to be used to ensure the safety of attendees, demonstrators, and officers assisting in the response. This philosophy stressed an adherence to community policing strategies that are focused and based on protecting the constitutional rights of demonstrators while ensuring officers' safety.

In preparation for the event, the TPD developed and distributed a standard operating procedure, produced specifically for this event. This standard operating procedure outlined the department's missions and general policing philosophy. Specific to their mission, during the 2012 RNC, the TPD sought to:

- Protect the First Amendment rights of all persons;
- Conduct all operations in a safe and efficient manner; and
- Ensure that public safety services remain in full effect in the non-event spaces for all affected jurisdictions.

To maintain uniformity and consistency of practices and protocols across the multiple agencies, TPD employed several strategies. It conducted training across the participating jurisdictions, provided officers with a pocket guide that referenced the department's use-of-force policy, held a training session for 1,900 crowd control officers, and provided all of the crowd control officers with identical uniforms.

These actions ensured that the officers supporting the TPD operated as one unit, following the same procedures as one another and acting under one mission. Such a strategy is imperative in large-scale events, where multiple agencies are involved.

Major Observations

During the event, CNA analysts observed discussions and noted key decisions, actions, and field operations as they related to critical functional areas, such as communications, intelligence, public information and media relations, and training.

From these observations, CNA identified a number of best practices and lessons learned.

Best practices reflect activities and actions that aided in the success of the event.

Lessons learned reflect areas for improvement and detail some activities or actions that would have improved operations and planning.

Following is a summary of the major observations, which are described in detail in the Quick-Look Report.

Best Practices

- **Pre-Event Planning:** Rigorous and robust planning prior to the event facilitated TPD's operations for several functional areas (e.g., training, tactical operations, logistics, communications, and traffic). Twenty-four subcommittees, an Executive Steering Committee, and a core planning team established effective operational plans, policies, and collaborative partnerships during the 28 months prior to the event that formed the basis for the successful execution of security operations. The TPD often cited the planning process and the operational plans that were developed as part of this multi-jurisdictional collaborative process as critical factors in ensuring the success of this event. Below are the key best practices that most influenced event-related security operations.

- **Pre-Event Training:** Training was disseminated in a number of different formats (e.g., scenario based, presentations, E-learning, and training videos) to ensure that officers clearly understood their roles and responsibilities. Training personnel was critical for ensuring that law enforcement officers accomplished their tasks while preserving the TPD's mission and policing philosophy. One example of the benefit that training provided was crowd control officers understanding their roles and expected behaviors in response to demonstrators exercising their freedom of speech.[20]

- **Personnel Recruitment:** The TPD recognized early in the planning process that event security would require a significant number of additional law enforcement

personnel. To satisfy this requirement, the TPD recruited more than 5,500 state and local law enforcement officers from across the State of Florida. This enabled the effective provision of security to over 80 venues, 60 critical infrastructure sites, hundreds of delegates and VIPs, and thousands of event attendees.

These additional law enforcement officers also provided a force reserve and the flexibility to meet potential/unanticipated challenges.

- **Communications and Situational Awareness:** The effective use of communications equipment and technology provided greater situational awareness for TPD Commanders. Extensive criminal intelligence capabilities and video surveillance technologies (e.g., fixed cameras, mobile cameras on sources in the field) allowed TPD Commanders to make strategic response and resource-allocation decisions based on real-time information. Essentially, the enhanced video capabilities allowed TPD Commanders to have a virtual presence or "eyes on the ground" directly from the command center.

- **Legal Affairs:** Training was provided to improve the officers' understanding of the legal and civil rights issues involved in this type of event (e.g., First Amendment rights and privileges) and helped to ensure that officers understood that their mission included protecting the rights and civil liberties of the demonstrators as well as the ticket-holding attendees (e.g., delegates and invited guests). Though the number of demonstrators was far less than expected, the TPD still responded to a number of demonstrations throughout the event to ensure public order. Senior command staff and officials worked directly with the demonstrator groups, and this tactic appeared highly effective in quickly reducing tensions by allowing protestors "to be heard." In addition, the accessibility of senior officers in the field smoothed crowd control issues and allowed for rapid adjustments of strategy.

- **Command and Control:** TPD and the supporting law enforcement agencies effectively coordinated command and control of the event through a number of operations centers, daily meetings, and a common communication radio network (see Figure 8.6). The implementation of the Incident Command System (ICS) allowed for multiple jurisdictions to perform their duties in operational synchronicity, and ensured that communications and situational awareness were maintained from the field through the chain-of-command to the Chief of the Department. ICS and the interagency partnerships among TPD, neighboring local jurisdictions, federal agencies, local businesses, and community organizations played a significant role in the operational success of the event as evidenced by the minimal arrests and the perceptions of both the public and the department.

- **Crowd Management:** The use of bicycle patrols to quickly manage and cordon off crowds was particularly beneficial. Officers on bicycles were used to quickly

(continued)

FIGURE 8.6 ▶ During the Republican National Convention, the Tampa Police Department 911 Emergency Communications Bureau was set up with 9 additional radio channels, 4 dedicated phone lines, and an RNC supervisor. The team monitored live video feeds, street cameras, and air service down links from the Tampa Police Department and the Hillsborough County Sheriff's Office. The information they gathered was then relayed to the numerous command centers and the 60 local, state, and federal agencies involved in the security operation. (Courtesy of Bill Serne/Tampa Police Department)

respond to demonstrators and provided a soft barrier along the demonstration routes. Officers on bicycles often rode to the front of the demonstrator marches and blocked traffic providing safe routes for these demonstrators to exercise their constitutional rights. Using bicycles to manage the crowds proved more efficient than having officers mounted on horses, while still providing a strong police presence (see Figure 8.7).

- **Intelligence/Counterterrorism/Counter Surveillance:** The 2012 RNC was the first time the 700-megahertz long-term evolution (LTE), a National Public Safety Broadband Network, was used by local law enforcement. This network provided officers with interoperable voice, video, and data communications allowing sources in the field to use iPhones, operated under this LTE network, to send, via a secure network, live video of demonstrations and other intelligence information.

Lessons Learned

The following are highlights of the key lessons learned:

- **Resource Allocation:** Obtaining and allocating personnel in an effective manner were issues that were apparent in both the planning and operational stages of the event. One issue that arose in planning for the event was that law enforcement planners and operators did not have a clear

understanding of the role the Florida National Guard would play in security operations. Confusion existed about the number of guardsmen the Department of Defense would provide and the tasks these guardsmen could fulfill. In addition to this, during the event, it quickly became apparent that not all venue security personnel were familiar with their assignments or their surroundings and as a result, there were inconsistencies in the security measures used at each checkpoint in the venue.

- **Personnel Tracking:** Although the Radio Frequency Identification (RFID) equipment experienced technical difficulties in tracking and logging of personnel throughout the event, these difficulties were minimally disruptive to the overall operation. After the event, however, these technical difficulties and the lack of personnel tracking caused inefficiencies in processing payroll. As a result, in order to track the hours logged working, payroll personnel resorted to using sign-in sheets, which were often incomplete.

- **Financial/Grant Management:** Substantial time is needed to apply for federal funds, clear budgets, and obtain approval to begin to obligate and expend funds. This process should be considered carefully as part of the planning process. More details on grant management processes and procedures are outlined in *Managing Large-Scale Security Events: A Planning Primer for Local Law Enforcement Agencies.*

FIGURE 8.7 ▶ Police bike patrols were used extensively during the Republican National Convention in Tampa, Florida. They travel in information throughout the Downtown Area, helping visitors find their way. Also, when demonstrators veered off the parade route bike officers rode ahead and blocked traffic on side streets to prevent accidents. The RNC bike patrol consisted of 200 officers who pedaled in for the event from 15 different Tampa Bay Area communities. (Courtesy of Bill Serne/Tampa Police Department)

- **Credentialing:** The credentialing application process and instructions provided were unclear and undefined. In addition, rather than distributing credentials at one central location, each agency was individually provided credentials to issue. While this method was intended to be more efficient, it delayed the credentialing process due to the large volume of credentials needed. In retrospect, TPD recognized that the distribution of these credentials at a central location would have likely cut down on

inconsistencies within the credential process and would likely have been a more efficient approach.

Overall, the TPD's operational response throughout the RNC was effective and aligned with its mission and planning objectives. Officers were prepared to deal with the incidents that arose and were able to maintain positive interactions with the demonstrators throughout the event.[21]

DECISION MAKING

This section provides a brief overview of selected milestones in the flow of thinking about decision making. Planning is essentially a decision-making process and some of the terms used in this portion of this chapter will be familiar due to the earlier discussions in the "planning" portion of this chapter. The synoptic planning model parallels a number of steps involved in the rational comprehensive decision-making process, and both Pugh decision-making matrix and paired comparisons are mainline decision tools.

In this section, the following are covered:

Rational Comprehensive and Sequencing Models

The earliest writings of decision making as a process are from the Frenchman, Nicolas de Caritat, Marquis de Condorcet (1743–1794).[22] In 1910, John Dewey (see Figure 8.8) developed

a sequence of five steps for his "reflective thinking" model that morphed into the classical rational comprehensive model of decision making through the work of Simon, Brim et al., and others.[23] Knight distinguished between risk and uncertainty in 1921, defining risk as knowing the probability of an adverse event happening and uncertainty as an unknowable risk.[24]

In 1960, Simon (1916–2001) adapted reflective thinking to a three-step model to make it suitable for use in the context of organizational decisions; 2 years later, Brim et al., elaborated on it as a six-step process:

1. identification of the problem,
2. obtaining necessary information,
3. production of possible solutions,
4. evaluation of solutions,
5. selection of a strategy for performance, and
6. implementation of the decision.[25]

From Dewey through Brim et al., the model remained sequential in the sense that each step occurred in the same order. The usual five or six steps in the rational comprehensive decision-making model are immediately recognizable as springing from the work of Dewey.

During the mid-20th century, Barnard imported the term "decision making" from the language of public administration and into business, where it was being discussed as "policy making" or "resource allocation."[26] The term quickly gained traction, perhaps because "policy making" could go on endlessly, but a decision implied the end of discussion and the beginning of the action phase.

Simon: Bounded Rationality

Beginning in 1947, Simon produced series of challenges to the rational comprehensive notion that decision makers behaved with rationality[27] (see Figure 8.9). He argued because decision makers did not acquire all of the relevant information about their decisions, the decisions were not fully rational. Instead, these decisions were sub-optimized by "bounded rationality." Simon described bounded rationality as:

> On one side, the individual is limited by those skills, habits, and reflexes which are no longer in the realm of the

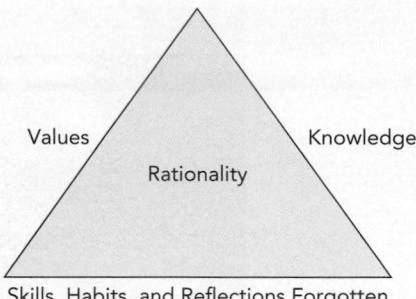

FIGURE 8.9 ▶ Simon's concept of bounded rationality.

conscious . . . on a second side, the individual is limited by his values and those conceptions of purpose which influence him in making decisions . . . and on a third side, the individual is limited by the extent of his knowledge that is relevant to his job.[28]

According to Simon, the consequence of bounded reality was "satisficing." It produced decisions with which the decision makers were not fully *satis*fied, but neither did it produce much sacri*ficing*; instead, it resulted in decisions that were "good enough."

Lindblom: Muddling Through/Disjointed Incrementalism

Lindblom also challenged the rational model of decision making with his "**muddling through**" approach in 1959.[29] Rather than making sweeping changes, decisions, plans, and policies are changed by making small, successive incremental changes to them, tending to promote the status quo. Muddling through and a later term "disjointed incrementalism" are synonymous. Based on his study of government institutions in the United States, Lindblom concluded the decision-making process is so fragmented and so complex, incorporating the interaction of various institutions, political entities, pressure groups, and individual biases, that rationality can have only a marginal effect. That is, the police administrator faces a set of limiting political factors, such as the mayor's wish to be re-elected, that prevent the decision-making process from being truly rational. For elected sheriffs, the political agendas can be so strong that rational decision making is inhibited.

Lindblom's **incremental model** asserts that decision making is serial—that it is limited by time and resources as it gropes along successive paths where means and ends are not distinct, where goals and objectives are ambiguous, and where rationality cannot consistently thrive. Contending that police managers and administrators "play things safe" and opt to move very slowly, in decision making, Lindblom[30] proposes that managers "muddle through" problems rather than analytically choosing decisions. Lindblom's incrementalism provides both the police administrator and the public with a number of safeguards against error:

> In the first place, past experience has given police chiefs knowledge about the probable consequence of any decision

they are considering. Second, chiefs need not attempt big jumps forward because they don't expect their decision to be a final resolution of a problem. Their decision is just a first step. . . . Third, Chiefs are in effect able to "feel their way forward" as they move to each successive step. Lastly, Chiefs can often remedy an error fairly quickly.[31] While Lindblom's now older characterizations are not flattering, some police leaders still find them to be "a description of reality."[32]

Although it was never an important challenge to the rational comprehensive model, in 1967, Etzioni produced a "third approach" to decision making that deserves mention. The first being the rational comprehensive and the second muddling through. His "third" approach was "mixed scanning." Decision makers at various points could use aspects of the rational comprehensive approach and at others rely on disjointed incrementalism. Mixed scanning was vaguely worded and difficult to operationalize. As a consequence, it never took hold.[33]

Allison: Political and Organizational Models

Allison's[34] analysis of the 1962 Cuban missile crisis led him to the conclusion that the rational decision-making model, although most widely used, was seriously flawed. He provided two models that ran counter to the rational comprehensive model:

First, the organizational process model is based on the premise that few government decisions are exclusively the province or "property" of a single organization. Illustratively, particularly when making major policy or other decisions, police agencies are subject to significant influences from entities in their immediate environment and in some instances even controlled by them. Just locally, there are mayors, city councils, district attorneys, courts, and business representatives, a small number of which cross the line from advocacy to improperly influencing or even controlling what the police do or not do.

Second, the government politics model holds that major government policies are rarely made by a single rational actor, such as the chief of police. Rather, policymaking and general decision making are the outcome of a process of bargaining among individuals and groups to support various interests. Implicit in both of the models is that the decision maker requires direction from his or her internal staff as well as support from other government agencies in the making of important decisions. This is especially true during crisis situations.[35]

Gore: The Gut Level Approach

In 1964, Gore[36] also challenged the rational comprehensive model by identifying the crucial element of humanism in decision making. He presents a **heuristic model**, appropriately referred to as "the gut-level approach," when considering action that may be taken. Many seasoned patrol officers assimilate their experiences as time passes, thus becoming "streetwise and develop the ability to anticipate events before they actually occur."

This streetwise dimension is captured in Gore's decision-making method for police administrators. In an antithesis to the rational model, Gore identifies a process by which a decision is the product of the maker's personality. Gore views the heuristic process as "a groping toward agreements seldom arrived at through logic . . . the very essence of those factors validating a decision are internal to the personality of the individual instead of external to it."[37] Whereas the rational method is concrete, formalized by structure and calculations, the heuristic concept is nebulous, characterized by "gut feelings reaching backward into the memory and forward into the future."[38]

For Gore, decision making is basically an emotional, nonrational, highly personalized, and subjective process. Therefore, the facts validating a decision are internal to the personality of the individual instead of external to it. The key word in this statement is "validating"; it is intended to convey a sense of personal psychological approval or acceptance. The optimum situation is to select the decision alternative that creates the least anxiety about or disruption to the individual's basic needs, wants, and desires. In effect, every "objective" decision should be modified to meet the emotional needs of the various members of the police department who will be affected by the decision. The passage from which this statement was taken provides additional insight into Gore's heuristic decision-making scheme:[39]

> Whereas the rational system of action evolves through the identification of causes and effects and the discovery of ways of implementing them, the heuristic process is a groping toward agreement seldom arrived at through logic. The very essence of the heuristic process is that factors validating a decision are internal to the personality of the individual instead of external to it. Whereas the rational system of action deals with the linkages between a collective and its objectives and between a collective and its environment, the heuristic process is orientated toward the relationship between that private core of values embedded in the center of the personality and its public counterpart, ideology. The dynamics of personality are not those of logic but rather those of emotion.[40]

In other words, although logic and reason may be the basic intellectual tools needed to analyze a given problem or to structure a series of solutions to a given situation, logic and reason may not prove to be completely effective in establishing intraorganizational agreement in connection with any given decision.[41]

Applauded for its contribution to the decision-making process, Gore's approach is also highly criticized as being too simplistic and nonscientific. Souryal[42] writes that "Gore's analysis is too unreliable. . . . It could complicate an existing situation, promote spontaneity, discredit the role of training and delay the advent of professionalism" in police organizations. This is an unfair assessment of the method. Gore views heuristic applications as adjuncts or alternatives to rational models. Further, some type of credibility must be assessed to that vague, unknown, and non-measurable entity we call experience, talent, streetwise, or a "sixth sense." It was these elements that Simon had so much trouble with in calculating his "bound and limited" argument regarding the rational model. In any event, Gore's contributions remain as an opposite of decision making based solely on figures, formulas, and mathematical designs.

Recognition-Primed Decision Making (RPD)

This is a model based on a more naturalistic view of decision making. While the previously discussed models focus on different courses of action and the selection of one course of action over others, RPD distinguishes itself by focusing more on the assessment of the situation, its dynamics, and the experience of the decision maker. Much like incrementalism and heuristic models, RPD asserts that formal models of decision making are not possible in real-life situations, where decision makers are under time constraints and face poorly defined tasks, dynamic conditions, and ill-structured goals. RPD contains elements of the incremental and heuristic models and considers how a police official's experience affects his or her decisions. In RPD, police officials are primed to act in a situation and do not wait for a complete analysis of the facts before acting. Instead, elements of the situation are recognized as typical and action is taken based on previous experience. RPD relies heavily on the concept of satisficing, in which a solution is not so much optimal as it is sufficient, given the circumstances.[43] In other words, decision makers utilizing RPD identify an option that will suffice in a given situation based on past experiences with similar situations, then try to elaborate and improve on that option. Of course, the RPD model brings to mind questions about how decision makers react when they encounter situations that are absolutely not typical. In these cases, the RPD model states that the decision maker must identify anomalies in the situation and obtain as much information about the anomaly as possible in order to make a decision. The RPD model does not allow for much creativity or ingenuity in a situation, and it certainly allows for previous mistakes to be repeated. However, research indicates that RPD is the dominant form of decision making used in command and control organizations.[44]

Thin-Slicing Theory

Gladwell, in his 2005 book *Blink*, described a model of decision making called "thin-slicing." The **thin-slicing theory** states that, in situations where snap decisions are required, whether by a police administrator, a line officer, or anyone else in a decision-making capacity, instantaneous decisions can often be the best, particularly when paired with training and expertise.[45] Thin-slicing is clearly an offshoot of the heuristic model, as Gladwell maintains those decisions that are made in an instant can be equally good, or even better, than those made deliberately and with a lot of information. Thin-slicing incorporates more rationality than traditional heuristic models. Unconscious decision making, which Gladwell describes as "a kind of giant computer that quickly and quietly processes a lot of the data we need in order to keep functioning as human beings."[46] This allows decision

makers to thin-slice, a rational response in which we find patterns based on very narrow slices of experience. According to Gladwell, our unconscious allows us to sift through situations that confront us, to the point that we throw out all irrelevant information and focus on the parts of the issue that are most relevant.

However, there is a dark side to rapid decision making which is clearly not rational and Gladwell incorporates this into his theory. Often, unconscious attitudes and prejudices sneak into the decision-making process, leading thin-slicing astray. Under extreme pressure, researchers have found that decision makers tend to fall back on stereotypes and prejudices. The best way to counter this type of bias, according to Gladwell, is to train decision makers to slow down, even slightly, and find ways to mitigate the effects of stereotypes and biases by changing the environment where decisions might occur. This may at first glance seem paradoxical, and some might argue that Gladwell's concept of thin-slicing is at odds with itself because the theory asks that the decision maker go with his or her first reaction, but set rules ahead of time for the way that he or she might think. Gladwell acknowledges this but asserts that those with enough training and expertise are more able to extract the most meaningful amounts of information from the smallest, thinnest slice of an experience and are able to control the environment in which rapid cognition takes place.[47]

THE USE OF COMPUTERS IN THE DECISION-MAKING PROCESS

In the early 1960s, some federal government agencies began using "modern" mainframe computers. The less costly, but still powerful, minicomputers appeared in 1964 and 1965. Initially, computers were used to automate labor-intensive tasks, such as payroll calculations. Around that time the phrase "garbage in, garbage out" gained currency, meaning that mistaken or poor quality input produced flawed results. In the mid-late 1960s, applications of computing to decision making largely centered on providing data to support decision, which had the collateral affect of reinforcing the rational comprehensive approach to decision making, as did many other subsequent computer applications. However, in the 1960s and even into the 1970s, the veil had not yet been lifted on the seemingly miraculous other things computers could do in the realm of sophisticated problem analysis and decision making.

Taking advantage of computer applications available now is particularly crucial to the future of intelligence-led/predictive policing and the research of the smart policing initiative.[48] Despite the advantages of powerful analyses, Maule issues a cautionary note:

Decision making is a vital activity. It determines the actions that individuals and organizations take and how successful these are, but we still have much to learn about it.

Many problems in how we make decisions have been attributed to limitations in how we memorize and process information, and computers are often used to overcome these restrictions. But because many computer systems have been developed without a full understanding of how people actually think, computers can lead people to make bad decisions. There are situations when it would have been better to follow gut reactions. Following your intuitions is much more difficult when you are sat in front of a computer! The trick is to know when and when not to use gut reactions, something that most decision makers are not taught.[49]

Currently, the field of computer science is focused on two broad, but related, fields of decision making (see Figure 8.10).

1. Decision systems, which are decisions made by a computer. It does so using any of several forms of artificial intelligence (AI) and relies on its own particular knowledge base and inference or reasoning programming to reach decisions that would otherwise have to be made by a human. As an illustration, many police departments direct incoming non-emergency calls by automation; and

2. Decision sciences have three sub-fields: Normative, descriptive, and decision support; they all rest on the rational model. For present purposes, the most important of these is decision support, which also has three sub-fields: decision analysis (DA), operational research (OR), and decision support systems (DSS) (see Figure 8.11).[50]

Together, the three sub-fields of decision support gives the police powerful tools to quickly and efficiently examine staffing patterns and needs, distribution of the field force, conduct social network analysis (SNA) to discover the connection between criminals and their patterns, analyze the cost-effectiveness of using DNA to solve property crimes, crime mapping, hot-spot analysis, and other important problems.[51]

As has been seen in the riots following a police shooting in Ferguson, Missouri, and the death of a Baltimore, Maryland, African-American male in police custody in 2015 (both discussed in greater detail in Chapter 4, Politics and Police Administration), planning was inadequate, the police were either not allowed to be effective in controlling the situation because of political considerations, and/or decision makers did not know what action should be taken. Using computer simulations, a 2008 study revealed what the optimal police responses should be when faced with a crowd control or riot situation, down to the placement of barricades. From decision support simulations, the on-scene commander can match crowd or riot behaviors with optimal response from pre-stored strategies to fit the tactical situation being faced.[52]

The Use of a Decision Tree

When using a decision tree model, the probabilities for various outcomes are calculated for each branch of the tree. In the example used in Figure 8.12, the first branch of the trunk has three possible outcomes: (1) arrest at the scene by a patrol officer, (2) no arrest at the scene, and (3) arrest at the scene by a detective. Note in the figure that the probabilities for those three events total 1.0, which is the mathematical value for certainty; all possible outcomes for that branch of the example are accounted for. The next-higher branch of the example decision tree deals with the various types of evidence obtained from investigation, and the final branches deal with the probability of arrest associated with the gathering of each type of evidence. Decision trees are very useful in analyzing situations and for reference when series of decisions that flow from one event are involved. For

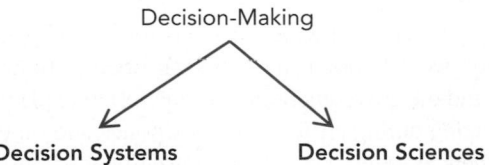

FIGURE 8.10 ▶ Decision Systems and Decision Sciences.

Decision Analysis (DA)	Operational/Operations Research (OR)	Decision Support Systems (DSS)
DA, popularly known as "applied decision theory" keeps breaking a decision problem into smaller sub-problems that may be more manageable. In doing so it considers factors like available information, alternatives, uncertainties and presents the results as a decision model. Needed, but missing information produces a model that is "satisfactory" or "sufficiently good."	Similar to DA, OR uses analytical and mathematical models for decision support. However, OR differs in that it relies on higher level mathematical modeling of questions or problems about the optimal way to manage scarce resources.	DSS is defined as interactive computer-based information systems intended to help users examine information data bases, e.g., mine for data on wanted suspects with outstanding warrants, and utilize data and models to solve problems.
Source: These points are loosely derived with restatement from Marko Bohanec, "Decision Making: A Computer Science and Information Technology Viewpoint," Interdisciplinary Description of Complex System 7, no. 2, (2009), pp. 28, 32–33.		

FIGURE 8.11 ▶ The Three Fields of Decision Support.[53]

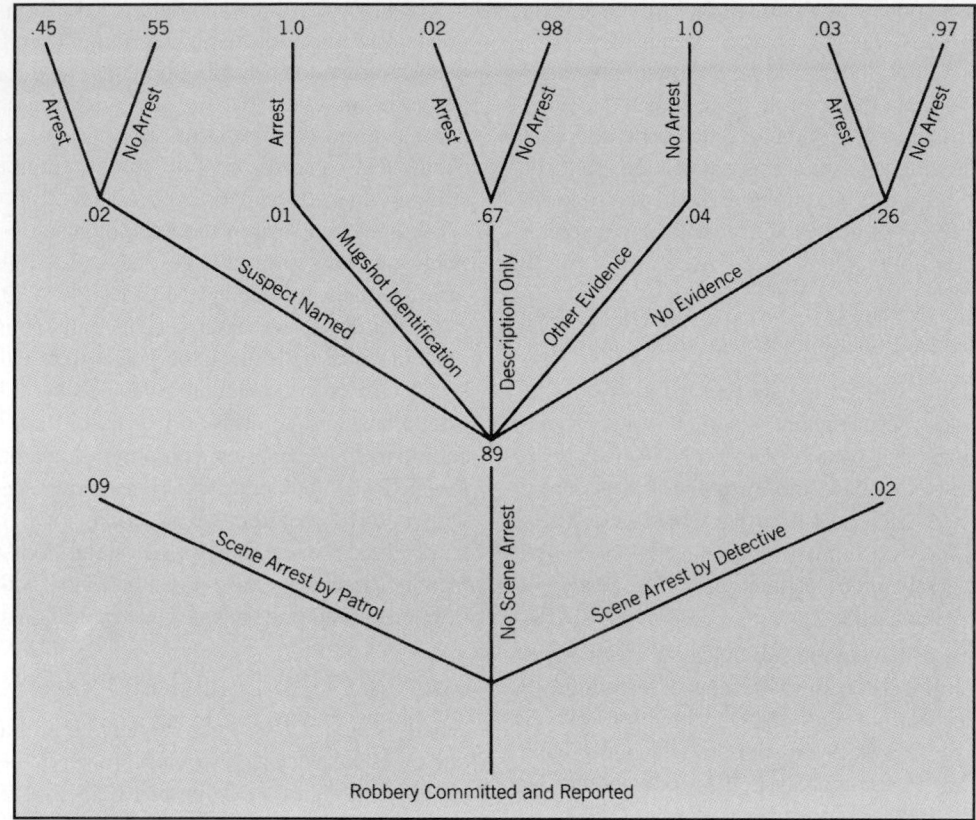

FIGURE 8.12 ▶ Decision tree of hypothetical probabilities of various outcomes in a robbery investigation.

example, decision trees would be useful to the commander of a detective bureau in formulating policy and guidelines on when to continue or inactivate an investigation based on the types of evidence that were involved in order to make the best use of investigative resources. In this regard, decision trees can be seen as a tool of operations research. If an administrator is facing a decision for which there are no actual data, a decision tree can still be useful in analyzing the situation, and the "probabilities" can be the administrator's own subjective estimations based on past experience. Decision tree models are commonly used in **e-learning software** programs that provide simulation training scenarios to police officers and executives. The program changes and alternatives appear as the student makes various decisions that alter the precise path incorporated into the gaming simulation. These types of simulation software programs represent the latest technology in police training relating to officer and executive-level decision making (see Figure 8.12).

For example, the RPD model is based on recognizing situations and knowing how to handle them.[54] Other types of alternative decision-making models come from notions popularized by best-selling books such as Gladwell's *Blink*.[55]

Alternative Decision-Making Models

Another attempt to outline various approaches to the decision-making process is Allison's[56] account of the 1962 Cuban missile crisis. He contends that the rational decision-making

model, although most widely used, is seriously flawed. Allison presents two additional models (the organizational process model and the government politics model) to explain the decision making during crisis events that police and other government agencies often face. The organizational process model is based on the premise that few government decisions are exclusively the province of a single organization. In other words, police agencies are dependent on information and advice from other government units (such as the mayor's office, the FBI, and the district attorney's office) to make major decisions that affect public policy. The government politics model purports that major government policies are rarely made by a single rational actor, such as the chief of police. Rather, policymaking and general decision making are the outcome of a process of bargaining among individuals and groups to support those interests. Implicit in both of the models is that the decision maker requires direction from his or her internal staff as well as support from other government agencies in the making of important decisions. This is especially true during crisis situations.[57]

Operational modeling
Other alternative models to decision making have evolved from the systems approach to management as described in Chapter 5, Organizational Theory. These techniques are vastly influenced by large, complex systems of variables. The application, collection, and analysis of data

from decision making within the organization are called **operations research**.[58] In response to a need for a management science that addressed complex problems involving many variables, such as government planning, military spending, natural resource conservation, and national defense budgeting, operations research employs the use of mathematical inquiry, probability theory, and gaming theory to "calculate the probable consequences of alternative choices" in decision making.[59]

These approaches are highly sophisticated elaborations of the rational model using quantitative techniques. The weakness of the methods is in their practicality to real-world situations in which time and resources are not directly structured to gather intelligence about every problem and possible alternative. Further, these models assume that human biases will not enter the decision-making process. The most critical aspect of the approaches appears to be in their overriding insistence that decision making is not a human activity but the product of some scientific, computerized, and unimpressionable robot that digests quantitative information.

Wildavsky[60] has continually warned that the application of decision making to costs, benefits, resources, and budgets frequently results in the adoption of meaningless data, and places unwarranted stimuli into the process.

DECISION MAKING DURING CRISIS EVENTS

Police agencies, like all government organizations and private entities, are not immune to the necessity of effective decision making during crisis events. Thus far in this chapter, we have examined decision making in law enforcement from the traditional aspects of planning, organizational needs, theoretical models, and administrative roles. However, two older major events still remain as prime examples of protracted crisis events in which law enforcement control of a situation was at best, slipping away: (1) the raid of the Branch Davidian Compound in Waco, Texas, in 1993 and (2) the FBI siege of the Weaver family at Ruby Ridge, Idaho, in 1992. These types of events span hours, days, and even months to end and must *not* be confused with active shooter situations requiring immediate action. The purpose of this analysis is to bring applications of the various decision-making models to reality. It is not intended as a critical commentary, but rather as an effort to identify the commonalities of the incidents and the lessons derived. It should not be taken lightly that each incident began with a sense of duty, good faith, honor, and courage yet ended in tragic losses and damaged agency reputations.

The Branch Davidians, Waco, Texas (1993)

During the early 1990s, a young, charismatic religious leader began to develop a group of followers known as the Branch Davidians. The group settled slightly northeast of Waco, Texas, and began building a well-fortified compound in which to protect themselves from the outside world and the impending "Last Judgment Day." Their spiritual leader, David Koresh (commonly referred to by followers as "the Lamb of God"), was a high school dropout with a perceived mystical ability to teach from the apocalyptic Book of Revelation in the New Testament.

Police investigations of the Branch Davidians did not begin until late in 1992, when Alcohol, Tobacco, and Firearms (ATF) agents were contacted by a postal driver who reported seeing hand grenades in a partially opened package delivered to the Waco compound. As a result of the investigation, an arrest warrant for Koresh was issued, along with a search warrant to seek out additional illegal weapons and explosives at the Waco compound.

In the early morning hours of February 28, 1993, ATF tactical teams totaling approximately 75 people stormed the Waco compound. The agents were met with a fusillade of heavy gunfire. In the resulting exchange, four ATF agents and six Branch Davidians were killed. The incident prompted a 51-day standoff between federal agents and the Branch Davidians. Immediately following the initial confrontation between ATF and the compound occupants, the FBI assumed control of the operation. While negotiations during the ordeal were targeted initially at a peaceful resolution, the FBI began preparations to re-enter the compound by force, using armored vehicles to break through heavily fortified walls and distribute a debilitating dose of CS tear gas. The gas was supposed to be nonlethal, would not permanently harm adults or children, and would not cause fire during the delivery stage. As time lingered and negotiations lulled, Attorney General Janet Reno gave orders to commence with the assault. At 6:00 A.M. on April 19, 1993, several M-60 military tanks, reconfigured with tear gas delivery booms, began breaking through the compound walls. Within hours of the operation, fire broke out. Fanned by 35-mile-per-hour winds, the fire raged, and the compound was rapidly incinerated. Seventy-two bodies were found among the remains, including several children.

The political flames of Waco linger. In 1999, the Texas Rangers and lawyers for the Waco survivors revealed a blatant cover-up by the FBI. For 6 years, the FBI insisted that the Branch Davidians burned their own compound and denied to Congress that its agents fired any flammable tear gas canisters in the attack on April 19, 1993. Renewed investigations revealed that not only did the FBI mislead Congress, but top decision makers may have overtly lied, finally admitting that the FBI did, indeed, fire at least two pyrotechnic M651 grenades at the Branch Davidian bunker. Even more troubling was the revelation that the U.S. military provided federal law enforcement agents with more than $1 million worth of support (supplying tanks, helicopters, aerial reconnaissance, munitions, and support personnel) during the standoff at Waco. At least 10 military advisers or observers attached to the U.S. Army's elite Delta Force were present at various times throughout the incident. The entire action came dangerously close to violating **the Posse Comitatus Act**, prohibiting the use of federal soldiers to act as police officers or in a law enforcement capacity within the borders of the United States. Further, Attorney General Reno admitted that her decision to allow the FBI to rush the Davidian compound was heavily based on tales of Koresh abusing children. Later, a Justice Department "clarification" said that there was no evidence of child abuse. According to Reno, the FBI convinced her that Koresh was a suicidal madman bent on destroying himself and others within the compound; however, she was never shown a letter by Koresh, dated just days before the attack, that promised that he would come out peacefully after completing his writing. The resulting publicity and trials caused serious questioning of the FBI's tactics, operations, and decision making.

The Weaver Family, Ruby Ridge, Idaho (1992)

In March 1992, federal prosecutors indicted Randy Weaver, a known white separatist, on a charge of selling two sawed-off shotguns to an undercover federal informant. The job of arresting Weaver, who had fled to his secluded and fortified retreat at Ruby Ridge, Idaho, was assigned to the U.S. Marshal Service. On August 12, 1992, marshals began their surveillance of the Weaver's cabin and surrounding terrain under the code name "Operation Northern Exposure."

Nine days later, on August 21, Randy Weaver; his 14-year-old son, Sam Weaver; and a family friend, Kevin Harris, followed their dog into the woods adjacent to the cabin. Deputy U.S. marshals surveilling the cabin were discovered, and gunfire was exchanged between the two groups. Sam Weaver and one U.S. marshal were fatally wounded. Confusion and speculation about who fired first and whose bullets killed the two victims continued to plague the investigation. In any event, information soon reached Washington, DC, that federal agents were under attack at Ruby Ridge and that assistance was badly needed. The FBI deployed its Hostage Rescue Team (HRT) to the location, beginning an 11-day standoff between the FBI and the Weaver family.

Under normal circumstances, the HRT snipers followed specific rules of engagement that dictated the use of deadly force only under the threat of "grievous bodily harm." Although the reasoning behind changing this operational policy at Ruby Ridge and who was responsible for it are unclear, FBI snipers were told that they "could and should fire at any armed adult male" in the cabin. Hence, on August 22, one day after the initial confrontation and the deaths of Sam Weaver and a U.S. marshal, FBI snipers fired on cabin occupants to protect a surveillance helicopter. The resulting shots struck Kevin Harris and Vicki Weaver (Randy Weaver's wife), who was standing just inside the cabin, holding her infant child. Although Mrs. Weaver died of her wounds, FBI personnel did not learn of her death until Randy Weaver surrendered 9 days later.

The actions of the FBI were debated in Congress, and a special Senate judiciary subcommittee was formed to investigate the incident. Both Randy Weaver and Kevin Harris were acquitted of murdering the U.S. marshal in the initial confrontation.

Analysis of Decisions Made During Protracted Crisis Events

The on and off-site decision makers in these crisis situations started out with a plan to follow a scripted step-by-step, rational model and adjust it if need be. However, the emotionality, stress, close attention by the national news media, the increasing situation complexity, and other factors may have resulted in impaired judgments about what to do. Arguably, any plans seemed successively overcome by rapidly occurring events and to some degree control became an illusion. Like disjointed incrementalism on steroids, events spiraled beyond the planning horizon, beyond any real control, and they took on a life of their own. Faced with escalating casualties and collapsing planning time, toward the end it seems possible that decision makers relied on their "gut-level" feeling.

Janis and Mann have outlined a decision-making model, based on psychological conflict, that emphasizes the decision-making process under stress.[61] Janis and Mann indicate that decision making involves "hot" emotional influences, similar to Gore's theory and the need to make a decision inherently becomes more stressful. When a decision maker is faced with an emotionally consequential, no-win choice, how he or she copes with the problem depends on two major factors: hope and time. This process causes great stress, as the factors of hope and time are rarely within the control and purview of the decision maker. This can be uniquely observed in protracted, high-stress incidents involving the police, such as those observed in Waco and Ruby Ridge.

When the decision maker has control of time and has hope that conciliation is possible, that person's efforts are more likely to follow the desired pattern of the "vigilant decision maker."[62] The vigilant model closely resembles the rational comprehensive model. The vigilant decision maker (1) thoroughly canvasses a wide range of alternatives; (2) surveys a full range of objectives to be fulfilled and the values implicated by choice; (3) carefully weighs the costs and risks of negative consequences as well as the positive consequences that could come from each alternative; (4) intensively searches for new information relevant to further evaluation of the alternatives; (5) correctly assimilates and takes account of new information or expert judgment to which he or she is exposed, even when the information or judgment does not support the course of action initially preferred; (6) re-examines the positive and negative consequences of all known alternatives, including those originally regarded as unacceptable, before making a final choice; and (7) makes detailed provisions for implementing or executing the chosen course of action, with special attention to contingency plans that might be required if various known risks materialize.[63]

While Janis is better known among students of politics, policy, and management for his earlier work on "groupthink,"[64] his development with Mann of the concept of the vigilant decision maker has provided a practical model for measuring administrative responsibility. Most notable is Nagel's work in applying the decision-making theories of Janis and Mann to the 1985 MOVE incident in Philadelphia.[65] In his highly critical work, Nagel identifies several decision-making paradoxes that, unfortunately, are not uncommon in similar incidents (e.g., the Symbionese Liberation Army [SLA] shoot-out in Los Angeles in 1968, the American Indian Movement [AIM] siege of Wounded Knee in 1977, the FBI shootings at Ruby Ridge, and the ATF raid on Branch Davidians in Waco).

These paradoxes are identified and elaborated on by Taylor and Prichard.[66] All the incidents have commonality. They were all police precipitated—that is, each incident grew from the police advancing on the homes of well-armed, openly defiant, and hostile groups of individuals. Each incident grew from earlier encounters with the police, often highly charged, emotional encounters involving everything from civil and slander suits against the police for harassment to police–group shootings. In all of the incidents, the police intelligence concerning the actual location of the assault and/or the number of suspects and their armaments were in gross error. To complicate the issue, the primary decision maker was not at the scene. In both the Waco and Ruby Ridge incidents, critical decisions were made in Washington, DC, several thousand miles away. Then, too, the incidents were characterized by an overreliance on technology. Decision makers believed that tear gas would not ignite and burn but rather force hostages and suspects from their barricaded positions. The illusion of invulnerability also impacted each incident—who would believe that suspects would not surrender to a large, powerful, tactically trained, well-armed group of federal agents? This certainly was the case in the ATF raid on the Branch Davidians in Waco. The overreliance on intellectual rationality failed as police decision makers underestimated the power and control of a charismatic leader in a relatively small, religiously inspired group. Further, the belief that police SWAT agents could act as an effective, highly specialized military unit performing a "surgical strike" on a bunker belonged more in the movies than in reality. Police officers and agents are simply not experienced, trained, or equipped to handle such encounters. Contrary to popular belief, highly trained police tactical units must rely on meticulous timing, superlative intelligence, surprise, and the ability to use deadly force effectively. None of these conditions existed in the protracted events of Waco and Ruby Ridge.

Finally, in each incident, the decision maker lost hope for a peaceful outcome. When such a condition occurs, the decision maker enters the downward spiral of "defensive avoidance."[67] The pattern is characterized by procrastination and delay, followed by passing the buck and other ways of denying personal responsibility, followed by bolstering and gaining superficial support from others. The distorted view produced by bolstering results in a spreading of responsibility and an exaggerated value of the chosen course of action. More often than not, the chosen course is a "do something" reaction. As Janis and Mann state, the process of defensive avoidance "satisfies a powerful emotional need—to avoid anticipatory fear, shame, and guilt."[68] Delay followed by haste can result in wishful thinking, oversimplification of the problem, and the selection of the force option. Confusion, catastrophe, and denial soon follow.

Handling Crisis Events in the Future

Several new directions for handling such crisis events in the future can be developed from the lessons of the past. These recommendations have been adopted as policy for the FBI Critical Incident Response Group, created in 1994 as a response to the Waco and Ruby Ridge encounters. Recommendations for protracted conflict can be summarized as follows:

1. Nagel strongly argues that policies to deal with such events must be institutionalized.[69] That is, they must be concrete, written directives that reflect the overall philosophy of the department or agency. These policies must not be changed arbitrarily during a crisis event or for a specific operational strategy. Further, policies must identify key players and decision makers during such events. Who is the primary decision maker? Who is in charge of operational management? Who is in charge of coordination, communication, logistics, and so on? These are critical positions that must be identified in writing, well before an incident occurs.

2. Police agencies must adopt a philosophy that clearly articulates the importance of the safety and security of human life during such incidents. The force option through the use of SWAT team assault, selective sniper fire, and tear gas distribution must be last resorts. The primary philosophy must emphasize a patient, no-force negotiation strategy rather than a tactical solution for outcome. This is not a new concept. Bolz and others have pressed for this type of departmental philosophy for the past 25 years.[70]

3. Police agencies must consider withdrawal as a strategy. Certainly, in most of these cases, the police could have arrested the primary leaders of these groups outside the confinement of a barricaded compound. The use of more modern surveillance equipment using forward-looking infrared (FLIR) and wall-penetrating radar technology could do much to increase the accuracy of intelligence and the development of an arrest plan before a barricaded standoff occurs.

4. Police executives must reconsider the role and use of SWAT teams. Their role must be limited to containment and deployment during search and arrest warrant executions. They should not automatically be deployed as a paramilitary group capable of executing high-risk operations requiring precision and exceptional teamwork unless their training skill level clearly establishes it. The routine comparison between police SWAT teams and military strike force teams (such as the Navy SEALS or Army Delta Force) must be broken. The rules of engagement for each unit are unique, as are their skills and outcomes when deployed.

5. Training for protracted conflicts must include the top-level decision makers as well as operational commanders and chiefs. Attorney generals, governors, city managers, mayors, councilpersons, and top police executives must be trained in coping with such conditions. Significant attention must be paid to the development of a policy that emphasizes the no-force negotiation option. Further, decision makers should be trained to recognize the characteristics of "defensive avoidance" and "groupthink" before courses of action are taken.[71] Mock scenarios and role playing should accompany the training.

6. During crisis events, outside and neutral referees or observers should assist in the situation. These individuals should be well versed in the no-force negotiation option and should act as "coaches" for the negotiation team.

These individuals should have no ownership or responsibility in the situation and should be paid a fee for their time only. These are not high-level consultants but rather well-trained, neutral observers with whom operational managers and top-level decision makers can review potential tactics and strategies. Outside observers must be protected from any type of potential ensuing liability through the agency involved. Their main purpose is to act as a "reality check and review" for actions to be taken by the police.

Decision making during these types of protracted events, when the suspects appear to be anything but rational, is always a very difficult task. It is also a very human endeavor, and, as such, mistakes will inevitably occur. Remember that the purpose of studying these cases is not to criticize the agencies involved (hindsight is always 20–20) but rather to offer students and police executives alternatives to past experiences and tactics. No one decision-making model guarantees success. However, we owe it to the dedicated men and women who died in these past incidents to ensure that future decision makers always attempt to maximize the two most important factors in the negotiation strategy: hope and time. This can be accomplished by the judicious use of the force options of direct assault, selective sniper fire, and tear gas dispersal.

GROUP DECISION MAKING

Research on group decision making reveals that this approach has both advantages and disadvantages over individual decision making. If the potential for group decision making can be exploited and its deficiencies avoided, it follows that group decision making can attain a level of proficiency that is not ordinarily achieved. The requirement for achieving this level of group performance seems to hinge on developing a style of leadership that maximizes the group's assets and minimizes its liabilities. Because group members possess the essential ingredients for the solution, the deficiencies that appear in group decisions reside in the processes by which group decisions are led and made. These processes can determine whether the group functions effectively or ineffectively. With training, a leader can supply these functions and serve as the group's central nervous system, thus permitting the group to emerge as a highly efficient entity.[72]

Group Assets in Decision Making

The following advantages are found in group decision making.

GREATER TOTAL KNOWLEDGE AND INFORMATION

The sum of information in a group is always greater than any one of its members. Thus, problems that require the use of knowledge (both internal and external to the police agency) almost always give groups an advantage over individual. If one member of the group, such as the police chief, has more knowledge on a subject than the others, they may still be an asset by filling any gaps that exist, adding their own thoughts, or critiquing what is being discussed.

GREATER NUMBER OF APPROACHES TO MAKING A DECISION

Some of us get into ruts in our thinking, especially when problems arise that have similarities to ones we've encountered in the past. Almost instinctively, like being on cruise control, we have a quick and easy answer and that might be true sometimes. It may also get in the way of finding more creative solutions that work better if the stakes warrant the expenditure of more time. Sometimes, we do not need the optimal decision; we just need one that is "good enough."

A group of police leaders may also have great "quick fixes," but their "fixes" may all be different. For example, one police administrator may insist that the best way to cope with the increasing number of robberies of local convenience stores in a community is to place the businesses under surveillance by specially trained police officers who can intervene effectively. Another police administrator might insist that the best way to reduce the number of robberies is through the implementation of crime prevention programs designed to use procedures that would make the businesses in question either less attractive or less vulnerable to robberies, for example, keep the amount of cash available to a minimum, put up cameras and height strips on the exit door, and remove large signs from the front of the store windows that block the view of passing patrol cars and other motorists. It is sometimes difficult to determine which approach or approaches would be most effective in achieving the desired goal. But undue persistence or allegiance to one method may imperil a decision group's willingness to be innovative.

PARTICIPATION IN PROBLEM SOLVING INCREASES ACCEPTANCE

Many effective solutions to problems require input, "shaping" or "tuning" by more multiple members of the group. When last checked, no one has cornered the market on wisdom. Group participation in forging a decision increases its acceptance and implementation. Such a solution may be more effective than a hypothetically better solution that lacks acceptance. For example, a decision to establish a crime prevention program in a crime-riddled neighborhood must have support from the chief to individual beat officers. Although other measures to reduce crime, such as increasing the number of patrol officers or more attention to juvenile gang activity, might have a more substantial impact, it is important to remember that most of the program participants must support the effort.

BETTER COMPREHENSION OF THE DECISION

Of necessity, when a Chief gives an order to be executed by subordinate commanders the attending details, standards, timetable, desired outcome, and other matters cannot or should not be ignored. If there is any ambiguity about the instructions being provided, a competent subordinate will quickly seek clarification. Thus, the chances for communication breakdowns are reduced greatly when the individuals who must work together in executing a decision have participated in making it. They not only understand the solution because they helped develop it but also are aware of the other alternatives that were considered and the reasons why they were discarded (see Figure 8.13).

Group Liabilities in Decision Making

Notwithstanding the benefits of group decision making, several liabilities are worth mentioning as a precautionary measure.

PEER PRESSURE

Peer pressure, whether it's articulated or unspoken, is major force for increasing conformity. The desire to be a good group member and to be accepted may become more important than arguing for a position which is contrary to that held by most of the members of the group. This may especially be true when a newly promoted member joins an established decision-making group, for example, the command staff, and may be hesitant to quickly jump into the discussion. This is understandable, but deprives the new member of an important developmental experience and "short-changes" the group.

INDIVIDUAL DOMINATION

In some groups, a dominant individual may emerge and capture a disproportionate amount of the influence in determining the final outcome. This does not necessarily equate to how much "air time" they get by talking frequently. Sometimes in groups, the most influential person is the one who patiently bides his/her time and waits to weigh in at exactly the most critical point of a discussion. In police circles, the influence of the chief's opinion is undeniable. Effective chiefs know they have two ears and one mouth and use them proportionately. They are excellent listeners, reining in a group with a few innocuous sentences to get things back on track only when the discussion has clearly gone far afield from its purpose.

FIGURE 8.13 ▶ Open communication and increased communication increases effective group decision making. (RosalreneBetancourt 2/Alamy Stock Photo)

Even there, the discussion may be useful, revealing to chiefs some of the things that are on the minds of their command staffs.

CONFLICTING SECONDARY GOALS: WINNING THE ARGUMENT

When groups are confronted with a problem, the initial goal is to obtain a solution. However, in the absence of a quick consensus solution, the appearance of several alternatives causes individuals to have preferences, and, once these emerge, the desire to support a particular position is created. Converting those with neutral viewpoints and refuting those with opposing viewpoints now enter the problem-solving process. This is a normal group dynamic and a time for everyone to keep their "eye on the ball." It's not about winning; the goal is forging a good solution.

GROUPTHINK

The theory of **groupthink** was first introduced by Irving Janis in 1972.[73] Groupthink is a psychological phenomenon that most often occurs in cohesive groups that are isolated from other political and decision-making bodies. This condition often occurs within police leadership circles, especially during crisis events. The political pressure and stress to make a decision, coupled with the presence of a strong leader, escalate the condition. Groupthink is most often characterized by a serious lack of methodical procedure that forces a misperception of the problem and a hurried search for answers. During groupthink, there is considerable focus on a shared rationalization that bolsters the least objectionable alternative as a decision, a suppression of unfavorable outcomes, and an illusion of unanimity and invulnerability. Indeed, Janis and Mann warn that the decision-making process may be so intense that more effort is expended on striving for concurrence than on finding an appropriate decision.[74] During such conditions, the chief should strive to remain impartial, listening to ideas and alternatives. He/she must encourage members of the command staff who have been quiet to express their thoughts about suggested decisions. The chief should play the devil's advocate, questioning some views expressed, for example, what might go wrong and what the possible adverse consequences might be to the proposed actions. Chiefs also must accept criticism of their own judgments as well as those proposed by the group. Janis and Mann are quick to point out that groupthink occurs not only during crisis times but also during rather mundane policymaking meetings.[75] It is incumbent that the Chief, as well as individual members of the group, be on guard for the signs and characteristics of groupthink. The best defense to such a condition is continual, open debate and discussion. This requires a leadership style which has earned the chief the trust of the command staff, which by experience has learned there are no repercussions from such discussions.

Factors That Can Serve as Assets or Liabilities in Group Decision Making

Depending on the skill of the Chief, some elements of group decision making can be either assets or liabilities.

DISAGREEMENT

Discussion sometimes leads to strong disagreement and fosters short-lived hard feelings among the command staff.

However, it is also the path to good decisions. The first of these outcomes of disagreement is a liability, especially with regard to the acceptance of solutions; the second is an asset, particularly where innovation is desired. A chief can treat disagreement as undesirable and thereby reduce both the probability of hard feelings and innovative thought. The skillful police administrator creates a climate for disagreement without risking hard feelings because properly managed disagreement can be a source of creativity and innovation. The chief's perception of disagreement is a critical factor in using disagreements. Other factors are the chief's permissiveness, willingness to delay reaching a solution, techniques for processing information and opinions, and techniques for separating idea elicitation from idea evaluation.

CONFLICTING VS. MUTUAL INTERESTS

Disagreement in discussions can take many forms. Occasionally, command staff members seemingly disagree with one another with regard to a solution, but when the disagreements are explored, it may be discovered that the solutions are in conflict because they are actually designed to solve slightly different aspects of the problem.

Analysis of a problem may reveal that it is actually the proverbial "hairball," a cluster of entwined problems. If possible, the best approach is to separate the problems into parcels, each of which can be resolved by a single solution. Failing this because of their uniqueness, each problem has to be fitted with an appropriate solution. Here the saying, "I thought I knew what this conversation was about, but I'm mistaken" comes into play. Chiefs, or a command member who has spontaneously taken the role of a gatekeeper, must keep the discussions focused or conflict instead of co-operation will arise. A gatekeeper guides the exchange of information in a discussion. Parenthetically, in politics, the gatekeeper is the person who gets access to his/her principal or "boss."

RISK TAKING

Groups are more willing than individuals to reach decisions that involve risk. Taking risks is a factor in the acceptance of change, but change may represent either a gain or a loss. The best protection against the latter outcome seems to be primarily a matter of the quality of a decision. In a group situation, this depends on the leader's skill in using the factors that represent group assets and avoiding those that make for liabilities.

TIME REQUIREMENTS

In general, more time is required for a group to reach a decision than for an individual to reach one. Some problems require immediate decisions in which case individual decisions are necessitated, such as a wounded officer down in the open with a barricaded subject still firing at the downed officer. The practice of moving a portion of a meeting or an entire meeting swiftly forward is likely to prevent a full discussion and have subsequent repercussions. A better tactic is to table the remaining portion of a meeting's agenda. Unskilled leaders tend to be either too concerned with reaching a solution and prematurely terminate a discussion or too anxious about getting input, allowing the discussion to digress and become repetitive.

WHO CHANGES

Unless it just immediately occurs, a consensus is reached because some members of a group change their views, not to just achieve consensus, but because they are persuaded by the points made by others. In group situations, who changes can be an asset or a liability. If persons with the most constructive views are induced to change, the endproduct suffers, whereas if persons with the least constructive points of view change, the endproduct is upgraded. Chiefs can potentially help upgrade the quality of a decision because their position allows them to elicit more information from a command staff member who has a strong idea but is in the minority. This "protection tactic" is a constructive factor because a minority viewpoint only has hope when the facts favor it.

Brainstorming is a type of group decision making developed initially in advertising to help trigger creativity. The idea behind brainstorming is to establish a group environment in which individuals can present any idea that seems to apply even remotely to the subject being considered with the understanding that criticism will be withheld unless it can somehow improve on the original idea.[76] Whiting identified specific procedures that improve the effectiveness of brainstorming sessions:

1. The sessions should last 40 min to an hour, although brief, 10- to 15-min sessions may be effective if time is limited.

2. Generally, the problem to be discussed should not be revealed before the session.

3. The problem should be stated clearly, but not too broadly.

4. A conference table may be the best setting because a certain level of closeness invites contributions.[77]

One of the most important aspects of brainstorming is an existing environment in which it can occur. Brainstorming requires a level of trust between individuals who work together, for example, they would not be ridiculed, which does not exist in an unstable organization.[78]

ETHICS AND DECISION MAKING

It is said that character is "What you do when someone isn't watching you." The difficulty of course is that we develop our defining character over time and likewise with ethics. None of us spring into the world fully formed; both are developmental processes.

Ethical behavior is difficult to define, and while ethics are not wholly based on feelings, religion, law, or science, individuals may take those things into account when defining their standards of behavior. Simply put, **ethics** are standards of behavior that dictate how humans are supposed to act within the roles that they find themselves in, whether that role is as a parent, friend, police administrator, supervisor, police officer, or private citizen. Ethics differ among individuals, depending on their personal values, cultural influences, or what they feel is the level of personal behavior that they should aspire to. Police administrators must identify ethical issues in decision making and develop strategies to confront ethical dilemmas. However, this process does not differ from the decision-making process used by any other individual.[79]

There are various ways to deal with ethical issues. One strategy for administrators is the following, developed by the Santa Clara University Markkula Center for Applied Ethics.[80] The first step in this framework is to recognize an ethical issue. Decision makers should ask themselves if there is something wrong personally, interpersonally, or socially and determine if the conflict, the situation, or the decision might be damaging to people or to the community. Then they should consider whether the issue goes beyond legal or institutional concerns and what it means to people who have dignity, rights, and hopes for a better life.

The next step in the framework is to get the facts, by determining what facts are relevant to the specific issue and what facts are unknown. Next, decision makers should decide what individuals and groups have an important stake in the outcome and should consider whether all stakeholders have been consulted or what they would say if they were consulted.

Law enforcement leaders should always evaluate alternative actions from various ethical perspectives when faced with an ethical dilemma. For instance, the utilitarian approach to ethics looks at which action is the one that will produce the greatest balance of benefits over harm. In this case, the decision maker asks which option will produce the most good and do the least harm. In approaching the decision using the rights approach, in which the ethical action is the one that respects the rights of all affected by the decision, one asks if everyone's rights and dignity will be respected, even if not everyone gets what he or she wants. The fairness approach, which defines an ethical action as one that treats people equally, or at least proportionately and fairly, requires that the decision maker ask which option is most fair to all stakeholders. The common good approach requires that an individual consider which option would help everyone involved participate more fully in society, and the virtue approach requires the decision maker to consider whether or not the action is one that embodies the habits and values of people at their best.

After decision makers carefully evaluate their options from one or more perspective, the framework requires that they make their decision based on which option they feel is the best or the right thing to do and then test it. After acting, it is important for decision makers to examine how it turned out for all concerned and to evaluate whether they would make the same decision if they had to do it all over again. Ethical decisions are not always the most cost-effective or popular ones, and they often cause some personal discomfort in the short term. However, by carefully evaluating the best course of action, a police administrator can avoid situations that may, over the long term, cause a great deal of personal stress, as well as remorse. Considering that ethical blunders in police administration tend to generate a great deal of negative publicity, taking the ethical route may also save police administrators from public shame or disgrace.

COMMON ERRORS IN DECISION MAKING

Analysis of the decision-making process indicates that certain types of errors occur at a higher frequency than others. Nigro and Nigro[81] have indicated that these errors are: (1) cognitive nearsightedness, (2) the assumption that the future will repeat the past, (3) oversimplification, (4) overreliance on one's own experience, (5) preconceived notions/confirmation bias, (6) unwillingness to experiment, and (7) reluctance to decide/procrastination.[82]

Cognitive Nearsightedness

A human tendency is to make decisions that satisfy immediate needs and to brush aside, ignore, or fail to consider the long-range implications. Implicitly, the hope is that the decision will "have legs' and be durable, but this actually is counting on being lucky. The odds for such good fortune to occur consistently across all decisions are poor.

Assumption That the Future Will Repeat Itself

In making decisions, police officials must try to forecast future conditions and events. Social upheavals, economic collapses, terrorist attacks, technological breakthroughs, droughts, famine, petulance, and epidemics and a host of other variables make forecasting a tough business. In relatively stable periods of history, the assumption can be made with reasonable assurance that conditions will stay approximately the same and the government, politics, the community, crime and other factors will be within the range of past experience. The present period is, however, far from stable. However, very rarely do dramatic changes occur without some warning signals. Attention to small "flutters" may provide valuable indicators about future conditions. The police administrator must make the effort to be aware of these trends and develop strategies to cope with them.

Oversimplification

People may address the symptom of a problem because the cause may be too complex to understand. It is also easier to understand a simpler solution: It is more readily explained to others and therefore more likely to be adopted. The decision maker looking for an acceptable answer may take the first simple one even in preference to a somewhat more complicated alternative with a much better outcome.

Overreliance on One's Own Experience

In general, law enforcement practitioners place great weight on their own previous experience and personal judgment. Although an experienced police executive should be able to make better decisions than a completely inexperienced one, a person's own experience may still not be the best guide. Frequently, another police executive with just as much experience has a completely different solution and is just as certain that his or her solution to a problem is the most satisfactory one. In fact, past success in certain kinds of situations may be attributable to chance rather than to the particular action taken. Thus, there is frequently much to be gained by counseling with others whose own experience can add an important and uniquely different dimension to the decision-making process.

Preconceived Notions/Confirmation Bias

Decisions purportedly based on facts may actually reflect the bias of some police executives. They are particularly diligent about finding information that supports their bias, as well as any that can be used to counter other anticipated views. Decision makers may only appear as if they are proceeding in an orderly fashion from consideration of the facts to the conclusions derived logically from them. Some cases of administrative policymaking suffer from a similar defect: They are supported by a dangerously thin foundation of facts and untested assumptions.[83]

Unwillingness to Experiment

The best way in which to determine the workability of a proposal is to test it on a limited scale. However, pressure for immediate, large-scale action may convince a police chief that there is no time to proceed cautiously with pilot projects, no matter how sound the case for a slow approach, because grant opportunities are evaporating for some other reason. Police executives may be reluctant to request funding and other needed support for the small-scale test implementations of new programs out of a concern that such prudence may create doubts about the soundness of the programs. In all fairness to the cautious police administrator, sometimes this assessment has merit.

Reluctance to Decide/Procrastination

Even when in possession of adequate facts, some chiefs try to avoid making a decision. They may procrastinate until the need for a decision is eliminated by events that occur or have "analysis paralysis," constantly seeking more information to assure themselves they are doing the right thing. Barnard speaks of the natural reluctance of some people to decide:

> The making of a decision, as everyone knows from personal experience, is a burdensome task. Offsetting the exhilaration that may result from a correct and successful decision is the depression that comes from failure or error of decision and in the frustration that ensues from uncertainty.[84]

IMPROVING DECISION MAKING

Recognizing some of these common errors in decision making can be a springboard for strengthening the ability to make good, ethical decisions in the future. Police executives fall into the trap of focusing on the outcome of a bad decision. Obviously, in the classic examples of Ruby Ridge and the Branch Davidians, the majority of us know *what*

happened but are unable to fully articulate *why* it happened. We know about the number of people killed but do not necessarily focus on the process that led the decision makers to take the actions that they did. By looking at mistakes on a personal level, as well as looking at mistakes made by contemporaries, police executives have an opportunity to capitalize on what did not work so well in the past. Mauboussin discusses this process at length and encourages all decision makers to take three steps toward better decision making: preparing, recognizing, and applying past mistakes to determine future courses of action.[85] Preparation is simply the process of gathering information about past mistakes and understanding why they happened. The goal, according to Mauboussin is "to recognize the kind of problem you face, how you risk making a mistake, and which tools you need to choose wisely."[86] Finally, Maubossin suggests applying what you have learned about past mistakes in decision making results in diminishing the opportunity for a repeat. Police executives should put together a mental toolbox of sorts to cope with situations as they come up. Filing away and flagging errors in decision making as they come up is an excellent way to avoid making the same mistake, no matter what the circumstances.

Chapter Summary

Summary by Learning Objective

1. **Explain what planning is expected to accomplish.**

   It is expected to (1) improve the analysis of problems; (2) provide better information for decision making; (3) help to clarify goals, objectives, and priorities; (4) result in more effective allocation of resources; (5) improve inter- and intradepartmental co-operation and coordination; (6) improve the performance of programs; (7) give the police department a clear sense of direction; (8) provide the opportunity for greater public support; and (9) increase the commitment of personnel.

2. **Define what a plan is.**

   Stated succinctly, planning involves linking present actions with future conditions.

3. **Discuss synoptic planning.**

   Synoptic planning, or the rational comprehensive approach, is the dominant tradition in planning. It is also the point of departure for most other planning approaches, which in general are either modifications of synoptic planning or reactions against it. The typical synoptic model is based on "pure" or "objective" rationality and attempts to ensure optimal achievement of desired goals from a given situation.

4. **Identify the specific elements of administrative, procedural, operational, tactical, and strategic plans.**

   (1) Administrative or management plans include formulation of the department's mission statement, goals, and policies; the structuring of functions, authority, and responsibilities; the allocation of resources; personnel management; and other concerns that are prevalent throughout the agency; (2) Procedural plans are the guidelines for the action to be taken under specific circumstances and detail such matters as how evidence is to be sent or transported to the crime laboratory, the conditions under which male officers may search arrested females and the limits thereto, and how to stop and approach traffic violators; (3) Operational plans describe specific actions to be taken by line units (patrol officers, precinct groups, and/or division teams); (4) Tactical plans involve planning for emergencies of a specific nature at known locations; (5) Strategic planning is an organizational management activity that is used to set priorities, focus energy and resources, strengthen operations, ensure that employees and other stakeholders are working toward common goals, establish agreement around intended outcomes/results, and assess and adjust the organization's direction in response to a changing

environment. This type of plan typically addresses events 3 to 5 years into the future.

5. **Discuss what planning can be expected to accomplish.**
   (1) Improve the analysis of problems; (2) Provide better information for decision making; (3) Help to clarify goals, objectives, and priorities; (4) Result in more effective allocation of resources; (5) Improve inter- and intradepartmental co-operation and coordination; (6) Improve the performance of programs; (7) Give the police department a clear sense of direction; (8) Provide the opportunity for greater public support; and (9) Increase the commitment of personnel.

6. **State Simon's concept of "bounded rationality."**
   Noting that human beings are "bounded" by a triangle of limitations, Simon said, "On one side, the individual is limited by those skills, habits, and reflexes which are no longer in the realm of the conscious . . . and on a second side, the individual is limited by his values and those conceptions of purpose which influence him in making decisions . . . and on a third side, the individual is limited by the extent of his knowledge that is relevant to his job."

7. **Explain Lindblom's incremental decision making.**
   Lindblom asserts that decision making is serial— that it is limited by time and resources as it gropes along a path where means and ends are not distinct, where goals and objectives are ambiguous, and where rationality serves no purpose. Contending that police managers and administrators "play things safe" and opt to move very slowly (incrementally) in decision making, Lindblom proposes that managers "muddle through" problems rather than analytically choosing decisions. In Lindblom's view, decision making that occurs through a series of

incremental steps provides the police administrator (and hence the public) with a number of safeguards against error.

8. **Describe Gore's decision-making process.**
   For Gore, decision making is basically an emotional, nonrational, highly personalized, and subjective process. Therefore, the facts validating a decision are internal to the personality of the individual instead of external to it.

9. **Explain the concept of the thin-slicing theory.**
   It occurs in situations where snap decisions are required, whether by a police administrator, a line officer, or anyone else in a decision-making capacity; instantaneous decisions can often be the best, particularly when paired with training and expertise.

10. **State the advantages of group decision making.**
    (1) Greater total knowledge and information; (2) Greater number of approaches to making a decision; (3) Participation in problem solving increases acceptance; (4) Better comprehension of the decision.

11. **Discuss the liabilities of group decision making.**
    (1) Social pressure; (2) Individual domination; (3) Conflicting secondary goals: winning the argument; (4) Groupthink.

12. **Explain the concept of brainstorming.**
    Brainstorming is a type of group decision making developed initially in advertising to help trigger creativity. The idea behind brainstorming is to establish a group environment in which individuals can present any idea that seems to apply even remotely to the subject being considered with the understanding that criticism will be withheld unless it can somehow improve on the original idea. The practitioners of brainstorming have been able to determine some specific procedures that improve the effectiveness of brainstorming sessions.

Chapter Review Questions

1. Explain the advantage of planning within a police department.
2. Why is it that some police administrators may not fully appreciate the importance of planning?
3. What is it that effective planning can be expected to accomplish?
4. Tankha identified four types of planning approaches based on their time orientation. What are they?
5. What are the key lessons learned by law enforcement officers participating in the Republican National Convention?
6. What is the purpose of the decision tree used in robbery investigations?
7. What are some of the important recommendations, developed in this chapter, for handling future protracted crisis events?
8. List the steps decision makers should take when confronted with an ethical issue?
9. What are the most common errors in decision making?

Critical Thinking Exercises

1. **Operational Plan.** In recent years, there has been a dramatic increase in prostitution in your community, primarily involving women and young girls from Central and South American countries. You suspect that many of them have been illegally trafficked into the United States and are being forced into prostitution. However, your patrol officers and vice squad officers have very little experience in identifying and dealing with the issue of sex trafficking. You have therefore made a decision to begin to train those officers who are most likely to come in contact with these victims so they will be able to more effectively identify and assist them. However, in order to do so, you need to answer to the following questions:

   a. What are the venues where sex trafficking victims are most likely to be found?

   b. What are the specific indicators that a woman who is engaged in prostitution has been trafficked and is being forced to engage in this practice against her will?

   c. Who can you turn to to assist in training your officers in better understanding the problem of sex trafficking in your community?

   d. Since you are aware that sex trafficking is a multi-jurisdictional problem how would you go about organizing a multi-agency task force to deal with the issue?

2. **Decision Making.** In recent years, there has been a national trend for police departments to require individuals being promoted to supervisory or managerial positions to have earned a college degree. However, the agency you have recently taken over as police chief has educational requirements for promotion which are the same as those required at the entry level, namely, a high school diploma. You have made a decision that in the future individuals will not be considered for promotion unless they have earned a college degree. However, before you can accomplish this objective you will have to address the following questions:

   a. What timeline, if any, would you recommend before putting this change into effect?

   b. Would you have a modified educational requirement for those applying for the position of sergeant (AA or AS degree) than you would for those applying for higher ranks such as lieutenant, captain, and major (BA or BS)?

   c. Will you impose limits on the number of courses an officer can take at one time so their school work will not interfere with their work responsibilities?

   d. Will you be reimbursing officers for their college tuition? If so, will there be a contractual obligation for them to stay with the agency for a specified period of time in order to compensate the agency for the financial aid it provided?

   e. Are you prepared to make adjustments in the work schedules if officers choose to take classes on campus as opposed to taking their courses online?

   f. Will you require your officers to major in certain academic disciplines such as criminal justice or criminology or will they have the latitude to major in other disciplines (e.g., business administration, public administration, psychology, education, and so forth)?

   g. Who will you involve in the decision-making process, for example; a committee composed of officers within the agency, police union representatives, the mayor, city manager, and citizens?

Key Terms

active shooter
administrative/management plans
brainstorming
e-learning software
ethics
groupthink
heuristic model
inactive planning

incremental model
operational plans
operations research
planning
posse comitatus
proactive planning
procedural plans
reactive planning

recognition-primed decision making (RPD)
strategic plans
SWAT
synoptic planning
tactical plans
thin-slicing theory

Endnotes

[1] Israel Stollman, "The Values of the City Planner," in *The Practice of Local Government Planning,* ed. Frank S. So et al. (Washington, DC: International City Management Association, 1979), p. 13.

[2] Ibid.

[3] Carol Weiss, *Evaluation Research: Methods of Assessing Program Effectiveness* (Englewood Cliffs, NJ: Prentice Hall, 1972), p. 7.

[4] John Hudzik and Gary Cordner, *Planning in Criminal Justice Organizations and Systems* (New York: Macmillan, 1983), p. 1.

[5] Charles M. Mottley, "Strategy in Planning," in *Planning, Programming, Budgeting: A System Approach to Management,* 2nd ed., ed. J. F. Lyden and E. S. Miller (Chicago: Markham, 1972), p. 127.

[6] See Sunil Tankha, Sustainable Corporations: Reconciling Wealth Creation with Global Sustainability, 15–16 (The Woodlands, TX: Houston Advanced Research Center, 1999. HARC is a non-profit organization founded in 1982). The authors have added the police context to the types of planning.

[7] The term "pure," or "objective rationality," is taken from the alternative planning models identified by Tony Eddison, *Local Government: Management and Corporate Planning* (New York: Harper & Row, 1973), pp. 19–23.

[8] The synoptic model is thoroughly discussed in Cushman, *Criminal Justice Planning.* Some of the following information relating to the model is paraphrased from that work.

[9] Patrick Slater, "Inconsistencies in a Schedule of Paired Comparisons," *Biometrika* 48, nos. 3/4, (December 1961):, p. 303.

[10] A good example of the statistical end is Kristi Tsukida and Maya R. Gupta, "How to Analyze Paired Comparison Data," UWEE Technical Report-2011-004, May 2011, Department of Electrical Engineering, University of Washington.

[11] Hudzik and Cordner, *Planning in Criminal Justice,* p. 196.

[12] Ibid.

[13] A number of sources identify plans according to their use; see O. W. Wilson, *Police Planning,* 2nd ed. (Springfield, IL: Charles C Thomas, 1962), pp. 4–7, and Vernon L. Hoy, "Research and Planning," in *Local Government Police Management,* ed. Bernard L. Garmire (Washington, DC: International City Management Association, 1977), pp. 374–375.

[14] This has been adapted from the After Action Report Washington Navy Yard September 16, 2013, Internal Review of the Metropolitan Police Department, Washington, DC, July 2014, pp. 28–30; http://www.policefoundation.org/wp-content/uploads/2015/05/Washington-Navy-Yard-After-Action-Report.pdf.

[15] The shooter in this incident, Aaron Alexis, 34 years old, was employed by Experts Inc., a subcontractor of Hewlett-Packard, as an independent contractor who provided information technology support services for the U.S. Navy at the installation. It was later learned that he may have been suffering from insomnia, pronounced bouts of anger, and possible psychological disturbances. It does not appear that he gave those who knew him or worked with him any prior warning or specific indication he planned on carrying out this shooting.

[16] The 117 officers that entered the building during the initial search for the shooter included officers and agents from DC Metropolitan Police Department (MPD); U.S. Park Police (USPP); Naval District of Washington (NDW) Police; Naval Criminal Investigative Service (NCIS); Metropolitan Washington Airports Authority; U.S. Marshalls Service (USMS); Navy Contract Service Guards; and U.S. Navy, Department of Defense (DOD).

[17] The police response to "active shooter" scenarios changed following the terrible events of the Columbine, Colorado, massacre on April 20, 1999. In the Columbine School shooting, Eric Harris and Dillon Klebold murdered 13 people on the school campus before they committed suicide, bringing the total to 15 people dead. The first responding patrol officers told horrific stories of arriving at the scene and hearing shots fired and victims screaming for over 10 min, yet had no training or advanced weaponry to enter the school and stop the killing. This event, more than any other, changed police responses to similar events now classified as "active shooter" situations.

[18] On November 5, 2009, a mass murder took place at Fort Hood, near Killeen, Texas. Nidal Malik Hasan, a U.S. Army major and psychiatrist, fatally shot 13 people, which included 12 U.S. soldiers and a civilian police officer working at the base, and injured more than 30 others. See "Soldier Opens Fire at Ft. Hood; 13 Dead," CBS News/AP, November 5, 2009; http://www.cbsnews.com/news/soldier-opens-fire-at-ft-hood-13-dead/ (accessed August 29, 2015).

[19] There are similarities in the nearly 100 school shootings (in the United States and Canada since 1966) that make them significantly different than those of the protracted crisis discussed earlier. Most of the victims are school-age children, some as young as 6 years old, who were shot *randomly*; the shootings have little, if any, logical reason or purpose other than causing massive carnage and human death; the suspects are for the most part, also students, or at least student age (11 to 22 years), working alone; the vast majority of the suspects are white males with a history of school issues, including social conflict, disenfranchisement, and/or mental problems; the suspect's actions were planned and well-thought-out, and in some cases even rehearsed, with suspects bringing guns to the school before their planned event. The suspects even made threats that they wanted to hurt people but were not taken seriously; the suspects had easy access to firearms and were often well-armed with multiple weapons and ammunition; and in most cases, the suspect(s) commits suicide or is killed by the police. The need to act quickly in these types of scenarios often precludes the use of SWAT teams that must be called out with some delay. Further, the presence of an active shooter at the scene also requires that responding patrol officers take action to save lives and human destruction rather than cordon off the area and wait.

[20]Examples of the training materials used in both the RNC and DNC are available as part of the Appendix in *Managing Large-Scale Security Events: A Planning Primer for Local Law Enforcement Agencies.*

[21]Tampa Police Department, *Command, Control, and Coordination: a Quick-Look Analysis of the Tampa Police Department's Operations During the 2012 Republican National Convention,* available at: https://www.cna.org/sites/default/files/research/2012-RNC-Quick-Look.pdf.

[22]Sven Ove Hansson, "Decision Theory: A Brief Introduction" (Stockholm: Department of Philosophy and the History of Technology, Royal Institute of Technology, August 19, 1994), p. 9.

[23]John Dewey, *Democracy and Education* (New York: The MacMillan Company, 1916).

[24]Leigh Buchanan and Andrew O'Connell, "A Brief History of Decision Making," *Harvard Business Review* (January 2006), p. 5. The page numbers used are from a PDF file, https://hbr.org/2006/01/a-brief-history-of-decision-making, accessed July 12, 2015.

[25]Hansson, "Decision Theory: A Brief Introduction," pp. 8–9.

[26]Buchanan and O'Connell, "A Brief History of Decision Making," p. 1.

[27]Herbert A. Simon, *Administrative Behavior: a Study of Decision-Making Processes in Administrative Organization* (New York: First Edition, MacMillan, 1947).

[28]Simon, *Administrative Behavior,* p. 40.

[29]Charles E. Lindblom, "The Science of Muddling Through," *Public Administration Review* 19, no. 2 (Spring 1959), pp. 79–88.

[30]Charles F. Lindblom, The Policy-Making Process (Englewood Cliffs, NJ: Prentice Hall, 1968), p. 209.

[31]Lindblom, "The Science of Muddling Through," p. 86.

[32]Jack Kuykendall and Peter Unsinger, *Community Police Administration* (Chicago: Nelson-Hall, 1975), p. 132.

[33]Buchanan and O'Connell, "A Brief History of Decision Making," p. 9.

[34]Graham T. Allison, *Essence of Decision: Exploring the Cuban Missile Crisis* (Boston: Little, Brown, 1971).

[35]Some of this discussion was excerpted from an excellent review of Allison's book by Robert B. Denhardt, *Theories of Public Organization* (Monterey, CA: Brooks/Cole, 1984), pp. 81–85.

[36]William J. Gore, *Administration Decision-Making: A Heuristic Model* (New York: John Wiley & Sons, 1964).

[37]Ibid., p. 12.

[38]Sam S. Souryal, *Police Administration and Management* (St. Paul, MN: West, 1977), p. 318.

[39]L. G. Gawthrop, *Bureaucratic Behavior in the Executive Branch* (New York: Free Press, 1969), pp. 98–99.

[40]Gore, *Administrative Decision-Making,* p. 12.

[41]Gawthrop, *Bureaucratic Behavior,* p. 99.

[42]Souryal, *Police Administration,* p. 319.

[43]C. Zsambock, and G. Klein, *Naturalistic Decision Making* (Mahweh, NJ: Erlbaum, 1997), p. 286.

[44]Ibid., p. 219.

[45]Malcom Gladwell, *Blink: The Power of Thinking without Thinking* (New York: Little, Brown, 2005), pp. 10–14.

[46]Ibid., p. 11.

[47]Ibid., p. 253.

[48]Relatedly, see Suhaib Alzou'bi et al., "Artificial Intelligence in Law Enforcement, A Review," *International Journal of Advanced Information Technology* 4, no. 4 (August 2014), pdf file pp. 1–9; http://airccse.org/journal/IJAIT/papers/4414ijait01.pdf (accessed August 14, 2015).

[49]John Maule, "Why the Computer Isn't Always Right," Leeds University Business School, United Kingdom, March 8, 2010, p. 1 http://business.leeds.ac.uk/about-us/article/why-the-computer-isnt-always-right (accessed August 14, 2015).

[50]These points are loosely derived with restatement from Marko Bohanec, "Decision Making: A Computer Science and Information Technology Viewpoint," *Interdisciplinary Description of Complex System* 7, no. 2, (2009), pp. 23–24.

[51]Several of the topics in this paragraph are taken from Tombul Fatih and Cakar Bekir, "Police Use of Technology to Fight Against Crime," *European Scientific Journal* 11, no. 10 (April 2015), pp. 290–292.

[52]Conference paper: Johan Schubert et al., "A Decision Support System for Crowd Control," Proceedings of the 13th International Conference Command and Control Research Technical Symposium, Seattle, Washington, June 2008, p. 1.

[53]Ibid., pp. 28, 32–33.

[54]Gary A. Klein, *Sources of Power: How People Make Decisions* (Cambridge, MA: MIT Press, 1998).

[55]In his book *Blink: The Power of Thinking without Thinking* (New York: Little, Brown, 2005) Malcom Gladwell examines: Why are some people brilliant decision makers, while others are consistently inept? Why do some people follow their instincts and win and others end up stumbling into error? How our brains really work—in the office, in the classroom, in the kitchen, and in the bedroom? And why are the best decisions often those that are impossible to explain to others?

[56]Graham T. Allison, *Essence of Decision: Exploring the Cuban Missile Crisis* (Boston: Little, Brown, 1971).

[57]Some of this discussion was excerpted from an excellent review of Allison's book by Robert B. Denhardt, *Theories of Public Organization* (Monterey, CA: Brooks/Cole, 1984), pp. 81–85.

[58]John Ott, "The Challenging Game of Operations Research," in *Emerging Concepts of Management,* eds. Max S. Wortmann and Fred Luthans (London: Macmillan, 1970), p. 287.

[59]Ibid.

[60]Aaron Wildavsky, *Speaking Truth to Power: The Art and Craft of Police Analysis* (Boston: Little, Brown, 1979), p. 84.

[61]Irving L. Janis and Leon Mann, *Decision Making: A Psychological Analysis of Conflict, Choice, and Commitment* (New York: Free Press, 1977).

[62]Ibid., chapter 1.

[63]Ibid., pp. 11–15.

[64]Irving L. Janis, *Victims of Groupthink* (Boston: Houghton Mifflin, 1972).

[65]John H. Nagel, "Psychological Obstacles to Administrative Responsibility: Lessons of the MOVE Disaster," *Journal of Policy Analysis and Management* 10, no. 1 (1991), p. 3.

[66]Robert W. Taylor and Leigh A. Prichard, "Decision-Making in Crisis: Police Responses to Protracted Critical Incidents" (paper delivered at the Academy of Criminal Justice Sciences Annual Meeting, Las Vegas, NV, March 13, 1996).

[67]The concept of "defensive avoidance" was first developed by Janis and Mann in *Decision Making*. However, Nagel uniquely applied the concept to reality in his article "Psychological Obstacles to Administrative Responsibility."

[68]Janis and Mann, *Decision Making*, p. 85.

[69]Nagel, "Psychological Obstacles," p. 21.

[70]The concept of a negotiated solution to crisis events has been developed over the past 25 years. See Frank A. Bolz and Edward Hershey, *Hostage Cop* (New York: Rawson, Wade, 1979); Ronald C. Crelinsten and Denis Szabo, *Hostage-Taking* (Lexington, MA: Lexington Books, 1979); Murray S. Miron and Arnold P. Goldstein, *Handbook for Hostage Negotiations: Tactical Procedures, Negotiating Techniques and Responses to Non-Negotiable Hostage*

Situations (New York: Harper & Row, 1979); and Robert W. Taylor, "Hostage and Crisis Negotiation Procedures" in *Police Civil Liability*, ed. Leonard Territo (New York: Hanrow Press, 1984).

[71]See Nagel, "Psychological Obstacles"; Janis and Mann, *Decision Making*; and Taylor and Prichard, "Decision-Making in Crisis."

[72]N. R. F. Maier, "Assets and Liabilities in Group Problem Solving: The Need for Integrated Function," *Psychology Review* 74, no. 4 (1967), pp. 239–248. Much of the information in this chapter dealing with the discussion of group decision making was obtained from this source.

[73]See Irving L. Janis, *Victims of Groupthink* (Boston: Houghton Mifflin, 1972).

[74]Janis and Mann, *Decision Making,* pp. 398–400.

[75]Ibid.

[76]W. Gortner, *Administration in the Public Sector* (New York: John Wiley & Sons, 1977), p. 124.

[77]C. S. Whiting, "Operational Techniques of Creative Thinking," *Advanced Management Journal* 20 (1955): pp. 24–30.

[78]John Schafer, "Making Ethical Decisions: A Practical Mode," *FBI Law Enforcement Bulletin,* May 2002.

[79]For more information about the framework for ethical decision making, visit www.scu.edu/ethics.

[80]Markkula Center for Applied Ethics, Santa Clara University, "A Framework for Thinking Ethically." See http://www.scu.edu/ethics/practicing/decision/framework.html (September 2, 2007).

[81]Much of the information in this chapter dealing with the discussion of common errors in decision making was obtained from F. A. Nigro and L. G. Nigro, *Modern Public Administration* (New York: Harper & Row, 1977), pp. 226–232.

[82]D. Katz and R. L. Kahn, *The Social Psychology of Organizations* (New York: John Wiley & Sons, 1966), p. 285.

[83]Ibid.

[84]C. Barnard, *The Functions of the Executive* (Cambridge, MA: Harvard University Press, 1938), p. 189.

[85]Michael J. Mauboussin. *Think Twice: Harnessing the Power of Counterintuition* (Boston, MA: Harvard Business Press, 2009), pp. 137–143.

[86]Ibid., p. xvi.

CHAPTER NINE

HUMAN RESOURCE MANAGEMENT*

Learning Objectives

1. List 10 functions a police human resource unit might perform.

2. Identify the main objective of the Equal Pay Act.

3. Describe how the Age Discrimination in Employment Act is applied to law enforcement agencies.

4. Explain the four major theories of discrimination.

5. Name two categories of sexual discrimination.

6. Summarize the protection afforded by the Pregnancy Discrimination Act.

7. Define *disability* and *reasonable accommodation.*

8. Briefly discuss the law enforcement exemption of the Genetic Information Nondiscrimination Act.

9. Briefly contrast exempt and nonexempt employees.

10. List the four reasons for which leave may be taken under the Family Medical Leave Act.

11. Briefly state how the economy affects recruiting applicants.

12. Define *validity* and *reliability.*

13. Explain the meaning of *discipline* and *progressive discipline.*

14. Identify the four possible outcomes in a professional standards/internal affairs investigation.

15. Explain how a discipline matrix works.

16. List four purposes of performance appraisals.

17. Name the five different purposes promotional testing can serve.

18. Describe the assessment center process.

19. Explain rank order, all-qualified, and banded promotional rosters.

20. Discuss the problem of identity loss that some officers experience in retirement.

*The content of this chapter should not be relied on for legal guidance, which should be obtained from a qualified attorney at law.

INTRODUCTION

THERE ARE SOME COMPELLING *reasons to have a strong working knowledge of human resource management: (1) at least 80 percent of a law enforcement agency's annual operating budget is spent on personnel and personnel support costs; (2) an agency competes in the same labor market with businesses and other police organizations; it should strive to become the law enforcement employer of choice; (3) some number of personnel problems can be traced back to faulty human resource management practices; (4) serious mistakes by weak selection processes and inadequate training are inevitably revealed by the actions of officers; (5) high turnover costs not only result in repetitive selection and training costs, but drive down the experience level of patrol officers—a threat to the quality of service delivery; (6) achieving and maintaining a diverse work force is a strong element in working effectively with the different populations in our communities; (7) there is a maze of local, state, and federal laws and regulations pertaining to public sector employees; failure to understand and follow them will bring adverse attention to an agency and can result in litigation by employees; (8) a department embroiled in job discrimination litigation puts the community at a significant disadvantage when trying to recruit potential employers to relocate there; for some potential employers, it will be sufficient to scratch your city or county off their list; (9) valid and reliable promotional practices will identify leaders (see Chapter 7, Leadership) who can help maintain a high level of agency performance; and (10) a community needs and deserves the best possible law enforcement agency, whose effectiveness and image ultimately rests on the people that represent it.*

FUNCTIONS OF A POLICE HUMAN RESOURCES UNIT

In small jurisdictions, human resources (HR)/personnel services will largely be provided by the city's or county's central personnel office. As law enforcement agencies become progressively larger, they take on additional HR responsibilities. Larger departments may have a HR division, but in many agencies, HR management is a function within their Administrative or Personnel and Training Divisions.

Depending on the size of a law enforcement agency and the division of responsibilities with the central personnel office, a police HR unit may have oversight of the following functions:

1. Complying with Peace Officers Standards and Training Commission (POST) requirements and guidelines;
2. Maintaining currency with federal job discrimination laws;
3. Developing agency HR policies, subject to executive approval;
4. Recruiting and selecting sworn and civilian personnel;
5. Monitoring turnover, retention, and diversity;
6. Providing or contracting for psychological services (e.g., entry screening and critical incident counseling);
7. Delivering or contracting for academy, in-service, advanced, and managerial training;
8. Conducting special studies (e.g., staffing, benefits, and compensation surveys);
9. Administering benefits programs (e.g., health and life insurance and workers compensation);
10. Preparing payroll;
11. Directing labor relations;
12. Coordinating drug testing;
13. Administering promotional testing;
14. Managing intern programs;
15. Advising commanders on personnel matters;
16. Coordinating the employee evaluation process;
17. Organizing promotions and awards ceremonies;
18. Coordinating off-duty work;
19. Directing Professional Standards/Internal Affairs efforts;
20. Acting as personnel records custodian;
21. Preparing content for the agency's website;
22. Conducting job exit interviews to identify factors associated with turnover; and
23. Serving as liaison to the central personnel office.[1]

In preparing this list, a number of local law enforcement websites were visited. The City and County of San Francisco Police Department has an unusual and very useful function for a large agency, an American with Disabilities Act (ADA) Coordinator who meets with personnel seeking an accommodation under that federal legislation, which is covered later in this chapter.

KEY FEDERAL LAWS PROHIBITING JOB DISCRIMINATION

In addition to the protections afforded by state laws, local ordinance, and civil service or merit commissions, there are several prominent federal laws prohibiting job discrimination. An overview of them is provided for general familiarity and not as a substitute for legal counsel. Some of these statutory laws are further referred to in a more specific context in subsequent sections of this chapter.

These laws discussed in this section are administered by the Department of Justice's **Equal Employment Opportunity Commission (EEOC)** and the **U.S. Department of Labor (USDOL)**. Despite the differences in the laws, the remedies available to plaintiffs are often similar or the same.

Job Discrimination Laws Administered by the Equal Employment Opportunity Commission:

THE EQUAL PAY AND THE LILLY LEDBETTER FAIR PAY ACTS

The Fair Standards Labor Act (FLSA, 1938) was amended in 1963 by the **Equal Pay Act (EPA)**. Its main objective is to eliminate discrimination in wages based on gender. Still, it was not until 1970 that a federal court ruled in *Schultz v. Wheaton Glass Company* that for EPA purposes, the job of a woman did not need to be identical to a man's, only substantially similar. Although there has been

progress, the EPA has never fully achieved its intended objective.

In 2009, the **Lilly Ledbetter Fair Pay Act (LLFPA)** was signed into law, overturning the Supreme Court's decision in *Ledbetter v. Goodyear Tire & Rubber Co.*, which held a discrimination charge under EPA had to be filed within 180 days of the date of the original compensation decision leading to the charge or within 300 days in jurisdictions that have a state or local law prohibiting the same kind of compensation discrimination. The LLFPA carried a retroactive effective date of May 28, 2007, and vindicated EEOC's position that each discriminatory paycheck was a new violation.

LLFPA provided a brief victory to Mary Lou Mikula, who was hired as a grants coordinator for the Allegheny (PA) County Police Department.[3] After being hired, Ms. Mikula began inquiring about an adjustment in pay because she was doing work equal to a similarly situated male, but making $7,000 less annually. Ultimately, she litigated and the suit was dismissed by the District Court because it was not filed within the time limits existing at that time. That decision was upheld by the 3rd Circuit Court of Appeals just as the LLFPA act passed. On a rehearing and facts considered within the recently passed LLFPA, the 3rd Circuit reversed itself and Mikula's case was remanded for further proceedings, where the court ruled for the employer on other grounds. Box 9.1 summarizes a pay suit filed under a state equal pay act.

AGE DISCRIMINATION IN EMPLOYMENT ACT (ADEA)

The **Age Discrimination in Employment Act, ADEA** (1967), only forbids age discrimination against people who are age 40 or older and work in organizations with 20 or more employees.[4] ADEA forbids age discrimination in any aspect of employment, including hiring, job assignments, promotions, layoffs, training, fringe benefits, and any other term or condition of employment. Harassment of older workers, such as continuing offensive remarks about their age, may rise to the level of creating a hostile working environment and may also be actionable.

In *Smith v. City of Jackson* (2005), the U.S. Supreme Court reviewed a case filed by Jackson (Mississippi) police officers who were 40 years of age and older, who sued under a theory

---

Quick Facts: Gender and Other Pay Disparities

A Presidential Proclamation (2016) noted the typical woman working full-time, year-round, only earns 79 cents for each dollar earned by a man. For women of color that figure is 60 cents and for Hispanic women 55 cents.[2]

Box 9.1 Officer Kristi Lougheed Wins Suit

Officer Lougheed was hired with 15 years of prior police experience by the Aberdeen, Washington, Police Department at Step 1, the lowest pay grade. She subsequently learned that some male counterparts, with less experience, were making more than she was. The Chief agreed at some point to move her to Step 2, which was only a modest increase, and Lougheed filed suit under the State of Washington's equal pay and anti-discrimination laws. A trial determined that Aberdeen had violated both laws and the city unsuccessfully appealed the decision. In mid-2015, Aberdeen agreed to pay Lougheed $375,000 for general damages, costs, litigation expenses, purge her personnel file of letters of reprimand, advance her to Step 4, and the Chief was to write a letter of apology.[5]

of disparate impact, alleging that their employer's new adopted pay plan was more favorable to younger officers and fell more harshly by comparison on older officers.[6] Factually, officers with less than 5 years tenure received higher raises than those with more service. The defendant, City of Jackson, argued that it had a legitimate, nondiscriminatory reason for the plan, desiring to raise starting salaries to the regional average. The Supreme Court affirmed the lower court's summary judgment in favor of the defendant, concluding that while there were other ways to achieve the city's goal, the method selected was not unreasonable.

Nassau County (New York) reached a voluntary settlement with the EEOC in 2008 on an age discrimination suit. Although protected by the ADEA, four Nassau County Police Department Marine Bureau officers with excellent records and no negative performance evaluations were transferred to precinct jobs that were less desirable and were replaced by younger officers. The plaintiff officers argued that the personnel actions were motivated by an attempt to get them to retire. The settlement included $450,000 in damages for the plaintiffs and other injunctive relief.[7]

ADEA has a public safety exemption provision to apply its provisions; local units of government can refuse to hire a person for a sworn position if the applicant is over their maximum age for hiring and the refusal to hire was part of a bona fide hiring or retirement plan and not a subterfuge to evade ADEA's purposes.[8] This position was reached in *Kannady v. City of Kiowa* (2010). It was undisputed that the City of Kiowa refused to hire the plaintiff because he was 45 years old and thus not eligible to participate in the state-operated Oklahoma Police Pension and Retirement System, which had a 45-year-old cutoff for membership since 1989. In response, Kannady filed an ADEA suit. The trial court dismissed the suit and upon appeal, the federal 10th Circuit Court of Appeals affirmed the District Court's decision.

Many states have also enacted age discrimination laws. In ten states there is no minimum number of employees required to sue for age discrimination, although the usual number specified by states often is in the 5 to 15 employee range. Some states also specify an age discrimination threshold younger than the federal threshold of 40.

TITLE VII (1972) OF THE CIVIL RIGHTS ACT OF 1964

Title VII prohibits discrimination in hiring, pay, promotion, firing, wages, job assignments, fringe benefits, and other terms and conditions of employment because of race, color, sex, national origin, or religion.[9] These five categories are referred to as **protected classes**. The law covers federal, state, and local governments, private employers with 15 or more employees, labor unions, and employment agencies. Although Title VII contains no references to lesbian, bisexual, gay, or transgender people (LBGT), EEOC asserts that they are included within the meaning of the "sex" class of Title VII.[10] In FY 2015, EEOC received 26,396 claims of sex discrimination

which represented 29.5 percent of all claims.[11] A key case on the way to EEOC's inclusion of LBGT people within the sex class of Title VII was *Barnes v. City of Cincinnati* (2005), the facts of which are summarized in Box 9.2.

Remedies for relief available to plaintiffs include (1) injunctive relief, a court order prohibiting future discrimination; (2) hiring, promotion, or reinstatement; (3) backpay with interest; (4) if discriminatorily denied a job or terminated and there is no current vacancy, frontpay will be ordered until a position is available. Frontpay may also be an appropriate remedy when employer–employee hostility would make a continuing employment relationship difficult; (5) compensatory damages, to make the victim financially whole for past losses and emotional distress; (6) attorney fees; (7) removal from personnel and all other files of discipline, adverse performance appraisals, and other actions related to the complaint ultimately filed, and (8) punitive damages, against nongovernmental entities, where the discrimination was undertaken with malice or reckless indifference.[12]

EEOC's enforcement of the law is based on four theories of discrimination. These theories apply both to Title VII violations and to the other job discrimination laws that EEOC administers:

1. ***Disparate treatment***—An applicant or officer may rightly believe that he or she has been dealt with unfairly by an employment decision. To rise to the level of a disparate treatment claim, the person must have been intentionally treated differently because of his or her membership in a protected class; the discrimination must be more than slight to be actionable.[13] Both compensatory and punitive damges can be awarded against a *nongovernmental employer*.

African-American police officers in Houston filed a Title VII suit alleging racial discrimination. The officers complained they were excluded from serving in four divisions that prohibited officers from wearing beards. The department's position was that those divisions would be most likely to respond to chemical, biological, radiological, or nuclear attacks and the bearded African-American officers could not safely wear respirators.

Quick Facts: Limits on Compensatory and Punitive Damages Vary By Size of Employer

For employers with 15–100 employees, the limit is $50,000.

For employers with 101–200 employees, the limit is $100,000.

For employers with 201–500 employees, the limit is $200,000.

For employers with more than 500 employees, the limit is $300,000.[14]

Box 9.2 The Probationary Sergeant Who "Lacked Command Presence"

Phillip Barnes (PB) joined the Cincinnati Police Department as an officer. On the Sergeants' examination some 10 years later, he was placed 18th among 120 officers who took it. He was promoted to Sergeant and, like other recently promoted Sergeants, placed on probation. PB was living as a pre-operative male-to-female transsexual, dressing as a man at work and a woman while off-duty, sometimes coming to work with arched eyebrows and lipstick on his face. This resulted in a reputation as a homosexual, cross dresser, or bisexual.

After reporting to District One on his first assignment as a Sergeant, a superior noted that PB had trouble completing documents, exercising judgment in the field, and completing assignments on time. Unlike other Sergeants on probation, PB was then evaluated by a different set of standards in a "new training program." A special six-page form was developed, used only for evaluating PB. He was not allowed to go to the field alone; was required to wear a microphone at all times; during the last weeks of his probationary period had to ride in a car with a camera in it, and was evaluated daily by seven Sergeants. One of the Sergeants who evaluated PB testified that the purpose of the program was to document every mistake he made so he could be failed on probation. The Sergeant also stated PB was targeted for failure although he was actually improving over the course of his probationary period.

This Sergeant warned PB that he was going to fail probation because he wasn't masculine enough. Prior to promotion a senior commander had counseled PB because he needed to stop wearing makeup and act more masculine, which was explained as an effort to correct grooming deficiencies.

Ultimately, a recommendation was made to fail PB during probation. This recommendation was rejected and instead PB was told to choose a mentor. At the beginning of that relationship PB got mediocre scores, which later collapsed to zeros in some categories as time passed. A second fail recommendation was made and accepted by the administration. PB was the only Sergeant to fail probation during an 8-year period.

Among the other characterizations of PB made during probation was that he lacked command presence, he failed to use proper radio procedures, his grooming and uniform appearance didn't meet standards, and he was dishonest on several occasions.

PB acknowledged that being a Sergeant was more difficult than he had expected, there was a difference in the duties of officer and Sergeant, and in some areas he did need to improve. At one point during probation, he sought help from the department's psychologist, stating problems during probation elevated his stress and that the problems would not have occurred but for his supervisors singling him out in the manner they did, which he found demeaning.

PB filed a sex discrimination suit under Title VII and prevailed at a jury trial The jury awarded him $150,000 in compensatory damages, $30,511 in back pay, and $140,000 in front pay. The District Court additionally awarded PB $527,888 in attorney fees and $25,837 in costs. The city appealed the case twice, both of which were denied. Phillip Barnes later became Philecia Barnes.

In *Stewart et al. v. City of Houston Police Department,* the District Court granted summary judgment to the defendant, the Houston Police Department, and the dismissal was afffirmed by the Appellate Court (2010).[15]

In *Endres v. Indiana State Police* (2003), a Baptist officer refused assignment as a full-time gaming commission agent at a casino because gambling violated his religious belief that games of chance were sinful.[16] The plaintiff requested other duties and was denied. The suit was dismissed with the court noting that juggling unpopular enforcement duties and the preferences of officers would be a daunting task to managers and create operational hardships.

Religious discrimination may also be litigated on Constitutional, as opposed to Title VII, grounds. An Orthodox Jewish Las Vegas detective, Steve Riback, sued his department (*Riback v, Las Vegas Metropolitan Police Department*) for religious discrimination because it would not allow him to grow a short beard or wear a yarmulke skullcap, even though he was on desk duty and not in contact with the public (see Figure 9.1). In 2009, this First Amendment case was settled with the plaintiff receiving $350,000, the right to grow a beard, and permission to wear a baseball cap in lieu of a yarmulke.[17] Newark Sunni Muslim police officers also successfully litigated a First Amendment claim, allowing them to grow beards in fulfillment of their religious practices (1999).[18] In its decision, the court noted that the department had already made an exception for African-American officers prone to develop infections from shaving (*Fraternal Order of Police Newark Lodge 12 v. City of Newark*).

2. ***Adverse impact***—Prior to 1965, the Duke Power Company hired only African-Americans into the lowest-paying job classifications, while Whites were hired into better-paying positions. The two races worked in segregated departments and promotions were made within those racially divided departments. Based on the enactment of the Civil Rights Act of 1964, Duke Power was later required to change its employment practices.

In 1965, new applicants and employees seeking transfer to traditional White classifications were required to have a high school education and pass two aptitude tests. The tests excluded

FIGURE 9.1 ▶ Detective Steve Riback reviews his religious discrimination suit against the Las Vegas Metropolitan Police Department. (Photograph by Steve Riback)

94 percent of the minorities, but only 42 percent of the majority group. At that time in Duke Power's home state of North Carolina, only 12 percent of African-Americans had a high school education. Willie Griggs, an African-American employee of Duke Power, filed a class action suit under the Civil Rights Act of 1964.

In *Griggs v. Duke Power Company* (1971), the Supreme Court found for plaintiff, Griggs. The tests and the high school education requirement continued past discriminatory practice and both requirements were not job related. Griggs established the principle that the absence of discriminatory intent is unimportant and it is the consequences that matters. Although Duke Power's requirements were seemingly innocuous, their impact fell more harshly on African-Americans, excluding them from better-paying positions, creating an adverse impact. An adverse impact is an employment practice that, although lacking any discriminatory intent and on its face appearing to be neutral, an employer is prohibited from using because it has an unjustified impact on members of a protected class.

In 1978, the EEOC developed **Uniform Guidelines for Employee Selection Procedures**. The purpose of the Guidelines was to create a single set of principles designed to help covered employers comply with federal laws prohibiting employment practices that discriminated on the basis of race, color, sex, religion, and national origin. As defined by EEOC, "selection procedure" means any measure, or combination of measures or procedures, used as a basis for any employment decision. The term includes the full range of evaluation techniques from traditional paper and pencil tests, performance tests, training programs, probationary periods, and physical, educational, and work experience requirements through informal or casual interviews and unscored application forms.

Using the example of a written promotional test, a rough rule-of-thumb method of assessing adverse impact is the "**4/5ths rule**."[19] If the passing rate on the test for any race, sex, or ethnic group is less than 4/5ths, or 80 percent, of the passing rate for the group with the highest passing rate, an adverse impact exists (see Table 9.1).

TABLE 9.1	EXAMPLE OF THE 4/5THS RULE APPLIED TO A POLICE PROMOTIONAL WRITTEN TEST[a]		
Test Data	White Candidates	African-American Candidates	Totals
Took Test	400	100	500
Passed	120	10	130
Failed	280	90	370
Passing Rate	30%	10%	26%

[a]Adverse impact calculation: 10% (lowest passing rate) ÷ 30% (highest passing rate) = 33.3%, substantially less than 80 percent, indicating an adverse impact. To avoid adverse impact in this example, the African-American passing rate would have to be a minimum of 24 percent.

In such a case the employer must defend its practices or under EEOC guidelines adopt a selection process that is equally valid and reliable, reasonably meets the employer's legitimate business needs, and is less discriminatory, or go to trial. The replacement selection process might be a different written test or it could be an entirely different process, such as an oral board.

Law enforcement agencies are sensitive to the problems of adverse impact. However, as noted above, under EEOC guidelines, all adverse impact is not illegal, although defending such practices imposes a substantial burden. That is a fight, even if winnable, in which most employers don't want to engage. It is likely to be costly, time-consuming, reduce prospects for increasing diversity, tarnish the image of the employer, and make economic development a harder task because employers are reluctant to relocate their businesses to a city or county that can't effectively govern itself. The flip side is that abandoning the results of a test with adverse impact may result in a suit by officers who passed the test.

In *Ricci v. DeStefano* (2009), the Supreme Court ruled that New Haven, Connecticut, couldn't simply dismiss the results of promotional tests for Fire Lieutenant and Captain that produced adverse impacts because it feared Title VII liability. The data for an adverse impact was clear—under the 4/5ths rule, the minority passing rate was 34 percent, only 59 percent of the passing rates for majority officers. The Court concluded that before being used the tests had been subject to "painstaking analysis," New Haven had turned a "blind eye" toward its validity evidence, and another process that met the employer's needs was not available at that time.

A case with a fact situation striking similarity to *Ricci* is *Joe Oakley v. City of Memphis*. The 40 plaintiffs in Oakley included a racially and gender-mixed group of candidates that litigated over a promotional test to police major that Memphis discarded amid concerns about Title VII litigation despite strong possibilities for its defense. Both the trial and appeals court found for the defendant city of Memphis and plaintiffs appealed to the Supreme Court. In the wake of its decision in *Ricci*, the Supreme Court remanded Oakley for further consideration. Upon reconsideration, the plaintiffs prevailed. Note should be taken that both the original trial and appeals court decisions were based on the prevailing decisions prior to *Ricci*.

> 3. ***Harassment***—Although technically harassment is a form of disparate treatment, EEOC recognizes it as a separate theory of discrimination.[20]

Harassment is a discriminatory, unwelcome action toward an individual on the basis of race, color, sex (including pregnancy), national origin, age, religion, disability, or genetic information. Unwelcome actions that may rise to the level of harassment include speech, touching, and other conduct that create an intimidating "hostile work environment" that employees reasonably should not have to endure. Mild teasing and occasional offhand comments will fall short of being recognized as creating a hostile environment; the conduct involved must be more severe or pervasive but need not be totally intolerable.[21] Gender harassment can occur without it being specifically sexual harassment[22] (e.g., "You're pigheaded like all other women").

A single significant act may constitute harassment. In *Chris Sanford v. Department of Veterans Affairs* (2009), the Associate Director grabbed the plaintiff's arm, turned him around, pushed him into a desk, and screamed at him.[23] The incident was sufficiently severe as to allow a claim of harassment to be made. However, the more usual situation is a pattern of continuing conduct. The more severe the harassing actions, the less need there is to show a pattern.

Sexual harassment is perhaps the most immediately recognizable form of harassment. The harasser may be an immediate supervisor, a supervisor in another unit, the agent of the employer, or an non-employee, such as a package delivery person. The victim and harasser may be of the same gender; a victim may also be someone other than the person being harassed who finds the conduct offensive. There does not have to be an economic injury to the victim before a claim can be filed and the harasser's attention must be unwelcome. It is helpful if the victim informs the harasser that the conduct is not wanted and uses the employer's complaint system to document the circumstances of each such encounter.[24] Although victims of sexual harassment can be men, they are most often women; in rare occasions, they may be very young. A 14-year-old girl working in a Wichita, Kansas, fast-food restaurant was sexually harassed by the store manager almost immediately after being hired. One day after work he insisted on driving her home. Instead, he took the girl to his home and sexually assaulted her. The manager was later sentenced to 8 years in prison. EEOC investigated and found that other girls were also sexually harassed, and sued the company, which settled the suit in 2002. The girl who was sexually assaulted received $150,000.[25]

Traditionally, **sexual harassment** has been categorized as (1) **quid pro quo**, from Latin, meaning an exchange or literally "something for something." It is constituted by unwelcome sexual advances, requests for sexual favors, and other verbal or physical conduct of a sexual nature when (A) submission to such conduct is either explicitly or implicitly a term or condition of an individual's employment or (B) submission or rejection of such conduct by an individual is used as the basis for employment decisions affecting that individual[26] and (2) **hostile environment**, which is created when the prohibited and unwelcome behavior has the purpose or effect of unreasonably interfering with an individual's work performance or by creating an intimidating, hostile, or offensive working environment.[27]

Examples of conduct that contribute to a hostile work environment include crude language; displaying sexually suggestive cartoons, calendars, posters, photographs, sex toys, or pornographic material; unnecessary touching; off-color, lewd, and obscene jokes; sexually suggestive gestures and body language; references to sexual activity and questions about another's sexual life; social invitations to discuss a promotion, raise, performance appraisal, or other terms and conditions of employment; and demeaning or offensive language, such as "babe," or "work spouse."[28] In determining whether such unwelcome conduct may have established a hostile environment, a variety of factors are considered, such as frequency, severity, and whether the conduct is intimidating or humiliating.

Box 9.3 Deputy Sues Sheriff, Alleges Sexual Harassment

Although the Sheriff avowed there would be no toleration of sexual harassment, he was self-described as a "touchy-feely person." Periodically, the sheriff had contact with a female deputy, making inappropriate or suggestive remarks and touching her in sexually aggressive ways. Subsequently, he insisted on hugging her when they encountered each other at work and would grab her buttocks. At one point, he required her to sit on his lap and forced a kiss on her lips, admonishing her that if she wanted a transfer or promotion, she had to choose him over her boyfriend. Some at work referred to the Sheriff as a "gropealope." These and other episodes made the plaintiff dread going to work. She resigned, filed suit, and prevailed at trial on appeal, the judgment of the trial court was affirmed.[29]

Employers have a substantial responsibility in curbing all forms of prohibited harassment. Table 9.2 illustrates common elements in a sexual harassment policy. Such policies often include the names, telephone numbers, and physical and e-mail addresses of those outside of the department to whom sexual harassment can be reported. Not shown in Table 9.2 are the specific procedures related to the policy.

4. *Retaliation*—Unlawful retaliation can take one of two forms: (1) retaliation for participation and (2) retaliation for opposition.

Under retaliation for participation, employers are prohibited from retaliating against a job applicant or an employee because he or she made a charge, testified, assisted, or participated in any manner in an investigation, proceeding, or hearing involving a covered job discrimination claim; for the employee's expression or conduct to be protected from retaliation, it must make reference to a protected class or type of prohibited job discrimination.[30]

Under retaliation for opposition, employers cannot discriminate against an applicant or employee who opposed covered job discrimination practices or said so in response to the employer's questions. Protection is afforded so long as the opposition is based on a reasonable and good faith belief that the practice opposed is illegal. In the event, the practice opposed is not prohibited, the employee is still protected. However, if such opposition is unreasonable, in bad faith, deliberately false, or malicious there is no protection.[31]

TABLE 9.2 SEXUAL HARASSMENT POLICY STATEMENT
Policy
All Departmental employees have a right to work in an environment free from unsolicited and unwelcome conduct of a sexual nature. Sexual harassment is against the law and is prohibited conduct that will not be tolerated in the department. Violations will be swiftly investigated and appropriate action taken at the earliest possible point. It may be necessary to transfer the accused to another position pending resolution.
In addition to being legally wrong, sexual harassment is also misconduct that undermines the integrity of the employment relationship. All employees have a responsibility to prevent the development of a department climate that allows, supports, promotes, condones, tolerates, or ignores sexual harassment and are required to report violations orally or written at the earliest possible opportunity.
Reports of misconduct may be made with any of the following: (1) any departmental supervisor, including outside of the normal chain of command; (2) the Internal Affairs Unit; (3) the city's Human Resource Department or EEO Officer; (4) any Assistant City Manager or the City Manager; (5) the State Civil Rights Commission; and (6) the federal Equal Employment Opportunity Commission.
All supervisors are responsible for preventing sexual harassment by: (1) monitoring the workplace on a daily basis; (2) ensuring that employees understand their rights and requirements to comply with the law and this policy; (3) taking immediate corrective action when misconduct is observed even if the involved employee is outside the normal chain of command; and (4) reporting allegations and observed misconduct in writing to the Office of the Chief of Police within 24 hours of occurrence. Reports shall be hand carried by the initiating supervisor to the Office of the Chief of Police in a sealed envelope bearing no outer details to protect privacy.

Source: Drawn, with restatement for brevity, from the policies of the Denver, Colorado; Santa Cruz, California; and Peoria, Illinois, Police Departments.

Quick Facts: Officer Sues for Retaliation, Actively Supported Wife's Disability Claim

A consent decree was entered into by the City of Colorado Springs and plaintiff Lance Lazoff in a retaliation case.[32] Both Mr. Lazoff and his wife were police officers. She filed an Americans with Disabilities Act (ADA) complaint, which he actively supported. Subsequently, he was denied promotion to Sergeant 16 times. The consent decree remedies included back pay and retroactive seniority.

THE PREGNANCY DISCRIMINATION ACT (PDA)

Pregnancy, childbirth, and related medical complications were not originally conceived of as discrimination issues. Still, some agencies developed policies to prevent such discrimination and the courts allowed litigation under the 1964 Civil Rights Act. To formalize what had previously been an ad hoc process and to promote uniformity of rights, the **Pregnancy Discrimination Act (PDA)** of 1978 was enacted. In some circumstances, the ADA, and the Family Medical Leave Act (FMLA) protections may also be envoked. The PDA is the primary law prohibiting discrimination against pregnant women and is applicable to businesses with 15 or more employees and all public employers.

Box 9.4 Pregnant Officer Fights Back After Lost Opportunity to Take Sergeant's Exam

In 2013, New York Police Department Officer Akema Thompson learned that the first Sergeant's test in 2 years was going to be on the same day as her baby's due date. She also knew that the civil service gave a makeup test. After an exchange of correspondence, the most accommodation she received was civil service would allow her to sit on a cushion on the regular date for the test, In that same year, 1,376 women nationwide had pregnancy discrimination cases resolved in their favor.

Thompson solicited the support of her union, the Patrolmen's Benevolent Association, which sent three letters warning that the denial would alter the trajectory of Thompson's career and was unlawful. Her request for a makeup test, which the civil service had scheduled, was once again turned down. In 2014, the Legal Momentum, a women's advocacy group, took her case pro bono and filed suit against the city for pregnancy discrimination. The case was settled out of court in 2015. Thompson received $50,000 and was allowed to take the make-up test, the Legal Momentum got $15,000, and the city stipulated that pregnancy and child-related conditions would be grounds for a make-up examination in the future.[33]

Broadly, the act makes it illegal to discriminate in employment practices against a woman because of pregnancy, childbirth, or medical conditions arising from such.[34] Hiring a pregnant woman is not required, but such an applicant must be treated equal to all other candidates. Women applying for pregnancy leave cannot be required to give more than the 30 days notice mandated by the FMLA. Poor performance and attendance problems by pregnant women need not be tolerated by an employer, but such employees cannot be held to a higher standard than any other employee. A woman cannot be forced from her job even if it exposes her to dangerous conditions although the employer should provide her with written notice of the hazards.

Box 9.5 Six Officers Sue for Pregnancy Discrimination

Six Suffolk County (New York) Police Department (SCPD) female officers sued their employer on pregnancy discrimination grounds in 2006 for denying women officers limited duty, desk-type jobs during their pregnancies. Until 2000, the SCPD provided access to such positions and then changed its policy to limit the use of such positions to officers injured on-duty. The SCPD also failed to provide bulletproof vests and gun belts that would fit pregnant women. The result was that women could not work for much of their pregnancies and were unpaid after exhausting their annual leave. The trial court found for the women in *Lochren et al. v. Suffolk County* and awarded damages and attorney fees. The plaintiffs appealed the amount of attorney fees and costs awarded to the Appeals Court, which discovered mathematical and other errors by the trial court, in awarding $578,704. The Appeals Court remanded those issues to the trial court. In 2010, the trial court awarded attorney fees and costs of $932,187.[35]

PREGNANT POLICE OFFICERS AND DEPARTMENTAL PRACTICES AND POLICIES

Findings from a major review of research studies lead to the question of whether existing law enforcement policies related to pregnant officers are sufficiently comprehensive and informative.

Some departments still lack policies regarding firearms training by pregnant officers. Although nonlead rounds are used by many law enforcement agencies, others still use leaded bullets. "Non-lead" rounds use no or very little lead and are sometimes called "green rounds" because they are also more eco-friendly. Lead toxicity is harmful to the fetus and exposure during pregnancy is associated with serious complications, including spontaneous abortion and hypertension. Well-ventilated indoor ranges can substantially mediate this problem. Noise toxicity is also related to acute disorders, including miscarriages. Lead and noise combined have a higher toxicity with significant consequences (e.g., heart lesions).[36]

Gun-cleaning solvents may not be safe and pregnant officers should not clean firearms. Heavy physical activity during the last trimester may injure the baby or the mother. Pregnant officers should not be tasered during training due to a risk of miscarriage. Chemicals at clandestine labs, haz-mat spills, and traffic accidents are also health risks, as are contact with potentially infectious subjects and violent assaults. Shift work and night duty are associated with preterm births.[37]

The International Association of Chiefs of Police (IACP) developed a policy, Pregnancy and Policing," in October 2010. Among its notable points: (1) women are important in policing as part of its diversity; (2) women should never have to choose between motherhood and livelihood; (3) there continue to be obstacles for women in law enforcement, including inadequate facilities and equipment; (4) male norms in place can create self-doubt, and (5) inadequate maternity policies and equipment for pregnant officers.[38] In 2011, The Women in Federal Law Enforcement (WIFLE) Foundation has also offered advisory pregnancy guidelines for federal law enforcement agencies.

The IACP properly notes that policies that automatically exclude women from regular duties from the onset of pregnancy are discriminatory, as are policies that afford no accommodation because it ultimately results in loss of seniority, health benefits, and pensions (see *United States of America v. Bill Sturch, Sheriff,*

Bryan County, Oklahoma, 2009). No accommodation policies also deny departments the opportunity to retain valuable women officers. Automatically placing women on light duty status when they become pregnant also create some potential disadvantages: loss of off-duty employment, may be unable to maintain state certification as a peace officer, may be illegally excluded from competing for promotion, and adversely effecting opportunity for productivity and thus a potentially negative performance evaluation.[39]

According to the IACP, a sound policy keeps trained and experienced female officers working as long as reasonably possible and does not compel light duty until medically necessary, defers types of training that could interfere with the pregnancy, preserves seniority and all other employment rights, recognizes pregnancy as a transient or temporary condition, is based on medically sound information and not stereotypes, and prevents Title VII liability. The IACP policy also avoids the use of assignments that have a likelihood of encountering toxic chemicals, or pose other health risks, for example, raids on meth labs, chemical spills, intensive traffic enforcement, prolonged air travel, high risk entries, SWAT Team duty, riot control, and prolonged stationary posts, all of which have a high possibility of producing trauma. The option to use maternity duty should be made available to the pregnant officer during the second trimester or when medically indicated and may include non-hazardous assignments, writing police reports, operating a radio, interviewing people, and clerical work.[40]

The IACP also recommends avoiding the following during maternity duty: alternating shifts, defensive tactics training, actual firearms training, patrol duties, extensive exposure to automobile exhaust fumes, standing for more than 30 min at a time, lifting more than 25 pounds, and exposure to high concentrations to toxins. During pregnancy, the department should seek a temporary weapon qualification exemption or arrange for an alternative firearms qualification.[41]

THE AMERICANS WITH DISABILITIES ACT (ADA) 1990

The **Americans with Disabilities Act (ADA)** was enacted in 1990 to guarantee equal opportunity to jobs for qualified individuals with disabilities and to provide covered individuals with other protections as well. The ADA

Quick Facts: ADA Suits Often Against the Police

Impressionistically, after looking at ADA suits involving the police from 2011 to 2015, there is not a lot of litigation involving officers suing their departments on the basis of ADA. In contrast, there are a number of ADA suits against the police for not accommodating a citizens' disabilities, e.g., physical or mental disabilities. Officers may also misinterpret what they see when they encounter people with disabilities. Assume that a car is stopped and the officer orders the driver out of the car. He has mobility problems and gropes for a cane, but the officer yells freeze to the deaf man, thinking he is reaching for a gun. Fearing for his life, the officer shoots, killing the driver.

Box 9.6 Rochester, Michigan, Police Department Settles ADA Complaint

In 2015, the Rochester Police Department (RPD) reached an out-of-court settlement with a deaf man who was arrested. His hands were cuffed behind him, so he could not sign or write a note. He was detained without access to a telecommunication device such as a TTY device or a video phone, and not provided an interpreter for his video arraignment. In addition to other terms, the RPD was required to implement measures to avoid another such incident.[42]

A TTY device allows a deaf person to send and receive typed messages. A Sorenson Video Relay Service (SVRS) "video phone" creates a high-speed connectom to an SVRS interpreting center. The interpreter appears on the device and the deaf person signs his/her message, which is relayed in English to the police.

Amendment Acts of 2008 provided broader protections to job seekers with disabilities and put in place less-restrictive interpretations of the law than those held by the courts. The law covers private employers, state and local governments, employment agencies, and labor organizations and is enforced by the U.S. Equal Employment Opportunity Commission.

Rochester, Michigan, is one of only a number of police departments that have been sued because they lacked the policies and equipment to properly handle deaf persons. With all of its resources and specialization, even the New York City Police Department entered into a settlement with the U.S. Department of Justice in 2009 to implement practices that would enhance effective communication when its officers are in contact with deaf persons.[43] ADA further requires easy access and use by covered individuals to a wide range of facilities, including banks, theaters, recreational opportunities, transportation, hotel/lodging, child care centers, voting centers, restaurants, and assistance at self-serve gasoline stations.

ADA legislation has had a significant impact on the hiring and other human resource practices of law enforcement agencies. It makes it unlawful to discriminate in all employment practices with respect to covered individuals, including recruitment, hiring, pay, firing, promotion, job assignments, training, leave, layoffs, and benefits. The law does not require that preferences be given to covered individuals.

In the employment context, a **qualified individual with a disability** is a job applicant or employee who meets legitimate skill, experience, education, or other requirements of an employment position that he or she seeks or holds.[44] The person must be able to perform the essential or core job functions versus the marginal requirements, with or without a **reasonable accommodation** for his or her disability by the employer; job requirements that screen out people with disabilities are legal only to the extent that they are job related and consistent with business necessity.[45] Examples of reasonable accommodations by employers include modifying equipment and facilities, redesigning jobs, modifying work schedules, and approving transfers to other vacant jobs that can be performed.[46] There are federal and some state tax credits for businesses to offset the cost of providing reasonable accommodations.

Accommodations cannot impose an "undue hardship" on employers, such as substantial expense. This is evaluated in terms of the employer's own circumstances. Accommodations will vary according to individual needs (e.g., an applicant may need a sign language interpreter during an interview, blind employees may need someone to read job instructions to them, and diabetics may need periodic breaks to eat properly and monitor their blood sugar and insulin levels).[47] Employers are not required to lower production or quality standards as an accommodation, nor must they provide one unless a request is made.[48]

With respect to an individual, a **disability** is (1) a physical or mental impairment that *substantially* limits one or more major life activities, (2) a record of such an impairment, or (3) a perception that a person has such an impairment.[49] Major life activities include but are not limited to by federal law, caring for one's self, performing manual tasks, seeing, hearing, eating, sleeping, walking, standing, lifting, bending, speaking, breathing, learning, reading, concentrating, thinking, communicating, and working.[50] Major bodily functions are also covered, including digestive, bowel, bladder, respiratory, circulatory, and reproductive functions.[51] Determining "substantial limitation" is a "common sense judgment"; the limitation need not totally prevent a major life activity nor rise to the level of a significant or severe restriction.[52] Although individuals may take "mitigating measures" to reduce or eliminate their impairment (e.g., insulin or use of a prosthetic limb), in ADA's view, the test of impairment is whether the person would have a substantial limitation of a major life activity without it.

GENETIC INFORMATION NONDISCRIMINATION ACT (GINA)

Passed in 2008, the **Genetic Information Nondiscrimination Act (GINA)** covers employers with 15 or more workers, labor unions, training programs, and employment agencies. It effectively extends the reach of Title VII of the Civil Rights Act of 1964. The law defines "genetic information" broadly; it includes information about an individual's genetic tests and the genetic tests and medical histories of "family members" (i.e., their diseases, disorders, and conditions). *Family members* means to the fourth degree (i.e., great-great-great grandparents). In addition to other provisions, GINA strictly limits the disclosure of genetic information and requires

---

Box 9.7 Police Chief Gave HIV Warning to EMS?

Perception of a disability played a central role in a West Virginia incident. Claude Green, Jr. had a heart attack while driving. Billy Snead, a passenger in the vehicle, was giving CPR to Green when Welch Police Chief Bowman arrived at the scene. It was alleged that Chief Bowman knew or believed Green was gay, pulled Snead away from giving CPR, falsely warning him that Green was HIV positive, and 10 min later repeated the warning to arriving EMS workers, who nonetheless performed CPR. Green died a short time later at the hospital after attempts to revive him failed.[53] Chief Bowman labeled the allegations a "bold-faced lie."[54] *The Estate of Claude Green, Jr. v. Robert Bowman* was settled out of court, the terms of which cannot be discussed.[55]

---

its storage in special medical files. The law provides for compensatory damages for violations, which make plaintiffs whole, restoring them, and punitive damages, which are intended to punish violators and deter future offenses.

Title I forbids the use of genetic information by health insurers. Excluded from the definition of genetic information are cholesterol and liver-function tests, the sex of a person, or his/her age. Blood tests are permitted to the extent that they are not designed to detect genotypes, mutations, or chromosomal changes.

Title II regulates the use of genetic information in the work setting. Employers cannot (1) use genetic information when making employment decisions about applicants and the terms and conditions of employment for employees (e.g., a law enforcement agency cannot refuse employment to applicants because they have a family history of cancer); (2) classify, segregate, or limit employees based on genetic information; (3) retaliate against someone who asserts opposition to actions or practices forbidden by GINA; or (4) request, require, purchase, or disclose genetic information about employees. For example, employers may not use a health risk questionnaire requesting family medical history unless an "exception" applies.

The law recognizes six narrow exceptions to acquiring genetic information: (1) the "water cooler" situation, when an employer overhears someone talking about a family member's illness; (2) accidental discovery acquisition through a newspaper obituary or other publicly available source (e.g., reading that an employee's mother died of heart failure); (3) voluntary participation in an employer's wellness program where the employee gives written consent; (4) when the information is required as part of a Family Medical Leave Act or similar state or local law provision to establish the medical necessity for which an employee is asking for leave (the Family Medical Leave Act is discussed in the next section of this chapter); (5) genetic testing that monitors the biological effects of toxic substances in the workplace, where program participation is voluntary or required by law; and (6) law enforcement agencies may request genetic information from employees to determine if they have contaminated forensic evidence and to identify human remains.

GINA took effect on November 21, 2009, and litigation involving it has been sparse during 2009–2015. There does not appear to be any GINA suits filed by police officers because of their department's disclosure of genetic information or against police departments by civilians for their disclosure of it.

Job Discrimination Laws Administered by the Department of Labor

The Fair Labor Standards Act (FLSA) was passed in 1938 and the U.S. Supreme Court upheld its constitutionality in 1941. It has been amended several times; most importantly for present purposes is that public employees became covered in 1986. It affects 130 million full-time and part-time private and public sectors employees.[56] In 1938, the federal minimum wage was 25 cents an hour; when adjusted for inflation it now equates to $8.56 hourly.[57]

The goal of the original **Fair Labor Standards Act (FLSA)** (1938) was to create jobs in a struggling economy in the belief that business employers would rather pay normal or "straight time" to new employees than pay overtime to existing workers—1.5 times their normal hourly rate—when they worked more than 40 hours a week.[58] In 1974, Congress amended the FLSA to make it applicable to public sector employees; 2 years later in *National League of Cities v. Usery*,[59] the Supreme Court held the amendment to be unconstitutional. Subsequently, the Supreme Court reversed itself on this issue in *Garcia v. San Antonio Metropolitan Transit Authority* (1985),[60] ruling that Congress did have the authority to apply FLSA to state and local governments.

The purpose of the FLSA is to establish national minimum wage, work hours, overtime pay, child labor, and required record-keeping standards. Of concern here are the work hours and overtime provisions pertaining to law enforcement agencies:

1. FLSA does not require holiday, vacation, or sick leave days; shift differential pay, hazardous duty compensation, overtime pay for working holidays, specific work schedules, fringe benefits, meal breaks, a written notice of the reason a person is fired, or any type of severance pay or package.[61] It also does not speak to job-sharing arrangements. Such things may be provided by a police department as part of its HR program or by written agreement with the officers' union.

Quick Facts: Youth Minimum Wage

Because of the pervasiveness of community policing and police youth programs, officers should be aware of the youth minimum wage so they do not mislead the youngsters with which they work.

A minimum wage of not less than $4.25 an hour is permitted for employees at least 16, but under 20 years of age during their first 90 consecutive calendar days of employment with an employer. Thereafter, such employees must be paid the minimum wage. If federal or state minimum laws are in conflict, employees are entitled to the higher of the two rates. Employers are prohibited from taking any action to displace employees in order to hire employees at the youth minimum wage. Also prohibited are partial displacements such as reducing employees' hours, wages, or employment benefits.

2. Nothing in the FLSA prevents employers from paying more than the national minimum wage of $7.75 an hour and 1.5 times it for each hour beyond a 40-hour work week. Some states have enacted a higher minimum wage. New York is committed to raising the minimum wage to $15 an hour by 2018. In 2014, by President Obama's Executive Order 13658, federal subcontractors must be paid $10.10 hourly.

3. Employees are grouped into two categories for purposes of overtime pay: (1) **nonexempt**—the group that is entitled to overtime pay and (2) **exempt**—the group that is not. Under the rule change effective December 1, 2016, to be classified as exempt, an employee must: 1) be paid a predetermined and fixed annual salary, 2) be paid more than $913 weekly or $47,476 annually, and 3) primarily perform bona fide executive, administrative, or professional ("white collar") duties as identified in the three-pronged "duties test:" 1) the *salary test*, which is covered above, 2) the *duty test*, which requires that the content of the job are directly related to the organization's management or general business operations and must be the principal, main, major, or most important duty of the employee, and 3) the *discretion and independent judgment test*, meaning the employee must exercise such judgment in matters of significance for the organization.[62] There are a number of exceptions to FLSA overtime provisions. Members of the "learned professions," such as medical doctors, lawyers, the clergy, registered nurses, pharmacists, teachers, and accountants are all examples. Coaches are exempt if they teach athletic concepts and skills, but athletic personnel who primarily recruit, have quality control responsibilities, or kindred positions are non-exempt.[63] If properly classified, exempt employees have no FLSA rights.

Quick Facts: Additional FLSA Information

The minimum salary for employees exempt because they are Highly Compensated Employees (HCE) was set at $134,000 annually. To automatically update the law, the $47,476 and $134,000 threshold salary points will be automatically updated every three years, starting on January 1, 2020.

Under FLSA, a person who: 1) is not protected by a civil service system and 2) serves on the staff of an elected official has no rights under FLSA. An elected sheriff has no FLSA rights nor does his personal staff, but the deputies do have such rights.[64] In Michael Souryavong, et. al. v. Lackawanna County (PA) and the Lackawanna Deputy Sheriff's Association (2015) the plaintiffs sought summary judgment against both defendants. On the issue that the county had failed to pay overtime ,the court granted the summary judgment, because there was no dispute as to the material facts. As to the suit against their own association for breaching the duty to fairly represent them, the court did not do so because there were material differences of facts.

Occasionally, an FLSA issue becomes involved in a larger one. In Anderson v. City of Los Angeles (2011) a police officer was fired because she failed to request compensation for working overtime and sued to be reinstated. The trial court order her reinstatement noting that no other LAPD officer had ever been discipline on those grounds. Her employer appealed the decision, arguing the case should have been returned for a disciplinary re-evaluation. Instead, the Appeal court noted that while the overtime was unauthorized, she made no compensation claim and there was no authority for the disciplinary action taken by the LAPD.

4. Employers with less than five law enforcement officers working during a 7-day week have a complete FLSA exemption from paying overtime for such weeks.[65] The law does not differentiate between full and part-time officers when counting the number of officers working.

5. Many private and public employers must pay overtime when the number of hours worked exceeds 40 hours during a week; for such employers, a "work week" may start on any day and consists of 7 consecutive 24-hour periods that total 168 hours. Law enforcement

TABLE 9.3 THRESHOLDS TRIGGERING OVERTIME COMPENSATION REQUIREMENTS FOR LAW ENFORCEMENT OFFICERS			
Work Period Days	Maximum Hours	Work Period Days	Maximum Hours
28	171	17	104
27	165	16	98
26	159	15	92
25	153	14	86
24	147	13	79
23	141	12	73
22	134	11	67
21	128	10	61
20	122	9	55
19	116	8	49
18	110	7	43

Source: Code of Federal Regulations, Title 29, Subtitle B, Chapter V, Subchapter A, Part 553, September 14, 2015.

employers have wider latitude before the overtime compensation requirement is triggered, as shown in Table 9.3. In contrast to a "work week," police employers can use a "work period" that ranges in length from 7 to not more than 28 consecutive days. "Work period" and paydays do not have to coincide.

6. Overtime compensation must be paid at least as 1.5 times the employee's normal hourly rate. In lieu of overtime pay, law enforcement employers can award compensatory time on the same basis; "comp time" acts as a bank of additional vacation or days off time. Officers can accrue up to 480 hours of comp time. Any hours worked beyond that accrual point must be compensated with pay. Officers may apply to take "comp time" off at any point, but agencies may consider their own operational needs and are not required to approve it as requested. However, agencies must allow officers to take comp time within a "reasonable period" following a denied request.

FLSA cases involving law enforcement officers as plaintiffs have not been substantial in recent years. Police officers were not entitled to compensation when putting on and taking off their uniforms and accompanying gear in *Bamonte, Cota, Perine et al. v. City of Mesa* (2010).[66] Although the officers were permitted, as a convenience, to change at the police station, there was no requirement to do so. The court contrasted the officers' situation with those working in a chemical plant who are mandated by the employer to change into and out of protective clothing on-site and who cannot safely perform their essential duties without doing so.

Adams et al. v. United States (2006) concluded that police officers commuting to and from work in an agency provided a "take-home car" are not entitled to be compensated under FLSA unless they perform some substantial police functions

(e.g., working a wreck, intervening in a violent assault, or apprehending an offender).[67] In *Cleveland et al. v. City of Elmendorf, Texas* (2004), the court decided that small law enforcement agencies employing fewer than five officers need not count the unpaid service of reserve officers in determining whether they are FLSA exempt.[68] Compensation for K-9 officers caring for their dogs off-duty has been litigated under a variety of fact situations. As held in *Bull v. Customs and Border Protection Service* (2007), *Lewallen v. Scott County, Tennessee* (2010), and other K-9 cases, the courts have generally been favorable to FLSA claims by such officers. In cases not favorable to the plaintiffs, they asserted overtime, but failed to keep records, began litigation too late, or their suits were otherwise defective.

In general, when officers are on standby duty in anticipation of being recalled to work, they are not entitled to FLSA overtime compensation if they are able to conduct personal business and have freedom of movement. The more restrictive the conditions a law enforcement agency places on its standby officers, the closer it moves toward having to pay FLSA overtime compensation (e.g., state police troopers being required to remain in state patrol barracks when on standby).

THE FAMILY MEDICAL LEAVE ACT

Enacted in 1993, the **Family Medical Leave Act's (FMLA)** intention is to help employees balance their career and family needs. States are allowed to enact more generous terms but cannot adopt more restrictive measures Although the federal government and a minority of the states had previously extended some benefits to same-sex partners, the Supreme Court's decision in *Obergefell v. Hodges* (2015) resulted in a substantial extension of those benefits. That decision rested on the equal protection clause of the 14th Amendment, which established a right to same-sex marriages. Among the new benefits for same-sex marriages are social security payments, FMLA

Box 9.8 FLSA and Virginia Laws Collide

Richmond police officers were generally scheduled to work 80 hours in a 14-day period. However, at times officers worked up to 86 hours during that period and were paid regular, not the higher overtime, wages. In 2011, Stacy Rogers, on behalf of herself and other similarly situated plaintiffs filed suit under Virginia State law, which required overtime pay after 80-hours working a 14-day period. As its defense, the city claimed that under FLSA standards overtime pay did not begin until more than 86 hours were worked in a 2-week period and federal law negates state law.

Because there was no difference in the facts before the court, the sole question for it to decide was did federal FLSA law trump the more generous provision of state law. Normally, the Supremacy clause of the Constitution invalidates a conflicting state law. However, when faced with that claim by Richmond, the court's responsibility was to determine what the intent of Congress was in enacting FLSA. With regard to the Virginia law, its potential trumping by the Supremacy Clause was not to be taken lightly inasmuch as the power of a state to establish labor standards is part of traditional state powers. Moreover, under a prior federal decision, there had to be "clear and manifest purpose of Congress" to trump the historic power of the states. Richmond did not establish such a purpose, nor could it show that Virginia State law was a "barrier" to the implementation of FLSA or why the city could not obey both FLSA and state law, the latter of which was properly regarded as more generous than the *minimum standard* established by FLSA.

The city's argument did not prevail and in a court approved settlement in 2012, the city agreed to pay $7.2 million to Richmond police officers for previously uncompensated overtime.[69]

leave to care for a sick spouse, and spousal benefits for someone married to a member of the armed forces.[70]

"Covered employers" must grant "eligible workers" a total of 12 work weeks of unpaid leave during any 12-month period for one or more of the following reasons:

1. the birth and care of the newborn child of the employee;
2. placement with the employee of an adoptive or foster care son or daughter;
3. care of an immediate family member, spouse, child, or parent, with a serious health condition; and
4. medical work when the employee is unable to work because of a serious health condition.

A "covered employer" is a business with at least 50 employees and all public sector organizations. An "eligible worker" is a person who has worked for the employer 12 continuous months and at least 1,250 hours immediately prior to the request for FMLA leave. Employers may require a medical certification of the condition of a

Box 9.9 Can Officers Get FLSA Overtime Pay for Attending Mandatory Counseling?

In *Gibbs and Drew v. City of New York Police Commissioner Bratton and others* (2015), the court had to determine if mandatory counseling to save one's job required FLSA overtime pay for inpatient and after regular work hours outpatient counseling. Gibbs joined the NYPD in 2009 and was later assigned to the 63rd Precinct in January 2010 as a police administrative aide. In June, she was referred to the Counseling Service Unit (CSU) for coming to work on several occasions with alcohol on her breath (AOB). She met with a CSU counselor who documented that she drank after work nearly every day, for the last few months she drank in the morning, and drank the night before and on the morning of her first visit to CSU. Diagnosed as alcohol dependent, she initially resisted a 28-day inpatient treatment but finally relented. The release report states her prognosis was extremely poor and she needed to be more open and honest. Gibbs was paid her regular rate during inpatient treatment. She returned to work. On three different later occasions Gibbs refused to participate in another 28 days impatient treatment. On her fourth refusal, her employment was terminated.

Because Drew, the second plaintiff, was non-sworn as a civilian employee at the Bronx Tow Pound lot, the particulars of her case do not warrant extensive comment here except to note that the court record, as far as it goes, reveals a successful recovery.

The court held that the extra hours spent in inpatient and outpatient counseling were not FLSA compensable. Those activities were not compensable because they were not part of the plaintiffs, indispensable primary duties. On another test, the court held that the counseling was not for the primary benefit of the employer. It did note that if Gibbs' rehabilitation had have been successful, the NYPD would receive some, but not a primary, benefit in that it would not have to go to the effort and expense of hiring and training a replacement.[71]

Box 9.10 Officer Files FMLA Suit Against Elkhart, Indiana

Officer Lee served with the Elkhart Police Department from 2005 until 2011. He shot a suspect in 2008 in connection with his police duties and in 2009 was present when another officer was shot. He did not make any FMLA claims in these incidents. In 2010, while on duty in uniform, he allegedly grabbed the breast of a restaurant employee hard enough that her cell phone was knocked from her front shirt pocket. Investigation into this allegation incident established: (1) Lee's supervisor knew of the restaurant incident and (2) there was another allegation of unwelcome sexual touching by Lee from a woman at a convenience store.

Lee's supervisor was reduced from Sergeant to Corporal for not reporting the restaurant incident and Lee received counseling and a five-day suspension. Another allegation also occurred in 2010 in which a woman reported that Lee, in uniform and on-duty, came to her house, said he had a warrant, and had sex with her. Lee denied these allegations and returned to counseling. At some point, the EPD was informed by the counselor Lee needed to take 7 to 10 days off. Lee was cleared to return to duty, but during his last visit to the counselor Lee said he wanted to be tested for PTSD. The counselor didn't see this as necessary and Lee said he would visit another health provider. The counselor then advised the department that Lee could not perform his duties safely.

During this time the Chief of Police was considering what disciplinary action would be appropriate in light of the second allegation. He ultimately decided to recommend termination to the Elkhart Board of Public Safety. After a 2-day hearing, the Board concluded that termination was appropriate.

Lee filed suit in 2012 claiming that he was denied FMLA rights and fired in retaliation because he tried to claim them and that some other rights were violated as well. When the city filed for summary judgment, he "substantially narrowed" his legal claims, focusing on the FMLA claim. The city's core defense was that when Lee finally made application for FMLA leave, he was already under the investigation which led to his termination. In 2014, the federal District Court found for the defendant City of Elkhart because (1) the city's treatment of Lee was more favorable than he would have received under FMLA. He was placed on administrative leave when being counseled and on the additional days off recommended by the counselor. As a result, no deductions were made to his sick and annual leave days; (2) Lee never established there was a denial of some benefit; and (3) Lee never challenged the Board of Public Safety hearing.

Lee appealed to the 7th Circuit Court of Appeals in Chicago. In 2015, the 7th Circuit affirmed the decision of the District Court, ending the litigation.[72]

covered family member or that of an employee. The employer may seek a second medical opinion about such certification. Employees seeking FMLA leave must give the employer 30 days notice except for "unforeseeable circumstances," in which case the employee must explain and provide answers to any questions about why the request was unforeseeable. The use of sick or vacation days may be permitted in conjunction with a request for FMLA leave; the use of those days does not count as part of the 12-week FMLA leave period.

The FMLA was amended in 2009 and added two additional circumstances in which FMLA leave may be requested:

1. because of a "qualified exigency" arising out of the fact that the spouse, child, or parent of a police officer is on active duty in the armed forces or has been notified of an impending call to active duty and

2. to care for a covered military service member's serious illness or injury if the eligible police officer is the child, spouse, parent, or next of kin of the service member.

In *Knussman v. State of Maryland* (1999), the principle was established that under FMLA, a man cannot be denied FMLA leave on the basis of gender to be the primary caretaker for a seriously ill family member.[73] The plaintiff was a 22-year veteran of the Maryland State Police whose wife was bedridden with several medical conditions following childbirth.

THE POLICE PERSONNEL SELECTION PROCESS

Figure 9.2 summarizes police applicant processing, selection, and training. The flow of this chapter substantially parallels this figure.

Applicants and Recruiting

Minimum standards for the employment of law enforcement officers are established by each state's **Police/Peace Officer Standards and Training Commission (POST)** or similarly titled agency. Employers may establish further or higher standards. Recruiting is the process of attracting a pool of candidates from which well-qualified applicants can be selected. The attractiveness of any pool of applicants can vary from one time to another. The economy has an impact on the number and quality of applicants for law enforcement positions; in a good economy the applicant pool is sometimes shallow, and in a down cycle, there are more quality applicants.[74] As the U.S. economy soured in 2007, the New York City Police Department received 54 percent more applications the next year and the FBI was sorting through 227,000 applications in 2009 for 3,000 openings.[75]

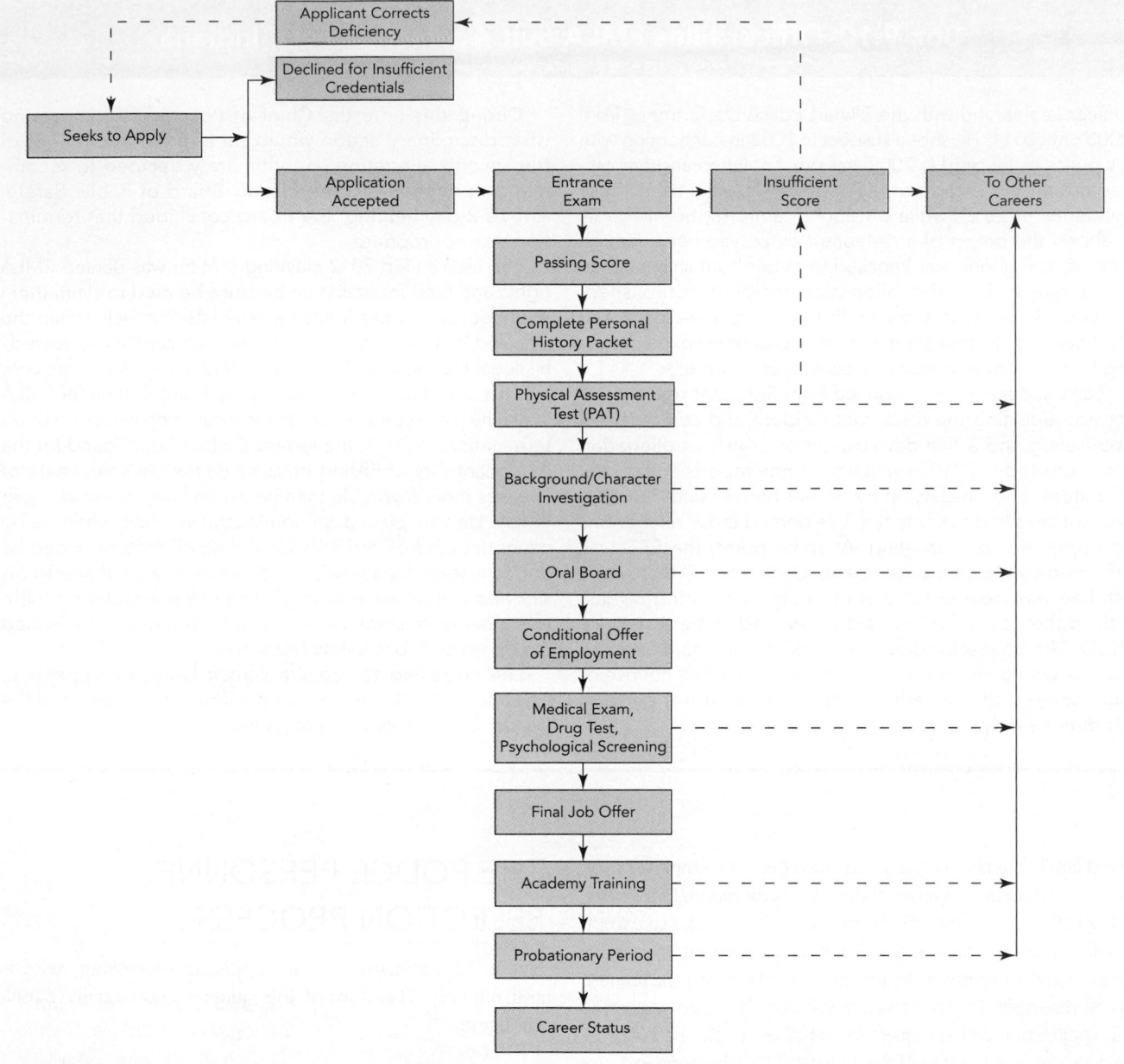

FIGURE 9.2 ▶ Applicant screening model.

A study of 850 California academy recruits explored their views about the recruiting process and revealed:[76]

1. The top two reasons for joining a law enforcement agency were a desire to serve and a sense of adventure and excitement, although most recruits were also influenced by health and retirement benefits.
2. The length of time it took to process their applications (54 percent) and the lack of personal contact and updates during the process (34 percent) were negative experiences.
3. The professional reputation of a potential employer (i.e., well-respected) was a major attractor (86 percent).

4. The least productive recruiting strategies were traditional ones, such as advertising in newspapers.
5. The most productive recruitment strategies were websites with information and online application forms followed by contacts with officers who were friends or family members or other employee referrals.
6. Recruits had long-term interest in law enforcement; 20 percent were interested in a police career in elementary school and 50 percent by the time they graduated from high school.

A study surveyed 205 North Carolina state and local law enforcement agencies.[77] Respondents classified their recruiting techniques as passive (35 percent), neutral (34 percent), and aggressive (31 percent). Overall, the agencies' preferred methods of recruiting were word of mouth (95 percent), newspaper ads (83 percent), targeting community college students (72 percent), and the Internet (63 percent). With nearly 70 percent of the departments employing passive or neutral recruiting efforts, it is not surprising that 68 percent of them had no waiting or backlog list of qualified candidates. Their techniques were simply not very successful. For them, if police recruiting was survival of the fittest, they would be an endangered species.

The California Peace Officers Standards and Training Commission recommends the following recruiting practices:[78]

1. Develop an overall plan that addresses a range of factors, including agency goals, the community's demographics, future number of officers needed, the skills that will be required, and diversity.

2. Profile the ideal candidate, review past successes, failures, and future opportunities, and identify best practices; one agency found that its most successful candidates were 27-year-olds, who had a stable employment history during the past 2 years, and at least 2 years of college.

3. Personalize the recruiting process; stay in contact with applicants, update them on their status with calls and letters, and let them know which staff members to call with questions.

4. Carefully select and train recruiters.

5. Build strong partnership with potential applicant pipelines (e.g., the military, educational institutions, and student associations).

6. Make officers recruiting ambassadors, provide them with excellent recruiting packets, and reward them for referrals and hires.

7. Streamline the recruiting process, cutting out bottlenecks; provide potential applicants with a self-administered form so they can decide if they have any disqualifiers.

8. Develop a plan to deliver recruiting messages using multiple means or channels.

9. Have an Internet presence that is easy to navigate with as few clicks as possible to accommodate the many people who use the Internet to sort through employment opportunities.

10. Use effective recruiting strategies, relying on proven techniques and being open to new possibilities. Thinking "outside the box," the Sacramento (California) Police Department began hosting a Law Enforcement Expo/Female Health and Fitness Challenge, with males allowed to participate. The orientation of the event significantly increased female hirings.

Recruiting strategies and the expenditure of any recruiting funds should be carefully considered in light of human resource objectives, and the results carefully scrutinized. A study of the recruiting practices of the Los Angeles Police Department (LAPD) found results that may vary elsewhere, but illustrate the point that successful recruiting requires careful thought. The site of a recruiting event yields differential results; as compared to recruiting on military bases, the LAPD produced three times the number of applicants at community colleges.[79] Recruiting at events that focused on employment (see Figure 9.3) produced more applicants than those at cultural celebrations and athletic events; events that charged an entry fee and advertised in advance were also productive.[80] Women are more likely than men to attend events.[81]

The cost of reaching applicants varies by the methods used and also may yield applicants with different characteristics. It costs

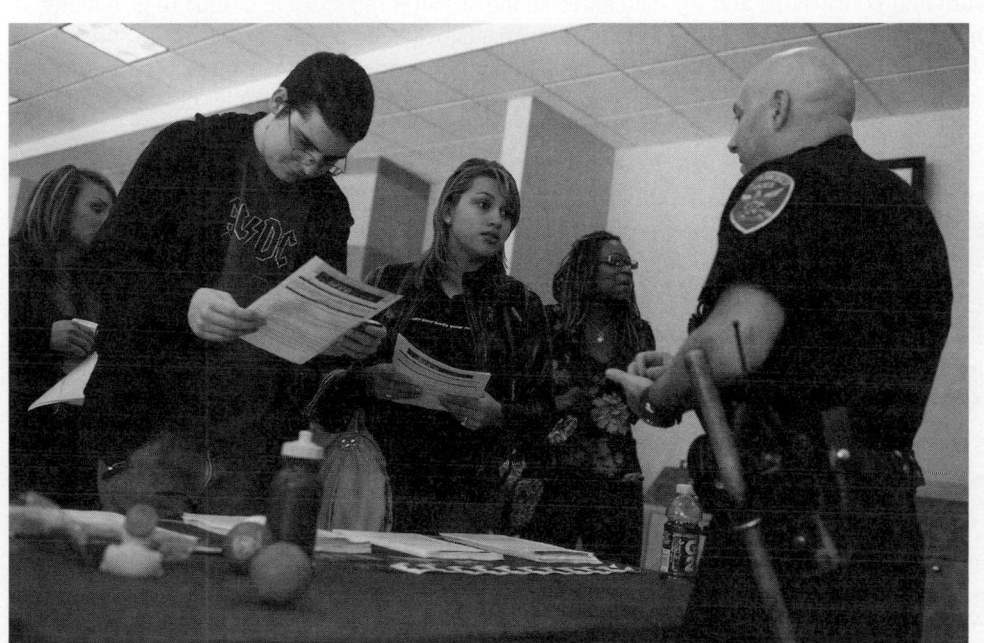

FIGURE 9.3 ▶ San Bruno, California: At a job fair, Skyline College students talk to a recruiter from the San Francisco Police Department. Job fairs benefit recruiters, giving them a chance to meet a variety of candidates from different backgrounds and it gives attendees a chance to "feel out" different police departments in attendance. (Justin Sullivan/Getty Images)

the LAPD $29 to attract each applicant from its e-government recruiting site and $1,012 from radio advertising.[82] Asian and Pacific Islanders report significantly more exposure to the Internet than do other racial and ethnic groups; African-Americans report more exposure to events, for example, job fairs and direct mail than do other groups.[83] The LAPD advertises on only one television station, an Asian language channel, where it broadcasts ads in Korean, Chinese, and Tagalog; it is a cost-effective effort at $147 per applicant.[84] The cost of recruiting efforts must also be evaluated in the context of keeping a law enforcement agency's "brand" before the public in a positive light.

By 2007, the EEOC began focusing more attention on recruiting efforts to determine to what degree they were unbiased or discriminatory. Recruiting messages cannot express a preference for any race, sex, color, ethnic group, or religion. Although most police departments depend, to a degree, on word-of-mouth recruiting by its officers, in a nondiverse department it might constitute a barrier to equal employment opportunity and limit diversity. Likewise, homogenous recruiting occurs when law enforcement agencies fail to use minority newspapers or Internet job sites such as Asian Nation, which might also be a barrier to equal opportunity.

The professionalization of policing has long been linked to college education for police officers. Only 1 percent of agencies require a college degree, 9 percent a 2-year degree, and another 8 percent, some college education; the high school degree is the basic educational credential for 81 percent of all agencies.[85] These requirements do not, however, reflect the actual numbers of police officers working in agencies who have some college to graduate or professional degrees.

The Entrance Examination

EEOC's Uniform Guidelines for Employee Selection requires that tests be valid and reliable. **Validity** means that a test actually measures what it is intended to measure and conclusions and decisions based on test scores are therefore appropriate and meaningful. The starting point to establish the validity of any test is a detailed job analysis.

A job description falls substantially short of being a job analysis because it is just a broad description of duties and responsibilities. Job analysis techniques can be used to identify (1) the important types of knowledge to test for on a written examination and the number of questions to be written for each knowledge area; (2) the skills to be measured in a single job simulation exercise, such as requiring an applicant to play the role of an officer who has been stopped by an elderly citizen who is hard of hearing, a little confused, and asking for directions. The importance of each skill needed for a job varies and each skill identified by the job analysis ordinarily has its own unique statistical weight. A series of job simulations may constitute an assessment center. Additionally, the job analysis can identify (3) the knowledge and skills to be tested by an oral board; and (4) the physical tasks police officers must perform in carrying out their duties. Validity gives tests the quality of being job related.

Reliability means that if the same test was given again or in a parallel form to the same group of people, they would score substantially the same. Reliability speaks to getting consistent, rather than random, results.

Larger municipalities and counties can develop their own entry tests. However, because establishing test validity and reliability can be time-consuming and technically challenging, many police entry-level tests are purchased or rented from test providers. Such providers include POSTs, Police Chief and Sheriff Associations, the International Personnel Management Association (IPMA), and private companies. Typical entry-level areas tested include reading comprehension, basic mathematical calculations, grammar, spelling, reasoning, memory, vocabulary, and clarity of expression (see Table 9.4).

Passing scores on entry-level tests for all jobs in local government have traditionally been set at 70 by local civil service/merit boards. The courts have been disinclined to alter that standard when it has been challenged. Jurisdictions allow a failed candidate to retake the test after the passage of time (e.g., 6 months). To avoid potential liability, test administrators make sure that all applicants take the test under the exact same conditions (e.g., everyone starts and stops at the same time, no one is allowed

---

TABLE 9.4 EXAMPLES OF VOCABULARY AND CLARITY OF EXPRESSION QUESTIONS ON AN ENTRY-LEVEL EXAMINATION

Vocabulary: Select the word that has the closest meaning to the word in bold print.
1. The suspect's employer **corroborated** her alibi.
   a. doubted
   b. verified
   c. contradicted
   d. denied

Clarity: Compare the two statements. Pick the one that is most clearly stated.
   a. The hairs were gathered in a clear envelope by the evidence technician.
   b. The hairs were gathered by the evidence technician in a clear envelope.

to use a cell phone, and lighting is adequate throughout the room). In large longitudinal studies published in 2009 and 2010, respectively, the passing rate on entry-level examinations for LAPD applicants was 84 percent versus 83 percent in Rochester, New York.[86]

Although entry-level tests are most often written or a job simulation exercise, assessment centers are also used. The key advantages to the written test are low cost, ease of administration, and rapid scoring. Entry-level tests cannot cover what applicants are expected to learn in the academy or on the job, only

the things the knowledge and/or skills they are expected to bring to the job.

To a passing score on any federal entrance examination, the federal government will add five points for an honorably discharged veteran and 10 points for a disabled veteran or a recipient of a Purple Heart Medal for a combat wound. If a veteran is unable to use the preference points a mother, widow/widower. or spouse is entitled to them for federal employment purposes. Some law enforcement agencies have provisions to add points to qualifying veterans who make a passing score.

Quick Facts: Long Odds to Be Hired by Las Vegas Metropolitan Police Department (LVMPD)

Las Vegas is a Mecca for gambling. Being hired by the LVMPD is a long shot proposition for applicants. Roughly only 10 of every 100 job seekers at the LVMPD satisfy all requirements and make it to working on the street. The entrance examination stage eliminates 23 percent of candidates. The physical fitness stage knocks out 40 percent of those taking it. But the real applicant killers are the background and polygraph tests stages where 70 percent are washed out. Some applicants lie on their application about their prior drug use. Occasionally the actual details of that use would not have disqualified them, but lying about it did.[87]

The Physical Assessment Test

The physical demands of police work are considerable at times. Illustratively, officers must have a level of strength and cardiovascular fitness to sustain themselves in a fight with a resisting subject or in pursuit of a subject fleeing on foot.[88] Physical fitness, condition, assessment, readiness, and agility tests are all intended to gauge the extent to which applicants can do so (see Figure 9.4). Physical assessment tests (PATs) are developed from a job analysis physical task inventory. The important tasks are translated into physical requirements by a qualified person, such

as an exercise physiologist, and a battery of tests is developed to measure those attributes (e.g., bench pressing weights or doing push-ups to determine upper-body strength, as well as timed runs to gauge cardiovascular condition and endurance).

Many agencies rely on the standards and testing protocols of outside providers for PATs for the same reasons they use their entrance examinations. PATs are **often** assessed on a fail/pass basis, with applicants being excluded from further participation at any point in which they cannot pass a subtest of the PAT. Table 9.5 summarizes a PAT test battery.

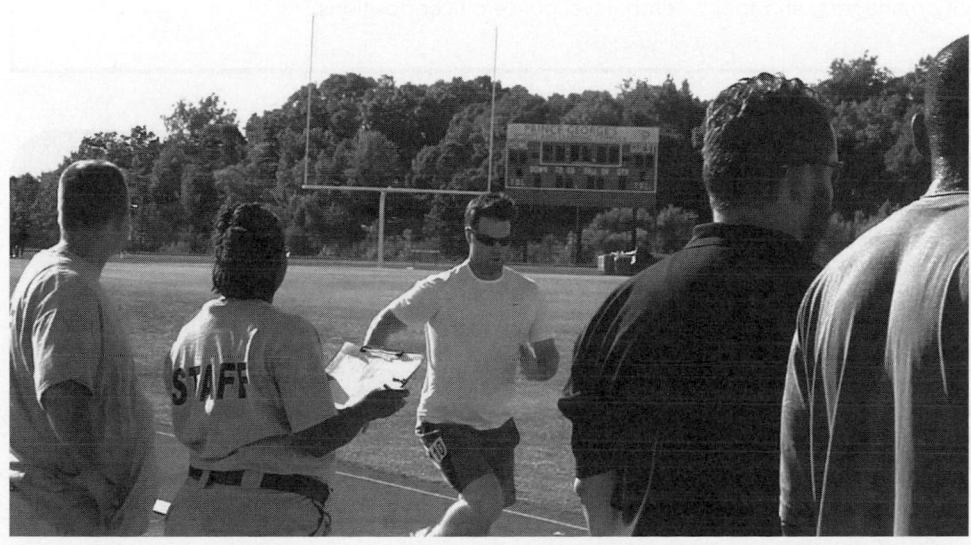

FIGURE 9.4 ▶ Police applicants participating in a physical assessment test. (Courtesy of Fit Force, Inc.)

TABLE 9.5 PAT TEST BATTERY							
Vertical Jump	Bench Press	Bench Press*	Sit Ups	Agility Run	300 Meter Run	Push Ups	1.5 Mile Run
11.0–20.5"	90–205 lbs.	57–93%	25–42	17.8–22.0 seconds	56–92 seconds	12–34	14:05–19:48

*Percent of current body weight
Source: FitForce

The EEOC prohibits requiring a medical examination before an applicant is offered a job contingent on passing it. Police departments have opted for two strategies to avoid liability if candidate injures him/herself or dies in association with the PAT: (1) applicants are advised of all activities and potential dangers and must sign a waiver to participate or (2) the candidate must provide a "medical certification," stating that a physician has examined the candidate and that he or she can participate. EEOC allows the medical certification because it is not a full medical examination and no specific medical data are provided with the certification. A study of the Rochester, New York, Police Department found that 61 percent of those tested passed the physical agility test.[89]

Women have successfully challenged some PATs on the basis that they produce a discriminatory adverse impact. *United States v. City of Erie* (Pennsylvania, 2005) illustrates this problem. A police lieutenant was assigned to develop a new PAT, although he had none of the needed specialized education, training, or experience. Nonetheless, he developed a series of tests with cut-off scores. During its use, from 1996 to 2002, 71 percent of the men taking it passed versus only 13 percent of the female applicants. There was no job analysis or validity evidence and the court held the test to be neither job related nor consistent with the employer's business needs.[90]

A 2005 study by the University of Kentucky addressed the question "What percentage of currently employed full-time

Box 9.11 Corpus Christi Sued for Physical Test Gender Discrimination

In 2012, the Corpus Christi, Texas, Police Department (CCPD) settled a suit by the U.S. Department of Justice involving gender discrimination in its PAT testing by agreeing to a consent decree. In 2011, 82 percent of male CCPD applicants passed the PAT, but only 33 percent of the women did so. Applying the previously explained EEOC 4/5ths "rule of thumb" to the CCPD case, the expected pass rate for women on the PAT should have been be at least 65.6% (0.80 × 82) or about twice what actually occurred. The 4/5ths rule is not a prima facie case but does invite more scutiny from many directions, including EEOC, those negatively effected, lawyers, law enforcement executives, city managers, and their human resources director.[91]

The CCPD consent decree required the city to pay $700,000 as back pay to female applicants who took and failed the challenged physical abilities test between 2005 and 2011 and who were determined to be eligible for relief. Also under the consent decree, some women who took and failed the challenged physical abilities test between 2005 and 2011 may receive offers of priority employment with retroactive seniority and benefits. Applicants interested in priority employment must pass the new, lawful selection procedure developed by Corpus Christi under the decree and meet other qualifications required of all applicants considered for entry-level police officer positions.[92]

Quick Facts: Colorado Springs Veteran Female Officers Sue Over Physical Test

Rebecca Arndt hasn't lost a single foot chase to a suspect in 16 years on the Colorado Springs, Colorado, Police Department (CSPD). Recently, because she did not run the department's distance test fast enough, the CSPD banned her from patrol duties. She is one of 12 decorated women who sued the CSPD in 2015 over a test that they say discriminates against women over 40 years of age. The recipient of many awards, Officer Arndt claims that "what they are saying is my work ethic and everything I've done up to now doesn't count."

None of the women filing suit has been injured making an arrest. One of the plaintiffs is the recipient of the CSPD's highest honor, the Medal Of Valor. According to the suit filed, the test is not normed or adjusted for gender or age, but is an absolute standard.[93] The CSPD intends to continue fitness testing for inservice police officers and there is wide community support to do so. In light of the pending trial in 2016, fitness testing has been temporarily suspended by the CSPD and the women have been returned to their regular duties.

sworn officers in Kentucky police departments could pass the Police Officers Professional Standards physical agility test (PAT)?" A survey was sent to 286 police departments and 155 (54 percent) responded. Among responding agencies only 22 did recurring PAT of currently employed police officers. After statistically analyzing responses, the study estimated that between 58.5 percent and 72.7 percent of all currently employed full-time Kentucky police officers could pass the test.[94]

The Lie Detection/Truth Verification Examination and Background/Character Investigation

The **Employee Polygraph Protection Act (EPPA**, 1988) is administered by the federal Department of Labor (USDOL) and restricts the use of the *polygraph* and other mechanism of lie detection with respect to employees. An employer shall not:

1. require, request, suggest, or cause an employee or prospective employee to take or submit to any lie detector test;

2. use, accept, refer to, or inquire about the results of any lie detector test of an employee or prospective employee; or

3. discharge, discipline, discriminate against, deny employment or promotion, or threaten to take any such action against an employee or prospective employee for refusal to take a test, on the basis of the results of a test, for filing a complaint, for testifying in any proceeding or for exercising any rights afforded by the Act.[95]

Included within the meaning of lie detector are the **computerized voice stress analyzer (CVSA**, see Figure 9.5) and the similar Layered Voice Analyzer, which uses its own patented technology.

The EPPA provides certain exceptions, including screening security services employees (e.g., guards for banks and armored cars), national defense and security, certain portions of the pharmaceutical industry, some business-conducted investigations involving theft and fraud, and law enforcement agencies.[96] A national study found that even when combining the use of polygraphs and CVSAs, only 29 percent of the law enforcement agencies responding to the survey used them in the selection process.[97]

Studies of the accuracy of the polygraph and the CVSA vary considerably; to some degree this is due to the research design, whether the subjects were students playing a role versus "real-world" applications, and the training and experience of examiners. A National Academy of Sciences analysis labeled the evidence supporting the polygraph weak and lacking scientific rigor.[98] Still, other studies place its accuracy between 64 percent and 98 percent; the reports of CVSA accuracy are similar to those of the polygraph.[99]

In several federal court circuits, there has been somewhat of a relaxation of the practice of automatically barring lie detection results, although the clear majority view is that the scientific evidence is not sufficiently substantial.[100] Some state courts admit lie detection evidence if the parties to a proceeding stipulate to its admission prior to the test being administered; New Mexico allows its admission in state courts as scientific evidence.[101]

Consistent with the EPPA, when a lie detector is used with police applicants it is primarily to verify the information on their detailed personal history questionnaire. In addition, applicants are asked an additional set of questions that are standard in each jurisdiction but vary somewhat across law enforcement agencies. Examples of these include whether they have ever used a different name or social security number, received an unfavorable work evaluation, been paid for work "under the table" or "off the books," used illegal drugs while working, falsified a time sheet, shoplifted

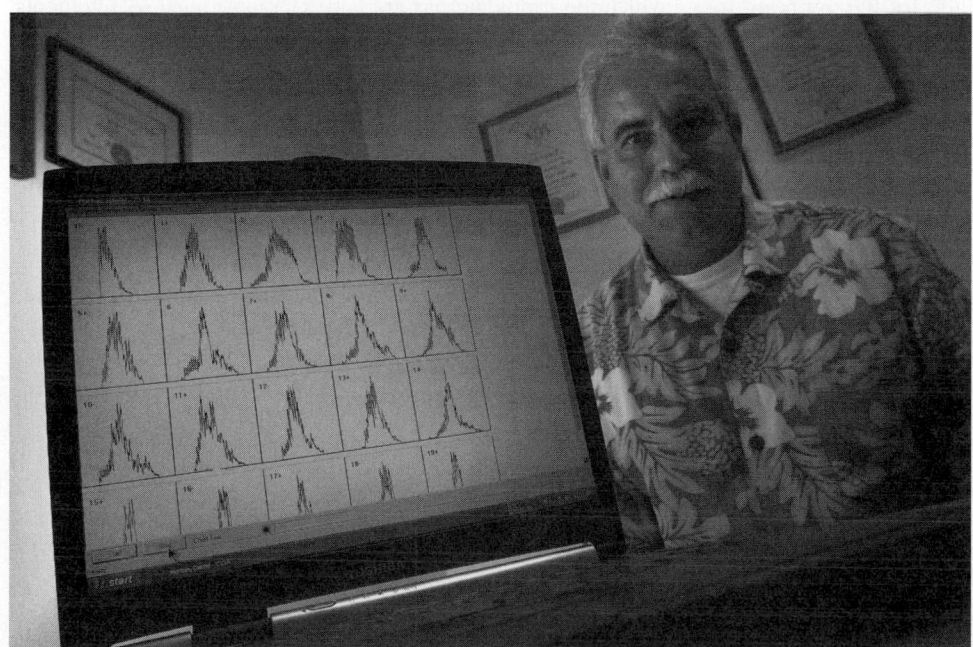

FIGURE 9.5 ▶ A San Diego Sheriff's Department Detective sits near a Computer Voice Stress Analyzer (CVSA) used to screen applicants seeking to be employed with that agency. The CVSA screening verifies statements made on the employment application and identifies areas that need further attention by the department's background investigators. (Dan Trevan/ZUMA Press/Newscom)

or switched price tags, been involved in a fight, carried a weapon illegally, driven without a license or insurance, received a major discipline on a previous job, or been involved with a group that advocates violence, hate, racial prejudice, terror, or subversive activities. Thus, a lie detector examination mechanism is primarily used to 1) verify personal history information and 2) probe for particular things that may require special attention by the background/character investigator.

During lie detection examinations, applicants may be disqualified for deception, using countermeasures, or admitting actions that disqualify them (e.g., thefts and acts of family violence). Except for these reasons or closely allied ones, eliminating a candidate solely on the basis of a lie detection examination is not a good practice. Two large studies placed the passing rate for polygraph examinations at 63 percent and 70 percent.[102]

In *Mullen v. County of Suffolk* (2007), a polygraph examiner determined that a police officer applicant to the Ocean Beach (New York) Police Department was deceptive in responding to questions about his drug involvement.[103] The applicant was disqualified from further consideration and appealed that decision. The court ordered the polygraph evidence reviewed. The record was independently evaluated by the Vermont State Police, which concurred with the initial findings, and the plaintiff's suit was dismissed.

The background/character investigation is a specialized type of investigation and one best learned through training and the guidance of more experienced personnel. Like other types of investigations, it requires strong attention to detail and executing all required steps. The first step is to review the applicant's personal history questionnaire and the findings of the lie detector examination. Combined, these documents will key the investigator to contradictions, inconsistency in details, admissions made that need to be discussed with the candidate, and other matters.

Prior to the initial meeting with the applicant, the investigator should prepare a series of questions to probe areas of concern and have information release forms ready for the applicant to sign (e.g., education, military, and credit). Any documents that the applicants are required to present should be copied and the originals returned to the applicant. The copies should be dated and countersigned by the applicant and the assigned investigator so it is clear where the documents came from and who received them. Documents that agencies commonly request from applicants include a current color photograph signed on the back, birth certificate/naturalization order, divorce decree, name change, social security card, restraining orders, selective service card (if subject to the draft), DD 214 record of military service, passport, driver's license, and POST training record if presently or previously serving as a peace officer in another state.

Even when presented with apparently genuine documents, verification of them is essential. An applicant submitted his documents, including an original DD 214. In the initial meeting with the applicant, the investigator asked about the 3-month employment gap between his honorable discharge from the Coast Guard and his application to the law enforcement agency. The man related he and his wife had taken an extended vacation to "see the country." Nonetheless, the investigator had the man sign a military records release form. Once received, the record showed that the applicant had been separated from the Coast Guard twice. The first DD 214 was accurate in all respects. However, there had been no extended vacation. Several weeks after being discharged the applicant reenlisted and shortly thereafter weeks later was drunk, beat his wife badly, and assaulted the military authorities who came to his on-base quarters to handle a domestic disturbance complaint. The applicant told the investigator that he gambled his DD 214 would be accepted at face value or that the record of his second enlistment and dishonorable discharge would never be discovered.

Other aspects of the background investigation include checking references and interviewing family, friends, roommates, coworkers, landlords, neighbors, spouse and/or a former spouse, and such others as the investigator feels necessary. Prior to writing the final report on the candidate, it might be necessary to have a second interview to resolve any lingering questions. A study found that 8 percent of the applicants making it to the background stage are eliminated.[104]

The Oral Board

Oral board panelists cannot ask whatever suits them and then simply subjectively evaluate applicants; in the past, such shoddy practices were so rampant that Doerner characterized police oral interviews as a fallible practice that had outlasted their usefulness,[105] and Gaines and Lewis concluded that they were the largest source of errors in making decisions about people.[106] The use of oral boards has improved substantially over the past several decades, although there are still some jurisdictions whose use of entry and promotional oral boards lags behind best and legal practices (see Box 9.12).

An applicant oral board often has three members, one of whom may represent the central personnel officer or community and two who are supervisors in the law enforcement agency to which the candidate has applied. To satisfy legal requirements, the questions asked must be job related and not be impermissible. "Tell us about your writing skills; how good do you think they are?" or "Would you describe a time when you got really angry?" would be established as job related by any competent job analysis. In contrast, "When is your baby due?" or "What provisions will you make for child care?" may lead to a charge that the Pregnancy Protection Act and Title VII were violated if the person is not hired and otherwise qualified.[107]

The length of an oral board varies across agencies but often falls in the 20 to 45 minute range. The members must be adequately trained in using a well-developed scoring system and the questions must have been validated. Although shorter training times are common, 8 hours of it, including the opportunity to evaluate multiple mock applicants, should provide the skills needed by panel members and a good level of defensibility if the adequacy of training is challenged. A good training method to calibrate the scoring by oral board members to the standards desired is to make digital motion pictures of the performance of six or so mock candidates and have experts make a written record of important behaviors noted and translate them into scores.

Box 9.12 The Police Consultant Who Couldn't Help

A sheriff hired a consultant to help the agency become accredited. At the first meeting of the sheriff, command staff, and the consultant, the first topic was the promotional system. It consisted of an oral board scored by three departmental supervisors. When the consultant asked why the question "How do you feel about emigrants?" was used, the sheriff said it was because people came to that county and his department had to deal with them. The consultant pointed out that "emigrants" meant people who left the county and that even if the language was corrected to "immigrants," the question was very vague, making it difficult to score with

any reliability. It was too akin to an ink blot test. The scoring instruction used by the board was simply a piece of paper labeled "The Scale" with numbers listed from 1 to 10 with no definitions of each point or an indication which were the high and low ends. Board members were selected by "seeing who was in the building" and they were not trained to be promotional raters. Each of the consultant's observations about the promotional system were loudly challenged by the sheriff, who fired the consultant on the spot, saying "I just don't think you're going to be able to help us." The consultant agreed with this assessment but for different reasons.

When the actual board members are evaluating the same motion pictures, the written behavioral comments and scores of the experts and the board members are compared with the goal of having the behaviors noted and scores converge during the training.

As questions are asked at an oral board, each member makes his or her own notes. When the candidate leaves the room, each member reviews his or her own notes and translates them into a whole number score. As a protocol, every score of board members on each skill involved, such as oral communication, must be within one point. When there are discrepancies greater than that, the panel discusses the applicant's behavior until the discrepancy is resolved.

A portion of a scoring sheet for oral communication is shown in Table 9.6. A training manual provided to each panel member gives substantial guidance as to the exact types of behavior that place an applicant in each score level.

Conditional Job Offer

The **conditional job offer (CJO)** is a letter from the employing agency to the applicant offering a job contingent upon there being a funded position available and the applicant passing the medical, drug, and psychological screening. A CJO is usually extended only to the best qualified/most competitive candidates.

An agency may not know exactly how many positions it has available because the new budget has not been finalized, and resignations, retirements, and terminations may be more or fewer than projected; thus, the need to condition the offer on a position being available.

The Medical Examination, Drug Test, and Psychological Screening

The purpose of this phase is to ensure that applicants can medically and psychologically perform the essential functions of a law enforcement officer. Some state POSTs have validated standards for medical, drug, and psychological screening. The exact sequence of these three tests varies and are often outsourced. In addition to the usual components of a health examination, an audio test is conducted to verify that candidates meet hearing standards. Vision is tested for acuity, narrowing, and color deficiency. Vision acuity must be correctable to a reasonable standard, such as 20/30. Drug screening is based on urine samples, although a handful of agencies use hair analysis, which can reveal drug use over a longer period of time.[108] The physical assessment test may be a surrogate for the medical examination; a study found that 95 percent of those who passed the PAT also passed the medical examination.[109]

TABLE 9.6 A PORTION OF AN ORAL BOARD SCORING SHEET FOR ORAL COMMUNICATION

To what extent did the applicant:
_____1. Speak in a clear voice.

_____2. Use voice volume appropriate to the situation.

_____3. Complete all sentences began.

_____4. Use correct grammar.

_____5. Avoiding distracting hand and/or other nonverbal body gestures.

_____6. Actively listen to the instructions to him/her at the beginning of the panel.

Psychological tests used in police selection vary, although the Minnesota Multiphasic Personality Inventory is commonly used. The 2001 revision of it was designated MMPI-2 (2001, 567 true-false questions). The 2008 revision is referred to as the MMPI-2-RF (Revised Form). It has 338 questions and can be administered in 30–50 min, about half the time for the MMPI-2. However, many users prefer to use it because there is more research data on it. The MMPI-2-RF is not a replacement for the MMPI-2; it is a revision of it.[110]

The Inwald Personality Inventory (IPI) was developed for use with public safety officers and is not used with other high-risk occupations. It has gained supporters over the past two decades and is designed specifically for use in law enforcement agencies. A study found that combining the results from the MMI-2, IPI, and Costa and McCrae's Neo Personal Inventory-Revised (Neo) contributed significantly to predicting recruit academy success.[111] Psychological tests may be followed by up to a 1-hour interview with a licensed clinical psychologist or a psychiatrist.

Box 9.13: Police Applicant Appeals Psychological Screening Conclusions

Plaintiff Jill Kavaleski applied for a job with the Boston Police Department, passed all hurdles, and was made a conditional job offer, contingent upon passing the medical and psychological screening. Phase 1 of the psychological screening was a group administration of the MMPI-2 and the Personality Assessment Inventory (PAI). Candidates are only passed along to Phase 2 of psychological screening if there are questions from Phase 1. In Phase 2, the plaintiff initially saw a first level screener, Dr. Brown, who told her the responses on the MMPI were too defensive to permit adequate psychological evaluation. The plaintiff then met with psychiatrist Dr. Reade, who notes she was thin, wore casual clothing, had messy hair, and was subdued and mildy depressed. She denied having eating problems and told Dr. Reade she was working out. Dr. Reade found her unacceptable.

At some later point, the plaintiff received a second conditional job offer from the Boston Police Department, requiring passing of the medical psychological screening. In her meeting with Dr. Reade, she was found to be a bright and hard

working woman, who was limited interpersonally. Apparently, therefore, she was again found unacceptable.

Some 6 months later, she again received a conditional job offer under the same conditions. She took the MMPI-2 and the PAI for a third time. Dr. Reade again had a negative opinion, seeing her as interpersonally stiff with a concrete cognitive style that was especially limiting. The conditional offer was revoked.

Plaintiff Kavaleski appealed to the city's Civil Service Commission (CSC). It concluded that Dr. Reade did not identify or substantiate any traits that would make Kavaleski unfit to serve as a police officer and that prior screenings (apparently referring to the first three of them) were subjective and/or amounted to opinion. The CSC directed she be placed at the head of the hiring list and authorized psychological retesting if (1) none of the prior screeners were involved and (2) it was video taped. Kavaleski passed and was hired. While she was in the academy the Boston Police Department appealed, but the court held for Kavaleski in 2014.[112]

The Formal Offer of Employment

At this point in the selection process, there is a completed file for each applicant documenting the results of the selection process. The appointing authority ultimately decides on those to whom a formal offer of employment will be made, although civil service rules, union contracts, and politics may influence those decisions. In larger law enforcement agencies, the names on the formal offer list will have been compiled by a staff member for the chief's or sheriff's approval. As the size of the agency decreases, the probability increases that the chief executive of the agency has a more personal hand in picking many of those to whom a job offer will be extended.

The Recruit Academy

Based on a single major analysis, 12 percent of those taking the entrance exam make it to the academy; there is no significant difference between the success rates of men and women in it. Those with at least some college enter the academy at a marginally higher rate than those with a high school degree, as do

applicants in their thirties compared to younger candidates. Among ethnic/racial groups, the ability to get into the academy ranged from 16 to 22 percent, with African-Americans lagging other groups.[113] Eighty-eight percent of males successfully completed academy training as compared to 81 percent of females.[114]

The length and content of the recruit academy/basic course is established by each state's Peace Officers Standards and Training Commission (POST). Individual law enforcement agencies can require training beyond the minimum established. The basic POST course in Texas is 618 hours, about 15.5 weeks, whereas the Austin Police Department operates a 32-week police academy with 1,280 hours on instruction. The national average for POST mandated entry training is 588 hours.[115]

Nationally, there are 626 academies providing entry-level training, employing 12,200 full-time instructors and about twice that number in part-time faculty.[116] Recruit academies must be certified by their state's POST. They may be operated by midsized to larger departments that allow smaller agencies to use a few seats at a nominal fee, by vocational/technical schools, community colleges, and by university police departments as a service to agencies in their region. If a state has a central police training facility, it may do some basic training, although the main effort of this type of facility is often focused on advanced/specialized courses. POSTs also require the completion of annual training to remain certified as a peace officer, with the national average being 24 hours.[117]

A study of 250 police academies concluded they failed to provide adequate training to investigate child sexual abuse.[118] The same criticism could also be made of preparation for other types of offenses (e.g., of white collar and organized crime, homeland security threats, human trafficking, and kidnapping). Almost any academy subject could benefit from additional training hours, but some useful topics simply cannot be squeezed into the overall time available. The academy's objective is to produce an adequate or better beginning generalist; within the resources available, often every additional hour added to one subject must be taken from some other subject area.

Police cadets socialize and drink more with their fellow recruits as compared with their previous circle of friends.[119] Scarfo found a significant relationship between education and police academy scores; however, military experience was not related to academy performance.[120] In a comparison between a traditional academy and one oriented toward community policing, more educated officers and women did better in the latter although overall recruits from both types of academies performed similarly.[121]

If a police academy is accredited with the Veterans Administration, veterans benefits can be used while attending it. A number of academies also have arrangements for trainees to earn college credits upon successful completion.

In 2010, the New York City Police Department began a $1.5 billion project to develop a new police academy that will also be used for advanced training.[122] When fully developed, the new facility will look like a small city, including five-story buildings, a tactical village with movable walls so cadets cannot memorize the course, and a firearms range. Outdoors, trainees will be put through trench collapse and other scenarios. The facilities provide the setting to make a shift from predominately classroom-based instruction to more hands-on scenario training. The first phase of construction was completed at a cost of $750 million. In January 2015, the first academy class began at the new facility with 800 trainees.

Probationary to Career Status

The probationary period is the last step in the entry-level selection process and the opportunity to observe the recruit under actual work conditions. In many jurisdictions, probationary periods can be extended, although most often that flexibility is not needed. The length of police probationary periods and when they start varies (see Table 9.7), although 1 year following graduation from the police academy may be typical. Nationally, 4 percent of probationary officers are rejected.[123]

Following completion of the recruit academy, a probationary police officer is placed in a field training program to prepare officers to function on their own. The national average length for POST-mandated field training programs is 147 hours[124] although many jurisdictions have longer ones.

Officers in training (OITs) ride with a **field training officer (FTO)** whose primary responsibility is to demonstrate skills from a checklist and then develop the OIT's proficiency to perform them by certain points in the program (e.g., perform 25 traffic stops correctly by the end of week 4). FTOs are experienced officers; in many states, they must complete a POST-required certification course to ensure they are qualified for their duties.

The Mesa, Arizona Police Department (MPD), has a nationally recognized 19-week FTO program.[125] OITs are rotated through the department's patrol districts and must be supervised by at least three different FTOs. Daily Observation Reports (DORs) are completed by FTOs and become the basis for the Sergeant's Weekly Report (SWR) on each OIT under his or her supervision. OITs may acquire the needed proficiencies before the end of the 19-week program. If so, they are allowed to ride solo, although the supervising sergeant continues to fill out SWRs. In the MPD and elsewhere, those successfully completing the OIT program will be recommended for career status.

TABLE 9.7 ILLUSTRATIVE PROBATIONARY PERIOD LENGTHS	
Law Enforcement Agency	**Length**
Anchorage, Alaska	One year from the end of field training period, but not longer than 18 months from the date of hire.
Marion, Iowa	One year from date of hire
St. Paul, Minnesota	One year from Police Academy graduation
Wauchula, Florida	6 months, beginning with the first day assigned to a Field Training Officer
Montpelier, Vermont	9 months, although the chief may extend it for 3 months. If the City fails to write a final probationary evaluation, the employee is deemed to have completed it satisfactorily

WORK GENERATIONS AND THE NEW RECRUITING

Recruits entering law enforcement have been shaped by forces such as their genetic predispositions and life experiences. After their academy training, the "locker room wisdom" is passed on to them, and they become socialized into the norms of the agency. In short, police work changes people. This section explores several generations of recruits who have entered law enforcement. While it is true that law enforcement agencies still change people and that, to a degree, each generation has changed policing, the more recent generations must be recruited with new messages attuned to their skills and values, as well as more generous benefits.

The Silent Generation

Born between 1925 and 1945, the **Silent Generation** is generally loyal, security conscious, and conforming.[126] They were born from the Great Depression until the end of World War II; as adults, many of the men served in the military and, like the women they married, they believe in the American way of life. The silent generation, with perhaps a rare exception, has passed through their law enforcement careers and retired. Recruiting members of this generation to jobs in police departments and supervising them did not present unusual challenges because of their experiences and values.

The Baby Boomers

Baby boomers have turned gray and are at or beyond normal retirement years, but are often reluctant to retire; 39 percent do not plan to retire until 66 or older and another 10 percent say they will never retire.[127] Born during 1946 to 1964, after millions of men and women returned home from the war, boomers grew up during a period of widespread social change. Early boomers personally experienced the unfolding of rock and roll, military service during the Vietnam War, civil rights demonstrations, the proliferation of drug use, assassinations, and all of the other manifestations of the turbulent 1960s (see Chapter 1, Evolution of Police Administration). With some college or more, boomers are better-educated and more liberal than their parents. As teenagers and young adults, they challenged conventional values, with the slogan "Never trust anyone over 30." Still, they were influenced by the strong work ethic of their parents. Ultimately goal and achievement oriented, the boomers are work focused and sacrificed, including some neglect of their families, to get ahead in their careers. Women had more career opportunities. Divorces were sometimes followed by second marriages to "start another family and get it right." Overall, 27 percent of baby boomers never married.[128]

Police departments did not hire boomers who admitted, or were discovered during the character/background investigation, to having used drugs. This eliminated some otherwise outstanding candidates, some of whom experimented with drugs while in the military. Eventually, departments softened their stance on drug use, although use of "hard" drugs was still an automatic disqualifier. Boomers were at the forefront as college education became more common in policing. Some supervisors routinely gave "college boys" lower performance appraisals than their less-educated counterparts. Sergeants were annoyed by the boomers' "disturbing tendency" to ask why things had to be done a certain way. To accommodate officers attending college, some received special work schedules, further irritating their routine-oriented supervisors. Authoritarian middle-managers were aggravated by the periodic written suggestions boomers submitted to improve operations, regarding them as a lack of respect for "proven methods." Eventually, the boomers proved their worth, even to skeptics, rising through the ranks to senior leadership positions with new styles of leadership. There are 30 million more boomers than the number of the next generation of workers, the "Xers."[129] When boomers finally retire it will create a loss of experience and institutional memory.

Generation X

Presently, **Generation X** makes up a large number of officers employed by police agencies. Many of them have retired and some are approaching or are in the tail end of their careers.[130] Birthed from 1965 to 1980, Xers are more ethnically diverse than boomers, grew up in families where both parents worked, and were the first generation of "latch-key" children.[131] More than one-half have divorced parents and one-third were physically or sexually abused, often by a stepparent.[132] Drive-by shootings, abortions, AIDS, school violence, and missing children were also part of their lives. Technologically, Xers tend to be computer fluent.

Early Xers grew to adulthood in a mixed economy; as toddlers their nation's economy was sound, but turned sour during the 1970s with stagflation. Stagflation, or a stagnant economy, is produced by a combination of a high unemployment and high inflation. It resulted in interest rates hitting 21.5 percent in 1980. As a result of stagflation, there was a noticeable migration of Xers back to their parents' homes to make ends meet.[133] The economic instability left Xers with concerns about their financial circumstances and retirement and with good reason: They are the first generation predicted to have a lower standard of living than that of their parents.[134] Xers marry later, delay having children, and expect their spouses to work; the women place a great emphasis on the family life many of them missed and are less inclined to sacrifice their families for career gain as the boomers did.[135] Rejecting the political platforms of the major parties, most Xers are independents (43 percent), followed by Democrats (30 percent) and Republicans (27 percent).[136] The three leading causes of death for Xers are automobile accidents, homicide, and suicide.[137]

Xers have been branded in various ways, including crybabies, grunge, and the lost generation. They have also been described in positive ways, including clear sighted, practical, intelligent, curious, good strategists and negotiators, seeing the whole person—not just the good or bad qualities, comfortable with diversity, and voracious learners.[138] There is some truth to these various characterizations because Xers are less homogeneous than boomers.

A Census Bureau study identified Xers' core values as equality, honesty, and respect in dealing with others, hard work, family values, and a sense of public service, which leads them to be high in volunteerism for social causes such as homelessness and social harmony.[139]

In the work setting, Xers have been restless; they welcome change and move from one employer to improve their financial circumstances and to be where they can make lasting contributions. At some point, Xers will run out of the number of times they can shift from one job to another and many settle down into something more like a conventional career as opposed to a succession of jobs with different employers. Managed properly they will go the extra mile and beyond to get things done well but will resist being micro-managed; given job autonomy, they are determined to succeed.[140]

Many police departments adapted their recruiting messages to attract Gen Xers, including (1) ensuring that the recruiting messages and their cultures are aligned to avoid turnover with repeated recruitment, screening, selection, and training costs; (2) communicating that policing is a noble, exciting public service career; (3) emphasizing that there are many career paths in law enforcement that will require life-long learning in order to be effective, giving them a sense of possibilities about their futures;[141] (4) highlighting that their sense of self-reliance is a substantial asset for them and their department; (5) illustrating how the Xers' skills at multitasking can be used; (6) underscoring that they will often be working without direct supervision, giving them desired flexibility and freedom in carrying out their job responsibilities;[142] and (7) giving them examples of how suggestions made by departmental members have improved operations.

As Xers entered law enforcement, some of their sergeants quickly noticed two characteristics that required attention: (1) their propensity to innovate occasionally made them somewhat resistant to supervision; sergeants lamented "I can tell them what to do until I'm blue in the face and they still do some part of the job their own damned way" and (2) their strong self-reliance and individuality led some patrol division Xers to emphasize a single or small number of duties, such as DUI enforcement, neglecting their broader responsibilities.

Generation Y: The Millenniums

Born during 1981 to 1994 and largely the children of baby boomers, **Generation Y** babies are entering our law enforcement agencies. The "Yers" have also been called the Millenniums, dot com babies, and "thumbers" because of the speed with which they can text message (see Figure 9.6). Less favorably, they have been tagged as Kids in Parents Pockets or "KIPPers," a slap at certain Yers prolonged dependence on their family of origin. Some of this dependency is created by overly supportive parents who get in the way of their children's journey to living as independent adults.

Raised in an era of gaming and rising modes of instant communication, social network sites (SNSs) have become a staple for Yers, including MySpace (2003), Facebook (2004), and Twitter (2006); they cruise Craigslist ads and subscribe to Internet dating services like Match.com (1995) and eHarmony (2005). Some SNSs target Yers, such as BrazenCareerist and MyYearBook, giving them forums to discuss their careers and workplace issues.

They are more optimistic than Xers, seek a better balance between work and the rest of their lives, have high expectations for their employers, enjoy diversity and challenges, prefer teamwork over individual efforts, feel a need to volunteer and fundraise, desire honest feedback about their job performance, and are unafraid to question authority. There is a trend toward traditional family values and Yers are spiritual about love, although not necessarily religious.[143]

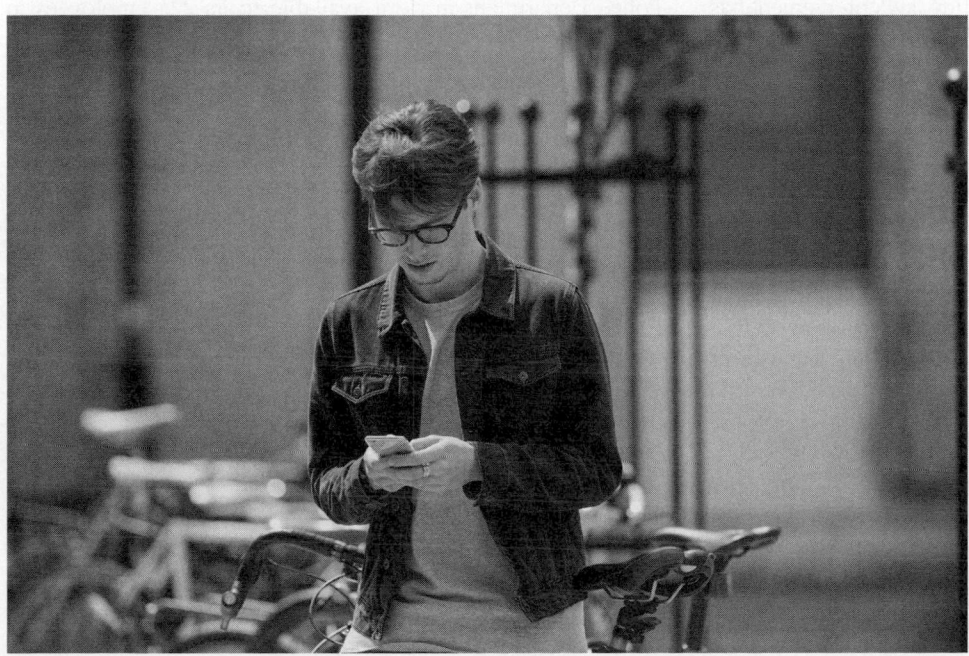

FIGURE 9.6 ▶ A Generation Y student using the "thumber technique" to text. (Biddy O'Neill/Corbis)

Quick Facts: Use of Social Networking Sites (SNS)

Research in 2014 by the Pew Research Center reveals SNS use in the United States is substantial: 76 percent of women and 74 of males use them. Eighty-five percent of those 18–49 are on SNS, but only 56 percent of those 65 or older are. In contrast, during an 18-month period between 2005 and 2006, the percentage of people 18–29 years old using SNS jumped from 9 percent to 49 percent.

SNS use is greater among those with a higher income, younger people, African-Americans, and Hispanics. Smartphones and tablets are key pieces of technology fueling the rise of SNS. A slight majority of SNS users, 52 percent, are on 2 or more sites.[144]

World-wide, the four most popular SNS are (1) Facebook (1,100,000,000 users), (2) Twitter (310,000,000,), (3) LinkedIn (255,000,000), and (4) Pinterest (250,000,000).[145]

Prensky coined the term "digital natives" to describe those raised in the immediate availability of information and images on the Internet. Later, the term came to be loosely defined as those born in 1980 and thereafter, a period which coincides with the beginning of Generation Y.

In 2015, the International Association of Chiefs of Police (IACP) released the results of a survey of 553 responding law enforcement agencies revealing 96 percent of them had an SNS presence. The most common use was for criminal investigations, for example soliciting leads for information or location of wanted persons (89 percent).[146]

Other uses made by law enforcement agencies using SNS include building a relationship and enhancing trust with the community being served, dissemination of information to protect the community, such as gas leaks in a neighborhood, school closings due to weather conditions, announcing where roadblocks will be set up in the future, recruiting, and missing persons information.

SNS can serve a key interest of governments generally and for police departments specifically in developing a reputation in the community for transparency.

Generations Z and Alpha

Generation Z, the "Zedders," fall in the birth range of 1995 to 2010. Although their profile is still emerging, their fascination with virtual realities may lead to impoverished social and interpersonal skills. Beyond Zedders is the **Alpha Generation**, which will be the best-educated of all of the generations and the most technologically sophisticated. Alphas are in their infancy with a birth cohort of 2011 to 2025.

The New Recruiting

The combination of Xers and Yers entering law enforcement has resulted in a better understanding that part of the process of recruiting officers might also be about recruiting their families, leading to the development of elaborate family information packages and videos about all aspects of a community, including job opportunities for spouses and departmental partnerships with children's day-care centers.

In addition to the usual benefits, such as life and disability insurance and deferred compensation plans, police recruiting tools have been elevated.[147] Although the practices of individual jurisdictions vary, officer incentives have become more varied[148] and may include relocation reimbursement; signing bonuses of $5,000 to $10,000; a stipend of $6,000 for graduation from the recruit academy and another $4,000 for completing the probationary period; allowing the use of GI Bill benefits while attending the academy; 45 or more college credits for academy completion; interest-free home loans up to $75,000 and forgiveness of home loans of up to $28,000 on the basis of 5 percent for each year of service;[149] increased vacation time and enhanced longevity pay and retirement systems. In some cities, officers retire with 20 years of service, based on 70 percent of the average of their three highest-paying years or 80 percent at 25 years. Some of these incentives "take a hit" in fiscally constrained environments; Los Angeles and Dallas are among large cities trimming such incentives.

Job flexibility and job sharing are used in law enforcement, but only to a small extent. Flexibility scheduling means that police departments present officers a choice of schedules within those established by the department; in contrast, job sharing means two or more officers share a single job.[150] Since 1999, the Orange County, California, Sheriff's Department has offered job sharing to its 4,000 members; the Huntington Beach, California, Police Department made it available to its 224 employees in 2001, and the Medina, Washington Police Department, allows 2 of its 12 members to job share. Job sharing reduces stress and absenteeism, increases job satisfaction, and allows valuable employees enough "wiggle room" to remain on the job.[151] For managing dwindling budgets and as a regular tool, job sharing may be attractive to personnel winding down their careers, as a prelude to their actual retirement. Used as a "decompression" period, job sharing would be beneficial in making the transition from work to retirement.

MILITARY CALL-UPS AND REINSTATEMENT

The substantial military commitments in Iraq and Afghanistan required the activation/call-up of National Guard and Reserve units as well as personnel in the Individual Ready Reserve (IRR), who do not participate in the two days a month "weekend drills" or the 14 days of annual training for unit members. While entire

National Guard and Reserve units are called to active duty, members of the IRR are activated individually based on the need for their special skills, such as helicopter pilots.[152] Law enforcement officers from both categories have been activated.

How many law enforcement agencies have experienced personnel call-ups is somewhat of a question; two national studies came up with different answers: 21 percent and 44 percent.[153] In a 40-officer department, the loss of four officers represents a 10 percent drop in staffing, creating operational difficulties and generating overtime costs. Even in departments where call-ups have been minimal, the loss of a single key person can create an impact: In Youngstown, Ohio the SWAT Team's only qualified sniper was activated.[154] Some agencies have officers who have been deployed several times on tours of up to 16 months.

Administered by the USDOL, the purpose of the **Uniformed Services Employment and Reemployment Rights Act** (USERRA, 1994) is to encourage noncareer participation in the uniformed military service by eliminating barriers to such service, minimizing the disruption of the lives of those called to active duty, and prohibiting discrimination against them. The Palm Beach County (Florida) Police Benevolent Association filed a grievance when a deputy on military leave was allowed to take a promotional test elsewhere, asserting that the collective bargaining agreement made no allowance for such a test. The arbitrator found for the Sheriff's Office; the provisions of USERRA supersede collective bargaining agreements.[155]

Under USERRA, a police officer called to active duty must give advance notice of his pending absence to the department unless it is precluded by military necessity or otherwise impossible or unreasonable. The cumulative period of absence with that department cannot be longer than 5 years, and service separation cannot be under dishonorable or other punitive conditions. The officer must report back to duty on a timely basis or file a timely application for reemployment unless impossible or unreasonable.[156] Table 9.8 summarizes the reporting back to duty timelines.

Quick Facts: The 5-Year Cumulative Absence

An employer is legally obligated to support up to a 5-year cumulative total of military service. However, not included in that total are: involuntary recall to active active duty, drills for reserve and national guard (active "reserve") participation, training, annual training, and additional training requirements determined and certified in writing by the Service Secretary concerned to be necessary for professional development or for completion of skill training or retraining.

When called to active duty, officers can keep their individual and family health insurance for up to 24 months, although they may be required by their department to pay up to 102 percent of the full premium. USERRA also provides guidelines for seniority, pension, and other rights of returning officers who are returning from active duty call-up. The "escalator principle" requires reemployment at the position officers would have attained but for their military service. If the officer is not qualified for the escalator position, the employer must provide the nearest approximation to it or if that is not possible, to the pre-military service position.

Assuming the example of a state trooper called to active duty who misses a promotional examination, her employer is required to give her a make-up exam and promote her with back-dated seniority to the point she reasonably would have been expected to be advanced in rank.[157] A federal court approved a jury award of double-pay, $300,000 for emotional distress, and promotion without testing for a New York City Fire Department promotional candidate who was denied an opportunity for a make-up exam when the absence was due to his military service.[158]

TABLE 9.8 USERRA REPORTING OBLIGATIONS FOLLOWING MILITARY SERVICE	
Length of Service	**Reporting Requirement**
Service of 1 to 30 days	The beginning of the first regularly scheduled work day or 8 hours after the end of the military duty, plus reasonable commuting time from the military duty station to home
Service of 31 to 180 days	application for reinstatement must be submitted not later than 14 days after completion of military duty
Service of 181 or more days	application for reinstatement must be submitted not later than 90 days after completion of military duty

(Based on information from U.S. Department of Labor, No author, Your Rights Under Userra The Uniformed Services Employment and Reemployment Rights Act, undated, p. 1, http://www.dol.gov/vets/programs/userra/aboutuserra.htm#knowyourrights, accessed September 17, 2015.)

The call-up of officers also raises some POST certification issues that should be included in an agency's policy on military activation. As an illustration, in Michigan, officers are not considered to have discontinued their law enforcement employment for license purposes, unless they voluntarily extended their active duty commitment. Upon return to their agencies, officers must provide a copy of their DD 214s (Certificate of Release or Discharge from Active Duty) or a DD 220 if the active duty lasts less than 90 days. If separated dishonorably, an investigation must be conducted to determine if the circumstances still allow POST licensing.

Activated officers may also be entitled to other rights under some state statutes and other federal laws (e.g., the federal **Servicemembers Civil Relief Act** [SCRA, 2003]). Some of SCRA's protections require that debts or leasing agreements entered into must pre-date the call to duty and the relief applying to them may be limited to the period during which the officer is on active duty or a short period thereafter. Key SCRA protections include (1) service members and their family members cannot be evicted from leased housing costing less than $2,932 monthly; (2) interest charged on debts cannot be greater than 6 percent; (3) if the officer receives permanent change of station orders, a housing lease can be terminated, if present at the new location for 90 days or more; (4) car leases can be terminated if the officer is called to duty for 180 days, or after entering the service, the officer executes a lease and is deployed outside of the continental United States for 180 days or more; (5) up to $250,000 of life insurance cannot be cancelled for nonpayment while on active duty; and (6) protections begin with the date of activation and may apply until as much as 180 days after return to civilian life.

Paul Sutton, a former police lieutenant, sued the City of Chesapeake, Virginia, claiming that contrary to USERRA he was denied reemployment after completing call-up service in the Coast Guard. Sutton had been employed with the police department from 1974 until he was activated in 2000. In 2007, he was denied reemployment and continued to serve on active duty until 2009, when he retired from the Coast Guard and litigated.

The federal court noted that Sutton had retired from the police department before going on active duty, cashing out his vacation and sick time, and that he began drawing a police pension. Sutton argued that his retirement should not be a barrier to reemployment. The court dismissed the suit, reasoning that to find for Sutton would be an expansion of rights beyond those contemplated by USERRA and his absence from the police department was greater than the law's 5-year limitation.

Despite some difficulties created by a call-up of officers, law enforcement agencies are proud of their service. Such officers exhibit a strong commitment to our nation and often return with sharpened or new skills that are relevant to the police setting. However, inevitably someone will attempt to take advantage of a situation. A police officer claimed he was being called to active duty. However, the officer went to another city in the state and took a high-paying job in business. The employing agency continued to deposit money into the officer's bank account, reaching $8,700 before the scheme was discovered. Convicted of fraud, the officer lost his job and served a jail sentence of 90 days.[159]

EARLY INTERVENTION SYSTEMS

In reaction to public concerns about police abuse of force and the number of complaints being generated by some officers, early-warning systems (EWSs) began appearing in the late 1980s. The police departments of New York City, Oakland, Kansas City, Miami, and Miami Dade were early leaders in this movement.[160] Some law enforcement executives speculate that perhaps 10 percent of their officers cause 90 percent of the problems. Leaving aside speculation, it is true that a relatively small number of officers cause a lot of an agency's problems. Research somewhat supports this belief. An 8-year study of the San Francisco Police Department showed that of its 2,200 officers, just 100, roughly 5 percent of all sworn personnel, were associated with 25 percent of the use of force reports.[161]

EWS were subsequently modified and "rebadged" as **Early Identification and Intervention Systems (EIIS)**. In some agencies, EWS had developed a negative image with rank-and-file members because the term "problem officer" was closely associated with the program. In contrast, EIIS is framed as being a support system for officers and includes them in decision making.

Well-operated EIISs assumed even greater importance following the passage of the federal Violent Crime Control and Law Enforcement Act (1994). The Act authorizes the Attorney General to file lawsuits to reform police departments engaging in a pattern or practice of violating citizens' federal rights. Suits may also be brought by the Attorney General under the Omnibus Crime Control and Safe Streets Act (1968) and Title VII (1972) for discrimination by law enforcement agencies on the basis of race, color, sex, or national origin if they receive federal funds.[162]

Presently, many agencies have substituted the use of Early Intervention System (EI or EIS) for the EIIS designation. Whatever terminology is used, it is clear what began as the early warning system (EWS) has continued to evolve and mature.

About 40 percent of law enforcement agencies use EIs.[163] While manual EIs may work well in smaller departments, in larger agencies, the systems must be automated to be effective because of the volume of daily work that must be entered and analyzed. The Seattle Police Department's policy on their EI system/program characterizes it in the following ways.[164] It (1) is a risk management strategy that is neither punitive nor disciplinary in nature, which is separate from, but does not replace, the disciplinary system, (2) seeks to identify and change at-risk behaviors, although employees remain fully accountable for following policy and other performance standards, (3) supports officers by supervisors coaching, mentoring, performance feedback, identification of pathways to improve job performance, which may include appropriate training, (4) regards early identification information as confidential, except as may be required by law, policies, or union contract, (5) requires Sergeants, managers, and commanders to review early intervention thresholds at least weekly for their subordinates, (6) allows leaders to develop assessments before the pre-established threshold value has been not yet been reached if potentially problematic behavior is identified, (7) requires other leaders to review assessment reports and take appropriate action, such as developing a mentoring plan, and (8) provides that officers may review their files and report inaccuracies immediately to their supervisor.

The Phoenix, Arizona Police Department's (PPD) EI system is transparent. Officers can access their EIIS status online at any time and see where they stand in relation to the threshold standards that would trigger an EI identification, allowing them to be self-monitoring.[165]

Whenever a Phoenix officer is "tagged" by the EI, a case manager is automatically notified electronically. Case managers review each file to make sure that the identification is not a "false positive," an error. Once contacted, the actual supervisor of the officer involved has 21 days to complete the intervention review.[166] Officers are part of the intervention review process, helping to design the responses that are most helpful to them.

Ten years ago, only 27 percent of the agencies responding to a national survey reported using EIs, although that number is thought to be much higher now.[167] The number of variables tracked in an EI largely depends on whether it is a manual or automated system. Common variables include use of force reports, the ratio of use of force reports to arrests, the number of force incidents in which its use is questionable, citizen complaints, the numbers of resist arrests, the frequency of high-speed pursuits, assignment history, and disciplinary record. An EI system has "threshold values" that when reached result in an officer being "tagged" by the computer (e.g., two sustained citizen complaints in a 3-month period or three in a year).[168]

The value of EIs is substantial: (1) it supports officers' desires to perform well, (2) it reduces the numbers of officers who might lose their jobs, (3) it protects the departments investments in its current workforce, (4) it reduces or eliminates potential for officers' at-risk behaviors to advance to a legal liability or it damages the department's reputation in, and relationship with, the community. EIs have produced dramatic results in curbing citizen complaints and related performance indicators—the New Orleans Police Department reported a 62 percent drop in a single year.[169] Significant results from using EIs have also been reported in other countries; in Victoria, Australia, a 71 percent reduction over a 12-month period was achieved.[170]

DISCIPLINE

If law enforcement executives are to be held accountable for the performance of their agencies, they must have ways to control them. This system of controls is well-understood and includes staff inspections to make sure that policies are being followed; line inspection at roll call to verify officers are adhering to grooming, uniform, and other standards; financial audits; periodic evaluation of programs and units; and stringent selection procedures.

Discipline is part of the control system and, in some agencies, the wooden application of sanctions for violations of standards of conduct has made discipline synonymous with punishment—far from its actual meaning and intention. **Discipline** is related to three Latin words: (1) *disciplina,* or instruction to a disciple; (2) *discipulus,* or pupil; and (3) *discere,*

or to learn, to acquire knowledge. Although discipline is often thought of as punishment, its core meaning is instruction. Police discipline serves important purposes: (1) modify/correct an officer's behavior, (2) to deter future misconduct by the officer and other officers, (3) to give departmental members notice that misconduct will not be condoned and to communicate this stance to the public, (4) ensure the proper operation of the police department, (5) reinforcement of department values and standards, (6) reinforcement of training, (7) manage liability risks, and (8) establish respect for the disciplinary system by fair and impartial administration of it.[171] Not all investigations into alleged police conduct results in a disciplinary action. There are four possible outcomes to such investigations:

1. Unfounded: The investigation indicates that the subject officer's alleged actions relating to the Department policy, procedure, rule, regulation, or directive in question did not actually occur;
2. Exonerated: The investigation indicates that the alleged actions of the subject officer were within the policies, procedures, rules, regulations, and directives of the Department;
3. Not Sustained: There was insufficient evidence to either prove or disprove the allegation; and
4. Sustained: The subject officer's actions were found, by a preponderance of the evidence, to have been in violation of the Department policy, procedure, rule, regulation, or directive in question.[172]

By way of comparison, the "preponderance of evidence" standard to sustain an allegation against an officer is the lightest burden of proof in civil cases. In some states, the higher standard of "a clear and convincing" evidence in a civil case must be demonstrated. In a few states, the highest burden of proof in both civil and criminal cases is required, "beyond the exclusion of any reasonable doubt," the meaning of which is that no other logical explanation of the facts in the case is possible except as posited by the plaintiff or district attorney.

Standards of Conduct and Progressive Discipline

The standards of conduct for police officers are set forth in their oath of office; their agency's policies, rules, and regulations; local ordinances; state statutes; federal laws; and consent decrees (e.g., prohibition against racial profiling). In addition to departmental discipline, an officer's POST license may be in jeopardy in some fact situations (e.g., acts of **moral turpitude**, conduct that is contrary to honesty, justice, or good morals). Law enforcement agencies use a system of **progressive discipline**, incrementally increasing more serious penalties for transgressions. A progressive discipline system may include many of the following steps:

1. Verbal counseling;
2. Oral reprimand;
3. Written reprimand;

4. Monetary fine;
5. Transfer/reassignment;
6. Suspension without pay;
7. Loss of promotional opportunity;
8. Demotion; and
9. Termination.[173]

In some situations, progressive discipline is not possible and termination is the only reasonable course of action (e.g., an officer steals money from the informant fund or drugs from the evidence room). In some jurisdictions, monetary (e.g., New Jersey) fines may be used in lieu of a suspension when the absence of an officer is detrimental to public health, welfare, or safety; when the fine is restitution; or when the officer agrees to the fine.[174]

Administration of Discipline

Of necessity, the chief executive of a law enforcement agency must delegate the authority for discipline to individuals in the chain of command and to the professional standards/internal affairs (PS/IA) unit. Many agencies have clearly specified rules about what misconduct may be handled by the first-line supervisor, within a division, at the bureau level, or those that must be referred to PS/IA. In addition to unit commanders being required to refer more serious misconduct to PS/IA, such action may also be called for when officers from different divisions are involved. Criminal acts by officers employed by smaller law enforcement agencies are often investigated by an external agency, such as a nearby larger department or the state police. Larger agencies will usually refer such acts to their own investigative unit.

Entities outside of the department may also be involved in the disciplinary process. In some jurisdictions, civilian review boards (CRBs), and unions evaluate law enforcement agencies' completed internal affairs investigations and the chief's disciplinary decisions and may offer their own recommendation as to the appropriate sanctions. CRB members are usually appointed by the relevant local official, such as a mayor. CRBs can be relatively "toothless," with only the power to make recommendations. Alternatively, CRBs can receive complaints directly from the public, have an investigative staff and subpoena power, and are able to make disciplinary decisions on the cases that fall within the scope of their authority. Independent monitors may be appointed by the mayor or other official or as part of a consent decree; they have no investigative power and their function is to scrutinize and report on the disciplinary process (e.g., why does it take so long to complete internal affairs investigations?). District attorneys do not want to prosecute police officers accused on a criminal act because they want to maintain a close working relationship with law enforcement agencies. In such cases, a special prosecutor may be temporarily hired for this purpose.

In addition to oral and written reprimands and suspensions, officers may lose privileges, such as (1) eligibility to work extra-duty assignments and grant provided overtime (e.g., driving while intoxicated checkpoints and patrol); (2) use of a take-home car; and (3) serving on specialty teams, such as scuba, search and rescue, canine, hostage negotiation, and SWAT.

All disciplinary actions are subject to review through the chain of command and may be appealed by the officer. Under collective bargaining agreements, disciplined officers may be able to grieve the action taken, potentially requiring a binding decision by a neutral arbitrator. A study analyzed 100 police cases selected at random from the Labor Arbitration Reports and compared them to another randomly selected 100 cases from non-law enforcement public agencies.[175] Law enforcement executives' disciplinary recommendations were sustained at a higher rate, suggesting better handling by them. An alternative explanation is that officers are held to a higher standard. A 5-year study of arbitrator discipline decisions involving the Houston Police Department revealed that the sanctions being sought were reduced by a net amount of nearly 50 percent.[176]

Because much misconduct is relatively minor (e.g., violating grooming standards, being late to roll call, not keeping the department informed of current address, telephone number, and internet address, writing on departmental walls, not providing a badge number and name to the person requesting it, maintaining desk in an unsatisfactory order, and ignoring a radio call), first-line supervisors play a primary role in the disciplinary process. This dictates that supervisors have substantial training in policies, forms, officers rights, and counseling techniques. On incidents referred to PS/IA, the first-line supervisor is no longer the key figure.

In cases of serious misconduct, the unit commander may immediately suspend officers pending the outcome of an investigation because (1) they are unfit for duty; (2) they would constitute a hazard to themselves or others if allowed to remain on the job; (3) the action is necessary to protect health, safety, order, or effective direction of services; or (4) they have been charged with a crime. Where immediate action is required in these situations, some law enforcement agencies often allow the first-line supervisor to place the officer on "temporary relief from duty," pending review by higher authority. Officers so relieved must ordinarily be advised of their duty status within 24 hours by the higher authority.

Officers may also be placed on administrative leave, with full pay and benefits, pending the completion of an investigation. In an unusual situation during 2010, an Arizona police chief was placed on administered leave as part of an on-going inquiry into his leadership, including inconsistency in handling disciplinary actions.[177]

A barrier to PS/IA investigations continues to be the "blue wall," or code of silence. Although 83 percent of officers responding to a national survey rejected the notion that a code of silence is necessary for good policing, 25 percent reported whistle-blowing was not worth it and 67 percent indicated that those who report misconduct by their peers would get the "cold shoulder."[178] Fifty-two percent of the respondents said that it was not unusual to turn a blind eye toward improper conduct by other officers and 61 percent disagreed with the statement that police officers always report serious criminal violations involving abuse of authority by fellow officers.[179]

One study concluded that officers with at least some college were not better behaved than those with a high school degree.[180] A larger Florida analysis indicated that high school graduates

TABLE 9.9 NATIONAL DISPOSITION OF USE OF FORCE COMPLAINTS	
Disposition	Percentage*
Not Sustained, insufficient evidence to support allegation	34
Unfounded, complainant factually wrong or did not occur	25
Exonerated, the incident occurred but the officer's action was lawful and proper	23
Sustained, sufficient evidence to discipline officer	8
Other disposition (e.g., complaint withdrawn)	9

*Does not add to 100 percent due to rounding.

Source: Matthew J. Hickman, *Citizen Complaints About Police Use of Force* [Washington, DC: Bureau of Justice Statistics, June 2006], p. 5.

made up about 50 percent of all law enforcement officers in the state but accounted for 75 percent of all disciplinary actions.[181] Among those who lost their POST certification, high school graduates were disproportionately represented also: 76 percent versus 12 percent for those with a bachelor's or higher degree.[182] An analysis of discipline in the New York City Police Department found no evidence of race, gender, or national origin bias.[183] In an unnamed large-city police agency, minorities were over-represented in documented complaints, specifically those initiated by fellow officers and supervisors.[184] In a year, use of force complaints nationally may average about 6.6 per 100 officers and one sustained complaint for every 200 officers (see Table 9.9).[185]

In 2015, Hickman and Poore completed a study of complaints against police use of force. Part of that study was a review of the literature, which revealed:

1. A relatively small proportion of officers are responsible for a large proportion of complaints, but this has generally been linked to arrest activity and other measures of productivity;

2. On-view incidents and more "proactive" policing assignments may be more likely to lead to complaints than dispatched calls;

3. Minority citizens complain in numbers disproportionately greater than their representation in the population served, and this is particularly true for black citizens;

4. Minority officers are disproportionately the subject of citizen complaints, as well as internal (police-initiated) complaints;

5. There is wide variation in sustain rates across agencies, some of which is attributable to structural differences, but also to idiosyncrasies in the processing of complaints;

6. In general, sustain rates are lower for physical force complaints as compared to other types of complaints; and

7. Internal (police-initiated) complaints tend to have higher sustain rates than citizen complaints.[186]

The Discipline Matrix

The perceived or actual unfairness of discipline is a long-standing problem in law enforcement agencies. In traditional disciplinary systems, this condition has been exacerbated because (1) fact situations may appear the same or similar on the surface, but the variance in individual circumstances leads to lesser or greater sanctions, which have gone unexplained and (2) variance in the disciplinary measures taken by supervisors was seen as part of the essential discretion they needed to deal with misconduct. As a matter of informal practice in many traditional discipline departments, a probationary officer late to roll call is not likely to "catch a break" while a veteran officer with "credits" in the agency may "get by with a hard look or word or two" from some supervisors.

A **discipline matrix** is a formal schedule for disciplinary actions, specifying both the presumptive or presumed sanction to be imposed for misconduct and any reduction or increase in the presumptive sanction for mitigating or aggravating factors (see Table 9.10).[187] Its primary purpose is to develop consistency in discipline, eliminating disparities and ensuring those who commit similar acts of misconduct will be sanctioned *equally*, as adjusted for *fairness* based on their mitigating and aggravated circumstances.[188] Discipline matrixes incorporate the concept of progressive discipline.

A matrix system identifies categories of conduct or perhaps more accurately, misconduct; a typical figure *number of categories* seems to be six (see Table 9.11, with categories A–F). As partially illustrated in Table 9.12, under each category are lists of what policies, procedures, rules, or regulations fall within it. Sanctions to be imposed are also associated with each category (see Table 9.12) and may run from Level 1 (least serious, oral or written reprimand) to the highest level, termination, which Table 9-12 does not illustrate.

In actual use multiple tables are used in a matrix system; for purposes of illustration Table 9.14 combines them, showing their interaction. If two or more charges against an officer arise from a single incident, a decision is made as to which one is the primary.

Matrix systems have been opposed by officers and unions when they have not been included in their development. In a few jurisdictions, there have been complaints by officers that supervisors have not been held to the same degree of

---

TABLE 9.10 ILLUSTRATIONS OF MITIGATING AND AGGRAVATING CIRCUMSTANCES

Mitigating circumstances may include, but are not limited to:

1. Willingness to accept responsibility and acknowledge wrongdoing;
2. The circumstances under which the rule was violated;
3. The culpable mental state of the officer in the commission of the violation;
4. Complimentary history, including awards, commendations and positive public recognition;
5. If minimal, the severity of the current offense and the lack of or minimal nature of any consequences caused by the current offense;
6. Prior work history, such as positive evaluations and/or work performance, or voluntary, advanced, job-related training; and/or
7. Minimal or lack of prior disciplinary history relative to the officer's years of service.

Aggravating circumstances may include, but are not limited to:

1. Injury or harm to a member of the public or an officer;
2. Endangerment to a member of the public or an officer;
3. The existence of an actual and demonstrable legal or financial risk to the department or the city (including, but not limited to, cases involving allegations of civil rights violations, unlawful search and seizure, excessive use of force or unlawful detention or arrest);
4. The supervisory or command rank of the officer who committed the violation. It is appropriate that the department have higher expectations for supervisors and commands officers and that they exercise greater judgement and restraint than subordinates;
5. The officer's prior disciplinary history;
6. Actual and demonstrable prejudice to the department;
7. Jeopardizing the department's mission and/or relationship with other agencies;
8. Loss or damage to city or private property;
9. A criminal conviction of the involved officer arising out of the underlying event;
10. Dishonesty on the part of the officer;
11. Prejudicial conduct regarding race, color, creed, national origin, ancestry, gender/sex (including pregnancy, childbirth, or caregiver status), sexual orientation, age, religion, political affiliation, physical or mental disability, military status, marital status, or other protected classifications;
12. Harassment or retaliatory conduct;
13. The culpable mental state of the officer in the commission of the violation; and/or
14. Unsatisfactory work history.

Source: These points are drawn with restatement and consolidation from the Denver Police Department, *Discipline Handbook*, revised September 6, 2012. pp. 23–24, https://www.denvergov.org/content/dam/denvergov/Portals/744/documents/handbooks/DPD_Handbook_Revised_9-6-2012.pdf, accessed May 13, 2016.

---

accountability. Other critics wonder about the fairness of rank being an aggravation factor. When all is said and done, matrix systems are a leap forward and traditional discipline agencies should take a close look at them.

Legal Aspects of Discipline

Disciplining police officers also has a legal component to it; illustratively, to prevent disciplinary abuses, many states have enacted police officer bill of rights legislation; content related to discipline is also commonly included in collective bargaining agreements; and except for narrow restrictions in some areas, officers retain all of their Constitutional rights. These and related topics are covered in Chapter 14, Legal Aspects of Police Administration.

PERFORMANCE APPRAISAL

Performance appraisals are sworn by and at. Supporters claim that they are essential and detractors label them as "annual rituals," a "global scourge,"[189] and are based on the erroneous assumption that the supervisors completing them have sufficient relevant information to complete them accurately and do so without any bias or prejudice.

Assuming that the performance of individuals does not vary greatly, it is reasonably expected that their ratings would remain relatively stable. However, a study of 6,000 business employees reporting simultaneously to two different bosses revealed ratings ranging from "very weak" to "outstanding." Sixty-two percent of those receiving "outstanding" evaluations from the first boss got lower scores from their other boss.[190] This finding may reflect that

TABLE 9.11 CATEGORIES OF CONDUCT IN A DISCIPLINE MATRIX

Category	Definition
A	Conduct that has a minimal negative impact on the operations or professional image of the department.
B	Conduct that has more than minimal negative impact on the operations or professional image of the department; or that negatively impacts relationships with other officers, agencies or the public.
C	Conduct that has a pronounced negative impact on the operations or professional image of the department; or on relationships with other officers, agencies, or the public.
D	Conduct that is substantially contrary to the values of the department or that substantially interferes with its mission, operations or professional image, or that involves a demonstrable serious risk to officer or public safety.
E	Conduct that involves the serious abuse or misuse of authority, unethical behavior, or an act that results in an actual serious and adverse impact on officer or public safety, or to the professionalism of the department.
F	Any violation of law, rule or policy which: foreseeably results in death or serious bodily injury to another person; or constitutes a willful and wanton disregard of department values; or involves any act which demonstrates a serious lack of the integrity, ethics or character related to an officer's fitness to hold the position of police officer; or involves egregious misconduct substantially contrary to the standards of conduct reasonably expected of one whose sworn duty is to uphold the law; or involves any conduct which constitutes the failure to adhere to any contractual condition of employment or requirement of certification mandated by law.

Source: Denver Police Department, *Discipline Handbook (2012)*, pp. 16–17.

TABLE 9.12 PARTIAL ILLUSTRATION OF RELATIONSHIP AMONG A CONDUCT CATEGORY A, POLICIES, LEVELS OF DISCIPLINE, AND SANCTIONS

Category A: Conduct that has a minimal negative impact on the operations or professional image of the department or that negatively impacts with other officers, agencies, or the public.

Policy Involved	1st Violation in Four Years	2nd Violation in Four Years	3rd Violation in Four Years
Giving testimonials, seeking publicity	Discipline level 1	Discipline level 2	Discipline level 3
Use of tobacco in police facilities	Discipline level 1	Discipline level 2	Discipline level 3
Personal appearance in court	Discipline level 1	Discipline level 2	Discipline level 3
Testifying in civil cases	Discipline level 1	Discipline level 2	Discipline level 3
Sanctions Table			
Mitigation	Not applicable	Oral reprimand	Written reprimand to 1 fined day
Presumptive	Oral reprimand	Written reprimand	2 fined days
Aggravated	Written reprimand	1–3 fined days	4–6 fined days

Source: Drawn from the Denver Police Department Discipline Handbook (2012), Appendix F, pp. 1–2.

one boss did not get as much effort as the other one; the duties were different and when working for one boss the duties were not a good fit for the skill set for the employee; or flaws in the performance appraisal system itself.

A majority of 393 constables, sergeants, and staff sergeants surveyed across 15 Canadian cities reported that their performance appraisal system was "deficient."[191] Officers did not receive regular feedback during the rating period, had little or no input into the evaluation, the supervisors were not sufficiently trained in evaluation, and personality often triumphed over actual performance criteria.

The truth is that getting a performance appraisal system to have real meaning requires a substantial organizational commitment, a stream of informal feedback, good supervisory record keeping, employee participation, validated forms, and rater training. In broad terms, the purpose of ratings is to (1) reinforce organizational values, (2) have a basis for impartial personnel decisions, (3) reinforce performance expectations, (4) stimulate performance, (5) identify the officers' training needs, and (6) extend recognition to those who perform their duties well. The results of performance appraisals are used to determine or influence:

1. pay raises;
2. eligibility for promotion;
3. shift bids/duty assignments;
4. career development decisions (e.g., attendance at the FBI National Academy);
5. eligibility for reinstatement;
6. layoffs/reduction in force decisions; and
7. terminations.

Officers satisfactorily completing their probationary periods are awarded career status and cannot be terminated except for serious misconduct. During financial emergencies, career-status officers can be furloughed indefinitely. Career-status officers are commonly rated once annually by their immediate supervisors. However, special circumstances may cause an evaluation to be written on an other than annual basis: (1) officer resignations and terminations and (2) transfers to another unit and promotions may trigger a probationary requirement for monthly or quarterly evaluations for a year.

In preparing a standard evaluation form, a supervisor considers notes he or she has made about the officer and the factors identified on the form such as adherence to safety procedures, relationships with coworkers and supervisors, report quality, commendations, complaints, attendance, and training.

Informally, some supervisors initially fill out the appraisal in pencil and at a preliminary meeting give the officer an opportunity to provide input that may alter the ratings. A similar practice is to give the officers to be rated a copy of the appraisal form and ask them to evaluate themselves. Before the actual rating conference, the supervisor's and officers' preliminary ratings are compared and discussed. By policy in many law enforcement agencies, officers headed toward an unsatisfactory rating must be advised of their deficiencies at least 90 days before the end of the rating period so they have an opportunity to improve.

Signing a performance appraisal is akin to signing a traffic ticket; the signature means that you have received a copy of it, not that you necessarily agree with it. Officers seldom formally appeal a performance appraisal; although they may ask that a statement prepared by them be attached to it for the record.

PROMOTIONS

Promotional tests can serve several objectives: (1) determining which candidates' names should be placed on the promotional roster; (2) reinforcing organizational change (e.g., when the Savannah, Georgia Police Department adopted community-oriented policing, all sworn personnel had to complete a 40-hour course in that philosophy. The next written promotional tests drew questions from the course material, communicating the message "you need to be on-board with COP if you plan to get promoted"); (3) refreshing familiarity with critically important policies, such as use of force and high-speed pursuits, by asking questions about them; (4) increasing the level of important knowledge in the organization through candidates studying the resource material for written tests; and (5) improving the candidates' understanding of their skill levels by their behaviors being tested in assessment centers, which roughly equate to a series of job simulations, and receiving feedback about their performance.

A dilemma for many law enforcement executives is the disparity between the limited number of promotional openings they have versus their large pool of well-qualified candidates. Even so, that pool might be more substantial were it not for the fact that some officers choose not to participate in promotional testing. Seventy percent of nonparticipating women and 51 percent of men do not want to be moved from their current assignment or shift.[192] They know that a transfer usually accompanies a promotion; by doctrine, a new supervisor should not lead those with whom they have worked as equals. Other reasons for nonparticipation include child-care/family responsibilities, not wanting supervisory responsibilities, and loss of overtime pay; overall, one in five potential candidates is simply not interested.[193]

Although infrequent, officers do cheat on promotional exams and supervisors sometimes help them to do so. An officer hired someone to take the Hudson County (New Jersey) Sheriff's Office's Sergeant's exam for him; both men were sentenced to prison terms on a variety of charges.[194] In Providence (Rhode Island), a chief directly or indirectly provided four favored candidates with an advance copy of the materials for a written exam, giving them more time to study, and also dictated who would score first, second, and third in the interview phase.[195]

With respect to the rules and testing processes used to identify those eligible for promotion, law enforcement officers want (1) clear and unambiguous guidelines, (2) the rules to be evenly applied to all candidates, (3) confidence in the integrity of the testing process, (4) a reasonable amount of material to study for a written test, and (5) prompt feedback on the results.[196]

The rules and practices that comprise the promotional system can be specified in departmental policy, civil service/merit rules, local ordinances, the city or county charter, or state statutes. Broadly, the promotional policy specifies who is eligible, what the steps in the promotional process are, how the final scores are calculated, and how officers passing the process will be selected from the eligibility roster. Policies must use carefully crafted language to avoid potential problems. A well-written promotional policy might specify that to be eligible for promotion to sergeant, "An officer shall have completed at least 36 months of continuous service with this agency on the date immediately preceding the administration of the written examination." In contrast, another policy might simply provide "Three years of police service must be completed to be eligible." Does that mean with the present agency? Could some of it be with another department? Do breaks in service affect eligibility? Assume an officer works for a department 32 months, then he resigns to work in at an insurance company. Eight months later he is rehired by his former agency. After completing 4 months of service, is the officer eligible for promotion?

Promotional tests are subject to the same EEOC validity and reliability requirements as are entrance examinations and physical assessment tests. Despite these requirements, some agencies attempt to prepare their own written promotional tests. There are reasons they should be reluctant to do so: (1) most frequently they will not have conducted a validity study, (2) the perception or actuality of the test "getting out" is substantial, (3) the skills to write good test items may not exist in the department, (4) command officers teaching part-time in a criminal justice program are often selected to prepare the test. Some agency officers taking the promotional exam will have taken classes from them and have a perceived or real advantage, and (5) if the test results are challenged under Title VII, the prospects for successfully defending them are often dim. If other types of promotional tests are prepared internally (e.g., an oral board or an assessment center), they face the same hurdles as do written examinations.

Regardless of what form a promotional test takes, the reading level of the materials must be closely monitored. On average, high school graduates read at a tenth-grade level; only 35 percent of them achieve a "proficient" or higher level of performance.[197] Most law enforcement agencies require a high school diploma as an entry-level education requirement. In those departments, if the promotional materials are written at more than a tenth-grade level, a court may find the test is not job related. A related matter is a review of the job analysis study before each promotional cycle begins. Roughly, if an agency has no major shifts in operational philosophy, does not significantly reallocate tasks or have other major transitions, a job analysis study might remain in use for 5 years. However, a committee should carefully review the study annually, record comments about its currency, and certify in writing that in the group's judgment, it can be relied upon for the next promotional cycle. A more conservative approach is to conduct the annual reviews and do a new job analysis study every 3 years.

Written Promotional Tests

Written promotional tests from test providers come in three basic models:[198]

1. *Off-the-Shelf/Stock*—Test providers have validity data from a large number of departments from across the country that can be "transported" or used with virtually all other law enforcement agencies. The provider gives clients a list of the five to eight books from which the questions are drawn. The clients buy enough copies to establish a lending library for candidates. Some candidates buy their own books and small study teams pool their money to do the same thing. The test questions are generic and can be used with the "Anywhere U.S.A." police department. Off-the-shelf/stock tests rent for about $15 per copy, with price breaks for larger orders. Additional sources of profit for providers include (a) a transportability study at a cost of roughly $1,500; (b) the sale or rental of candidate study guides, around $7.50 each; and (c) administration and/or scoring services.

2. *Custom-Developed*—The provider may have validity data from a large-scale study on which the test is based or can validate the test for use in a single agency. When the knowledge areas and the number of questions to come from each area are known, the test developer sits down with a liaison committee from the agency and they decide from which sources the test questions will come. This allows many questions to come from sources unique to the agency, such as the policy manual and training materials.

Custom test developers also write scenario questions that incorporate local information (see Table 9.13). Too many scenario questions on a test require more time to complete the test. An overly long test creates the danger that test fatigue will occur and applicants will not be able to perform at a level that reflects their actual knowledge. As a rule of thumb, 15 to 20 short scenario questions is probably a reasonable limit for a 100-item test.

Custom developers also charge a fee for a job analysis studies. If a sergeants test is going to be developed, all sergeants will be asked to complete the job analysis questionnaire. Job analysis fees vary widely depending on the number of job incumbents in the target position, but the fees range from several thousand dollars for a single rank in one department to over $100,000 for a state-wide study. Custom test questions cost $35 to $60 each, with a minimum number, such as 75, plus a base fee of $250 to several hundred dollars more. Like off-the-shelf/stock providers, custom test providers provide other services, such as administration and scoring, for additional fees.

TABLE 9.13 SCENARIO QUESTION USING LOCAL INFORMATION

Thirty-year-old Wilbur is 6'5" tall. He weighs 295 pounds. Wilbur is a mean drunk. He has a history of fighting in bars. Tonight, Wilbur is drunk in Charlie's Tavern on Hancock Avenue. Patrons there have seen Wilbur pick a fight. Wilbur is in the restroom. Milford comes in and sits at the bar. He is a timid man. Milford is 31 years old and 5'4". He weighs 140 pounds. Wilbur returns to the bar. He sees Milford. He reaches for the front of Milford's shirt. Then he pulls back his fist. He screams "I'm going to hit you hard! You'll be 6 months older when you quit rolling!" Milford passes out. He falls to the floor. Wilbur's actions violate which of the following offenses?
a. Menacing
b. Battery
c. Terrorist threats
d. Assault

3. *Semi-Custom Tests*—These exams include stock questions plus some custom-written items. Providers may require that if a client selects this option, he or she must agree to use a minimum number of custom questions, such as 10 or 25, plus the base fee and charges for other services.

Study guides should be provided to all candidates taking a written test. It is also essential that law enforcement agencies conduct seminars on how to study and take multiple-choice exams. All sessions of seminars should be video recorded and placed on the department's intranet for four primary purposes: (1) candidates can review their own session to refresh their recollection, (2) those unable to attend can have access to the same information, (3) different questions will arise if there are multiple training sessions; everyone should have access to the same information, and (4) if controversies or litigation exist, the videos might be useful in defending the agency's practices. Although some argue that a video record may be used to bolster a plaintiff's case, they may also guide the agency to making a pre-trial settlement, which avoids costly litigation and leads to mistake-free seminars.

The contents of a study guide often have the following elements: (1) information about the test; (2) study tips; (3) strategies for taking multiple choice tests; (4) creating a good study environment; (5) sample questions; and (6) the list of source materials from which the test is drawn.

Less frequently, two other elements are included in a study guide: (1) a copy of the test plan (see Table 9.14) and (2) copies of all source material. While many test providers simply supply a list of books, a test plan is narrower and more specific. If one purpose of written testing is to increase the level of knowledge in the agency, narrowing the amount of material to be studied encourages it by making preparation less formidable. Including all source material eliminates the need for the agency to establish a lending library and places everything candidates need to know in a single volume. In addition to permission costs to reprint all copyrighted material, which can range from $300 to as much as $800, printing each all-inclusive study guide of 350 to 425 pages ranges from $16 to $22. Besides its fairness to all candidates, the use of an all-inclusive study guide cuts down on complaints and grievances. Those who perform poorly on the written test often make the comment. "It's my own. Everything I needed was handed to me." Study guides do not inflate the results of the written test. Scores, typically range in the low 30s to the lower-mid-90s.

Promotional practices are not normally addressed in a collective bargaining agreement in detail. Union contracts often specify that a promotional vacancy must be filled within 60 or 90 days if the position is not abolished. Likewise, contacts may specify the study time allowed before the promotional test is administered. Most test providers recommend 60 to 90 days, and unions push for a 30- to 45-day period to get their members promoted quicker. Sixty days is actually ample study time if an all-inclusive study guide is provided, but 90 days provides a humane safety buffer for candidates who need operations, get married, go on vacation, have deaths in the family, emergencies, and become a primary caregiver under FMLA, or other related events.

Oral Boards and Assessment Centers

Promotional oral boards are conducted in the same manner as entry-level oral boards, although the questions are different, and therefore require no further elaboration. An *assessment center* is both a process and the place where the process is conducted. Such places might be a hotel, a technical school or community college, a civic center, or National Guard installation.[199] Police facilities are not a good choice for testing; to candidates, they reek of the possibility of command influence and lack a factually neutral feeling.

Assessment centers were first used to select German Army officers during World War I; during World War II, the British War Officer Selection Boards (WOSBs) employed them to find competent officers. The United States Office of Strategic Services (OSS), the forerunner of the Central Intelligence Agency, utilized them to screen for agents who could be infiltrated into enemy territory to gather intelligence. The first large-scale test of assessment centers in this country was carried out by AT&T.[200] By the mid-1980s, American law enforcement agencies began using assessment centers.

Assessment centers are an attractive alternative to written tests because they produce less or no adverse impact. As compared to both written tests and oral boards, assessment centers are more difficult to administer, use a great amount of officers' time, and are more costly. A sergeants assessment center for the

TABLE 9.14 PORTION OF A TEST PLAN

2015 Columbus (Georgia) Police Department Sergeant Written Test Plan

KNOWLEDGE NUMBER	KNOWLEDGE AREA	APPROX. NUMBER OF QUESTIONS	SOURCE MATERIALS‡
K1	Basic legal standards (including state statutes; arrest, search and seizure laws; court procedures; warrants; rules of evidence; legal terms and definitions; legal rights of accused; civil liability)	10	• Bill of Rights • Columbus Consolidated Government Code. Selected portions of Chapter 14. • Georgia State Statutes, Title 16. Selected Portions including: 5-20; 5-21; 5-23; 5-23.1; 5-24; 5-40; 5-41; 5-42; 5-72; 10-2; 10-20; 10-93; 10-94; 11-30; 11-31; 11-33. Title 17, 4-20. • Peace Officer Standards and Training Council. *Rules of Evidence*. Pages 2.3-1-2.3-15
K2	Correct and safe use of equipment	9	• CPD Policies and Procedures. 3-3: Firearms; 3-4: Discharging of Firearms; 3-11: Responsibility and Accountability of Police Equipment; 3-12: Permanently Assigned Vehicles; 3-14: Vehicle Operations; 3-15: Operations of Motor Vehicles While Responding to Requests for Police Services
K3	Investigative concepts, principles, methods, procedures, and practices (including crime scene search, physical evidence, and modus operandi of criminals)	21	• Swanson, CR, Chamelin, NC, & Territo, L (2012). Criminal Investigation. Boston: McGraw Hill. Pages 37-78. • CPD Policies and Procedures. 5-2: Criminal Process; 6-5: Property and Evidence Procedures; 7-1: Criminal Investigation; 7-2: Collection and Preservation of Evidence.
K4	Interview and interrogation concepts, principles, and practices	6	• CPD Policies and Procedures. 2-6: Inter-department Investigations; 5-2: Criminal Process; 7-1: Criminal Investigation • US Department of Transportation (2006). *DWI Detection and Standardized Field Sobriety Tests*. Pages VI-1 to VI-6.
K5	Columbus Police Department policies and procedures	10	• CPD Policies and Procedures. 1-7: Disciplinary Action; 3-1: Non-Deadly Force/Less Lethal Munitions; 3-2: Deadly Force; 3-7: Required Court Attendance; 3-10: Off-Duty Employment; 3-16: Motor Vehicle Pursuit; 3-17: Hot Pursuit, Extradition, and Fugitive Warrant; 3-25: Guidelines for the Release of Information; 4-4: Performance Evaluations; 4-8: Drug and Alcohol Testing Policy.
K6	Leadership and Motivation concepts, practices, and principles	17	• Iannone, NF & Iannone, MP (2014). Supervision of Police Personnel. Upper Saddle River, NJ: Prentice-Hall. Pages 33-56; 147-155.
K7	Interpersonal and organizational communication concepts, principles, and practices	10	• Swanson, CR, Territo, L, & Taylor, RW (2012). Police Administration. Upper Saddle River, NJ: Prentice-Hall. Pages 434-466.
K8	Counseling and discipline concepts, principles, and practices (including administrative principles and practices)	17	• Whisenand, Paul M (2014). *Managing Police Organizations*. Upper Saddle River, NJ: Pearson Education. Pages 171-188, 262-276.

NOTES:

1. Questions may be drawn from any source cited regardless of the alignment of knowledge areas and sources shown above.
2. The number of questions drawn from each knowledge area is based on the 2010 job analysis conducted by the Carl Vinson Institute of Government. The number of questions on the actual written promotional test may vary somewhat from the exact number of questions shown in this test plan. Any such variation, if necessary, would be minor.
3. For the purposes of developing a test plan, the following K areas were merged due to similar source material: Investigative concepts (merged with Crime Scene Search, Physical Evidence, and Modus Operandi of Criminals); Leadership (merged with Motivation); Counseling and Discipline (merged with Administrative principles and practices).
4. Total number of questions is 100.

Dallas Police Department processed 208 candidates at an average cost of $764.[201]

An **assessment center** consists of several exercises or job simulations designed to elicit behaviors from candidates that are established to be important to job success by a job analysis. At least one of the exercises must require candidates to interact with someone else. Usually panels of three trained assessors make notes about the behaviors and assign whole number scores to the behaviors tested. Behaviors are also referred to as dimensions or competencies.[202] Examples of dimensions are shown in Table 9.15. Several exercises are required so that candidates have multiple opportunities to have their behavior assessed by panels staffed by different teams of assessors.

Assessors must at least hold the rank for which a candidate is competing. Customarily, other law enforcement agencies allow their supervisors to serve as assessors for other departments with the tacit understanding that the favor will be returned. Assessor panels should reflect diversity. Departments should not use their supervisors in their own assessment centers because charges of favoritism, bias, and prejudice will discredit the process. Most often, assessors are paid no fee, although their travel, hotel, and meal costs are covered by the department hosting them.

Some law enforcement agencies do not host assessors well and have them evaluate too many candidates each day, which can lead to rating errors. Good hosting etiquette includes having per diem checks ready for the candidates on the first day of their training, arranging transportation to the agency's bank to cash them, the hotel room charge being directly billed to the department's account, bringing in varied and quality lunch meals, allowing assessors in departmental cars to fill up at the police motor pool, and arranging special tours of the city. Depending on the length of exercises, which influences the time needed to properly assess the candidates, assessors can reasonably see 8 to 12 candidates a day.

Table 9.16 provides examples of assessment center exercises; it assumes that the candidate is seeking promotion to the rank of sergeant. In each example, the candidate has just been promoted to sergeant and this is "day one" in that rank. The types of exercises illustrated could be used for any rank. The length

of time each exercise takes depends on its complexity; the times indicated are approximations.

A minimum of two, but usually three, trained raters observe each exercise, making their own notes during the exercise, and making their individual ratings after the candidate leaves the room (see Table 9.17). The individual ratings are then discussed by the assessor panel and the final whole number scores for that exercise formed in the same manner as described for entry-level oral boards. Each candidate's overall score is formed by combining the scores from each of the exercises (see Table 9.18).

The number of exercises used in an assessment center is not a fixed requirement. Some assessment centers use six or so short exercises of perhaps 5 to 8 min each, while others might have three or four exercises that each last 15 or 20 min. Short exercises require little or no time for candidates to prepare. Often they are simply given a single sheet of paper with a few lines of information immediately before they begin the exercise.

The longer exercises require that candidates have more time to prepare. A typical cycle is 30 min of candidate preparation time followed by 15 or 20 min before the assessor panel. For purposes of illustration, a candidate may assume the role of a just-promoted sergeant. On his/her "first day" as a "sergeant," the candidate arrives at work and finds a stack of papers to review. At the end of 30 min, the "sergeant" is to go to the "lieutenant's" office" to discuss what he/she has learned during the review period (i.e., an assessment center staff member will come get the "sergeant" from the preparation station and take him/her to the assessor panel). The staff member knocks on the "lieutenant's" door and announces, "Your new sergeant is here to see you." A role player previously trained for 8 to 16 hours for the "lieutenant's" part assumes the role of the lieutenant and greets the candidate directing him/her to sit at in front of the "lieuteant's" desk. The lieutenant then asks a standard series of questions. The "meeting" ends when time expires or, when asked, the sergeant says he/she has nothing left to add. The length of time spent in the exercise room is not an assessed factor, only what the candidate accomplished. This information should also included in the instructions to the assessors and candidates.

TABLE 9.15 SHORT DEFINITIONS OF VARIOUS DIMENSIONS

Perception: Being able to identify the key elements of a situation, the importance of these elements, and their relationship to one another.

Oral Communication: Clear, unambiguous, composed, and effective expression of one's self through oral means and gestures. Included are active listening, appropriate eye contact, and the use and interpretation of nonverbal communication, such as hands, facial, and body movements/positioning.

Written Communication: Preparing written documents that are well-organized, flow logically, have clear meaning, and use correct grammar and spelling.

Decisiveness: Willingness to take action, make a decision, commit to a course of action, and accept responsibility for those actions.

Judgment: Making sound and logical decisions based on factual information.

Planning and Organizing: Effectively and efficiently establishing a direction and sequence of prioritized actions for self/others to complete a task/accomplish a goal.

Leadership: Getting ideas accepted and the direction, guidance, and control of the activities of others, interrelating individual/departmental needs, monitoring performance, delegation, control, and follow-up.

TABLE 9.16 EXAMPLES OF ASSESSMENT CENTER EXERCISES	
Type	**Brief Description**
Press Conference (PC)	The candidate must brief "members of news media" on an incident. Assessors may play the role of news media members or others may do it. Length: 5 min.
Role Play (RP): Citizen Meeting	The sergeant meets with agitated citizen who wants to complain about one of the sergeant's subordinates. A role play can be conducted with any subject matter. Variations include meeting with an officer who is a declining performer and selecting members of a robbery investigation task force from a pool of candidates. Length: 20 min.
In-Basket (IB)	The candidate replaces a sergeant who was killed in an accident while on vacation, had a heart attack and took a medical retirement, or is otherwise gone. His/her in-basket has been filled up pending the appointment of a replacement. The new sergeant must go through a stack of papers and make dispositions and write necessary memos. Length: 45 min to 3 hours.
The Written Problem Analysis (WPA)	The sergeant's boss has delegated a problem to be solved (e.g., abuse of sick leave). A packet of information about the problem is on the sergeant's desk. A memo must be written to the boss explaining the situation and making a recommendation. Length: 45 min to 2 hours.
Leaderless Group Discussion (LGD)	The candidate and four other sergeants have been assigned to discuss a problem (e.g., a large home subdivision has been hit with four to seven car burglaries in four of the last 10 days). A leader for the group has not been designated. Each candidate has the same packet of information. The group must come up with a consensus strategy to attack this problem. The LGD is hard to score and is unpopular with officers because it doesn't square with actual practice where someone is always in charge. Put differently, it lacks "face validity" to candidates. The use of LGDs appears to have been on the wane in industry and policing. Length: 45 to 60 min.
Video-Based	A DVD is made showing an officer making traffic stops and performing other duties. The sergeant is asked to identify the policy violations committed and write a memo to his/her Lieutenant. This format may also be used with other scenarios. Video length: 7 to 12 minutes followed by a 25 to 30 minute period to write the memo.

The sergeant's preparation ("prep") station is set up like an office and includes staple removers, pads of papers, sticky notes, a dictionary, other accoutrements, and sometimes a telephone and/or computer. The telephone can be used to simulate the lieutenant calling him to add information or a requirement for their meeting. This call must be made at the same point in each candidate's preparation time. Many assessment centers allow candidates to bring their policy manual for reference and place a countdown timer on their desk so they know how much preparation time they have left. The candidate's policy manual must be checked before an exercise's preparation period begins to avoid allegations or the possibility someone had access to unauthorized material.

TABLE 9.17 EXAMPLE OF AN ASSESSMENT CENTER RATING SCALE		
Rating	**Definition of Behavior**	**Extent to Which Behavior Falls Short/ Exceeds Normally Expected Standards**
1	*Unable to perform.* Completely unacceptable. Improvement required in every aspect of the dimension.	Completely unacceptable
2	*Needs much improvement.* Definite improvement needed in nearly all aspects of the dimension.	Clearly below acceptable
3	*Needs some improvement.* Approaches, but falls short, of acceptable on this dimension. Some aspects of standards met, but improvement needed.	Marginally unacceptable
4	*Satisfactory, Adequate.* Performs consistently at acceptable level on this dimension.	Acceptable
5	*Effective.* Consistently better than acceptable performance on this dimension, characteristically above acceptable standards.	Above acceptable
6	*Outstanding.* Demonstrates high degree of proficiency on this dimension. Far exceeds normally expected standards consistently.	Outstanding

TABLE 9.18 SERGEANTS ASSESSMENT CENTER SCORE SUMMARY SHEET

Candidate Name: Joe Jones

Candidate Identifier: Badge 181

Dimensions/ Exercises	Role Play 1	In-Basket	Press Conference	Role Play 2**	Average	Dimension Weight***	Total
Perception	6,5,6	5,5,5	4,5,5	6,5,5	5.16	8.23	42.46
Oral Communication	5,6,5	NM*	5,5,5	6,6,5	5.33	7.93	42.26
Written Communication	NM*	4,4,5	NM*	5,5,4	4.50	6.71	30.19
Decisiveness	5,6,5	5,5,5	3,4,4	4,5,5	4.66	7.33	34.15
Judgment	4,5,5	5,5,4	3,3,4	5,5,5	4.41	8.15	35.94
Planning & Organizing	5,5,5	5,6,5	3,4,4	6,6,5	4.91	6.82	33.48
Leadership	5,5,6	NM*	4,3,3	5,5,5	4.55	8.41	38.26
						Overall score:	256.7

*Not Measured.

** After Role Play 2 candidates returned to their office with the requirement to write a summary memo to their Lieutenant.

***Statistical importance of dimension to doing the job of a captain as derived from the job analysis study.

Likewise, backpacks should not be allowed in the preparation room. The staff member administering the exercise also keeps time but is not in the room while the candidate prepares. In lieu of a telephone call, the staff member may knock on the door and announce "Here is a another piece of paper the lieutenant wants you to look over for the meeting." Like the telephone call, the paper must be delivered at the same time for each candidate (e.g., 6 min into the exercise).

Most commonly, the only feedback candidates get about their assessment center performance is a letter telling them how they scored on each dimension in the assessment center and where their overall score places them on the eligibility list. In the "Cadillac" of feedback, after candidates have received their feedback letter, they can sign up for a feedback session. Supervisors from other law enforcement agencies are trained in providing feedback, including ones that were assessors in that assessment center. Each feedback session lasts 30 to 60 min, during which time the candidate can review everything—literally every piece of paper—in his or her file. The videos from the interactive exercises are shown to the candidates; this vividly illustrates the scores given to the candidates and they can see the specific skills they need to improve upon. This approach uses feedback as a staff development opportunity and appears to reduce the number of disgruntled candidates.

Selection from the Promotional Roster

In selecting those to be promoted from a promotional roster, law enforcement executives are usually restricted in their choices by civil service/merit rules or other measures (e.g., the city charter or state law). All candidates on a **rank order** roster are listed from high to low based on their final passing scores. A rule of three can be used, meaning that for a single promotional vacancy, any one of the top three candidates can be selected. A variation is to use a rule of 5 or 10. When someone is promoted under the rule of three, the fourth-ranked candidate often becomes part of the next top three. This has the same effect on rules of 5 or 10.

Various jurisdictions provide that an otherwise eligible person cannot be passed over more than twice during the life of a promotional roster, although this rule does not appear to be common. Absent such a provision a person ranked first on a promotional list may "die on it" if others are chosen for

Quick Facts: Assessor Goes from Dumb Ass to OK

At a "Cadillac" feedback session a sergeant's candidate was going through his file page by page. While looking at the assessors' notes taken during one of his exercises, he read aloud a comment written by one particular assessor and exclaimed "What a dumb ass! I never said that! He asked "Do we know who Assessor C was? The feedback person replied, "I'm the dumb ass." When he later reviewed the video of that exercise and saw he actually said what was in the assessor's notes, he turned to the feedback person and said, "Well, I guess I'm the dumb ass now and you're OK."

nondiscriminatory reasons.[203] Depending on the applicable provisions of a promotional system, a candidate passed over for promotion may or may not be entitled to a reason, although the latter seems to be more usual.

An unknown number of agencies use an **all-qualified** promotional roster. It allows the executive to pick anyone on the list, which is alphabetized and the appointing authority does not know what the test scores were. From a risk management perspective, this provides an opportunity to virtually eliminate adverse impact in promotions because the chief or sheriff can ensure diversity when selecting from the promotional roster. However, the premise of a valid and reliable test is that higher scores are reasonably expected to be associated with higher performance of important job attributes. Stated somewhat differently, the primary purpose of testing is to make useful distinctions between people. All qualified lists simply separate the unqualified from the qualified and toss out the finer distinctions that undergird the notion of merit.

Banded promotional rosters are widely used. Their essence is placing candidates with similar scores into groups, called bands. The most common method of doing so is through any of several statistical processes. As a general rule, the highest ranking band must be exhausted before selections are made from the next highest band.

There are two types of bands:

1. *Fixed bands*—All officers in the top band must be promoted before anyone in the next-highest-ranked band can be offered a promotion. There are two exceptions to this: (a) some systems provided that if no candidates in the top band accept a promotional offer, then someone from the next-highest band may be selected. For example, the last state police trooper in the top band might decline a promotion because it would mean moving her family to the far end of the state. There may also be a provision that if two promotional opportunities are declined, the candidate's name is struck from further consideration from the life of the list, and (b) court orders to correct past discrimination may exist, functionally requiring either that lower-scoring minorities are "lifted into the top band" or are otherwise selected off of the promotional list.

2. *Sliding bands*—The width of the band is adjusted when all members holding the top score are exhausted. If the range of the scores in the top band is 88–93, then when all those with 93 are promoted, the bottom of the range is adjusted by including all of those who scored an 87. The promotion of those with the top score first is not required.

Banded systems have been criticized on the grounds that they invite bias, favoritism, and politics into promotional decisions. These fears loom larger when the chief executive and command staff do not enjoy the trust of the rank and file. Where collective bargaining is allowed, philosophical differences almost naturally exist about promotional decision making. The unions want their members treated equally and those responsible for making the decisions want some discretionary authority. A properly conceived banded system dispenses with at least the intensity of some of these fears by a written policy that clearly identifies the factors that will be used when making selections from within a band.

Using a strict rank order list to make promotions from is fraught with danger. In *Bridgeport Guardians v. City of Bridgeport*,[204] 68 percent of whites taking the test passed versus 30 percent of African-Americans, creating an adverse impact. Despite this impact, Bridgeport insisted on relying on a rank order list and litigation ensued. The court essentially saw this reliance as a pretext for discrimination and ordered the use of a banding system, which reduced, but did not totally eliminate, the adverse impact and reasonably met the employer's needs.

As was the case with new hires, the final step in the selection process for supervisors is the probationary period or "**working test**." Most of those promoted will successfully complete the probationary period for two reasons: (1) while promotional tests do not totally eliminate "false positives" (those who test well, but cannot do the job), they reduce the frequency with which that happens and (2) law enforcement agencies are reluctant to revert probationers to their previously held rank.

RETIREMENT COUNSELING

Retirement is not given much thought by newly hired officers. It is decades away and they are focused on beginning their careers and getting on the streets "doing police work." Unless a law enforcement agency provides retirement counseling, these eventually-gray officers will arrive at retirement unprepared. Although many departments provide the counseling, the quality of it is not documented.

Officers may benefit in the long run from their agency offering retirement counseling with the content geared to the different stages of their career. In the earliest stage the content might emphasize the value of participating in a supplemental retirement account, the difference between a disability in the line of duty pension versus one that is not service connected, and in states where applicable, that a pension earned while married is divisible property. Later-stage counseling might include subjects such as changes in survivor benefits, tax exposure for withdrawals from supplemental retirement accounts, cost-of-living-adjustments (COLAs), and the effect of taking Social Security benefits at different ages.

Police unions and associations appear to have done a good job in keeping their members informed about matters affecting their retirement, particularly by providing up-to-date information on their websites. As the federal Pension Protection Act (PPA) of 2006 made its way through Congress, their websites carefully followed its progress. Parenthetically, for state and local police officers, the PPA eliminated the 10 percent penalty for early withdrawals from certain types of tax-sheltered savings plans and allows up to $3,000 in annual tax credits when health insurance costs are deducted directly from qualified plans.

Retirement creates challenges for police officers and can be stressful.[205] The Chief of the Lake Oswego, Oregon Police Department died unexpectedly from an apparent heart attack the night before his retirement ceremony.[206] Although the relationship between the chief's imminent retirement ceremony and heart attack is not certain, the proximity of the two events suggests that it may have been more than mere coincidence.

A common retirement problem is the loss of professional identity. Many people, when asked who they are, respond with both their names and what their job is. Retirement punches a hole in that identity, leaving officers unable to define themselves as anything other than what they were. Lacking plans to retire to something, some former officers become bored, drink more heavily, develop health problems, become despondent, and commit suicide.[207]

Important relationships may be disturbed as stressed retirees struggle with redefining themselves; they are more often at home, aimless, restless, and sometimes agitated.[208] A lack of long-term financial planning (e.g., the failure to create a supplemental pension or other streams of income such as rental property) may create financial pressures as retirees come to grips with the fact that their pension does not go as far as they thought it would.

The general consensus is that people fare better in retirement when, instead of just retiring from, they are retiring to something (e.g., a new job, devoting time to hobbies, travel, a family business, or learning a new skill like making jewelry or knives). In addition to other benefits, retirement counseling can implant the notion to simultaneously celebrate the end of one career while embracing the opportunity to reinvent oneself.

Quick Facts: The Embarrassed Sergeant "Jake"

A few months after his sergeant retired one of his detectives called to ask if he could swing by for a visit. The wife answered the call and said, "Sure, he's out back in the garage, just walk out there."

When the detective arrived "Jake" was seated in the garage weaving a basket. Several baskets that looked to be recently completed hung on the wall. He looked up at the detective and said "You're not going to tell anyone about this are you?" Jake was assured not a word would be said and the detective complimented him on the quality of his designs and workmanship. Perhaps 10 months later another detective came into the station and told several people "I saw Jake selling baskets at a craft fair and bought one. He does a hellava good job." Later Jake bought a loom and over time became an accomplished fabric weaver. Jake lived to be 88, perhaps due just to good genes. However, some that knew him thought perhaps his enthusiasm for weaving may have helped carry him that far.

Chapter Summary

Summary by Learning Objective

1. List 10 functions a police human resource unit might perform.

Any 10 of these 23 function will satisfy this objective. A police human resources (HR) unit may have oversight of the following functions:

1. Complying with Peace Officers Standards and Training Commission (POST) requirements and guidelines;
2. Maintaining currency with federal job discrimination laws;
3. Developing agency HR policies, subject to executive approval;
4. Recruiting and selecting sworn and civilian personnel;
5. Monitoring turnover, retention, and diversity;
6. Providing or contracting for psychological services (e.g., entry screening and critical incident counseling);
7. Delivering or arranging for academy, in-service, advanced, and managerial training;
8. Conducting special studies (e.g., staffing, benefits, and compensation surveys);
9. Administering benefits programs (e.g., health and life insurance, and workers compensation);
10. Preparing payroll;
11. Directing labor relations;
12. Coordinating random drug screening;
13. Administering promotional testing;
14. Managing intern programs;
15. Advising commanders on personnel matters;
16. Coordinating the employee evaluation process;
17. Organizing promotions and awards ceremonies;
18. Coordinating off-duty work;
19. Directing Professional Standards/Internal Affairs efforts;
20. Acting as personnel records custodian;
21. Preparing content for the agency's website;

22. Conducting job exit interviews to identify factors associated with turnover; and
23. Serving as liaison to the central personnel office.

2. **Identify the main objective of the Equal Pay Act.**
Its main objective is to eliminate discrimination in wages based on gender.

3. **Describe how the Age Discrimination in Employment Act is applied to law enforcement agencies.**
ADEA has a law enforcement exemption provision; local units of government can refuse to hire a person for a sworn position if the applicant is over their maximum age for hiring and the refusal to hire was part of a bona fide hiring or retirement plan and not a subterfuge to evade ADEA's purposes.

4. **Explain the four major theories of discrimination.**
   1. *Disparate treatment*—An applicant or officer may rightly believe that he or she has been dealt with unfairly in an employment decision. To rise to the level of a disparate treatment claim, the person must have been intentionally treated differently because of his or her membership in a protected class; the discrimination must be more than slight to be actionable. Both compensatory and punitive damages can be awarded against a *nongovernmental employer*;
   2. **Adverse Impact**—An applicant or officer may rightly believe that he or she has been dealt with unfairly in an employment decision. To rise to the level of a disparate treatment claim, the person must have been intentionally treated differently because of his or her membership in a protected class; the discrimination must be more than slight to be actionable;
   3. *Harassment*—Although technically harassment is a form of disparate treatment, EEOC recognizes it as a separate theory of discrimination. Harassment is action toward an individual on the basis of race, color, sex (including pregnancy), national origin, age, religion, disability, or genetic information. Unwelcome actions that may rise to the level of harassment include speech, touching, and other conduct that create an intimidating "hostile work environment" that employees reasonably should not have to endure. Mild teasing and occasional offhand comments will fall short of being recognized as creating a hostile environment; the conduct involved must be more severe or pervasive, but need not be totally intolerable; and
   4. *Retaliation*—Unlawful retaliation can take one of two forms: (1) retaliation for participation, meaning an employer retaliated against a job applicant or employee because he or she made a charge, testified, assisted, or participated in any manner in an investigation, proceeding, or hearing involving a covered job discrimination claim; for the employee's expression or conduct to be protected from retaliation, it must make reference to a protected class or type of prohibited job discrimination and (2) retaliation for opposition, which prohibits employers from discriminating against an applicant or employee who opposed covered job discrimination practices or said so in response to the employer's questions. Protection is afforded so long as the opposition is based on a reasonable and good faith belief that the practice opposed is illegal. In the event, the practice opposed is not prohibited, the employee is still protected. However, if such opposition is unreasonable, in bad faith, deliberately false, or malicious there is no protection.

5. **Name and explain two categories of sexual discrimination.**
Traditionally, sexual harassment has been categorized as (1) quid pro quo, from Latin, meaning an exchange or literally "something for something." It is constituted by unwelcome sexual advances, requests for sexual favors, and other verbal or physical conduct of a sexual nature when (a) submission to such conduct is either explicitly or implicitly a term or condition of an individual's employment or (b) submission or rejection of such conduct by an individual is used as the basis for employment decisions affecting that individual and (2) hostile environment, which is created when the prohibited and unwelcome behavior has the purpose or effect of unreasonably interfering with an individual's work performance or by creating an intimidating, hostile, or offensive working environment.

6. **Summarize the protection afforded by the Pregnancy Discrimination Act.**
Broadly, the act makes it illegal to discriminate in employment practices against a woman because of pregnancy, childbirth, or medical conditions arising from such. Hiring a pregnant woman is not required, but such an applicant must be treated equal to all other candidates.

7. **Define *disability* and *reasonable accommodation*.**
With respect to an individual, a disability is (1) a physical or mental impairment that *substantially*

limits one or more major life activities, (2) a record of such an impairment, or (3) a perception that a person has such an impairment. In general, a reasonable accommodation is any change in the work environment or in the way things are customarily done that enables an individual with a disability to enjoy equal employment opportunities.

8. **Briefly discuss the law enforcement exemption of the Genetic Information Nondiscrimination Act (GINA).**
Law enforcement agencies may request genetic information from employees to determine if they have contaminated forensic evidence and to identify human remains.

9. **Briefly contrast exempt and nonexempt employees.**
Employees are grouped into two categories for purposes of overtime pay: (1) nonexempt—the group that is entitled to overtime pay and (2) exempt—the group that is not.

10. **List the four reasons for which leave may be taken under the Family Medical Leave Act.**
The four are as follows:

    1. the birth and care of the newborn child of the employee;
    2. placement with the employee of an adoptive or foster care son or daughter;
    3. care of an immediate family member, spouse, child, or parent, with a serious health condition; and
    4. medical work when the employee is unable to work because of a serious health condition.

11. **Briefly describe how the economy affects recruiting applicants.**
In a good economy the applicant pool is shallow, and in a down cycle, there are more quality applicants.

12. **Define *validity* and *reliability*.**
Validity means that a test actually measures what it is intended to measure and conclusions and decisions based on test scores are therefore appropriate and meaningful. Reliability means that if the same test was given again or in a parallel form to the same group of people, they would score substantially the same. Reliability speaks to getting consistent, rather than random, results.

13. **Explain the meaning of *discipline and progressive discipline*.**
Discipline is related to three Latin words: (1) *disciplina*, or instruction to a disciple; (2) *discipulus*, or pupil; and (3) *discere*, or to learn, to acquire knowledge. Although discipline is often thought of as

punishment, its core meaning is instruction. Progressive discipline is incrementally increasing more serious penalties for transgressions.

14. **Identify the four possible outcomes in a professional standards/internal affairs investigation.**
(1) Unfounded, (2) exonerated, (3) not sustained, and (4) sustained.

15. **Explain how a discipline matrix works.**
A discipline matrix is a formal schedule for disciplinary actions, specifying both the presumptive or presumed sanction to be imposed for misconduct and any reduction or increase in the presumptive sanction for mitigating or aggravating factors.

16. **List four purposes of performance appraisals.**
There are seven purposes; any four responds to the objective:

    1. pay raises;
    2. eligibility for promotion;
    3. shift bids/duty assignments;
    4. career development decisions (e.g., attendance at the FBI National Academy);
    5. eligibility for reinstatement;
    6. layoffs/reduction in force decisions; and
    7. terminations.

18. **Name the five different purposes promotional testing can serve.**
These are (1) determining which candidates' names should be placed on the promotional roster; (2) reinforcing organizational change; (3) refreshing familiarity with critically important policies, such as use of force and high-speed pursuits, by asking questions about them; (4) increasing the level of important knowledge in the organization through candidates studying; and (5) improving the candidates' understanding of their skill levels by their behaviors being tested in assessment centers.

19. **Describe the assessment center process.**
An assessment center consists of several exercises or job simulations designed to elicit behaviors from candidates that are established to be important to job success by a job analysis. At least one of the exercises must require candidates to interact with someone else. Usually, panels of three trained assessors make notes about the behaviors and assign whole number scores to each of the behaviors tested.

20. **Explain rank order, all-qualified, and banded promotional rosters.**
In the rank order promotional roster: (1) All candidates on a rank order roster are listed from high to low based on their final scores. A rule of three can

be used, meaning that for a single promotional vacancy, any one of the top three candidates can be selected. A variation is to use a rule of 5 or 10. When someone is promoted under the rule of three, the fourth-ranked candidate often becomes part of the top three. This has the same effect on rules of 5 or 10. An all-qualified promotional roster allows the executive to pick anyone on the list, which is alphabetized and the appointing authority does not know what the test scores were. Banded promotional rosters are widely used. Their essence is placing candidates with similar scores into groups, called bands. The most common method of doing so is through any of several statistical processes. As a general rule, the highest ranking band must be exhausted before selections are made from the next highest band.

21. Discuss the problem of identity loss that some officers experience in retirement.
Loss of professional identity is a common retirement problem. Many people, when asked who they are, respond with both their names and what their job is. Retirement punches a hole in that identity, leaving officers unable to define themselves as anything other than what they were. Lacking plans to retire to something, some former officers become bored, drink more heavily, develop health problems, become despondent, and commit suicide.

Chapter Review Questions

1. What are five compelling reasons to have a working knowledge of human resource management?
2. What is the purpose of EEOC's Uniform Guidelines for Employee Selection?
3. Under FLSA, at what rate is overtime compensation paid?
4. Except for "unforeseeable circumstances" an employee seeking FMLA leave must give the employer how many days notice?
5. A California study revealed the top two reasons for joining a police department. What were they?
6. For police applicants, what are the top two negative experiences?
7. What is the primary responsibility of a Field Training Officer (FTO)?
8. Hickman and Poore's review of the literature of police use of force produced seven findings. What are four of them?
9. Why are police promotional assessment centers an attractive alternative to the use of written promotional tests?

Critical Thinking Exercises

1. Re-read Quick Facts: Colorado Springs Veteran Female Officers Sue Over Physical Test. Looking at the facts of the case, how do you evaluate the plaintiff's chances of prevailing and for what reasons?
2. Re-read Box 9.12, "The Police Consultant Who Couldn't Help." For what reasons do you think the Sheriff fired the consultant? Also, the consultant agreed with the sheriff's assessment that he was not going to be able to help, but for different reasons than the Sheriff professed. What reasons do you think the police consultant had in mind when he agreed with the Sheriff that he could not be helpful?

Key Terms

adverse impact
Age Discrimination in Employment Act (ADEA)
all-qualified list
Alpha generation
Americans with Disability Act (ADA)
assessment center
baby boomers

banded list
change officers' at-risk
computerized voice stress analyzer (CVSA)
conditional job offer (CJO)
disability
discipline
discipline matrix

disparate treatment
early intervention system
Employee Polygraph Protection Act (EPPA)
Equal Employment Opportunity Commission (EEOC)
exempt Employee
Equal Pay Act (EPA)

Fair Labor Standards Act (FLSA)
Family Medical Leave Act (FMLA)
field training officer (FTO)
4/5ths rule
Generation X
Generation Y
Generation Z
Genetic Information
   Nondiscrimination Act (GINA)
harassment
hostile environment
Lilly Ledbetter Fair Pay Act (LLFPA)
moral turpitude
nonexempt employees

normed
officer in training (OIT)
Peace Officers Standards and Training
   Commission
Pregnancy Discrimination Act
progressive discipline
protected class
qualified individual with a
   disability
quid pro quo
rank-order list
reasonable accommodation
reliability
retaliation

Servicemembers Civil Relief Act
   (SCRA)
sexual harassment
silent generation
Title VII
Uniform Guidelines for Employee
   Selection Procedures
Uniformed Services Employment and
   Reemployment Rights Act
   (USERRA)
U. S. Department of Labor
validity
working test

Endnotes

[1] These functions were originally taken on June 22, 2010, from 31 different police websites across the country that described their HR responsibilities. We did not keep a list of those agencies, but for the current edition we visited the websites of 16 local law enforcement agencies during August 31–September 1, 2015, to verify the list was still valid.

[2] A Proclamation by the President of the United State, Office of the Press Secretary, The White House, Washington, D.C., April 11, 2016, https://www.whitehouse.gov/the-press-office/2016/04/11/presidentialproclamation-national-equal-pay-day-2016, accessed May 7, 2016.

[3] Amy Onder, "Ledbetter Law Leads to Equal Pay Victory," *HR Magazine*, Vol. 54, Issue no. 12, (December 2009), p. 58, http://connection.ebscohost.com/c/articles/47554472/ledbetter-law-leads-equal-pay-victory, (accessed September 1, 2015).

[4] The statements in this paragraph are drawn from U.S. Equal Employment Opportunity Commission, Age Discrimination, p. 1, http://www.eeoc.gov/laws/types/age.cfm,(accessed August 31, 2015).

[5] Kyle Mitten, "City to Pay $375K as Part of Lougheed Settlement." The Daily World (Aberdeen, Washington), April 9, 2015, p. 1, http://thedailyworld.com/news/local/city-pay-375k-part-lougheed-settlement, (accessed August 31, 2015).

[6] U.S. 288 (2005).

[7] Equal Employment Opportunity Commission, "Nassau County Police Department to Pay $450,000 for Age Bias," p. 1, October 23, 2008, http://www.eeoc.gov/eeoc/newsroom/release/archive/10-23-08.html, (accessed September 1, 2015).

[8] See 29 United States Code, Section 623 (j)(1)(A).

[9] No author, Laws Enforced by EEOC, Equal Employment Opportunity Commission, http://www.eeoc.gov/laws/statutes, p. 1, (accessed September 1, 2015) and No author, Title VII of the Civil Rights Act of 1964, Equal Employment Opportunity Commission, http://www.eeoc.gov/laws/statutes/titlevii.cfm, (accessed August 31, 2015). This second source is the actual text of Title VII.

[10] No author, "Facts About Discrimination in Federal Government Employment Based on Marital Status, Political Affiliation, Status as a Parent, Sexual Orientation or Transgender (Gender Identity) Status, Equal Employment Opportunity Commission, p. 1.,http://www.eeoc.gov/federal/otherprotections.cfm, (accessed August 31, 2015). No author, "What You should Know About EEOC and the Enforcement Protections for LGBT Workers," Equal Employment Opportunity Commission, p. 1., http://www.eeoc.gov/eeoc/newsroom/wysk/enforcement_protections_lgbt_workers.cfm, (accessed August 31, 2015). No author, Remedies for Employment Discrimination, Equal Employment Opportunity Commission, http://www.eeoc.gov/employees/remedies.cfm, (accessed August 31, 2015).

[11] No author, "EEOC Releases Fiscal Year 2015 Enforcement and Litigation Data (Equal Employment Opportunity Commission: Washington, D.C., February 11, 2016), p, 1, http://www.eeoc.gov/eeoc/newsroom/release/2-11-16.cfm, (accessed March 1, 2016).

[12] No author, *EEOC Training Institute Resources Guide: Employer Responsibilities* p. B-2 to B4, No author, Remedies for Employment Discrimination, Equal Employment Opportunity Commission, http://www.eeoc.gov/employees/remedies.cfm, (accessed August 31, 2015), and Barbara L. Johnson, "Types of Damages Available in Employment Cases," American Bar Association, 2011 Conference, Toronto, Canada, August 4, 2011.

[13] Loc.cit.

[14] No author, Remedies for Employment Discrimination, Equal Employment Opportunity Commission, http://www.eeoc.gov/employees/remedies.cfm, August 31, 2015.

[15] *Stewart et al. v. City of Houston Police Department*, No. 09-20680, U.S. Court of Appeals for the Fifth Circuit (2010).

[16] Benjamin P. Endres, Jr. and the *United States of America v. Indiana State Police*, No. 02-1247, United State Court of Appeals for the 7th Circuit 349 F.ed 922, U.S. App Lexis 23570 (2003).

[17] Carri Geer Thevenot, "Las Vegas Police Settle Officer's Lawsuit Over Religious Clothing," *Las Vegas Review-Journal*, January 23, 2009.

[18] *Fraternal Order of Police v. City of Newark*, 170 F.3d 359 (3d Cir, 1999).

[19]41 Code of Federal Regulations (CFR) 60 3.1(D), 1978.

[20]Laurie Wardell and Michael K. Fridkin, *Title VII and Section 1981* (Chicago: Chicago Lawyers' Committee for Civil Rights Under the Law, October, 2009), p. 15.

[21]*Jackson v. County of Racine*, 474 F.3d 493 (7th Cir. 2007).

[22]*Hall v. Gus Construction Co.*, 842 F.2d 1010, 46FEP, Cases 57 (8th Circuit), 1988.

[23]*Chris Sanford v. Department of Veterans Affairs*, EEOC Appeal No. 0120082632 (2009).

[24]U.S. Equal Employment Opportunity Commission, Facts About Sexual Harassment, July 22, 2002, p. 1, http://www.eeoc.gov/facts/fs-sex.html, (accessed September 2, 2015).

[25]U.S. Equal Employment Opportunity Commission, Fourteen-Year-Old Reports Sexual Harassment and Assault at Kansas Fast Food Restaurant, undated, p. 1, http://www.eeoc.gov/youth/case3.html, (accessed September 2, 2015).

[26]U.S. Equal Employment Opportunity Commission, Policy Guidance on Current Issues of Sexual Harassment, March 19, 1999, p. 2, http://www.eeoc.gov/eeoc/publications/upload/currentissues.pdf, (accessed September 2, 2015) and Federal Code of Regulations, Title 29, Subtitle B, Chapter XIV, Part 1604, 1604.11, Sexual Harassment, August 31, 2015, https://www.google.com/webhp?sourceid=chrome-instant&ion=1&espv=2&ie=UTF-8#q=Federal+Code+of+Regulations%2C+Title+29%2C+Subtitle+B%2C+Chapter+XIV%2C+Part+1604%2C+1604.11%2C+Sexual+Harassment%2C+August+31%2C+2015, (accessed September 2, 2015).

[27]Policy Guidance on Current Issues of Sexual Harassment, p. 2.

[28]On some of these points see *Robinson v. Jackson Shipyards*, 760 F.Supp 1486, Cases 971 (M.D. Fla), 1991.

[29]*King v. Macmillan,* U.S. Court of Appeals for the 4th Circuit, 594 F.3d 301 (2010).

[30]Wardell and Fridkin, Title VII and Section 1981, p. 24.

[31]Ibid.

[32]Civil Action No. 07-cv-02560-LTB-CBS, *The United States of America and Lance Lazoff v. City of Colorado Springs, Colorado,* in the United States District Court of Colorado (2008).

[33]Drawn with restatement from Rachel L. Swarns, "Pregnant Officer Denied Chance to Take Sergeant's Exam Fights Back," The New York Times, August 9, 2015.

[34]No author, Laws Enforced by the EEOC (Washington, DC: U.S. Equal Employment Opportunity Commission: Washington, DC, 2010), p. 1., http://www.eeoc.gov/laws/statutes, (accessed September 4, 215).

[35]See *Lochren et al. v. County of Suffolk,* No. 08-2723-cv, United States Court of Appeals, 2nd Circuit (2009) and *Sandra L. Lochren, Sara A. Macdermott, Patricia O'brien, Kelly Mennella , Christine Blauvelt, and Miriam Riera, plaintiffs, v. County of Suffolk, defendants,* United States District Court, e.d. New York, March 23, 2010.

[36]The content in this paragraph is drawn from Fabrice Czarnecki, M.D., "The Pregnant Officer," *Clinics in Occupational and Environmental Medicine,* Vol. 3, Issue No. 4, (August 2003), pp. 641–648 and Karen J. Kruger, Fabrice Czarnecki, and Gary W. McLhinney, "Pregnancy and Policing: Are They Compatible?" Paper presented at the 2008 International Association of Chiefs of Police Annual Meeting, San Diego.

[37]Loc. cit.

[38]Drawn from Colonel Deborah J. Campbell, New York State Police, Karen J. Kruger, Funk and Bolton, and Randall H. Carroll, Chief of Police (Retired), speakers, Bellingham, Washington, "Pregnancy & Policy: A New Policy Makes Them More Compatible," International Association of Chiefs of Police, October 2010, 28 pp., 1–28, http://www.aele.org/los2010kruger-pregnancy.pdf, (accessed September 4, 2015) and no author, Pregnancy Guidelines for Federal Law Enforcement, May 1, 2011, Wifle Foundation, 8 pp, http://www.wifle.org/pdf/PregnancyGuidelines.pdf, (accessed September 4, 2015).

[39]Loc. cit.

[40]Loc. cit.

[41]Loc. cit.

[42]Settlement, The United States of America and the Rochester. Muchigan, Police Department, August 24. 2015, http://www.ada.gov/rochester_pd_sa.html, (accessed September 4, 2015).

[43]Settlement Agreement Between the United States of America and the New York City Police Department, November 18, 2009.

[44]No author, Americans with Disabilities Act, Information for Law Enforcement, December 1, 2008, www.ada.gov/policeinfo.htm, (accessed September 4, 2015).

[45]Loc. cit.

[46]U.S. Equal Employment Opportunity Commission, *Disability Discrimination,* undated, http://www.eeoc.gov/laws/types/disability.cfm, (accessed September 6, 2015). Parenthetically, while the EEOC may or may not note the date a document is effective or placed on the Internet, it does note when documents are outdated.

[47]Loc. cit.

[48]Loc. cit.

[49]Americans with Disabilities Act (1990) as Amended (2008, effective January 1, 2009), Section 12103((1).

[50]Ibid., Section 12103(2).

[51]U.S. Equal Employment Opportunity Commission, *Questions and Answers on the Final Rule Implementing the ADA Amendments Act of 2008 the ADA Amendments Act* undated, p. 1, http://www.eeoc.gov/laws/statutes/adaaa.cfm, (accessed September 6, 2015).

[52]Loc. cit.

[53]No Author, *ACLU Sues West Virginia Police Chief Who Blocked Life-Saving Measures for Gay Heart Attack Victim Assumed to Be HIV Positive,* American Civil Liberties Union March 2, 2006, www.aclu.org/news/aclu-sues-west-virginia-police-chief-who-blocked-life-saving-measures-gay-heart-attack-victim, (accessed September 6, 2015).

[54]The Associate Press, W.Va. Police Chief Denied Gay Man CPR, March 3, 2006, No longer available on the Internet. Parallel content is found at no author, "Police Chief Sued for Denying Gay Man CPR," USA Today, March 3, 2006, http://usatoday30.usatoday.com/news/nation/2006-03-02-cpr-suit_x.htm, (accessed September 6, 2015).

[55]The case was filed by the Charleston, WV ACLU Office. It does not appear in any legal index. A July 1, 2010 call by "Mike" Swanson to the ACLU in Charleston confirmed the basic facts in this case, but no other information could be provided.

[56]The points in this short paragraph, except for the last sentence, are taken from no author, Wage and Hour Division History, U.S.

Department of Labor, 2009, p. 1, http://www.dol.gov/whd/about/history/whdhist.htm, (accessed September 9, 2015).

[57]No author, Minimum Wage Since 1938, CNN Money, 2015, p. 1, http://money.cnn.com/interactive/economy/minimum-wage-since-1938, (accessed September 9, 2015).

[58]Michael E. Brooks, "The Fair Standards Labor Act and Police Compensation, *FBI Law Enforcement Bulletin*, Vol. 73, No. 6, (June 2004), p. 1 and Ted H. Bartlestone, "Issues to Consider in Defending Overtime Claims Under the Fair Labor Standards Act," *Journal of the Missouri Bar*, (November/December, 2009), p. 290.

[59]U.S. 833 (1976).

[60]U.S. 528 (1985).

[61]U.S. Department of Labor, "Handy Reference Guide to the Fair Labor Standards Act," November 2014, p. 2., http://www.dol.gov/whd/regs/compliance/hrg.htm, (accessed September 9, 2015).

[62]See U.S. Department of Labor. Fact Sheet, May 2016, https://www.dol.gov/whd/overtime/final2016/overtime-factsheet.htm, accessed June 21, 2016.

[63]No author, Guidance for Higher Education Institutions on Paying Overtime Under the Fair Labor Standards Acr, Wage and Hour Division, United States Department of Labor, May 18, 2016, p. 7.

[64]See No author, Fact Sheet: Final Rule to Update the Regulations Defining and Delimiting the Exemption for Executive, Administrative, and Professional Employees, Wage and Hour Division, United States Department of Labor, May 2016, no page numbers, https://www.dol.gov/whd/overtime/final2016/overtime-factsheet.htm, accessed June 21, 2016.

[65]Loc. cit.

[66]*Fred Bamonte, Javier Cota, Ricardo Perine and other similarly situated employees v. City of Mesa (AZ)*, 598 F. 3rd 1217 (2010).

[67]*Stephen S. Adams, et al. v. United States*, 471 F. 3d 1321 (2006).

[68]*David A. Cleveland, Mark S. Vojodich, Andres W. Aston, Brian Benavides v. City of Elmendorf, Texas*, 388 F.3d 522 (2004).

[69]*Rogers v. City of Richmond*, 851 F.Supp 2d 983 (2012) and Lisa Casabona, "Richmond, Virginia Settles Overtime Suit with City Police Officers for $7 M+," Thompson Information Services, August 23, 2012, p. 1, http://smarthr.blogs.thompson.com/2012/08/23/richmond-va-settles-overtime-lawsuit-with-city-police-officers-for-7m, (accessed September 10, 2015).

[70]Brian Taylor, "Government Extending Federal Benefits to All Married Same-Sex Couples," NPR (National Public Radio), July 9, 2015, pp. 1–2, http://www.npr.org/sections/thetwo-way/2015/07/09/421489372/government-extending-federal-benefits-to-all-married-same-sex-couples, (accessed September 11, 2015).

[71]*Gibbs and Drew v. City of New York Police Commissioner Bratton and Others*, 2015 U.S. Dist. Lexis 7960 and 24 Wage and Hour Cas. 2d (BNA) 274

[72]*Lee v. City of Elkhart*, 2015 U.S. App. LEXIS 3712 (7th Cir. Ind., Mar. 10, 2015) Prior history: *Lee v. City of Elkhart*, 2013 U.S. Dist. LEXIS 57624 (N.D. Ind., Apr. 22, 2013).

[73]*Knussman v. State of Maryland*, No. B-95-1255 (D. MD. February 2, 1999).

[74]MaCherie Placide, "In Search of the Best," Paper presented at the Annual Meeting of the Midwest Political Science Association, Chicago, April 3–6, 2008 addresses the quality of recruits and recruiting difficulties. Also see Jeremy M. Wilson and Justin A. Heinonen, "Police Workforce Structures: Cohorts, the Economy, and Organizational Performance," *Police Quarterly*, Vol. 15, Issue 3, (September 2012), pp. 283–307.

[75]Kevin Johnson, "Police Agencies Buried in Resumes," *USA Today*, March 12, 2009.

[76]No author, *Recruitment and Retention Practices* (Peace Officers Standards and Training Commission: Sacramento, April 2006), drawn with restatement from p. viii. and 25–26. A national study of 49 state police agencies produced similar results; parenthetically, Hawaii has no state police force per se. See Thomas S. Whetstone, John C. Reed, Jr., and Phillip C. Turner, "Recruiting: A comparative Study of the Recruiting Practices of State Police Agencies," International Journal of Police Science and Management," Vol. 8, Issue 1, (Spring 2006), pp. 52–66.

[77]Douglas L. Yearwood, *Recruitment and Retention Study Series* (North Carolina Criminal Justice Analysis Center: Raleigh, North Carolina, April 2003), p. i.

[78]*Recruitment and Retention Practices*, pp. xi and 25–26. Also see no author, *POST Recruitment Strategic Planning Guide* (Peace Officers Standards and Training Commission: Sacramento, 2009).

[79]Nelson Lim et. al., *To Protect and Serve: Enhancing the Efficiency of LAPD Recruiting* (Santa Monica, CA: The Rand Corporation, 2009), p. xviii.

[80]Ibid., p. xvii.

[81]Ibid., p. 39.

[82]Ibid., p. 40.

[83]Ibid., p. 39.

[84]Ibid., pp. 42 and 40.

[85]Matthew Hickman and Brian Reaves, *Local Police Departments, 2003* (Washington, DC: Bureau of Justice Statistics, May 2006), p. 9.

[86]Lim et. al., *To Protect and Serve: Enhancing the Efficiency of LAPD Recruiting*, p. 60 and Michelle Comeau and John Klofas, *The Police Recruiting Process: Rochester: N.Y.*, p. 5.

[87]Kevin Johnson, "Long Odds to Join Las Vegas Force," USAToday, August 2, 2007, http://usatoday30.usatoday.com/news/nation/2007-08-01-vegascops_N.htm, (accessed September 14, 2015).

[88]See W. Payne and J. Harvey, "A Framework for the Design and Development of Physical Employment Tests and Standards," Vol. 53, Issue 7, (July 2010), pp. 858–871.

[89]Comeau and Klofas, *The Police Recruiting Process: Rochester: N.Y.*, p. 7.

[90]*United States v. City of Erie*, 411 F.Supp.2d 524 (2005).

[91]No author, "Justice Department Settles Sex Discrimination Lawsuit Against City of Corpus Christi, Texas, Police Department," U.S. Department of Justice Press Release, September 109, 2012, p. 1, http://www.justice.gov/opa/pr/justice-department-settles-sex-discrimination-lawsuit-against-city-corpus-christi-texas, (accessed September 15, 2015).

[92]Loc. cit.

[93]Kassondra Cloos, "Lawsuit: Colorado Springs Female Police Officers Allege Discrimination in Physical Fitness

Test," The Gazette (Colorado Springs, Colorado), May 1, 2015, pp. 1–2, http://gazette.com/lawsuit-colorado-springs-female-police-officers-allege-discrimination-in-physical-fitness-test/article/1550705, (accessed September 15, 2015).

[94]Charles Nathan Brown, Survey of Physical Agility Testing and Officer Fitness Levels in Kentucky Police Departments, Martin School, University of Kentucky, Spring 2005, p. 111.

[95]No author, Fact Sheet #36: Employee Polygraph Protection Act of 1988, U.S. Department of Labor, July 2008, http://www.dol.gov/whd/regs/compliance/whdfs36.pdf, (accessed September 16, 2015).

[96]Code of Federal Regulations (CFR) 801.10, current to July 2, 2010.

[97]Hickman and Reaves, *Local Police Departments*, p. 8.

[98]No author, *Polygraph Testing May Be Flawed for Security Screening*, National Academy of Sciences, October 8, 2002, p. 1.

[99]Charles Swanson, Neil Chamelin, Leonard Territo, and Robert Taylor, *Criminal Investigation* (New York: McGraw-Hill, 2006), pp. 218–219.

[100]*United States, Petitioner v. Edward G. Scheffer* 523 U.S. 303 (1998). Also see Christopher Domin, "Mitigating Evidence? The Admissibility of Polygraph Results in the Penalty Phase," *University of California, Davis, Law Review*, Vol. 43, No. 4, (April 2010), pp. 1461–1490 and Leonard Saxe and Gershon Ben-Shakhar, "Admissibility of Polygraph Tests: The Application of Scientific Standards Post-Daubert," *Psychology, Public Policy, and Law*, Vol. 5, Issue 1, (March 1999).

[101]Ibid.

[102]Lim et al., *To Protect and Serve: Enhancing the Efficiency of LAPD Recruiting*, p. 61.

[103]*Thomas J. Mullen v. County of Suffolk, Supreme Court of the State of New York*, D16143 (2007).

[104]Lim et al., *To Protect and Serve: Enhancing the Efficiency of LAPD Recruiting*, p. 60.

[105]William G. Doerner, "The Utility of the Oral Board in Selecting Police Academy Admissions," *Policing: An International Journal of Police Strategies and Management*, Vol. 20, Issue 4, (1997), pp. 777–785.

[106]Larry Gaines and Bruce Lewis, "Reliability and Validity of the Oral Board in Police Promotions," *Journal of Criminal Justice*, Vol. 10, Issue 5, (1982), pp. 403–420.

[107]This section draws on the 38 years of experience of Charles Swanson in designing oral boards, job simulations, and assessment, as well as training promotional panel members from over 26 states.

[108]T. Mieczkowski, "Drug Testing The Police: Some Results of Urinalysis and Hair Analysis in a Major U.S. Metropolitan Police Force," *Journal of Forensic Medicine*, Vol. 3, (June 2004), pp. 115–122.

[109]Comeau and Klofas, *The Police Recruiting Process: Rochester: N.Y.*, p. 8.

[110]Martin Sellbom, Gary L. Fischler, and Yossef S. Ben-Porath, "Identifying the MMPI-2 Predictors of Police Integrity and Misconduct," *Criminal Justice and Behavior*, Vol. 34, No. 8, (August 2007), pp. 985–1004. Also see Jane Framingham, Minnesota Multiphasic Personality Inventory (MMPI),

PsychCentral, 2015, p. 1, http://psychcentral.com/lib/minnesota-multiphasic-personality-inventory mmpi/?all=1, (accessed September 16, 2015).

[111]John T. Chinall and Paul Detrick, "The Neo PI-R, Inwald Personality Inventory and the MMPI-2 in the Prediction of Police Academy Performance: A Case for Incremental Validity," *American Journal of Criminal Justice*, Vol. 27, No. 2, (March 2003), pp. 233–248.

[112]*Boston Police Department v Jill Kavaleski, et al., J.V. Kavaleski v Julia Reade, M.D., et. al*, Opinion No. 128315 Docket Number, SUCV2009-04978-C, Superior Court of Massachusetts at Suffolk, 2014 Mass. Super. Lexis 133, 2014.

[113]Lim et al., *To Protect and Serve: Enhancing the Efficiency of LAPD Recruiting*, pp. 61, 69–70.

[114]Matthew Hickman, *State and Local Law Enforcement Training Academies-2002* (Washington, DC: Bureau of Justice Statistics, 2005), p. iii.

[115]Hickman and Reaves, *Local Police Departments*, p. 9.

[116]Ibid.

[117]Hickman and Reaves, *Local Police Departments*, p. 9.

[118]Lawrence W. Daly, "Police Officers Do Not Receive Adequate Training to Prepare Them to Handle Child Sexual Abuse Investigations," *Issues in Child Abuse Accusations*, Vol. 15, Issue 1, (Winter 2005), p. 1.

[119]Patricia Obst and Jeremy Davey, "Does the Police Academy Change Your Life?" *International Journal of Police Science and Management*, Vol. 5, Issue 1, (2003), p. 31.

[120]Stephen J. Scarfo, "Validity Study Relationship Between Police Academy Performance and Cadet Level of Education and Cognitive Ability," *Applied H.R.M. Research*, Vol. 7, No. 1, (2002), p. 39.

[121]Allison Chappell, "Police Academy Training: Comparing Across Curricula," *Policing: An International Journal of Police Strategies and Management*, Vol. 31, No. 1, (2008): p. 52.

[122]Nadine Post, "Police Academy to Set Stage for Scenario-Based Training," *ENR: Engineering News-Record*, Vol. 264, Issue 6, (February 22, 2010).

[123]Hickman and Reaves, Local Police Departments, 2003, p. 8 and James Hannah, "Military Call-Ups Strain Police Forces in Ohio and Elsewhere," *The Enquirer* (Cincinnati, Ohio) February 20, 2003.

[124]Ibid., p. 9.

[125]For more details, including forms, see www.Mesaaz.gov/police/FTO

[126]Francis L. McCafferty, "The Challenge of Selecting Tomorrow's Police Officers from Generations X and Y," *The Journal of the American Academy of Psychiatry and Law*, Vol. 31, No. 1, (2003), p. 81. This note is only for the qualities of the silent generation. As a separate matter, McCafferty uses a 1930–1948 birth range for this group. Our own reading of sources led us to use a 1925–1945 range.

[127]Population Division, U.S. Census Bureau, "Selected Characteristics of Baby Boomers," (Washington, DC:, U.S. Census Bureau, 2009), from unnumbered PowerPoint presentation. Also see Jim Harter and Sangeeta Agrwal, "Many Baby Boomers Reluctant to Retire," Gallup Poll, January 20, 2014, p. 1, http://www.gallup.com/poll/166952/baby-boomers-reluctant-retire.aspx, accesssed May 13, 2016.

[128]Ibid.

[129]Commission on Peace Officers Standards and Training (POST), Recruitment & Retention (Sacramento, CA: POST, 2006), p. viii.

[130]Eric P. Werth, "Adult Learning: Similarities in Training Methods and Recruits Learning Characteristics," *The Police Chief*, Vol. LXXVI, No. 11, (November 2009), p. 1, online access.

[131]"The Challenge of Selecting Tomorrow's Police Officers from Generations X and Y," p. 80.

[132]Ibid., p. 80.

[133]Melinda Crowley, Generation X Speaks Out on Civic Engagement and the Decennial Census: An Ethnographic Approach (Washington, DC: U.S. Census Bureau, June 17, 2003), p. 2.

[134]"The Challenge of Selecting Tomorrow's Police Officers from Generations X and Y," p. 80.

[135]Ibid., p. 80. Also see Marisa Dinatale and Stephanie Boraas, "The Labor Force Experience of Women from Generation X," *Monthly Labor Review*, Vol. 125, No. 3 (March 2002), pp. 3–15.

[136]Elwood Carlson, 20th-Century Generations, *Population Bulletin*, Vol. 64, No. 1, (2009), computed from Table 4, p. 11.

[137]"The Challenge of Selecting Tomorrow's Police Officers from Generations X and Y," p. 80.

[138]Ibid., p. 82.

[139]Generation X Speaks Out on Civic Engagement and the Decennial Census: An Ethnographic Approach, pp. 10–16.

[140]"The Challenge of Selecting Tomorrow's Police Officers from Generations X and Y," p. 82.

[141]Tamara Erickson, "Don't Treat Them Like Baby Boomers," *Business Week*, Issue 4097, (August 25, 2008), p. 1, online access.

[142]Neil Simons, "Leveraging Generational Work Styles to Meet Business Objectives," *Information Management*, Vol. 44, Issue 1, (January/February 2010), p. 29.

[143]"The Challenge of Selecting Tomorrow's Police Officers from Generations X and Y," p. 81.

[144]No author, "Social Networking Fact Sheet," Pew Research Center, undated, but contents reveal it was written in late 2014 or 2015, http://www.pewinternet.org/fact-sheets/social-networking-fact-sheet, (accessed March 2, 2016) and Maeve Duggan, Nicole B. Ellison, Cliff Lampe, Amanda Lenhart, and Mary Madden, "Social Media Update, 2014," Pew Research Center, January 9, 2015, p.1, http://www.pewinternet.org/2015/01/09/social-media-update-2014, (accessed March 2, 2016).

[145]No author: "Top 15 Most Popular Social Networking Sites," eBizMBA Rank, March 2016, p. 1, http://www.ebizmba.com/articles/social-networking-websites, (accessed March 2, 2016).

[146]No author, "2015 Social Media Survey Results," International Association of Chiefs of Police, 2015, p. 1, http://www.iacp.org/portals/0/documents/pdfs/2015SocialMediaSurveyResults.pdf, (accessed March 2, 2016).

[147]See Christopher D. Licher, Devon Reister, and Christopher Mason, *Vermont Statewide Law Enforcement Study* (Chicago: I/O Solutions, Inc., 2006).

[148]See *Major Cities Chiefs and the Federal Bureau of Investigation, National Executive Institute, Retention: Understanding the Generations, Recruitment, and Selection*, Employee • Leadership Development, 2007.

[149]Liz Martinez, Real Life Recruiting, Officer.com, online access, August 2006, pp. 2–3.

[150]Lisa Perrine, "Job Sharing: A Viable Option for Law Enforcement?" *The FBI Law Enforcement Bulletin*, Vol. 78, No. 3, (March 2009), pp. 14–15.

[151]Lisa Perrine, "Is Job Sharing a Viable Option for Law Enforcement?" (Sacramento: California Commission on Police Standards and Training), 2007 Paper for Command College 41, p. 5.

[152]Donna Leinwand, "IRR Call-Up Puts Lives in Disarray," *USA-Today*, August 5, 2004, Also see Leonard Territo, "Military Combat Veterans: What They Mean to Your Department," The Florida Police Chief, August 2008, pp. 26–31. This comprehensive article also discusses the psychological issues facing returning Veterans and the necessity for re-entry psychological evaluation of returning police officers.

[153]Hickman and Reaves, *Local Police Departments*, 2003, p. 4.

[154]Hannah, "Military Call-Ups Strain Police Forces in Ohio and Elsewhere."

[155]Palm Beach County Sheriff's Office and PBC PBA, AAA Case No. 32-390-100713-04, 121 LA (BNA) 1624 (Smith, 2005; Reported 2006).

[156]United States Code, Sections 4301 to 4335, December 19, 2005.

[157]Code of Federal Regulations (CFR) 1002.193(6), current to July 1, 2010.

[158]*Fink v. City of New York*, 129 F.Supp.2d 511 (E.D. N.Y. 200 (1)).

[159]Missy Diaz, "Former Fla. Officer Gets 90 Days for Faking Military Call-Up," PoliceOne.Com, August 26, 2007. www.PoliceOne.com

[160]Samuel Walker, *Early Intervention Systems for Law Enforcement Agencies: A Planning and Management Guide* (Washington, DC: Office of Community Oriented Policing Services, 2003), p. 48.

[161]Susan Sward and Elizabeth Fernandez, "The Use of Force/Counting Without Consequence/Police System of Tracking is Outdated, Often Ignored, SFGate.com, February 6, 2006. SFGate is the online version of the San Francisco *Chronicle*. The study covered 1996–2004.

[162]No Author, *Conduct of Law Enforcement Agencies, Civil Rights Division, U.S. Department of Justice*, current to July 7, 2010. www.Justice.Gov.

[163]Tami Abdollah, Los Angles Daily News, "Early Warning Systems Aim to Identify Problem Officers, September 7, 2014, p. 1, http://www.dailynews.com/government-and-politics/20140907/early-warning-systems-aim-to-id-troubled-police-officers, accessed March 2, 2016.

[164]Ibid., p. 2.

[165]Ibid.

[166]Ibid.

[167]Samuel Walker, *Early Warning Systems: Responding to the Problem Officer*, (Washington, DC: Office of Justice Programs, July 2001), p. 2.

[168]*Early Intervention and Personal Assessment FAQs*, Phoenix (AZ) Police Department, p. 5.

[169]Walker, *Early Warning Systems: Responding to the Problem Officer*, p. 3.

[170]Stuart MacIntyre, Tim Prenzler, and Jackie Chapman, "Early Intervention to Reduce Complaints," *International Journal of Police Science and Management* 10, no. 2 (Summer 2008), 238–250.

[171]Denver Police Department, *Discipline Handbook (2012)*, pp. 13–14.

[172]Ibid., p. 13

[173]No Author, *Internal Affairs Policy and Procedures*, N.J. Office of the Attorney General, November 2000, p. 11–20.

[174]Ibid.

[175]Helen LaVan, "Public Sector Employee Discipline: Comparing Police to Other Public Sector Employees," *Employee Responsibilities and Rights Journal*, Vol. 19, No. 1 (March 2007), pp. 17–30.

[176]Mark Iris, "Police Discipline in Houston: The Arbitration Experience," *Police Quarterly*, Vol. 15, No. 2, (June 2002), pp. 132–151.

[177]Lisa Halverstadt, *The Arizona Republic*, July 9, 2010.

[178]David Weisburd et al., *Police Attitudes Toward Abuse of Authority: Findings From a National Study* (Washington, DC: Bureau of Justice Statistics, 2000), 5.

[179]Ibid.

[180]Jennifer Manis, Carol A. Archbold, and Kimberly D. Hassell, "Exploring the Impact of Police Officer Education Level on Allegations of Police Misconduct," *International Journal of Police Science and Management*, Vol. 10, Issue 4, (Winter 2008), pp. 509–523.

[181]No Author, "For Florida Police, Higher Education Means Lower Risk of Disciplinary Action," *Law Enforcement News*, October 31, 2002, pp. 1 and 10.

[182]Ibid.

[183]James J. Fyfe et. al., "Gender, Race, and Discipline in the New York City Police Department," paper presented at the Annual Meeting of the American Society of Criminology, Washington, DC, 1998.

[184]Jeff Rojek and Scott H. Decker, "Examining Racial Disparity in the Police Discipline Process," *Police Quarterly*, Vol. 12, Issue 4, (December 2009), pp. 388–407.

[185]The data is for 2002. Matthew J. Hickman, Citizen Complaints About Police Use of Force (Washington, DC: Bureau of Justice Statistics, June 2006), p. 1.

[186]Matthew J. Hickman and Jane E. Poole, "National Data on Citizen Complaints about Police Use of Force: Data Quality Concerns and the Potential (Mis)use of Statistical Evidence to Address Police Agency Conduct," Draft unpublished paper dated January 26, 2015, https://nacole.org/wp-content/uploads/Hickman.National-Data-on-Citizen-Complaints-about-Police-Use-of-Force_Data-Quality-Concern-and-the-Potential-Mis-Use-of-Statistical-Evidence-to-Address-Police-Agency-Conduct.DRAFT_.pdf, (accessed September 17, 2015). Hickman has previously published on police misconduct.

[187]With modification, from Samuel Walker, Conference Report, "The Disciplinary Matrix: An Effective Police Accountability Tool?" January 2003, University of Nebraska at Omaha.

[188]Ibid., with modification.

[189]Bernd Debusmann, "Performance Reviews-A Global Scourge," June 1, 2010. Online access http://blogs.Reuters.com/great-debate, p. 1.

[190]Ibid., p. 2.

[191]Larry M. Coutts and Frank W. Schneider, "Police Officer Performance Appraisal Systems: How Good Are They?" *Policing: An International Journal of Police Strategies and Management* Vol. 27, Issue 1 (2004), pp. 67 81. Also see David Lilly and Sameer Hinduja, "Police Officer Performance Appraisal and Overall Satisfaction," *Journal of Criminal Justice*, Vol. 35, Issue 2, (March/April 2007), pp. 137–150.

[192]Thomas Whetstone and Deborah G. Wilson, "Dilemmas Confronting Female Police Officer Promotional Candidates," p. 69, in Jim Ruiz and Don Hummer, *Handbook of Police Administration* (Boca Raton, FL: CRC Press, 2008).

[193]Ibid.

[194]No Author, Former Police Officer Convicted in Hudson County Promotional Exam Cheating Case, N.J. Office of the Attorney General, March 6, 2006 press release.

[195]Gregory Smith, "Ex-Chief Who Helped Officers May Face Pension Cut," *The Providence (R.I.) Journal*, June 12, 2007.

[196]These points are repeatedly mentioned by agency personnel to Charles Swanson.

[197]Mark Schneider, "National Assessment of Educational Progress," February 22, 2007. http://NCES.ed.gov

[198]Ibid.

[199]For the most current standards see No Author, Guidelines and Ethical Consideration for Assessment Center Operations, *International Journal of Selection and Assessment* Vol. 17, No. 3, (September 2009), pp. 243–252.

[200]This history is recited in numerous publications; for example, see Kris Hogarty and Max Bromley, "Evaluating the Use of an Assessment Center Process for Entry Level Police Officer Selections in a Medium Sized Agency," *Journal of Police and Criminal Psychology*, Vol. 11, No. 1, (March 1996), p. 27.

[201]George C. Thornton and Michael J. Potemra, "Utility of Assessment Center Promotion of Police Sergeants," *Public Personnel Management*, Vol. 39, No. 1, (Summer 2010), p. 57.

[202]On the relationship of dimensions and exercises, see Filip Lievens, Stephen Dilchert, Deniz S. Ones, "The Importance of Exercise and Dimension Factors in Assessment Centers," *Human Performance*, Vol. 22, Issue 5 (November 2009), pp. 375–390.

[203]For example, see *Oliver v. Scottsdale*, 969 F.Supp.564 (D.Ariz. 1996).

[204]F.2d 1140 (2nd Cir. 1991).

[205]On this point see Jim Ruiz and Erin Morrow, "Retiring the Old Centurion: Life After a Career in Policing: An Exploratory Study," *International Journal of Public Administration*, Vol. 28, Issue 13/14, (December 2005), pp. 1151–1186.

[206]Rick Bella, *The Oregonian*, OregonLive.com, Lake Oswego Police Chief Dan Duncan Dies," May 20, 2010.

[207]Michelle Perin, "Police Suicide," *Law Enforcement Technology*, Vol. 34, Issue 9 (September 2009), pp. 8, 10, 12, 14, and 16.

[208]Organizational culture and workload remain as key stressors; see P. A. Collins and A. Gibbs, "Stress in Police Officers: A Study of the Origins, Prevalence, and Severity of Stress-Related Symptoms with a County Police Force," *Occupational Medicine*, Vol. 53, No. 4, (2003), p. 256. The findings are based on a sample of 1,206 officers.

This section addresses three core issues of managing law enforcement agencies that if mismanaged invariably lead to thorny problems: communication within the organization, the leaders' relationship with a unionized workforce, and obtaining financial resources and being a good steward of them.

In an earlier chapter it was asserted that communication was a crucial skill. This assertion was justifiable by a single sentence: Without communication, no new activities can be initiated and programs in progress cannot be steered. An agency that cannot be guided is akin to a ship without a rudder and renders leadership ineffective. Illustratively, the most common complaints that police officers have about their immediate supervisors is a lack of communication. Where this deficiency exists, officers lack clarity about what they are to do and it shakes confidence in their supervisors, sometimes leading to them having less influence with those they supervise. Chapter 10. "Organizational and Interpersonal Communication" examines these issues, including how to communicate effectively, the dangers when both senders and receivers miscommunicate, the importance of the grapevine, effective use of e-mail, using social networking site for organizational purposes, proper use of such venues when officers are posting personal thoughts, cross-gender, multicultural, and trans generation, communication, as well as the special attention that is required when relating to people with disabilities.

Chapter 11, "Labor Relations" traces the multiple forces that led to the creation of public sector collective bargaining. Among these forces were the maladaptive personnel practices used in some law enforcement agencies, such as uncompensated court appearances on off-duty days. There is no national public sector collective bargaining law. As a result, it was developed in a number of different states whose respective laws have both similar and different provisions for the bargaining process.

The traditional "big stick" in private sector collective bargaining has been the right of many categories of employees to strike, withhold their services. This right is very limited or non-existent for public sector employees.

Although in the early days of police collective bargaining there were some strikes, they were notable exceptions and not widespread. This was followed by a period of unofficial job actions by officers, such as work slowdowns, for example, to put pressure on their unit of government by depriving it of revenue, officers only wrote traffic tickets for the most egregious violations. Deprived of the right to strike, states have provided various ways of resolving bargaining impasses short of the strike. However, unofficial job actions still occasionally occur. Chapter 11 also examines how the collective bargaining relationship is established, administered, its impact on police administration, involvement in the political process, and its setbacks in the last several years.

Frederick Mosher (1913–1990) was one of the preeminent scholars of public administration. One of his concise observations was not the least among the qualifications of an administrator is his ability as a tactician and gladiator in the budget process, which underscores the importance of Chapter 12, "Financial Management." While Mosher's statement has always been true, it assumed even greater importance for law enforcement executives from December 2007 to 2009, a period that is called the Great Recession.

During this period the American economy went into a deep economic recession and its affect on many police agencies was profound. As an illustration, this chapter contains a case study of Stockton, California, where the police department was cut so severely that it could only respond to crimes-in-progress calls many hours of some days. The city went bankrupt and among the measures taken were substantial cuts to police pensions. Other common cost-cutting measures across the country included lay-offs, closing precincts and selling police patrol boats, motorcycles, mounted patrol horses, and helicopters, and slashing overtime spending. Some municipalities simply closed their police departments and contracted with the county for such services. The cuts went well beyond fat and muscle into hitting bone.

Although the Great Recession nominally ended in 2009, the recovery has been slow and may take a decade or more if there are no intervening economic problems. Some cuts to police budgets may never be restored because citizens are asking questions such as did we really need the police department we had. Financial management is much broader than someone adding and subtracting figures in different columns. Chapter 12 examines a full range of financial management information from what a budget is, budgeting as a political process, and budget formats and strategies.

ORGANIZATIONAL AND INTERPERSONAL COMMUNICATION

Learning Objectives

1. Identify five types of downward communications within an organization.

2. List the order of effective communication from most effective to least effective.

3. Discuss the steps necessary to eliminate some of the missteps in e-mail communications within an organization.

4. Discuss the recent trends by police departments to use social media with the public.

5. Discuss what a law enforcement agency can do to insure a more culturally aware workforce.

6. List the five categories of people with disabilities that law enforcement officers are most likely to come in contact with.

INTRODUCTION

RESEARCH IN RECENT YEARS *has indicated that communication is the number one problem in management and that lack of communication is the employees' primary complaint about their immediate supervisors. There are many components to the communication process and it is essential for police administrators to understand not only what they are but also why they are so important. These include (1) what important steps are involved in the communication process? (2) describe those barriers that can impede the communication process, (3) the variety of organizational systems of communication for familiarization with the many forms of organizational electronic communication, (4) the role of social media in law enforcement communication, (5) the ways in which social media can be used by law enforcement to communicate with the public, (6) a cautionary tale for officers who are posting on social media websites while representing themselves as law enforcement officers, (7) the role of the public information officer in organizational communication, (8) the importance of interpersonal communication and how police managers can become more effective communicators, (9) different ways in which males and females communicate, (10) important variations in cross-cultural communication, (11) the difference in communication styles and needs of those* *officers are classified as Generation X and Generation Y (Millennials), and (12) how best to communicate with people with disabilities.*

THE COMMUNICATION PROCESS

An explanation of communication begins with the basic problem that it cannot be examined as an isolated event. Communication is a process, so it must be understood as the totality of several independent and dynamic elements. An aggregate **communication** can be defined as the process by which senders and receivers interact in both professional and social contexts.

Steps in the Communication Process

To understand the steps in the communication process, assume that a midnight shift lieutenant informs a midnight shift patrol sergeant that there has been a dramatic increase in the number of burglaries in the sergeant's patrol sector during the past month and then suggests it might be the result of inattention on the part of the sergeant and the sergeant's subordinates. The following are the steps that are occurring in this communication process:

Sender—The sender (in this case, the lieutenant) is attempting to send a spoken message to the sergeant. The perceived authority and credibility of the sender are important factors in influencing how much attention the message will receive. Because of the authority and rank of the lieutenant, it is very likely the patrol sergeant will not ignore the message.

Message—The heart of the communication event is the message—a purpose or an idea to be conveyed. Many factors influence how a message is received. Among them are clarity, the alertness of the receiver, the complexity and length of the message, and how the information is organized. The patrol lieutenant's message might have commanded even more attention if the lieutenant had said

clearly, "I need to talk to you about last month's dramatic increase in burglaries in your patrol sector."

Channel (medium)—Several communication channels, or media, are usually available for sending messages in organizations. Typically, messages are spoken (as in this case), written (increasingly electronically), or a combination. When a message is spoken, it is typically accompanied by nonverbal signs, such as a frown, smile, or hand gesture.

Receiver—A communication is complete only when another party receives the message and understands it properly. Perceptual distortions of various types act as filters that can prevent a message from being received as intended by the sender.

Feedback—Messages sent back from the receiver to the sender are referred to as **feedback**. Without feedback, it is difficult to know whether a message has been received and understood. The feedback step also includes the receiver's reactions. If the receiver—in this case, the patrol sergeant—takes appropriate action as intended by the lieutenant, then the message has been received satisfactorily. Effective interpersonal communication involves an exchange of messages between two people. The two communicators take turns being receivers and senders.

Environment—A full understanding of communication requires knowledge of the environment in which messages are transmitted and received. The organizational culture (attitudes and atmosphere) is a key environmental factor that influences communication. It is easier to transmit controversial messages when trust and respect are high than when they are low.

Noise—Distractions, such as noise, have a pervasive influence on the components of the communication process. However, within this context, **noise** can also mean anything that disrupts communication, including the attitudes and emotions of the receiver, such as stress, fear, negative attitudes, and low motivation[1] (see Figure 10.1).

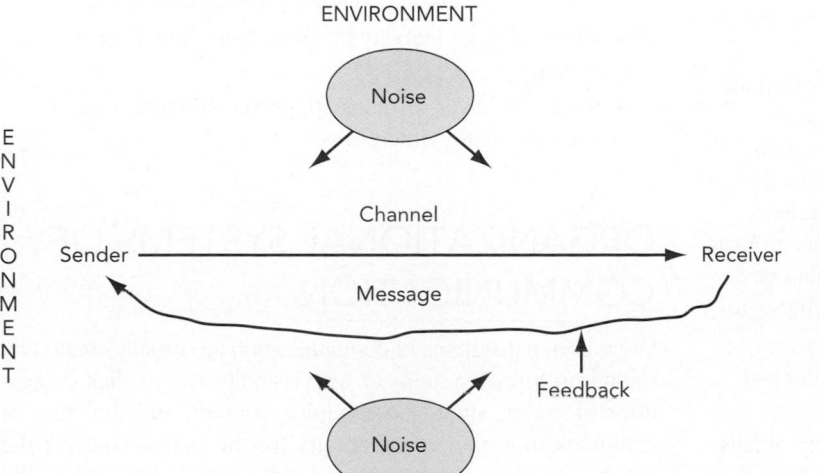

ENVIRONMENT

FIGURE 10.1 ▶ A basic model of the communication process. *Source:* Dubrin, Andrew J., *Human Relations: Interpersonal, Job-Oriented Skills,* 8th edition, © 2004. Reproduced by permission of Pearson Education, Inc., Upper Saddle River, New Jersey.

Quick Facts: What Happens When Senders and Receivers Both Miscommunicate?

In 2009, Harvard Professor Henry Louis Gates, an African-American, was arrested at his home by Cambridge (Massachusetts) Police Sergeant James Crowley.

A neighbor saw two African-American men with backpacks on pushing against the door to the Gates home and called the police, thinking there was a burglary in progress. However, the neighbor had misread the situation. The two men at the door were actually Dr. Gates and his limo driver who were trying to open a jammed door. Before the police were on the scene, the limo driver had departed and Dr. Gates was inside his home.

Sgt. Crowley arrived with a man unknown to him in the house. The man refused to come outside and so Sgt. Crowley entered the home. Dr. Gates, a Harvard Professor, showed Sgt. Crowley identification that established he lived there. At some point, an angry Dr. Gates followed Sgt. Crowley outside of the home and there was a confrontation between the two men. Gates was arrested for disorderly conduct, a charge that was later dismissed.

President Obama was critical of the arrest, calling it "stupid," but later invited both men to the White House. An independent report on the incident concluded that the arrest could have been avoided and was caused by a mutual "misunderstanding and failed communication."[2]

COMMUNICATION BARRIERS

Barriers to communication, or communication breakdowns, can occur at any place in the system. Barriers can be the result of improper techniques on the part of either the sender or the receiver.

The sender hinders communications when the following conditions occur:

- The sender is not clear about what the message is intended to accomplish.
- The sender assumes incorrectly the receiver has the knowledge necessary to understand the message and its intent and does not adapt the message to the intended receiver. For example, experienced criminal justice instructors who teach at the community college and university level understand that when they have a class comprised primarily of pre-service students, as opposed to in-service police practitioners, the way in which the material is presented, if done correctly, is quite different even when the same textbook is being used. They will also tell you that among the more challenging classes to teach are those comprised of an almost equal number of pre-service and police in-service students.
- The sender uses a communication medium not suited for the message. For example, some messages are better transmitted face-to-face, others in writing, while others most effectively transmitted with the use of visual aids. Still others are best taught with direct, hands-on experience. Figure 10.2 displays a scale of sensory perceptions that can be useful as a guide in determining which medium of communication is most effective for a particular message.
- The sender does not develop a mechanism for receiving feedback to determine if the message was understood correctly.
- The sender does not interpret feedback correctly or fails to clarify the message on the basis of feedback from the receiver.

- The sender uses language that causes the receiver to stop listening, reading, or receiving.
- The sender analyzes the audience improperly.
- The sender's background, experiences, and attitudes are different from those of the receiver, and the sender does not take this into account.

The receiver hinders communication when the following occur:

- The receiver is a poor listener, observer, or reader and therefore misinterprets the meaning of the message.
- The receiver jumps to conclusions.
- The receiver hears or sees only certain parts of the message.
- The receiver tends to reject messages that contradict beliefs and assumptions.
- The receiver has other concerns or emotional barriers, such as being mentally preoccupied.

Some other barriers to communication are as follows:

- Noise, temperature, and other physical distractions
- Distance or an inability to see or hear the message being sent
- Sender–receiver relationship, power structure, roles, and personality differences

ORGANIZATIONAL SYSTEMS OF COMMUNICATION

Organizational systems of communication are usually created by setting up formal systems of responsibility and explicit delegations of duties, such as the nature, content, and direction of communication that are necessary for the performance of the group. Consequently, formal communication is required by the organization and follows the accepted pattern of hierarchical

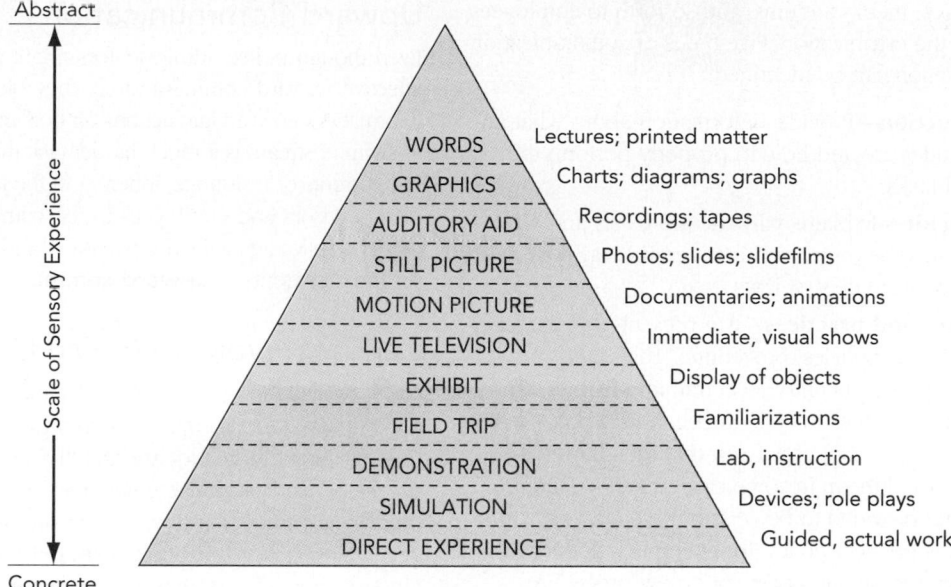

FIGURE 10.2 ▶ Scale of sensory perception.

structure. Delegated authority and responsibility determine the path that communication should take, whether upward or downward. Messages that travel through the formal channels of any organization can follow routine patterns; they may be expected at a given time or presented in a standard form and receive a regularized degree of consideration.[3]

Most police managers prefer a formal system, regardless of how cumbersome it may be, because they can control it and because it tends to create a record for future reference. However, motivational factors of the individual and organizations affect the flow of communication. Employees typically communicate with those who help them achieve their aims and avoid communicating with those who do not assist or who may retard their accomplishing those goals. They direct their communications toward those who make them feel more secure and gratify their needs and away from those who threaten or make them feel anxious or generally provide unrewarding experiences. In addition, employees communicate in a manner that allows them to increase their status, belong to a more prestigious group, attain more power to influence decisions, or expand their control.

Multi-Level and Multi-Agency Communication

The moving transaction identified as organizational communication can occur at several levels and can result in understanding, agreement, good feeling, and appropriate behavior; the converse may also be true.[4]

Downward Communication

Law enforcement agencies substantially rest on classical management theories with emphasis on control, chain of command, and downward flow of information. **Downward communication** is used by management for sending orders, directives, goals,

---

Quick Facts: The Boston Nuclear Attack Warning That Went Awry

In 2005, an FBI Agent was called out of a meeting with approximately 100 local government officials, as well as some consultants. When the Agent returned, he reported in what was described as "heavy detail" an uncorroborated threat report that two Iraqis and four Chinese chemists might be conspiring to launch some sort of nuclear attack on Boston.

The story quickly hit the newspapers and produced an uproar. After several days of investigation, the FBI concluded that the report was false. An unnamed FBI source blamed the uproar on officials in the meeting because information was leaked and some of them responded by saying the federal government was trying to make them scapegoats.[5]

policies, procedures, memorandums, and so forth to employees at lower levels of the organization. Five types of communication within an organization can be identified:[6]

1. **Job instruction**—Provides information about what an officer's duties are and how to properly perform the associated tasks;

2. **Job rationale**—Explains why the job exists and why the tasks must be performed in a certain way, for example, officer safety or laws.

3. **Procedures and practices**—Are presented in the form of departmental policies, procedures, rules, and regulation during the entry level training. As these are updated or new ones issued, officers must acknowledge in writing their receipt and assert that they have read and understood them. In some cases inservice training may also be provided to be certain the employee understands the new policy, for example, adoption of a more restrictive pursuit policy, or a new procedure dealing with how to appropriately handle calls dealing with domestic violence that involves police officers.

4. **Feedback**—Supervisors provide officers with information about their performance, both about what they are doing right as well as areas which need improvement. This is done informally in conversations and formally during the written performance appraisals. The goal for employees is to have a clear understanding of what they need to do going forward.

5. **Indoctrination**—Orients new officers to the norms of the department and assists in assimilating them into the department. Orientation is also provided for all officers in law enforcement agencies when new programs are introduced, such as the shift from traditional policing to community-oriented policing.[7]

Most Effective to Least Effective Downward Communication

Studies of the flow of communications within complex organizations repeatedly demonstrate that each level of management can act as a barrier to downward communication.[8] In perhaps the best-controlled experimental research in downward communication, Dahle[9] proved the efficacy of using oral and written media together. His findings indicate the following order of effectiveness (from most effective to least effective):

1. Oral and written communication combined
2. Oral communication only
3. Written communication only
4. The bulletin board
5. The organizational grapevine

In the final analysis, attempts at disseminating information downward in an organization should not depend exclusively on a single channel.

Upward Communication

Even though police administrators might appreciate the need for effective upward communication, they often do not translate the information received into action.[10] It becomes apparent at once that to swim upstream is a much harder task than to float downstream. But currents of resistance, inherent in the temperament and habits of supervisors and employees in the complexity and structure of modern police agencies, are persistent and strong. In the following section, deterrents to **upward communication** are examined.

Barriers Involving Police Organizations

The physical and other types of distances between superior and subordinate impedes upward communication in several ways. If there is a central headquarters building as well as a number of precincts/districts, police chiefs may wonder if the officers "out there" really understand what the Chief's communications mean and what actions the officers should take. Moreover, the precinct/district officers may read a message or new policy and conclude that headquarters is really out of touch with what they are dealing with "out here." Likewise, when the command staff is seldom seen, they forfeit some credibility with street officers.

Barriers Involving Superiors

The attitudes of superiors and their listening behaviors play a vital role in encouraging or discouraging communication upward. If, in listening to a subordinate, a supervisor seems anxious to end the interview, impatient with the subordinate, or annoyed or distressed by the subject being discussed, a major barrier to future communication may be created.

There is always the danger that a supervisor may assume the posture that "no news is good news" when, in fact, a lack of complaints or criticism might be a symptom that upward communication is operating at a dangerously low level: officers have "learned" the messages they send up the chain of command die someplace but they don't know why.

Supervisors may also assume, often incorrectly, that they know what subordinates think or feel and believe that listening to complaints from subordinates, especially complaints about departmental policies or even specific supervisors, is an indication of disloyalty. This attitude tends to discourage officers with justifiable complaints from approaching their superiors.

One of the strongest deterrents to upward communication is a failure of management to take action on undesirable conditions previously brought to their attention. The result is that subordinates lose faith both in the sincerity of management and in the value of communication.

To avoid this, leaders must provide feedback to subordinates as to why something was not done or what was done with the complaint or criticism.

Barriers Involving Subordinates

Communication can flow more freely downward than upward because a superior is free to call in an officer and talk about a problem at will. Officers do not have the same freedom to intrude on the superior's time and are discouraged from circumventing the chain of command by going over the superior's head directly to the Chief. Even memos from officers that are marked "To Chief Smith, Through the Chain of Command" may be problematic for the officer submitting the memo. If a memo merits attention from senior commanders, it will be referred up the chain of command. Thus, neither the system available nor the rewards offered to the subordinate for upward communication equal those for downward messages.

Horizontal Communication

When an organization's formal communication channels are not open, the informal horizontal channels are almost sure to thrive as a substitute.[11] If there is a disadvantage in **horizontal communication**, it is that it is much easier and more natural to achieve than vertical communication and, therefore, it often replaces vertical channels rather than supplementing them. Actually, the horizontal channels that replace weak or nonexistent vertical channels are usually of an informal nature. There are, of course, formal horizontal channels that are procedurally necessary and should be built into the system. Formal horizontal channels must be set up between various bureaus and divisions for the purposes of planning, interwork task coordination, and general system maintenance functions, such as problem solving, information sharing, and conflict resolution.

We can begin by acknowledging that horizontal communication is essential if the subsystems within a police organization are to function in an effective and coordinated manner. Horizontal communication among peers may also furnish the emotional and social bond that builds esprit de corps or a feeling of teamwork. Psychologically, people seem to need this type of communication, and police managers would do well to provide for this need and thus allow peers to solve some of their own work problems together (see Figure 10.3).

Suppose, for example, that patrol sergeant A is having great difficulty communicating certain mutually beneficial information to detective sergeant B because the police department requires strict adherence to the chain of command in transmitting information. As indicated in Figure 10.3A, sergeant A would have to go up through the various hierarchical complexities of the patrol division and back down through the detective division to communicate with sergeant B. The time being wasted and the level-to-level message distortion occurring in the classically managed organization was recognized by Fayol[12] in 1916. Fayol proposed the creation of a horizontal bridge (see Figure 10.3B) that would allow more direct communications between individuals within an organization. The major limiting factor to the use of Fayol's bridge is a loss of network control and the subsequent weakening of central authority and the random transmission of messages throughout the system.[13]

Despite the need for formal horizontal communication in an organization, there may be a tendency among peers not to formally communicate task-related information horizontally. For instance, rivalry for recognition and promotion can cause competing subordinates to be reluctant to share information. Subordinates may also find it difficult to communicate with highly specialized people at the same level as themselves in other divisions.

In the main, then, formal horizontal communication channels are vital as a supplement to the vertical channels in an organization. Conversely, the informal horizontal channels, although socially necessary, can be detrimental to the vertical channels. They may also introduce false or distorted information into the agency.[14]

The Grapevine

The best-known system for transmitting informal communication is the **grapevine**, so-called because it meanders back and forth like a grapevine across organizational lines. The grapevine's most effective characteristics are that it is fast, it can be highly selective and discriminating, it operates mostly at the place of work, and it supplements and relates to formal communication. These characteristics can be divided into desirable or undesirable attributes.

The grapevine can be considered desirable because it gives management insight into employees' attitudes, provides a safety valve for employees' emotions, and helps spread useful information. Dysfunctional traits include its tendencies to spread rumors and untruths, its lack of responsibility to any group or person, and its uncontrollability. Attributes of the grapevine—its speed and influence—may work either to the good or to the detriment of the organization. The actual operation of the grapevine can be visualized in four ways (see Figure 10.4):[15]

1. **The single strand**—A tells B, who tells C, who tells D, and so on.
2. **The gossip chain**—A seeks and tells everyone, thus becoming the organizational Paul Revere.
3. **The probability chain**—A communicates randomly to D and F, then with the laws of probabilities, D and F tell others in the same manner.
4. **The cluster chain**—A tells three selected others; perhaps one of them tells two others and one of these tells one other person.

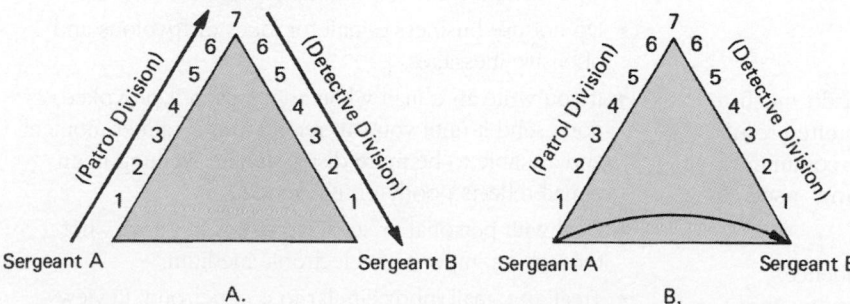

FIGURE 10.3 ▶ Horizontal lines of communication: (A) message path from sergeant A to sergeant B following the usual structured channels; (B) message path from sergeant A to sergeant B following Fayol's bridge.

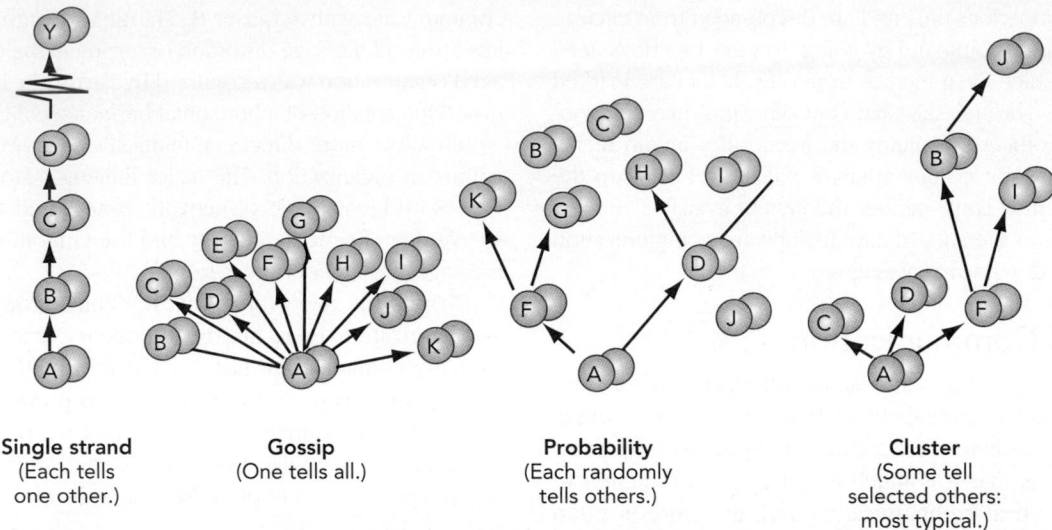

Single strand	Gossip	Probability	Cluster
(Each tells one other.)	(One tells all.)	(Each randomly tells others.)	(Some tell selected others: most typical.)

FIGURE 10.4 ▶ Grapevine patterns. *Source:* John W. Newstrom and Keith Davis, *Organizational Behavior: Human Behavior at Work,* 9th ed., p. 445. © 1993 McGraw Hill Companies. Reproduced with permission from The McGraw Hill Companies.

The grapevine is a permanent factor to be reckoned with in the daily activities of management, and no competent manager would try to abolish it. Rather, the astute manager should analyze it and consciously try to influence it.[16]

ORGANIZATIONAL ELECTRONIC COMMUNICATION

In recent years, the nature of organizational communication has changed dramatically, mainly because of breakthroughs in electronic communication technology, and the future promises even more changes. Decades ago, electric typewriters and photocopying machines were considered cutting-edge technology. The photocopier, for example, made it possible for a police manager to have a typed report distributed to large numbers of personnel in an extremely short period of time. Personal computers accelerated the process. E-mail networks, the Internet, and corporate intranets have carried communication technology even further and it is imperative that police managers continue to avail themselves of the latest communications technology as it develops.

Tips for Successful E-Mail Use

The following suggested tips if followed would do much to eliminate the unfortunate consequences that too often results from violations of commonsense etiquette in the communication process when this technology is being used in correspondence.

- Maintain professionalism in e-mail correspondence. People who do not know you will form an impression based on what they read. As in any other business correspondence, business etiquette does not change when a message is digitized.

- Avoid flowery prose, which lengthens the message without adding value. Write in a sparse, tight manner. Limit the e-mail to a single topic and group the content in short paragraphs that are sequenced logically.

- Don't slow the system down with very large attachments, and avoid using the blind copy (BC) line; it suggests that there is something to hide.

- Respond to e-mail promptly, even if only to acknowledge initial receipt and that a more detailed response will follow.

- Check e-mail frequently but do not allow it to interrupt other scheduled tasks.

- Read and reread your e-mails for quality, tone, grammar, spelling, and punctuation before sending them. Do not rely solely on grammar or spell check to catch errors. Moreover, spell check may change the spelling of words, giving the message a different or no meaning.

- Remember that e-mail is not private correspondence and can easily become public without intent or consent. It is a permanent record of written communication.

- Do not use business e-mail for jokes or frivolous and offensive messages.

- If you write an e-mail while angry, even if provoked, don't send it until you can reread it in a calmer moment and are able to be more dispassionate. Venting in an e-mail reflects poorly on the sender.

- Deal with personal or sensitive issues in person, not through an impersonal electronic medium.

- Treat an e-mail inbox similar to a paper one: Review the document, act on it, and move on.

- The agency's e-mail is very effective in getting information to a number of people in an expeditious fashion and to quickly, involve others, but do not send copies to persons who do not need to receive it.

- Use caution when responding to e-mails. How something is said in an e-mail language is just as important as what is said, no matter how emotional the issue or the contents of the e-mail received.[17]

The Use of Technology in Police Administration

A television ad proclaims "This is not your father's Buick," implying that today's version is substantially improved. Likewise, the current generation of technology tools available to law enforcement leaders is also more advanced. Chiefs and the command staff can use teleconferencing to hold meetings with law enforcement executives in several states and to discuss matters with their own far-flung precinct commanders. They can also Skype on an individual basis with anyone who has that capability on their smart phone or personal computer. A wide range of databases can be tapped into to obtain a variety of administrative information, such as (1) model law enforcement policies on the use of force, high-speed pursuits, and domestic violence by police officers from the International Association of Chiefs of Police (IACP); (2) the details of the jail certification program operated by the National Sheriffs' Association; (3) a publication on how to measure performance in the modern police organization issued by the National Institute of Justice (NIJ), (4) police leadership challenges in a changing world, a monograph from the National Criminal Justice Reference Service (NCJRS). Both NIJ and NCJRS have substantial publication lists of interest to students, scholars, and other publications from the Combatting Terrorism Center, located at West Point (New York), the home of the U.S. Military Academy, (5) data and studies from the National Highway Traffic Safety Institute, and (6) the police-related studies at the Centers for Disease Control (CDC). In light of the public and media attention devoted to police use of deadly force, the CDC's series "National Violent Death Reporting System" is illuminating. The databases listed here is not exhaustive; instead it is offered as an example of the breadth of information available to law enforcement administrators.

The Use of Teleconferencing and Cell Phones

The ubiquitous use of cellular telephones has also made it even easier for police managers to communicate with one another and their subordinates. Capabilities such as Twitter, Facebook, YouTube, and Nixle have all revolutionized how police organizations effectively reach the public when seeking help with an investigation, warning of impending mega storms, what streets will be closed during parades, and other matters. Free Wi-Fi "hot spots" allow the public to access to the social media capabilities police use without the cost of using their cellular networks.

However, as already suggested, these rapid technological advances are not without their side effects and psychologists are beginning to associate some problems with these communication advances. Police managers may unwittingly drop out of the organizational grapevine and miss out on very important informal communication that takes place. Moreover, the use of electronic communication at the expense of face-to-face meetings and conversations makes it more difficult to build a strong culture, develop solid working relationships, and create a mutually supportive atmosphere of trust and cooperativeness.

SOCIAL MEDIA AND LAW ENFORCEMENT COMMUNICATION

American law enforcement can learn a great deal about social media from the corporate sector because businesses have already encountered some of the same challenges in this new environment and have more experience dealing with it than police departments. However, police departments are not corporations, businesses nor even run-of-the-mill government agencies; they have unique powers and responsibilities along with a unique relationship with the public. Police need their own models, their own best practices, and their own discussions and philosophies about how to incorporate social media to achieve their distinct purposes.[18]

Social Media Management

Three factors should be considered in the process of social media management, namely, (1) selecting the right personnel to run the program, (2) having a good understanding of voice and tone, and (3) the role of the public information officer with the press (previously discussed in Chapter 4, Politics and Police Administration).[19]

Selecting the Right Personnel

Finding the right personnel to manage a social media program is critical. While some agencies have chosen a centralized approach with tight controls over who within the department has access to post information from a single agency account, others have chosen a decentralized approach and have allowed the creation of multiple users, each with sub-accounts, to distribute information. Both approaches are dramatically different and have their own unique sets of benefits and risks. Regardless of which approach an agency chooses to use, though, the selection of the right personnel involved cannot be overemphasized. Social media management is really no different than many areas of police work: Having the right people in the right places can make all of the difference.

Having personnel in place who are already familiar and comfortable with the platforms will save time and training costs. A person familiar with the technology will be able to step into the technical side of the role very easily, and they will accordingly have more time available to devote to content development and other necessary tasks.

However, if it were as simple as that, agencies could simply authorize access to the social media passwords to any 21-year-old officer fresh out of the academy. Instead, a second key consideration is the selection of personnel who command a grasp of the "big picture" for the agency. It is important to find employees who have an understanding of the local politics and current events; who have an understanding of broad issues of department concern and the agency's official stance on them; and who have a level of foresight about the important issues that are likely to be forthcoming in the near future. This point cannot be overstated, as everything broadcast on social media, even down to a single 140-character tweet, amounts to a press release. And anything broadcast, if written in the wrong manner or with the wrong words, can instantly and irreparably bring negative attention to the agency.[20]

The Importance of Voice and Tone

Once the right people are in place, special consideration should be given to the agency's social media voice and tone. As any public information officer will attest, the way in which a message is delivered often has more impact on the audience than the actual words used. This is also true in the messages sent via social media. Consistency in voice is key; each agency, particularly those using multiple posters, should strive for uniformity with how messages are conveyed. This can give the department an online identity that the public comes to recognize, appreciate, and depend upon. By way of example, consider an agency that has two employees who share posting duties on the official department Twitter account. One employee may choose to tweet, "If you drink and drive tonight, we will arrest you, tow your car, and throw you in jail. Don't drink and drive." The other employee may take a softer approach, and choose to tweet, "If you are going out tonight, have fun, but please be safe and designate a non-drinking driver!" While there's nothing inherently wrong with either tweet, having both messages come from the same agency account on consecutive weekend nights will confuse followers and can even be off-putting. Having a consistent message, delivered in a reliable voice that remains the same day-in and day-out, regardless of who actually authors it, makes the agency seem more professional and dependable.

Many agencies choose to use a stoic and unemotional tone in their social medial platforms, a sort of 21st-century "just the facts, ma'am" approach. Consider, though, that several departments have had great social media success by relaxing the tone slightly when appropriate and by choosing to show some personality and even humor at times. Just like in-person interactions at a block party or at a local park, online social interactions give departments the chance to show the human side of their personnel. Agencies have long recognized that communities who get to know their officers usually like them, as well. With the current commonality of online "friendships' and other interactions, getting to know a department virtually can have the same effect.

A tone that always projects professionalism, competence, and confidence is fundamental. However, an agency really can go the extra mile and win over the public by remaining approachable and human on their social media channels. Messages that show compassion, empathy, and humor are more often shared or retweeted, leading to a broader audience and more exposure to the agency's humanity. This, in turn, often leads to an increased follower base.[21]

THE USE OF SOCIAL MEDIA WITH THE PUBLIC

The Police Executive Research Forum (PERF) conducted a national survey to determine the extent to which police departments are sharing information and developing relationships with their communities using social media.[22] What they discovered was that 80 percent of those agencies responding said that they use social media to share information with the public. As a matter of fact, more than 2,800[23] law enforcement agencies in the United States have social media accounts and that number is growing every day.[24]

Following is specific information provided by several law enforcement officials regarding their agency's use of social media.

Sacramento, California Police Department (SPD)

The SPD is active on Facebook and Twitter and also have used YouTube. The SPD uses the Internet to interact with the public. They post "dumb crook" stories, which are very popular. Once members of the public visit the site, many of them look at other information. They also post all their press releases, including commendations to their employees as well as posting anniversaries of officers' deaths, which gets a considerable amount of attention as well (see Figure 10.5).

They also put video clips on their Facebook page, for example, crime prevention videos. In the last couple of years, there has been a significant increase in the amount of rapes committed (see Figure 10.6). The SPD analyzed the reports and found that at least 90 percent of the suspects and victims knew each other and as a result decided to find a way to educate the public about date rape and other types of rape in which the perpetrator is not a stranger. They have partnered with Women Escaping a Violent Environment (WEAVE) and started a campaign to post educational messages about the consequences of committing any kind of rape. The messages were designed for different groups of people. One targeted 16- to 25-year-olds, while another targeted those who were 25 years and older.

Los Angeles County, California Sheriff's Department (LASD)

The LASD reports that as technology changes, the public *expects* them to communicate in new ways. They now have the ability to instantly send out notifications when emergencies or other situations arise that the public should be aware of and to do so using the most effective technology available. The agency has also made major upgrades in their website and frequently sends

FIGURE 10.5 ▶ The home page of the Sacramento, California Police Department's website, available at: http://portal.cityofsacramento.org/Police.

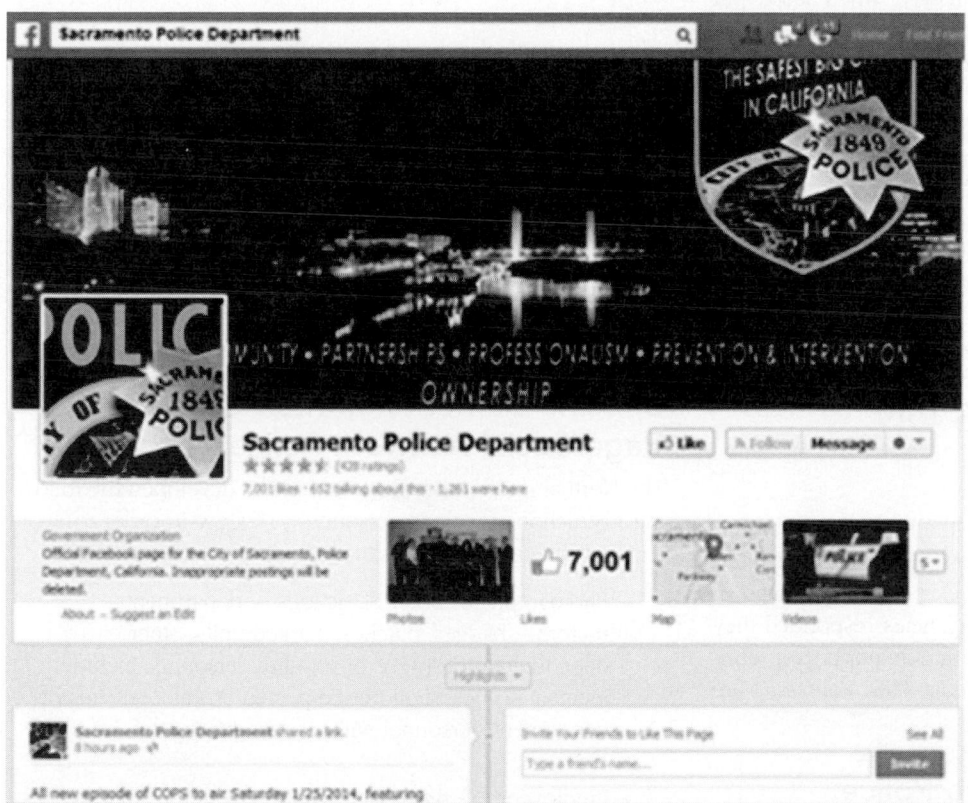

FIGURE 10.6 ▶ The Facebook page for the Sacramento, California Police Department, available at: https://www.facebook.com/pages/Sacramento-Police-Department/137481202396.

department messages using systems popular with the public including Nixle, as well as Twitter, Facebook, and YouTube.

They realized that the general public usually does not have much of an opportunity to interact with the police unless they see them while on patrol or they do something wrong. But by using technology such as Nixle, Facebook, and Twitter messages, they are able to engage citizens who would like to have more interaction with the department.

These new forms of communication allow them to release news stories themselves instead of relying solely on traditional media outlets. One might expect this to lead to an antagonistic relationship with the local news media because they are no longer dependent on them anymore for communications. But in reality, they found it actually resulted in a closer relationship with the media. The media still likes to be the first ones to report police-related stories, so they are often given the story first. In addition, the agency still works closely with the media to provide accurate information. The overall effect is that most of the local media are reporting law enforcement stories in a more balanced and factual way.

Boston, Massachusetts Police Department (BPD)

Recently, the Police Commissioner noticed teens standing around the yellow tape at crime scenes and sending text messages. The commissioner thought that there might be a way for the agency to harness the information these individuals were gathering at the crime scene. The agency created an advertising campaign in which it set up the software that would be needed to develop a "text-to-tip" line. The program was so well received that people were texting in tips from across the country not just from Boston and they also saw a dramatic increase in the volume of calls to their 1-800 tip line.

Today, the BPD has developed a blog to help them communicate with the public and they have seen an incredible response to that. Their blog, bdnews.com, gets about 70,000 visitors a month. They have reached that number through the application of a variety of publicity techniques, including printing the websites on the side of all police vehicles. Having a very visible website has helped the agency avoid any of the confusion that can occur when people put up fake websites, in an effort to make it appear that they are the actual BPD website. The BPD has benefitted from having the blog as a forum to put out news about the department before the local papers. When people are getting their police news—both good and bad—straight from the law enforcement agency, it provides a higher level of assurance that the public is receiving accurate information and avoiding some of the sensationalizing that sometimes occurs when news agencies are racing to "break" the story.

ISSUES REGARDING OFFICERS' PERSONAL POSTINGS ON SOCIAL MEDIA SITES

Of those police agencies responding to the PERF survey on this topic, 57 percent reported that they have had issues, disputes, or controversies resulting from employees' personal postings on social media sites, and 58 percent of agencies responded they now have policies regarding what may or may not be appropriate for employees to post on social media sites. Following are some examples:

Albuquerque, New Mexico Police Department (APD)

The APD now has an officer specifically assigned as part of his/her job description to monitor all of the agency's officers who have Facebook accounts. The agency recently drafted a four-page social media policy for its officers as a result of one of its gang unit officers caught describing his job on Facebook as "human waste disposal." Officials found the post after the officer shot and killed a suspect in an incident that got a lot of media attention.

The new policy allows officers to identify themselves as Albuquerque officers, on the Internet but what they write is under close watch.

Under the provisions of the department's new policy, the chief must approve all photos depicting the department before they are posted. Anything from vulgar posts to divulging information about investigations can result in a verbal reprimand or even termination.[25]

Arlington, Texas Police Department (APD)

The APD reported that an officer who was at the scene at a critical incident took photographs with his personal camera. Later this officer posted these pictures and messages to his social media page. To deal with the situation, the Austin Police Department cited a policy of unbecoming conduct which prevents officers from bringing the city into disrepute. He was ultimately suspended for his actions. Since then, they have developed a social media policy.

Social media issues also are involved in recruiting and hiring personnel. The APD evaluates numerous people during the hiring process and inevitably some of them will present themselves poorly through media outlets. Their postings reflect on their character and provide the agency with a much better idea about whether a particular candidate has the qualities they are looking for in an officer. The APD also reports learning quite a bit about applicants based on the friends they have when they post and what they are doing online. When the agency does this, they consider the totality of the circumstances such as the age of the applicant when the posting was made. A single posting on Facebook in poor taste will not automatically eliminate someone from their hiring process but if there is a consistent pattern of behavior or something that raises a red flag, it lets the agency know that they need to dig a little deeper during the background investigation.

Specific Elements of Internet Sites/Web Page/Social Network Police Policy

The Northampton Police Department has developed the following instructions for their personnel to follow in order to avoid some of the embarrassing situations discussed thus far.

- Photographs or other depictions of departmental uniforms, badges, patches, marked units, other departmental property, or on-duty personnel, including incident scenes, shall not be posted on Internet sites by department personnel without the approval of the Chief of Police.

- Employees are prohibited from posting, transmitting, and/or disseminating any pictures or videos of official departmental training, activities, or work-related assignments, without the expressed, written permissions of the Chief of Police.

- Employees shall treat as confidential, all the official business of the department.

- No employee shall release, either directly or indirectly, information concerning crimes, accidents, or violations of ordinances and/or statutes to persons outside the department, except as authorized by departmental policy under Public Information Function.

- No employee should gossip about the affairs of the department with persons outside the department.

- No sexual, violent, racial, ethically derogatory material, comments, pictures, artwork, video, or other references may be posted along with any department-approved reference.

- Employees shall not post any material on the Internet that brings discredit to or may adversely affect the efficiency or integrity of the Northampton Police Department. In disparage or harass, another department or city employee, as well as any other citizen.

- Employees should consider the possible adverse consequences of Internet postings, such as future employment, cross-examination in criminal cases, and public, as well as private, embarrassment.

- Employees are reminded to exercise good judgment and demonstrate personal accountability when choosing to participate on social networking sites such as Facebook, MySpace, and Twitter. Use of these types of sites while on duty shall be restricted to official departmental business only.

- Employees becoming aware of or having knowledge of a posting or of any website or web page in violation of the provision of this policy are strongly encouraged to notify his/her supervisor immediately for follow-up action.

THE EVOLUTION OF POLICE–MEDIA COMMUNICATION IN THE DIGITAL AGE

There is little dispute that both law enforcement and the news media play essential roles in a democratic society and are, to a great extent, mutually dependent. The media provides the police with broad access to the public, and the media relies on the police for a steady stream of stories to fill the endless space and time requirements of their respective mediums. Although much of the coverage is focused on the crime du jour, investigative reporters may delve into issues about budgets, resource allocations, policies, procedures, allegations of police misconduct, political infighting, or other controversies.[26]

The quality of police–media communication varies from department to department, and even from day to day within a department. For many, police–media communications are often characterized as tense and adversarial. Even agencies that enjoy generally positive relationships with the media in their markets find themselves at odds from time to time. From the law enforcement perspective, some argue that the media's "watchdog" role conveys inherent distrust, which sets up a defensive posture from the start. Others maintain that in pursuit of the "scoop," oriented reporters care little about issues of privacy or accuracy and even less whether disclosing certain information may impede an investigation.

From the journalists' point of view, the police are among the organizations that especially bear watching, since they have enormous power and history is replete with examples of police corruption. Also, members of the media believe the police withhold far more information than they need to—or should—and but for the watchful eye of the media, would likely keep the public in the dark about everything from crime and police misconduct to how taxpayer money is spent and what procedures are used to do the job of law enforcement.[27]

Despite advances that enable police to communicate directly with large segments of the public, much—if not most—of their time and resources are still devoted to traditional media relations activities. And until recently, this made sense. Not long ago, when a police agency wanted to communicate with a large number of citizens, the traditional mass media was pretty much the only game in town. Departments had little if any funding for public information campaigns and rarely attracted enough people to a community meeting to considerate critical mass. The news media not only controlled the mass distribution channels but also influenced how public viewed the police.[28] The books and articles that address police public information programs have invariably focused almost exclusively on ways the police could improve media relations.[29] Most highlight the media's dissemination and perception-shaping roles, and therefore, stress the importance of courting the local media for coverage. While good media relations still make good sense, it has taken on new qualities, new players, and the necessity to fully understand today's media technology.

Today's Media Technology and the Public Information Officer

Nearly every news organization has a 24-hour assignment editor or news director watching wires and rival television newscasts and reading Web logs and feeds. Even non-24/7 outlets, such as alternative papers and weekly editions, still demand access to information about incidents that occur outside normal business hours. Public Information Officers (PIOs) can exploit this by developing their own news-producing feeds online that can become the official message of an agency during routine days, as well as crises[30] (see Figure 10.7).

Real Simple Syndication Feeds—Subscribers to Real Simple Syndication (RSS) feeds automatically receive notification when a web site they follow is updated; they also choose the type of content to which they want to be alerted.[31] For example, RSS users who subscribe to CNN's site can elect to receive notification only when a new story post that contains the word *police* or their town name. They do not have to manually check each site of interest or stay logged on and click "refresh" every few seconds. RSS feeds take away all of this work. Similarly, journalists can avoid being inundated with news releases and story ideas by controlling and monitoring the feeds. This proves especially helpful in large markets where reporter with different assignments can subscribe to separate feeds from the same web site; a crime reporter can opt to learn about arrests

FIGURE 10.7 ▶ A Public Information Officer is on call 24 hours a day, 7 days a week in order to handle media requests for police-related information. (Courtesy of Colorado State Patrol)

and investigations, while a school reporter may select only juvenile intervention programs.

Twitter—Twitter claims that it has 175 million accounts and 600 million people who visit or "follow" one or more of those accounts from daily to monthly. For the most part, Twitter postings are about someone's daily activities and personal news, with details that sometimes are mundane. Followers can view a user's postings, also known as "tweets." In contrast, when a PIO is posting updates, readers can see organizational events in real time.

Among social networking sites, Twitter is unique in that it limits postings to 140 characters; forcing postings to be short and to the point. During times of crisis communication, PIOs can take advantage of this; instead of preparing, editing, and distributing a full news release, they simply can use Twitter to put the basic facts into a single, short message. Further, PIOs can continue to provide information in a timely manner through regular updates and, if necessary, schedule a full news conference and prepare a news release, all from a command post or office.[32]

Nixle—Nixle is the first social networking company to include government agencies as part of their target audience. Daily, Nixle processes messages from 8,000 public safety and government agencies. Examples of law enforcement agencies using Nixle are the Spring Hill (Tennessee) Police Department, the Pocatello (Idaho) Police Department, the Indiana State Police, the Lyon County (Minnesota) Sheriff's Office, and the West Milford (New Jersey) Police Department.

Nixle's inclusion of government agencies has earned it some unique partners. In 2008, Nixle became the first public networking site to partner with the National Law Enforcement Telecommunications System (NLETS). Because of this relationship, Nixle can house its servers in NLETS'

secure facilities, resulting in an enhanced level of security and reliability for municipal agencies.[33]

Similar to Twitter, Nixle requires users to confine their messages to a 140-character message. Anyone can set up a network and send messages about their activities, breaking news, or other details. However, Nixle offers users the opportunity to have their own network that allows them to send secure instant emergency messages to all users in a designated geographic area.[34] This works well in communicating directly to those who need the information quickly. Users simply log in, enter their message, and then select the area on a map affected by the incident. The message goes only to users who choose to accept alerts in those areas. This ability to limit information distribution to those who need it offers a substantial advantage for other networking sites. Reducing the number of messages ensures that readers pay attention relevant to them.

Nixle has demonstrated its usefulness to law enforcement: For example, an elderly resident in a California community failed to return home after she went out for a brief walk. Local police quickly sent out a description to all subscribers within one-half mile of her home and a short time later expanded the message to include more information and more subscribers within a larger search area. The woman was found safe and returned to her family.[35]

YouTube—YouTube has one billion active users each month.[36] Many departments use it to publish recruiting videos and news conferences. The primary attraction to YouTube is that agencies can have a department profile and create and post videos for free. This allows large agencies to focus media dollars on "slick" productions and smaller ones to establish a Web presence. In addition, PIOs can use YouTube to promote new initiatives that are sometimes difficult to have covered in the traditional media.[37]

Facebook —Facebook reports that it has 1.44 billion monthly active users,[38] more than half logging on once a day looking for some type of information. As in the case with other sites, the potency of Facebook is harnessed by understanding how it works. Law enforcement agencies provide information and videos about news, arrests, and promotions, and academy class graduation, as well as other content. Visitors to the site choose to follow an agency by becoming a "friend." Especially important in organizations, friends can opt to receive instant notification when the agency posts new information and content, and they can respond with their own comments.

To illustrate, a law enforcement agency can post a Friday afternoon status update reminding friends of checkpoints targeting drunk driving. Every friend will get this information as they make plans for Friday night activities and, thus, hopefully will remember to use a designated driver. Similarly, a single posting can spread AMBER Alerts and other breaking news around the world, both to citizens and to the media. PIOs no longer need to e-mail, fax, and call numerous outlets to promote a story and then wait hours or days for them to air or publish it.[39]

INTERPERSONAL COMMUNICATION

The information available about how to communicate persuasively and effectively is extensive.[40] In this section, we focus primarily on creating the high-impact communication that contributes to effective leadership. Both formal and informal leaders must be persuasive and dynamic communicators. Effective **interpersonal communication** skills often help informal leaders be selected for formal leadership positions.

Suggestions for becoming effective communicators can be divided into the following two categories: (1) speaking and writing and (2) nonverbal communication. We will also discuss certain basic principles of persuasion.

Speaking and Writing

Many people are already familiar with the basics of effective spoken and written communication, yet the basics, such as writing and speaking clearly, maintaining eye contact, and not mumbling, are only starting points. Most effective leaders have extra energy in their communication style. The same excitement is reflected in both their speaking and their writing styles. Kouzes and Posner underscore the importance of colorful language in communicating a vision (one of the leader's most important functions) in these words:

Language is among the most powerful methods for expressing a vision. Successful leaders use metaphors and figures of speech; they give examples, tell stories, and relate anecdotes; they draw word pictures; and they offer quotations and recite slogans.[41]

Group members and other constituents generally have more exposure to the spoken words of leaders, yet clearly the increased use of e-mail, printed memos, and the written word exerts considerable influence. The following are some suggestions for dynamic and persuasive oral and written communication.

Be Credible

Attempts at persuasion, including inspirational speaking and writing, begin with the credibility of the message sender. It has long been recognized that credibility is a powerful element in the persuasive process. If the speaker is perceived as highly credible, the attempt at persuasive communication is more likely to be successful.[42] The perception of credibility is influenced by many factors. Being trustworthy heavily influences being perceived as credible. A leader with a reputation for lying will have a difficult time convincing people of the merits of a new initiative. Being perceived as intelligent and knowledgeable is another major factor contributing to credibility.

Gear the Message to the Listener

An axiom of persuasive communication is that a speaker must adapt the message to the listener's interests and motivation. A review of the evidence concludes that the average intelligence and experience level of the group is a key contingency factor in designing a persuasive message. People with high intelligence tend to be more influenced by messages based on strong, logical arguments. Also, bright people are more likely to reject messages based on flawed logic.[43]

Persuade Group Members on the Benefits of Change

Sometimes, a leader is constrained by the unwillingness of agency members to accept the leader's initiatives for change. To counter this "slowness of spirit," the leader must explain to agency members how they will benefit from what is being proposed.

For example, let us assume that the head of a law enforcement agency has decided to radically modify the agency's policy on high-speed pursuits (a topic discussed in much greater detail in Chapter 14, Legal Aspects of Police Administration). In the past, the agency has had a very liberal policy that allowed officers considerable latitude to pursue fleeing motorists irrespective of the violation, but the agency head is now seriously considering restricting the policy, so that officers will only be permitted to pursue known dangerous felons.

Selling agency members is quite often done more effectively when the persuader takes the time to build consensus rather than to change the policy through administrative fiat. Instead of trying simply to order a change without any discussion, it might be more effective to win over key personnel within a reasonable time frame. Persuasion guru Jay Conger notes that successful persuasion often requires ongoing effort and suggests that the following sequence be followed:

- At the first meeting, appeal to them to consider the initiative carefully.
- At the second meeting, after they have had the opportunity to think about the modification, see if the key members have concluded that it is necessary to make adjustments in the policy.
- At the final meeting, it is imperative to have all the key members to reach a consensus. If a consensus cannot be obtained and the final decision has been made to modify the policy, it is important that key personnel understand the importance of not undermining the policy with their constituents.[44]

Use Heavy-Impact and Emotion-Provoking Words

Certain words used in the proper context give power and force to a presentation. Used comfortably, naturally, and sincerely, these words project the image of a self-confident person with leadership ability or potential.

Closely related to heavy-impact language are emotion-provoking words. An expert persuasive tactic is to sprinkle one's speech with emotion-provoking—and therefore inspiring—words. Emotion-provoking words bring forth powerful images. For example, the chief executive must convince agency personnel that the existing policy on high-speed pursuits increases the likelihood of "death" and/or "injury" to them, as well as to "innocent" third parties, the fleeing motorist and, in some cases, "innocent" passengers in the fleeing vehicles. It will also result in "lawsuits" against the officer and the agency and, in some rare cases, when a death has occurred, officers have been criminally charged, convicted, and sent to prison.

Back Up Conclusions with Data

A message either spoken or written will be more persuasive if it is supported with solid data. Published sources provide convincing data for arguments. Supporting data for many arguments can be found in incidents from the agency's history, professional journals, in government studies, in scholarly research, in books, on the Internet, on TV, and in newspapers. Specific examples and statistics can be extracted from those various documents to support the previously discussed significant changes in the agency's high-speed pursuit policy. For example, the National Law Enforcement Officers Memorial Fund has reported that the second-leading cause of deaths of law enforcement officers were auto accidents (the leading cause was officers being shot in the line of duty).[45] These figures do not include the many thousands of police officers who have been seriously injured and disabled as a result of

automobile accidents, many of which occurred during high-speed pursuits for what turned out to be, in many cases, minor traffic violations or misdemeanors.

Minimize Vocalized Pauses and Parasitic Words/Junk Words

The use of words and phrases that dilute the impact of a speech, such as "you know," "you know what I mean," as well as the distracting unintentional utterances such as "umm" and "uhhhh-hhh," should be minimized. The use of parasitic words (also known as "junk words") conveys the impression of low self-confidence—especially in a professional setting—and detract from a sharp communication image. The word "like" has emerged as one of the words used most frequently, especially by young people. For example, "the test was like so hard"; "the weather was like so bad"; and "I am like so tired." All of these vocalized pauses and parasitic or junk words make the job of listening a challenge and diminish the credibility of the speaker.

An effective way to decrease the use of these distracting vocalized pauses and extraneous words is to tape record or video record one's own side of a conversation and then play it back. Many people are not aware that they possess these shortcomings as a part of their speech.

It is always important to speak with precision and convey the impression of being articulate, well informed and confident.

Write Crisp, Clear Memos and Reports, Including a Front-Loaded Message

According to Mercer, high achievers write more effective reports than do their less-highly achieving counterparts. Mercer examined the writing (memos, letters, and reports) of both high achievers and low achievers. He observed that the high achievers' writing was distinctive in that it had more active verbs than passive verbs, more subheadings and subtitles, and shorter paragraphs.[46]

Writing, in addition to speaking, is more persuasive when key ideas are placed at the beginning of a conversation, an e-mail message, a paragraph, or a sentence. Front-loaded messages are particularly important for leaders because people expect leaders to be effective communicators.

Use a Power-Oriented Linguistic Style

A major part of being persuasive involves choosing the right linguistic style, which is a person's characteristic speaking pattern. According to communications specialist Deborah Tannen, linguistic style involves such aspects as amount of directness, pacing and pausing, word choice, and the use of such communication devices as jokes, figures of speech, anecdotes, questions, and apologies.[47] Linguistic style is complex because it includes the culturally learned signals by which people communicate what they mean, along with how they interpret what others say and how they evaluate others. The complexity of linguistic style makes it difficult to offer specific prescriptions for using one that is power-oriented. However, there are several components of a linguistic style that will, in many situations, give power and authority to the message sender. Some of these, as observed by Tannen and other language specialists, are the following:

- Downplay uncertainty. If you are not confident of your opinion or prediction, make a positive statement anyway, such as saying, "I know this new restrictive high-speed pursuit policy will reduce deaths, injuries, and litigation."
- Keep an open mind and accept verbal opposition to ideas, especially at staff meetings, rather than becoming upset and defensive.
- Emphasize direct rather than indirect talk, such as by saying "I need your report by noon tomorrow" rather than "I'm wondering if your report will be available by noon tomorrow."
- Speak without expressing uncertainty, for example, "I will have my portion of the strategic plan completed by no later than the Wednesday before Thanksgiving." This will give the staff time to sift through the information.
- Know exactly what is needed. The chances of selling an idea increase to the extent that it is clarified in the mind of the presenter. The clearer and more committed the person is at the outset of the session, the stronger he or she will be as a persuader and the more powerful the language becomes.
- Strive to be confident when making statements, but be sensitive to the possibility of unintentional criticism being directed toward those who preceded you and who may still have powerful friends and supporters within the agency. For example, if an agency head says that "I believe that our new high-speed pursuit policy will significantly reduce injuries and deaths to our officers and citizens, as well as result in a reduction in liability to our agency," then it is an idea that is being attacked and not one's predecessor who may have been reluctant to implement a more conservative high-speed pursuit policy.[48]

Despite these suggestions for having a power-oriented linguistic style, Tannen cautions that there is no one best way to communicate. How one projects power and authority is often dependent on the people involved, the organizational culture, the relative rank of the speakers, and the other situational factors. The power-oriented linguistic style should be interpreted as a general guideline.

Nonverbal Communication

Effective leaders are masterful nonverbal as well as verbal communicators. Nonverbal communication is important because leadership involves emotion, which words alone cannot communicate convincingly.

One research study concluded that when communicating about *feelings* 55 percent of the message is non verbal, 38 percent is tone of voice, and 7 percent is the actual words spoken.[49] If true, you miss 97 percent of a message about feelings by just focusing on the words spoken. Leaving aside whether the percentages are about right and they are applicable to presentations not about feelings, it remains true that effective leaders are masterful nonverbal as well as verbal communicators. Nonverbal communication is important because leadership involves emotion, which words alone cannot communicate convincingly.[50]

A self-confident leader not only speaks and writes with assurance but also projects confidence through body position, gestures, and manner of speech. Not everybody interprets the same body language and other nonverbal signals in the same way, but some aspects of nonverbal behavior project a self-confident, leadership image in many situations. For example:

- Using an erect posture when walking, standing, or sitting. Slouching and slumping are almost universally interpreted as an indicator of low self-confidence.
- Standing up straight during a confrontation. Poor posture may be a sign of low self-confidence and poor leadership qualities.
- Speaking at a moderate pace, with a loud, confident tone. People lacking in self-confidence tend to speak too rapidly or very slowly.
- Smiling frequently in a relaxed, natural-appearing manner
- Maintaining eye contact with those around you
- Gesturing in a relaxed, nonmechanical way, including pointing toward others in a way that welcomes rather than accuses, such as using a gesture to indicate "You're right" or "It's your turn to comment."[51]

A general approach to using nonverbal behavior that projects confidence is to have a goal of appearing self-confident and powerful. This type of autosuggestion makes many of the behaviors seem automatic. For example, if you say to yourself, "I am going to display leadership qualities in this meeting," you will have taken an important step toward appearing confident.

External image also plays an important role in communicating messages to others. People have more respect and grant more privileges to those they perceive as being well dressed and neatly groomed. An old adage is "you don't get second chance to make a first impression." Self-confidence is projected by such items as the following:

- Neat uniform or suit with appropriate accessories and polished shoes
- Clean fingernails
- Well-maintained hair
- Good oral hygiene

A subtle mode of nonverbal communication is the use of time. Guarding time as a precious resource will help project an image of self-confidence and leadership. A statement such as "I have 15 min to go over this with you on Thursday at 4 P.M." connotes confidence and control. Other ways of projecting power through the use of time include such behaviors as being prompt for meetings and starting and stopping meetings on time.

GROUP VS. INTERPERSONAL COMMUNICATION

For our purposes, interpersonal communication is defined as the sharing of information between two persons. **Group communication** involves interaction among three or more individuals in a face-to-face situation. The three people have a common need that is satisfied by the exchange of information.[52] However, there are important variables that can affect the group communication process. These include the following:

Size of the Group

The definition of group communication does not set limits on the ultimate size of the group. However, practical considerations inherent in the definition do define a maximum number of people who would be able to interact effectively. Individuals attending a professional sporting event may have a commonality of interest, but their opportunities for face-to-face interaction is likely limited to those seated in their immediate area and while standing in line at the refreshment stand. If we compare the Super Bowl, with an attendance of 100,000 people, to a group of five fans planning a tailgate party before the game, it is easy to see that the size of the group is a factor in determining the ability of individuals to communicate with each other.

Numerous scholars have examined the dynamics of group communications.[53] Various research has determined that the range between 3 and 20 is a natural size for purposes of defining group interactions.[54] Once the size of the group exceeds 20 people, the ability of individual members to influence each other diminishes. The nature of the gathering takes on more of the characteristics of a mass meeting or conference, in which one person may influence the group but the ability of individual members within the group to influence each other is limited. The size of the group has a direct bearing on the type of communication involved. Therefore, we will limit our discussion of communication to groups that do not exceed 20 individuals. Once the size of the group involved in the communication process has been determined, group interaction must be addressed.

Group Interaction

It is generally accepted by leading scholars that there are four phases in **group interaction**: (1) orientation, (2) conflict, (3) emergence, and (4) reinforcement.[55]

In the *orientation* phase, group members attempt to get to know each other and discover the problems that face the group. This may occur as strangers meet in a group for the first time, or it may happen with people who know each other and attend periodic meetings, such as roll call before the beginning of patrol shifts. In the latter situation, group members already know each other, and the orientation is aimed at common problems facing the group. These problems could range from new shift hours to planning a social gathering after the shift.

The second phase, *conflict,* involves disagreement among the members of the group. This phase is characterized by an atmosphere of polarization and controversy. Using the previous two examples, patrol officers may be sharply divided concerning the benefits of the new shift hours or have strong feelings regarding the location of the social gathering.

During the *emergence* phase of group interaction, there is more emphasis on positive statements. This phase allows dissenting members to save face by moving toward the majority's position. Officers who oppose the new shift hours may begin to find other benefits not previously discussed. Similarly, the location for the social gathering may be a third alternative that is acceptable to all members.

The final phase is *reinforcement*. In this phase, group members comment on the positive aspects of the group and its problem-solving ability.

The preceding discussion focused on the dynamics that normally occur in a problem-solving group; however, this interaction is usually present in most groups.[56] A police officer may determine what phase a group is in by listening to the types of comments being made by members of the group, and then use that information to express personal views in the most effective manner. Group interaction is an important aspect of any organization. Law enforcement officers need to understand these group dynamics in order to carry out their duties effectively. Once a group has been established, certain communication networks begin to emerge.

CROSS-GENDER COMMUNICATION

Generally, an examination of the differences in the ways men and women communicate would be confined to scholarly books in the area of linguistics or perhaps to books in the popular market that examine male/female relationships. However, it is essential that police supervisors who must evaluate the actions of their subordinates understand that men and women in our society often communicate quite differently and may solve problems in dramatically different ways. A failure to understand these differences can result in erroneous evaluations of police officers' actions and even result in unfair criticism by fellow officers and superiors.

The following scenario was witnessed by one of the authors.

A young woman pulled up to the gas station to fill up her car. While at the pump, her boyfriend pulled up behind her in his vehicle. They had had a dispute the evening before and she walked out on him. He had been driving around looking for her when he observed her pulling into the filling station. Initially, she did not see him pull up. He exited his car, walked up to her from behind, forcefully turned her around and slapped her across the face. An off-duty police officer in plainclothes and in his personal car was filling up his car at an adjoining pump and witnessed the assault. He immediately identified himself as a police officer and advised the man he was under arrest. The officer requested that the filling station attendant call for a patrol unit. Prior to the arrival of the patrol unit, the assailant was placed in the front seat of the off-duty police officer's car unhandcuffed. Two uniformed officers arrived in separate police cars. One was a male, and the other was a female. The off-duty officer explained to the uniformed officers what he had witnessed and requested their assistance in filling out the necessary paperwork and transporting the assailant to the county jail. However, as the officers were conversing, the assailant, who was still agitated, was loudly expressing his anger at his female companion, who had apparently been out with another man the evening before. The female officer walked over to the assailant and in a very conciliatory way attempted to calm him down, which did not work. After a couple of minutes, the male officer became agitated with the prisoner still "running his mouth." He walked over to the assailant and, in very close physical proximity, said very angrily, "If you don't shut your damn mouth, your ass is really going to be in trouble." At that point, the man became quiet.

Now let us assume that this scenario was being witnessed by a traditionally trained male supervisor. He might believe that the female officer should have been less conciliatory and more assertive and that her failure to be more assertive could have been interpreted as a sign of weakness by the arrested man, thereby encouraging him to become more belligerent. The supervisor might have assessed the male officer's approach as being more effective because he did, in fact, get the individual to quiet down and there were no further difficulties. However, let us assume, on the other hand, as sometimes happens, that the individual being arrested was sufficiently agitated that, when the agitated male officer spoke to him, he in turn responded angrily and decided he would rather fight than go peaceably to jail. If this had occurred, the outcome could have been quite different, and someone could have been injured or perhaps even killed.

The fact of the matter is that the female officer was behaving in a way that women in our society learn to behave when attempting to resolve a conflict—namely, in a nonconfrontational, conciliatory, and nonphysical manner. In fact, this technique is recommended and employed in conflict resolution in many facets of police work. There is some merit to the old proverb that "a soft word turneth away wrath."

Insights into the differences between the ways males and females communicate are important for police supervisors. Supervisors lacking such insight might unfairly judge the actions of the female officer. Worse yet, if a female officer is criticized, she may believe that, in order to be accepted by her peers and her supervisor, she has to be overly aggressive, more confrontational, and more physical. This is not to suggest that assertiveness is not a positive quality for police officers to possess. However, like anything else, too much can lead to unfortunate consequences.

COMMUNICATION WITH OTHER CULTURES

The United States has been considered a melting pot (or, as some have characterized it, a salad), for many races and cultures throughout its history. With the increase of Southeast Asian refugees and especially the rapidly increasing Hispanic population, the problem of communicating with persons who do not speak English as a primary language is critical within the law enforcement community.[57]

Development of a cross-cultural training course titled "Survival Spanish for Police Officers" began in mid-1986 at Sam Houston State University in Texas in a cooperative effort between the police academy and a faculty member of the university's Spanish department. The course grew from a minor part of the language component when it became apparent that cultural barriers were just as important as the language barrier and had to be addressed in more detail.

Even with the awareness that minority populations continue to expand in the United States, the ability to communicate with them will continue to be a problem for many law enforcement agencies unless a concerted effort is made to address the problem such as being done by the New York City Police Department.

For many New York officers, their second language is simply part of their culture. Officer Michael Belogorodsky, a native of Ukraine, helped investigate a suspected con artist who had targeted non-English speakers by posing as a travel agent. After speaking in Russian with several alleged suspects, police arrested a 40-year-old man and charged him with stealing more than $26,000 from a dozen people (see Figure 10.8).

In Chicago, the nation's second-largest police force with roughly 13,000 officers, some 3,835 speak additional languages, most commonly Spanish, Polish, and German. The department is also in its first year of requiring officers to take a 24-hour Spanish course during their academy training.

Quick Facts: Hispanics as the Fastest Growing Minority

The Hispanic population of the United States as of July 1, 2012, was 53 million making people of Hispanic origin the nation's largest ethnic or racial minority. Hispanics constituted 17 percent of the nation's population. The percentage of Hispanic-origin people in the United States who were of Mexican background was 65 percent. Another 9.4 percent were of Puerto Rican background, 3.8 percent Salvadoran, 3.6 percent Cuban, 3.0 percent Dominican, and 2.3 percent Guatemalan. The remainder was of some other Central American, South American, or other Hispanic/Latino origin.

The projected Hispanic population of the United States in 2060 is 128.8 million. According to this projection, the Hispanic population will constitute 31 percent of the nation's population by that date.[58]

FIGURE 10.8 ▶ The presence of a bilingual officer at the scene of an incident is often useful in assisting victims, obtaining important information, and effectively resolving conflicts. (Seth Wenig/AP Images)

The Los Angeles Police Department gives raises to as many as 3,305 officers who become fluent in another language—one-third of the department. And in Dallas, where 358 members speak Spanish and another 20 or so speak Asian languages, officers can earn an extra $150 a month after they become certified that they are fluent in another language.

In Lexington, Kentucky, officers spend a year practicing Spanish and are then sent to Mexico to improve their language skills and learn about the culture. The department's Spanish speakers have increased from two to more than 100, according to the Vera Institute.

Recent census data shows more than 20 percent of Americans speak a language other than English and 12 percent are foreign-born. Many smaller cities are also attracting increasing numbers of immigrants. Managing that change is a challenge for law enforcement.

Other Multicultural Issues

The term **culture** can be applied to various population categories. However, it is normally associated with race and ethnicity. It is this diversity that both enriches and obstructs a law enforcement officer's involvement and interaction with other persons, groups, and cultures.

Officers should remember that most minorities have developed a sharp sense for detecting condescension, manipulation, and insincerity. There is no substitute for compassion as the foundation, and sincerity as its expression, in carrying out law enforcement services equally and fairly.

The first contact minorities have with law enforcement officers will either confirm or dispel suspicion as to how they will be treated. Proper pronunciation of a person's surname is an excellent place to begin contact with him or her. Surnames have histories and meanings that allow for conversation beyond the

---

Quick Facts: Multi-Culturalism and the New York City Police Department

One-third of NYPD employees can speak a second language. Of those, 785 are certified linguists, or expert translators, in 63 languages, including Bengali, Dari, Farsi, Arabic, and Urdu. Bilingual officers do everything from intelligence gathering to undercover work to community outreach. But New York police do not rely solely on their own officers. Nearly all of the city's 76 precincts and most transit facilities are equipped with a dual-handset phone that can get a third-party translator instantly. There are software applications (Apps) that allow the officer to speak English into the phone and then the words are spoken or displayed on the phone in Spanish.[59]

introduction. In working with immigrant, refugee, or native populations, it is helpful to learn a few words of greeting from those cultures. This willingness to go beyond what is comfortable and usual conveys the officer's intent to communicate.

Listening is fundamental to human relationships. The principles and manner of listening, however, differ among cultures. Asians and Pacific Islanders, for example, deflect direct eye contact in conversation as a sign of patient listening and deference. These groups therefore consider staring to be impolite and confrontational. Many Western cultures, on the other hand, value direct eye contact as a sign of sympathy or respect. Misunderstanding in the communication process will occur if some allowance is not made for these differences. Multicultural issues must be understood by all law enforcement officers. Understanding that "different" does not mean "criminal" will assist officers attempting to communicate in an environment that continues to be increasingly diverse.

Consider the following hypothetical scenario.

A cab driver from Nigeria runs a red light. An officer pulls him over in the next block, stopping the patrol car at least three car lengths behind the cab. Before the police officer can exit the patrol car, the cabbie gets out of his vehicle and approaches the officer. Talking rapidly in a high-pitched voice and making wild gestures, the cab driver appears to be out of control, or so the officer believes.[60]

As the officer steps from his car, he yells for the cab driver to stop, but the cabbie continues to walk toward the officer. When he is about 2 feet away, the officer orders the cabbie to step back and keep his hands to his sides. But the cab driver continues to babble and advance toward the officer. He does not make eye contact and appears to be talking to the ground.

Finally, the officer commands the cab driver to place his hands on the patrol vehicle and spread his feet. What began as a routine stop for a traffic violation culminates in charges of disorderly conduct and resisting arrest.

This scenario is present in some encounters that take place daily in the United States between law enforcement personnel and people of other cultures. A simple traffic violation escalates out of control and becomes more than a matter of miscommunication and common sense. It represents—different cultures—colliding and producing unnecessary outcomes.

To understand the final outcome, we need to examine the breakdown in nonverbal communication. First, most Americans know to remain seated in their vehicles when stopped by the police. But the cab driver exited his cab because he wanted to show respect and humility by not troubling the officer to leave his patrol car. The suspect relied on his own cultural experience, which conveyed a completely different message to the officer, who viewed it as a challenge to his authority.

The cab driver then ignored the command to "step back." Most likely, this did not make any sense to him because, in his eyes, he was not even close to the officer. The social distance for conversation in Nigeria is much closer than in the United States. For

Nigerians, it may be less than 15 inches, whereas 2 feet represents a comfortable conversation zone for Americans.

Another nonverbal communication behavior is eye contact. Anglo Americans expect eye contact during conversation; the lack of it usually signifies deception, rudeness, defiance, or an attempt to end the conversation. In Nigeria, however, people often show respect and humility by averting their eyes. While the officer saw the cabbie defiantly "babbling to the ground," the Nigerian believed he was sending a message of respect and humility.

Most likely, the cab driver was not even aware of his exaggerated gestures, high-pitched tone of voice, or rapid speech. But the officer believed him to be "out of control," "unstable," and probably "dangerous." Had the cab driver been an Anglo American, the officer's reading of the cabbie's nonverbal behavior would have been correct.

One of the primary results of a breakdown in communications is a sense of being out of control, yet in law enforcement, control and action are tantamount. Unfortunately, the need for control combined with the need to act often makes a situation worse. "Don't just stand there. Do something!" is a very Anglo American admonition.

With the cab driver, the officer took control using his cultural common sense when it might have been more useful to look at what was actually taking place. Of course, in ambiguous and stressful situations, people seldom take time to truly examine the motivating behaviors in terms of culture. Rather, they view what is happening in terms of their own experiences, which is ethnocentric—and usually wrong.

Law enforcement professionals need to develop cultural empathy. They need to put themselves in other people's cultural shoes to understand what motivates their behavior. By understanding internal cultures, they usually can explain why situations develop the way they do. And if they know their own internal cultures, they also know the reasons behind their reactions and realize why they may feel out of control.

Here's another scenario.

During face-to-face negotiations with police at a local youth center, the leader of a gang of Mexican American adolescents suddenly begins to make long, impassioned speeches, punctuated with gestures and threats. Other members of the group then join in by shouting words of encouragement and agreement.

A police negotiator tries to settle the group and get the negotiations back on track. This only leads to more shouting from the Chicano gang members. They then accuse the police of bad faith, deception, and an unwillingness to "really negotiate."

Believing that the negotiations are breaking down, the police negotiator begins to leave, but not before telling the leader, "We can't negotiate until you get your act together where we can deal with one spokesperson in a rational discussion about the issues and relevant facts."

At this point, a Spanish-speaking officer interrupts. He tells the police negotiator, "Negotiations aren't breaking down. They've just begun."

Among members of certain ethnic groups, inflammatory words or accelerated speech are often used for effect, not intent. Such words and gestures are a means of getting attention and communicating feelings.

For example, during an argument, it would not be uncommon for a Mexican American to shout to his friend, "I'm going to kill you if you do that again." In the Anglo culture, this clearly demonstrates a threat to do harm. But in the context of the Hispanic culture, this simply conveys anger. Therefore, the Spanish word *matar* (to kill) is often used to show feelings, not intent.

In the gang scenario, the angry words merely indicated sincere emotional involvement by the gang members, not threats. But to the police negotiator, it appeared as if the gang was angry, irrational, and out of control. In reality, the emotional outburst showed that the gang members wanted to begin the negotiation process. To them, until an exchange of sincere emotional words occurred, no negotiations could take place.

Each culture presents arguments differently. For example, Anglo Americans tend to assume that there is a short distance between an emotional, verbal expression of disagreement and a full-blown conflict. African-Americans think otherwise.[61, 62] For African-Americans, stating a position with feeling shows sincerity. However, White Americans might interpret this as an indication of uncontrollable anger or instability and, even worse, an impending confrontation. For most African-Americans, threatening movements, not angry words, indicate the start of a fight. In fact, some would argue that fights do not begin when people are talking or arguing but rather when they stop talking.

Anglo Americans expect an argument to be stated in a factual–inductive manner. For them, facts presented initially in a fairly unemotional way lead to a conclusion. The greater number of relevant facts at the onset, the more persuasive the argument.[63]

African-Americans, on the other hand, tend to be more affective–intuitive. They begin with the emotional position, followed by a variety of facts somewhat poetically connected to support their conclusions. African-Americans often view the mainstream presentation as insincere and impersonal, while White Americans see the Black presentation as irrational and too personal. Many times, arguments are lost because of differences in style, not substance. Deciding who's right and who is wrong depends on the cultural style of communication and thinking used.

Differences in argumentative styles add tension to any disagreement. As the Chicano gang leader presented his affective–intuitive argument, other gang members joined in with comments of encouragement, agreement, and support. To the police-negotiator, the gang members appeared to be united in a clique and on the verge of a confrontation.

Sometimes, Anglo Americans react by withdrawing into a superfactual–inductive mode in an effort to calm things down. Unfortunately, the emphasis on facts, logical presentation, and lack of emotion often comes off as cold, condescending, and patronizing, which further shows a disinterest in the views of others.

Because of naive assumptions, the criminal justice community seldom views cross-cultural awareness and training as vital, yet as society and the law enforcement workforce become more diverse, the ability to manage cultural diversity becomes essential. Those agencies that do not proactively develop cultural knowledge and skills fail to serve the needs of their communities. More importantly, however, they lose the opportunity to increase the effectiveness of their officers.

Unfortunately, cross-cultural training in law enforcement often occurs after an incident involving cross-cultural conflict. If provided, this training can be characterized as a quick fix, a once-in-a-lifetime happening, when in reality it should be an ongoing process of developing awareness, knowledge, and skills.

At the very least, officers should know what terms are the least offensive when referring to ethnic or racial groups in their communities. For example, most Asians prefer not to be called Orientals. It is more appropriate to refer to their nationality of origin, such as Korean American, assuming that the officer is positive about their nationality of origin.

Likewise, very few Spanish speakers would refer to themselves as Hispanics. Instead, the term "Chicano" is usually used by Mexican Americans, while the term "Latino" is preferred by those from Central America. Some would rather be identified by their nationality of origin, such as Guatemalan or Salvadoran.

Many American Indians resent the term "Native American" because it was invented by the U.S. government. They would prefer being called American Indian or being known by their tribal ancestry, such as Crow, Menominee, or Winnebago.

The terms "Black American" and "African-American" can usually be used interchangeably. However, "African-American" is more commonly used among younger people.

Law enforcement executives need to weave cross-cultural awareness into all aspects of law enforcement training and realize it is not enough to bring in a "gender expert" after someone files sexual harassment charges or a "race expert" after a racial incident occurs. 3-hour workshops on a specific topic do not solve problems. Cross-cultural issues are interrelated; they cannot be disconnected.

Developing a Culturally Aware Workforce

What can the law enforcement community do to ensure a more culturally aware workforce? To begin, law enforcement professionals must know their own culture. All personnel need to appreciate the impact of their individual cultures on their values and behaviors. Sometimes, the best way to gain this knowledge is by intensively interacting with those who are culturally different. However, law enforcement professionals must always bear in mind that culture, by definition, is a generalization. Cultural rules or patterns never apply to everyone in every situation.

The next step is to learn about the different cultures found within the agency and in the community. However, no one should rely on culturally specific "guidebooks" or simplistic "dos and don'ts" lists. While such approaches to cultural awareness are tempting, they do not provide sufficient insight and are often counterproductive.

First, no guidebook can be absolutely accurate, and many cover important issues in abstract or generic terms. For example, several nations constitute Southeast Asia. Therefore, when promoting cultural awareness, law enforcement agencies should concentrate on the nationality that is predominant within their respective communities—that is, Vietnamese, Laotian, Cambodian, and so on. At the same time, these agencies should keep in mind that cultures are complex and changing. Managing cultural diversity also means being able to adjust to the transformations that might be occurring within the ethnic community thus necessitating the incorporation of this information into both police academy training as well as in-service training courses.

Second, relying on a guidebook approach can be disastrous if it does not provide the answers needed to questions arising during a crisis situation. It is much more useful to have a broad framework from which to operate when analyzing and interpreting any situation. Such a framework should focus on internal, not just external, culture. Knowing values, beliefs, behaviors, and thought patterns will assist law enforcement professionals to avoid catastrophic misunderstanding.

Law enforcement professionals should also understand the dynamics of cross-cultural communication, adjustment, and conflict. When communication breaks down, frustration sets in. When this happens, law enforcement reacts. This presents a potentially dangerous situation for officers because of the emphasis placed on always being in control. Understanding the process of cross-cultural interaction gives a sense of control and allows for the development of coping strategies.

Finally, law enforcement professionals should develop cross-cultural communicative, analytic, and interpretive skills. Merely having a casual familiarity about the history and religion of a particular culture or ethnic group will not in and of itself allow police officers to communicate effectively or understand someone from that group. Although the ability to communicate effectively is often best learned through experience, police officers can also gain valuable insights into the various facets of these groups by inviting respected leaders from these groups to participate in police academy training or specifically designed in-service training course. All related training should be designed to provide insights into important characteristics of these groups. These can also be accomplished by reading authoritative books about these groups or by listening to lectures from experts in the field. All of these combined will assist law enforcement officers in analyzing and understanding the ways in which people of different cultures or ethnic groups communicate and resolve conflict.

COMMUNICATING ACROSS GENERATIONS

In the communicating process the biggest stumbling block does not always result from gender or cultural differences. It can also result from differences in the way the various generations communicate. In Chapter 9, Human Resource Management, certain important characteristics were discussed about the various generations; however, this chapter focuses primarily on the communication characteristics of the two generations that make up most of the employees in police departments today—namely, **Generation X** (those born between 1965 and 1980) and **Generation Y** or **Millennials** (born between 1981 and 1994).

Some Generalizations

There are certain characteristics each of these two groups have in their communication style, and it is important for each group to be aware of the differences so miscommunications are less likely to occur. The following represent what can best be described as some broad but useful generalizations about the communication styles of these two groups.

Generation X

The generation of officers who have grown up with sophisticated communications technology are most certainly different from previous generations. Their way of thinking has been characterized as having an information age mindset. Some of the characteristics of this mindset include:

- **Computers are not technology**—Officers falling into this category have never known life without computers and the Internet. To them computers are unquestioned part of their life.

- **The Internet is considered better than TV**—In recent years, the number of hours spent watching TV by this group has declined, supplanted by time spent online. Among the reason for the changes are interactivity and the use of the Internet for socializing.

- **Doing is more important than knowing**—Knowledge is no longer perceived to be the ultimate goal, particularly in light of the fact that the half-life information is so short. Results and actions are considered more important than the accumulation of facts.

- **Learning more closely resembles Nintendo than logic**—Nintendo symbolizes a trial-and-error approach to solving problems; losing is the fastest way to mastering a game because losing represents learning. This contrasts with the problem-solving approaches of previous generations, who employ a more logical, rule-based approach.

- **Multitasking is a way of life**—Generation X officers appear to be quite comfortable when simultaneously engaged in multiple activities, such as listening to music, texting, and talking on the phone. **Multitasking** may also be a response to information overload.

- **Typing is preferred to handwriting**—Generation X officers prefer typing to handwriting and many admit their handwriting is atrocious. Penmanship has been superseded by keyboard skills.

- **Staying connected is essential**—Generation X officers stay in touch both on and off duty via multiple devices, as they move throughout the day. Cell phones, smart phones, personal digital assistants (PDAs), netbooks, Blackberries, tablets and pads, and computers ensure that they remain connected anyplace and anytime. As the network becomes more ubiquitous, increasing numbers of Generation Xers participate in real-time dialogues from anywhere using a variety of devices.

- **There is zero tolerance for delays**—Having grown up in a culture that places a strong demand on immediacy, Generation Xers have little tolerance for delays. They expect services to be available 24/7 in a variety of modes (cell phone, texting, social media (Facebook, Twitter, e-mail, camera phone, SKYPE, and in person) and that responses will be quick.[64] This generation is equally comfortable giving feedback to others.

- **They are comfortable in multicultural settings**—This group tends to work well in **multicultural settings** and takes a pragmatic approach to accomplishing tasks.[65]

- **They have a need for effective mentoring**—A mentoring program is essential. They seem to like feedback on their performance and appreciate the opportunity to create new ways to accomplish tasks. It is important to inform Generation Xers of the agency's expectations and how their progress will be measured. They work best when they are informed of the desired outcome and given specific instructions on how to achieve it.[66]

Generation Y/ Millennials

Many officers from Generation Y, also called Millennials, are increasingly assuming positions as supervisors and in middle management. This is a generation that has been raised in one of the most child-centric times in our history. Perhaps because they were showered with attention and felt high expectation from their parents, they display a great deal of self-confidence, to the point that they have sometimes been characterized as having an attitude of entitlement. They are certainly the most technically literate generation ever because they have spent their entire lives working with the Internet, computer, cell phones, Blackberries, PDAs, netbooks, digital readers, and so on.

Like Generation X officers, they are good multitaskers, having juggled sports, school, and social interests as children and can be expected to work hard. Millennials seem to expect structure in the workplace. They acknowledge and respect positions and titles and want a relationship with their superiors.

Because Generation Yers are new to the professional workplace, no matter how smart and confident they are, they are definitely in need of mentoring. Also, they will respond well to the personal attention. Because they appreciate structure and stability, mentoring Millennials should be more formal, with set meetings and a more authoritative attitude on the mentor's part.

They prefer lots of challenges but also need the structure to back it up. This means breaking down goals into steps, as well as offering any necessary resources and information they will need to meet the challenge. Consideration should be given to **mentoring** Millennials in groups because they work well in team situations. In this kind of a setting, they can act as each other's resources or peer mentors.[67]

Quick Facts: Millennials Will Benefit and Suffer Due to Their Hyperconnected Lives

A survey was taken by the Pew Research Center's Internet & American Life Project and Elon University's Imagining the Internet Center to determine the impact on millennials of being hyperconnected.

The survey question about younger users was inspired by speculation over the past several years about the potential impact of technology on them. Looking toward the year 2020, respondents to this survey were fairly evenly split on whether the results will be primarily positive or mostly negative. They were asked to read two statements and select the one they believe is most likely to be true and then explain their answers.

Some 55 percent agreed with the statement:

In 2020, the brains of multitasking teens and young adults are "wired" differently from those over age 35 and overall it yields helpful results. They do not suffer notable cognitive shortcomings as they multitask and cycle quickly through personal- and work-related tasks. Rather, they are learning more and they are more adept at finding answers to deep questions, in part because they can search effectively and access collective intelligence via the Internet. In sum, the changes in learning behavior and cognition among the young generally produce positive outcomes.

Some 42 percent agreed with the opposite statement, which posited:

In 2020, the brains of multitasking teens and young adults are "wired" differently from those over age 35 and overall it yields baleful results. They do not retain information: they spend most of their energy sharing short social messages, being entertained, and being distracted away from deep engagement with people and knowledge. They lack deep-thinking capabilities; they lack face-to-face social skills; they depend in unhealthy ways on the Internet and mobile devices to function. In sum, the changes in behavior and cognition among the young are generally negative outcomes.

A third alternative was not offered—that young people's brains would not be wired differently—but some of the respondents make those arguments in their elaborations. They often noted that people's patterns of thinking will likely change, though the actual mechanisms of brain function will not change.[68]

Generational Differences in Formal and Informal Styles of Communication

A particular problem area is that involving forms of address. For example, informal talk or an over familiarization with superiors from Generation Y (Millennials) may be offensive and seem somewhat disrespectful to Generation X officers. In many instances, the younger officers who engage in this informal conversation do not mean to be disrespectful but just have a more informal and casual style of communicating with friends and co-workers.

One thing is certain: Some things are important to nearly all employees, regardless of age. Simple gestures like listening, acknowledging what others have said, and acting on their suggestions when appropriate are all signs of respect. People tend to appreciate being addressed with a "hello" or a "good-bye" or being greeted by name. Saying something like "yo, dawg" (meaning a friend and not a member of the canine variety) is probably not going to be appreciated by all generations.

The best solution is to try to be considerate of the views of members of other generations. If someone from another generation says something problematic, or their manner or tone is causing a problem, efforts should be made to discuss it openly to resolve the situation.[69]

Generational Lingo

A Millennial employee may use a term such as "phat" (excellent or great) and mean it as a compliment. However, an older co-worker may hear it as "fat" and take it as an insult. This is not meant to be an insult. However, unless it is understood, intergenerational communication can jeopardize workplace morale and productivity when employees of different generations miscommunicate.[70]

Preference to Texting as a Major Means of Communication

Millennials, especially those at the younger end of the age spectrum, clearly prefer to communicate via texting rather than either face-to-face or telephone contact.

There are those in law enforcement who are arguably concerned that the increasing immersion and preference for this form of communication, especially if started at an early age, could possibly negatively impact the normal development of intellectual interpersonal skills. This could include a reduced pursuit of deep knowledge and understanding of important

social and political issues in favor of superficial "sound bites," failing to develop important negotiation skills; how to accurately assess body language, facial expressions, emotional vocalizations, how to empathize with others, patience, and, most important, self-reflection. All of these qualities are critically essential for law enforcement officers to possess in order for them to be able to intelligently and effectively intervene in a wide variety of conflicting situations, especially those that have enormous potential for danger. It is absolutely essential that officers possess the necessary skills to safely diffuse such situations. There also comes concern that the excessive immersion into technology could also reduce the development of one's observational skills. For example, it is very common to see individuals so involved in the texting process that they are totally oblivious to their surrounding environment. Most of us have seen people on TV walking into water fountains and into doors while texting. Also, increasingly many drivers are now texting and driving thereby jeopardizing their own personal safety and the safety of others.

Assuming these concerns are valid then law enforcement agencies will have to make important changes in their training regimes, mentorship, as well as their supervisory and leadership styles. We are in the very early stages of fully understanding this phenomenon and simply recognizing it and assessing it is insufficient. The emphasis must be placed on how to rectify any shortcomings that might result in order to provide officers with the vast array of skills they need to effectively communicate with a variety of people and resolve conflicts in an intelligent and equitable manner.[72]

Creeping Computerese

Technology is not just changing the ways we communicate but is also changing the words or phrases with which we communicate. Items of computerese, which many see as acceptable in e-mail or instant messaging, are starting to find their way into nonelectronic communication as well. Computerese, such as *btw* (by the way) or *imo* (in my opinion), may be acceptable to some number of people in an e-mail; however, for many others, especially older people, it may not be acceptable or even understandable if included in professional writings or even e-mails. Computer emoticons (e.g., animated smiley faces used in e-mails) to indicate humor, for example, are more likely to be acceptable to younger generations.[73]

What Is Said Is Not Always What Is Heard

Regardless of the generational category an employee falls into, it is important to understand that what is said needs to be completely understood by each generation. It is advisable to anticipate intergenerational miscommunications as much as possible and tailor all messages to be as clear as possible to all generations.[74]

Learning how to communicate across the generations can eliminate many of the misunderstandings. If a Generation X manager says, "We need to get this report written," another Generation X employee would correctly interpret this as a nicely stated command. On the other hand, if that same Generation X manager made the same statement to a Millennial, the Millennial could well hear this comment as an observation and not as an

---

Quick Facts: Generational Variations

According to the Pew Research Center, cellphone owners between ages 18 and 24 exchange an average of 109.5 texts a day or more than 3,200 texts per month. However, a third of U.S. adults also prefer texting to talking on the phone.[71]

order. Thus, cross-generational communication is not always clear. It is important to understand that what a person in one generation hears may not be what the person of another generation means to communicate.

COMMUNICATING WITH PEOPLE WITH DISABILITIES

Thus far, all of our discussions about communications, both organizationally and interpersonally, have been based on the assumption that we are dealing with individuals who do not have special needs that would affect their ability to engage in normal communication. However, there are in fact literally millions of individuals living in the United States who have special needs and law enforcement officers must be aware of the most effective means of communications in dealing with such individuals.

Within the special need groups are individuals who are blind or visually impaired, deaf or hard of hearing, mobility impaired, speech impaired, or have cognitive disabilities.

The following are some suggestions that will assist law enforcement officers in more effectively communicating and dealing with individuals they encounter who have special needs.

Individuals Who Are Blind or Visually Impaired

- Speak to the individual as you approach him or her.
- State clearly who you are; speak in a normal tone of voice.
- When conversing in a group, remember to identify yourself to the person to whom you are speaking.
- Never touch or distract a service dog without first asking the owner's permission.
- Tell the individual when you are leaving.
- Do not attempt to lead the individual without first asking. Also, allow the person to hold your arm, thus allowing him/her to control their own movements.
- Be descriptive when giving directions; verbally give the person information that is visually obvious to individuals who can see. For example, if you are approaching steps, mention how many steps.
- If you are offering a seat, gently place the individual's hand on the back or arm of the chair so that the person can locate the seat.[75]

Individuals Who are Deaf or Hard of Hearing

- Before speaking, get the person's attention with a wave of the hand or a gentle tap on the shoulder.
- Face the person and do not turn away while speaking.
- Try to converse in a well-lit area.

- Do not cover your mouth or chew gum.
- If a person is wearing a hearing aid, do not assume he or she can hear you clearly.
- Minimize background noise and other distractions whenever possible.
- When you are communicating orally, speak slowly and distinctly. Use facial expressions to reinforce what are you saying.
- Use visual aids whenever possible such as pointing to printed information on a citation or other document.
- Generally, for those who are deaf or hard of hearing, only one-third of spoken words can be understood by speech reading.
- When communicating in writing, keep in mind that some individuals who use sign language may lack good English reading and writing skills.
- If someone with a hearing disability cannot understand you, write a note to ask them what communication aids or service are needed.
- If a sign language interpreter is requested, be sure to ask via a note which language the person uses. American Sign Language (ASL) and Signed English are the most common.
- When interviewing a witness or a suspect or engaging in any complex conversation with a person whose primary language is sign language, a qualified interpreter is usually needed to ensure effective communication.
- When using an interpreter, look and speak directly to the deaf person and not to the interpreter.
- Talk at your normal rate or slightly slower if you normally speak fast.
- Only one person should speak at a time.
- Use short sentences and simple words.[76]
- If you telephone an individual who is hard of hearing, let the phone ring longer than usual. Speak clearly and be prepared to repeat the reason for the call and who you are.
- If you do not have a Text Telephone (TTY), dial 711 to reach the national telecommunications relay service, which facilitates the call between you and the individual who uses a TTY.

Individuals with Mobility Impairments

- If possible, put yourself at the wheelchair user's eye level.
- Do not lean on a wheelchair or any other assistive device.
- Never patronize people who use wheelchairs by patting them on the head or shoulders.
- Do not assume the individual wants to be pushed— ask first.

- Offer assistance if the individual appears to be having difficulty opening a door.
- If you telephone the individual, allow the phone to ring longer than usual to allow extra time for the person to reach the telephone.

Individuals with Speech Impairments

- If you do not understand something the individual says, do not pretend that you do. Ask the individual to repeat what he or she said and then repeat it back.
- Be patient. Take as much time as necessary.
- Try to ask questions that require only short answers or a nod of the head.
- Concentrate on what the individual is saying.
- If you are having difficulty understanding the individual, consider writing as an alternative means of communicating, but first ask the individual if this is acceptable.[77]

Individuals with Cognitive Disabilities

About three out of every 100 people have developmental disabilities, so it is likely that a law enforcement office will at some point come in contact with an individual who has this disability. A successful interaction with a person who has developmental disabilities can yield accurate and useful information while, at the same time, protecting his or her rights as an individual.[78]

- If you are in a public area with many distractions, consider moving to a quiet or private location.
- Be prepared to repeat what you say, orally or in writing.
- Offer assistance completing forms or understanding written instructions and provide extra time for decision making. Wait for the individual to accept the offer of assistance; do not "over-assist" or be patronizing.
- Be patient, flexible, and supportive. Take time to understand the individual and make sure that the individual understands you.[79]

Chapter Summary

Summary by Learning Objectives

1. **Identify five types of downward communications within an organization.**

   1. **Job instruction**—communication relating to the performance of a certain task.
   2. **Job rationale**—communication relating a certain task to organizational tasks.
   3. **Procedures and practices**—communication about organization policies, procedures, rules, and regulations.
   4. **Feedback**—communication appraisal of how an individual performs the assigned task.
   5. **Indoctrination**—communication designed to motivate the employee.

2. **List the order of effective communication from most effective to least effective.**

   1. Oral and written communication combined;
   2. Oral communication only;
   3. Written communication only;
   4. The bulletin board;
   5. The organizational grapevine.

3. **Discuss the steps necessary to eliminate some of the unfortunate missteps in e-mail communications within an organization.**
   Maintain professionalism in e-mail correspondence, as in any other business correspondence; business etiquette does not change when a message is digitized; Respond to e-mail promptly, even if only to

acknowledge initial receipt and that a more detailed response will follow; Check e-mail frequently, but do not allow it to interrupt other scheduled tasks; Read and reread e-mails for quality, tone, grammar, spelling, and punctuation before sending them. Do not rely solely on spell check to catch errors; Remember that e-mail is not private correspondence and can easily become public without intent or consent. It is a permanent record of written communication; Do not use business e-mail for jokes or frivolous messages; Deal with personal or sensitive issues in person, not through an impersonal electronic medium; Use business e-mail as a means to get information to a number of people in expeditious fashion and to quickly involve others but do not send e-mails to persons who do not need to receive it; Use caution when responding to e-mails. How something is said in e-mail language is just as important as what is said. No matter how emotional the issue or the contents of the e-mail received and the resultant need to verbalize emotions, do not vent and send; and treat an e-mail inbox similar to a paper one: Review the document, act on it, and move on.

4. **Discuss the recent trends by police departments to use social media with the public.**
   The Police Executive Research Forum (PERF) conducted a national survey to determine the extent to which police departments are sharing information and developing relationships with their communities with the application of social media. What they discovered was that 80 percent of those agencies

responding said they use social media to share information with the public. As a matter of fact, more than 2,800 law enforcement agencies in the United States have social media accounts and that number is growing every day.

5. Discuss what a law enforcement agency can do to insure a more culturally aware workforce.

To begin, law enforcement professionals must know their own culture. All personnel need to appreciate the impact of their individual cultures on their values and behaviors. Sometimes, the best way to gain this knowledge is by intensively interacting with those who are culturally different. However, law enforcement professionals must always bear in mind that culture, by definition, is a generalization. Cultural rules or patterns never apply to everyone in every situation.

The next step is to learn about the different cultures found within the agency and in the community. However, no one should rely on culturally specific "guide-books" or simplified "dos and don'ts" lists. While such approaches to cultural awareness are tempting, they do not provide sufficient insight and are often counterproductive.

6. List the five categories of people with disabilities that law enforcement officers are most likely to come in contact with.

1. Individuals Who are Blind or Visually Impaired;
2. Individuals Who are Deaf or Hard of Hearing;
3. Individuals with Mobility Impairments;
4. Individuals with Speech Impairments; and
5. Individuals with Cognitive Disabilities.

Chapter Review Questions

1. Discuss the steps in the communication process.
2. What are some of the barriers that result because of improper techniques used on the part of either the sender or receiver?
3. What have psychologists said about the potential problems associated with an administrator's dependence upon technology in the communication process?
4. Why is it necessary for departments to monitor what their officers may be posting on their personal social media sites?
5. What is the role of the public information officer in organizational communication?
6. What suggestions were made for becoming an effective communicator?
7. What are the major differences between the way that female and male officers communicate, especially during conflict resolution?
8. What are the main issues in communication between law enforcement and citizens from other cultures, and how are law enforcement agencies trying to address these changes?
9. What are the major characteristics of the ways Generation X officers communicate?
10. What are the major characteristics of the ways Generation Y (Millennial) officers communicate?
11. What are some of the possible long-term consequences of preferring texting as a major means of communication?

Critical Thinking Exercises

1. Cross-Cultural Communication. Your community has recently received a major influx of immigrants from a non-white, non-Judeo-Christian country.

a. There have been some unfortunate clashes between your uniformed police officers and some young males from this community.

b. You believe that many of these clashes have resulted because of a failure of your officers as well as members of this recently arrived immigrant community to understand important aspects of each other's culture.

c. Who would you turn to provide the necessary training so your officers can become familiar with important aspects of the recently introduced culture in order to reduce some of the unfortunate misunderstandings and confrontations that have recently occurred?

d. How would you go about identifying leaders within the newly arrived immigrant community who would be in a position to serve as a useful conduit with your agency in order to assist the recently arrived immigrants to better understand the expectations of your agency both in its personal and professional interactions?

2. Communication Across Generations. Your agency is now recruiting officers primarily from Generation Y/Millennials and you note a big difference in their interpersonal communication styles from previous generations as well as what appears to be their lack of skills necessary to resolve personal and professional conflicts. Following are some examples of how these perceived deficiencies are showing up in the organization.

a. In some cases, the style of informal communication used by Millennials is viewed by older officers as being disrespectful.

b. Also, because Millennials prefer texting as their principal means of communication many older officers believe that this has resulted in their failing to develop the skills necessary to assess and resolve interpersonal and professional conflict. This assessment has been supported by the police academy director and staff who say in a number of recent cases where recruit officers were intentionally exposed to verbal abuse and aggressive behavior in role playing situations some of them broke down and cried. This applied to both male and female officers. The police academy director and some academy staff members believe that this is attributable in part to their constant use of impersonal electronic communication instruments. There is also some concern that the dependency on this form of communication has contributed to their inadequacies in developing the face-to-face skills necessary to effectively resolve hostile conflicts.

How would you go about working with older officers in your agency so they have a better understanding of the communication styles of Millennials? Also, how would you go about being certain that newly employed Millennials have the skills necessary to assess, identify, and effectively resolve confrontational situations?

Key Terms

communication	grapevine	multicultural settings
culture	group communication	multitasking
downward communication	group interaction	noise
feedback	horizontal communication	upward communication
Generation X	interpersonal communication	
Generation Y	mentoring	

Endnotes

[1] A. J. DuBrin, *Human Relations: Interpersonal Job-Oriented Skills,* 8th ed. (Upper Saddle River, NJ: Prentice Hall, 2004), pp. 42–46.

[2] Krissah Thompson, "Arrest of Harvard's Henry Louis Gates Jr. Was Avoidable, Report Says," *Washington Post,* June 30, 2010; Katie Zezima, "Officer and Professor Faulted for Confrontation at Home," *New York Times*159 Issue 55088, (July 1, 2010), p. 21. Op.

[3] P. V. Lewis, *Organizational Communication: The Essence of Effective Management* (Columbus, Ohio: Grid, 1975), p. 36.

[4] Ibid., pp. 36–37.

[5] Siobhan Gorman, "How Boston Terror Warning Went Awry," *National Journal* 37, No. 8 (February 19, 2005), p. 542.

[6] Ibid., pp. 37–38.

[7] D. Katz and R. L. Kahn, *The Social Psychology of Organizations* (New York: John Wiley & Sons, 1966), p. 239, as cited in Lewis, *Organizational Communication,* p. 38.

[8] R. L. Smith, G. M. Richetto, and J. P. Zima, "Organizational Behavior: An Approach to Human Communication," in *Readings in Interpersonal and Organizational Communication,* 3rd ed., ed. R. C. Huseman, C. M. Logue, and D. L. Freshley (Boston: Holbrook Press, 1977), p.11.

[9] T. L. Dahle, "An Objective and Comparative Study of Five Methods of Transmitting Information to Business and Industrial Employees" (Ph.D. dissertation, Purdue University, 1954), as cited in Smith et al. "Organizational Behavior," p. 12.

[10] E. Planty and W. Machaver, "Upward Communications: A Project in Executive Development," *Personnel* 28 (January 1952), pp. 304–319.

[11] R. K. Allen, *Organizational Management through Communication* (New York: Harper & Row, 1977), pp. 77–79.

[12] H. Fayol, *General and Industrial Administration* (New York: Pitman, 1949), p. 34.

[13] Allen, *Organizational Management,* p. 78.

[14] Ibid., pp. 78–79.

[15] K. Davis, "Management Communication and the Grapevine," *Harvard Business Review* (September–October 1953), pp. 43–49, as cited by Lewis, *Organizational Communication,* p. 41.

[16] Lewis, *Organizational Communication,* pp. 41–42.

[17] James D. Sewell, "Handling the Stress of the Electronic World," *FBI Law Enforcement Bulletin,* August 2003, p. 14.

[18] Edward F. Davis III, Alejandro A. Alves and David Alan Sklansky, *Social Media and Police Leadership: Lessons from Boston* New Perspectives in Policing Bulletin (Washington, DC: U.S. Department of Justice, National Institute of Justice, 2014.) NCJ 244760, p. 2.

[19] Dennis Burns and Zach Perron, "Considerations for Social Media Management and Strategy," *The Police Chief* (April 2014), 30–32.

[20] Ibid., p. 31

[21] Ibid.

22The Police Executive Research Forum (PERF) is a professional organization of progressive chief executives of city, county, and state law enforcement agencies. In addition, PERF has established formal relationships with international police executives and law enforcement organizations from around the globe. PERF's membership includes police chiefs, superintendents, sheriffs, state police directors, university police chiefs, public safety directors, and other law enforcement professionals. Established in 1976 as a nonprofit organization, PERF is unique in its commitment to the application of research in policing and the importance of higher education for police executives.

23Numbers throughout this paper that represents certain online metrics, such as the number of likes, shares or retweets received, or the number of agencies present on social media, may change frequently and are accurate as of December 2013.

24See IACP Center for Social Media Directory, http://www.iacpsocialmedia.org/Directory.aspx.

25"Facebook Detail?" *American Police Beat*, (June 2011), p. 16.

26Darrel W. Stephens, Julia Hill, and Sheldon Greenberg, *Strategic Communication Practices: A Toolkit for Police Executives*, Community Oriented Policing Services, U.S. Department of Justice (September 2011), p. 23–24.

27Ibid., p. 23.

28Ibid.

29E. M. Morley and M. J. Jacobson, "Building a Successful Public Information Program," *Police Chief Magazine* vol. 74, no. 12 (2007); (accessed June 2015), www.policechiefmagazine.org/magazine/index.cfm?fuseaction=display&article_id=1345&issue_id=122007; S. Braunstein and W. Cheek. (eds). *Best Practices in Law Enforcement Public Information* (Alexandria, VA: IACP, 2006); M. Motschall and L. Cao. 2002. "An Analysis of the Public Relations Role of the Police Public Information Officer." *Police Quarterly* 5, no. 2 (2002), 152–180. doi: 10.1177/109861102129198084; R. Surette, 2001. "Public Information Officers: The Civilianization of a Criminal Justice Profession." *Journal of Criminal Justice* 29, no. 2, (March-April): 107–117. doi:10.1016/0047-2352(95)00023-J.

30Patrick Davis, "The Public Information Officer and Today's Digital News Environment," *FBI Law Enforcement Bulletin*, July 2010, p. 3.

31David Scott, *The New Rules of Marketing and PR: How to Use News Releases, Blogs, Podcasts, Viral Marketing, and Online Media to Reach Your Buyers Directly* (New York, NY: John Wiley and Sons, 2007), 191.

32"The Public Information Officer," pp. 4–5.

33Ibid., p. 5.

34Http://www.nixle.com; accessed June 16, 2015.

35"The Public Information Officer, p. 5.

36Ibid., p. 6

37Ibid., p. 7.

38Ibid.

39Ibid.

40Andrew J. Dubrin, *Leadership* (New York: Houghton Mifflin, 2004), pp. 364–371, 373, 374.

41James M. Kouzes and Barry Z. Posner, *The Leadership Challenge: How to Get Extraordinary Things Done in Organizations* (San Francisco: Jossey-Bass, 1987), p. 118.

42Roberta H. Krapels and Vanessa D. Arnold, "Speaker Credibility in Persuasive Work Situations," *Business Education Forum* (December 1997), pp. 24–25.

43Stephen P. Robbins and Phillip L. Hunsaker, *Training in Interpersonal Skills: Tips for Managing People at Work* (Upper Saddle River, NJ: Prentice Hall, 1996), p. 115.

44Refer to Jay A. Conger, *Winning 'Em Over: The New Model for Management in the Age of Persuasion* (New York: Simon & Schuster, 2001).

45From 2000 through 2009 469 deaths. "Causes of Law Enforcement Deaths," From the National Law Enforcement Officers Memorial Fund website, available from http://www.nleomf.org/facts/officer-fatalities-data/causes.html

46Michael W. Mercer, "How to Make a Fantastic Impression," *HR Magazine*, March 1993, p. 49.

47Deborah Tannen, "The Power of Talk: Who Gets Heard and Why?" *Harvard Business Review* (September–October 1995), pp. 138–148.

48Ibid, "How You Speak Shows Where You Rank," *Fortune*, February 2, 1998, p. 156 "Frame Your Persuasive Appeal," *Executive Strategies*, September 1998, p. 7 "Weed Out Wimpy Words: Speak Up without Backpedaling, Qualifying," *Working Smart*, March 2000, p. 2.

49Albert Mehrabian and M. Wiener, "Decoding Inconsistent Communications," *Journal of Personality and Social Psychology* 6 (1947), pp. 109–114.

50Several of these suggestions are from *Body Language for Business Success* (New York: National Institute for Business Management, 1989), pp. 2–29 and "Attention All Monotonous Speakers," *Working Smart*, March 1998, p. 1.

51Several of these suggestions are from *Body Language for Business Success* (New York: National Institute for Business Management, 1989), pp. 2–29 and "Attention All Monotonous Speakers," *Working Smart*, March 1998, p. 1.

52Harvey Wallace, Cliff Roberson, and Craig Steckler, *Written and Interpersonal Communication Methods for Law Enforcement* (Upper Saddle River, NJ: Prentice Hall, 2001), pp. 39, 40. Reprinted by permission of Pearson Education, Inc., Upper Saddle River, NJ.

53See Michael Burgoon, Judee K. Heston, and James McCroskey, *Small Group Communication: A Functional Approach* (New York: Holt, Rinehart & Winston, 1974), pp. 2–3, 12, 39.

54See Robert Ardrey, *The Social Contract* (New York: Atheneum, 1970), p. 368, where the author theorizes that the range for a natural group is 11 or 12, and Marvin E. Shaw, *Group Dynamics* (New York: McGraw-Hill, 1971), which places the maximum number of persons at 20.

55B. Aubrey Fisher, "Decision Emergence: Phase in Group Decision-Making," *Speech Monographs* 37 (1970), pp. 53–66.

56Field, "The Abilene Paradox," p. 89.

57Spanish is not the only language that officers will encounter. For a discussion of law enforcement agencies' experiences with Chinese, see C. Fredric Anderson and Henriettee Liu Levy, "A Guide to Chinese Names," *FBI Law Enforcement Bulletin*, March 1992, p. 10.

58Source: "Profile America Facts for Features," *U.S. Census Bureau News*, U.S. Department of Commerce, Washington, DC, July 30, 2013 (accessed June 2015) http://www.census.gov/newsroom/releases/archives/facts_for_features_special_editions/cb13-ff19.html; U.S. Census Bureau, 2011 American Community Survey: Table B03001 (accessed June 2015); http://factfinder2.census.gov/faces/tableservices/jsf/pages/procudtview.xhtml?=table; Population Projections (accessed June 2015) http://www.census.gov/newsroom/releases/archives/population/cb08-123.html.

59Colleen Long, "Police Departments Offer Raises, Immersion Programs for Bilingual Cops," Associated Press, March 11, 2010. Writers Cristian Salazar in New York and Jeff Carlton in Dallas, and AP photographer Bebeto Matthews in New York contributed to this report.

60This section is adapted from Brian K. Ogawa, *Focus on the Future: A Prosecutor's Guide for Victim Assistance* (Washington, DC: National Victim Center, 1994).

61G. Weaver, "Law Enforcement in a Culturally Diverse Society," *FBI Law Enforcement Bulletin*, September 1992, pp. 3–7. (This discussion of cross-cultural diversity in communication was taken with modification from this source.)

62Thomas Kochman, *Black and White Styles in Conflict* (Chicago: University of Chicago Press, 1981).

63Edmund Glenn, D. Witmeyer, and K. Stevenson, "Cultural Styles of Persuasion," *International Journal of Intercultural Communication* 1 (1977), pp. 52–66.

64Diana Oblinger, "Boomers & Gen-Xers, and Millennials: Understanding the New Students," *Educause Review* (July/August, 2003), p. 40.

65Diane Thielfoldt and Devon Cheef, "Generation X and the Millennials: What You Need to Know About Mentoring the New Generations," *Law Practice Today* (2010).

66Ibid.

67Ibid.

68Janna Anderson and Lee Rainie, "Millennials Will Benefit and Suffer Due to Their Hyperconnected Lives," Pew Research Center, February 29, 2012; (accessed June 15, 2015), http://www.pewinternet.org/2012/02/29/millennials-will-benefit-and-suffer-due-to-their-hyperconnected-lives/.

69Linda A. Panszczyk, *HR How-to: Intergenerational Issues* (Chicago, IL: CCH KnowledgePoint, 2004), p. 168.

70Ibid., pp. 168–170.

71"Texting 911 for Help Could be a Lifesaver," *Tampa Bay Times*, May 24, 2014, p. 14A.

72For a more detailed discussion of this topic see Sherry Turkle, "The Flight From Conversation," *The New York Times*, April 21, 2012, page SR1 of the New York edition; Sherry Turkle, "The Tethered Self: Technology Reinvents Intimacy and Solitude," *Continuing Higher Education Review* 75 (2011), pp. 28–31; Sherry Turkle, "The Creep of Social Media Raises Big Questions," *The New York Times*, updated June 20, 2012, The Opinion Pages.

73Ibid., p. 170.

74Ibid., pp. 170–171.

75U.S. Department of Labor, Office of Disability Employment Policy; the Medial Project, Research and Training Center on Independent Living, University of Kansas, Lawrence, KS; and the National Center for Access Unlimited, Chicago, IL. About 9 percent of the American population is either deaf or hard of hearing. And as baby boomers reach their senior years, the percentage is going to increase. So the chance of an officer dealing with a deaf person or someone who is hard of hearing is a distinct possibility, which the officer should be prepared to deal with. Retrieved from; *http://www.dol.gov/odep/pubs/fact/comucate.htm* (accessed February 17, 2014).

76Amaury Muragado, "Dealing with the Deaf," *Police Beat*, September 20, 2013; (accessed February 17, 2014) http://www.policemag.com/channel/careers-training/articles/2013/09/dealing-with-the-deaf.aspx.

77U.S. Department of Labor, Office of Disability Employment Policy.

78Police Officer's Guide for Working with People with Developmental Disabilities and Achieving Positive Outcome, Community Mental Health for Central Michigan; (accessed February 17, 2014) http://www.thearcofmidland.org/wordpress/wp-content/uploads/2013/11/A-Police-Officers-Guide-for-Working-with-People-with-Developmental-Disabilities-and-Achieving-Positive-Outcome.pdf.

79U.S. Department of Labor, Office of Disability Employment Policy.

CHAPTER ELEVEN

LABOR RELATIONS

Learning Objectives

1. Identify the seven significant factors that led to public sector collective bargaining.
2. Discuss the ways in which police unions impact the community.
3. Explain briefly the differences between the three models of collective bargaining.
4. Identify who generally serves on management and union teams during negotiations.
5. Describe the four potential major types of job actions a police union can take and the appropriate administrative actions that can be taken in response by police administrators.
6. Understand why many police departments around the country are facing funding cutbacks.

INTRODUCTION

NO SINGLE FORCE IN *the past 60 years has had a greater impact on the administration of police agencies than collective bargaining by officers. Police unions represent a major force with which police managers must reckon. It is important for the police administrator to possess the following information in order to enhance their effectiveness in dealing with police unions: (1) the historical aspects of the creation of police unions in the United States, (2) the impact police unions have had on their communities and their respective agencies, (3) the general structure of laws governing collective bargaining for law enforcement officers, (4) how a bargaining relationship is formed, (5) the various job actions that police unions will sometimes take when they are dissatisfied with the negotiation process or other political issues arising in the community, (6) the most efficient ways for police administrators to handle job actions, and (7) how to most effectively respond to the most recent funding cutbacks.*

UNIONIZATION OF THE POLICE: A HISTORICAL PERSPECTIVE

From 1959 through the 1970s, a number of events combined to foster public-sector collective bargaining. These significant forces were (1) the needs of labor organizations, (2) the reduction of legal barriers, (3) police frustration with the perceived lack of support for their "war on crime," (4) personnel practices in police agencies, (5) salaries and benefits, (6) violence directed at the police, and (7) the success of other groups.[1]

The Needs of Labor Organizations to Expand Their Membership

The attention of labor organizations was devoted almost entirely to obtaining members from the private sector until the 1960s. However, because of this exclusive focus on the private sector the opportunity to gain new members was limited. Therefore, unions looked at the possibility of organizing public employees in order to increase their membership rolls. Illustratively, in 1965, there were 10.6 million employees in local, state, and federal governments, who were almost entirely non-unionized.[2] With barriers to the unionization of public employees falling, combined private and public sector unions peaked in 1979 with 21 million members.[3]

In the decades following 1979, union membership declined. By 2014, the total number of unionized employees fell to 14.6 million.[4] Some 35.7 percent of public sector employees were unionized in 2014 with members from education and protective services being most numerous.[5] Overall, the share of the total workforce that is unionized has fallen to 11.3 percent, a 97-year low.[6]

There are multiple reasons for the reduction in union membership[7]: (1) new laws that rolled back the power of unions in states such as Indiana, Michigan, New Jersey, and Wisconsin with right to work laws. Such laws allow people to be employed without an obligation to join the applicable union, commonly called a union "closed shop"; (2) manufacturers have been expanding into the 25 states with right to work laws[8]; and (3) the growth in sectors such as retail and restaurants, where unions have little presence.

The Reduction of Legal Barriers

Although workers in the private sector had been given the right to bargain collectively under the federal National Labor Relations Act of 1935, it was another quarter-century before the first state enacted even modest bargaining rights for public employees. Beginning with the granting of public-sector collective bargaining rights in Wisconsin in 1959, many of the legal barriers that

---

Quick Facts: The Boston Police Strike of 1919 and Its Aftermath

The first campaign to organize the police started shortly after World War I, when the American Federation of Labor (AFL) reversed a long-standing policy and issued charters to police unions in Boston, Washington, DC, and about 30 other cities. August Vollmer and many other police chiefs promptly condemned this move. Following the logic of the military analogy, they insisted that policemen had no more right to join a union than soldiers and sailors and therefore no right to affiliate with the AFL.

Boston Police Commissioner E.U. Curtis refused to recognize the police union, forbade the rank and file to join it, and filed charges against several union officials. Commissioner Curtis called on the union to give up its charter and when it refused it suspended more than a dozen policemen. As a result, three-quarters of the force went out on strike. On orders from Governor Calvin Coolidge, the Commonwealth fired the strikers and destroyed the union. This action was hailed by President Woodrow Wilson, who claimed that policemen had the same obligation as soldiers branded the walkout "a crime against civilization." By 1920, efforts to organize the police in America effectively ended for the next 40 years.[9]

had been erected in the wake of the Boston police strike of 1919 began to tumble (see Figure 11.1).

Other states that also extended such rights to at least some classes of employees at an early date included California (1961) and Connecticut, Delaware, Massachusetts, Michigan, Oregon, Washington, and Wyoming, all in 1965. Many other states followed this lead, particularly from 1967 to 1974.[10] President John F. Kennedy granted limited collective bargaining rights to federal workers in 1962 by Executive Order 10988. The courts, too, were active in removing barriers; for example, in *Atkins v. City of Charlotte* (1969), the U.S. District Court struck down a portion of a North Carolina statute prohibiting public employees from being or becoming a union member as an infringement on the First Amendment right to free association.[11] While *Atkins* involved firefighters, the federal courts reached similar conclusions involving Atlanta police officers in *Melton v. City of Atlanta* (1971)[12] and a Colorado deputy sheriff in *Lontine v. VanCleave* (1973).[13]

Police Frustration with the Perceived Lack of Support for Their War on Crime

Historically, the police have felt isolated in their effort to control crime. This stems from two factors: (1) perceived public hostility and (2) the impact of the due process revolution.

Perceived Public Hostility

As an illustration of this historic, a 1967 survey of a larger city police department revealed that over 70 percent of the officers had an acute sense of citizen hostility or contempt.[14] In contrast, a survey conducted by the National Opinion Research Center that same year revealed that 77 percent of the respondents felt the police were doing a "very good" or "pretty good" job of protecting people in their neighborhoods.[15] These data notwithstanding, the police saw the public as hostile, and the most persuasive "evidence" of this emerged in the attempts to create civilian review boards, which carried several latent messages to

police officers. First, it created anger with its implied allegation that the police could not, or would not, keep their own house in order. Second, it fostered the notion that politicians were ready to "throw the police to the wolves" and thus were part of "them." However, the previously high public opinion of the police presently has declined dramatically in recent years. A 2015 Gallup poll found confidence in the police at its lowest in two decades, a mere 52 percent, matching the level in a 1991 poll taken after African-American motorist Rodney King was beaten by Los Angeles police officers.[16] Perhaps the string of unarmed African-American men killed by the police during 2014 and 2015 has had a similar effect on public opinion.

The Impact of the Due Process Revolution

Particularly among street-level officers, the reaction of the police to the whirlwind of Supreme Court decisions, discussed in Chapter 4, Politics and Police Administration, was one of dismay at being "handcuffed" in attempts to control crime. It tended to alienate the police from the Supreme Court and to contribute to a general feeling that social institutions that should support the police effort in combating crime were, instead, at odds with that effort.

Personnel Practices in Police Agencies

Past practices become precedent, precedent becomes tradition, and tradition in turn becomes the mighty anchor of many organizations, sometimes impeding change. By the late 1960s, the tendency to question the appropriateness of certain traditions was pervasive. Police rank-and-file members were no exception. This tendency was heightened by the increased educational achievement of police officers. Although management's general performance was often judged to be suspect, traditional personnel practices were the greatest concern, as these directly affected the individual officer.

Quick Facts: Did the Report Really Need Attention That Quick?

A 1960s police officer had worked the evening watch. He was assigned a late call and was 3 hours late getting off. He turned his incident report into the then-on duty patrol sergeant because his supervisors were gone. The sergeant reviewed it and signed and the tired patrol officer headed home, 14 miles away.

Shortly after he got home, the sergeant called and said he just noticed something in the report that needed to be changed and ordered the officer back to the station. He dismissed the officer's point that the matter was not critical and

could wait until he came back on duty. The sergeant insisted that the officer needed to return to the station. The officer was in a difficult situation: tell the sergeant he wasn't going to do it and risk discipline for failure to obey an order or simply return to the station. He returned as instructed.

Several years later the officer was trying to decide whether or not to vote for unionization. His decision to vote for union representation was influenced, in part, by the inconsiderate actions of the sergeant who made him come back to the station.

Among the practices that were most distasteful to rank-and-file members were: the requirement to attend, unpaid, a 30-min roll call immediately before the 8-hour tour of duty; uncompensated court attendance during off-duty time; short-notice changes in shift assignments; favoritism in both work assignments and selection for attendance at prestigious police training schools; and arbitrary disciplinary procedures.

Gradually, the gap between officers and management widened. Officers began turning to employee organizations to rectify collectively the shortcomings of their circumstances. Subsequently, the solidarity of police officers was to prove a great benefit to employee organizations.

Salaries and Benefits

As did other government workers in the 1960s, police officers felt their salaries, fringe benefits, and working conditions were not adequate. In 1961, mining production workers were averaging $111 a week in earnings, lithographers $114, tire and inner-tube producers $127, and telephone line construction workers $133,[17] whereas the pay of police officers averaged far less. Even by 1965, the salary range for patrol officers in the larger cities—those with more than 100,000 in population—was only between $5,763 and $6,919 annually.[18] The rank-and-file members believed increasingly that, if what was fairly theirs would not be given willingly, they would fight for it. In New York City, the Patrolmen's Benevolent Association (PBA) was believed to have been instrumental, from 1958 to 1969, in increasing entry-level salaries from $5,800 to $11,000 per year; obtaining longevity pay, shift differential pay, and improved retirement benefits; and increasing the death benefit from $400 to $16,500.[19] In 1968, the Boston PBA, in negotiating its first contract—which required mediation—obtained increased benefits for its members, such as an annual increase of $1,010; time and a half for all overtime, including court appearances; and 12 paid holidays.[20] However, in recent years, police unions have been called upon not only to fight for pay raises for their members but also to oppose and effectively deal with threatened pay cuts, reductions in pension benefits, and forced layoffs (discussed in greater detail later in this chapter).

Violence Directed at the Police

In 1964, there were 9.9 assaults per 100 officers; in 1969, this figure rose to 16.9. Before 1968, the killing of police officers by preplanned ambushes was unheard of; in that year, there were seven such incidents.[21] The escalating violence had considerable psychological impact on the police, who saw themselves as symbolic targets of activists attacking institutional authority. Rank-and-file members began pressing for body armor, special training, the placement of special weapons in police cars, and sharply increased death benefits. The Islamic State has recently encouraged jihadists to kill American police officers, raising the specter that ambushes of the police may increase, even as many are calling for the demilitarization of the police.

The Success of Other Groups

During the 1960s, the police witnessed mass demonstrations on college campuses that used many of the tactics associated with the Civil Rights movement. The college campus protests were against the Vietnam War. Among the campus demonstrations that were highly publicized were the University of Chicago (1965), Columbia University (1968), and San Francisco State College (1969). By 1970, campus demonstrations reached the point that, within 10 days of President Richard Nixon's announcement that he was expanding the Vietnam War and invading enemy sanctuaries in Cambodia, a total of 448 campuses were either shut down or otherwise affected by campus unrest.[22] One lesson the police learned from this is that collective action can produce results.

THE IMPACT OF POLICE UNIONS ON THE COMMUNITY

There is little question that the presence of a police union in a community has an impact upon both the police department and the community it serves. There are essentially four areas that need to be examined in order to fully understand and appreciate the impact of police unions, both within their respective agencies and in the community. These include (1) the impact on discipline and accountability, (2) the impact on the police subculture, (3) the impact on city or county finances, and (4) the impact on politics.

Impact on Discipline and Accountability

The impact of police unions on discipline and accountability is arguably the issue that causes the greatest concern among community activists, public officials, and many police executives. The impact is felt in several different ways.[23]

For example, police unions play a role in reinforcing the norms of police subculture. One of the most important aspects of this involves the **code of silence**, which results in the refusal of officers to testify against other officers who are accused of misconduct. The code has been widely cited as perhaps the most familiar obstacle to the effective investigation of alleged allegations of misconduct against officers.[24] Missing from these discussions, however, is any analysis of the extent to which the police union sustains the code of silence by (1) providing tangible support for accused officers in the form of experienced legal representation, (2) providing moral support for accused officers through organized group solidarity, and (3) negotiating a contract that inhibits thorough investigations of misconduct. As an example, there are specific provisions in many collective bargaining agreements that inhibit investigations. Police union contract provisions typically specify detailed procedures for the investigation of alleged misconduct, including the time, place, and manner of interviews or interrogations. Many, if not most of these provisions represent legitimate due process protections for employees. These include the right to notice of charges, the right to legal representation, the right to a hearing, and the right to an appeal, among others.[25]

About 14 states also have state Police Officers Bills of Rights (POBR), which contain provisions similar to those in police union contracts. In their content analysis of these statutes, there are a few provisions that inhibit accountability. For example, the Maryland POBR prohibits questioning of officers by investigators who are not sworn officers. Such a prohibition precludes the investigation of complaints by an independent citizen oversight agency.[26]

Police unions have had a major impact on the development of citizen oversight agencies, whether in the form of civilian review board or police auditors, or some other arrangement. Most famously, pressure by the local police unions was responsible for the demise of the two major civilian review boards in the 1960s, in New York City and Philadelphia.[27]

Impact on the Police Subculture

Another important area of policing is the so-called police subculture. The Christopher Commission report on the Los Angeles Police Department released in 1991, for example, contains a chapter with "LAPD Culture" in the title. The report does not, however, contain any substantive discussion of that culture or the role of the local union in maintaining it.[28] The related issues of the police subculture and of organizational cultures within police departments have not yet received sufficient scholarly attention.[29]

A Community Oriented Policing (COPS) report argues that "failing to understand and respect the culture of the agency" is one of the major factors explaining the failure of police chiefs to be effective and retain their jobs. This conclusion represents a recognition of the importance of the police culture and the fact that local police cultures vary, but like other references to this phenomenon, it is based on anecdotal evidence.[30] There is an expression in policing that "culture eats policy for lunch," thus suggesting when there is a conflict between culture and policy, culture will prevail.

The Relationship Between Police Unions and the Police Subculture

We can formulate three tentative hypotheses regarding the relationship of police unions to the police subculture: (1) following Herbert's discussion, the police subculture is a multi-dimensional phenomenon, of which the police union is only one aspect or influence; (2) there are great differences in the informal cultures among police departments, and the relative influence of the police union varies from department to department; and (3) the differences in local police subcultures have some significant and measurable difference in all aspects of policing, including overall management practices, accountability and discipline, police officer interactions with citizens, and local politics.

The idea of a distinct police subculture originated in the 1950s and early 1960s, emphasizing group solidarity, hostility to the public, secrecy and toleration of misconduct, and even violence against citizens.[31] Much has changed for the better in policing since publication of the works that defined the police subculture. At that time, African Americans and Hispanics were grossly under-represented among sworn officers, and women were not employed on a basis equal to men. In the past 45 years, the composition of the rank-and-file has changed dramatically as a result of both equal employment opportunity considerations and a significant rise in educational levels of officers.[32] One index of the growing diversity of the rank-and-file is the prevalence of nonunion employee associations based on race, ethnicity, and gender.

As a result, the entire concept of a distinct police subculture needs consideration. Herbert has described a complex, multidimensional view of the police subculture that is far more sophisticated than the original concept.[33] There is evidence of very different attitudes on the part of African-American officers compared with Whites, particularly on the issue of the use of force.[34] In some departments, African-American associations have been publicly critical of positions taken by both management and police unions that tend to be dominated by White males. A significant body of research, however, has found no meaningful differences on the street behavior among White, African American, Hispanic, or female officers. The exception to this rule is that female officers appear to be far less involved in serious misconduct, repeated misconduct, and as recipients of citizen complaints.[35] (See Chapter 10, Organizational and Interpersonal Communication for the possible reasons for gender differences.)

Impact on City or County Finances

Until the most recent funding cutbacks faced by many communities police unions have been generally successful in negotiating good salary and fringe benefit packages for their members. The resulting contract provisions undoubtedly have some significant impact on the finances of cities and counties. The nature of this impact is not known, however. It is believed that police (and sometimes firefighters) negotiations set the standard for negotiations by other municipal employees, although this proposition has not been researched. It is not known to what extent negotiated police salaries and benefits force cities and counties to reduce expenditures for other services such as streets, parks, and libraries.[36]

On the positive side, it is generally accepted that the advent of police unionism in the late 1960s and early 1970s resulted in significant improvements in police salaries and fringe benefits. This in turn has helped to improve the relative attractiveness of law enforcement as a career. It should be noted that the President's Crime Commission on Law Enforcement and Administration of Justice released in 1967 reported both lagging salaries and benefits and an inability of some agencies to attract qualified recruits.[37] It might also be noted that 20 years later, a report on police education found that the educational levels of police recruits had risen dramatically in the two previous decades.[38]

Impact on Local Politics

Police unions are well-organized, may have substantial financial resources, and possess political clout. Police unions regularly endorse or oppose political candidates for office, support or oppose proposed ordinances or referenda, and influence city or county budgets.

THE GENERAL STRUCTURE OF LAWS GOVERNING COLLECTIVE BARGAINING FOR LAW ENFORCEMENT OFFICERS

Without question, the broadest grant of rights to law enforcement officers exists in **collective bargaining** agreements. Under collective bargaining agreements, the wages and benefits of law enforcement officers are guaranteed for the duration of the agreement. Most significantly, officers who dispute a decision of their employer concerning working conditions usually have the right to appeal that decision through a grievance procedure that culminates with a final and binding decision by a neutral third party.

Under the terms of the federal National Labor Relations Act, state governmental bodies and their political subdivisions, such as cities and counties, are excluded from the definition of "employer" and are not brought within the scope of that federal law. As a result, laws regulating collective bargaining for state, county, and city law enforcement officers have developed on a state-by-state basis and, occasionally, on a local basis. Most states that allow public sector collective bargaining have created a Public Employees Relations Commission (PERC) to administer the enabling law.

Although public employee collective bargaining laws in each state are different, the general thrust of the laws can be summarized by three simplified models: the binding arbitration model, the meet and confer model, and the bargaining not required model.[39]

Binding Arbitration Model

In states following the **binding arbitration model**, public employees are granted the right to select exclusive representatives for the purposes of bargaining with their employers. In such states, the public employer and the labor organization are required to bargain in good faith until impasse, then to submit any unresolved disputes to a process known as "interest arbitration," in which a neutral third party selected by the parties makes a final and binding resolution of those issues.

In binding arbitration, the neutral third party decides what the terms and conditions of the new collective bargaining agreement will be, usually using standards established by state statute. For example, Michigan's collective bargaining law contains standard language governing the right of law enforcement labor organizations to binding arbitration, a right that is always accompanied by a ban on the right of law enforcement officers to strike:

> It is the public policy of this state that in public police and fire departments, where the right of employees to strike is by law prohibited, it is requisite to the high morale of such employees and the efficient operation of such departments to afford an alternate, expeditious, effective and binding procedure for the resolution of disputes, and to that end the provisions of this act, providing for compulsory arbitration, shall be literally constructed.[40]

There are three general types of binding arbitration laws, reflecting differences in the latitude given arbitrators to render decisions. Under the first type, known as an "issue-by-issue" law, an arbitrator has the obligation to render a decision on each issue independently and to craft an award on each issue that best accomplishes the purposes of the arbitration statute. Under the second type of law, known as "final offer, issue-by-issue," each party submits a final offer on each issue. The arbitrator then renders a decision on each issue independently, but must award the final offer made by one of the parties, and is not free to craft a compromise position that has not been specifically proposed by either party. The third type of law, known as "total package" arbitration, requires the arbitrator to select the most reasonable of the total packages submitted by each party, even if selected elements of that party's total package might not have been awarded by the arbitrator on an issue-by-issue basis. All states with binding arbitration require an arbitrator to analyze a set of criteria established by statute, usually including factors such as the wages and benefits paid in comparable jurisdictions, the cost of living, and an employer's ability to pay.[41]

Employers have challenged binding arbitration laws under a variety of theories, including arguments that binding arbitration is an unconstitutional delegation of legislative authority and that binding arbitration inappropriately interferes with a city or county's home rule status. Almost uniformly, such challenges have not been successful, with courts upholding binding arbitration as a rational means to bring about the resolution of bargaining disputes involving law enforcement officers.[42]

Meet and Confer Model

Labor leaders commonly refer to the **meet and confer model** as "collective begging" because it confers little or no bargaining rights on employees. There are variations in meet and confer models, but most commonly they permit the governmental employer and the employees representative to meet and discuss "permissible" topics, such as wages, benefits, and working conditions. Some topics, such as pensions, may be specifically excluded from discussion. The governmental employer has the final decision on any topics discussed and there is no neutral impasse resolution mechanism.

Meet and confer laws may be established by state statute or local enactments. They may describe how officers select their representatives, the obligation to freely exchange information, meet for reasonable periods of time, bargain in good faith, and that agreements be in writing and approved by a majority of the officers being represented and the governing body. Under the least labor friendly meet and confer laws, neither the governmental employer nor the employees are required to meet. Such meetings are often only an opportunity, not a requirement.

Bargaining Not Required Model

The third model for police-sector collective bargaining laws, the **bargaining not required model**, is found in states that do not statutorily require or, in some cases, allow collective bargaining for law enforcement officers. In some of these states, bargaining laws have been enacted by the state legislature, only to be declared unconstitutional later by the courts (Indiana, for example, has such a history) or even have the bargaining rights rescinded by a state's governor. In the majority of such states, a statewide collective bargaining statute covering law enforcement officers has never been enacted. In some states where collective bargaining has not been granted on a statewide basis, certain cities and counties within the state have voluntarily chosen to bargain with their law enforcement officers.[43]

Unfair Labor Practices

States with collective bargaining almost always have statutes that list a number of labor practices deemed to be "unfair." The usual list of unfair labor practices includes the following:

- A refusal to bargain in good faith over subjects that are mandatory for bargaining[44]

- Interference, restraint, or coercion of employees because employees have exercised their collective bargaining rights
- The "domination" of a labor organization by an employer
- The failure to furnish information relevant to the collective bargaining process
- Inappropriate "interference" by an employer with the internal activities of a labor organization
- Discrimination against employees who have exercised their collective bargaining rights[45]

The usual form of challenging any of these practices is through the filing of an "unfair labor practice" or "prohibited practice" complaint with the state agency responsible for administering the collective bargaining laws. Most states have a relatively quick statute of limitations—some as short as six weeks—for the filing of such complaints.[46]

Categories of Collective Bargaining Topics

Where a law enforcement employer is obligated to bargain collectively, the bargaining topics over which bargaining may be conducted are generally classified under one of three categories—mandatory, permissive, or illegal topics of bargaining.[47] Mandatory subjects of bargaining—usually those described as topics pertaining to wages, hours, and terms and conditions of employment—must be bargained if raised by either side.[48] Permissive subjects of bargaining—usually falling under the general heading of "management rights"—are those over which bargaining may occur but is not compelled.[49] Illegal subjects of bargaining are those over which the employer is forbidden by law from bargaining.[50] The distinction among the categories of bargaining subjects is particularly important when interest arbitration is the last step in the bargaining process because only mandatory subjects of bargaining may generally be referred to interest arbitration.[51]

Where the obligation to bargain exists, it has importance, not only when negotiations for an actual contract are being conducted, but also during the term of the contract and after the contract expires. The obligation to bargain is continual, a characteristic that can significantly limit an employer's flexibility in making certain decisions. If a matter is a mandatory subject for bargaining, an employer cannot make changes in past practices affecting the matter without first negotiating with the labor organization representing its officers.[52] This restriction applies whenever a labor organization has been certified as the bargaining representative for employees. The continuing duty to bargain can even invalidate an employer's efforts to change its past practices through enacting a charter amendment.[53]

Two cases from the state of Washington provide a good example of this so-called continuing duty to bargain. In one case, the collective bargaining agreement covering a city police department had expired when the employer decided to change from a fixed-shift system, in which shifts were selected by seniority, to a system in which shifts rotated every few months. In the second case, the employer made changes in the method of allocating standby assignments. Even though a contract was in effect at the time of the changes, the contract did not address the method of standby assignment allocation. In both cases, the employers were held to have committed unfair labor practices by making the changes without first negotiating with their respective unions. The Washington State **Public Employment Relations Commission** held that, absent a clear waiver of the union's right to bargain, the continuing duty to bargain prohibited the implementation of any changes in such mandatorily negotiable hours of work issues.[54]

A labor organization can waive the right to bargain over changes in past practices in one of two ways: by "inaction" and by "contract." A waiver by inaction occurs when the labor organization has knowledge that the employer intends to make a change in past practice (or has actually made such a change) but does not demand to bargain over the change in a timely manner.[55] Even a 6-week delay in demanding the right to bargain has been held to waive bargaining rights.[56] In order to have a labor organization's demand to bargain held untimely, the employer generally must establish that it provided actual and timely notice of its intended action.[57]

A waiver by contract exists when the labor organization has contractually given the right to the employer to make changes in mandatory subjects of bargaining. To be effective, "contract waivers" must be specific and clearly articulated. For example, a management rights clause that generally gives the employer the right to establish hours of work would likely not be specific enough to allow the employer the unilateral right to change work shifts or to change from fixed to rotating shifts.

For bargaining rights to exist mid-contract, the labor organization must establish that the past practice the employer is intending to change has been consistent and long-standing.[58] The labor organization must also establish that there has been an actual change in past practices in order to demand bargaining during the term of the contract. In one case, the police association in New York City was attempting to bargain over a department directive that banned "hog-tying" of suspects. The court ruled the directive was not negotiable because the labor association failed to prove the existence of a past practice that allowed hog-tying, resting its decision on testimony that hog-tying was not taught during training and on the word of the supervisor of the patrol force that, in 41 years of service, he had never seen hog-tying used in the department.[59] In addition, an employer's right to make changes in mandatory subjects of bargaining can also be limited by a collective bargaining agreement. Contractual clauses typically labeled "maintenance of benefits" or "existing conditions" forbid an employer from changing wages, hours, or working conditions. The contract covering Buffalo, New York police officers contains an example of such a clause:

All conditions or provisions beneficial to employees now in effect which are not specifically provided for in this Agreement or which have not been replaced by provisions of this Agreement shall remain in effect for the duration of this

Agreement, unless mutually agreed otherwise between the Employer and the Association.[60]

Maintenance of benefits clauses enhance a labor organization's ability to prevent changes in past practices. When under the general continuing duty to bargain, a labor organization has the ability to demand only that an employer bargain to impasse over changes in past practices that are mandatory negotiable; a maintenance of benefits clause allows a labor organization simply to refuse to agree to the change, even if the employer is willing to bargain over the issue. This distinction is particularly important in states where the bargaining process does not culminate with binding arbitration but, instead, allows an employer to unilaterally implement its last best offer on a bargaining issue.

When a topic is mandatory for bargaining, the employer must negotiate about the topic with the labor organization, not with individual union members. For example, because discipline is mandatorily negotiable, an employer would violate its bargaining obligation if it entered into a "last chance" agreement with a troubled employee unless the employee's labor organization also was a party to the agreement.[61] This ban on one-on-one contracts with individual union members is a strong one and has invalidated a wide variety of employer agreements with individual union members, including the payment of a signing bonus,[62] a contract with the newly hired officers that they will repay the costs of their training if they quit to go to work for another law enforcement employer,[63] and an agreement with a probationary employee to extend the probationary period.[64]

ESTABLISHING THE BARGAINING RELATIONSHIP

The Process

Assuming the existence of a legal provision for collective negotiations, the process of establishing a bargaining relationship is straightforward, although fraught with the opportunity for disputes. The mere fact that most members of a police department belong to a single organization does not mean that it automatically has the right to represent its members for the purpose of collective bargaining.[65] Those eligible to be represented may, in fact, select an organization to which they already belong for this purpose, or they may select another one. This choice must be made, however, in ways that conform to the legislation providing the collective bargaining if the employee organization hopes to gain certification by the **Public Employment Relations Commission** (PERC).

The union begins an organizing drive, working to get 30 percent of the class or classes of employees it seeks to represent to sign authorization cards, of which Figure 11.2 is typical. Once this goal is reached, the union notifies the police department. An election is held, and the union must get 50 percent plus one officer to prevail. If management believes that the union has obtained a majority legitimately and that it is appropriate for the

FIGURE 11.2 ▶ A typical authorization card. *Source:* Reprinted with permission from the International Union of Police Associations.

class or classes of officers to be grouped together as proposed by the union, it will recognize the union as the bargaining agent of the officers that it has sought to represent. Once recognized by the employer, the union will petition the PERC or another body responsible for administering the legislation for certification. In such cases, the PERC does not check the authorization cards but only the appropriateness of the grouping of the officers. If the grouping is deemed appropriate by the PERC or a similar administrative body, then the employee organization is certified as the bargaining representative.

If the employee organization is not recognized by management, it can petition the PERC for an election; the petition must be accompanied by signed and dated representation cards from 30 percent of the group of employees the union seeks to represent. A secret vote is then held at the direction of the PERC, with the ballot including the union or unions that are contesting the right to represent the officers, along with the choice of no union. The union that receives a majority of the votes from among the officers who are eligible to be represented by the employee organization and who actually cast ballots is then certified. Alternately, a majority of those casting ballots might vote for no union. In the event that no majority is achieved, a runoff election is necessary.

The Opportunity for Conflict

In establishing the bargaining relationship, there is ample opportunity for disputes to develop. Management may undertake a campaign to convince officers they are better off without the union at the same time that the union is mounting its organizing drive. The employee organization may wish access to bulletin boards, meeting space, and mailing lists to publicize the advantages of unionizing to the officers, all of which management may not wish to provide. The decision as to what is an appropriate grouping of officers for the purposes of collective bargaining, technically referred to as "unit determination," is profoundly significant and one about which management and the union may have sharp differences.

Questions such as the following may arise: Are lieutenants part of management and therefore not eligible for representation by the union for purposes of collective bargaining? Should civilian radio dispatchers be part of the same bargaining unit as uniformed officers? Should detectives be in a bargaining unit by themselves? These decisions are important because they can affect the operation of the police department and can determine, to some degree, the dynamics of the employee organization. They can impact the scope of bargaining and affect the stability of the bargaining relationship, or they can even be decisive in the outcome of a representation election.[66]

Both the union and management are pragmatic when it comes to defining the appropriate bargaining unit. In general, both might prefer a broad unit, the union, because the numbers will give it strength, while management resists the proliferation of bargaining units because each one that is recognized officially must be bargained with separately. Here, too, despite a similar orientation, disputes can arise. The union may know that it has the support of only one category of employees (e.g., detectives) and seeks to represent them as a single bargaining unit.

Management may feel that particular union is too militant and, consequently, favors, as a part of a hidden agenda, the inclusion of detectives in a wider unit as a means of promoting the election of a more moderate union that is also seeking to represent employees. What constitutes an appropriate unit may be defined by state law. The most common method of unit determination, however, is for the PERC or a similar administrative body to make decisions on a case-by-case basis, applying certain criteria stipulated in the legislation.[67] Among the criteria often identified are the desires of the employees, the "community of interests" shared by the employees, the need to avoid creating too many bargaining units, the effects on efficiency of operations, and the history of labor relations in the police department.

NEGOTIATIONS

Selection of the Management and Union Teams

Figure 11.3 depicts a typical configuration of the management and union bargaining teams. The union's chief negotiator will usually not be a member of the bargaining unit; rather, he or she will be a specialist brought in to represent it.

This ensures a certain level of expertise, wider experience, an appropriate degree of objectivity, and an autonomy that comes from knowing, once the bargaining is over, he or she will not be working daily for the people sitting across the table. It is not automatic that the union president will be a member of the bargaining team, although customarily a union officer is, and often it is the president. Accompanying the union's chief negotiator and president will be two or three team members who have conducted in-depth research on matters relating to the bargaining issues and who will have various types of data, facts, and documents—such as wage and benefit surveys, trends in

the consumer price index, and copies of recent contracts for similarly sized jurisdictions—with them. Although there will be only several union research team members at the table, they will have had assistance in gathering their information from others in the union. Unless the union's chief negotiator is an attorney, there will seldom be an attorney sitting at the table with the union's team.

The chief negotiator for management may be the director of labor relations or the human resources director of the unit of government involved or may be a professional labor relations specialist. Some jurisdictions prefer the latter because, if there are acrimonious occurrences, once the bargaining is over the director of labor relations can step back into the picture and assume a relationship with the union that is unscarred by any incidents. The chief of police should not appear at the table personally, but a key member of the command staff who has his or her confidence should. The appearance of the chief at the table makes the task of leadership more difficult; to appear there on equal footing with the union's bargaining team on one day and then to step back atop the organizational hierarchy on the next requires greater adjustments by both the chief and the union members than the creation of any benefits associated with his or her presence are worth.

The way in which issues are presented, and the flexibility that both sides have, will impact strongly on how the bargaining sessions will go. Perhaps equally important are the decisions made as to who will represent each side at the table, and in what role. The proper training of all involved in the negotiation process is absolutely essential.

Personality Types to Be Avoided

There are certain personality types that should not be called upon to participate in the negotiation process. This includes individuals with "axes to grind," as well as those with sarcastic,

| Assistant City Manager (Legal Matters) | Human Resources Representative (HR Policy) | Lead Negotiator (City's Positions) | Scribe (Recorder) | Senior Police Commander (Chief's Representative) |

| Union Vice President (Union Policy/Research) | Union Secretary (Recorder) | Union Treasurer (Finance/Research) | Lead Negotiator (Union's Positions) | Union Executive Board Member (Financial Specialist) | Union Executive Board Member (Newest member-training for him/her) |

FIGURE 11.3 ▶ The management and union bargaining teams. Although the composition of management's and the union's bargaining teams varies somewhat from one jurisdiction to another and even within jurisdictions over time, the configuration shown here approximates the "typical" municipal situation. Occasionally, a member of the city council also sits in as an observer. Source: Courtesy of Chuck Foy, past president of the Arizona Conference of Police and Sheriffs Local 7077 and past president of the Peoria [Arizona] Police Officers Association.

acrid, or abrasive personalities. The purpose of bargaining is to produce a bilateral written agreement to which both parties will bind themselves during its lifetime. This is not only a profoundly important task but also one that is sufficiently difficult without including people on either side who have an agenda other than negotiating in good faith or whose personalities create yet another obstacle. For these reasons, management must exercise careful consideration in deciding who will represent the police department at the table and, if necessary, influence the selection of the city's other representatives.

Preparing for Negotiations

Management can ill afford to simply wait until the employee organization prepares its demands and presents them; effective action requires considerable effort on management's part before it receives the union's proposal. Management's negotiating team must be selected, agreement with the union obtained on the site where the negotiations will take place; the bargaining schedule established in conjunction with the union; and various types of data and information gathered, tabulated, and analyzed. Although final preparations for negotiating will begin several months before the first bargaining sessions, the preparation process is a continuous one; management should begin preparing for the next negotiations as soon as these are completed. The demands not obtained by the union in the past year may be brought up again in this year's bargaining sessions, and management should be prepared for this.

Various types of records should be kept and summaries made of such factors as the union membership; the types and outcomes of grievances; the costs of settling grievances; the numbers, kinds, and consequences of any contract violations by the employee organization; the subject matters brought before the union–management committee during the life of the expiring contract and the disposition of them; and the themes reflected in the union's newsletter. Additionally, just as the employee organization's bargaining team is doing, the management team must be familiarizing itself with changes in the consumer price index and the provisions of recent contracts in similarly situated jurisdictions and conducting its own wage and benefit survey or cooperating with the union on one.

From all of these sources, and others, it is essential that management do three things. First, it must develop fairly specific anticipations as to what the union will be seeking and the relative importance of each demand to the union. Second, it must develop its position with respect to the anticipated preliminary demands it believes the union will present. Third, it must develop the objectives it seeks to achieve during the forthcoming process of bilateral determination. If it is not already an institutionalized practice, arrangements should be made to have the union submit its demands in writing prior to the first scheduled round of negotiations. These demands may be submitted either in the form of a proposed contract or as a "shopping list," which simply lists the demands being made. The presentation of the demands in writing before the first bargaining session allows for a more productive use of the time allotted for the first negotiating session.

If management has done a good job, there will be relatively few surprises when the proposed contract is submitted. Surprises do not indicate that management's preparation was wasted; the knowledge gained through the process of anticipating the union's demands adds to the negotiating team's depth of understanding and overall confidence, key ingredients of bargaining table success. It is difficult to know precisely when management's bargaining team is prepared, but the employee organization will easily detect and capitalize on a lack of preparation.

The Negotiating Sessions

The publicity and attending atmosphere preceding the negotiating sessions focus considerable attention on them and can be barometers of or may influence how the sessions unfold. However, prebargaining publicity is also part of attempts to influence public opinion, to impress the public or rank-and-file members with the city's or union's resolve, and to create a façade behind which both sides can maneuver for advantage. Thus, one should not be too encouraged or discouraged about the content of such publicity; it should be considered and evaluated but not relied on solely as an informational source.

The number of bargaining sessions can run from one to several dozen, lasting from 30 min to 10 or more hours, although half-day sessions are more common, depending on how close or far apart the union and management are when they begin to meet face to face. Traditionally, any means of making verbatim transcripts, such as the use of a stenographer or tape recorder, have generally been excluded from the bargaining sessions, as it was believed that they tended to impede the progress of negotiations because people would begin speaking for the record.

In a related vein, the enactment of Florida's "sunshine law" opened up many previously closed government meetings to the general public, including bargaining sessions, and stirred up some controversy. Advocates of the legislation argued it opened up government to the people, making it both more responsive and responsible. With respect to its application to collective negotiations, critics of the law maintained the real bargaining would be done secretly, the scheduled public bargaining sessions would be merely a ritualistic acting out of what had been agreed on privately, and real negotiating would be difficult because both sides would tend to "play to the audience." This last point is underscored by one negotiator's wry observation that bargaining under the sunshine law was like "a Roman circus with kibitzers."[68]

At the first meeting, friendly conversation might be passed across the table, or there may be merely strained greetings before the formal session begins. Much like the prenegotiations publicity, this may or may not reflect how the session will go. Friendly conversation might suggest that rapid and amicable bargaining will follow but instead no mutually acceptable positions will be reached because the friendly conversation has veiled only thinly the hostility or aggressiveness of one or both sides, which quickly comes to the fore. On the other hand, strained greetings might reflect the heavy responsibility each party to the negotiations feels, and quick progress may follow.

In the initial session, the chief negotiator for each party will make an opening statement; management's representative will often go first, touching on general themes, such as the need for patience and the obligation to bargain in good faith. The union's negotiator generally will follow this up by voicing support for such sentiments and will outline what the union seeks to achieve under the terms of the new contract. Ground rules for the bargaining may then be reviewed, modified as mutually agreed on, or developed. The attention then will shift to the terms of the contract that the union is proposing, and the contract will be examined thoroughly in a "walk-through," during which time management will seek to learn what the union means by particular wording. This is a time-consuming process but of great importance because both parties need to have a common understanding of what it is they are attempting to commit each other to, or there will be frequent unresolved conflicts and many complex and expensive grievances filed during the lifetime of the contract. For purposes of illustration, the union may have proposed that "vehicles will be properly maintained to protect the health and safety of officers." Discussion of this proposal may reveal that their expectations are much more specific:

1. This is to apply to all vehicles, including marked, semimarked, and unmarked.

2. Each patrol vehicle, whether marked, semimarked, or unmarked, will be replaced at 60,000 miles.

3. All vehicles will be equipped with radial tires.

4. Plexiglas protective shields will be installed between the front and rear seats.

5. Shotguns or rifles in locking mounts accessible from the front seat will be provided in all marked and semimarked cars.

6. First-aid kits of a particular type will be placed in all vehicles.

7. Comprehensive blood body fluid pathogen protection kits will be provided.

For bargaining purposes, the union will have categorized each clause in the proposed contract as being (1) "expendable," meaning that under certain circumstances it will be withdrawn as a symbol of good faith; (2) a "trade-off," indicating that it will be dropped as total or partial payment for obtaining some other benefit; (3) "negotiable," meaning that the benefit needs to be obtained in one form or another; and (4) "non-negotiable," meaning that the benefit is wanted exactly as proposed.[69] Management will study the information gained from the walk-through for several days and then both parties will return to the table. Management then will respond to the union's proposal by indicating which clauses it has (1) "accepted," (2) "accepted with minor modification," (3) "rejected," and (4) wished to make its own proposals and counterproposals. Management cannot simply reject a clause out of hand; to do so would not constitute bargaining in good faith. Instead, it must give a reason for the rejection that is reasonable, such as an actual inability to pay.

Having been told formally of management's position on the contract proposed, the bargaining begins, concentrating on the items upon which agreement can be reached immediately or fairly rapidly. Such an approach helps foster a spirit of mutualism that can be useful in dealing with the issues about which there are substantial differences. As bargaining enters the final stages, the issues that must be dealt with usually become fewer but also more difficult in terms of securing agreement.

At such points, "side trips" may threaten to make the sessions unproductive. These side trips might involve wild accusations, old recriminations, character assassinations, or discussion of a specific clause in philosophical or intellectual terms as a means of not dealing with the concrete realities that may be threatening and anxiety provoking for one or both parties. At these times, a caucus or even a slightly longer space of time than ordinary until the next session may give enough time for tempers to calm or for more perspective to be gained. At other times, the police union may feel the need to "up the stakes" by engaging in picketing as a form of political pressure.

Ultimately, unless a total impasse is reached, agreement will be obtained on the terms of a new contract. The union's membership will vote on the contract as a whole. If approved by the membership, the contract then goes before the necessary government officials and bodies, such as the legislative unit that appropriates the funds, for its approval.

GRIEVANCES

Why Grievances Are Inevitable

There is a notion that, once the bargaining is completed and an agreement signed, the most difficult part of labor relations has been passed through and easy times are ahead. Such a notion is natural. Bargaining is high drama, with a great deal of attention focused on it by the news media and the community. The production of an agreement acceptable to both the union and management is, in fact, a significant achievement. Beyond it, however, is the day-to-day administration of the contract during its lifetime. Because the contract outlines the duties and rights of each party in its dealings with the other, it is ironically the basis not only for accord but also for conflict:

It would, of course, be ideal for all concerned, including the public, if in the negotiation of the agreement both parties were able to draft a comprehensive document capable of foreseeing and forestalling all potential disputes which might arise during its life. Unfortunately, such crystal-ball vision is usually lacking, particularly when the parties are pressured to obtain agreement in a period of negotiation tensions and time deadlines. It is not humanly possible in a new collective bargaining relationship to draft such a perfect document.

Therefore, it is inevitable that questions will arise concerning the interpretation and application of the document drafted in the haste and pressure of contract negotiations. What is the meaning of a particular clause of the agreement? How does it apply, if at all, to a set of facts which occurred after the agreement was signed? These questions are not at all uncommon in any contractual relationship.[70]

The Definition of a Grievance

Whereas in common usage a **grievance** is a complaint or an expression of dissatisfaction by an employee with respect to some aspect of employment, what can be grieved formally is usually defined within the contract itself. Grievances may be limited to matters discussed specifically in the contract, that are primarily contract-related, or that pertain to the job, as is seen in these clauses from three different agreements:

1. A grievance is defined as a complaint arising out of the interpretation, application, or compliance with the provisions of this agreement.

2. For the purpose of this agreement, the term "grievance" shall mean the difference of dispute between any police officer and the city, or a superior officer in the chain of command, with respect to the interpretation, application, claim or breach, or violation of any of the provisions of this agreement, or with respect to any equipment furnished by the city.

3. A grievance, for our purposes, shall be defined as any controversy, complaint, misunderstanding, or dispute arising between an employee or employees and the City, or between the Brotherhood and the City.

The Grievance Procedure

The grievance procedure is a formal process that has been the subject of bilateral negotiations and is detailed in the contract. It involves seeking redress of the grievances through progressively higher levels of authority and most often culminates in binding arbitration by a tripartite panel or a single neutral. A typical sequence of steps includes the following:

Grievances shall be presented in the following manner and every effort shall be made by the parties to secure prompt disposition of grievances:

Step 1. The member shall first present his/her grievance to his/her immediate supervisor within 5 days of the occurrence which gave rise to the grievance. Such contact shall be on an informal and oral basis, and the supervisor shall respond orally to the grievance within 5 working days.

Step 2. Any grievance which cannot be satisfactorily settled in Step 1 shall be reduced to writing by the member and shall next be taken up by his/her division commander. Said grievance shall be presented to the division commander within 5 working days from receipt of the answer in Step 1. The division commander shall, within 5 working days, render his/her decision on the grievance in writing.

Step 3. Any grievance not satisfactorily settled in Step 2 shall be forwarded, in writing, within 5 working days to the chief of police, who shall render his/her written decision on the grievance within 5 working days.

Step 4. If the grievant is not satisfied with the response of the chief of police, he/she will forward his written grievance within 5 working days to the city manager, who will have 10 working days to reply, in writing.

Step 5. If the grievance has not been settled to the satisfaction of the grievant in Step 4, the matter will be subject to arbitration. An arbiter will be selected, without undue delay, according to the rules of the American Arbitration Association. The arbiter will hold an arbitration hearing. When the hearing has ended, the arbiter will be asked to submit his/her award, in writing, within 15 days. His/her decision shall be final and binding on both parties.[71]

Because the union must share equally the cost of arbitration with management, the decision to take a grievance to the last step is customarily the prerogative of the union rather than the individual officer who is grieved.

Enumerated in the agreement are not only the steps of the grievance procedure but also such matters as the manner of selecting the tripartite panel or the single neutral, along with their duties and powers. If the panel is used, management and the union each appoints one member, and those two appoint the third; where the two cannot agree on the neutral, the contract may provide for the referral of the choice of a chairperson to a designated agency,[72] such as the Federal Mediation and Conciliation Service, or a state agency. Where a single arbitrator is used, a variety of techniques are employed in selection, ranging from agreement on the person by the union and management on a case-by-case basis, to the appointment of a permanent arbitrator during the lifetime of the contract, to having an outside agency submit a list of qualified arbitrators from which management and the union take turns eliminating names until only one remains or they agree to accept any of some number remaining, such as three.

The arbitration hearing is quasi-judicial, with more relaxed rules of evidence than are found in either criminal or civil proceedings. The burden of proof is on the grieving party, except in discipline cases, where it is always on the employer. The parties may be represented by legal counsel at the hearing, and the format will generally include obtaining agreement on what the issue is, an opening statement by each side (with the grieving party going first), examination and cross-examination of witnesses, and closing arguments in the reverse of the order in which the opening statements were made.

Arbitration Issues and Decision Making

Despite the many types of matters that can be and are grieved, the largest single category of cases, about 90 percent of the total, brought to an arbitration hearing are those involving discipline against an officer. Some arbitration decision making is not difficult because one side, perhaps the union, chooses to take a losing case to arbitration, because of its symbolic importance, and the need to appear supportive of union members. This rationale can also be applied on management as well in order to show support for managers.

If an employee is found to have done what he or she has been accused of, the arbitrator may then consider certain factors that might mitigate the severity of the penalty, including the officer's years of service to the department; the provocation, if any, that led to the alleged offense; the officer's disciplinary history, including the number, types, and recency of other violations; the consistency with which the applicable rule is enforced; and the penalties applied for similar offenses by other officers.[73]

One study of arbitrated police grievances reveals that the officer involved in the grievance was assigned to uniformed patrol 84 percent of the time, another police officer was involved in the incident slightly more than half the time (56 percent of the cases), the grieving officer's supervisor supported him or her 14 percent of the time, and in exactly three-quarters of the cases the involved officer had a clean disciplinary record.[74] Given that police unions must be selective in terms of the cases they take to arbitration, the results are not too surprising: The union won 77 percent of the grievances.

A key advantage of arbitration is the speed with which issues are heard and a decision is made, as compared with seeking resolution of the dispute in court. The deadline for issuance of the award may be established by statute; the parties; a government authority, such as the PERC; the arbitrator, if he or she is acting as an independent; or the body appointing the arbitrator.[75] The AAA requires arbitrators to render their decisions in writing within 30 days of (1) the conclusion of the hearing; (2) the receipt of the hearing transcript, if one has been made; or (3) the receipt of posthearing briefs.[76] In general, except in such instances as fraud or bias by the arbitrator, the hearing officer's decision, where binding arbitration is provided for, will not be reviewed by the courts.

JOB ACTIONS

Job action is a label used to describe several types of activities in which employees may engage to express their dissatisfaction with a particular person, event, or condition or to attempt to influence the outcome of a matter pending before decision makers, such as a contract bargaining impasse. Job actions carry the signal, "We are here, organized, and significant, and the legitimacy of our position must be recognized." Four types of job actions are recognizable: the vote of confidence, work slowdowns, work speedups, and work stoppages.

The Vote of Confidence

The **vote of confidence**, which typically produces a finding of no confidence, has been used somewhat sparingly in law enforcement. Such a vote is how rank-and-file members signal their collective displeasure with the chief administrator of their agency. Although such votes have no legal standing, they

sometimes generate a great deal of negative publicity that causes a police chief to make a decision to resign.

Work Slowdowns

Although officers continue to work during a **work slowdown**, they do so at a leisurely pace, causing productivity to fall. As productivity drops, the unit of government employing the officers comes under pressure to restore normal work production. This pressure may be from within the unit of government itself. For example, a department may urge officers to write more tickets, so more revenue is not lost. Or citizens may complain to politicians and appointed leaders to "get this thing settled," so the police will answer calls more rapidly and complete the reports citizens need for insurance purposes. In New York City, police officers protesting stalled contract negotiations staged a ticket-issuing slowdown that resulted in a loss of $2.3 million in just two months. This action also produced strong conflict within the rank-and-file among officers who did and did not support the slowdown. In order to counter New York City Police Department pressure to stop the ticket slowdown, the Patrolmen's Benevolent Association—which represents the city's 29,000 officers—picketed outside traffic courts, denouncing what it called the administration's traffic ticket quota policy.[77]

The adoption of new technologies in a police department, intended to speed up police responses, also offers the opportunity to create a work slowdown. For example, several years ago before department-issued cell phones were regularly provided to police officers, 150 police officers in Alexandria, Virginia turned in their department-issued pagers to protest a pay scale that lagged behind those of neighboring jurisdictions. The pagers were used to call in off-duty officers in specialized units, such as homicide and hostage negotiations, when needed. Detective Eric Ratliff, president of Local 5, International Union of Police Associations, said, "I won't sugar-coat it. The response time of specialized units . . . will be slower. What this does is take us back to the early '80s, before we had pagers, which is basically where our pay is."[78] In East Hartford, Connecticut, the police union contract approved by the city council included a provision to pay officers required to carry pagers an extra $1,500 annually, avoiding the wholesale return of pagers that Alexandria experienced.[79]

Work Speedups

Work speedups are an acceleration of activity, resulting in the overproduction of one or more types of police services. The purpose is to create public pressure on elected and appointed government leaders to achieve a union-desired goal. The purpose of a work speedup may be to protest a low pay increase proposed by the employer, to force the employer to make more or particular concessions at the bargaining table, or to pressure the employer to abandon a policy change that adversely affects union members. Examples of speedups include "ticket blizzards" and sudden strict enforcements of usually ignored minor violations, such as jaywalking, littering, or smoking in prohibited areas. The intent with this type of job action is to so anger the public that citizens will direct their hostility toward public officials—via angry e-mails, phone calls, letters, etc.—who are likely to be in a position to solve or at least ameliorate the problem so the issue causing their dissatisfaction can be resolved politically in their favor.

Work Stoppages

The ultimate **work stoppage** is the strike, which is the withholding of *all* of labor's services. This tactic is most often used by labor in an attempt to force management back to the bargaining table when negotiations have reached an impasse. However, strikes by public employees are now rare. In 1969, public employee strikes peaked at 412.[80] Today, there are fewer than 50 a year and police strikes by police unions have all but disappeared in the past 30 years. The reasons for the sharp decline in strikes include the extension of collective bargaining rights to many public employees, state laws prohibiting strikes, the fines that may be levied against striking unions and employees, and the fact that striking employees may be fired. In 1981, President Ronald Reagan fired 11,000 air traffic controllers and it remains a potent lesson for unionists. Additionally, the climate starting in the 1990s and continuing today has not been favorable to unionism. This is so because of the growing conservatism in this country and the view that the unions are adept at getting what they want at "our expense" are also factors that make both private and public unions less likely to strike.[81] In states where public-sector bargaining is not allowed, tough laws affecting strikers have made public employees think long and hard before striking. Even in those states, many public employers know what they have to do in order to reap the benefits of a well-trained and seasoned workforce, and they do so to prevent the labor unrest that would impede economic development. Companies are not likely to relocate to cities that cannot govern effectively, for example, manage their own workforce well. Without these relocations, a city's budget becomes increasingly tight because tax revenue is flat or falling; residents and business are hit with increased and new taxes, and they begin to leave to find more hospitable locations in which to live and work.

Briefer work stoppages may affect only specialized assignments or involve a large number of police officers but not all of them. Epidemics of the **blue flu**, as they are often characterized, can last only a few days. Work stoppages of this type are an important police labor tactic. While, like strikes, these briefer collective actions may be intended to force management back to the table, they are also used occasionally to punctuate the extreme displeasure of officers with a policy (e.g., one unreasonably restricting moonlighting by officers) or with particular actions by officials inside and outside the department (e.g., the decision of a district attorney to prosecute a police officer on what is seen as a public image-enhancing but "thin" case).

Police Unions: The Political Context

Although union job actions frequently center on economic factors, unions also take stances on other issues. In the 1990s, in Washington, DC, Ron Robertson, president of the local Fraternal Order of Police, asked the federal government to take over the police department because the public and officers were in a "killing field."[82] Two days prior to Robertson's request, an officer working alone was shot four times and killed as he sat in his patrol car at a traffic light outside a nightclub. The city's inability to staff two officers to a car had been a continuing union concern.

While contract negotiations were ongoing between the state and the State Police Association of Massachusetts (SPAM), the association opted at the last minute not to air an ad that blamed (now former governor) Governor Weld for the death of a state trooper gunned down by a convicted murderer who had been released early by the parole board. In the midst of the state–SPAM negotiations, Governor Weld reappointed one of the members of the parole board. This member had voted for the murderer's early release, prompting the preparation of the ad. Despite the fact that the ad was not aired, a controversy ensued. Weld aides asserted the union's tactics were designed to make the governor capitulate to the union's demands, and one of the governor's political allies, a state senator, called the ad "the lowest." The union responded by stating the state senator was "intruding into the collective bargaining process and acting beyond his realm."[83]

When Riverside County, California deputies beat two suspected undocumented Mexican immigrants after a well-documented high-speed chase seen on the evening news, the AFL-CIO took strong exception. AFL-CIO Executive President Linda Chavez-Thompson said, "The movement will not tolerate this kind of brutality, nor will we excuse officers because the situation [was] volatile. . . . This is not a question of immigration rights, but of basic civil and human rights."[84]

The Lautenberg Amendment to the federal "Brady Bill" gun control legislation retroactively denies anyone convicted of a domestic violence misdemeanor from having a gun. When applied to police officers and federal agents, this law ends their careers. Women's rights groups have supported the law because it denies a firearm to "cops who batter." Police unions have been angered by the retroactive application of the law, claiming it is unfair to take away an officer's livelihood with no advance notice. The Grand Lodge of the Fraternal Order of Police filed a lawsuit challenging the constitutionality of the law, a move supported by a number of unions, including the Detroit Police Officers Association.

Police unions also use high-visibility, high-impact tactics to further their objectives. Fraternal Order of Police Lodge 89 in Prince George's County, Maryland, spent $7,000 to erect billboards assailing what they saw as County Executive Wayne Curry's inaction on rising crime and an understaffed police department. Other police unions have used radio stations to broadcast 30- to 60-second messages designed to "bring heat" on politicians by mobilizing the public to their side. Some police unions also have in-state toll-free numbers that can be automatically connected to the offices of key legislators, so members can lobby for their bills. When a sheriff spoke against the FPBA before a legislative committee, the FPBA campaigned against him in the next election; the incumbent was defeated, thus showing strong political muscle by the union.

Administrative Reaction to Job Actions

Anticipatory Strategies There are no simple answers for what police administrators should do in the face of a job action. A short period of ignoring a work slowdown may see its natural dissipation, or it may become more widespread and escalate. Disciplinary action can effectively end a job action, or it might simply aggravate the situation further, causing the job action to intensify and become more protracted. In choosing a course of action, one must read the environment, assess the situation, review alternatives, decide on a course of action, implement it, monitor the impact, and make adjustments as necessary. In short, it is a decision-making process, albeit a delicate one.

The best way to handle job actions is for both management and the union to take the position that they have mutual responsibilities to avoid job actions. This may not, however, be uniformly possible; a union leadership that is too cooperative with management might, for example, be discredited by rank-and-file members or negotiations fall short of militant union members, however unrealistic, may result in job actions, such as a sick out.[85]

Among the steps that can facilitate the bargaining process and reduce the possibility of labor strife are the following:

- The appropriate city officials (both appointed and elected), union leaders, and management must be trained in the tenets and practices of collective bargaining, particularly as they relate to mutual trust and the obligation to bargain in good faith.

- Formal and informal communications networks should be used freely within city government, the police agency, and the union for the transmission of messages between them. The timely sharing of accurate information is essential to good labor relations in that it reduces the opportunity for misinformation or non-information to create distance and build barriers.

- On a periodic basis, key managers from the police department, along with the staff and its labor relations unit, should meet with union leaders and the representatives, including elected officials, of the city who are responsible for the implementation of its labor relations program. This strengthens existing communications networks, it allows new networks to open, and it is a continuing affirmation of the mutualism that is central to the process of collective bargaining.

- Well before any job actions occur, management must develop and publicize the existence of a contingency plan that contemplates as many of the problems as reasonably can be foreseen with respect to each type of job action. For example, in planning for a job action, one must consider such things as how the rights and property of those not participating in the job action will be protected.[86] What security measures are to be invoked for government buildings and property? What are the minimum levels of personnel and supplies required? What special communications arrangements are necessary? Does the city's insurance cover potential liabilities to employees and property? What legal options exist, who has authority to invoke them, and under what circumstances? What coordination arrangements are needed with other police departments and government agencies? What effect will various job action policies have on labor relations after the job action? How will nonparticipating officers and the public react to various policies? Can an employee participating in the job action who is injured on the picket line be placed on sick leave? Do such employees accrue sick leave and retirement credit for the time they are out?

- In attempting to determine the possibility of various job actions, management must assess the philosophy, capabilities, strengths, weaknesses, and propensities of the union—its officers, negotiators, legal counsel, and members. That, along with an estimate of the financial resources of the union, will be useful in anticipating the actions in which it is likely to engage and toward which planning can be directed. Although the hallmark of good planning is that it provides for future states of affairs, management is most likely to underestimate the union's capabilities, and the planning bias should therefore be toward an overstatement of what is possible.

During the Job Action

Police managers must appreciate the long-range implications of any job action such as the "blue flu." The officers involved in the job action are engaging, as is the employer, in a power struggle that has an economic impact on both parties. The union is not attempting to divest itself of its employer, and for both legal and practical reasons, the employer cannot unilaterally rid itself of its relationship with the union; at some point in the very near future, it is most likely that they will resume their former relationship.[87] Considering this, managers must be temperate in their private and public remarks regarding officers involved in the job action; emotionally laden statements and cynical characterizations regarding these individuals may provide a degree of fleeting satisfaction, but at some cost to the rapidity with which antagonisms can be set aside and the organization restored to its normal functioning. The union leadership and the rank-and-file membership have the same obligation; in the face of either management or the union not fulfilling its obligation, it becomes even more important that the other side be restrained in its remarks, or the ensuing trail of recriminations and biting comments will lead only to hostility and a degeneration of goodwill, both of which will have negative effects on future relations.

Maintaining a Fair and Balanced Posture Managers should strive to maintain a fair and balanced posture on the subject of the job actions, and their dominant focus should be on ending it. In addition, the following points should be noted:

- No reaction to a job action should be taken without first anticipating the consequences of a reaction from the union and the officers involved. For example, the decision to seek an injunction ordering the officers to terminate the action and return to work could result in the officers disobeying the order and forcing a confrontation with the court issuing the order. A public statement that all officers involved in the action will be fired places the chief in the difficult position after the conflict is terminated of either firing participating officers or losing credibility with his or her employees.

- All management responses to a job action should be directed toward terminating it only, not toward an ulterior purpose, such as trying to "bust" the union. There have been job actions in which the employer's real objective was to destroy the union, an objective that frequently results in aggravated hostility between the employer and the union, between the chief and the officers participating in the action, and among the officers themselves. The long-range effect of this approach is to injure the morale of the police department, affecting the quality of police services and ultimately the service to the public.[88]

For a department whose workforce is depleted by a job action, personnel are a scarce resource, and not to invest in communications efforts is a natural temptation tinged heavily by the reality of other needs that must also be considered. To be borne in mind, however, is the perspective that the effective use of some personnel in communications efforts may shorten the job action.

It is essential during a job action that communications be rapid, accurate, consistent, and broadly based. Employees not participating in the job action can be kept informed by the use of the daily bulletin, briefings, or other devices. Letters can be sent to the homes of job action officers, informing them of the applicable penalties for their actions, the status of negotiations, and management's present position with respect to these issues. Facsimile letters for this and other actions should already have been prepared as part of the development of the contingency plan.

Personal appearances by police managers before neighborhood groups, professional associations, civic clubs, and similar bodies can be useful in maintaining calmness in the community, in providing one means of informing the public of special precautionary measures they can take to protect themselves, and in galvanizing public opinion for management's position. Care must be taken to ensure that in this effort the needs of lower-socioeconomic groups are not overlooked. Special attention must be given to how they will be informed and how their needs will be listened to.

In the Aftermath At some point, the job action will collapse or an agreement will be reached, or both sides will agree to return to the bargaining table on the return of personnel to the job. Often, a tense atmosphere will prevail for some time. Employees who did not participate in the job action will resent any threats made and any damage to their personal property. Those who walked out will view those who continued to work as not having helped maintain the solidarity necessary for effective job actions. Union members dissatisfied with what the job action did or did not produce may engage in the petty harassments of nonparticipants, display thinly veiled contempt for management, or surreptitiously cause damage to city property. Management's posture during the job action can in part reduce the tensions inherent in the post job action adjustment period, but it cannot eliminate the need for responsible action by the union or overcome the intransigence of a subversely militant union.

As soon as an agreement ending the job action is reached, a joint statement with the union should be released, announcing the settlement and highlighting its key features, and letters should be sent to the homes of all officers, urging them to put aside the matter and return to the business of public service with renewed commitment. All personnel in the department should take particular care not to discriminate between those who were involved in the job action and those who were not.

Other items of business that must be handled after a job action relate to whether the employees participating are to be disciplined, although the union will typically insist on amnesty for all involved officers as a precondition to returning to the job; in addition, it must be determined what disciplinary measures are to be taken against those who destroyed private or public property during the course of the job action; what measures are to be taken against those who undertook various actions against officers who did not participate; and the securing of a union commitment not to act in any way against those employees who did not participate and to actively discourage such actions by union members.

There has been some experimentation with reconciliation meetings of parties to promote goodwill. Experience has demonstrated that, in most cases, the wounds are so fresh and the feelings so intense that it simply creates the opportunity for an incident. In one notable instance, a reconciliation party resulted in each of the groups remaining separated for 2 hours. Finally when each group reached the buffet table, a fight broke out.[89]

LABOR-MANAGEMENT RELATIONS IN THE FACE OF FUNDING CUTBACKS

In the wake of the recent economic crisis and cuts in government funding, police departments have had to seriously reevaluate the way they operate. Many police chiefs do not see the budget cuts of the past few years as a temporary inconvenience but rather as a "new normal."[90]

Quick Facts: A Paradigm Shift Because of Budget Cutbacks

In the past, police agencies in many jurisdictions were immune to budget-cutting even when other government agencies were being cut because no elected official wanted to be seen as a politician whose decisions resulted in the firing of police officers. But the "new normal" is that police department budgets are no longer considered untouchable, and in many cities, police departments account for the largest share of municipal operating spending. Therefore, when the most recent economic crisis hit, politicians realized that police budgets, like all other budgets, had to be carefully re-examined for possible reductions.

Setting New Priorities

Many police chiefs are faced with significant cuts in funding while at the same time having enormous responsibilities, such as combating terrorism. Many of these chiefs have decided that keeping patrol officers is their top priority, so they have been forced to cut what some consider "special programs," such as community policing initiatives and special units that focus on gangs or drug crime. This is one of the types of decisions that must be made in response to communities' growing fiscal crises. However, others have resisted that trend, believing that the huge gains in crime fighting that occurred during the 1990s and 2000s were as a direct result of the community policing and problem-oriented policing programs.

Some police chiefs are also looking at the state of policing from a broader perspective and are asking whether the police are "pricing themselves out of the market." This is so because some community services that have been traditionally provided by the police agencies are increasingly being taken over by the private security industry, at a lower cost.[91]

Other police chiefs are, for example, trying to cope with budget cuts by making their departments more efficient by using technology as a force-multiplier. Some communities have made the decision to consolidate their police departments with larger agencies while others have completely abolished their police departments and made a decision to contract for police services with their state police or local sheriff's department. Others are discussing possible changes in the entire mission of police agencies. Thus, there has been a good deal of new thinking about what the police should do and how they should do it. Police managers are also carefully analyzing every dollar that is spent, and there is a greater sense of urgency about ensuring that police resources are being allocated efficiently.

A New Reality Regarding Budgets

Today, chiefs and union officials understand that they share the common goal of protecting the public and wanting officers to be as effective as possible. At the same time, some previously negotiated collective bargaining agreements may have established benefits and working conditions that are problematic in today's more austere economic times. Therefore, when a mayor, city manager, or city council instructs a police chief to start making plans for a 5- or 10-percent budget cut, the chief may, for example, try to convince the police union to help achieve the savings

by asking officers to contribute more to their retirement fund and/or agreeing to reduce pay and benefits. In this way, the chief may be able to avoid making layoffs while still maintaining the strength of the workforce. However, sometimes even a union's willingness to accept these reductions may not be sufficient to meet the externally imposed budget cuts. For example, recently San Jose, California police budget cuts forced the layoffs of 66 officers because of a $115 million budget shortfall. This was so even though the police union had agreed to a 10-percent pay cut. However, the savings were not sufficient enough to avoid the layoff of an additional 156 officers[92] (see Figure 11.4). The only positive news was that because of the high quality of San Jose, California police officers dozens of these police officers that were laid off were hired by other California police departments who were not facing the same economic crisis that San Jose was.

Nevertheless, not all unions are so inclined and some take the position that management should not be asking workers to give back benefits they worked so hard to obtain. In some cases, a majority of union members, especially those with seniority, prefer to keep all of the benefits they have negotiated, even if it results in recently hired officers having to be laid off.

Similarly, a chief facing budget cutbacks may wish to reassign employees from one unit to another, or change their shifts, or make other decisions that the chief believes are in the best interest of the departments' overall effectiveness and efficiency. But a union may refuse to compromise on work rules negotiated in the past.[93]

In other cases, retired police officers have seen their pensions dramatically reduced because their communities were no longer able to meet their fiscal obligations.

SPECIFIC RECOMMENDATIONS ON HOW BEST TO DEAL WITH BUDGET REDUCTIONS

A meeting with police executives and labor officials was held by the Police Executive Research Forum (PERF). The goal was to determine how they were dealing with some of the Draconian cuts that they were being forced to make. Following are some summaries of their reactions to these cuts as well as how they are addressing them.[94]

FIGURE 11.4 ▶ San Jose, California police officers display collective sadness and support for one of their officers who as just notified he was being laid off as a result of budget cuts. (Patrick Tehan/Mercury News)

Los Angeles, CA Assistant Chief Michel Moore:

You Cannot Eliminate 800 Employees and Be as Effective as You Were Before

In Los Angeles, we have eight bargaining units. The primary one is for officers but there are also separate unions for our command officers and our civilian work force. Our civilian work force has taken a huge hit during the economic downturn. About two and a half years ago, we had 3,600 civilian employees, but those numbers have since been reduced to 2,800, and these 800 positions were not just vacant positions that had not been filled.[95]

We know we cannot eliminate 800 people and continue to be as efficient and effective as we have been before. For example, backlogs are developing and service delays are being encountered. Service curtailment is something we have been looking at for the last couple of years. We will continue to strategize and prioritize about what police services we can cut. We now have to operate within a framework of this a "new normal" in terms of the type of work we can provide to the city.

Columbus, OH Deputy Chief Tim Becker:

We Have Cut Civilian Jobs, and Have Been Forced to Move Officers into Those Roles

With all the agencies being downsized, I think we need to look at what part of our job we can afford to cut. We are trying to do as much as we were doing a year ago, but we have 120–130 fewer officers today than we had this time last year. So assuming we were being efficient last year, we cannot continue carrying out all our responsibilities with the same level of efficiency.

We have also had to cut a lot of civilian positions. Generally, politicians like to keep the number of sworn officers up but they do not talk about keeping the number of civilians up. This is so even though many civilians are performing very crucial roles within our agencies. We have had to move sworn officers into these roles, but they are probably less efficient at performing some of these tasks. Also they cost more because of higher salaries, as well as leaving fewer officers available to act in an enforcement capacity.[96]

Quick Facts: Communities File for Bankruptcy and Pensions Are Going Up in Smoke

Some cities are now unable to pay pensions of retirees. In a drastic move that wipes out the contracts of police, firefighters, teachers, and other town employees. Cuts have been made in pension checks by as much as 50 percent. The small Rhode Island town of Central Falls found itself unable to pay for retiree pensions and health care premiums and filed for bankruptcy with U.S. Bankruptcy Court in Boston.[97] Other cities filing bankruptcy include San Bernardino and Stockton, California, and Jefferson County, Alabama. In 2013, Detroit became the largest city to declare bankruptcy, which was based on debts totaling $7 billion.[98]

Philadelphia, PA Commissioner Chuck Ramsey:

Budget Cuts May Be Imposed, But We Still Must Get the Job Done

I am not anti-union at all. But I do think that we have to find some common ground in this climate of a significant economic downturn. The labor issue that is probably most problematic and of concern to me is operational flexibility—the ability to deploy people as you need them, at the time that you need them. People will tell you, "Sure, you can do that"—but at time-and-a-half, at double-time-and-a-half, at pay levels we cannot afford. Ninety-seven percent of the police budget in Philadelphia is for personnel. That leaves me 3 percent to do everything else.

When budgets are tightened, there will be cuts in certain overtime categories. The increased cost of overtime payment is one area in which we have taken a tremendous hit in our budget. But when you have a smaller force to work with, the only way to deliver high-quality service is to have the limited number of officers available to work overtime. It puts you in a terrible position when you have to make these cuts but still have to get the job done.

Having said all that, I will add that I would still rather have a small, well-trained, well-equipped police force than a very large, ill equipped and poorly trained police department.

Camden, NJ Deputy Chief Mike Lynch:

We Need to Remember that We Are Public Servants Working for the Community

To overcome some of the challenges we are facing, I think it is important to have a discussion about the "market value" of the police, how we market to our constituency, and who that constituency is. We are clearly losing the battle of public perception, particularly when it comes to issues like pension reform. Immediately after 9/11, there was no doubt that public opinion of police officers spiked upward but that has since subsided.

The fact is that we are currently being viewed by some as greedy public servants who want more and want to give less. So our conversations about this needs to continue. The good news is that if we put our heads together as a team, we can develop a clearly, defined message that transforms the public perception into something that will benefit everyone.

In other words, we cannot lose focus of why we are here. We have talked a lot about contracts, salaries, pensions, and benefits, all of which are very important issues that affect everybody from a Commissioner down to the newest officer in your organization. However, we need to make sure that we do not lose focus of why we are here to begin with, which is to work as police officers and as public servants, serving the community.

Darryl Clodt, Sergeant at Arms, Las Vegas, NV Police Protective Association:

Labor and Management Must Come Together to Fight for Funding

I think one measure of our success is being able to help elect people in government who are going to vote for our needs and be there to support the issues of greatest concern to us.

Our economy is weak and our property taxes are down almost 25 percent. The lost tax revenue takes away a quarter of our operating budget. It is difficult and we have recognized that. Over the last several years, we have had to make some concessions.

The prior union leaders are going to be remembered for the agreements they reached that have given us what we have today. I will be remembered—for what we will be able to hang on to for our membership.

I think we may have to change our thinking and not view our interactions as a battle but rather change our philosophy to one in which labor and management stand together to accomplish the mutual objectives of servicing the public.

Chapter Summary

Summary by Learning Objectives

1. **Identify the seven significant factors that led to public sector collective bargaining.**

   These significant forces were (1) the needs of labor organizations, (2) the reduction of legal barriers, (3) police frustration with the perceived lack of support for their war on crime," (4) personnel practices in police agencies, (5) salaries and benefits, (6) violence directed at the police, and (7) the success of other groups.

2. **Discuss the ways in which police unions impact the community.**

   It Can Impact on Discipline and Accountability
   Police unions play a role in reinforcing the norms of police subculture. One of the most important aspects of this involves the **code of silence**, which results in

the refusal of officers to testify against other officers who are accused of misconduct.

It Can Impact on the Police Subculture
We can formulate three tentative hypotheses regarding the relationship of police unions to the police subculture: (1) the police subculture is a multi-dimensional phenomenon, of which the police union is only one aspect or influence; (2) there are great differences in the informal cultures among police departments, and the relative influence of the police union varies from department to department; and (3) the differences in local police subcultures have some significant and measurable difference in all aspects of policing, including overall management practices, accountability and discipline, police officer interactions with citizens, and local politics.

It Can Impact of City or County Finances

Until the most recent funding cutbacks faced by many communities, police unions have been generally successful in negotiating good salary and fringe benefit packages for their members. The resulting contract provisions undoubtedly have some significant impact on the finances of cities and counties. The nature of this impact is not known, however. It is believed that police (and sometimes firefighters) negotiations set the standard for negotiations by other municipal employees, although this proposition has not been researched. It is not known to what extent negotiated police salaries and benefits force cities and counties to reduce expenditures for other services such as streets, parks, and libraries.

It Can Impact on Local Politics

Police unions are well-organized, may have substantial financial resources, and possess political clout. Police unions regularly endorse or oppose political candidates for office, support or oppose proposed ordinances or referenda, and influence city or county budgets.

3. **Explain briefly the differences between the three models of collective bargaining.**

Binding Arbitration Model

In the binding arbitration model, public employees are granted the right to select exclusive representatives for the purposes of bargaining with their employees. In such states, the public employer and the labor organization are required to bargain in good faith until impasse, then to submit any unresolved disputes known as "interest arbitration," in which a neutral third party selected by the parties makes a final and binding resolution of those issues.

Meet and Confer Model

There are variations in meet and confer models, but most commonly they permit governmental employer and the employees representative to meet and discuss "permissible" topics, such as wages, benefits, and working conditions. Some topics, such as pensions, may be specifically excluded from discussions. The governmental employer has the final decision on any topics discussed and there is no neutral impasse resolution mechanism.

Bargaining Not Required Model

The third model for police-sector collective bargaining laws, the **bargaining not required model**, is found in states that do not statutorily require or, in some cases, allow collective bargaining for law enforcement officers.

4. **Identify who generally serves on management and union teams during negotiations.**

On the Management Team: Assistant City Managers (Legal Matters); Human Resources Representative (HR Policy); Lead Negotiator (City's Positions); Scribe (Recorder); Senior Police Commander (Chief's Representative).

On the Union Team: Union Vice President (Union Police Research); Union Secretary (Recorder); Union Treasurer (Finance/Research); Lead Negotiator (Union's Positions); Union Executive Board Member (Financial Specialist); Union Executive Board Member (Newest member—training for him/her).

5. **Describe the four potential major types of job actions a police union can take and the appropriate administrative actions that can be taken in response by police administrators.**

The Vote of Confidence

Such a vote is how rank-and-file members signal their collective displeasure with the chief administrator of their agency. Although such votes have no legal standing, they sometimes generate a great deal of negative publicity that causes a police chief to make a decision to resign.

Work Slowdown

Although officers continue to work during a slowdown, they do so at a leisurely pace, causing productivity to fall. As productivity drops, the unit of government employing the officers comes under pressure to restore normal work production. This pressure may be from the unit of government itself.

Work Speedups

Work speedups are an acceleration of activity, resulting in the overproduction of one or more types of police services. The purpose is to create public pressure on elected and appointed government leaders to achieve a union-desired goal.

Work Stoppages

The ultimate work stoppage is the strike, which is the withholding of *all* of labor's services. This tactic is most often used by labor in an attempt to force management back to the bargaining table when negotiations have reached an impasse. However, strikes by public employees are now rare.

6. **Understand why many police departments around the country are facing funding cutbacks.**

In the wake of the recent economic crisis and cuts in government funding, police departments have had to seriously reevaluate the way they operate. Many police chiefs do not see the budget cuts of the last few years as a temporary inconvenience but rather as a "new normal."

Chapter Review Questions

1. What were the consequences of the Boston Police Strike of 1919 on the efforts by the police to organize?
2. What three hypotheses have been formulated to explain the relationship between the police unions and the police subculture?
3. What are considered unfair labor practices?
4. Explain the process involved in establishing the bargaining relationship.
5. What personality types should not be part of the bargaining team on either side?
6. What steps are involved in the grievance process?
7. Describe five anticipatory strategies police administrators can employ to reduce the possibility of job actions.
8. What have been some of the most significant effects of the reduction of funding for law enforcement agencies?

Critical Thinking Exercises

1. **Mandatory Wearing of Body Armor.** Most police departments have a mandatory policy which requires their officers to wear department-issued body armor. However, there are some officers who are resisting it because they say it is too hot, too uncomfortable, and it limits their upper body mobility.

   a. What course of action should a chief take if an officer will not wear body armor no matter how many times he/she is told to wear it?
   b. If the police chief decides to take disciplinary action against an officer to force compliance to wear the body armor, will the union have a legal grievance claiming that it should not be mandatory?
   c. What arguments would you provide to these reluctant officers to convince them that it is in their best interest to wear the body armor?
   d. If an officer is not wearing body armor and is shot and killed in the line of duty, should the benefits his or her family would have derived be withheld?

2. **Police Officers' Statutory Bill-of-Rights.** There has been an increase in concerns by police unions in your state that the rights of law enforcement officers are not always observed in the internal officer investigation process. The police unions in the state generally believe that what it needed is a statutory bill-of-rights specifically for police officers.

   a. You are to review the existing statutory bill-of-rights of the following states: California, Delaware, Florida, Illinois, Louisiana, Maryland, Minnesota, Nevada, New Mexico, Rhode Island, and Wisconsin.
   b. When you complete your review, you are to identify which elements of each of these statutory bill-of-rights you feel would provide the best balance to protect managerial prerogatives, while at the same time providing protection for the individual rights of police officers.

Key Terms

bargaining not required model
binding arbitration
blue flu
code of silence
collective bargaining

grievance
job action
meet and confer model
Public Employment Relations
   Commission

vote of confidence
work slowdowns
work speedups
work stoppages

EndNotes

[1]These themes are identified and treated in detail in Hervey A. Juris and Peter Feuille, *Police Unionism* (Lexington, MA: Lexington Books, 1973).

[2]Data 360; http://www.data360.org/dsg.aspx?Data_Set_Group_Id=228 (accessed June 21, 2015).

[3]Gerald Mayer, "Union Membership Trends in the United States," *Congressional Research Service*, p. CRS -10, August 31, 2004; http://digitalcommons.ilr.cornell.edu/cgi/viewcontent.cgi?article=1176&context=key_workplace (accessed June26, 2015).

[4]Union Members Summary, Economic News Release, Department of Labor, Bureau of Labor Statistics, January 23, 2015, p. 1; http://www.bls.gov/news.release/union2.nr0.htm (accessed June 26, 2015).

[5]Ibid.

[6]Steven Greenhouse, "Share of the Work Force in a Union Falls to a 97-Year Low, 11.3%," *The New York Times*, January 23, 2013; http://www.nytimes.com/2013/01/24/business/union-membership-drops-despite-job-growth.html?_r=0 (accessed June 26, 2015).

[7]Loc. Cit., with additions by the authors. National Right to Work Legal Defense Foundation; http://www.nrtw.org/b/rtw_faq.htm (accessed June 26, 2015).

[8]Ibid.

[9]Robert M. Folgeson, *Big-City Police* (Cambridge, MA: Harvard University Press, 1977), 193–195.

[10]Public Service Research Council, *Public Sector Bargaining and Strikes* (Vienna, VA: Public Service Research Council, 1976), pp. 6–9.

[11]296 F. Supp. 1068, 1969.

[12]324 F. Supp. 315, N.D. Ga., 1971.

[13]483 F. 2d 966, 10th Circuit, 1973.

[14]President's Commission on Law Enforcement and Administration of Justice, *Task Force Report: The Police* (Washington, DC: U.S. Government Printing Office, 1967), p. 144.

[15]Ibid., p. 145.

[16]Suzannah Gonzales, "Opinion Poll: Confidence in Police Hits a 22-Year Low," *The Columbus Dispatch*, June 20, 2015; http://www.dispatch.com/content/stories/national_world/2015/06/20/confidence-in-police-hits-22-year-low.html (accessed June 26, 2015).

[17]From various tables, U.S. Department of Labor, *Employment and Earnings* 8, No. 4 (October 1961).

[18]Bureau of the Census, *Statistical Abstract of the United States, 1975* (Washington, DC: U.S. Government Printing Office, 1975), p. 162.

[19]John H. Burpo, *The Police Labor Movement* (Springfield, IL: Charles C Thomas, 1971), p. 34.

[20]Albert, *A Time for Reform*, p. 29. Several studies have reported that market forces other than unions explain better the rise in public employees' salaries than does union activity.

[21]The data were extracted from the Federal Bureau of Investigation's *Uniform Crime Reports* (Washington, DC: U.S. Government Printing Office, 1965, 1970).

[22]William W. Scranton, *Report of the President's Commission on Campus Unrest* (Washington, DC: U.S. Government Printing Office, 1970), p. 18.

[23]Samuel Walker, "The Neglect of Police Unions: Exploring One of the Most Important Areas of American Policing," *Police Practice and Research* 9, No. 2 (May 2008), pp. 102–107. (This discussion has been adapted from this source.)

[24]Christopher Commission, *Report of the Independent Commission to Investigate the Los Angeles Police Department* (Los Angeles, CA: City of Los Angeles, 1991), p. 120, available from http://www.parc.info; Human Rights Watch, *Shielded from Justice* (New York: Human Rights Watch, 1998); Mollen Commission Report (New York: Mollen Commission, 1994), p. 53, available from http://www.parc.info; J.H. Skolnick and J.J. Fyfe, *Above the Law* (New York: Free Press, 1993), pp. 108–112.

[25]H. A. Juris and P. Feuille, *Police Unionism* (Lexington: Lexington Books, 1973), pp. 142–145.

[26]K. Keenan and S. Walker, "An Impediment of Police Accountability? An Analysis of Statutory Law Enforcement Officers' Bill of Rights," *Boston University Public Interest Law Journal* 14 (2005), pp. 189–243.

[27]S. Walker, *Police Accountability: The Role of the Citizens Oversight* (Belmont, CA: Wadsworth, 2001).

[28]Christopher Commission, *Report of the Independent Commission*, 1991, pp. 97–106.

[29]B. Armacost, "Organizational Culture and Police Misconduct," *George Washington Law Review* 72 (2004), pp. 515–547.

[30]S. Greenberg, "Police Chief Selection and Survival: Looming Crisis in America's Major Police Departments," in *Police Labor-Management Relations* 1 Vol. 1, pp. 47–57 (Washington, DC: Office of Community Oriented Policing Services, Department of Justice, 2006), p. 51.

[31]J. H. Skolnick, *Justice Without Trial* (New York: MacMillan, 1994); W. Westley, *Violence and Police* (Cambridge, MA: MIT Press, 1970).

[32]S. Walker, "Racial Minority and Female Employment in Policing: The Implications of 'Glacial' Change," *Crime and Delinquency* 31, No. 4 (1985), pp. 555–572.

[33]S. Herbert, "Police Subculture Reconsidered," *Criminology* 36, No. 2 (1998), pp. 343–368.

[34]D. Weisburd et al., *Police Attitudes Toward Abuse of Authority: Findings from a National Study* (NCJ 181312) (Washington, DC: Department of Justice, 2000), available from http://www.njcrs.gov

[35]National Academy of Sciences, *Fairness and Effectiveness in Policing: The Evidence* (Washington, DC: National Academy Press, 2004), chap. 4; S. Walker and C. M. Katz, *The Police in America: An Introduction*, 6th ed. (New York: McGraw-Hall, 2008); S. Walker et. al., *The Color of Justice: Race, Ethnicity, and Crime in America*, 4th ed. (Belmont, CA: Wadsworth, 2007), chap. 4.

[36]Juris and Feuille, *Police Unionism*, pp. 53–55.

[37]President's Commission on Law Enforcement and Administration of Justice, *Task Force Report: The Police* (Washington, DC: Government Printing Office, 1967), pp. 163–178.

[38]D. L. Carter, *The State of Police Education* (Washington, DC: Police Executive Research Forum, 1989).

[39]Will Aitchison, *The Rights of Law Enforcement Officers*, 5th ed. (Portland, OR: Labor Relations Information Systems, 2004), pp. 8–11, 18–21. (This discussion and accompanying references were adapted from this source with permission.)

[40]See §423.231 et seq., Michigan Comp. Laws Annotated (West, 1994).

[41]*Hillsdale PBA v. Borough of Hillsdale*, 644 A. 2d 564 (N.J. 1994).

[42]*Municipality of Anchorage v. Anchorage Police Department Employee's Association*, 839 P.2d 1080 (Alaska 1992); *City and County of San Francisco*, 43 Cal. Rptr.2d 421 (Cal.App. 1995); *City of Detroit v. Detroit Police Officers' Association*, 294 N.W.2d 68 (Mich. 1980); *City of Richfield v. Local 1215, Intern. Ass'n of Fire Fighters*, 276 N.W.2d 42 (Minn. 1979); *Medford Firefighters' Association v. City of Medford*, 595 P.2d 1268 (Or. App. 1979). But see *County of Riverside v. Superior Court*, 30 Cal. 4th 278 (Cal. 2003) (binding arbitration violates unique provision of California state constitution); *Salt Lake City v. Inter. Assn. of Fire Fighters*, 563 P.2d 768 (Utah 1977) (overturns binding arbitration as unconstitutional delegation of legislative authority).

[43]This "local option" has been adopted by such cities as Phoenix, Arizona; Boise, Idaho; Denver, Colorado; and San Antonio, Texas. In states that follow the meet and confer model, there usually exists a local option to allow interest arbitration as the last step in the bargaining process. For example, even though for years California followed the meet and confer model, cities in California such as Oakland and San Jose had local laws providing for interest arbitration.

[44]For example *Village of Dixmoor*, 16 PERI ¶2038 (Ill. SLRB Gen. Counsel 2000).

[45]For example *California Correctional Peace Officers Association v. State California*, 25 PERC 32,015 (Cal. PERB ALJ 2000).

[46]*Borough v. Pennsylvania Labor Relations Board*, 794 A.2d 402 (Pa.Cmwlth. 2002).

[47]A good early discussion of bargaining topics can be found in Clark, *The Scope of the Duty to Bargain in Public Employment, in Labor Relations Law in the Public Sector* 81 (A. Knapp ed. 1977).

[48]*Portland Firefighters Association v. City of Portland*, 751 P.2d 770 (Or. 1988).

[49]If an employer chooses to agree to include a permissive subject of bargaining in a collective bargaining agreement, and finds the provision to its distaste, it may simply refuse to include the provision in a subsequent agreement. *Paterson Police Local v. City of Paterson*, 432 A.2d 847 (N.J. 1981).

[50]*City of Portland*, 8 PECBR 8115 (Or. 1985).

[51]*City of Buffalo*, 13 NPER NY-13036 (N.Y. PERB 1990).

[52]*County of Perry*, 19 NPER IL-124 (Ill. LRB 2003).

[53]*Plains Township Police Bargaining Unit v. Plains Township*, 33 PPER ¶33,019 (Pa. LRB ALJ 2001).

[54]*City of Bremerton*, PEB ¶45,352 (Wash.) (CCH, 1987).

[55]*City of Iowa City*, 17 NPER IA-26005 (Iowa PERB ALJ 1995) delay of 90 days in filing unfair labor practice charge); *County of Nassau*, 35 NYPER ¶4583 (NY PERB ALJ 2002); *City of Reading*, 17 NPER PA-26132 (Pa. LRB ALJ 1995)); *City of Philadelphia*, 13 NPER PA-22042 (Pa. LRB Hearing Examiner 1991) (six-week delay between filing of unfair labor practice charge and violation of duty to bargain did not render the charge untimely).

[56]*Throop Borough*, 16 NPER PA-25012 (Pa. LRB ALJ 1993).

[57]*Law Enforcement Labor Services, Inc. v. City of Luverne*, 463 N.W.2d 546 (Minn.App.1990).

[58]*Peekskill Police Association*, 35 NYPER ¶3016 (N.Y. PERB 2002).

[59]*Caruso v. Board of Collective Bargaining of the City of New York*, 555 N.Y.S.2d 133 (A.D. 1990).

[60]Quoted in *Model Law Enforcement Contract, 1993 Edition* (Portland, OR: Labor Relations Information System, 1993).

[61]*Washington State Patrol*, 3 (8) Public Safety Labor News 7 (Wash. PERC 1995).

[62]*City of Grosse Pointe Park*, 14 MPER ¶32051 (Mich. ERC 2001).

[63]*City of Mt. Vernon*, 23 GERR 667 (New York) (BNA 1986).

[64]*Howard County*, 1 (9) Public Safety Labor News 5 (Fishgold, 1993).

[65]William J. Bopp, *Police Personnel Administration* (Boston: Holbrook HSS, 1974), p. 345.

[66]See Richard S. Rubin et al., "Public Sector Unit Determination Administrative Procedures and Case Law," Midwest Center for Public Sector Labor Relations, Indiana University Department of Labor Contract J-9-P-6–0215, May 31, 1978.

[67]In this regard, see Stephen L. Hayford, William A. Durkee, and Charles W. Hickman, "Bargaining Unit Determination Procedures in the Public Sector: A Comparative Evaluation," *Employee Relations Law Journal*, 5, No. 1 (summer 1979), p. 86.

[68]Donald Slesnick, "What Is the Effect of a Sunshine Law on Collective Bargaining: A Union View," *Journal of Law and Education* 5 (October 1976), p. 489.

[69]Charles W. Maddox, *Collective Bargaining in Law Enforcement* (Springfield, IL: Charles C Thomas, 1975), p. 54.

[70]Arnold Zack, *Understanding Grievance Arbitration in the Public Sector* (Washington, DC: U.S. Government Printing Office, 1974), p. 1.

[71]Maddox, *Collective Bargaining*, p. 109.

[72]Zack, *Understanding Grievance Arbitration*, p. 4.

[73]Maurice S. Trotta, *Arbitration of Labor–Management Disputes* (New York: Amacon, 1974), p. 237, with changes.

[74]See Helen Lavan and Cameron Carley, "Analysis of Arbitrated Employee Grievance Cases in Police Departments," *Journal of Collective Negotiations in the Public Sector* 14, No. 3 (1985), pp. 250–251.

[75]Zack, *Understanding Grievance Arbitration*, p. 32.

[76]Ibid.

[77]Michael Cooper, "Police Picket Traffic Courts, as Pact Protests Go On," *The New York Times*, January 27, 1997, p. B3.

[78]Peter Finn, "Police Officers Send Pointed Message: More Than 150 Pagers Turned in to Protest Alexandria Pay Scale," *The Washington Post*, January 24, 1997, p. B6.

[79]Stephanie Reitz, "Council Approves Police Contract in East Hartford," *Hartford Courant*, March 19, 1997, p. B1.

[80]Jack Rabin, Thomas Vocino, W. Bartley Hildreth, and Gerald J. Miller, eds., *Handbook of Public Sector Labor Relations* (New York: Marcel Dekker, 1994), p. 6.

[81]On these and related points, see Robert P. Engvall, "Public Sector Unionization in 1995 or It Appears the Lion King Has Eaten Robin Hood," *Journal of Collective Negotiations in the Public Sector* 24, No. 3 (1995), pp. 255–269.

[82]*Detroit Free Press*, February 8, 1997.

[83]Don Aucoin, *Boston Globe*, September 27, 1997.

[84]http://204.127.237.106/newsonline/96apr22/beatings.html

[85]On September 29, 1976, Richard M. Ayres presented a paper, "Police Strikes: Are We Treating the Symptom Rather Than the Problem?" at the 83rd International Association of Chiefs of Police meeting, Miami Beach, Florida. Although it is not quoted here, some of his themes may be identifiable, and his contribution in that regard is acknowledged.

[86]This list of questions with modifications and additions is drawn from Charles C. Mulcahy, "Meeting the County Employees Strike," in *Collective Bargaining in the Public Sector*, pp. 426–430. See also Carmen D. Saso, *Coping with Public Employee Strikes* (Chicago: Public Personnel Association, 1970).

[87]Harold W. Davey, *Contemporary Collective Bargaining* (Englewood Cliffs, NJ: Prentice Hall, 1972), p. 195.

[88]John H. Burpo, *Labor Relations Guidelines for the Police Executive* (Chicago: Traffic Institute, Northwestern University, 1976), p. 14, with modifications and additions.

[89]Lee T. Paterson and John Liebert, *Management Strike Handbook* (Chicago: International Personnel Management Association, 1974), p. 42.

[90]Labor-Management Relations in Policing: Looking to the Future and Finding Common Ground, *Critical Issues in Policing Series* (Washington, DC: Police Executive Research Forum, October 2011), p. 1.

[91]Chris Stein, "As Cities Lay Off Police, Frustrated Neighborhoods Turn to Private Cops," *Christian Science Monitor*, April 5, 2105; http://www.csmonitor.com/USA/2013/0405/As-cities-lay-off-police-frustrated-neighborhoods-turn-to-private-cops (accessed June 27, 2015).

[92]John Woolfolk, "66 Officers Turn in Badges in San Jose's First Police Layoffs," *San Jose Mercury News,* June 30, 2011; http://www.mercurynews.com/san-jose-police/ci_18384442 (accessed June 26, 2015).

[93]Labor-Management Relations in Policing, p. 1.

[94]Some of the specific recommendations made at the 2011 PERF meeting and discussed herein have been slightly edited in order to reduce some unintentionally awkward wording. However, the authors have made every effort possible to be faithful to the original transcription that was itself also summarized from much more detailed discussions by these chiefs and labor union representatives.

[95]Ibid., pp. 1–2.

[96]Ibid., p. 3.

[97]"Town files Chapter 11, pensions go up in smoke," *American Police Beat* (September 2011), p. 51.

[98]"Bankrupt Cities, Municipalities List and Map," *Governing the States and Localities*, November 7, 2014, p. 62; http://www.governing.com/gov-data/municipal-cities-counties-bankruptcies-and-defaults.html (accessed June 26, 2015).

CHAPTER TWELVE

FINANCIAL MANAGEMENT

Learning Objectives

1. State the five ways in which the Great Recession affected many law enforcement agencies.

2. Identify seven strategies used by law enforcement agencies to counter fiscal stress.

3. Give three definitions of the budget.

4. Explain why budgeting is inherently a political process.

5. Define operating and capital budgets.

6. Identify the key objectives of citizen-centric reports.

7. Provide five quick budgeting tips.

8. List and briefly describe the four major steps in the budget cycle.

9. Identify six common ways in which a police budget can be adjusted.

10. Describe the nature of the line item budget.

11. Identify the feature that is increasingly found in program budgets.

12. Provide three reasons why cost measures for performance budgets/performance-based budgets are carefully selected.

13. Explain how service level and zero line item budgeting work.

14. Explain hybrid budgets and why they exist.

15. Identify eight different jobs a volunteer could do in a law enforcement agency.

INTRODUCTION

THIS CHAPTER IS IMPORTANT *to the development of police leaders for the following reasons: (1) Budgeting does not occur simply in a police context; it occurs within a larger framework of state laws and regulations, city or county charters, local ordinances, guidance from city/county chief executives, finance officers, legislative bodies, regulations, the terms of collective bargaining agreements, citizen and special interest groups, the political climate, and the financial markets. Complete police administrators must understand the larger context and their own departmental budgeting practices to be effective, (2) Essentially, three things fuel law enforcement agencies: funding, people, and information; continuous learning about all three is essential; (3) Responsibilities in the budget process increase as the rank ladder is climbed; learning now prepares one for the future. Moreover, some agencies solicit budget input from all levels of the agency. In those instances, your knowledge of the budget will serve you well from the beginning of any career in law enforcement; (4) The budget process is closely watched by more senior appointed and elected officials, police associations and unions, auditors, and the news media; to a large degree the measure of police administrators is how well they prepare, present, and execute their department's budget; (5) A reputation as a good financial manager is a major asset when facing cutbacks or seeking appropriations for new programs.*

THE ECONOMY AND POLICE BUDGETS

The Great Recession began in December 2007 and was the longest since the 1930s.[1] It was officially declared over in 2009, yet recovery is slow, uneven, and economic indicators continue to be mixed. All of this is consistent with the rule of thumb that recovery from a major recession takes roughly a decade. In 2015, some police departments had slivers of their cuts restored, but conservatives and Tea Party members continue to argue for smaller and more efficient government. Some citizens are asking, "Can we really afford the police department we used to have?" It seems likely that as we progress slowly toward a recovery of some sort that policing may also be on the path to becoming institutionally different. With deep cuts in staffing, many law enforcement agencies are actually a thin blue line and unpredictable events, such as landslides, wildfires, tornadoes, rioting, floods, hurricanes (see Figure 12.1), terrorist attacks, and protracted union strikes may stretch agencies too far. Moreover, cutting staffing and overtime funding are incompatible strategies. Technology is a force multiplier for law enforcement agencies, but if staffing cuts are severe enough technology cannot overcome the absence of officers.

The Great Recession affected many law enforcement agencies because it (1) introduced fiscal distress, (2) reduced their resources, (3) forced law enforcement executives to make painful decisions, (4) left a lingering impact on many agencies, and (5) provided useful and sometimes painful lessons about financial management.

Stockton: Bankrupt and Only Responding to Crimes in Progress Many Hours of the Day

Fourteen months after the onset of the recession, CNN found that 84 percent of cities surveyed were in financial trouble and that number was expected to rise to 92 percent by the end of the year.[2] The states also had their financial problems. Between 2009 and 2012, state budget shortfalls amounted to $376 billion; state debts soared; and just in 2010 alone, 39 states made mid-budget year cuts totaling $18.3 billion.[3]

How did all of this indebtedness happen? Broadly, although the specifics vary somewhat from one situation to another, falling property values and increasing unemployment figures caused tax revenues to decline, consumer spending slowed, people relocated to find greener economic pastures, mortgage foreclosures, loan defaults, and personal bankruptcies spiked, and many businesses reduced the number of employees or were forced to close their doors. In some jurisdictions, plaintiffs received large settlements or were awarded substantial judgments for police misconduct, resulting in budget tightening. In the 10 years before 2014, lawsuits against the police cost Chicago taxpayers $521 million.[4] In just 2014 and 2015 that figure was $106 million for settlements, judgments, legal fees, and other related expenses.[5] That amount was an additional staggering expenditure for Chicago, already saddled with billions of dollars in unfunded pension obligations, mental health clinic shutdowns, reduced library hours, and higher fees for water, parking, and other services.[6] Elsewhere, a few cities discovered their municipal charters prohibited reducing police salaries.

Stockton provides a case study of the complexities of local government financial management. It a city of 300,000 located

FIGURE 12.1 ► New Orleans, Louisiana, 2 days after Hurricane Katrina struck (2005). A sheriff's deputy helps an elderly man, too weak to lift his bottle of water, take a drink. (FEMA/Win Henderson)

in Northern California's San Joaquin Valley. In the decade leading up to 2007, it became an economic engine. Just a few years later it filed for bankruptcy. Unemployment reached 18 percent, Nearly 30,000 children lived below the poverty line and crime increased substantially;[7] It became one of the most dangerous California cities in which to live.[8] In 2013, the city manager reported: "There are still an unacceptable number of hours in a day when police will only respond to crimes in progress."[9] In 2009 and 2011, Stock led Forbes list of "America's Most Miserable Cities."[10] No single factor propelled the city into insolvency in 2012; instead, it was a volatile mix of factors:

1. A widespread, but undue optimism, that the "good" economic times would continue unabated, a prime example of the danger of linear thinking. Some investors and analysts generally saw Stockton as an extreme case

of fiscal mismanagement, described by one as a "slow moving train wreck."[11]

2. Voters in California in 1978 used the initiative and approved Proposition 13 to cap property taxes at 1 percent of the appraised value and other initiatives further constrained the governmental finances (see Quick Facts: What is the Initiative? and the accompanying informational link). Although distant in time, Proposition 13 is one of the root causes that cumulatively, along with other events, propelled Stockton and other California cities into dire fiscal straits.

3. Starting in the mid-1990s, the city began attracting buyers from San Francisco and the Bay area who were seeking bargain homes.[12] This surge drove *median*

Quick Facts: What Is the Initiative?

California and 21 other states include the initiative and referendum in their state constitutions; South Dakota was the first to do so, in 1898.[13] These states are for the most part concentrated in the West. Initiatives allow voters to propose *new* laws. During any given year in California, a dozen initiatives may appear on the ballot. The initiative is a process that allows citizens with sufficient valid petition signatures to bypass their legislatures and place proposed statutes, and in some states new Constitutional amendments, on the ballot for determination by popular vote. It is *direct democracy* (See Quick Facts: James Madison and Direct Democracy), as opposed to representative democracy. In contrast, the subject of a referendum is an *existing* law that is subject to approval or repeal by voters.

There are two types of referendums: (A) the legislative referendum, in which the legislative body refers a law to voters for their approval or disapproval and (B) the popular referendum, which allows voters, with valid petitions, to place on the ballot the approval or repeal of an existing act of their legislature.

Informational Link: 50-State Interactive Initiative MAP

This link connects with an excellent interactive 50-state map that displays information about where each state stands with initiative and referendum, along with the applicable histories. Visit: http://www.iandrinstitute.org/statewide_i%26r.htm.

Quick Facts: James Madison and Direct Democracy

James Madison (1751–1836) was America's fourth President. He believed, like many of his contemporaries, in *representative democracy* and was suspicious of *direct democracy*, of which the modern day initiative is an example. Madison regarded direct democracy as the "tyranny of the masses."

Some officials and citizens believe that too much use has been made of the initiative in California, usurping the role of the legislature to some degree. Two examples of the use of the initiative follow. The first example was a victory for animal rights activists and kindred spirits, while the second one was defeated.

1. Proposition 2, which went into effect in 2015. It required that all chickens must be confined in spaces sufficient for them to turn freely, stand up, sit down, and unfold their wings. Now, all eggs sold in California must come from chickens housed in that manner. At least four states have filed suit on the basis it is an unreasonable restraint of interstate commerce[14] and

2. Proposition 23, defeated in 2000, would have required "None of the above" to be included on all election ballots. The proposal seemingly comes from a Richard Pryor comedic movie, *Brewster's Millions* (1985). On the other side of the Jordan River, James Madison must be shaking his head.

home prices from $110,000 to nearly $400,000 between 2000 and 2006.[15] Permits for new home construction soared to nearly 3,000 annually and the additional property taxes seemingly made Stockton a wealthy municipality.[16] The California home market began its ugly crash in 2007 and 2 years later Stockton's home values retreated to their 2000 level, by 2010 there were only 152 building permits issued.[17] The housing collapse hit Stockton in two ways: (1) Upside down on their mortgages, many people lost their homes to foreclosures[18] and other property owners simply walked away from their mortgages and fled to other jurisdictions, depriving the city of property tax revenue and (2) the decline in population negatively impacted local businesses, to a discernible degree. As times continued to worsen Stockton became a ghost town at night with boarded up businesses and rubbish in the streets (see Figure 12.2).[19]

4. As the national financial markets plummeted, so did Stockton's return on investments, which were used for a variety of purposes, including pension payouts. In 2007, the city borrowed $125 million and invested it in Calpers (California Public Employees Retirement System, a state agency that manages pension and health funds).[20] Calpers lost money in the market downturn, reducing the value of Stockton's investment in 2010 to $93 million.[21] Stockton was left with both bond and pension liabilities: the combined pension liabilities became a major driver in Stockton's insolvency.

FIGURE 12.2 ▶ Crumbling sidewalks and shuttered businesses line a downtown street in Stockton as hard times hit the city.
(Kevin Bartram/Reuters/CorbisKevin Bartram/Reuters/Corbis)

5. The turbulent and sometimes swift changes in financial markets and Stockton's own economic crisis complicated making accurate planning and fiscal decisions. Illustratively, as Stockton prepared its 2012 budget, it had already announced a fiscal emergency in the two prior budget years and made substantial cuts in an attempt to remain solvent.[22] The city had reduced the police department by one-fourth, the fire department by 30 percent, slashed other departments as well, and workers who kept their jobs had their pay cut by as much as 22 percent.[23] Stockton also defaulted on three sets of bonds, losing control of three parking garages and an 8-story building that was to have been the new city hall and still faced a deficit. Since 2009, the city had cut its budget $90 million.[24]

6. In times of plenty Stockton spent freely and made compensation commitments that just a few years later became unsustainable.[25] The starting point appears to have been 1996, when Stockton gave firefighters full health care coverage for life and it spread to other public safety employee groups.[26] Even if revenues decreased compared to the previous year, employee salaries would still automatically increase by 2.5 to 7 percent and unionized employees would get a pay increase that could not be less than comparable cities.[27] Although Stockton cut positions and implemented other measures, it was still accumulated annual deficits starting in 2007, steadily pushing the city toward the brink.

To meet its pension funding requirements, the city needed an annualized return on investments of 7.75 percent, but its bonds only paid 5.46 percent, leaving the city to fund the difference, which eventually it could not[28] and fell $41 million deeper into debt.[29] Stockton was further rocked when it calculated a terrible truth: Retiree health benefit costs were increasing even faster than pensions. Moreover, these health care costs were taken from the annual operating budget, further constraining what Stockton otherwise might have been able to allocate elsewhere. By 2011, the projected liability for future/post employment health care was $544 million, entirely unfunded.[30] If bankruptcy had not happened when it did, it is clear than just salaries and pensions and health care liabilities would have forced Stockton into it within a very short time horizon.

Stockton exited federal bankruptcy in late 2014, but still deeply in debt. The saddest part of the saga of Stockton is what happened to those who worked for the city in good faith for years, earned a pension, and retired. Under California state law the pensions of public employees cannot be cut. However, the federal bankruptcy court ruled otherwise and Stockton pensioners suffered as their income in their "Golden Years" was substantially slashed and their health care was quickly phased out. Some retirees discovered that health care insurance would cost as much as roughly one-third to one-half of their new monthly retirement earnings.

The Stockton bankruptcy case study illustrates the point that policing is affected by the currents of the society in which it is embedded.

Law Enforcement Agencies and Fiscal Stress

Law enforcement agencies have been using the following strategies in some combination to counter fiscal stress: (1) freezing new hires and eliminating positions; (2) cancelling recruit and many advanced training classes;[31] (3) requiring officers to take furlough/unpaid days off; (4) reducing salaries;[32] (5) closing precincts;[33] (6) delaying the purchase of replacement vehicles; (7) selling helicopters;[34] (8) closing police stations to the public;[35] (9) slashing police programs;[36] (10) eliminating mounted patrol, motorcycle, accident investigation, burglary, and marine patrol units;[37] (11) laying off officers and slashing overtime funding; (12) achieving reductions in force by not filling vacancies created by attrition; (13) replacing sworn officers with fewer and less-expensive civilians; and (14) increasing the numbers and breadth of assignments for volunteers.

The financial management skills of law enforcement executives have been severely tested by the circumstances of our economy for almost a decade. Even their best efforts have sometimes not been sufficient. Hundreds of small towns have abolished their police departments.[38] Typically, these small towns contract with the state police or a sheriff's office for minimal law enforcement services or consolidate with another law enforcement agency.

For many police departments, all fat had been trimmed and the continuing cuts were well into muscle and bone, affecting service delivery, such as increased response time, in ways that citizens can feel. Slashed budgets are particularly vulnerable to deficit spending because there are so many "budget busters" that cannot be foreseen—for example, natural disasters,[39] such as hurricanes, tornadoes, earthquakes, floods, mudslides, and wildfires. Other budget busters include searches for missing children, hunters, and seniors who walk away from their care situations protracted strikes, complex investigations involving serial offenders, unforeseeable surges in the price of gasoline, terrorist attacks, demonstrations, and the cost of using private labs to process key evidence in significant cases. In many of these examples, cutting staffing and reducing overtime funds in the police budget are not compatible strategies because the need to respond to special circumstances quickly overspends the overtime budget. In very small departments, the budget may be "busted" by lesser events, such as having to replace a copier machine or buying a new patrol car because of an accident. Without question, the deep cuts resulted in some people becoming crime victims, some criminals escaped investigation and prosecution due to elimination of positions, and police work became more dangerous because of less or no backup on calls where it previously had been provided (See box 12.1).

Police executives are not going to be criticized about financial management when unforeseeable "budget busters" occur. However, when mistakes are made on basic matters, budget appropriators are typically unsympathetic. A state police commissioner failed to request $4 million to train the new troopers the state legislature had authorized hiring. To express its displeasure, the state legislature froze trooper hiring for 1 year.

Box 12.1: Two Examples of Under Supported and Overloaded Investigators

Southwest Missouri Cyber Crimes Task Force

The Task Force was crippled by budget cuts and may be forced to disband. Its work: investigating online predators targeting Missouri children and selling child pornography.[40] Last year, the Governor vetoed $1.5 million to support cyber units across the state and was characterized as being "anti-law enforcement." However, scarce resources may have actually accounted for the Governor's decision.

The Oakland, California, Police Department

In 2015, the OPD only had eight detectives in its robbery investigation unit and they were charged with investigating more than 3,300 crimes or a staggering 419 cases a year each. As a practical matter, only 20 percent of all robbery cases were investigated and few of those were solved. Consequently, the Alameda County District Attorney's Office was only able to bring charges in just 231 or less than one percent of all robbery cases.[41]

Quick Facts: The Distinction Between Budgeting and Accounting

Some police personnel are dismissive about budgeting, claiming it's "accountant's work." The claim reveals a lack of information about how the two concepts are related.

Budgeting is prospective, future oriented; accounting is retrospective, past oriented.[42]

POLITICS AND FINANCIAL MANAGEMENT

Anything done by government involves the expenditure of public funds.[43] Budgeting is inherently a political process because elected members of city councils, county commissions, state legislatures, and the Congress express their preferences when they vote on appropriations. Appropriators consider their own views, as well as those expressed by constituents, political donors, the news media, police unions, polls, special interest groups, lobbyists, and colleagues, as well as deals made to secure support for their own interests. Politics do not stop when a budget is adopted; in some circumstances, the politics can actually intensify during the time a budget is executed (see Figure 12.3).

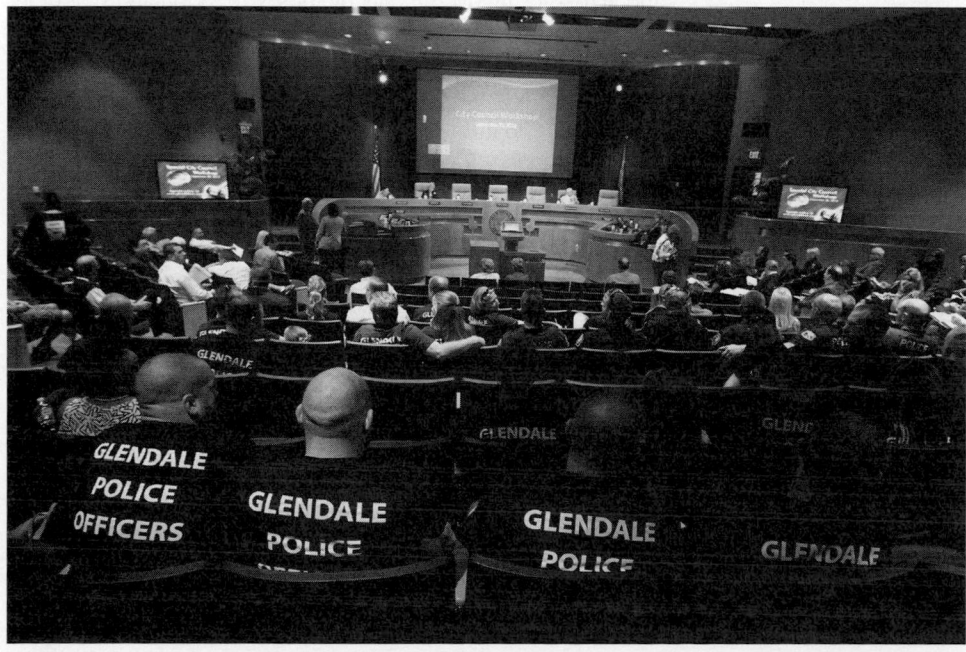

FIGURE 12.3 ▶ Glendale, Arizona, police officers attended a 2012 city council meeting during which a $20 million budget cut was discussed. The cuts were not as deep as feared; the police department lost 19 of 425 sworn and 14 of 152.5 civilian positions. (Ross D. Franklin/AP/Corbis)

This is especially true when a law enforcement agency has scarce resources and must cut back or end different services. Some citizens and groups effected by such decisions will try to get their preferred services restored.

STATE AND LOCAL INFLUENCES ON FINANCIAL MANAGEMENT

Cities and counties are under the authority of their respective state governments, which have considerable authority over them, including their financial management. Local governments cannot be created, nor can they levy taxes or deliver services without the prior approval of the state. Following the economic crash of 1929, thousands of local governments went bankrupt because they could not meet their financial obligations. As a result, many states passed laws that regulate local finance in such areas as revenue sources, tax collection, level of permissible indebtedness, budgeting procedures, and audits. Typically, states prohibit cities and counties from borrowing to fund annual operating budgets; historically such borrowing signaled bankruptcy was on the near horizon.[44] States also require detailed financial reports from local governments, which are carefully studied for signs of fiscal weakness.

In addition to whatever requirements the state establishes, local financial management is guided by a maze of other guidelines, including the city or county charter, ordinances, executive orders, regulations, and customary practices. The form of local government shapes who the dominant figures are in finance. In a strong mayor system, the mayor is the key player, whereas in the weak mayor form, the council is the predominant force. In a mayor–city manager system, the manager holds great power. These generalizations are affected by other factors, such as how much influence a long-serving finance director has accrued and the degree to which a city council is more or less activist in scrutinizing and revising the mayor's or city manager's budget.

KEY BUDGET TERMS

Every year, the most important statement governments make is the approval of their budgets because it reveals in financial terms what their priorities are. There are different ways to define a budget. For example, it is a plan expressed in dollars, it is the use of financial resources to meet human needs, and it is a contract between those who appropriate the money and those who execute the budget.[46]

A budget year is called a **fiscal year (FY)**, and it may coincide with the calendar year. Often, a FY runs from July 1 of one year until June 30 of the next year. A budget, which begins on July 1, 2018, and ends on June 30, 2019, is called the FY '19 budget. Some local units of government have changed their fiscal year to October 1 of 1 year until September 30 of the next year to coincide with the federal budget year and the funding of its grant programs. At various times, the Congress has considered adopting a biennial budget but never changed to one. In 1940, 44 states were using a **biennial budget**, which covers a 2-year period, by 2015 only 19 states were using one.[47,48]

Budgets can also be defined as operating and capital:[49]

An **operating budget** usually covers a 12-month period and consists of annually recurring costs such as salaries, fringe benefits, uniforms, crime scene supplies, ammunition, training, telephone service, gasoline, and kindred expenses. Operating budgets are overwhelmingly funded by a city or county's annual stream of revenues into its general fund, with a few exceptions such as grants and donations. As its name suggests, the general fund contains a local government's revenues that are not obligated to other funds. Both operating and capital budgets must be approved by the appropriate legislative body which authorizes appropriations, such as a city council, county commissioner, state legislature, or the congress.

Capital budgets were introduced in the United States during the 1940s and the use of them slowly spread.[50] Capital budgets are made up of individual "high cost" capital improvement projects (CIPs). There is variation in local government capital budgeting practices across the United States. As an example, there is no generally accepted definition of a capital budget because the definition of what is a "capital" item varies by state, and across local governments by their size, population, or other factors. For example, in Minnesota, state guidance on capital budgets for small units of local government is different than for large ones. Over the next two decades capital budget expenditures will be higher as aging/inadequate facilities are replaced and the population increases, creating further police service demands.

Quick Facts: State Control of Local Government Finance

There are four broad category areas in which states commonly exert at least some control of local government finance by law or regulation: (1) budgeting practices and format, (2) raising revenue, (3) indebtedness and debt management, and (4) fiscal reporting requirements to the state.[45]

Quick Facts: Origination of the Term "Budget"

"Budget" comes from the French *bougette*, meaning a leather bag. Originally, it referred to the bag in which the Chancellor of the Exchequer carried budget documents to the English Parliament. Later, it came to mean the documents themselves.[51] The first Exchequer budget was taken to Parliament in 1284 and the office still exists.

A single car may be identified as a capital expense in one jurisdiction while in another it may be part of the separate operating budget. This is usually because jurisdictions are operating on different financial thresholds that determine into which budget an item goes. As an example, in many small jurisdictions the cost of purchasing an automobile is automatically in the capital budget. In contrast, in New York City, unless the cost of purchasing a car is more than $35,000, its cost goes into the annual operating budget. The advantage of placing an item in the capital budget is that it can be paid for over multiple years as opposed to 1 year in an annual operating budget.

Illustrations of CIPs include the purchase of land, major rehabilitation of buildings, construction of new facilities, sewer, gas, and water lines, bridges, dams, parks, and airports. Equipment and machines, such as increasingly sophisticated computers and vehicles, firearms, and forensic laboratory equipment, may also be in the capital budget. The $250,000 Rapid Hit 200, which completes DNA testing in 90 min, as opposed to 2 days, would be in the capital budget of almost all local governments.

CIPs vary in terms of the number of years over which they are paid off and each of them are reviewed annually and adjusted. The subsequent maintenance of many newly acquired capital items, for example, cars, buildings, and a new police station comes out of the operating budget. Some CIPs may be required as a matter of law, such as a court order to a county to build a new jail for the Sheriff's Office/Department because the existing one is antiquated and continuously overcrowded.

Unlike operating budgets, capital items are not an annually recurring expense because once paid for the item no longer appears in the budget. Commonly, capital items are paid for by multiple sources, including revenues, grants, and donations. Some jurisdictions have a preference to "pay as you go" as much as possible, but very large projects, such as purchasing a helicopter for surveillance and rescue, may force counties to issue a bond, creating an indebtedness. Bond investors are repaid semiannually over a fixed number of years.

A number of cities and counties have a combined operating and capital budget that the legislative body considers, usually over several meetings. The Government Finance Officers Association (GFOA) recommends that when a combined operating and capital budget is used, the operating and capital budgets should be distinctly separated.[52]

THE BUDGET CYCLE

At its heart, the **budget cycle** is a stream of four sequential steps that are repeated at about the same time every year in a jurisdiction: (1) preparation and submission of the budget by all of a city or county's departments, which includes getting input from stakeholders, such as citizens and advisory boards (see Box 12.2); (2) review and approval by the legislative body,

---

Box 12.2: Citizen-Centric Reports (CCRs)

Citizens in the United States generally have multiple opportunities to learn about and provide input on budget priorities and appropriations. Such opportunities are enhanced by a technique loosely referred to as a "citizen guide," citizen-centric report, "performance report" or some similar title. The key objectives of citizen-centric reports are to increase the transparency of government and citizen participation in governance. The contents vary, but frequently incorporate color pie and bar graphs to summarize information about the budget, the accomplishments of the jurisdiction, and a survey of local citizens on their satisfaction with the city or county's services. Citizen guides are widely distributed in print and are often available on the city or country's website. The advantage of surveying citizens is that instead of a jurisdiction just *telling* people what the city or county has done, it is in a *listening* mode to the perceptions of citizens and may discover new opportunities or conditions that need correction.

Used precisely, a "Citizen-Centric Report" (CCR) refers to an initiative by The Association of Government Accountants (AGA) to give citizens numbers that they can understand. In plain language and limited to four pages, the AGA's CCR format answers four questions for citizens: (1) Strategic Objectives/what are we chartered (required) to do? This explains the mandated services to be provided; (2) How are we doing? This page is a performance report of key missions and services and AGA encourages that public input, such as a survey, be used to gather data. A usual survey question is, "How much confidence do you have in your police department?" This question is used with other departments as well; (3) What are the costs for servicing citizens and how is it paid for? On this third page, cost data is linked to the service delivery outcomes so citizens understand what each service costs; and (4) The last page covers challenges moving forward: What's next and future challenges, which summarizes emerging conditions and the economic outlook.

The more elaborate reports may also incorporate information from the International City/County Management Association's (ICMA's) National Citizen Survey (NCS), which asks questions in eight different community domains to determine citizen perceptions. Users jurisdictions can get data about their own community as well as comparative data for comparable jurisdictions. NCS may be used in lieu of the local survey or as a supplement.

Law enforcement agencies may be able to hone their annual and other reports by discovering new ideas for them by studying the features of citizen-centric and other citizen guides on the internet.

(continued)

Box 12.2 (*Conclusion*)

Informational Link: Palo Alto, ICMA, and Citizen-Centric Reports

The City of Palo Alto has an excellent annual report to citizens, "FY 2015 Performance Report, The National Citizen Survey, and Citizen Centric Report." Visit Palo Alto's site (CityofPaloAlto.org) and search for more recent performance reports.

Also, go to ICMA.org and search for "The National Citizen Survey" to read more about this important subscription service and the eight domains: community engagement, education and enrichment, recreation and wellness, economy, built environment, natural environment, safety, and mobility.

AGA's CCR initiative is intended to foster innovative means of communicating between governments and their citizens AGA's survey can also be customized for local needs. Information about the CCR, including the AGA's format, is found at Agacgfm.org.

which usually involve public hearings and occasionally heated exchanges; (3) execution of the budget, meaning doing the actual things for which the funds were appropriated, including any budget adjustments after the budget is approved; and (4) the audit and evaluation.[53] An audit is an independent evaluation of something, for example, a law enforcement agency's control of its petty cash fund, its annual expenditures, or its performance on key indicators, such as use of force incidents. Many of these four activities are going on simultaneously because different budget activities overlap or are "scrambled" together.[54] For example, while a sheriff's, or police department is executing this year's budget, last year's budget is being audited and the next year's budget is being prepared.

Well before a police department starts preparing its budget, the F/FSD has been at work preparing the revenue forecast for the city, documenting the assumptions departments are required to make during budget preparation, such as percentage increases for gasoline or equipment service, and other data, including the budget preparation manual. These manuals focus on the technical aspects of putting the budget together and include definitions, forms, and the **budget calendar** (see Figure 12.4).

The city or county manager then sends the budget manual to the department heads with specific guidelines on services to be emphasized and specific fiscal guidance as to the amount the budget may increase or must decrease, the upper percentage of employees raises, limits on new positions and programs, and other fiscal data. Often, the budget message from the city or county manager, the budget preparation manual, and past budgets are available online, along with any software needed to prepare the budget. Budget workshops can be held by the F/FSD to explain the process and establish uniformity in the budget process across departments.

Before sending out the budget preparation manual, city and county managers usually meet with their mayor and council or commission informally or formally to get their views on budget priorities to avoid major conflict later in the budget process. Many jurisdictions conduct strategic planning and budget workshops at various points in the budget process to get citizen and city council or county commission input early in the process, especially with respect to goals, priorities, and target budget figures. These measures do not guarantee there won't be conflict later, but they do reduce some potential for it. Occasionally, differences arise in budgeting over seemingly minor programs (see Quick Facts: Geese Police Restored in Budget).

Step One: Budget Preparation in the Police Department

In small police departments, those with roughly 10 or fewer officers, the chief's role in budget preparation is often limited.[55] Most frequently, strong mayors or city managers will have several conversations with such chiefs about their department and formulate the budget themselves or delegate its preparation. In larger departments with seven or eight layers of hierarchy, the budget process is more formal. In medium-sized and larger departments, the chief's budget is shaped by the guidance given by a city or county manager and, in that context, is a top-down process. However, to know what the actual needs are, the lowest-ranking supervisors in the department, sergeants or corporals may be involved in identifying them and, in that regard, the budget is a bottom-up process. Some departments go further and solicit budget input from non-ranking patrol officers, the usual entry-level position.

The budget is built by reviewing, sometimes revising, and then combining the budget requests from smaller units to form much of the budgets of bureaus or divisions. The single most important element in a police budget is people and their support costs, such as salaries, medical insurance, life insurance, and pension benefits, as well as overtime and training. In many departments, personnel and personnel support costs may consume 80 or more percent of the budget, limiting what cuts can be made before staffing is reduced.

In a tight budget year, some chiefs cut back on training dollars. This might make the budget work, but it is a poor strategy. Any chief who submitted a budget without dollars in it for preventive maintenance of the police fleet would be criticized; yet, training is the preventive maintenance on people. It keeps personnel fresh and at the cutting edge, prevents litigation or can be a defense to it, and is a means of importing new ideas and techniques into the police department. As to delaying the purchase of replacement vehicles, officers operating vehicles with 100,000 and more miles are using cars that may be

Action	Responsibility	Deadlines
Budget kickoff: Budget manual and city manager's transmittal letter (the "budget call") distributed to all departments, often done in a meeting with additional comments[a]	City manager	October 1, 2017
Department heads issue their budget message to immediately subordinate unit commanders (e.g., deputy chiefs or majors in charge of bureaus or divisions)	Police chief	October 15, 2017
City holds budget preparation workshops; police representatives—may be mix of civilians and sworn personnel—involved in preparing police budget attend	F/FSD holds workshop	October 22–23, 2017
Recommended budgets for all police bureaus or divisions developed with justification and submitted to police budget office	Bureau/division commanders	February 1, 2018
Recommended bureau or division budgets reviewed with the respective commanders	Police budget office with bureau or division commanders; chief may participate	February 18–22, 2018
Bureau or division budgets consolidated into overall department budget	Police budget office	March 1, 2018
Overall police budget reviewed by chief	Chief, bureau or division commanders, police budget office	March 4–15, 2018
Police department budget approved for submission to city manager or F/FSD	Chief	March 18, 2018
City manager meets separately with department heads to review their budget requests	City manager, police chief, other department heads	April 1–12, 2018
Department budgets revised per city manager's guidance	Chief, police budget office	April 15–May 10, 2018
City manager forwards recommended budget to city council	City manager	May 16, 2018
City council as a whole or through its finance/ways and means committee reviews departmental budgets	City council	May 17–31, 2018
City manager and departments present their respective budgets separately to city council and respond to questions	City manager, department heads, city council	June 3–14, 2018
City council holds public hearings on city budget[b]	City council	June 17–21, 2018
City council approves budget and it becomes effective	City council	July 1, 2018

FIGURE 12.4 ▶ A police department's FY '19 budget calendar.

[a]Budget calendars vary widely in local government. This figure omits the handling of capital improvement projects (CIPs) and advanced financial topics, such as the submission of departmental earnings estimates, setting the tax millage rate, and forums for getting citizen input on priorities and programs.

[b]The number of public hearings required may be set in the city/county charter, by local ordinance, or by state law.

Quick Facts: Geese Police Restored in Budget

The Eatontown, New Jersey, city finance staff cut the budget $12,000 by eliminating the "Geese Police," a dog that chased the geese from Wampum Memorial Park. The city council's president expressed anger at the cut. One council member said the program was very effective, the cut would reduce park use, and the budget should be amended to fund the Geese Police.[56]

On the "left coast," There is an Oregon business, "Geese Guys," who use highly trained border collies to humanely eliminate high concentrations of Canada Geese from parks and other public areas. A single Canada Goose produces several pounds of "poop" daily. When there are larger populations of them, this creates a health hazard and eyesore, both of which reduce public use of such facilities. Because some number of animal control departments are located within the organizational structure of law enforcement agencies, "geese herding" becomes their responsibility.

dangerously worn out, no matter how well they have been maintained. These ideas are easily written, but when chiefs are confronted with 25 percent cuts in their budgets or end up where Stockton did after bankruptcy solid ideas perish under the weight of ugly realities.

When the chief meets with bureau or division commanders to review their budget requests, it is an opportunity to reward the "faithful" and to informally discipline those who are seen as "not toeing the party line" and are therefore "disloyal." In lean budget years, however, it is harder to reward the faithful and easier to harm a wayward subordinate.

Chiefs are also concerned with budget strategy and making the best case for funding. If solid justifications cannot be made for programs, they should not be included in the request lest it set budget analysts in the F/FSD on a quest to also find other programs to cut. As a matter of strategy, chiefs may include some "fat" in the budget, so that they can withstand a certain degree of reductions. The fat is not wasteful spending; it represents new positions or programs the department would like to have and would make good use of but whose loss would not endanger the delivery of important services.

In fiscally strained years, when transmitting the budget to the finance director or city manager, the chief's cover letter will detail what cuts were necessarily made in his/her proposed budget for the next year and what their probable impact will be and other difficulties created by budget cuts, for example, reduced response times, increased citizen dissatisfaction of their perception of the police and with police services, lower clearance rates, and future difficulties in recruiting. When a city or county's revenues are more robust, the Chief or Sheriff will cite accomplishments from the current budget, illustrated by success stories, and will call attention to the importance of new initiatives, and the lost opportunities and ills likely to arise if these initiatives are not funded. No matter what is happening in terms of the amount of crime, chiefs and sheriffs have an explanation that seemingly justifies a budget increase: If crime is up, more personnel and programs are needed to reduce it; if things are going well, new funding will help keep crime in check.

Step Two: Budget Review and Approval

At some point, the city manager will meet with the police chief to review the department's request. Prior to that meeting, the F/FSD will have reviewed the budget and had discussions about it with the mayor or city manager. How the meeting goes with the city manager depends on many factors, including the chief's reputation as a fiscal manager, his/her relationship with the city manager, the priorities and direction given by the city council, and the confidence the public has in the chief and the police department. Even recent events can affect the outcome. For example, assume that a chief has a street crimes unit whose tactics often include using decoys who are similar to the types of victims being targeted by predatory criminals (e.g., indigents, the elderly, and lone females). If in the past week, an offender was killed attempting to rob a decoy, the newspapers, and public sentiment may run toward disbanding this "killer" unit. No matter how effective the unit is, the question may become how much "bad press" can the city afford to have? Ultimately, the city manager and chief come to an understanding about the department's request. That understanding is reflected in the budget the city manager recommends to council.

When making their budget "pitch" to the city council, chiefs should be able to anticipate questions. For example, if the U.S. Department of Justice has just released a study on how the use of body cameras leads to a reduction in complaints against officers, the chief is likely to get this question: "Why aren't there body cameras in your budget?" If there is a large foreign population, law enforcement executives should be prepared to

---

Quick Facts: Quick Budget Tips

Although there are many considerations in budgeting, these are five quick tips:

1. **Don't Grasp Your Favorite Projects too Tightly.** Keep an eye on the big picture of what your core needs are and be flexible;

2. **Over Reliance on Workload Measures Can Create Problems.** If you relied on workload measures to justify prior budget increases, be prepared to counter downsizing questions when statistics take a fall. Such statistics may actually be 1-year anomalies;

3. **Keep Personnel as Your Top Priority.** You can lose positions faster than you acquired them and this is category to be defended, if possible,

because it accounts for the bulk of your operating budget;

4. **Under-Promise and Over-Deliver.** This is a well-known consultants' saying and it's true for budgeting too. Appropriators have long memories and they will remember and perhaps punish your department budgetarily for broken promises; and

5. **Paint a Realistic Picture of the Likely Results from Proposed Budget Cuts.** Don't overstate the "doom and gloom." Appropriators do need to know that cuts in patrol officer staffing will mean longer response times, fewer timely arrivals at crimes in progress scenes, and that there will be increasing citizen complaints about slow service.[57]

Quick Facts: Elite New York Police Department's (NYPD) Street Crimes Unit (SCU) Disbanded

The NYPD's SCU was elite, comprised of between 100 and 150 officers. Officers voted who came into the unit because their lives depended on each other. The SCU was particularly effective in detecting those who surreptitiously carried guns despite the strict gun laws. The almost legendary successes of the SCU became a prime factor in its downfall.

Against the advice of the unit's commanding officer, it was expanded by roughly another 300 officers. It is believed the quality of unit personnel was reduced by this decision. In 1999, there was a wrongful fatal shooting while young and inexperienced SCU officers searched for a rapist suspect. The suspect, perhaps thinking the plainclothes officers were robbers, tried to move his wallet, which was mistaken for a move to draw a weapon.

Although the officers were indicted for murder, they were acquitted. In the backlash that followed SCU was disbanded and as of 2015 had not been reactivated despite some calls to do so in a city where gun crimes and violence are on the rise.[58] At budget hearings before their city councils, chiefs must tread a narrow path. If they attempt to persuade council members to restore cuts made by city managers,

the chiefs risk alienating their "bosses." Conversely, if the cuts have gone too deep, chiefs as a matter of public safety may feel obliged to appeal for some funds to be restored (see Figure 12.5). Safer than initiating the appeal on their own, experienced chiefs may plant key questions with friendly members of council so that the discussion can be had without them openly spearheading the discussion. City managers know this game and can tolerate it, versus having their chiefs openly defy them. Generally, even council members who favor increasing the police budget may be reluctant to do so if it means voting for a tax increase.

Following several years of severe major budget cuts, one chief wrote a "budget impact" statement, explaining in detail to the city council what the effect of mandated as a result of the planned cuts of 110 positions and several programs.[59] This statement became a means of building budget support and mediating criticisms by citizens of slow service by the police department. One immediate result was that through public donations the mounted patrol continued to operate, albeit at about half its previous number of officers.

---

field a question such as: "What provisions have you made for pro-immigration reform demonstrations?" (see Figure 12.6.) In the final analysis, in some years chiefs, no matter how skilled they are or how good a presentation they made, simply have to be political realists and gracefully take their "budgetary lumps."

Table 12.1 shows the operating budget approval process for a police department's patrol function for FY 2016. The first column, "ORG" refers to the organizational unit (01474), which refers to the Patrol Division; each unit in the police department has a different "Org" number. "OBJ" is the number of the object of expenditure for each budget line; the object of expenditure for

FIGURE 12.5 ▶ New York City Police Commissioner Bill Bratton (2nd right) speaks to the media in his department's Joint Operations Command Room in 2016. The federal government announced plans to cut nearly $300 million from its national Urban Area Security Initiative grant program. In past years the Joint Operations Command Room was in part funded by grants from this source and Commissioner Bratton was speaking against the cuts and urging the $300 million be kept in the grant program. (Andrew Burton/Getty Images)

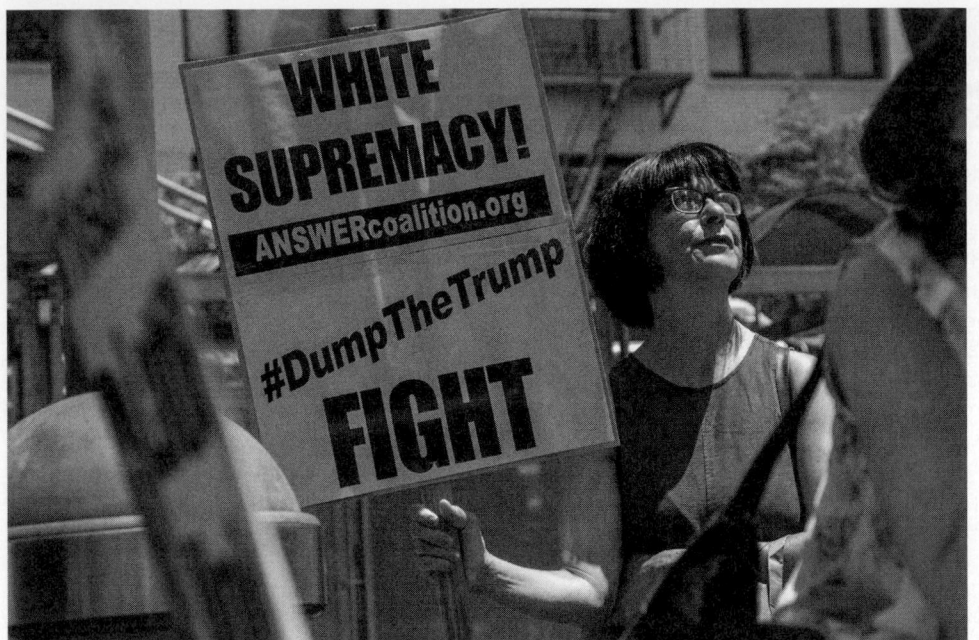

FIGURE 12.6 ▶ A 2015 demonstration in San Francisco by immigrants and their supporters against Presidential candidate Donald Trump, whose remarks about the shooting death of Kathryn Steinle by an undocumented Hispanic man who was just released from custody and previously been deported multiple times inflamed many people. (Santiago Mejia/Demotix/Corbis)

"6003" is "Payroll-Regular." The columns labeled "FY 2012 Actual" to "FY 2014 Actual" give the mayor and council members a quick 3-year summary of patrol's budget trend. "FY 2015" is the current budget year and that budget was still being executed. "FY 2016

Mayor Proposed" is the budget recommendation of the mayor to the city council, which, as the legislative body, has the final authority on budgets. The city council agreed with the mayor on most lines in the patrol budget, but came to different conclusions

TABLE 12.1 FY 2016 OPERATING BUDGET APPROVAL PROCESS

This table shows the operating budget approval process for one police department unit, the Patrol Division

ORG	OBJ	Police Patrol	FY 2012 Actual	FY 2013 Actual	FY 2014 Actual	FY 2015 Budget	FY 2016 Mayor Proposed	FY 2016 Council Approved	Percent Change
01474	6003	Payroll—Regular	4,283,889	4,428,791	4,612,450	4,497,410	4,510,787	4,510,787	0.30%
01474	6008	Special Officers/Events	67,297	90,414	149,508	60,480	122,823	112,823	86.55%
01474	6009	Payroll—Supplementary	202,006	226,554	188,437	240,000	140,000	140,000	-41.67%
01474	6020	Payroll—Overtime	137,398	204,775	127,687	84,000	125,000	125,000	48.81%
01474	6021	Court Time Travel	—	—	—	1,960	—	—	-100.00%
01474	6022	Shift Differential	113,690	125,089	117,547	124,460	124,460	124,460	0.00%
01474	6024	Callback	659,794	551,044	441,546	425,000	393,000	383,000	-9.88%
01474	6058	Uniform Maintenance	64,991	69,774	72,282	64,800	69,600	69,600	7.41%
01474	6156	Prisoner Meals	5,358	6,557	2,665	2,500	2,500	2,500	0.00%
01474	6302	Equipment Service	19,533	20,198	10,360	19,600	19,600	19,600	0.00%
			5,553,956	5,723,198	5,722,482	5,520,210	5,507,770	5,487,770	-0.23%

on two others. The budget format used in Table 12.1 is a "line item," discussed in more detail in a later section of this chapter.

Step Three: Budget Execution

This section deals with three key aspects of **budget execution**: (1) budget execution objectives, (2) budget execution adjustments, and (3) budget execution control.

BUDGET EXECUTION OBJECTIVES

Budget execution is the action phase of budgeting, the phase in which plans reflected in the police budget are put into operation.[60] During this phase, police chiefs:

1. must rigorously pursue achieving the goals of the agency;

2. document service gaps, the variance between the types and amounts of service delivery planned for versus actual demand;

3. provide timely information on expenditures, program accomplishments, and milestones for any CIP projects to senior appointed and elected officials, as well as the legislative body, such as city council, which appropriated the budget;

4. publicize police department successes; and

5. maintain budget execution control, a responsibility which is shared with the F/FSD and discussed in a subsequent section.

Budget Adjustments

It is said that people plan and fate laughs; like other types of plans, budgets must be monitored and adjusted as needed. Budget adjustments may increase or decrease a police department's budget. Any financial changes proposed for an adopted budget must be approved by the legislative body that adopted it, e.g., city council or county commission. In some states if the change reaches a certain dollar threshold, it requires the approval of the state.

There are six common methods of adjusting the budget: (1) accepting grants and donations; (2) transferring funds from one category to another, subject to any approval that is needed. A department head may have limited authority to do so and for larger transfers the approval of the legislative body, such as city council, is required; (3) seeking a supplemental budget some months into the execution phase because of unforeseeable conditions or other grounds, for example, when it is clear that anticipated demands for police services are outstripping resources. An example of this is when a smaller community suddenly becomes a college spring break destination; (4) freezing expenditures when the city's or county's revenue collection may be slower than anticipated; (5) delaying expenditures due to signs of revenue shortfalls; and (6) the city council or county commission may reallocate funds from one department to another, reduce the budget in just one or a few departments or by an across the board cut such as 3.5 percent (refer back to Figure 12.3). Some of these methods and related topics are discussed more fully in a later section of this chapter.

The Oregon Department of Revenue recognizes the following reasons for changing an approved budget, some of which exist in its State Statutes:

1. An occurrence or condition that was not known at the time the budget was prepared requires a change in financial planning.

2. A pressing necessity creates a need for prompt action.

3. Unexpected funds are made available by another unit of federal, state or local government (see Figure 12.7).

4. A request for services or facilities is received and the cost will be paid for by a private individual, corporation or company, or by another governmental unit, and the amount of the request could not have been known or known for certain at the time the budget was prepared.

5. Proceeds from the involuntary destruction, involuntary conversion, or sale of property have necessitated the immediate purchase, construction or acquisition of different facilities to carry on governmental operations.

6. A sufficiently greater amount of ad valorem taxes than estimated are received during the fiscal year such that the difference will significantly increase the level of government operations that can be funded by those taxes in the current year.

7. A local option tax is approved by the voters and produces revenue that can be used in the current budget year.

8. Less income from taxes and other mechanisms is produced, requiring the governing body to reduce appropriations.[61]

BUDGET EXECUTION CONTROLS

Even if the budget is not changed during its execution, budget controls are crucial to public accountability for the use of resources entrusted to the unit of government involved. Means of control are specified by state law and regulations, city/county charters and ordinances, and the policies and procedures established by the F/FSD, and the police chief.

Budget controls serve several purposes: (1) ensuring that laws, regulations, and accepted accounting procedures are followed, (2) making sure the funds are expended for the purposes authorized by the appropriators, (3) protecting resources from mismanagement or fraud,[62] (4) eliminating waste to preserve public funds, (5) preventing deficit spending, (6) identifying problems so responsibility can be fixed and remedial action taken, and (7) identifying gaps in control procedures that must be rectified.

The single most important aspect of both external and internal controls is separating the responsibility for various functions, which promotes the benefits of specialization and limits the ability of a few people to misuse or corrupt the system. Thus, for example, the purchasing department obtains competitive bids for equipment, but a different office, accounts payable, actually writes the checks, the police department verifies the delivery of the equipment, and a separate inventory control office accounts for the placement and use of the equipment.[63]

CITY COUNCIL AGENDA REPORT

DEPARTMENT: Administrative Services

MEETING DATE: March 17, 2015

PREPARED BY: Buffy Bullis, Finance Division Manager

AGENDA LOCATION: CC-5

TITLE: Acceptance of Fiduciary Management of the 2015-2016 High Intensity Drug Trafficking Area (HIDTA) Grant

OBJECTIVE: To approve the Finance Department's fiduciary oversight of the 2015-2016 HIDTA Grant and other related fiduciary responsibilities. In addition, to authorize the Chief of Police to execute the necessary grant documents.

BACKGROUND: Drug trafficking continues to be a problem for many communities within our country. In response to this national problem, law enforcement agencies across the United States have joined forces to combat drug trafficking. In Southern California, the Los Angeles High Intensity Drug Trafficking Area (LA HIDTA) serves as a means for coordinating various multi-jurisdictional task force activities which integrate federal, state, and local law enforcement resources for one common purpose: fighting and preventing drug trafficking.

As part of the financial requirements, a local jurisdiction must be responsible for the grant award and compliance, the receipt of funds, the disbursement of funds based on approved expenditures, and full accounting disclosure based on Generally Accepted Accounting Principles (GAAP).

ANALYSIS: Since 2007, the City of Monrovia has accepted fiduciary responsibility for managing the financial reporting and administration of this grant. As fiduciary, the City is a conduit for the grant funds. Authorized representatives from the LA HIDTA task forces submit approved invoices for payment and the City of Monrovia, in turn, issues payment and draws down funds from federal offices for reimbursement of monies paid.

The administration of this grant has a zero cost impact to the City's General Fund. The City will receive $120,000 to cover administrative and personnel costs necessary to properly account for the grant funds. In addition, if other additional related fiduciary responsibilities are undertaken, the City will receive appropriate reimbursement for any costs incurred.

According to the federal grant requirements, City Council approval is required before the City of Monrovia is allowed to accept fiduciary responsibility. In addition, grant guidelines require City Council to appoint an authorized official to execute the necessary documents. The Chief of Police will be designated as the authorized official.

If the City Council does not approve the acceptance of fiduciary management over the HIDTA grant, the ability for the LA HIDTA task forces to continue to combat drug trafficking will be substantially delayed until an alternate fiduciary is located.

ENVIRONMENTAL IMPACT: There is no environmental impact resulting from the acceptance of fiduciary management responsibility for this grant.

CC-5

FIGURE 12.7 ▶ Budget Adjustment Document for City Council Approval (Courtesy City of Monrovia, California). http://www.cityofmonrovia.org/sites/default/files/fileattachments/city_council/meeting/1869/cc-5.pdf

FIGURE 12.7 ▶ *(conclusion)*

FISCAL IMPACT: Approving the Finance Department's responsibility as fiduciary over the 2015-2016 HIDTA Grant will have a zero cost impact to the City's General Fund. The City will receive $120,000 to cover administrative and personnel costs incurred to properly account for the grant funds. The City will also be reimbursed for costs associated with performing other related fiduciary responsibilities.

OPTIONS: The City Council has two options:

1) Approve the Finance Department's fiduciary management of the 2015-2016 HIDTA Grant and other related fiduciary responsibilities. This option is recommended as it will allow the LA HIDTA task forces to continue their efforts to combat drug trafficking within the Southern California region.

2) Decline approval of the Finance Department's fiduciary oversight of the 2015-2016 HIDTA Grant and other related fiduciary responsibilities.

RECOMMENDATION: Staff recommends approving the acceptance of responsibility for fiduciary oversight of the 2015-2016 HIDTA Grant.

COUNCIL ACTION REQUIRED: If the City Council concurs, the appropriate action would be a motion to approve the acceptance of fiduciary oversight of the 2015-2016 HIDTA Grant and other related fiduciary responsibilities, and authorize the Chief of Police to execute the necessary documents.

External Controls.

External control is the control exercised on a police department's budget from outside of the police department. Each city or county's F/FSD is the primary external control agent for the police and other departments. The control methods here are illustrations; the full range of controls is much richer.

One universal method of external control is the allotment system. The F/FSD breaks each department's budget into portions, called **allotments**, which are amounts of money made available to the departments for specific periods of time, such as for a month or a 3-month period, called a quarterly allotment.

Allotments allow the F/FSD to time the availability of funding in the police department to the actual need for their expenditure. Therefore, allotments may vary in their amount from 1 month or quarter to another. This allows governments to invest funds not immediately needed. Freezing expenditures and cutting the budget are also external budget control measures.

In jurisdictions and particularly where there has been fraud or abuse in agencies, the F/FSD may conduct a "pre-audit" of transactions before purchases are made. The F/DSD periodically generates financial reports, such as Table 12.2, which they send to all departments. These budget status reports play a significant

TABLE 12.2 A PORTION OF A POLICE DEPARTMENT'S BUDGET STATUS REPORT, DECEMBER 31, 2016

Line Item	Approved	To Date Expended	Encumbered	Balance	% Expended
Salaries	$1,710,788.00	$848,161.05	$0.00	$862,626.95	49.58%
Training	$15,000.00	$5,374.47	$6,098.00*	$9,625.53	35.83%
Professional Services	$6,000.00	$2,000.00	$0.00	$4,000.00	33.33%
Travel	$8,500.00	$3,500.57	$1,500.25	$4,999.43	41.18%
Dues and Sub-scriptions	$3,100.00	$1,800.00	$0.00	$1,300.00	58.06%
Utilities	$35,000.00	$17,213.81	$0.00	$17,786.19	49.18%
Office Supplies	$22,000.00	$7,688.93	$634.39	$14,311.07	34.95%
Printing	$8,300.00	$4,187.23	$0.00	$4,112.77	50.45%
Uniforms	$38,000.00	$18,725.13	$0.00	$19,274.87	49.28%
Totals	$1,846,688.00	$908,651.19	$8,232.64	$938,036.81	49.20%

*Before a contract is signed or a purchase order issued, the F/FSD first determines if the funds are available in the budget. If they are, the amount involved is encumbered, meaning that it is held in reserve for payment upon delivery of the services or goods and is not part of the available balance in the budget.

role in monitoring expenditures. The final element in external control is audit and evaluation, discussed later in this chapter, as it is also the fourth and last component of the budget cycle.

Internal Controls.

The objectives of a police department's financial control system include: 1) safeguarding access to, and use of, organizational assets, 2) verifying financial transactions (such as cash payments from the informant fund), 3) encouraging operational efficiency, and 4) fostering adherence to fiscal policies. Altogether, the fundamental purpose of internal controls is to prevent mistakes before they happen and to rectify them when they occur.

Examples of internal controls include breaking the overall budget for the police department into smaller, more easily managed amounts based on units or activities, often referred to as cost centers (see Figure 12.8). Expenditures must be authorized in advance by appropriate documentation and authorizations.

Internal controls are crucial not only in the budget context but for the operation of the police agency as well. Illustrations of operational controls include policies on the use of tasers, impact weapons, pursuits, and use of deadly force.

Step Four: The Audit and Evaluation

Stated simply, an **audit** is a check on something; Governments audit themselves on an on-going basis throughout the FY. Historically, annual audits were of a department's budget, expenditures, and financial management practices—a financial audit

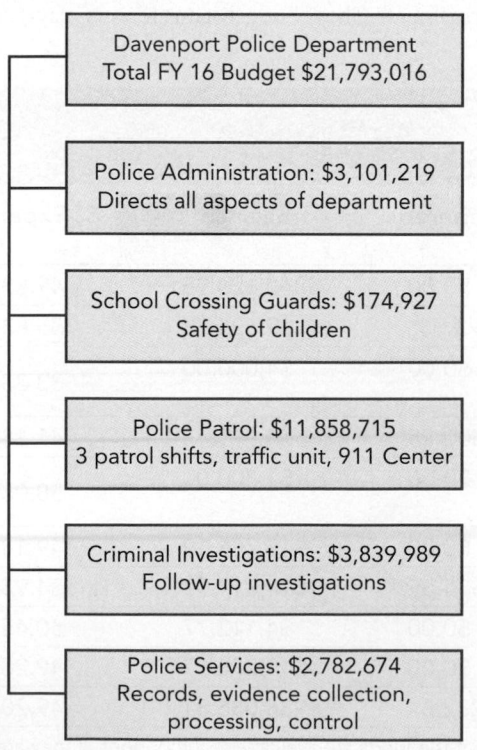

Davenport Police Department
Total FY 16 Budget $21,793,016

Police Administration: $3,101,219
Directs all aspects of department

School Crossing Guards: $174,927
Safety of children

Police Patrol: $11,858,715
3 patrol shifts, traffic unit, 911 Center

Criminal Investigations: $3,839,989
Follow-up investigations

Police Services: $2,782,674
Records, evidence collection, processing, control

FIGURE 12.8 ▶ Major cost centers in the Davenport, Iowa, Police Department's FY '16 budget.

(**FA**). In most states, the annual FA is submitted to the Office of State Auditor, where it is reviewed and any needed follow-up action taken. Financial auditors systematically collect and examine records and reports, conduct interviews, and otherwise rely on competent evidence to determine whether:

1. Required financial records and reports were made in a timely and complete form;

2. Public funds were subject to any waste, fraud, or abuse;

3. Unauthorized charges to the budget or reimbursements from the budget were made;

4. Computations were accurate;

5. Unauthorized transfers from one budget category to another were made;

6. Procurement requirements were followed; and

7. Expenditures were at or less than the approved budget.

Although there was some earlier movement, another type of annual audit began stirring in the late 1970s, determining how good of a job an agency was doing—a **performance audit (PA)**. Today, in many jurisdictions, an "audit" often encompasses both financial and performance components. Because financial audits have a longer history, the standards for them are well established and they have a fixed focus to them.[64] The U.S. Government Accountability Office's (GAO) guidelines for both FAs and PAs are contained in its Government Auditing Standards (2012), commonly referred to as the "Yellow Book." It notes that the focus of a PA is variable, according to the purpose stated for its execution. PAs may focus on some aspect of a police department's performance (e.g., compliance with legal mandates, program effectiveness and results, or a prospective analysis, such as the future value of advanced training in conflict de-escalation for police officers).[65]

The essence of all audits is that an independent party who has no stake in the outcome of the audit does the checking. To ensure the independence of auditors, some jurisdictions elect them, in others the legislative body, such as a city council or county commission, may appoint the auditor or a firm specializing in auditing governments will be retained.

Before an audit report is submitted in any unit of government, it is discussed with the chief of police and any errors of fact, representation, interpretation, or conclusion are corrected. If there is still content for which the auditor and the chief have differing opinions, the chief may write a **letter of exception**, setting forth the reasons why he or she believes that the audit report is wrong or manifestly unfair. After the city council reviews the audit report, the chief may be directed to appear before the council to answer questions, or the council may simply task the city manager or finance director to make sure that the police department takes any needed corrective action. No one enjoys criticisms because they identify weaknesses, yet a wise chief knows that correcting deficiencies is a pathway to enhanced performance and makes any needed changes without rancor.

Quick Facts: Audit Leads to Police Chief's Arrest

In 2015, an audit was performed of the Greensburg (Indiana) Police Department's Evidence Room. Thirteen property receipts for cash were found, but no cash. According to subsequent court documents, the chief stole $73,000 from it and gambled it away. She lost another $57,000 of family money gambling that was intended to partially replace the missing cash. Her gambling problem also led her to charge $30,000 on a credit card. The chief was arrested for one count of felony theft and another of official misconduct and plead guilty.[66]

BUDGET FORMATS

At the beginning of the 20th century there was nothing resembling the budget cycle previously described in this chapter. The power center in budgeting was the legislative body and its respective committees. Budgeting was a chaotic process because there was no central point, such as a budget office, where budget requests from departments were reviewed or revised. Moreover, committees, rather than a legislative body as a whole, often had the authority to appropriate funds for departments. Lump sum budgets were requested by the departments without any supporting details and sent directly to the legislature. There was no uniform system of accounts because each department used its own method, and audits were either not done or decades went by between them.[67]

It is not surprising that legislative bodies had little interest in giving up their central role in budgeting. When President Taft submitted an executive budget for FY 1914, Congress received it coldly and practically ignored it.[68] However, strong reform forces

were at work. In 1899, the Model Municipal Corporation Act, which proposed an executive budget under a mayor, received significant national attention. Executive budgets were also called for by New York Bureau of Municipal Research's *Making a Municipal Budget* (1907) and the National Municipal League's model 1916 city charter. Between roughly 1915 and 1925,[69] the executive budget and standard budget cycles and formats gained considerable use in local government. These appeared in the federal government with the passage of the 1921 Budget and Accounting Act.

These events are important because they (1) explain why substantial emphasis was placed on the control orientation in the early stages of budget reform and (2) underscore that budget control remains at the heart of budget execution, regardless of the type of budget format used. The sections that follow address six major types of budget formats: (1) line item, (2) program, (3) performance, (4) PPBS and zero-based, (5) priority based, and (6) hybrid. Additionally, service level, zero line item, and target budgeting are briefly discussed.

The Line Item Budget

The **line item**, or object of expenditure, is the oldest and simplest budget format; it remains widely used today, although it is most closely associated with the period from 1915 to just after World War II. The line item is the basic system on which all other budget formats ultimately rest because of its excellence as a control device. It gets its name from its nature: The amount that is requested, recommended, appropriated, and expended is associated with a particular item or class of items which appears as a separate numbered line in the budget.

Table 12.3 is an example of line item budget for the Borough of Colwn, incorporated in 1682. "Borough" is one of the legal classes of cities in Pennsylvania and Colwn is a bedroom community of 0.3 miles located adjacent to Philadelphia. The police department consists of a full-time Chief and nine part-time officers that provide 24-hour police coverage.

TABLE 12.3 THE 2015 LINE ITEM BUDGET FOR THE BOROUGH OF COLWN, PENNSYLVANIA	
410.122 • Salary—Police Chief	67,480.00
410.130 • Salary - Police Officers	0.00
410.135 • Salary—Part-time Police	269,680.00
410.137 • Police Overtime	5,000.00
410.145 • Salary—Crossing Guards	73,700.00
410.156 • Health\RX Insurance	108,924.00
410.157 • Dental Insurance	3,732.00
410.158 • Life Insurance	6,000.00
410.159 • Medicare	35,000.00
410.160 • Health/RX Deductibles	5,040.00
410.16-Fica	10,000.00
410.162 • Unemployment Compensation	15,000.00

(continued)

TABLE 12.3 (CONCLUSION)	
410.163 • Training	1,000.00
410.165 • Police Pension MMO	11,500.00
410.191-Cleaning Allowance	550.00
410.210 • Office Supplies	1,200.00
410.231 • Vehicle Fuel—Gasoline	24,000.00
410.238 • Uniforms—Officers and Crossing Guards	5,000.00
410.242 • Police Supplies	5,000.00
410.249 Ammunition	500.00
410.310 Professional Services—Animal Control	3,000.00
410.321 • Communication Telephone	2,000.00
410.351 • Automobile Liability Insurance	8,000.00
410.352 • General Liability Insurance	52,500.00
410.353 • Police Professional Liability Insurance	44,000.00
410.354 • Worker's Compensation Insurance	56,496.00
410.355 • Commercial Crime	22,375.00
410.374 • Vehicles - Maintenance	7,500.00
410.420 • Dues, Subscript. & Memberships	500.00
410.750 • Capital Purchases - Other Equip	50,000.00
410.900 • Miscellaneous Police Expenses	2,000.00
Ttal 410.000 • Police Protection	896,733.00

(Courtesy of the Borough Of Colwn) http://colwynborough.com/wp-content/uploads/2015-Final-Adopted-General-Fund-Budget.pdf, pp. 3–4.

Some limited workload indicators for past years and the forthcoming budget may also be included as part of a line item budget, although they are not used in a classical, or "pure" line item budget format. Such workload indicators may include one or a few of the following (1) arrests by various categories, (2) calls for service, (3) response times for emergency calls, (4) traffic citations issued, (5) accident investigations, (6) criminal investigations, (7) Uniform Crime Reports Part 1 Offenses per capita, and clearance rates.

In police departments large enough for functional specialization, there is an overall line item budget and that budget is broken down into smaller line item budgets for the various organizational entities (cost centers; refer to Figure 12.8, such as patrol, investigation, and crime prevention. These smaller budgets further facilitate control and serve as the basis of allocations within the police department. Cost centers can be used with any budget format. Table 12.4 summarizes the advantages and disadvantages of the line item budget format.

The Program Budget

The roots of the **program budget** spring from work by the (New York) Bureau of Municipal Research, which called for a new budget format in 1907. The term *program budget* was not established at that time, but its elements were clearly defined: "For each department, the budget shall be separated to show the kinds of services to be provided."[70] The next year New York City adopted a program budget. Both DuPont and General Motors used program budgeting during the 1920s and it was used by the federal government beginning in 1942. Program budgets were "center stage" from the 1940s until the 1960s, although they continue to be used.

For present purposes, a basic police program budget is a planning tool that links the expenditures for each program to the achievement of goals. Its basic components include (1) a program structure, (2) the attachment of goals to each program, and (3) a line item budget for control. Program budgets have increasingly added another feature: Objectives to Meet Goals. This feature identifies the activities that must be undertaken to achieve the goals.

Table 12.5 is a portion of a program budget for the Clovis Police Department. It shows the name of the program (Youth Services Section), its five goals, and the four objectives to reach the goals. A line item budget for the Youth Section immediately followed and totaled $790,900. Just two lines in the budget, regular salaries and benefits, totaled $490,100. In as much as the line item budget has been previously discussed, another such formatted budget is not repeated.

TABLE 12.4 ADVANTAGES AND DISADVANTAGES OF A LINE ITEM BUDGET	
Advantages	**Disadvantages**
• Focus is on controlling expenditures • Simplest format • Expenditures organized around categories or object of expenditures (e.g., SWAT Training, Paper for Copy Machines, or Gasoline) • Easy to prepare, present, and understand • Every item or class of items for which expenditures made is controlled • Control systems prevents overspending budget • "Behind" all other budget formats there is a line item budget for control	• Perpetuates the status quo: Once items become a line in the budget, they tend to stay there, creating inertia • No specific, measurable goals, without which police agencies have nothing to drive toward and measure their accomplishments/performance • No program structure (e.g., "DUI Enforcement" or "Abatement of Open-Air Drug Markets) • Budget changes tend to be incremental, small changes up or down in various categories • Inhibits reviews of what the valuable activities in the police department are versus the need to downsize, recombine, or eliminate some units that exist simply by the weight of tradition • Long-range planning is neglected • Limited information is provided to decision makers

Table 12.6 summarizes the advantages and disadvantages of a program budget.[71]

The Performance Budget/Performance-Based Budget (PB/PBB)

The (New York) Bureau of Municipal Research quickly improved on its program budget format by advocating that each program should now be accompanied by cost data, such as the cost for sweeping each mile of road. Such data is now included in what is called performance measures (PMs). The 1912 Taft Commission on Economy and Efficiency also called for a budget with cost data for the type of work being done. The weight of these two recommendations led to the adoption of what is now called a **performance budget or a performance-based budget (PB/PBB).** The absence of computer systems made implementing the PB/PBB labor intensive and it soon developed a reputation for being costly to implement, and unwieldy. Many cities that were early adopters of PB/PBB, such as New York City, tried it briefly and quickly dropped it.

In the 1930s, during the Depression, some cities (e.g., San Diego) made brief use of PB, although generally there was little experimentation with it until the 1950s. Faced with a large debt from World War II, the federal government sought to achieve

TABLE 12.5 CLOVIS, POLICE DEPARTMENT 2016 BUDGET FOR YOUTH SERVICES SECTION PROGRAM
2015–2016 Goals
1. Provide youth-related services that reduce the need to utilize the resources in patrol.
2. Deter and prevent juvenile crime by holding youth accountable through the Juvenile Work Program.
3. Maintain a 15 percent recidivism rate for juveniles referred to the Diversion Program.
4. Keep the City clean of graffiti.
5. Provide opportunities for youth to get involved in positive activities.
Objectives to Meet the Goals:
1. Plan and coordinate proactive police operations to identify, prevent, and break up juvenile parties where there is underage drinking and/or drug use.
2. Conduct on-going investigations to identify, arrest, and prosecute juveniles that commit drug- and alcohol-related offenses.
3. Provide youth leadership opportunities through the Police Explorer Post and Youth Leadership Institute for City of Clovis Youth.
4. Remove graffiti within 24–48 hours after the initial report.

(Courtesy City of Clovis, California, http://www.ci.clovis.ca.us/Portals/0/Documents/Finance/2015-2016%20Annual%20Budget.pdf, p. 136).

TABLE 12.6 ADVANTAGES AND DISADVANTAGES OF A PROGRAM BUDGET	
Advantages	**Disadvantages**
• Focus is on achieving broad police goals • Links programs, expenditures, and goals (e.g., 85% of citizens will feel safe) • Budget justifications are concrete • Appropriators can easily shift resources from one program to another • An excellent management tool for police chiefs • Because of goal orientation, easier to explain to public and garner their support	• More Labor intensive to develop than line item budgets • Some police goals are hard to measure. • Ineffectual program may be difficult to reduce or cut due to political champions of it. • Lacks a full system of performance metrics, such as number of new gang graffiti eradicated within 24 hours of discovery • Doesn't reveal the relative priority of each program.

greater spending efficiency. In 1949, the Commission on the Organization of the Executive Branch (the "Hoover Commission") recommended a performance budget and Congress passed the Reorganization Act that same year requiring its use. PB/PPB was used in the federal government in the1950s and part of the 1960s.

During the 1960s, the federal adoption of the Planning, Programing Budgeting System ended its use of PB/PBB and that format also lost momentum in state and local government. PPBS is discussed later in this chapter. PB/PBB regained some traction in state budgeting not later than the 1990s and also in local governments, but as the Great Recession played havoc with budgets, some jurisdictions retreated to a line item budget because there was simply less revenue over which to preside.[72] As the Great Depression receded, there was renewed interest in state and local government in PB/PBB and some of its techniques. To some degree, this interest was fed by the government transparency movement.

Presently, all 50 states and Puerto Rico use some form of performance measures in their budgets; however, only three states use a "pure" form of the new PB/PBB.[73] The remaining states use some PMs in conjunction with their primary budget format, such as the line item.

In local governments under 25,000, the new PB/PBB is often not practical because of limited resources and perhaps the expertise to implement it. However, the most significant contribution of PB/PBB may not be its pure form, but the substantial interest it has generated in PMs. Measuring what you are doing becomes the pathway to improved public service and being a better steward of resources allocated to the police department. Even in smaller jurisdictions there may be linkages between the budget and the outcomes produced, even if they are not robust. However, even measurements of "Planned For" versus "Actual" for different activities, e.g. number of burglaries investigated, is useful. Jurisdictions have to start where they are with what they have and improve going forward. As jurisdictions grow in size, their use of PMs increases. Mayors are less likely to use PMs than city managers.[74] While descriptions of PB/PBB continue to vary, a common set of elements is: 1) a program/activity structure; 2) goals (multi-year effort to reach) and/or objectives (one year or less to achieve); 3) a description of the strategies to be used to achieve the goals/objectives; 4) the resources (allocations/expenditures) connected to the program/activity; 5) use of PMs; and 6) a line item budget undergirding it for control.

The actual wording of PMs is dependent on what measurement they are trying to express. However, there are basic categories of PMs: 1) input: the resources (e.g., dollars and number of positions) that are used in a program/activity to deliver services to the public; 2) output: as a result of using the inputs, what was produced, such as the number of fatal auto/pedestrian collisions investigated; and 3) outcome/impact: changes in the number of such collisions and their clearance rate.[75]

Many law enforcement simply use PMs without reference to the basic categories, but which are illustrations of them. Examples include effectiveness (To what extent was the goal/objective achieved?), efficiency (creating the lowest cost for providing a given unit of output, such as the average hourly cost for operating the Police Harbor Patrol Boat) and quality (This measure often determines to what degree are citizens satisfied with the quality, accuracy, or timeliness of police service.

As currently practiced, the cost measures for PB/PBB are carefully selected because (1) good measures are difficult to develop, (2) cost accounting requires a high level of expertise, for example, determining the average cost is for an officer to respond to a call for service, and (3) it is expensive to collect and analyze the data for them. As a result, measures are often based on available data and costs may be stated in lump sum amounts instead of the average cost for producing a unit of work.

Table 12.7 shows the PB/PBB 2015 Police budget of Prince William County for its Support Service program. Some number of PB/PBB include data to compare their jurisdiction to the average of some number of similarly sized police departments or cities in their state, for example, clearance rates for Uniform Crime Reports Part I offenses. The outcome measure may specify that a police department must be in the upper third or half as compared to the other similarly situated cities. Table 12.8 summarizes the advantages and disadvantages of PBB.

The Support Services Division provides support services to the Office of the Chief, the Financial and Technical Services Division, the Operations Division and the Criminal Investigations Division. Located within the Support Services Division are the Administrative Support Bureau, the Personnel Bureau, the Animal Control Bureau, the Criminal Justice Academy, and Public Safety Communications (which is jointly administered with the Department of Fire & Rescue).

TABLE 12.7 THE PRINCE WILLIAM COUNTY, VIRGINIA, PB/PPB BUDGET FOR SUPPORT SERVICES IN THE POLICE DEPARTMENT

Key Measures	FY 12 Actual	FY 13 Actual	Trend	FY 14 Adopted	FY 15 Adopted
OSHA recordable incident rate among police employees	9.3	10.6	↑	—	≤10.8
Animal control effectively protects citizens and animals (community survey)	88%	88%	↔	88%	88%
Total number of identifications made from fingerprint impressions	310	385	↑	250	250
Sworn turnover rate without retirement and terminations	4.4%	4.6%	↑	4.2%	4.7%
Discrepancies found from audit of property evidence material	0	0	↔	0	0

↑ Trending Upward ↔ Stable ↓ Trending Downward

Support Services Program Activities & Workload Measures

	FY 12 Actual	FY 13 Actual	FY 14 Adopted	FY 15 Adopted
Administrative Services Bureau	$6,011,981	$6,254,422	$5,469,274	$5,652,057
Property received entered into systems within 48 hours	95%	100%	95%	100%
Permits and licenses reviewed	1,928	3,254	2,000	2,800
Records Section	$1,528,531	$1,510,346	$1,549,930	$1,596,118
Service requests	36,616	36,861	25,000	36,000
Forensics Services Section	$1,412,237	$1,524,190	$1,543,249	$1,595,915
Fingerprint packages recovered	1,233	1,284	1,500	1,300
Personnel Bureau	$1,634,788	$1,407,058	$1,491,820	$1,616,434
Applications reviewed	—	4,143	—	4,200
In-Service Training Section	$2,707,097	$2,490,813	$2,795,031	$3,263,862
Total hours of in-service training	—	42,625	—	48,000
Compliance with VA mandatory training standards	100%	100%	100%	100%
Basic Recruit Training Section	$3,593,670	$1,554,051	$2,125,502	$2,986,826
Total hours of basic training	—	21,200	—	42,000
Supervisors and field training officers reporting satisfactory preparedness of recruits	100%	96%	95%	95%
Animal Enforcement Section	$990,620	$1,250,600	$1,053,598	$1,136,414
Calls for Animal Control services	10,351	9,631	11,600	9,500
Animal Care Section	$838,400	$784,375	$844,964	$841,636
Animals entering shelter	5,867	5,558	5,500	5,500
Animals adopted	38%	43%	36%	40%

(Courtesy Prince William County, Virginia). http://www.pwcgov.org/government/dept/budget/SiteAssets/Pages/default/11—PS-Police.pdf, p. 412

The Planning, Programming Budgeting System (PPBS), and Zero-Based Budgeting (ZBB)

During the 1960s, federal government used the **Planning, Programming Budgeting System (PPBS)**. PPBS's dominant feature was planning and required extensive use of cost-effectiveness data. The process was cumbersome and unpopular with the federal agencies using it; PPBS made almost no headway in state and local government and by the very early 1970s it disappeared.

Another short-lived budget format in its pure form was **Zero-Based Budgeting (ZBB)**, developed at Texas Instruments in the early 1970s and introduced into the federal government in 1977 by President Carter. Pure ZBB requires that every governmental program or activity must justify its entire existence

TABLE 12.8 ADVANTAGES AND DISADVANTAGES OF A PERFORMANCE-BASED BUDGET

Advantages	Disadvantages
• Focus is on costs and performance measures. • As presently practiced, the limited and carefully selected cost measures substantially reduces expensive cost accounting techniques. • Provides sufficient data to decision to strengthens oversight by appropriators. • Performance measures assist police chiefs in allocating resources, a plus in strategic planning and management, as well as being able to demonstrate being responsive to the community, e.g. adding more school crossing guards at the request of the Parent Teacher Association (PTA). • Performance measures can be useful in program evaluation. • Chiefs can use on-going performance measurement data to guide and control current programs, identify deviations, and "keep things are on track." • Like Citizen Centric Reports, PBB makes government more transparent, enhancing government openness, which is associated with greater citizen satisfaction.	• May measure what is easy rather than what is important. • Expensive if extensive cost measures are used. • Can tell whether current programs are being done right, but not whether the right things are being done. • How do you determine if the results are "good enough"? Benchmarking? Ad hoc comments by appropriators, citizens, special interest groups? Citizen Centric Reports? • Additional resources dedicated to successful programs do not guarantee even better results. • May be time consuming to distinguish between poorly performing police programs that are under resourced and those that must be abandoned. • Some poorly stated performance measures may imply quotas and provoke public controversy, e.g., number of traffic citations to be issued.

each new operating budget year. In ZBB, each program or activity requested in a budget is organized into a decision package (DP) and includes three alternative funding levels: eliminated or reduced, current, and enhanced. No program or activity is considered essential; its existence must be tightly justified. New service DPs could also be submitted. Police chiefs who used ZBB prioritized their DPs and appropriators determined what DPs would be funded at what level but tended to carefully consider their Chiefs' priorities. The massive paperwork required doomed ZBB as a budgeting process and it also faded, although here and there a less comprehensive use of DPs can be found as part of program or performance budgeting.

Today, the use of pure ZBB is seldom encountered, although remnants are still found, e.g., service level budgeting and zero line item budgeting. **Service level budgeting (SLB)** assumes, unlike ZBB, that programs and activities have previously been justified. The key question is at what level should they be funded? Departments using SLB prepare a required number of packages for their programs and activities, each package describe a different level of service and cost for appropriators to consider. In "**zero line item budgeting**" departments receive a blank budget request form with zeros filled in for each line item, instead of last year's budget or actual expenditures as the starting point. Departments must rebuild their budgets from the ground up and justify each line,[76] but do not use decision packages.

The Hybrid Budget

Budget formats can be described with a great deal more purity than actually exists in many real-world applications. The lone exception may be the line item because so many of the numerous smaller jurisdictions use it and even in larger cities and counties where more advanced formats are used the line item is still relied on for

control. The reason for this lack of "pure" formats is that each jurisdiction, and by extension its police department, uses a system that makes sense to it. History, unique city charter provisions, state laws and local ordinance, past practices, the preferences of key people in the budgeting process, and other variables contribute to the reality that many budgeting systems incorporate features from one or more formats. The test of a budget format is how it's constructed, not what it's labeled. Many budgets are **hybrid budgets**, incorporating features of several different types of budget formats. There are also different philosophies that can be attached to the budget formats. As an illustration, "target budgets" is when agencies are given a target amount that their budget cannot exceed unless compelled by special circumstances.

ASSET FORFEITURE, GRANTS, POLICE FOUNDATIONS AND DONATION PROGRAMS, AND THE WIDE USE OF VOLUNTEERS

This section provides more detailed information about some of the common ways budget adjustments can be made, as well as several other topics, such as asset forfeitures and the wide use of volunteers.

Asset Forfeiture

In 11th-century England, horses, carts, and other property involved in a fatal accident were deemed *deodand* (literally, to be given to God) and forfeited to the king for "pious use"; the practice was abandoned by an act of Parliament in 1846 due to the seizure of trains involved in fatal accidents.[77] Generally, property can be subject to forfeiture in the United States if it is (1) contraband, (2) the proceeds of criminal activity, (3) used to facilitate criminal activity, or (4) connected to criminal enterprise.[78]

In addition to their own state forfeiture laws, state and local law enforcement agencies were long able to retain, unless otherwise directed by state laws, 80 percent of their seizures by asking the federal government under the Equitable Sharing program to "adopt" their seizures.[79] After 9/11 to 2014, state and local law enforcement agencies made 61,998 cash seizures totaling $2.5 billion.[80] In 2015, the U.S. Department of Justice barred state and local law enforcement agencies from using federal law to seize almost all types of assets unless it was under warrant or involved criminal charges. A few exceptions to this policy exist, such as illegal firearms, explosives, and child pornography.[81]

State laws regulating forfeitures have not changed much since 2015. Generally, such laws have not been required a search warrant as a pre-condition to seizing assets. However the U.S. Department of Justice's action may foreshadow similar actions by some states. State forfeitures may follow a criminal conviction or be by civil forfeiture, which is independent of criminal proceedings.[82] The standard of proof for forfeiture cases varies by state and in some states by the type of asset seized. States laws that regulate the distribution of forfeitures may be restricted or generous. Some allow none or 100 percent of the assets to be retained by the police. Missouri is one of eight states where asset forfeitures go to education and that distribution has not reduced police asset seizures.[83] Because of these variations asset forfeitures were not included in the earlier section on budget adjustments.

Allowing a portion of or all assets forfeited to go to the police has fairly raised the criticism that it gives the police an incentive to focus on forfeitures (see Figure 12.9). There may be some validity to that criticism. In a budget reviewed for this chapter, a performance measure was to increase forfeiture cases by a certain number. Other jurisdictions may not be so frank as to openly espouse such an increase, but the possibility exists that under fiscal stress a police department may be under pressure to essentially help fund itself.

Grants

The largest amount of grant funds flowing to the police has always been through the federal government. However, the dollar amount of federal grants to law enforcement agencies has been trending downward since 1996. Although a number of federal agencies, such as the Department of Homeland Security and the National Highway Traffic Safety Administration, provide grants for law enforcement agencies, the U.S. Department of Justice has provided a wider array of grant opportunities, such as those for community-oriented policing, reduction of gun and gang crimes, DUI abatement, enhancement of crime analysis, acquisition of new technologies, reduction of violence against women (including stalking and human trafficking), enforcement of protective orders, and date and domestic violence.

Some large corporation foundations have an interest in the police; the Met Life Foundation makes grants nationally to support innovative partnerships between community groups and the police to promote neighborhood safety and neighborhood revitalization.

One of the most spectacular awards to a law enforcement agency by a community foundation was made by the Caruth

FIGURE 12.9 ▶ City of Tenaha, Texas, which serves a community of 1,000. In a single year Tenaha seized nearly $1.2 million in cash, mostly from out-of-town motorists. (San Antonio Express-News/ZUMA Press/Alamy Stock Photo)

Quick Facts: Black Asphalt

A private intelligence network has assisted law enforcement agencies across the country in seizing assets. The **Black Asphalt Electronic Networking & Notification System** has allowed agencies to share information about drivers, both criminal and innocent, including social security numbers, addresses, tattoos, and hunches about which drivers to stop. The driving force behind it also made a movie in 1989, Desert Snow, which trained law enforcement officers in recognizing potential stops.[84]

Foundation in 2008. The Dallas Police Department (DPD) received $9.5 million from it to train a new generation of leaders for the 21st century, leading to the creation of the Caruth Police Institute (CPI). An endowment for perpetual support was created with $6 million and the remaining $3.5 million was dedicated to startup costs. In 2010, CPI graduated the first class—23 DPD Lieutenants, who completed a 6-week course taught by leading national experts. The graduates reported that the course taught them to think differently and to set higher goals. Even the smallest foundations, which may restrict applicant eligibility to one county, make police awards. Illustratively, the Harrison County (Indiana) Community Foundation funds small police projects, often for the acquisition of a single piece of equipment.

Police Foundations and Donations

Nonprofit police foundations have proliferated over the past 30 years, literally dotting the landscape from Los Angeles to New York City. Their prominence is such that the International Association of Chiefs of Police (IACP) has a Police Foundations Section. Police foundations are a conduit from the public and businesses that wish to promote excellence in their police departments through the donation of money, goods, and services.[85] The goal is to provide resources unavailable to departments through the budget process. Most police foundations serve multiple purposes, such as promoting wellness, recognizing valorous officers, and making purchases of equipment and newer technology, such as license plate scanners. In Indianapolis during 2015, the Police Foundation was raising $200,000 to help officers injured in the line of duty. CompStat may have never been or its development delayed without a $15,000 check from the New York City Police Foundation, which was ready 2 days after the request was initiated.[86] Police foundations in smaller jurisdictions have a narrower focus and may be limited to a single purpose. The Jackson, Mississippi, Police Foundation funds one-time purchases such as noise decibel readers to enforce the noise pollution ordinance; the foundation also engages in advocacy for the Jackson Police Department (JPD), orchestrating an agreement with a local hospital to perform police physicals, saving the JPD $100,000.[87]

Donations to law enforcement agencies are widely varied. Two examples of good corporate citizenship illustrate this point. When four police officers were killed in Lakewood in 2009, all of the Papa John's Pizza restaurants in the state of Washington gave 100 percent of 2 days' receipts to the families of the slain officers.[88] Law enforcement agencies also rally to help their own when tragedy strikes. In the "home department" where the tragedy occurred, officers and civilian employees personally make donations and hold fund-raising activities to help the families of officers killed in the line of duty. In 2010, QualComm and Leap Wireless International gave 200 cell phones and 2 years of service to the San Diego Police Department. Among the units that had been facing a loss of cell phones were child abuse, sex crimes, narcotics, and auto theft.[89] Individually, actor David Spade donated $100,000 to the Phoenix, Arizona, Police Department to help purchase new firearms. Another sign of hard times are police websites, like that for Oshkosh, Wisconsin, which prominently feature a donations section advising readers how to help the department by making donations.

Wide Use of Volunteers

Police departments have long been aware of the advantages of involving volunteers. Often, this was limited to Reserve/Auxiliary police and a few other positions. In the midst of budget slashes, many agencies have, and seem likely to continue, a much more robust use of qualified volunteers. The volunteers often have diverse backgrounds in business, are well-qualified retirees, or simply may be local citizens who want to help make a difference in their community. Among the uses made of volunteers are:

- Bilingual services, including verbal and document translations
- Coordinate neighborhood watch programs
- Crime prevention activities
- Maintaining computer systems
- Counsel victims of domestic abuse
- Parking enforcement
- Crime scene protection
- Vacation checks
- Bike registration
- Traffic control
- Legal research
- Crime analysis
- Purchasing
- Editing/Writing departmental publications, for example, newsletters and brochures
- Administration of volunteer program
- Recruiting volunteers, especially those with specific skill sets
- Planning departmental events
- Communications and Records assistance

Quick Facts: Volunteers in Police Service

VIPS has been an important catalyst to the movement toward broader use of volunteers. The International Association of Chiefs of Police (IACP) manages and implements the Volunteers in Police Service (VIPS) Program in partnership with the Bureau of Justice Assistance, U.S. Department of Justice. VIPS is administered by individual agencies and its origin was in President George W. Bush's 2002 State of the Union Address.

The VIPS Program provides support and resources for agencies interested in developing or enhancing a volunteer program and for citizens who wish to volunteer their time and skills with a community law enforcement agency. The program's ultimate goal is to enhance the capacity of state, local, campus, tribal, and territorial law enforcement to utilize volunteers. The VIPS staff shares information and resources with law enforcement agencies that want to expand their programs, increase the use of volunteers in existing programs, help citizens learn about and become involved in VIPS program.[90]

Chapter Summary

Summary by Chapter Objective

1. **State the five ways in which the Great Recession affected many law enforcement agencies.**

The Great Recession: (1) introduced fiscal distress, (2) reduced their resources, (3) forced law enforcement executives to make painful decisions, (4) left a lingering impact on many agencies, and (5) provided useful and sometimes painful lessons about financial management.

2. **Identify seven strategies used by law enforcement agencies to counter fiscal stress.**

Any seven of the following 14 strategies fully responds to this objective:
(1) freezing new hires and eliminating positions; (2) canceling recruit and many advanced training classes; (3) requiring officers to take furlough/unpaid days off; (4) reducing salaries; (5) closing precincts; (6) delaying the purchase of replacement vehicles; (7) selling helicopters; (8) closing police stations to the public; (9) slashing police programs; (10) eliminating mounted patrol, motorcycle, accident investigation, burglary, and marine patrol units; (11) laying off officers and slashing overtime funding; (12) achieving reductions in force by not filling vacancies created by attrition; (13) replacing sworn officers with fewer and less expensive civilians; and (14) increasing the numbers and breadth of assignments for volunteers.

3. **Give three definitions of the budget.**

Those definitions are (1) a plan expressed in dollars, (2) the use of financial resources to meet human needs, and (3) a contract between those who appropriate the money and those who execute the budget.

4. **Explain why budgeting is inherently a political process.**

Budgeting is inherently a political process because elected members of city councils, county commissions, state legislatures, and even Congress express their preferences when they vote on appropriations. The appropriators' personal views and those of their constituents, political donors, the news media, police unions, polls, special interest groups, lobbyists, colleagues, and other entities often shape these decisions, as well as deals to secure support for their own interests. Politics do not stop when a budget is adopted; in some circumstances, the politics can actually intensify during the time a budget is executed.

5. **Define operating and capital budgets.**

Most operating budgets are for a single fiscal year, although some jurisdictions use the 2-year biennial operating budget. Operating budgets are for recurring expenses, such as salaries, gasoline, paper, uniforms, and kindred items. Except for grants and donations, the operating budget is overwhelmingly funded by the general fund.

The definition of what goes into the capital budget varies widely. This is because the threshold for placing items in a capital budget is not uniform. In one city, it might be $2,500 or less, while in another, the cost must exceed $35,000. Capital budgets are for larger cost "big ticket" items which last multiple years, are an aggregation of capital improvement projects (CIPs), may necessitate issuing a bond and going into debt, although some jurisdictions have a pay-as-you-philosophy, are reviewed and adjusted annually, bond debt is paid on semi-annually to investors and after it is retired, there are no recurring capital budget costs for it. However, in the case of a new police station or other facility, the maintenance cost for it comes out of the operating budget.

Some CIPs may be required as a matter of law, such as a court order to a county or a consent decree to build a new jail for the Sheriff's Office/Department because the existing one is antiquated and continuously overcrowded.

Some local governments have moved away from having separate operating and capital budgets and combine them in a single document. Appropriators usually consider the operating portion first and the capital section last, usually over a series of meetings.

6. **Identify the key objectives of citizen-centric reports.**

The key objectives of citizen-centric reports are to increase the transparency of government and citizen participation in governance

7. **Provide five quick budgeting tips.**

   1. Don't grasp your favorite projects too tightly.
   2. Over-reliance on workload measures can create problems.
   3. Keep personnel as your top priority.
   4. Under-promise and over-deliver.
   5. Paint a realistic picture of the likely results of proposed budget cuts.

8. **List and briefly describe the four major steps in the budget cycle.**

The **budget cycle** has four sequential steps that are repeated at about the same time every year in a jurisdiction: (1) preparation and submission of the budget by all of a city or county's departments, which includes getting input from stakeholders, such as citizens and advisory boards; (2) evaluation and appropriation by the legislative body, which may involve public hearings and occasionally heated exchanges; (3) execution of the budget and supplemental budgets, which means actually doing the things for which public funds have been appropriated; and (4) the audit, which is an independent evaluation of something, for example, a law enforcement agency's control of its petty cash fund, its annual expenditures, or its performance on key indicators, such as use of force.

9. **Identify six common ways in which a police budget can be adjusted.**

These common methods are (1) accepting grants and donations, (2) transferring funds from one category to another, subject to any approval that is needed. A department head may have limited authority to do so and for larger transfers the approval of the city council and in some cases the state is required, (3) seeking a supplemental budget some months into the execution phase because of

unforeseeable conditions or other grounds, for example, when it is clear that anticipated demands for police services are outstripping resources. An example of this is when a community suddenly gets caught "on the radar" of students in Spring break and couldn't anticipate the traffic congestion and accidents, the volume of visitors, and the substantial increase in calls for service, (4) freezing expenditures when the city's or county's revenue collection may be slower than anticipated, (5) delaying expenditures due to signs of revenue shortfalls, and (6) the city council or county commission reallocates funds from one department to another or reduces the budget in just one or a few departments or by an across the board cut such as 3.5 percent.

10. **Describe the nature of the line item budget**

Every amount that is requested, recommended, appropriated, and expended is associated with a particular item or class of items that appear as a separate numbered line in the budget. It's wide use is because it provides excellent budget control.

11. **Identify the feature that is increasingly found in program budgets.**

Program budgets have increasingly added "Objectives to Meet Goals." It identifies the activities that must be undertaken to achieve the goals.

12. **Provide three reasons why cost measures for performance budgets/performance-based budgets are carefully selected.**

Cost measures for PB/PBB are carefully selected because (1) good measures are difficult to develop, (2) cost accounting requires a high level of expertise, for example, determining what the average cost is for an officer to respond to a call for service, and (3) it is often expensive to collect and analyze the data for them.

13. **Explain how service level and zero line item budgeting work.**

Both are variants of ZBB. Service level budgeting (SLB) assumes, unlike ZBB, that programs and activities have previously been justified. The key question is at what level should they be funded? Departments using SLB prepare a required number of packages for their programs and activities, each package describes a different level of service and cost for appropriators to consider. In "zero-line item budgeting" departments receive a blank budget request form with zeros filled in for each line item, instead of last year's budget or actual expenditures as the starting point. Departments must rebuild their budgets from the ground up and justify each line, but do not use decision packages.

14. **Explain hybrid budgets and why they exist.**

Hybrid budgets are not a "pure" budget format and incorporate features from two or more different formats. Many budgets are hybrids because of history, unique charter provisions, state laws local ordinances, past practices, the preferences of key people in the budget process, and for other reasons. It seems likely that the line item budget is used in a "pure" form more than any format. It dominates the budgets of the numerous small jurisdictions and in larger cities and counties that use a more advanced format, the line item budget is also there for control.

15. **Identify eight different jobs a volunteer could do in a law enforcement agency.**
   Any eight of the following 19 jobs fully responds to this objective:

   Bilingual services, including verbal and document translations

   Coordinate neighborhood watch programs

   Maintaining the agency's website/keeping it updated

Crime prevention activities

Maintaining computer systems

Counsel victims of domestic abuse

Parking enforcement

Crime scene protection

Vacation checks

Bike registration

Traffic control

Legal research

Crime analysis

Purchasing

Editing/Writing departmental publications, for example, newsletters and brochures

Administration of volunteer program

Recruiting volunteers, especially those with specific skill sets

Planning departmental events

Communications and Records assistance

Chapter Review Questions

1. In terms of financial management, how did the economic crash of 1929 a effect the relationship of states with their local units of government?

2. What is a fiscal year? Give examples of two different fiscal years.

3. Before appearing before city council to present their departments' budgets chiefs may plant questions with a friendly member. Why?

4. What are financial and performance audits? Why are performance audits more varied in their approach?

5. What is the focus of a line item budget versus a program budget?

6. Why is it argued that law enforcement agencies should not receive any portion of the assets that are forfeited as the result of their investigative actions?

Critical Thinking Exercises

1. Assume that you were the Chief of Police in Stockton from the time that city had substantial revenues until the court issued its adverse ruling on pensions in that jurisdictions. From an overall financial management situation, what things did you learn?

2. Read the section on performance audits. Assume you are a Sergeant in the Patrol Division. One of your officers hands you a report to approve that only states in the narrative section that the "Subject was injured while resisting arrest and transported to the hospital." What information do you think is missing?

Key Terms

allotments	budget cycle	operating budget
audit	budget execution	performance audit (PA)
benchmarking	capital budget	performance budget (PB)
biennial budget	capital improvement project (CIP)	Planning, Programming Budget
Black Asphalt	fiscal year (FY)	System (PPBS)
budget	Great Recession	program budget
budget adjustment	letter of exception	results-based budget (RBB)
budget calendar	line item budget	zero-based budget (ZBB)

Endnotes

[1] See No author, "Longest Recession Since 1930s Ended in June 2009, Group Says," Los Angeles Times, September 20, 2010, p. 1, http://articles.latimes.com/2010/sep/20/business/la-fi-recession-20100920, accessed May 27, 2016.

[2] Tahmi Luhby, "84% of Cities in Money Trouble," CNN, February 4, 2009, p.1, http://money.cnn.com/2009/02/04/news/economy/city_troubles/?postversion=2009020418, accessed May 27, 2016.

[3] Robert Jay Dilger, State Government Fiscal Stress and Federal Assistance (Washington, DC: Congressional Research Service, February 4, 2014), unnumbered summary page at the front of the document and National Governors Association and the National Association of State Budget Officers, "The Fiscal Survey of States," (Washington, DC: National Association of State Budget Officers, 2011), p. Xiii.

[4] Nick Wing, "We Pay a Shocking Amount for Police Misconduct, and Cops Want Us to Accept It. We Shouldn't," Huffington Post, May 29, 2015, p. 1, http://www.huffingtonpost.com/2015/05/29/police-misconduct-settlements_n_7423386.html, accessed May 27, 2016.

[5] Andrew Schroedter, "Chicago Police Misconduct-A Rising Financial Toll," Better Government News, January 31, 2016, p. 1. http://www.bettergov.org/news/chicago-police-misconduct-%E2%80%93-a-rising-financial-toll, accessed May 27, 2016.

[6] Charles Thomas, "City Council Passes Budget, Praises Mayor," ABC/WLS-TV Chicago, November 16, 2011, pp. 1-2, http://abc7.com/archive/8433801, accessed May 28, 2016.

[7] No author, U.S. Bureau of Labor Statistics Data, "Databases, Tables, and Calculations By Subject," May 28, 2016, p. 1, http://data.bls.gov/timeseries/LAUMT064470000000004?data_tool=XGtable, accessed May 28, 2016, Kevin Parrish, "In Stockton, Nearly 30,000 Youngsters Live Below the Poverty Line," Recordnet.com, July 29, 2013, p. 1, http://www.recordnet.com/article/20130729/A_NEWS/307290312, accessed May 28, 2016, and John Rudolph, "Stockton's Poor Mired in Violence After Police Cuts, Recession," Huffington Post, March 19, 2012, p. 2, http://www.huffingtonpost.com/2012/03/18/stockton-poor-poverty-crime-california_n_1346096.html, accessed May 28, 2016.

[8] For a period of several years Stockton was in the top 4 of the highest crime plagued cities in California. Conditions have improved and Stockton should be recognized for the improvements made.

[9] Alan Greenblatt, "What It's Like Living in a Bankrupt City," NPR (National Public Radio), September 6, 2013, p. 2, http://www.npr.org/2013/09/06/219313881/what-its-like-living-in-a-bankrupt-city, accessed May 28, 2016.

[10] Kurt Badenhausen, "America's Most Miserable Cities," Forbes, February 6, 2009, p. 1, http://www.forbes.com/2009/02/06/most-miserable-cities-business-washington_0206_miserable_cities.html, Accessed May 29, 2016 and Kurt Badenhausen, "In Pictures: America's Most Miserable Cities," Forbes, February 2, 2011, p. 1, http://www.forbes.com/2011/02/02/stockton-miami-cleveland-business-washington-miserable-cities_slide_2.html, accessed May 29, 2016.

[11] Jim Christie, "How Stockton Went Broke: A 15-Year Spending Binge," Reuters, July 3, 2012, p. 2, http://www.reuters.com/article/us-stockton-bankruptcy-cause-idUSBRE8621DL20120703, accessed May 28, 2016.

[12] Ibid., p. 2.

[13] No author, "Initiative, Referendum, and Recall, National Conference of State Legislatures, September 20, 2012, p. 1, http://www.ncsl.org/research/elections-and-campaigns/initiative-referendum-and-recall-overview.aspx, accessed May 29, 2016.

[14] See Dan Charles, "How California's New Rules Are Scrambling the Egg Industry," NPR (National Public Radio), December 29, 2014, pp. 1-3, http://www.npr.org/sections/thesalt/2014/12/29/373802858/how-californias-new-rules-are-scrambling-the-egg-industry

[15] S. Evans, B. Kosenko, and M. Polyakov, "How Stockton Went Bust: A California's Decade of Policies and the Financial Crisis that Followed," U.S. Common Sense, May 24, 2012, p. 5, http://uscommonsense.org/research/how-stockton-went-bust-a-california-citys-decade-of-policies-and-the-financial-crisis-that-followed, accessed May 29, 2016. U.S. Common Sense is a 501©3 non-profit, non-partisan entitydedicated to "opening up" or making government more transparent.

[16] "How Stockton Went Bust: A California's Decade of Policies and the Financial Crisis that Followed,"p. 5.

[17] Loc. Cit.

[18] "How Stockton Went Broke: A 15-Year Spending Binge," p. 3.

[19] Joe Goldeen, "Thieves Taking Advantage of Abandoned Rural Homes," Recordnet.com, February 10, 2008, p. 1, http://www.recordnet.com/article/20080210/A_BIZ/802100302, accessed May 29, 2016.

[20] "How Stockton Went Bust: A California's Decade of Policies and the Financial Crisis that Followed," p. 4.

[21] "How Stockton Went Bust: A California's Decade of Policies and the Financial Crisis that Followed,"p. 14.

[22] Taves and White, "On The Mend, But Going Bust," p. 4.

[23] Evans, Kosenko, and Polyakov, "How Stockton Went Bust: A California City's Decade of Policies and the Financial Crisis That Followed," p. 2.

[24] Billy Hamilton, 'The Ask': What's at Stake in Stockton's Bankruptcy? State Tax Notes, 65, July 30, 2012, p. 2. State TaxNotes is the publication of a non-profit organization created in 1970 to provide tax news and analysis to tax specialists around the world, see Taxanalysts.com.

[25] Evans, Kosenko, and Polyakov, "How Stockton Went Bust: A California City's Decade of Policies and the Financial Crisis That Followed" p. 7. 26.

[26] Rich Danker, "Rich Danker: How Bad Pension Accounting Sunk Stockton," San Jose Mercury News, August 20, 2012, p. 1. http://www.mercurynews.com/ci_21358657/rich-danker-how-bad-pension-accounting-sunk-stockton (accessed July 3, 2015).

[27] Evans, Kosenko, and Polyakov, "How Stockton Went Bust: A California City's Decade of Policies and the Financial Crisis That Followed", p. 9.

[28]Ibid., p. 11.

[29]Ibid., p. 9.

[30]No Author, "Stockton Bankruptcy Court Looks at Pension Cuts," Calpensions, May 19, 2014, p. 2, http://calpensions.com/2014/05/19/stockton-bankruptcy-judge-looks-at-pension-cuts/ (accessed July 8, 2015).

[31]WSLS10 (Television), Angela Hatcher, "Losing Troopers: Virginia State Police Hit Hard by Budget Cuts," online access, p. 3, WWW2.WSLS.com, November 11, 2008.

[32]Dustin Gardiner, "Phoenix Imposes Cuts on Police Pay in Late, Tense Session." The Republic, May 8, 2014, http://www.azcentral.com/story/news/local/phoenix/2014/05/08/phoenix-imposes-cuts-police-pay-late-tense-session/8838737, accessed May 25, 2016. The police were not singled out for a pay cut. The council voted for a 1.6% pay cut for all employees to save $16.5 million in expenditures.

[33]Todd South, "Police Satellite Precincts Closing," *Chattanooga (TN) Times Free Press*, online access, February 4, 2010, TimesFreePress.com

[34]Jeff Brady, "Facing Budget Gap, Colorado City Shuts Off Lights," National Public Radio, February 14, 2010, online access, NPR.org

[35]Matt Bartosik, "Police Station: Sorry, We're Closed," NBCChicago.com, on-line access, July 29, 2009.

[36]Arlington (VA) Proposed Fiscal Year 2011 Budget Proposal.

[37]Maxine Bernstein, "Portland Police Propose Cutting Mounted Patrol and Leaving Some Positions Vacant to Balance Budget," PortlandLive.com, on-line access, January 14, 2010.

[38]In Minnesota alone in the past few decades, more than 100 small towns have disbanded their police department, merged with another one, or turned to their sheriff for services," See Tom Robertson, "Cass Lake Abolishes Police Force, Seeks Enforcement Deal with County," MPR News Q: Minnesota's On-Line News Source," August 1, 2008, online access, August 1, 2008.

[39]See Vicki Wilson, "Being Prepared for Disasters," *Government Finance Review*, Vol. 23, No. 6, (December 2007), pp. 22–26 and Timothy McKeon, "Lessons from Recent Natural Disasters," *Municipal Finance Journal*, Vol. 27, No. 4, (Winter 2007), pp. 27–53.

[40]Michelle Friedrich, "Funding Cuts Cripple Cyber Crimes Task Force," Standards-Democrat, February 9, 2015, p. 1, http://www.standard-democrat.com/story/2164589.html (accessed July 9, 2015).

[41]Mike Blasky, "Oakland Police: Too Many Robberies, Too Few Detectives," Contra Costa Times, May 13, 2015, p. 1, http://www.contracostatimes.com/breaking-news/ci_28109602/oakland-police-too-many-robberies-too-few-detectives (accessed July 9, 2015).

[42]Robert D. Lee, Ronald W. Johnson, and Philip G. Joyce. *Public Budgeting Systems* 8th Edition (Boston: Jones and Bartlett, 8th Edition, 2008), p. 17.

[43]Roland N. McKean, *Public Spending* (New York: McGraw-Hill, 1968), p. 1.

[44]Robert J. Landry III and Cynthia S. McCarty, "Causal Factors Leading to Municipal Bankruptcies," *Municipal Finance Journal*, Vol. 28, No. 1, (Spring 2007), p. 21.

[45]Jack Rabin, Encyclopedia of Public Administration and Public Policy, (Boca Raton, Florida: CRC Press, 2003), p. 1154.

[46]Aaron Wildavsky, *The Politics of the Budgetary Process*, 2nd edition, (Boston: Little, Brown, 1974), pp. 1–4.

[47]Ron Snell, "State Experiences with Annual and Biennial Budgeting, National Conference of State Legislatures, April 2011, p. 1, http://www.ncsl.org/research/fiscal-policy/state-experiences-with-annual-and-biennial-budgeti.aspx, accessed July 10, 2015. Also see Jessica Tollestrup, Biennial Budgeting: Options, Issues, and Previous Congressional Action, Congressional Research Service, February 2, 2015, http://www.ncsl.org/research/fiscal-policy/state-experiences-with-annual-and-biennial-budgeti.aspx (accessed July 12, 2015).

[48]Bryan Leonard, "Are Biennial Budgets Better?" State Budget Solutions, April 18, 2011, http://www.statebudgetsolutions.org/publications/detail/are-biennial-budgets-better (accessed July 11, 2015).

[49]See David R. Shock, "Capital Budgets: The Building Blocks for Government Infrastructure," *Government Finance Review*, Vol. 23, No. 3, (June 2007), pp. 16–22.

[50]Jill Wendorf, "Capital Budgeting from a Local Government Perspective," *SPNA Review* Volume 1, Issue No. 1, (May 2001), p. 76, (accessed July 13, 2015).

[51]A. E. Buck, *The Budgets in Governments Today* (New York: Macmillan, 1945), p. 5.

[52]No author, "Presenting the Capital Budget in the Operating Budget Document," Government Finance Officers Association, October 2008, p. 1, http://www.gfoa.org/presenting-capital-budget-operating-budget-document (accessed July 13, 2015).

[53]Robert D. Lee, Ronald W. Johnson, and Philip G. Joyce, *Public Budgeting Systems* (Boston: Jones and Bartlett, 8th Edition, 2008), p. 17.

[54]Ibid, p. 53.

[55]Because sheriffs are elected and police chiefs appointed, there are some differences in city and county budgeting because as an elected official, a sheriff would be more independent. See LaFrance T. Casey and MaCherie, "Sheriffs' and Police Chiefs' Leadership and Management Decisions in the Local Law Enforcement Process," *International Journal of Police Science and Management*, Vol. 12, issue 2, (Summer 2010), pp. 238–255.

[56]Sherrry Conohan. "Geese Police Fall Victim to Borough Budget Axe," Atlanticville (Manalapan, New Jersey, March 5, 2004, pp. 1-2, http://atl.gmnews.com/news/2004-03-05/Front_page/009.html (accessed July 16, 2015).

[57]Barry Reynolds, "Five Simple Rules for Managing Your Police Agency's Budget," Policeone.Com News, August 7, 2014, pp. 1-2, http://www.policeone.com/police-leader/articles/7429369-5-simple-rules-for-managing-your-police-agencys-budget, accessed July 16, 2015. The names of some points made by Barry Reynolds and commentary have been restated without losing their meaning.

[58]Thomas A. Reppetto, "The Elite Unit the NYPD Must Revive to Fight Gun Crime," New York Post, January 11, 2015, p. 1, http://nypost.com/2015/06/11/the-nypd-needs-to-revive-its-elite-anti-gun-unit, accessed March 3, 2016.

[59]Police Chief Bruce G. Roberts, letter to the city of Ft. Lauderdale Commission, April 1, 2004.

[60]Robert D. Lee and Ronald Johnson, *Public Budgeting Systems* (Gaithersburg, MD: Aspen, 1998), p. 265.

Also see the execution phase of the budget in No Author, North Carolina Budget Manual (Office of the State Budget and Management: Raleigh, North Carolina), January 1, 2015.

[61]No author, Local Budgeting Manual (Oregon Department of Revenue: Eugene, Oregon, 2012), p. 65.

[62]See Jeffrey C. Steinhoff, "Forensic Auditing: A Window to Identifying and Combating Fraud, Waste, and Abuse," Journal of Government Financial Management, Vol. 57, No. 2, (Summer 2008), pp. 10–18.

[63]The organizational placement of procurement, purchasing, payment of invoices, and property control varies. They may be clustered in a F/FSD or spread out over several departments. In very small units of government, one or two people working in the same office may perform these functions. For purposes of this text, we use a F/FSD that encompasses all of these functions, although in actual practice there are many variations.

[64]Mark Schelker, "Public Auditors: Empirical Evidence from U.S. States," Center for Research in Economics, Management, and the Arts (CREMA: Basel, Switzerland, 2008), p. 9.

[65]No Author, Conducting Performance Audits in Accordance with the Yellow Book (San Diego: Office of the City Auditor, 2009), pp. 4–6.

[66]Briefly summarized from Steve Jefferson, "Former Greensburg Police Chief Pleads Guilty to Charges," March 5, 2015, pp. 1-2, http://www.wthr.com/story/28128743/former-greensburg-police-chief-arrested-following-audit (accessed July 17, 2015).

[67]Allen Schick, Budget Innovation in the States (Washington, DC: Brookings Institution, 1971), pp. 14–15.

[68]A. E. Buck, The Budget in Governments of Today (New York: Macmillan, 1945), p. 5.

[69]In 1913, Ohio became the first state to adopt the executive budget.

[70]No Author, Purpose and Methods of the Bureau of Municipal Research (New York: Bureau of Municipal Research, 1907), p. 25.

[71]John Worrall, Asset Forfeiture (Washington, DC: Center for Problem-Oriented Policing, 2008), p. 5.

[72]Robert O'Harrow, Jr., Sari Horwitz, Steven Rich, "Holder Limits Seized-Asset Sharing Process That Splits Billions with Local, Stat, Police," The Washington Post, January 16, 2015, p. 1,http://www.washingtonpost.com/investigations/holder-ends-seized-asset-sharing-process-that-split-billions-with-local-state-police/2015/01/16/0e7ca058-99d4-11e4-bcfb-059ec7a93ddc_story.html (accessed July 20, 2015).

[73]See Richard D. Young, "Performance Based Budget Systems, Public Policy and Practice, Vol. 2, No. 2, January 2003, about p. 4 of an unnumbered online copy, http://ipspr.sc.edu/ejournal/performancebudgets.asp and No author, "Budget Processses Spotlight: How States Use

Performance Data," (The National Association of State Budget Officers: Washington, DC: August 4, 2015.

[74]David H. Folz, Reem Abdelrazek, and Teonsoo Chung, "Thr Adoption, Use, and Impacts of Performance Measures in Medium-Size Cities: Progress Toward Performance Management, University of Tennessee, undated paper, although the data for it was gathered in 2004, p. 5.

[75]Among the resources on PMs is the State of Washington's, Office of Financial Management, Budget Division, "Performance Measurement Guide, August 2009.

[76]No author, Zero-Based Budgeting: Modern Experiences and Current Perspectives (Government Finance Officers Association: Calgary, Canada, 2011), p. 7.

[77]William Pietz, "Death of the Deodand," Res: Anthropology and Aesthetics, Vol. 31, Spring 1997, pp. 97-98.

[78]John Worrall, Asset Forfeiture (Washington, DC: Center for Problwm-Oriented Policing, 2008), p. 5.

[79]Michael Sallah, et. al., "Stop and Seize," The Washington Post, September 6, 2014, p. 3, http://www.washingtonpost.com/sf/investigative/2014/09/06/stop-and-seize/ (accessed July 20, 2015).

[80]"Holder Limits Seized-Asset Sharing Process That Splits Billions with Local, Stat, Police," p.1.

[81]Asset Forfeiture, p. 3.

[82]Pamela Delaney and Donald Carey, "Police Foundations: Partnerships for the 21st century," The Police Chief 74, No. 8 (2007), p.1 of online copy. Editor: FNs 41-49 deleted

[83]No author, "Policing For Profit, Missouri Profile," The Institute for Justice, undated, but citations suggest no earlier than 2008, https://www.ij.org/asset-forfeiture-report-missouri (accessed July 20, 2015).

[84]"Stop and Seize," p. 1

[85]Pamela Delaney and Donald Carey, "Police Foundations Partnerships for the 21st Century," The Police Chief, Vol. 74, No. 8, (2007), p.1.

[86]Pamela Delaney and Donald Carey, "Police Foundations: Partnerships for the 21st Century," The Police Chief, Vol. 74, No. 8, 2007, p. 2, http://www.policechiefmagazine.org/magazine/index.cfm?fuseaction=display_arch&article_id=1237&issue_id=82007, accessed May 30, 2016.

[87]Adam Lynch, "Police Foundation Eyeing Safe City Role," Jackson (Miss) Free Press, March 31, 2010.

[88]Television station KREM (Seattle, Washington, KREM.com), December 9, 2009.

[89]San Diego Mayor Jerry Sanders, Press release, March 18, 2010.

[90]No author, VIPS-Volunteers in Police Service, International Association of Chiefs of Police, undated, p. 1, http://www.theiacp.org/VIPS (accessed July 7, 2015).

PART 4   Organizational Issues

Chapter 13 | Stress and Police Personnel
Chapter 14 | Legal Aspects of Police Administration
Chapter 15 | Organizational Change

Some 50 years ago the police were described as a "terra incognita," an unknown land. Empirical research on this unknown land was sparse and there needed to be empirical research on every subject connected with it. Since that time we have learned much about policing, but there is still a great deal to learn. In the intervening years there has been a proliferation of studies on the subject of Chapter 13, "Stress and Police Personnel." Under stress, the body changes, for example, the heart rate accelerates, blood pressure increases, pupils dilate, and the mouth goes dry. Unsurprisingly, the greatest stressor for police officers is killing someone in the line of duty. Chapter 10 identifies: the remarkably numerous affects stress has on our bodies, the symptoms of post-traumatic stress syndrome, the maladaptive use of alcohol and drugs by officers

Chapter 14, "Legal Aspects of Police Administration," addresses the ever-changing landscape of laws, which are enacted by legislative bodies and interpreted by court decisions. Police enforcement of criminal laws is typically sound because it is an everyday activity. In contrast, while high speed pursuits, use of force, and kindred incidents are not uncommon across police agencies, officers understanding of the civil liability created by mistakes in these areas is less perfected.

Police leaders at every level must also be aware that their decisions or lack of appropriate action can also result in civil liability. For example, if an officer has been repeatedly disciplined for excessive use of force, but remains on the department assigned to field duties, and subsequently shoots someone several times, crippling them for life, when the use of deadly force is not authorized, the employing agency will be faced with a civil suit claiming that but for the agency wrongfully continuing to employ the officer, the plaintiff would not have suffered the life changing injury. In such a fact situation the department would have the difficult task of defending the officer's action and may settle out of court.

Depending on the particulars of a situation, officers and their leaders, in addition to civil liability, are further exposed to two other risks: (1) being charged with a criminal act and (2) loss of their certification from the state's Peace Officers Standards and Training Commission or similarly titled body, ending their law enforcement careers. Thus, the content of this chapter is central to the welfare of persons having contacts with officers and maintaining public confidence, as well as officers and their leaders, their families their agency, and their police profession. Although the fate of the officers involved in the death of Freddie Gray in Baltimore is unknown at this writing, their prosecution should be regarded as an object lesson: exposure to these risks is an occupational risk in law enforcement.

Chapter 15, "Organizational Change," may well not have been an important topic when the policing philosophy in America was "aggressive preventive patrol in all areas at all times diminishes the opportunity for crimes to be committed." This philosophy held sway until roughly the advent of community policing. A whole series of refinements of community policing, as well as newer philosophies and programs, moved the importance of understanding organizational change into the important category. To no small extent other factors such as news events, political decisions, and technological innovations also propel changes in law enforcement agencies.

The Italian historian, government official, and thinker Machiavelli (1469–1527) observed in *The Prince* "There is nothing more difficult to take in hand, more perilous to conduct, or more uncertain of success than to lead in the introduction of a new order of things." President John Kennedy (1917–1963) concluded, "Trying to change the federal bureaucracy has the same affect as punching a curtain." Separated by four centuries two remarkable men reached the same conclusion: changing organizations is hard, uphill work that may not turn out well. Among the topics this chapter details is when changes should not be made, different change strategies, and how to heighten the possibilities when introducing change.

CHAPTER THIRTEEN

STRESS AND POLICE PERSONNEL

Learning Objectives

1. Explain why police officers are more prone to stress than individuals in many other occupations.
2. Describe the perceptual, cognitive, and behavioral disturbances resulting from an officer's use of deadly force.
3. Discuss some of the questions that police administrators must address in terms of drug use by police officers.
4. Describe some of the negative physical consequences associated with the use of steroids.
5. Discuss the indicators that would suggest a police officer is considering suicide.
6. Examine the role the police psychologist plays in a psychological health wellness initiative.

INTRODUCTION

FOR THE PAST 45 *years, the topic of stress and its relationship to police work has been extensively studied by both the social science community and the police profession. As a result, there is now an abundance of police stress–related information available to the law enforcement executives to assist them in fully understanding and developing programs designed to reduce stress among their personnel.[1] Police administrators should be aware of the following stress-related information: (1) how stress is defined by the medical and social science community, (2) the relationship between diseases of adaptation and job-related stress, (3) the ways in which personality type can impact positively or negatively upon job performance, (4) why the use of deadly force by police officers is consistently listed as the number one stress inducer, (5) the negative physical and psychological impacts of alcohol, drugs, and steroids on police performance, (6) the multiple aspects of police suicide and what can be done to prevent it, (7) police domestic violence and the ways in which police departments can and should react to it, (8) the sources of work satisfaction that are stress reducers, (9) stress reduction management techniques, (10) the police psychologist's role in a psychological health wellness initiative, and (11) the functions and value of an employee assistance program.*

WHAT IS STRESS?

Hans Selye, the researcher and theorist who pioneered the physiological investigation of stress, defines **stress** in the broadest possible terms as anything that places an adjustive demand on an organism (see Figure 13.1). Identified as "the body's nonspecific response to any demand placed on it," stress can be either positive (eustress) or negative (distress; see Table 13.1).[2] According to this distinction, many stressful events do not threaten people but provide them with pleasurable challenges. Illustrations of eustress include driving at top-end speeds, gambling, free climbing mountains, and sky diving. Arguably, volunteers for "high-speed" military units such as the U.S. Navy's SEAL Team 6, the U.S. Army's Delta Force, and SWAT Police Teams or undercover drug detectives may fall into this category. Fledgling entrepreneurs also face many stressful situations; some entrepreneurs crack under the distress and others experience eustress and succeed spectacularly. Illustratively, Bill Gates dropped out of college to pursue his computing interests and was the co-founder of Microsoft in 1975, and as of 2013 enjoyed an annual income of $11.5 billion.[3]

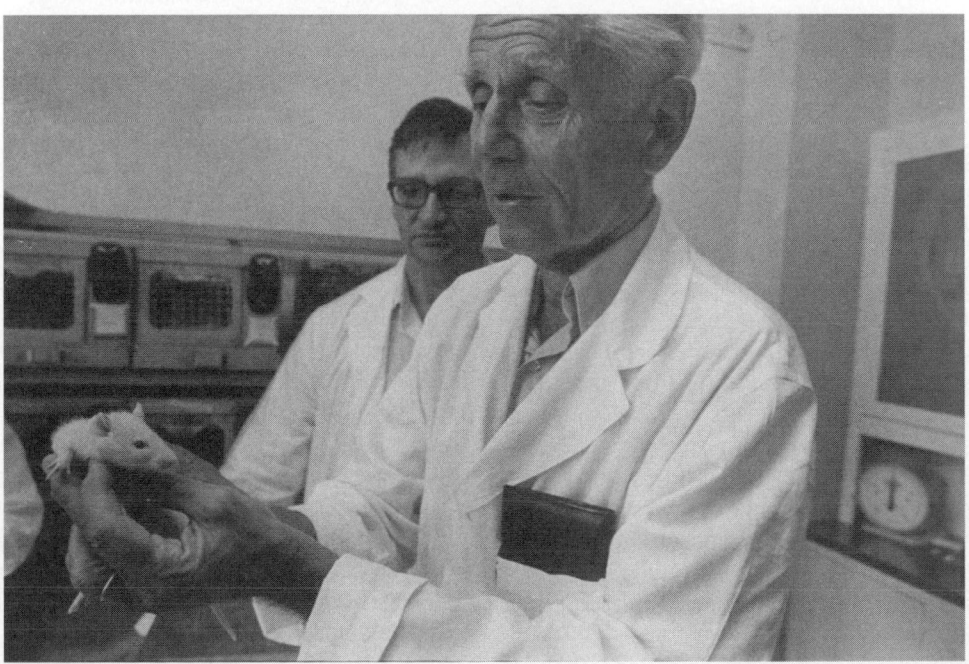

FIGURE 13.1 ▶ Dr. Hans Selye holds one of the many rats studied in meticulous detail to work out the actual nature of the mammalian stress response. (John Olson/The LIFE Images Collection/Getty Images)

TABLE 13.1 CHANGES TO THE BODY AT THE ALARM STAGE	
Heart rate increase	Blood flow increases to heart, lungs, and large muscles
Blood pressure increase	Perspiration, especially to palms
Large muscle groups tense	Digestive secretions slow
Adrenaline rush	Dry mouth due to saliva decrease
Increase blood sugar	Bowel activity decreases
Hypervigilance	Extremities become cool
Pupils dilate	Sphincters tighten
Increased hearing acuity	More white blood cells enter the bloodstream
Increased blood clotting	Cholesterol remains in the blood longer
Increased metabolism	Dilation of the lung passages and increased respiration

Source: Wayne Anderson, David Swenson, and Daniel Clay, *Stress Management for Law Enforcement Officers*, 1st edition, © 1995, p. 37. Adapted by permission of Pearson Education, Inc., Upper Saddle River, NJ.

Biological Stress and the General Adaptation Syndrome

Selye formulated the **general adaptation syndrome (GAS)** to describe how stress, on the biological level, can incapacitate an individual. The GAS encompasses three stages of physiological reaction to a wide variety of stressors: environmental agents or activities powerful enough in their impact to elicit a reaction from the body. These three stages are as follows:

- Alarm
- Resistance
- Exhaustion

The **alarm stage**, sometimes referred to as an emergency reaction, is exemplified on the animal level by the so-called fight-or-flight syndrome. When an animal encounters a threatening situation, its body signals a defense alert. The animal's cerebral cortex flashes an alarm to the hypothalamus, a small structure in the midbrain that connects the brain with body functions. A powerful hormone called adrenocorticotropic hormone (ACTH) is released into the bloodstream by the hypothalamus and is carried by the bloodstream to the adrenal gland, a part of the endocrine, or ductless gland, system. There, ACTH triggers the release of adrenaline, which produces a galvanizing, or energizing, effect on the body functions. The heart pounds, the pulse races, breathing quickens, the muscles tense, and digestion is inhibited. The adjustive function of this reaction pattern is readily apparent—namely, preparing the organism biologically to fight or to run away. When the threat is removed or diminished, the physiological functions involved in this alarm, or emergency reaction, subside, and the organism regains its internal equilibrium (see Table 13.1).

If the stress continues, however, the organism reaches the **resistance stage** of the GAS. During this stage, bodily resources are mobilized to deal with the specific stressors, and adaptation is optimal. Although the stressful stimulus may persist, the symptoms that characterized the alarm stage disappear. In short, the individual seems to have handled the stress successfully.

Under conditions of prolonged stress, the body reaches a point where it is no longer capable of maintaining resistance. This condition characterizes the **exhaustion stage**. Hormonal defenses break down, and emotional reactions that appeared during the alarm stage may reappear, often in intensified form. Further exposure to stress leads to exhaustion and eventually to death.[4]

DISEASES OF ADAPTATION AND RECENT MEDICAL FINDINGS

There is considerable agreement that some types of stress can worsen the symptoms of almost any condition, but recent medical research suggests there is little evidence that stress is the exclusive or the principal cause of any disease. For decades, it was accepted by the medical community that stress led to the overproduction of stomach acid, which caused duodenal ulcers. Stress does increase the amount of acid produced in the stomach, and there is no doubt that, once a person has a duodenal ulcer, acid makes the ulcer hurt. However, medical science has determined that the ulcer is not caused by stress but rather by a bacterial infection, curable with antibiotics. Doctors also once believed that the inflammatory bowel diseases—Crohn's disease and ulcerative colitis—were caused by stress. They now know that these diseases are caused by inherited tendencies toward abnormal inflammation in response to gut bacteria. Also, there is little evidence that stress causes asthma, although some patients have flare-ups more often at times of stress.[5]

The Role of Stress in Heart Disease

The role of stress in heart disease has received the most attention over the years, and with good reason. Like our ancestors, we all occasionally face the single, sudden, and extreme stressors that the stress response has evolved into in order to protect us from dangerous situations. However, unlike our primitive ancestors, the acute stressor is not caused by an approaching wild animal's intent on devouring us or the belief that we will soon be dead because we have been hexed by the local witchdoctor. Instead, it might result from a road rage situation when an angry motorist is attempting to run us off the road or perhaps someone is attempting to forcibly enter our home. Our response to such sudden and extreme stressors can protect us, but it can also trigger a powerful hormonal release that can have dire consequences if a person already has heart disease.

Perhaps even more important are the persistent, chronic, low-grade stressors experienced by almost everyone in a modern society, such as the recurring tension in dealing with an unpleasant supervisor, co-worker, spouse, or child; or worrying about how to pay the bills this month. These chronic stressors, like sudden and acute stressors, can also affect the most common and lethal form of heart disease we face—atherosclerosis, sometimes called "hardening" of the coronary arteries.

Coronary atherosclerosis deforms artery walls and can ultimately block blood flow, starving the heart muscle of the oxygen it needs. Plaques of atherosclerosis cause symptoms in two ways. First, if the plaques grow large enough to significantly obstruct the flow of blood, the heart will not get the blood supply it needs when it is forced to work harder—for example, by exercise or by anger or fear. The heart is not actually damaged, but pain can occur whenever the heart is again forced to work hard. Second, plaque can rupture, either when the heart is working hard or even when a person is at rest and at peace. Plaque rupture causes a blood clot to form that suddenly and often completely stops the flow of blood through the artery.

Chronic stressors also contribute to heart disease indirectly if they lead us to overeating, under-exercising, or smoking. Stress is a toxic emotional and physical response; anger, hostility, depression, and anxiety are examples of such toxic responses. Anxiety, for instance, involves apprehension combined with palpitations, fatigue, and shortness of breath. Some people respond to chronic stressors with remarkable equanimity. Others spend a substantial fraction of their day experiencing one or more of the toxic reactions. This is influenced in part by our genes but is also controllable with stress-management techniques (discussed later in this chapter). In addition, if these toxic reactions are not controlled they can be fatal. Also there is growing evidence that heart disease is more likely to occur and at an earlier age.[6]

Major Stressful Life Events

Sudden, major stressful life events can sometimes cause catastrophic results in people with an underlying heart disease which they did not know they had because it had never before caused symptoms. This could then result in the sudden outpouring of adrenalin resulting from a specific highly stressful event such as a police officer responding to an officer in need of assistance, or a felony in progress call. This can cause a plaque of atherosclerosis to rupture, which in turn can generate dangerous heart rhythms and sudden death.

In a paper published over 45 years ago in the *Annals of Internal Medicine*, internist and psychiatrist George Engel reconstructed the events in the hours before 170 people died suddenly. Particularly for women, Engel found that the most common trigger for sudden death was a major loss—of a spouse or self-esteem. For men, sudden danger (a constant companion for law enforcement officers) more often was a trigger. Subsequent evidence supports Engel's thesis. For example, sudden deaths increased immediately following the Northridge earthquake in southern California in 1994, and after September 11, 2001—and not just in New York City.

STRESS AND PERSONALITY TYPE

The classification of personalities into major categories can be a very useful tool in assessing personality types. However, when discussing them it is important to remember that almost no one fits entirely into a single category but simply possesses a majority of the characteristics associated with that specific personality type.[8]

Type A Personality

- Under constant stress, much of which is self-generated
- Continuous pressure to accomplish
- Hostile and demanding
- Always in a hurry; sense of time urgency
- Continuing impatience
- Intense and ambitious
- Believes time should be used "constructively"

Quick Facts: Too Much Happiness Can Kill You

Sudden death can also follow a triumph or a happy ending to a long struggle. These include the reported sudden deaths of a number of individuals, including a just-released prisoner upon returning home, a man who had just scored his first hole in one, and an opera singer who was receiving a standing ovation. Even joy can disrupt silently diseased arteries.[7]

- Has difficulty relaxing and feels guilty when not working
- Compelled to challenge, and not understand, another type A personality

The qualities underlying type A characteristics include the following:

- Constant state of being "on guard"
- Hypermasculinity
- Constantly working against time
- Lack of insight into one's own psychological needs

The physiological implications are as follows:

- Seven times as likely to develop heart disease
- Higher cholesterol and triglyceride (blood fat) levels (sudden stress increases triglyceride; prolonged stress increases cholesterol)
- Clotting elements have greater tendency to form within coronary arteries
- Excess accumulation of insulin in blood

Type B Personality

- Less competitive and less rushed
- More easygoing
- Better able to separate work from play
- Relatively free of a sense of time urgency
- Ambitions are kept in perspective
- Generally philosophical about life

Type C Personality

- Appear to be quiet and introspective but are actually frustrated and suppress their anger
- They are at increased risk of developing cancer
- They are non-emotional, non-assertive and appease others to the point of self-effacement and self-sacrifice
- They suppress their own desires even if there is something they dislike
- Their lack of assertiveness results in tremendous stress and sometimes leads to depression
- They tend to be introverted, respectful, eager to please, and compliant
- They love details and can spend a lot of time trying to find out how things work and this makes them very suitable for technical jobs[9]

Type D Personality

- Have a negative outlook toward life and are pessimistic
- Might become socially withdrawn as a result of fear of rejection, even if they like to be around people

- They are famous for suppressing their emotions thus making them vulnerable to depression
- Like the type A personality, they are also more likely to develop cardiovascular problems[10]

Workaholic Personality

- This phrase was coined in 1968
- Similar to type A
- Has an addiction to work
- When absent from the job, may experience withdrawal symptoms similar to those of withdrawal from other addictions
- Is agitated and depressed when not working
- May account for up to 5 percent of the working world
- Typical workaholics
  - Readily buck the system; often bucked by the bureaucracy
  - Display well-organized hostility toward the system's imperfections
  - Obsessed with perfection in their work
  - Haunted by deep-seated fear of failure; will "play to win" at all games
  - Prefer labor to leisure
  - Constantly juggle two or more tasks (called multitasking)
- Many are overachievers and "get things done"
- Takes its toll and may result in:
  - Gastrointestinal problems
  - Cardiovascular disease
  - Divorce

The Pitfalls of Being a Workaholic— Police Work Addiction

The following is a cautionary tale based upon an actual case, using a fictitious name, which describes the pitfalls of being a workaholic.

Great leaders lead by example, and Police Chief William Smith was no exception. He was totally selfless and always available, arriving at work each morning before 8:00 and not leaving until everyone else had gone home. It was not uncommon to find him working on Saturday or Sunday. The deputy chief told those assembled at the church that he was actually reluctant to leave each night before the chief. Everyone felt sad that Chief Smith left a young family and even sadder that he should pass away in the prime of his life.[11]

Certainly, police officers are expected to put aside all other needs when duty calls, and, without question, duty does call. Commanders and officers alike must sustain an endless capacity to meet this demand. Communities hold fast to the expectation that the police will do all that can be humanly done and, at times, much more than should be expected of mere humans.

Therein lies the great challenge for law enforcement officers and supervisors—maintaining a healthy balance in meeting *reasonable* responsibilities to the job, to themselves, and to their families.

Perhaps Chief Smith represents an extreme example of the dangers inherent in the work-addicted lifestyle. However, literature on work addiction asserts that work constitutes the drug of choice for some 30 percent of the population, for whom working is so vital to their emotional well-being that in fact they have become addicted to it.[12] While the actual mortality rate for work addiction may be low, the social lethality of this behavior proves overwhelming. These unfortunate individuals are predisposed to involve themselves—and their families—in a life not unlike that of Chief Smith's. Clearly, work addicts (or workaholics, the more common descriptor) cannot assess what is important in healthy lifestyle choices and, thus, experience a diminished quality of life. Regrettably, they do not suffer alone. They unwittingly share this pain with their families and colleagues alike.

Workaholics are married to their work. Their vows to love and honor their spouses above all "others" no longer hold meaning or possibility. No spouse and no family can compete with this all-consuming obsession.

Workaholics themselves are a key contributor to the unhealthy family patterns resulting from work addiction for a number of reasons. First, they may have grown up in a dysfunctional family system where role models taught unhealthy patterns of relating to others. Research indicates that the family origin contributes greatly to the development of the workaholic, and the roots of the workaholic's perfectionism often lie in childhood experiences.[13] In these dysfunctional homes, families reward children for good performance, not for who they are. They give praise and conditional love whenever children perform a certain way or meet certain high expectations. In adulthood, this same need for perfection is the basis for the obsession for work—everything must be done properly and always at a very high level of competence and perfection.

Second, the need for workaholics to feel dominant and "in control" may make them less able to relate to peers. They may interact more easily with older and younger people or those of lower status or socioeconomic level than themselves. This need for continually being in control of themselves and in charge creates tension in family relationships. The one constant involved in this work mind-set devalues the quality of social interactions. Loved ones have a reasonable expectation that time spent together is time well spent and, therefore, they should not be made to feel that such time comes at the expense of personal productivity. Loved ones can sense when the workaholic is "just going through the motions." The same holds true for relationships with peer groups and clients. People have a strong sense for those who are too busy to make time to properly address issues. Conflict becomes inevitable, and everyone "gets drawn into the act by waltzing around the workaholic's schedule, moods, and actions."[14]

The self-imposed behavior of work addiction also causes physical symptoms. Excessive pumping of adrenaline resulting in abnormal blood pressure, heart trouble, stomach sensitivity, nervousness, and the inability to relax under any circumstances are commonplace. Workaholics report feeling pressure in their chests, dizziness, and lightheadedness.[15] Obviously, any long-term stress that manifests such symptoms as these can result in dangerous health consequences of many types. Chief Smith's protracted work addiction led to serious illness and his ultimate, untimely death.

Those people obsessed with work share the traits of others with such addictions as substance abuse, food dependencies, or sexual compulsions. A classic definition of a workaholic describes "a person whose need for work has become so excessive that it creates noticeable disturbance or interference with bodily health, personal happiness, and interpersonal relations, and with smooth social functioning."[16] The unique difference between work addiction and other addictions, however, is that supervisors often sanction work addiction. Supervisors and peers admire this so-called work ethic, and it can be both financially and professionally rewarding.

Workaholics become gradually more emotionally crippled as they become embroiled with the demands and expectations of the workplace. They are "addicted to control and power in a compulsive drive to gain approval and success."[17] The obsession with work grows out of the workaholic's perfectionism and competitive nature. As with other addictions, work is the "fix," the drug that frees the workaholic from experiencing the emotional pain of the anger, hurt, guilt, and fear in the other areas of the workaholic's life. Workaholics constantly focus on work, seeking to meet their personal emotional needs through their professions.

With this information in mind, law enforcement supervisors must understand the dangers that work addiction presents. These supervisors also must remember that they have an ethical responsibility to intervene when they observe the telltale signs of the work-addicted personality.

Perhaps the poet Robert Frost had Chief Smith in mind when he observed, "By working faithfully 8 hours a day, you may eventually get to be boss and work 12 hours a day." Certainly, expectations run high in the law enforcement profession. Establishing and maintaining relationships creates tremendous demands on time, resources, and energy; life balance easily becomes lost. The wise boss must understand and accept this reality.

STRESS IN LAW ENFORCEMENT

Police work is highly stressful—it is one of the few occupations in which an employee is asked continually to face physical dangers and to put his or her life on the line at any time. The police officer is exposed to violence, cruelty, and aggression and is often required to make extremely critical decisions in high-pressure situations.

The Highest Police Stressors

In order to assess which events generate the most stress for police officers, Violanti and Aron distributed a 60-item Police Stress Survey (PSS) to a random sample of 110 officers in a

Quick Facts: The Deadly Effects of Stress on Police Officers

More law enforcement officers are likely to be killed by job-related stress than are killed by criminals. For every police officer slain by an assailant in the line of duty, countless others succumb to the insidious, long-range effects of job-induced pressures including alcoholism, drug abuse, domestic violence, posttraumatic stress disorder, and even suicide.[18]

large New York State police department.[19] Ninety-three percent of those sampled ($N = 103$) completed the PSS and returned it. The results of the survey reveal that the single-most-potent stressor was killing someone in the line of duty (79.38%) and close behind was the killing of a fellow officer (76.38%).

The empathy police officers have for victims is revealed by the fact that the fourth-most-potent stressor was handling child abuse cases (69.24%), which ranked ahead of other well-known stressors, such as engaging in high-speed chases (63.73 percent), using force (60.96%), responding to felony-in-progress calls (55.27%), and making death notices (52.59%).[20]

Quick Facts: The Use of Deadly Force as a Major Source of Stress for Police Officers

Available data indicate that between 400 and 450 criminals are killed each year by police officers in the United States.[21] Some of these killings are in self-defense, some are accidental, and others are to prevent harm to others. The sources of stress attached to an *officer-involved shooting* (OIS) are multiple, and include: the officer's own psychological reaction to taking a life; the responses of his or her law enforcement peers and the officer's family; the rigorous examination by departmental investigators and administrators, and increasingly federal investigators who are trying to determine if there have been any civil rights violations; the possible disciplinary action resulting in suspension, demotion, or dismissal; the possibility of criminal prosecution and imprisonment; the possibility of civil litigation; and negative media attention.[22]

Perceptual, Cognitive, and Behavioral Disturbances Resulting from the Use of Deadly Force

Many police officers who have been involved in a deadly force shooting episode have described one or more alterations in perception, thinking, and behavior that occurred during the event,[23] and these are similar to those reported in military personnel following a firefight. Most of the following reactions can be interpreted as natural adaptive defensive reactions of an organism under extreme emergency stress:

- *Distortions in time perception* are most common, with the majority of officers recalling the shooting event as occurring in slow motion, although a smaller percentage reported experiencing the event as speeded up.

- *Sensory distortions* are also common and most often involve *tunnel vision,* in which the officer is sharply focused on one particular aspect of the visual field, typically the suspect's gun or weapon, while blocking out everything in the periphery. Thus, such distortions are also very common for officers who are engaged in high-speed pursuits. Similarly, "*tunnel hearing*" may also occur, in which the officer's auditory attention is focused exclusively on a particular set of sounds, most commonly the opponent's voice, while background sounds are excluded. Sounds may also seem muffled or,

in a smaller number of cases, louder than normal. Police officers have reported not hearing their own or other officers' gunshots. Thus, overall perceptual clarity may increase or diminish.

- *A sense of helplessness* may occur during the shooting exchange, but this may be underreported due to the potential stigma attached. A small proportion of service members report they "froze" at some point during the event: again, either this is an uncommon response or personnel are understandably reluctant to report it, especially in a culture like law enforcement, which places a premium on physical courage and disparages those who show any degree of timidity in the face of danger. In a series of interviews with police officers,[24] it was found that most of these instances of "freezing" really represented the normal *action-reaction gap* in which officers make the decision to shoot only after the suspect has engaged in clearly threatening behavior. In most cases, this brief evaluation interval is a positive precaution to prevent the premature shooting of someone who does not pose a threat to the officer. But in situations where the ostensibly prudent action led to a tragic outcome, this cautious hesitation by an officer may well be viewed retrospectively by him or her as a fault: "If I hadn't hesitated to shoot, maybe my partner would still be alive."

- *Disturbances in memory* are commonly reported in shooting exchanges. About half of these involve impaired recall for at least some of the events during the shooting; the other half involve impaired recall for at least part of the officer's own actions; this, in turn, may be associated with going-on-automatic response. More rarely, some aspects of the event may be recalled with unusual clarity, sometimes characterized as a *flashbulb memory*. Over a third of the cases involve not a total loss of recall but a distortion of memory, to the extent that the shooter's account of what happened differs markedly from the report of other observers at the scene; in such cases, they might be unfairly accused of lying.

Five Basic Phases of the Post-Shooting Reaction

1. The first phase occurs prior to the shooting itself and consists of *concern about being able to pull the trigger* when the time comes and not freezing up and letting one's fellow officers down.

2. The second phase is the *actual killing experience*, which is often done reflexively, with officers describing themselves as "going on automatic."

3. The third stage is that of *exhilaration* that comes from having been able to put one's training into action. This exhilaration, fueled by the release of huge amounts of adrenalin, can create a high or rush, which in some cases can give rise to what the military has characterized as "combat addiction." It has been described as the kind of "adrenalin overdosing" that can negatively impact a police officer's nervous system and lead to adverse reactions later on (i.e., hesitating to use deadly force when it is clearly justified or overreacting to situations that do not justify the use of deadly force).[25]

4. The fourth phase[26] is what police psychologists[27, 28] have called the *recoil, remorse, and nausea* phase. This follows the rush of exhilaration and is often associated with a close-range kill; this is the more common type of response experienced by police officers who tend to confront their adversaries in close quarters, rather than from a distance, which is often the case with military personnel.

For police officers, feelings of guilt or self-recrimination may be especially likely in cases where the decision to shoot was less than clear-cut or where the suspect's actions essentially forced the officer into using deadly force, such as botched robberies, violent domestic disputes, or **suicide by cop (SbC)**.[29] SbC occurs when an individual who intends to take his or her life uses the police to assist in accomplishing that objective by threatening to injure or kill the police officer, typically with a gun or some other similar deadly weapon (see Figure 13.2).

During the recoil/remorse phase, law enforcement service members may seem detached and preoccupied, going through the motions of their job duties, and operating on what could be characterized as "behavioral autopilot." In addition, they may be hypersensitive or even annoyed to well-meaning probing and congratulations by peers who make comments such as "Way to go, killer—the dirt bag deserved it."

Also, during this recoil phase, a variety of posttraumatic symptoms (discussed earlier) may be seen, most of which will resolve themselves in a few days or weeks.[30] Some of these will represent general posttraumatic reactions similar to those experienced by psychological trauma workers.[31]

5. The fifth phase,[32] *rationalization and acceptance*, can be a long process, and many law enforcement officers wrestle with this single event for a lifetime. As the officer begins to come to terms with the shooting episode, a similar resolution or acceptance phase may enure, wherein the officer assimilates the fact that the

FIGURE 13.2 ▶ A man, armed with what police would later learn were unloaded guns, confronted Chicago police officers. When the man refused to drop his guns and threatened to kill the officers, he was shot and killed. (The Shelby Star, Lee McLeod/AP Images)

use-of-deadly-force-action was necessary and justified in this particular instance. Even under the best of circumstances, resolution may be partial rather than total, and psychological remnants of the experience may continue to haunt the officer periodically, especially during future times of crisis. But in most cases, the officer is eventually able to return to work with a reasonable sense of confidence.[33]

However, in the worst cases, sufficient resolutions may never occur, and the officer enters into a prolonged posttraumatic phase, which may effectively end the officer's law enforcement career. In less severe cases, a period of temporary stress disability allows the officer to seek treatment, to eventually regain his or her emotional and professional bearings, and to ultimately return to the job. Still other officers return to work right away but continue to perform marginally or dysfunctionally until their actions are brought to the attention of superiors.[34]

POST-SHOOTING INTERVIEW

An important question about post-shooting interviews is what the agency's policy should be as it relates to how, where, and when it should be conducted. It is very clear that the event itself can have very serious consequences on the officer's recollection of what happened and in some cases a failure in this area may result in the officer being unfairly accused of lying. The International Association of Chiefs of Police (IACP) Police Psychological Services has provided guidelines suggesting that investigators should give officers time to recover after the incident before they conduct detailed interviews, with this recovery time ranging from a few hours to overnight.[35] Other experts have also supported this recommendation and suggested that officers would be better able to provide more accurate and thorough statements if they are allowed to wait at least 24 hours before questioning, thereby giving the officers time to rest and recuperate.[36]

Many agencies have embraced this suggestion and implemented policies requiring officers to wait before giving an interview or speaking to an investigator about an officer-involved shooting (OIS). In this respect, these departments have made a decision to treat their officers differently than civilian witnesses or suspects who are normally interviewed as soon as possible after the incident. The rationale for this differential treatment is the fact that sometimes victims who are seriously injured may die, witnesses may disappear, and suspects may flee.

Prior research has consistently determined that individuals' memories react strangely to stressful or traumatic events. This includes both officers and civilians alike who may experience serious perceptual and memory distortions.[37] The question is how to best minimize this phenomenon.

To this end, it might be best for agency protocol to allow for case-by-case flexibility when determining the timing and structure of interviews following an OIS. Investigators must remain sensitive to personnel who have likely just experienced one of the most traumatic events in their life while striving to obtain the most accurate information possible about the incident. For example, because investigators need precise details it may be advantageous for them to give the officers and civilian witnesses an initial walk-through of the incident without engaging in intensive probing detail which has been customary in the past. This walk-through may function as the "rehearsal" interview that helps trigger better memory recall later on. One expert has highlighted the value of this time delay in the interview process, stating that interviewers can consider ". . . enough brief information during an immediate on-scene 'walk-through' to get the investigation started."[38]

POSTTRAUMATIC STRESS DISORDER (PTSD)

PTSD can be traced back to antiquity. It was called "soldier's heart" during the American Civil War, "shell shock" in the First World War and "battle fatigue" in the Second World War. In the Korea War, it was called "operational exhaustion." It was not until the Vietnam War that the term "posttraumatic stress disorder" was created when the American Psychiatric Association added the term to its list of recognized mental disorders.[39]

The Clinical Classification

In clinical classification, a *syndrome* is defined as a set of symptoms and signs that occur in a fairly regular pattern from patient to patient, under a given set of circumstances, and with a specific set of causes (even though individual variations may be seen).[40] By this definition, **posttraumatic stress disorder**, or **PTSD**, is a syndrome of emotional and behavioral disturbance that follows exposure to a traumatic stressor or set of traumatically stressful experiences that is typically outside the range of normal, everyday experience for that person. As a result, there develops a characteristic set of symptoms.[41]

Symptoms of Posttraumatic Stress Disorder

Anxiety. The subject describes a continual state of free-floating anxiety or nervousness. There is a constant gnawing apprehension that something terrible is about to happen. He or she maintains an intensive hypervigilance, scanning the environment for the least hint of impending threat or danger. Panic attacks may be occasional or frequent.

Physiological Arousal. The subject's autonomic nervous system is always on red alert. He or she experiences increased bodily tension in the form of muscle tightness, tremors, restlessness, fatigue, heart palpitations, breathing difficulties, dizziness, headaches, and gastrointestinal or urinary disturbances. About one-half of PTSD subjects show a classic startle reaction: surprised by an unexpected door slam, telephone ring, sneeze, or even just hearing their name called, the subject may literally "jump" out of his seat and then spend the next few minutes trembling with fear and anxiety.

Irritability. There is a pervasive chip-on-the-shoulder edginess, impatience, loss of humor, and quick anger over seemingly trivial matters. Friends get upset, coworkers shun the subject, and family members may be verbally abused and alienated. A particularly common complaint is the patient's increased sensitivity to children's noisiness or the family's bothering questions.

Avoidance and Denial. The subject tries to blot out the event from his or her mind and avoids thinking about the traumatic event. Also the subject shuns news articles, radio programs, or TV shows that are reminders of the incident. "I just don't want to talk about it," is the standard response, and the individual may claim to have forgotten important aspects of the event. Some of this is a deliberate, conscious effort to avoid reminders of the trauma; part of it also involves an involuntary psychic numbing that blunts most incoming threatening stimuli. The emotional coloring of this denial may range from blasé indifference to nail-biting anxiety.

Intrusion. Despite the subject's best efforts to keep the traumatic event out of his or her mind, the horrifying incident pushes its way into consciousness, often rudely and abruptly, in the form of intrusive images of the event by day and frightening dreams at night. In the most extreme cases, the individual may experience dissociative flashbacks or reliving experiences in which he seems to be mentally transported back to the traumatic scene in all its sensory and emotional vividness, sometimes losing touch with current reality. More commonly, the intrusive recollection is described as a persistent psychological demon that "won't let me forget" the terrifying events surrounding the trauma.

Repetitive Nightmares. Even sleep offers little respite. Sometimes, the subject's nightmares replay the actual traumatic event; more commonly, the dreams echo the general theme of the trauma but miss the mark in terms of specific content. For example, an individual traumatized in an auto accident may dream of falling off a cliff or having a wall collapse on them. A sexual assault victim may dream of being attacked by vicious dogs or drowning in a muddy pool. The emotional intensity of the original traumatic experience is retained, but the dream partially disguises the event itself. This symbolic reconfiguration of dream material is, of course, one of the main pillars of Freudian psychoanalytic theory.[42]

Impaired Concentration and Memory. The subject complains of having gotten "spacey," "fuzzy," or "ditsy." He or she has trouble remembering names, tends to misplace objects, loses the train of conversations, or can't keep their mind focused on work, reading material, family activities, or other matters. The subject may worry that he or she has brain damage or that "I'm losing my mind."

Sexual Inhibition. Over 90 percent of PTSD subjects report decreased sexual activity and interest; this may further strain an already stressed-out marital relationship. In some cases, complete impotence or frigidity may occur, especially in cases where the traumatic event involved sexual assault.

Withdrawal and Isolation. The subject shuns friends, neighbors, and family members and just wants to be left alone. He has no patience for the petty, trivial concerns of everyday life—bills, gossip, news events—and gets annoyed at being bothered with these piddles. The hurt feelings this engenders in those he rebuffs may spur retaliatory avoidance, leading to a vicious cycle of rejection and recrimination.

Impulsivity and Instability. More rarely, the trauma survivor may take sudden trips, move from place to place, walk off his job, disappear from his family for prolonged periods, uncharacteristically engage in drunken binges, gambling sprees, or romantic trysts, make excessive purchases, or take dangerous physical or legal risks. It is as if the trauma has goaded the subject into a "what-the-hell—life-is-short" attitude that overcomes their usual good judgment and common sense. Obviously, not every instance of irresponsible behavior can be blamed on trauma, but a connection may be suspected when this kind of activity is definitely out of character for that person and follows an identifiable traumatic event. Far from taking such walks on the wild side, however, the majority of trauma survivors continue to suffer in numbed and shattered silence.

CUMULATIVE CAREER TRAUMATIC STRESS (CCTS)

In contrast to the condition posttraumatic stress disorder just discussed, officers may also experience trauma symptoms sporadically throughout a career as a result of being routinely exposed to many traumatic events over a period of time. This is classified as **Cumulative Career Traumatic Stress** (CCTS).[43]

The symptoms of CCTS are similar to PTSD, but rather than presenting suddenly as a result of a single traumatic event directly experienced by the officer, such as a shooting, the officer may experience one or a combination of symptoms sporadically throughout a career as he or she is exposed to a myriad of traumatic events over a period of years. The trauma symptoms that are experienced fail to fit the duration criteria of PTSD but are nonetheless frequently experienced and left unacknowledged. This in turn creates the potential to cause a slow and subtle deterioration of the officer's psychological and emotional stability. For example, an officer who has responded to a fatal motor vehicle collision may experience nightmares or flashbacks of the scene for a few days after the incident. This is especially true of those fatal traffic accidents that result in the death of a small child. Several months later, the officer may respond to another motor vehicle fatality or similar scene that brings back memories of the previously investigated serious collision.

Many times throughout a career, an officer may be involved in incidents that threaten his or her physical safety or which directly threatens the officer's life.[44] These events are typically quickly forgotten and are often viewed as a "part of the job." This cycle repeats itself throughout the officer's career. As past events are hopefully forgotten, new events trigger additional trauma symptoms and may exhume old memories.[45] CCTS involves the sporadic experience of trauma symptoms such as intrusive thoughts and memories of troubling incidents (via flashbacks or nightmares), emotional numbing, moodiness, anxiety, avoiding reminders of an incident/s, loss of hope, hyper-vigilance, memory and/or concentration problems, sleeping and/or eating problems, disconnection from family and friends, and hyper-arousal (e.g., jumpiness, easily startled), among others. These symptoms typically will not last for more than a few days to a week but may be re-experienced at a later time either alone or in conjunction with other trauma symptoms.

There are a number of ways in which CCTS might adversely affect the officer. These include psychological problems, impaired job performance, marital/family problems, and diminished physical health to name a few. Implicit in the process of understanding why an officer may be experiencing the adverse reactions of CCTS is the understanding that these symptoms are normal reactions to the abnormal and unique demands of policing.

ALCOHOL, DRUGS, AND STEROID USE BY POLICE OFFICERS

Alcoholism and Police Officers

Alcohol abuse among police officers is a serious and widespread problem, with some studies estimating that it affects one-quarter of all police officers in the United States Research has revealed a strong connection between occupational stress and alcohol and drug abuse but also a strong sub-culture among police officers that encourages drinking both for social and stress-reduction purposes. Alcohol consumption among police officers is also correlated with officer suicides and domestic violence, and many departments are beginning to recognize the liability in allowing this problem to go untreated.[46]

The Impact of the Police Culture and Character Traits on the Development of Alcoholism

Paradoxically, despite the significantly high risk for alcoholism and other related problems, law enforcement officers remain one of the most difficult groups to reach with intervention and prevention services, due largely to the insular and clannish nature of the police culture.[47]

Several researchers have also linked negative coping mechanisms with both alcoholism and drug abuse in law enforcement personnel[48] and suggest these negative coping skills may be embedded in character traits (specifically, tough-mindedness, and aggressiveness) typically associated with the "beat cop," which

many departments may still look for in recruits despite a rapidly changing social environment. Another researcher suggests that these character traits are "constant predictors of superior police performance" in a traditional, reactive law enforcement setting. However, the current trend in law enforcement is away from the reactive practices of patrol, rapid response, and investigation and toward a more proactive, community-oriented approach. The new skills required for this new approach include "problem solving, flexibility, good interpersonal and communication abilities, and a demeanor that is *authoritative* rather than authoritarian."[49]

Thus, officers who cling to the "old school" mind-set may suffer future shock in a rapidly evolving social climate. Even in the midst of social change, many police departments today continue to embrace many of the traditions of a bygone era, including the acceptance of drinking.[50] Factors such as the availability of alcohol both inside and outside of work, lack of departmental policies on drinking (or if they do exist, lax enforcement), lack of support mechanisms to help members deal with the stress, and—not by far the least—peer pressure, all contribute to the problem of drinking among police officers.[51] Bandura's Social Learning Theory[52] would view drinking as a *social cue* of the cultural group or subgroup with which one is involved. In the case of police work, drinking has been a time-honored way of "taking the edge off" the stresses of the job since the first New York City patrolman set out on their nightly rounds in the 1840s.

It has been suggested further that policing is especially conducive to alcoholism. Because police officers frequently work in an environment in which social drinking is commonplace, it is relatively easy for them to become social drinkers. The nature of police work and the environment in which it is performed provide the stress stimulus.

Traditionally, police departments adhered to the "character flaw" theory of alcoholism. This outdated philosophy called for the denunciation and dismissal of the officer with an alcohol problem. Today, police departments attempt to rehabilitate officers by employing a number of preventive and intervention programs.

Drug Use by Police Officers

Drug abuse by police officers has garnered a great deal of attention and as a result of this condition, police administrators have had to grapple with such issues as the following:

- What positions will the employee unions or other employee organizations take if drug testing is proposed?

Quick Facts: The Cost of Problem Drinking

Problem drinking in the United States costs employers a staggering $10.7 to $20.7 billion per year in accumulated sick pay, lost productivity, accidents, and the consequences of bad workplace decisions. Some 60% of job absenteeism is attributable to alcoholic and other troubled employees, and these employees miss work 16 times more frequently than do their non-troubled colleagues. Moreover, nearly 90% of all industrial accidents are attributed to workers with either substance abuse or mental health issues.[53]

- Who should be tested for drugs? Entry-level officers? Regular officers on a random basis? All officers before they are promoted? Personnel assigned to high-profile units, such as bomb disposal and special tactics and response?

- When does a supervisor have "reasonable suspicion" of a subordinate's drug use?

- Who should collect urine or other specimens and under what conditions?

- What criteria or standards should be used when selecting a laboratory to conduct the police department's drug-testing program?

- What disciplinary action is appropriate when officers are found to have abused drugs?

- What duty does an employer have to rehabilitate employees who become disabled as a result of drug abuse?[54]

In recent years, issues concerning the testing of sworn officers for drugs have been debated and litigated. In the early days of such litigation, court rulings were sometimes wildly contradictory, with most courts striking down such requirements, typically on the basis that it was an unwarranted intrusion into officers' constitutional right to privacy.[55] Nevertheless, three major principles have emerged from the many random drug cases decided by the courts. The first is that drug testing—both on the basis of reasonable suspicion and when conducted on a random basis—does not violate the federal Constitution. The second is that, although drug testing may not violate federal Constitutional rights, it may not be permissible under the constitutions of some states. The third principle is that, in states that have granted collective bargaining rights to police officers (see Chapter 11, Labor Relations), drug testing cannot be unilaterally implemented by the employer. Instead, it must be submitted to the collective bargaining process.

The selection of officers for drug testing must be truly random and part of a clearly articulated drug-testing policy. The courts will not support the police department's operation of a nonrandom drug-testing program except when there is reasonable suspicion to test for the presence of certain drugs.[56] This generally involves a urine drug screen for the following drugs:

- Cannabinoids (Marijuana, Metabolite)
- Benoyldcgonine (Cocaine, Metabolite)
- Opiates (Codeine, Morphine, Hydrocodone, Hydromorphone, Oxycodone)
- Amphetamines (Amphetamine, Methamphetamine)
- Phencyclidine
- Barbiturates (Phenobarbital, Secobarbital, Pentobarbital, Butalbital, Amobarbital)
- Benzodiazepenes (Oxazepam, Nordiazepam, Alpha OH-Alprazolam, Temazepam)
- Propoxyphene
- Methadone
- Ecstasy
- Anabolic steroids[57]

Anabolic Steroids

Steroids are a group of chemical substances that have certain structural similarities. **Anabolic-androgenic steroids** (AASs) constitute a subgroup of this category that includes the physiological (normal) human male hormone testosterone as well as related compounds with similar functions. These compounds have legitimate medical uses but are frequently abused for illegitimate, recreational uses (bodybuilding, weightlifting, or "bulking up," as well as enhancing athletic performance). AASs should not be confused with other types of "steroids," such as corticosteroids. This latter group of drugs, including hydrocortisone and prednisone, is prescribed widely for legitimate medical purposes (for example, skin creams to treat rashes, in asthma inhalers). Corticosteroids do not cause increases in muscle mass, have almost no abuse potential, and are almost never sold on the illicit market. Therefore, for our purposes, references to steroids mean specifically AASs, which are the type of steroids that are used illicitly.[58]

Controlled Substances

AASs are controlled substances and are prescribed by physicians for certain specific, legitimate medical reasons. These include the treatment of a condition known as hypogonadism (abnormally low testosterone production in men), cancer (to suppress certain kinds of tumors), a rare genetic condition called angioneurotic edema, AIDS wasting syndrome, and some forms of anemia (low red blood cell counts). The U.S. Federal Drug Administration (FDA) lists specific allowable "indications," or uses, for all regulated drugs. The legitimate uses of AASs are minimal as noted; for example, an officer who states that a physician provided them for "elbow pain" would be using them inappropriately.

Illicit "Benefits" of AASs

AASs can be taken orally, by injection, as a skin patch or cream, or sometimes by placing them between the cheek and gum. When combined with a high-protein diet and vigorous weightlifting, AASs "work." That means that they stimulate the formation of muscle tissue and are known to cause enlargement of muscle fibers. It is widely understood that testosterone (the major natural male AAS hormone in normal, healthy men) stimulates an increase in fat-free muscle mass while at the same time decreasing fat. Doses of AASs that exceed the normal production rate of testosterone can amplify this effect, resulting in supernormal gains in lean muscle mass and strength.

Adverse Physical Effects of AAS

Anabolic steroids can cause temporary or permanent medical problems. Some known medical problems associated with AAS use are as follows:

For men:

- Breast enlargement
- Testicular atrophy with consequent sterility or decreased sperm count
- Impotence
- Enlarged prostate

For women:

- Breast diminution
- Clitoral enlargement
- Facial hair growth
- Deepened voice
- Menstrual irregularities
- Excessive body hair
- Baldness

For both sexes:

- Abscess at the site of injection
- Increased risk of heart disease, stroke, or obstructed blood vessels
- Liver tumors, jaundice, and peliosis hepatitis (blood-filled cysts)
- Pre-teens and teenagers: accelerated bone maturation, leading to permanently short stature
- Increased or severe acne[59]

Researchers now know a great deal about the long-term dangers of AAS use in individuals and the evidence of potential dangers has been steadily increasing. These potential dangers have been reported in recent scientific publications. For example, one study of older champion power lifters (most or all of whom had likely used AASs) found that their death rate was almost five times as great as that of a comparison group of men of the same age in the general population. The reasons for death in the older power lifters included both medical problems such as heart disease and psychiatric problems such as suicide.[60]

Adverse Psychological Effects of AAS

Users of AASs can experience adverse psychological symptoms during use, abuse, or withdrawal. Symptoms differ depending on the drug's absence or presence in the body but can manifest itself in the following ways:

- Mania or hypomania (high-energy levels associated with increased self-confidence, increased activity, impaired judgment, and reckless behavior)
- Psychosis—loss of touch with reality (for example, paranoia or delusions of grandeur; infrequent)
- Aggression and violence (in both sexes). This condition is also known as **roid rage**.

The following actual case illustrates the dangers associated with the use of steroids by law enforcement officers.

Several years ago, a uniformed deputy sheriff in Oregon was on his way to work in his personal car when it started to overheat. He stopped at a nearby feed store and requested assistance from the proprietor in getting some water for his radiator. She told him where the water was. After filling his radiator, he asked her if he could use her telephone in order to call the Sheriff's Office, because he was going to be late to work. (This was a time before cell phones were as readily available as they are today.) He called his supervisor to advise him he was going to be late because he was having car problems. When he completed the phone call the proprietor told him in a sarcastic way, "I should start charging you cops because of all the times you come in here to use my phone." He became angry at her for what he perceived as her sarcastic and disrespectful comment but left without saying anything. The following day, still angry about her comment, he returned to the feed store. He was off duty on the way to the gym and was wearing workout clothes. As would later be learned, he was a heavy user of steroids and at the time of this incident was experiencing what is characteristically referred to as "roid rage." He was also armed with his .357 magnum service revolver. He confronted the woman about her sarcastic remarks the day before and then forced her at gunpoint into his personal car. After driving a short distance, the women tried to escape and the deputy shot her in the back. After shooting her, he dumped her injured body from the car onto the street. When members of his agency responded to the assaulted woman she told them what had happened. They immediately proceeded to the deputy's house and arrested him. One of the first things he said upon being arrested was "It was those steroids. It was those steroids." The follow-up investigation revealed that the deputy had a perfect work record and there was absolutely no evidence of any anger management issues on his part. However, a blood test revealed that he had been using heavy doses of three different types of very powerful steroids and had 50 times the level of testosterone that would normally be expected to be found in the male body. He was subsequently found guilty at trial and sentenced to 20 years in prison. As a result of the gunshot wound the victim's spinal cord was irreparably damaged and she remains today a wheelchair-bound paraplegic.

Symptoms Associated with Withdrawal of AAS:

- Long-term AAS abusers can develop symptoms of dependence and withdrawal on discontinuation.
- Withdrawal sometimes leads to severe depression and thoughts of suicide, in addition to medical effects, especially in individuals who have taken AASs for months or years.

Typical Issues Addressed in Police Steroid Testing Policies

Negligent Retention: Agencies have a duty and a right to maintain fit officers and to protect the public from impaired officers. They must exercise reasonable means at their disposal to ensure that officers are fit. Both national and local standards regarding the use of AASs support the idea that officers abusing such substances could be at risk for impairment and could even be involved in criminal activity related to the use of these substances.

Employees' Rights: *National Treasury Employees* v. *Von Raab* is a landmark U.S. Supreme Court case in which employees carrying firearms were required to submit to drug testing.[61] The Court approved the testing program due to the extraordinary hazards of drug use in these officers. No specific guidelines for testing were put forth, but purely random testing is constitutional according to various courts. However, in the mid-1980s, the Boston Police Department adopted a random drug-testing program that was struck down in 1991 by the Massachusetts Supreme Judicial Court.[62] Therefore, the acceptability of random drug testing is highly variable in different jurisdictions and likely depends on union and/or employment contracts.

Detection: To act against an officer, an agency must have reasonable suspicion that the officer is abusing substances or must have an agency-wide random drug-testing schedule. Agencies may not single out an officer for "random" drug testing in the absence of information to suggest use, dealing, and/or impairment.

Testing: Virtually, all testing for AASs is on urine specimens. Courts have accepted gas chromatography/mass spectrometry (GC–MS) urine test results. Levels of most AASs in the blood are generally too low to be easily tested. Detection of AASs in hair samples appears possible but is still in an experimental stage of development.

Collection: Although most of the focus of drug testing is on sample analysis, proper collection and chain-of-custody procedures are also of paramount importance. It does not make sense to employ high-quality, expensive laboratories to analyze samples that have been improperly collected. In drug testing appeal cases, the first challenge is usually to the collection process. Collection procedures should be thorough enough to withstand legal scrutiny and accurate enough to ensure that drug-using officers are properly identified.

Determination of Legitimate Use: If an individual is found using an illicit substance and cannot provide evidence of a legitimate prescription for a medically necessary condition, a fitness-for-duty evaluation is likely needed to ascertain whether the officer is using or abusing the substance in such a way as to jeopardize public safety. The most likely legitimate uses in which a working officer might be prescribed AASs would be for treating hypogonadism. The standard treatment of hypogonadism is the use of a testosterone patch or gel, both of which are highly unlikely to be abused. Injectable and sometimes oral preparations are the common choices of AAS abusers.

Research suggests that individuals taking AASs in excess of 100–200 mg of testosterone per week are outside the bounds of therapeutic use. Upon reaching a dose of 300 mg of testosterone per week, they are somewhat more likely to exhibit aggressive behaviors, which starts to take place more frequently.[63]

Determining the amount taken may be difficult; therefore, it might be necessary to establish a policy that disallows any level of use above therapeutic levels, since it would be difficult to predict aggressive, inappropriate behaviors.

POLICE SUICIDE

Suicide is a very real problem for law enforcement officers and their families. Most studies have shown that the number of officers lives lost to suicide exceeds those killed in the line of duty. A number of potential risk factors are unique to law enforcement. Law enforcement officers are regularly exposed to traumatic and stressful events. Additionally, they work long and irregular hours, which can lead to isolation from family members. Negative perceptions of law enforcement officers and discontent with the criminal justice system also play a role in engendering cynicism and a sense of despair among some officers. A culture that emphasizes strength and control can dissuade officers from acknowledging their need for help. Excessive use of alcohol may also be a factor, as it is for the population in general. Also, suspended police officers and those who are under investigation are 6.7 times more likely to kill themselves.[64]

Need for a Cultural Change in Law Enforcement

Unfortunately, in many law enforcement departments, the culture toward mental wellness or addressing emotional problems of any kind is one of disdain and avoidance. The presumption within this culture is often that the mere presence of an emotional problem indicates a weakness on the officer's part. That perception leads to the even more dangerous perception that being open about these issues can make the officer vulnerable, even to the point of losing his or her job. Significant progress in curbing officer suicide and enhancing officer mental wellness is only achievable if the culture does an about-turn toward openness and support for all aspects of officer health and wellness, particularly mental health.[65]

Also, to more effectively deal with this issue, it has been recommended that the chief executive should be proactive and speak directly to their officers about mental wellness and officer suicide. Hearing from the chief personally and candidly carries a tremendous amount of weight. In particular, police chiefs or others who have triumphed over their own mental health issues should champion this subject and share their own success stories. In addition, one of the executives' most important tasks in this effort is to be held accountable for the review, improvement, and auditing of mental wellness and suicide prevention policies and practices. Police chiefs should appoint and personally oversee a specific employee to begin such an agency review, including identification of resources needed and implementation deadlines. Such an assessment tool or "checklist" could include items such as those found in Table 13.2.

TABLE 13.2 SUGGESTED CHECKLIST FOR COMPREHENSIVE MENTAL WELLNESS AND SUICIDE PREVENTION PROGRAMS

Policy/Practice Review	To Do
Does your agency treat officer mental and physical safety and wellness equally?	A mental resiliency check is like a cholesterol check. Make sure that your officers are mentally fit.
Do you and your officers know the early warning signs of depression, other mental illness, and suicidal behavior?	Implement effective education and training initiatives, and aggressively (and routinely) publicize how officers can get the mental health assistance they need.
Do you have an effective Employee Assistance Program (EAP), peer support group, a consortium approach, or other mental health providers dedicated to law enforcement? Do you have a relationship with a local hospital with trusted doctors to treat officers?	Know what mental health assistance is available to your department, and find out how you can improve the quality of mental health services delivered to your officers.
What are your mental health intervention protocols for at-risk officers and after critical incidents?	Make sure that these protocols are effective and consistent.
Do your training programs from academy recruits to retirees include routine training on mental wellness and stress management? Do you incorporate these curricula at critical incident training?	Invest in this training throughout an officer's career. It is as important as firearms training or wearing body armor.
If you officers have a union, is the union on board with your mental wellness program?	The union might be the go-to contact for a line officer. Work with your unions to foster support for mental wellness programs.
Do you have clear guidance on confidentiality law and rules?	Confidentiality laws are complex and a failure to comply with them can have serious ramifications. Educate your agency.
Does employee self-reporting result in discipline or negative consequences, either intentional or unintentional? Do officers fear that self-reporting will result in discipline or even job loss? Do you have clear guidance on the laws and policies that govern when an officer's firearm must be removed due to mental health issues?	Fear of self-reporting may be one of the greatest barriers to achieving a healthy department. Change your culture so that officers are encouraged to self-report. When an officer sees another officer getting help without having his or her gun and badge taken away, it is very reassuring.
Are the policies in your department addressing suicide adequate?	Be sure you have an established notification and funeral policy in place for officers who die by suicide, to include outreach, education, support for family members and fellow officers, and media coordination.

Source: Breaking the Silence on Law Enforcement Suicides, Community Oriented Policing Services, U.S. Department of Justice, July 2013, p. 6.

Stressors That May Contribute to Suicide or Mental Illness

While by no means an exhaustive list, the following identifies some of the stressors and indicators that officers encounter, which may cause officers to consider suicide or contribute to the development of mental illness:

- Accumulation of chronic stresses and daily hassles
- Exposure to horrific events or acute stresses
- Negative relationship events, including divorce or loss of major relationship; death of a spouse, child, or best friend, especially if by suicide; infidelity or domestic violence
- Shift work, as officers on midnight shifts may be at higher suicide risks because of abnormal sleep patterns, which can impair their ability to make rational decisions
- High expectations of the profession, followed by perceived futility or social isolation

- Significant financial strain, such as inability to pay mortgages or car payments
- Diagnosis of serious or terminal illness
- Significant change in routine, such as a change of duty or pending or existing retirement[66]
- An internal affairs investigation resulting in disciplinary action that could be career ending

Indicators of Police Officers Who May be Contemplating Suicide

- Talking about wanting to die, seeking revenge, feelings of hopelessness, being trapped, being a burden to others, or in unbearable pain
- Increased risk-taking behavior or recklessness
- Looking for a way to kill oneself
- Emotionless, numb, angry, agitated, anxious, enraged, or showing extreme mood swings
- Giving away valued possessions
- Socially isolated or withdrawn
- Weight gain or loss
- Sleep deprivation or sleeping too much
- Cutting themselves
- Increased consumption of alcohol or drugs[67]

Intervention Protocols

Identify, evaluate, and routinely audit mental health providers that screen and provide services to officers at risk.

To identify early warning signs of mental health issues, mental illness, and suicidal behavior and implement successful intervention programs, departments must identify, evaluate, and routinely audit their mental health providers. These providers are the linchpin to the delivery of effective mental health care to officers in need. Symposium participants identified the types of providers typically used by law enforcement, and some of their respective benefits and drawbacks. Participants also made recommendations respective to each type of service to enhance the delivery of these services.

Whoever the providers are, be sure to not only identify and evaluate their services but also routinely audit their quality and to track how often their services are used. This data is essential to obtaining necessary funding and to deploying effective resources where needed.

Peer Support Personnel

Specially trained peer support personnel were recognized as critical mental health resources, as officers in crisis may be far more willing to talk to colleagues than to mental health professionals. Peer support services should be reviewed to ensure that the participants are formally trained: (1) to recognize warning signs of officers with mental illness or at-risk for suicide; and (2) to effectively refer appropriate cases to the professionals. Make sure that the officers selected for the peer support groups are the best officers for the job and enforce accountability and oversight of its members. Consider including retirees who bring extensive experience on the job and can speak to the many challenges of the profession. Finally, ensure that written confidentiality guidelines are clear. And if an agency does not have a peer support group, starting one should be considered.

Employee Assistance Programs (EAP)

EAPs (discussed in greater detail later in this chapter) provide no-cost, confidential assistance to an agency's employees (and sometimes their families) on health and wellness issues that impact work performance, such as stress management, substance abuse counseling, domestic problems, and mental health concerns.

Reinforce family connections

Families are a key resource to any successful early intervention program. Programs and information are important for family members in order for them to understand how they can support their significant other.

POLICE DOMESTIC VIOLENCE

Given the stressful nature of police work, it is not surprising that officers sometimes have difficulty keeping what happened to them at work separate from their home lives. "Leave it at the office" is a common admonition to officers. While the intent of this message is clear, it is often hard to do so consistently and unfortunately, it sometimes manifests itself in domestic violence.[68]

The International Association of Chiefs of Police (IACP) Model Policy on Police Officer Domestic Violence defines it as follows:

It is any reported, founded, and/or prosecuted incident of domestic violence wherein a sworn police officer is the suspected offender. It is also an act of violence (threatened or actual) perpetrated by a police officer (on or off duty) or any police department employee upon his or her intimate partner. "Partner" refers to any individual (opposite or same sex) the officer has dated, cohabitated with, married, and/ or has a child in common.[69] These definitions may be limited to the definitions in the law of each state. While not the focus of this policy, other forms of family violence (for example, child and elder abuse) should be addressed in a parallel manner.[70, 71]

It is not known how many acts of **domestic violence** police officers commit in their own homes. The reasons for the nonreporting of such incidents include victims with low esteem who think they "got what they deserved," threats from their attackers of more severe physical harm if the victims do call the police, and the belief that fellow officers will not take action against "one of their own."

Early Warning and Intervention

Of critical concern to departments is how to screen and select new officers to minimize the risk of hiring officers who may engage in domestic violence.[72] To understand the connection among the various forms of family violence, it is essential to investigate whether a candidate has a history or likelihood of engaging in child abuse, domestic violence, or elder abuse. The process of investigating candidates must be handled in two stages: (1) pre-employment screening and investigation and (2) postconditional offer of employment.

Pre-Employment Screening and Investigation

All candidates should be asked about any history of perpetrating child abuse, domestic violence, or elder abuse and past arrests or convictions for such crimes. They should be asked whether they have ever been the subject of a civil protective order. If the candidate answers positively to any of these questions or the department uncovers any information in the background check that indicates a history of violence, the candidate should be screened out of the hiring process.

During the background investigation, a check should be made for restraining orders issued in any jurisdiction where the candidate has lived.

Post-Conditional Offer of Employment

If the candidate's background investigation does not indicate a history of child abuse, domestic violence, or elder abuse, the department should proceed with a psychological examination, which should include indicators of violent or abusive tendencies. This portion of the screening process should be conducted by an experienced clinical psychologist or psychiatrist. (see Chapter 9, Human Resource Management, for a more detailed discussion.)

Zero-Tolerance Policy

Departments must make it clear to all officers that the department has a zero-tolerance policy on domestic violence, and the department should share this information with family members of the officer. Departments should look to develop a line of communication directly with the domestic partners of recruits and officers. For example, a department can hold a family orientation day prior to graduation from the police academy. Family members should be provided with instructions on whom to contact within the department if any problems arise. The dual purpose of establishing such contact is to underscore the

department's zero-tolerance policy, even with high-ranking members of the organization and to provide victims with an avenue for direct communication with a department employee who is trained in handling such calls.

Department Responsibilities

An individual or a family member of an officer may recognize early indicators of potential violence, such as issues of power and control. The power and control might take the forms of restricting contact with family and friends, requiring the partner to turn over his or her paycheck, and limiting activities outside the home. Victims may communicate their concerns "informally" at first, such as with calls to an officer's supervisor. These informal contacts must be treated with care, since this is a critical opportunity for a department to provide intervention using early intervention and prevention strategies. The model policy calls for a formal system of documenting, sharing, and responding to information from concerned partners and family members.

Departments need to provide officers and their families with nonpunitive avenues of support and assistance before an incident of domestic violence occurs. Departments must establish procedures for making confidential referrals to internal or external counseling services with expertise in domestic violence. These referrals can be made on the request of an officer or family members or in response to observed warning signs.

Officers will not be entitled to confidentiality anytime they or family members disclose to any member of the department that an officer has engaged in domestic violence. Confidentiality should be extended to partners or family members who report an officer as a matter of safety. A report of such criminal conduct must be treated as an admission or a report of a crime and investigated, both criminally and administratively.

Departments must understand that other officers may become involved in domestic violence situations by engaging in inappropriate activities that interfere with cases against fellow officers who are engaged in acts such as stalking, intimidation, harassment, or surveillance of victims, witnesses, and/or family members of victims or witnesses. If this occurs, these officers must be investigated and sanctioned and/or charged criminally where appropriate.

Supervisory Responsibilities

Typically, an abusive person engages in certain patterns of behavior. These may include repeated actions of increasing control directed at his or her partner preceding an incident of physical or criminal violence.

The early indicators of potential violence are not limited to home life; the department may detect warning signs in an officer's behavior prior to a domestic violence incident. Supervisors must receive specific training on warning signs and potential indicators of violent or controlling tendencies. Warning signs that may indicate a likelihood of violent behavior include increased use of force in arrest situations, drug/alcohol problems, frequent tardiness or absences, verbal disputes, physical altercations, and other aggressive behavior.

When supervisors become aware of a pattern of controlling or abusive behavior exhibited by officers, the supervisors have a responsibility to document the information and notify their immediate ranking supervisor, who will then inform the chief in accordance with the department's chain of command. After making proper notification, supervisors should inform officers that the behaviors have been documented. A recommendation can be made to officers that they participate voluntarily in a counseling or support program to address the identified issue or behavior.

In cases in which behavior violates departmental policy, a department can seize the opportunity to mandate participation in a batterer intervention program in addition to any appropriate sanctions.

Early prevention and intervention strategies employed by a department at this phase of the continuum have tremendous potential not only to reduce future violence but also to save victims' lives and officers' careers. The services that can be made available include the following:

- Employee assistance program referral (discussed later in this chapter)
- Internal professional counseling (police psychologist)
- External professional counseling (contract/referral)
- Advocacy support from local agencies
- Peer support program (with clear reporting and confidentiality guidelines)

The department will need to ensure that the quality and expertise of these resources are sound. Collaboration with local domestic violence victim advocacy organizations is recommended.

Police Officer Responsibilities

As part of a department's zero-tolerance policy, all officers need to understand their responsibility to report definitive knowledge they have concerning domestic violence on the part of an officer. Departments must be prepared to investigate and possibly sanction and/or charge criminally any officer who fails to report such knowledge or to cooperate with an investigation.

In addition, all officers need to know they will be investigated and sanctioned and/or charged criminally if they engage in activities such as stalking, surveillance, intimidation, or harassment of victims or witnesses in an attempt to interfere with investigations of other officers accused of domestic violence.

In the event that an officer is the subject of a criminal investigation and/or a protective or restraining order, the officer is responsible for informing his or her supervisor and providing copies of the order and timely notice of court dates regardless of the jurisdiction.

Incident Response Protocols

A department's response to 911 calls involving police officer domestic violence immediately sets the tone for how a situation will be handled throughout the remainder of the continuum. Further, the unique dynamics between the offending and responding officers (e.g., collegiality and rank differential) often make on-scene decisions extremely difficult.

A department must take the following actions, all of which are critical steps in responding to allegations of domestic abuse by police officers:

Communications officer/dispatcher documentation—When a call or report of domestic violence involves a police officer, the dispatcher should have a standing directive to document the call and immediately notify both the on-duty patrol supervisor and the chief of police. This directive ensures that key command personnel receive the information and prevents the call from being handled informally.

Patrol response—Any officer arriving at the scene of a domestic violence call or incident involving a police officer must immediately request the presence of a supervisor at the scene, regardless of the involved officer's jurisdiction.

On-scene supervisor response—The on-scene supervisor has responsibilities for the following:

- Securing the scene and collecting evidence
- Ensuring an arrest is made where probable cause exists
- Removing weapons in the event of an arrest
- Considering victim safety
- Notifying the police chief or sheriff if the incident occurs outside the officer's jurisdiction

The on-duty supervisor must respond to the call and assume all on-scene decision making. Leaving the decision making to officers of lesser or equal rank to the suspect officer puts the responding officer in a difficult situation. The presence of a ranking officer on the scene resolves this problem. The policy recommends that, in police officer domestic violence cases, no fewer than two officers, with at least one of senior rank to the accused officer, be present. This is also the case when serving arrest warrants and civil protective orders.

Crime scene documentation—Recanting or reluctant witnesses and victims are not uncommon when domestic violence occurs. Police on the scene of a 911 call must take specific actions to document all evidence, including color photographs/videotape of injuries, overturned/damaged furniture, interviews of neighbors and family members, and threats from the officer. Documentation of this evidence will be essential to the successful prosecution of the case with or without the victim's presence in court.

Arrest decisions—Policies on arrest for domestic violence incidents vary among state, county, and local jurisdictions. In all cases, responding officers should base arrest decisions on probable cause. When a crime has been committed, an arrest will be made, as in all other cases. The on-scene supervisor is responsible for ensuring an arrest is made if probable cause exists or for submitting written documentation to explain why an arrest was not made. All officers need sufficient training to enable them to determine which party is the primary (i.e., dominant) aggressor in domestic violence situations. Every effort should be made to identify the primary aggressor to avoid the unwarranted arrest of victims.

Weapon removal—If an arrest is made, the on-scene supervisor will relieve the accused officer of his or her service weapon. Some police officers may have several weapons at their home. Where multiple weapons are present, removing only the service weapon of the officer leaves the victim entirely vulnerable to further violence. While federal, state, and local laws vary on how and when such weapons can be removed, police have broad powers to remove weapons in certain circumstances, particularly if an arrest is being made. Where application of the law is questionable, the on-scene supervisor should suggest that the officer in question voluntarily relinquish all firearms. The supervisor can also simply ask victims if they want to remove any weapons from the home for safekeeping by the department. When no arrest has been made, the on-scene supervisor should consider removing the accused officer's weapon as a safety consideration.

After weapons are removed, decisions need to be made about how long they will or can be held. Where court orders of protection are in place, these orders may also affect decisions on gun removal or seizure.

When the accused officer is the chief, director, or superintendent of the department, a specific protocol must be in place to document and report the incident to the individual who has direct oversight for the chief, director, or superintendent.

When police respond to a domestic violence incident involving an officer from another jurisdiction, all responding officers, investigators, and supervisors will follow the same procedures to be followed if responding to a domestic violence complaint involving an officer from their own department. The on-scene supervisor will notify the chief of police from the accused officer's department verbally as soon as possible and in writing within 24 hours of the call.

Departments may be faced with domestic violence situations where the victim is a police officer. If this occurs, standard domestic violence response and investigation procedures should be followed. The department should take steps to protect the privacy of the officer and make referrals to confidential counseling services. The department should not allow the reported incident to impact negatively on the assignments and evaluation of the victimized officer.

If both the victim and the offender in a domestic violence situation are police officers, the protocols established by the department should remain substantially the same. Safety of the victim should be the paramount concern. In the event that an order of protection has been issued, a department will need to make careful decisions concerning work assignments for accused officers pending administrative and criminal investigations. Gun removal in this situation becomes extremely complex. In the development of the policy, individual departments should seek legal guidance to ensure that the rights of all concerned are protected.

Department follow-up—The department or supervisor should require a debriefing of all officers involved in a response to the scene of a police officer domestic violence case and may include communications officers. At the debriefing, the department's confidentiality guidelines should be reviewed. In addition, a command-level **critical incident** management review of every domestic violence case involving an officer should be conducted.

The department must take responsibility for conducting an assessment to determine the potential for further violence on the part of the accused officer. A specifically trained member of the command staff should review a domestic violence lethality checklist (discussed later in this chapter) of risk factors with the accused officer. In addition, the evaluation should be supplemented by interviews with the victim, witnesses, and family members. Information gained from the assessment should be used to determine appropriate sanctions, safeguards, and referrals. The command officer assigned as the victim's principal contact should discuss the risk factors with the victim as part of safety planning.

DOMESTIC VIOLENCE LETHALITY ASSESSMENT FOR FIRST RESPONDERS

Law enforcement agencies are increasingly providing their first responders with a **domestic violence lethality assessment form** and accompanying them with instruction to assist them in more systematically evaluating the extent to which someone may be in grave danger of being seriously injured or killed (see Figure 13.3).

Purpose of the Lethality Assessment: This evidence-based Lethality Assessment form is a user-friendly, straightforward instrument that predicts danger and lethality in domestic incidents between intimate or former intimate partners to a high degree. Research shows that **only 4% of intimate partner murder victims ever used domestic violence (DV) services.** This Assessment encourages victims in high danger to seek domestic violence program services to prevent serious injury or death.

Step 1—Fill out the Assessment Form with the victim.

Step 2—If any of the first three answers are yes, ask the victim to call the agency's local advocacy agency and ensure that they make contact. You may need to dial the number for them if they are upset.

Step 3—If they talk to someone, check the box that they spoke to a hotline counselor.

Step 4—If they answer yes to one of the first three questions but do not want to speak to a hotline counselor right away, note the victim's safe phone number to call.

SANTA CLARA COUNTY DOMESTIC VIOLENCE
LETHALITY ASSESSMENT FOR FIRST RESPONDERS

Date:	Case #:	
Officer:	Agency:	
Victim:	Offender:	
Victim's Safe Numbers to Call: Home: Cell: Work:	Would you like to provide names/phone numbers of 2 people that can reach you? 1. 2.	

Is the victim monolingual/limited English proficient? If yes, what language do they speak?
☐ Check here if the victim did not answer any of the questions.

If the victim answers YES to any of questions 1–3, please call the appropriate domestic violence crisis hotline and have the counselor speak with the victim.

1. Has your current or previous partner ever used a weapon against you or threatened you with a weapon?	☐ Yes ☐ No ☐ No Answer
2. Have they threatened to kill you or someone else?	☐ Yes ☐ No ☐ No Answer
3. Do you think your current or previous partner might try to kill you?	☐ Yes ☐ No ☐ No Answer

If the answers to the above questions are NO but at least 4 of the questions below are YES please contact the hotline.

4. Do they have a gun or can they easily get one?	☐ Yes ☐ No ☐ No Answer
5. Have they ever tried to choke/strangle you?	☐ Yes ☐ No ☐ No Answer
6. Are they violently or constantly jealous or try to control most of your daily activities?	☐ Yes ☐ No ☐ No Answer
7. Have you left or separated from your partner after living together or being married?	☐ Yes ☐ No ☐ No Answer
8. Are they unemployed?	☐ Yes ☐ No ☐ No Answer
9. Have they tried to commit suicide?	☐ Yes ☐ No ☐ No Answer
10. Do you have a child that he knows is not his?	☐ Yes ☐ No ☐ No Answer
11. Do they follow or spy on you or leave threatening messages?	☐ Yes ☐ No ☐ No Answer

12. Is there anything else that worries you about your safety? If yes, what concerns do you have?

Officers are encouraged to call the hotline whenever they believe the victim is in a potentially lethal situation regardless of the victim's responses to the questions above.

Check one:	☐ Victim screened in based on responses ☐ Victim screened in based on the belief of officer	☐ Victim did not screen in
Did the victim speak with the hotline counselor?	☐ Yes	☐ No

NORTH COUNTY HOTLINE: **YWCA Support Network** **1-800-572-2782** **FAX: 408-295-0608**		**CENTRAL COUNTY HOTLINE:** **Next Door Solutions** **408-279-2962** **FAX: 408-441-7562**
	SOUTH COUNTY HOTLINE: **Community Solutions** **1-877-363-7238** **FAX 408-782-9469** 54	

PLEASE FAX THIS DOCUMENT TO THE APPROPRIATE DOMESTIC VIOLENCE AGENCY

FIGURE 13.3 ▶ Santa Clara County Domestic Violence Lethality Assessment for First Responders. *Source:* Domestic Violence Protocol for Law Enforcement, Police Chiefs Association of Santa Clara County, California, March 2014, p. 54.

Step 5—If the victim answers yes to the first three questions, or a significant number of follow up questions are yes, but they refuse to speak to a hotline counselor advise the victim that in your opinion, he/she is in high danger for lethality and you highly encourage them to seek DV program services.

Step 6—Provide them with a DV resource card and case number,

Step 7—Fax all Lethality Assessment forms to the appropriate DV organization listed on the bottom of the form regardless of the answers or whether or not the victim answered any of the questions.[73]

POLICE OFFICER HOMICIDES AND SUICIDES

Police departments should not underestimate the potential for domestic violence situations involving their police officers as well as high-ranking police administrators to escalate not only into suicides but also into homicides.

The following summarized news stories show the potential for such a tragic event.[74]

Case 1

The Tacoma, Washington, Police Chief, killed his wife and then himself during a violent domestic dispute. Two weeks prior to the incident the chief had arrived at his estranged wife's house and attempted to gain entry. She called the Sheriff's Department and told the Sheriff's operator her estranged husband was attempting to forcibly enter the house. She also advised them that he was the Chief of the Tacoma, Washington, Police Department, and that he was armed. The Sheriff's Department did not respond to take a report even though it was their agency's standard procedure to do so. Two weeks after this initial encounter when the news broke about the Chief's divorce battle and allegations of his forcible attempt to gain entry into the house occupied by his wife, city officials still insisted that the Chief was doing a good job. City Attorney Robin Jenkinson rejected an internal proposal by other city officials that the Chief be disarmed feeling this was a civil matter. The following day the Chief shot his wife and himself.

Case 2

A 33-year-old Police Deputy Inspector shot his 38-year-old wife several times, killing her. It happened during an argument the couple had in their car. The officer had earlier approached his wife in a cafeteria and ordered her into the car. He later committed suicide. During the month prior to the homicide, the wife told friends she felt threatened and afraid. However she never filed any claims or notified the police. He was well known as a campaigner against domestic violence, and only weeks earlier had received praise for his efforts in the protection of women.

Case 3

A county Sheriff's Office jailer shot his 4-year-old son, his wife, and then himself. The jailer called 911 and informed the dispatcher of the situation prior to turning the weapon on himself. Shortly after the killings, the Sheriff said that the jailer had been in good spirits and had not exhibited signs of depression or agitation at any time prior to the homicides. Last week, the Sheriff investigated allegations made by the jailer's wife, accusing the sheriff's office of not acting on information regarding abuse at the hands of her husband. The wife's father said Friday that he contacted County officials multiple times to report domestic abuse, but officials did not act. He alleges that his daughter was the victim of physical abuse and said that he had witnessed his daughter with black eyes.

THE STRESS OF SMALL TOWN POLICING

Much of the research that has been done on the study of police stress in recent years has been done on large and medium-sized police departments. However, law enforcement officers in smaller agencies are also exposed to stressful situations but there are certain aspects of their job that create uniquely stressful situations precisely because of the small size of their community.

Police officers who live and work in small towns almost never have an opportunity to decompress. Precisely because they are well known to the residents, business owners, and others in the community, officers cannot separate on-duty and off-duty time. Essentially, small town police officers live in a "fishbowl." Off-duty trips to the store frequently become job related because everyone seems to know the officers and their family vehicles. Spouses and family members often come under close observation. For example, residents who observe an officer's family member violating traffic laws may believe that they are doing so because other officers in the community will likely not issue them a traffic citation. Taking their children to school becomes complicated when other parents wonder out loud why officers are not at work or when a school administrator asks for advice about an unruly child or parent. All of this "off-duty" interaction contributes to the stress of the small town police officer.[75]

In addition to these daily stressors, small town police officers often find themselves in the unenviable position of being the only officer on duty. The nearest backup may be in a town or county many miles away. The level of stress that these officers feel as a result of responding to potentially dangerous calls for service creates even greater stress than for officers in larger communities who have back up at their immediate disposal. In addition, because of their isolation they cannot readily share the stressful experience with another officer. Their first opportunity to express their anxiety could be at their shift change several hours later. The passage of time can have negative long-term effects on an officer's ability to decompress from the incident and the accumulated stress that it has produced.[76]

Also in small town policing, officers generally live and work in the community that they serve. In these tight-knit localities, the officers often know the residents. Thus, for example, if a traffic accident occurs resulting in a serious injury or fatality, the responding officer will likely know the people who are involved. This familiarity with the victims, unlike dealing with strangers, can be very traumatic for the officer and if the incident is serious enough could contribute to the development of PTSD.

It is true that police officers in smaller communities do not typically handle the volume of dangerous or hazardous events as police officers in large or medium-sized agencies. However, as suggested herein, they are not as stress free as some would imagine, plus they have stressors that are not normally experienced by police officers in larger and medium-sized agencies.

THE IMPACT OF SHIFT LENGTH ON PERFORMANCE, HEALTH, QUALITY OF LIFE, SLEEP, FATIGUE, AND EXTRA-DUTY EMPLOYMENT

In the past, most law enforcement agencies had traditionally deployed their patrol officers based on a 40-hour work week in which personnel work five consecutive, 8-hour shifts, followed by 2 days off.[77] However, in recent years, an increasing number of agencies have moved to some variant of a compressed work-week (CWW) schedule in which officers work four 10-hours shifts per week or three 12-hour shifts (plus a time adjustment to make up the remaining 4 hours of the standard 40-hour work-week). While this trend toward CWWs has dramatically increased in recent years there have been few, if any, rigorous scientific studies examining the advantages and disadvantages associated with these work schedules for officers and their agencies.

Recently, a study was funded by the U.S. Department of Justice to examine any potential issues associated with CWW. This was done by implementing a randomized block experiment in Detroit (MI) and Arlington (TX), in which the blocks include site (i.e., Detroit, Arlington) as well as shift (day, evening, and midnight) in order to examine the effects of the three shift lengths on various outcomes. Work performance was measured using both laboratory simulations and departmental data. Health, quality of life, sleep, sleepiness, off-duty employment, and overtime hours were measured via self-report measures including surveys, sleep diaries, and alertness logs. Fatigue was measured using both objective, laboratory-based instruments, and subjective reports of sleepiness.

The results revealed no significant differences between the three shift lengths on work performance, health, or work–family conflict. There were, however, important differences where the other outcomes were concerned. Officers working 10-hour shifts, for example, averaged significantly more sleep and reported experiencing a better quality of work life than did their peers working 8-hour shifts. And officers working 12-hour shifts experienced greater levels of sleepiness (subjective measure of fatigue) and lower levels of alertness at work than those assigned to 8-hour shifts. The results suggest that CWWs are not likely to pose significant health risks or result in worsened performance and that 10-hour shifts may offer certain benefits not associated with 8-hour shifts, whereas 12-hour shifts may have some disadvantages over 8-hour shifts. Importantly, those on 8-hour shifts averaged significantly less sleep per 24-hour period and worked significantly more overtime hours than those on 10- or 12-hour shifts. As such, a 10-hour shift may be a viable alternative to the traditional 8-hour shift in larger agencies; however, caution is advised when considering 12-hour shifts due to increased levels of self-reported fatigue/sleepiness and lower levels of alertness. Indeed, researchers have noted that individuals tend to underestimate their levels of fatigue, so officers may be more fatigued than they reported while working 12-hour shifts. Additionally, past research has shown increased risks for accidents with increasing numbers of hours worked. It is for these reasons that caution should be exercised when agency leaders consider adopting 12-hour long shifts. Finally, the reduced levels of overtime usage for those working 10- and 12-hour shifts suggests the possibility for cost savings for agencies employing compressed schedules. These findings are consistent with many past findings; however, the lack of randomized controlled trials has limited the utility of past studies.

SLEEP DEPRIVATION AS A STRESS INDUCER

Although sleep deprivation is often not thought of as a stress factor, it can be a significant factor in the creation of stress. For example, sleep deprivation can cause the following to occur in police officers:

- Increased mood swings
- Impaired judgment
- Decrease in adaptability to certain situations
- Heightened sense of threat
- Increased anxiety or depression
- Increased chances of mental illness (e.g., officers may develop posttraumatic stress disorder or bipolar disorder)
- Reduced eye–hand coordination
- Weight gain
- Pain (e.g., backaches and headaches)
- Inability to relax (e.g., cause restless sleep and provoke heightened alert response)
- Gastrointestinal problems (e.g., loss of appetite or abdominal distress)
- Damage to the cardiovascular system (e.g., causing heart disease, arteriosclerosis, or congestive heart failure)
- Use of more sick leave
- Inappropriate uses of force more frequently

- More vehicle accidents
- More accidental injuries
- Greater difficulty in dealing with the community members and other law enforcement agencies
- Higher likelihood of dying in the line of duty[78, 79] because of fatigue-related factors

Sleep Deprivation Is Comparable to Excessive Drinking

A sleep deprivation study found that not sleeping for 17 hours impaired a person's motor skills to an extent equivalent to having an alcohol toxicity of 0.05 percent. Not sleeping for 24 hours was equivalent to a toxicity level of 0.10 percent.[80] This level of deprivation would impair speech, balance, coordination, and mental judgment.

Sleep Deprivation Can Cause Work-Related Accidents

One study found that four out of eight officers involved in on-the-job accidents and injuries were impaired because of fatigue.[81] Such accidents include automobile crashes that were due to officers' impaired eye–hand coordination and propensity to nod off behind the wheel. Other work-related injuries come from accidents that occur when officers have impaired balance and coordination.

Despite the impact of fatigue, many officers continue to work double shifts, triple shifts, and second jobs. Some work well over 1,000 hours of overtime a year. Excessive work with inadequate rest over a long period of time can make officers sleep-deprived—53 percent of officers report an average of 6.5 hours of sleep or less.[82]

STRESS REDUCTION MANAGEMENT TECHNIQUES

Some police officers think that stress is just "a fairy tale—something that those who can't hack it can blame for their problems." Thus, the first step is for officers to recognize that unchecked stress can cause them to be sick more frequently, to engage in self-destructive behaviors (such as substance abuse or suicide), to live life less fully, to lose their families, and simply to be more uncomfortable every day than they need to be. The second step for officers is to monitor their own bodies and actions for stress, even though this capacity for self-awareness and introspection is difficult for some people to develop. Simply put, officers need to be in touch with what they are feeling, to think about what they have said and done, and to ask, "Why?" The final step is to eliminate or reduce stress by engaging in the so-called **stress inoculation activities**:

- Exercise rigorously for 20 to 30 min at least three times per week
- Maintain a proper diet, including minimizing the intake of foods high in salt and cholesterol

- Develop leisure interests and hobbies, such as hiking, tying fishing flies, rock climbing, gardening, collecting stamps, writing poetry and fiction, learning a foreign language, and photography—in other words, learning new things that excite and refresh the mind
- Meditate and pray
- Avoid maladaptive responses to stress, such as smoking and drinking
- Establish support groups
- Develop a network of friends, including people outside the department
- Monitor yourself; refer yourself for help before you have to be referred; you will avoid some problems, reduce others before they become entrenched, and get more out of the helping process
- Use relaxation techniques, such as biofeedback, yoga, progressive muscle relaxation, tai chi, imagery, and breathing exercises
- Make sure that your career and other expectations are consistent with your actual situation[83]

THE POLICE PSYCHOLOGIST'S ROLE IN A PSYCHOLOGICAL HEALTH WELLNESS INITIATIVE

The role of a police psychologist in psychological health wellness initiatives can vary on a number of dimensions, mostly determined by the individual needs of the department or agency hiring the psychologist or contracting for the psychologist's services. However, there are specific ways in which a psychologist can function more effectively if the goal of the relationship with the department involves fostering a comprehensive psychological health and resiliency initiative.[84]

In order for a psychologist to be an effective part of a psychological health initiative, there must be clarity on the part of the department, the officers, and the psychologist on the functions being served. For example, delineating the role of the psychologist as evaluator for fitness for duty from that of the psychologist providing officer support, resources, and consultations is important in building relationships. The police psychologist will ideally have the ability to work with training units on developing wellness trainings at the primary prevention level on a variety of topics that can help officers to buffer stress. In addition to standard stress management and suicide awareness trainings, officers can often make use of primary prevention training to develop skills in the areas that can lead to a cumulative buildup of stress for an officer. At the secondary level, the police psychologist who successfully collaborates with other department officer resources, such as peer support teams, chaplaincy programs, and veteran assistance and reintegration programs, will enhance the connections between these efforts and the psychologist's services.[85]

More specifically, police psychologists must exhibit their willingness to work as a team by first of all demonstrating great respect for the natural healing resource of the police brotherhood. Peer supporters are the specially trained colleagues of other officers. They play an important role in the first-line response to officers who are experiencing stress, distress, or impairment. If the police psychologist can earn the respect, trust, and collegiality of the peer support providers, then peer support will act as a natural bridge to the psychologist when the peer encounters an officer in need of the special services available only from the mental health provider. Psychologists will need to play an important role in facilitating such collaborations. A consultation and client-centered approach is the hallmark of effective psychological assistance and central to the training of psychologists. Such skills can be extremely valuable in the effort to foster teamwork and establish a psychological health initiative.[86]

A police psychologist can and should perform the traditional roles of providing an assessment of a potentially suicidal individual if the officer has reached the stage of obvious impairment, as well as implementing or arranging the appropriate type of tertiary prevention. However, the police psychologist who adopts a focus on "problem solving for people in crisis" in carrying out these professional activities can do much to reduce the stigma associated with using both secondary and tertiary suicide prevention programs and, in that way, help to prevent an officer from becoming impaired and suicidal. A police psychologist is a specialist in stress management and helps to reverse the downward cascade of poorly managed stress before it becomes distress, impairment, and ultimately problem behaviors (e.g., suicidal thoughts or acts, substance abuse, or dysfunctional relationship dynamics on the job or at home). Police officers are natural problem solvers who do not like to ask for help, but they are smart enough to seek out the experts and the specialists for DNA analysis, complex data analysis and management, or whatever else it takes to get the job done. Consulting with a police psychologist regarding the maintenance of the officer's most important "piece of equipment"—his or her health and wellness—is just smart police work. The police psychologist who can serve as a consultant to the officer in this way can serve a valuable role.[87]

EMPLOYEE ASSISTANCE PROGRAMS

Although their evolution has been slow in development, a variety of employee assistance services are currently available within police departments.[88] The growth of **employee assistance programs (EAPs)** in the law enforcement field can be traced back to the early 1950s.[89] Many programs, such as those initiated in Boston, New York, and Chicago, were created to deal primarily with alcohol abuse.

In the 1970s, agencies such as the Los Angeles Sheriff's Office, the Chicago Police Department (see Figure 13.4), and the San

Chicago Police Department		**Employee Resource E06-01**	
PROFESSIONAL COUNSELING SERVICE/EMPLOYEE ASSISTANCE PROGRAM			
ISSUE DATE:	21 February 2012	**EFFECTIVE DATE:**	21 February 2012
RESCINDS:	Version dated 01 June 2011; A04-16		
INDEX CATEGORY:	Personnel Support		

I. **PURPOSE**

This directive:

    A. states Department policy regarding members who may seek counseling assistance.

    B. outlines:

        1. the scope of the Professional Counseling Service/Employee Assistance Program (EAP).

        2. policy regarding confidentiality.

    C. provides:

        1. information for general counseling and referral services.

        2. procedures for crisis intervention.

    D. describes the services available to Department members and their families.

II. **POLICY**

    A. The Department is committed to ensuring the safety and well-being of all members and their families whenever possible. The Department recognizes that members may experience personal difficulties which may impact their personal and professional lives. The Department supports and encourages members in securing quality, confidential assistance.

FIGURE 13.4 ▶ Professional counseling service/Employee assistance program. Courtesy Chicago, Illinois Police Department, 2015.

(continued)

In keeping with this commitment, the Department has established the Professional Counseling Service/EAP, staffed with clinical professionals and trained peer counselors who provide confidential counseling and consultation.

B. The Professional Counseling Service/EAP is structured around a concept of confidentiality which mandates that **no information, including identifying factors, identifying biographical material, clinical notes, or therapy issues, be reported to or requested by the Department.** Individual members may expect, and will be granted, complete privacy when voluntarily seeking counseling assistance through the Professional Counseling Service/EAP. Refer to the Department directive entitled **"Professional Counseling Confidentiality"** for a full explanation of the confidentiality policy, including exceptions.

III. GENERAL INFORMATION

A. The Professional Counseling Service/EAP unit of the Chicago Police Department is staffed by sworn and civilian counselors and requires the **voluntary** involvement of Department members or their families who are seeking counseling. The Professional Counseling Service is not located in a police facility.

B. To request counseling services, the _Professional Counseling Service / EAP_ may be contacted **24 hours a day, 7 days a week.**

C. The Professional Counseling Service/EAP is component of the _Bureau of Administration_ and is administered by a Director.

D. All of the services offered by the Professional Counseling Service/EAP are available to Department members, a member's immediate or extended family, and retired sworn members.

E. All counseling services provided by the Professional Counseling Service/EAP are **free of charge.** Referrals to a private therapist, specialist, outside agency, or hospital, however, are for profit, non-Department providers which may charge a fee. Information regarding referral sources, credentials, programs, and the level of care provided may be obtained by the Professional Counseling Service/EAP. Counselors from the Professional Counseling Service will conduct follow-up sessions with the members after they receive counseling services from an outside agency to ensure the quality or care provided by the outside agency is satisfactory to the member.

F. The _Professional Counseling Service/EAP_ can be contacted by letter, telephone, or in person for information regarding a counseling appointment.

G. Communications between the Professional Counseling Service/EAP and the counseled member will be confidential as outlined in the Mental Health and Development Disabilities Act and shall not be subject to disclosure in any judicial, administrative, or legislative proceedings as described in _Chapter 740, Illinois Compiled Statutes, Section 110/3._ Communications between a counseled member and a professional counselor are protected from discovery in federal cases under Federal Rule of Evidence 501.

IV. SERVICES AVAILABLE

A. The Professional Counseling Service/EAP has been established to provide confidential supportive assistance, including peer counseling and referral services, for all Department members. Comprehensive services include:

1. 24-Hour Crisis Intervention Services,
2. Stress Management Training,
3. Alcohol and Substance Abuse, Support Service and Prevention Training,
4. Peer Support,
5. Couples Counseling,
6. Individuals Counseling,
7. Family Crisis Intervention,
8. Grief Counseling.
9. Communication Skills,
10. Anger Management and Conflict Resolution,
11. Traumatic Incident Stress Management,
12. Referrals to Pastoral Counseling,
13. _Anonymous and Confidential Depression and Alcohol Screening_, and
14. Gambling and Debt Management.

B. The services provided by the Professional Counseling Service/EAP Unit are designed and tailored to meet the unique needs of each and every Department member, members of their family, or retired members seeking assistance. This is accomplished by maintaining a network of quality resources (i.e., treatment facilities, self-help and support groups, and stress management training) which allows the unit to respond promptly to the needs of individuals.

C. Alcoholism and Other Addictions Services Unit

This Unit is administered by a supervisor who reports to the Director, Professional Counseling Service. The Unit is staffed by certified alcoholism and other drug abuse counselors who are specially selected and trained Department members.

1.   The Alcoholism and Other Addictions Unit will:

    a. provide services to Department members and/or their families who may be experiencing difficulty wilh problems related to alcoholism or other addictions. In an emergency, the unit can be contacted 24 hours a day, 7 days a week.

    b. serve as a resource to command and supervisory personnel and other Department units whose function involves interaction with employees experiencing impairment due to alcoholism or other addictions.

    c. be responsible for that portion of supervisory training that focuses upon employee impairment due to alcoholism or other addictions.

2.   When an employee is identified by Department supervisory personnel as possibly having problems related to alcoholism and/or other addictions, a counselor will be available to evaluate and provide appropriate support services and/or guidance.

3.   When a disciplinary action / investigation has been initiated against a member impaired by alcoholism or other addiction(s), involvement in an Alcoholism and Other Addictions Services Unit program will not delay the disciplinary or investigative processes.

D. Traumatic Incident Stress Management Program

This program provides Department members the opportunity to understand and put into perspective the emotional and/or psychological impact of a traumatic incident. The debriefing process is not a critique of any assignment or action taken by the officer.

1.   The referral procedure to the Traumatic Incident Stress Management Program for sworn members is outlined in the Department directive entitled "**<u>Traumatic Incident Stress Management Program</u>.**"

2.   The Traumatic Incident Stress Management Program is also available to non-sworn members, their families, and retired members. To request services contact the *Professional Counseling Services/EAP*.

V. DEPARTMENT REFERRALS TO THE PROFESSIONAL COUNSELING SERVICE

A. Department command and supervisory personnel have the authority and the responsibility to make members under their supervision aware of the Professional Counseling Service/EAP when appropriate.

B. Department members will he assured that any consultation at the Professional Counseling Service/EAP will be confidential.

C. In a crisis or emergency situation, supervisors will recommend immediate intervention by the *Professional Counseling Service / EAP* **24 hours a day, 7 days a week.**

D. Recommendations or referrals to the Professional Counseling Service/EAP will not be used as a substitute for the disciplinary process.

E. Unit commanding officers and/or supervisors may contact the Professional Counseling Service for information about the counseling program or the referral process.

F. The procedures contained in this directive do not relieve unit commanding officers of their responsibility to counsel members as set forth in existing Department directives.

(Items indicated by *italics/double underline* were revised)

Authenticated by: RMJ

Garry F. McCarthy
Superintendent of Police

11-052/12-003 AMR/PMD

PHONE BOOK ENTRIES:

1. **Professional Counseling Division**
312-743-0378

2. **Anonymous and Confidential Depression and Alcohol Screening**
800-900-7401

ADDENDA:

1. E06-01-01 - Crisis Intervention
2. E06-01-02 - Professional Counseling Confidentiality

FIGURE 13.4 ▶ *(continued)*

Francisco Police Department expanded their programs to include problems not related to alcohol. In 1980, mental health professionals began providing personal and job-related counseling services to FBI personnel. Mental health professionals were also used to assist FBI managers with a variety of employee-related matters. By 1986, many of the largest police departments in the United States had formed "stress units" or other sections to provide help for officers having personal or occupational difficulties. In the early 1990s, the U.S. Customs Service provided stress-management training for both its supervisory and its non-supervisory personnel throughout the country.[90] The majority of law enforcement agencies with 100 or more officers now have written policies regarding providing counseling assistance services for their officers.[91]

Chapter Summary

Summary by Learning Objective

1. **Explain why police officers are more prone to stress than individuals in many other occupations.**

   It is one of the few occupations in which an employee is asked continually to face physical dangers and to put his or her life on the line at any time. The police officer is exposed to violence, cruelty, and aggression and is often required to make extremely critical decisions in high-pressure situations.

2. **Describe the perceptual, cognitive, and behavioral disturbances resulting from an officer's use of deadly force.**

   (1) *Distortions of time perception* are most common, with the majority of officers recalling the shooting event as occurring in slow motion, although a smaller percentage reported experiencing he even as speeded up; (2) *Sensory distortions* are also common and most often involve *tunnel vision*, in which the officer is sharply focused on one particular aspect of the visual field, typically the suspect's gun or weapon, which blocks out everything in the periphery; (3) *A sense of helplessness* may occur during the shooting exchange, but this may be underreported due to the potential stigma attached; (4) *Disturbances in memory* are commonly reported in shooting exchanges. About half of these involve impaired recall for at least some of the events during the shooting; the other half involve impaired recall for at least part of the officer's own actions; this, in turn, may be associated with going-on-automatic response.

3. **Discuss some of the questions that police administrators must address in terms of drug use by police officers.**

   (1) What positions will the employee unions and other employee organizations take if drug testing is proposed? (2) Who should be tested for drugs? Entry-level officers? Regular officers on a random basis? All officers before they are promoted? Personnel assigned to high-profile units, such as bomb disposal and special tactics and response? (3) When does a supervisor have "reasonable suspicion" of a subordinate's drug use? (a) who should collect the urine or other specimens and under what conditions? (b) what criteria or standards should be used when selecting a laboratory to conduct the police department's drug-testing program? (c) what disciplinary action is appropriate when officers are found to have abused drugs? (d) what duty does an employer have to rehabilitate employees who become disabled as a result of drug abuse?

4. **Describe some of the negative physical consequences associated with the use of steroids.**

   For men: (1) breast enlargement; (2) testicular atrophy with the consequent sterility or decreased sperm count; (3) impotence; (4) enlarged prostate. *For women:* (1) breast diminution; (2) clitoral enlargement; (3) facial hair growth; (4) deepened voice; (5) menstrual irregularities; (6) excessive body hair; (7) baldness. *For both sexes:* (1) abscess at the site of injection; (2) increased risk of heart disease, stroke, or obstructed blood vessels; (3) increased or severe acne; (4) liver tumors, jaundice, and peliosis hepatitis, (blood-filled cysts); pre-teens and teenagers: accelerated bone maturation, leading to permanently short stature.

5. **Discuss the indicators that would suggest a police officer is considering suicide.**

   Indicators that a police officer is contemplating suicide are talking about wanting to die, seeking revenge, feelings of hopelessness, being trapped, being a burden to others, or in unbearable pain; increased risk-taking behavior or recklessness; looking for a way to kill oneself; emotionless, numb, angry, agitated, anxious, enraged, or showing extreme mood swings; giving away valued possessions; socially isolated or withdrawn; weight gain or loss; sleep deprivation or sleeping too much; cutting themselves; and increased consumption of alcohol or drugs.

6. **Examine the role the police psychologist plays in a psychological health wellness initiative.**

   The police psychologist will ideally have the ability to work with training units on developing wellness trainings at the primary prevention level on a variety of topics that can help officers to buffer stress. In addition to standard stress management and suicide awareness trainings, officers can often make use of primary prevention training to develop skills in the areas that can lead to a cumulative buildup of stress for an officer. At the secondary level, the police psychologist who successfully collaborates with other department officer resources, such as peer support teams, chaplaincy programs, and veteran assistance and reintegration programs, will enhance the connections between these efforts and the psychologist's services.

Chapter Review Questions

1. Describe the three stages of the general adaptation syndrome (GAS), as described by Hans Selye.
2. According to recent medical findings, what is the relationship between diseases of adaption and stress?
3. What is posttraumatic stress disorder (PTSD)?
4. How does cumulative career traumatic stress (CCTS) differ from posttraumatic stress disorder?
5. What are the major characteristics of the type-A personality, type-B personality, type-C personality, type-D personality, and workaholic?
6. What are the five basic phases of the post-shooting reaction?
7. What recommendations were made regarding the post-shooting interview of police officers?
8. Alcohol-related problems manifest themselves in police officers in a number of ways. What are they?
9. Describe some of the issues that police administrators must deal with in terms of drug use by police officers within their agencies.
10. What are some of the indicators that an officer might be contemplating suicide?
11. What are some things police departments can do to curtail incidents of domestic violence among their officers?
12. If a police supervisor notices a pattern of controlling or abusive behavior in an officer, what steps should be taken?
13. What role can the police psychologist play in the health and wellness of individual law enforcement officers in an agency?
14. What services are available to the employees within the Chicago Police Department Employee Assistance Program (EAP)?

Critical Thinking Exercises

1. **Cumulative Career Traumatic Stress (CCTS).** During the past 30 years, there has been a surge of public and professional attention focused on the psychological and physical effects of continuous exposure to traumatic stressors. Typically, individuals who are routinely exposed to cumulative career traumatic stress acquire this condition over a period of years. These include police officers, firefighters, and emergency medical services personnel. You should answer the following questions:
   a. How does CCTS differ from posttraumatic stress disorders?
   b. What are the behavioral manifestations of CCTS?
   c. In what ways may CCTS adversely affect a police officer in his/her job performance?[92]
   d. What intervention counseling strategies would you suggest be employed in dealing with officers suffering from CCTS?

2. **Homicide-Suicide in Police Families.** Police officers work in an occupational culture in which they must sometimes use considerable force to control a situation. Unfortunately some officers may resort to the use of force in attempting to resolve conflicts at home and this might explain why the rate of domestic violence is significantly higher for police officers than it is for the general population. You should answer the following questions:
   a. What are the factors that are most likely to make police officers disproportionately at risk for homicide-suicide?
   b. What is the best course of action a police department can take to anticipate and then prevent homicide-suicide among its police officers?[93]
   c. Of what value is a domestic violence lethality assessment scale for first responders having calls involving police officers who are involved in domestic violence situations?

Key Terms

alarm stage
anabolic steroids
cumulative career stress
domestic violence lethality
assessment form
employee assistance programs (EAPs)
exhaustion stage

general adaptation syndrome (GAS)
posttraumatic stress disorder (PTSD)
resistance stage
roid rage
stress
stress inoculation activities
suicide by cop (SbC)

type A personality
type B personality
type C personality
type D personality
workaholic personality

Endnotes

[1] For a complete review of the most current programs and techniques being used by police departments see: Leonard Territo and James D. Sewell, *Stress Management in Law Enforcement*, 3rd ed. (Durham, NC: Carolina Academic Press, 2013).

[2] H. Selye, *Stress without Distress* (Philadelphia: Lippincott, 1974), p. 60.

[3] Julia La Roche, "Here's How Much 10 of the Richest People in the World Made Per Minute in 2013," *Business* Insider, December 19, 2013; (accessed June 11, 2015), http://www.businessinsider.com/what-warren-buffett-makes-per-hour-2013-12.

[4] Selye, *Stress without Distress*, pp. 35–39.

[5] Anthony L. Komaroff, "The Usual Suspect," *Newsweek*, 25 (February 2009), pp. 52–53.

[6] Ibid.

[7] Ibid.

[8] M. Farouk Radwan, "A B C D Personality Types," *Segen's Medical Dictionary*, 2012.

[9] Ibid.

[10] Ibid.

[11] Gerard J. Sloan and Jean M. Casey, "Police Work Addiction: A Cautionary Tale," *FBI Law Enforcement Bulletin* (June 2003), pp. 13–17. (This discussion of workaholics was adapted from this article.)

[12] B. E. Robinson, *Chained to the Desk* (New York, NY: New York University Press, 1998), p. 3.

[13] B. Killinger, *Workaholics: The Respectable Addicts* (Buffalo, NY: Firefly Books, 1991).

[14] Supra note 1, 75.

[15] Supra note 2.

[16] W. E. Oates, *Confessions of a Workaholic* (New York, NY: Abingdon Press, 1971), p. 4.

[17] Supra note 2, 6.

[18] For a complete review of the ways in which these various factors have deadly effects upon police officers see: Territo and Sewell, *Stress Management in Law Enforcement*.

[19] John M. Violanti and Fred Aron, "Police Stressors: Variations in Perceptions among Police Personnel," *Journal of Criminal Justice* 23, No. 3 (1995), pp. 287–294.

[20] Ibid., p. 347.

[21] FBI "Crime in the United States 2013," Expanded Homicide Data Table 14, *Uniform Crime Report*, Department of Justice, Federal Bureau of Investigation, Washington, DC, 2013; (accessed June 11, 2015), http://www.fbi.gov/about-us/cjis/ucr/crime-in-the-u.s/2013/crime-in-the-u.s.-2013/offenses-known-to-law-enforcement/

expanded-homicide/expanded_homicide_data_table_14_justifiable_homicide_by_weapon_law_enforcement_2009-2013.xls.

[22] C. Baruth, "Pre-critical Incident Involvement by Psychologists," in *Psychological Services for Law Enforcement*, eds. J. T. Reese and H. A. Goldstein (Washington DC: USGPO, 1986), pp. 413–417.

[23] Alexis Artwohl, "Perceptual and Memory Distortion During Officer-Involved Shootings," *FBI Law Enforcement Bulletin* (October, 2002), pp. 18–24. (This discussion was adapted from this article.)

[24] Ibid., pp. 18–24.

[25] Bruce A. Rodgers, *Psychological Aspects of Police Work: An Officer's Guide to Street Psychology* (Springfield, IL: Charles C Thomas, 2006).

[26] D. A. Grossman, *On Killing: The Psychological Cost of Learning to Kill in War and Society* (New York: Little, Brown, 1996).

[27] E. Nielsen, E. "Traumatic Incident Corps: Lessons Learned," in *Critical Incidents in Policing*, eds. J. Reese, J. Horn & C. Dunning (Washington DC: US Government Printing Office, 1991), pp. 221–226.

[28] M. B. Williams. "Impact of Duty-related Death on Officers' Children: Concepts of Death, Trauma Reactions, and Treatment," in *Police Trauma: Psychological Aftermath of Civilian Combat*, eds. J. M. Violanti & D. Paton (Springfield: Charles C Thomas, 1999), pp. 159–174.

[29] Suicide by Cop (SbC) refers to an individual who wishes to die and uses the police to affect the goal. For more details see D. B. Kennedy, R. J. Homant, and R. T. Hupp, "Suicide by Cop," *FBI Law Enforcement Bulletin* (August, 1998), pp. 21–27.

[30] W. Anderson, D. Swenson, and D. Clay, *Stress Management for Law Enforcement Officers* (Englewood Cliffs: Prentice Hall, 1995).

[31] M. A. Borders and C. H. Kennedy, "Psychological Interventions After Disaster in Trauma," in *Military Psychology: Clinical and Operational Applications*, eds. C. H. Kennedy and E. A. Zillmer (New York: Guilford, 2006).

[32] Grossman, *On Killing*.

[33] L. Miller, *Practical Police Psychology: Stress Management and Crisis Intervention for Law Enforcement* (Springfield, IL: Charles C Thomas, 2006).

[34] L. G. Bender and others, *Critical Issues in Police Discipline: Case Studies* (Springfield, IL: Charles C Thomas, 2005).

[35] Geoffrey P. Alpert, John Rivera, and Leon Lott, "Working Toward the Truth in Officer-Involved Shootings: Memory,

Stress, and Time," *FBI Law Enforcement Bulletin*, May 2012, 5 and 6."/>

[36]D. Grossman and B. K. Siddle, *Critical Incident Amnesia: The Physiological Basis and the Implications of Memory Loss During Extreme Survival Situations* (Millstadt, IL: PPCT Management Systems, 1998).

[37]Alpert, op cit., pp. 5–6.

[38]Alexis A. Artwohl, "Perceptual and Memory Distortions in Officer-Involved Shootings," *FBI Law Enforcement Bulletin*, October 2002, 22.

[39]Mark Thompson, "Unlocking the Secrets of PTSD," *Time*, March 26, 2015; p. 42.

[40]Laurence Miller, "Stress, Traumatic Stress, and Posttraumatic Stress Syndromes," in Leonard Territo and James D. Sewell, editors, *Stress Management in Law Enforcement*, 3rd ed. (Durham, NC: Carolina Academic Press, 2013), 13–16.

[41]American Psychiatric Association, *Diagnostic and Statistical Manual of Mental Disorders* (4th ed., text revision). (Washington DC: American Psychiatric Association, 2000); C. L. Meek, "Evaluation and assessment of post-traumatic and other stress-related disorders," in *Post-traumatic Stress Disorder: Assessment, Differential Diagnosis, and Forensic Evaluation*, ed. C. L. Meek (Sarasota, FL: Professional Resource Exchange, 1990), 9–61; H. Merskey, "Psychiatric Aspects of the Neurology of Trauma," *Neurologic Clinics*, 10 (1992), pp. 895–905; L. Miller, "Civilian Posttraumatic Stress Disorder: Clinical Syndromes and Psychotherapeutic Strategies," *Psychotherapy* 31 (1994), pp. 655–664; L. Miller, *Shocks to the System: Psychotherapy of Traumatic Disability Syndromes* (New York: Norton, 1998); L. Miller, "Ego Autonomy and the Healthy Personality: Psychodynamics, Cognitive Style, and Clinical Applications," *Psychoanalytic Review* 85, (1998), pp. 423–448; L. Miller, *Counseling Crime Victims: Practical Strategies for Mental Health Professionals* (New York: Springer, 2008); L. Miller, *Criminal Psychology: Nature, Nurture, Culture* (Springfield, IL: Charles C Thomas, 2012); H. C. Modlin, "Traumatic Neurosis and Other Injuries," *Psychiatric Clinics of North America* 6 (1983), pp. 661–682; R. S. Parker, *Traumatic Brain Injury and Neuropsychological Impairment: Sensorimotor, Cognitive, Emotional, and Adaptive Problems in Children and Adults* (New York: Springer-Verlag, 1990); H. Weiner, *Perturbing the Organism: The Biology of Stressful Experience* (Chicago: University of Chicago Press, 1992).

[42]L. Miller, *Freud's Brain: Neuropsychodynamic Foundations of Psychoanalysis* (New York: Guilford, 1991); L. Miller, *Criminal Psychology: Nature, Nurture, Culture* (Springfield, IL: Charles C Thomas, 2012).

[43]Ellen K. Marshal, "Cumulative Career Traumatic Stress (CCTS): A Pilot Study of Traumatic Stress in Law Enforcement," in Leonard Territo and James D. Sewell, Editors, editors, *Stress Management in Law Enforcement*, 3rd ed. (Durham, NC: Carolina Academic Press, 2013), 372–373.

[44]C. Alexander, "Police Psychological Burnout and Trauma," in J. M. Violanti & D. Paton, editors, *Police Trauma: Psychological Aftermath of Civilian Combat* (Springfield, IL: Charles C Thomas, 1999), 54–64; P. Bonifacio, *The Psychological Effect of Police Work* (New York: Plenum

Press. 1991); J. T. Fennel, "Psychological Stress and the Peace Officer, or Stress—a Cop Killer," in G. Henderson, editor, *Police Human Relations* (Springfield, IL: Charles C Thomas, 1981), 170–179.

[45]T. H. Blau, *Psychological Services for Law Enforcement* (New York: John Wiley & Sons, 1974); C. M. Davidson, I. Fleming, & A. Baum, "Post-traumatic Stress as a Function of Chronic Stress and Toxic Exposure," in C. E. Figley, editor, *Trauma and Its Wake: Traumatic Stress, Theory, Research, and Intervention* (New York: Brunner/Mazel, 1986), 57–77; C. M. Dunning, "Postintervention Strategies to Reduce Police Trauma: A Paradigm Shift," in J. M. Violanti & D. Paton, editors, *Police Trauma: Psychological Aftermath of Civilian Combat* (Springfield, IL: Charles C Thomas, 1999), 269–289.

[46]James Genovese, "Alcoholism Among Law Enforcement Personnel: Its Unique Challenges," The Milestone Group, n.d., (accessed May 31, 2015) http://www.milestonegroupnj.com/?page_id=348.

[47]Ed. Donovan, "Programs Need Caring Touch to Reach Law Enforcement Enforcers," *Alcoholism & Drug Abuse Weekly* 6, No. 35 (1994), pp. 3–4.

[48]P. Shanahan, *A Study of Attitudes and Behaviours: Working in the Police Force Today and the Role of Alcohol* (Sydney, Australia: Elliott and Shanahan Research, 1992); Elliot and Shanahan Research, *Alcohol and Other Drugs in the Workplace: A Benchmark Survey Comparing two Victorian Organisations* (Sydney: Elliot and Shanahan Research, 1994); J.M. Violanti, "Coping in a High Stress Police Environment," *Journal of Social Psychology* (1993), pp. 717–730; J. D. Davey, P.L. Obst, & M.C. Sheehan, "It Goes with the Job: Officers' Insights into the Impact of Stress and Culture on Alcohol Consumption within the Policing Occupation," *Drugs, Education, Prevention, and Policy* 8, No. 2 (2001), pp. 141–149;

[49]R.C. Lumb & R. Breazeale, "Police Officer Attitudes and Community Policing Implementation: Developing Strategies for Durable Organizational Change," *Policing and Society* 13, No. 1 (2002), pp. 91–106.

[50]Davey et al., "It Goes with the Job."

[51]Ibid.

[52]A. Bandura, *Social Foundations of Thought and Action: A Social Cognitive Theory* (Englewood Cliffs, NJ: Prentice-Hall, Inc., 1986)

[53]Ibid.

[54]*Newlun v. State Department of Retirement Systems*, 770 P. 2d 1071 (Wash. App. 1989). Relatedly, *McElrath v. Kemp*, 27 Govt. Emp. Rel. Rep. (BNA) 605 (D.D.C. 1989), deals with an alcoholic employee who had relapses after being treated and was terminated but was reinstated later.

[55]Will Aitchison, *The Rights of Police Officers*, 3rd ed. (Portland, OR: Labor Relations Information System, 1996), pp. 228–233, is the source of the information in this paragraph, with restatement by the authors.

[56]*Delaraba v. Nassau County Police*, 632 N. E. 2d 1251 (N.Y. 1994).

[57]Cincinnati, Ohio Police Department, Administrative Regulation #52 (06/07), Manual of Rules and Regulations: 15.110 Alcohol and Drug Testing of Department Personnel, revised 02/26/15, p. 6 (accessed June 11, 2015), http://www.cincinnati-oh.gov/police/assets/File/Procedures/15110.pdf.

[58]Kim R. Humphrey, Kathleen P. Decker, Lin Goldberg, Harrison G. Pope Jr., Joseph Gutman, and Gary Green, "Anabolic Steroid Use and Abuse by Police Officers: Policy and Prevention," *The Police Chief* 75, No. 6 (2008), 66–74.

[59]Adapted from C. Swanson, L. Gaines, and B. Gore, "Use of Anabolic Steroids," *FBI Law Enforcement Bulletin* 60, No. 8 (1991), 19–23.

[60]M. Parssinen et al., "Increased Premature Mortality of Competitive Powerlifters Suspected to Have Used Anabolic Agents," *International Journal of Sports Medicine* 21, No. 3 (April 2000), pp. 225–227.

[61]*National Treasury Employees Union* v. *Von Raab*, 489 U.S. 656 (1989).

[62]*Guiney* v. *Police Comm'r of Boston*, 411 Mass. 328 (1991).

[63]Hall et al., "Psychiatric Complications of Steroid Abuse," 285–286.

[64]Melanie Hamilton, "Special Report on Police Suicide: Cop Killer," *Police* 27, No. 5 (2003), p. 18.

[65]*Breaking the Silence on Law Enforcement Suicides*, Community Oriented Policing Services, U.S. Department of Justice, July 2013, pp. 4–17. The remainder of the discussion of police suicide was obtained from this document with modifications.

[66]Ibid.

[67]Office of the Surgeon General and National Action Alliance for Suicide Prevention, 2012 National Strategy for Suicide Prevention: Goals and Objectives for Action (Washington, DC: U.S. Department of Health and Human Services, September 2012: 19) (accessed June 11, 2015), http://www.armyg1.army.mil/hr/suicide/docs/10%20Sep%202012_NSSP_Final.pdf.

[68]L. D. Lott, "Deadly Secrets: Violence in the Police Family," *FBI Law Enforcement Bulletin* , November 1995, pp. 12–15. This discussion was adapted from this article.

[69]Police Officer Domestic Violence, Concepts and Issues Paper, Developed by the International Association of Chiefs of Police, April 1999.

[70]These definitions may be limited to the definitions in the laws of each state. While not the focus of this policy, other forms of family violence (for example, child and elder abuse) should be addressed in a parallel manner.

[71]In order to access the Model Policy on Police Officer Domestic Violence, as well as the accompanying Concepts and Issues Paper log onto www.theiacp.org and click on Publications (under Information Resources) then scroll down to "Police Officer Domestic Violence Information," this will lead you to links to each of the two documents.

[72]André Ivanoff, "Police Suicide Study Recommends Additional Training, Counseling," *Columbia University Record* 20, No. 2 (September 16, 1994) (accessed June 11, 2015), http://www.columbia.edu/cu/record/record2002.14.html.

[73]Domestic Violence Protocol for Law Enforcement, Police Chiefs Association of Santa Clara County, California, March 2014, p. 55.

[74]John M. Violanti, "Homicide-Suicide in Police Families: Aggression Full Circle," *International Journal of Emergency Mental Health* 9, No. 2(2007), pp. 101–102.

[75]Dennis Lindsey and Sean Kelly, "Issues in Small Town Policing: Understanding Stress," *FBI Law Enforcement Bulletin* 73, No. 7 (2004), p. 4.

[76]Ibid.

[77]Karen L. Amendola, David Weisburd, and Edwin E. Hamilton, *The Impact of Shift Length in Policing on Performance, Health, Quality of Life, Sleep, Fatigue, and Extra-Duty Employment*, Final Report Submitted to the National Institute of Justice, December 12, 2011. (This discussion was adapted from the abstract of this document appearing on pg. iv.)

[78]B. J. Vila and D. J. Kenney, "Tired Cops: The Prevalence and Potential Consequences of Police Fatigue," (pdf, 6 pages) *National Institute of Justice Journal* 248 (2002), pp. 16–21.

[79]U.S. Department of Justice, Office of Justice Programs, "How Fatigue Affects Health" (Washington, DC: National Institute of Justice, The Research, Development, and Evaluation Agency of the U.S. Department of Justice, January 6, 2009) (accessed May 5, 2010) http://www.ojp.usdoj.gov/nij/topics/law-enforcement/stress-fatigue/health.htm.

[80]D. Dawson and K. Reid, "Fatigue, Alcohol and Performance Impairment," *Nature* 388 (1997), p. 235.

[81]B. J. Vila, *Tired Cops: The Importance of Managing Police Fatigue* (Washington, DC: Police Executive Research Forum, 2000).

[82]D. J. Dijk, D. F. Neri, J. K. Wyatt, J. M. Ronda, E. Riel, A. Ritz-De Cecco, R. J. Hughes, A. R. Elliott, G. K. Prisk, J. B. West, and C. A. Czeisler, "Sleep, Performance, Circadian Rhythms, and Light-Dark Cycles During Two Space Shuttle Flights," *American Journal of Physiology* 281 (2001), pp. R1647–R1663.

[83]Many of these factors are identified in Robert W. Shearer, "Police Officer Stress: New Approaches for Effective Coping," *Journal of California Law Enforcement* 25, No. 4 (1991), pp. 97–104.

[84]Scott Allen, Christine Jones, Frances Douglas, and Daniel Clark, "A Comprehensive Approach to Destigmatizing Mental Health Issues in Law Enforcement," *The Police Chief* 81 (March 2014), pp. 34–38.

[85]Ibid., p. 36.

[86]Ibid.

[87]Ibid., p. 37.

[88]Max Bromley and William Blount, "Criminal Justice Practitioners," in *Employee Assistance Programs*, ed. William R. Hutchison, Jr., and William G. Emener (Springfield, IL: Charles C Thomas, 1997), p. 400.

[89]J. T. Reese, *The History of Police Psychological Service* (Washington, DC: U.S. Department of Justice, 1987).

[90]C. Milofsky, E. Astrov, and M. Martin, "Stress Management Strategy for U.S. Customs Workers," *EAP Digest* 14, No. 6 (1994), pp. 46–48.

[91]Bromley and Blount, "Criminal Justice Practitioners," p. 401.

[92]For a more detailed discussion see Ellen K. Marshall, "Cumulative Career Traumatic Stress (CCTS): A Pilot Study of Traumatic Stress in Law Enforcement," in *Stress Management in Law Enforcement*, 3rd edition, eds., Leonard Territo and James D. Sewell (Durham, NC: Carolina Academic Press, 2013), 371–382.

[93]For a more detailed discussion, see John M. Violanti, "Homicide-Suicide in Police Families: Aggression in Full Circle," in *Stress Management in Law Enforcement*, 3rd edition, eds., Leonard Territo and James D. Sewell (Durham, NC: Carolina Academic Press, 2013), 303–316.

LEGAL ASPECTS OF POLICE ADMINISTRATION

Learning Objectives

1. Explain the three general categories of torts. How do they differ?
2. Define "acting under the *color of state law*." How does this statement relate to Section 1983 actions?
3. Explain and describe a *Bivens* action.
4. List and describe the negligence theories applicable to police supervision and management.
5. Describe procedural and substantive due process.
6. Explain a *Brady* violation?
7. Explain when rules infringing on the free speech of officers might be upheld.
8. Describe the circumstances in which an officer may use deadly force?
9. List the four elements that must be proven in order to sue the police for negligence in a high-speed pursuit.
10. Describe how a department can reduce liability in high-speed pursuits.
11. Relate the focus of most training programs regarding emotionally disturbed persons.
12. Describe the balancing test related to alcohol and drug testing in the police workplace.

INTRODUCTION

ONE OF THE PRIMARY *characteristics of our nation's law is its dynamic nature. Rules of law are developed by legislation, regulation, and by court decision. In this chapter, we talk about the fluid nature of our lawmaking system as it applies to police and police executives. It is important to understand the legal aspects of police administration because: (1) police officers understand criminal law because they deal with it on a daily basis; however, they have a relatively poor understanding of civil law; (2) civil law addresses private injuries that lead to liability and subsequent monetary damages due to negligence; (3) the major areas of litigation against the police fall under Title 42, U.S. Code, Section 1983, and usually involve negligent hiring, negligent assignment and retention, negligent supervision, and/or negligent training; (4) police officers have constitutional rights that are enjoyed by all citizens within the United States including the rights and liberties that address privacy, free speech, search and seizure, and self-incrimination; and (5) most civil actions against the police arise from the misuse of firearms and deadly force, use of force, high-speed pursuits, and police handling of emotionally disturbed persons. Finally, police officers are held to a different and higher standard of conduct both on and off the job. Even when their actions do not arise to the level of a criminal complaint, they still might receive discipline that can result in termination and loss of career. These types of behaviors and officer actions most often violate departmental policy addressing conduct unbecoming an officer, sexual conduct, residency requirements, religious beliefs or practices, moonlighting, and alcohol and drug testing.*

The reader should view the material that follows as instructive background rather than as an authoritative basis for action. Police administrators should always seek qualified legal counsel whenever they face a problem or a situation that appears to have legal ramifications. A primary objective of this chapter is to make police administrators more capable of quickly determining when they face such a problem or situation.

LIABILITY FOR POLICE CONDUCT

One of the most troubling legal problems facing police officers and police departments in recent years has been the expanded impact of civil and criminal **liability** for alleged police misconduct. It is commonplace to hear police spokespersons complain that law enforcement officers are widely hampered by the specter of being undeservedly sued for alleged improper performance of duty. Although one can argue that the magnitude of police misconduct **litigation** may be overstated, the amount of litigation appears to be increasing and is apparently accompanied by a movement toward larger monetary damage awards.

Basic Types of Police Tort Actions[1]

Law can be divided into two parts: criminal law and civil law. Police officers and other criminal justice practitioners are generally more familiar with criminal law because they deal with it on a daily basis. Each "piece" of the law addresses a specific type of action. For instance, criminal law focuses on crimes, whereas civil law applies to torts.

Barrineau defines a crime as a public injury, an offense against the state, punishable by fine and/or imprisonment. It is the violation of a duty one owes the entire community; the remedy for a breach of such duty is punishment (fine or imprisonment) imposed by the state. Crimes are exemplified in the FBI Crime Index (generally speaking, they are murder, aggravated assault, robbery, rape (sexual battery), burglary, larceny over $200.00, auto theft, and arson), wherein each crime is composed of specific elements and has an affixed penalty.

On the other hand, a **tort** is a private injury inflicted on one person by another person for which the injured party may sue in a civil action. Such action may bring about liability that leads to an award of money damages. Tort actions encompass most personal injury litigation. The injured party initiates the lawsuit and is called the **plaintiff**. The sued person is called the **defendant** and is often referred to as the *tort feasor*.[2]

One example of a tort action brought against police officers is an allegation of criminal behavior, such as assault and battery (police brutality). More commonly, they are civil actions brought about by claims of false arrest, false imprisonment, invasion of privacy (through illegal search and seizure), negligence, defamation, or malicious prosecution.[3] Most of the suits against police officers fall into three general categories: negligence torts, intentional torts, and constitutional torts.[4]

NEGLIGENCE TORTS

Our society imposes a duty on individuals to conduct their affairs in a manner that does not subject others to an unreasonable risk of harm. This responsibility also applies to criminal justice practitioners. If a police officer's conduct creates a situation recognizable as dangerous by a reasonable person in like circumstances, the officer will be held accountable to those injured as a result of his or her conduct.

In **negligence** suits, defendants are not liable unless they foresaw or should have anticipated that their acts or omissions would result in injury to another. The key in negligence suits is the standard of the reasonably prudent person, also referred to as **reasonableness**. Was the care provided at the same standard that a reasonably prudent person would observe under a given set of circumstances?[5] Examples of negligence involving police officers often arise from pursuit driving incidents in which the officers violate common traffic laws, such as speeding, running a stop sign, or failing to control their vehicles, resulting in the injury or death of another person.

INTENTIONAL TORTS

An intentional tort is the voluntary commission of an act that to a substantial certainty will injure another person. It does not have to be negligently done to be actionable. Intentional torts are therefore *voluntary* and *deliberate* acts, such as assault, false arrest, false imprisonment, and malicious prosecution.

CONSTITUTIONAL TORTS

The duty to recognize and uphold the constitutional rights, privileges, and immunities of others is imposed on police officers and other criminal justice practitioners by statute, and violation of these guarantees may result in a specific type of civil suit. Most of these suits are brought under Title 42, U.S. Code, Section 1983, in federal court.

In our system of government, there are court systems at both federal and state levels. However, federal courts are intended to be courts of somewhat limited jurisdiction and generally do not hear cases involving private, as opposed to public, controversies

unless a question of federal law is involved or the individuals involved in the lawsuit are residents of different states. Even then, the suit can be decided in a state court if both parties to the controversy agree to have the dispute settled there. As a result, most tort suits have been brought in state courts.

Title 42, U.S. Code, Section 1983

A major trend in the area of police misconduct litigation is the increase in the number and proportion of these suits that are being brought in federal court. The most common legal vehicle by which federal courts can acquire jurisdiction of these suits is commonly referred to as a **1983 action**. This name derives from the fact that these suits are brought under the provisions of Section 1983 of Title 42 of the U.S. Code. This law, passed by Congress in the aftermath of the Civil War and commonly referred to as the Civil Rights Act of 1871, was designed to secure the civil rights of the recently emancipated slaves. It prohibits depriving any person of life, liberty, or property without due process of law. Specifically, Section 1983 states:

> Every person who, under color of any statute, ordinance, regulation, custom, or usage of any State or Territory, subjects, or causes to be subjected, any citizen of the United States or any other person within the jurisdiction thereof to the deprivation of any rights, privileges, or immunities secured by the Constitution and laws, shall be liable to the party injured in an action at law, suit in equity, or other proper proceeding for redress.[6]

After 90 years of relative inactivity, Section 1983 was resuscitated by the U.S. Supreme Court in the landmark case *Monroe v. Pape* (1961).[7] In this case, the Court concluded that, when a police officer is alleged to have acted improperly (e.g., in conducting an illegal search), that officer can be sued in federal court by alleging that he or she deprived the searched person of his or her constitutional right under the Fourth Amendment to be free from unreasonable searches and seizures. A critical element of Section 1983 is that the violation must have occurred while the officer was acting "under color of State law"—that is, while the officer was on duty and acting within the scope of employment as a sworn police officer. Unless there is direct

---

Quick Facts: Americans for Effective Law Enforcement (AELE)

The Americans for Effective Law Enforcement (AELE) is a non-profit agency founded in 1967, and today it is one of the most highly respected sources of legal advice and training for police officers. The AELE holds workshops on legal issues that affect police officers and administrators, such as the use of force, sudden and in-custody death, and discipline and internal investigations. Officers and administrators who attend special training courses are eligible to earn Certified Litigation Specialist credentials, which honor those who pursue litigation-related studies and increase their understanding of public agency litigation. The AELE is also a resource for officers and administrators facing legal action. The agency can offer legal advice or refer officers to local attorneys or expert witnesses. The AELE also offers monthly newsletters, including the *Law Enforcement Liability Reporter* and the *AELE Monthly Law Journal*, both available on its website at www.aele.org. The website also offers an extensive law library, organized by topics of interest to law enforcement officers.

personal participation by police supervisory personnel, they are not generally liable for Section 1983 damages, even if there are broad allegations of failure to properly train and supervise police officers who are liable in the Section 1983 lawsuit.[8]

Bivens Action

Section 1983 is the primary civil rights statute involved in litigation against municipal and state police officers. However, the statute rarely applies to federal agents (such as officials of the FBI, Secret Service, and Drug Enforcement Administration) because its terms require that the plaintiff be acting under "color of State law." Federal officials can be sued under one of two complaints. The first is a **Bivens action** for a violation of constitutional rights. The *Bivens* action applies only to the individual, not to the government. The second is a tort action against the United States under the Federal Tort Claim Act (FTCA).[9] Both actions can be combined into one lawsuit.

Essentially, a *Bivens* action is a judicially created counterpart to a Section 1983 tort action. The Supreme Court has permitted suits against federal officials (not, however, against the United States) for violations of constitutional rights that would otherwise be the subject of a Section 1983 action against a state or local officer. Its name is derived from the landmark case *Bivens v. Six Unknown Federal Narcotics Agents* (1971), wherein the Supreme Court held that a cause of action for violation of the Fourth Amendment (search and seizure clause) can be inferred from the Constitution itself.[10] Hence, federal courts have jurisdiction to hear federal question cases involving suits against federal employees in their individual capacities.[11]

In summary, there are three basic types of tort actions that can be brought against police for misconduct: traditional state law torts, Section 1983 torts, and *Bivens* torts. It is important to understand these classifications because the type of tort action brought will determine who can be sued, what kind of behavior will result in liability, and which immunities might be available to the defendants.

WHO CAN BE SUED?

At common law, police officers were held personally liable for damage caused by their own actions that exceeded the boundaries of permissible behavior. This rule applied even if the officer was ignorant of the boundary established by the law. As unjust as many of such results may seem, the rule establishes one of the traditional risks of policing.

A more difficult question concerns whether the supervisors of the officer and/or the government unit by which he or she is employed can be sued for that individual's misbehavior. Generally, an effort to impose liability on supervisors for the tortious conduct of their employees is based on the common-law doctrine of *respondeat superior*. That doctrine, also called **vicarious liability**, developed along with the growth of industrial society and reflected a conscious effort to allocate risk to those who could afford to pay for the complaint of damages.[12]

As could be expected, the growing area of negligence as a Section 1983 cause of action has caused concern within police supervisory ranks. The courts have supported several negligence theories applicable to police supervision and management. The following is a discussion of important negligence cases and subsequent legal development in this area.[13]

Negligent Hiring

The law enforcement administrator and the local government entity have a duty to "weed out" those obviously unfit for police duty. Further, the courts have held that an employer must exercise a reasonable standard of care in selecting persons who, because of the nature of their employment (such as policing), could present a threat of injury to members of the public.[14] Further, in 1997, the Supreme Court held that law enforcement and government entities could be held liable under Section 1983 if the plaintiff's injury was an obvious and direct consequence of a bad hiring decision on the part of an agency. In this case, an officer was hired by a local police department *after* it was discovered that the officer had lied on his original application and had been convicted of a felony, barring him from police service under state regulatory agencies.[15]

Negligent Assignment, Retention, and Entrustment

Police administrators who know or should have known of individual acts or patterns of physical abuse, malicious or threatening conduct, or similar threats against the public by officers under their supervision must take immediate action. If an internal investigation sustains an allegation of such serious conduct by an officer, appropriate action by a police chief could be suspension—followed by assignment to a position with little or no public contact—or termination. A police chief failing to take decisive action when required could be held liable for future injuries caused by the officer. In addition, entrustment of the "emblements of office" (e.g., a badge, a gun, or a nightstick) subjects a municipality and appropriate administrators of a municipal agency to liability whenever injury results from the known misuse of such emblements. In other words, administrators and supervisors have a duty to supervise errant officers properly.[16]

Negligent Direction and Supervision

The administrator and/or supervisor have the duty to develop and implement appropriate policies and procedures. Therefore, a written manual of policies and procedures is an absolute must. This manual must provide clear instruction and direction regarding the position of police officer, be widely disseminated, and be accompanied with training so that all officers understand the significance of the manual.[17] Further, the courts have held that supervisors must "take corrective steps" where evidence indicates that official policy is being abridged and/or the public is being placed at an "unreasonable risk" because of the actions of a police officer. Inaction on the part of the police supervisors and/or administrators is enough to establish negligence if there is a pattern or custom of police abuse and accession to that custom by police supervisors and/or administrators.[18] For example, the failure of a police sergeant to order the termination of a high-speed pursuit of a minor traffic violator through a congested downtown business area that results in serious personal injuries or deaths to members of the public is sure to bring litigation based on an allegation of failure to supervise (see Figure 14.1).

Negligent Training

The local unit of government and the administrator or supervisor of a police department have an affirmative duty to train their employees correctly and adequately. In a recent landmark case (*City of Canton v. Harris*), the Supreme Court limited the use of inadequate police training as a basis for Section 1983 actions. The Court held that inadequate police training may form the basis for a civil rights claim "where the failure to train amounts to **deliberate indifference** to the rights of persons with whom the police come in contact" and that such official indifference amounts to "policy or custom." Therefore, it is incumbent on the plaintiff to prove that the training program is inadequate as to the expected duties of an officer and that the deficiency of training is closely related to the ultimate injury.[19]

The two areas of negligence that have been the greatest sources of litigation under Section 1983 in recent years have been negligent supervision and negligent training. Incidents arising out of the use of deadly force and use of force, and pursuit driving have certainly raised significant questions regarding training and are covered later in this chapter.

A second difficult question with respect to who may be sued for damages caused by police misconduct concerns the liability of the police department and the government unit of which the

department is a part.[20] Individuals pursuing damage claims under Section 1983 against local government officials and state officials who are sued in their individual rather than official capacities will have to overcome the defense available to such parties of "qualified, good-faith immunity." Such official immunities are not creatures of Section 1983; they arose from traditional, common-law protections that were historically accorded to government officials. Basically, the good-faith immunity doctrine recognizes that public officials who exercise discretion in the performance of their duties should not be punished for actions undertaken in good faith. Imposing liability on public officials in such situations would inevitably deter their willingness to "execute . . . [their] office with the decisiveness and the judgment required by the public good."[21]

Over the years, the courts have struggled to develop a test for good faith. In 1975, the Supreme Court articulated such a test that considered both the official's state of mind when he or she committed the act in question (the subjective element) and whether the act violated clearly established legal rights (the objective element).[22]

However, seven years later, the Supreme Court decided that the subjective element of the text should be dropped, leaving only the standard of **objective reasonableness**.[23] Now a court must determine only whether the law at issue was "clearly established" at the time the challenged action occurred. Furthermore, if the plaintiff's allegations do not show a violation of clearly established law, a public official asserting good-faith immunity will be entitled to dismissal of the lawsuit before it proceeds further.[24]

The immunities available to state and local officials are generally designed to protect individuals from liability arising out of the performance of official acts. With the Eleventh Amendment providing similar protection to the states, the question of the immunity of a local government was raised. Initially, the

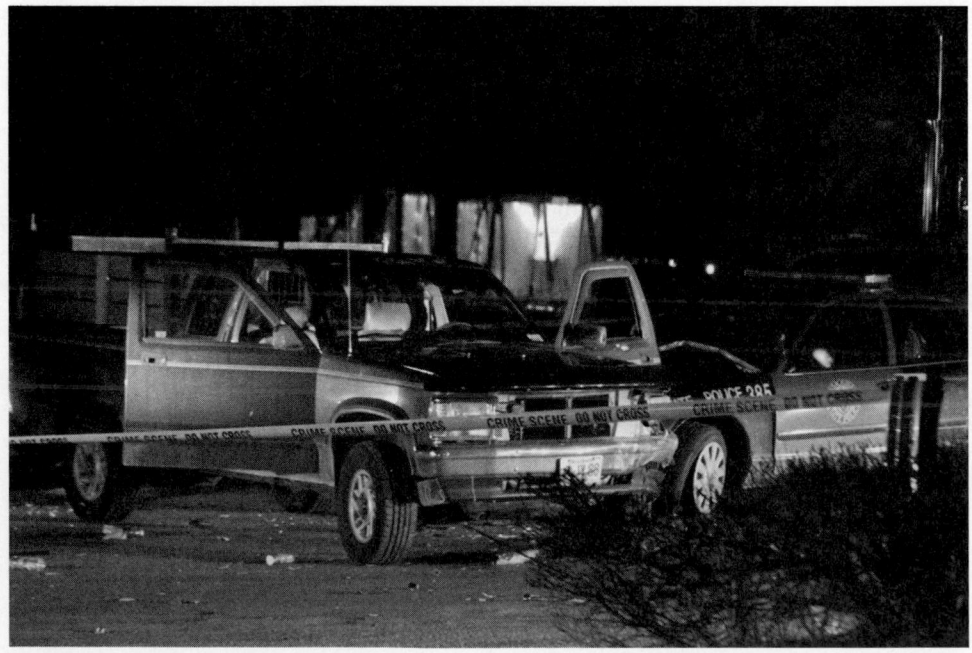

FIGURE 14.1 ▶ The failure to provide direction and/or supervision during police incidents (e.g., barricaded felons, hostage situations, police chases) can result in a negligence tort action. (Kevin Wiles Jr/Demotix/Corbis)

Supreme Court concluded that Congress had not intended to apply 42 U.S.C. 1983 to municipalities, thereby giving municipalities what is called "absolute," or unqualified, immunity from suit.[25] On re-examination of this issue in the 1978 case *Monell v. Department of Social Services*,[26] the Court decided that Congress had intended for Section 1983 to apply to municipalities and other local government units. The Court further concluded that, although certain other immunities were not available to a municipality in a Section 1983 lawsuit, the municipality could not be held liable solely because it employed an individual who was responsible for Section 1983 violations. The Court made it clear that local government entities will be liable under Section 1983 only when that government's policies or official procedures can be shown to be responsible for the violation of federally protected rights.

Unfortunately, the *Monell* decision did not fully articulate the limits of municipal liability under Section 1983. The result has been considerable litigation to establish when a deprivation of federally protected rights actually results from enforcement of a municipal policy or procedure and at what point an official's actions can be fairly treated as establishing the offending policy.[27]

More recently, the Supreme Court has held that "single acts of police misconduct" do not, by themselves, show that a city policy was involved in the alleged tortious act.[28] Generally, a plaintiff must show a pattern of negligence or deliberate indifference by the agency.[29]

Box 14.1: Police Training and Liability: An Officer's Perspective

by Ryan M. Getty, Ph.D.

Police have wanted to be become a profession rather than a trade for some time. That elevation of status and responsibility comes with standardized training and a formal education. Police in every state have had basic training academies since the 1960s. However, the lack of requirements for a minimum of a college education to become an officer has eluded police since the first national recommendation in the early 1900 by August Vollmer.[30] Many scholars insisted, and some even today, that individual police officers do not need a college degree to be a good officer. One academic remarked that, "it is doubtful whether a course in university lectures [would be] much practical value for police officers."[31] This still seems to be the prevailing sentiment since only two states (Minnesota and Wisconsin) require a minimum of an associate's degree to be a police officer, and no state requires a full 4-year degree.[32] Instead, police have relied upon ever-increasing hours within the police academy. Once graduated from an academy, officers are taught how to apply those teachings under the watchful eyes of field training officers. Virtually all law enforcement agencies have a field training program either by policy or by state law. New officers must pass through the field training portion of training before they can be released to police by themselves. Field training programs can be as brief as a month or two for experienced, lateral hires and up to 9 months for new, academy graduates. This depends a great deal on departmental policy and to some extent, individual state laws.

The two most popular field training programs are the San Jose (CA) model and the Reno (NV) model or the Police Training Officer (PTO) program.[33] The San Jose model was developed in the early 1970s, primarily as a result of a negligence lawsuit. It is highly standardized (e.g., regimented) and relies on officers completing numbered tasks over time while the field training officer demonstrates, models, and tests the probationary officer's knowledge through standardized checklists and Likert-like scales while the Reno model is problem-based learning centered upon John Dewey's philosophy of learning.[34] Again, it is up to the individual agencies which model they will adopt. Some states like California allow for the adoption of either while other states only mandate a "field training program." Regardless of the program, both train officers in an attempt to perform duties in a careful and direct manner, adhere to policy, safeguard the Constitutional rights of citizens, and avoid civil (and criminal) liability.

Beginning at some of the earliest lessons in the academy, officers are taught about police behavior, police tactics, and civil liability. Prior to graduation, candidate officers are usually tested on policy and procedure, state laws, and common policing theory, as well as mandatory courses on the use of force, use of firearms and less lethal weapons, pursuit driving, and tactics of arrest. Some states have included mandatory in-service classes that begin shortly after graduation, and continue every one to 2 years on specific topics, often recommended or even required by state accreditation bureaus.

However, no matter how well trained, no law enforcement officer (or department) is protected from being sued. Lawsuits are an inherent risk born of dealing with people in an adversarial role such as arresting and using force. These two functions of policing are most likely to cause suit.[35] According to the U.S. Department of Justice, the vast majority of police contact with citizens that end in force being used is minor.[36] However, there need not even be forced used in order for an officer and their agency to be sued. Violation of civil rights can take many forms.

Lawsuits happen! There is a place and time for legitimate legal remedies but those "classic" actions against an officer and department are to an extent anticipated and with some departments, budgeted for because of the nature of police work. However, there seems to be a more insidious trend that tends to undermine justice in the name of expediency and public pressure. These are not cases where police officers have clearly acted improperly, used excessive force, or violated the law. No one is more concern about abusive and rogue officers than police officers themselves. Good officers

(continued)

want bad officers out of the police service. Rather, these are events that most officers conduct almost every day . . . frisking a vagrant or panhandler, stopping a traffic violator, or arresting a drunk and disorderly person. Due primarily to the expanding popularity of social media coupled with the mass availability of video recording, the typical officer is being videoed simply "doing their job." Hundreds of thousands of videos of officers making an arrest or a traffic stop can be found on the Internet . . . unfortunately, with derisive tag lines. A simple search of "officer misconduct" on YouTube yielded a whopping 40,600 video results. Because the videographer and most citizens have no idea what the police actually do, or their legal responsibilities or liabilities, these videos often lead to defensiveness on the part of the police officer and manager; fundamental fairness for the officer and justice wane to political and public pressure and outcry. Unfortunately, there is no research explaining administrative and policy reactions as a result of the newer social media or video recordings. However, what those in law enforcement know anecdotally is that what was once seen as a "routine" arrest could suddenly become a social media uproar, disenchantment with the department, and the loss of police legitimacy within a community. Because the context, as well as the officer's thoughts and intuition cannot be videoed and therefore justified, the community has been shown only one side of an incident, at one specific time and from one specific camera angle. There seems all too often to be a new "legal system" of judgment by popular decree and there are no legal due process remedies against public opinion and perception. What was once a physical mob mentality has become a social media mob mentality that could escalate into violence and property loss. The reality of policing is that arrests sometimes become violent and various tactics and weapons are used. To the casual, untrained observer, it often appears to be way too much force, and again, this does not include those times when errant officers clearly beat a suspect, or hit a suspect with handcuffs on, or slam a suspect into a car door. These are everyday events, the vast majority of the "40,600 YouTube hits" that culminate in "police misconduct" by the public, but routine activity for the officer. Indeed, police supervisors and internal affairs investigators often spend countless hours viewing public videos and effort to sort out routine activity versus excessive force; and fortunately, only a fractional percentage of these incidents ever find their way into a frivolous lawsuit against an officer or a department or a sustained complaint against an officer. Police officers are not trained on how to "look good" while making an arrest. Perhaps someday, drama will become part of the basic academy.

SCOPE OF LIABILITY

In general, state tort actions against police officers provide a greater scope of liability than do the Section 1983 and *Biven* suits. That is, in tort actions under state law, a greater range of behavior is actionable.

The types of torts under state law that commonly are brought against police officers can be categorized as intentional or negligence torts. An intentional tort is one in which the defendant knowingly commits a voluntary act designed to bring about certain physical consequences. For example, the tort of assault is the purposeful infliction on another person of a fear of a harmful or offensive contact. If X points an unloaded pistol at Y, who does not know the pistol is unloaded, X has created in Y an apprehension that Y is about to experience a harmful contact from a bullet. X voluntarily lifts the pistol and points it at Y, fully expecting that it will cause Y to be apprehensive about being hit by a bullet. Thus, X is liable to Y for the intentional tort of assault.

The tort of negligence involves conduct that presents an unreasonable risk of harm to others that, in turn, is the proximate cause of an actual injury. Whereas in an intentional tort, the consequences following an act must be substantially certain to follow, in the tort of negligence the consequences need only be foreseeable. When X drives through a stop sign, even if unintentionally, and hits the side of Y's car, X's behavior presents an unreasonable risk of harm to others and is the proximate cause of the damage to Y's car. Although X would have been negligent for "running the stop sign" even without hitting the other car, he or she would not have committed the tort of negligence in that no injury was caused.

The Supreme Court has limited the scope of liability in reference to negligence as an element of deprivation of constitutional rights in Section 1983 and *Bivens* actions. In *Daniels v. Williams* (1986), the petitioner sought to recover damages as a result of injuries sustained in a fall caused by a pillow negligently left on the stairs of the city jail in Richmond, Virginia. The Court held that the petitioner's constitutional rights were "simply not implicated by a negligent act of an official causing *unintentional* loss or injury to life, liberty, or property."[37] This case has had a profound impact on limiting Section 1983 and *Bivens* actions to intentional torts; hence, the sheer volume of such cases has significantly decreased in past years. It is important to note, however, that the Supreme Court "has not changed the rule that an intentional abuse of power, which shocks the conscience or which infringes a specific constitutional guarantee such as those embodied in the Bill of Rights," still implicates serious liability.[38]

As noted earlier in this chapter, many lawsuits against police officers are based on the intentional torts of assault, battery, false imprisonment, and malicious prosecution.[39] Suits against police officers for intentional torts can be brought as state tort actions, Section 1983 suits, or *Bivens* suits. Although suits against police officers for negligence torts can be brought as state tort actions, the issue is not so clear-cut with regard to Section 1983 and *Bivens* suits.

Generally, damages assessed in civil litigation for negligence are ordinary (compensatory) damages that are paid by the employing government entity (or its liability insurance carrier) on behalf of the defendant officer. Therefore, as a general rule, the individual employee is not required to pay ordinary damages that result from a civil negligence suit. This is so because, normally when government employees are performing their duties within the scope of employment, they are deemed to be the agents or representatives of the employing agency and therefore not personally liable for their acts. However, where punitive damages are assessed for conduct that is grossly negligent, wanton, or reckless, individuals who have been responsible for such acts are personally liable and, generally speaking, these assessments are not absorbed by the employing government entity or by liability insurance. Thus, law enforcement employees who act in reckless, wanton, or grossly negligent manners will be subject to and personally liable for punitive damage awards.

In this constantly changing area of the law, the Supreme Court has established a rule that police are entitled to "qualified" immunity for acts made in good faith that can be characterized as "objectively reasonable." In *United States v. Leon*,[40] the Court focused on the objectively ascertainable question of whether a reasonably well-trained officer would have known that the act committed was illegal. Subsequently, following that logic the Court held that, if police personnel are not "objectively reasonable" in seeking an arrest warrant, they can be sued personally for many damages, despite the fact that a judge has approved the warrant. In fact, the Court stated that a judge's issuance of a warrant will not shield the officer from liability if a "well-trained officer in [his] position would have known that his affidavit failed to establish probable cause and that he should not have applied for the warrant."[41] However, the Court modified its position in a later case when an FBI agent conducted a warrantless search of a resident's home for a fugitive by holding that an alleged unlawful warrantless search of an innocent third party's home does not create an exception per se to the general rule of qualified immunity. The Court held that the relevant question is whether a reasonable officer would have believed the search lawful once the clearly established law and the information possessed by the agent were taken into consideration and, if the answer is yes, whether the agent is protected by qualified immunity from civil liability.[42] This standard was upheld in 2001 and 2009.[43]

As with many areas of the law, lower courts have somewhat modified this landmark decision. In 1987, a U.S. district court found that qualified immunity protects all but the plainly incompetent or those who knowingly violate the law.[44] And in 1992, a federal court ruled that law enforcement officers are protected by immunity from "bad guesses in gray areas" but are liable for "transgressing obviously bright lines of law,"[45] essentially leading the way for protective immunity for officers honestly attempting to do their job. This was affirmed again in *Pearson et al. v. Callahan* in 2009.[46] Still, whereas public officials exercising discretion (e.g., judges and prosecutors) have absolute immunity for their unreasonable acts, the only person in the system left to sue for damages for a wrongdoing will be the police officer, unless his or her acts can be attributed to the policy or procedural custom established by the employing government agency.

TRENDS IN TORT LIABILITY FOR POLICE SUPERVISORS AND ADMINISTRATORS

Although there has been a reluctance to hold police supervisors and administrators liable for the misbehavior of their subordinate officers, some courts have been increasingly willing to extend liability to these officials where the plaintiff has alleged negligent employment, improper training, or improper supervision.[47]

Under negligent employment, a police official can be held liable for his or her failure to conduct a thorough investigation of a prospective employee's suitability for police work if he or she hires an applicant with a demonstrated propensity "toward violence, untruthfulness, discrimination, or other adverse characteristics."[48] Of course, under this theory, the injuries suffered by the plaintiff would have been the result of the negative trait that had been demonstrated by the individual before employment as an officer. If the negative trait is not demonstrated until after employment, a party injured by the officer may be able to sue a police official successfully for negligently retaining the officer or otherwise failing to take appropriate remedial action. In some circumstances, the official may not be able to dismiss an officer who has demonstrated unfitness, but the official still might be found liable if he or she negligently assigns the unfit officer to duties where the public is not protected adequately from the officer's particular unfitness. Finally, the official is potentially liable for negligently entrusting a revolver to an officer who has a history of alcohol or other drug abuse or the misuse of a weapon.

Suits alleging that police officials have improperly trained a police officer have been particularly successful where firearms were involved in inflicting the injury. Courts have stressed that the "law imposes a duty of extraordinary care in the handling and use of firearms"[49] and that "public policy requires that police officers be trained in the use of firearms on moving and silhouette targets and instructed when and how to use them."[50] Suits alleging lack of necessary training are also becoming increasingly successful in cases involving the use of physical force to overcome resistance, the administration of first aid, pursuit driving (see Figure 14.2), and false arrest.[51]

Another emerging theory of recovery against police officials is an allegation of failure to properly supervise or direct subordinate officers. This type of suit is typically brought where officials have failed to take action to rectify a recurring problem exhibited in the conduct of police operations by subordinates.[52] An interesting development in this area concerns the situation in which the police department issues a written directive that establishes a policy more stringent than the law requires. In several cases involving such a situation, the courts have held that the written directive establishes a standard of conduct to which police officers must conform or face the possibility of civil liability for their actions.[53]

The last area to which courts have given increased attention concerns cases in which it is alleged that the police officer failed to provide needed medical care to people with whom the officer

FIGURE 14.2 ▶ Police officers responding to hostage and/or barricaded suspect situations often require specialized training in crisis negotiations and the use of firearms. In this case, a man was taken hostage at a local television station while the suspect shouted demands from the control room. After hours of skilled negotiations by local detectives, the hostage was released without harm, avoiding potential liability stemming from the incident.
(Roberto Pfeil/AP Images)

came in contact.[54] Although the incidents giving rise to such allegations can occur in a variety of situations, they seem to occur with greatest frequency when the plaintiffs have been in custody or have been mistakenly thought to be intoxicated when they actually were suffering from a serious illness. These cases are based on four categories of recovery: (1) failure to recognize and provide treatment for injury, (2) failure to provide treatment on request, (3) failure to provide treatment on recognition of an injury, and (4) negligent medical treatment. Suits in the first three categories may allege either negligent conduct or intentional behavior. Court rulings suggest that police officers who ignore classic signs of illness, such as a heart attack, are depriving arrestees of their Fourteenth Amendment right to receive medical care as a pretrial detainee. To prove that an officer is subject to liability because he or she failed to provide medical treatment requires a showing that the officer acted with deliberate indifference to the serious medical needs of an arrestee.[55] Recent cases have affirmed that holding.[56] Some courts have held that police officers do not have a duty to care for injured persons with whom they come in contact,[57] although such a holding is not likely to occur when the injured person is in their custody.

MISUSE OF FIREARMS AND DEADLY FORCE

There is no topic that weighs heavier on the mind of police administrators today than that of the misuse of firearms and deadly force by police officers. Because of the 2014–2015 incidents in Ferguson, Missouri; Charleston, South Carolina; Cincinnati, Ohio; Baltimore, Maryland; and more, departments are keenly aware that not only is there tragedy in the lives lost due to potential misuse of force, but there is also massive liability. It's not small thing that departments (and by proxy, their communities) have to pay out millions in damages due to such events, but even worse, such questionable shootings erode trust, put officers on edge, and can affect police/community relations for years.

To be clear, in the spate of high-profile officer shootings that made the news in 2014 and 2015, not all of them involved explicit wrongdoing by the officers at the time of the shootings. In a few cases, the officers perhaps failed to deescalate a situation properly, leading to a confrontation where deadly use of force was necessary. In other cases, the facts backed the officers' actions. It's also worth noting that use of force is applied in about 1.9 percent of the nearly 40 million police/citizen contacts over the period of one year.[58] However, even one "bad" police shooting is too many—and, hence, there are far too many.

Unfortunately, in the past, police officer training has too often focused on the issue of how to shoot and not when to shoot. Many times when a problem does arise relating to the use of deadly force, it is not that the officer failed to qualify at the police pistol range or that the weapon malfunctioned but that the officer made an error in judgment.

The police chief and his or her legal counsel must question whether this error in judgment was merely a human error resulting from the pressure of the moment or whether the police department failed to provide proper guidelines to the officer. If proper guidelines were made available to the officer, did the police department incorporate these guidelines into its formal training program?

Let us examine what areas a use-of-deadly-force policy should cover and the formalized mechanisms by which officers can be trained to understand this policy.

Tennessee v. Garner (1985)

Until 1985, the courts nationwide had not established a standard of law regarding the use of deadly force. Likewise, law enforcement agencies had not developed a standard, written directive that would establish national guidelines. While most large police agencies had established use-of-deadly-force policies, those policies certainly were not consistent in form or content.[59]

On March 27, 1985, all this started to change when the Supreme Court ruled unconstitutional a Tennessee law that permitted police officers to use deadly force to effect an arrest.[60] The Tennessee statute on the police use of deadly force provided that if, after a police officer has given notice of an intent to arrest a criminal suspect, the suspect flees or forcibly resists, "the officer may use all the necessary means to effect the arrest."[61] Acting under the authority of this statute, a Memphis police officer shot a juvenile, Garner, as he fled over a fence at night in the backyard of a house he was suspected of burglarizing. The officer ordered him to halt, but he failed to stop. The officer then fired a single shot and killed him. The officer used deadly force despite being "reasonably sure" that the suspect was unarmed and believing him to be 17 or 18 years old and of slight build. The suspect's father subsequently brought an action in federal district court, seeking damages under 42 U.S.C.S. 1983 for asserted violations of his son's constitutional rights. The district court held that the statute and the officer's actions were unconstitutional. The court of appeals reversed and the Supreme Court affirmed the Court of Appeals' decision.

The Supreme Court held that the Tennessee statute was unconstitutional insofar as it authorized the use of deadly force against, as in this case, an apparently unarmed, nondangerous, fleeing suspect. Such force may not be used unless necessary to prevent the escape and the officer has probable cause to believe that the suspect poses a significant threat of death or serious physical injury to the officer or others. The Court's reasoning was as follows:

1. Apprehension by the use of deadly force is a seizure and subject to the Fourth Amendment's reasonableness requirement. To determine whether such a seizure is reasonable, the extent of the intrusion on the suspect's rights under that amendment must be balanced against the government interests in effective law enforcement. This balancing process demonstrates that, notwithstanding probable cause to seize a suspect, an officer may not always do so by killing him or her. The use of deadly force to prevent the escape of all felony suspects, whatever the circumstances, is constitutionally unreasonable.

2. The Fourth Amendment, for purposes of this case, should not be construed in light of the Common-Law rule allowing the use of whatever force is necessary to effect the arrest of a fleeing felon. Changes in the legal and technological context mean that the rule is distorted almost beyond recognition when literally applied to criminal situations today.

   Whereas felonies were formerly capital crimes, few felonies are now. Many crimes classified as misdemeanors or nonexistent at Common Law are now felonies. Also, the Common-Law rule developed at a time when weapons were rudimentary. The varied rules adopted in the states indicate a long-term movement away from the Common-Law rule, particularly in the police departments themselves; thus, that rule is a dubious indication of the constitutionality of the Tennessee statute. There is no indication that holding a police practice, such as that authorized by the Tennessee statute, will severely hamper effective law enforcement.

3. While burglary is a serious crime, the officer in this case could not reasonably have believed that the suspect—young, slight, and unarmed—posed any threat. Nor does the fact that an unarmed suspect has broken into a dwelling at night automatically mean he or she is dangerous.

Graham v. Connor (1989)

Another landmark case related to the use of force started innocuously enough: Dethorne Graham, a maintenance worker in North Carolina, asked a friend to drive him to a convenience store when he felt a diabetic episode creeping up on him. He went into the store in search of orange juice to offset an insulin reaction. Once in the store, he purchased his juice quickly, then ran out to the car to drink it. A patrol officer sitting outside saw him dart from the store and into the car and suspected that Graham had just committed a robbery. The car was stopped, and despite the pleas of the driver and Graham, the officer forced Graham out of the car, where Graham lost consciousness. Graham was immediately cuffed, at one point, he gained consciousness and begged officers to check his wallet for an ID card that detailed his medical condition. Their reaction was to slam his head into the hood of a car. Graham suffered injuries that included a broken foot, cuts, bruising, and a long-term ringing in his ear. He sued under Section 1983, and the Supreme Court ruled in his favor, establishing a major three-prong test of reasonableness for all use-of-force cases in the future:

- First, what was the severity of the crime that the officer believed the suspect to have committed or was committing at the time of the encounter?
- Second, did the suspect present an immediate threat to the safety of officers or the public?
- Third, was the suspect actively resisting arrest or attempting to escape?

Graham also offered one of the most important narratives about police use of force, from Chief Justice William Rehnquist:

The reasonableness of a particular use of force must be judged from the perspective of a reasonable officer on the scene, rather than with the 20/20 vision of hindsight. The calculus of reasonableness must embody allowance for the fact that police officers are often forced to make split-second judgments—in circumstances that are tense, uncertain and rapidly evolving—about the amount of force that is necessary in a particular situation. The test of reasonableness is not capable of precise definition or mechanical application.[62]

It is interesting, using the perspective on reasonableness to consider some of the more prominent use-of-force cases from the past several years. Though the emotion from these cases may run high—the *Graham* decision makes clear that the **standard of reasonableness** emanates from *the officer's perception at the time of the crisis that results in the shooting.* It is possible that this decision may be revisited in the wake of the rash of high-profile use-of-force incidents—but as of this writing, *Graham v. Connor* remains the dominant test for use-of-force considerations.

Evaluation of Written Directives

As suggested earlier, when an alleged wrongful death case is being evaluated, the adequacy of the police department's policy must be considered. Generally speaking, an adequate policy addresses the following topics: defense of life and fleeing felons, juveniles, shooting at or from vehicles, warning shots, shooting to destroy animals, secondary guns, off-duty weapons, and registration of weapons (see Figure 14.3).

DEFENSE OF LIFE AND FLEEING FELONS

State laws and departmental policies still remain fairly diverse even after *Garner*, although with narrower bounds. No longer can these provisions leave officers virtually untethered, as in the extreme case of one small American town whose only gun guidance to its officers was the homily "Never take me out in anger; never put me away in disgrace."[63]

The range of firearms policies hereafter is likely to be from the "defense-of-life" regulations, which permit shooting only to defeat an imminent threat to an officer's or another person's life. At the other extreme, a minimal compliance with the *Garner* rule permits shooting at currently nonviolent, fleeing suspects who the officer reasonably believes committed a felony involving the threat but not the use of violence. Both approaches are currently employed by many large police departments.

The defense-of-life approach significantly reduces the possibility of wrongful death allegations.

JUVENILES

For the most part, police departments do not instruct their officers to make a distinction between adults and juveniles in using deadly force, unless it is readily apparent that the individual is a juvenile. This is not based on a callous disregard for youthful offenders; rather, it is based on the pragmatic view that an armed juvenile can kill with the same finality as an armed adult. Further, it is often difficult, if not impossible, to tell if an offender is a juvenile or an adult.

SHOOTING AT OR FROM VEHICLES

The trend in recent years has been to impose severe limitations on police officers shooting at or from vehicles except as the ultimate measure in self-defense or the defense of another when the suspect is using deadly force by means other than the vehicle.

Some of the reasons presented against shooting at or from vehicles are difficulty in hitting the target, ricochets striking innocent bystanders, population densities, difficulty in penetrating the automobile body and steel-belted tires, inability to put a stop to the vehicle's momentum even when the target suspect is hit, damage that might result from causing the vehicle to go out of control, difficulty in hitting a moving target, and striking of an innocent passenger in the fleeing vehicle.[64]

There is little question that, if a motorist is trying to run a police officer down and the officer has no reasonable means of escape, then the officer has every right to defend his or her life. What often happens, however, is that the officer starts shooting at a vehicle when he or she is no longer in danger. For example, if a vehicle attempts to run a police officer down and the officer is able to take evasive action and get out of harm's way, under the provisions of many police departments' policies, the officer is no longer permitted to shoot at the vehicle because the officer is no longer in danger. Naturally, if the driver turns the vehicle around and goes back toward the officer, the officer once again has the right to protect his or her life.

FIGURE 14.3 ▶ Two Special Weapons and Tactics (SWAT) officers watch a third SWAT officer use a one-man door ram, which appears to be a Broco's Enforcer model. Manual rams are used to achieve rapid forced entry into a premise, for example, officers have search and arrest warrants for drug offenses and they reasonably believe that those inside are flushing drugs down the toilet. (Photo courtesy of the National Tactical Officers Association. www.ntoa.org)

WARNING SHOTS

There seems to be a general consensus among administrators that department policies should prohibit warning shots, as they may strike an innocent person. Privately, however, officials might fear something else: Officers shooting at and missing a suspect may claim that they were merely firing a warning shot and attempt to avoid answering for their actions. In addition, police officials point out that warning shots rarely accomplish their purpose, especially if suspects know that officers will not or cannot shoot them.[65]

SHOOTING TO DESTROY ANIMALS

Police departments generally allow their officers to kill an animal in self-defense, to prevent substantial harm to the officer or others, or when an animal is so badly injured that humanity requires its relief from further suffering. A seriously wounded or injured animal may be destroyed only after all attempts have been made to request assistance from the agencies (i.e., humane society, animal control, or game warden) responsible for disposal of animals. The destruction of vicious animals should be guided by the same rules set forth for self-defense or the defense and safety of others.[66]

SECONDARY GUNS

Police officers in the United States are all conspicuously armed with a revolver or semiautomatic handgun. This fact is recognized and for the most part approved by our citizenry. A second fact not commonly known is that many police officers also carry a concealed secondary weapon. There are stated reasons for the practice: Officers are concerned about being disarmed (with sound justification) during a confrontation, officers are less likely to be caught off guard when confrontation is not anticipated, and officers can less conspicuously be prepared to protect themselves during routine citizen stops. Regardless of the rationale, the practice is considered acceptable by knowledgeable police officials but treated by many police administrators as something understood but not formally admitted.

A major criticism of backup weapons is that they may be intended as "throwaways" in the event an officer shoots an unarmed suspect. In order to protect the officer from such allegations, it is generally recommended that there be a strict policy of registering all backup guns with the department.[67]

OFF-DUTY WEAPONS

The rationale for officers to be armed while off duty is based on the assumption that police officers within their own jurisdictions are on duty 24 hours a day and are therefore expected to act in their official capacity if the need to do so occurs. This, for the most part, was the policy of many police departments. Until recently, an officer who failed to comply with this regulation was subject to disciplinary action if a situation occurred that needed police action, such as responding to a robbery in progress, and the officer could not respond because he or she was unarmed.

Many police departments now make being armed while off duty optional but still compel their officers to register with the department any weapons they choose to wear off duty and to qualify regularly with the weapons. Most police departments also designate the type of ammunition the officers may carry in all weapons they use, regardless of whether they are used on duty or off duty.[68]

REGISTRATION OF WEAPONS

Most police departments require their officers to use only department-approved weapons on and off duty and further require that the weapons be inspected, fired, and certified safe by the departments' armorers. Further, the firearms must be registered with the departments by make, model, serial number, and ballistics sample.[69]

Familiarization with the Department's Policy

It does a police department little good to have an adequate use-of-deadly-force policy if its officers are not familiar with all aspects of that policy. Following are some examples of formalized administrative means by which officers can become familiar with their agencies' policies:

- *Recruit training*—Instructions dealing with the deadly force policy should be incorporated into the unit of instruction dealing with firearms training. As suggested earlier, the judgmental aspects of using deadly force are as important as the hands-on skill development of police officers in firearms training. Such a unit of instruction should involve a discussion of the numerous situations that officers will typically encounter and what course of action would keep these officers in strict compliance with their departments' policies and minimize wrongful deaths.

- *Field training officer*—The field training officer to whom a rookie officer is assigned immediately upon graduation from the police academy is responsible for continuing the training process started by the police academy and for evaluating the suitability of the rookie for police work. Such programs frequently incorporate training features designed to reinforce topics covered in the formal classroom setting of the academy. This component of the training program should be examined to be certain it deals with the topic of police use of deadly force.

- *Roll-call training*—A part of this training, which typically occurs just prior to the officers going on patrol, can be spent in reviewing newly developed departmental policies, procedures, and regulations, including those dealing with the use of deadly force.

- *In-service training*—In-service training classes typically range from one to five days (see Figure 14.4). It is quite clear that the *Garner*[70] decision has resulted in many police departments rethinking and rewriting their use-of-deadly-force policies. The importance of the *Garner*

FIGURE 14.4 ▶ Police use of deadly force requires extensive training in firearms techniques that can be validated and documented by qualified personnel. Virtual and simulation training programs provide real-world police encounters that hopefully decrease the number of officer-involved shootings as well as the subsequent number of police litigations. (Sgt Parker Gyokeres/ U.S. Air Force photo)

Quick Facts: Body-Worn Cameras and Use of Force

Early research on body-worn cameras indicates that the use of the technology may reduce use-of-force incidents by up to 50 percent.

Source: Tony Farrar, "Self-awareness to being watched and socially desirable behavior: A field experiment on the effect of body-worn cameras on police use-of-force." *Police Foundation.* Retrieved August 5, 2015 from: http://www.policefoundation.org/content/body-worn-camera

---

decision will not be fully appreciated if a police department merely rewrites its policy and hands it out to its officers with no explanation. It is imperative that some explanation be provided, preferably by legal counsel, so that there is no misunderstanding about what this policy means. This familiarization and orientation can occur in conjunction with the firearms requalification training that officers have to go through regularly, or it can be treated within the context of an in-service training course.[71]

POLICE USE OF FORCE AND LESS-LETHAL WEAPONS

Law enforcement agencies must walk a careful line in American society. While police officers are responsible for maintaining peace and order, this is complicated by a multitude of factors unique to each and every situation. When an officer responds to a call for service or reacts to observed criminal behavior in the field, that officer must either quell the disturbance or apprehend a suspect, sometimes through the use of force. Police use of force is most often justifiable and legal, particularly when overcoming resistance during arrests or in course of protecting themselves or others from harm.[72]

There is a general, usually unrealistic, societal expectation of increasingly more technical and sophisticated weapons available to police agencies. This is propagated in the entertainment industry. Television and big-screen productions tend to display deadly force in black and white; the evil doer misses or inflicts minor wounds while heroes are incredibly accurate and kill painlessly and from great distances. Less-lethal weapons in the entertainment arena can be viewed through a similar lens. The public, raised on science fiction like Star Trek©, expects phaser-like weapons that can incapacitate without causing permanent harm or death. Viewers watch as the fictitious recipient is usually rendered unconscious from a single application of a less-lethal weapon and recovers almost immediately. This creates a massive discrepancy between reality and the portrayal of **less-lethal weapons** in popular media. While less-lethal weapons are used without the intent to cause permanent injury or death, they still have the potential to cause death or serious injury. However, these weapons are ordinarily less harmful and hence, less lethal than the projectiles fired from firearms.[73] Common less-lethal weapons used in policing include chemical weapons such as oleoresin capsicum (OC) or pepper spray, bean-bag guns, net guns that shoot a web around suspects, and controlled energy devices (CEDs).

TASERS®

A CED is a device designed to deploy electricity throughout the body of the target to temporarily cause loss of muscle control. Throughout the history of law enforcement in America, there have been many devices that loosely fit this description, including "cattle prods" or "stun guns." Such devices allow electricity to be deployed on contact with the skin or within close distances. Over the past several years, the technology for these devices has become more advanced, allowing the user to apply the device more accurately and from greater distances. Although greatly accepted as a less-lethal weapon option by many local, county, state, and federal police agencies, they have also been met by community concerns about safety, misuse, and overuse. TASER® International[74] is the company best known for producing CEDs. Their product has become so well-known that the name "TASER®" has become synonymous with "CED," much like the name "band-aid" is to a plastic bandage.[75]

According to the Government Accounting Office, TASERS® are now used by more than 10,000 law enforcement agencies across the United States.[76] TASERS® shock a person with 50,000 volts and create intense pain and discomfort by involuntary constrictions of skeletal muscles in order to gain compliance on the part of the suspect. A person being shocked or "tased" is conscious and the event is designed to last for five seconds or less; however, the newest version of the weapon is designed to produce up to three cycles of five seconds (15 seconds). While application of the electrical current is possible by contacting the end of the device to the skin, the uniqueness of the TASER® weapons lies in its ability to be applied from greater distances. Powered by high-pressure air probes that are similar to darts, the probes are fired while tethered to the handheld device on wire that can reach from 15 to 31 feet. However, in order for the device to be effective in gaining compliance, both probes must strike the target, preferably with a spread of about 1 foot between the probes.

Liability and Less-Lethal Weapons

While empirical research on police use of force has increased over the last 50 years, only limited attention has been paid to use-of-force encounters wherein the police used "less-lethal weapons" generally, and the TASER® specifically. Alpert and Dunham have focused on use-of-force encounters and police injuries and have demonstrated that the greatest likelihood of officer injury occurs when they attempt to control a suspect by punching, kicking, take-down, wrestling, and joint locks.[77] These types of incidents account for almost 70 percent of injuries. Research findings also reveal a higher likelihood of injury to the suspect when officers use canines, bodily force, and impact weapons (e.g., batons and riot sticks) as well. Generally, research reveals that few problems occur when healthy subjects are shocked or "tased" for less than 15 seconds.[78] Even though the bulk of research shows that the use of less-lethal weapons reduces injury, there have been several highlighted incidents across the nation that have peaked interest in the use of such weapons and influenced public opinion (see Figure 14.5).[79]

Most departments using TASERS® place the weapon within their continuum of force policy and provide extensive training on the use of the weapon. Most importantly, recent research[80] using data from 12 local police departments representing more than 24,000 incidents found that the use of physical force (e.g., striking, wrestling, and come-along holds) by police increased the odds of injury to both suspects and officers. Conversely, the use of less-lethal weapons (such as OC spray or TASERS®) decreased the odds of injury to suspects and officers. When used appropriately as trained, and controlled through use-of-force policy, the employment of less-lethal weapons (such as OC spray and TASERS®) against healthy suspects reduces injury overall; by reasonable

FIGURE 14.5 ▶ The use of pepper spray against Occupy protestors at UC Davis in California in 2011 raised public debate about police use of less-lethal weapons. (JASNA HODZIC/epa european pressphoto agency b.v./Alamy Stock Photo)

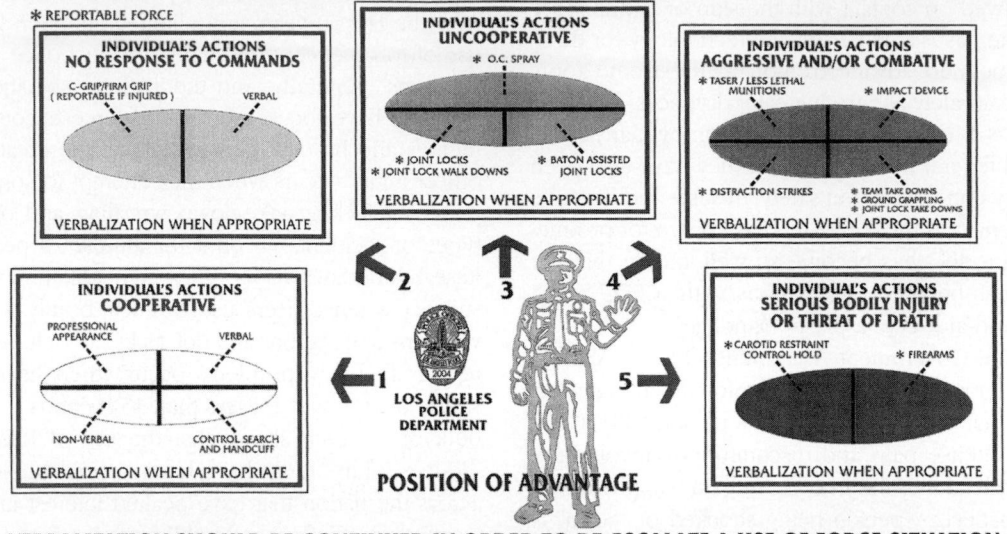

extension, the use of less-than-lethal weapons also reduces the number and severity of potentially successful liability claims brought against the police.[81] To further reduce liability, officers should follow many of the suggestions designed to reduce liability during use-of-deadly-force encounters as proscribed above, be well-trained on each type of less-lethal weapons, be familiar with policies relating to their use, and receive periodic in-service training to update their skills and the usage of such devices.

POLICE LIABILITY AND HIGH-SPEED PURSUIT

The legal theory underlying most pursuit-related lawsuits is that the police were negligent in conducting a pursuit.[82] A negligence action is based on proof of the following four elements: (1) the officer owed the injured party a duty not to engage in certain conduct, (2) the officer's actions violated that duty, (3) the officer's negligent conduct was the proximate cause of the accident, and (4) the suing party suffered actual and provable damages.[83] Negligence litigation focuses on the alleged failure of an officer to exercise reasonable care under the circumstances.

Duty Owed

Courts first determine the duty owed in a pursuit situation by examining the officer's conduct in light of relevant laws and department regulations. With the exception of some police departments that prohibit all pursuits, police officers have no duty to refrain from chasing a criminal suspect, even when the risk of harm to the public arising from the chase is foreseeable and the suspect is being chased for a misdemeanor.[84] In *Smith v. City of West Point*,[85] the court stated that police "are under no duty to allow motorized suspects a leisurely escape."[86] However, police do have a duty of care with respect to the manner in which they conduct a pursuit. This duty is derived from state statutes, court decisions defining reasonable care, and departmental pursuit policies.

Statutes in most jurisdictions confer a special status on police and other authorized emergency vehicles, exempting them from certain traffic regulations, such as speed limits, traffic signals, and a right of way.[87] Statutes exempting emergency vehicles from ordinary traffic regulations generally make the privilege conditional on (1) the existence of an actual emergency, (2) the use of adequate warning devices, and (3) the continued exercise of due care for the safety of others. Whether a government unit or its officers can be held liable depends in large part on the construction of such statutes. As a general rule, police drivers are not liable for negligence as a matter of law solely because they disregard a traffic regulation during an authorized emergency run. However, these statutes provide no protection against liability for an officer's reckless driving. Drivers of emergency police vehicles have a statutory duty to drive with due regard for the safety of others.

Court decisions defining the reasonable care standard constitute a second source from which to derive a duty owed by police pursuit drivers. Most courts have translated the reasonable care

Quick Facts: The Statistics of Police Pursuits and Chases

A recent National Highway Traffic and Safety Administration (NHTSA) analysis revealed that over 11,500 people, including 6,300 fleeing suspects, were killed in police pursuits from 1979 to 2013; that is an average of 329 a year—nearly one person a day. The number also includes more than 5,000 innocent bystanders and passengers killed, and countless more injured as a result of high-speed and dangerous pursuits often initiated by the police for minor traffic infractions. In addition, State of California records of 63,500 police chases from 2002 through 2014 revealed:

• Most chases ended quickly—76 percent were over within five min.

• The vast majority (a whopping 89 percent) were initiated for vehicle-code violations or traffic infractions, including speeding, vehicle theft, reckless driving, and

missing license plate or expire registration (nearly 5,000 cases).

• Only 5 percent of the cases were developed in an effort to arrest a suspected for a violent crime (e.g., robbery, kidnapping, assault, or murder). Only 168 cases out of over 63,500 cases in 13 years (less than 003 percent) sought a known suspect for murder.

• Nearly a 1,000 cases were initiated for safety violations like not wearing a seat belt or not wearing a helmet for motorcycle rider.

• In 90 cases, police chased suspect for "driving too slowly."

Source: Thomas Frank, "High Speed Police Chases Have Killed Thousands of Innocent Bystanders," USA Today (July 30, 2015). See: http://www.usatoday.com/story/news/2015/07/30/police-pursuits-fatal-injuries/30187827/

standard into a duty to drive with the care that a reasonable, prudent officer would exercise in the discharge of official duties of a similar nature.[88] "Reasonable care" is a relative term depending on the exigencies of the situation and the degree of care and vigilance reasonably dictated by the circumstances of the chase.

A third source from which to derive a duty owed by police pursuit drivers is department policy. A law enforcement organization's policies, procedures, and training material concerning high-speed pursuits are generally admissible as evidence in lawsuits against the department or its officers for the negligent operation of a pursuit vehicle.[89] For example, in order to ascertain the standard of care applicable to a particular pursuit situation, a court could admit into evidence a police department regulation defining the proper speeds at which police cars responding to emergency calls were supposed to enter intersections when proceeding against red traffic signals. Depending on the jurisdiction involved, departmental pursuit policies may be merely a guideline to assist juries in determining the reasonableness of pursuit conduct, or they may actually constitute a duty owed, the violation of which would be considered negligent.

Proximate Cause

Liability must be based on proof that police conduct in breaching a duty owed was the **proximate cause** of a pursuit-related accident. Proximate cause is difficult to establish in cases involving the intervening negligence of other drivers, such as a case in which a fleeing motorist collides with an innocent person. In such cases, some courts impose liability on the officer and the department if the accident was a foreseeable consequence of police negligence.[90] For example, if police pursue without activating their emergency/flashing lights and siren and an innocent citizen enters an intersection without being warned of the pursuit and collides with the pursued vehicle, the police may be

liable because the accident was the proximate and foreseeable result of their failure to adequately warn other drivers of the pursuit. In *Nelson v. City of Chester, Ill.*,[91] the court held that the city's breach of its duty to properly train its police officers in high-speed pursuit might be found to be the proximate cause of the pursued driver's death, notwithstanding the contributing negligence of the pursued driver.

Legal barriers to civil actions, such as immunity, have been removed in many jurisdictions by a combination of legislation and judicial decisions, even though the extent of immunity continues to vary.[92] Statutes in most states have limited sovereign immunity to discretionary as opposed to ministerial decisions. Accordingly, the decision to pursue is viewed as discretionary, rendering the public entity immune, but the manner of pursuit is a ministerial decision for which there is no general grant of immunity. *Rhodes v. Lamar*[93] used this bifurcated approach to hold that the decision to institute a pursuit is a discretionary decision for which a sheriff enjoyed sovereign immunity, but liability was not precluded if the pursuit was conducted in a manner that violated a reasonable duty of care. In *Fagan v. City of Vineland*, the Court of Appeals allowed the municipality to be sued directly under Section 1983 when the pursuit causing a constitutional tort was pursuant to municipal policy or custom. Furthermore, the court allowed the municipality to be held liable for lack of training its officers in high-speed pursuit even if none of the officers involved in the pursuit at issue violated the Constitution.[94]

Federal Civil Rights Act

Pursuit-related liability under the federal Civil Rights Act, 42 U.S.C. 1983, requires proof that an officer's conduct violated a constitutionally protected right.[95] In *Cannon v. Taylor*,[96] the Court of Appeals for the Eleventh Circuit concluded that "a person injured in an automobile accident caused by the negligent, or even grossly negligent, operation of a motor vehicle by a police officer acting in the line of duty has no Section 1983 cause of action for violation of a federal right."[97] The Supreme Court in *County of Sacramento v. Lewis* decided that a police officer does not violate the Fourteenth Amendment's guarantee of substantive due process "by causing death through deliberate or reckless indifference to life in a high-speed automobile chase aimed at apprehending a suspected offender."[98] The only violation of substantive due process occurs when there is a purpose to cause harm unrelated to the arrest. Automobile negligence actions are grist for the state law mill, but they do not rise to the level of a constitutional deprivation.[99] The common thread running through the cases is that negligent conduct during a pursuit does not suffice to trigger jurisdiction under Section 1983. However, a municipality can be held liable under Section 1983 if there was no or inadequate high-speed pursuit training for its officers, even when the officers involved with a pursuit were not individually negligent.[100]

Certain techniques employed by police during a pursuit may raise constitutional issues cognizable under 1983. For example, in *Jamieson By and Through Jamieson v. Shaw*[101] the court held that the constitutionally permissible use-of-force standard set forth by the Supreme Court in *Tennessee v. Garner*[102] was violated when a passenger in a fleeing vehicle was hurt when the vehicle hit a so-called deadman roadblock after officers allegedly shined a bright light into the driver's eyes as the vehicle approached the roadblock. In *Bower v. County of Inyo*,[103] a high-speed pursuit of over 20 miles ended when the fleeing suspect was killed when his vehicle hit a tractor-trailer that police had placed across the road as a roadblock. The Court of Appeals held that police use of a roadblock could constitute a constitutional violation of substantive due process if it was designed as an intentional deathtrap where the approaching driver does not have a clear option to stop because the roadblock is concealed around a curve or inadequately illuminated. The Supreme Court went further in stating that the deceased driver was unreasonably "seized" when the roadblock was placed completely across the highway in a manner likely to kill the driver and that the police officers were liable under the Fourth Amendment and Section 1983 for the use of excessive force.[104]

Factors Determining Liability

Pursuit-related litigation usually involves an inquiry into whether the manner in which the pursuit was conducted was reasonable under the circumstances of that case. Each pursuit situation is different and requires a particularized assessment. Following is a brief discussion of certain factors that most frequently determine the extent of pursuit-related liability.

PURPOSE OF PURSUIT

This factor relates to the need or reason for a pursuit. Does the purpose of the pursuit warrant the risks involved? What is the nature and seriousness of the suspected offense? Is the fleeing motorist suspected of committing a serious crime or only a misdemeanor? Was the motorist already operating the vehicle in a reckless and life-threatening manner before the pursuit started or had the motorist committed a minor, nonhazardous traffic violation prior to the pursuit but then started driving in a reckless and life-threatening manner after the pursuit was initiated? Is there a need for immediate apprehension or has the suspect been identified so that apprehension at a later time is possible?

DRIVING CONDITIONS

This factor involves a general assessment of equipment, the weather, roadway and traffic conditions, and the experience and personal ability of the drivers involved in the chase.

USE OF WARNING DEVICES

The use of adequate visual and audible warning devices, such as flashing lights and a siren, not only is a statutory mandate for most pursuit situations but also ensures to the greatest extent possible that other vehicles and pedestrians are alerted to approaching emergency vehicles and to the need to yield the right of way.

EXCESSIVE SPEED

Whether a particular speed is excessive depends on the purpose of the pursuit, the driving conditions, and the personal ability of a police driver to control and effectively maneuver the vehicle. Speed when crossing an intersection against a light or sign is an especially critical consideration, since statistics suggest that most pursuit-related collisions occur at intersections.[105] Liability may be based on the failure to sufficiently decrease speed when approaching an intersection so that a complete stop can be made to avoid a collision.

DISOBEYING TRAFFIC LAWS

Pursuit vehicles are statutorily obligated to use due care for the safety of others when disobeying traffic laws, such as operating a vehicle on the wrong side of the road, passing on the right, going the wrong way on a one-way street, passing in a "no passing" zone, or proceeding against a traffic signal. These dangerous and high-risk driving situations should be avoided because police are generally held liable for any resulting accidents.[106]

ROADBLOCKS

Special care is required when using roadblocks to ensure that innocent persons are not placed in a position of danger and that the fleeing motorist is afforded a reasonable opportunity to stop safely.[107] To reduce the risk of liability, it is recommended that roadblocks be used only when authorized by a supervisor and only as a last resort to apprehend a fleeing motorist who is wanted for a violent felony and who constitutes an immediate and serious threat. Although the Supreme Court stated that a roadblock could be a Fourth Amendment unreasonable seizure granting

Section 1983 liability,[108] the Court of Appeals for the First Circuit qualified the definition of "seizure" to apply to roadblock accidents constituting a "misuse of power" as opposed to the "accidental effects of otherwise lawful governmental conduct."[109]

TERMINATION OF PURSUIT

Every police department's pursuit policy has a provision dealing with termination of pursuit. When officers are expected to terminate varies considerably, depending on the agency's philosophy. Some agencies allow their officers very broad latitude, while others greatly restrict officers' actions. Policies generally fall into one of three models:[110]

1. *Judgmental*—Allowing officers to make all major decisions relating to initiation, tactics, and termination.
2. *Restrictive*—Placing certain restrictions on officers' judgments and decisions.
3. *Discouragement*—Severely cautioning or discouraging any pursuit, except in the most extreme situations.

However, despite these variations in department policies, a noticeable trend has been emerging. Increasingly, police departments are permitting their officers to pursue only individuals who are known to have committed dangerous felonies—that is, murder, felonious assault, rape, robbery, kidnapping, and so on. This trend is occurring because it is becoming increasingly difficult to justify pursuits that result in injuries and the death of innocent third parties, as well as the injuries and death of police officers. Another reason for the dramatic shift in these policies has been because of the enormously high-monetary judgments imposed by juries for injuries to innocent third parties.

Alpert[111] and Beckman[112] show that the vast majority of pursuits are for traffic violations and/or misdemeanors and not felonies. The issue of when the violator would eventually stop was addressed by Alpert.[113] He interviewed 146 inmates who had fled from the police and who were confined to jails in three cities: Omaha, Nebraska; Miami, Florida; and Columbia, South Carolina. Over 70 percent of the suspects said that they would have slowed down "when I felt safe" whether the pursuit was on a freeway, on a highway, or in a town. The phrase "when I felt safe" was interpreted by the respondents as outdistancing the police by 2.2 blocks on surface streets, 2.3 miles on highways, and 2.5 miles on freeways. Fifty-three percent of the suspects responded that they were willing to run at all costs from the police in a pursuit, and 64 percent believed that they would not be caught; however, 71 percent said that they were concerned with their own safety, and 62 percent stated that they were concerned with the safety of others while engaged in a chase.[114]

Thus, law enforcement agencies that allow their officers broad discretion in pursuit can expect a greater number of arrests of violators who flee. However, they can also expect to have more uninvolved third parties injured or killed, as well as more police officers injured and a greater number of lawsuits. Conversely, those departments that have more restrictive policies can expect more conservative results. The final decision is ultimately left to the chief administrator of the agency.

Departmental Responsibility for Liability Reduction

To reduce the risks and liability associated with vehicular pursuits, law enforcement organizations must carefully evaluate their pursuit policies, training, supervision, and postincident evaluations. Liability reduction is accomplished through sound management controls and a reduction in the number of pursuit-related accidents.

POLICY DEVELOPMENT

The function of a well-written pursuit policy is to state the department's objectives, establish some ground rules for the exercise of discretion, and educate officers as to

---

Box 14.2: Dallas, Texas Police Department Institutes a Restrictive Vehicle Pursuit Police

The Dallas Police Department has one of the most restrictive vehicle pursuit policies in the United States, and the policy appears to be saving officers' and citizens' lives. Since the policy was enacted at the beginning of 2007, individual officers and the police unions have been critical, indicating that the policy is "soft on criminals" and encourages traffic violators not to stop for the police. Several officers indicated that the policy actually undermined their ability to "catch criminals." However, the policy has dramatically decreased the numbers of officers and citizens killed and injured in the city of Dallas as the result of a police vehicle pursuit, and crime rates remain among the lowest in Dallas for decades. The policy is still at odds with many officer's desires to chase down the bad guys, but for newer officers, the policy is just the way things have always been.

Note that the policy places the entire decision on the officer. The highlighted area indicates that the officer must be able to immediately articulate why he or she is engaging in a chase and that the immediate need to apprehend the offender (via a police pursuit) outweighs the safety of other members of the community who might be endangered by the chase.

(continued)

Dallas Police Department General Order
301.00 Emergency Vehicle Operation

Revised 09/18/15

301.07   Vehicle Pursuits

A. Purpose - The purpose of this policy is to establish guidelines for making decisions with regard to vehicular pursuits.

B. Philosophy - General Order 906.01 B., states "protection of human life is a primary goal of the police department; therefore, police officers have a responsibility to use only the degree of force necessary to protect and preserve life." Initiating or participating in a vehicular pursuit presents a danger to the officers involved, the suspect, and the general public. Accordingly, the decision to initiate a pursuit must be based on the pursuing officer's conclusion that the immediate danger to the officer, public and suspect created by the pursuit is less than the immediate or potential danger to the public should the suspect remain at large.

C. Definition - A Pursuit is defined as an active attempt by an officer in an authorized emergency vehicle to apprehend a fleeing suspect in a motor vehicle who is attempting to elude the officer. A suspect is considered to be fleeing upon making any overt action intended to avoid arrest. For the purpose of this order, violators who follow all traffic regulations after an officer initiates a traffic stop and are merely failing to yield to the authorized emergency vehicle are not considered to be fleeing. The term "Chase" will be considered synonymous with "Pursuit".

D. Decision to Initiate Pursuit

   1. The decision to pursue must be based upon facts and circumstances known to the officer.
   2. In deciding whether to pursue, an officer must take the following pursuit risk factors under consideration:
      a. road, weather and environmental conditions.
      b. population density, vehicle and pedestrian traffic.
      c. relative performance capabilities of both the authorized emergency vehicle and the suspect's vehicle.
      d. seriousness of the offense.
      e. presence of other persons in the police vehicle.
      f. age of offender.
      g. whether or not the offender's identity is known, and
      h. any circumstance under which the pursuing officer will be unable to maintain control of the emergency vehicle.
   3. An officer may initiate a pursuit under the following circumstances:
      a. When the officer has probable cause to believe that a felony involving the use or threat of physical force or violence has been, or is about to be, committed, and the officer reasonably believes that the immediate need to apprehend the offender outweighs the risk to any person of collision, injury or death, or
      b. to assist another law enforcement agency that has initiated a pursuit under the same circumstances.
      c. All other pursuits are prohibited.
   4. Officers will not pursue a motorist whose only offense is driving while intoxicated if the actions of the driver escalate beyond merely failing to yield to the emergency vehicle.

E. Manner of Operation While in Pursuit

   1. The emergency warning lights, siren, and emergency vehicle headlights will be used at all times while operating Code 3.
   2. Only police vehicles equipped with operable emergency warning lights and sirens will participate in the pursuit of a fleeing vehicle.
   3. Unmarked vehicles without roof mounted emergency warning light systems will not become involved in a pursuit. Supervisors in unmarked vehicles will follow the chase using a Code 1 response.
   4. If a pursuit is initiated by a motorcycle, the motorcycle will abandon the pursuit when a four-wheel unit with roof mounted emergency warning light systems joins the pursuit.
   5. Vehicles with passengers (prisoners, witnesses, suspects, complainants or other non-police personnel who have not signed a waiver of liability) will not become engaged in pursuits.
   6. Paddy Wagons will not become engaged in pursuits.

---

specific factors they should consider when conducting a vehicular pursuit. Where feasible, a comprehensive policy statement should give content to terms such as "reasonable" and "reckless" and provide officers with more particularized guidance. A policy should be tailored to a department's operational needs, geographical peculiarities, and training capabilities. A written policy also provides a basis for holding officers accountable for their pursuit-related conduct.

TRAINING

Lack of adequate training may contribute to many pursuit-related accidents. The natural tendency for many police drivers is to become emotionally involved and therefore lose some perspective during a pursuit. They are also required to drive different police vehicles with unique handling characteristics under various road and weather conditions. It is easy to lose control of a vehicle that is driven beyond its or the driver's capabilities, and law enforcement organizations can be held liable for failing to provide adequate driver training to prepare officers to handle vehicles safely in pursuit situations.[115] The extent and type of training required depend on a department's operational needs and objectives. A minimal level of cost-effective training can be accomplished by emphasizing defensive driving techniques and carefully instructing officers about departmental pursuit policies and relevant state regulations concerning the operation of emergency vehicles.

SUPERVISION

Police departments are responsible for providing adequate supervision of officers involved in a pursuit. Experts who have studied the emotionalism and psychology associated with pursuits recommend that, as soon as possible after a pursuit has been initiated, a supervisor who is not in any of the pursuit vehicles be tasked with the responsibility of supervising the pursuit.[116] The supervisor who is not immediately involved is in a better position to oversee objectively the pursuit and decide whether it should continue and under what circumstances. The supervisor should track the location of the pursuit, designate the primary and secondary pursuit vehicles, and maintain tight controls on the desire of other officers to get involved or parallel the action. Effective communication between the pursuing vehicles and the supervisor is essential. The failure to transmit information concerning the location of a pursuit, the offense for which the pursuit was initiated, and other information required by departmental policy, such as the speed of vehicles, traffic conditions, and whether the pursued vehicle is ignoring traffic lights and signs may contribute to a subsequent accident because the supervisor lacks sufficient knowledge to order a pursuit terminated.

EVALUATION AND DOCUMENTATION

Law enforcement organizations should provide for an ongoing process of evaluation and documentation of pursuit-related incidents. All pursuits, including those successfully terminated without an accident, should be routinely critiqued to determine whether departmental policy was followed and the extent to which any policy modification, training enhancement, or other remedial action is warranted.

VEHICLE PURSUITS AND THE USE OF DEADLY FORCE

In an interesting mix of case law, the Supreme Court decided (2014) that police officers have an affirmative duty to end "grave risks" to the community. In *Plumhoff v. Rickard,* the Court straddled both vehicle pursuit and use-of-deadly-force case law. The case involves several West Memphis (AR) police officers who ended a high-speed vehicle pursuit by firing their weapons 12 times at a man fleeing from them in a vehicle. The court, in this decision, held that the officers' actions were reasonable in that the police chase caused a "grave public safety risk" to the wider community. As a result, the use of deadly force to end dangerous vehicle pursuits is justified in cases where the "totality of the circumstances" would make such action reasonable under *Graham v. Connor.*[117]

LIABILITY AND EMOTIONALLY DISTURBED PERSONS

Forty percent of persons suffering from serious mental illness will be arrested at least once during their lifetime. For this reason, it is imperative that progressive law enforcement agencies assume responsibility for evaluating potentially dangerous situations and recognizing those individuals suffering from various forms of mental illness. These individuals are commonly referred to as **emotionally disturbed persons (EDPs)**.[118]

Police responses to EDPs are determined to some degree by the manner in which the contact is initiated. The largest percentage of police officer contacts with EDPs are a result of on-the-street observations of bizarre, disruptive, or abnormal behavior. These encounters often end in an arrest of the subject for a relatively minor charge (e.g., disturbing the peace, disorderly conduct, vagrancy, or loitering), especially if alcohol use can be easily detected (see Figure 14.6). In other cases, the police receive complaints on an EDP as a result of a family disturbance or neighborhood problem. In either event, officers are often confronted by an individual with whom they have had prior contact (perhaps multiple prior contacts) and one who might suddenly and without provocation burst into a violent confrontation, endangering everyone at the scene. As a result, many police departments are beginning to address this issue through basic and advanced training. For example, the Washington State Criminal Justice Commission has developed a unique curriculum focused on five key areas:

1. Recognizing abnormal behavior and mental illness (neuroses, psychoses, and psychopathic/sociopathic behavior);

2. Dealing with suicidal subjects (true versus parasuicidal behavior);

3. Developing crisis intervention skills (legal considerations in subject committal, tactical responses to handling the EDP, and responses to mental disturbance calls);

4. Developing awareness and knowledge of community services (interim facilities, hospital and emergency services, and community care homes); and

5. Recognizing and caring for Alzheimer's patients (physical cues and behavior).[119]

FIGURE 14.6 ▶ Police officers often encounter vagrants near public buildings, business entrances, and parks. Removing emotionally disturbed people, homeless vagrants, and panhandlers is often a very delicate issue. (Mark Boster/Los Angeles Times/Getty Images)

Other departments have also developed specialized in-service courses designed to provide more information to officers. The Monterey County Police Chief's Association has developed a Crisis Intervention Team (CIT) Academy in San Jose, California. The academy has distinguished itself through community collaboration and is well respected as a training model by the legislature and law enforcement community in California. The CIT Academy provides a 40-hour intensive training course that includes role playing, interactive participation of people with mental illness (consumers), identification of various symptoms and signs of medication use by consumers, crisis negotiation skills and tactics, panel discussions and feedback, visits to interim-type housing facilities, suicide and crisis training, and a constant review of all countywide protocols and incident procedures.[120] The training focuses on developing the most useful tool available to officers on the street: the ability to communicate in a nonthreatening manner.

The effective training of police officers in dealing with EDPs should result in two significant changes. First, there should be fewer incidents in which the use of force is necessary, thereby increasing officer safety. Second, effective training will provide a strong defense to litigation, should the department become entangled in litigation arising from the handling of an EDP.

Case law on the subject is still evolving. In 2015, the Supreme Court declined to expose two San Francisco police officers to liability under the Fourth Amendment after they shot a mentally ill woman who was brandishing a knife and making death threats. The incident occurred in August 2008, when a San Francisco city social worker called police after he was threatened by Teresa Sheehan when he went to check on her at the group home where she lived. When Sheehan refused

to open the door to the officers, they let themselves in with the key provided by the social worker, and the officers were confronted with Sheehan, who was holding the knife. The officers called for back-up but decided that Sheehan presented an imminent threat and entered her room before back-up arrived, with their guns drawn. After Sheehan could not be subdued with the use of less-lethal weapons (pepper spray), the officers opened fire, wounding Sheehan. She later sued for claimed violations of the Fourth Amendment and the Americans with Disabilities Act (ADA), a 1990 law that requires government programs to take steps to accommodate the disabled.

In *City and County of San Francisco vs. Sheehan*, the Court ruled that the officers did not violate the Constitution on their first entry into Sheehan's room and that the use of force on entering the second time was "reasonable," but it did not address whether the two officers were liable on Sheehan's constitutional claim that the Fourth Amendment required them to accommodate her mental condition. Hence, no landmark case exist that could have documented and established officer's duties under similar circumstance involving EDPs and the ADA—officers were immune to that specific claim.[121] However, the Department of Justice generally holds that Title II of the ADA includes all operations and activities of a police department, including the provision of reasonable accommodations during an arrest. So despite the lack of clarity from the Supreme Court and the inconsistency among lower courts related to whether the ADA requirement of reasonable accommodation applies to arrest, "a law enforcement agency may be subject to an enforcement action by the DOJ if reasonable accommodations are not provided during an arrest when dealing with a subject who is mentally ill."[122]

Box 14.3: Portland Police and Oregon Try to Impact Police Handling of Emotionally Disturbed Persons

Amid a rash of highly controversial shootings throughout the State of Oregon, the legislature passed Senate Bill 111 (SB 111) in late 2007, to be in force by the end of 2008. The law requires each county in the state to develop a plan regarding the use of deadly physical force by law enforcement officers. The purpose of the committee composed of various law enforcement executives within each of Oregon's 36 counties was to develop a deadly physical force plan to meet specific criteria:

• Develop proper training on the use of deadly force for police officers on a local and state-wide basis.

• Provide mechanisms for support for officers, civilians, and families of a community involved in a deadly force incident.

• Develop a specific process or protocol for investigating a deadly force incident.

• Determine whether the use of deadly force complied with applicable federal, state, and local law as well as the individual police department police.

• Stimulate research and interest on the issue of police use of deadly force.

Unfortunately, Oregon continues to suffer under the specter of questionable police use of deadly force. On January 29, 2010, an unarmed Aaron M. Campbell was shot in the back by members of the Portland Police Bureau SWAT team as he exited his apartment complex. Campbell, a person with a violent past including weapons charges and resisting arrest, had reportedly been suicidal after the death of his sister. During a bungled communication, officers mistakenly believed that Campbell made threatening gestures and the ensuing 50 rounds fired by the police was caught on video and widely dispersed on YouTube (see:—http://www.youtube.com/watch?v=_iwyd4ZHBUc).

The questionable shooting sparked an outrage in the city, with numerous public demonstrations and the firing of Chief of Police Rosie Sizer on May 12, 2010, in part for $1.6 million settlement for yet another questionable police-involved death. James A. Chasse, a skid-row bum with a history of mental illness was chased by police after allegedly urinating on the street. Witnesses indicated that police officers tackled, tased, and kicked Chasse as he laid defenseless on the ground. He died in the backseat of a police cruiser from injuries that included 26 breaks to 16 ribs and a punctured lung.

It is precisely these types of questionable incidents that cause significant strain between the police and public, and demand that police act appropriately in handling emotionally disturbed persons. The Portland Police Bureau remains under a Federal Consent Decree since 2012.

Source: See http://www.leg.state.or.us/07reg/measpdf/sb0100.dir/sb0111.c.pdf (Retrieved July 20, 2010); 'Why James Chasses' Story Matters to Portland,' *The Oregonian*, May 11, 2010; "Man Shot and Killed by Police, KPTV.com (February 1, 2010), see http://www.kptv.com/news/22383908/detail.html; Carol Cratty, "Portland Police, Justice Department Agree on Excessive Force Reform," *CNN* (December 17, 2012), see: http://www.cnn.com/2012/12/17/justice/portland-police-justice-department/.

FEDERAL CONSENT DECREES

The violent beating of Rodney King by several police officers in Los Angeles in 1991 shook the consciousness of the United States and set in motion one of the most sweeping mechanisms for controlling the police outside of civil litigation. After a high-speed pursuit stemming from a speeding violation, no less than 20 officers from the California Highway Patrol (the agency initiating the pursuit), the Los Angeles School District, the Los Angeles County Sheriff's Office, and the Los Angeles Police Department

Quick Facts: Officer Sues the Suspect

In an interesting turn of events, a white Chicago police officer counter-sued the estate of Quintonio LeGrier, an African-American teenager shot dead by the officer the day after Christmas, 2015. The officer, Robert Rialmos alleged that the 19-year-old LeGrier assaulted him with a baseball bat and caused him to suffer extensive trauma and post-traumatic stress. He argues that he had no other choice but to use deadly force against the teenager to save his life. He is seeking more than $10 million in damages. In the first-of-its-kind lawsuit, the officer's emotional as well as operational actions are considered in this controversial case involving police use of deadly force—one of many that have riddled the Chicago Police Department.

Source: Catherine E. Shoichet, Jeffrey Acevedo, and Tony Marco, "Chicago Cop Who Killed Quintonio LeGrier Sues Teen's Estate for $10 million" (Chicago, IL: CNN, February 9, 2016). See: http://www.cnn.com/2016/02/07/us/chicago-police-officer-sues-quintonio-legrier-estate/

responded to incident. Four LAPD officers were charged with the assault of King with a deadly weapon and the use of excessive force, as they were videotaped hitting, kicking, and tasing King. The ensuing trial ended with deadlocked jury and the acquittal of the officers. The incident triggered the 1992 Los Angeles riots in which 53 people were killed, 2,000 more were injured and millions of dollars of property damage occurred. The then Governor Pete Wilson activated the California National Guard in an effort to restore order.

As a result, the largest crime bill in the history of the United States, the 1994 Violent Crime Control and Law Enforcement Act was passed by Congress and signed into law by President Bill Clinton. The law provided for 100,000 new police officers, over $9.5 billion in funding for prison and another $6.1 billion in funding for community prevention programs. The law also funded the development of the Community Oriented Policing Services office within the U.S. Department of Justice (COPS Office) for another $14 billion aimed at not only hiring but also significantly training police officers in community policing programs aimed at bringing the police and minorities closer together. The law also gave, for the first time in American history, the federal government under the guidance of the U.S. Department of Justice, the power to sue local and state jurisdictions over a "pattern and practice" of policing that violated federal law or the U.S. Constitution. The impact of such suits has been dramatic in policing over the past two decades. The suits essentially compel the defendant jurisdiction to change their practice through what is commonly known as a **federal consent decree**. Specific agencies agree to demanded changes over specified timeframes that are formalized in a "memoranda of understanding" and enforced by external and neutral federal monitors that oversee the changes and subsequent compliance by the agency.

The first case of federal suit or consent decree was brought against the Pittsburgh (PA) Police Department in 1997 for a "pattern and practice" of police abuse, particularly against the black community.[123] Since that time, nearly 30 cities have entered into consent decrees with the Department of Justice, including a large variety of agencies such as Los Angeles Police Department (CA), Cincinnati and Cleveland Police Departments (OH), New Orleans Police Department (LA), Portland Police Bureau (OR), Detroit Police Department (MI), the New Jersey State Police, the Virgin Islands Police Department, Seattle Police Department (WA), Albuquerque Police Department (NM), and Missoula Police Department (MT). The importance of these consent decrees cannot be overstated in reforming rogue police agencies and department.[124] Transformational change within police cultures is difficult at best and in many instances, changing patterns of abuse and excessive force as well as abhorrent behavior requires significant time and focused external effort. Police agencies, as well as individual officers, must be accountable for their actions; federal consent decrees have made such an impact.[125]

Box 14.4: Police Sexual Violence (PSV): An Emerging Law Enforcement Issue

By John C. Liederbach and Robert W. Taylor

Police sexual violence (PSV) has emerged as a critical issue for law enforcement agencies. PSV is the most egregious form of police sexual misconduct and involves sexual harassment and violence—including rape and violent sexual assaults—perpetrated by police officers against victims who are most often women. The PSV issue has surfaced within the context of recent high-profile cases that clearly demonstrate the problem. The city of San Diego (CA), for example, recently (2015) paid $5.9 million to settle a civil lawsuit involving a former San Diego Police Department officer who groped a woman in a public restroom while on-duty. The officer was found guilty of 12 different sex-related charges perpetrated against five different woman during a previous criminal trial.[126] Other cases in Los Angeles (CA), Eugene (OR), Nassau County (NY), Houston (TX), Milwaukee (WN), and Chicago (IL) have also raised the specter of PSV. The International Association of Police Chiefs (IACP) has recognized PSV as an important problem for police agencies and has held official roundtable discussions and published policy recommendations that describe sex-related misconduct as an issue that "warrants the full attention of law enforcement leadership."[127]

Police work affords ample opportunities to rogue police officers to perpetrate acts of sexual deviance and violence. Opportunities for sex-related misconduct derive from the context of the job. Police commonly patrol alone and largely free from any direct supervision. Police commonly encounter citizens who are vulnerable, usually because they are victims or criminal suspects. Police–citizen interactions often occur in the late-night hours that provide low-public visibility and ample opportunities to those officers who are able and willing to take advantage of them to commit acts of sexual deviance and to perpetrate sex crimes.[128]

Cases of sex-related police misconduct and crime have been described as "hidden" offenses that are likely to go unreported; and hence, difficult to document and study. However, there is a limited but growing line of empirical research designed to identify and describe the problem of PSV. One of the earliest studies on the phenomenon is authored by Kraska and Kappeler.[129] They use published opinions of the federal district courts in Section 1983 actions to identify and describe cases that mostly involved the use of strip or body cavity searches by police; but also, less commonly involved sexual assaults or rape. Other studies use

(continued)

published court opinions to focus on PSV liability under state tort law, and the Section 1983 liability of individual officers engaged in PSV,[130] Walker and Irlbeck identify what they refer to as the national problem of "driving while female."[131] Police in these cases use the pretext of alleged traffic violations to sexually harass or abuse female drivers. A follow-up report also includes victims of sexual misconduct who were prostitutes or teenagers involved in police "explorer" programs. Rabe-Hemp and Braithwaite explore recidivism among police who perpetrate sex crimes. Their findings suggest that PSV is a "pattern prone" offense that often involves recidivist officers who victimize multiple persons; and, that many police accused of sex crimes manage to escape penalties and maintain police certification by moving from one jurisdiction to another.[132]

A 2014 national-scale study of PSV identifies and describes cases in which police officers were arrested for criminal offenses associated with sex-related misconduct through a content analysis of published newspaper articles. The study identified 548 arrests of police officers across the United States for sex-related crimes from 2005 to 2007. The most serious offense charged in over 20 percent of these cases was forcible rape ($n = 117$). There were also 107 cases of forcible fondling, 59 cases involving statutory rape, 54 cases involving forcible sodomy, and 39 cases involving child pornography. The study found that victims of sex-related police crime are typically female and younger than 18 years of age. The study overall demonstrates that the most egregious forms of PSV are not isolated events, a situation that presents considerable challenges to law enforcement executives.[133]

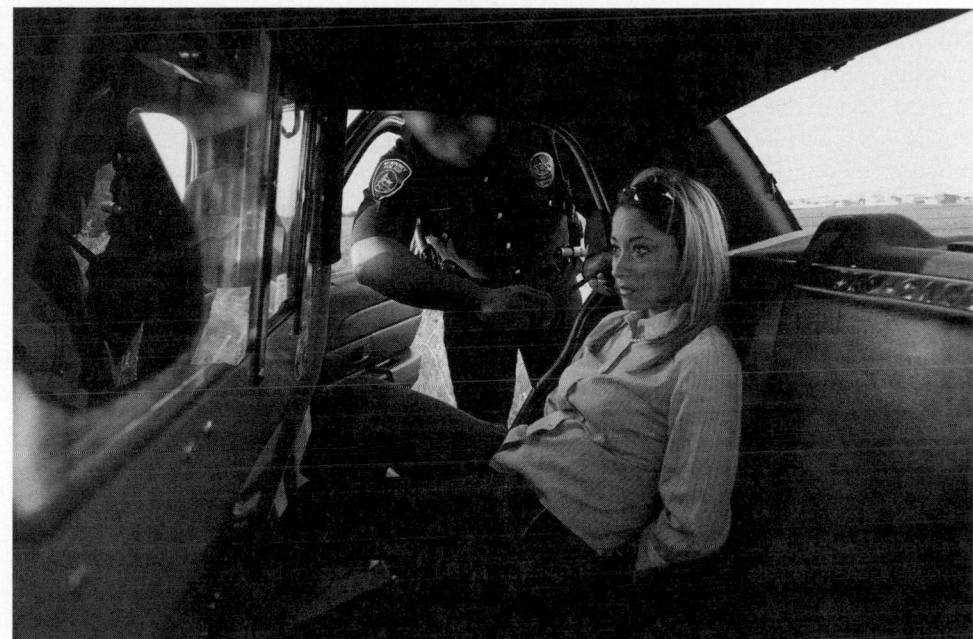

Police Sexual Violence (PSV) often occurs while the officer is working alone at night, with little or no direct supervision, and often hidden from public view. Victims of PSV are usually those who are most vulnerable to police power and abuse, oftentimes suspects of drug or alcohol-involved crimes such as DUI, or prostitutes or adult entertainment dancers who work late at night. (Jeremy Woodhouse/Blend Images/ Getty Images)

ADMINISTRATIVE DISCIPLINE: DUE PROCESS FOR POLICE OFFICERS

The Fifth and Fourteenth Amendments to the Constitution state that "no person shall be . . . deprived of life, liberty, or property, without **due process** of law."

Liberty and Property Rights of Police Officers

There are two general types of situations in the disciplinary process in which an employee of a law enforcement agency can claim the right to be protected by the guarantees of due process.[134] The first type involves those situations in which the

disciplinary action taken by the government employer threatens **liberty rights** of the officer. The second type involves a threat to **property rights**.

Liberty rights have been defined loosely as rights involving the protection and defense of one's good name, reputation, and position in the community. It has, at times, been extended further to include the right to preserve one's future career opportunities as well. Thus, when an officer's reputation, honor, or integrity is at stake because of government-imposed discipline, due process must be extended to the officer.[135]

It should be noted that the use of the "liberty rights" approach as a basis for requiring procedural due process has proven extremely difficult. The Supreme Court further restricted the use of this legal theory by holding that it can be utilized only when the employer is shown to have created and publicly disseminated a false and defamatory impression about the employee.[136]

The more substantial and meaningful type of due process guarantee is that pertaining to the protection of one's property. Although the general concept of property extends only to real estate and tangible possessions, the courts have developed the concept that a person's property also includes the many valuable intangible belongings acquired in the normal course of life, such as the expectation of continued employment. However, not all employees are entitled to its protection.

The courts have consistently held that an employee acquires a protected interest in a job (property interest or right) only when it can be established that there exists a justifiable expectation that employment will continue without interruption except for dismissal or other discipline based on just or proper cause. This expectation of continued employment is sometimes called "tenure" or "permanent status."[137]

Federal courts have been inclined to read employment laws liberally so as to grant property rights whenever possible. For example, the Fifth Circuit Court of Appeals found that a city employment regulation that allowed termination "only for cause" created a constitutionally protected property interest.[138] A federal district court held that a Florida statute (Section 112.532), known as the "Law Enforcement Officers' and Correctional Officers' Bill of Rights," created a property interest in employment because of its disciplinary notice provisions.[139] That approach is consistent with those of other jurisdictions in which state statutes have been interpreted to give property interests in a job to local government employees.[140]

Once a liberty or property right has been established, certain due process guarantees attach to protect the employee. The question becomes, what process is due?

The question of due process for police officers falls into two categories: **procedural due process** and **substantive due process**. The former, as its name implies, refers to the legality of the procedures used to deprive police officers of status or wages, such as dismissal or suspension from their job. Substantive due process is a more difficult and elusive concept. Simply, substantive due process is the requirement that the basis for government disciplinary action be reasonable, relevant, and justifiable.

Procedural Due Process

One of the 20th century's preeminent administrative law scholars, Kenneth Culp Davis, identified 12 main elements of a due process hearing:

(1) timely and adequate notice, (2) a chance to make an oral statement or argument, (3) a chance to present witnesses and evidence, (4) confrontation of adverse witnesses, (5) cross-examination of adverse witnesses, (6) disclosure of all evidence relied upon, (7) a decision based on the record of evidence, (8) a right to retain an attorney, (9) a publicly compensated attorney for an indigent, (10) a statement of findings of fact, (11) a statement of reasons or a reasoned opinion, and (12) an impartial deciding officer.[141]

The courts have not examined all the trial elements in the context of the police disciplinary process. However, some cases have held that police officers must be informed of the charges on which the action is based,[142] be given the right to call witnesses,[143] be confronted by the witnesses against them,[144] be permitted to cross-examine the witnesses against them,[145] be permitted to have counsel represent them,[146] have a decision rendered on the basis of the record developed at the hearing,[147] and have the decision made by an impartial hearing officer.[148]

A question that has proven particularly troublesome for the courts is whether due process requires that an evidentiary hearing be held before the disciplinary action being taken. In *Arnett v. Kennedy*, a badly divided Supreme Court held that a "hearing afforded by administrative appeal after the actual dismissal is a sufficient compliance with the requirements of the Due Process Clause."[149] In a concurring opinion, Justice Powell observed that the question of whether a hearing must be accorded before an employee's removal "depends on a balancing process in which the government's interest in expeditious removal of an unsatisfactory employee is weighed against the interest of the affected employee in continued public employment."[150] In *Mathews v. Eldridge*, the Supreme Court set forth the competing interests that must be weighed to determine what process is due to (1) the private interest that will be affected by the official action; (2) the risk of an erroneous deprivation of such interest through the procedures used and the probable value, if any, of additional or substitute procedural safeguards; and (3) the government's interest, including the function involved and the fiscal and administrative burdens that the additional or substitute procedural requirement would entail.[151]

In 1985, the Court further clarified the issue of pretermination due process in *Cleveland Board of Education v. Loudermill*.[152] The Court found that public employees possessing property interests in their employment have a right to "notice and an opportunity to respond" before termination. The Court cautioned that its decision was based on the employees also having an opportunity for a full posttermination hearing. Therefore, assuming that a public employee will be able to challenge the termination in a full-blown evidentiary hearing after the fact, pretermination due process should include an initial check against mistaken decisions—essentially, a determination of whether there are reasonable grounds to believe that the charges against the employee are true and support the proposed action. The Court went on to describe an acceptable pretermination procedure as one that provides the employee with oral or written notice of the charges against him or her, an explanation of the employer's evidence, and an opportunity to present his or her side of the story. The Court reasoned that the government interest in the immediate termination of an unsatisfactory employee is outweighed by an employee's interest in retaining employment and the interest in avoiding the risk of an erroneous termination.[153] In 1997, the Court ruled that public employees do not have the right to a hearing before suspension without pay as long as the suspension is short, the effect on pay is insubstantial, and the employee is guaranteed a postsuspension hearing.[154]

Thus, it is clear that public employees who can legitimately claim liberty or property right protections of due process for their jobs are guaranteed an evidentiary hearing. Such a hearing should be conducted before disciplinary action is taken unless the pre-discipline protections just mentioned are provided, in which case the full-blown hearing could be postponed until afterward.

For administrators with a collective bargaining relationship with their employees, where minimal procedural safeguards are provided in contractual grievance provisions, that avenue of relief may provide an acceptable substitute for constitutionally mandated procedural rights.[155]

Substantive Due Process

As mentioned earlier, due process requirements embrace substantive as well as procedural aspects. In the context of disciplinary action, substantive due process requires that the rules and regulations on which disciplinary action is predicated be clear, specific, and reasonably related to a valid public need.[156] In the police environment, these requirements present the greatest challenge to the commonly found departmental regulations against conduct unbecoming an officer or conduct that brings discredit on the department.

The requirement that a rule or regulation be reasonably related to a valid public need means that a police department may not intrude into the private matters of its officers in which it has no legitimate interest. Therefore, there must be a connection "between the prohibited conduct and the officer's fitness to perform the duties required by his position."[157] In addition, the conduct must be of such a nature as to adversely affect the morale and efficiency of the department or have a tendency to destroy public respect for and confidence in the department.[158] Thus, it has been held that a rule prohibiting unbecoming conduct or discrediting behavior cannot be applied to a police officer's remarks that were highly critical of several prominent local figures but were made to a private citizen in a private conversation in a patrol car and were broadcast accidentally over the officer's patrol car radio.[159]

The requirements for clarity and specificity are necessary to ensure that (1) the innocent are not trapped without fair warning, (2) those who enforce the regulations have their discretion limited by explicit standards, and (3) where basic First Amendment rights are affected by a regulation, the regulation does not operate unreasonably to inhibit the exercise of those rights.[160]

The courts' applications of these requirements to unbecoming conduct and discrediting behavior rules have taken two courses. The first course, exemplified by *Bence v. Breier*, has been to declare such regulations unconstitutional because of their vagueness. In its consideration of a Milwaukee Police Department rule that prohibited "conduct unbecoming a member and detrimental to the service," the court found that the rule lacked

inherent, objective content from which ascertainable standards defining the proscribed conduct could be fashioned. Like beauty, their content exists only in the eye of the beholder. The subjectivity implicit in the language of the rule permits police officials to enforce the rule with unfettered

discretion, and it is precisely this potential for arbitrary enforcement which is abhorrent to the Due Process Clause.[161]

The second course taken by the courts has been to uphold the constitutionality of the regulation because, as applied to the officer in the case at hand, it should have been clear to him that his behavior was meant to be proscribed by the regulation. Under this approach, the court is saying that there may or may not be some circumstances in which the rule is too vague or overbroad, but the rule is constitutional in the present case. Thus, it should be clear to any police officer that fleeing from the scene of an accident[162] or making improper advances toward a young woman during the course of an official investigation[163] constitutes conduct unbecoming an officer or conduct that discredits the police department.

Many police departments also have a regulation prohibiting neglect or dereliction of duty. Although on its face such a rule seems to possess some of the same potential vagueness and over breadth shortcomings characteristic of the unbecoming conduct rules, it has fared better in the courts because the usual disciplinary action taken under neglect-of-duty rules nearly always seems to be for conduct for which police officers could reasonably expect disciplinary action. The courts have upheld administrative sanctions against officers under neglect-of-duty rules for sleeping on the job,[164] failing to prepare for planned demonstrations,[165] falsification of police records,[166] failure to make scheduled court appearances,[167] failure to investigate a reported auto accident,[168] and directing a subordinate to discontinue enforcement of a city ordinance.[169] The courts have refused to uphold disciplinary action against a police chief who did not keep 8-to-4 office hours,[170] and against an officer who missed a training session on riot control because of marital problems.[171]

Damages and Remedies

In determining an employee's entitlement to damages and relief, the issue of whether the employer's disciplinary action was justified is important. For example, when an employee's termination was justified but procedural due process violations occurred, the employee can recover only nominal damages in the absence of proof of actual compensable injuries deriving from the due process violation. On proof of actual injury, an employee can recover compensatory damages, which would include damages for mental and emotional distress and damage to career or reputation.[172] However, injury caused by the lack of due process when the termination was justified is not compensable in the form of back pay.[173]

CONSTITUTIONAL RIGHTS OF POLICE OFFICERS

Police officers have the same individual rights that all citizens within the United States are afforded under the U.S. Constitution. Even though they have been given significant training, held to a higher standard of conduct, and are subject to public and legal scrutiny, they still enjoy the same protections afforded to everyone else in our society.

Free Speech

The First Amendment of the U.S. Constitution prohibits Congress from passing any law "abridging the freedom of speech." It has been held that the due process clause of the Fourteenth Amendment makes this prohibition applicable to the states, counties, and cities as well.[174]

Although freedom of speech is one of the most fundamental of all constitutional rights, the Supreme Court has indicated that "the State has interests as an employer in regulating the speech of its employees that differ significantly from those it possesses in connection with regulation of the speech of the citizenry in general."[175] Therefore, the state may place restrictions on the speech of its employees that it could not impose on the general citizenry. However, these restrictions must be reasonable.[176] Generally, disputes involving the infringement of public employee speech will be resolved by balancing the interests of the state as an employer against the employee's constitutional rights.[177]

There are two basic situations in which a police regulation or other action can be found to be an unreasonable infringement on the free speech interests of an officer. The first is when the action is overly broad. A Chicago Police Department rule prohibiting "any activity, conversation, deliberation, or discussion which is derogatory to the Department" was ruled overly broad because it prohibited all criticism of the department by police officers, even if the criticism occurred in private conversation.[178] The same fate befell a New Orleans Police Department regulation that prohibited statements by a police officer that "unjustly criticize or ridicule, or express hatred or contempt toward, or . . . which may be detrimental to, or cast suspicion on the reputation of, or otherwise defame, any person."[179]

The second situation in which a free speech limitation can be found unreasonable is in the way in which the government action is applied. The most common shortcoming of police departmental action in this area is a failure to demonstrate that the statements by the officer being disciplined adversely affected the operation of the department.[180] Thus, a Baltimore police regulation prohibiting public criticism of departmental action was held to have been applied unconstitutionally to a police officer who was president of the police union and who had stated in a television interview that the police commissioner was not leading the department effectively and that "the bottom is going to fall out of this city."[181] In this case, no significant disruption of the department was noted. However, when two officers of the Kinloch, Missouri Police Department publicly complained of corruption within city government, the court held that the "officers conducted a campaign . . . with complete disregard of chain of command motivated by personal desires that created disharmony among the 12-member police force."[182] Because the allegations were totally unfounded and were not asserted correctly through channels instituted by state "whistle-blower" procedures, the dismissals were upheld.

A more recent basis for enforcing employees' First Amendment freedom of speech is that of public policy. The Court of Appeals for the Eighth Circuit held that discharging an employee who violated the police department's chain of command by reporting misconduct to an official outside of the city violated the employee's First Amendment rights. The court reasoned that the city's interest in maintaining discipline through the chain-of-command policy was outweighed by the public's vital interest in the integrity of its law enforcers and by the employee's right to speak out on such matters.[183] Generally, speech about corruption or criminal activity within the officer's law enforcement agency is very likely to be given protection under the First Amendment, especially when such speech is protected by a state "whistle-blower statute."[184] Central to a successful claim under a whistle-blower statute is that the employee show that discipline resulted from the employee's reporting of a violation of the law. Essentially, there must be an element of retaliation against the employee for publicly reporting illegal conduct.[185] The employee need only have a reasonable belief that illegal conduct has occurred and need not have absolute proof of the illegality.[186]

It appears that one's right to speak openly about the policies of a police department may well depend on four important factors: (1) the impact of the statements on the routine operations of the department, (2) the truth of the statements, (3) the manner in which the statements are made regarding existing policy orders involving chain-of-command and state whistle-blower regulations, and (4) the position occupied by the officer. For instance, statements made by dispatchers, clerks, and first-line officers in a large department that have relatively little impact might be given much more tolerance than supervisory or command personnel complaining of departmental policy because the degree of influence, validity, and credibility significantly increases with rank.

Other First Amendment Rights

A basic right of Americans in our democratic system of government is the right to engage in political activity. As with free speech, the government may impose reasonable restrictions on the political behavior of its employees that it could not impose on the citizenry at large. It is argued that, if the state could not impose some such restrictions, there would be a substantial danger that employees could be pressured by their superiors to support political candidates or causes that were contrary to their own beliefs under threat of loss of employment or other adverse action against them for failure to do so.[187]

At the federal level, various types of partisan political activity by federal employees are controlled by the Hatch Act. The constitutionality of that act has been upheld by the Supreme Court.[188] Many states have similar statutes, which are usually referred to as "little Hatch" acts, controlling political activity by state employees. The Oklahoma version of the Hatch Act, which was upheld by the Supreme Court,[189] prohibited state employees from soliciting political contributions, joining a partisan political club, serving on the committee of a political party, being a candidate for any paid political office, or taking part in the management of a political party or campaign. However, some states, such as Florida, specifically prohibit local governments from limiting the off-duty political activity of their employees.

Nonpolitical associations are also protected by the First Amendment. However, it is common for police departments to prohibit officers from associating with known felons or other persons of bad reputation on the basis that "such associations may expose an officer to irresistible temptations to yield in his obligation to impartially enforce the law, and . . . may give the appearance that the community's police officers are not themselves honest and impartial enforcers of the law."[190] Sometimes, the prohibition is imposed by means of a specific ordinance or regulation, whereas in other instances, the prohibition is enforced by considering it conduct unbecoming an officer. Of course, if the latter approach is used, the ordinance or regulation will have to overcome the legal obstacles discussed earlier, relating to unbecoming conduct or discrediting behavior rules.

As with rules touching on the other First Amendment rights, rules prohibiting associations with criminals and other undesirables must not be overly broad in their reach. Thus, a Detroit Police Department regulation that prohibited knowing and intentional associations with convicted criminals or persons charged with crimes except in the course of an officer's official duties was declared unconstitutional because it proscribed some associations that could have no bearing on an officer's integrity or the public's confidence in an officer. The court cited as examples an association with a fellow church member who had been arrested on one occasion years ago and the befriending of a recently convicted person who wanted to become a productive citizen.[191]

The other common difficulty with this kind of rule is that it is sometimes applied to situations in which the association has not been demonstrated to have had a detrimental effect on the performance of the officer's duties or on the discipline and efficiency of the department. Thus, one court has held that a police officer who was a nudist but was fully qualified in all other respects to be a police officer could not be fired simply because he was a practicing nudist.[192] On the other hand, another court upheld the firing of a police officer who had sexual intercourse at a party with a woman he knew to be a nude model at a local "adult theater of known disrepute."[193] The court viewed this behavior as being of such a disreputable nature that it had a detrimental effect on the discipline and efficiency of the department. In 2005, the Supreme Court determined that the police department could terminate an officer for selling a sexually explicit videotape of himself, in which he identified himself as a police officer. The Court ruled that, even though the activities of the officer took place outside the workplace, the department "demonstrated legitimate and substantial interests of its own that were compromised by the officer's speech" and the activities did not fall under free speech protections.[194]

The First Amendment's protection of free speech has been viewed as protecting means of expression other than verbal utterances.[195] That issue as it relates to an on-duty police officer's personal appearance was addressed by the Supreme Court decision in *Kelley v. Johnson*,[196] which upheld the constitutionality of a regulation of the Suffolk County, New York Police Department that established several grooming standards for its male officers. The Court in *Kelley* held that either a desire to make police officers readily recognizable to the public or a desire to maintain an esprit de corps was a sufficiently rational justification for the regulation. The issue of personal grooming and style continues to be a subject of hot debate in departments across the nation, particularly as officers move closer to their constituencies through community policing endeavors.

Searches and Seizures and the Right to Privacy

The Fourth Amendment to the U.S. Constitution protects "the right of the people to be secure in their persons, houses, papers, and effects, against unreasonable searches and seizures." This guarantee protects against actions by states and the federal government.[197] Generally, the cases interpreting the Fourth Amendment require that, before a search or seizure can be effectuated, the police must have **probable cause** to believe that a crime has been committed and that evidence relevant to the crime will be found at the place to be searched. Because of the language

---

Quick Facts: Police Membership in Hate Groups

In 2015, a police officer was forced to resign in San Francisco because of racist text messages, and a police officer and a lieutenant in the Anniston, Alabama police department were terminated following the discovery of a YouTube video that showed their participation in a neo-Confederate, white supremist group called the *League of the South (LOS)*. In both of these cases, the officers had extensive Facebook pages which depicted their racist perspectives on all minorities, and members of the gay, lesbian, and transgender population. The Anniston case, the group was identified by the Southern Poverty Law Center as a "hate group" which strongly supported the city's action. However, at the heart of the matter is whether an officer can be terminated for his or her own personal perspectives of race or their membership in a "civic club" even if that club, although legal and lawfully formed, expresses extreme bigotry, racism and hate (e.g., the KKK, neo-Nazi groups, and Skinheads). The answer is cleared when a policy exists within the department that prohibits actions of racism or hate that would violate the spirit of the U.S. Constitution and/or embarrass the department. In these cases, as well as in many others, racial bigotry cannot and will not be tolerated in police organizations.

in the Fourth Amendment about "persons, houses, papers, and effects," for years the case law analyzed what property was subject to the amendment's protection. However, in *Katz v United States* (1967)[198] the Supreme Court established a two-pronged test that accounted for both property and the *privacy expectations* of a person.[199] The two prongs are: 1) the person has an expectation of privacy, which is a subjective test and 2) the expectation of privacy is reasonable in the fact situation. This test has been used in decisions that affect not only police officers, but employees in other sectors of our economy as well. In this section we examine how these decisions have specifically impacted officers' right to privacy with respect to departmental supplied lockers, communication devices (such as cell phones and radios), and equipment generally.

In a case involving a police officer suspected of gambling, the Supreme Court held that the use of a pen register did not require the same constitutional safeguards as those surrounding a wiretap. The pen register uses a "trap-and-trace" device that records phone numbers and the duration of each call but does not capture any type of communication between parties. The Court reasoned that no warrant or probable cause was needed, as the Fourth Amendment was applicable to captured communication only and that there was no reasonable expectation to privacy regarding the actual phone number.[200]

The Fourth Amendment usually applies to police officers when at home or off duty as it would to any other citizen. In general, police officers cannot sustain a reasonable privacy expectation claim when using government issued/departmental lockers,[201] communications devices, and other equipment, for example, cars, desks, and filing cabinets. Many police agencies reinforce the applicable court decisions by formal policy, noting that all departmentally owned items such as lockers, desks, and cell phones may be opened and inspected at any time by an appropriate representative for both routine inspection as well as in the course of an investigation. Some agencies even go into such detail as to require the use of a department-issued lock on lockers, and prohibit the use of secondary/private locks. Further, in a landmark case in 2010, the Court ruled unanimously that a search of a police officer's personal, and sometimes sexually explicit, text messages on a city-owned pager was constitutional, even though it was conducted without a warrant.[202] By extension of previous case logic, cell phone communications and e-mail on a city-owned cell phone or computer would also not be protected material and the officer does not have a constitutional right to privacy regarding these devices. Again, there appears not to be an expectation of privacy for officers when using government-owned devices or equipment.

Another situation involves the ordering of officers to appear at a lineup. Requiring someone to appear in a lineup is a seizure of his or her person and, therefore, would ordinarily require probable cause. However, a federal Appeals Court upheld a police commissioner's order to 62 officers to appear in a lineup for the purpose of identifying officers who had allegedly beaten several civilians. The court held that, in this situation, "the governmental interest in the particular intrusion (should be weighed) against the offense to personal dignity and integrity." Because of the nature of the police officer's employment relationship, "he does not have the full privacy and liberty from police officials that he would otherwise enjoy."[203]

To enforce the protections guaranteed by the Fourth Amendment's search-and-seizure requirements, the courts have fashioned the so-called *exclusionary rule*, which prohibits the use of evidence obtained in violation of the Fourth Amendment in criminal proceedings. However, in a series of cases, the Supreme Court has redefined the concept of "reasonableness" as it applies to the Fourth Amendment and the exclusionary rule. In *United States v. Leon* and the companion case of *Massachusetts v. Sheppard*, the Court held that the Fourth Amendment "requires officers to have reasonable knowledge of what the law prohibits" in a search.[204] In essence, *Leon* and *Sheppard* began to develop the concept of "totality of circumstances" confirmed in *Illinois v. Gates*—that is, that evidence cannot be suppressed when an officer is acting "under good faith" whether or not a warrant issued is good on the surface.[205] These cases have far-reaching implications in civil actions against police officers, in that officers enjoy the benefits of qualified immunity when they are acting in good faith and under the belief that probable cause does exist.[206] Indeed, the Court has held that only a clear absence of probable cause will defeat a claim of qualified immunity.[207]

Finally, the exclusionary rule and the previously mentioned cases have an important bearing on disciplinary hearings involving the police. In *Sheetz v. Mayor and City Council of Baltimore*, the court held that illegally seized drugs in the possession of an officer could be used in an administrative discharge proceeding against that officer.[208] The Court reasoned that only a bad-faith seizure would render the evidence inadmissible because the police are not motivated to seize illegally for the purpose of use in an administrative discharge proceeding; hence, the exclusionary rule was not applicable, and the officer's firing was upheld.

Right Against Self-Incrimination

On two occasions, the Supreme Court has addressed questions concerning the Fifth Amendment rights of police officers who are the subjects of investigations. In *Garrity v. New Jersey*,[209] a police officer had been ordered by the attorney general to answer certain questions or be discharged. The officer testified, and the information gained as a result of his answers was later used to convict him of criminal charges.

The Fifth Amendment protects an individual from being compelled "in any criminal case to be a witness against himself."[210] The Supreme Court held that the information obtained from the police officer could not be used at his or her criminal trial because the Fifth Amendment forbids the use of coercion of this sort to extract an incriminating statement from a suspect.

In *Gardner v. Broderick*,[211] a police officer had declined to answer questions put to him by a grand jury investigating police misconduct on the grounds that his answers might tend to incriminate him. As a result, the officer was dismissed from his job. The Supreme Court ruled that the officer could not be fired for his refusal to waive his constitutional right to remain silent. However, the Court made it clear that it would have been proper for the grand jury to require the officer to answer or face discharge for his refusal, as long as the officer had been informed that his answers could not be used against him in a criminal case and the questions were related specifically, directly, and narrowly to the performance of his official duties. The Court felt that this approach was necessary to protect the important state interest in ensuring that the police officers were performing their duties faithfully.

In its ruling, the Supreme Court set forth a basic standard for disciplinary investigations of police officers. Referring to *Garrity*, the Court ruled that although a police agency can conduct an administrative investigation of an officer, it cannot in the course of that investigation compel the officer to waive his or her privilege against self-incrimination. As it has been interpreted, *Garrity* requires that before a police agency can question an officer regarding an issue that may involve disciplinary action against the officer for refusal to answer questions, the agency must do the following:

1. Order the officer to answer the questions.
2. Ask questions that are specifically, directly, and narrowly related to the officer's duties.
3. Advise the officer that the answers to the questions will not be used against the officer in criminal proceedings.[212]

If the officer refuses to answer appropriate questions after being given these warnings and advisement, then he or she may be disciplined for insubordination.

As a result of these cases, it is proper to discharge police officers who refuse to answer questions that are related specifically and directly to the performance of their duties and who have been informed that any answers they do give cannot be used against them in a criminal proceeding.[213]

Historically, it was not uncommon for police departments to make use of polygraph examinations in the course of internal investigations. The legal question that has arisen most frequently is whether an officer can be required to submit to such a procedure under threat of discharge for refusal to do so. There is some diversity of legal authority on this question, but the majority of courts that have considered it have held that an officer can be required to take the examination.[214]

An Arizona court overturned a county merit system commission's finding that a polygraph examination could be ordered only as a last resort after all other investigative efforts had been exhausted and held that

> a polygraph is always proper to verify statements made by law enforcement officers during the course of a departmental investigation as long as the officers are advised that the answers cannot be used against them in any criminal prosecution, that the questions will relate solely to the performance of official duties, and that refusal will result in dismissal.[215]

The use of polygraph examinations as a viable tool for internal affairs investigations was further strengthened by a state court in 2008.[216] The Massachusetts appeals court found that the Plymouth police department did not violate the state's statute by requiring a police officer who was accused of sexually molesting two minors to take a polygraph test for suspicion of criminal misconduct. After refusing to take the examination, the officer was terminated for "just cause."

On the other hand, a more recent decision of the Florida Supreme Court held that the dismissal of a police officer for refusing to submit to a polygraph test constituted "an unjust and unlawful job deprivation." Further, the court recognized that granting to public employers a carte blanche authority to force employees to submit to unlimited questioning during a polygraph test would conflict with the employees' constitutional right of privacy and would abrogate their protection against self-incrimination.[217]

Further, the use of a polygraph test to screen job applicants for police jobs has fallen under severe criticism. In 1987, a federal judge declared the test to be both unconstitutional and unreliable and ordered the city of Philadelphia to reconsider the applications of individuals denied positions because of their failure to pass a polygraph test. Conversely, the court of appeals reversed the district court holding and stated that the use of polygraph tests for pre-employment screening did not violate either equal protection or substantive due process.[218]

As a result of these cases and the resulting ambiguity concerning polygraph testing and the Fifth Amendment, most jurisdictions have limited the use of the polygraph by statute and/or administrative regulation. Also, most agencies have developed extensive internal policies to limit the use of the polygraph and to expressly detail circumstances in which the test may be used to corroborate officer statements.

OTHER GROUNDS FOR DISCIPLINARY ACTION

Although police officers enjoy the same constitutional rights as other citizens within the United States, they are clearly held to a different standard of conduct both on and off the job. In many cases, their actions do not rise to the level of a criminal complaint yet still become the grounds for disciplinary actions that may result in termination and loss of career.

Conduct Unbecoming an Officer

By far, the largest number of police disciplinary cases arise under rules prohibiting conduct unbecoming an officer. These rules have traditionally been vague and overly broad in order to control officers both on and off duty.[219] Most "conduct unbecoming" regulations have been challenged for being unconstitutionally vague.[220] The basis of this claim rests in the concept of reasonableness as applied to the misconduct.[221] In a leading case, the California Supreme Court held that the permissible application of a "conduct unbecoming" regulation turns on whether the officer could reasonably anticipate that his or her conduct would be the subject of discipline:

> *We construe "conduct unbecoming" a city police officer to refer only to conduct which indicates a* lack of fitness *to*

perform the functions of a police officer. Thus construed, [the rule] provides a sufficiently specific standard against which the conduct of a police officer in a particular case can be judged. Police officers . . . will normally be able to determine what kind of conduct indicates unfitness to perform the functions of police officer.[222]

A wide variety of conduct has been held to fall appropriately within the scope of a "conduct unbecoming" regulation. It is important to note that the regulation must reasonably warn the officer of what type of conduct would be considered unbecoming and that said conduct would tend to affect the officer's performance of his or her duties adversely or cause the department to fall into public disrepute.[223] Some of the activities that commonly fall within the scope of a "conduct unbecoming" regulation and that have been upheld by the courts include associating with crime figures or persons with a criminal record,[224] verbal abuse and swearing,[225] off-duty drinking and intoxication,[226] criminal conduct,[227] dishonesty,[228] fighting with coworkers,[229] insubordination,[230] and a number of improprieties involving sexual activity, including promiscuity and fraternizing with known prostitutes.

One of the more interesting and recent cases involving "conduct unbecoming an officer" involved the Federal Bureau of Investigation in 2009. In *Doe v. U.S. Department of Justice*,[231] Doe argued that the FBI failed to show that his off-duty misconduct affected the "efficiency of the service" of his employment. The FBI's Office of Responsibility developed an investigation revealing that Doe had videotaped his personal sexual activities with women, including two women in his division, and that he might have done so without their consent. Doe was terminated for "unprofessional conduct"—conduct unbecoming an agent of the Federal Bureau of Investigation. Although an external review by the Merit Systems Protection Board (MSPB) supported the FBI's decision to fire Doe, the Federal Circuit Court of Appeals ruled that the FBI failed to address how Doe's off-duty and personal conduct negatively impacted the agency's "ability to perform" its mission. Further, the court ruled that the FBI failed to point out a violation of a specific internal policy that fit the circumstances of the conduct. Consequently, the MSPB's decision was reversed and remanded, and John Doe continues to be a Special Agent with the FBI. The case appears to reaffirm the concept that cases resting on "conduct unbecoming an officer" must not be overly vague, must indeed violate specific policies, and the behavior must be shown to negatively impact the agency in some manner.

Brady Violations

In a landmark 1963 case (*Brady v. Maryland*),[232] the U.S. Supreme Court ruled that the suppression of any evidence by the prosecution favorable to the accused violates the due process clauses of the Fourth and Fourteenth Amendments of the Constitution. As a result, prosecutors were compelled to disclose to the defense any and all evidence that might be exculpatory for the accused—meaning any evidence that could possibly clear the suspect must be presented to the defense. Such evidence could include physical evidence, fingerprints, DNA, photographs, and the alike, which conflicts with the prosecutor's evidence, and any evidence that could impeach the credibility of a prosecution witness.

More importantly for police administrators, in a follow-up case, *Giglio v. United States* and other *Brady* progeny cases,[233] the Court extended that obligation to share exculpatory

---

Box 14.5: Female Police Officers Still Have to Fight for the Right to Breastfeed on Duty, Despite Federal Law that Permits It

A police officer in Washington, DC has raised concern about the lack of private lactation rooms for female officers.

In a case that challenges gender stereotypes and perceptions of police officers, female officers in many police departments have had to fight to have a secure, clean place to pump milk for their babies.

In 2011, the Affordable Care Act amended the Fair Labor Standards Act to hold that employers must provide a place, *other than a restroom*, that is shielded from view and free from intrusion in order for employees to express breast milk. However, police agencies have been slow to adapt to this change. The Metropolitan Police Department in Washington, DC, led by Cathy Lanier, was still directing employees as late as 2014 to bathroom stalls for the purposes of pumping—an unsanitary and unsavory practice that also had the effect of humiliating lactating police officers.

Officers have also reported that supervisors required them to log in and out when they pumped, taking note of the amount of time that they spent and requiring them to take leave when they pumped outside of their lunch hour. This is not illegal but does create difficulties for female police officers with young children.

The federal law is clear on the availability of private and appropriate lactation rooms, however—but many female officers feel that they will be retaliated against or mocked if they press the issue. For now, many police moms are forced to seek space in restrooms, utility closets and even patrol cars in order to provide milk for their infants.

Source: Emily Miller, "DC police department violates federal breastfeeding law." November 12, 2014. Retrieved on August 7, 2015 from: http://www.myfoxdc.com/story/27370521/dc-police-department-violates-federal-breastfeeding-law information with the defendant to include information concerning the credibility of the prosecution's witnesses, including individual police officers. As a result, police agencies must disclose to the prosecution, who must disclose to the defense, any exculpatory or impeachment evidence that demonstrates that a witness is lying about specific facts in a case or is generally unworthy of belief. Evidence of this nature is often referred to as "*Brady* material." Failing to disclose such evidence is a "*Brady*" violation that can lead to dismissal of the criminal case and civil (U.S. Code 42, Section 1983) cases brought against the individual prosecutor, the police department, and the officer for violation of the suspect's constitutional rights.

LYING

Brady cases have had a dramatic effect on the credibility of individual police officers as witnesses. Because the prosecution is bound to reveal any possible impeachment evidence regarding its own witnesses, an officer's internal affairs records and any documented report where the officer lied or was untruthful must be presented as *Brady* material. Such officers simply cannot testify in court without being impeached; hence, their ability to work as a police officer is seriously compromised. For this reason, many police departments now have policies that terminate an employee for lying.

Social network sites

Although past incidents of lying and untruthfulness form the basis for impeaching the individual officer under *Brady*, there are indeed other issues that warrant discussion. Postings on social network sites have recently been entered into evidence in successful attempts to discredit police officers. Take, for example, officers who have posted racy and/or nude photos of themselves on their Facebook page, or pictures of officers taking drugs or drinking excessively on YouTube, or statements by officers that are offensive, racist, and show extreme bias on Twitter or a local blog. These examples show not only poor judgment on the part of the officer, but in the worst case, provide potential evidence for impeachment during a trial. While the behavior does not comport to *Brady* technically, this type of material can still be used to impeach the officer's credibility. As a general rule, the following "tips" are offered for police using social networking sites:

- *No nudity or sexually explicit pictures*—This includes pictures of you or you with a friend who is disrobed. Understand that your Facebook pictures and YouTube videos can easily be presented in court.
- *No drug taking or excessive alcohol postings*—Keep private "partying" photos to a minimum.
- *No gun glorification*—Keep your weapon and other police equipment off your social networking sites, and keep pictures of you in uniform off your social network sites.

- *Avoid bashing the department and keep rumors quiet*—Not only does this alleviate issues previously discussed that may indeed "interfere with the official business of the department," but also protects you from potential civil actions if the statements are found to be untrue.
- *Restrict personal information and manage your privacy settings*—Remember that suspects use the computer as well and that personal information relating to your address and family may place you in harm's way.[234]

Sexual Conduct and Sexual Orientation

The cases in this area tend to fall into two general categories: cases involving adultery and cases involving homosexuality. Most cases are in general agreement that adultery, even though committed while the police officer is off duty and in private, created a proper basis for disciplinary action.[235] The courts held that such behavior brings adverse criticism on the agency and tends to undermine public confidence in the department. However, one case involving an Internal Revenue Service agent suggests that to uphold disciplinary action for adultery, the government would have to prove that the employing agency was actually discredited; the court further stated that the discreditation would not be presumed from the proof of adulterous conduct.[236]

More recently, the Supreme Court justices appeared to be divided on the issue of extramarital sexual activity in public employment. In 1984, the Court of Appeals for the Sixth Circuit held that a Michigan police officer could not be fired solely because he was living with a woman to whom he was not married (a felony under state law). In 1985, the Supreme Court denied review of that decision over the strong objection of three justices who felt the case "presented an important issue of constitutional law regarding the contours of the right of privacy afforded individuals for sexual matters."[237]

In cases involving sexual improprieties that clearly affect an officer's on-the-job performance, the courts have had far less controversy. In a series of cases, the courts have consistently supported the disciplinary action attached to the department's "conduct unbecoming" regulation, including cases in which officers were cohabiting or in which the sexual activities were themselves illegal (e.g., public lewdness, child molestation, sexual activity with prostitutes, and homosexuality).[238] In fact, the courts have upheld internal regulations barring the employment of spouses, in part because of the concern for an officer's work performance.

The issue of homosexual activity as a basis for discharge was presented to the Supreme Court. Oklahoma had a law permitting discharge of schoolteachers for engaging in "public homosexual activity." The lower court held the law to be facially overly broad and therefore unconstitutionally restrictive. The Supreme Court affirmed the decision.[239] Another federal court held that the discharge of a bisexual guidance counselor did not deprive the plaintiff of her First or Fourteenth Amendment rights. The counselor's discussion of her sexual preferences with teachers and other personnel was not protected by the First Amendment.

Her equal protection claim failed because she did not show that the heterosexual employees would have been treated differently for communicating their sexual preferences.[240]

In an equally important federal case involving 13 lesbian deputies terminated from the Broward County, Florida Sheriff's Department, the Supreme Court held that homosexuals are not a suspect class accorded strict scrutiny under the equal protection clause and, therefore, the dismissal did not deprive the plaintiffs of any constitutional or equal protection right.[241] However, in 2003, the Supreme Court ruled that state sodomy laws are unconstitutional,[242] nullifying many police departments' argument that homosexuality is a criminal violation that is a viable basis for discharging a police officer.

Although there has yet to be a clear reversal of previous court rulings on gay and lesbian protections in the workplace, there have been a number of decisions made at the circuit court level that support discrimination (including discrimination against trans-gender individuals) as sex discrimination. In addition, the Supreme Court ruling in *Obergefell v. Hodges* on June 26, 2015, legalizing same-sex marriage tends to support the equality of gay and lesbians in the workplace. As a result of this shifting tide of legal opinion, the Equal Employment Opportunity Commission developed a statement following the ruling:

> discrimination against an individual because of that person's sexual orientation is a violation of Title VII. The Commission accepts and investigates charges alleging sexual-orientation discrimination in employment.[243]

Residency Requirements

A number of local governments have established requirements that all or certain classes of their employees live within the geographical limits of the jurisdiction. These residency requirements have been justified by the governments imposing them as desirable because they increase employees' rapport with and understanding of the community. When police officers were concerned, it has been asserted that the presence of off-duty police has a deterrent effect on crime and results in chance encounters that might lead to additional sources of information.

Before 1976, challenges to the legality of residency requirements for public employees dotted the legal landscape. In 1976, the Supreme Court, in *McCarthy v. Philadelphia Civil Service Commission*, ruled that Philadelphia's residency requirement for firefighters did not violate the Constitution.[244]

Since the *McCarthy* decision, the legal attacks on the residency requirements have subsided. The cases now seem to be concerned with determining what constitutes residency. The most obvious means of attempting to avoid the residency requirement (by establishing a second residence within the city) appears doomed to failure unless the police officer can demonstrate that he or she spends at least a substantial part of his or her time at the in-city residence.[245] A strong argument has been made that in areas where housing is unavailable or prohibitively expensive, a residency requirement is unreasonable.[246] In upholding the application of such requirements, courts have focused on the issues of equal enforcement and the specificity of the local residency standard.[247]

Moonlighting

Traditionally, the courts have supported the authority of police departments to place limits on the outside employment of their employees.[248] Police department restrictions on moonlighting range from a complete ban on outside employment to permission to engage in certain endeavors, such as investments, rental of property, teaching of law enforcement subjects, and employment designed to improve the police image. The rationale in support of moonlighting prohibitions is that "outside employment seriously interferes with keeping the [police and fire] departments fit and ready for action at all times."[249]

However, in a Louisiana case, firefighters offered unreputed evidence that moonlighting had been a common practice before the city banned it; during the previous 16 years, no firefighters had ever needed sick leave as a result of injuries suffered while moonlighting, there had never been a problem locating off-duty firefighters to respond to an emergency, and moonlighting had never been shown to be a source of fatigue that was serious enough to impair a firefighter's alertness on the job. Under these circumstances, the court ruled that there was not a sufficient basis for the prohibition on moonlighting and invalidated the ordinance.[250]

It is important to note that, in several cases involving off-duty, moonlighting officers (as private security guards or store detectives), the same legal standards imposed on sworn officers acting in the capacity of their jobs apply. The Court has held that off-duty officers act "under color of State law" and are subject to Section 1983 liability while working in a private security or "special patrolman" capacity.[251] Therefore, it follows that police agencies and departments may be liable under the same ramifications, opening up a new wave of future litigation involving police officer off-duty employment.

Alcohol and Drug Testing

It is common for police departments to require that their officers not be under the influence of any intoxicating agent while on duty. Even in the absence of such specific regulation, disciplinary action has been upheld when it was taken against an officer who was suspected of being intoxicated while on duty by charging him or her with neglect of duty or violation of a state law.[252]

Regulations that prohibit being under the influence of an intoxicating or mind-altering substance have been upheld uniformly as reasonable because of the hazardous nature of a police officer's work and the serious impact his or her behavior or misbehavior is sure to have on the property and safety of others. The necessity to require a clear head and rational action, not confused by alcohol or drugs, is clear.[253] A Louisiana court upheld a regulation that prohibited an officer from consuming alcoholic beverages on or off duty to the extent that it caused the officer's behavior to become obnoxious, disruptive, or disorderly.[254]

Effective enforcement of regulations against an officer being under the influence of drugs or alcohol will occasion situations when a police supervisor or administrator will order an officer to submit to one or more tests to determine the presence of the prohibited substance in the subject's body. It has been held that a firefighter could be ordered to submit to blood sampling when reasonable grounds existed for believing that he or she was intoxicated and that it was permissible to discharge the firefighter for his or her refusal to comply with the order.[255] More recently, the courts have also been asked to review police department policies that require officers to submit to urinalysis for the purpose of determining the presence of drugs or alcohol. In *United States v. Jacobsen*, the Supreme Court defined the concept of search and seizure:

> A "search" occurs when an expectation of privacy that society is prepared to consider reasonable is infringed. A "seizure" of property occurs when there is some meaningful interference with an individual's possessory interests in that property.[256]

According to the Supreme Court, removing urine from an individual's body is a search within the meaning of the Fourth Amendment. Consequently, when a government agency tests an employee's urine, due process must be applied, which involves providing probable evidence of illegal activity. In the case of public employer drug testing, the search is justified from the beginning, when "reasonable grounds exist for suspecting that the search will turn up evidence of work-related drug use."[257]

A reasonable search depends on a "balancing test" set forth by Justice Sandra Day O'Connor:

> A determination of the standard of reasonableness applicable to a particular class of searches requires balancing the nature and quality of the intrusion on the individual's Fourth Amendment interests against the importance of the governmental interest alleged to justify the intrusion. In the case of searches conducted by a public employer, we must balance the invasion of the employee's legitimate expectations of privacy against the government's need for supervision, control, and the efficient operation of the work place.[258]

The Supreme Court has ruled on two cases that have become landmarks for drug testing in the public sector. In *Skinner v. Railway Labor Executives' Association*, the Court upheld a mandatory drug testing program in cases in which the government had no reasonable suspicion about any particular public employee but had a substantial interest in maintaining public safety.[259] In a case even more important to police agencies, the Court considered in *National Treasury Employees Union v. Von Raub* whether the U.S. Customs drug testing program was constitutional. The customs service drug-tested employees who sought a promotion to positions that required seizing or safekeeping illegal drugs, carrying firearms, or handling classified documents. The Court held that such employees have a "diminished expectation of privacy" and that drug testing is a minimal intrusion that is far outweighed by the government's interests to keep the public and citizenry safe.[260]

The prevailing view appears to be that totally random, unscheduled drug testing is unacceptable but that particular officers can be required to submit to urinalysis if there exists a "reasonable suspicion" that the officer has been using a prohibited substance or is involved in an incident involving citizen safety.[261] For instance, in 2007, the New York Police Department instituted a new drug and alcohol policy regarding critical incidents involving the police. If an officer fires his or her weapon either on or off duty or is involved in a traffic accident that causes injury or death, a portable breathalyzer test is automatically given as a condition of employment. If the breathalyzer test concludes a blood alcohol level of 0.08 or greater, the officer is immediately placed on administrative leave and an Internal Affairs investigation is opened.[262] More importantly, advanced alcohol and drug testing is then conducted through blood tests or urinalysis. The results of such compulsory tests are appropriate evidence for introduction in administrative discharge proceedings.[263]

Decisions involving other government employees and similar kinds of personal intrusions (e.g., strip searches of prison guards) seem to support the view that random testing is unreasonable under the Fourth Amendment.[264] However, without a definitive decision from the Supreme Court on random drug testing, lower federal court decisions concerning public agency personnel appear to allow random drug testing without reasonable suspicion of individual drug abuse if (1) an employer knows that drugs are used in the workplace, (2) the testing will not totally disrupt the employee's privacy expectation, and (3) the jobs are "safety-sensitive" in nature.[265]

In an attempt to skirt the issue of mandatory or random testing, some departments have incorporated drug testing as a "usual and customary" part of a required medical examination. For instance, the Philadelphia Police Department requires a medical examination for all individuals attempting to secure employment under the following conditions: (1) when an officer is first hired, (2) when an officer is transferred to a "sensitive" position (i.e., vice and narcotics division, SWAT, and hostage negotiation teams), (3) when an officer is promoted to a higher rank, and (4) when an officer returns to duty after an extended period of time (e.g., long illness, disability, or suspension). Drug abuse is viewed as a medical malady and is subject to disclosure, similar to the findings of other tests that show spinal problems, poor vision, hearing loss, and the like. Hence, drug testing can be viewed as a routine part of the medical examination for pre-employment to a new position.

Chapter Summary

Summary by Learning Objectives

1. **Explain the three general categories of torts. How do they differ?**

   Negligence, intentional, and constitutional torts are the three general categories of torts. Negligence torts focus on whether an individual conducted his or her affairs in a manner that does not subject others to an unreasonable risk of harm. Intentional torts are the voluntary commissions of an act that has a substantial certainty to injure another person—it does not have to be negligent. Constitutional torts deal with the duty to recognize and uphold the constitutional rights, privileges and immunities of others.

2. **Define "acting under the color of state law." How does this statement relate to Section 1983 actions?**

   "Acting under color of state law" means that when the action under question occurred, the individual officer was on-duty and acting within the scope of his or her employment. It extends the Title 42, U.S. Code, Section 1983 civil rights statute to apply to plaintiffs in municipal and state police officers only; it does not relate to federal officers (such as agents with the FBI or DEA), as they act under federal jurisdiction.

3. **Explain and describe a *Bivens* action.**

   A Bivens action applies to federal officials, and it is a judicially created counterpart of Title 42, U.S. Code, Section 1983 that allows federal courts to hear federal litigation cases involving suits against federal employees in their individual capacities. In this manner, agents of the federal government (e.g., FBI, DEA, U.S. Marshall Service, and ICE) can be sued by individuals

4. **List and describe the negligence theories applicable to police supervision and management.**

   Negligent hiring means that employers must exercise a reasonable standard of care in not selecting persons who, because of the nature of their job, could present a threat of injury to members of the public. Negligent assignment, retention, and entrustment means that police administrators who know of or should have known of individual acts or patterns of behavior by police officers that could threaten the public must take immediate action to remedy said situation or be subject to liability. Negligent direction and supervision means supervisors have the duty to develop and implement appropriate policies and procedures. Negligent training deals with the fact that the local or state unit of government, acting through their administrator of a police department, have an affirmative duty to train their employees (officers) correctly and adequately.

5. **Describe procedural and substantive due process.**

   Procedural due process refers to the legality of the procedures used to deprive police officers of status or wages, such as dismissal or suspension from their job. Substantive due process is the requirement that the basis for government disciplinary action be reasonable, relevant, and justifiable.

6. **Explain a *Brady* violation.**

   Police agencies must disclose to the prosecution, who must disclose to the defense, any exculpatory or impeachment evidence that demonstrates that a witness is lying about specific facts in a case, or is generally unworthy of belief. Evidence of this nature is often referred to as "*Brady* material." Failing to disclose such evidence is a "*Brady*" violation that can lead to dismissal of the criminal case and civil (U.S. Code 42, Section 1983) cases brought against the individual prosecutor, the police department, and the officer for violation of the suspect's constitutional rights.

7. **Explain when rules infringing on the free speech of officers might be upheld.**

   When there are reasonable motives for a department to infringe upon those rights; when those motives are not overly broad; and when statements by employees adversely affect the operation of a department.

8. **Describe the circumstances in which an officer may use deadly force?**

   An officer may use deadly force only in defense of life and against fleeing felons who the officer reasonably believes committed a felony involving the threat of violence.

9. **List the four elements that must be proven in order to sue the police for negligence in a high-speed pursuit.**

   The officer owed the injured party a duty not to engage in certain conduct; the officer's actions violated that duty; the officer's negligent conduct was the proximate cause of the accident; and the suing party suffered actual and provable damages.

10. **Describe how a department can reduce liability in high-speed pursuits.**

    To reduce risks and liabilities associated with vehicular pursuits, law enforcement organizations must carefully evaluate their pursuit policies, training, supervision, and post incident evaluations.

11. Relate the focus of most training programs regarding emotionally disturbed persons.

The primary focus of most training programs regarding emotionally disturbed persons (EDPs) is recognizing behavior that indicates that officers are dealing with EDPs and communicating with those persons in a non-threatening manner.

12. Describe the balancing test related to alcohol and drug testing in the police workplace.

The balancing test relating to alcohol and drug testing involves balancing the nature and quality of the intrusion of the individual's Fourth Amendment protections against the importance of the governmental interest that justifies the intrusion.

Chapter Review Questions

1. What are the three general categories of torts?
2. Explain the meaning of "acting under the color of state law" as it relates to U.S. Code 42, Section 1983 actions.
3. What is a *Bivens* action?
4. What are the primary negligence theories applicable to police supervision and management?
5. Describe procedural and substantive due process.
6. What is the major three-prong test of reasonableness for all use-of-force cases in the future established in *Graham v. Connor*?
7. What are federal consent decrees and how important are they in reforming the police?
8. What is PSV?
9. Discuss the importance of the 2015 landmark case, *Obergefel v. Hodges*.
10. Identify when department rules and policies might infringe on the free speech of officers.
11. What is a *Brady* violation?
12. Describe the circumstances when an officer can use deadly force.
13. Identify the four elements that must be proven in order to sue the police for negligence in a high-speed pursuit.
14. Describe a police department's responsibility in reducing liability in high-speed pursuits.
15. Identify the desired outcomes of effective training of police officers in dealing with emotionally disturbed persons.
16. List the *Garrity* warnings; why was this case so instrumental in investigating police officers of wrongdoing?
17. Why is "conduct unbecoming an officer" such a controversial issue?
18. Describe the "balancing test" as referred to in alcohol and drug testing in the workplace.

Critical Thinking Exercises

1. Do you think body-worn cameras will have the effect of increasing or decreasing *Brady* violations? Why or why not?
2. Should a police officer have the right to use personal social media platforms, like Facebook and Twitter, to give his or her opinion of the police department even though those opinions might be critical of their department? Do you think that an officer's right to be critical of a department or an incident, specifically one that might involve racist or bigoted officers be protected under their First Amendment rights? Why or why not?
3. Visit the AELE Law Enforcement Legal Center website at http://www.aele.org/. Navigate to their "Special Issues in Law Enforcement" section at http://www.aele.org/hotissues.html. Do you think that these legal updates are something that the average patrol officer is aware of? Do you think that it's necessary for patrol officers to know these legal updates? Why or why not? If you were an administrator or executive of a law enforcement agency, how would you make sure that patrol officers kept abreast of such information?

Key Terms

1983 action	liability	procedural due process
Bivens action	liberty rights	property rights
defendant	litigation	proximate cause
deliberate indifference	negligence	reasonableness
due process	objective reasonableness	standard of reasonableness
emotionally disturbed persons (EDPs)	plaintiff	substantive due process
federal consent decree	police sexual violence (PSV)	tort
less-lethal weapon	probable cause	vicarious liability

Endnotes

[1] Much of this section is adapted, with additions, from H. E. Barrineau III, *Civil Liability in Criminal Justice* (Cincinnati: Anderson, 1987), pp. 3–5.

[2] Ibid., p. 3.

[3] False arrest is the arrest of a person without probable cause. Generally, this means making an arrest when an ordinarily prudent person would not have concluded that a crime had been committed or that the person arrested had committed the crime. False imprisonment is the intentional illegal detention of a person. The detention that can give rise to a false imprisonment claim is any confinement to a specified area and not simply incarceration in a jail. Most false arrests result in false imprisonment as well, but there can be a false imprisonment after a valid arrest also, as when the police fail to release an arrested person after a proper bond has been posted, the police unreasonably delay the arraignment of an arrested person, or authorities fail to release a prisoner after they no longer have authority to hold him or her. "Brutality" is not a legal tort action as such. Rather, it must be alleged as a civil (as opposed to a criminal) assault and/or battery. Assault is some sort of menacing conduct that puts another person in reasonable fear that he or she is about to have a battery committed on him or her. Battery is the infliction of harmful or offensive contact on another person. Harmful or offensive contact is contact that would be considered harmful or offensive by a reasonable person of ordinary sensibilities. See Clarence E. Hagglund, "Liability of Police Officers and Their Employers," *Federation of Insurance Counsel Quarterly* 26 (summer 1976), p. 257, for a good discussion of assault and battery, false arrest, false imprisonment, and malicious prosecution as applied to police officers.

[4] Although a fourth category (strict liability tort action) does exist in the wider body of law, such a general category is rare in police officer litigation. Therefore, for the purposes of this book, strict liability actions are not discussed. Under strict liability, one is held liable for one's act, regardless of intent or negligence. The mere occurrence of certain events will necessarily create legal liability. A good example of such cases is often found in airplane disasters in which the air transportation company is strictly liable for the passengers' health and well-being, regardless of other factors.

[5] *Black's Law Dictionary*, 4th ed. (St. Paul, MN: West, 2004), p. 470.

[6] Title 42, U.S. Code, Section 1983.

[7] See *Monroe v. Pape*, 365 U.S. 167, 81 S. Ct. 473 (1961). The plaintiff and his family sued 13 Chicago police officers and the city of Chicago, alleging that police officers broke into their home without a search warrant, forced them out of bed at gunpoint, made them stand naked while the officers ransacked the house, and subjected the family to verbal and physical abuse. The court held that the definition of "under color of State law" for Section 1983 purposes was the same as that already established in the criminal context and concluded that, because Section 1983 provides for a civil action, the plaintiffs need not prove that the defendants acted with a "specific intent to deprive a person of a federal right" (365 U.S. at 187). The court also

held that municipalities (such as the city of Chicago, in this case) were immune from liability under the statute, although the Supreme Court later overruled this part of *Monroe v. Pape*, holding that municipalities and other local governments are included among "persons" open to a Section 1983 lawsuit. See *Monell v. Dept. of Social Services of the City of New York*, 436 U.S. 658, 98 S. Ct. 2018 (1978). (Citations to case opinions give the volume number in which the opinion is located followed by the name of the reporter system, the page number, the court if other than the Supreme Court, and the year in which the opinion was rendered.)

[8] The resuscitation of Section 1983 hinges on the misuse and abuse of power imbued to individuals acting as police officers. All municipal and county law enforcement officers take an oath to uphold and enforce the laws of a specific state in which their municipality resides. Therefore, municipal police officers are squarely within the confines of Section 1983. "Misuse of power," possessed by virtue of state law and made possible only because the wrongdoer is clothed with the authority of state law, is action taken "under the color of law." *United States v. Classic*, 313 U.S. 299, at p. 326, 61 S. Ct., 1031, at p. 1043 (1941) as quoted in *Monroe v. Pape*. Thus, private citizens cannot be sued under Section 1983 unless they conspire with state officers. (See *Slavin v. Curry*, 574 F. 2d 1256 [5th Cir. 1978], as modified by 583 F. 2d 779 [5th Cir. 1978].) Furthermore, if a state officer has immunity to a Section 1983 lawsuit, private citizens who conspired with him or her do not have "derivative immunity" to the lawsuit. (See *Sparks v. Duval County Ranch Co., Inc.*, 604 F. 2d 976 [5th Cir. 1979], at p. 978.) In addition, see *Sanberg v. Daley*, 306 F. Supp. 227 (1969), at p. 279.

[9] Most tort actions against the U.S. government must be brought under the FTCA. The FTCA is a partial waiver of sovereign immunity, with its own rule of liability and a substantial body of case law. Federal employees can be sued for violation of constitutional rights and for certain Common-Law torts. For more information, see Isidore Silver, *Police Civil Liability* (New York: Mathew Bender, 1987), section 1.04, from which this material is taken.

[10] See *Bivens v. Six Unknown Federal Narcotics Agents*, 403 U.S. 388, 91 S. Ct. 1999 (1971). See also Silver, *Police Civil Liability*, section 8.02.

[11] Silver, *Police Civil Liability*, Section 8.02.

[12] See William L. Prosser, *Handbook of the Law of Torts*, 4th ed. (St. Paul, MN: West, 1971), p. 69, for a good discussion of the philosophical basis for and development of the doctrine of vicarious liability.

[13] Although this list does not include all types of negligence theories regarding 1983 action against police supervisors and managers, it does provide a starting point in understanding this issue. This part has been adapted from Barrineau, *Civil Liability*, pp. 59–60.

[14] See *Peter v. Bellinger*, 159 N.E. 2d 528 (1959); *Thomas v. Johnson*, 295 F. Supp. 1025 (1968); *McKenna v. City of Memphis*, 544 F. Supp. 415 (1982), affirmed in 785 F. 2d 560 (1986); *McGuire v. Arizona Protection Agency*, 609 P. 2d 1080 (1908); *Di Cosal v. Kay*, 19 N.J. 159, 450 A. 2d 508

(1982); *Pontiac v. KMS Investments*, 331 N.W. 2d 907 (1983); and *Welsh Manufacturing Division of Textron, Inc. v. Pinkertons, Inc.*, 474 A. 2d 426 (1984).

[15]See *Board of the County Commissioner of Bryan County v. Brown*, 117 S. Ct. 1383 (1997).

[16]See *Moon v. Winfield*, 383 F. Supp. 31 (1974); *Murray v. Murphy*, 441 F. Supp. 120 (1977); *Allen v. City of Los Angeles* (No. C-9837), LA Sup.Ct. (1975); *Stengel v. Belcher*, 522 F. 2d 438 (6th Cir. 1975); *Dominguez v. Superior Court*, 101 Cal. App. 3d 6 (1980); *Stuessel v. City of Glendale*, 141 Cal. App. 3d 1047 (1983); and *Blake v. Moore*, 162 Cal. App. 3d 700 (1984).

[17]See *Ford v. Breiser*, 383 F. Supp. 505 (1974); *Dewel v. Lawson*, 489 F. 2d 877 (10th Cir. 1974); *Bonsignore v. City of New York*, 521 F. Supp. 394 (1981), affirmed in 683 F. 2d 635 (1st Cir. 1982); *Webster v. City of Houston*, 689 F. 2d 1220 (5th Cir. 1982), reversed and remanded on the issue of damages in 739 F. 2d 993 (5th Cir. 1984); and *District of Columbia v. Parker*, 850 F. 2d 708 (D.C. Cir. 1988), cert. denied in 489 U.S. 1065, 109 S. Ct. 1339 (1989).

[18]See *Marusa v. District of Columbia*, 484 F. 428 (1973); *Webzster v. City of Houston*, supra note 22; and *Grandstagg v. City of Borger*, 767 F. 2d (5th Cir. 1985), cert. denied in 480 U.S. 917, 107 S. Ct. 1369 (1987).

[19]*City of Canton v. Harris*, 389 U.S. 378, 103 L. Ed. 412, 109 S. Ct. 1197 (1989), at pp. 1204–1205; *Merritt v. County of Los Angeles*, 875 F. 2d 765 (9th Cir. 1989); *Owens v. Haas*, 601 F. 2d 1242 (2nd Cir. 1979), cert. denied in 444 U.S. 980 (1980).

[20]Prosser, *Handbook of the Law of Torts*, pp. 977–978.

[21]*Scheuer v. Rhodes*, at p. 240.

[22]*Wood v. Strickland*, 420 U.S. 308, 95 S. Ct. 992 (1975).

[23]*Harlow v. Fitzgerald*, 457 U.S. 800, 102 S. Ct. 2727 (1982).

[24]*Mitchell v. Forsyth*, 472 U.S. 511, 105 S. Ct. 2806 (1985).

[25]*Monroe v. Pape*, supra note 7.

[26]436 U.S. 658, 98 S. Ct. 2018 (1978).

[27]See, for example, *Rookard v. Health and Hospitals Corp.*, 710 F. 2d 41 (2d Cir. 1983).

[28]*Oklahoma City v. Tuttle*, 471 U.S. 808, 105 S. Ct. 2427 (1985); but see *Pembauer v. Cincinnati*, 475 U.S. 469, 106 S. Ct. 1292 (1986).

[29]M. S. Vaughn et al., "Assessing Legal Liabilities in Law Enforcement: Police Chief's Views," *Crime and Delinquency* 47, No. 1 (January 2001): 22.

[30]August Vollmer, "Police Schools," *Journal of the American Institute of Criminal Law and Criminology, 8 (3) 1917.*

[31]L. F. Fuld, "University Lectures for Police," *Journal of the American Institute of Criminal Law and Criminology, 8(3) 1917, p. 464.*

[32]James Conser, R. Paynich, and T. Gingerich, *Law Enforcement in the United States*, 3rd ed. (Burlington, MA: Jones & Bartlett Learning, 2013).

[33]J. Scott, "Survey: The Status of Field Training," *The Police Chief*, LXXVII (November 2010).

[34]S. Pitts, R. W. Glensor, and K. Peak, "The Police Training Officer (PTO) Program: A Contemporary Approach to Post-Academy Recruit Training," *The Police Chief*, 74 (August 2007).

[35]Victor Kappeler, *Critical Issues in Police Civil Liability*, 4th ed. (Long Grove, IL: Waveland Press, 2006).

[36]U.S. Department of Justice, *Contacts between Police and the Public* (Washington, DC: Bureau of Justice Statistics, 2011).

[37]*Daniels v. Williams*, 474 U.S. 327, 106 S. Ct. 662 (1986).

[38]*New v. City of Minneapolis*, 792 F. 2d 724, at pp. 725–26 (8th Cir. 1986). See also *McClary v. O'Hare*, 786 F. 2d 83 (2nd Cir. 1986).

[39]Hagglund, "Liability of Police Officers," p. 257.

[40]*United States v. Leon*, 468 U.S. 897, 104 S. Ct. 3430 (1984).

[41]*Malley v. Briggs*, 475 U.S. 335, 106 S. Ct. 1092 (1986).

[42]*Anderson v. Creighton*, 483 U.S. 635, 107 S. Ct. 3034 (1987).

[43]*Saucier v. Katz*, 533 U.S. 194, 121 S. Ct. 2151 (2001). See also *Pearson et al. v Callahan*, 07-751 (494 F3d 891) (January 21, 2009).

[44]*Malley v. Briggs*, 475 U.S. 335, 341 (1986).

[45]*Maciarello v. Summer*, 973 F. 2d 295, 298 (1992).

[46]*Pearson et al. v Callahan*, 07-751 (494 F3d 891) (January 21, 2009).

[47]Schmidt, "Recent Developments."

[48]Ibid., p. 198.

[49]*Wimberly v. Patterson*, 183 A. 2d 691 (1962), at p. 699.

[50]*Piatkowski v. State*, 251 N.Y.S. 2d 354 (1964), at p. 359.

[51]Schmidt, "Recent Developments," p. 199.

[52]*Fords v. Breier*, 383 F. Supp. 505 (E.D. Wis. 1974).

[53]*Lucas v. Riley*, Superior Court, Los Angeles County, CA (1975); *Delong v. City of Denver*, 530 F. 2d 1308 (Colo. 1974); *Grudt v. City of Los Angeles*, 468 P. 2d 825 (Cal. 1970); *Dillenbeck v. City of Los Angeles*, 446 P. 2d 129 (Cal. 1968).

[54]*AELE Law Enforcement Legal Defense Manual*, "Failure to Provide Medical Treatment," Issue 77-6 (1977).

[55]*Watkins v. City of Battle Creek*, 273 F. 3d 682, 685–86 (6th Cir. 2001).

[56]*Carter v. City of Detroit*, 480 F. 3d 305, 310, 311 (6th Cir. 2005).

[57]*AELE Law Enforcement Legal Defense Manual*, "Failure to Provide Medical Treatment."

[58]International Association of Chiefs of Police. "Emerging Use of Force Issues: Balancing Public and Officer Safety." March 2012. Retrieved on August 2, 2015 from http://www.theiacp.org/portals/0/pdfs/emerginguseofforceissues041612.pdf.

[59]Kenneth James Matulia, "The Use of Deadly Force: A Need for Directives in Training," *The Police Chief* (May 1983), p. 30.

[60]Kenneth James Matulia, "A Balance of Forces: Model Deadly Force and Policy Procedure," *International Association of Chiefs of Police*, (1985), pp. 23, 24. See also *Tennessee v. Garner*, 471 U.S. 1, 105 S. Ct. 1694 (1985). While this citation is relatively old, many of the basic positions held here are reiterated in the Commission on Accreditation for Law Enforcement Agencies (CALEA), Model Policy for Use of Force and Use of Deadly Force (2010).

[61]*Tennessee v. Garner*, supra note 17.

[62]*Graham v. Connor*, 109 s Ct. 1865, 1872 (1989).

[63]*Tennessee v. Garner*, supra note 179.

[64]Matulia, "A Balance of Forces," p. 72.

[65]Catherin H. Milton, Jeanne Wahl Halleck, James Lardnew, and Gray L. Albrecht, *Police Use of Deadly Force* (Washington, DC: Police Foundation, 1977), p. 52.

[66]Matulia, "A Balance of Forces," p. 52.

[67]Ibid., p. 77.

[68]Ibid.

[69]Ibid., p. 78.

[70]471 U.S. 1, 105 S. Ct. 1694 (1985).

[71]Matulia, "A Balance of Forces," p. 78.

[72]C. Mesloh, M. Henych, and R. Wolf, Conducted Electrical Weapons and Resolution of Use of Force Encounters. In M.W. Kroll, and J.D. Ho (eds.), *Taser® Conducted Electrical Weapons: Physiology, Pathology and Law* (New York: Springer Science and Business Media, 2009). Much of this section on TASERS and the Police Use of Less-Lethal Weapons has been adapted from Ross Wolf, "TASERS and Electronic Control Devises," LETN Video: *Electronic Control Devices* Courseware 111-0510 (Carrollton, TX: Critical Information Network, 2010).

[73]C. Mesloh, R. Wolf, M. Henych, and F. Thompson, "Less Lethal Weapons for Law Enforcement: A Performance-Based Analysis." *Law Enforcement Executive Forum* 8(1) (2008), pp. 133–149.

[74]See TASER International at: www.taser.com

[75]Ross Wolf, "TASERS and Electronic Control Devises," LETN Video: *Electronic Control Devices* Courseware 111-0510 (Carrollton, TX: Critical Information Network, 2010).

[76]U.S. General Accounting Office, TASER Weapons: Use of TASERS by Selected Law Enforcement Agencies (Washington, DC: USPO, 2005).

[77]Geoffrey P. Alpert and Roger G. Dunham, *Understanding Police Use of Force: Officers, Suspects, and Reciprocity* (Cambridge, NY: Cambridge University Press, 2004). See also Geoffrey P. Alpert, "Police Use-of-Force, Less Lethal Weapons, and Injuries: Findings from a National Study," *Police Quarterly*, Forthcoming, 2010.

[78]Ibid.

[79]Incidents involving TASERS that have caused death and serious injury continue to dot the newspapers across the United States and Canada. For a discussion of concerns involving less-lethal weapons and a description of specific highlighted events, see a series of reports by Amnesty International (London: Amnesty International) at — www.amnestyusa.org: 1) "USA Amnesty International's Continuing Concerns about TASER Use (2006); Excessive and Lethal Force? Amnesty International's Concerns about Deaths and Ill-Treatment Involving Police Use of TASERS (2004); USA: Police Use of Pepper Spray—Tantamount to Torture (1997) and the American Civil Liberties Union (ACLU) at—www.aclu.org: (1) Pepper Spray Update: More Fatalities, More Questions (1995) and (2) Stun Gun Fallacy: How the Lack of TASER Regulation Endangers Lives (2005).

[80]See John M. MacDonald, Robert J. Kaminski, and Michael R. Smith, "The Effect of Less-Lethal ON Injuries in Police Use-Of-Force events," *American Journal of Public Health*, 99, No. 12 (December 2009), pp. 2260–2274 and M. R. Smith, R. J. Kaminski, J. Rojek, G. P. Alpert, and J. Mathis, "The Impact of Conducted Energy Devices and Other Types of Force and Resistance on Police and Suspect Injuries," *Policing: An International Journal of Police Strategies and Management*, 30 (2007), pp. 443–426.

[81]Geoffrey P. Alpert, "Police Use-of-Force, Less Lethal Weapons, and Injuries: Findings from a National Study," *Police Quarterly*, Forthcoming, 2010.

[82]Daniel L. Schofield, "Legal Issues of Pursuit Driving," *FBI Law Enforcement Bulletin*, May 1988, pp. 23–30. This discussion was adapted from this source.

[83]Richard G. Zivitz, "Police Civil Liability and the Law of High-Speed Pursuit," *Marquette Law Review* 70, No. 237 (1987), pp. 237–279.

[84]*Jackson v. Olson*, 712 P. 2d 128 (Or.App. 1985).

[85]457 Do. 2d 816 (Miss. 1985).

[86]Ibid., at p. 818.

[87]See generally Annotation, "Emergency Vehicle Accidents," *American Jurisprudence, Proof of Facts* (St. Paul, MN: West, 1985), p. 599.

[88]See *Breck v. Cortez*, 490 N.E. 2d 88 (III. App. 1986).

[89]See generally Annotation, "Municipal Corporation's Safety Rules or Regulations as Admissible in Evidence in Action by Private Party against Municipal Corporation or Its Officers or Employees for Negligent Operation of Vehicle," *American Law Review*.

[90]See *Fiser v. City of Ann Arbor*, 339 N.W. 2d 413 (Michigan 1983).

[91]733 S.W. 2d 28 (Mo. App. 1987).

[92]For a general discussion of immunity, see David Charlin, "High-Speed Pursuits: Police Officer and Municipal Liability for Accidents Involving the Pursued and an Innocent Third Party," *Seton Hall Law Review* 16, No. 101 (1986). While this citation is relatively old, many of the basic positions held here are reiterated in the Commission on Accreditation for Law Enforcement Agencies (CALEA), Model Policy for Police Pursuits (2010).

[93]490 So. 2d 1061 (Fla. App. 1986).

[94]*Fagan v. City of Vineland*, 22 F. 3d 1283 (3rd Cir. 1994).

[95]42 U.S.C. 1983 provides in relevant part: "Every person who, under color of any statute, ordinance, regulation, custom, or usage, of any State of Territory, subjects or causes to be subjected, any citizen of the United States or other person within the jurisdiction thereof to the deprivation of any rights, privileges, or immunities secured by the Constitution and laws, shall be liable to the party injured in an action at law, suit in equity, or other proper proceedings for redress."

[96]782 F. 2d 947 (11th Cir. 1986).

[97]Ibid., at p. 950.

[98]See *County of Sacramento v. Lewis*, 98 F. 3d 434 (1998).

[99]Ibid.

[100]See *Allen v. Cook*, 668 F. Supp. 1460 (W.D. Okla. 1987). See also *Fagan v. City of Vineland*, supra note 202.

[101]772 F. 2d 1205 (5th Cir. 1985).

[102]471 U.S. 1, 105 S. Ct. 1694 (1985). The Supreme Court held that the use of deadly force to apprehend an unarmed fleeing felon was an unreasonable seizure which violated the Fourth Amendment.

[103]817 F. 2d 540 (9th Cir. 1987). In *City of Miami v. Harris*, 490 So. 2d 69 (Fla. App. 1985), the court held that a city can be liable under 1983 for a pursuit policy that is adopted with a reckless disregard of whether such policy would cause loss of life without due process.

[104]*Brower v. County of Inyo*, 489 U.S. 593, 109 S. Ct. 1378 (1989).

[105]A discussion of empirical studies regarding pursuits is set forth in Geoffrey P. Alpert, "Questioning Police Pursuits in Urban Areas," in R. G. Dunham and G. P. Alpert (eds.), *Critical Issues in Policing: Contemporary Readings* (Prospect Heights, IL: Waveland Press, 1989), pp. 216–229.

[106]*Jackson v. Olson*, supra note 192.

107See Annotation, "Municipal or State Liability for Injuries Resulting from Police Roadblocks or Commandeering of Private Vehicles," 19 *American Law Review* 4th 937.

108*Brower v. County of Inyo*, supra note 212.

109*Horta v. Sullivan*, 4 F. 3d 2 (1st Cir. 1993), at p. 10.

110Edmund Fennessy, Thomas Hamilton, Kent Joscelyn, and John Merritt, *A Study of the Problem of Hot Pursuit by the Police* (Washington, DC: U.S. Department of Transportation, 1970).

111Geoffrey P. Alpert, "Questioning Police Pursuit in Urban Areas," *Journal of Police Science and Administration* 15 (1987), pp. 298–306.

112Eric Beckman, "Identifying Issues in Police Pursuits: The First Research Findings," *The Police Chief* (July 1987), pp. 57–63.

113Geoffrey P. Alpert, *Police Pursuit Policies and Training* (Washington, DC: U.S. Department of Justice, Office of Justice Programs, National Institute of Justice, May 1997), pp. 1–8.

114Ibid.

115See, for example, *Nelson v. City of Chester, Ill.*, 733 S.W. 2d 28 (Mo. App. 1987); *Biscoe v. Arlington County*, 738 F. 2d 1352 (D.C. Cir. 1984).

116Alpert, "Questioning Police Pursuits in Urban Areas," pp. 227–228.

117*Plumhoff v. Rickard*, 188 L. Ed. 2d 1056 (U.S. May 27, 2014).

118International Association of Chiefs of Police, *Dealing with the Mentally Ill: Concepts and Issues* (Alexandra, Va.: IACP Law Enforcement Policy Center, December 1, 1997).

119Washington Criminal Justice Training Commission (WCJTC), *Crisis Intervention Skills: Abnormal Behaviors, Mental Illness, and Suicide* (Seattle: WCJTC. 2000).

120Michael Klein, "Law Enforcement's Response to People with Mental Illness," *Law Enforcement Bulletin* (February 2002), pp. 12–16.

121*City & Cnty of San Francisco v. Sheehan*, 575 U.S. ___ (2015)

122Michael J. Oh."Encountering Mentally Ill People and Potential Liability under the Americans with Disabilities Act". *Police Chief Magazine* (July 2014).

123Robert C. Davis, Christopher W. Ortiz, Nicole J. Henderson, Joel Miller, and Michelle K. Massie, *Turning Necessity into Virtue: Pittsburgh's Experience with a Federal Consent Decree* (Washington, DC: Vera Institute of Justice, September 2002).

124Joe Domanick, "Police Reform's Best Tool: A Federal Consent Decree," *The Crime Report* (July 15, 2014).

125Police Executive Research Forum (PERF), *Civil Rights Investigations of Local Police: Lessons Learned* (Washington, DC: PERF, July 2013). Available online at: http://www .policeforum.org/assets/docs/Critical_Issues_Series/ civil%20rights%20investigations%20of%20local%20 police%20-%20lessons%20learned%202013.pdf

126D. Littlefield, "Arevalos Victim Settles for $5.9 Million." *San Diego Union-Tribune* (September 25, 2014).

127International Association of Chiefs of Police *Addressing Sexual Offenses and Misconduct by Law Enforcement: Executive Guide* (Washington DC: Alexandria, VA: International Association of Chiefs of Police, 2011), p. 1.

128Phillip Matthew Stinson, Sr., John C. Liederbach, Steven L. Brewer, and Brooke E Mathna, "Police Sexual Misconduct:

A National-Scale Study of Arrested Officers. *Criminal Justice Policy Review*. April 2014. Published On-LineDOI 10.1177/0887403414526231.

129Peter B. Kraska and Victor E. Kappeler, "To Serve and Pursue: Exploring Police Sexual Violence Against Women. *Justice Quarterly* 12, No. 1, (1995), pp. 85–111. Published online: DOI:10.1080/07418829500092581

130See Michael S. Vaughn, "Police Sexual Violence: Civil Liability Under State Tort Law," *Crime and Delinquency* 45, No. 3 (1999); and Sarah Eschholz and Michael S. Vaughn, "Police Sexual Violence and Rape Myths: Civil Liability under Section 1983," *Journal of Criminal Justice* 29, No. 5, (2001). Published online: DOI:10.1016/ S0047-2352(01)00104-0

131Samuel Walker and Dawn Irlbeck, *Police Sexual Abuse of Teenage Girls: A 2003 Update on Driving while Female.* (Omaha, NE: University of Nebraska at Omaha, Department of Criminal Justice, Police Professionalism Initiative, 2003).

132C.E. Rabe-Hemp and J. Braithwaite, "An Exploration of Recidivism and the Officer Shuffle in Police Sexual Violence, *Police Quarterly* 16, No. 2 (2013). DOI: 10.1177/1098611112464964

133Phillip Matthew Stinson, Sr., John C. Liederbach, Steven L. Brewer, and Brooke E Mathna. Ibid.

134See, generally, Joan Bertin Lowy, "Constitutional Limitations on the Dismissal of Public Employees," *Brooklyn Law Review* 43 (summer 1976), p. 1; Victor G. Rosenblum, "Schoolchildren: Yes, Policemen: No—Some Thoughts about the Supreme Court's Priorities Concerning the Right to a Hearing in Suspension and Removal Cases," *Northwestern University Law Review* 72 (1977), p. 146.

135*Wisconsin v. Constantineau*, 400 U.S. 433, 91 S. Ct. 507 (1970); *Doe v. U.S. Department of Justice*, 753 F. 2d 1092 (D.C. Cir. 1985).

136*Codd v. Velger*, 429 U.S. 624, 97 S. Ct. 882 (1977). See also *Paul v. Davis*, 424 U.S. 693, 96 S. Ct. 1155 (1976), which held that injury to reputation alone does not constitute a deprivation of liberty. See also *Swilley v. Alexander*, 629 F. 2d 1018 (5th Cir. 1980), where the court held that a letter of reprimand containing untrue charges that was placed in an employee's personnel file infringed on his liberty interest.

137See *Board of Regents v. Roth*, 408 U.S. 564, 92 S. Ct. 2701 (1972); *Perry v. Sinderman*, 408 U.S. 593, 92 S. Ct. 2694 (1972); *Arnett v. Kennedy*, 416 U.S. 134, 94 S. Ct. 1633 (1974); *Bishop v. Wood*, 426 U.S. 341, 96 S. Ct. 2074 (1976). Also see Robert L. Rabin, "Job Security and Due Process: Monitoring Administrative Discretion through a Reasons Requirement," *University of Chicago Law Review* 44 (1976), pp. 60–67, for a good discussion of these cases; see also *Bailey v. Kirk*, No. 82-1417 (10th Cir. 1985) and Carl Goodman, "Public Employment and the Supreme Court's 1975–76 Term," *Public Personnel Management* 5 (September–October 1976), pp. 287–289.

138*Thurston v. Dekle*, 531 F. 2d 1264 (5th Cir. 1976), vacated on other grounds, 438 U.S. 901, 98 S. Ct. 3118 (1978).

139*Allison v. City of Live Oak*, 450 F. Supp. 200 (M.D. Fla. 1978).

140See, for example, *Confederation of Police Chicago v. Chicago*, 547 F. 2d 375 (7th Cir. 1977).

141Davis, *Administrative Law*, p. 242.

[142]*Memphis Light Gas & Water Division v. Craft*, 436 U.S. 1, 98 S. Ct. 1554 (1978).

[143]*In re Dewar*, 548 P. 2nd 149 (Mont. 1976).

[144]*Bush v. Beckman*, 131 N.Y.S. 2d 297 (1954); *Gibbs v. City of Manchester*, 61 A. 128 (N.H. 1905).

[145]*Morrissey v. Brewer*, 408 U.S. 471, 92 S. Ct. 2593 (1972).

[146]*Goldman v. Kelly*, 397 U.S. 254, 90 S. Ct. 1011 (1970). See also *Buck v. N.Y. City Bd. of Ed.*, 553 F. 2d 315 (2d Cir. 1977), cert. denied in 438 U.S., 98 S. Ct. 3122 (1978).

[147]*Morrissey v. Brewer*, supra note 70.

[148]*Marshall v. Jerrico, Inc.*, 446 U.S. 238, 100 S. Ct. 1610 (1980); *Hortonville J.S.D. No. 1 v. Hortonville Ed. Assn.*, 426 U.S. 482, 96 S. Ct. 2308 (1976); *Holley v. Seminole County School Dist.*, 755 F. 2d 1492 (11th Cir. 1985).

[149]94 S. Ct. 1633, 416 U.S. 134 (1974), at p. 157.

[150]Ibid., at pp. 167–68.

[151]96 S. Ct. 893, 424 U.S. 319 (1975), at p. 335.

[152]105 S. Ct. 1487, 470 U.S. 532 (1985).

[153]Ibid., at p. 1494.

[154]See *Gilbert v. Homar*, 520 U.S. 924 (1997).

[155]*Gorham v. City of Kansas City*, 590 P. 2d 1051 (Kan. S. Ct. 1979); *Winston v. U.S. Postal Service*, 585 F. 2d 198 (7th Cir. 1978).

[156]*Bence v. Breier*, 501 F. 2d 1185 (7th Cir. 1974), cert. denied in 419 U.S. 1121, 95 S. Ct. 804 (1975).

[157]*Perea v. Fales*, 114 Cal. Rptr. 808 (1974), at p. 810.

[158]*Kramer v. City of Bethlehem*, 289 A. 2d 767 (1972).

[159]*Rogenski v. Board of Fire and Police Commissioners of Moline*, 285 N.E. 2d 230 (1972). See also *Major v. Hampton*, 413 F. Supp. 66 (1976), in which the court held that an IRS rule against activities tending to discredit the agency was overbroad as applied to a married employee who had maintained an apartment for illicit sexual liaisons during off-duty hours.

[160]*Grayned v. City of Rockford*, 92 S. Ct. 2294, 408 U.S. 104 (1972), at pp. 108–109.

[161]*Bence v. Breier*, supra note 81, at p. 1190.

[162]*Rinaldi v. Civil Service Commission*, 244 N.W. 2d 609 (Mich. 1976).

[163]*Allen v. City of Greensboro, North Carolina*, 452 F. 2d 489 (4th Cir. 1971).

[164]*Petraitis v. Board of Fire and Police Commissioners City of Palos Hills*, 335 N.E. 2d 126 (Ill. 1975); *Haywood v. Municipal Court*, 271 N.E. 2d 591 (Mass. 1971); *Lewis v. Board of Trustee*, 212 N.Y.S. 2d 677 (1961). Compare *Stanton v. Board of Fire and Police Commissioners of Village of Bridgeview*, 345 N.E. 2d 822 (Ill. 1976).

[165]*DeSalvatore v. City of Oneonta*, 369 N.Y.S. 2d 820 (1975).

[166]*Marino v. Los Angeles*, 110 Cal. Rptr. 45 (1973).

[167]*Guido v. City of Marion*, 280 N.E. 2d 81 (Ind. 1972).

[168]*Carroll v. Goldstein*, 217 A. 2d 676 (R.I. 1976).

[169]*Firemen's and Policemen's Civil Service Commission v. Shaw*, 306 S.W. 2d 160 (Tex. 1957).

[170]*Martin v. City of St. Martinville*, 321 So. 2d 532 (La. 1975).

[171]*Arnold v. City of Aurora*, 498 P. 2d 970 (Colo. 1973).

[172]*Carey v. Piphus*, 435 U.S. 247, 98 S. Ct. 1042 (1978).

[173]*County of Monroe v. Dept. of Labor*, 690 F. 2d 1359 (11th Cir. 1982).

[174]*Gitlow v. New York*, 268 U.S. 652, 45 S. Ct. 625 (1925).

[175]*Pickering v. Board of Education*, 88 S. Ct. 1731, 391 U.S. 563 (1968), at p. 568.

[176]*Keyishian v. Board of Regents*, 385 U.S. 589, 87 S. Ct. 675 (1967).

[177]*Pickering v. Board of Education*, supra note 100.

[178]*Muller v. Conlisk*, 429 F. 2d 901 (7th Cir. 1970).

[179]*Flynn v. Giarusso*, 321 F. Supp. 1295 (E.D. La. 1971), at p. 1299. The regulation was revised and later ruled constitutional in *Magri v. Giarusso*, 379 F. Supp. 353 (E.D. La. 1974). See also *Gasparinetti v. Kerr*, 568 F. 2d 311 (3rd Cir. 1977), cert. denied in 436 U.S. 903, 98 S. Ct. 2232 (1978).

[180]*In re Gioglio*, 248 A. 2d 570 (N.J. 1968); *Brukiewa v. Police Commissioner of Baltimore*, 263 A. 2d 210 (Md. 1970); *Kannisto v. City and County of San Francisco*, 541 F. 2d 841 (9th Cir. 1976), cert. denied in 430 U.S. 931 S. Ct. 1552 (1977). Compare *Magri v. Giarusso*, supra note 104; *Hosford v. California State Personnel Board*, 141 Cal. Rptr. 354 (1977); and *Simpson v. Weeks*, 570 F. 2d 240 (8th Cir. 1978).

[181]*Brukiewa v. Police Commissioner of Baltimore*, supra note 105.

[182]*Perry v. City of Kinloch*, 680 F. Supp. 1339 (1988).

[183]*Brockell v. Norton*, 732 F. 2d 664 (8th Cir. 1984).

[184]See *Perez v. Agostini*, 37 F. Supp. 2d 103 (D.P.R. 1999); *Dill v. City of Edmond, Oklahoma*, 155 F. 3d 1193 (10th Cir. 1998); *Cahill v. O'Donnell*, 7 F. Supp. 2d 341 (S.D.N.Y. 1998); *Hadad v. Croucher*, 970 F. Supp. 1227 (N.D. Ohio 1997); *Saunders v. Hunter*, 980 F. Supp. 1236 (M.D. Fla. 1997); *Forsyth v. City of Dallas, Texas*, 91 F. 3d 769 (5th Cir. 1996); and *Glass v. Dachel*, 2 F. 3d 733 (7th Cir. 1993).

[185]Adapted from Will Aitchison, *The Rights of Law Enforcement Officers*, 4th ed. (Portland, Oregon: Labor Relations Information System, 2000), p. 298.

[186]See *Lytle v. City of Haysville*, 138 F. 3d 857 (10th Cir. 1998), and *Frederick v. Department of Justice*, 73 F. 3d 349 (4th Cir. 1996).

[187]*Broaderick v. Oklahoma*, 413 U.S. 601, 93 S. Ct. 2908 (1973), and *Reeder v. Kansas City Bd. of Police Comm.*, 733 F. 2d 543 (8th Cir. 1984).

[188]*United Public Workers v. Mitchell*, 330 U.S. 75, 67 S. Ct. (1947): *U.S. Civil Service Commission v. National Association of Letter Carriers*, 413 U.S. 548, 93 S. Ct. 2880 (1973).

[189]*Broaderick v. Oklahoma*, supra note 112.

[190]*Sponick v. Detroit Police Dept.*, #15396, 49 Mich. App. 162, 211 N.W.2d 674 (Mich. App. 1973).

[191]*Sponick v. City of Detroit Police Department*, 211 N.W. 2d 674 (Mich. 1973), at p. 681. But see *Wilson v. Taylor*, 733 F. 2d 1539 (11th Cir. 1984).

[192]*Bruns v. Pomerleau*, 319 F. Supp. 58 (D. Md. 1970). See also *McMullen v. Carson*, 754 F. 2d 936 (11th Cir. 1985), where it was held that a Ku Klux Klansman could not be fired from his position as a records clerk in the sheriff's department simply because he was a Klansman. The court did uphold the dismissal because his active KKK participation threatened to cripple the agency's ability to perform its public duties effectively.

[193]*Civil Service Commission of Tucson v. Livingston*, 525 P. 2d 949 (Ariz. 1974).

[194]*City of San Diego v. John Roe*, 543 U.S. 77, 125 S. Ct. 521 (2005).

[195]See, for example, *Tinker v. Des Moines School District*, 393 U.S. 503, 89 S. Ct. 733 (1969).

[196]425 U.S. 238, 96 S. Ct. 1440 (1976).

[197]*Mapp v. Ohio*, 367 U.S. 643, 81 S. Ct. 1684 (1961).

[198]*Katz v. United States*, 389 U.S. 347, 88 S. Ct. 507 (1967).

[199]*Ibid*.

[200]*Smith v. Maryland*, 442 U.S. 735, 99 S. Ct. 2577 (1979), and *Chan v. State*, 78 Md. App. 287, 552 (1989). The "expectation to privacy" clause was developed in *Katz v. United States*, supra note 12, a case that involved warrantless electronic surveillance of a public telephone booth. The Court said that "the Fourth Amendment protects people, not places. What a person knowingly exposes to the public, even in his own home or office, is not subject to Fourth Amendment protection. But what he seeks to preserve as private, even in an area accessible to the public, may be constitutionally protected. . . . There is a two-fold requirement, first that a person have exhibited an actual expectation of privacy, and second that the expectation by one's society is prepared to recognize it as reasonable/legitimate."

[201]See *People v. Tidwell*, 266 N.E. 2d 787 (Ill. 1971).

[202]See *Ontario v. Quon* 529 F.3rd 892 (2010).

[203]*Biehunik v. Felicetta*, 441 F. 2d 228 (2nd Cir. 1971), cert. denied in 403 U.S. 932, 91S.Ct. 2256 (1971).

[204]*United States v. Leon*, 468 U.S. 897, 104S.Ct. 3430 (1984), and *Massachusetts v. Sheppard*, 468 U.S. 981, 104 S. Ct. 3424 (1984).

[205]*Illinois v. Gates*, 462 U.S. 213, 103 S. Ct. 2317 (1984).

[206]The concept of the "good faith-reasonable belief" defense as either a qualified or an absolute immunity has significant case history. See Isadore Silver, *Police Civil Liability* (New York: Matthew Bender and Company, 1987), chapters 4 and 7.

[207]See *Floyd v. Farrell*, 765 F. 2d 1 (1st Cir. 1985); *Malley v. Briggs*, 475 U.S. 335, 106 S. Ct. 1092 (1986); *Santiago v. Fenton*, 891 F. 2d 373 (1st Cir. 1989); and *Hoffman v. Reali*, 973 F. 2d 980 (1st Cir. 1992).

[208]*Sheetz v. Mayor and City Council of Baltimore, Maryland*, 315 Md. 208 (1989).

[209]385 U.S. 493, 87 S. Ct. 6126 (1967).

[210]The states are bound by this requirement as well. *Malloy v. Hogan*, 378 U.S. 1, 84 S. Ct. 489 (1964).

[211]*Gardner v. Broderick*, 392 U.S. 273, 88 S. Ct. 1913 (1968).

[212]These procedural rights in police disciplinary actions have often been referred to as the "Garrity Rights." They were developed through a series of cases; see *Lefkowitz v. Turley*, 414 U.S. 70, 94 S. Ct. 316 (1973), and *Confederation of Police v. Conlisk*, 489 F. 2d 891 (1973), cert. denied in 416 U.S. 956, 94 S. Ct. 1971 (1974). Further, as the rights appear here, see Aitchison, *The Rights of Law Enforcement Officers*, p. 118.

[213]See *Gabrilowitz v. Newman*, 582 F. 2d 100 (1st Cir. 1978). Cases upholding the department's authority to order an officer to take a polygraph examination include *Eshelman v. Blubaum*, 560 P. 2d 1283 (Ariz. 1977); *Dolan v. Kelly*, N.Y.S. 2d 478 (1973); *Richardson v. City of Pasadena*, 500 S.W. 2d 175 (Tex. 1973); *Seattle Police Officer's Guild v. City of Seattle*, 494 P. 2d 485 (Wash. 1972); *Roux v. New Orleans Police Department*, 223 So.2d 905 (La. 1969); *Coursey v. Board of Fire and Police Commissioners*, 234 N.E. 2d 339 (Ill. 1967); *Frazee v. Civil Service Board of City of Oakland*, 338 P. 2d 943 (Cal. 1959); and *Hester v. Milledgeville*, 777 F. 2d 1492 (11th Cir. 1985). Cases denying the department's authority include *Molino v. Board of Public Safety of City of Torrington*, 225 A. 2d 805 (Conn. 1966); *Stape v. Civil Service Commission of City of Philadelphia*, 172 A. 2d 161 (Pa. 1961); and *Farmer v. Fort Lauderdale*, 427 So. 2d 187 (Fla. 1983), cert. denied in 464 U.S. 816, 104 S. Ct. 74 (1983).

[214]*Eshelman v. Blubaum*, supra note 141, p. 1286.

[215]*Farmer v. City of Fort Lauderdale*, supra note 141.

[216]*Furtado v. Town of Plymouth*, 451 Mass. 529, 888 N.E.2d 357 (Mass. 2008).

[217]*Faust v. Police Civil Service Commission*, 347 A. 2d 765 (Pa. 1975); *Steward v. Leary*, 293 N.Y.S. 2d 573 (1968); *Brewer v. City of Ashland*, 86 S.W. 2d 669 (Ky. 1935); *Fabio v. Civil Service Commission of Philadelphia*, 373 A. 2d 751 (Pa. 1977).

[218]*Anderson v. City of Philadelphia, Pennsylvania*, 668 F. Supp. 441 (1987), reversed by 845F. 2d 1216 (3rd Cir. 1988).

[219]See Aitchison, *The Rights of Law Enforcement Officers*, pp. 58–62.

[220]See *Bigby v. City of Chicago*, 766 F. 2d 1053 (7th Cir. 1985), cert. denied in 474 U.S. 1056, 106 S. Ct. 793 (1986); *McCoy v. Board of Fire and Police Commissioners* (Chicago), 398 N.E. 2d 1020 (1979); *Davis v. Williams*, 588 F. 2d 69 (4th Cir. 1979); *Parker v. Levy*, 417 U.S. 733, 94 S. Ct. 2547 (1974); *Bence v. Brier*, 501 F. 2d 1184 (7th Cir. 1974), cert. denied in 419 U.S. 1121, 95 S. Ct. 1552 (1977); and *Gee v. California State Personnel Board*, 85 Cal. Rptr. 762 (1970).

[221]Whether or not reasonable people would agree that the conduct was punishable so that an individual is free to steer a course between lawful and unlawful behaviors is the key to "reasonableness." See *Cranston v. City of Richmond*, 710 P. 2d 845 (1986), and *Said v. Lackey*, 731 S.W. 2d 7 (1987).

[222]*Cranston v. City of Richmond*, supra note 148.

[223]See *City of St. Petersburg v. Police Benevolent Association*, 414 So. 2d 293 1982, and *Brown v. Sexner*, 405 N.E. 2d 1082 (1980).

[224]*Richter v. Civil Service Commission of Philadelphia*, 387 A. 2d 131 (1978).

[225]*Miller v. City of York*, 415 A. 2d 1280 (1980), and *Kannisto v. City and County of San Francisco*, 541 F. 2d 841 (1976), cert. denied in 430 U.S. 931, 97 S. Ct. 1552 (1977).

[226]*McIntosh v. Monroe Police Civil Board*, 389 So. 2d 410 (1980); *Barnett v. New Orleans Police Department*, 413 So.2d 520 (1982); *Allman v. Police Board of Chicago*, 489 N.E. 2d 929 (1986).

[227]*Philadelphia Civil Service Commission v. Wotjuski*, 525 A. 2d 1255 (1987); *Gandolfo v. Department of Police*, 357 So.568 (1978); *McDonald v. Miller*, 596 F. 2d 686 (1979).

[228]*Monroe v. Board of Public Safety*, 423 N.Y.S. 2d 963 (1980).

[229]*Redo v. West Goshen Township*, 401 A. 2d 394 (1979).

[230]*Brase v. Board of Police Commissioners*, 487 N.E. 2d 91 (1985).

[231]See *John Doe v. U.S. Department of Justice*, 565, F.3d 1375 (Fed Cir. 2009).

[232]See *Brady v. Maryland*, 373 U.S. 83 (1963).

[233]See *Giglio v. United States*, 405 U.S. 150 (1972) and expansion of the *Brady* duty in *United States v. Agurs*, 427 U.S. 97 (1976), *United States v. Bagley*, 473 U.S. 667 (1985), *Kyles v. Whitley*, 514 U.S. 419 (1995), and *Youngblood v. West Virginia*, 547 U.S. (2006).

[234]Adapted from Richard Weinblatt, "Top 10 Social Networking Tips for Police," Policeone.com (August 25, 2009). Retrieved on July 24, 2010.

[235]*Major v. Hampton*, 413 F. Supp. 66 (1976).

[236]*City of North Muskegon v. Briggs*, 473 U.S. 909 (1985).

[237]*National Gay Task Force v. Bd. of Ed. of Oklahoma City*, 729 F. 2d 1270 (10th Cir. 1984).

[238]See *Whisenhund v. Spradlin*, 464 U.S. 964 (1983), and *Kukla v. Village of Antioch*, 647 F. Supp. 799 (1986), cohabitation of officers; *Coryle v. City of Oil City*, 405 A. 2d 1104 (1979), public lewdness; *Childers v. Dallas Police Department*, 513 F. Supp. 134 (1981); and *Fout v. California State Personnel Board*, child molesting; *Fugate v. Phoenix Civil Service Board*, 791 F. 2d 736 (9th Cir. 1986), sex with prostitutes; and *Doe v. Commonwealth Attorney*, 425 U.S. 901, 96S. Ct. 1489 (1976), *Smith v. Price*, 616 F. 2d 1371 (5th Cir. 1980), and *Bowers v. Hardwick*, 478 U.S. 186, 106 S. Ct. 2841 (1986), sodomy as a state law prohibiting homosexuality.

[239]*Bd. of Ed. v. National Gay Task Force*, 729 F. 2d 1270 (10th Cir. 1984), affirmed in 470 U.S. 903, 105 S. Ct. 1858 (1985).

[240]*Rowland v. Mad River Sch. Dist.*, 730 F. 2d (6th Cir. 1984), cert. denied in 470 U.S. 1009, 105 S. Ct. 1373 (1985).

[241]*Todd v. Navarro*, 698 F. Supp. 871 (1988).

[242]*Lawrence v. Texas*, 539U.S. 558, 123 S. Ct. 2472 (2003).

[243]"What you should know about the EEOC and the enforcement protections for LGBT Workers." Retrieved August 6 from: http://www.eeoc.gov/eeoc/newsroom/wysk/enforcement_protections_lgbt_workers.cfm

[244]*McCarthy v. Philadelphia Civil Service Comm.*, 424 U.S. 645, 96 S. Ct. 1154 (1976).

[245]*Miller v. Police of City of Chicago*, 349 N.E. 2d 544 (Ill. 1976); *Williamson v. Village of Baskin*, 339 So.2d 474 (La. 1976); *Nigro v. Board of Trustees of Alden*, 395 N.Y.S. 2d 544 (1977).

[246]*State, County, and Municipal Employees Local 339 v. City of Highland Park*, 108 N.W. 2d 544 (1977).

[247]*Hameetman v. City of Chicago*, 776 F. 2d 636 (7th Cir. 1985).

[248]*Cox v. McNamara*, 493 P. 2d 54 (Ore. 1972); *Brenkle v. Township of Shaler*, 281 A. 2d 920 (Pa. 1972); *Hopwood v. City of Paducah*, 424 S.W. 2d 134 (Ky. 1968); *Flood v. Kennedy*, 239 N.Y.S. 2d 665 (1963). See also *Trelfa v. Village of Centre Island*, 389 N.Y.S. 2d 22 (1976). Rules prohibiting law enforcement officers from holding interest in businesses that manufacture, sell, or distribute alcoholic beverages have also been upheld. *Bock v. Long*,

279 N.E. 2d 464 (Ill. 1972); *Johnson v. Trader*, 52 So.2d 333 (Fla. 1951).

[249] Richard N. Williams, *Legal Aspects of Discipline by Police Administrators*, Traffic Institute Publication No. 2705 (Evanston, IL: Northwestern University, 1975), p. 4.

[250] *City of Crowley Firemen v. City of Crowley*, 264 So. 2d 368 (La. 1972).

[251] See *Rojas v. Alexander's Department Store, Inc.*, 654 F. Supp. 856 (1986), and *Reagan v. Hampton*, 700 F. Supp. 850 (1988).

[252] *Reich v. Board of Fire and Police Commissioners*, 301 N.E. 2d 501 (Ill. 1973).

[253] *Krolick v. Lowery*, 302 N.Y.S. 2d 109 (1969), at p. 115, and *Hester Milledgeville*, 598 F. Supp. 1456, at p. 457, n. 2 (M.D. Ga. 1984), modified in 777 F. 2d 1492 (11th Cir. 1985).

[254] *McCracken v. Department of Police*, 337 So. 2d 595 (La. 1976).

[255] *Krolick v. Lowery*, supra note 229.

[256] 466 U.S. 109, 104 S. Ct. 1652 (1984), at p. 1656.

[257] *National Federation of Federal Employees v. Weinberger*, 818 F. 2d 935 (1987). See also related cases: *National Treasury Employees Union v. Von Raab*, 816 F. 2d 170 (1987),

and *Lovvorn v. City of Chattanooga, Tennessee*, 846 F. 2d 1539 (1988).

[258] *O'Connor v. Ortega*, 480 U.S. 709, 107 S. Ct. 1492, (1987).

[259] 489 U.S. 602, 109 S. Ct. 1402 (1989).

[260] Supra note 195.

[261] *City of Palm Bay v. Bauman*, 475 So.2d 1322 (Fla. 5th DCA 1985). Officers can be required to submit to urinalysis if there is a "reasonable suspicion" that the officer has been using a prohibited substance (including alcohol), see *Jackman v. Schembri*, 635 NYS.2d 30 (A.D. 1995)[1996 FP72].

[262] The New York Policy was challenged and upheld in *Lynch v. City of New York*, 589 F.3rd 94 (2d Cir. 2009).

[263] *Walters v. Secretary of Defense*, 725 F. 2d 107 (D.C. Cir. 1983).

[264] *Security of Law Enforcement Employees, District Counsel 82 v. Carly*, 737 F. 2d 187 (2d Cir. 1984); *Division 241 Amalgamated Transit Union v. Suscy*, 538 F. 2d 1264 (7th Cir. 1976) cert. denied in 429 U.S. 1029, 97 S. Ct. 653 (1976); *McDonnell v. Hunter*, 612 F. Supp. 1122 (S.D. Iowa 1984), affirmed in 746 F. 2d 785 (8th Cir. 1984).

[265] For a comprehensive review of the cases in this area, see Gregory P. Orvis, "Drug Testing in the Criminal Justice Workplace," *American Journal of Criminal Justice* 18, No. 2 (spring 1994), pp. 290–305.

CHAPTER FIFTEEN

ORGANIZATIONAL CHANGE

Learning Objectives

1. Explain why change occurs in law enforcement agencies.
2. Discuss five situations when change should not be initiated.
3. Analyze three models of change in organizations.
4. Discuss the role of the rank and file in organizational change.
5. Explain why organizational change sometimes fails.
6. Describe how to make organizational change succeed.
7. Describe the role of technology in police organizational change.
8. Discuss a few ways in which policing may change in the coming years.

INTRODUCTION

IT HAS LONG BEEN *said in policing circles that cops hate two things: change; and the way things are! That old adage is humorous but also adeptly sums up the organizational frustrations for many police officers and executives. Law enforcement is notoriously slow to change, but when things do happen, it often results in longstanding cultural norms, creating uncertainty and tension.*

Organizational change is stressful, even in the best of circumstances. But in law enforcement, change often requires both structural and cultural adjustments that impact an organization's legitimacy, officer morale, union or association relationships, and community relations. And organizational change in policing is a phenomenon that is occurring at warp speed. For instance, outrage over the deaths of several unarmed black men in 2014 and 2015 has led to calls to adopt principles of fair and impartial policing, examine use of force and hiring policies, demilitarize crowd control measures, improve community relations, and expand the role of technology. Furthermore, generational issues within the workforce are driving massive changes in police culture as well.

Police administrators in the current climate and the near future must understand and adapt to these factors in order to lead their organization successfully. This chapter discusses elements of organizational change, including (1) what drives change in law enforcement; (2) what limits change in law enforcement; (3) models of organizational change; (4) the role that politics plays in organizational change; (5) the role of officer culture in organizational change; (6) the role of technology in organizational change; (7) why change sometimes fails; (8) how to increase the chances of organizational success; and (9) the future of policing.

WHY CHANGE OCCURS

In any organization, there can be any number of catalysts for change. Law enforcement agencies, however, are in a unique position when it comes to change: they sit at a complex intersection of social issues, politics, and community service. Each of those facets both influence and are influenced by changes in policing organizations. This is why police administrators face particularly stressful and difficult challenges when making decisions related to organizational change. The following provides some concrete examples as to "why" police agencies change.

Reaction to Crisis

After September 11, 2001, the mission of police organizations in America—particularly those in major metropolitan areas—fundamentally changed. Never before had police departments been charged with securing the nation by preventing the next terrorist attack on the homeland. Historically, that was the role of the federal government and did not include state and local police agencies. As discussed in Chapter 3, the Posse Comitatus Act actually made it illegal for federal troops to be used in law enforcement purposes primarily because their role was relegated to national security interests; blurring the role between police and the military was prohibited. However post-9/11, police agencies began to take a much more active role in anti-terrorism by gathering intelligence, monitoring communities for terror activity, militarizing their SWAT operations, and equipping fusion centers with the technology to allow the analysis of massive amounts of data and information.[1]

Further, we are currently witnessing a major crisis that may again, fundamentally change policing. The 2014-15 shootings of unarmed black men by local police, such as Michael Brown, Samuel DuBose, and Walter Scott, as well as the in-custody deaths of Sandra Bland, Freddie Gray, and Eric Garner have caused a major public outcry and prompted calls for police agencies to re-examine the way they do business. External constraints as well as internal self-reviews have prompted significant changes in policing, from training to internal investigations to public outreach. In the wake of these incidents, departments are struggling to address inherent bias within officer culture, de-escalation techniques, and community relations—all of which could have major implications related to organizational structure and procedure. (See Box 15.1.)

As discussed in the previous chapter, the Civil Rights Division of the U.S. Department of Justice has the right to sue police agencies anywhere within the jurisdiction of the United States under the 1994 Violent Crime Control and Law Enforcement Act. While forced change is rarely seen as a positive influence in policing, the impact of a federal consent decree on police reform has not gone unnoticed.[2] For those agencies currently under such "memorandums of understanding," the ability of an external entity to monitor rogue police cultures and agencies and develop a set of "best practices" has been the pathway to change. Effective policing should not be violent and should not be biased but rather imbue from the *Bill of Rights* those guarantees and liberties to which every police officer in this country swears their first and most important oath . . . to uphold U.S. Constitution.

Box 15.1: Actions in Wake of Police–Community Unrest

Police confront protestors in Baltimore, Maryland, following the funeral of Freddie Gray in Baltimore in April, 2015. (MICHAEL REYNOLDS/epa european pressphoto agency b.v/Alamy Stock Photo)

An Associated Press analysis identified at least 40 measures passed by 24 states that addressed issues highlighted by the events in Ferguson, MO, in the summer of 2014:

Body Cameras: Sixteen states passed measures that directly addressed officer worn cameras that can record interactions with an individual during a specific incident as well as general interactions with the public. Some states (Arizona, Maryland, and Louisiana) merely created committees to further study the issue or recommend policies on how the cameras should be used by local and state agencies, while other states (Illinois and Oregon) passed rigorous laws setting standards for when police must use the cameras and how long the videos must be stored. Other states (Colorado, Connecticut, South Carolina, and Texas) approved various grant programs to help local agencies purchase cameras and associated equipment and still other states (Florida, North Dakota, and Oklahoma) passed laws limiting the access of camera videos to the public. Finally, some states (North Carolina, Alaska, and Washington) simply did not address the issue or had previous legislation that governed the use of body worn cameras by police.

Citizen Cameras: Several states (California and Oregon) affirmed the right of citizens to video or take photos of police officers conducting business or acting while on duty. Other states (Colorado and Connecticut) passed laws that held police agencies liable for interfering with citizens filming, taking videos, or photographing police officers in the scope of their duty.

Use of Deadly Force—Chokeholds: As a reaction stemming from the death of Eric Garner by an NYPD officer in Staten Island, New York, in July 2014, some states (Nevada, Tennessee, Illinois, and the District of Columbia) have laws that severely limit the police use of the carotid artery chokehold, or any other type of choke hold unless the officer is in a "life-or-death" situation. These laws classify chokeholds as "the use of deadly force."

Military Equipment: Concerned that some tactical weaponry such as riot gear, grenade launders, assault rifles, and armored vehicles, for example—are transferred from the U.S. Department of Defense with little oversight or justification creating a culture of aggression within police agencies and forces, several states (Montana, New Jersey, and New York) passed laws prohibiting local police to acquire former military equipment without specific authorization and oversight. These laws severely restrict the acquisition of military equipment by police and stem from President Barack Obama's special report entitled, *Review of Federal Support for Local Law Enforcement Equipment Acquisition*, December 2014.

Training for Police Officers: Forty-nine states have commissions that develop, implement, and administer training curriculum for police. These entities now require inclusion of issue-specific courses in basic as well as in-service police training focused on de-escalation. The two most cited areas of training include (1) *crisis intervention training* that prepares officers to better respond to situations involving people with mental health problems and alternatives to lethal force when interacting with potentially dangerous people in the community; and (2) *racial bias training* providing police officers with tools to help them reduce the effect of bias on their decision-making particularly during arrest. One state (Montana) enacted legislation that provided counseling for officers found to have engaged in race-based traffic stops and dictated that state training courses must "stress understanding and respect for racial and cultural differences and the development of effective, noncombat methods of carrying out law enforcement duty in a racially and culturally diverse environment" (Montana State Law, Section 44-2-117). Further, several states (Colorado, Connecticut, Maryland, Rhode Island, and Illinois) passed legislation that either addressed and curtailed racial bias or profiling by police or required racial demographic data on subjects to be collected regularly and reported to state agencies for oversight.

Source: Associated Press, "State Actions in Wake of Ferguson's Upheaval." August 2, 2015, and National Conference of State Legislatures (NCSL), *Law Enforcement Overview* (May 29, 2015). See: http://www.ncsl.org/research/civil-and-criminal-justice/law-enforcement.aspx.

Fluctuating Crime Rates

As crime rates fluctuate, police organizations often adapt to address these primary indicators of safety and concern. Increasing the number of patrol officers to combat rising crime rates may involve significant organizational change—perhaps a tactical unit or special program was shifted in order to free-up personnel for such a change. Agencies may adapt new strategies—like hotspots policing—to attack a specific problem, requiring dedicated units, new task forces and partnerships, new technology, additional training, additional community outreach, and a new outlook on crime reduction altogether. Conversely, if crime rates decrease dramatically, specialized units may be disbanded altogether or reorganized to tackle another problem.

Technological Advances

Rapid change is often associated with the introduction of new technology. Witness the complex and rapid change that has occurred in global society over the past two decades with the introduction of the Internet or the impact on lives due to new innovations in medicine in just the last 5 years. Consider the discussions in Chapter 2 relating to Compstat, intelligence-led policing, evidence-based policing, and GIS—and how they fundamentally changed the way police organizations go about doing their job.[3] Currently, and as discussed in Chapter 4, body worn cameras are being touted as the next instrument of change within policing—and the technology will certainly require major resource commitments from agencies, infrastructure adjustments, policy and procedural changes, and new organizational considerations.

Funding and Economic Decline

Budgetary concerns obviously affect any organization—and in policing, money can be tied to every level of organizational effort. In a survey by the Police Executive Research Forum (PERF) in 2010, 78 percent of police agencies surveyed reported that they had experienced budget cuts as a result of the recession that began in 2008; by 2012, 51 percent reported that they were *still* experiencing cutbacks due to lingering effects of the downturn.[4] One significant result of the 2008 recession has been the steady and rapid decline of employee benefits to police officers across the nation. Despite market rebounds, by 2015, many pension plans were still struggling as a result of the massive losses sustained in the economic collapse that devastated stock and real estate holdings on which many pension funds were dependent upon. Coupled with an ever-aging workforce, police agencies witnessed an unprecedented number of retirements that further stressed the situation. For instance, in San Diego and other California communities, police officers facing a slashing of work and retirement benefits simply quit—or retired before change legislation was enacted causing further negative impact on already stressed funds. Department across the country, and especially in hard-hit California, massive reductions in pension plans approved as a result of economic crisis continues to hamper recruitment efforts.[5] Chapter 12(Financial Management) highlights similar issues in other communities.

Unfortunately, economic decline for most cities interprets into fewer officers for the police department. Dwindling numbers of police have several negative effects on a community: (1) More proactive programs that focus on crime-specific areas are reduced, as well as more community-based strategies give way to the primary, reactive police mission of answering calls for service at the patrol level; (2) Reactive policing usually results in higher crime rates as little if any proactive work is focused on crime-specific issues; (3) The reduction of community-based programs often hinder larger efforts to improve relationships between the police and different sectors of the community, particularly minority areas; (4) This leads to a vicious downward cycle of maintaining the reactive functions of patrol over more progressive strategies that attempt to improve police transparency, legitimacy, and organizational change; and (5) The resulting end is often highlighted by community distrust and anger toward the police.

More obvious effects can be seen in program cuts and organizational shifts as a result of budget adjustments. In 2010, PERF's research revealed that 32 percent of agencies reported freezing recruitment of new officers, and 23 percent had implemented officer layoffs. Fifty-eight percent of agencies in 2010 reported a reduction of services to the community; in a 2012 follow-up, that number had dropped to 44 percent. Furthermore, 45 percent of police agencies had discontinued or significantly reduced specialty units as a result of a poor local economy; and 51 percent of agencies reported that they were eliminating or cutting back on plans to acquire new technology.[6] (See Box 15.2.) Considering that technology plays a crucial role in the advancement of policing and that most cutting-edge policing strategies require sophisticated information systems to be monitored and hence, evaluated—and that technology is the inherent cornerstone of a much-demanded implementation of body worn cameras across the country—it becomes obvious that organization change within policing often requires significant economic funding.

Politics

Chapters 1 and 4 documented the historical linkages and issues of politics in policing in the United States and clearly the professional era of policing argued successfully to eliminate politics out of law enforcement. However, this has rarely been the case. The reality is that law enforcement agencies are legitimate governmental entities given the authority to enforce the laws of the government—making them inherently political. Police

organizations are impacted greatly by what goes on in voting booths, city halls, district attorneys' offices, state legislatures, and the White House.

The most obvious organizational effects from political meddling often occur in agencies where leadership is elected—namely sheriff's offices. In those cases, when a new sheriff is elected, an organization can experience tremendous turnover and major structural change to accommodate a new leader's agenda or mandate. However, elections can greatly change law enforcement agencies that *are not* led by elected officials. For instance, the election of new mayors and the subsequent appointment of new city managers can result in incumbent police chiefs being replaced in order to better fit with an incoming administration's agenda—or, simply because of personality clashes. Police chief positions are largely political appointments, with the chief serving at the pleasure of city officials. If a mayor or city manager is, for example, unhappy with the performance of the police department, they may dismiss the chief and seek change through the administration of a new leader. There can

---

Box 15.2: The Effect of Economic Downturn on Police Agencies

After the recession of 2008, law enforcement agencies felt the effects of tightened budgets for years. A 2012 Police Executive Research Forum survey revealed the organizational consequences of the crisis.

CHANGE IN DEPARTMENT STRUCTURE	% OF POLICE AGENCIES THAT ARE IMPLEMENTING THE CHANGE
Discontinuing or significantly reducing **specialty units**	45%
Consolidating units	25%
Consolidating services with other departments	22%
Reducing public access hours at district stations	18%
Closing/consolidating **district stations**	8%
Contracting out for services	7%
Demoting staff in certain ranks	4%
Privatizing some police services	3%

REDEPLOYMENT STRATEGY	% OF DEPARTMENTS THAT ARE IMPLEMENTING THE CHANGE
Altering **shift times**	44%
Changing **patrol levels in** defined areas	34%
Handling **crime scene processing with** patrol officers	32%
No longer sending **investigators** immediately for certain crimes	30%
Alternative **call handling** strategies (phone or Internet)	25%
Changing **investigative priorities**	24%
Changing **response policies** for calls for service	19%

Source: Police Executive Research Forum. "Policing and the Economic Downturn: Striving for Efficiency Is the New Normal." February 2013. See: http://www.policeforum.org/assets/docs/Critical_Issues_Series/policing%20and%20the%20economic%20downturn%20-%20striving%20for%20efficiency%20is%20the%20new%20normal%202013.pdf.

be real expenses to this type of political change. It can be unsavory and kill officer morale when unqualified or marginally competent people with unbridled ambition successfully use politics to their personal advantage at the considerable expense of others or when the use of politics interferes with the timely and effective implementation of a new or exciting strategy.

Political meddling from outside of the city organizational structure can also have significant impact. For example, a newly elected District (County) or State's Attorney may signal change in prosecutorial decisions that greatly impact policing in that community. Illustratively in Dallas (Texas), a newly elected district attorney suddenly closed a digital forensics lab inside the Dallas Police Department. The closure was not due to financial issues, but rather the political whims of the newly elected DA, whose office in the past had funded the lab.

The lab had been processing digital evidence for police agencies in the entire Metroplex area of over 7 million people, relating to homicide, sexual abuse, child pornography, and various financial crimes.[7] The closure meant that police agencies were left scrambling to find other resources for the processing of digital evidence, forcing organizational changes from small movements like increasing overtime limits for detectives with backlogged cases, to more substantial impacts like adding significant personnel to new units within the department or assembling task forces to process digital evidence for growing numbers of cases.

A Changing Workforce

Conventional wisdom would dictate that the aging sector of the workforce—namely the *Baby Boomers*, who are those born between 1946 and 1964—is leaving policing in large numbers, as they reach retirement age. However, the 2008 economic downturn has actually slowed their retirement in some communities—as pension funds scramble to catch up, and as the cost of living rises, many older police officers are hesitant to leave.[8] Policing, as with other public sector positions, has witnessed this trend more acutely than the private sector. Previous generations of police officers have managed to adapt to the traditional organizational structure without too many issues. The leadership of most police organizations are still very much indoctrinated in a paramilitary model of leadership. However, some policing scholars believe that dramatic change in the workforce of American policing is about to occur.

Contemporary employees, who include *Gen Xers* (1965 through 1980) and *Millenials* (1981 through 1994), are fundamentally different than their predecessors—not content to plow through monotonous paperwork, conform to a stagnant set of rules and regulations, and/or endure the hardship of working for an incompetent manager simply for the sake of getting a paycheck. These employees have been described in the literature as very conscientious, self-assured, and value-centered. Studies have shown Gen Xers and Millenials to be more likely to thrive in collaborative environments than Baby Boomers (1945 through 1964), better at recognizing the value of technology and embracing it as a vital part of their work; more accepting of diversity as a strength in the workplace; and better at multitasking in their jobs.[9]

However, they also lack many of the attributes that current police agencies value highly: namely, the ability to focus on a key issue or see a project through to its end. To deal with such issues, and to fully capitalize on the more positive qualities these generations bring, police agencies may need to change their organizational training model to focus on mentoring and coaching over a longer term than a traditional training academy. Gen Xers and Millenials also have a tendency to want to see career progression much more quickly than their predecessors. For current officers and managers, 20 years was not an abnormal amount of time to ascend to a leadership rank in police agencies. However, the contemporary generation of police wants much faster-growing careers and expects to move up through the ranks much more quickly. Faced with a slow-moving organization structure and bureaucracy, traditionally without many employee incentives, retention of officers will be problematic—an issue that has never confronted most police agencies. The contemporary generation will be much more likely to leave in pursuit of career fulfillment outside of law enforcement.[10] In response, police organizations today may have to institute career pathway programs that emphasize opportunities and delineate ways to achieve them and work with police unions and associations to adapt the promotional process to this new, shifting paradigm of employees. Further, contemporary police officers are also much more interested in accommodations in the workplace that improve their quality of life and their family's quality of life than their predecessors. Contemporary officers often seek more of a work/life balance and identify things like maternity/paternity leave and flexible scheduling as important

---

Quick Facts: The Race Gap in America's Police Departments

According to a recent article in the New York Times, the percentage of white police officers is more than 30 points higher than in the communities they serve. Minorities make up only a quarter of police forces across the county. Therefore, more than three quarters of the cities on which the Census Bureau has collected data have a police department that is disproportionately white relative to the local community population.

Source: Jeremy Ashkenas and Haeyoun Park, "The Race Gap in America's Police Departments," *The New York Times* (April 8, 2015).

to them as paid overtime and vacation. In the future, police agencies that have traditionally been wedded to the 24/7 law enforcement practice over 365 days, with newer officers bearing the burden of the midnight shift and adapting to the complexities of "seniority," may find the significant challenges in keeping the most qualified candidates to the profession. One chief recently lamented as a top recruit left his department after graduating first in the academy, "He didn't want to work nights . . . how can you expect to be a police officer and not work nights?"

Another significant difference from past generations that will undoubtedly be a challenge to police agencies in the future is the bureaucratic structure of command control. As explained in Chapters 5 Organizational Theory and 6 Organizational Design, chain of command and management requires written documents that pass through ranks of progressive responsibility of an organization, with direction following, again in writing down through the organization. By design, these steps take time and reflection with a focus on preserving organizational order and control. Today's contemporary employees demand immediate feedback—a result of technological capabilities like instant text messaging, the ubiquity of email, and social media—mainstays in everyday life of contemporary employees. Today's officers expect much more timely responses with coherent and rationale for decisions than their predecessors and will most certainly impact officer morale, employee retention and productivity, and police organizational dynamics in the future.[11]

As the demographics of the country change, police organizations will also change to become more diverse.[12] (See Figure 15.1.) Population shifts in and of themselves don't necessarily drive this change. For example, a recent examination by the Associated Press of Census Data found that 49 out of 1,400 police departments served majority Hispanic populations; in many cases, these departments served communities that were vastly majority (over 80 percent) Hispanic. However, the demographic make-up of those departments was still well over 50 percent white.[13] Police agencies have long struggled with recruiting minority applicants. The events of 2014 and 2015 have highlighted, once again, the imbalance of power between races within our country. As citizens and government alike begin to focus on this issue in the future, recruitment and retention strategies that focus on minorities, ethnicities, and lifestyles will force organizational change. Nothing heralds this change more than the Supreme Court actions ruling to legalize and recognize same-sex marriages in the landmark case, *Obergefell v. Hodges*. Organizationally, this ruling required that accommodations be made to allow employees to add their same-sex spouses to employer insurance policies, broadened the application of existing leave policies, and opened the availability of retirement and pension benefits to same-sex spouses. While it is too soon to assess the impact that this ruling may have on overall police demographics and organizational change, it does seem likely that police organizations—long considered to be socially conservative—may be headed for massive organizational and cultural change. The Supreme Court ruling directly points to public agencies that

FIGURE 15.1 ▶ New York Police Department (NYPD) Chaplin Iman Khalid Latif offers the opening prayer at the NYPD's Muslim Officers Society scholarship dinner. Founded in 2009 to promote patriotism and advance the interests of its members, the Society is recognized by the NYPD as an employee organization for sworn and civilian personnel. Such organizations reflect the continuing movement of law enforcement agencies toward a diverse workforce. (Courtesy of New York Police Department)

will be more inclusive of gay employees, particularly since sweeping legal rulings related to discrimination against lesbian, gay, bi-sexual, and transgender (LGBT) employee hiring and promotional practices are on the immediate horizon in the wake of the Equal Employment Opportunity Commission's 2015 statement that such discrimination is illegal under federal law.[14]

A New Paradigm Shift

As discussed in Chapter 2, Policing Today paradigms are ways or models of conducting business and they often have an accompanying set of rules and procedures. Max Weber's bureaucratic model can be thought of as a paradigm; when new paradigms are developed, they have the potential for causing significant organizational change. Police scholars have identified several major and important paradigm shifts in policing over the past three decades. These certainly include (1) the advent of new technology to include vast information and communication systems that have broaden the police role from crime fighter to a much more intelligence-driven, national security-oriented police officer backed by fusion centers and array of federal task forces; (2) individual identification by DNA, which has created demands for new skills, training, and procedures in criminal investigation, especially in the areas of evidence identification, collection, preservation, and processing, as well as quantum leaps in clearing decades-old cold cases and exonerating those who were erroneously convicted in the past; and (3) the shift from the traditional, reactive model of policing characterized by random-moving police cars responding to calls for service to the widespread adoption of community-based, predictive police models that are evaluated through rigorous evidence-based techniques. It is too soon to say that the uprising of community outrage over police-involved shootings and in-custody deaths of African Americans in Ferguson, Missouri; Baltimore, Maryland; and Cleveland, Ohio, has contributed to yet another tangible paradigm shift—though it may be on the horizon as body worn cameras and an emphasis on de-escalation training and fair and impartial policing practices become the emphasis of the day.

Regardless, however important these new policing perspectives and strategies may be to improving police legitimacy and to crime reduction, they have exacerbated already existing staffing shortages in state and local law enforcement agencies, strained technology and training budgets, and forced agencies to "do more with less."

WHEN CHANGE SHOULD NOT BE MADE

Because change is a perilous process, some thought should be given to whether it should be undertaken in the first place. Among the conditions that indicate contemplated change should be delayed are as follows:

1. The knowledge, skill, or other resources needed to carry out the change effectively do not exist inside the department.
2. An appropriately experienced external **change agent** is not presently available.
3. The effort of making the change is greater than any benefits to be derived. Former Georgia Governor Zell Miller expressed this as "the juice isn't worth the squeezing." This principle can also be stated as "all motion isn't progress; some of it is just thrashing around."
4. Collateral damage, such as abandonment by key supporters or significant union opposition, may lead chiefs to use their limited stack of "political chips" on another issue of greater concern to them and the community.
5. Too much change is already underway in the department and the nature of the change is not sufficiently important to make now, versus its potential for personnel to feel confused about priorities or conclude that the organization is becoming unstable.

ORGANIZATIONAL CHANGE MODELS

There is an old story about a boy who wanted his dog to have a short tail. But rather than hurt the dog by cutting the tail off all at once, the boy sliced an inch off at a time. This story illustrates what is described as "pain level" associated with gradual and radical change strategies in public organizations. One camp maintains that it is better to implement change swiftly (radical change) and get the upheavals that follow done and over with; the other camp wants to implement changes incrementally over time (gradual change) so that personnel have an opportunity to adjust to new realities and requirements. Proponents of radical change argue that when change is gradual, unanticipated events can derail the effort before it can be completed and that it gives opponents time to organize themselves to thwart further implementation. Kurt Lewin's three-step model on organizational change is a general model of the likely impact on police members when authoritarian and participative strategies using wide input and involvement are used as the basis for gradual radical organizational change; as noted in Chapter 7, leadership is not a spectator sport. Regardless of whether change is gradual or radical, the chief cannot sit passively on the sidelines to see how it turns out—he or she must actively help lead the change.

While some changes can be accomplished through the pronouncement by chiefs, especially in very small departments, larger departments are more complex and therefore require greater planning, the use of more sophisticated techniques, and wide involvement to garner crucial input and support before moving forward to the implementation phase. This often involves the use of organizational development (OD). In Chapter 5, Organizational Theory, the OD process was defined and described. To briefly review, OD is an applied behavioral science method of changing organizations through long-term efforts designed to improve the work culture and work processes.

In this section, two models of **directed change** are presented. The first one, **Lewin's three-step model**, was selected because it is one of the oldest, simplest, and yet, the most durable. The second model, the **traditional action research model**, represents a fairly typical change process. If the second one seems somewhat familiar, it may be due to the fact that planning was covered in an earlier chapter (see Chapter 8, Planning and Decision Making). The traditional action research model is simply a special type of planning. Both Lewin's three-step model and the Traditional Action Research Model rely on the use of organizational development (OD). In addition, the **Burke-Litwin model** of change, a more practical than theoretical exercise, will be presented.

Kurt Lewin's Three-Step Model on Organizational Change

This model involves three sequential steps (see Figure 15.2):

1. *Unfreezing*—Officers, like all other people, get into their "comfort zones." Before change can occur, they have to be "unfrozen" from the perceptions and behaviors that are presently part of who they are and how they approach their jobs. Often, this is

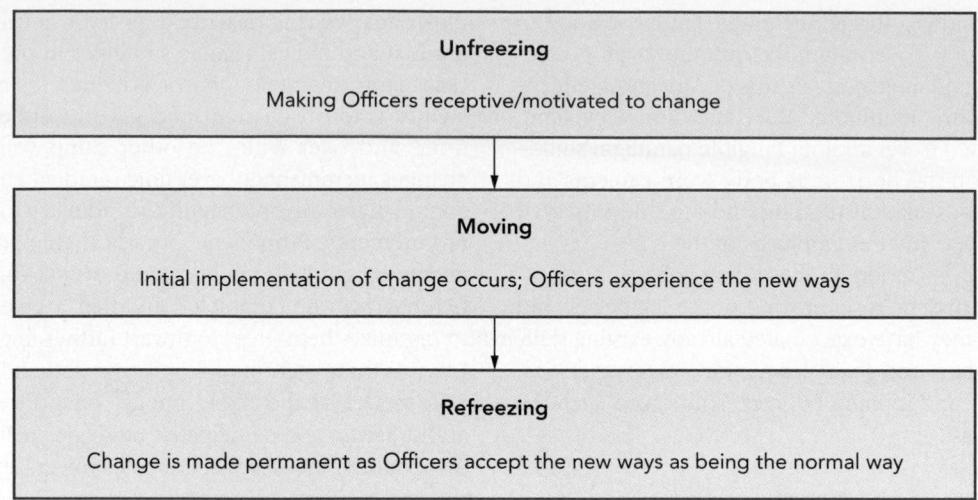

FIGURE 15.2 ▶ Kurt Lewin's three-step model on organizational change.

accomplished by creating a sense of urgency that the present way of doing things is deficient in some way and that a shift to some new procedures will produce better results more efficiently. This tactic is known as "disconfirmation" because, to some degree, it invalidates what is presently being done. The heart of unfreezing is making people be receptive to change.

2. *Moving*—This is a transitional phase in which officers actually experience the changes that were planned; there will be less resistance if officers are, to the maximum extent possible, included in the planning process and feel that they have some impact in shaping events. While chiefs do make top-down decisions that constitute major change, such as to begin using Compstat, there is ample room to involve sworn and civilian personnel from across the agency on the details of implementation, such as the design of forms to capture data and what types of data are most useful for planning various types of operations. The use of officers on task forces or committees cannot be symbolic or gratuitous; such motives will be "sniffed out" immediately and provoke an unpleasant set of dynamics for the chief to preside over.

3. *Refreezing*—The purpose of this phase is for officers to make permanent the changes they experienced in the previous phase, part of the normal way in which they see things, think about them, and behave. Some of the refreezing can be accomplished by appealing to the professionalism of officers—"When we get this thing fully up and running, everybody in the state will be looking at us, wondering how we got so far ahead of them." However, drawing upon the lessons learned from the shift from traditional policing to community policing, resistance tapered off and refreezing occurred faster when departmental awards were realigned with community policing goals, such as recognition for enrolling 25 businesses in a crime prevention program. Thus, as part of any large-scale change process, the use of awards to reinforce the desired behaviors should be carefully considered.

Traditional Action Research Model

There are many organizational development (OD) change models; however, most of them approximate the traditional action research model with the following five steps (see Figure 15.3):

1. *Recognizing the need for change*—Without this awareness, it is simply "business as usual" for police agencies. The change awareness may come from the need to implement the provisions of a Supreme Court decision or a consent decree entered into in partial settlement of a civil liability suit. The department's planning and research unit may have identified lapses in performance that need to be addressed or unusual opportunities on which to capitalize, such as the availability of federal grants to implement community policing programs or to upgrade crime scene investigation capabilities. Individual officers, supervisors, command staff members, or the union may make written recommendations in the form of memos or completed staff work that leads to change. Additionally, any of the situations discussed in the earlier section "Why Change Occurs" can take place, such as a new chief being hired with a mandate to make specific changes in the department's operating philosophy, organizational structure, programs and policies, and procedures.

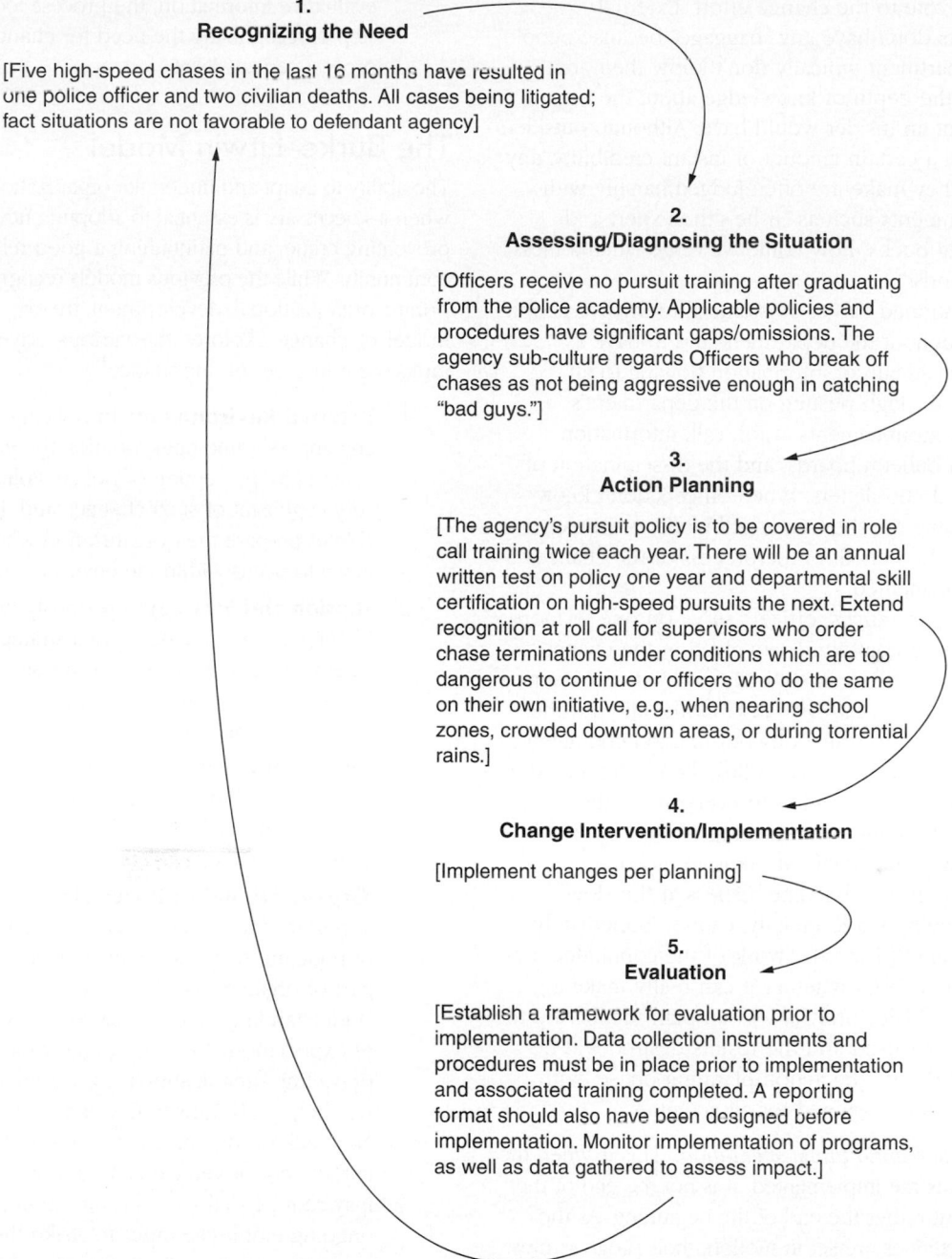

1.
Recognizing the Need

[Five high-speed chases in the last 16 months have resulted in one police officer and two civilian deaths. All cases being litigated; fact situations are not favorable to defendant agency]

2.
Assessing/Diagnosing the Situation

[Officers receive no pursuit training after graduating from the police academy. Applicable policies and procedures have significant gaps/omissions. The agency sub-culture regards Officers who break off chases as not being aggressive enough in catching "bad guys."]

3.
Action Planning

[The agency's pursuit policy is to be covered in role call training twice each year. There will be an annual written test on policy one year and departmental skill certification on high-speed pursuits the next. Extend recognition at roll call for supervisors who order chase terminations under conditions which are too dangerous to continue or officers who do the same on their own initiative, e.g., when nearing school zones, crowded downtown areas, or during torrential rains.]

4.
Change Intervention/Implementation

[Implement changes per planning]

5.
Evaluation

[Establish a framework for evaluation prior to implementation. Data collection instruments and procedures must be in place prior to implementation and associated training completed. A reporting format should also have been designed before implementation. Monitor implementation of programs, as well as data gathered to assess impact.]

FIGURE 15.3 ▶ Traditional action research model.

2. *Assessing/diagnosing the situation*—Two fundamental tasks in assessing the situation must be executed flawlessly: (a) determining the opportunity or the problem—care must be taken to make sure that attention is given to the real problem and not a symptom of it and (b) determining the gap or difference between what is now happening and what the department would like to have happen. In order to accomplish these twin objectives, data must be gathered. Sources of such data include 911, training, and other records, surveys of personnel and clients, and reviews of disciplinary records and litigation trends.

3. *Action planning*—The gap or difference between what is happening and what is desirable is the zone of impact, where meaningful change can occur if something significant is selected to work on. The chief must decide who will be in charge of the change process. Internal candidates for this responsibility know the organization, its capabilities, and its personnel but may lack the necessary skills to lead an effective intervention or may not have the

time to devote to the change effort. External consultants don't have any "baggage" because people in the department typically don't know them, but they lack the depth of knowledge about the department an insider would have. Although outsiders come with a certain amount of instant credibility, any missteps they make are often judged harshly with biting comments such as "If he's the expert and making big bucks, how come we've got such a mess on our hands?"

As mentioned earlier, it is crucial to involve people from throughout the department and to have a continuous stream of information flowing to all personnel through posting on the department's intranet, announcements at roll call, information posted on bulletin boards, and the dissemination of memos and newsletters. When officers don't know what is going on, the rumor mill works overtime, seldom to the benefit of the process or the changes being implemented.

In many instances, officers serve on one or more task forces or committees involved in the change. For example, officers may be appointed to a steering task force, which has overall responsibility for the change, or the information coordination committee, which is charged with providing the continuing and timely flow of information to everyone in the department. Many lower-ranking officers are field-oriented and may chafe at being in meetings, particularly if they become restless at the slow progress being made initially, cannot immediately see any benefit from the work of the committee, or have doubts about whether it can really make a difference.[15] Ultimately, a written plan identifying the process to be used and the results desired will be produced during the action planning phase, with responsibilities assigned for all activities.

4. *Change Intervention/Implementation.* This is when the action plans are implemented. It is not the end of the process but rather the end of the beginning. As the various activities are set in motion, their progress must be carefully monitored against the time lines and standards established during the previous phase.

5. *Evaluation.* This is best accomplished by a series of informative, scheduled reports, and periodic personnel checking through observation and conversations with personnel involved at various levels of the department. The two most common needs during this time are (a) the need to further articulate or increase the level of detail in plans and (b) the need to initiate corrective action because the time lines initially set were too ambitious and cannot be met or the activities have somehow otherwise gotten off track (e.g., an equipment supplier cannot make delivery as previously agreed upon). As the decision makers receive

evaluative information, the process loops back to step 1, recognizing the need for change, and the process repeats itself.

The Burke–Litwin Model

The ability to adapt and undertake organizational transformation when it's necessary is essential to adopting new policing models, preventing crime, and maintaining a good relationship with the community. While the previous models recognize this and incorporate organizational development theory, the Burke–Litwin model of change explores the various drivers of change and ranks them in order of importance[16].

1. **External Environment:** In policing, this would encompass crime rates, politics, the economy, and the community perception of police. Police leaders must be very cognizant of such changes and, indeed, should be able to prepare their organization when such shifts begin to occur within the environment.

2. **Mission and Strategy:** Previously discussed in Chapter 2, these changes are a strategy as a reaction to external forces. Police executives should recognize the necessity for changes in strategy and be able to articulate those to staff.

3. **Leadership:** The ways in which changes are perceived and implemented by line officers and law enforcement staff largely depends on the actions and attitudes of police leaders.

4. **Organizational Culture:** This is extraordinarily important for law enforcement. Culture is a huge part of policing, with traditions and procedures an integral part of organizational and even personal identity. Understanding that culture comes with a certain set of expectations from the organization and that prevailing organizational values must be respected will help with transition. Changes that can feel like an attack on organizational culture (for example: the curtailment of vehicle chases in many jurisdictions) may require dialogue through multiple channels and ongoing employee input to strike the right balance between culture and organizational need.

5. **Structure:** Police leaders will need to assess the impact on relationships, responsibilities, and division of labor that a change will have.

6. **Systems:** These are the policies and procedures related to both people and operations of the organization.

7. **Management Practices:** How do managers/police executives work within the mission and strategy of the organization? Does the way that they treat and direct officers and other personnel reflect the agency's overall values, mission, and strategies?

8. **Work Unit Climate:** Often, a change will impact the immediate working environment of officers or other employees—this can include work hours (such as a

shift change), personnel (redeployments), or locations. In these cases, police executives will need to manage such change sensitively, as it may evoke a range of responses from personnel.

9. **Task Requirements and Individual Skills/Abilities:** Are there personnel with appropriate skill sets within the organization to carry out the necessary change? If not, will training be sufficient, or should outside consultants or new team members be brought in?

10. **Individual Values and Needs:** Organizational dynamics are greatly affected by individual personnel. When implementing change, it is critical to recognize the ways that individual styles, skills, abilities, and attitudes may come together in order to both capitalize on their potential and mitigate their risks.

11. **Motivation Level:** Are employees motivated to make a change? Or is the change an unpopular or misunderstood one? Recognizing and maintaining (or augmenting, if necessary) that the level of motivation throughout a change is critical to success.

12. **Individual and Overall Performance:** It is crucial to understand the level of performance in key areas such as productivity, budgetary adherence, crime reduction and be able to establish baselines to measure the effects of change.

Various Levels of Change

Not all change is momentous. However, the wider the scope of the change and the greater the number of people significantly impacted are, the more difficult it is to implement, sustain, and institutionalize it. For example, assume that historically in a department the ranking patrol supervisor at the scene of a serious crime was in charge of the scene. A new policy is issued; stating whenever detectives are dispatched to the scene of a serious crime, they are in command of all aspects of conducting the on-site investigation. Usually, this would affect the job of patrol sergeants and, although they would grouse at the loss of authority, the change would be implemented without any significant turbulence or opposition. In fact, some sergeants would simply say, "It's fine by me; it's one less thing I have to worry about." But when there is large-scale directed change, "more people are going to be ticked off and eating Rolaids." While some policy changes can be made without controversy, others will provoke opposition; an excellent example of this is when an agency goes to a very restrictive high-speed chase policy and rank-and-file officers feel that their "hands are being tied when it comes to catching bad guys."

When automobiles started becoming more commonplace, police chiefs assigned their best officers to traffic duty because they would be coming into contact with wealthy and professional citizens who could afford the cars. In a sense, police professionalism had its first modest start in traffic units; officers assigned there considered themselves elite. Once in a while, that leftover manifestation of this fact still appears.

Recently, a consultant finished a major organizational study of a police department with 200 sworn officers. One of his recommendations was that the traffic division (TD) be eliminated and all personnel from the TD be transferred to the patrol division. However, in order to maintain a high level of ability to investigate serious personal injury and fatality accidents, each patrol division shift would be assigned several of the best qualified TD accident investigators, who would continue to specialize in the same jobs they formerly held. The rest of the TD officers would be assigned to patrol duties. The reason for the recommendation was that the TD, whose members considered themselves the elite of uniformed officers, had become increasingly dysfunctional over a period of years. Among the indicators of this was that no traffic unit worked past 10:00 P.M., meaning that TD officers were not working during some of the prime hours for driving while intoxicated (DWI) enforcement. Moreover, compared with similarly sized cities, the TD officers generated fewer cases, despite having more personnel, used more sick leave than other officers in the department, and were often antagonistic to personnel in other divisions. They were often characterized as prima donnas by other officers in the department because of their reluctance to handle any other types of police incidents other than traffic accidents and traffic law enforcement. The change was implemented but not without great upheaval. Some TD officers and supervisors attempted to have the change killed before it was implemented by politicians who began to voice various concerns, pro and con, about the change. Some experienced TD officers left to take jobs in police departments in several nearby, smaller municipalities. The chief, who had risen through the ranks internally and had only recently been appointed, felt that the "change was long overdue, but messy." The mayor, who had appointed the chief, dismissed the controversy by noting that "You can't make an omelette without breaking a few eggs; we can't have a few malcontents trying to make policy." Slowly, things changed. DWI arrests went up because there were more officers working during the prime enforcement hours for them, response times to calls for service improved slightly because there were more patrol officers on duty to answer calls, and the number of traffic accidents declined marginally each month.

As the positive aspects of the change were "kicking in," a radical shift occurred that no one had foreseen. After some discussion and study, the city's voters approved merging their police department under the sheriff's office, which had a traffic unit. The benefits of the city police department having gone through a hard, large-scale organizational change were lost when the two agencies actually combined operations 18 months later. Under the sheriff, the former TD officers remembered who had supported the elimination of their division and made life difficult for them whenever they could, although slowly that behavior seemed to lessen over time. Thus, in large organizational change, there can be some lingering unanticipated difficulty for years beyond when the change actually happens.

THE ROLE OF THE POLICE CULTURE IN ORGANIZATIONAL CHANGE

The dominant mindset of police departments, police reformers, appellate judges, and criminal justice scholars—in short, of nearly everyone who thinks about policing and its problems–is, and always has been, that policing needs strong, top-down management. However, in many ways, police officers necessarily collaborate in the shaping of their work environment.[17] Partners assigned to the same patrol car discuss how they should spend their time and the best ways of responding to known problems in familiar places. Teams of officers plan undercover stings. At a more indirect level, police officers have a say in organizational planning and policy making through strongly supported police unions as well as identity-based caucuses of police officers' groups such as minority officers, women officers, or gay or lesbian officers. And even without pressure from below, wise sergeants, lieutenants, and captains—like wise supervisors in any occupation—find ways to enlist the rank and file in the process of cooperative problem solving. Arguments for systematically involving frontline employees in workplace decision making have gained extraordinarily broad currency over the past several decades, in the public sector and the private sector alike—but not in policing. This is so despite the increasing frequency with which police executives speak in terms of team management, shared organizational outcomes, and aligning police managerial systems with the private sector employment relations practices.[18,19]

Three overlapping arguments are commonly made for involving rank-and-file officers in the decision-making process:

- It heightens morale and commitment.
- It develops democratic skills and habits.
- It makes for better decisions.

Scholars addressing this issue emphasize how police decision making could be improved by securing what is called *diffused and seminal intelligence* of the police culture, *craft knowledge, street knowledge,* or *context-specific knowledge.*[20] It includes not only the kind of micro-level sociological understanding all good officers acquire about their beats but also a hands-on feel for best practices, innovative ideas for improving those practices, and a thorough, nuanced understanding of their fellow offices—who can be trusted, who shirks responsibility, who cuts corners, and who is prone to violence. Thus, line officers can collectively offer not only richer and more nuanced *answers* to central problems of policing but also distinctive and important *questions*—questions different than, and complementary to, the ones typically posed by police executives and typically pursued by scholars.

In addition, if the policy is strongly opposed by the rank-and-file members of the agency, they could decide to flex their political muscle in opposition to it as reflected in the following Box 15.3.

WHY ORGANIZATIONAL CHANGE EFFORTS SOMETIMES FAIL

While organizational change is ubiquitous and necessary, it is also tenuous. As any organization prepares itself to manage the challenge of a planned change, it must be aware of the various threats that might be present that could inhibit the success of the change effort. Despite proper strategy selection, elaborate planning and resourcing, and strong administrative commitment, evaluation research shows that many attempts at major organizational change fail.[21]

Threats to the success of a planned organizational change can take many forms, both internal and external to the organization. External threats to change initiatives can present themselves as budgetary setbacks, a lack of support or misunderstandings from citizens, or opposition by a newly elected politically powerful official. Internal threats to change initiative also come in many forms. These include, but are not limited to, a lack of leadership commitment, a conflicting organizational culture, or as earlier suggested in this chapter, a lack of support, or understanding from the employees involved in the change.[22]

Box 15.3: Change Successfully Blocked by Rank-and-File Officers Labeling It a "Quota System"

The Ogden (Utah) City Council decided to drop a controversial police performance evaluation plan that included 18 factors, including a score for the number of traffic tickets given. This followed a period during which the wife of an officer who drove a van used to display signs critical of the traffic quota and Mayor Godfrey. Within hours, the officer was placed on administrative duty, although the police chief maintains this was due to other alleged actions by the officer. A 2-day "blue-flu" was also used, with officers calling in "sick" during it. City officials agreed to meet with the officers to discuss the ticket quota system and after the meeting decided to rescind the ticket quota system.

Source: "Ogden Rescinds Ticket Quota for Police," The Associated Press and Local Wire, August 16, 2006.

Models Regarding Change

There are three models regarding officer receptivity to planned organizational change:

1. A life experiences/life chances model
2. An officer/organizational subculture model
3. An organizational/structural model

The first model, the life experiences/life chances model, examines the influence of officers' ascribed and achieved status attributes, as measured by their socio-demographic and work experience characteristics. Although sparse, the extant literature suggests that some officer socio-demographic and work experience characteristics (race, gender, education, and years of service) are associated with their receptivity to change[23] and that female, minority, college-educated, and less-experienced officers are more open to organizational changes. Because policing has traditionally been a field dominated by White males and not requiring a college degree, the presence of women, minorities, and college-educated officers among the more recent recruits to the profession constitutes a form of organizational change aimed at diversifying and professionalizing the ranks. Such officers tend to be less wedded to more traditional models of policing and, likewise, are less integrated into the police subculture.[24]

The second rival model, the subculture of policing model, addresses the effects of officers' work orientation on their receptivity to planned organizational change. In particular, the influence of officer cynicism, traditionalism, as well as their crime-control and service work orientations. Those officers who most adhere to elements of the subculture of policing (i.e., have high scores on measures of cynicism, traditionalism, and a strong crime control orientation) are least receptive to organizational change, especially those that involve service activities and partnerships with community members to solve non-crime-related social problems. Conversely, those who hold a strong social orientation are most receptive of such change.

The final model, the organizational/structural model, asserts that officers' receptivity to change is a function of their perceptions of the extent to which their agency is prepared for such a change. This model also examines the association between officer receptivity to change and their perceptions of agency readiness with regard to the adequacy of officer training, administrative commitment, resource distribution, and reorganization.

Additionally, new research has found that a person's reaction to organizational change can be "so excessive and immediate, that some researchers have suggested it may be easier to start a completely new organization than to try and change an existing one."[25] In a police agency, this obviously isn't possible, but it does illustrate the difficulty in getting officers to accept change. The field of neuroscience offers some insight into this, finding that there are three main approaches to change that can actually trigger negative chemical and neurological changes in people:

1. Under preparation for change which means that it comes as a surprise to personnel.
2. Motivation for change via either expressed or implied threat.
3. Leading change from the top of an organization without involving or communicating with lower ranks.

All of these approaches can induce limbic responses in people, affecting basic emotions and drives. Any or all of these can trigger fear, anxiety, and anger about their social status, their autonomy, their relationships with others, and about fairness and certainty within their jobs. Scientific studies have shown that these feelings activate the same circuitry in the brain that physical threats—such as pain—do.[26] Change, in these circumstances, can be literally painful and organizationally counterproductive.

WAYS TO MAKE ORGANIZATIONAL CHANGE SUCCESSFUL

To accomplish organizational change, the police manager needs a combination of will and skill to seize the opportunity to make the needed changes. The basic recommendations that follow can help managers seize opportunities for change in their departments.

Use Coaching as a Tool to Facilitate Organizational Change

Coaching, when provided by a carefully selected peer or supervisor, can be an invaluable tool for assisting officers in accepting change. If done properly, it can provide officers with increased awareness and information about the benefits of the change (i.e., requiring a 2-year college degree for promotion to sergeant and a 4-year bachelor's degree for a promotion to the rank of lieutenant and above). It can also give officers an opportunity to express any negative emotions they might be feeling about the change and provide them with the opportunity to express precisely why they are opposed to the new

---

Quick Facts: The Brutal Fact: About 70 Percent of All Change Initiatives Fail

Just how hard is organizational change? Research suggests that between 50 and 80 percent of the time, the major results that were anticipated are *not* produced. Most initiatives—installing new technology, downsizing, restructuring, or trying to change organizational culture—have very low success rates.

Source: Nitin Nohria and Michael Beer, "Cracking the Code of Change." *Harvard Business Review*, May–June 2015.

policy.[27] If properly handled, coaching can give the officers inclined to resist the change an opportunity for self-evaluation and a chance to consider how the organizational change could affect them in a very positive way.

Once an administrator has made a decision to implement a change and has moved into an action stage, carefully selected coaches who support the change process should work with potentially resistant individuals as they move through the change process. The coach can provide social and emotional support for the change process and can help the individual being coached accept the change in such a way as to make it easier to be implemented.

Individual and group coaching is just one tool for facilitating the change process in organizations; however, it should be given serious consideration. The organization as a whole must find ways of informing its employees about the benefits of the new program, ways of raising an awareness of the pros and cons of changing or not changing, and ways of reinforcing and supporting employees as they go through the change process.[28]

Coaching can be a critical part of this change process because it focuses on the individual's own agenda. It can also provide an effective process to assist officers in dealing with all the other changes they or their police organizations feel necessary to implement.[29]

Set Flexible Priorities

Police managers should plan their reform agendas very carefully but be prepared to change plans quickly. Effective managers always juggle their plans, putting some on hold while pursuing others. Priorities may vary with the manager's personal interests, the recent political history of the department, or new pressures being put on the department. They may also vary with issues largely unrelated to the police, such as a municipal election that has resulted in a shift in political power. There are reform agendas that will improve police performance, agendas that will heal community conflicts, and agendas that will advance personal careers. These are not always the same.

In any given situation, there may be issues that police managers feel are very important but they have found that their ideal goals are strategically impossible to accomplish. Thus, police managers should set potentially achievable goals. This is not to advocate timidity in setting such goals but merely to counsel against overreaching folly.[30]

Assemble Resources

In order to effect successful organizational change, police managers should accumulate political and other resources to strengthen their credibility and persuasiveness. It is important to have as many allies as possible. How these resources are accumulated, and which ones are chosen, depend very much on the personal style of the players in question. Police chiefs, for example, are often faced with the choice of whether to build support in the community, in the department, with local elected officials, or some combination. Because community coalitions shift, however, it is important to seek a broad base of support from citizen leaders, media, prosecutors, state legislators, and others.[31]

Seize Opportunities

With priorities set and resources in line, a police manager should be ready for a wide range of opportunities for change. These opportunities can be defined as events that can throw the spotlight on police policy and provide a "case in point" justification for an organizational change proposal.

Ironically, opportunities often come disguised in crises, and managers must resist the initial impulse to think first of damage control. In some cases, it may be advantageous for managers interested in change to embrace a crisis and make the most of it. Several generic kinds of events provide opportunities to capitalize on crises to achieve reform.

For example, dramatic tragedies can sometimes provide an opportunity for making needed improvements in department procedures. In one department, the death of an officer who employed an improper tactic in a traffic stop led to the development of a training course on traffic stop safety, as well as expanding the training on other officer survival skills. Other crime-related crises can also be used to bolster requests for additional police officers and financial resources. The dramatic death of an officer or uninvolved innocent third party during a high-speed pursuit for a minor traffic violation may provide an opportunity for a chief law enforcement officer who supports a more conservative pursuit policy to impose restrictions that had been heretofore resisted by rank-and-file officers.

Local or nationwide studies of a police department or policing in general on similar related issues can provide support for the chief's reform agenda. Even if a report is critical, the chief may be able to use its conclusions for the benefit of the department.

Budget crises and fiscal restraint—even layoffs—provide opportunities for questioning traditional practices and making hard choices. As a matter of fiscal necessity, for example, many departments have reordered their priorities, adopted various forms of call screening, and started to refer some kinds of calls to nonpolice organizations. For a chief who has long argued that the police cannot do everything, dramatic news about city tax shortfalls which have become endemic in recent years can provide the political opportunity to make needed changes.[32]

Create Opportunities

No matter how skillfully a police manager seizes opportunities, major items on the reform agenda may still have to be left unaddressed because of political or other reasons. The times may be so sensitive or so complex that no naturally occurring event opens a window for them. However, in some rare cases, police reformers have created their own opportunities by initiating publicity concerning police problems. However, such actions should be undertaken only after consultation with the city manager or mayor to avoid having important individuals being publicly "blindsided" or "embarrassed."

In highly publicized situations, police at various ranks have tried to create public debate through leaks or whistle blowing, with attendant press coverage. More quietly, some top executives have sought to freshen their agencies by airing out some of their own dirty laundry in order to provoke the press into demanding reforms sought by the executives themselves. Another way to call attention to departmental problems is to launch an internal investigation or commission a study. Clear proof of misconduct provides a firm excuse for radical changes, and investigations are often the best way to produce that proof. Studies can be used to make people remember an old problem or to demonstrate the existence of a new one.[33]

Follow Through

In all these seized and nurtured opportunities, reform depends on more than just a single press conference. Announcing a planned change or signing an executive order is not usually enough to make change happen. Without a concerted follow-up effort, many or most reforms may die.[34]

Another important model that helps us understand the organizational transformation process is proffered by Dr. John Kotter. Kotter's process is logical and detailed, making it an ideal way to categorize change in police agencies. The **Kotter Model of Successful Change** is composed of eight steps as diagrammed in Figure 15.4:

1. **Establish a sense of urgency:** Most change in law enforcement is inherently urgent, particularly when it involves a reaction to a crisis—like rising crime rates—or a paradigm shift to quell community distrust of police. Nonetheless, police leaders should examine the environment that has led to the need for change, identify and discuss potential problems and opportunities, and create a catalyst for the change.

2. **Form a powerful coalition:** Police leaders should bring community organizers, police union or association leaders, and diverse group of informal leaders from throughout the agency together to develop strategies to achieve change.

3. **Create a vision:** What will the transformation look like? The coalition should identify a means to direct the change effort.

4. **Communicate the vision:** Use formal and informal channels of communication to ensure that everyone understands the new vision and strategies. The coalition responsible for guiding the change should use their formal and informal leadership to teach new behavior and lead by example.

5. **Empower others to act on the vision:** Remove obstacles to change by removing or revising structures, policies, and procedures that may undermine the new vision.

6. **Plan for and create short term wins:** Planning for tangible improvements in performance will allow officers and other staff to see results; for example, in implementing a new community policing program, a department can hold a community event where a good turnout will be noticeable to employees. In that case, the department can credit employees with their role in the positive turnout, further creating buy-in to the change.

7. **Consolidating improvements and creating still more change:** Continuing to refine and reinvigorate the processes behind the change by taking opportunities to use increased buy-in from personnel to make additional tweaks to systems, policies, and procedures.

8. **Institutionalizing new approaches:** Emphasize the links between the organizational change and any benefits/successes as a result of that change. Prioritize leadership development and succession planning to continue to vision and strategies put in place; anchor changes in organizational culture.[35]

FIGURE 15.4 ▶ Kotter's Eight Step Model of Successful Change.
See http://tie575changemodel.wikispaces.com/Kotter%27s+8-step+model.

INFORMATION TECHNOLOGY AND CHANGE

We have previously discussed the ways in which technology can drive change; recall in Chapter 2, Policing Today that GIS, CompStat, and fusion centers have revolutionized policing. Technology, as a driver of change, is extraordinarily powerful—so much so that there is an entire field of change management theory that deals with information technology (IT). Morton's theory of change management, for example, looks at how change should occur with IT as an impetus. Morton asserts that it is critical that such change be made after several issues have been accomplished: First, people issues must be resolved through training and education, so that individuals have time to grapple with, and take on expanded roles utilizing the new technology. Second, management processes that redistribute power and control must be presented and accepted within the organization. Third, the organizational structure must change in order to provide effective administration and management for the new technologies. Fourth, new strategies must be developed and accepted within the organization that develops a long-term plan for future technology in relation to the overall goals and objectives. And finally, after the previous steps have been accomplished, the new technology is implemented.[36] Essentially, Morton advocates for groundwork being laid, organizationally speaking, before a change is undertaken. Technological changes, particularly, evoke that limbic response in people; they fear it will complicate their jobs, or that they won't know how to operate or adapt to the technology. Worse yet, they may fear that their job is in jeopardy to the implementation of new technology. Police officers often feel similarly, however, that they manifest their dissatisfaction with statements associated about hindering their interaction with the community, or that this change will make it more difficult to "catch criminals," or that the change is simply another "duty" on top of an already full day of answering calls for service, citizen interactions, meetings, and report writing.

Some of these technological transformations are not specific to policing; social changes that have been facilitated by technology have had an impact on organizational change. Changes in the way that we, as a society, communicate have had a major hand in police organizational change. For instance, recalling our discussion on generational issues earlier in this chapter that instant messaging and web connectivity have created a generation of people who are used to tech-based communication, instant feedback, and immediate gratification. These are expectations often carried into the workplace. Some agencies have embraced this phenomenon—for example, using virtual roll calls where officers can be briefed before their shifts via email and check in using mobile devices. Other departments have implemented secure applications for personnel to give constant and continuous feedback and suggestions to supervisory and command staff.[37] And, the impact of social media cannot be overstated; social media has revolutionized the way police interact with each other as well as the community. Patrol, crime control strategies, community relations, personnel management, and the functions of the public information officer (PIO) are all vastly impacted by today's social media technology. For instance, PIO officers once responded to media requests, coordinated press conferences, and directed media mobilizations to crisis events; now, social media has allowed police departments to control their message, to get in front of potentially negative stories by offering their version of events before the media can break the story, and to inform the media of staging areas and other events with a simple Tweet or Facebook post. Social media has singlehandedly allowed PIO officers to transform from reactive entities to proactive public relations-style units.

Social media has also transformed the way police organizations communicate with the public. In years past, engaging the community meant deploying personnel into neighborhoods as

time and budgets allowed—perhaps holding crime watch meetings, hosting community events, or even conducting "knock and talk" programs where officers went door to door to assess problems and solicit tips and solutions. While those programs are all still enormously valuable, social media has allowed police agencies to fill-in the gaps and give communities the opportunity to have a dialogue with police agencies. Sometimes that dialogue is negative—but that in and of itself can be valuable feedback in identifying areas where police need to increase outreach and improve their interaction with citizens. Frequently, though, social media yields tips on crimes, gives the public insight into day-to-day law enforcement processes, and creates goodwill. These functions have all led to changes within police organizations—from the way internal affairs handles citizen complaints to the way that community affairs offices get the word out about specific events or informing the public of dangerous situations, wanted and suspicious persons, or even critical incidents like terrorist attacks and natural disasters.

Social media has also transformed the job of police recruiting offices. A decade ago, police recruiters traveled extensively to find new applicants and relied on background checks to ensure that they were a good fit for their agencies. Today, recruiters can make connections with potential recruits through social media advertising and direct messaging; background checks now include a thorough vetting of an applicant's social media sites. Applicants who post inflammatory content, express viewpoints that run counter to law enforcement values, and who have had the lack of foresight to remove photos of themselves in intoxicated states or compromising positions are now weeded-out before these characteristics become apparent in their work—and before they can embarrass the departments that hire them.

As discussed in Chapter 2, "Policing Today" and Chapter 10 "Organizational and Interpersonal Communication," social media has also caused some systemic changes within departments; policies and procedures have had be carefully updated to balance free speech of employees with the best interests of the organization. Never before have police organizations had to be so concerned with what their officers were saying in their off time—now with a screenshot and a share button, racist/sexist/classist ramblings or shared memes from an off-duty officers can become a major story in local, state, and even national news, causing major heartburn and damaging legitimacy for law enforcement institutions. Ten years ago, social media policies could probably not be found in more than a couple of police agencies' standard operating procedures in the United States. Today, just under 72 percent of all police departments in the United States have some sort of social media policy to guide and direct operations.[38]

Technology has also driven transformational change in the arena of crime control. The very nature of many crimes has changed as a result of new technology. For instance, people don't carry as much cash as they used to, forcing criminals to resort to identity theft and cybercrime to line their pockets. Many departments have found themselves scrambling to identify tech-savvy personnel to work on these complex issues and crimes, and having to restructure financial crimes units to keep up with the caseloads. Tools like GPS trackers have changed the way auto theft and other burglary investigators do business; surveillance cameras can now give clear pictures of criminal activity, enhancing the potential for suspects to be caught. Complex banking and security software can make organized crime and money laundering perpetrators much more easily identifiable to investigators—though the downside to this is that it may push the commission of such crimes to organizations such as Russia and China. For small departments without any type of experience in international locations, that reality will certainly engender some organizational adaptation.

The final area to consider when discussing technology as an impetus for change in a police organization is that of infrastructure. Unfortunately, many planners do not see the whole scope of technology change or implementation. Any major IT change requires connectivity, and connectivity requires infrastructure like bandwidth, cellular/microwave towers, generators, servers, hardware, and software. The demand for broadband access in a major city police department is staggering, considering that the massive needs required by police IT entities (e.g., dispatch, patrol officer's cell phones, wireless computers in patrol cars, downloads of dash-cam footage, downloads of body camera footage, fusion center computing, GIS, closed circuit cameras, crime mapping, websites, and crime watch apps). Increasing speed and broadband access will most likely be critical for a police agency to implement a necessary change or expansion of IT. The accompanying budgetary increase for such change may be staggering, adding to the stress of implementation. For example, a patrol station that is in an area of town surrounded by hills or tall buildings may not accommodate a microwave tower (or tower array) necessary for the massive amount of data that comes with police IT needs. Rural departments may not have the proper fiber optic infrastructure to accommodate fast Internet connectivity. However, despite the challenges that infrastructure can present, technology has the potential to truly revolutionize the way police organizations function in our rapidly changing society.

POLICING IN THE FUTURE: EVERYTHING CHANGES

For students of criminal justice—or even just consumers of current events—the term "post-Ferguson" is probably one that has become ingrained in the consideration of policing and police administration. As has been discussed throughout this text, that particular event in Ferguson, Missouri—followed by additional instances of use of force or in-custody deaths against African Americans by police—has become a flashpoint for the discussion about the future of policing. (See Box 15.4.) And indeed, it's difficult to forecast the future of the police organization without acknowledging the effects of Ferguson. In a nutshell, police organizations will have to become more

responsive to the communities that they serve. They will have to strive to become a reflection of those communities, and they will have to work hard to eliminate bias in their ranks and gain the trust of the community through cooperation, communication, and—in some instances—some measure of reconciliation. This will absolutely run counter to the command and control style of policing that some agencies are used to, and it will require major ideological transformations in law enforcement. Training, recruitment, and crime control practices will all be touched by these shifts—making this both an exciting and challenging time to be in the field of law enforcement.

But beyond that, the infusion of contemporary employees into the workplace, the effects of complex economic and social drivers, and advances in technology will all combine to change the landscape of law enforcement. In very short order, policing will evolve and change, with experts predicting the most change in the following areas:

1. **Predictive policing:** Advances in IT and infrastructure improvements will take intelligence-led policing to the next level. Real-time analytics will allow intelligence to be drawn from data about crime and crime trends—allowing police to see patterns that may be actionable for purposes of crime prevention and response.[39]

2. **Changes in traditional police response:** Economic realities combined with technological opportunities may mean that police no longer respond to certain non-violent property crimes. Victims may be able to report minor burglaries and thefts via online portals, and burglar alarm calls may require secondary verification before police are dispatched.

3. **Next Generation 9-11:** New capabilities in smart phones and internet protocol (IP)-enabled dispatch systems mean emergency services infrastructure may be enhanced in the near future. This can improve response time, enhance dispatch efficiency through better geo-location, allow for text and photo-based reporting, and give better service to disabled citizens.[40]

4. **Body Worn Cameras:** These cameras (as well as police vehicle dash-cameras) are seen as a panacea for use-of-force incidents and will likely become ubiquitous in police agencies in the coming years, though it remains to be seen what effect they will really have on police–citizen encounters.

Police leadership will also see major changes in the coming years. In a 2014 Police Executive Research Forum survey, 61 percent of police chiefs who participated said that their agencies would be experimenting with some kind of organizational structure change in the coming 2 to 5 years. In many cases, this involves a new emphasis on developing future leaders, through career pathway opportunities and

Box 15.4: Inner Cities, The Police, and the Way Forward

The immediate facts and controversies surrounding the use of police deadly force in Ferguson (MO) an by officers indicted in Baltimore (MD) received a great deal of attention from the media and the U.S. Department of Justice. For present purposes, these and other related events fueled three results: 1) Many individual law enforcement agencies initiated a sweeping reappraisal of their own policies. 2) The final report from President Obama's Task Force on 21st Century Policing (2015) recommended a number of changes, including: (a) improving trust and legitimacy in policing; (b) using technology and social media to engage the community in dialogue; (c) adding more community-based policing efforts to involve larger percentages of minority populations in our communities; (d) officers should use deadly force only as a last resort; (e) increasing police transparency; (f) using unbiased, independent investigations for all police-involved shootings and/or in-custody deaths; (g) ending racial and ethnic profiling; (h) officers should wear body cameras; (i) fundamental changes in police training to include an emphasis on de-escalation, crisis intervention, and other less or no-force alternatives to arrest; and (j) programs to increase officer wellness and safety, such as design of optimum work shifts and greater analysis of data from police deaths and "near misses"; and 3) The Ferguson, Baltimore, and other recent police use of force incidents generated further interest among scholars in race, crime, and policing.

In 2015, an African American Harvard faculty member, Dr. Orlando Patterson offered his thoughts on policing and inner cities. He dismissed claims that rising racism or police violence was the cause of inner city problems. Labeling such claims a "gross oversimplification" he provided an analysis that started with the demographics of inner cities. Patterson noted that 80 to 85 percent of inner city residents range from the working poor to those who are solidly middle middle class, most of whom are church going, law abiding, and typically socially conservative, and have dreams for their children's future.

However, Patterson concludes that simultaneously in inner cities a minority of the population is problematic, ranging from 12 to 28 percent of the population. Characteristically this group is younger (16–24 years of age), not in school, frequently unemployed, have few job skills, and some exist by engaging in illicit activities. Their numbers may be swelled by older people who elect a street life. Patterson calls attention to a volatile intermixing of: (1) "concentrated poverty," disaffected young people, ages 16 to 24, and a small vein within the minority of the population which has a propensity for violence and destruction and revels in the "thug culture" and (2) uncontrolled police actions such as racial profiling and violent confrontations. The thug culture is reinforced by contemporary conditions of urban decay, like poverty, unemployment, single parenting, and a chemically toxic, neurologically injurious environment. Violence often occurs as the thug culture collides with an equally aggressive police subculture.

According to Patterson, there is a way forward. Federal and state programs that work (e.g., Head Start, nurse–family partnerships, after-school programs, and My Brother's Keeper program) aimed at reducing youth crime, particularly in regard to black youth, must be implemented immediately in inner cities. New educational programs that provide contemporary job training, enhanced life skills, short-term employment, and badly need male role models must be initiated. The private sector must foster new jobs and careers in the inner city as well as for those in outlying areas. Part of the way forward cannot be provided by business, governments, or non-profit organizations. Patterson maintains that "there is one long-term, fundamental change that can come only from within the black community: a reduction in the number of children born to single, usually poor, women, which now stands at 72 percent. Its consequences are grim: greatly increased risk of prolonged poverty, child abuse, educational failure, and youth delinquency and violence, especially among boys, whose main reason for joining gangs is to find a family and male role models."

Source: Orlando Patterson, "The Real Problem with America's Inner Cities," The New York Times (May 9, 2015).

specialized leadership training that highlights developing and building relationships with communities over tactical considerations.

Organizations may also begin to experiment with flatter bureaucratic structures that impose fewer communication barriers, allow quicker response and adaptation, and establish clear lines of responsibility. Middle management positions tasked mainly with information sharing may be able to be streamlined, particularly since e-mail and cell phones make communication between front-line officers and administration quick and virtually painless[41].

Ultimately, this is a challenging time for police officers and administrators alike as they navigate issues in police legitimacy, procedural justice, technology, and community relations. It's hard to say what the outcome of all these transitions will be, but it's worth noting that the public absolutely demands that police undertake them. Therefore, it's not a question of whether all of the disparate 18,000 law enforcement agencies across this country undergo some level of change—it's a question of how well the leaders and the officers will embrace their future, as they transform to earn and maintain community trust and keep crime at bay.

Chapter Summary

Summary by Learning Objective

- **Explain why change occurs in law enforcement agencies.**

  Change occurs in reaction to a crisis; due to fluctuating crime rates; because of technological advances; due to funding changes and economics; because of politics; because of changing workforces; and because of changing paradigms or models of policing.

- **Discuss five situations when change should not be initiated.**

  1. The knowledge, skill, or other resources needed to carry out the change effectively do not exist inside the department.
  2. An appropriately experienced external change agent is not presently available.
  3. The effort of making the change is greater than any benefits to be derived.
  4. Collateral damage, such as abandonment by key supporters or significant union opposition, may lead chiefs to use their limited stack of "political chips" on another issue of greater concern to them and the community.
  5. Too much change is already underway in the department and the nature of the change is not sufficiently important to make now, versus its potential for personnel to feel confused about priorities or conclude that the organization is becoming unstable.

- **Analyze three models of change in organizations.**

  Kurt Lewin's three-step model on organizational change involves three sequential steps: (1) *unfreezing*, or making people be receptive to change; (2) *moving*, or the transitional phase in which officers actually experience the changes that were planned; and (3) *refreezing*, where officers make permanent the changes they experienced in the previous phase.

  The TRAC model recognizes the need for change; assesses and diagnoses the situation; involves action planning; implements and intervenes; and includes ongoing evaluation.

  Finally, the Burke-Litwin model ranks various drivers of change from most to least important: the external environment; mission and strategy; leadership; organizational culture; structures; systems; management practices; work unit requirements;

tasks and skills; individual values and needs; motivation level; and individual and overall performance.

- **Discuss the role of the rank and file in organizational change.**

  Line officers can collectively offer not only richer and more nuanced *answers* to central problems of policing but also distinctive and important *questions*—questions different than, and complementary to, the ones typically posed by police executives and typically pursued by scholars. In addition, if the policy is strongly opposed by the rank-and-file members of the agency, they could decide to flex their political muscle in opposition to it.

- **Explain why organizational change sometimes fails.**

  Threats to the success of a planned organizational change can take many forms, both internal and external to the organization. External threats to change initiatives can present themselves as budgetary setbacks, a lack of support or misunderstandings from citizens, or opposition by a newly elected politically powerful official. Internal threats to change initiative also come in many forms. These include, but are not limited to, a lack of leadership commitment, a conflicting organizational culture, or as earlier suggested in this chapter, a lack of support or understanding from the employees involved in the change. There is some research that also points to neurological resistance to change, as it evokes feelings such as fear, alienation, and other negative emotions.

- **Describe how to make organizational change succeed.**

  Coaching, when provided by a carefully selected peer or supervisor, can be an invaluable tool for assisting officers in accepting change. Additionally, police managers should plan their reform agendas very carefully but be prepared to change plans quickly. In order to effect successful organizational change, police managers should accumulate political and other resources to strengthen their credibility and persuasiveness. Police managers should also seize opportunities, create opportunities and always follow through. Additionally, John Kotter described eight additional steps to success in organizational change: Establish a sense of urgency; form a powerful coalition; create a vision; communicate the vision; empower others to act on the vision; plan for and create short-term wins; consolidate improvements and create still more change; and institutionalize new approaches.

• **Describe the role of technology in police organizational change.**

Technology is a major impetus for change in police organizations. It has changed the way crime is analyzed (e.g., fusion centers, GIS); the way agencies communicate with the public (social media); the ways police agencies establish legitimacy (body worn cameras); and more. It also affects internal budgets, internal administration, and internal policies and procedures.

• **Discuss a few ways in which policing may change in the coming years.**

Law enforcement organizations will have to respond to citizen calls for transparency and fair and impartial policing through training, technology, and administrative policies and procedures. Predictive policing, enabled by technology, will allow quicker responsiveness. New modes for police responsiveness—including innovative dispatch systems—will also come online. Police organizations will also evolve to include specialized leadership training for its commanders and may become flatter structures as communication capabilities decrease the need for multiple levels of administration.

Chapter Review Questions

1. Identify seven recurring reasons why change occurs in law enforcement agencies.
2. Identify actions that many states have taken to address issues in wake of recent police-community unrest.
3. Explain the importance of the 2015 landmark case, *Obergefell v. Hodges*.
4. State five reasons when change should not be made.
5. What are the three steps in Kurt Lewin's model on organizational change?
6. What are the five steps in the traditional action research model?
7. What are the eleven drivers of change identified in the Burke-Litwin model?
8. What are the most common overlapping arguments commonly made for involving rank-and-file employees in workplace decision making?
9. Why do organizational change efforts sometimes fail?
10. What are ways to make organizational change succeed?
11. Identify the eight steps in Kotter's model for successful change.
12. Discuss and identify Mortons theory of change management involving information technology.
13. According to Orlando Patterson, what are the real problems confronting America's inner cities?
14. Identify the four areas where experts predict that the most change will occur in policing in the future.

Critical Thinking Exercises

1. Envision a change that you would make in your local law enforcement agency. Using the Burke–Litwin Model of Change, describe how you would implement your ideas.
2. Visit the website for the Police Executive Research Forum—PERF (policeforum.org) to browse publications and documents about police organizations that have adopted major changes in their organization. Do you think that similar changes could be made within any law enforcement agency or are certain agencies more adaptive to change than others? Why or why not?
3. Search the Internet to find articles and literature on organizational change in the private sector. Why is creating organizational change so difficult? Do you think that change is easier in the private sector versus the public sector? Why or why not?

Key Terms

Burke-Litwin Model
change agent
directed change

Lewin's three-step model
Kotter Model of Successful Change

Obergefell v. Hodges
traditional action research model

Endnotes

[1]Robert W. Taylor and Charles R. Swanson, *Terrorism, Intelligence and Homeland Security* (Upper Saddle River, NJ: Pearson, 2015). See specifically Part III: Responding to the Challenges of Terrorism.

[2]Joe Domanick, "Police Reform's Best Tool: A Federal Consent Decree," The Crime Report (July 15, 2014).

[3]Brian A. Jackson, Victoria A. Greenfield, Andrew R. Morral, and John S. Hollywood, *Police Department Investments in Information System Technology*, (Santa Monica, CA: RAND Corporation, 2014).

[4]Police Executive Research Forum. "Policing and the Economic Downturn: Striving for Efficiency Is the New Normal." February 2013. Retrieved on July 17, 2015 from http://www.policeforum.org/assets/docs/Critical_Issues_Series/policing%20and%20the%20economic%20downturn%20-%20striving%20for%20efficiency%20is%20the%20new%20normal%202013.pdf,

[5]http://www.bloomberg.com/news/articles/2015-01-26/pensions-hobble-police-hiring-as-san-diego-seeks-boots-on-street.

[6]Police Executive Research Forum (PERF), ibid.

[7]Tanya Eiserer. "Dallas DA disbands digital forensics lab after 8 months." WFAA, July 31, 2015. Retrieved on July 31, 2015 from: http://www.wfaa.com/story/news/local/dallas-county/2015/07/dallas-das-digital-forensics-lab-shuttered-after-8-months/31/30968707/.

[8]James P. Henchy. "Ready or Not, There They Come: The Millenial Generation Enters the Workforce."

[9]Anthony Batts, Sean Michael Smoot, and Ellen Scrivner."Police Leadership in a Changing World." National Institutes of Justice: New Perspectives in Policing. July 2012. Retrieved on July 5 from: https://www.ncjrs.gov/pdffiles1/nij/238338.pdf.

[10]Bob Moritz. "The US Chairman of PwC on Keeping Millenials Engaged." Harvard Business Review, November 2014.

[11]Anthony Batts, Sean Michael Smoot, and Ellen Scrivner. "Police Leadership in a Changing World." National Institutes of Justice: New Perspectives in Policing. July 2012. Retrieved on July 5 from: https://www.ncjrs.gov/pdffiles1/nij/238338.pdf.

[12]"Diversity in Law Enforcement: A Literature Review." U.S. Department of Justice Civil Rights Division Office of Justice Programs and US Equal Employment Opportunity Commission. January 2015. Retrieved July 27, 2015 from: http://www.cops.usdoj.gov/pdf/taskforce/Diversity_in_Law_Enforcement_Literature_Review.pdf.

[13]Eileen Sullivana and Jack Gillam. "Analysis: Hispanic police officers scant in police forces despite growing populations." Fort Worth Star Telegram, September 8, 2014. Retrieved on July 19, 2015 from: http://www.star-telegram.com/news/local/community/fort-worth/article3872396.html.

[14]"What You Should Know About EEOC and the Enforcement Protections for LGBT Workers." Equal Employment Opportunity Commission. Retrieved July 25, 2015 from: http://www.eeoc.gov/eeoc/newsroom/wysk/enforcement_protections_lgbt_workers.cfm.

[15]Hans Toch and J. Douglas Grant, *Police as Problem Solvers* (Washington, DC: American Psychological Association, 2005), p. 342.

[16]W. Warner Burke and George H. Litwin. "*A Causal Model of Organization Performance and Change.*" Journal of Management, Volume 18, No. 3 (1992): pp. 523–545.

[17]David Alan Sklansky and Monique Marks, "The Role of the Rank and File in Police Reform," *Policing and Society 18*, no. 1 (March 2008): pp. 1–6. (This discussion was adapted with permission from this source.)

[18]E. McLaughlin and K. Murji, "Resistance Through Representation: 'Storylines,' Advertising and Police Federation Campaigns," *Policing and Society 8*, no. 4 (1998):, pp. 367–399.

[19]M. Silvestri, "'Doing' Police Leadership: Enter the 'new smart macho,'" *Policing and Society 17*, no. 1 (2007): pp. 38–58.

[20]H. Toch and J. D. Grant, *Police as Problem Solvers: How Frontline Workers Can Promote Organizational and Community Change*, 2nd ed. (Washington, DC: American Psychological Association, 2005).

[21]John K. Cochran, Max L. Bromley, and Matthew J. Swando, "Sheriff's Deputies' Receptivity to Organizational Change," *Policing: An International Journal of Police Strategies & Management 25*, no. 3 (2002): pp. 507–529. (This discussion was adapted from this source.)

[22]R. Aragon, "Community-Oriented Policing: Success Insurance Strategies," *The FBI Law Enforcement Bulletin* 66 (1997): pp. 8–18.

[23]A. J. Lurigio and W. G. Skogan, "Winning the Hearts and Minds of Police Officers: An Assessment of Staff Perceptions of Community Policing in Chicago," *Crime and Delinquency* 40, no. 3, (1994):, pp. 315–330.

[24]John K. Cochran, Max L. Bromley, and Matthew J. Swando, "Sheriff's Deputies' Receptivity to Organizational Change," *Policing: An International Journal of Police Strategies & Management 25*, no. 3 (2002): pp. 507–529.

[25]Walter McFarland. "This is Your Brain on Organizational Change." Harvard Business Review, October 16, 2012.

[26]Ibid

[27]Richard C. Lumb and Ronald Breazeale, "Police Officer Attitudes and Community Policing Implementation: Developing Strategies for Durable Organizational Change," *Policing and Society* 13, no. 1 (2002): p. 99.

[28]Ibid.

[29]Richard C. Lumb and Ronald Breazeale have developed a training program to prepare supervisors to address and resolve problems before they affect either employees or the organizations. The results of this study can be found in Ibid., pp. 100 and 101.

[30]Lawrence W. Sherman, Albert M. Greenfield Professor of Human Relations in the Department of Sociology and director of the Fels Center of Government, University of Pennsylvania, and Anthony V. Bouza, former chief of police, Minneapolis, Minnesota, in *Local Government Police Management*, 4th edition (Washington DC: International City/County Management Association, 2003), p. 440.

[31]Ibid., p. 440.

[32]Ibid., pp. 440, 441.

[33]Ibid., p. 441.

[34]Ibid., p. 441.

[35]This section was adapted from John P. Kotter. "Leading Change: Why Transformation Efforts Fail." Harvard Business Review, January 2007.

[36]Michael Morton. "The Corporation of the 1990s: Information Technology and Organizational Transformation." Oxford University Press, 1991.

[37]Anthony Batts, Sean Michael Smoot, and Ellen Scrivner."Police Leadership in a Changing World." National Institutes of Justice: New Perspectives in Policing. July 2012. Retrieved on July 5 from: https://www.ncjrs.gov/pdffiles1/nij/238338.pdf.

[38]International Association of Chief of Police. "IACP Center for Social Media: 2014 Survey Results." Retrieved on July 26, 2015 from: http://www.iacpsocialmedia.org/Resources/Publications/2014SurveyResults.aspx.

[39]Police Executive Research Forum."Future Trends in Policing." 2014. Washington, DC: Office of Community Oriented Policing Services.

[40]Christopher Moraff. "8 Ways American Policing Could Change This Year." NextCity Politics. Retrieved on July 18, 2015 from: https://nextcity.org/daily/entry/police-technology-changes-2015.

[41]Police Executive Research Forum."Future Trends in Policing." 2014. Washington, DC: Office of Community Oriented Policing Services.

GLOSSARY

1983 action: a tort action by which federal courts obtain jurisdiction of suits that involve the deprivation of any rights, privileges, or immunities secured by the Constitution by an individual acting under color of any statute, ordinance, regulation, custom, or usage of any state.

4/5ths rule: a rule of thumb used to determine whether adverse impact has occurred, not a legal standard.

active shooter: describes an individual who is still at the scene of an event and actively engaged in continuing to attempt to injure or kill people at the scene.

administrative theory: also called management theory and the principles approach, sought to find "universal" principles of management that could be used in any setting; also see traditional organizational theory.

administrative/management plans: this includes formulation of the department's mission statement of values, goals, and policies and procedures; the organizational structure, the functions, authority, and responsibilities of the positions; the allocation of resources; sick leave, vacation time, court appearance, and other related topics.

adverse impact: an employment practice, which although lacking any discriminatory intent and on its face appearing to be neutral, an employer is prohibited from using because it has an unjustified impact on members of a protected class.

advocates: leadership style described by Downs; such leaders promote everything under their control.

affiliation needs: the desire to be accepted and liked.

Age Discrimination in Employment Act (ADEA): (1967), forbids age discrimination in any aspect of employment for those 40 or older.

air raid wardens: persons in WW II who patrolled to make sure that during "black outs" no lights were showing that could assist enemy submarines in identifying targets if they shelled our coast. Also used to prevent enemy submarines or aircraft from using lights to assist in their navigation. Police and civic groups shared this duty across the country.

alarm stage: the component of general adaptation syndrome that puts the body on a "fight-or-flight" alert by releasing hormones that produce an energizing effect on the body.

all-hazard: able to support operations during an emergency that is either human-made or natural.

allotments: small amounts into which a budget is broken and given to the police department monthly or quarterly, instead of giving all of it at once to the police department.

all-qualified list: promotional roster method in which anyone on the list can be selected in any order.

Alpha generation: born 2011–2025, projected to be best-educated and most technologically sophisticated.

al-Qaeda: a radical Islamic, Middle Eastern terrorist organization formally led by the late Osama bin Laden and Ayman al-Zawahiri; it was responsible for the attacks against the United States on September 11, 2001.

Americans with Disability Act (ADA): (1990), provides equal opportunity to jobs for qualified persons with a disability as well as other protections. Job requirements that screen out people with disabilities are legal only to the extent they are job related and consistent with business necessity.

anabolic steroids: a group of synthetic hormones usually derived from testosterone, that promote storage of protein and the growth of muscle tissue.

Argyris, Chris: developed maturity–immaturity model postulating that traditional organization forms get in the way of workers' development.

assessment center: consists of several exercises or job simulations designed to elicit from candidates the behaviors found to be important to job success by the job analysis.

audit: an independent verification by someone who has no stake in the outcome; audits can be financial or programmatic.

authentic leadership: (1) being deeply aware of how you think, behave, and are seen by others; (2) awareness of your own and others' values/moral perspectives, knowledge, and strengths; (3) understanding the context in which you operate; and (4) being grounded by confidence, hopefulness, optimism, resiliency, and high moral character.

authoritarian/autocratic: a leadership style; makes all decisions, closely controls work, a micromanager, "my way or the highway."

authority: Weber identified three sources: charismatic, traditional, and rational legal. In police departments, it is a formal grant to a position, the incumbent uses it to accomplish organizational goals. Also see power.

baby boomers: born 1946–1964, many still employed by law enforcement agencies, reaching the end of their careers; grew up in era of widespread social change.

banded list: promotional roster method in which candidates with similar scores are grouped together.

bargaining not required model: the model for police-sector collective bargaining law in which collective bargaining is not statutorily required by the state.

behavioral systems theory: sees organizations as made up of the behavior of individuals and groups, wanted to make organizations more democratic and participative. Founded by Lewin.

benchmarking: the practice of comparing one's organizational performance to those that are recognized leaders in the field or otherwise relevant competitors.

biennial budget: a 2-year police budget.

bifurcation: the "flash-point" when chaos overcomes normal conditions in an agency and forces it in a new direction in terms of priorities and tactics. See cosmology.

big five: the traits approach produced long lists of traits; using meta-analysis, five broad trait categories were identified into which the longer lists of traits could be fitted: surgency, conscientiousness, agreeableness, adjustment, and intellectance. See Big Two.

big two: a refinement of the Big Five: stability and plasticity.

binding arbitration: a judgment made by a neutral third party to settle a dispute between labor and management, in which both parties agree in advance to abide by the result.

***Bivens* action:** a judicially created counterpart to a 1983 action that gives the federal courts jurisdiction over torts involving federal officials.

Black Asphalt: the short name for a particular company that teaches police agencies how to identify enforcement opportunities that provide opportunities for subsequent asset forfeitures..

Black Codes: laws quickly adopted in southern states following the Civil War to repress African Americans.

Black September Organization (BSO): terrorist group.

blue flu: a job action in which officers organize mass absences on the pretext of sickness for the purpose of protest against their employer.

bootlegger: someone who smuggled illegal alcohol during prohibition; also referred to people who hid a flask in their boot or held one to their leg with a garter.

Boston Police Strike: 1919 police strike that killed the possibility of police unionization until the 1960s.

brainstorming: this is a type of group decision making developed initially in advertising to help trigger creativity. The idea behind brainstorming is to establish a group environment in which individuals can present any idea that seems to apply even remotely to the subject being considered with the understanding that criticism will be withheld unless it can somehow improve on the original idea.

budget adjustment: during the course of executing a police department's budget it may be adjusted upward or downward by only by the action of the local legislative body, such as a city council or county commission. There are six common methods of making budget adjustments.

budget calendar: a schedule of events for the preparation and approval of a budget.

budget cycle: a four-step, sequential process repeated annually in government.

budget execution: the action phase of budgeting, budget implementation.

budget: a government's priorities expressed in financial terms, a plan stated in financial terms, the use of resources to meet human needs, a contract between the appropriators and those who execute the budget.

buffering: stores inputs (e.g., gasoline) to avoid disruption of services if supply is interrupted; also see negative entropy.

bum blockades: police-staffed blockades established by some cities during the Depression to turn immigrants away at the city limits who would be a drain on local government resources if allowed to enter.

bureaucratic model: organizational form often called classical, mechanistic, and a closed system; comprised of eight characteristics.

Burke-Litwin Model: a change model that recognizes and incorporates organizational theory by exploring and ranking the various drivers of change.

business concerns: owners are the primary beneficiaries.

butterfly effect: small, helpful, self-initiated acts have a ripple effect, causing others to become energized and helpful.

caliphate: an Islamic state in which the political and religious leader are the same.

capital budget: groups together multiple large-scale, nonrecurring projects such as the construction of a new police station and has a multi-year time horizon, often 5 years.

capital improvement project (CIP): a single capital improvement project, a component of a capital budget.

CAPS: **C**hicago **A**lternative **P**olicing **S**trategy; one of the largest and most comprehensive community policing initiatives in the United States, conducted by the Chicago Police Department during the 1990s.

carpetbaggers: Northerners who came to the South following the Civil War, so called because their suitcases were cheaply made of second-hand carpet.

Challenge of Crime in a Free Society: 1967 government report calling for improvements across the criminal justice system.

change agent: an individual or a group from within or outside the police department that stimulates, guides, facilitates, and stabilizes the change process.

chaos theory: an organizational state of nonequilibrium produced by a crisis event that exceeds anything we can imagine. See cosmology and bifurcation.

charismatic leadership: Charisma was originally thought to be a gift of abilities from above; failures cannot be charismatic, nor can leaders proclaim themselves to be such. Charismatic leaders have seven traits, including having an innovative vision, inspiring and developing followers, and leading their departments to superior performances.

Chavez, Cesar: farm worker and later civil rights activist, fought for better working conditions and pay for migrant pickers.

citizen oversight: This is a process by which people who are not sworn officers are involved in some way in the review of citizen complaints against police officers.

city council: Acts as the chief legislative and policy making body of a city.

city manager movement: style of city government that began in Stanton, Virginia, in 1908.

city manager: A professional administrator who is recruited for certain skills and training and is appointed by the city council.

city-county consolidated governments: a city and county that have merged into one unified jurisdiction, having the powers and responsibilities of both a municipal corporation (city) and the administrative division of a state (county).

Civil Rights Act of 1964: federal law that invalidated Jim Crow laws; Title 7 forbade discrimination by businesses, unions, and federal agencies on the basis of sex, race, color, religion, or national origin in hiring, promoting, and firing. Title 7 did not apply to state and local governments until 1972. See Equal Employment Opportunity Act of 1972.

climbers: leadership style described by Downs; such leaders invent new functions for their units.

code of silence: refusal of officers to testify against other officers who are accused of misconduct.

CODEFOR: **C**omputer **O**ptimized **DE**ployment—**F**ocus **O**n **R**esults; one of the first experiments in the CompStat process, used in Minneapolis, Minnesota, designed specifically to reduce crime and improve the efficiency and effectiveness of the police department.

coding: to prevent overload, an organization codes or prioritizes messages so that important messages get to the right place quickly; citizens with minor problems wanting to talk to the Chief find themselves redirected and talking to some other official.

cognitive maps: accumulated sense making produces "mental understandings" that help us navigate our world. See sense making.

collective bargaining: negotiation between an employer and a labor union, usually regarding issues such as wages, benefits, hours, and working conditions.

colors: outlaw motorcycle gang patches and insignias that represent the club's name and chapter; usually wore on a denim jacket or vest.

Commission on Accreditation of Law Enforcement Agencies (CALEA): created in 1979 with the support of police associations, this private body accredits law enforcement agencies that meet its list of standards.

commonweal organizations: the public at large is the beneficiary (e.g., law enforcement agency).

communication: the process by which senders and receivers interact in both professional and social contexts.

Community-Oriented Policing Services (COPS): a federal grant program.

community-oriented policing: early 1980s policing philosophy that essentially provided custom-tailored police services to neighborhoods and business districts. Used interchangeably with problem-oriented policing (POP).

community policing: a policing philosophy that focuses on general neighborhood problems as a source of crime; community policing is preventive, proactive, and information-based.

CompStat: a police methodology using the most accurate and timely information to identify crime and social problems within a given geographic area and then to develop strategies designed to stop or prevent them from occurring in the future; CompStat holds police administrators accountable for their decisions, tactics, and strategies aimed at reducing crime.

computerized voice stress analyzer (CVSA): a lie detection mechanism.

conceptual skills: the ability to understand and interrelate various parcels of information that seem unrelated or whose meaning or importance is not immediately apparent.

conditional job offer (CJO): an employment offer made contingent on passing a medical screening.

conservers: leadership style described by Downs; such leaders exhibit bias toward maintaining things under their control.

cosmology: chaos event that overwhelms us; beyond the worse conditions we could imagine; problems of magnitude, complexity, and durability on a scope not seen by us before.

counterproductive work behavior (CWB): behavior that has a detrimental effect on relationships with coworkers and/or the efficiency of operations.

crime analysis: the organization of massive quantities of raw data and information relating to reported crime in an effort to identify trends and patterns and then to forecast specific events from the statistical manipulation of these data.

critical infrastructure and key resources (CI/KRs): the important facilities, buildings, and installations that provide basic services within a community, such as transportation and telecommunications systems, water and power lines, electronic data systems, key bridges and waterways, emergency facilities, and private sector industries and businesses, that are essential for the defense and security of the United States.

culture: the beliefs and behaviors characteristic to a particular ethnic, racial, or other population.

cumulative career stress: this is distress that often results from officers being exposed routinely to traumatic events over an extended period of time, sometimes years.

decentralization: the process of distributing the administrative functions or powers of an organization among all levels of the structure.

deep web: a secret part of the World Wide Web, not accessible through regular Internet browsing or search engines; accessible from dynamic websites that require the use of an application program called "Tor" that allows encrypted conversations.

defendant: the person or organization being sued; also called a tort feasor.

deliberate indifference: a legal standard that involves more than negligence; the conscious or reckless disregard of the consequences of one's acts or omissions.

democratic: a leadership style; encourages individual and group participation, "let's talk about it."

detainer: a written request issued by ICE to a local jurisdiction requesting 48 hours advanced notice before a person in their custody is released so ICE may take him/her into its custody. Compliance with a detainer is a voluntary "immigration hold" because it is not a legal document such as a court order or a warrant.

Dillinger, John: bank robber killed in Chicago by FBI agents in 1934, marking the end of the lawless era.

directed and saturation patrols: more of a police tactic than a style, directed patrol usually involves the directing of patrol officers to specific locations during their patrol shift; saturation patrol concentrates *additional* officers on specific locations at specific times in an attempt to efficiently deploy officers as well as deter and prevent crime.

directed change: a carefully planned, formal action designed to bring about a new condition.

disability: under ADA: (1) physical or mental impairment that substantially limits one or more major life activities; (2) a record of such impairment; and (3) a perception of such impairment.

discipline matrix: a formal schedule for disciplinary actions, specifying both the presumptive or presumed sanction to be imposed for misconduct and any reduction or increase in the presumptive sanction for mitigating or aggravating factors.

discipline: the core meaning is to teach or instruct.

disparate treatment: an EEOC theory of discrimination; a member of a protected class is intentionally discriminated against in an employment decision.

domestic violence lethality assessment form: used to assist law enforcement officers in objectively assessing the potential dangers to a victim of domestic violenc.

double-loop learning: causes organizations to reconsider whether they are pursuing the right

downward communication: communication used by management to send orders, directives, goals, policies, and so on, to employees at lower levels of the organization.

due process: a guarantee of fairness in legal matters that requires that all legal procedures set by statute and court practice must be followed for every individual, so that there is no prejudicial or unequal treatment.

dustbowl: term for dried-out prairie states, where good topsoil blew away; many immigrated from those states to seek a better life. See okies.

early intervention system: a non-punitive way for a police department to identify and change officers' at-risk behaviors that could result in legal liability or damage its relationship with the community. It is therefore a tool to support officers and a tool to manage the department.

Earth Liberation Front (ELF), Animal Liberation Front (ALF): the two most infamous, single-issue, ecoterrorist groups active in the United States; they are responsible for significant destruction of property caused by arson and vandalism and sometimes resort to more violent means to express their message.

e-government: provides citizens with on-line access to many governmental services.

e-learning software: computer-based training software designed to incorporate case studies and simulation in the learning experience.

emotional skills (ES): The ability to accurately perceive and appraise your own emotions and those of others, to regulate your own emotions, and to do so while adapting and responding to the needs of others.

emotionally disturbed persons (EDPs): individuals suffering from various forms of mental illness that may complicate interactions with police officers.

employee assistance programs (EAPs): programs made available by employers to help employees having personal or occupational difficulties.

Employee Polygraph Protection Act (EPPA): limits the use of lie detectors by employers, provides a law enforcement exception.

entropic process: open systems concept; all organizations face the prospect of moving toward decline, disorganization, and death.

equafinality: there are multiple ways to achieve goals.

Equal Employment Opportunity Act of 1972: law that amended Title 7 of the Civil Rights Act of 1964 to include state and local units of government.

Equal Employment Opportunity Commission (EEOC): a unit within the U.S. Department of Justice (USDOJ) that administers several key job discrimination laws. EEOC recognizes four theories of discrimination.

Equal Pay Act (EPA): (1963), prohibits wage discrimination based on gender.

ethical leadership: consistent demonstration of moral values though personal actions, in interpersonal communications, and the communication of values to followers. Two components: (1) moral person and (2) moral manager.

ethics: rules and standards governing conduct.

evidence-based policing (EBP): theory of policing that grew out of 1998 article by Larry Sherman, who argued that police practices should be based on the best evidence available.

evidence-based policing: a style of policing using the best available research to guide, manage, and evaluate police operations within a community.

exception principle: routine matters should be handled at the lowest possible organizational level that they can be properly addressed, and unusual events, above or below standards, should be brought to the attention of higher-level managers.

exempt Employee: not entitled to overtime pay under FLSA.

exhaustion stage: the point in general adaptation syndrome when resistance can no longer be maintained and the body's defenses against stress begin to break down.

Fair Labor Standards Act (FLSA): (1938, private sector; 1985, public sector), establishes national minimum wage, work hours, overtime pay, child labor, and record-keeping requirements.

Family Medical Leave Act (FMLA): (1993), provisions to help employees balance their career and family needs. Mandates unpaid leave by covered employees for eligible workers for up to 12 weeks during any 12-month period for four specific reasons.

federal consent decree: a federal lawsuit against a city or state jurisdiction that has an established "pattern and practice" of violating the Constitutional rights of people within their jurisdiction.

feedback: messages sent from the receiver to the sender in a communication.

field training officer (FTO): guides the field training of a recent basic/academy graduate; see officer in training.

fiscal year (FY): the 12-month period usually covered by a budget; also see biennial and capital budgets as exceptions.

force-field analysis: a decision-making tool developed by Lewin. Also see behavioral systems theory.

Forces Act: federal legislation (1870) to combat Ku Klux Klan.

Fosdick, Raymond: author who played a major role in the Cleveland Foundation Study.

Freedmen's Bureau: federal agency that provided assistance to African Americans after the Civil War.

frontier closing: 1890—the official date set by the federal government for the "closing of the frontier," a key point in the transition from a rural to an urban society.

functional structure: a modified line and staff structure that brings together trained specialists and specialized resources under a single manager to accomplish a core responsibility.

functional supervision: one person supervises a function, even if it cuts across several organizational units.

fusion centers: data centers within police agencies that serve as intelligence hubs and clearinghouses for all potentially relevant homeland security and crime information that can be used to assess local terror threats and aid in more traditional anti-crime operations.

Garfield, President: U.S. president assassinated by frustrated patronage seeker; event gave momentum to passage of Pendleton Act.

general adaptation syndrome (GAS): the biological and physiological reactions, caused by stress, that may eventually incapacitate an individual.

Generation X: born 1965–1980, the largest generation working in law enforcement presently; grew up in mixed economy; first-generation latch key children; tend to be computer fluent. Many departments adapted their recruiting practices to attract Gen Xers.

generation x: those born between 1965 and 1980.

Generation Y: born 1981–1994, largely the children of baby boomers, recently entering law enforcement agencies. Tend toward traditional family values; spiritual, but not necessarily religious.

generation y: those born between 1981 and 1994.

Generation Z: born 1995–2010, the "Zedders," little known about them; fascination with virtual realities may lead to impoverished social and interpersonal skills.

Genetic Information Nondiscrimination Act (GINA): (2008), limits the use of genetic information, provides a law enforcement exemption.

geographic information systems (GIS): the integration of automated database operations and high-level mapping to analyze, manipulate, and manage spatial data, particularly relevant to crime analysis and forecasting.

grapevine: a system of informal information that meanders across organizational lines.

"great man" theories: two contrasting views: (1) events that must be responded to produce the great man and (2) great men are "born leaders," exceptionally endowed; one of two branches of traditional leadership theory, the other being the traits approach.

Great Recession: a major downturn in the American economy that began in December 2007 and was officially declared over in 2009, although the recovery has been slow.

Greensboro Massacre (N.C.): brutal and widely seen 1979 attack on African Americans by KKK and American Nazi Party.

grievance: an official expression of dissatisfaction brought by an employee or an employee organization as the initial step toward resolution through a formal procedure.

group communication: interaction among three or more individuals in a face-to-face situation where all parties have a common need that is satisfied by the exchange of information.

group interaction: a process which has four phases: orientation, conflict, emergence, and reinforced.

groupthink: decision making by a group, characterized by a lack of both creativity and individual responsibility.

Gulick, Luther: coined the most famous acronym of administration: POSDCORB.

harassment: a discriminatory, unwelcome action toward an individual on the basis of race, color, sex (including pregnancy), national origin, age, religion, disability, or genetic information.

Sexual harassment is perhaps the most well-known type of harassment.

Harrison, President: U.S. president accused of "prostitution of the public service."

hate crimes: harms (usually violent crimes) committed against an individual because of his or her perceived race, religion, ethnicity, gender, and/or sexual orientation.

Hawthorne effect: people being studied behave differently because they like the attention they get; part of a study by the human relations school at the Hawthorne Electrical Plant.

Herzberg, Frederick: developed motivation-hygiene theory.

heuristic model: a simplified, gut-level method of decision making that emphasizes internal personality attributes of the decision maker.

Hispanic American Police Command Officers Association (HAPCOA): established 1973, HAPCOA provides training and other opportunities for its members.

homegrown terrorism: instances where U.S. citizens and residents convert to radical Islamic extremism and conduct terrorist acts.

homeostasis: when an organization is "in balance."

horizontal communication: communication among peers.

horizontal differentiation: an organizational design that is structured based on activity rather than rank.

hostile environment: created when the prohibited and unwelcome behavior has the purpose or effect of unreasonably interfering with the individual's work performance or by creating an intimidating, hostile, or offensive working environment.

hot-spots policing: a geographically based approach to crime-fighting focused on in-depth analysis of "places" and times, and deploying police officers to those locations that account for the majority of calls for service and crime in a community.

human relations school: saw traditional organizational theory as ignoring the human element and sought changes; helped set the stage for the emergence of organizational humanism; see Hawthorne effect.

human relations skills: the capacity to interrelate positively with other people.

hybrid budget: budget formats that incorporate features from one or more other budget formats versus being purely one type of format.

immaturity versus maturity: see Argyris.

improvised explosive devices (IEDs): Homemade explosive devices and bombs, these "booby-trap" explosives are designed to cause extensive bodily injury or death and are usually located along roads or streets in conflict areas. IEDs are responsible for the majority of the casualties of U.S. troops in Iraq and Afghanistan.

inactive planning: this type of planning is based on the assumption things will continue to be as they are and will be "business as usual." Its time orientation is rooted in the present under the assumption that it is better than the past and not as dangerous as the uncertainty of the future. There is no systematic scanning of the environment to detect new opportunities.

incremental model: this model contends that police managers and administrators "play things safe" and opt to move very slowly (incrementally) in decision making.

informal organization: an unofficial structure within an organization, often based on personal relationships, that has its own goals, communications, and behavior patterns.

intelligence: data and information that have been evaluated, analyzed, and produced with careful conclusions and recommendations for future decision makers and policymakers.

intelligence-led policing (ILP): arising from the 9/11 terrorist attacks, ILP is a relatively new policing style focused on offenders, not crime incidents, using intelligence analysis to prevent crime.

internal subsystems: in open systems theory, the internal unifying forces of an agency that prevent fragmentation of the organization and transform inputs into outputs.

International Association of Chiefs of Police (IACP): a professional organization of chiefs of international, federal, state, and local police agencies of all sizes.

International Association of Police Women (IAPW): organization founded in 1969, roots in organization date back to 1926.

interpersonal communication: the process of message transmitting between two people to create a sustained shared meaning.

Islamic State (ISIS): a radical Islamic terrorist group that quickly rose in the Middle East in 2014; previously known as the Islamic State in Iraq and the Levant (ISIL) (The Levant is a geographical region on the edge of the Eastern Mediterranean Sea composed of Syria, Jordon, Lebanon, and Israel and more recently referred to as ISIS or the Islamic State in Iraq and Syria).

isomorphism: resource-dependent agencies tend to mirror the complexities and demands of their environments; when agencies receive signals from important others, they develop responsive policies and programs.

jihad: a "holy war," a concept perverted by radical Islamists to justify a physical war against the West; a perversion of the concept proscribed in the Holy Qur'an and *not* representative of mainstream Islam.

Jim Crow laws: southern laws that repressed African Americans, enacted 1880–1960, followed the Black Codes.

job action: a label used to describe several types of activities in which employees may engage to express their dissatisfaction with a particular person, event, or condition or to attempt to influence the outcome of a matter pending before decision makers, such as a contract bargaining impasse.

judiciary: This is a system of courts of law that administer justice.

Kansas City Preventive Patrol Study: part of the trilogy of research and experiments that rocked policing in the early 1970s.

King, Martin Luther Jr., Reverend: distinguished leader in the Civil Rights movement.

KKK: Ku Klux Klan, organization founded as a social club in 1866, quickly turned to terrorizing African Americans.

Knapp Commission: studied corruption in the NYCPD, identifying meat- and grass-eaters.

Kotter Model of Successful Change: an eight-step process model that identifies a logical and ideal way to implement successful change in police agencies.

laissez-faire: a leadership style; takes passive, "hands-off" approach, reluctantly use the authority of one's position, "whatever."

leader member exchange (LMX): theory by Dansereau, Graen, and Haga; those who are like the leader go to the in-group, those unlike the leader go to the out-group, and those about whom the leader is unsure, go to the try-out bin (1975). See life cycle LMX theory (1995).

leader: can be contrasted with manager: (1) management is the content of a job, being a leader is how you get it done; (2) one person may be a leader, manager, both, or neither; and (3) a leader is identified by the position he or she occupies in the department's hierarchy. Leaders and managers can be differentiated by the variables identified in Table 7.1. See leadership.

leadership neutralizers: as described by Kerr and Jermier, those who make leadership ineffective or impossible.

leadership substitutes: as described by Kerr and Jermier, those who diminish or take the place of formal leadership.

leadership: (1) relating the police department to the larger/external environment and (2) influencing officers to use their energies willingly and appropriately to achieve the department's goals.

least preferred coworker (LPC): Fiedler's theory that, underlining LPC is the assumption that how leaders treat their LPC is an indicator of their leadership preference. The relationship of that preference has three situational variables: (1) task structure, (2) leader-follower relations, and (3) the power position of the leader determines group effectiveness.

less-lethal weapon: As their name reflects, less-lethal weapons are used without the intent to cause permanent injury or death. Common less-lethal weapons include chemical weapons such as oleoresin capsicum (OC) or pepper spray, bean-bag guns, net guns that shoot a web around suspects, and controlled energy devices (CEDs) like Tasers.

letter of exception: a letter written by a chief of police to whatever office authorized the audit contesting one or more findings by the auditor.

Lewin, Kurt: founder of behavioral systems theory. Also see force-field analysis.

Lewin's three-step model: a change model that has three sequential steps: (1) unfreezing, (2) moving, and (3) refreezing.

Lexow Committee: committee that in 1894–1895 examined corruption in the New York Police Department.

liability: legal responsibility for a person's or an organization's acts or omissions.

liberty rights: rights involving the protection and defense of one's good name, reputation, and position in the community.

Lilly Ledbetter Fair Pay Act (LLFPA): (2009), law that states that each discriminatory paycheck is a new violation.

line and staff structure: an organizational structure that retains basic elements from line structure but adds auxiliary and administrative support units.

line item budget: budget whose focus is on controlling expenditures; each object of expenditure has a separate line in the budget.

line structure: the oldest, simplest, and clearest form of organizational design; authority flows from the top to the bottom of the organization in a clear and unbroken line.

litigation: a lawsuit or another question to the court that resolves a legal matter or question.

lone wolf (wolves): a violent attack by a single perpetrator (or small group), acting alone, without any direction, or assitance from an organization or outside group.

lynching: initially a severe beating, later synonymous with illegally hanging someone; initially meant rough justice.

machine politics: see political machine.

management systems: as described by Likert, a continuum of four leader styles.

manager: See leader.

managerial grid: Blake and Mouton's theory that balances two considerations: (1) concern for people and (2) concern for task to produce five distinct leadership styles.

Maslow, Abraham: developed the five-level hierarchy of human needs.

matrix (or grid) structure: an organizational design that assigns members of functional areas to specific projects, such as a task force.

McGregor, Douglas: developed Theory X and Theory Y, two contrasting sets of assumptions about workers.

McVeigh, Timothy: individual convicted of the Oklahoma City bombing and murders, executed in 2001; he stated that he wanted to get revenge for Ruby Ridge and Waco.

Mechanistic organizational structure: Mechanistic organizational structures are set up to run like a machine, tightly controlled, error free and producing a sustained, unflawed output. They incorporate many of the features of the bureaucratic structure, for example, a hierarchy, chain of command, and specialization, and much of the communication is vertical or top-down. Mechanistic organizations are also called "closed systems" because their boundaries are conceived of as being fairly impermeable to outside influences. Many theorists use mechanistic, closed system, and bureaucracies synonymously.

meet and confer model: referred to by some as "collective begging" because the laws or agreements establishing it confer little or no rights on employees. In the meet and confer model least friendly to employees, neither the employer nor the employees are required to meet. Such meetings are an opportunity, not a requirement.

mentoring: individuals selected to train, as well as provide role models to individuals new to a particular position.

military model: police theory that there is a war against crime and the police are front-line soldiers.

moral manager: ethical leadership concept, a fair and principled decision maker, who is altruistic, cares about people and the larger society.

moral person: ethical leadership concept, proactively strives to reinforce followers' ethical behavior.

moral turpitude: conduct contrary to honesty, justice, or good morals.

motivation-hygiene theory: two sets of factors, motivators and hygiene; hygiene factors, if met, don't motivate someone, but unmet they are a source of dissatisfaction. See Herzberg.

muckrakers: journalists and writers who exposed corruption and other abuses.

multicultural settings: the organizational environment in which there are individuals from numerous cultures and racial and religious backgrounds.

multitasking: engaging in multiple activities such as listening to music, working on the computer, and talking on the phone.

mutual benefit association: an association whose primary beneficiary is its members (e.g., a police union).

narco-terrorism: acts of insurgency by narcotics and drug traffickers aimed at influencing the policies of a specific government or society through violence and intimidation; the violent disruption of legitimate governmental services and security in a specific area.

Nation, Carry: WCTU activist, gained notoriety for "hatchitations," ripping alcohol kegs open with her axe.

National Academy (NA): institution founded in 1934 by FBI to train state and local law enforcement officials.

National Advisory Commission on Civil Disorders: government report on riots in 1968; also known as the Kerner Commission after the group's Chair.

National Association of American Asian Law Enforcement Commanders (NAAALEC): founded in 2002, an organization fostering leadership, fraternal enrichment, and advancement.

National Association of Women Law Enforcement Executives (NAWLEE): established to address the unique needs of women holding senior positions in law enforcement.

National Commission on Law Observance and Law Enforcement: first comprehensive national study of police, 1929.

National Criminal Justice Reference Service (NCJRS): online reference source for criminal justice students, scholars, practitioners, and the public.

National Organization of Black Law Enforcement Executives (NOBLE): founded in 1976, NOBLE works toward the elimination of racism and bias with the law enforcement field.

National Prohibition Act: see Volstead Act, prohibition.

National Sheriffs Association (NSA): chartered in 1940, the NSA, like other professional organizations, provides education, training, and information resources to its members.

natural soldiering: the natural inclination of workers not to push themselves.

needs hierarchy: five levels of needs that explain human motivation; see Maslow.

negative entropy: the capacity to resist decline or death, see buffering.

negligence: the failure to exercise the care toward another person that a reasonable person would do in the same circumstances; also includes taking action that a reasonable person would not take; negligence is accidental.

neighborhood-oriented policing: a style of community policing fostered by Lee P. Brown in Houston, Texas, that focused on crime and social problems in select neighborhoods or districts.

networked organizations: organizations that are heavily dependent on informational technology, often comprised geographically dispersed units, horizontal communication accounts for most message traffic, their existence is panned and bound together by contract, may be single purpose or continuous in operation. Units are not part of same organization; they are autonomous, but collaborative. See virtual organizations.

new public management (NPM): began in 1980s, called for greater use of business practices to achieve greater efficiency.

noise: anything that disrupts communication, including the attitudes, the emotions of the receiver, such as stress, fear, negative attitudes, and low motivation.

nonexempt employees: entitled to overtime pay under FLSA.

normative decision-making theory: leadership model by Vroom, Yetton, Jago; not a general model of leadership; narrowly focuses on three leadership approaches to decision making and provides the greatest probability for a good decision, contingent upon follower characteristics.

normed: a norm is a statistical average of performance by a well-defined population. In the case involving the Colorado Springs Police Department suit by women who did not run a distance in an absolute time, a normed score for the plaintiffs would be the average time on the run for women in various age groups, i.e., adjusted for both gender and age.

Obergefell V. Hodges: The 2015 supreme court landmark case recognizing and legalizing same-sex marriages across the united states.

objective reasonableness: A court-developed standard imposed under the Fourth Amendment "reasonableness" inquiring as to whether an officer's actions are "objectively reasonable" in light of the facts and circumstance of a specific incident. Would a reasonable officer confronted with the same or similar circumstances make the same decisions and conduct the same actions under review? The "objective reasonableness" test acknowledges that police officers are often forced to make split-second decisions under highly stressful conditions relating to the amount of force necessary in a particular incident.

objectives, programs, and policies. See single-loop learning.

officer in training (OIT): a recent academy graduate under the supervision of a field training officer.

Okies: term for immigrants from dust bowl states, many of them from Oklahoma.

open systems theory: a grouping of separate, but interdependent components that work together to achieve common goals.

operating budget: a recurrent budget for salaries, fringe benefits, uniforms, training, telephone service, and kindred expenses.

operational plans: often called "work plans" and describe specific actions to be taken by line units, such as, patrol officers, precinct group, and/or other division teams.

operations research: the application, collection, and analysis of data from decision making within an organization.

organic organizations: organic organizations recognize that they have permeable boundaries and are therefore co-dependent with the larger environment in which they are embedded. Knowing they face an unstable environment, organic organizations are adaptable and "nimble on their feet. Organic and open systems are used synonymously. Mechanistic and organic organizations can be thought of as opposite ends of a continuum.

organizational citizenship behavior (OCB): the extra things followers do that are not required but contribute to organizational effectiveness. See POB.

organizational development (OD): a change management process.

organizational humanism: 1950–1960s movement by theorists that called for the softening or elimination of many of the features of the bureaucratic model; see human relations school.

organizing: the process of determining the formal structure of task and authority relationships best suited to accomplish a mission.

path-goal theory (PGT): theory by House, 1996; revised his 1971 theory. The essence of PGT is that for leaders to be effective, they must engage in leader behaviors that compensate for the deficiencies of their subordinates, enhance their performance, and are instrumental to their individual and work unit performance and satisfaction.

patronage: in the worst sense, rewarding voters for their loyalty rather than their ability; useful in appointing qualified supporters who can help politicians implement their policies.

Peace Officer Standards and Training Commissions (POSTs): organizations that played an important role in police professionalization.

Peace Officers Standards and Training Commission: (POST), a state level organization that sets standards for police employment, basic and annual training, special certifications (e.g., use of radar, license revocations and other matters).

Peel, Sir Robert: driving force behind the London Metropolitan Police (1829).

Pendleton Act: federal legislation (1883) establishing the U.S. Civil Service Commission.

performance audit (PA): ordinarily a study to see how well a subunit or the whole organization is achieving its performance objectives. With some questionable shootings in 2014 and 2015, some audits are examining whether officers are following their use of force policies and writing all of the reports they should with the detail needed in them to constitute a professional report. One such study concluded that the officers were not writing all of the reports they should to keep use of force statists low and often simply wrote short passages, like arrested person was injured while resisting arrest and transported to the hospital.

performance budget (PB): also referred to as a performance-based budget (PBB), which focuses on results-based budgeting (RBB). In theory, a PB has four characteristics.

personalized power needs: the desire to be in control for selfish, self-aggrandizing reasons.

Pinkerton National Detective Agency: a private detective agency that excelled at tracking down outlaws.

plaintiff: the injured party that initiates a legal action.

Planning, Programming Budget System (PPBS): a budgeting innovation used in the federal government from the mid-1960s to the early 1970s; little use of it in state and local government.

planning: a process that links present actions to future conditions.

Police Administration: book authored by O.W. Wilson, known for many decades as the "Bible" of police administration, reasserted professional model of policing.

Police Executive Research Forum (PERF): group formed to do research and public policy work of interest to the larger jurisdictions founding it.

police sexual violence (PSV): an egregious form of sexual misconduct that involves sexual harassment and violence, including rape and other sexual assault, perpetrated by police officers against women.

political machine: a tightly controlled political party headed by a boss or small autocratic group whose purpose was to repeatedly win elections for personal gain, often through graft and corruption.

politics: In the negative sense, this refers to attempts to impose external, partisan political influence on the operation of a police department.

Politics: the process of acquiring and maintaining control over a government, including its policies, administration, and operations.

Politics: Used in a positive sense, means the governance of the city.

Popular Front for the Liberation of Palestine (PFLP): terrorist organization.

POSDCORB: planning, organizing, staffing, directing, coordinating, reporting, and budgeting; also see Gulick.

positive organizational behavior (POB): a broader cluster of organizational behaviors that contribute to its overall success; OCB is included within POB by some researchers. See OCB.

posse comitatus: prohibits the use of federal soldiers to act as police officers in a law enforcement capacity within the borders of the United States.

posttraumatic stress disorder (PTSD): a psychological reaction that occurs after experiencing a highly stressful event outside the range of normal human experience.

power motivation: see affiliation, personalized power, and socialized power needs.

power: when a formal grant of authority is made, some power inherently accompanies it, to maintain standards, correct deficiencies, and discipline as needed. However, even with authority and power, leaders may not be able to compel others to perform. To a significant degree, power is a grant made by the led to the leader. Also see authority.

predictive policing: a proactive policing style that uses information and analytical tools to prevent crime while using the fewest police resources possible.

Pregnancy Discrimination Act: PDA (1978), the Act makes it unlawful to discriminate against women in employment practices because of pregnancy, childbirth, or medical conditions rising from such.

principle of hierarchy: a requirement that each lower level of the organization be supervised by a higher level.

proactive planning: this is the attempt to change or anticipate events in the future that are likely to occur.

probable cause: Arising from the Fourth Amendment, probable cause is the standard by which a police officer has the authority to make an arrest, conduct a personal or property search, or to obtain a warrant for arrest; a set of facts and circumstances that would lead a reasonable person to believe that a crime has occurred and that a specific person is responsible for that crime.

problem-oriented policing: originally branded by Herman Goldstein, this style of policing addresses reoccurring social problems within a community through an innovative, four-step model called SARA.

procedural due process: the legality of the procedures used; in this case, to deprive police officers of status or wages.

procedural plans: the guidelines for the action to be taken under specific circumstances and address such matters as the use of force, high-speed pursuits, evidence handling, K-9 teams, sexual predators, domestic violence, hate crimes, cold case investigation, and form of management and dozens of other matters that permeate the agency.

profession: several definitions; see Table 1.1.

program budget: focuses organized around programs/activities, has line item budget for control.

progressive discipline: slowly increasing the severity of sanctions unless a higher level is immediately required (e.g., termination).

prohibition: national prohibition officially lasted from 1919 to 1933.

property rights: rights involving the protection of one's property; in some cases, an individual's right to his or her job is considered a property right.

prosecutor: This is the public officer within a jurisdiction who represents the citizenry of a state or county who charges and prosecutes individuals who are alleged to have committed a crime.

protected class: a Title VII (1972) designation, race, color, sex, national origin, or religion.

proximate cause: an event that directly results in another event, particularly injury due to negligence or an intentional, wrongful act.

Public Employment Relations Commission: an administrative body, often on a state level, responsible for administering legislation related to union bargaining.

public interest organizations: These are organizations such as the American Civil Liberties Union (ACLU) and the National Association for the Advancement of Colored People (NAACP), which play an important role in police accountability, especially as it relates to allegations of police misconduct.

qualified individual with a disability: job applicant or employee who meets the employer's legitimate requirements for the position sought or held and is able to perform the essential/core functions with or without a reasonable accommodation by the employer.

quid pro quo: "something for something," a category of sexual harassment.

racial profiling: This is the consideration of race as a key factor in police decisions to stop and interrogate citizens.

Rand Criminal Investigation Study: part of the trilogy of research and experiments that rocked policing in the early 1970s.

rank-order list: promotional roster method in which candidates are listed in their rank order. Selections are usually made from the list using a rule of 3, 5, or 10.

ration books: to divert as much food as possible to support service members fighting in WW II, national food rationing was instituted in the United States in 1942. Each person was issued a book of stamps that established the amounts of various types of foods he/she could have. Also see victory gardens.

rational model: this model assumes that people are motivated predominately by "economic incentives" and will, therefore, work harder given the opportunity to make more money.

rational-legal authority: authority is granted by the organization to the occupant of a position who uses it to accomplish organizational goals, a Weber-supplied concept.

reactive planning: this is the reaction to problems that have presently occurred and are being addressed or are presently happening and require a response. It is both past and present oriented.

reasonable accommodation: employers may tell applicants what the selection process consists of and whether they will need a reasonable accommodation by the employer. Examples of selection accommodations include large-print examinations and scheduling a wheelchaired applicants' interview on the first floor rather than the second floor where there is no elevator. After a conditional job offer is extended, employers may ask whether a reasonable accommodation is needed for any aspect of the job (e.g., modifying the equipment the person will use).

reasonableness: a standard applied to many legal questions in which it must be determined if conduct or action was reasonable in the eyes of the court.

recognition-primed decision making (RPD): method of decision making that focuses on the assessment of the situation, its dynamics, and the experience of the decision maker.

reformation period: reformers sought to free policing from political abuses and corruption; had two needs: arouse apathetic public and a conceptual model to drive it.

reformatted bureaucracy: a shift from close adherence to traditional organizational theory/closed system views to a neoclassical or neo-Weberian view that includes open systems precepts.

reliability: if the same test or a parallel form is given to the same group, substantially the same results will occur; results are not random.

residency requirements: rules from the Depression era, stating that before hiring, person had to live in a community six months or a year; intent was to protect jobs for local tax-paying residents.

resistance stage: the second step in general adaptation syndrome, exemplified by specific responses to continued stress by the body in order to optimize adaptation.

results-based budget (RBB): see performance budget.

retaliation: one of four EEOC theories of discrimination; two types: (1) retaliation for participation and (2) retaliation for opposition.

roid rage: an outburst of violent or aggressive behavior caused by taking large doses of anabolic steroids.

Ruby Ridge: 1992 Idaho standoff involving Weaver family and a friend and federal agents; fatalities on both sides; Weavers were seen by far-right groups as martyrs to federal government.

sanctuary movement: Some people fleeing violence in Central America during the 1980s entered this country illegally. To prevent them from being returned to their home country some sympathetic churches gave them sanctuary, hiding and caring for them. This practice spread to city and counties and soon officials in those jurisdictions placed limits on the amount of assistance their public safety agencies could provide to the federal government with respect to illegal immigrants.

SARA: a cyclical, four-step problem-solving methodology designed to enhance community policing: **S**canning, **A**nalysis, **R**esponse, and **A**ssessment.

scientific management: finding the "one best way" to accomplish a task; see F. W. Taylor and traditional organizational theory.

sector policing: an innovative and proactive approach to structuring law enforcement crime-fighting strategies, personnel deployment, allocation of resources, and accountability to a geographical zone or area.

sense making: how people and organizations process their experiences and what they do with them. See cognitive maps.

servant leadership: as described by Greenleaf, primary orientation is the theory that leaders should first be servants, meeting the legitimate needs of their followers.

service organizations: a organization whose specific clientele is the primary beneficiary (e.g., clients of a community health center).

Servicemembers Civil Relief Act (SCRA): (2003), provides protections to service members, including those called to active duty; key provisions apply to leasing arrangements, the amount of interest that debtors can charge, and life insurance.

sexual harassment: a specific type of harassment, two categories: (1) quid pro quo and (2) hostile environment; violates Title VII.

sheriffs: Usually elected, with a custodial role in the detention of prisoners and serving as bailiffs in the court.

silent generation: born 1925–1945, loyal, security conscious, and conforming are key attributes. Almost entirely retired from law enforcement.

single-loop learning: allows organizations to make corrections and continue operations; see double-loop learning.

Singleton, Benjamin "Pap": former Tennessee slave, promoted founding African American townships in Kansas after the Civil War.

situational leadership: leadership model by Hersey and Blanchard; relates the behavior of the leaders to the maturity of followers, identifies the most probable successful leader behaviors for each level of maturity.

skill: how knowledge gets translated into action.

slave patrols: groups that hunted down fugitive slaves, administered impromptu punishments as they saw fit, and dispersed slave meetings; continued through the end of the Civil War.

snatch racket: 1920s and 1930s gangster term for kidnappings.

social media: a type of internet-based resource integrating user-generated content with user participation.

social skills (SS): the ability to express oneself in social situations; the ability to "read" social situations; recognizing different social roles and expected behavior; and interpersonal problem solving; closely related to ES.

socialized power needs: the desire to have a positive impact on the department's operations and administration.

span of management: the number of personnel a supervisor can personally manage effectively.

speakeasies: illegal bars during federal prohibition.

specialization: a division of labor wherein specific jobs and tasks are allocated to meet different responsibilities with those specially qualified or trained to perform them.

spiritual leadership: leadership divided into two camps: those who are more overtly religious and those who define spirituality in another way. People can be spiritual without being religious, seeking meaning in their lives. Spiritual in this sense means having a closer connection with one's higher values and morality. Spiritual leadership taps into followers' higher-order needs (e.g., challenging work that is socially meaningful). See spiritual survival.

spiritual survival: (1) transcendence, a sense of being called to a profession and (2) membership, a sense of belonging.

spoils system: see patronage.

standard of reasonableness: in *Graham v. Connor,* the Supreme Court held that the standard of reasonableness emanates from the officer's perception at the time of the crisis that resulted in the use of deadly force.

station house sergeants: as described by Van Maanen, such sergeants work inside, have a strong conformity orientation, are immersed in the police department's management culture, and make contacts that can help career.

strategic plans: typically longer in duration than other kinds of planning, usually planning for events 3 to 5 years into the future.

street sergeants: as described by Van Maanen, such sergeants have a distaste for office procedures, are action oriented, are more likely to be investigated and sued, and may not advance beyond middle management.

street-level bureaucrats: government workers in direct contact with clients who use discretion on how to implement public policy (e.g., police officers and field social workers).

stress: anything that places an adjustive demand on the organism.

stress inoculation activities: activities that help eliminate or reduce stress.

strong mayor: In this form of government, the mayor is elected to office and serves as the chief executive of the city.

structure: an organizational design that assigns members of functional areas to specific projects, such as a task force.

substantive due process: the requirement that the basis for government disciplinary action be reasonable, relevant, and justifiable.

suicide by cop (SbC): a situation involving an individual who wishes to die and uses the police to affect that goal.

SWAT: special weapons and tactics police teams often used by the police during critical incidents such as barricaded felons, hostage situations, and felony search warrants.

synoptic planning: also known as the rational comprehensive approach and is the dominant tradition in policing.

systematic soldiering: keep production rates low so quotas don't increase.

tactical plans: these involve planning for emergency of a specific nature at known locations.

Tannenbaum and Schmidt: authors who identified a theory of leader styles (1958), revising it to a full situational leadership theory (1973).

Taylor, F. W.: father of scientific management.

team policing: an attempt to reshape how police resources were used by reducing specialization and enlarging the role of uniformed patrol officers. Part of the trilogy of research and experiments that rocked policing in the 1970s.

technical skills: skills that are essential to doing a job; vary by level within a police organization (e.g., identifying physical evidence versus preparing a budget).

temperance movement: late 19th century anti-alcohol movement; church based.

tenure: This is a period, or term, during which a position is held.

terrorism: the threat of and/or use of violence to achieve a specific set of political objectives or goals.

Theory X–Theory Y: see McGregor.

thin-slicing theory: the concept that instantaneous or quick decisions made by well-trained and experienced administrators may often be better than those made more deliberately and with significantly more information and time.

Title VII: (1972), law that amends the Civil Rights Act of 1964; prohibits job discrimination in employment based on race, color, sex, national origin, or religion.

Tor network: Synonymous for the "deep web:" see deep web.

tort: a private injury inflicted on one person by another person, for which the injured party may sue in a civil action.

traditional action research model: a five-step change model consisting of the following: (1) recognizing the need for change, (2) assessing/diagnosing the situation, (3) action planning, (4) the intervention, and (5) evaluation.

traditional organizational theory: has three stems, bureaucracy, scientific management, and administrative theory; the centerpiece of organizational theory during 1900–1950.

traditional policing: a style of policing based on response to calls for service after the activity has occurred; traditional policing is reactive and incident driven, often utilizing random moving patrol cars.

traits approach: relatively stable predispositions to behave in a certain way; since roughly 1910, there has been interest in identifying the traits leaders have. Also see great man theory.

transactional leadership: leadership style that gives something (rewards) to get something (performance by followers). TLers appeal to the self-interest of followers. A basic system of reciprocity. Followers are motivated by lower levels of Maslow's needs hierarchy.

transformational leadership: leadership style that inspires followers to "elevate their game," go beyond self-interests, and make more and larger contributions than they had originally intended. In the process, transformational leaders help them to grow personally and professionally, to develop their own capabilities for leadership. Transformational leaders appeal to followers' ideals and values, aligning them with the organization's.

Two Medal of Honors: "Teddy" Roosevelt (1858–1919) and Mary Edwards Walker.

type A personality: the personality type characterized by an intense and ambitious mindset, which puts the person under constant stress and physiological strain.

type B personality: the personality type characterized by a more easygoing state of mind than the type A personality.

type C personality: the personality type characterized as non-emotional, non-assertive, quiet, and introspective but actually frustrated and suppresses anger.

type D personality: the personality type characterized as pessimistic and socially withdrawn and as a result fears rejection.

U. S. Department of Labor: administers some job discrimination laws in addition to other responsibilities.

undocumented immigrant: An individual who does not qualify for admission into the United States has entered the country illegally by crossing the border without full inspection or has violated the terms of legal admission.

unequal badge: term that describes African American officers in some southern communities who, until the early 1960s, only walked beats in African American business and entertainment districts; by custom, African American officers were often not allowed to arrest Caucasians because an "ugly incident" leading to rioting might occur.

Uniform Guidelines for Employee Selection Procedures: "Uniform Guidelines," 1978, developed by EEOC to create a single set of selection principles designed to help covered employers comply with federal laws prohibiting employment decisions that discriminated against members of protected classes.

Uniformed Services Employment and Reemployment Rights Act (USERRA): (1994), encourages noncareer participation in the uniformed military service by eliminating barriers to such service, minimizing the disruption of the lives of those called to service and prohibiting discrimination against them.

untouchables: Treasury agents under Elliot Ness assigned to Chicago who couldn't be corrupted.

upward communication: communication used by lower-level employees.

validity: quality of a test that means it actually measures what it is intended to measure.

vertical differentiation: an organizational design based on levels of authority within an organization.

vicarious liability: a legal doctrine also known as "respondent superior" imposing liability on supervisors and managers for the tortious conduct of their employees.

victory gardens: small household gardens planted during WW II for personal consumption so more food could be used in war effort.

virtual organizations: organizations that arise spontaneously to an urgent need; there is no planning or contract; participation is voluntary and members can withdraw at any time; there is not a command and control structure; they usually disappear when the single purpose that brought them together is accomplished.

Vollmer, August (Gus): father of modern law enforcement.

Volstead Act: National Prohibition Act; see prohibition.

vote of confidence: reflects how rank and file members signal their collective displeasure with the chief administrator of their agency.

Waco: Texas city where, in 1993, there was a 51-day federal siege of the Branch Davidian Compound led by David Koresh; ended with federal fatalities and perhaps 75 or more Branch Davidian deaths; federal authorities were sharply criticized, but no wrongdoing was found.

Watergate Scandal: petty burglary that ultimately led to President Nixon's resignation.

Weber, Max: founder of modern sociology whose name is synonymous with bureaucracy.

Whitman, Charles: man who committed the first mass murders on a college campus at the University of Texas in 1966.

Wickersham Commission: see National Commission on Law Observance and Law Enforcement (1929).

Wilson, O.W.: chief of several jurisdictions; studied under Vollmer; his *Police Administration* has been regarded as the "Bible" of police administration for decades.

work slowdowns: officers continue to work but do so at a leisurely pace causing productivity to fall.

work speedups: an acceleration of an activity resulting in over production of one or more types of police services.

work stoppages: the ultimate work stoppage is the strike, which is withholding all of labors' services.

workaholic personality: this personality type is similar to a type A, and can result in serious physical and psychological consequences.

working test: the probationary period for a position.

zealots: leadership style described by Downs; such leaders have narrow interests, focus almost entirely on them.

zero tolerance policing: ZTP was based on the premise that when small infractions of the law are ignored, it creates a climate conducive to more serious crimes being committed. The extension of this thinking was ZTP, which required non-discretionary enforcement for all crimes.

zero-based budget (ZBB): in pure form, every program in a budget starts from "zero" and must be justified each year. Three alternative service levels are prepared for each program. As practiced in less stressful economic times, departments "have" 75 or 80 percent of their prior year's budget and use from there.

zero-tolerance policing (ZTP): a focused police strategy built on the philosophy that visible signs of social decay often lead to more serious crimes in a specific neighborhood; emphasis then, should be on strict enforcement of the law for even minor crimes of disorder.

INDEX